MANAGEMENT

...ned on or before
...te below.

MANAGEMENT

John Naylor

Principal Lecturer in Management
Liverpool John Moores University

FINANCIAL TIMES
PITMAN PUBLISHING

FINANCIAL TIMES
MANAGEMENT

LONDON • SAN FRANCISCO
KUALA LUMPUR • JOHANNESBURG

Financial Times Management delivers the knowledge,
skills and understanding that enable students,
managers and organisations to achieve their ambitions,
whatever their needs, wherever they are.

London Office:
128 Long Acre, London WC2E 9AN
Tel: +44 (0)171 447 2000
Fax: +44 (0)171 240 5771
Website: www.ftmanagement.com

A Division of Financial Times Professional Limited

First published in Great Britain in 1999

© Financial Times Professional Limited 1999

The right of John Naylor to be identified as Author
of this Work has been asserted by him in accordance
with the Copyright, Designs and Patents Act 1988.

ISBN 0 273 62532 2

British Library Cataloguing in Publication Data
A CIP catalogue record for this book can be obtained from the British Library

10 9 8 7 6 5 4 3 2 1

Typeset by Pantek Arts, Maidstone, Kent.
Printed and bound in China

The Publishers' policy is to use paper manufactured from sustainable forests.

Contents

Preface

Aims of the book

This book aims to offer an excellent package to support students following courses in management. These may be within an undergraduate programme or among those offered at postgraduate level to those who come from other disciplines. Its intention is to be comprehensive and thorough, yet flexible, readable and interesting. Theory is explained and applications are discussed. From this source, students can both learn about, and develop skills in, management.

The complexity of management as a field of study is reflected in the range of approaches taken to its presentation. From among these, we can pick out four:

- *Management as a process*

  Variants of the sequence of planning, organising, implementing and controlling can be found in management thought from the earliest days. In this book, Parts 3 to 7 represent stages of this process. The constraints of book design inevitably lead to a sequential presentation. Yet, the management process should really be seen as a number of loops. In practice, not only is there neither beginning nor end, but managers are engaged in several stages simultaneously. As we shall see in Chapter 1, this way of presenting management does not constitute a descriptive theory, even less a prescriptive one. It merely offers a useful way of sorting and examining ideas.

  One further comment concerns the division of chapter topics among the process stages. The sequence could be changed. For instance, control could be discussed much earlier than in the last two chapters. Further, the discussion of organising is divided rather arbitrarily into large and small groups. The split was made because of the amount of material to be covered under the general heading of organising people.

- *Themes in management*

  A less structured approach is to use current themes and controversies as the basis of book design. The starting point is to examine what questions are of greatest concern to the modern manager. In this book, we select four of these: globalisation; ethics and social responsibility; quality; and enterprise. This selection does not mean that other issues are ignored. Questions such as diversity, gender and governance could have warranted their own chapters. The limited space, however, kept the list to four and other issues are included at appropriate points.

  The book is designed to relate the chosen themes to the management process. They are, therefore, set out in Part 2 and then referred to again at appropriate points throughout.

■ *Management skills*

It has been recognised that knowing about management is not enough. Learners are interested in developing their skills. These can lie in administrative or interpersonal aspects of the managerial role or in the ability to manage oneself or one's career. In recognising the importance of skills, the book takes many opportunities to demonstrate how things are done. Examples include: appraising the state of an organisation and environment; choosing appropriate forecasting techniques; preparing a mission statement, objectives and plans; examining the ethics within a decision; using techniques to assess and improve quality; avoiding decision traps; designing an organisation structure; recruiting; communicating and making a communications plan; working out a payment scheme; setting up control systems; anticipating and coping with cultural differences; nurturing enterprise; and learning.

Summarising and presenting ideas are important skills. Through its use of hundreds of examples, students are encouraged to create and use diagrams as support for investigation, thinking and presentation. Styles very from the formal flow and block diagrams to the apparently less formal mind maps and rich pictures. The book shows that they all have their place.

■ *Critique*

With the overwhelming weight of material about management, there is a danger in not standing back and taking a detached, critical look. Without this perspective, one might conclude that the only controversies in the field were about the efficacy of one theory as opposed to another. A critical perspective, on the other hand, sees through what is so often taken for granted. For instance, in discussing communication in Chapter 18, we might assume that the problem is to find ways of making the transmission of information from one person to another as clear, accurate and efficient as possible. Yet, a more detached view asks whether this assumption is sustainable. It may be that managers do not want to tell the whole story. While espousing openness and sharing, they may practice obfuscation and manipulation.

The discussion of theory is developed in Chapter 1. Nevertheless, the book is not a comprehensive critique of management. In referring, however, to alternative perspectives on processes such as communication and control, and practices such as marketing, it points out that there are alternative viewpoints. Students are encouraged to question theory and what is taken for granted. Then they can resist swallowing simple dogma such as 'managers' right to manage'.

■ *A combination of approaches*

As shown in the Plan of the Book, the design of the book combines the above approaches. Having established a context for management in Part 1, and set out the four themes in Part 2, the book then follows the stages of the management process. Readers with different backgrounds, or with different learning needs, may follow a different sequence. It is possible, for instance, to start with organising and study planning and control later. To assist with alternative routes, each chapter has been set out in a standard way, introduced by clear objectives showing the material that is to be covered.

Student learning features

While fitted into the sequence explained above, every chapter stands on its own. Key features are as follows:

- learning objectives immediately establish the purpose of the chapter;
- the opening case study provides a context for discussion and draws attention to the practical implications of key concepts;
- these concepts are laid out in sections with clear headings;
- there are numerous examples and references, including useful web site addresses;
- the conclusion of each chapter draws the themes together;
- a 'Quick check up' test challenges the student to assess whether objectives have been met at a basic level;
- chapter questions are structured to test knowledge, explore practical applications and stimulate further investigation;
- the closing case builds on the work covered in the chapter and raises points for discussion;
- the opening and closing cases use real life examples. They are short enough to be digested quickly yet are especially written to focus on relevant issues;
- other examples and illustrations are highlighted in text boxes or, if sufficiently brief incorporated in the text;
- the cases and examples are deliberately varied to cover different perspectives, nations, and size and types of organisation.

Support material for lecturers

This book comes as part of a teaching package and the following supplementary material is available:

- *Web site support* A regularly updated web site can be found on **http://www.ftmanagement.com**. This contains downloadable versions of diagrams from the book and extra OHPs to aid preparation and presentation of classes;
- *Password protected areas* In addition, lecturers who adopt the text can gain access to Password protected areas. To request a registration form and password, send an e-mail to register@ftmanagement.com. This address also has the facility for e-mail transmission on specific queries;
- *Lecturer's Guide* a resource manual containing lecture notes and suggestions for tutorial work and assignments;
- *PowerPoint Lecturer's Guide* an electronic version of the above.

Acknowledgements

Many people have contributed to this work. In particular, I would like to thank present and past members of the management teaching team at John Moores University. They have supported and guided my ideas over many years. An especial debt is owed to colleagues who provided detailed comments on parts of the book: Nick Hawkins, Mike Kennedy, Martin Parnell, Brian Whorrall and Maurice Yolles.

At Financial Times Management, Beth Barber, Michelle Graham, Pradeep Jethi, Sadie McClelland and Andrew Mould were valuable points of contact and sources of encouragement throughout the project. My thanks goes to them and others in the team who worked behind the scenes.

Financial Times Management brought in seven reviewers who commented anonymously as the book was being written. Their details appear below. Although always interesting and constructive, I have not been able to incorporate every suggestion. On the other hand, I hope each reviewer will find something of themselves in the ideas and the way they are expressed:

Professor William Conradie, Rand Afrikaans University, South Africa
Professor Peter Kähäri, Swedish Institute of Management, Stockholm
Dr F.J. van de Linde, Erasmus University, Rotterdam
Benny Loke, Temasek Polytechnic, Singapore
Louise McArdle, Department of Organisation Studies, University of Lancashire
Dr John Mackness, The Management School, Lancaster University
Chris Prince, Director of Programmes, Nottingham Business School, Nottingham Trent University

There are two personal acknowledgements. I extend a warm thanks to my wife, Maureen, who cheerfully added an extra share of domestic duties to the responsibilities of her career. Finally, the book is dedicated to my mother, Mary Naylor, who was always an inspiration.

John Naylor
Summer 1998

Plan of the book

PART 1 — MANAGEMENT IN CONTEXT

CHAPTER 1 Management and the manager's job

CHAPTER 2 The development of management ideas

CHAPTER 3 Outside the organisation: Understanding the environment

CHAPTER 4 Inside the organisation: Adapting to change

PART 2 — THEMES IN MANAGEMENT

CHAPTER 8 Enterprise

CHAPTER 7 Managing for quality

CHAPTER 6 Social responsibility and ethics

CHAPTER 5 Global business: Bridging nations and cultures

PART 3 — PLANNING AND DECISION MAKING

CHAPTER 9 Planning: Coping in an uncertain environment

CHAPTER 10 Strategic management: looking to the long term

CHAPTER 11 Decision making: Choosing from alternatives

PART 4 — ORGANISING LARGE GROUPS

CHAPTER 15 Human resource management

CHAPTER 14 Managing organisational change

CHAPTER 13 Organisational design: Matching the situation

CHAPTER 12 Organisations: Principles, models and outcomes

PART 5 — ORGANISING SMALL GROUPS

CHAPTER 16 Leadership and motivation

CHAPTER 17 Groups and teams

CHAPTER 18 Communication in management

PART 6 — IMPLEMENTING POLICIES AND PLANS

CHAPTER 22 Managers and information

CHAPTER 21 Innovation: From ideas to customer benefits

CHAPTER 20 Marketing: Managing relations with customers

CHAPTER 19 Operations management

PART 7 — CONTROLLING

CHAPTER 23 Control systems

CHAPTER 24 Control and change

Part 1

MANAGEMENT IN CONTEXT

Management is the art of getting others to do all the work. *Anon*

A theory can be proved by experiment; but no path leads from experiment to the birth of a theory. *Albert Einstein, German physicist*

A body seriously out of equilibrium, either with itself or with its environment, perishes outright. *George Santayana, American philosopher*

Always design a thing by considering it in its larger context – a chair in a room, a room in a house, a house in an environment, an environment in a city plan. *Eero Saarinen, Finnish architect*

PART 1 MANAGEMENT IN CONTEXT	CHAPTER 1 Management and the manager's job	CHAPTER 2 The development of management ideas	CHAPTER 3 Outside the organisation: understanding the environment	CHAPTER 4 Inside the organisation: adapting to change

PART 2 THEMES IN MANAGEMENT	CHAPTER 8 Enterprise	CHAPTER 7 Managing for quality	CHAPTER 6 Social responsibility and ethics	CHAPTER 5 Global business: bridging nations and cultures

The four chapters of Part 1 provide the foundation, background and context for the study of management. It is defined in Chapter 1, which considers a range of descriptions based on roles, styles and abilities. The function of theory is also investigated, showing that practising management is more than merely the application of common sense. Finally, there is consideration of what it is like to be a manager and how personal ideas about the nature of management work and careers are developed.

Chapter 2 offers a historical context. It outlines the development of management ideas, mainly through the twentieth century. Students who have already met these ideas may prefer to skip this material, although even they may benefit from the extra historical detail compared with other sources.

Chapters 3 and 4 use the open systems idea of the organisation in a complex environment. They promote the idea of the organisation achieving a 'fit' if it is to succeed. Chapter 3 presents the environment as layered and shows how managers interpret and forecast its behaviour. In Chapter 4, these changes are presented as challenges to which the organisation must adapt. Whether and how the adaptation occurs is strongly influenced by the prevailing culture.

1

Management and the manager's job

Chapter objectives

When you have finished studying this chapter, you should be able to:

- describe and define management, illustrating the elements of the definition;
- explain why we talk of organisations as wholes;
- classify the manager's job according to roles, styles and required abilities;
- argue for the value of theory in the management discipline, refuting the argument that it is merely applied common sense; explain and illustrate how myths of management are created;
- outline what it takes to become a successful manager and what people are seeking in their careers;
- suggest why managing diversity is becoming more important.

A tale of two city schools[1]

It matters how a school is run. Claremont Junior School is in Moss Side, Manchester, one of the United Kingdom's most run-down areas. The district, having many dilapidated terraced houses with no gardens, has a reputation for crime and drugs. The pupils are mostly poor: 56 per cent take free lunches; 83 per cent are from ethnic minority families; many live with one parent in rented housing or units for the homeless; some are refugees; a quarter speaks English as an additional language. According to those who cite poverty and class as the main reason for educational failure, the place is bound to be a dump. Not so. The 1997 inspection report found, 'Claremont Junior is a good school with some excellent features'. The 228 pupils had a positive attitude and were well behaved.

About a mile away, in a similar neighbourhood, stood Princess Primary School. In 1996, inspectors found its hitherto separate junior department to be a 'failing' school. It required special measures to counteract the unacceptable standard. Some staff were seconded to other schools to improve their skills; experienced teachers replaced them. The junior and infant schools were amalgamated. The head of the infant department, which had received a more favourable report, took charge. After a year, a return visit recognised 'considerable gains' in teaching quality. Yet they had come too late. Manchester City Council wielded the axe. In spite of progress, standards remained unsatisfactory. Furthermore, finances were seriously in the red and parents were sending their children elsewhere. Numbers were down to 30 per cent of total capacity.

Figure 1.1 shows how achievement differed between the two schools. Claremont's leavers were close to the national average while those from Princess clearly under achieved. Clear differences appeared in most other subjects. Standards at Claremont in information technology, physical education and religious education were high. Inspectors rated opportunities in music as excellent; the school's steel band is well known.

Teachers' organisations and others argue for more money, small classes and new buildings to resolve such problems. Yet the two schools suggest otherwise. Claremont has a two-storey Victorian building, although in good condition; Princess's smart new one replaced another burnt down a few years ago. Claremont spends less than the national average on each child yet achieves below average class sizes; Princess's classes were smaller and its costs were well above the mean.

Could the explanation lie among lazy teachers? At Princess the report found, 'The teachers work hard and have an adequate

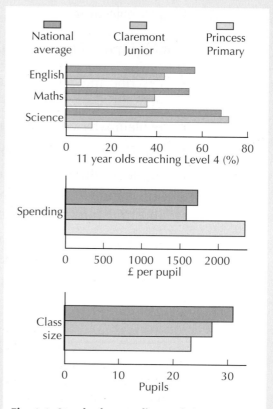

Fig. 1.1 Standards, spending and sizes – two Manchester schools

knowledge of the subjects ... but their expectations of the pupils are often too low'. Low achievement was blamed on an overall lack of structure. There was no clear curriculum and little monitoring of what pupils were learning. At Claremont, teachers were also 'a very committed and hard working team'. They gave all pupils, from the brightest to those with learning difficulties, suitable work, including regular homework. Teachers planned lessons carefully, kept detailed records for each child, and reviewed the curriculum every three years. Even the 'dinner ladies' (who supervise the lunchtime break) were clear about discipline policies, ensuring a consistent approach across the school. Staff did not see planning as a burden, recognising that it avoided crisis management. Over at Princess, crises were common. Teachers spent much time keeping order and were tempted to give easy work to avoid child frustration and misbehaviour. They only gave homework if parents asked for it.

Low expectations often dog failing schools. On the whole, teachers, pupils and parents at Princess believed that improvement was impossible. Community relations were distant; many parents showed little concern about development so long as their children seemed happy. Parents were more involved at Claremont and most were keen for their children to do well. Continuity of leadership strengthened such links. Destruction of the old building had caused great disruption for Princess; yet the school had also had eight heads in 12 years. In the same period, Claremont had experienced one change at the top.

Introduction

Management makes a difference. Claremont Junior shows how inner-city schools can offer a good education. In its last years, even Princess Primary showed that recovery is possible. Whether schools succeed depends on good leadership, a clear curriculum, sound planning and monitoring, and high expectations.

Naturally, picking examples to make a point is easy. The comparison may be harsh on Princess Primary. The fire that destroyed the previous buildings may have had more impact than we could guess; the two neighbourhoods, although both in central Manchester, may be very different. The snapshot of the case study catches only part of the story. Yet such variations are seen in many human activities. Well-managed organisations out-perform the competition. Good planning, organising, implementing and controlling yield rewards. Openness to pressure from a demanding environment helps to set standards and keep managers on their toes. These are the essentials of management and form the framework of this book.

Plan of the book

The 24 chapters are divided into seven parts. We can regard the opening two as foundation, explaining the background to management and picking out themes. The first part, starting with this chapter, creates a context for the study. It shows what management is, where its ideas come from, and sets out the broad notion of managing organisations as to do with adapting a complex system to a changing environment. The second part covers four themes that affect, in different ways, all managers. Clearly, globalisation, social responsibility and ethics, quality and enterprise have their impact in many organisations, including schools. Examples in

United Kingdom primary schools include: changing populations through migration; professional standards of teachers; raising attainment targets; and the need for heads to manage (and stretch) budgets.

The last five parts of the book are built around planning, organising (taking up two parts), implementing and controlling. This view of management as a cyclical process is explained below. Although the plan of the book suggests a route backwards and forwards through the parts, the book can be used in other ways. Each chapter, designed as a sandwich of text between two relevant case studies, can be studied on its own or used for reference. Links can be made in many ways, with the index helping to plot alternative routes.

This chapter

To begin the study of the context of management, this chapter considers the following questions:

- What is management?
- What do managers do and what skills, styles and capabilities do they need?
- How do managers learn and develop?
- Why study management as a discipline? Can theories about management enhance learning and enlighten practice?
- What are people looking for when embarking on a management career?

What is management?

One explanation of management is that it is a process – the planning to monitoring cycle we mentioned above. This, however, is what engages all members of the organisation. What is the purpose of management in particular? The following definition brings out its main features:

> *Management is the process of achieving organisational objectives, within a changing environment, by balancing efficiency, effectiveness and equity, obtaining the most from limited resources, and working with and through other people.*

As can be seen, the definition has five key elements that can be explained as follows:

- *... achieving organisational objectives ...*
  An objective is a target or aim to be striven for. As we see in later chapters, individuals and organisations are more successful if they aim for outcomes that are both challenging and achievable. Targets are means by which the individual can plan and co-ordinate work with others. Through them, leaders of an organisation communicate its overall aims in order to mobilise effort. Business people involved in sport find that each domain can illuminate the other. Graham Westley, whose career with Queens Park Rangers was cut short by an injury, now heads the family business founded by his grandfather and manages

Kingstonians, a non-league club. He finds that ' ... sport's clear focus on results, both short-term in relation to the next match and long-term with regard to the season and beyond ... ' is useful in business. His experience of football encouraged him to make results more visible. In turn, this made the staff of his service company more competitive. Meanwhile, business experience helped in establishing commercial targets for the football club.[2]

Comparing the two schools in the opening case makes it clear that matching targets to the ability of each child was a significant element of the success achieved at Claremont. Doing this consistently throughout the school meant that each teacher could provide good quality learning linked to what had gone before.

■ *... within a changing environment ...*

We shall see in Chapter 3 how the changing world outside an organisation imposes new demands and problems, whether they concern shortage of raw materials, rising energy prices, new customer requirements or tougher competitive policies of rivals. A key part of the management function is to maintain an awareness of such changes and prepare responses to them. Senior managers spend a great deal of their time learning about, and interpreting, the environment. While saying that two rival organisations may face a common environment is easy, this notion of interpretation is important. The Manchester schools served similar catchment areas. Yet they interpreted and responded to the educational needs of their pupils in different ways.

■ *... balancing efficiency, effectiveness and equity ...*

Trying to achieve the three Es of the management balance, *see* Fig. 1.2, is a dilemma. Success against one criterion is often at the expense of another. Efficiency is a measure of how well resources are transformed into outputs. We are encouraged to compare results in terms of how much resource is used in producing them. We can see this among the things we buy: washing machine suppliers state the energy consumption per cycle; car manufacturers must state fuel consumption under standard test conditions; audio equipment manufacturers stress minimal distortion losses. In these cases, efficiency is being assessed by comparing an output with the use of a key resource or input. But what if the washer does not wash very well, the car is too small or the hi-fi not powerful enough? They may be very efficient but incapable of doing what we want. We have overemphasised efficiency at the expense of effectiveness.

Effectiveness, then, is an assessment of how far a stated objective is achieved. Often, a focus on 'getting the job done' is important, for example when managing a crisis. War, the ultimate crisis, requires leaders who believe in 'winning at all costs'. Even in such dire circumstances, however, good generals consider how to conserve and deploy their resources. A manager's overemphasis on effectiveness leads to a loss of efficiency in terms of wasted resources. On the other hand, too much stress on efficiency may mean that the task does not get done at all. The right balance is a management decision.

Equity is the third ingredient of the mixture of Es. This concerns the distribution of outputs among recipients. Many public sector and not-for-profit organisations place equity at the core of their objectives. In principle, hospital staff or social workers ensure that they treat all clients fairly according to their needs, no matter how well off they are. Managers in the private sector are not always so concerned with treating everyone the same, although they must not discriminate unfairly. If goods are expensive and some people cannot afford them, that is not a normally a reason to withdraw them. Yet private companies are involved with questions of equity. Many accept they must consider the interests of those affected by their activities. For instance, they must not abuse monopoly positions. Sometimes, regulators such as OFGAS strive to maintain equitable energy prices to protect the budgets of poor families. The extent of this social responsibility is a theme picked up in Chapter 6.

The blend of the three Es is a changing choice for all organisations. This is illustrated in primary schools. When controlled closely by local authorities, their mission was clear. They were expected to achieve the best results for the children in a defined district using resources, such as staff levels, set down by the authority. More recently, as management powers have been devolved to them, schools have become engaged in competition. They have abandoned the notion of clear catchment areas; schools try to avoid admitting difficult children; heads are tempted to appoint inexperienced (yet cheaper) teachers; there is competition for resources. The balance among the three Es has clearly shifted towards efficiency.

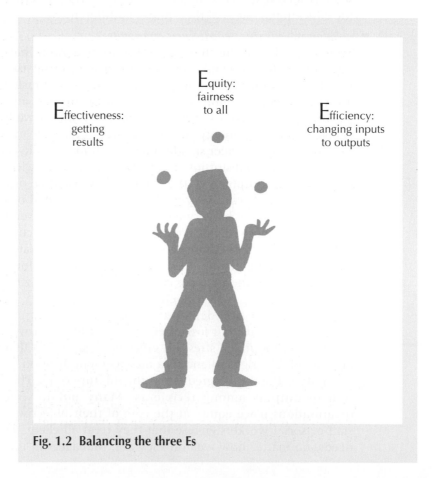

Fig. 1.2 Balancing the three Es

■ *... obtaining the most from limited resources ...*

Recognising that resources are limited is more than a question of using them most efficiently. Managers have to recognise that they have to be found and obtained. Where materials are scarce, innovating may be better. This means adapting products and processes to use fewer or alternative resources. Concerns over raw materials mean more emphasis on less wasteful processes, recycling and improved product designs. Rising labour costs, especially when compared with competitors in developing countries, press managers into finding ways of deploying staff more efficiently.

Squeezing more from resources is not the only route to success. Another way to offer value for money is to increase value. Westley's service business, for example, is ready to respond to any customer's needs irrespective of time scale and inconvenience. In addition, staff have many skills, rather than one, and can usually respond to any problem the customer faces. Service like this does not come cheap but is much appreciated. The business increased its sales from £1 million to £20 million in the six years to 1997, while the number of staff rose from 50 to 700.[3]

■ *... with and through other people.*

Management is primarily a social process, often defined as 'getting things done through people'. There is always a danger of presenting management as a set of techniques, such as for optimising plans or controlling production rates. Yet people put all plans into effect. In the primary school, teachers cooperate in developing the curriculum. In this way they learn about what happens in classes and departments other than their own. At the same time, they build a shared commitment to the plans which makes it easier to make them work. This is why the staff at Claremont Junior were so positive about their planning. They saw that it avoided the wasteful work incurred in a crisis. We shall find throughout the book many examples of work that require cooperation to make it happen. This takes us back to one element of the management cycle – organising. Texts on management stress this area because organising both huge enterprises and small work groups presents such difficulties yet offers so much potential.

▬ Talking about organisations ...

We noted the danger of presenting management as a set of techniques independent of the people involved. Similarly, we often talk of organisations behaving with a life of their own. A typical example is the quotation shown in Exhibit 1.1.[4]

Some experts object to discussing organisations in this way, pointing out that words such as *system*, *Scania* and *company* are abstractions. Although defined in law and vested with legal powers, organisations can only act through the behaviour of managers and members who make individual responses to, say, environmental stimuli or instructions received from others. Extending the argument, the same experts say that the idea of the 'interests of the organisation' is a falsehood. What is really meant are the interests of whichever individual, group or coalition happens to wield power.

Exhibit 1.1 Organised behaviour

'Scania is aiming to achieve an entirely integrated design and production process in its core European and Latin American manufacturing operations. When a $300 million investment programme under way in Latin America is complete, the result should be a "global truck" – identical vehicles and components that can be sold and serviced in most world markets, excluding the United States.

'The system, based on maximising the standardisation of parts, has enabled Scania to produce trucks with the smallest number of components of any in the industry. It has also been the key to the company's record – until a recent profits collapse – as the world's most profitable maker of heavy trucks.'

Reification

So, talking of an organisation 'investing in Latin America' or 'standardising components' is reification. This means giving a reality to abstract notions that they do not possess. In this argument, organisational behaviour can be neither more nor different to the collection of members' actions. This is what Margaret Thatcher meant in her famous remark, 'There is no such thing as Society. There are individual men and women and there are families.'[5]

There is, however, a counter-argument. Speaking of the attributes and behaviour of organisations is a useful way to summarise observations, make comparisons, and develop new ideas and theories. We could hardly make progress if we ruled offside any discussion of organisations in general, or of named ones, such as the BBC or European Commission. Furthermore, there is some sense in which organisations act as wholes. As we see in Chapter 4, the notion of collectivity is expressed in culture. A little like bees in a hive, individuals feel bonded through sharing common values and ways of doing things. The fact that they work *together* shows that organisations have meaning. Studying the behaviour of wholes, known as *holism,* is a feature of systems thinking outlined in Chapter 2.

Organisations, like systems, tend to be nested. That is, within a large one we find smaller ones, and, within each of those, there may be smaller ones still. Curiously, Thatcher's remark allowed one level, the family, yet not another, society. Convention has it that levels are linked in a hierarchy with managers as bosses and subordinates lower down. This, however, is but one way of arranging relationships. For example, many have noted the advantages to be gained from subcontracting, the pattern that tends to prevail on building sites. Now, new organisational forms are emerging to try to reap these advantages. One example is Powerscreen, an engineering company based in Northern Ireland, detailed in Exhibit 1.2.[6]

Talking about the cells at Powerscreen, and comparing the performance of conventional and networked organisations, is a practical short cut. It would be tedious and pedantic continually to refer to individuals acting together when we really mean the workgroup. Yet we must bear in mind that organisations do nothing without the action of people. The role of managers is to focus and direct that effort.

Exhibit 1.2 A company as a network of cells

Fewer than half of Powerscreen's 2500 workers are on the company's payroll. Independent teams provide the labour while the company supplies the space, machinery and components. Each work group of between 10 and 20 people is a registered business. The groups specialise in tasks such as welding, fitting or painting. Each year, the two sides agree prices for work, standards for quality and scrap. Group leaders arrange work schedules after the weekly production meeting. They are also responsible for tasks from catering to bookkeeping. The latter task is subcontracted to an accountant who handles the payroll calculations, including arrangements for tax payments, for a weekly fee of 25 pence per person.

Two of Powerscreen's subsidiaries make specialist tractors in cooperation with John Deere, the giant United States manufacturer of farm equipment. The plant in Northern Ireland, where 130 workers are arranged in nine teams, shows 28 per cent lower labour costs than its sister in Gloucestershire which does not use cells. Managers can also be sure in advance of the labour costs per built engine.

Managerial roles

Besides studying a process, another way to examine management is to find out what managers do. It turns out they do a variety of activities that we call roles. One study that has become well known was carried out by Mintzberg in the 1960s. He was concerned that 'classical' descriptions of management in terms of functions did not correspond to what happened in practice. So while we might *think* of management as the ordered sequence of planning, organising, doing and controlling, it seemed to him to be much more interactive and complex than this. So Mintzberg shadowed managers, keeping detailed records of what they did. From the results, he identified ten roles that most managers appeared to occupy from time to time.[7] Grouped into three classes, the roles are set out in Fig. 1.3.

- *Interpersonal roles*
  Most people in organisations engage in much interpersonal contact. When acting as manager, a person plays three identifiable parts – figurehead, leader and connecter.

- *Informational roles*
  All managers act as focal points for information. Through it they enhance their understanding of the organisation and the environment. As nerve centres and disseminators, they assist their staff to achieve their objectives. They are frequently nominated as speakers ('spokespersons') to provide and control information flows to outsiders.

- *Decisional roles*
  Managers are engaged both in change and 'running the business'. For the former, they act as entrepreneurs, stimulating and pushing through change. As we shall see in Chapter 8, this role is often called *intrapreneur*. When running the business, they fill roles of disturbance handler, resource allocator and negotiator.

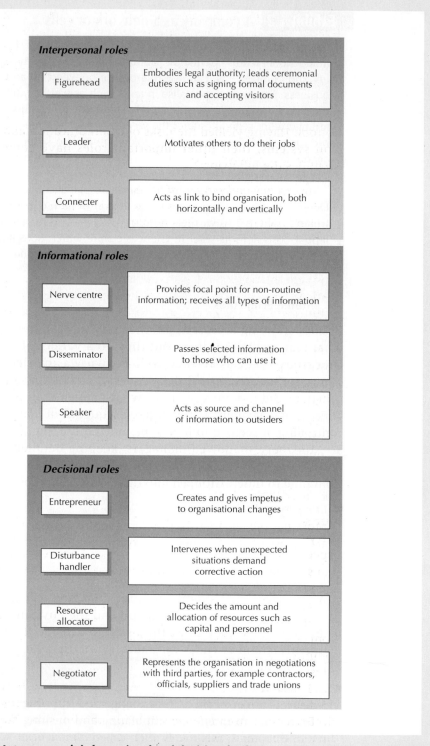

Fig. 1.3 Interpersonal, informational and decisional roles

In his list, Mintzberg generalises about all managers, especially those near the top who formed the subjects of his research. Others have narrowed the perspective to look at the roles of those carrying out named functions, such as Human Resource Management or Marketing, or at different levels. Middle managers are a group that have come under scrutiny. For instance, enthusiasts for 'downsizing' as a cost-cutting measure during recession subsequently found that removing middle managers left organisations lacking an often critical resource. Middle managers, it turned out, did rather more than link decisions at the top with actions at the bottom. Having yielded the tasks of communication and co-ordination to information systems, their other important roles have come to the fore. Dauphinais identifies the following:[8]

■ *Creators and implementors of strategy*
These are quick responses to developments within the framework of organisational goals. Middle managers gain early knowledge of internal problems and shifts in the marketplace.

■ *Influencers*
Middle managers' roles are at junctions of up and down and sideways communication. Their core responsibilities require them to manage key tasks or functions yet their position enables them to influence people above, below and at the same level.

■ *Key sources of stability*
Although they may resist needed change, middle managers can use their experience to consolidate and integrate the improvements that change may bring.

■ *Drivers of continual change*
As we shall see in later chapters, project and team work have grown to match the need for change. Middle managers largely participate in, and control the outcomes of, such activities.

Management styles

Our second perspective on the nature of management examines how managers carry out their jobs. This is the area of management style, often called the 'softer' aspect of the job. It contrasts the 'harder' facet concerned with formal structures and systems. Pitcher identified three stereotypes that can be used to describe managers. Figure 1.4 shows their characteristics.[9]

Looking at managerial styles yields important insights into how people behave in organisations. For instance, Pitcher found that conflict arises in work teams, not from clashes of ideas, but from differences in character. The three types can hardly communicate with each other. They perceive the world differently, ask different questions and, therefore, hear different answers. Looking across the lists in Fig. 1.4, we can see why. When serious encounters funny it thinks: 'Irresponsible, childish'. When a cerebral technocrat meets an intuitive artist, there is an image of, 'Dreamer, not of this world'. When the wise and humane artisan comes across the intensely analytical technocrat, it perceives a brain without a heart.

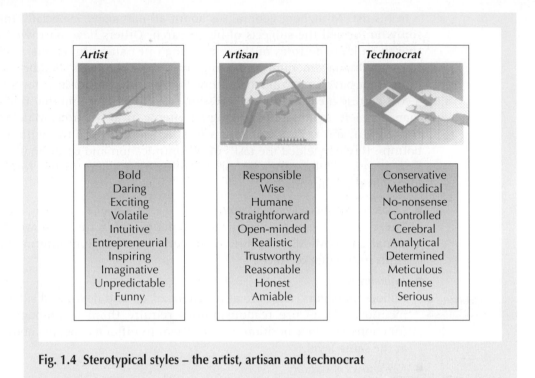

Fig. 1.4 Sterotypical styles – the artist, artisan and technocrat

The rise of the technocrat

Pitcher rues the advance of the technocrat in modern corporations. Nowadays many people explain their ideas of the ideal manager with the terms listed in the third column of Fig. 1.4. In effect, being a technocrat has become the desired state; it has become *the* definition of management. Following this trend, there are consequences including the way managers are selected, trained and promoted and the design of courses in business schools. The development of the technocrat is particularly noticeable in France, *see* Exhibit 1.3.[10] Yet, as we argue later in the book, organisations need a rich mixture of people if they are to succeed. To squeeze out the artist and ignore the artisan would only impoverish them.

There is another lesson in Pitcher's work. Setting out stereotypes (often referred to as *ideal-types*), is a common practice in behavioural science. If you objected that many people display mixed characteristics, you would be right. Experts recognise this but use the ideal-types to set up scales to compare one person or group with another. Therefore, expecting managers to display a mix of all three features, we can say that people are 'more technocratic' or 'more artistic' in their styles. As with many aspects of management, it pays to read and listen with such ideas in mind. The extracts quoted in Exhibit 1.4 suggest the three types at work. They also show how managers mix it, for the first and third are taken from the same chief executive's report.[11] Furthermore, in the second, we see the head of IBM as artist, using imagery and rhetorical tricks to appeal to a wide audience from investors to employees. Yet the rest of his speech, not included here, makes sufficient references to dollars, margins, percentages and the like to satisfy any meticulous analyst.[12]

Exhibit 1.3 Sustaining technocracy in France

Many authors have noted national differences, not only in management practice but also in the way people perceive the role of manager. In France, the development of senior managers begins in the specialist schools. Management is a state of mind. It also means identification with a particular group – the French managerial class. Being a member of the *cadre* often means graduation from one of the thirty or so *grandes écoles*, especially *l'École Polytechnique (l'X) or l'École Nationale d'Administration (ÉNA)*. One study found that, of the 100 chief executives in France, 36 came from l'X or ÉNA. Their graduates also enter government, either as civil servants or, eventually, as ministers.

Unlike Anglo-Saxons, the French do not see management as centred on communication and interpersonal skills. Drive and initiative are not stressed. They prefer analysis of problems, handling ideas and evaluating solutions.

Exhibit 1.4 Language and content reveal style

The technocrat

' ... Global in Hungary in 1994 signalled our intention to expand into Central Europe. We believe that there are good prospects for growth in this region, where there has been very little investment in retailing and distribution.

The technocrat uses analysis to justify what has been happening. Growth prospects and previous lack of investment justify the policy.

' ... we invested £8m in Savia ... in southern Poland ... we [are] to buy the two retailing businesses of the US retailer, Kmart in the Czech Republic and Slovakia ... We will then be operating in four countries in Central Europe which form a coherent geographical region. This will give us advantages as we develop the supply chain and other aspects of the business.

The investments look sensible and are grouped to build a network. This matches both conventional expectations of what supermarkets should do and the declared strategy.

'In accordance with our strategy of developing a European retailing business, with Kmart, we will have invested £340m in France and Central Europe. We expect to invest further in the future.'[11]

The artist

'But I believe that we have made enormous progress over the past four years – in part because of the grit and determination and talent and teamwork of IBM employees, and because we set a strategic direction for the company that was right for us, right for our industry, and, most importantly, right for our customers. Information technology will revolutionise every institution in our society – government, schools, post offices, libraries and, of course, every form of commercial enterprise ... [It will happen] only when industry stops worshipping technology for its own sake and starts focusing on real value for its customers..'[12]

The artist plays down technical detail in favour of imagery such as 'grit and determination', and strong persuasion. Note how 'right for ... ' appears thrice.

The messages about the future are vague, recognising that it is unknowable, especially in this industry.

The artisan

'We have worked more closely than ever with our customers, suppliers, and staff this year to provide better quality products, better value for money, improved customer service and more attractive stores ... a very satisfactory performance, which has strengthened our already strong trading base.

'Competition continued to be fierce throughout the year. Price continues to be at the forefront of the customer's mind and to be one of the key determinants of where people choose to shop. To meet their expectations, we have continued to keep prices low across the board and in two important areas, bakery and produce, we introduced new initiatives to significantly reduce prices.'[11]

The craft tradition is conservative, rooted in extensions of what is known. Tesco has succeeded through its policies of steady improvement in value, opening stores and so on. Note the use of 'continued' in the second paragraph.

Different cultures

Setting up scales and placing different managers (or groups of managers) on them is a useful way of unravelling questions of why managers behave so differently. Thinking in terms of artist, artisan and technocrat may yield useful insights when comparing Anglo-Saxon and French styles. Yet there is a trap. The scales have been developed from research carried out in the West, in this case French Canada. Take the case of Japan. Exhibit 1.5 draws on work by Morikawa, a Japanese economic historian.[13] After a first read, we may conclude that, compared with Europeans, Japanese managers are less the technocrat and more the artisan. Yet such notions may have no meaning in that country. We are using a theory whose applicability is untested. The most important differences may arise from other attributes – such as traditions of group loyalty. The question of checking theories adequately is considered later.

■ Management abilities

Our last perspective on what management is examines what managers should be capable of. Taking up the definition of management given earlier in the chapter, we see that those who succeed get things done, either alone or, more often,

Exhibit 1.5 The rise of the Japanese managerial enterprise

Large managerial enterprises emerged in Japan in the 1930s. After the war, they were critical in reconstruction and achieved rapid economic growth. In contrast to the former *zaibatsu*, diversified family-owned companies, the new enterprises were run by salaried managers promoted from within. They had close and trusting relationships with the people in their businesses, having a particular understanding of the capabilities of their engineers. In the process of transplanting and improving leading-edge production methods, this was vital.

through and with others. Bearing this in mind, Eccles and Nohria suggested that what distinguishes good managers is their ability to take 'robust action.'[14] It means the ability to fulfil management roles under pressure and when situations are unclear. There are seven features:

■ *Acting under uncertainty*
  Rarely able to wait for full information, managers have to withstand uncertainty and ambiguity. This does not mean taking blind guesses. Instead, it requires managers to recognise and cope with the gaps in their knowledge.

■ *Preserving flexibility*
  Keeping one's options open does not show a lack of commitment but ensures that there is room left for further change and decision. Actions should increase the options available to a decision maker, not reduce them.

■ *Political awareness*
  Since the actions of one interact with those of others, a good manager will be aware of their agendas. This does not imply rivalrous behaviour with destructive effects. Politics can be seen in a positive light. Constructive conflict, where parties recognise different interests yet are committed to find solutions that benefit both, is a healthy process.

■ *Timing*
  Having a sense of timing is important to success. This applies as much to strategic decisions, for example entering new markets neither too early nor too late, as to scheduling daily activities. In the role of speaker, a manager may have to announce news to several people and groups. Deciding the sequence can affect the way they receive the message.

■ *Judgement*
  Much information received by managers is qualitative. Interpreting it involves subtle judgement as opposed to formal calculation. The technocrat may abhor the idea, arguing that using judgement disguises incompetence in handling data. The artisan, on the other hand, argues that judgement grows from experience. Formal data can rarely do more than map choices and rule out seriously unfavourable options.

■ *Using rhetoric effectively*
  As we shall see in Chapter 18, communication in organisations is not simply a question of sharing information. For several reasons, including practicality and confidentiality, managers cannot share all information about decisions with all who are affected. Therefore, they have both to inform others of decisions and persuade them that they are justified. Using appropriate rhetorical skills, *see* Exhibit 1.6,[15] helps in persuasion and builds flexibility for the next action.

■ *Running multiple agendas*
  Good managers can link actions from several agendas. Rather than focus on one task at once, keeping 'several balls in the air' enables a good manager to apply a sense of timing to take opportunities. This then allows several actions to fall into place simultaneously.

Exhibit 1.6 Understanding the world through talking about it

Rhetoric is concerned with how language is used to influence the ways people think and act. We often use the term to mean trickery, as in empty-, mere-, inflammatory- or powerful rhetoric. Scholars, however, are concerned with what happens, not whether it is good or bad.

' ... management has a lot to do with the use of language, both in the sense of how language is used *in* organisations and in the sense it is used in ways – such as business books and journalism – that *span* organisations ... In a nutshell, managers live in a rhetorical universe – a universe where language is constantly used not only to communicate but also to *persuade*, even to *create*.'

Studying management

The study of management involves an interplay between theory and practice. Yet the mixture makes many students uneasy, especially if they already have experience of being a manager. 'After all, it's practical, not theoretical,' one might say, 'And isn't it all applied common sense?' In reply, we can consider two aspects of these concerns – the nature of theory and the seemingly obvious nature of management ideas.

The value of theory

To talk about theory and practice suggests a separation of the two that does not really exist. Every successful practical person, from farmer to film maker or painter to politician, cannot proceed without a framework of theory. Sometimes this is explicit – the things they learn when being trained – while other times they develop the theory intuitively. We all build on experience and, as we advance, we consolidate it into a personal theory of our world. This helps us to understand the world without having to remember the details of every case.

The trouble is that some of it can be wrong. If we never take the trouble to learn from others, we will believe the earth is flat. Take the tale of the inductivist turkey, originally told by Bertrand Russell, shown in Exhibit 1.7. The turkey in the story

---

Exhibit 1.7 Turkey talk

Feeding on the first morning was at 9. A cautious inductivist, the turkey drew no conclusion. It collected data and studied variables. At the weekend or in the week, on warm days or cold, whether rain or shine, feeding occurred at 9. Satisfied at last, the turkey drew the inductive inference, 'They always feed me at 9.'

Then came 24 December. The turkey was no more. With true premises and inductive inference, it had reached the wrong conclusion.

---

asked the wrong question. Just as we often do from our limited perspective, it asked the narrow, 'When does feeding happen?' instead of the broad, 'Why does feeding happen?' If the turkey had shared its theories with others long since on the dinner table, it may have thought again.

We can draw out two broad points about good theory and the way it is formed. First, a good theory makes a proposition, builds on observations, explains something and is *shared*. Only by presenting our theories of the world, and comparing them with others, do we develop useful, robust ones that work. Second, there is nothing wrong with induction. Billsberry explains that the theories we meet in management books are all inductivist in nature.[16] For example, we can take the well-known theory of motivation developed by Herzberg, explained in Chapter 16. Adding to existing knowledge, it allowed him to explain the satisfaction of workers. Having shared the ideas, work by others has strengthened the theory so we know it can be applied in many cases. Yet we can never prove it to be right for all cases. Christmas Eve may come.

So how could we, as managers, use theories such as Herzberg's? The answer is to do so cautiously. Every situation is unique. So avoid the trap of blindly applying a theory developed in one set of circumstances to another. We must understand the theory, understand our circumstances, and check that the theory can be applied. Variations require us to take a critical view. This is not to praise one and rubbish another, but to learn to compare theories and situations to see where they can come together. That is why a good management course blends theory and practice.

Description and prescription

Another way to look at theory is to compare two types, descriptive and prescriptive:

- Descriptive theories refer to the world as it is. Based on observations, they may say things such as, 'Multinational enterprises usually have decentralised personnel functions'.

- Prescriptive theories make statements about the world as it ought to be. They may say things such as, 'Multinational enterprises should decentralise their personnel functions'.

While you may think that the statements amount to the same in practice, the differences are important. The former makes no judgement and recognises that there is never a best way that applies in all cases. The latter tells all organisations in a particular category what is best. Many managers prefer prescription. Would it not help if they could be told what to do? – 'Have you a problem with arrangements in your Personnel Department? Then reach for the *Universal Guide to Personnel Management*.'

Although what are sometimes called 'airport books' offer guidance like this, Mintzberg and colleagues warn against it. To them, ' ... no prescription works for all organisations. Even when a prescription seems effective in some context, it requires a sophisticated understanding of exactly what the context is and how it functions. ... one cannot decide reliably what should be done in a system as complicated as a contemporary organisation without a genuine understanding of how that organisation really works'.[17] They then point out that a science student is interested in how a molecule works, not in knowing how it *ought* to work. Why should a management student want something so different?

In the main, the theories presented in this book are of the descriptive type. Along the way, however, there are examples of the prescriptive, for example in Chapter 19. Some operations planning processes are so well established that it is sensible to say, 'This is the way things should be done'. Even in such cases, however, we should follow the warning given above. Always check that a theory does apply before applying it!

Are management ideas obvious?

The comment that statements about management are obvious often follows a reading of research studies. For example, the conclusions of Chapter 16 on motivation may seem trite: 'People work better if the work is interesting'; 'They are driven to satisfy meaningful goals'; or 'People's perceptions of a reward are influenced by their prior experience'. Aren't these statements so self-evident that going through lengthy studies to arrive at them is a waste of time? To examine this problem, we can draw on a neat argument presented by Vecchio, given in Exhibit 1.8.[18]

Illusions

Through giving erroneous, yet plausible, results, Vecchio cleverly destroys the idea that behavioural phenomena are obvious. How does this confusion happen? It comes from being human. When someone tells us something about behaviour, we often respond with a defensive reaction similar to, 'Naturally, I could have guessed that'. It is common in daily life. We hear, 'June and Jack are getting a divorce', 'Telecom shares have fallen again', or 'The washing machine's broken'. We reply, 'I knew it couldn't last'. This is the advantage of hindsight. Hindsight is logical. Survival is helped by persuading ourselves that we are so much in control of our surroundings.

As humans, we are clever at rationalising, that is building *post hoc* explanations. Buckley and Chapman draw on social anthropology which reveals how groups 'reorganise' their history. They attribute present successes to forethought in the past. It is common among managers, who make random events seem planned or recast good luck as strategic thinking.[19] Eccles and Nohria showed how, in one company, two contrasting explanations of the world coexisted. Rational statements about the past demonstrated how the company was well run while managers faced the problem of coping with the chaos of the moment and the future, *see* Exhibit 1.9.[20] Notwithstanding this justification, however, hindsight is delusion. How can we avoid it? We must rely not on intuition but on the application of sound theory and healthy skepticism.

Mintzberg's myths: what management is not

The relevance of delusion to management becomes clearer when we realise how the subject is full of myths. Summarising many studies including his own, Mintzberg points to four widely held notions of managerial work that do not withstand scrutiny.[21]

Exhibit 1.8 Obvious ... isn't it?

During the Second World War, the research branch of the United States War Department conducted several studies on soldiers' attitudes, morale and feelings of frustration. In total, some 600 000 servicemen were interviewed. So extensive were the results that the final summary, which appeared in 1949, occupied four volumes. On publication, the report was much criticised in the popular press. One charge dwelt on the obvious nature of the findings, citing the conclusion that many soldiers were unhappy during the war. Questions were raised over whether such surveys were justified.

One review listed typical findings. How novel do you find the following results? And would you make comments similar to those on the right?

Results

1. During the fighting, servicemen were more desirous of returning home than they were after the fall of Germany.

2. Soldiers from the southern states stood the tropical climate of the south Pacific better than northerners.

3. Less well educated men adjusted better to army life than did the better educated. This was especially shown by the incidence of minor psychological disorders.

4. Black soldiers from the South preferred to serve under white officers also from the South than under northerners.

5. Those who had been brought up in rural areas adjusted better to army life than those from urban areas.

Comments

1. Would anyone be surprised to find that soldiers wanted to avoid being killed?

2. This could be easily predicted by differences in upbringing and climate.

3. Of course, the army requires obedience and unquestioning acceptance in its harsh daily life. Low intelligence aids adjustment.

4. Naturally, under the rigid social divisions of the South, both parties would know where they stood.

5. Clearly, rural recruits would have experienced a rougher life, including sleeping in the open.

Two points follow. First, if we go along with the comments, we are agreeing with the 1949 critics. The results were obvious and the whole enterprise a waste of time. Second, if this is the basic data to be used for developing principles in, say, how to manage an army in the field, then normal officers already have enough expertise to go ahead.

The snag is these statements are precisely the opposite of the published findings. These showed that: soldiers preferred to remain abroad while the war was on but were most anxious to return once it had ended; southerners were no better at adjusting to the heat of the South Pacific than were northerners; poorly educated men found adjustment more difficult, and so on. In each case, however, we can immediately reach for new explanations. For instance: patriotism and commitment were motivators during the war, but, once it was over, homesickness was the strong emotion; urban life, with its pressure on personal space and freedom was a better preparation for being in the army than was a rural upbringing. Had we listed these true results and comments first, we would also have said they were obvious.

| Exhibit 1.9 | Making sense of the past |

'[Planning] gave people in the company a framework for thinking about the activities they were engaged in, and a sense of mastery over these activities. In essence ... it allowed people to get a grasp on an uncertain and constantly changing environment.

'What was more important, however, was that this rhetoric of rationality did *not* interfere with the way managers acted. The plans were sufficiently flexible ... not constraining ... guidelines to action rather than as objective descriptions of the company's reality.'

■ *Managers engage in reflective, systematic planning*
The work pace for all is unrelenting. In the European Union, about a quarter take work home several times a week with another third staying behind after normal hours. In Japan, annual hours seem stuck at around 2100; working late has been a traditional way of displaying loyalty to boss and company.[22] During the working day, one study found half of managers' activities lasted less than nine minutes. Another reported working for half an hour without interruption happened only every other day. 'Free' time is immediately grabbed by subordinates. For supervisors, one study found an average of 48 seconds per encounter. Managers do plan but do so implicitly, during the framework of daily work; it is no wonder that many plans stay in their heads.

■ *Managers have few regular duties to perform*
Figure 1.3 includes some roles, such as figurehead, connecter, nerve centre and negotiator that many managers perform routinely. A chief executive is expected to receive dignitaries, officiate at Christmas parties and hand out retirement watches. Much external, 'soft' information only comes to them because of their access to business and social networks. To support the work of others, they must pass it on regularly. These are all regular duties.

■ *Senior managers need an assembly of information best provided by a formal information system*
Typical results show that managers spend between 66 and 80 per cent of their time in oral communication. Most managers skim periodicals and do not reply to all correspondence. Only about one sixth of the post is important. Senders know this so may send e-mail, follow with a letter and ring to check it has arrived! Another research result is that managers cherish gossip, hearsay and speculation. Through building broad pictures, they use it to anticipate the behaviour of others. Unfortunately, the extensive use of verbal, informal information makes delegation of many tasks difficult. There is no dossier of data ready to be passed to subordinates.

All in all, most managers see written material as a burden. It is, however, worth noting that the French seem to be an exception. In France there is emphasis given on written communication using correct and elegant language.[23]

■ *Management is a science and a profession, or, if not, it is rapidly becoming one*
Observations of managers at work show this to be untrue. True they make decisions *about* new technology or about the application of science to new products.

Yet the way they make decisions is complex, fragmented, often superficial and rarely recorded or followed up.

Sources of myth

How do myths like these grow? Ignorance is a critical factor. Adopting the general view of management as applied common sense means that many organisations do not spend on anything but limited management training. One report on United Kingdom graduate recruitment (not necessarily for management positions) showed that employers look for people with personal and interactive attributes set out in Exhibit 1.10.[24] Rarely do such studies mention the advantages of learning about management, although more recent reports have begun to call for awareness of enterprise. Additionally, many employers prefer their managers to learn through specific on-the-job training and in-company courses rather than through broad studies of the management discipline. This further restrains any interest in management as an object of serious study. Essentially uneducated, with fewer than 20 per cent in the United Kingdom having degrees,[25] managers are prey to the fad, the quick fix and the myth.

Exhibit 1.10 Employers' preferred attributes of graduates

Personal attributes

- Intellect – being able to analyse, criticise and synthesise and think things through.
- Knowledge – including the ability to acquire it.
- Willingness to learn throughout life.
- Flexibility and adaptability.
- Self-regulation – discipline, time-keeping, coping with stress, juggling priorities.
- Motivation – self-starting, tenacity, determination, finishing.
- Self-assurance – self-confidence, self-awareness, self-belief, self-sufficiency, self-direction and self-promotion.

Interactive attributes

- Communication – formal and informal, with all types of people, using information technology.
- Team working – including being in more than one team, adjusting roles as needed.
- Using interpersonal skills to share ideas, influence people and interact with outsiders.

Becoming a successful manager

Management is a complex job. It is no surprise to find that managers come from many backgrounds and display a wide range of personal attributes and abilities. Given the complexities of theory and the difficulties of accumulating experience, we may ask how managers reach their positions. The answer is that they come by many routes.

■ The school of hard knocks

Learning from experience is important, whether one has 'risen from the ranks' or entered a fast track training scheme after graduation. Unfortunately, such experience can be bruising to the individual and wasteful for the organisation. Snell's study among United Kingdom managers identified what they had found to be 'hard knocks'. We list examples in Exhibit 1.11.[26] Although these traumas meant that managers learned to avoid the same errors twice, they involved unnecessary psychological distress. Consequently, Snell argued for better learning practices both on and off the job.

■ Seeing oneself as a manager

The many abilities required of a manager present serious challenges. Whether one chooses to take them on depends on what Schein calls a 'career anchor'.[27] This is the self-concept we all have, consisting of three elements: talents and abilities that we perceive; our basic values; and, most important, an evolving set of needs and motives related to our career. Although the anchor develops and changes with experience, we can also see it as a stabilising element. It represents the values and motives that we will not give up when making a career choice.

Schein reports how research in the United States of the 1970s and 1980s identified eight categories of career anchors. Figure 1.5 shows how beliefs about general management or technical competence dominate them.

More recently, shifts in career anchors have been noted. For example, changes in employment practices have caused problems for those anchored in security. On

---

Exhibit 1.11   Classes at the school of hard knocks

- Making a big mistake;
- Becoming overstretched by a difficult task;
- Feeling threatened;
- Finding oneself stuck in an impasse or dilemma;
- Being treated unjustly at work;
- Losing out to another;
- Being attacked personally.

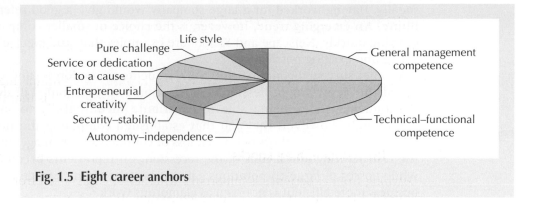

Fig. 1.5 Eight career anchors

the other hand, individuals seeking autonomy will be more favoured. There has been a rise in the 'life style' group as more graduates see their careers as part of a wider 'system of life'. Some look to follow two or more careers simultaneously while others see the possibilities of switching at an appropriate time. An important point with all anchors is that we are usually unaware of them until confronted by a career decision such as, 'Shall I move home for a job with more money or stay in my present occupation, knowing that it fulfils my need for autonomy?'

Students have their career anchors changed by their university experience. This is clear among those at business school, influenced by learning about companies covered in the curriculum. Universum, a leading Swedish recruitment consultancy, conducts an annual study of final year students at 36 Western European business schools.[28] When asked about first employers, graduates stressed social aspects of their careers, *see* Fig. 1.6. They looked for task variety, interesting colleagues and international experience. Multinationals, especially the leading consulting and accounting firms, such as McKinsey and Arthur Andersen, were favoured by more than half. They offered careers with opportunities to grow per-

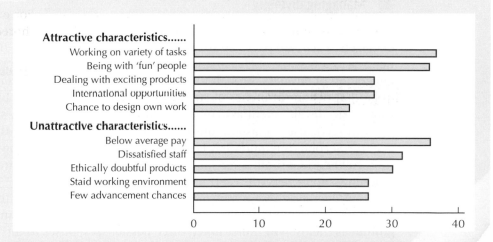

Fig. 1.6 First employers – attractive and unattractive characteristics

sonally. Having worked for a large company would give a good reference for the future. An emerging trend, however, is the choice of smaller companies that are growing quickly. Netscape and Yahoo! are examples that students feel would offer varied and exciting possibilities.

Another survey, this time of 140 MBA students at London Business School, also noted the desire for professional satisfaction and personal skill development. Respondents added being able to contribute meaningfully to society. Overwhelmingly, however, they felt that established companies did not offer such opportunities. The authors point to a loss of confidence in management, following the restructuring and layoffs of the recession. Entrepreneurs become cult heroes while bosses of large corporations gain, at best, grudging recognition. Making a business more efficient is not seen as glamorous work.[29]

Cultural differences

As with other aspects of management, we must beware of assuming that career anchors and attitudes are universal. For instance, respondents to a Universum study of graduates from eight East European business schools placed competitive salary much more highly than their counterparts in the West. Further they were interested in specialisation, while Westerners wanted to be generalists. They did not favour careers with consulting firms.[30]

Further afield, becoming a top manager in Japan is very different from the experience of most Europeans. Storey and colleagues compared the origins and development of managers in the United Kingdom and Japan.[31] Firms in the former are not alone in a 'sink or swim' attitude to early managerial development and stick to the notion that the individual is responsible for his or her career. In Japan, employers accept more responsibility for development and direction of careers. Being a successful European manager probably means gathering a wide range of role experiences, frequently with different employers. The convention in Japan is to change roles less often and stay with the same organisation for life.

■ Managing diversity

Coping with cultural differences has become one of the most difficult problems for managers. There are two reasons. First, as explained in Chapter 5, the world is experiencing a new wave of globalisation. This means not only more trade but increasing integration of business through the growth of the multinational corporation. It used to be that distant branches of such enterprises were managed by expatriates on short-term development assignments. Now, leading companies, such as Unilever, want to recognise the aspirations of all their staff and draw on the global pool of talent.[32] Second, migration has created significant minority groups in many countries. At the same time, some long settled minorities, whose aspirations have been until now suppressed, are asserting their rights to being different.

Taken together, these trends mean that managers are faced with an increasingly diverse workforce. Staff and colleagues do not come from the same cultural background as themselves. Adler noted three possible responses to this pressure:[33]

- *Parochial*

  This is the most common response, captured by the phrase. 'Our way is the only way'. The organisation does not recognise differences and therefore makes no provision. Any problems that occur are attributed to other causes.

- *Ethnocentric*

  Here, 'Our way is the best way'. Managers recognise diversity but try to min-imise its effects by maintaining a single corporate culture. Usually this means domination by people from the original country. Others are admitted provided they accept this ascendancy.

- *Synergistic*

  The least common of the three, this organisation trains its managers to recog-nise cultural differences and use diversity to advantage. The idea is to combine the best.

This classification can explain the different attitudes between West and East European graduates. Accepting the increasingly diverse nature of the people they will work with, Westerners stress the importance of some international experience in the development of their careers. In the East, attitudes are more parochial. Aspirations are limited to gaining good positions in local firms or local branches of multinationals. There is, therefore, more emphasis on salary and specialised com-petence with little mention of international experience.

Conclusion: studying management, becoming a manager

We began by showing that management is important. The difference between good and failing schools, or between successful and ordinary companies, is often due to relative advantages beyond their control. Schools have different catchment areas; companies face forces such as governments about which they can do little. Having said that, however, given reasonable parity of conditions, the best man-aged organisation will succeed.

To understand what management is, it is tempting to rely on a definition. Ours develops from the idea of 'getting things done through people' to clarify aspects such as the 'things'. Yet to define management in this way is only to look at it from one angle. Other approaches find clues by looking at how managers behave. Studying roles, styles, capabilities and what managers do, or do not do, also helps us to understand.

We are not just in the business of understanding. Studying management is also about seeing ourselves as managers and improving our chances of becoming a suc-cessful one. While many managers report that they learn most of their skills at the school of hard knocks, studying the discipline has its place. It helps us avoid the worst mistakes and enhances our rate of learning at that hard school. Theory and practice are complementary. Good theory is practical. It helps us look ahead and avoid or mitigate errors. At the same time, practice develops theory. It allows test-ing and refinement and a deeper understanding of how it can be used. Becoming a successful manager involves personally integrating the two.

Diversity means that managers have to become more sensitive to cultures other than their own. We noted how graduates are increasingly valuing international experience. Not only must they understand different behaviour, but they should recognise the contrasting ways different people think about management. In other words, both practice and theory are grounded in culture.

Quick check up *Can you ...*

- Define management;
- Outline the purpose of objectives;
- Name the three Es of the management balance;
- Define reification;
- List Mintzberg's managerial roles;
- List Dauphinais' roles of middle managers;
- Name Pitcher's three management styles;

- Distinguish descriptive and prescriptive theories;
- Refute Mintzberg's four management myths;
- Explain career anchors and how they develop;
- Show why managing diversity is becoming more important.

Questions

Chapter review

1.1 Summarise Pitcher's managerial styles, illustrating each with your own examples.

1.2 Define management, giving an example for each phase of the definition.

1.3 Do you agree with Lewin's statement that there is nothing so practical as a good theory?[34]

1.4 Is management just applied common sense?

Application

1.5 From your knowledge of head teachers in schools, assess how good they were in occupying Mintzberg's roles.

1.6 Given that, in a management career, you will occupy each of Mintzberg's managerial roles, which do you think you will be good at and which others are your weak points? Explain the implications of your analysis for career choice.

Investigation

1.7 Carry out a 'semi-structured' interview with a practising manager to test Mintzberg's myths. The idea is to use his categories to find out how the manager feels about the job yet not to lead the interviewee into giving the answers you may appear to want.

1.8 Conduct interviews with a few fellow students to investigate their career anchors and preferences. Start by listing names of favoured employers before trying to establish why they have been chosen

Winning formula[35]

Formula One has become one of the most slickly marketed sports, closer to brands on wheels than grease and gear boxes. Counting recordings, the claimed television audience for each of the 17 races amounts to about 3 billion in 202 countries. The industry was created by Ferrari, Fangio and Fittipaldi, Senna, Surtees and the brothers Schumacher, Hill, Hunt and Hill again. Or was it the engineers? It was none of these. The *business*, as opposed to the racing teams, has been built by Bernie Ecclestone.

Selling motorcycles, cars and property made Ecclestone a considerable sum. Then, after a crash at Brand's Hatch, he gave up his hobby of driving to buy, in 1970, the Brabham racing team. This gave him membership of FOCA (Formula One Constructors' Association) which elected him president in 1985. He used his position to transfer control of the sport from FISA to FIA (Fédération Internationale de l'Automobile). The latter, of which he is a vice-president, has rules that more closely match his views of the way the sport should be organised. Although his public persona is of a reserved man, Ecclestone is at the centre of all that happens in the sport. At the track, he spends his time behind the tinted windows of his executive coach cum mobile office known as 'The Kremlin'. He has, however, been known to use a helicopter to check the size of a crowd against the gate receipts declared by a circuit.

Ecclestone has built Formula One in two ways. First he managed to persuade the rival teams to work together in the commercial domain. Now FOCA offers each track a fixed sum in exchange for exclusive rights to advertising, gate receipts and, above all, television coverage. These are then marketed by companies controlled by Ecclestone. Teams receive money for appearances and winning races as well as from their own sponsorship deals. His second success has been based on sensing and developing the value of television coverage. Unlike the glimpses caught by track side spectators, the television audience dwells on each car as the camera follows it. Foreshortened long shots seem to slow the car down; close-ups reveal every detail. Even the smallest label on a driver's helmet is legible. Ecclestone's companies control every frame shot, including practices, pit stops and interviews.

Digital television offers even greater prospects. Not only will many viewers pay to watch races, they may even be able to switch from camera to camera to follow the perspective of their favourite. There are worries. Bans on tobacco advertising in France, Germany and the United Kingdom, currently ineffective, are being tightened. The Jordan team receives 60 per cent of its sponsorship funds from Benson and Hedges; Marlboro is said to spend £50 million. The worldwide television audience has started to fall. Typically, Ecclestone is contemplating changing the rules to make races more exciting. Shortening cars, shrinking aerofoils and requiring tyres with treads will slow the cars and ease overtaking.

Estimates of the worth of the Formula One business vary, for it is a complex network of interlinked contracts. Before a planned stock market flotation, one source suggested £2 billion with Ecclestone's share about one half. This would place him, in his late sixties, among the world's richest people. In 1996, he paid himself, as head of Formula One Promotions & Administration, a salary of £55 million. Yet his position has been challenged, notably by the European Commission. It is concerned by the close and secretive relationships among Ecclestone's companies. Granting exclusive broadcasting rights may breach competition law.

Questions

1 Case studies give you a chance to check over ideas put forward in the chapter, especially to see how they work out in practice.

   Examine the extent to which Ecclestone's activities are covered by Mintzberg's managerial roles. What does your comparison say about the man and the model?

2 Most of the cases in the book are based on real companies, people or events. You should be able to find out more from the press, journals and the Internet. See whether you can collect further information about Bernie Ecclestone to assess which managerial style he uses.

3 Another way to use a case study is to compare its subject with another. Select a 'management profile' article from a business journal or newspaper. Compare the profile with Ecclestone's, commenting on the two people's management traits.

Bibliography Billsberry, Jon (1996) *The Effective Manager* (London: Sage) extends and broadens many of the issues raised in this chapter. Leading authors Peter Drucker, Charles Handy and Henry Mintzberg have produced both popular and serious works on management that you should find in the library.

References

1. *Inspection Report: Princess Junior School*, 30 April–3 May 1996; *Inspection Report: Claremont Junior School*, 13–17 January 1997; School inspection reports for Manchester are on: http://www.open.gov.uk/ofsted/htm.pri352.htm; 'Moss Side Story', *The Economist*, 22 November 1997, 32–3
2. Westley, Graham (1997) 'It's a game of two halves', *Independent on Sunday*, 13 April.
3. *Ibid.*
4. Carnegy, Hugh (1997) 'Generic engineering: Hugh Carnegy looks at Scania's global approach to truck manufacture', *Financial Times*, 6 January.
5. Thatcher, Margaret (1993) *The Downing Street Years*, London: HarperCollins, 626.
6. Murray Brown, John (1997) 'An organism made up of many cells', *Financial Times*, 7 May.
7. Mintzberg, Henry (1971) 'Managerial work: analysis and observation', *Management Science*, October, B97–110.
8. Dauphinais, G. William (1996) 'Who's minding the middle managers?', *HR Focus*, **73** (**10**) October, 12–13
9. Pitcher, Patricia (1997) 'Artists, craftsmen and technocrats' in Mintzberg, Henry, Quinn, James Brian and Ghoshal, Sumantra, *The Strategy Process*, revised European edition, London: Prentice-Hall, 578–85.
10. Barsoux, Jean-Louis and Lawrence, Peter (1991) 'The making of a French manager', *Harvard Business Review*, **69** (**4**) July–August, 58–67.
11. Tesco plc (1997) *1996 Annual Report and Accounts*,2; http://www.tesco.co.uk/report96, 2.
12. Gerstner, Lou V. (1997) 'Address to stockholders', Annual General Meeting, Dallas, Texas, 29 April.
13. Morikawa, Hidemasa (1995) 'The role of managerial enterprise in post-war Japanese economic growth: focus on the 1950s', *Business History*, **37** (**2**) April, 32–43.
14. Eccles, Robert G. and Nohria, Nitin with Berkley, James D. (1992) *Beyond the Hype*, Boston, Mass.: Harvard Business School Press, 40–4.

15. *Ibid.*, 8.
16. Billsberry, Jon (1996) 'There's nothing so practical as a good theory: how can theory help managers become more effective?' in Billsberry, Jon (ed.) *The Effective Manager,* London: Sage, 1–5.
17. Mintzberg, Quinn and Ghoshal (1997) *op. cit.,* xi.
18. Vecchio, Robert P. (1995) *Organisational Behaviour,* Third edition, Fort Worth, Tex.: The Dryden Press, 22–3.
19. Buckley, Peter J. and Chapman, Malcolm (1996) 'Wise before the event: the creation of corporate fulfilment', *Management International Review,* **36** Special Issue, 95–110.
20. Eccles and Nohria (1992) *op. cit.,* 53.
21. Mintzberg, Henry (1997) 'The manager's job' in Mintzberg, Quinn (1997) and Ghoshal, *op. cit.,* 23–7.
22. Jack, Andrew, Rich, Motoko and Terazono, Emiko (1995) 'Daily grind of the 7 to 9 – The working week is becoming longer', *Financial Times,* 18 January, 16.
23. Barsoux and Lawrence (1991) *op. cit.*
24. Harvey, Lee, Moon, Sue and Geall, Vicki (1997) *Graduates' Work: Organisational change and students' attributes,* Centre for Research into Quality, University of Birmingham, 63–73.
25. Taylor, Robert (1995) 'Only 20 per cent of managers have degrees', *Financial Times,* 19 June, 11.
26. Snell, Robin (1989) 'Graduating from the school of hard knocks', *Journal of Management Development,* **8** (**5**), 23–30.
27. Schein, Edgar H. (1996) 'Career anchors revisited: implications for career development in the 21st century', *The Academy of Management Executive,* **10** (**4**) November, 80–8.
28. Universum International (1997) *The European Graduate Survey 1997,* http://www.universum.se/international/surveys/egs-97/
29. Ghoshal, Sumantra and Sull, Donald (1997) 'Loss of faith in managers: The brightest and best no longer aspire to a management career', *Financial Times,* 6 June, 18.
30. Universum International (1997) *op. cit.,* http://www.universum.se/international/surveys/ces-96/8.html
31. Storey, John, Edwards, Paul and Sisson, Keith (1997) *Managers in the Making: Careers, development and control in corporate Britain and Japan,* London: Sage.
32. Interview with Richard Greenhalgh, head of management development at the Anglo-Dutch company Unilever, in Jackson, Tony (1997) 'Perspective: The myth of the global executive', *Financial Times,* 8 October.
33. Adler, Nancy J. (1983) 'Organisational development in a multicultural environment', *Journal of Applied Behavioural Science,* **19** (**3**) Summer, 349–65.
34. Lewin, Kurt (1945) 'The research centre for group dynamics at Massachusetts Institute of Technology', *Sociometry,* **8**, 126–36.
35. 'Mr Formula One', *The Economist,* 15 March 1997, 92; Brierly, David and Alexander, Robert (1997) 'Formula One flotation may spin off course', *The European,* 22 May, 3; Rubin, David (1997) 'Formula One's man of mystery', *Independent on Sunday,* 21 December; Tucker, Emma and Griffiths, John (1997) 'Formula 1 TV deal could run into Brussels barrier', *Financial Times,* 23 December, 1.

The development of management ideas

Chapter objectives

When you have finished studying this chapter, you should be able to:

- justify taking a historical perspective on management ideas;

- explain the origins and key features of three strands of the classical perspective;

- show how the human relations movement grew from a combination of systematic studies, philosophy and external pressures;

- describe how operations research developed from modelling skills assisted by the invention of the computer;

- present the applications of systems as an integrating perspective that has not been fully realised;

- explain the notion of 'contingency' and how managers can reconcile approaches that focus on the universal or the particular.

The pajama game

[Scene: A sewing machinist addresses the production superintendent at the Sleep-Tite pajama factory: Illinois, USA, about 1950.]

"Trouble, why your wonderful Hines set a rate on this here elastic job so low ... Took me an hour and a quarter to get out my last bundle. Goddamn it if it isn't a crime and a shame what I put up with around this dump."

The setting of rates and the reaction by the operators is a routine you have to go over again and again, forever and ever, apparently, as long as there shall be garment plants, superintendents, sewing-machine operators, piece-rates and broken needles. You study carefully and set the rate, say 49½ cents a dozen for hemming. She says she can't make nothing on that rate. She says she's been here on the line for twenty-three years and no young squirt time-study man is going to push her around. You tell her there's a lot of factors involved (what would we do without those involved factors?), and that management wants to meet the operators half way and continue to enjoy mutual confidence for the highest production, Sleep-Tite quality, and the highest earnings based on output and ability. The operator says she can't buy no groceries on mutual confidence and is going to work at the Packing Plant unless something can be done about that rate. The other girls in the unit glare at management and exchange significant looks and talk so much about it all day that production goes off twelve dozen. You promise to analyse the situation and make an "eight-hour study" to check for any factors that might have been overlooked (or involved).

Next day the time-study man takes an all day study and finds that he forgot to allow one-half minute per hour for "grasp scissors with left hand, clip estimated two threads per dozen, return and release scissors to position on machine table", and this raises the rate 0.0015 per doz. ...

You [eventually] agree to raise the rate from 49½ cents per doz. to 50½. Two weeks later the operator is running away with the rate and making $1.33 an hour, within 17 cents of the machinist, who is the best machinist in the area and knows more about a Singer sewing machine than the Singer people.'

Introduction

The thoughts expressed by the superintendent in the opening case could have been pondered by any manager anywhere. In *The Pajama Game*,[1] Bissell captured impressions of bullying management, wily workers, chaos, breakdowns, fiddles and scams, and impossible production and sales targets. There is a sense of conflict yet also of a game, a break in the monotony of manual mass production. It is a game in which both sides cooperate, they take up roles and speak their lines, knowing always that they have to make a deal.

In the extract, we see references to 'management', an obscure power to whom the superintendent refers to justify his position. The author takes a critical view of the time-study man, adjusting arbitrarily determined rates. Yet we also are given hints of the humanity of the actors. 'Mutual confidence' is mentioned. Workers show both their pride and their artfulness, the superintendent the same. They are human beings separated by hierarchy.

In such business situations we find managers acting according to mixtures of ideas, theories and principles. How can a manager, or a student of management, make sense of it all? We each carry with us a set of attitudes and beliefs about the nature of management and organisations. These lead to generalisations and hypotheses that enable us to say, 'Such and such an action will have the following consequences.' We learned in Chapter 1 how our practical actions are tied to our theories. The two are inseparable. Yet where do these theories originate?

An important source of theory is experience, both our own and of others. We may have learnt from others through novels, plays and films as well as from informal contacts. Yet there are also those authorities who have conducted systematic studies of management. As we saw in Chapter 1, studying their work takes our understanding of management beyond the level of applied common sense. It provides a rich framework within which we can criticise and develop our own ideas and, in turn, improve our practice. In this chapter, then, we shall look at the more important strands of management theory as they have grown and interacted since the discipline first received serious attention.

A historical perspective

Studying the history of management and the development of management theory is fruitful. While not becoming engaged in studying the past for its own sake, a historical perspective helps us because:

■ it clarifies our view of the present;

■ it allows us to explain the way things are;

■ it instils a sense of causation;

■ it underlines the importance of interpretation in social science.

Studying management is like studying history in that both are processes going beyond the gathering of facts. There is interaction between the facts and the practitioner. As Carr argues, 'To enable man to understand the society of the past, and to increase his mastery over the society of the present, is the dual function of history.'[2] The history of management, combining facts and interpretation, contributes to our ability to understand, and therefore succeed, in the present. Further, in recognising how the present is a product of the past, the idea that the future is strongly influenced by current decisions also becomes embedded. This notion of causation or teleology, events being connected as a series through time, is as basic to the study of history as to the practice of management.

We must be cautious, also. All events in the past are interpreted according to current attitudes. Historical patterns may now seem logical although events were not connected at the time. Therefore, while this chapter presents a time-line covering the past hundred or so years of management thought, the selections of important trends and events and the connections that are made among them are to some extent arbitrary. In each era, scholars and practitioners have asked new questions and faced new problems and have proposed new (or recycled) approaches to their resolution. Further, there have been other ideas, authors and events whose significance we have yet to discover.

Understanding the background to current theory should not be left to historians. Management is an interdisciplinary field. It draws on the work of, among others, anthropologists, economists, engineers, geographers, information scientists, lawyers, mathematicians, political scientists, psychologists, sociologists and statisticians.

The history of management thought starts from a search for a universal theory. Yet we see that no single theory is accepted today. Instead we have theories devised and developed at different times with applications to different aspects of the management role. We shall discuss five approaches that have become well known and accepted:

- Classical
- Human Relations
- Management Science
- Systems
- Contingency.

The classical perspective

One can trace reference to management principles and problems back to medieval times or earlier. For instance, authors refer to Confucius[3] or Machiavelli.[4] From their writings on government, servants, leadership or the conduct of war authors pick out statements about questions of management today. This is unsound. Authorities of the distant past were discussing the government of city states, directing armies or the running of traditional enterprises. We are separated from that era by the industrial revolution, a period that transformed everything. The context of management changed considerably. Business developed from small cottage industries to large industrial organisations employing many thousands of staff at one site. With its scale, the factory system posed challenges that had, except military activities, been little experienced in earlier generations. Problems arose in areas such as operational co-ordination, organisation structure, communication and control. The ideas that emerged were responses to these problems and many remain relevant today.

The views that we can call the classical perspective really developed at around the end of the nineteenth century. They result from attempts by proponents, mainly American engineers, to establish general principles upon which management practice could be based. We can identify three sub-categories for further study, namely scientific management, bureaucracy and administrative principles. The pioneers of these strands each sought means of improving management practice in different areas, namely operations, organisational structure and the general processes of management.

Scientific management

In their search for ways of improving business performance, advocates of scientific management focused on operations. These are the many routine tasks that any large organisation finds itself engaged in. Pioneers with a scientific bent learned that detailed investigations and experiments would discover the best ways of carrying them out. Further, they argued that such an approach was rational since the benefits to be gained from even minor improvements in each process would outweigh the costs of the studies.

At the end of the nineteenth century, many industrial plants were mechanised. Yet they still employed thousands of staff to feed and unload the machines, shift materials and so on. It was in such a context that scientific management was born. The movement's pioneer was F.W. Taylor, see Exhibit 2.1.[5] This Taylorism was founded on six key ideas:

- *Observation*
  Systematic observation, including making detailed timings with stopwatches, enabled Taylor and his staff to analyse each aspect of the production process. Studies showed up the inefficiencies in allowing each worker to decide for himself the way tasks were carried out. For instance, in the yard of the iron works, labourers engaged to unload wagons brought their own shovels to work. Yet varying material densities meant that a shovelful of iron ore weighed some 15 kg compared with 2 kg for loose coal. It was clear to Taylor that using the same shovel for each task could not be the best way of working.

Exhibit 2.1 F.W. Taylor: the father of scientific management

Frederick Winslow Taylor (1856–1915) was born into a Quaker family in Philadelphia. He was destined to follow his father into the law but an eye problem prevented him attending Harvard University. Instead he started as a labourer in a local machine shop and in four years learned the trades of pattern maker and machinist. Recovered from the eye condition, he took a degree in mechanical engineering at night school while rising quickly to the post of chief engineer at the Midvale Steel Works.

During his training, Taylor had observed the inefficiency and lack of cooperation that characterised large plants. Restrictive practices (Taylor's 'systematic soldiering') were rife. Poorly trained and ill equipped workers were left to decide for themselves how tasks were to be carried out. He became committed to stamping out such inefficiencies.

At Midvale, and later at Bethlehem Steel, measurement and experiment became Taylor's watchwords. He changed the role of supervisor, issuing each with a stopwatch and detailed instructions on how to break down tasks into measured work elements. Scientific study would also match each worker to the most suitable job. Payment was to be by results; Taylor was committed to raising the living standards of his workers provided they cooperated in the new ways of doing things.

In the highly influential *Principles of Scientific Management* (1911), Taylor published for the first time a book on the detailed processes of manual work. His inventiveness was also seen in engineering, where he took out more than one hundred patents. Beyond this, Taylor applied himself to sport. He was United States doubles champion in 1881, invented a spoon-shaped tennis racquet and persuaded the baseball authorities to switch from under-arm pitching to the more efficient over-arm style.

■ *Experiment*

From observations, often running into many thousands, Taylor developed a science of work and devised experiments to discover optimal methods. Studies ranged from attempts to eliminate unnecessary movements to varying the frequency and length of rest breaks. In the yard of the iron works, for instance, experiments suggested that the optimal shovel load for sustained work was 10 kg. This implied that, for each grade of material to be shovelled, the supervisors had to arrange for an appropriate size of shovel to be provided.

■ *Standardisation*

Having collected data and established optimal methods of working, managers had to publish instructions to be followed by the workers. Taylor's early expertise as a machinist enabled him to establish optimal cutting speeds and depths as well as best sizes and shapes for the metal cutting tools. Using the correct tool under the right conditions caused productivity to increase. Standardisation implied that managers had to equip all workplaces with proper tools and ensure that they were used effectively.

■ *Selection and training*

Taylor argued for care in matching of staff to tasks. In a famous 'pig-iron study' at the Bethlehem Steel Corporation, Taylor investigated the job of loading railway wagons with 42 kg blocks of iron. A group of 75 men was employed to carry the 'pigs' up a 12-metre incline. Each normally made some 300 trips in a ten-hour day, loading some $12\frac{1}{2}$ tonnes. Selecting one of the strongest and fittest, followed by instructing him in correct techniques of lifting and carrying, Taylor showed how output could be increased to $47\frac{1}{2}$ tonnes. Others were then selected and trained, although only one in eight could achieve the top rate. Taylor reported that this remarkable four-fold increase was preferred by the labourers; the new methods left them feeling less fatigued and enabled them to earn 60 per cent more pay.

■ *Payment by results*

Taylor believed that workers were primarily motivated by pay. Therefore, piecework systems were at the centre of scientific management schemes. In traditional schemes the rate per piece was figured out by rule of thumb and negotiation between supervisor and worker. Instead, Taylor and his followers experimented with differential piecework plans. For instance, having found out the best method, a piecework rate may be set for the average worker. Output higher than this may be rewarded with an enhancement of, say, 20 per cent. Thus, the standard rate may have been 10 pence per unit up to 20 units and 12 pence after that.

■ *Cooperation*

Taylor felt that cooperation was the most important need if the fruits of success were to be distributed equitably. Perrow[6] summarised the view as follows: the argument between labour and management over how to divide any surplus between higher wages and profits should be replaced by constructive discussion about increasing the size of the surplus itself. In short, it was rational for both sides to cooperate in applying scientific principles to the study of work.

Exhibit 2.2   The Gilbreths: time and motion and psychological studies

Following a successful career in building, Frank Gilbreth (1868–1924) turned to consultancy in his middle age, becoming converted to scientific management. Using film cameras and special charts to build on his experience, he identified 17 basic human motions which he called *therbligs* (a name coined from his own). These were used in the training of bricklayers and soldiers and the rehabilitation of the disabled. The focus was less on times than on the elimination of unnecessary movements.

Lilian Gilbreth (1878–1972) was more interested in psychological aspects of work, yet, after her husband's death, she carried on his studies and seminar programme and eventually became professor at Purdue University.

Two of the Gilbreths' 12 children published *Cheaper by the Dozen* describing how both family and household were organised for maximum efficiency.

While Taylor is often called the 'father' of scientific management, he was hardly alone in innovation and publication of new ideas. A colleague, Henry Gantt, gave his name to the Gantt Chart – a bar graph widely used to plan and sequence events along a time line. Frank and Lilian Gilbreth (*see* Exhibit 2.2) were also innovators, working on the idea of 'motion study'.

The legacy

Scientific management pointed the way towards improved productivity. Yet its failings quickly became apparent. It did not consider the social context of work and the workers' psychological needs for attachment to the work process itself. They frequently felt exploited, an attitude that contrasts with the rational harmony that Taylor had advocated. Less scrupulous managers took up the ideas of work measurement, using the notorious 'time and motion man' for beating down workers' pay and limiting their scope. A strike at Watertown Arsenal led to an investigation by the United States' House of Representatives. Because of its report, the Senate banned the use of Taylor's methods in defence establishments.

As students, however, we should not deride the approach. It was developed in an age of mass manual production with emphasis on the quantity, as opposed to quality, of output. The stress on detailed management control of every aspect of a job now looks old fashioned. Yet the attention to work design, worker development, fair rewards and cooperation have echoes in much modern management literature. What has happened since is that definitions of ideas of development, fairness and cooperation have shifted. They are based less on managerial rationality and more on broader ideas of equity.

■ Bureaucracy

Whereas scientific management gained by making a detailed analysis of operational processes, especially manual tasks, the study of bureaucracy looked at the problem of managing the organisation as a whole. Advocates, led by Weber (*see* Exhibit 2.3), took up the scientific management notion that there is one best way to do a job: they argued that there must be one best way to run an organisation.

| Exhibit 2.3 | Max Weber and the ideal-typical bureaucracy |

While best known as a sociologist, Max Weber (1864–1920) lectured in law, then economics before obtaining a chair in sociology. He was an evolutionist who saw man in society moving towards greater reasoning in the light of acquired knowledge. Rationality would replace blind faith or unquestioning assumptions based on age-old tradition.

Weber developed the difficult concept of the *ideal-type*. This is a pure model of part of social reality with which some element of that reality could be compared. It is, as it were, a lens used to focus and clarify the area under study. While Weber was not the first to use the term *bureaucracy*, it was he who discerned its qualities in terms that we can recognise today. Some followers have taken Weber's discussion as prescriptive, that is a statement of the way organisations ought to be. For instance, it must be hierarchical, rules must be clear and comprehensive, and so on. This contrasts with his intention of it being a starting point for debate and comparison.

Weber argued that the most efficient organisation parallelled a machine, its rules and controls being the equivalent of the shafts and rods of the mechanism. This was the *rational-legal* model of organisation, distinguished from the *charismatic* (dominated by the leader) and *traditional* (run on custom and practice) models. Weber worked at a time when many organisations were managed by families with their practices serving personal rather than organisational goals. He saw the need for impersonal, rational management in charge of his ideal organisation, the *bureaucracy*.

The elements of a bureaucracy are:

1 *Division of labour* with clear definitions of authority and responsibility as official duties.

2 *Organisation of positions into a hierarchy*, with each under the authority of a higher position.

3 *People are assigned to positions* in the hierarchy according to qualifications, assessed by examination or training and experience.

4 *Decisions and actions are recorded in writing* with files providing continuity and memory over time.

5 *The management and ownership* of the organisation are separated.

6 *All are subject to rules and procedures*, applied impersonally and equally to all to ensure predictable behaviour.

Weber believed that the rational-legal organisation would be both more efficient in operation and more adaptable to change than any other. The system was rational in that competent managers made decisions according to clear criteria; it was legal because they had been appointed by legitimate processes. Yet the notion of bureaucracy has become discredited in modern times, becoming associated with stifling rules and endless red tape. As with Taylorism, however, we should not be too critical. The emphasis in Weber's time was on improving efficiency and consistency whereas for some modern organisations the stress is on innovation and flexibility.

Furthermore, there are many organisations today that incorporate most of Weber's elements. For instance, the notion of impersonally applied rules is fundamental to any dealings with personal issues. This applies as much to clients in the social security office as to employees looking for promotion. It is in complex, rapidly changing environments that zealous adherence to rules leads to a downfall.

Management principles

A different, yet related, approach to the question of running whole organisations examined the practice of management itself. Perhaps the best known among the advocates of general principles applied to practice was Fayol, *see* Exhibit 2.4. Others such as Follett made contributions that we shall include in this discussion.

In the hundred or so pages of *General and Industrial Management*[7], Fayol examined three themes: the abilities required of managers; general principles of management; and elements of management. Writing in French, he used the term *administration* to refer to the management process. In the foreword to the 1967 edition, Urwick supported the use of the English *administration*, too. To Urwick, *management* had too many other uses: there were connotations of higher levels in the hierarchy together with a suggestion of deviousness or manipulation. Urwick noted that Fayol's intention had been to describe management as a function carried out by those whose work involved his principles and elements. These days, however, the word administration has moved towards describing the carrying out of instructions, especially in government. On the other hand, management is commonly used to describe Fayol's processes. Meanwhile, the term *management* has entered the French language.

Exhibit 2.4   Henri Fayol: establishing general principles of management

Henri Fayol (1841–1925) graduated in mining engineering from the famous École Nationale in St. Étienne at the age of nineteen. The first years of his career were devoted to resolving problems of mining, especially fire hazards. Then, on promotion, he worked on geological questions, publishing a theory of coal deposition. In 1888, Fayol was appointed directeur général (managing director) of the ailing Commentry-Fourchambault mining and iron making group which he saved and developed into Comambault, one of France's most successful companies. Retiring in 1918 at the age of 77, he devoted his last years to spreading his theory of management.

The classic *Administration industrielle et générale* appeared in 1916, although the book had little influence in the English speaking world until translations appeared. A few copies were available in the United Kingdom in 1929, although it was not until 1949 that Pitman published the work in book form throughout the English speaking world. It was based on his broad experience.

Fayol saw his work as complementing that of Taylor. He argued that his five basic functions and fourteen principles of management were applicable in any organisational setting. In his view, these basic ideas of management were waiting to be discovered and elaborated. They appear in developed and adapted form in much modern management teaching.

Exhibit 2.5 Fayol's fourteen principles of management

Division of work	This produces more and better work using the same effort.
Authority and responsibility	Authority is the right to give orders and have them followed. It is matched by responsibility, the accountability for exercise of authority.
Discipline	Maintained by good superiors, clear and fair agreements and appropriate sanctions.
Unity of command	Dual command leads to tension and disorder and is a perpetual source of conflict.
Unity of direction	Established by sound organisation with plans coming from one person.
Subordination of individual to group interest	Good leadership, fairness and supervision ensure that people follow the organisation's goals rather than their own.
Remuneration	It should be fair and encouraging yet not excessive. (Fayol then detailed various schemes for workers and higher managers.)
Centralisation	Both centralisation and decentralisation are necessary; the question is how to establish the proportions which will optimise the use of people's capacities.
Scalar chain	The path followed by authority up and down the hierarchy can be disastrously lengthy in large organisations. Fayol set out principles under which horizontal links could be maintained.
Order	Everyone and everything should be in its place. This not only implies a sense of tidiness and discipline but also, in the case of personnel, of selection of staff to match abilities with job needs.
Equity	Treating all employees fairly encourages loyalty.
Stability of tenure	Instability of tenure is both the cause and effect of inefficiency.
Business strength	Initiative comes from combining the initiative of all. A manager should encourage its use among subordinates.
Esprit de corps (team spirit)	In spite of unity of command, personnel must not be arbitrarily split up; contacts, both within and between departments should be encouraged to avoid misunderstandings and disputes.

Abilities required of personnel

Fayol's first theme is analysis of the abilities required of personnel at different levels and in different types of organisation. His intention is to show that while many people are engaged in the process called management, they are involved to different degrees. He distinguishes management from other abilities required of people in organisations, concluding with the following definition:

■ *to manage is to forecast and plan, to organise, to command, to co-ordinate and to control.*

By identifying the required abilities, and then defining management by subdividing it, Fayol pointed to the need for, and the possibility of, teaching management as a discipline. The principles would naturally form a framework for the curriculum.

General principles of management

Fayol set out fourteen principles although not with the intention of making a complete list. They were, he said, the ones that he had had to apply most frequently. They are summarised in Exhibit 2.5. In studying the items, we should focus less on the detail of each, and more on recognising two features of the approach. First, there is the attempt to generalise, to extract from the manager's job common features that can be studied and, for example, used as the basis of selection, training and assessment. This is the start of a long tradition of attempting to define the management task leading to what may now be called generic competences. Second, in attempting to be universal, the principles are couched in very general terms. Fayol intended them to be flexible, adaptable to every need. In being so general, however, they can be criticised for not being *operational*. They cannot readily be converted into practical action in any particular case.

Elements of management

The elements are drawn directly from Fayol's definition of management. He gives details of: good planning on a business and national scale; organising materials and personnel at all levels, including the use of organisation charts, defining jobs and training people to fill them; the knowledge and personal qualities needed to give commands; means of achieving co-ordination; and the timeliness of control with related sanctions.

Fayol's writings now seem old-fashioned and can be criticised for being grounded in the experience of someone whose career was confined to one organisation. As with others of his era, however, we should recognise the originality of the ideas and the different context in which they were developed. Many can be traced through to today, although the ideas have frequently been reinvented and re-labelled.

Mary Parker Follett[8], *see* Exhibit 2.6, was another who saw management as a generic function to which can be attached general principles. Her work can be

---

Exhibit 2.6 Mary Parker Follet: looking forward with new ideas

Mary Parker Follett (1868–1933) was born near Boston and educated at Radcliffe College (now part of Harvard) and Cambridge. Her early work was in political science and social work and it was only in her fifties that she began to be involved in lecturing and writing on business administration. She never worked in business but took ideas which she had developed on the health of society and applied them to the task of creating healthy organisations. She wrote on conflict, power and leadership, explaining how the former should not be hidden within the rational organisation but be resolved through processes aimed at joint accommodation rather than imposed solutions.

Follett knew Taylorism well, having joined the Taylor Society. Yet she did not approve of seeing workers as hired hands to be optimised. For her, managers and workers all had reason, feelings and character.

Grieving for the loss of a friend in 1926, Follett moved to London to work. Her 1933 lectures series at the London School of Economics was on *The Problem of Organisation and Co-ordination in Business*. She died later that year, during a brief visit to Boston.

seen as part of the classical tradition yet it provided a bridge to later ideas. She investigated questions of power and responsibility but also recognised the needs, abilities and aspirations of employees.

The management task is to integrate all the specialist functions of the bureaucracy. Echoing Taylor, Follett stressed the need for systematic record keeping and learning from experience. Simultaneously, she criticised the inhumanity of hierarchical structures, arguing that people were more important than machines. Follett saw conflict not as something to be avoided but as a 'fact of life'. Conflict was based on difference and without difference there would be no progress. She argued against the conventional idea of power, which is the idea of one person having it 'over' another. Instead, Follett argued that power should be pooled, built around transactions and mutual influence. She continually interpreted situations as wholes, taking the broad picture and examining the linkages between the elements. In taking both the humanist stance and looking at the broad picture, Follett foresaw future trends in management thought.

The human relations perspective

We have seen how the emphasis in the classical approach was on principles, science and structure. The human aspects of work and organisation had not been ignored but relegated to a secondary issue in the campaign to increase the efficiency of enterprises. It was during the 1920s that scholars and innovators turned their attention more towards the behaviour of employees within organisations. They became concerned with human relations.

Three factors, pictured in Fig. 2.1, brought this change about:

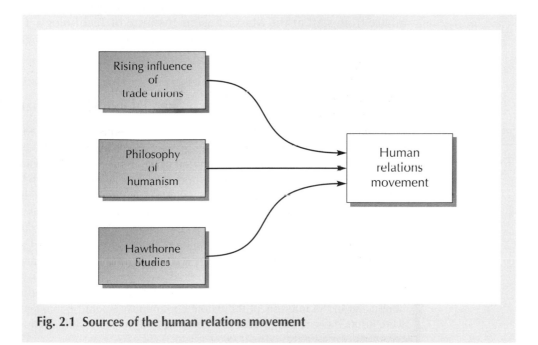

Fig. 2.1 Sources of the human relations movement

- The rising influence of trade unions in many countries. The scale of mines, manufacturing plants and service industries from docks to railways meant that unions could readily organise, especially after governments had legislated to grant them the necessary freedoms. Meanwhile, workers became angry at the exploitative application of 'time and motion' studies by unreasonable employers and the boom and bust cycles that affected many industries. It is not surprising that more enlightened employers became attracted by human relations ideas. More contentment among workers would mean they would be less likely to join and support trade union activities.

- Industrial humanism as a philosophy had been gaining ground for many years. It had origins among philanthropic employers, among them the Rowntree family, *see* Exhibit 2.7.[9] Industrial humanism did not approve of paternalistically caring for workers' welfare, a view that justified the continuation of managers deciding what was in their best interests. Following Follett, it held that all employees were human with associated rights, aspirations and needs and these should be a major concern. The manager's role was to engage with the worker in making decisions. Work should flow from motivation, not from command.

- Researchers began to pay attention to issues beyond the methods and techniques that had been the cores of scientific management. This change of perspective was partly the result of puzzling results from the studies themselves. Perhaps the best-known example is the series beginning with the illumination experiments conducted from 1924 to 1927 by engineers at the Hawthorne Plant of the Western Electric Company. (For details see this chapter's closing case.) Their inconclusive results prompted a series of further experiments and studies lasting until about 1933. The complete series became known as the Hawthorne Studies.

  The follow-up studies were initiated by the company's own managers with advice from staff at the Massachusetts Institute of Technology. There were three broad phases: the relay assembly test room; the interview programme; and the

Exhibit 2.7   Seebohm Rowntree: influential industrial humanist

B. Seebohm Rowntree (1871–1954) attended the Friends' School in York and Owen's College, now the University of Manchester. His chemistry degree had practical benefit at his family's York Cocoa Works, yet he spent much time studying social issues. When made labour director he focused his work on improving democratic relations at work, an attitude that many regarded as risky. All rules in the factory had to be approved by managers and workers; shop stewards were elected with the chief among them paid by the company; foremen could not be appointed without consultation; disciplinary cases could go to a joint appeal committee. There were welfare and training departments and, in 1906, the company introduced a generous pension scheme.

Rowntree constantly argued that workers were more than hired hands. They were citizens and, because of this, they were entitled to demand that industry should be conducted in the interests of the whole community. Scientific management methods were justified because they generated more surplus to share with employees.

bank wiring observation room. Elton Mayo, of Harvard Business School, became involved in 1928. It is often said that the main guidance over the following years was given by Mayo and another Harvard professor, Fritz Roethlisberger.[10] While Mayo took an interest in the interviews, there is some doubt as to the degree to which he was directly involved in all phases.[11] The importance of this work is such that we shall look at it further.

■ The Hawthorne Studies

The relay assembly test room

The boring, repetitive work of relay assembly involved women who put together telephone relays from many small parts. Two women friends were asked to select four others for a trial. The six worked in a special room where observers could watch the process, listen to and consult with them and keep them informed of experimental progress. During the 13 periods of the experiment, lasting from 2 to 31 weeks, the researchers evaluated changing conditions. These were patterns and times of rest breaks and length of the working day. Simultaneously they monitored factors such as diet, physical health and sleep habits.

The experiment was designed so that the last two periods meant a return to the nominal conditions experienced earlier. Period 12 resembled Period 3 which itself was similar to the conditions measured before the experiment began. There were no morning and afternoon rest breaks. Yet, apart from a slight dip in the output at the start of Period 12, production rose to a new record. The average weekly output was up from less than 2500 to more than 2900 units. Periods 7, 10 and 13 also had nominally the same working conditions, with break and snack in the morning and a break in the afternoon. Weekly output figures were 2500, 2800 and 3000 respectively. Apart from the dip already mentioned, production in the RATR rose steadily throughout the two years of the trials.

Mayo later explained the results as follows:

> I have often heard my colleague Roethlisberger declare that the major experimental change was introduced when those in charge sought to hold the situation humanly steady ... by getting the cooperation of the workers. What actually happened was that six individuals became a team and the team gave itself wholeheartedly and spontaneously to cooperation in the experiment. The consequence was that they felt themselves to be participating freely and without afterthought, and were happy in the knowledge that they were working without coercion from above or limitation from below...
>
> Here then are two topics which deserve the closest attention ... – the organisation of working teams and the free participation of such teams in the task and purpose of the organisation.[12]

Mayo's discussion has the advantage of hindsight, as we discussed in Chapter 1. Yet at the time the result remained mysterious. Even today, authors dispute how the RATR results should be interpreted. What was so special about the RATR? How did it compare with the work outside? It was to try to answer these questions that the interview programme began.

The interview programme

The RATR outcomes seemed to point to the influence of supervision. Interviews were aimed at eliciting workers' feelings about their supervisors as well as their conditions of work. More than twenty thousand were conducted during this period, ended by the onset of the Great Depression. At first, they followed a pre-pared schedule but were changed in the light of responses that found some of the questions irrelevant. The style became less directive and more open-ended. Subjects were encouraged to talk about any aspect of the work that concerned them. Confidentiality was assured.

Information on many aspects of working life was gained. Further, many wel-comed the opportunity to talk to a sympathetic listener in a friendly atmosphere. This finding pointed the way to the development of personnel management and associated counselling services. According to Mayo, however, the most important outcome was the recognition of the power of groups.

In one case, members of a work group were invited to talk about fatigue. They said that they did most of their work in the morning and 'took it easy' in the after-noon. In contrast, the boss thought that the group worked hard all day. Although he was well respected, he knew nothing of the practice. The researchers arranged for engineers to quietly measure the electric current used throughout the day as a means of indirectly measuring activity. The results supported the women's state-ment. Together with other incidents, this observation showed how, in Mayo's words, 'the working group as a whole actually determined the output of individ-ual workers by reference to a standard ... that represented the group conception of a fair day's work. This standard was rarely, if ever, in accord with the standards of the efficiency engineers.'[13]

The bank wiring observation room

The researchers returned to experiment to continue their investigation of groups. Here, a group of 14 men – wiremen, solderers and inspectors – connected tele-phone cables to switchgear. The men formed their own informal subgroups with leaders emerging by consent. The group set norms, including output standards. In spite of pay inducements, the men decided to produce much less than the amount they were capable of. The group pressure upon individuals was much stronger than the financial incentives offered by management.

Overview of Hawthorne

Taken as a whole, the Hawthorne Studies generated new ideas that contributed greatly to management theory and practice. Quite what the results were, and how they should be interpreted, remains controversial. For instance, it has been pointed out that the RATR workers were all young unmarried women living, bar one, with their parents. The bank wiring group was all male. Responses have, therefore, been explained by traditional power differences between the sexes.[14] In another interpretation, Greenwood and others challenge those interpretations that shift money from the centre of the stage. They point out that, interviewed many years later, one ex-participant acknowledged how simply joining an experimental group meant a substantial rise in income.[15] One theme, however, became clear almost from the start and dominates the difficulties with interpretation. It is impossible to conduct experiments or make detailed inquiries without influencing the attitudes and behaviour of those being studied. This is widely known as the *Hawthorne effect*.

The human relations movement

The human relations movement gathered momentum from the Hawthorne Studies. Additionally, the Depression stimulated people's humanitarian efforts. At work, it was increasingly believed that the search for increased productivity was being held back by the lack of attention to workers' concerns and needs for job satisfaction. The naive view was that contented staff would produce more.

Deeper insights came from Maslow and McGregor. We shall look at Maslow's work in more detail in Chapter 17. It is sufficient to note here that he drew insights into human behaviour from his psychology practice, proposing that human motivation be caused by the desire to satisfy a hierarchy of needs. Douglas McGregor (1906–64) drew on his own psychological training and management consultancy experience. He built upon Maslow's ideas in formulating his *Theory X and Theory Y*. These were not theories in themselves, more labels describing typical management attitudes. Exhibit 2.8 summarises the two ideal-types.[16]

McGregor used his theories to challenge both the classical and the early human relations perspectives. To him they were both coercive, the former seeking to systematise incentives and punishments, the latter looking for other variables to push up output. Neither Taylor nor the managers at Western Electric started by

---

Exhibit 2.8 Douglas McGregor: Theory X and Theory Y describe managers' beliefs

Theory X managers believe:
- The average person inherently dislikes work and will avoid it if at all possible.
- Therefore, most people must be coerced, directed or threatened to get them to put in adequate effort for the organisation.
- The average person prefers direction, avoids responsibility, is unambitious and desires security above everything.

Theory Y managers believe:
- The expenditure of effort, both physical and mental, is natural.
- Control and direction are not the only means of bringing about effort; a person will exercise self-control and self-direction when committed to the task in hand.
- The average person is prepared both to accept and seek responsibility.
- Many people have the capacity to demonstrate imagination, ingenuity and creativity in the organisational context.
- In most industrial jobs, employees' intellectual potential is only partially tapped.

recognising that the worker may have at least as much to contribute as the manager. In contrast, Theory Y managers seek to enrol employees in a wider and deeper range of questions. Under the right conditions, Theory Y managers could rely on staff to exercise self-direction and control and apply their intellect to problems as they arise. In advocating training policies aimed at creating Theory Y conditions, McGregor was taking both a pragmatic and a moral position.

■ Organisational behaviour (OB)

The OB, or behavioural science, perspective has linked the practical concerns of the human relations movement with all the behavioural sciences, for instance: anthropology, medicine, political science, psychology and sociology. Although set in organisations, OB is not necessarily managerial in its orientation. In what many would regard as the core purpose of science, many who work in OB have as their goal the gathering of knowledge for its own sake. The benefits of this work may not become apparent until much later. At the same time, leading researchers have influenced modern management practice and we shall draw on their work throughout the book.

The management science perspective

Whereas OB covers the application of social sciences to enterprise, management science draws on the natural sciences. Scholars in fields such as physics and mathematics began to see that management problems had many features related to their own. Applications were therefore stimulated by the development of new techniques as well as new problem situations. We mentioned earlier in the chapter how the problems of scale arose with growth of business enterprises themselves. This ignores any learning that may have taken place, for example from military experience. Many leading figures in management and consultancy, such as Lyndale Urwick (1891–1983), had experience in the services that they transferred to the civilian sphere. It was in wartime that the two grew closer.

During the Second World War, groups of scientists, especially mathematicians, were assembled by governments to solve military problems. These frequently included, for example, *logistics*. Warfare demands the rapid movement of large quantities of personnel, weapons, equipment and stores. It is not surprising that successful solutions readily found application to large-scale business. The approach, named *operations research (OR)*, requires the expression of a problem in mathematical terms, the manipulation of the data to produce a result and the translation of the result back into management practice.

Further explanation and examples are left to Chapter 19. Operations management applies a wide range of OR techniques that have been developed to optimise the supply of goods and services. They range from forecasting to stock control and queue management to scheduling. While many mathematical techniques have been known for a long time, OR had to await the development of computers for its major impact.[17] Exhibit 2.9 describes how a classic OR problem was solved at the dawn of the information era; this would nowadays take seconds on a moderate computer.

Exhibit 2.9 | OR applications had to await the computer

Transportation studies were carried out by the UK National Coal Board from the mid-1950s. Solutions required desk-top calculators and much effort; a 60 colliery to 60 customer problem took 3 days to solve! The Central Electricity Generating Board conducted similar studies at around the same period. Efficient movement from pit to power station was the focus. A regional model with 135 mines and 32 stations needed 71 iterations even though the most efficient numerical procedures were used.

Such problems were ready made for the nascent computing facilities. By the late 1960s, British Petroleum was one of the largest computer users in the country. Most of its usage was devoted to OR, working on forecasting, marketing, supply and so on.

As mentioned above, management science has been applied to many aspects, especially operations. We should also recognise, however, that the approach traditionally focuses on quantitative aspects, playing down the significance of attitudes and behaviour and the problems of implementing solutions in complex organisations.

Integrating perspectives

The three perspectives we have considered so far each grew out of problems and attitudes of their time. They differ not just because of their diverse origins but are concerned with distinct aspects of the management problem. Scientists call this *reduction*. It may be satisfactory for those interested in the advancement of knowledge. It enables them to establish general, fundamental truths about elements of the world. *Reductionism* is not so good for managers faced with coping with a stream of interrelated problems. They want the world to be fitted together rather than taken apart.

▤ The systems approach

The systems approach is a set of ideas that have grown up to counter the reductionist trend. It began when scholars in apparently different fields recognised common patterns that may be investigated using similar techniques. For instance: the flow of traffic on a busy road resembles the flow of water along a channel or waves up a beach; networks, from telephone companies to the connections in the brain, have fascinating commonalities; political instability can be analogous to the weather. Pioneers, such as von Bertalanffy,[18] began the search for the common patterns, aiming to develop a general systems theory. This could be applied in many spheres, from economics to ecology or biochemistry to business. Some success has been achieved, notably in work on complexity and control. Yet the goal of an overarching model that would describe patterns in different fields has not been reached.

The approach is, of course, built around the idea of *system*. When we observe something we call a system, we tend to speak of it as a whole. Although remaining wary of reification (*see* Chapter 1), we ascribe to the whole system attributes that cannot be attached to any particular part. It is as though the system behaves in a way that is different from simply a sum of the behaviour of all its parts. It is said to have *emergent properties*. Naturally, if we knew enough about each element and link in detail, we could predict the behaviour of the whole system. But that is rarely possible, except with the simplest of systems. In real life, we talk about the whole as in: the band; the crowd at the match; the United Nations; the flock of sheep; Rome; and so on. The idea that the whole is greater than the sum of the parts is called *synergy*. This gives the study of systems its importance.

■ *A system is a set of parts which are connected and behave together in significant ways.*

Central to the idea of system, captured by this definition, are the significant connections or *relationships* among the components. It is as though the arrangement of these parts, and the way they work together, are at least as important as the parts themselves. For the manager, what are the key features of systems thinking?

- Holism – the notion that the whole of the system behaves in a way which is greater than the sum of its parts.

- Open system – the recognition that the system interacts with other systems in order to survive and succeed. In the above example, we cannot understand the band without knowing about the audience, the venue, and so on. Similarly, the match crowd interacts with the teams.

    This is an antidote to the classical perspective. It frequently saw organisations as closed systems where all behaviour could be accounted for by events that took place within the plant, office, business or whatever. Open systems thinking, however, recognises that interactions with external factors, the *organisation's environment*, are very important.

- Hierarchy – each system consists of parts that are themselves systems. This goes beyond Weber's notion of bureaucratic hierarchy to see it as 'systems within systems'. The elements of these smaller systems may be people. They could equally well be any physical or abstract element, from plant to patents or inventory to instructions, that make the organisation tick. When we see that the elements themselves are made up of systems, we may call them *subsystems*.

    The notion of hierarchy makes us sensitive to the possibility of complexity both in relation to subsystems and to systems of which the system under investigation is a part. The depth of investigation, that is the degree of resolution of these systems, will depend on the relevance it has for our investigation.[19]

- Boundary – the notional line that separates the system from those elements outside it. For a business organisation, what is owned by it and who is employed by it are usually easy to define. But what of charitable organisations that rely on volunteers? What about groups of organisations that, from time to time, cooperate with each other? The boundary in these cases is not easy to draw.

- Significance – the use of *significant* in the definition is important. Systems definitions are subjective, depending on the purpose of the observer. Just as a marine biologist sees a shoal as part of a wider ecosystem, so the captain of a trawler sees it as profit and the European Union official as an excuse to write regulations in ten languages. Awareness of the effect of different viewpoints helps us to understand ideas such as stakeholders.

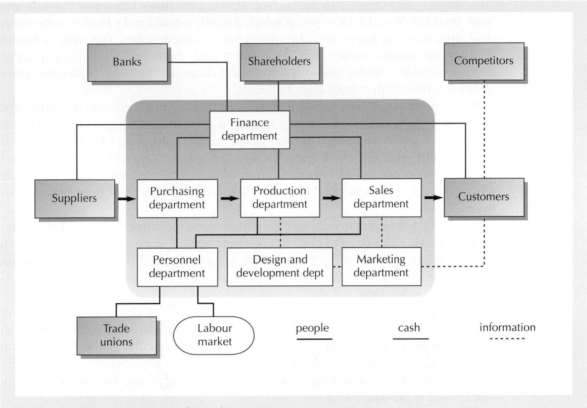

Fig. 2.2 Business seen as a transformation system

Figure 2.2 illustrates the systems view of a business. Within the boundary, various subsystems (departments) interact with each other. Together they make up a *transformation system*. This converts inputs into outputs. In turn, these are exchanged with elements of the environment, each of which has a different view about what the business is for.

We noted that the search for general systems theory has only been partially successful. Instead, different thinkers have taken the idea of system and used it in different ways. We shall summarise four lines of thought before picking them up again later in the book. They are: socio-technical systems, systems and control, systems and chaos, and systems as methodology.

■ Socio-technical systems

Trist and Bamforth, with others at London's Tavistock Institute, carried out a series of studies into the relationships between the social and technical subsystems of an organisation. Their famous studies in the UK coal mining industry of the late 1940s coincided with the change from traditional methods to large-scale mechanisation.[20]

The customary method of coal-getting involved teams of about four miners working together. They hewed coal from a short section of the face and loaded it into wagons for transport to the surface. It was sometimes known as the 'tub and stall' method. Typically, the group selected itself, rotated tasks between members and shared bonus payments. The quiet, the confined spaces, the risks to health and mortal dangers meant that there was a high degree of mutual dependence among members. Social ties were strong and these tended to be replicated above ground, where miners lived close to the pit.

New equipment, long-wall seam cutters, conveyors and hydraulic roof supports, demanded great change in the way mining was organised. The work pattern was changed to three specialised shifts – preparation, cutting and loading. Forty or more miners were dispersed along the face rather than confined in the short faces or stalls. Supervision and communication were difficult because of the noise and dust caused by the new machines. Productivity levels that had been planned for were not realised.

The Tavistock researchers helped to relieve some negative features of the long-wall method. They devised the 'composite longwall' arrangement under which specialisation was reduced. Responsibility was returned to multi-skilled work teams. The work was found more satisfying and more efficient than with the earlier version of longwall.

The important lesson from the Tavistock Studies is the strong interaction between the social and technical subsystems. The *socio-technical systems* approach recognises that any work system has these key components. When the technical system is changed, for example in an attempt to increase efficiency or safety, there will be social consequences and reactions. Good managers will look at these before the change is introduced.

■ Systems and control

Cybernetics is the study and application of the idea of control. Engineering control systems always include regulators to maintain them at their desired states. Examples include: the steam engine governor invented by James Watt seen on top of many steam engines; central heating thermostats; voltage regulators in battery-charging systems; and level controllers in water closets. All these dynamic systems are controlled according to Wiener's recognition of feedback: 'the difference between the pattern and the actually performed motion is used as a new input to cause the part regulated to move in such a way as to bring the motion closer to that given pattern.'[21] Feedback loops back information about output to change the system to close any output gap.

Contributions to the theory of control include Ashby and Beer. Ashby is known for his work on self-regulating systems and the Law of Requisite Variety.[22] This says that, in order for a system to maintain stability within a changing environment, it must match the variety of the environment within itself. With more external uncertainty, that is more possible states in the environment, there must be more variety, that is a greater number of possible responses. Complexity demands flexibility. Beer took up the theory of control to design organisations along cybernetic lines.[23] More details of his work appear in Chapter 23.

Systems and chaos

The control approach has been challenged because it suggests that organisations should continuously strive towards equilibrium. Feedback loops help them to correct deviations from the chosen path. Belief in cause and effect interactions among system elements suggests that managers, having predicted the future, can take steps to control it. But is the search for stability justified? What if feedback control is so strong that the organisation cannot change?

Building on the theoretical work of Gleick,[24] Stacey has pioneered the application of *chaos theory* to management.[25] He argues that most organisations are *chaotic.* This means they operate in a zone of bounded instability. It is a region between being stable and predictable and being unstable and falling apart. The future of an organisation is bounded and it will display regular patterns of behaviour. Yet the detailed outcomes of these patterns cannot be predicted. This implies that, with the long-term future essentially unknowable, any manager's attempts at close and rational control are likely to flounder. 'Muddling through' is likely to be a more effective approach. A more detailed discussion of chaos theory is given in Chapter 24.

Systems as methodology

The term methodology refers to a way of approaching questions or problems. It is broader than a technique, which is a specific process to be applied once a problem or task has been clearly specified. Managers are familiar with techniques for scheduling vehicles, finding optimal stocks levels or assessing the health of a balance sheet. Yet, in attempting to manage complexity, managers quickly find that problems are not so well defined. No one is saying, 'Hey! Solve this!' In reality, they are told, 'Customers are uneasy about the delivery schedules,' or, 'The quality of our service seems to be suffering.' To proceed, managers have to both select and define problems as well as resolve them. This is aided by a methodology which, if appropriate, gives pointers to the way through the confusion.

Methodologies have been matched to problem settings. On the one hand, there are relatively clear-cut (called 'hard') situations characterised by agreed goals and clear data. OR techniques have been extended to cope with these circumstances.[26] On the other hand, Checkland's methodology[27] is focused on 'soft' systems where the goals are unclear and there is little quantitative data to go on. More specialised methodologies are designed for tasks such as information systems planning.[28]

The attempted integration of relevant disciplines under the systems banner, followed by spawning of several new directions, reflects one theme of our history. As with the classical view, systems set out to be universalistic. Yet, in delving into the complexity of each case, it recognises its uniqueness and acts accordingly. This tension between the universal and the particular is the basis of the contingency view.

The contingency perspective

The universalists saw management ideas and skills as transferable across all sorts of organisation. Once one had found the 'one best way' all could learn from it. In contrast, others pointed to the special nature of each case and how it differed. This view, which has been matched by the 'case method' in management education, says that there are no universal principles. The way to learn is to study and experience as many circumstances as possible.

The contingency perspective comes to terms with these opposing views. It recognises both commonality and uniqueness but proceeds with care in the way both are interpreted. General principles can only be transferred from one case to another once it has been established that the cases are sufficiently similar. The contingency approach is well established in many aspects of management. For instance, links between organisation structure and other variables have been studied by Burns and Stalker, Lawrence and Lorsch, Woodward, Williamson and Mintzberg. As detailed in Chapter 13, these scholars sought to find the best structure to match different factors whether within the organisation or its environment. Another study that received much attention was the search for excellence.

■ Excellence

In their attempt to identify characteristics from successful companies that could be generalised and from which all could learn, Peters and Waterman studied 62 major United States companies.[29] There were interviews supported by literature reviews spanning 25 years. Those that had performed excellently during the period 1961 to 1980 were selected for further investigation. What characteristics did they display that were not generally shown by the remainder? The outcome was the well-known list of eight excellence characteristics:

- *A bias for action* – getting on rather than being slowed by analysis.
- *Close to the customer* – learning from the people served.
- *Autonomy and entrepreneurship* – fostering innovators and risk takers.
- *Productivity through people* – participation is the basis of rising standards.
- *Hands on, value driven* – all know what the company stands for, leaders get involved at all levels.
- *Stick to the knitting* – focus on business you know well.
- *Simple form, lean staff* – a few headquarters staff to run a large business through a simple organisation structure.
- *Simultaneous loose–tight properties* – being as decentralised as possible while centralising the things that really matter.

One could hardly argue with the items in the list. Yet they have many problems that take us back to Fayol. Items are couched in such general terms that it is difficult to apply them in any particular case. Therefore they tend to support and reinforce decisions that managers make, rather than help them reach them in the first place. A further twist to the contingency tale began to emerge almost as soon as the list appeared. Carroll pointed out how the authors had ignored contingencies such as industry, technology and government support in the analysis of the sample.[30] Others showed that companies in the list, including IBM for example, were already beginning to fail.[31]

The snag may lie in the way the list was publicised and received. Hitt and Ireland[32] underscore the contingency perspective in showing how managers should use new ideas such as proposed by Peters and Waterman. They should not regard them as 'quick-fixes' but as stimuli for further investigation, *see* Exhibit 2.10.

Exhibit 2.10 **How to avoid the quick-fix mentality[32]**

Keep abreast of good literature, especially that on putting theory into practice.
Ensure that decisions follow careful analysis and not unreasoned argument.
Introduce new ideas readily, but first test them on a small scale.
Be sceptical of simple ideas; test them thoroughly.
Continually check the impact of current actions on future results.

Conclusion: looking backwards and forwards

We end with a diagram. Figure 2.3 lays out the key points roughly along a time line representing the twentieth century. It both provides a useful summary and makes a valuable teaching point. As a summary, the diagram refers to some trends of management thought in the twentieth century. It identifies key actors and events referred to throughout the chapter. Lines suggest the main influences among these various elements. Note that the start and finish dates for the major 'movements' are somewhat arbitrary. This particularly applies to their termination, for it is clear that all have an influence down to the present day.

The teaching point concerns the discipline of drawing the diagram itself, for in doing so, we go beyond summarising. We are made to recognise the way we choose, group and interpret historical events, trends and figures and the weight we give to each. In expressing the complexity of history in this form, it shows our selectivity in what we have covered and hints at what is missing.

What is missing? We have not covered themes that have had a strong influence on management. For example, modern management wrestles with issues of culture, globalisation, quality, information, ethics and enterprise. Furthermore, this chapter has been ethnocentric, focusing on the development of thought in one, predominantly Anglo-Saxon, culture. How the best companies and managers are learning from other sources will be discussed in later chapters.

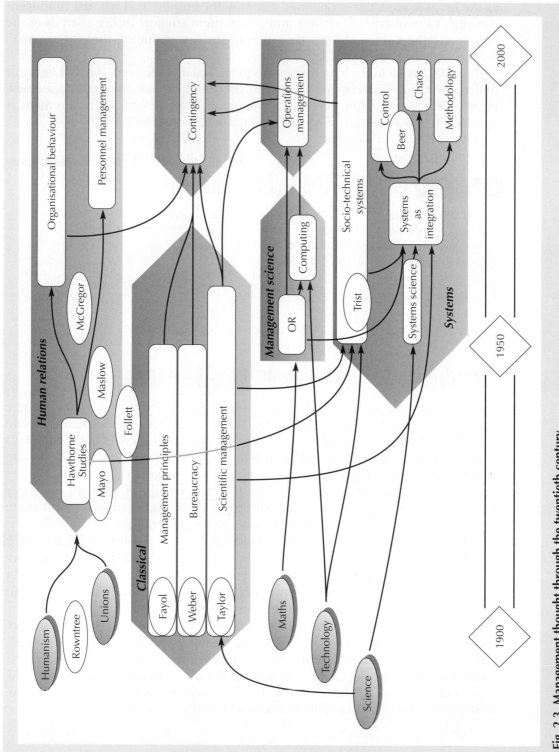

Fig. 2.3 Management thought through the twentieth century

Quick check up   *Can you ...*

- Name five well-known schools of management thought;
- List six key ideas of Taylorism;
- Identify the six elements of bureaucracy;
- State Fayol's definition of management;
- Name three trends that led to the rise of the human relations movement;

- Define Theory X and Theory Y;
- Outline the operations research process;
- List the key features of systems thinking;
- Define cybernetics;
- State the principles of contingency theory.

Questions

Chapter review

2.1 Why should managers be aware of the origins of ideas?

2.2 What is classical about the classical perspective?

2.3 Explain why the Hawthorne Studies were so significant and remain so today.

Application

2.4 What do the developments in management thought during the second half of the twentieth century tell us about the possibility of developing a universal theory of management?

2.5 Analyse the opening case from the classical, human relations and systems perspectives.

Investigation

2.6 Using interviews, report on how far managers and their colleagues subscribe to the different schools of thought.

2.7 Prepare a short paper on the writing of one key figure mentioned in the text. Show how it related to the time it was written and how far it is relevant today.

CLOSING CASE

Illumination at Hawthorne[33]

During the 1920s in the United States, manufacturers of industrial lighting equipment sought to promote their products as productivity aids. To this end, they formed the Committee on Industrial Lighting, with Thomas Edison as honorary chairman, to oversee experiments.

One site chosen for the tests was the Hawthorne Plant of the Western Electric Company. Up to four work groups underwent a series of tests while three others acted as controls. In a typical test, the illumination level was increased. As expected, output went up. Then, illumination was put up again. Productivity increased once more. So far the results tallied with the expectations of the engineers and the CIL.

To check on the results, however, the lighting was cut from the maximum to the intermediate level. Productivity continued to rise. Finally, when levels were returned to those prevailing before the experiment, output went up again. Throughout a series of similar trials, work-rates would tend to rise whether the work conditions were made better or worse.

One final observation was made. The work-rate in the control groups also tended to rise when the experimental room was made brighter. And when the latter's illumination was cut from 10 to 3 foot-candles, the control room's output went up once more. The experiments seemed to lead nowhere. As Mayo commented later:

> The conditions of scientific experiment had apparently been fulfilled – experimental room, control room; changes introduced one at a time; all other conditions held steady.[33]

The engineers refused to accept defeat. They set up more tests which eventually formed the series known as the Hawthorne Studies.

Questions

1 What was happening in and around the lighting test room?

2 Could you propose an experiment that could have checked your suggestions?

Bibliography Mullins, Laurie J. (1996) *Management and Organisational Behaviour,* Fourth edition, Financial Times Pitman Publishing, describes and evaluates a wide spectrum of approaches. Otherwise, a student should find in the library one of the many editions of works by Fayol, Follett, Mayo or Taylor. To read one is rewarding.

ferences

1. Bissell, Richard (1955) *The Pajama Game*, Harmondsworth: Penguin,107–8. The book led to a famous musical hit.
2. Carr, E.H. (1964) *What is History?* Harmondsworth: Pelican, 55.
3. Dawson, Miles Menander (1932, ed.) *The Wisdom of Confucius*, Boston, Mass.: International Pocket Library. This is one of the many pocket books of sayings that are in print.
4. Machiavelli, Nicolo (c.1505) *The Prince*. A translation by W.K. Marriott is available on: http://daemon.ilt.columbia.edu/academic/digitexts/machiavelli
5. Nelson, Daniel (1980) *Frederick W. Taylor and the Rise of Scientific Management*, Madison, Wis.: University of Wisconsin Press.

6. Perrow, Charles (1979) *Complex Organisations: A critical essay*, New York, Scott, Foresman and Company, 64.

7. Fayol, Henri (1916) *Administration Industrielle et Générale*; English translation, *General and Industrial Management* (1967) London: Pitman.

8. Graham, Pauline (1995, ed.) *Mary Parker Follett – Prophet of Management: a celebration of writings from the 1920s*, Boston, Mass.: Harvard College.

9. Urwick, L. and Brech, E.F.L. (1959) *The Making of Scientific Management: Volume 1, Thirteen pioneers*, London: Pitman, 58–70.

10. For example, Daft, Richard L. (1993) *Management*, Third edition, Orlando, Fla.: Dryden, 52.

11. Smith, J.H.(1975) 'The significance of Elton Mayo', foreword to Mayo, Elton (1975) *The Social Problems of an Industrial Civilisation*, London: Routledge & Kegan Paul, xvi.

12. Mayo (1975) *op. cit.*, 64.

13. Mayo (1975) *op. cit.*, 70.

14. Stead, B.A. (1978) *Women in Management*, New York: Prentice Hall, 190.

15. Greenwood, Ronald C., Bolton, Alfred A. and Greenwood, Regina A. (1983) 'Hawthorne a half century later: relay assembly participants remember', *Journal of Management*, **9**, Fall/winter, 217–31.

16. McGregor, Douglas (1960) *The Human Side of Enterprise*, New York: McGraw-Hill, 33–48.

17. Ranyard, J.C. (1988) 'A history of OR and computing', *Journal of the Operational Research Society*, **39** (**12**) 1073–86.

18. von Bertalanffy, Ludwig (1950) 'An outline of general systems theory', *The British Journal for the Philosophy of Science*, **1** (**2**).

19. The systems message is not expressed as follows:
    Great fleas have little fleas upon their backs to bite 'em,
    And little fleas have lesser fleas, and so *ad infinitum*.

20. Trist, E.I. and Bamforth K.W. (1951) 'Some social and psychological consequences of the longwall method of coal getting', *Human Relations*, **4**, 1–38.

21. Wiener, Norbert (1948) *Cybernetics or Control and Communication in the Animal and Machine*, Cambridge, Mass.: MIT Press, 6.

22. Ashby, Ross (1956) *An Introduction to Cybernetics*, New York: John Wiley.

23. Beer, Stafford (1994) *Brain of the Firm*, Second edition, London: Wiley.

24. Gleick, J. (1988) *Chaos: The making of a new science*, London: Heinemann.

25. Stacey, Ralph D. (1996) *Strategic Management and Organisational Dynamics*, Second edition, London: Financial Times Pitman Publishing.

26. Pidd, M. (1996) *Modelling in Management Science*, London: Wiley.

27. Checkland, Peter (1981) *Systems Thinking, Systems Practice*, London: Wiley.

28. Partanen, Karl and Sovalainen, Vesa (1995) 'Perspectives on executive information systems', *Systems Practice*, **8** (**6**) December, 551–76.

29. Peters, Thomas J. and Waterman, Robert H. (1989) *In Search of Excellence: Lessons from America's best-run companies*, London: Harper & Row.

30. Carroll, Daniel T. (1983) 'A disappointing search for excellence', *Harvard Business Review*, **61** (**6**) November–December, 88.

31. Editorial (1984)'Who's excellent now?', *Business Week*, 5 November, 76–8.

32. Hitt, Michael A. and Ireland, R. Duane (1987) 'Peters and Waterman revisited: the unended quest for excellence', *Academy of Management Executive*, **2** (**2**) May, 91–8.

33. Mayo (1975) *op. cit.*, 61.

3

Outside the organisation: understanding the environment

Chapter objectives

When you have finished studying this chapter, you should be able to:

- explain why and how managers filter environmental information and focus their attention on key factors;

- model the environment in its operating and wider layers;

- describe the main components of the operating environment, demonstrating how they continuously interact with the organisation;

- use the PEST categories to describe the wider environment;

- present the international environment as an extra dimension that adds complexity to transactions;

- summarise the main methods of forecasting and their contribution to making sense of change.

The decline of Fokker[1]

Fokker aircraft became famous during the First World War. The company's plants in Germany built more than 4000 biplanes and triplanes. While slower than allied aircraft such as the Sopwith Camel, Fokker machines had superior manoeuvrability and armament, underpinning the successes of aces such as von Richthofen, The Red Baron.

After the war, Anthony Fokker returned to his native Netherlands to set up manufacturing. Technical superiority was maintained until the 1930s when the firm gradually fell behind leaders such as Lockheed and Boeing. After the Second World War, the Dutch government, determined to reestablish an independent aircraft industry, subsidised reconstruction and also supported the development costs for the F-27 Friendship and F-28 Fellowship aeroplanes. Yet, in spite of holding the lead in specialised markets, Fokker rarely made a profit and the government was pressed into cash injections and complex lease arrangements to keep the company afloat.

Around 1990, Fokker had one third of the world's small regional jet market (70 to 120 seats). This segment was badly hit after the Gulf War, with sales falling by two thirds in the five years to 1994. Competition also became more intense. McDonnell Douglas and Boeing cut prices of their overlapping (100 to 150 seat) ranges; the Franco-Italian competitor ATR formed an alliance with British Aerospace; Brazil, China and Indonesia proceeded with setting up their own industries.

Deutsche Aerospace (DASA), part of Daimler-Benz, bought a controlling interest in 1993 as part of its strategy of building an integrated aerospace company. Yet DASA was itself badly hit by the falling market. It lost DM1.5 billion from 1992 to 1994.

Costs are a problem for European manufacturers. Aircraft sales are usually made in United States dollars. Most of Fokker's costs arose in guilders or deutschmarks. The early 1990s saw these currencies strengthened against the dollar by some 20 per cent. Jobs were cut from 13 000 to 7900 in an effort to keep costs down. Suppliers, such as Shorts of Northern Ireland, Rolls-Royce and companies in the DASA group, were asked to cut prices and have payments delayed. Yet losses mounted. Fokker lost an estimated $840 million in 1995, more than 20 per cent of turnover or about $5 million on each sale.

Jurgen Schremp, head of Daimler-Benz, made a personal appeal to the Dutch prime minister for more subsidies to protect jobs and save the company. Other firms, including Shorts' Canadian parent Bombardier and the Korean Samsung, considered acquiring stakes. Yet little was forthcoming. Fokker was declared bankrupt in March 1996 and liquidated on 3 June 1997.

One industry analyst was quoted as saying that Fokker should not have existed for 30 years. It was too small for an industry dominated by giants.

Introduction

We can define the environment of an organisation in systems terms. It consists of *all those elements that lie outside its boundary with which it interacts.*[2] These interactions range from trade in the marketplace, where there are exchanges of products for money and pressures of competition, to less tangible influences within, say, the political arena. The number of factors that could be involved is huge.

■ Tossed like a blade of straw among powerful currents or steered like a majestic ship more powerful than the tides? What metaphor describes the process of directing the organisation through this complex and ever changing environment? We see in the opening case how Fokker thrived for many years, then struggled. Could it have survived independently? We cannot tell. Yet we can see that it was overcome by powerful forces of fall in demand and rising competition that it could do little to resist. This is the impact of the business environment. It presents the organisation with a context in which to succeed, often expressed as a set of *opportunities*. Simultaneously, it poses challenges that must be faced and coped with. Without appropriate responses, these *threats* may lead to the organisation's downfall.

We begin to examine how organisations respond to these external forces in Chapter 4. First, however, we must look at how managers learn about and make sense of them.

Sensing the environment

Is the message that managers must continually study a vast quantity of external information to succeed? No, just as human sensory organs are designed *both* to collect *and* filter out information, so must managers. Their approach is selective, they habitually study only those aspects of the environment that are relevant to them. Figure 3.1 outlines this process.

The upper half of the diagram shows the process of finding out. It has two phases related to a manager's need to say:

■ this is the way the environment is; and

■ this is the environment's impact on the organisation.

Therefore, both description and interpretation are required. First, managers identify what they need to know and collect the appropriate information. Second, managers interpret the information by relating it to the needs of the job and the organisation. Also, since so much of the management task is forward looking, interpretation must include an element of forecasting. More than knowing about the way the environment is, they want to know how it will be.

The lower half of the diagram concerns learning. This is a theme we shall return to in Chapter 24, so we shall only mention it briefly here. The learning process controls the way we find out. Instead of relying on intuition to drive their scanning of the environment, managers should assess how effective their selection has been and what they can do to improve it.

Where should one start? Another aspect of learning is to gain from the knowledge of others. This is often incorporated into patterns or models that can be applied to problems. Here, we can begin with a conventional framework for describing the environment. Using a well-tried approach enables us to make progress and helps comparison with the work of others. Yet we should bear in mind that managers perceive the environment from their individual perspectives. Their views are influenced by position, problems, prejudices and habits.

The Fokker case shows how being purposeful works. It is a brief description of some events leading to the company's downfall. Here, information has been

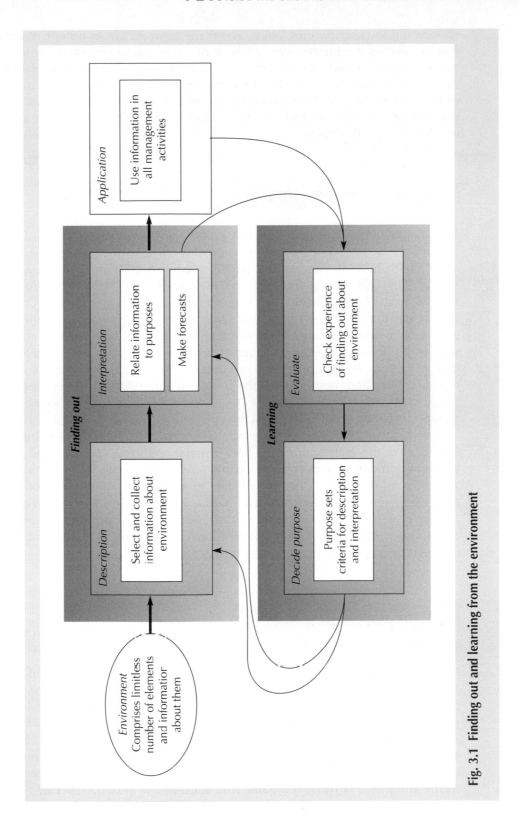

Fig. 3.1 Finding out and learning from the environment

chosen to illustrate teaching points about the business environment. Yet the case has been condensed from sources whose purpose was to spread and interpret the news for their readers. Their interest may have been as investors, employees, customers and so on. Anyhow, each observer selected and used data and made sense of it in different ways. Recognising this point tells us we should bear in mind *why* we are carrying out our analysis. We can then select what is relevant, a key part of developing our understanding.

Describing the environment

We have just noted the value of using a framework for our description. It is useful to think of the environment as having two layers, illustrated in Fig. 3.2. The *operating environment* is formed by specific elements that have clear and direct interactions with the organisation, often on a day-to-day basis. These are shown in Fig. 3.2 as customers, distributors, suppliers, competitors, investors and regulators. Remember that the list is typical, but may be longer or shorter, depending on the organisation and the manager's involvement. Successful organisations understand very well their operating environments and collect information on all elements so that they can respond quickly to changes. The *wider environment* is the set of broader dimensions that establish the context within which the operating environment exists. We refer to these factors as wider because their influence is often indirect, occurring gradually over a long period.

Figure 3.2 also includes the international environment, drawn as a third dimension. Shown this way, it illustrates how international issues permeate all aspects of the environment. In aircraft manufacture, for example, both the operating and the wider environments are global. Competition, supplies, innovation or political pressure can originate anywhere in the world. For other international companies, trading environments in different countries are so different that they manage, in effect, different businesses in these locations. A company that does not recognise different international influences is unlikely to succeed.

The operating environment

Customers

'First know your customer' is a valuable adage for the market-oriented organisation. Serving the needs of customers is its key purpose and if they are not satisfied, the organisation will fail. Usually, the identity of the customer is clear. For example, retail clothing shops deal with individual shoppers. They pay money in exchange for the supply of goods. Other cases are more complicated. If I buy Coca-Cola from a supermarket, I am a customer of that store yet what is my relationship to the Coca-Cola Company? The product will almost certainly have been supplied to the store by a bottling company with a licence to mix the special syrup with water, sugar and gas. Cadbury-Schweppes performs this function in the United

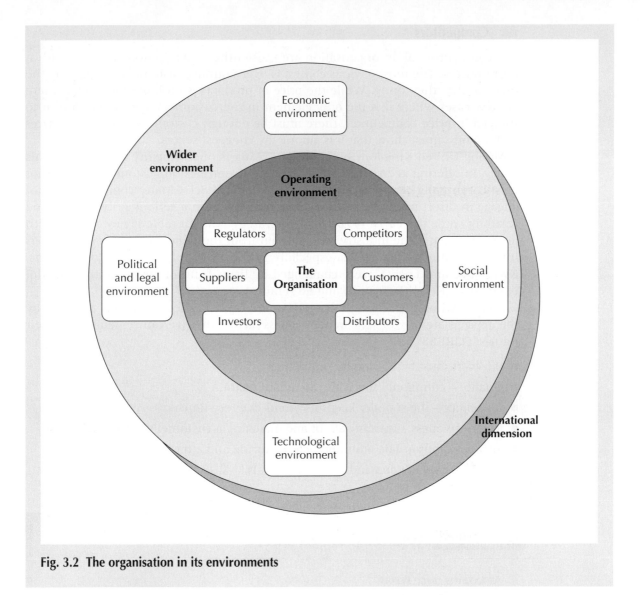

Fig. 3.2 The organisation in its environments

Kingdom. Further, I may have bought the drink for consumption by someone else. The Coca-Cola Company is faced with a difficult problem. Most consumers are not customers. Where should it focus its marketing effort? It needs to make sure that sufficient bottlers and distributors make Coca-Cola available while, simultaneously, cooperating with them in persuading individuals to consume it.

The difference between customers and consumers is highlighted in many public and personal service organisations. Here the latter become clients, patients or students, who often do not pay for the services they receive. For the supplying organisation, the problem is to show that the needs of the clients are being satisfied while the paying authority is receiving value for money.

Getting to know who customers are and what they want is the core task of marketing, explained in Chapter 20.

■ Competitors

The competitors of an organisation are those other organisations that vie with it for resources. The most obvious contest is over winning customers and gaining the revenue that they bring. While the price of products is an important factor, there are few cases where it is the only element in the customers' choice. For a firm to succeed in price competition, there must be enough customers sensitive to prices and the firm must show that it is among the cheapest sellers.

Among United Kingdom supermarkets, Asda is one company that pursues this policy. In offering keen prices every day, it concentrates on customers who do not trust continually changing promotions, *see* Exhibit 3.1.[3] Many companies do not engage in direct price competition; there has not been a serious price war in food retailing since the early 1970s. Asda's strategy is vulnerable if newcomers with lower costs enter the industry. Competition from these *limited assortment discounters* intensified during the 1990s, especially in the North of England. Local chains, Kwik Save and Locost, were challenged by firms from other EU countries: Aldi (Germany), Netto (Denmark) and Ed (France).

Usually, winning customers depends on more than price. Success is achieved by the appropriate mix of six competitiveness factors that we can remember by their initials, PQRRSS:

- Price – it must be not too far out of line.
- Quality – commonly this is the dominant factor.
- Reliability – the supplier keeps its promises every time.
- Responsiveness – learning about and matching a customer's particular needs.
- Service – appropriate attention before, during and after the sale.
- Speed – to satisfy demand faster than rivals.

Exhibit 3.1 Asda: competing on price?[3]

Asda turns price screw

Asda ... is demanding price cuts from suppliers to pass on to its customers, in an attempt to strengthen its market position.

It has written to selected suppliers demanding that they turn promotional deals into permanent price reductions. ...

In the letter, the Leeds-based company states its intention to operate permanent prices 'below those prevailing in the market place'. Customers resented 'yo-yo' pricing, the letter added. ...

... the letter is in line with the strategy ... of offering better value to its relatively poor customers who are based in the urban North of England.

The company has a policy of reducing promotional discounts, which it believes lead to distrust of its pricing.

It has about 300 promotional discounts a month now, compared with about 1000 a few years ago.

The balance among PQRRSS varies from firm to firm and from time to time. In the Fokker case, we can see that the company could not succeed in gaining customers by offering low-priced aircraft. The value of Fokker aircraft to customers lay in their quality and reliability and the strong after-sales network that the company maintained.

Competition is not restricted to profit-making businesses. We see that universities compete with each other to attract students who, in most European countries, either pay a fixed price or do not pay fees at all. Perceived quality and responsiveness are important in applicants' decision making. Further, competition for all organisations is not confined to gaining customers. Other resources, from raw materials to capital investment and from personnel to ideas and innovations, have to be contended for.

Given the importance of the competitive environment, it is not surprising that companies spend effort in gathering information on rivals' behaviour. Some of this is easy to obtain. The leading chain of department stores, John Lewis Partnership, claims to be 'Never knowingly undersold'. To help in keeping this promise, it employs 'Undersold Officers' at each store. They regularly visit all other local shops to check that no one is beating its prices. Similarly, it is good practice for manufacturers to buy competing goods, for hotel managers to stay at rivals' premises, for editors to read opponents' publications and even for chefs to eat out. Some organisations go beyond this kind of surveillance to engage in *benchmarking*. With the cooperation of partners, who may be direct rivals but are usually in related industries, they exchange information on processes, methods and products. ICL has compared its training methods with the Royal Mail and airlines have studied motor racing pit stop practices to try to shorten aircraft turnaround times. Other companies have searched worldwide for guides to the best ways of managing research and development effort.[4] The aim is to improve competitiveness, but not at the partner's expense.

Regulators

Regulators are elements outside the organisation that have power to control, legislate or directly influence its policies and practices. Industry regulators, the so-called 'watchdogs', became well known in the United Kingdom as utility companies were transferred from state to private ownership. OFFER, OFGAS, OFTEL and OFWAT regulate electricity, gas, telecommunications and water companies. Broadly speaking, their role is to balance the interests of customers and companies in industries where competition is absent or limited. Yet there are many more regulators than these and we shall look at some examples. They can be placed into three groups: statutory and voluntary regulators and self-appointed advocates.

Statutory regulators are set up by governments to ensure that legislation is followed, the rights of individuals are protected and the interests of the nation as a whole are advanced. Most aspects of organisational life are affected. Examples covering most organisations include: the Equal Opportunities Commission, which   oversees the application of relevant legislation in personnel management; the Health and Safety Executive, which supervises products, processes and work practices; Trading Standards departments, which take action where breach of consumer protection legislation is suspected. Many countries have equivalent establishments. There are other bodies whose role is confined to particular industries. Examples include the Civil Aviation Authority, the Independent Broadcasting Authority and the Nuclear Inspectorate. We should also recognise other regulators with international jurisdiction. These are set up within trading blocs, such as the competition monitoring offices within the EU, or because of specific international treaties or agreements. IATA, the International Air Transport Authority, regulates many aspects of the air transport industry from safety to routes and prices; the International Organization for Standardization works to assist free trade through the registration of common standards; the International Telecommunication Union works towards common technical standards and assists in planning regional interconnections.

Voluntary regulators are those established by groups of firms in certain fields or industries. Trade associations may perform this function although they are frequently formed to share information among members and combine to exert pressure on governments. In most countries concerted action to, say, control supplies or prices is illegal so these voluntary regulators cover other issues. The United Kingdom Press Complaints Commission was established by newspaper companies to study complaints and apply moral pressure to non-compliant publications. The intention was to forestall the setting up of a statutory body. One role of professional associations, for instance in accounting, engineering, law and medicine, is to regulate the behaviour of members.

Self-appointed advocates are outside interest groups whose power or influence is so great that they constrain an organisation's actions. They do not have official status. We shall see in Chapter 6 how associations such as Greenpeace call for higher ethical standards and influence the policies of large organisations such as Shell. Groups of customers, such as the Post Office Users' National Council, exert pressure over prices and service standards. The verdicts of consumers associations, now cooperating across Europe, influence the sales of products and indirectly set standards. Trades unions have often succeeded in regulating employment practices.

Given the importance of regulators to many organisations, many respond by appointing managers with the responsibility of dealing with them. In firms from financial service to utility companies for example, there are compliance departments whose role is to ensure that there is no breach of rules and codes of practice. Health and safety and equal opportunities questions are often dealt with by specialists in the personnel department.

■ Suppliers

Suppliers provide resources of all kinds. For retailers, the cost of goods bought for resale can amount to more than three quarters of all costs. Consequently, the buying department occupies a significant role. Being able to source the best goods at keenest prices is a key success factor. This applies especially to the limited assortment discounters, where the ability to put the lowest price goods on the shelf is the dominant competitive factor. Supplies cover more than raw materials, however. The organisation needs capital goods, from vehicles and equipment to land and buildings; other organisations supply the funds to finance these acquisitions; yet others provide personnel, either as employment agencies or direct employers of subcontract staff.

Many organisations argue that it is best not to rely on one supplier of whatever resource is being obtained. Either use several simultaneously or, in major purchases, make each contract the subject of open tender. Having a sole supplier brings with it the risk associated with too much dependence and severe problems if that company goes out of business. Motor assemblers, such as Volkswagen, had a tradition of sourcing key electrical components from two or three manufacturers, so-called *multiple sourcing*. The end of Fokker threatened those airlines that had committed themselves to operating only that company's aircraft (although it would be expected that spares would be available for at least ten years.)

The trend in modern supply chains, however, is to integrate and deepen the supplier–organisation links. Sharing information, often through direct computer connections, leads to savings in stock levels and improved service through just-in-time deliveries. Common efforts in product improvement are also being fostered. Therefore, the trend in industries such as car assembly, therefore, is towards *single sourcing*. In aircraft, it may seem less risky to buy from more than one manufacturer, but buying from more than one entails extra internal costs in pilot training, maintenance, scheduling and so on. British Airways, for example, keeps with Boeing jets to avoid these *switching costs*.

▨ Distributors

Distributors handle the organisation's products and ensure that they reach the customer. Their function is to add value to the product by ensuring that it is available at the right place and in quantities that the customer wishes to buy. In some industries such as cars, and in some countries, manufacturers have built networks through granting exclusive dealerships. Under this system, one dealer has the right to all sales in each area. It is justified by reference to the need to supply spares and after sales service yet has been challenged since competition is restricted. There are two arguments. First, other organisations are prevented from dealing in cars. Second, new entrants to the market have difficulty in having their vehicles displayed and sold. In the UK, Daewoo has bypassed these problems by setting up sales outlets in very small premises and contracting servicing to the specialist repairers, Halfords.

Access to crowded distribution channels is a constraint on the growth of small and medium-sized companies with good ideas. In service industries, franchising is one way of overcoming this problem. An innovator can achieve rapid exploitation of a new idea before imitators enter the market. Many restaurants, hotels, film processors, printers and household service companies are franchise operations. Each business is owned and managed locally, paying fees and royalties to the franchisor in exchange for supplies, technical support, marketing and so on.

Deepening of linkages with suppliers has been mentioned already. The same trend is occurring in distribution. Information on sales made anywhere in the world can be transferred through information systems to all stages of the supply chain. This enables raw material suppliers, component manufacturers, assemblers and shippers to balance production and demand much more readily than in the past. The integrated supply chain can be seen as behaving as a single organisation even though each stage consists of separate businesses.

■ Investors

The final element of our model of the operating environment is the group of investors. These range from banks and similar institutions which provide short-term finance, or liquidity, to sustain the business on a daily basis, to shareholders and lenders of long-term capital whose commitment is expected to last for years. Governments are often willing to provide grants and loans if in their national interest. EU membership restricts such action, however, if it can be shown to damage businesses elsewhere.

For sources of long-term capital, national differences are clearly seen. The United Kingdom and United States have well-developed stock markets with ready flows of funds for new investment. On the other hand, different traditions and the illiquid stock markets in Germany and Italy mean that banks provide more long-term finance as loans. Loans among business groupings are also common in Japan and South Korea. The effect is that companies based in these countries appear to have higher debt ratios, say 4:1, than those in the United Kingdom and United States, where the norm is not to exceed a 1:1 debt:equity ratio.

■ Managing the operating environment

A summary of the operating environment is shown in Fig. 3.3. This outlines the core of Fig. 3.2 with links representing flows of products, cash, operating information and influence. Operating information, being the day-to-day flows of data related to the exchange of products and cash, is separated from 'influence' to suggest that the latter is different in kind. Besides the formal links among elements of the system, there is much unstructured, or haphazard, information passing among elements of the system. Examples range from advertising by competitors to political pressure exerted by regulators. In combination, all the flows of Fig. 3.3 represent the dynamics of the system, enabling it to 'operate'.

We have already described examples of how organisations handle links with their operating environments by allocating specialists to roles from marketing to conformance. These *boundary spanning roles* usually focus on one aspect of the environment. This gives us clues as to how the vast quantity of information is coped with. The distribution manager concentrates on distribution or the financial accountant on relations with investors. Their interest in, and view of, the operating environment is purposeful; it is based on a key principle of management – the value of specialisation. Together, these managers handle the complexity faced by the organisation every day.

Two questions arise from this discussion. First, there is the overview. What pulls the organisation together? How do managers ensure that the operating team is effective, that it is achieving the best results and will continue to do so if environmental elements change? Second, managers should be seeking to anticipate change to be ready with responses. To do so they need to develop a deeper understanding of factors beyond the immediate perspective that, nevertheless, will affect the way things will be in the future. They require a view, so to speak, of the world over the horizon. Such broader and deeper understanding comes from investigation of the wider environment, which sets the context in which operating environment actions occur.

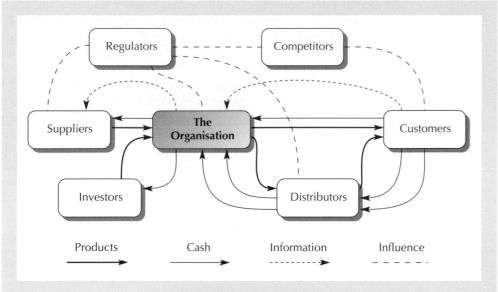

Fig. 3.3 Operating environment showing links between elements

The wider environment

Elements in the wider environment can influence the organisation in ways whose scope differs from the behaviour we have discussed above. While the boundary between the two environmental layers is artificial and rather arbitrary, we can separate them by the following:

■ *Operating environment*
  The organisation is engaged in regular, two-way interaction with other elements of its operating environment. There are exchanges of products, money, information and influence as shown in Fig. 3.3.

■ *Wider environment*
  The organisation is influenced by elements in the wider environment, either directly or through changes in its operating environment. Influence is usually one-way; only the largest organisations can exert much sway over the wider world and even then the effect will be limited.

The aircraft industry will illustrate this point. Shorts, the component supplier, will have seen Fokker as a key element of its operating environment. Fokker's own customers will be, from Shorts' point of view, part of the wider environment that influences demand for components and spares. After the failure of Fokker, Shorts will look to aircraft operators as a market for spares, probably for the next ten years. It will establish direct links with them, which means bringing them into its operating environment. The fall in demand, a key factor precipitating the crisis, was clearly beyond the control of either company and therefore in their wider environments. The timing of the fall depended on the withdrawal of support by the Dutch government. It could be that Fokker had become too used to treating the government as part of its operating environment. It failed to appreciate the international and national political forces that caused the state to say, 'Enough is enough'. The different perspectives of Fokker and Shorts, with the change in the latter, are illustrated in Fig. 3.4.

How do we identify and make sense of the wider environment? We made a start in the above case by recognising the government, the demand for travel that influences demand for aircraft and the acquisition activity of DASA. Rather than list items as they occur to us, various classifications have been proposed. Their advantage is that they act as check lists, ensuring that our view is comprehensive. Using this approach, it is common to think of the environment as made up of political,

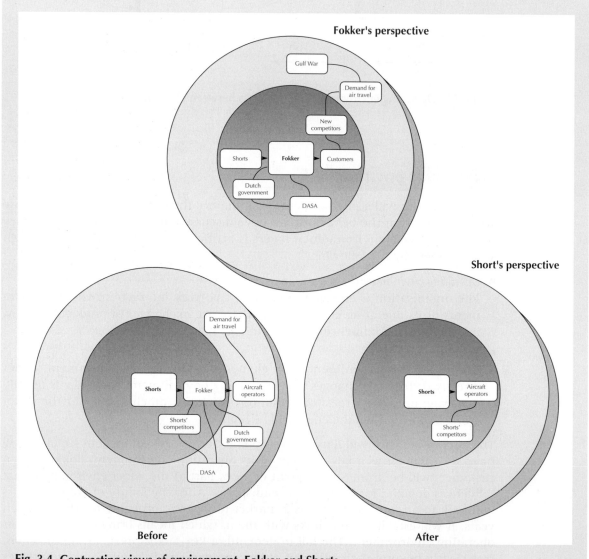

Fig. 3.4 Contrasting views of environment, Fokker and Shorts

economic, social and technological factors. PEST is a useful acronym here; others use STEP, EPTS and so on.

■ The political environment

The political environment of organisations comprises both the formal legal framework established by governments to regulate their behaviour and the often more complex and subtle relationships between governments and organisations involving power, pressure and influence. Especially for large organisations operating in more than one country, awareness of and sensitivity to these influences can be very important in achieving success. It is said, for example, that the main reason for the growth of Lonrho, the United Kingdom based mining and trading company with main operations located in Africa, was its political sensitivity. This stemmed from a network of personal links between Lonrho's one-time chief executive, 'Tiny' Rowland, and the heads of states south of the Sahara. He had established these with up-and-coming politicians during the colonial period.

Before looking at the international dimension, let us note three aspects of government–organisation links in one country:

- *The legal system* establishes a framework for operations. Even in nominally 'free' markets, there are many controls on behaviour. Some laws state what organisations must do: paying taxes and minimum wages; recruiting fairly; meeting safety standards. Other laws prescribe limits, stating what they must not do: banks must not allow balances to fall below defined levels; effluent producers have toxicity limits; publications of all kinds are censored; charitable and religious organisations have the scope of their activities restricted.

- *Governments encompass attitudes* that either favour or hinder different types of organisation and organisational behaviour. When *laissez-faire* views prevail, companies may find it easier to pursue policies such as growth by merger without the state mounting an investigation. At such times the government may lose interest in providing financial support, as Fokker found to its cost. Interventionist governments, on the other hand, press the national interest upon companies. In France of the 1990s, President Chirac's government followed Gaullist habits of intervention by creating large national groups. For instance, fearing the impact of international competition, Chirac forced the 1996 combination of the defence companies Aerospatiale and Dassault to form a group larger than British Aerospace or DASA. This merger was against the wishes of the profitable, privately owned Dassault.[5]

- *Government seeks to create a favourable economic and social environment.* This raises business confidence and, consequently, the willingness to invest and grow. For example, the favourable economic environment of the United Kingdom, coupled with efforts to welcome and integrate visiting managers and their families, are seen as the main reasons why the United Kingdom has received up to half the investment into the European Union by companies from South-East Asia.

Since governmental influences vary from country to country, international organisations face extra problems compared with those operating within one state. They must bear *political risk*. This is the threat of loss of assets, income or control through political actions of host governments, or indeed others. Revolutionary governments seize assets of companies and individuals associated with previous regimes; sanctions are sometimes imposed by leading powers (often the United States) in pursuit of their own national interests. The 1996 Helms-Burton Act[6] barred foreign companies having links with Cuba from trading in the US. Similar sanctions have been introduced in relation to business links in Cyprus, Iraq, Libya, Serbia and so on.

The effect of political risk can be seen in eastern Europe. After the 'velvet revolution' of 1989, Czechoslovakia was quick to establish a market economy, central bank and remove exchange controls. It established or extended its legal code covering company activities including a formal framework for joint ventures. Internal tensions were alleviated by a peaceful split between Slovakia and The Czech Republic. The former underwent a shift to the political left and began to lag, while the latter proceeded to 'Westernise' its institutions. It became particularly well placed to receive inward investment and was expected to be in the 'first wave' of Eastern countries joining the EU.

International alliances

A notable change in the international political framework is the growth of international trade alliances. The two most important are the EU and the NAFTA:

■ With 15 member nations in 1997, and a queue of applicants, the European Union is the most developed and integrated grouping in the world. Common decisions cover agriculture, economics, energy, fishing, trade, transport and the physical environment. Beyond economic cooperation, members have agreed to work together in foreign policy and aspects of justice and home policy. Presently, all, except the UK, accept the 'Social Chapter' on workers' rights. However, in view of the Labour Government's intention to ratify the Treaty of Amsterdam, this should be amended by 1999. The single market, formally completed for 1993, means that there are few constraints on moving products or assets among members. Some other countries, such as Norway, Iceland and Liechtenstein, are in the economic zone but not the EU.

Many see the need for a single currency as the next step in consolidating the single market. This would require close integration of national economic policies from control of government borrowing to taxation on products where different rates now account for large price differences across boundaries. Whatever the next step, harmonisation offers benefits of scale to many industries and opportunities to grow and become stronger. For others, there are threats. The EU plans to end, in 1999, duty-free shopping during air and sea travel between member states. Companies from manufacturers to transport providers must adapt. Duty free accounts for more than one quarter of the worldwide sales by Parfums Paco Rabane and over FF100 million of turnover at the shops of Aeroports de Paris.[7]

■ The North American Free Trade Agreement was signed in 1992 by Canada, Mexico and the United States. Its initial policies cover: phased abolition of tariffs on agricultural products and cars; access to Mexican operations for other road hauliers; and the raising of many standards in Mexico, including legal protection for patents and copyright.

Other groupings either exist (such as the Economic Community of West African States) or are proposed. Few have been successful. In some cases, member governments are rivalrous and unstable and the community's purpose is limited by stagnation of intra-regional trade. The ECOWAS countries, for example, rely on exporting agricultural and mineral products to the industrialised countries in exchange for manufactured goods. Furthermore, they suffer from poor infrastructure. Sub-Saharan Africa, excepting South Africa, has some 10 per cent of the world's population and less than 1 per cent of its telephone lines.[8]

Blocs can be welcomed by companies and other organisations as ways of reducing risk for those who operate within them. Yet there are two dangers. First, economic competition may develop into greater tension between the alliances. Such difficulties have shown themselves in disputes between the EU and the United States over subsidies to both agriculture and new passenger aircraft. Boeing, for example, alleges that the support given by European governments to the Airbus Industrie consortium amounts to unfair competition. The second danger is that alliances may further develop into three powerful trading blocs – America, Europe and the Pacific Rim. Whatever their form, they will have profound effects on the management of international operations.

Many organisations have to cope with a political environment rendered more complex by the overlapping and conflicting responsibilities of different authorities. SNCB, the Belgian state railway, is encouraged by the EU to plan and invest in high-speed lines as part of the development of the European transport infrastructure. Such investments are to cut travel times between Brussels and Amsterdam, Cologne, London or Paris by more than an hour. Simultaneously the national government seeks to rein in public spending while trying to satisfy regional aspirations. Railway investments in competing Flanders and Wallonia have to be balanced in spite of marked differences in costs and benefits of investment in the two parts of the country.[9]

■ The economic environment

The economic environment influences both the costs and revenues associated with operating in different locations. Within a national economic system, we can examine the general health and stability of the economic system using measures such as: general demand; per capita income; inflation; interest rates; and employment. When interest rates are high, for instance, consumers are less willing to borrow to make purchases and demand falls. This has strong effects in house buying markets, in turn influencing demand for goods and services associated with moving house. Examples range from removal services themselves to sales of interior decorating and other materials.

Advantages of different nations

There is more to the economic environment, however, than general measures of the economy. Porter presents a framework for comparing the characteristics of nations.[10] He argues that competing firms with different home bases have different advantages, summarised by the four factors shown in Fig. 3.5. A home base in the

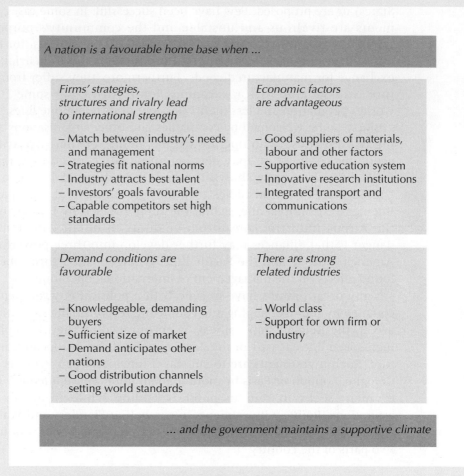

A nation is a favourable home base when ...

Firms' strategies, structures and rivalry lead to international strength

– Match between industry's needs and management
– Strategies fit national norms
– Industry attracts best talent
– Investors' goals favourable
– Capable competitors set high standards

Economic factors are advantageous

– Good suppliers of materials, labour and other factors
– Supportive education system
– Innovative research institutions
– Integrated transport and communications

Demand conditions are favourable

– Knowledgeable, demanding buyers
– Sufficient size of market
– Demand anticipates other nations
– Good distribution channels setting world standards

There are strong related industries

– World class
– Support for own firm or industry

... and the government maintains a supportive climate

Fig. 3.5 Factors behind the relative advantages of nations

right nation does not guarantee success since it is up to firms to seize opportunities presented. On the other hand, being based in the wrong nation raises problems. Firms seeking to build new strategies, engage in new activities, establish regional headquarters, or make acquisitions in other countries should look for nations that present a favourable pattern. Rather than seek quiet backwaters, Porter argues that ambitious companies should base themselves in national environments where standards are high. Figure 3.5 enables us to pick out the special national factors behind the success of Italian shoe manufacturers. Throughout the industry there are medium-sized family companies with a history of vigorous competition; local support comes from world class leather suppliers and designers enhanced by the mutually supportive industries such as gloves and handbags.

As with the political environment, study of the economic environment becomes more complex and risky for international transactions. The missions of many charities, including the International Red Cross, Médecins sans frontières and Oxfam, take them into areas where the 'business' infrastructure is weak. In 1994, conflict in Rwanda caused the displacement of refugees into neighbouring countries, say Tanzania or Zaire, whose governments were themselves facing economic difficulties. Regional offices of the charities in these border areas had often relied for international links on the dependable banking and communication systems within Rwanda. After the collapse, even taken-for-granted activities such as transferring money became very difficult. The only way to pay local staff was to send messengers from Europe with sufficient United States dollars to be exchanged through informal markets.

The Rwandan example, though easily recognised by managers with similar field experience, is atypical. Government policies, especially within blocs, aim towards stable exchange rates and converging economic indicators. It is believed that business investment and growth will be helped by calm economic conditions. Advocates of European monetary union, for instance, make this case.

■ The social environment

Sometimes called *societal* or *sociocultural,* the social environment refers to the elements that make up and give unique identity to what we broadly call society. A general description is helped by looking at demographic, geographic and cultural factors.

Demographic factors

Demographers study the make-up of populations. Changes generally take place slowly but can have profound effects on two important elements of the operating environment, namely the supply of staff and the demand for products. The most significant are as follows:

■ *Population.* Clearly, demand for products will be affected by changes in population. Many European countries, for example, have static or slowly declining numbers while in some less-developed nations the population is increasing by up to 3 per cent per annum. Within the national average, changes at local level can differ substantially. For instance, from 1991 to 1995, the population of England and Wales rose by 1.4 per cent. Yet some districts grew at more than five times this rate: Forest Heath, the Suffolk district around Newmarket, recorded 13 per cent and Bracknell, 9 per cent. In contrast, Scunthorpe lost 4.6 per cent of its people with Ipswich next at 4 per cent.[11] The implications for service providers from schools to supermarkets are clear.

■ *Age structure.* After birth rates decline, the age structure of the population shifts. With fewer babies and more old people, the demand for all kinds of products changes. Apart from the immediate changes in midwifery and geriatric care services, there are other trends that come through more slowly. Mothercare, part of the Storehouse group, used to specialise in clothes for expectant mothers and young children. Following the seminal fall in the United Kingdom birth rate during the 1970s, the company slowly extended its children's wear range to cover ages up to 12 years old. The increase in the numbers of healthy retired people creates new markets for holidays and leisure activities, especially at off-

Table 3.1 The ageing population of the United Kingdom

	1901	1931	1961	1991	2011
Total (millions)	38.2	46.0	52.8	57.8	61.2
School (5–15)	n.a.	n.a.	17.2%	13.6%	13.5%
65–74	3.3%	5.3%	7.5%	8.8%	8.8%
75–84	1.2%	1.8%	3.6%	5.4%	5.4%
85+	0.2%	0.3%	0.7%	1.6%	2.4%
Total 65+	4.7%	7.4%	11.8%	15.8%	16.6%

peak periods. Further, as Table 3.1 shows,[12] a further rise in the numbers of very old people is expected. Japan's population is ageing more quickly. The 15 per cent now over 65 is expected to reach 26 per cent by 2025. Japan's largest cosmetics company, Shiseido, finds its fastest growing lines are lotions to smooth wrinkles and resist baldness.[13]

Changes in age structure compound population shifts to influence the supply of labour. High unemployment rates will disguise scarcity of people in certain areas and occupations. Recognising emerging employee shortages, McDonald's set up its ReHIREment programme. This encourages older people to join the company while at the same time overcoming practical barriers to their employment.[14]

■ *Income distribution.* In democratic countries, shifts in income distribution are part of the battleground of party politics. There are many countries, however, where differentials are much higher than in Europe. Brazil is among the world's richest countries yet has many of its poorest people. Egypt, a nominally poor country, is a leading market for exported Mercedes-Benz cars.

Geographic factors

In examining geographic factors, the manager is trying to find out whether operating at one location is superior to another. Relevant questions are: location of raw materials, sources of energy and labour; location of markets; transport infrastructure; availability of sites; and climate. Different factors matter to different firms. When planning a new store, a supermarket chain evaluates accessibility, competition, the cost of land and the local population. Financial sector firms are attracted to London because of the large numbers already there. Access to markets, availability of experienced employees, and the infrastructure of communications, language and jurisdiction are backed up by excellent social and entertainment resources. These positive features outweigh high costs, frequently rising rents and poor local transport.[15]

Cultural factors

Under the heading of culture, we examine the values and attitudes of people – especially as customers or employees – and how these affect the organisation. One difficulty is that these issues are so much part of the taken-for-granted that we fail to recognise them at all! To overcome this, we can start by examining how values and attitudes are changing in our society and then move on to study others. Learning about other cultures leads to reflection on our own. Here we shall note some main changes, leaving intercultural comparisons until Chapter 5.

It has become commonplace to argue that society is changing at a pace never seen before. In these dangerous, 'turbulent times',[16] everything in society is challenged and transformed. New realities do not fit the old order. Some offer assistance through predicting where we are going, others tell us how to cope. Yet, as we investigate further in Chapter 24, whether our age is any more irregular, erratic and discontinuous than any other is doubtful. Social change is normal. And, since all parts of social and cultural life are interconnected, change is widespread. Exhibit 3.2 lists some areas where our attitudes and values change.

Exhibit 3.2 Challenging cultural changes

- **The individual:**
  The nature of self; gender; notions of responsibility; privacy; housing; health; ageing.

- **The social person:**
  Effects of one's behaviour on others; attitudes to smoking, drinking, driving; leisure; mass behaviour – concerts, crowds, trades unions; the structure of society – wealth, place, race; religion; the law.

- **The family:**
  What constitutes a family; single parents; role of grandparents and who is responsible for them; parenthood and the 'housewife'; rights of children.

- **Employment:**
  Attitudes to work and employment; women as employees and leaders; pressure for equal opportunity; retirement.

- **Organisations:**
  Function and power of organisations; privatisation; employers or exploiters?

- **Mankind and the environment:**
  Attitudes to the 'rights' of animals; the purpose of the countryside; pollution and waste; the function of cities; congestion.

- **Intellectual life:**
  The function of education – training or enlightenment? The arts; media; control of science and technology.

- **The nation:**
  Political system; attitudes to monarchy, presidency etc; nationalism.

- **Europe:**
  Economic fortress; integrated harmony; centralisation versus sovereignty; currency.

The technological environment

Technology is the application of knowledge to products and processes. Clearly, advances can affect both aspects. For example, the development of scanning systems, using light or ultrasound, has applications in fields as diverse as medicine and retailing. The processes of diagnosing heart problems or counting groceries at the checkout have been transformed by scanning. Suppliers have been able to offer new products to support these innovations, both in the equipment itself and in associated machines from couches and conveyors to computers for processing the information.

It has been argued that one benefit of large scale is the ability to develop technology more quickly. This comes from more spending on research and the faster accumulation of operating experience. Companies from pharmaceutical manufacturers to innovative service providers have followed this policy. Yet it is important to distinguish between transferable and embedded knowledge.[17] The former, incorporated in products, publications or even the minds of individuals, can move quickly. A rival can buy and dismantle a machine to discover its parts and method of operation; information on innovations appears in publications from patent applications and learned journals to instruction books; technologists with needed expertise can be recruited. Embedded knowledge, on the other hand, is neither written down nor possessed by individuals; it is embedded within teams or even whole organisations. While it is easy to buy a Toyota car, dismantling it will yield few clues about how its production has been organised.

Recognising the transferable nature of much knowledge, organisations draw on the technological environment as a source of product and process innovation. They maintain close contacts with equipment suppliers and research organisations. Woollen carpet weavers, for example, have access to process innovations through both the Wool Industry Research Association and loom manufacturers such as Cobbles. Since the knowledge is shared, each does not require large scale to benefit from the developments. There is more on technology and innovation in Chapter 21.

Technological innovation does not, so to speak, stand around awaiting ready applications. Winning firms are those that recognise the possibilities presented by new ideas and apply them both quickly and in imaginative ways. The bar coding of consumer products began for improving the management of retail stocks. Leading companies, however, soon saw the opportunities presented by collecting detailed information on each customer. Hence the creation of loyalty cards. Their dual functions are to reward customers according to how much they spend and to capture detailed information on what each is buying. Therefore promotions can be targeted and stores can ensure that more of the goods bought by high spending customers are on display. Personalisation and improved service levels are keys to customer retention. This race to apply innovations does not stop. Extensions of self-service to self-billing have been pioneered by Albert Heijn, in The Netherlands, and Safeway in Britain. Even the bar code may not survive. Its one-dimensional form limits the information to one serial number. It may be replaced by new patterns containing up to 2000 characters, or by cheap radio-sensitive chips.[18]

■ The international dimension

Through the examples of operating and wider environments, we have seen different issues that must be confronted when the organisation has interests in more than one country. The international dimension is best seen not as yet another environment but as a number of layers suggested in Fig. 3.2. Each layer represents a nation or region and contains all the PEST factors. Therefore, there are multiple political, economic, social and technological environments. Their similarities and differences have implications for all organisations.

A first glance at the PEST factors may suggest that it is technology that displays the greatest similarity across the world and, therefore, poses least problems in its management on a global scale. Harmonisation of products is a trend that has been picked out by authors such as Levitt.[19] He saw large-scale production of standardised items as so cheap that it is better to treat the world as a single market than as many separate ones. Levitt went beyond recognising the harmonisation of products and production systems. For him, differences in cultural preferences, national standards and tastes, and even business organisations themselves, were remnants of the past.

Levitt cited as evidence changes in automatic washing machines in Europe from the 1960s. Hoover, a United States owned company with a strong market share in the United Kingdom, sought to increase its sales in other countries. It analysed carefully each national market and tried to adapt its products to match local preferences. For instance, German and Swedish consumers were used to tall, wide and strong-looking casings, stainless steel drums, 6 kg capacity and high spin speed. In Sweden, water heating was not normally required. In Germany, however, it was demanded as users preferred to wash at temperatures higher than available from the domestic system. Italians, on the other hand, expected smaller, brightly coloured casings, enamelled drums with only 4 kg capacity and lower spin speed. The effect on Hoover's policy was that it had to bear extra costs to meet just some variations in preference. To these had to be added trade tariffs as the United Kingdom did not join the EEC until 1971. In retrospect, Levitt argued that there was already ample evidence of the 'cheap and cheerful' Italian models, including Indesit and Zanussi, making headway in all markets, including Germany and Sweden. Hoover ought to have standardised production on a simple model and used promotion to overcome previously apparent differences between markets. Today, the European market for automatic washers displays much greater homogeneity.

To counter Levitt's convergence argument, one can point to its narrow focus on some manufactured goods. Yet, remembering that technology is concerned with both products and processes, many differences are visible throughout the world. Even the technology of cultivation, from the hand-held hoe to the deep plough, is deeply embedded in local factors from physical conditions and labour costs to family structures and cultural patterns. Differences in other of the PEST environments are perhaps more obvious. Whether they are converging or diverging, and how international organisations cope with trends, are questions raised again in Chapter 5.

Interpreting the environment

Interpretation is the second stage shown in Fig. 3.1. Successful organisations display the ability to link the gathering of information to their purposes. This can be done by focusing attention on key success factors. How are they selected?

Key factors have the following characteristics:

■ they are expected to have a continuing influence on the project, department or organisation;

■ changes affect the relationships between the organisation and others in the environment;

■ their influence is substantial – they are worth much money.

Examples vary from manager to manager, firm to firm and industry to industry. We can illustrate the need for identifying key success factors by referring to a case that went wrong. Gilad and others[20] describe a pharmaceutical company project. The managers were considering whether to engage in a large-scale pilot production run of a new nutritional product. Judgements had to be made on market potential and competitors' strategies. Exhibit 3.3 lists items of environmental information thought by managers to be relevant, the asterisks identifying the most important.

The study brought out several problems with the collection of information in the lists: it turned out to be difficult to learn about competitors' technologies; managers were more satisfied with their marketing intelligence than technical intelligence; senior managers were more likely to find gaps in information, reflecting the filtering that often takes pace in hierarchies. Overconfidence in assessment of their firm's technical competence meant that, as events unfolded, the managers were surprised by competitors launching low cost products or dropping prices. Furthermore, access to the United States market was hampered by restrictions imposed by the Food and Drug Administration, an environmental question that did not figure in the original success factor list.

Exhibit 3.3 New product pilot project: relevant environment information

Market
Who are the competitors? *
Market size, present and future *
Competitors' prices *
Who might enter the market?
Substitutes and competing products
Competitors' track records
Competitors and our customers
Consumers' views of new product v rivals

Technical
Total costs for rival products *
Raw material supplies *
Competitors' development efforts *
Competitors' costs for new products *
State of technology *

Other
Links between competitors and parent companies

■ Forecasting

Noting that key factors have an important impact over a long period, managers need to go beyond descriptions of the present environment towards anticipation of the future. There are various forecasting methods whose application depends on whether data is quantitative or qualitative.

Quantitative methods

These are models that process historical data using numerical techniques. We shall look at causal and time-series modelling.

- Causal models attempt to establish patterns of relationships that decide the behaviour of the variables in question.

For instance, the modeller may be looking at sales from DIY stores. Rather than extrapolate trends from the past, a practice that in such cases is unreliable, the starting point may be the recognition that annual sales are closely related to the numbers of people who move home. Since such data is available, and house moves tend to precede the increased spending on carpets, curtains, finishes and furnishings, this approach gives a better forecast. A feature of the wider environment (house moves) is used to explain how sales, in the operating environment, behave.

Causal models can combine information on several variables to forecast the behaviour of others. The makers of Dettol, the leading domestic disinfectant and antiseptic, found that sales were strongly related to four factors shown in Exhibit 3.4. Of these, the first two were beyond the company's control but could be studied and forecast. With that information, it was possible to optimise prices and spending on advertising.[21]

- Time series models are based on the simple notion that the future depends on the past.

Exhibit 3.4 Factors affecting sales of Dettol

The study sought the main factors affecting the sales of Dettol. Sales were found to have statistically significant relationships with:

- real personal disposable income (purchases tended to fall when consumers had relatively less money);
- the seasons (sales of all disinfectants and antiseptics are higher in the warmer months);
- price (adjusted for inflation);
- the weight of advertising.

With the first two factors being outside the company's scope, the effects of price and advertising are of greatest interest. The study measured their effect. Price elasticity was estimated at −0.44 and advertising elasticity at 0.19. This data, coupled with cost figures, enabled the company to show that raising both price and advertising expenditure increased profits.

Lacking known relationships that could be built into a causal model, historical data is combined to make the forecast. For example, sales of a national newspaper for the next three months can, lacking significant changes in policy such as a price war, be predicted by examining recent trends. Those whose sales are growing should continue to grow, and so on.

Many time series do not display obvious patterns, any trends being masked by seasonal and random variations. In Fig. 3.6, the sales of a gift product are shown by the heavy line. In this case, an upward *trend* with *seasonal variations* and *random irregularities* is clearly seen. There are statistical techniques to *decompose* these and less obvious cases. This means breaking the changes down into components shown along the base of the graph. The trend and fluctuations can then be forecast separately. Due to their nature, random changes cannot be forecast.

Qualitative methods

Qualitative methods bring together the experience, intuition and value systems of experts to forecast the long-term future. We can mention three here:

■ *Delphi method*

The Delphi method is named after the Greek oracle, *see* Exhibit 3.5. A series of surveys draws together expert opinion. The experts, about ten in number not necessarily assembled in one place, are asked to speculate on questions about their field in (say) ten or more years time. If there is no accord after this first stage, all are circulated with each other's responses. Then follows a second

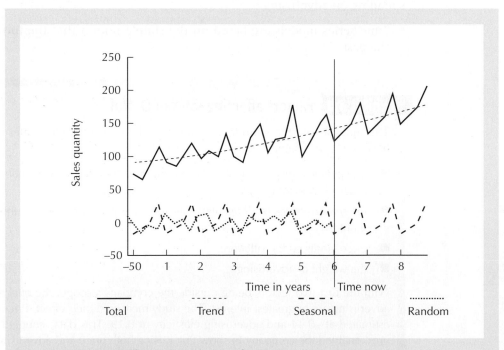

Fig. 3.6 Sales graph illustrating mixture of patterns

Exhibit 3.5 **Consulting the oracle**

In ancient Greece, enquirers about personal issues or affairs of state visited sacred sites, or oracles. Here answers, often ambiguous, came via priests from the utterances of priestesses of the deity. Delphi, whose shrine was dedicated to Apollo, was the most celebrated. Here, a conical stone, the *omphalos*, marked the centre of the Earth.

---

round in which a move towards consensus is anticipated. Rounds continue as necessary. Questions asked may be, for example, 'What do you think the average size of long-range passenger aircraft will be in 2020?' or 'What changes will there be in steel production methods before the middle of the next decade?'

Delphi methods are part of the family of jury methods gathering expert opinion. A related approach invites senior managers to forecast the business environment. They meet in a workshop setting away from the normal workplace with support from background data, statistical trends and so on.

■ *Sales force surveys*

Using the opinion and contacts of sales people themselves can enrich quantitative forecasts. Representatives spend much time with customers, hear about developments and gain a feel for the actions of competitors. Data is assembled using jury methods, general meetings or questionnaires.

■ *Customer surveys*

While many customer surveys gather quantitative data, approaches using customer panels are used to give an early feel for changes in attitudes or the likely acceptance of new product ideas. This is one of the functions of market research, discussed in Chapter 20.

Good forecasting combines technique and judgement. Nowhere are the problems thrown into sharper focus than in investment. Hindsight so often yields better performance:

> *PDFM, a United Kingdom subsidiary of the Union Bank of Switzerland, manages pension funds worth about £50 billion. In January 1995, it decided that shares in London and New York were overvalued and the market crash was imminent. Additionally, it expected United Kingdom inflation to rise in the months up to the 1997 election. Consequently, managers switched some 15 per cent of its assets into cash and up to 6 per cent into index-linked government bonds to hedge inflation. Figure 3.7 shows what happened in the financial markets over the following eighteen months. The London share market advanced by one third (New York was even stronger) while interest rates and inflation remained low. Keeping out of shares may have cost the funds more than £2 billion. Compared with rivals, they underperformed by a large margin.[22]*

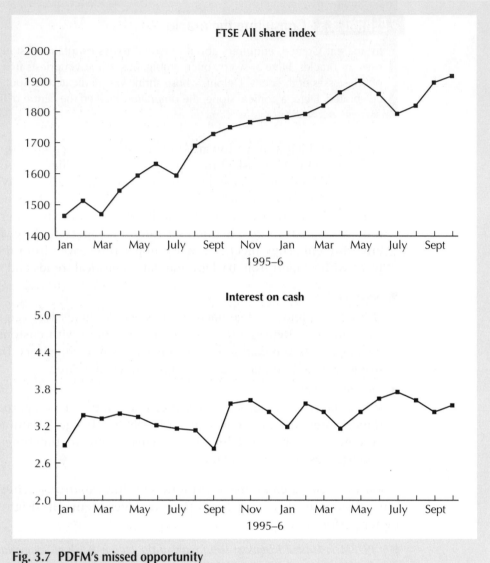

Fig. 3.7 PDFM's missed opportunity

Conclusion: interpreting the changing environment

This chapter has covered two parallel themes, the nature of the changing environment and how managers can make sense of it in the context of their jobs. The connections between the themes were brought out in Fig. 3.1. This suggests that people do not relate to the environment in a haphazard way. What they see, investigate and interpret is selected on the basis of intuition and experience.

The problem for managers is that reliance on information that has been of value in the past is no guard against the unexpected. Key success factors will change as the organisation moves into new territories. Hence a manager needs to review whether the right information is being obtained. Studying the wider environment can yield important clues.

The layered model of the environment, shown in Fig. 3.2, helps in understanding and coping. The operating environment contains elements with which there is continual interaction. Yet it is difficult, under the pressure of day-to-day affairs, to spot fundamental influences causing upheavals in the operating environment. These are found in the wider environment. Furthermore, for firms that have interests in more than one nation, the international environment adds extra layers of complexity.

Whatever the data, managers want to use it to anticipate the future. There are many methods of forecasting to help this process. Both quantitative and qualitative, their purpose is to give a good sense of what is to happen and hence support decision making.

Quick check up *Can you ...*

- Define environment;
- Distinguish between operating and wider environments;
- List six main elements of the operating environment;
- Give instances of boundary spanning roles;

- Name the four PEST elements;
- Outline how managers determine key environmental elements;
- Identify two classes of quantitative forecasting model;
- Give examples of three qualitative forecasting methods.

Questions

Chapter review

3.1 What elements of the operating environment are identified in the text? Suggest another that may be relevant.

3.2 How can one distinguish between the operating and wider environments?

3.3 Outline the types of forecasting set out in the chapter and suggest a role for each.

Application

3.4 What are the main elements of the operating environment for a hospital, a furniture retailer or a local newspaper? Use a diagram to sketch the key flows.

3.5 Suggest some key success factors in relation to the environment of Fokker.

Investigation

3.6 Investigate how a manager finds out about the business environment. Find out what types of information are collected and from what sources.

The international ambitions of Luxottica[23]

In May 1995, Luxottica became the world's largest supplier of spectacle frames. It achieved this through the bold step of acquiring, for $1.3 billion, United States Shoe Corporation. This company retailed shoes, clothing and frames, but Luxottica was only interested in the LensCrafters division. This subsidiary, with turnover greater than Luxottica's own total sales, was the largest optical retailer in the world and aiming for 50 per cent of the United States market. Luxottica quickly sold the footwear business to the specialist Nine West for $600 million and is reorganising the clothing arm with a view to selling. Vertical integration has meant expansion in frame production. Before the merger, 5 per cent of LensCrafters' sales were of Luxottica products, now the figure exceeds 50 per cent.

The present chairman, Leonardo del Vecchio, founded Luxottica in 1961. His innovation was to integrate manufacture and distribution so that, in the 18 countries where the firm operates, it controls the distribution network. It has strengths in design and marketing of high quality products. Until the move into United States retailing, it had focused on producing 12.8 million frames each year from four factories in north-east Italy. By 1996, 91 per cent of sales of 2373 billion lire (£841 million) were outside Italy, with some 70 per cent in the United States. Having avoided the Milan bourse, one quarter of the company's shares are listed on the New York stock exchange with the rest being retained by the family company Leonardo Finanziaria.

Luxottica is not a well-known brand as sales are under other names, mostly designer labels such as Giorgio Armani, Brooks Brothers and Yves St Laurent. It had thought that branding would influence sales through independent retailers but the growth of the quick-service optical superstores and imports of cheap frames from South-East Asia threatened its position. The company also expressed the wish to get closer to its customers.

Sunglasses also present an opportunity, especially in the US. The premium market, for pairs costing more than $30, is expanding. Using athletes to endorse the products is common, with Ray Ban, Revo and Oakley being well known. New entrants include the privately owned Japanese camera company Nikon, which is imitating the marketing of athletic shoes. One quarter of United States adults own four or more pairs, each designed for a different activity. Using its technical expertise, Nikon gears lenses to different sports.

Leonardo Finanziaria has joined with the Benetton company to buy and merge leading supermarket chains in Italy.

Questions

1 Using the categories explained in this chapter, draw up lists of factors in the environment that may influence Luxottica's future. If necessary, add items from your business knowledge.

2 What are the key factors to which Leonardo del Vecchio should pay attention?

Bibliography

Beyond the texts on the business environment mentioned in the references, the following give broad views of the business environment: Lynch, Richard (1997) *Corporate Strategy*, London: Financial Times Pitman Publishing; Hutton, Will (1996) *The State We're in*, London: Vintage; and Toynbee, Arnold and Ikeda, Daisaku (1989) *Choose Life: A Dialogue*, Oxford, OUP.

References

1. Smit, Barbara and Studemann, Frederick (1996) 'Struggling Fokker grounded as Daimler cuts the engine', *The European*, 25 January, 17; 'The lesson in Fokker's fall', *The Economist*, **338 (7950)** 27 January 1996, 55–6; 'Bombardier away: regional jets', *The Economist*, **338 (7954)** 24 February 1996, 69–70; van der Krol, Roger (1996) 'Fokker goes into bankruptcy', *Financial Times*, 16 March, 1; 'Inevitable end', *Flight International*, **149 (4515)** 20 March 1996, 3; Hetzel, Helmut (1997) 'Fokker ade: das Ende einer Legende', *Die Presse*, 18 April.
2. Some authors refer to this as the *external environment*. This enables them to use *internal environment* to refer to elements inside the organisation. These extra labels are muddled and are not used here.
3. Bruce, Rupert (1994) 'Asda turns price screw', *Independent on Sunday: Business*, 13 March, 1.
4. Trapp, Roger (1994) 'Benchmarking moves on to bench testing', *Independent on Sunday: Business*, 9 January, 13.
5. Milner, Mark and Duval-Smith, Alex (1996) 'Divine right of Chirac leaves aircraft firms cursing union', *Guardian*, 31 August, 24.
6. Cuban Liberty and Democratic Solidarity (Libertad) Act, 1996,104–14, 110 Stat. 785. This act imposes United States law on people who are neither nationals nor residents concerning their conduct outside the US.
7. Sullivan, Ruth (1995) 'Clock ticks as famous names look to the future', *The European*, 19 October, 10.
8. Holman, Michael (1995) 'A continent in transition', *Financial Times*, Survey of International Telecommunications, 3 October, xxxviii.
9. Southey, Caroline (1995) 'Controversy threatens rail network', *Financial Times*, 28 June, iii.
10. Porter, Michael E. (1991) *The Competitive Advantage of Nations*, London: Macmillan.
11. Office for National Statistics (1996) *Monitor PP1*, London: ONS.
12. Central Statistical Office (1996) *Annual Abstract of Statistics*, London: HMSO, 8.
13. Dawkins, William (1995) 'Gold streaks highlight Japan's grey waves – Shiseido's fastest growing products are aimed at the aged', *Financial Times*, 7 January, 11.
14. Marmer, Charles (1995) 'Unlock the potential of older workers', *Personnel Journal*, **74 (10)** October, 56–63.
15. Society of Property Researchers (1992) *London as a Business Location*, SPR, c/o RICS Research Officer, 12 Great George Street, London SW1P 3AD, 1–2.
16. Drucker, Peter (1981) *Managing in Turbulent Times*, London: Pan, 10.
17. Badaracco, J.(1991) *The Knowledge Link: How firms compete through strategic alliances*, Boston, Mass.: Harvard Business School Press.
18. Gooding, Claire (1995) 'Bar codes get high-tech links', *Financial Times*, 4 October, vi; Foremski, Tom (1995) 'Supermarkets checkout systems', *ibid*. v.
19. Levitt, Theodore (1983) 'The globalisation of markets', *Harvard Business Review*, May–June, 92–102.
20. Gilad, Benjamin, Gordon, George and Sudit, Ephraim (1993) 'Identifying gaps and blind sports in competitive intelligence', *Long Range Planning*, **26 (6)**, 107–13.

21. Cannon, Tom (1992) *Basic Marketing*, Third edition, London: Cassell, 156–71.

22. Murphy, Paul and Springett, Pauline (1996) 'Pensions giant bets £10bn on markets crash', *Guardian*, 18 September, 1; also 'Alarm over share collapse gamble', *Idem, ibid.* 18.

23. Jennings, Suzanne L. (1994) 'Niches within a niche', *Forbes*, **153** (**9**), 25 April, 122; Hill, Andrew (1995) 'A name right out of the blue – Profile: Luxottica', *The Financial Times Survey of Europe's most respected companies*, 19 September, IV; Morais, Richard C. (1996) 'Luxottica's golden spectacles', *Forbes*, **157** (**10**), 20 May, 98–9; Betts, Paul (1997) 'Case study: Luxottica and Parmalat', *Financial Times*, 22 October; http://www.luxottica.it/

Chapter 4

Inside the organisation: adapting to change

Chapter objectives

When you have finished studying this chapter, you should be able to:

- identify types of environmental change and the different problems they pose for organisations;

- outline the population ecology perspective on adaptation, suggesting limitations of organisational–organism analogies;

- present and illustrate the principal ways that organisations achieve fit with their environments;

- compare small and large organisations in their search for fit, showing why the latter rely on forecasting;

- define organisational culture and show how it can be seen as having visible and invisible layers;

- demonstrate how artefacts can be used as a route to holistic understanding of culture;

- comment on the application of categories of culture;

- show why cultural change may be needed and explain why this change is difficult to achieve.

Leg godt (play well): can Lego adapt?[1]

Lego is the only European toy company in the world's top ten and one of the best-known of all brands. Fourteen billion plastic pieces are produced each year to meet the rising demand from 133 countries. Some 180 billion have been supplied since 1949 when Lego's founder, Ole Kirk Christiansen, and his son switched from wooden toys to injection moulded plastic bricks. Now the family is one of Europe's wealthiest.

The early design was a close imitation of the British Kiddikraft. It was improved in 1955 when the completely hollow bricks had the familiar tubes moulded inside. This single innovation meant that the bricks interlocked much better and was the foundation for future success. Exports to the United Kingdom started in 1960, by which time Kiddikraft, which had given up bricks because they did not sell, did not claim any trade infringement. The final breakthrough in the acceptance of Lego System as an educational toy came in 1963 when the material specification was changed. Cellulose acetate, which could shrink and discolour, was replaced by the acrylic ABS. Fundamentals have not changed since. Now, most patents have expired and Lego itself attracts copies. None lasts long because the company has such a lead in marketing, design and manufacture – brick dimensions have tolerances of some 5 microns (0.005 millimetres). In addition, Lego vigorously defends its intellectual property of trademarks, designs and remaining patents.

Registration of the company in Switzerland meant that detailed figures were not released until the family decided to do so in 1995. For 20 years, annual profit growth had exceeded 10 per cent. In 1995, however, it fell 34 per cent to £65 million, recovering to £68 million the following year. Growth in the estimated $1.2 billion turnover is tailing off; German sales fell by 3 per cent in 1995. Lego has 70 per cent of the construction toy market. Possibly matching different ways of bringing up children, construction accounts for 8 per cent of

toys sold in Germany, 5 per cent in the United Kingdom and 1.5 per cent in Spain. Yet parents who favour educational toys have begun to accept that many electronic toys and personal computers contribute to the expansion of their children's skills. Children are no longer raised on conkers and tag, but Playstations and video machines. Competition for the toy budget, especially at Christmas, is severe.

'Age compression' describes the trend among children, especially in smaller families, to grow up faster than previous generations. Or, at least, this is the perception of both parents and offspring. In the 1960s, the basic Lego bricks were sold to ages four to ten, now children over six say they are not 'cool'. In response, the firm segments its offering by moving from Duplo, through trains, zoos and farms, on to classic models, broadened to include themes from pirates to space, and finally Technic. The last range includes motors containing chips and software control. In 1997, recognising that two thirds of sets are bought for boys, the company introduced a new range, Scala, aimed at girls over six years old.

In response to these changes, Lego is diversifying. It is aiming to increase sales in East Asia. There are to be new products with the Lego name. Plans are to reduce, in ten years, the reliance on sales of Lego System from 95 to 75 per cent. The brand is to be used on both clothes from high quality manufacturers and a range of playground equipment from the Danish maker, Kompan. Facing the challenge from software in the 'imaginative play' market, Lego has a joint venture with Mindscape. This US company is producing interactive software designed around the idea of visiting and rebuilding a Lego town. Later, on-screen virtual Lego will enable children to design before assembling their toys.

There are to be more theme parks. Starting with a few models on a patch of waste ground, the original Legoland was built in response to demands to see the Billund factory. Some 25 million people have visited the site. Many cities have written asking for their own versions. A second park opened at Windsor in 1996, receiving 1.5 million visitors in its first year. Another is planned for San Diego in 1999. Plans are for 15 sites by 2050. Each costs more than £50 million.

The slow diversification shows the company's reluctance to move away from the business it knows best. There is a family atmosphere among the 9200 employees, underscored by the private ownership and the fact that the present chief, Kjeld Kirk Kristiansen, is the founder's grandson. The family, and company, are focused on doing the right things for children. While models of knights and pirates are sold, there are no twentieth century military references. This non-violent theme dates to the 1940s when Kristiansen's mother stopped the company from selling a wooden toy pistol.

Mr Kristiansen concedes that the company had been guided too much by the success of the past. He recognised, by 1994, that quicker response to events was needed. Under a change project called Compass, senior managers were encouraged to halve their time in formal meetings. Less effort was to be spent on control and more time on coaching employees' skills. More autonomy was to be given to managers in key markets such as Germany, Japan, the United Kingdom and the United States. They would decide the mix of products to be pushed and choice of packaging. Product development, historically the exclusive domain of Billund, is to be decentralised and accelerated. Marketing staff worldwide will contribute to plans at an early stage.

Introduction

The question posed in the opening case – Can Lego adapt? – is faced by all organisations. For some, it is permanently on the agenda while, for others, it is asked only intermittently. How often depends on changes in the environment. In general, more changes mean that more adaptation is required.

Lego was founded by people who had the insight and drive to pick and develop a winning formula. For almost fifty years it has built on that same formula, entering new geographic markets, broadening the product range and improving quality. With success leading to success, it never had to question if there may be an end or when the end might be. The signs in recent years, however, show that there are threats to Lego's hegemony. For the post-industrial age, parents begin to value imaginative, as opposed to manual, skills. Construction toys face information technology. Software arrives in the kindergarten.

Naturally, the Kristiansens and the Lego company do not have to take any notice of this. The business, after all, is a private one. It does seem that, for several years, belief in the 'winning formula' caused them to resist change. They were not asking the adaptation question. Taking up a point from Chapter 3, we see that it is not the *fact* of environmental change that is important. Instead, it is the way the managers recognise and interpret the change and incorporate it into their business. At one extreme, they can ignore it and run the risk of following into oblivion makers of Bayko, Kiddikraft bricks, Meccano (almost) and Trix. At the other extreme, they can seek to match every whim and fad, risking the loss of focus suffered by almost all of Lego's rivals in the top ten. Lego has to find the balance. It has to understand the shifts to which it chooses to respond. Then it must match them with appropriate actions.

The chapter considers two features of this discussion. First, we study how organisations cope with the dynamic environment. Second, we probe more deeply into the organisation to investigate they respond, or do not respond. This is the effect of organisational culture.

Coping with the uncertain environment

The organisation without problems exists within a stable environment. With regular customers, no new competitors, fixed technology, quiet social conditions and so on, this fortunate organisation can hone its internal processes to maximum efficiency and hit its budget every year. Problems come from changes. If these are small, being random variations or seasonal fluctuations (*see* Fig. 3.6), that is disturbances that take place *within limits*, the organisation will cope through various operational mechanisms. It will maintain flexible operating capacity, switch resources, carry stocks, allow queues to form, regulate demand, and so on. While these fluctuations remain as variations around a mean, operating procedures can be developed. Coping becomes a matter of routine. On the other hand, if the change is permanent or in large steps, routine responses will not work. Major surgery is called for.

Types of change

Rhenman[2] distinguished between the two types of environmental change using the terms reversible and irreversible.

- *Reversible changes* are cyclical and random disturbances whose effect can be countered by planned operational responses. Most reversible changes relate to behaviour in the operating environment. For instance, a hospital plans its outpatients' surgeries through estimating the average time required per patient and issuing appointments to them. Disturbances arise from patients arriving early or late, or not showing at all. Furthermore, each treatment lasts for a different time. The department, therefore, uses queues to even out the flow. Visitors do not like queues, but will accept them provided they are well managed and not too long.

- *Irreversible changes* are permanent changes in the environment that require more fundamental responses within the organisation. Their origin can usually be traced to developments in the wider environment. Frequently, new and unknown conditions occur of which there is no previous experience. Then the organisation cannot rely on standardised responses. Over recent years, capacity planning for United Kingdom hospital maternity units, including related pre- and post-natal care functions, has been subject to many such changes. They include examples of all the PEST categories: decentralisation of planning and control structures in the Health Service with a rise in competition among units; shifts in resources allocated to midwifery services; steady decline in the birth rate accompanied by changed attitudes towards home deliveries; and new techniques in gynaecology.

Rhenman's categories encourage us to relate each disturbance to origins and possible effects. A broader view of the totality of changes was taken by Duncan.[3] He suggested two dimensions to assess the overall impact of the changes faced by an organisation. These were:

■ *Simplicity versus complexity*

A simple environment contains a few important factors and has little variety. In contrast, a complex environment is made up of many factors and displays greater diversity. We can illustrate these factors by comparing schools. Let us say, for a moment, that each child is seen as an element of the environment, a customer so to speak. Looking at no other factors, we say that larger classes are more complex just because there are more children. Smaller classes are simpler. In addition, we can consider diversity. In a selective school, or one with streaming, the teacher is faced with pupils with a narrow ability band. The teacher faces a simpler environment than if the children were not streamed. Some claim benefits from more efficiency under this 'simpler' selective system. We should, however, note that others point to disadvantages from a wider, societal perspective.

■ *Static versus dynamic*

The degree of environmental stability is the second cause of uncertainty. There are few environments that are unchanging, although there are often managers that treat them this way. We can see great differences in the dynamics of nations, markets, industries and companies. For instance, in urban areas with stable population, enrolments in primary schools vary little from year to year. Short of any other information, a good predictor is to use last year's registrations. One could not rely on a similar approach in countries with fluctuating rates of birth and infant mortality or considerable migration.

Duncan proposed that uncertainty arises from the way these dimensions come together. The most uncertain environments are those that are both complex and dynamic. If either comes into play, there is moderate uncertainty. Vecchio quotes studies that suggest the static–dynamic relationship is of greater importance in determining the level of perceived uncertainty.[4] Figure 4.1 summarises these relationships.

When conditions are uncertain, the following tasks become more difficult:

■ identifying key factors in the environment;

■ forecasting the environment;

■ evaluating the impact of potential changes;

■ knowing the costs of making the wrong choices.

For some managers, the last point is reassuring. Although wrong decisions are made, no one will ever suspect! Put another way, the foggy environment hides successes and mistakes! This is a problem examined more fully in Chapter 22. Information has value associated with the quality of decisions that it supports; it

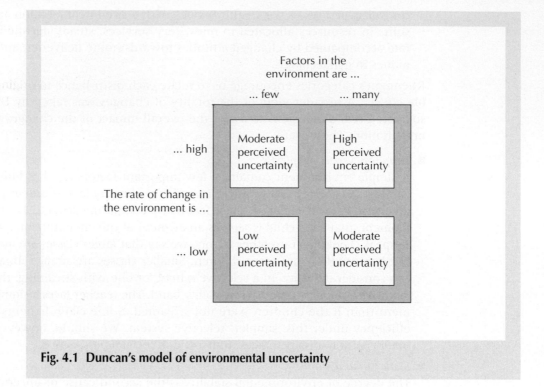

Factors in the
environment are ...

... few   ... many

... high

Moderate
perceived
uncertainty

High
perceived
uncertainty

The rate of change in
the environment is ...

... low

Low
perceived
uncertainty

Moderate
perceived
uncertainty

Fig. 4.1 Duncan's model of environmental uncertainty

also has costs linked to the effort expended in obtaining it. Uncertainty hampers good estimates of these values and costs.

It is useful to bring together the views of Rhenman and Duncan. We can recognise that organisations must respond to environmental changes if they are to survive. The easiest problems arise from reversible effects in relatively static and simple environments; irreversible changes in dynamic–complex situations pose greater problems.

We can illustrate these questions by looking back to the Lego case at the start of the chapter. The company is choosing to diversify away from a near-complete dependence on the Lego System. In so doing, it is facing greater complexity and dynamism, that is greater uncertainty. The above ideas help us to analyse the case in more detail.

Table 4.1 presents a set of notes prepared from the case study. Naturally, there will be more issues in practice, but space is restricted and the table will suit our purposes. The first column of the table lists, in order of appearance, the environmental changes mentioned. The second column categorises the environments according to where they fit in Fig. 3.2. An interpretation of each for reversibility and uncertainty completes the table. Study of the entries suggests that, for Lego, deeper problems arise in the wider environment. It has become used to managing its operating environment. For instance, it knows a great deal about the construction toy market: managers are familiar with competitors, customers and the monthly sales pattern leading up to Christmas. They can cope with fluctuations there. Similarly, the company faces many infringements of its property rights each

Table 4.1 Appraisal of Lego's environments

Item mentioned in study	Environmental category	Reversibility	Uncertainty
World's Top Ten	Operating – competition	Reversible	Moderate
Rising demand	Operating – market	Irreversible but slow	Moderate
Copies	Operating – competition	Reversible	Moderate
Intellectual property law	Wider – political	(Static)	None
Swiss company law	Wider – political	(Static)	None
Culture and toy market (D, GB, E)	Operating – market	(Static)	None
Parents' preferences	Wider – social	Irreversible	High in long term
Electronic toys	Wider – technology	Irreversible	High
Competition	Operating – competition	Reversible	Moderate
Christmas	Operating – market	Reversible	Low
Age compression	Wider – social	Irreversible	Moderate
East Asia	Wider – economic	Irreversible	Moderate
Clothes' industry	Wider – economic	Irreversible	High
Playground industry	Wider – economic	Irreversible	Moderate
Information industry	Wider – economic	Irreversible	High
Theme park industry	Wider – economic	Irreversible	Moderate
Cities' requests	Wider – economic	(Static)	Low
Key markets (D, J, GB, USA)	Operating – market	Reversible	Moderate

year. Such matters are mostly routine to the legal department. On the other hand, the irreversible changes mentioned demand more fundamental responses. Yet, in facing them, Lego is moving into untested territory. Uncertainty, rated at moderate or high in the fourth column, means that the company must find new ways of relating to the new opportunities and threats.

Organisations and environments

Managers must recognise and respond to uncertainty in the environment. As noted in Chapter 2, Ashby's Law of Requisite Variety[5] has been applied to this question. To survive, a system must match the variety of the environment within itself. As the variety (or uncertainty) increases, so must the complexity of the organisation. This implies that most organisations become more complex as they grow, for the growth means that they have to cope with more factors in their environments. Successful selection of environments and adaptation of the organisation to them lead to continuing prosperity. These ideas have been encapsulated in the *population ecology perspective*.[6]

▓ The population ecology perspective

This extension of systems ideas is analogous to Darwin's theory of evolution. Figure 4.2 summarises the process of creation of new organisations and the 'natural selection' that determines whether they are to survive. As shown in Chapter 8, new organisations are continually created. By analogy with Darwin, we can call this step *mutation*, suggesting that, while each is born out of what has gone before, it has its unique form and purpose. The process of *selection* follows. If the organisation is able to mirror the environment, often called finding a suitable opportunity or *niche*, it will survive and, perhaps, grow. Growth within the niche depends on the size of the niche and the number of other occupants. Maybe the niche can be expanded. The history of companies that have grown from small beginnings over recent years demonstrates that they found niches that were large, unoccupied or expandable. IKEA, Lego, Microsoft, Tesco and Virgin are but a few examples.

The population ecology perspective also takes us into later development. The third stage, *survival*, is never guaranteed. Organisations must continue to fight if they are to achieve everlasting life. An organisation may outgrow its niche, or predators may enter and it may be forced out. Some fail at this stage. Therefore managers must be prepared to adapt, to ward off predators and to find and develop new niches. Examples range from the corner grocer threatened by the predator supermarket to Lego which in turn outgrew the Danish, the Nordic and then the European construction toy markets.

Developments discussed here have focused on growth of an entity through time. More important to the population ecologists are emerging patterns of chronological and spatial distribution. Rather than look at individual location decisions, such as where a plant, bank or shop may decide to set up, ecologists look at the developing patterns of whole industries. Actions of each individual firm are clearly affected by the choices of those who have come before. Just as we see clusters of development through time, as in 'Industrial Revolutions', so they appear geographically. From the Potteries to the Ruhr, or the Po Valley to Silicon Valley, firms cluster in emerging networks. Lomi notes how photographs of Europe taken at night show concentration patterns that give no clue about political frontiers.[7]

The danger with analogies

There is value in seeing organisational change as a continual, responsive process capable of being modelled using ecological techniques. There are, however, dan-

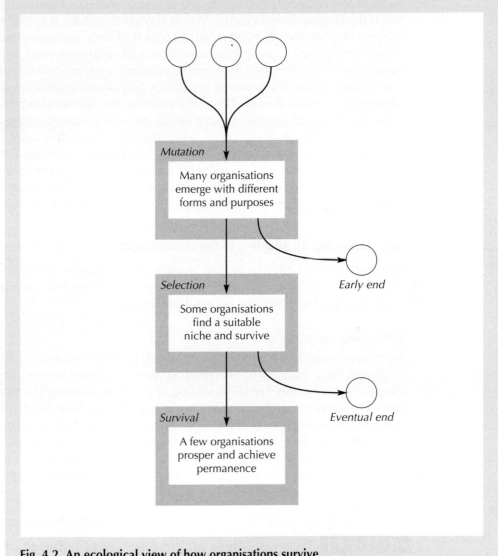

Fig. 4.2 An ecological view of how organisations survive

gers in using natural systems as analogies of organisations. In seeing correspondence between two systems, we are applying knowledge about one to explain something about the other. Analogies, therefore, use one system as a likeness of another. Problems arise when, seeing the first as having *some* features in common with the second, we carelessly assume that other features are also similar. It is to be hoped that the days are gone when introductory management texts opened with a comparison of the organisation to the human organism. It had a brain (the board), muscles (the workers and machines), a skeleton (the structure), nerves (information system) and so on. The analogy becomes an untested model.

Drawing conclusions from connections must be done with care. A more rigorous comparison between two systems should discover important differences. The

Darwinian perspective is a subtle and plausible picture of *some* aspects of organisational development and change. Yet, as shown in Exhibit 4.1, living and organised systems display such important differences that only tenuous connections can be made. Seeing the business environment as ecological may yield some insight but is hardly useful in answering managerial questions such as, 'What shall we do next?'.

A further difference between organisms and organisations lies in the way they respond to external change. Through evolution, the species survives through adapting slowly from generation to generation. Natural selection means that organisms with the best mutations do better. The organisation, on the other hand, has some power in relation to the world around it. It possesses, in its armoury, weapons to change the environment. Faced with a mismatch between the environment and itself, the organisation can try to change either to bring them more into line. Achieving fit through these two approaches is the subject of the next sections.

Achieving fit: adapting to the environment

There are several internal actions available to managers to counter the effects of uncertainty on the organisation. These are: forecasting and planning; information management; flexibility and boundary extension.

Forecasting and planning

Most large organisations expend great effort on forecasting and planning as means of coping with uncertainty. Forecasting aims to reduce uncertainty. For instance, Chapter 4 noted how causal modelling of markets could help a planner to receive early warnings of trends. Planning is needed in larger firms to ensure not only that needed change occurs but that it takes place at the rate required to match the environment. More than one plan may be necessary. Sometimes, as a result of unexpected events, managers face a crisis. Effective organisations plan for such occasions through *crisis management*. They prepare contingency plans to be called

---

Exhibit 4.1 **Generalisations on the differences between organised and living systems**

Organisations	*Organisms*
Abstract entities: described using economic and socio-psychological terms.	Concrete entities: described using physical and sometimes psychological terms.
Structure is chosen at start up, acquired in stages and can be changed at will.	Structure is inherited, mainly predetermined and changes little.
Life span can be unlimited.	Death is certain.
Parts are exchangeable and dispensable; boundary is flexible.	Usually complete with boundaries clearly defined.
Problems are defined socially.	Problems are defined clinically.

upon when needed. In other cases, managers find that forecasts are so uncertain that they do not justify a single plan. In that case they prepare alternatives from which one will be selected as matters become clearer.

Information management

Information management is vital both when managers are forming an initial appraisal of an environment or when they scan to look for signs of change. Just as forecasters try to improve techniques to give early warnings, so managers strive to obtain both accurate and early information. This can yield great advantages. The story of Rothschild making a fortune, however, is probably exaggerated, *see* Exhibit 4.2.[8]

Flexibility

The structure of an organisation should allow it to make the required responses to external change. In a historic study, Burns and Stalker[9] compared the flexibility required of a successful organisation with the uncertainty of the environment:

■ *Organic structure*
An organic structure is characterised by few rules and regulations, stresses teamwork, and decentralises decision making to the level of employees doing the work.

■ *Mechanistic structure*
A mechanistic structure features clearly defined tasks, many rules and regulations, requires little teamwork and tends to centralise decision making.

Exhibit 4.2 **First with the news from Waterloo**

Throughout the Napoleonic wars, Nathan Mayer Rothschild (1777–1836) implemented the British government's banking commitments. NM had a network of agents carrying out tasks such as funding the French opposition and delivering coin to Wellington's army. Family connections were spread across Europe. His communications were known to be good. For instance, contractors at Dover and Calais kept speedy vessels at the ready with post-boys making the land connections.

The Battle of Waterloo occurred on 18 June 1815. There are many conflicting accounts of Rothschild's actions in relation to the battle. Writers talk of NM being present at the scene or of carrier pigeons bringing back news; others suggest that, in London, he either pretended that Wellington had lost so as to depress securities prices, or started to sell so as to suggest that he knew of disaster.

According to Cowles' official family biography, NM probably received the news through a *Gazette Extraordinary* published in Brussels and sent post haste to arrive on the morning of the 20th. He went with a companion to rouse Lord Castlereagh, the Foreign Secretary, with the news. But Foreign Office officials were sceptical because they had just heard of the English defeat in the minor battle of Quatre Bras on the 17th. Frustrated, NM left immediately for the stock exchange and began to buy large quantities of bonds. Wellington's despatches from Waterloo arrived some forty hours after Rothschild's copy of the *Gazette*.

They found that in conditions of rapid change, the organic structure is more successful; the mechanistic structure, corresponding to Weber's idea of bureaucracy, works best in stable environments. As with other models, we should note that Burns and Stalker are describing ideal types. These establish a scale or continuum along which real organisations can be placed and can be seen to move. For instance, one of Lego's responses to market uncertainty is to decentralise Billund's marketing decisions concerning packaging and balance of the product line. This is a shift towards the organic end of the scale. There is more on the work of Burns and Stalker in Chapter 13.

To respond to uncertainty in the operating environment, there are many possible tactics. Production managers are used to carrying stocks and maintaining some spare capacity. Finance managers use insurance to guard against some bad debts and hedge against disadvantageous foreign currency movements. Incorporating such flexibility is costly and is often not called into play. Yet it guards against the unexpected.

Mergers

One way of reducing external uncertainty, especially in the operating environment, is to take direct control. Facing the risk of loss of supplies, the organisation can buy the source; fearing loss of outlets – buy the distributor; threatened by competition – buy the rival; spotting a new technology – buy the licence; finding an opportunity overseas – buy a local company. Control through ownership is attractive for the certainty it imposes upon the uncertain. Although such practices are sometimes banned by governments because they are anti-competitive, they are, none the less, permitted if they appear to be in the national interest. From the government's point of view, home industry consolidation can dampen down uncertainty in the domestic business and enable firms to face international competition more effectively.

The terms merger, takeover and acquisition describe three variants on the theme of boundary expansion although distinctions are often blurred.

- Merging firms usually combine to form a new one. Each party to the merger may join because it seeks to cut uncertainty in its environment.
- In a takeover, one firm buys another in order to absorb it.
- After an acquisition, the target company often maintains its identity as a subsidiary company.

All three processes were seen when the United Kingdom clearing banks, encouraged by the government, consolidated during the 1960s. As a result, in 1970, three of the 'Big Four' British clearing banks were in the world's top twenty – Barclays (4), NatWest (7) and Midland (20). By 1995, however, mergers and growth elsewhere, especially Japan, meant that their rankings fell. Barclays (22) and NatWest (26) remained independent while Midland had been acquired by Hong Kong and Shanghai Banking Corporation.

Japanese banks are often parts of large conglomerates called *keiretsu*. These form huge internal markets, producing, trading and distributing a wide range of goods and services. Many transactions are internal to the *keiretsu*, therefore avoiding the uncertainties of the market. Mitsubishi is one such example whose branded goods are well known in many countries. Its bank is number six in the world.

■ Achieving fit: adapting the environment

The alternative approach to fit is changing the environment. After all, to fit a square peg in a round hole, either the peg or the hole, or indeed both, can be worked on. To dampen external uncertainty, managers can try to steer events along planned courses or at least fight to resist unfavourable outcomes. The possible countermeasures are advertising and promotion; public relations; lobbying; bargaining; boundary extension; and supra-organisational groups.

Advertising and promotion

Advertising has now become a central plank of many organisations' attempts to manage, that is limit the uncertainty of, their market environments. As in many developed countries, spending on advertising in the United Kingdom is dominated by detergent, cosmetic, beer and car companies. Their production is characterised by high start-up or fixed costs and low variable costs per unit. This means that it pays suppliers to run plant as close as possible to full capacity and use advertising to push the product towards consumers. In such mature markets, advertising is less about attacking than defending. That means that maintenance of sales at planned levels is the overall objective. Advertising reduces uncertainty in the production and distribution environment.

Promotion refers to the final steps in the selling process. In the early days, Toyota's production workers were sent out to sell door to door during times of slack demand. Again, the company was putting its efforts into managing the environment. For more on marketing, *see* Chapter 20.

Public relations

Public relations processes are similar to those found in advertising and promotion except that the goal is to influence public opinion about the organisation rather than directly manage demand for products. Clearly, the two are connected as people will be more willing to deal with companies with good reputations. British Telecom's operating licence requires it to compete fairly. Yet the Consumers' Association found that BT's staff were giving misleading information about rivals' costs and services. In response to resulting criticism from the industry regulator, BT established a special compliance department to ensure that its performance was above reproach. Tasks include checking of all advertisements, training of staff and setting up procedures to be followed in cases of doubt. BT feels it will gain through being seen publicly to meet standards.[10]

Lobbying

Lobbying can be seen as public relations focused on a narrow section of opinion. Usually the targets are groups in authority such as Members of Parliament or local authorities. Many organisations, often in combination, employ professional lobbyists to ensure that their view is heard. A combination of public relations and lobbying can be a powerful factor in persuading governments to accept arguments from interest groups. Much of this process, sometimes called *politicking*, is legitimate. Organisations seek to explain the problems and difficulties caused by government policies. United States' car manufacturers fought hard to slow the introduction of exhaust emission measures, especially in the state of California. Under the original proposals, small cars were favoured. The United States companies needed time to adapt, pointing out the employment effects if advantage was given to importers.

Bargaining

An important outcome of a bargain is the removal of uncertainty, especially if the result is some kind of long-term contract. For instance, during periods of high inflation, unions are unwilling to enter into wage agreements lasting more than one year. When inflationary expectations are low, two and three year agreements become acceptable. Managers concede a little extra in return for being able to plan for labour costs. Other forms of bargain with similar effects cover long-term supplies of raw materials or undertakings to purchase outputs. Supply chains in some industries have developed in recent years into complex networks of long-term bargains. They include single-sourcing agreements and undertakings to exchange operational information. A key benefit for managers is the removal of uncertainty.

Benefits of such bargains tend to be undermined if basic assumptions prove to be wildly inaccurate. Ghana's Volta Dam project,[11] *see* Exhibit 4.3, was guaranteed by the construction of a foreign-owned aluminium smelter to take most of the electric power. In retrospect, the government's political needs made it blind to the risks it faced.

Boundary extension

Mergers were identified as means of adapting to uncertainty through internalising an important part of the environment. There are more subtle means of exercising some controlling influence without ownership. One means is to establish favourable links with other organisations through individuals. Representatives of important constituencies, such as major customers or banks, can be co-opted on to boards of directors. In parallel, senior managers may take up roles on other company boards or community groups. Through such *interlocking directorships* individuals reduce

---

Exhibit 4.3 **The Volta Dam scheme: subverted by the volatile environment**

Construction of the Volta Dam began in the 1960s. It was part of a scheme to stimulate rapid industrialisation. Desperate for both foreign investment and exports, the Ghanaian government needed a guaranteed market for electricity to make the project work. An aluminium smelter, with capacity of 200 000 tonnes per annum, would provide this guarantee and consume local bauxite ore. Yet the reduction of uncertainty has proved dear. First, the electricity tariff was fixed before the global rise in energy prices. Then it was found that local ores were too expensive to work and the Volta Aluminum Company (a subsidiary of Texas-based Kaiser Aluminum) imported richer bauxite from North America. Then, a 1983 drought shut the plant for two years. Finally, weak demand meant that Kaiser had too much capacity worldwide. Production in Ghana through the 1990s was little more than half of plant capacity.

uncertainty by sharing and spreading common interests and learning of board-level strategies such as acquisition.[12] The practice is more common in France, Germany and Japan than in the United Kingdom or United States.

Strategic alliances are long-term agreements among organisations which can take many forms. One of their functions is to exchange resources or information. Again, as with other forms of agreement, alliances can serve to cut uncertainty. A joint venture in a developing country can combine the local knowledge of the home partner with the technical knowledge of the foreign firm. In combining in this way, each avoids risks in its environment. The gradually developing cooperation between Honda and Rover enabled the former to overcome its inexperience of operating in the European arena while the latter could learn about best practice products and manufacturing processes.

Supra-organisational groups

Supra-organisational groups are formed among organisations with interests in common. They recognise that members can achieve more through working in concert than by acting on their own. At one end of the scale are international organisations such as the International Maritime Organization, the Organization of Petroleum Exporting Countries, the International Labour Organization, or the World Council of Churches. They help in regulation, price fixing, information sharing or spreading the word. Echoes exist at a smaller scale in local communities. Chambers of Commerce and Trades Councils bring firms and unions together to discuss local issues, although their influence varies according to tradition and official support. The voluntary sector is characterised by small organisations which gain from group membership. The National Pistol Association lobbies for its members' rights while sports 'governing bodies' are in fact committees elected by member organisations.

Groups use many of the tactics already mentioned: advertising and promotion; public relations and lobbying; bargaining; and boundary extension. They prosper when members see continuing membership as being in their own interests and wither when the motivation for joining fades. Among small firms, some of the strongest voluntary organisations bring direct operating benefits. Buying and market groups in retailing, such as the Spar network of food wholesalers and retailers, bring scale economies to members. Membership of the Wool Industry Research Association gives access to innovations in process technology. The strength of Chambers of Commerce, on the other hand, has declined in the United Kingdom. Their moderate budgets limit their functions to lobbying, information sharing and social events. In France, chambers do have important local functions. They raise levies and offer financial incentives for training and development.

■ Adaptation and size

Not all the adaptation strategies are available to every organisation. Size is a major factor deciding which is most applicable. Rather like David against Goliath, the small firm prospers through its internal flexibility, a feature that larger ones find difficult to replicate. Instead, giant firms rely more on modelling and forecasting the future. Reliance solely on forecasting, however, itself creates a difficulty which is set out in Exhibit 4.4.

Small firms survive through flexibility...

... while large ones need plans and countermeasures.

Fig. 4.3 Survival of the small and large

Exhibit 4.4 Bridging gaps between forecasts and outcomes

To predict the future, a forecaster must, following Ashby's Law, have a model that matches the complexity of the environment. This is not a reasonable prospect. Complexity is always going to be too great and, in any case, it is impossible to test the model.

The complete model is unnecessary if the forecaster has countermeasures powerful enough to control the environment. In other words, when a gap emerges between the forecast and 'reality' then the organisation changes the latter! For this to work, the planner needs to know what sort of change is possible so that the countermeasures can be put in place. (We do not know if the enemy is going to attack but if an attack occurs, we will be ready.)

The future, then, is partly predicted by the model and partly adjusted to fit the model.

Lacking internal flexibility, can large organisations rely on the combination of forecasts and countermeasures? The problem with reliance on the latter is that even they have to be part of the forecast. The organisation has to know the kinds of gaps that might arise before it can be sure it is ready with responses. Of particular concern are events with immediate impact arising in the operating environment. Lack of flexibility requires the large organisation to combine forecasting and countermeasures against these events. At the same time, as problems in the wider environment unfold more slowly, it adapts either by internal change or by evolving new countermeasures. If it behaves as though it can permanently cope with change through forecasts and existing countermeasures, it will be doomed. Fokker failed through inflexibility combined with being unable to control a key environment, the Dutch government.

Adaptation strategies are summarised in Fig. 4.4. Here each is placed according to whether it is concerned with internal or external adaptation and whether it is relevant to small or large organisations. There is no fixed rule. For example, advertising is available to all but, from the point of view of attempts to *manage* the environment, it is only relevant to those who can commit vast resources to it. At the other end of the scale, flexibility is most appropriate to small firms whose only hope of influencing the environment is through supra-organisations such as

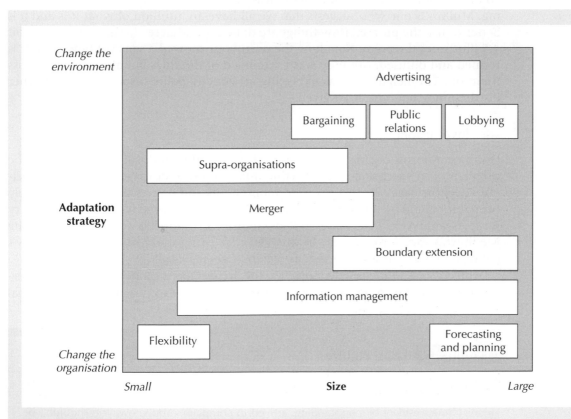

Fig. 4.4 Adaption strategies for different sizes of organisation

industry associations. In between, merger and boundary extension have aspects of both internal and external change.

The organisation's culture

So far we have discussed methods of coping with uncertainty and avoided, except for a mention of scale, a search for reasons why one path or another is followed. These lie in the organisation's culture which interacts with all other internal aspects – physical resources, formal structure and process technology – to give it its identity. Culture can be defined as follows:

> *Culture is the set of policies, values, beliefs and attitudes shared by the organisation's members.*
>
> *Values are fundamental principles that people have regarding what is right or wrong, important or unimportant, and so on.*
>
> *An attitude is a persistent inclination to feel and behave in a certain way towards a person or object.*

To define culture in such an analytic way tends to lose some of its holistic meaning. Mullins is one who suggests that we all have an intuition of what it is and it is better to use the phrase, 'How things are done around here'[13]. The story in Exhibit 4.5 illustrates the point. Note how the neighbour showed a sense of how culture is formed and diffused. Not only was I reminded of the rules but also of how to pass them on. The neighbour was expecting an equally polite response that, in other districts, may not have been given.

Investigating

Quite what forms organisational culture is a difficulty. In this it compares with the problem of the archaeologist collecting information to describe a prehistoric society. A century ago, the focus was on monuments and objects that had deliberately been left behind by our forebears. Now, with the development of technique, every scrap is analysed. Fish bones tell us about early imports to Britain from the Mediterranean, for example. In this view, knowing more of the Roman army's eating habits can be as important as reading Caesar's *Gaul*.

Denied access to the people, however, the archaeologist cannot interpret discoveries through the producers' eyes. We need, instead, to follow the social

---

Exhibit 4.5 Local culture

One afternoon a few days after moving into our new house, I made a bonfire of a heap of garden waste that had accumulated while the place was empty. After an hour or so, a neighbour, resident of long standing, arrived to complain. 'You know, you shouldn't be making all that smoke,' he said, politely. 'We don't do that sort of thing in Queen's Park.'

anthropologist, who proceeds both to observe and interpret. What is important in an organisation, and is captured by the 'Way we do things round here' definition, is the way people in the workplace understand the world. Linstead argues, 'The point is not simply to explain as an external observer what is happening, but to understand what the group members think is happening as an insider.'[14] It is, after all, the way group members interpret the world that leads to their unique response to it.

To make a start, we can recognise levels of analysis based on what we can see. At the surface are those elements that can be observed, the artefacts of the 'organisation society' under investigation. These include: symbols; language; stories; and activities. They can be collected, compared and assembled into a description of the organisation. Without interpretation, however, such data has little value. An example can be taken from the widespread introduction of single-level lunch rooms at workplaces:

> *A casual observer of such a change may applaud, 'This is a welcome representation of democratisation.' Note how the observer sees the act not only as an event but also as a* symbol *of a shift in values. Additionally, personal views on democracy are tossed in for good measure. Yet is it evident that the change symbolised this? It could have been forced by the canteen losing money; it may have been part of a settlement of a wider dispute; it could be the stated policy of a new parent company. In any case, the decision to reorganise the lunch arrangements had to be taken by managers. Making the 'concession' can also be interpreted as an expression and reinforcement of managerial control; 'They did this to demonstrate that they could.'*

Beneath the 'culture visible' at the surface, there is the invisible layer of beliefs, values and basic assumptions, *see* Fig. 4.5.[15] Values were incorporated, for example, in the 'that sort of thing' statement of Exhibit 4.5. Certain types of behaviour, including making smoke when the neighbours may have their washing out, were not favoured generally and especially in this neighbourhood. Beliefs are created by combining values with experience of the organisation to establish 'facts' about the way processes work. For example, experience may suggest that closing an hour or two early on the day before a holiday does not affect work output. In planning to make this concession next time, a manager is combining belief in its limited cost with the value that it is a good idea to treat staff in this way if possible. Other managers may not agree; in other words, they either have different experiences or do not share the same values.

Underlying assumptions are the unconscious premises that are learned by the organisation's members and taken for granted. All have world views that act like personal lenses through which they perceive what goes on around them. To some extent, membership of an organisation causes them to share these world views. Being part of the group, therefore, affects not only the way they perceive the world but also how they think about it.

■ Artefacts: the culture visible

The process of recognising and interpreting culture can start from identifying its special artefacts: symbols; language; stories; and activities.

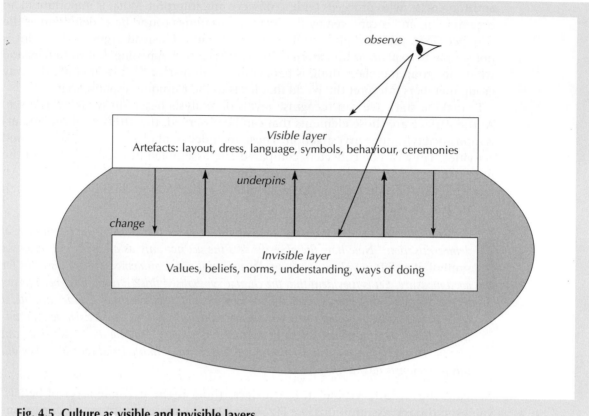

Fig. 4.5 Culture as visible and invisible layers

Symbols

Symbols are articles, actions or events that convey meaning. We noted in the above example of the dining room how the same action can have different meanings. Therefore, to enrich our understanding of the 'way things are done round here', we must go beyond finding out the important symbols, to investigating the interpretations people put on them. In his wry observation of institutional life, Parkinson compared chaotic departments such as publishing and research, which flourished in shabby and makeshift surroundings, with the splendid headquarters. Here you sit in a chromium armchair consoled by a receptionist 'with a dazzling smile for any slight but inevitable delay … A minute later you are ankle deep in the director's carpet, plodding sturdily towards his distant, tidy desk. Hypnotised by the chief's unwavering stare, cowed by the Matisse hung upon his wall, you will feel that you have found real efficiency at last.'[16]

Note the artefacts mentioned by Parkinson – chromium chair (*chic* in the 1950s), receptionist, delay, carpet, *distant* desk, *tidy* desk, stare, Matisse! It may be that the director does not mean to intimidate, to express power, but these symbols are taken by lesser mortals as expressions of that lofty position in the hierarchy. What is more, to the extent that subordinates replicate the same imagery (within their budgets) suggests they accept the relationship that is somehow captured by the thickness of carpet, area of office, tidiness of desk, number of secretaries and so on. In other words, the status symbols at the workplace serve a function akin to the organisation chart in maintaining the *status quo*.

Effective managers can be good at using symbols positively. Richard Branson, of The Virgin Group, regularly joins in the activities of his businesses, meeting crew aboard aircraft or trains, or driving a courier motorcycle. Michael Eisner, when chief executive of Disney, joined with fellow managers in entertaining all staff to Christmas parties at the theme parks. Other mass-service organisations use symbols, uniforms, badges and photographs to reward staff who have performed good service. To the outsider, these activities may seem trivial. Yet their importance lies in the effect they have inside. Note also the likelihood of unintended signs and symbols. What is your response to empty desks or others stacked high with paper, untidy signs and notices, or rubbish lying around?

Language

Pehr Gyllenhammar, when president of Volvo, wrote the description of leadership given in Exhibit 4.6.[17] We can examine what he wrote in two ways. At one level, we can use it as a definition. It states, in five categories, what leadership is and then explains why it is needed. Taken as a rational exposition to someone who is interested in knowing about the subject, this is useful. But is that all? No, the message contains more than explanation. It is full of symbolism conveying meaning at deeper levels. Possibly he thought of the Volvo employees in his audience. This elaboration, designed to persuade, justify and legitimise, is rhetoric.

We can comment on a few of the instances in the quotation. These fit in with three common uses of rhetoric by managers identified by Gowler and Legge.[18] They are hierarchy, accountability and achievement.

- *Hierarchy*
  Relationships within many organisations tend to be less formal than outsiders think and insiders may want. With their position subject to erosion, managers often use

Exhibit 4.6 Plain speaking and rhetoric

In 22 years at the top of Volvo, Pehr Gyllenhammar became one of the best-known and admired figures in Sweden. He developed the company's international reputation both for products and worker-friendly production techniques. Long-term resentment over his autocratic style came to a head when Gyllenhammar announced a plan to merge with Renault. Lacking widespread support among institutional shareholders, the project became a fiasco and he was ousted at the end of 1993. Years earlier, Gyllenhammar had written:

'Leadership is giving support, explanations, and interpreting information so employees can understand it. Leadership is developing consensus. Leadership is sometimes the ability to say "stop", to draw a line, to take the heat out of a conflict, to conclude a debate and get down to negotiations. Leadership is having the courage to put a stake on an idea, and risk making mistakes. Leadership is being able to draw new boundaries, beyond the existing limits of ideas and activities. Only through this kind of leadership can we keep our institutions from drifting aimlessly, to no purpose.'

rhetoric to reinforce their roles in the hierarchy. Note how Gyllenhammar's 'giving support, explanations and interpreting information' can be interpreted ambiguously. On the one hand, actions of training and nurturing can only be regarded as good for all. On the other hand, leaders are there precisely because of their superior ability, especially at simplifying information so the (less able) employees can understand it. By referring to hierarchical ideas in this matter-of-fact way, the rules of, and indeed existence of, hierarchy are reestablished.

■ *Accountability*
Extending the notion of accountability throughout the organisation creates and sustains a culture of responsible conduct and legitimates sanctions against those who do not follow the rules. This idea is contained within phrases such as 'interpreting information', 'developing consensus' and 'keeping our institutions from drifting aimlessly'.

■ *Achievement*
This theme concerns the duty of managers to achieve results. Within the capitalist system, varying degrees of achievement, are rewarded differentially according to a rough and ready share out. The notion of achievement is fundamental to risk, opportunity and inequality. By embedding ideas such as 'having the courage to put a stake on an idea', the quotation applauds the person who is prepared to seize a chance in spite of having to 'risk making mistakes'. Going 'beyond the existing limits of ideas', which is innovation, is also a trait to be rewarded.

We noted in Chapter 1 how managers spend most of their time communicating and how a greater part of that communication was oral. Courses in interpersonal skills espouse plain speaking as the ability to communicate efficiently about management matters at the surface level. Yet, as Exhibit 4.6 illustrated, many messages contain rhetoric that works at a deeper level. Put another way, the message has both intentions and implications. It both instructs and persuades.

Figure 4.6 sets out the plain speaking–rhetoric scale. It suggests that, as intentions and implications are usually combined, most of us operate somewhere in the middle. We also move about on the scale, depending on the needs of the circumstances. There are many more interpretations of the implied content of language.

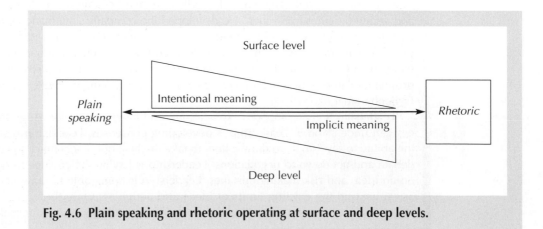

Fig. 4.6 Plain speaking and rhetoric operating at surface and deep levels.

For example, the use of jargon or 'group speak' enables one to express membership of a group and prove expertise and commitment. More on the content and context of communication is given in Chapter 16.

Stories

Besides illustrating a point about quality, the story in Exhibit 4.7 tells us something about the development of organisational myth. I have heard it in presentations and conversations from buyers who were sure that the events, although with different numbers, happened to someone in their own organisation. I took to asking people to give more details and learnt that they never knew but could refer me to someone who might. From these observations, I do not know whether such incidents are common or that they do not happen at all. In either case we have a simple story told to audiences who are ready to believe. It is about a time when many organisations changed their shared views about quality. Truth and myth are indistinguishable.

Organisations abound with stories. Along with the language with which they are told, their many functions include: confirmation of the role of management; clarification of how to deal with aspects of work from awkward customers to fiddling expense accounts; and understanding of what it takes to be a successful manager within the particular organisation. Lego's story of the wooden gun is significant in that it was a mother figure, combining notions of family-as-producer and family-as-consumer, who vetoed its sale. This myth has a continuing influence on the company's policy.

Heroes and villains are identified in stories. Sometimes a hero who falls from grace turns into a villain as news filters out about mistakes and the good times are forgotten. Volvo, after the fall of Gyllenhammar, is one of many companies that have had to reinterpret their past after the end of a leader and a shift in policy. Stories about the old and new are elaborated in their retelling during such times.

Activities

Manager's actions are a form of communication and, just as language has both intended and implied meaning, so do actions. Of particular interest in understanding culture are rituals. These can be deliberately planned events, or ceremonies, designed to influence an audience. Otherwise, there can be informal activities that take on significance because they are often repeated and become part of the 'way things are done'.

Exhibit 4.7 Quality as a story

A European company ordered some semiconductor components from a Japanese supplier. The order stated something like, '10 000 items required, with a defect rate of 0.02 per cent'. The consignment duly arrived in two containers. The larger carried 9998 good components and the smaller held the two defects, clearly labelled. The supplier could not understand why the customer wanted the defects but they were sent all the same.

Ceremonies are special events that display and reinforce an organisation's values. They may occur regularly, as in the annual staff awards (the 'Oscars') or presentations to people with long or meritorious service. University awards ceremonies combine the two in acknowledging graduates and giving honorary degrees for service to university or community. Otherwise, ceremonies are used to launch new initiatives or to mark turning points.

Rituals are more mundane than ceremonies. They are patterns of repeated behaviour that are not especially designed but, nevertheless, convey layers of meaning. Sometimes they become elaborated into ceremonies as shown by the process of initiation. At the Université Catholique de Mons in Belgium, new students as a group have to spend a week of humiliation before their seniors before they are accepted into student life. Other organisations have less formal initiation rituals where new members are subjected to jokes and tricks to demonstrate their naïveté. As in many factories, apprentices at Crewe Locomotive Works were sent to the stores with notes for 'Red oil for a red lamp' or 'A left-handed screwdriver'. Naturally, the storekeeper would make them wait a long time, telling other callers what they were waiting for, and then send them to another department where what the victim was looking for was sure to be in stock.

These examples show that rituals, while often difficult to understand, should not be thought of as pointless (as in 'empty ritual'). Initiations and regular habits, such as 'the office always goes out for lunch on a Friday', sustain bonds among people at the workplace. Managers also incorporate ritual into routine, cyclical processes such as budgeting.

▨ Difficulties with interpretation

The focus on artefacts brings with it two dangers:

- *Confusing artefacts and culture*
  Artefacts are elements that are relatively easy to observe and compare between organisations. It is tempting, therefore, to treat them as 'data' in the same way as figures on a balance sheet or pie charts summarising market share. The data then becomes a description of the culture. We should guard against this trap, reminding ourselves of the aim to understand what the group members think is happening as insiders. Artefacts are not the culture. Seeing through them enables us to understand the deeper levels.

- *Artefacts as a screen*
  The surface and deeper layers were presented here as simplifications. Having to use artefacts as a route to investigating deeper levels should not mean their value is discounted. They are not just manifestations or symbols of a 'real world' beneath the surface layer. We should not dismiss the totem pole as a mere representation of something more profound. Understanding culture means understanding culture as a whole; values, beliefs and their symbolic representation are all parts of the same system.

▨ How to investigate

Our purpose should be to reach the underlying assumptions held by the organisation and its members. Exhibit 4.8, based on Schein,[19] sets out these assumptions as questions. As our discussion shows, it would be naive to expect to gain answers merely by administering a questionnaire! The approach should be to study:

- symbols and how they are used to convey information;
- the value placed on artefacts;
- the relationships between language and concepts such as hierarchy, control and motivation;
- stories and the development of myths, heroes and villains;
- how communicative media are used;
- mental processes such as interpretation and understanding;
- social processes such as initiation, development and change.[20]

▨ Categories of organisational culture

Various proposals for classifications of culture have been put forward. Among the best known is that of Handy who suggested four types, namely: power, role, task and person.[21]

Exhibit 4.8 Questions on organisational culture

What is the relationship to the environment?	How are values captured in the corporate mission statement and how widely are they recognised and supported? Is the aim to grow and dominate or to occupy a niche position?
What do managers assume about reality?	Is the stress in decision making on rational argument using data or is it intuitive? Is consensus sought?
What are attitudes to the past and the future?	Do people focus on the future and reject the past; focus on the past and forget the future; or try to span the gap from past to future?
What beliefs are there about humans at work?	What is the view about motivation? How are employees motivated? What controls are apparent? What sort of rules apply?
What are the relationships among people at the workplace?	How do people cooperate? What is the attitude to conflict: healthy and creative or harmful and destructive? How is power legitimated and exercised?

■ In the *power culture* there is a central source of power connected radially to all members of the organisation. It is often found in small organisations whose entrepreneurial spirit is sustained by the energy of the founder and links of trust and empathy between this person and all others. As the organisation grows, key individuals are appointed to maintain links but these operate in a similar personal way to the founder. There are few rules and procedures. Decisions are taken on hunch and influence.

■ The *role culture* works by rationality. It is the epitome of Weber's bureaucracy. The roles which are the collection of tasks and duties that have to be performed, are fixed. Individuals can be 'slotted into' these roles and so the organisation moves on independently of who they are. Power derives from formal position. For the employee, stability is the watchword and the organisation offers psychological and contractual security.

■ In the *task culture*, management is seen as resolving a continuous stream of problems. Since each job, or project, is of varying size and scope, the purpose of the organisation is to bring together groups of people who can cope with them. The emphasis is, therefore, on adaptation, work teams and, possibly, a matrix structure, *see* Chapters 12 and 13. Power resides within the groups and is more dependent on expertise than on formal position.

■ *Person cultures* have individuals as their central concern. Examples are groups of professionals – lawyers, doctors and so on – who gather to share office space and administration costs, yet perform their own tasks according to personal decisions and professional standards. Autonomy is important and power is shared or allocated only by consent – for instance one partner may be senior because of greater investment in developing the group as a business.

In his books, Handy takes an increasingly bleak view of organisations and our relationships with them. Ironically, he proposed a way to find out which sort of organisation a person works for. Handy suggested one should ask, 'What do you do for a living?"[22] Answers can be matched with his cultural types as shown in Exhibit 4.9.

Such models of culture, combined with quick tools for diagnosis, are helpful for those who seek a snap analysis or want to draw general conclusions across a broad swathe. The problem is that they present ideal types that are rarely matched in practice as a university example will show:

> *Handy suggests that university departments are person cultures. He paints a picture of individuals committed to scholarship and drawn together by common intellectual interest. This ignores the 'reality' of many departments where, for example, financial stringency has led to higher officials exercising tight control on resources. Implied in this change is a swing towards a task culture as specialist staff are made responsible for budgetary control, resource allocation and so on. Meanwhile, some professors whose reputation enables them to win external funds and spend these on their projects, build teams of research assistants who depend on them for career continuation.*

In this example, we have a mix of Handy's types. We can try to get by with statements such as, 'It's mainly a person culture but it does have aspects of …'. Far better, when studying one organisation, to avoid general models and approach with an open mind.

> ### Exhibit 4.9 Quick cultural diagnosis of a person's organisation
>
> 'I work for Alpha (a person)'.
>
> The respondent defines his job as being employed by an individual. Suggests a power culture.
>
> 'I'm a _____ Manager with Beta Corporation'.
>
> Having mentioned a job title in a large organisation, the person is clearly a member of a role culture.
>
> 'I'm with Gamma Company working on the _____ Project'.
>
> Now the individual doesn't mention role but project. This suggest a task culture with teams.
>
> 'I am a solicitor (priest, colonel, opera singer)'.
>
> Person culture organisations consist of people who are what they do.

Culture change

Should and can culture be changed? We can start to answer this question by examining where difficulties begin to arise as the result of irreversible change. Culture is the accumulation of the past yet the organisation needs to move forward. Figure 4.7 shows the effect of emerging gaps between values and the rest of the organisation or the environment. We can look at internal and external problems.

Internal gaps

Of the many possible reasons for organisational inefficiency, one of the most intractable is where its processes and structures do not match its culture. For instance, a firm may undergo rapid expansion. The 'way things were done' when output was lower may not suit the new requirement for mass production. Employees may have been brought up to value personal contact with colleagues and customers, yet the new economic order may require specialisation in such dealings. Internal inefficiency may show itself in waste, frustration, soured relations and unrest.

External gaps

External gaps appear when an organisation no longer fits the niche it has found for itself. Figure 4.7 points out two areas. First, there is a problem in the economic relationship between the organisation and the environment. It could be that the products are no longer required or the firm continues to buy the wrong raw materials. Second, a gap emerges between the values of the organisation and those of the region or nation where it operates. The United Kingdom newspaper proprietors, led by Rupert Murdoch, faced battles with the trade unions over recognition. New technology offered business opportunities to the companies who introduced new working practices. The new culture did not find support among the traditional trade unions. In Sweden, Toys'R'Us, the United States based retailer, experienced a long dispute when it decided to stick to its no-union policy.

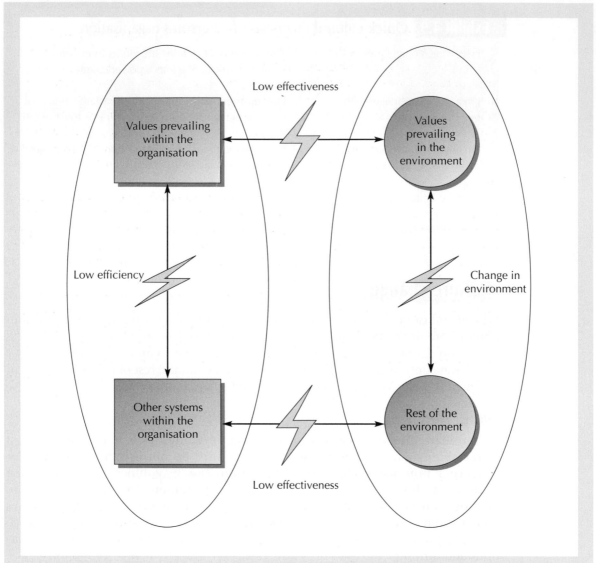

Fig. 4.7 Loss of efficiency and effectiveness comes from cultural mismatch

The campaign became a national cause. The question of how closely an international firm should fit in with the local 'scene' is one that is addressed in Chapter 5.

We see from these examples that match between system and environment goes beyond finding appropriate markets and products. It requires that an organisation's value system matches both its own policies and its environment. Culture gaps can be large, especially after takeovers or mergers. We frequently see rapid turnover of senior managers after such changes, not because of their incompetence but because they do not like the new ways of doing things. The CIBC Wood Gundy case that closes the chapter is a good example of this effect.

■ Changing culture

Clearly, cultures change and, unless there is a major disturbance, they will change slowly. Burnes suggests that this may not be sufficient. The need for efficiency means that matters are too pressing. He reports a survey showing that, in one five-year period, a quarter of the United Kingdom's leading companies had been involved in a deliberate culture change programme through shaping the beliefs, values and attitudes of employees.[23] A common example is the introduction of 'customer care' programmes in firms that were reorganising or, during this period, undergoing privatisation. These programmes included training in the processes of dealing with customers as well as attempts to implant the notion that the customer comes first.

Without any follow-up studies, we cannot know how effective the culture change programmes are. They run the risk of developing widespread cynicism and direct resistance. In any case, have managers the right to try to control what employees think and feel? Should their attitudes be directed towards economic ends? The answer is surely negative. Not only do they not have the right but they are unlikely to succeed. People are influenced so much by life outside the workplace.

Organisational culture should, therefore, not be regarded as a component like technology or structure. These can be changed to suit circumstances. Culture is different; it is best regarded as the 'way things are'. In the holistic system, any change will affect the culture and the culture will affect or constrain the change. Understanding is required not so that culture can be manipulated but so that the impacts of other changes can be recognised and evaluated. Cultural change is intimately bound up with the process of organisational change, a subject to which we return in Chapter 14.

Conclusion: change is necessary but difficult

Mismatch between the organisation and the environment leads to problems. Depending on the type of change, reversible or irreversible, the problems can be handled by routine processes or more fundamental adaptations. Uncertainty, growing from change and complexity, compounds the problems because managers find it difficult to recognise and interpret what is happening.

Essentially, the fit between the organisation and its environment is maintained by adaptation, either of the environment or of the internal structure. Large firms have a choice but those that assume they have perfect information and have a battery of countermeasures to resist external change will eventually fail. Small firms, on the other hand, know that they must continuously change themselves or disappear.

Culture, or 'the way we do things round here', is a powerful subsystem of every group. It may be the source of innovation and change but so often it develops to reinforce existing ways of doing things and hence resists change. The example of one of Europe's most successful family businesses, Lego, illustrates the danger of relying on, and being guided by, successes of the past.

Managers may be attracted to the idea of manipulating culture. Like tearing down statues, they may work on changing the artefacts of a culture where they want radical remodelling. We should recognise that culture is more than the arte-facts, it is a powerful, integrated system of artefacts, values, beliefs and fundamental assumptions. To improve the business, managers should work directly on altering processes and practices and not attempt to manipulate these values, beliefs and assumptions. Understanding culture gives clues as to the best ways to introduce and nurture changes so that they will be sustained.

Quick check up *Can you ...*

- Name Rhenman's categories of change;
- Use a diagram to show Duncan's change dimensions;
- Summarise the population ecology perspective;
- Distinguish four ways of adapting to the environment;

- Illustrate six ways of adapting the environment;
- Match the means of adaptation to organisational size;
- Compare formal and informal defini-tions of culture;
- Identify four types of artefact;
- Give examples of each of Handy's cultural types.

Questions

Chapter review

4.1 What are the main sources and types of change originating in the environment?

4.2 Outline the population ecology perspective on growth and change. What use could it be to someone who advises small firms?

4.3 Explain Handy's categories of organisational culture, naming an organisation you know which fits each case.

Application

4.4 List and explain the artefacts described in the Lego case. What is the cultural signifi-cance of Legoland to staff, customers and others?

4.5 In what ways would a culture that accepts change differ from one that resists it?

Investigation

4.6 Study an organisation that has recently undergone a change programme or initiative. Show why the change was introduced and explain what cultural implications could be seen.

Cultures clash at CIBC Wood Gundy[24]

Following 1987 deregulation, most Canadian banks bought brokerage firms. In no case has a merger been easy. Banks are hierarchical with formal reporting relationships and planned career paths; investment houses are partnerships, led by dealers who put their own money at risk and see themselves as prima donnas. Canadian Imperial Bank of Commerce was the most active in growth and acquisition. It lured staff from rivals, causing legal disputes. Furthermore, it bought various dealers in New York and Toronto, among them Wood Gundy in 1988.

The purpose of the merger was to offer clients a full service range. According to John Hukin, President of CBIC Wood Gundy, 'If we come through the door with our total capability, where we can look at a piece of the balance sheet from senior debt down through equity, we can solve any problem.' The creation of teams to achieve this has not been easy. Bureaucratic bankers and entrepreneurial brokers have different outlooks and do not work well together. Partners at brokerage houses risk their own money yet may achieve returns of 80 per cent or more. The stars take up to $300 000.

Only the trading room, run by Wood Gundy people, and the administrative office have worked well. Hukin's task has been to integrate, to impose a bank structure on the flexible trading business. There are now many committees including a nine-person executive. The deal makers from Wood Gundy used to spend as little time as they could on administration. Now they use up a day a week in discussions. There are tensions and jostling for power. Individuals were required to share costs and risks with the return limited to 20 per cent. From December 1995, the payment of any bonus more than $50 000 had to be spread over later years.

Job titles have been made uniform with senior bank directors and brokerage partners all becoming managing directors. There are 300 in all, spread throughout the world. In November 1995, they were brought to Toronto for a conference aimed at developing harmony. Yet so many attended, and the presentations were so focused on administration, that participants were dissatisfied. Questions to Hukin and the CIBC chief executive, Al Flood, had to be submitted in writing. One recalled, 'There were so many people, and so many I'd never seen before in my life.'

In the first year after the takeover, CIBC Wood Gundy is said to have lost $65 million. By 1996, however, the division was prospering. Its underwriting fees, brokerage commissions and earnings from foreign exchange and capital markets accounted for about a third of the bank's net income.

Staff have been leaving, especially some rising stars in their thirties. CIBC has been offering income guarantees to replacements but these antagonise current people. In the second half of 1995, more than 25 senior staff left the company, mostly to join smaller, entrepreneurial partnerships. The monthly *Investment Executive* surveyed issues such as image, morale and pay issues among retail representatives from the eight largest firms in the industry. CIBC Wood Gundy came last on morale measure and led in only one category – legal and compliance. In response, focus groups met to discuss the question of how to organise the business so that it felt more like a partnership. Ed King, chairman from 1988 and now retired, commented, 'If we have to discuss how to structure ourselves, are we really a partnership any longer?'

Meanwhile, the parent company is intent on further growth. It had been the world's 19th largest bank in 1970. Twenty five years later, mergers among rivals had pushed it down to 65th. Arguing for government approval for further Canadian consolidation, some bankers' leaders argue that international competitiveness depends on scale. Referring to international rankings, one said, 'The further you fall the less people are likely to include you in transactions.'

Questions

1 Explain the sources of change that caused first CIBC, and then CIBC Wood Gundy, to adapt.

2 What artefacts are described in the case study?

3 How can the artefacts be used to understand what went on at the division after the merger?

Bibliography Burnes, Bernard (1996) *Managing Change*, 2nd edn, London: Financial Times Pitman Publishing, includes useful chapters on culture and managing change. The works by Handy and Schein given in the references are among the more important works in the field. Linstead, Stephen and others (1996, eds) *Understanding Management*, London: Sage, supplies a critical view of current orthodoxy.

References

1. Marsh, Peter (1996) 'Lego builds its future: the Danish toymaker is expanding its empire', *Financial Times* 16 March; Marsh, Peter (1996) 'Management: one step ahead of the pack', *Financial Times*, 13 May; Bowen, David (1996) 'The house Kirk built: this is the toy that charmed the kids that pestered the parents that bought the bricks that built the firm that made the Danes a billion', *Independent on Sunday*, 24 March; Lawson, Mark (1996) 'The brick gets slick: once the bastion of educational values, even Lego has succumbed to the theme park', *Guardian*, 30 March; Luger, Fritz (1996) 'Lego will in 15 Landeren Themenparks bauen', *Der Standard*, 20 March; Castello, M. 'Lego estudia un parque tematico en el area de Barcelona', *Expansion*, 15 April; Richards, Hale (1997) 'Business Portrait: master builder and his wall of Lego: Kjeld Kirk Kristiansen', *The European*, 24 April; Barnes, Hilary (1997) 'Lego looks at girl power to spice up sales', *Financial Times*, 23 January; http://www.lego.com

2. Rhenman, Eric (1973) *Organisation Theory for Long Range Planning*, London: Wiley-Interscience, 16.

3. Duncan, R.B. (1972) 'The characteristics of organisational environments and perceived environmental uncertainty', *Administrative Science Quarterly*, **17**, 313–27.

4. Vecchio, Robert P. (1995) *Organisational Behaviour*, Third edition, Fort Worth, Tex.: Harcourt Brace and Company, 597.

5. Ashby, Ross (1956) *An Introduction to Cybernetics*, New York: John Wiley.

6. Sharfman, M. and Dean, J. (1991) 'Conceptualising and measuring the organisation environment: a multidimensional approach', *Journal of Management*, **17**, 749–68.

7. Lomi, Alessandro (1995) 'The population ecology of organisational founding', *Administrative Science Quarterly*, March, **40** (**1**), 111–44.

8. Cowles, Virginia (1973) *The Rothschilds – A family of fortune*, London: Weidenfeld and Nicholson, 47–9.

9. Burns, Tom and Stalker, G.M. (1961) *The Management of Innovation*, London: Tavistock.

10. Bannister, Nicholas (1996) 'Rebuke stings BT's sentinel', *Guardian*, 10 September, 18.

11. Morse, Laurie (1994) 'Drought threatens Ghanaian aluminium smelter', *Financial Times*, 1 September, 3; 'Kaiser averts Ghana smelter shutdown', *Financial Times*, 17 September, 11.

12. Haunschild, Pamela R. (1993) 'Interorganisational imitation: the impact on corporate acquisition activity', *Administrative Science Quarterly*, December **38** (**4**), 564–92.

13. Mullins, Laurie J. (1996) *Management and Organisational Behaviour*, London: Financial Times Pitman Publishing, 711.
14. Linstead, Stephen (1996) 'Understanding management: culture, critique and change', in Linstead, Stephen *et al.* (eds) *Understanding Management*, London: Sage, 14.
15. Schein, Edgar H. (1985) *Organisational Culture and Leadership: A dynamic view*, New York: Jossey-Bass, proposes two hidden layers – values and beliefs, and basic assumptions – but space does not allow such a detailed discussion.
16. C. Northcote Parkinson (1957) *Parkinson's Law, or the Pursuit of Progress*, London: John Murray, 84.
17. Gyllenhammar, Pehr G. (1977) *People at Work*, Reading, Mass.: Addison-Wesley, 161–2.
18. Gowler, Dan and Legge, Karen (1996) 'The meaning of management and the management of meaning', in Linstead *et al.* (eds) *op. cit.,* 34–50.
19. Schein (1985) *op. cit.*
20. Based on Linstead (1996) *op. cit.,* 19.
21. Handy, Charles B. (1986) *Understanding Organisations,* Fourth edition, Harmondsworth: Penguin, 188.
22. Handy, Charles B. (1978) *Gods of Management*, London: Pan, 44.
23. Burnes, Bernard (1996) *Managing Change,* Second edition, London: Financial Times Pitman Publishing, 116.
24. 'International Company News: Lehman sues to stop CIBC poaching staff', *Financial Times*, 26 May 1995; McQueen, Rod (1996) 'CIBC exodus: cultures clash', *Financial Post*, 10 June; Blackwell, Richard (1996) 'Indecent proposals: big or bigger', *Financial Post*, 24 June.

Part 2

THEMES IN MANAGEMENT

The new electronic interdependence recreates the world in the image of a global village. *Marshall McLuhan, Canadian sociologist*

A task becomes a duty from the movement you suspect it to be an essential part of that integrity which alone entitles a man to assume responsibility. *Dag Hammarksjöld, Swedish United Nations Secretary-General*

Our rockets can find Halley's comet and fly to Venus with amazing accuracy, but ... many Soviet household appliances are of poor quality. *Mikhail Gorbachev, Russian President*

If Enterprise is afoot, Wealth accumulates whatever may be happening to Thrift; and if Enterprise is asleep, Wealth decays, whatever Thrift may be doing. *John Maynard Keynes, British economist*

PART 1 MANAGEMENT IN CONTEXT	CHAPTER 1 Management and the manager's job	CHAPTER 2 The development of management ideas	CHAPTER 3 Outside the organisation: understanding the environment	CHAPTER 4 Inside the organisation: adapting to change
PART 2 THEMES IN MANAGEMENT	CHAPTER 8 Enterprise	CHAPTER 7 Managing for quality	CHAPTER 6 Social responsibility and ethics	CHAPTER 5 Global business: bridging nations and cultures
PART 3 PLANNING AND DECISION MAKING		CHAPTER 9 Planning: coping in an uncertain environment	CHAPTER 10 Strategic management: looking to the long term	CHAPTER 11 Decision making: choosing from alternatives

Part 2 introduces four themes frequently encountered in the study and practice of management. Awareness of the issues, and competence at coping with them, are important to every manager. Chapter 5 shows how the forces promoting globalisation of business seem, in the past half century, to have overcome those resisting it. In the 'second global economy' commerce is dominated by multinational enterprises. Their emergence raises questions of how they should organise and operate as well as problems for the individual manager. How can a person work well in different cultural environments, making the necessary adjustments?

Whatever the size of the organisation, the issue of social responsibility has become important. Chapter 6 introduces this theme, setting it in its ethical context. Managers should be able to recognise and resolve dilemmas through the application of ethical ideas.

Thanks to the work of pioneers such as Deming and Juran, who honed their ideas in the fertile ground of the post-war Japanese economy, the importance of quality has been recognised by leading organisations. Chapter 7 shows how concern with quality means more than ensuring that products meet standards. It is both a philosophy, illuminating all management practice, and a set of techniques with wide application.

The dominance of multinational organisations overshadowed the role of entrepreneurs in building businesses. Willing to take risks and innovate, entrepreneurs often create tomorrow's success stories. Although entrepreneurs are often to be found in small organisations, their contribution to large ones is also vital if stagnation is to be avoided. Chapter 8 studies what it takes to be an entrepreneur and how they can succeed.

5

Global business: bridging nations and cultures

Chapter objectives

When you have finished studying this chapter, you should be able to:

- compare the forces promoting and resisting the globalisation of business activities;

- show how the presence of multinational enterprises makes the second global economy differ from the first and debate what sorts of world groupings might emerge;

- name some leading MNEs, outlining where they are based and where they operate; link MNEs to the process of globalisation;

- explain key features of MNEs, showing why and how they have grown and, in particular, why they engage in foreign direct investment;

- illustrate how managerial attitudes within MNEs can differ;

- address the problems of managing in different cultures, explaining the benefits and limitations of cross-cultural research applied to management;

- suggest the key issues in cultural adjustment for a manager being posted abroad and how a firm can improve the rate of success.

Exports keep up Scotch distillers' spirits[1]

Few United Kingdom manufacturers have a greater need to export than distillers of Scotch whisky. Of total sales of some £2 billion, 90 per cent is sold abroad. Most sales, measured by volume, are blends from several distilleries with Johnny Walker Red Label, J&B Rare and Ballantine's being the leading whiskies in the world. The smaller volume, more expensive 'single malts' are identified by source and year of distillation. They are matured in oak casks and bottled for sale some 10, 12 or even 20 years later. Leaders are Glenfiddich, The Glenlivet and Glenmorangie. Balancing supply, demand and stock over decades is a major problem. To cut risk, some independent companies have diversified into other spirits. Highland Distilleries have launched Gloag's Gin, for example.

Many distilleries are small operations by world standards. Some 80 per cent of capacity is owned by larger companies with other interests. These owners commonly provide international distribution without which the brand would not survive. William Lawson, in the Bacardi group, is known for Glen Deveron malt; it exports 90 per cent of its £22 million turnover, mainly to Europe. Morrison Bowmore, which exports 60 per cent of its products including Bowmore, is a subsidiary of the Japanese drinks company Suntory. Highland Distilleries has cross-shareholding with Rémy-Cointreau.

The industry jealously guards its name. To qualify as 'Scotch', a whisky must be distilled in Scotland, although it can be bottled elsewhere. Major markets have been in the Anglo-Saxon world. Smaller companies have relied for too long on the leaders, such as Guinness (with Johnny Walker and the United Kingdom leader, Bell's), to promote the idea of Scotch as a drink. Forty-nine per cent of Guinness' £2000 million turnover comes from spirits. It spends some £500 million each year on marketing its stout, lager, Bell's whisky, Gordon's Gin and other brands.

Yet sales of Scotch in the United States have fallen by 60 per cent since 1980. Failure to continually recruit new, younger drinkers meant that Scotch has increasingly borne the burden of an 'oldie' image. Gin, sherry, port and Dutch jenever also suffer, although to a lesser extent. Young people often choose a different drink from their parents. In expanding markets, such as France, Greece, Italy and Spain, it is easier to present Scotch as a more fashionable product. One survey showed that, in a given month, 70 per cent of the UK's 55–64 age group drink it compared with only 6 per cent of the same group in Spain.

Overseas markets are reached through international distributors. These provide support in local markets but there can be difficulties. Macallan-Glenlivet exports three quarters of its output. Sales, of nearly £19 million, are dominated by 'The Macallan' whose chief markets are Italy, the United States and Japan. Dispute with the Italian distributor meant that almost one year's sales were lost in that country. Another feud, between William Grant and its French ex-agent Marie Brizard, had to be settled in court.

Glenmorangie is a family-controlled company with 30 per cent of its £39 million turnover coming from its flagship malt. Other malts include Glen Moray, Martin's 20-year-old (particularly strong in Portugal) and several private labels, such as Old Glen for the Asda supermarket chain. In the middle 1990s, new senior managers brought a new focus to its strategy. Multiple export markets had led to a proliferation of products. There were 9 brands, 41 bottles, 27 closures, 40 packages, 73 labels and 74 shipping cases! These have been halved and other overheads reduced.

The new emphasis is on developing the strong brands, introducing new products and opening new international markets. One move has been to introduce new luxury 'finishes'. These are achieved by moving the malt to former port, sherry or madeira casks for the last two of the twelve-year maturation period. Sub-brands, which command a premium of up to 25 per cent, are thus created in a short time.

Wooden casks are used during maturation although evaporation means loss of the so-called 'angels' share'. Even if new wood is used, its selection is important. Glenmorangie has wood management skills. The casks, or 'hogs', use finely grained white oak, seasoned in Kentucky. A 15 000-cask sampling programme has enabled the company to relate taste to the way the oak is treated. This knowledge was used in the development of the new finishes.

Glenmorangie serves its mature international markets through agents: Brown-Forman in the US; Kokubu in Japan; and Bacardi-Martini or Moët Hennessy for Europe and elsewhere. Many customers buy small quantities and are difficult to reach. Like several competitors, Glenmorangie now has an Internet page and plans to sell directly through it. Unlike most others, however, it foresees growth in new countries. It has recently established joint ventures in India and China. In India, bottling will be carried out by the long established Mohan Meakin distillery. In China, Glenmorangie will help its partner with quality improvement of the local Chinese spirit. Bottling of Scotch will also take place.

Commentators see entering developing countries as a high-risk strategy. Yet the current consumption of Scotch in China is lower than in Stirling, the Scottish town of 28 000 inhabitants.

Introduction

International business is simply that which takes place across national boundaries. At first we may think just of trade, as with the exporting of whisky from Scotland. Then, however, we recognise the presence of foreign firms in most countries. These companies, often among the largest in the world, have made investments in foreign operations that go beyond simply trading from their home base. Foreign investment tends to be handled by the large multinational enterprises. Of these, the top 500 are responsible for about 80 per cent of the flow of capital for investment.

Although almost all of the largest companies are international, to operate across frontiers is not the preserve of this group. Many Scotch distillers, with sales of perhaps £10 million, sell their products to fans and collectors in many countries. In service industries, small specialist companies, from courier services to publishers, operate and have offices or outlets in more than one country. One popular method of development is the international joint venture. This combines, for instance, local know-how of one company with the technical know-how of another. Glenmorangie is following a typical joint-venture strategy in China. Its partner, located in a spirit drinking region, knows its country's PEST factors. The Scottish company, on the other hand, brings a unique product along with technical skills.

Is Scotch a 'global' product? Broadly speaking, it is not changed from market to market. That is part of the product's appeal. Yet there are differences of detail, of tradition, of brand image, of competition, of distribution, and so on. These affect demand in different markets. For example, the Japanese government has been criticised by the World Trade Organization for protecting local 'shochu' producers. Taxes on imported whisky and brandy are seven times the rates on the potato-based spirit whose 1996 market share was 74 per cent.[2] In India, Bagpiper whisky, number four in the world, provides stiff competition. We can, therefore, see similarities among Scotch markets and consumers as well as differences. Which come into play when companies face decisions on international operations?

This chapter provides answers to these questions. It starts by investigating *globalisation*, the trend towards increased integration of business activities throughout the world. Then we look into the companies that have both stimulated and benefited from this trend to examine why and how they become international and why they go beyond trading to investing in foreign countries. Finally, in spite of global trends, substantial differences between countries remain. The question of managing in different cultures must be addressed.

Globalisation

The term globalisation refers to the process of integration on a world scale. Some authors define it solely as a business policy. For example, Rugman and Hodgetts see it as:

> *The production and distribution of products and services of a homogenous type and quality on a worldwide basis.*[3]

As discussed later in the chapter, this policy is a response to the needs of large companies to both gain economies of scale and take opportunities throughout the world. In contrast, other authorities see globalisation as the convergence of multiple forces in the international PEST environments, summarised in Exhibit 5.1. These are, as Perlmutter argues, 'but the first steps on a rocky road to building a global civilisation.'[4]

Exhibit 5.1 Convergent forces support global harmonisation

- Accommodation among political systems –
    openness and transparency among nations,
    willingness to cooperate.
- Open world economy –
    recognition of interdependency,
    reduction of trade barriers.
- Increased awareness and respect for other cultures –
    sharing of ideas,
    convergence of consumer tastes.
- Developments in communications –
    investment in freight and passenger systems,
    growth of the digital world.
- Common concerns for consequences –
    ecological effects,
    rich versus poor.

The reference to a rocky road underlines that it is not clear what kind of civilisation is emerging. There are many difficulties and paradoxes. For instance, we know of the Westernisation of tastes in many countries of Asia, the Middle East and Africa. Rashly, we may see these as 'harmonisation'. At the same time, however, we recognise the assertion and reassertion of ethnic, religious and cultural differences. These are manifest within and between nations and also on a wider scale. Western industrialism and commercialism meet Islamic fundamentalism and Confucianism. The obstacles to harmonisation are powerful, *see* Exhibit 5.2. The two effects go side by side. Isolationism, tried by countries such as Albania, Burma and North Korea, does not work. Autonomy and difference can only be sustained within a framework of worldwide cooperation. Countries, companies and individuals increasingly accept the need to do business with each other.

The second global economy

Making known, and extolling, the scale and scope of worldwide business has become common. The point is often made that the turnover of leading companies matches the output of leading nations. The leaders are crudely compared with nations ranked around twentieth in terms of gross national product (GNP), close to Austria or Belgium. The phenomenon of vast international business is regarded as new. Yet, as Kobrin points out[5], the world economy between 1870 and 1914 was at least as open and convergent as it is today. Levels of international trade and investment before 1914 – measured both relatively and absolutely – were only recently surpassed. It could be said that recent growth in world business has been simply a return to the state of affairs before the calamities of the two world wars.

Exhibit 5.2 **Divergent forces oppose global harmonisation**

■ Geography –
uneven distribution of natural resources,
different and shifting climates.

■ Income –
contrasting stages of economic development,
rich and poor within nations.

■ Education –
difficulties of catching up,
flows of the brightest out of poorer countries.

■ Culture –
conflict among ethnic and cultural groups,
rejection of dominant values.

■ Language –
rising divergence *within* languages such as English.

This somewhat rosy view is tempered by those who point to uneven development and the advantages that protectionism brought to some countries.[6]

In any case, history is not repeating itself. This 'second global economy' differs greatly from the first. Obviously, there are now many more national markets and the flows of goods and money are broader and deeper. Most important, however, is the change in organisation of international transactions. A century ago, the mechanism was the market; goods were traded through markets and foreign investments made directly by share and bond holders. Nowadays, these mechanisms are being supplanted by the international business that uses internal supply channels to replace trade and transfer of funds to replace investment markets. Internationally planned and controlled production has become a key characteristic. Some 38 000 international businesses with 207 000 affiliates now manage about a third of the total productive assets in the private sector. Their worldwide sales are about $5500 billion, roughly the GNP of the United States. World trade breaks down roughly into: one third among divisions of the same company; one third among international businesses; and only one third not linked with one of these companies.[7]

> The terms multinational and transnational, enterprise and corporation are used interchangeably when referring to organisations operating across frontiers. Hence we have MNE, TNE, MNC and TNC. This text sticks to MNE.

The integrated international business, often called the *multinational enterprise (MNE)*, has advantages within the second global economy that parallel those possessed by the international trader in the first. In his classic article 'The Globalisation of Markets',[8] Levitt argued that the global corporation wins by harnessing *technology*. This 'drives consumers relentlessly towards the same common goals – alleviation of life's burdens and the expansion of discretionary time and spending power.' The truly global company is reluctant to adjust to local differences, only doing so after testing consumers with standardised products of the highest quality. Standardisation allows for low cost supply at huge scale. Therefore, we have standard products: aero-engines from Rolls-Royce; shoes from Nike; chips from Intel; globally marketed pharmaceuticals, pesticides and agrochemicals; and drinks from Guinness to Glenmorangie.

Who are the multinational enterprises?

The introduction mentioned that a business does not have to be huge to be multinational. On the other hand, most of the largest are multinational. Table 5.1 lists the top 25 businesses measured by 1997 results.[9] Almost all these are heavily committed to international operations.

What does Table 5.1 tell us? Looking first at the industries, we can see companies that fit well with the picture of the second global economy. They supply products whose demand is high in many corners of the world and have built their size through the internalisation of markets: the petroleum companies control all stages from oil wells to the service station; the motor and engineering companies work by exploiting their technical innovations and process skills on the world

Table 5.1 The world's 25 largest corporations by turnover

Rank	Company	Nation	Industry	Sales $ bn
1	General Motors Corporation	US	Motor vehicles	168
2	Ford Motor Company	US	Motor vehicles	146
3	Mitsui & Co., Ltd	J	Trading	144
4	Mitsubishi Corporation	J	Trading	140
5	Itochu Corporation	J	Trading	135
6	Royal Dutch/Shell Group	NL/UK	Petroleum	128
7	Marubeni Corporation	J	Trading	124
8	Exxon Corporation	US	Petroleum	119
9	Sumitomo Corporation	J	Trading	119
10	Toyota Motor Corporation	J	Motor vehicles	108
11	Wal-Mart Stores, Inc.	US	General merchandisers	106
12	General Electric Company	US	Electronics; electrical equipment	79
13	Nissho Iwai Corporation	J	Trading	78
14	Nippon Telegraph & Telephone	J	Telecommunications	78
15	IBM Corporation	US	Computers	75
16	Hitachi, Ltd	J	Electronics; electrical equipment	75
17	AT&T Corp.	US	Telecommunications	74
18	Nippon Life Insurance Company	J	Insurance	72
19	Mobil Corporation	US	Petroleum	72
20	Daimler-Benz AG	D	Motor vehicles	71
21	British Petroleum	UK	Petroleum	69
22	Matsushita Electric	J	Electronics; electrical equipment	68
23	Volkswagen	D	Motor vehicles	66
24	Daewoo Group	SK	Motor vehicles	65
25	Siemens AG	D	Electronics; electrical equipment	63

stage; the service providers – telecommunications, retailing and insurance – match the high demand for these functions in and between the world's major economies. Six of the twenty-five are Japanese trading companies. These firms act as the distribution ends of combines of manufacturers, each of which can be a huge company in its own right. Commanding such a large proportion of trade both within and between Japan and other states, these companies are typical organisations of the second global economy.

Measuring size by turnover, however, overstates the importance of trading companies that combine high turnover with small margins. Another view is to look at employment. After all, in many observers' eyes, 'a big company' is one with many employees. Table 5.2 gives the top ten, noting the ranks that the companies gain in the turnover list. Note that only two firms appear in both top tens – Ford and General Motors. It is no wonder that they have for long been seen as the archetypal MNEs.

There are many European enterprises in the leading turnover list. Table 5.3 includes the ranking and nation of registration of the EU leaders. 154 of Fortune's Top 500 are registered in an EU member state. As has been mentioned, commitments to international activities and investments vary. For instance Royal Dutch/Shell achieves 24 per cent of its turnover in the United States, British Petroleum gains 28 per cent and the Belgian food company Delhaize 'Le Lion' (310th in the 500) reaches 65 per cent. It employs almost 50 000 people in that country. The French postal service (13th) and German railways (14th) and postal service (16th) are high in the employment list as monopoly providers of labour intensive services within large economies. Clearly, they have limited global interests.

Table 5.2 The world's 10 largest corporations, by employees

Rank by sales	Company	Nation	Industry	Employees 000
29	US Postal Service	US	Mail	887
11	Wal-Mart Stores	US	General merchandisers	675
1	General Motors	US	Motor vehicles	647
86	PepsiCo	US	Beverages	486
146	Rao Gazprom	R	Energy	399
25	Siemens	D	Electronics; electrical equipment	379
2	Ford Motor	US	Motor vehicles	372
147	United Parcel Service	US	Delivery	336
61	Sears Roebuck	US	General merchandisers	335
16	Hitachi	J	Electronics; electrical equipment	330

Table 5.3 The EU's 25 largest corporations, by turnover

Rank	Nation	Company	Industry	Sales $ bn
6	NL/UK	Royal Dutch / Shell Group	Petroleum	125
20	D	Daimler-Benz	Motor vehicles	72
21	UK	British Petroleum	Petroleum	70
23	D	Volkswagen	Motor vehicles	67
25	D	Siemens	Electronics; electrical equipment	64
28	D	Allianz Holding	Insurance	57
31	NL/UK	Unilever	Food	52
32	I	Fiat	Motor vehicles	51
35	I	IRI	Telecommunications	49
39	F	Elf Aquitaine	Petroleum	47
42	D	Veba Group	Trading	45
48	F	Electricité de France	Electricity	44
50	D	Deutsche Telekom	Telecommunications	42
51	NL	Philips Electronics	Electronics; electrical equipment	41
52	F	Union des Assurances de Paris	Insurance	41
56	D	Deutsche Bank	Commercial banking	39
57	D	RWE Group	Electricity	39
58	I	ENI	Petroleum	38
63	F	Renault	Motor vehicles	36
64	NL	ING Group	Insurance	36
66	D	BMW	Motor vehicles	35
67	F	Crédit Agricole	Commercial banking	35
70	F	Total	Petroleum	35
72	F	Peugeot	Motor vehicles	34
74	D	Hoechst	Chemicals	34

Location of multinational enterprises

Tables 5.1 to 5.3 suggest some geographical distribution of the leading MNEs. It is hardly surprising that their headquarters are to be found, for the most part, in the nations with the strongest economies. This spread is illustrated in Fig. 5.1, showing how almost 90 per cent of the Top 500 companies have their homes in the European Union, Japan or the United States. Trade and investment among these regions dominate world commerce and are, in turn, dominated by MNEs. Figure 5.2[10] illustrates export flow between regions; there are similar strong links for investments. Heaviest flows are typically among countries that are part of a cluster, that is in the same region. Some authors see the clusters crystallising into the three members of the *triad*[11] – the EU, Japan and its neighbours, and NAFTA. Between them, triad countries account for 80 per cent of all foreign investment flows.

Links within each region are strengthening. The EU and NAFTA countries trade heavily with each other. Japan's foreign investment is weighted towards other countries in South-East Asia. For instance, 60 per cent of Matsushita's overseas production is in neighbouring countries; a tenth of this output is exported to Japan, a proportion that is rising. Japan is a key source of foreign investment in China and its foreign aid programme is focused on poorer countries in the region.[12]

Governments display a mixed response to such developments. On the one hand, they seek the benefits of foreign capital and technology and frequently offer incentives to capture new facilities and the jobs that go with them. On the other hand,

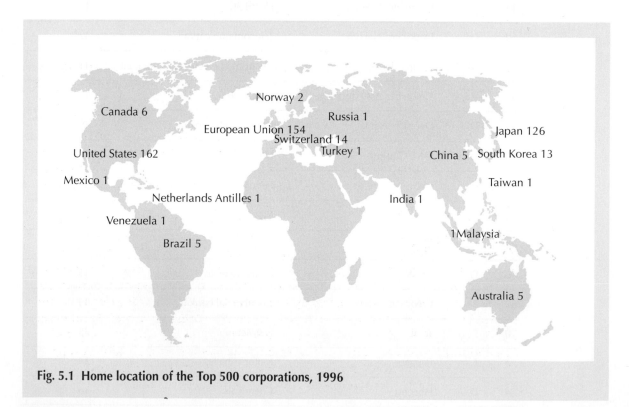

Fig. 5.1 Home location of the Top 500 corporations, 1996

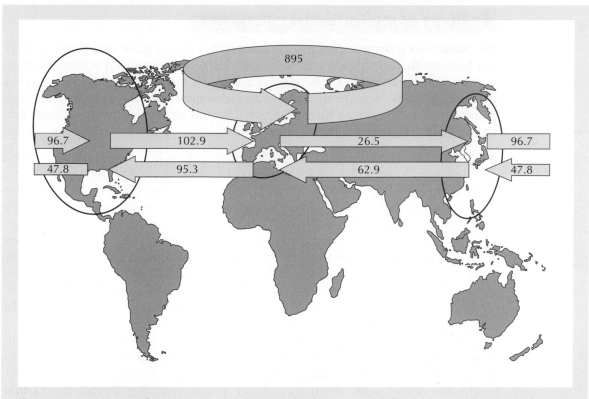

Fig. 5.2 Exports among the EU, Japan and the United States, 1992 ($ billions)

they fear the threat to sovereignty implied by the ceding of control of key industries to foreign owners. Therefore, we see within two or three years the United Kingdom government welcoming investments by Ford, General Motors, Honda, Nissan and Toyota while simultaneously watching the sale of the locally-owned Jaguar and Rover. Ambiguous attitudes to trade blocs are part of the same dilemma. On the one hand, the EU single market offers the possibility of scale economies to producers in many of its industries. On the other hand, EU members, both separately and in unison, sometimes try to use trade barriers to protect key industries, such as agriculture or aircraft manufacture, from worldwide competition.

The development of the triad clusters underscores the point that we do not know what sort of global civilisation is emerging. The optimist may argue that, led by the most efficient MNEs, trade barriers will continue to be dismantled and the benefits of the best technology will be spread among all countries. The pessimist will fear that the richer blocs will be satisfied with less than optimum performance in their own industries, boosted by the removal of internal barriers. 'Fortress Europe' will be matched by 'Fortress Asia' and 'Fortress America'. Limited outward investments from these economic strongholds will be targeted on neighbouring or 'client' states. Latin America will look north, Eastern Europe will look west and the Pacific Rim will look to Japan. The effect, in the pessimistic scenario, will be for the triad fortresses to expand into these regions.

Features of multinational enterprises

The MNE is an enterprise that has its headquarters in one place (the *home* country) but has operations in others (the *host* countries). Note that this is a form of international business in that it is involved both in trade and investment across frontiers. We have seen that the MNE harnesses the twin forces of globalisation and technology to achieve its ends. From this statement we can derive three key characteristics of these organisations:

■ MNEs must respond to environments in both their home and host countries. Many aspects are replicated from country to country. For example, in the operating environment, globalisation of markets means that an MNE will meet the same competitors in each nation or region. This applies as much to Sony and Toshiba as it does to BP and Royal Dutch/Shell. Yet different traditions and histories of competition, combined with the presence of local competitors, can have subtle or substantial effects. The malt whisky market is hardly uniform. We noted the varying strengths of each Scotch in different countries and how they face diverse competitors. Figure 5.3 suggests how all aspects of the environment can change from country to country although there may be links among suppliers, distributors, customers and competitors.

   The wider environment also has a variable influence. For instance, the way products are used varies from place to place. Germans prefer to wash clothes in very hot water while Brazilians wash their clothes (and themselves) in cold. This distinction, with variations in water quality and other factors, means that the soaps and detergents on sale are not the same.

■ The strength of the MNE is drawn from its pool of resources. These range from the tangible assets of plant and facilities to the intangible assets of information, trademarks, patents and designs. Capital can be made available for projects and, given the general strength of the business, funds can be obtained at advantageous rates. Furthermore, there are the knowledge and skills of the personnel. They know how to supply and make things, how to buy and sell. Many international developments are based on applying the knowledge in new markets. Pilkington, the glass maker based in North-West England, gained a technological advantage from its float glass process. It used a system of licensing, followed by direct investment, to ensure rapid and widespread application of its knowledge while it was protected by patents. The flow of royalties enabled it to become one of the world's leading glass companies. At a smaller scale, Glenmorangie's entry to China and India is based on its process expertise.

■ The MNE can plan and control all its resources. Sometimes it can do this in a decentralised manner, allowing local subsidiaries to work closely with their environments. In other cases it is very centralised, setting targets and making detailed plans from headquarters. Development of global products, from Proton Cars to Pepsi-Cola tends to be centralised. At the other extreme, the managers and editors of newspapers in the News International Group are expected to fit them to the needs of local markets. We saw in Chapter 4 how Lego decided to change the balance between global and local as it found it needed to adapt its product range and packaging to suit local needs.

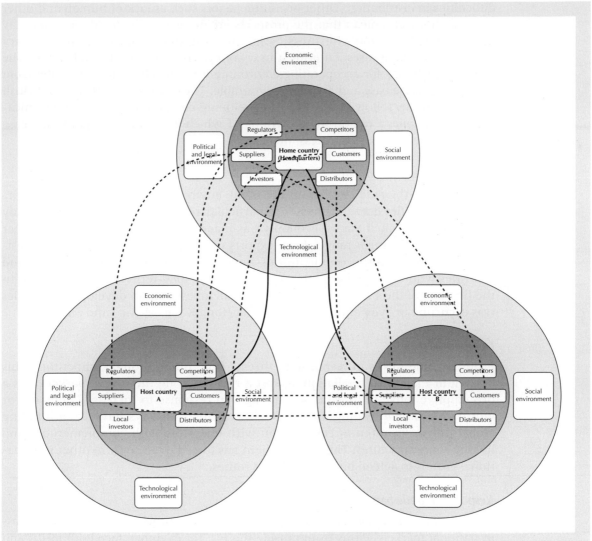

Fig. 5.3 Different operating environments may have linked elements

Becoming a multinational enterprise

Why become an MNE?

The following six points summarise the reasons why firms might become MNEs. Clearly they do not all apply in each case although more than one will often have an effect.

Avoiding reliance on home base

There may be difficulties in the home country. For example, the market could be highly competitive or subject to constraints imposed by government controls or difficulties in distribution. Other operating factors such as lack of human and other resources may also mean that the prospects are not good. Finally, the market may suffer from the nation's business cycle, meaning that income and profits vary widely. In all these cases, entering a new country is a form of diversification. The company will look for an operating environment whose characteristics differ from those of its home base and are more favourable. Throughout the 1990s, the British government has followed a policy of developing competition in telecommunications. This implies a cap on the growth of BT which in turn has sought to increase its unregulated overseas business interests.

Taking opportunities abroad

In contrast to the *push* away from the home environment, the *pull* factors of foreign opportunities draw businesses to particular regions. The strength and steady growth of the United States' economy has made it attractive to firms from other countries. Involvement ranges from exports of all types of goods to direct investments. More recently, opportunities have begun to be taken in Japan and countries whose size and growth rates suggest that long-term benefits will flow. In the first half of the 1990s, more than half of all investment in developing countries was occurring in five nations: Brazil, China, Hong Kong, Mexico and Singapore.

Competitiveness

Firms become MNEs in response to threats from international competitors. This behaviour may be in retaliation against a rival entering the home market or as a pre-emptive move to forestall a challenge. In response to increased demand for worldwide travel, leading airlines such as British Airways have been building global networks, often in cooperation with operators with complementary and linking route structures. This development has forced rivals to form other multinational groups to defend business on their routes.

Response to trade barriers

Trade barriers are designed to prevent overseas competitors from achieving success in national markets. Firms from outside the EU, for example, face both tariffs and quotas. Japanese-made cars are subject to a 'voluntary' quota of 12 per cent market share. This arrangement is supposed to be temporary, allowing time for local industry to increase its efficiency to match world standards. In response, Japanese companies have built plant within the bloc, mostly in the United Kingdom. If cars are assembled from more than 80 per cent of locally made components, the plant output does not count against the quota.

Operational improvements

Direct control of operations in a foreign country can result in service improvements and reduced costs. This is the advantage of the MNE compared with trading in the market or using agents. Provided business is of sufficient scale, direct control enables more rapid response to customers, selection of the most efficient pattern of production and distribution, and elimination of intermediate traders and inventory holders.

Application of knowledge

Innovatory firms have the potential to reap benefits from their developments. These can be in all aspects of business from products to processes. One way of rapidly exploiting these inventions on a world scale is to allow others the right to use them in their own regions. The licence is a contract to exchange expertise for royalties. In the short term the licensor gains cash flow while the innovation is still fresh and has not attracted imitators. The problem in the longer term is that the licensee can build its own business strength and learn too much about the innovation. Quick service restaurants, such as McDonald's, are based on a particular kind of process knowledge – knowing how to deliver good service every time. They have spread across the world by issuing franchises. Market share in each target country is built quickly by this method, a move that forestalls competitors. Yet the continuing success of the leading companies means that it is now better for them to invest directly in the restaurant facilities. In manufacturing, the case of Pilkington was mentioned above. It eventually found its glass process to be so successful that it was better to make investments in foreign ventures rather than merely issue licences.

■ The internationalisation process

There are four main methods of engaging in international business – trading, licensing, cooperating and investing. These are sometimes presented as a set of stages through which most home businesses develop into MNEs.[13] As some of our examples will show, however, an organisation may start with any of the methods and proceed by using others. Figure 5.4 shows some of these routes. The business may not start out with the intention of becoming an MNE. Yet, as Fig. 5.4 shows from left to right, this is a likely development if the initial forays pay off and the business gathers strength and experience in international affairs. The four main policies are listed in the left margin of the figure. Their sequence represents an increased degree of control over foreign operations. Given the need of large corporations both to control their activities and strongly influence their operating environments, the expanding MNE moves towards the lower right-hand corner of the diagram.

Trading, or export–import

A home company will frequently make a start in international business through trade, either exporting or importing. Exporting may result from push or pull factors in the home or target environments. Since net prices obtained in export markets are often lower than at home, selling abroad will be attractive only if it can be done at low cost. Scotch whisky producers, for example, find that their revenue from exports is around 25 per cent lower than at home. There are, in addition, many risks and difficulties facing the exporter. A small firm in Liverpool manufactures battery-powered locomotives that can haul loads along metre-wide passages in mines and other excavations. The owner's fluency in Spanish and local knowledge enables him to gain export opportunities in Bolivian silver mining. This is, however, an erratic industry in a volatile country so there are risks from currency fluctuations and payment delays or defaults.

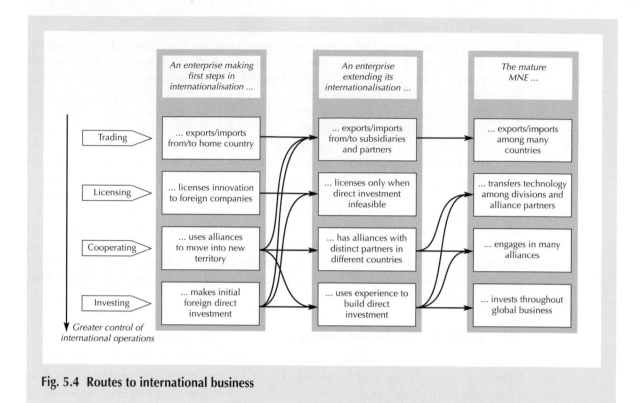

| An enterprise making first steps in internationalisation ... | An enterprise extending its internationalisation ... | The mature MNE ... |

Trading → ... exports/imports from/to home country → ... exports/imports from/to subsidiaries and partners → ... exports/imports among many countries

Licensing → ... licenses innovation to foreign companies → ... licenses only when direct investment infeasible → ... transfers technology among divisions and alliance partners

Cooperating → ... uses alliances to move into new territory → ... has alliances with distinct partners in different countries → ... engages in many alliances

Investing → ... makes initial foreign direct investment → ... uses experience to build direct investment → ... invests throughout global business

↓ Greater control of international operations

Fig. 5.4 Routes to international business

Importing reflects exporting in that the company acts as a foreign agent or customer for the exporter. The activity could be to exploit an opportunity in the home market, such as the rising demand for foreign wines, clothes or authentic 'ethnic' products. On the other hand, the stimulus may be to reduce operating costs through a search for cheaper raw materials or semi-finished goods.

Once an enterprise has become an MNE, its operations in different countries will themselves engage in international trade. The ability of the MNE to rationalise and coordinate these activities and use them to avoid trade restrictions is one of its strengths.

Licensing

As we have seen, licensing involves trade in intellectual property. This can be items that are formally recognised in law, such as patents, designs, works of art and trade marks. Knowledge can also go beyond this if it consists of skills and experience that the purchaser of the licence would otherwise take too long to acquire. Some organisations, from research arms of universities to the entertainment conglomerates of Hollywood, trade almost entirely in intellectual property, looking to worldwide exploitation for their profits. A notable example is the Victoria and Albert Museum which has entered international business via the licensing route, *see* Exhibit 5.3.[14]

> ### Exhibit 5.3 *Inspiring Design* brings licence income to the V&A
>
> The Victoria and Albert Museum is constantly on the look out for extra revenue to pay for the care and display of its 5 million artefacts. The museum's name is famous, especially in the United Sates and Japan. Recognising this, the V&A set up, in 1994, a licensing project *Inspiring Design* intended to generate revenue and further spread awareness of its collection. It is a world leader in licensing, issuing more than 80 in little over a year.
>
> More than 80 per cent of the licensed goods are sold abroad. They include textiles, gifts, wall coverings, jewellery, china and glass. In a typical three-year rolling agreement, V&A Enterprises allowed the Welsh tie-maker Frank, Theak and Roskilly access to its William Morris archives to reproduce patterns. The initiative coincided with the centenary of Morris' death when a large exhibition was being held. FT&R supplies silk ties and accessories for sale through the V&A's shop and mail-order catalogue. A different range is sold through Marks & Spencer and other leading fashion shops. The link has helped FT&R to recover from a decline. Sales rose from £7.5 million in 1992 to £11 million four years later.

A franchise is a form of licensing in which the core organisation provides its franchisees with detailed support. This ranges from materials to marketing, products to processes and trade marks to training.

Cooperating, or forming strategic alliances

A strategic alliance could be an agreement between two firms to exchange technical know-how for other resources. Here it would be similar to a licence agreement. In general, however, strategic alliances involve all types of cooperation between two or more partners for mutual benefit. Applied to international business, a frequent arrangement is for one party to offer product and process expertise and, possibly, capital, while the other is a local company, bringing with it relevant political, market and management experience. Alliances are generally for experienced companies willing to commit themselves to long-term links. T1 New Media is a subsidiary of Bertelsmann, Germany's largest media group and number 283 in the Fortune 500. In 1996, it announced a cooperation agreement with Mitsui. Initially, the deal was to license and market each other's products. It gave Bertelsmann improved access to the Asian market, where Mitsui could use its trading expertise. Meanwhile, the latter was looking for a distributor for its multimedia products in Germany.[15]

Joint ventures are special types of alliance where the partners establish jointly-owned facilities. Political restrictions and high risks mean that they are a common method of joining the race to set up business in China. The French companies Cerestar (starch derivatives), Air Liquide (oxygen) and the Italian Marcegaglia (steel) were just three £100 million projects announced in June 1996.[16] Although on a smaller scale, Glenmorangie's moves into China, reported in the opening case, have an eye on long-term benefits.

Investing

Joint ventures span the cooperating and investing categories because they involve international flows of capital. The current surge of such projects is fuelled by MNEs' urgent desire to achieve global coverage while also limiting risk. Beyond the joint venture, however, is the establishment of a wholly-owned subsidiary. This gives the MNE complete control and may bring savings in terms of shortening of channels of distribution and reduced operating costs. Local awareness is achieved not through partnerships but by direct employment of local managers.

Investments can be to buy current businesses or to build new facilities on green-field sites. Ford Motor Company has displayed both policies. It built its European business through investment in new plant over some 70 years and recently acquired Jaguar. Leading retailers, including IKEA, Marks & Spencer and Toys'R'Us have concentrated on direct investment as their preferred means of entering foreign markets, although there can be variations. M&S has 350 stores in 31 overseas countries yielding 15 per cent of annual sales. Most are wholly owned and have been set up from scratch. Expansion into the Union States, however, was through the 1988 acquisition of the up-market Brown Brothers which also has 55 outlets in Japan. Commentators suggest that the company has had poor returns from its $750 million outlay. The Australian market is to be entered through franchises in the Sydney area.[17]

Foreign direct investment

It is important to distinguish between foreign direct investment (FDI) and other forms of overseas financial holdings. For the latter, an organisation may purchase bonds or financial securities in the expectation of gaining a profit when they are sold. It may also hold currencies in cash to simplify trade and hedge against rate fluctuations during the life of a sale or purchase contract. FDI, on the other hand, means active management of foreign facilities. Why should firms engage in such investments as opposed to exporting and importing? To answer this question, Dunning compared firm-specific and location-specific advantages.[18] Firm-specific advantages (FSAs) are those 'knowledge' factors that the firm can protect and use to resist the establishment of rivals. Location-specific advantages (LSAs) arise from the country's geographical position – for instance, distance from resources and markets – and its endowment in terms of infrastructure, information, skilled labour, cheap power and so on. The interplay of the two types of advantage suggests the best development policy for each firm.

Figure 5.5 shows how Dunning combined the ideas. Let us say that a firm has an FSA, such as a patent, yet its home country is not well suited for its exploitation. It may lack sufficient skilled labour or other costs may be too high. This places the firm in the top right-hand cell of the diagram, suggesting that outward FDI may be the best policy. If, on the other hand, home firms have no FSA, or there are simply no firms, then inward FDI is likely when the location is favourable. Furthermore, FSAs and LSAs together imply exporting; having neither means importing will be successful. A weakness of the model is that it takes no account of licensing or

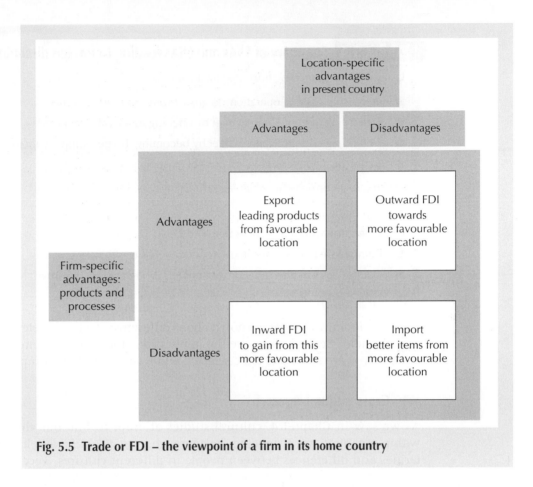

Fig. 5.5 Trade or FDI – the viewpoint of a firm in its home country

joint-venturing. Dunning saw these as second-best policies for firms that are pre-vented from trading or exercising full control. Yet their advantages, especially in terms of the speed with which they can bring results, should be recognised.

Exhibit 5.4 pulls together the above discussion, summarising why firms undertake FDI. LSAs explain the waves of investment from East Asian firms into the United Kingdom. The 1996 decision of Hyundai to build a £1 billion semiconductor plant at Dunfermline, Scotland is a typical example. Reasons given were: the threat of trade barriers; market benefits from being close to customers; and production costs lower than Korea, considering government regional assistance grants.[19]

Managing in different cultures

A consequence of engaging in international business is that managers are immedi-ately faced with colleagues and rivals from different cultures. Unfortunately, they are often badly prepared for these encounters, having been presented with racial and national stereotypes from when they were children. The rest of the chapter examines two aspects of this difficult area. First, there is the field of cross-cultural

---

Exhibit 5.4 Summary of FSAs and LSAs leading to foreign direct investment

Using and strengthening firm-specific advantages:

- Increasing scale of operations to grow profits and reduce costs.
- Defending current home market by opening in a rival's backyard.
- Defending current export market by becoming 'home' company there.
- Acquiring knowledge by purchase of existing business.

Seeking location-specific advantages:

- Exploiting fast growing markets.
- Operating within an economic bloc.
- Being close to customers means speedy service.
- Cutting costs in new location: materials, labour, energy, transport.

---

research, looking at what is known about differences and how relevant they are to management. Second, there are the implications for staffing of international operations. How are managers to be selected and trained for these 'outposts' of MNEs?

Cross-cultural research

As we saw in Chapter 4, cultural studies attempt to find out about individuals within organisations. Extending the approach, *cross-cultural studies* look for the similarities and differences between people in different cultures. Vecchio warns us of the difficulties of this work and hence the danger in placing great reliance on many of the results.[20] These arise from two issues, defining cultures and measurement. Comparisons are often made between managers in different nations, taking for convenience the national boundary as a basis for defining culture. Yet, as Denfeld Wood points out, differences between individuals within one culture may be greater than shown by those from different ones.[21] Differences arise from gender, social class, education, age, religious background and so on. Given that culture is a *shared system of meaning*, this begs the question of what a national culture is!

Vecchio's second concern is with the application of theory to measurement. He is concerned with the use of theories and techniques that had developed in the West for the study of Western workers. 'It is probably incorrect to assume that ideas and constructs … are equally appropriate for explaining the behaviour of workers in all other countries.'[22] More specifically, Riordan and Vandenberg report on two scales developed in the United States to assess self-esteem and satisfaction with supervision. They concluded that Koreans used different frames of reference when responding to the scale items and, therefore, different scores could not be interpreted.[23]

In spite of these difficulties, studies continue. They parallel the continuing problem of managing MNEs, especially if formed by merger or acquisition. Different cultural approaches to handling conflict can lead to failure unless shared meanings are achieved quickly.[24] Furthermore, managers are less concerned with research than with action. Consequently, they often see differences as sources of learning as well as obstacles to be overcome. German and United Kingdom companies each now invest huge sums in the other nation. Marsh reports on how interaction among managers is leading to a *rapprochement* between the German industrial perspective and 'long-termism' and the British emphasis on finance and the short term. German managers are conscious of technical competence and position in the hierarchy while their British counterparts prefer less structure and the freedom to use initiative.[25] In summary, we can quote Hofstede: 'There is something in all countries called management, but its meaning differs to a larger or smaller extent from one country to the other, and it takes considerable historical and cultural insight into local conditions to understand its processes, philosophies, and problems.'[26]

■ Management attitudes

Perlmutter was concerned with assessing the degree of multinationality of an enterprise. How could one tell whether a firm was 'truly' multinational as opposed to one having a few overseas operations? He concluded that there were no feasible operational or financial measures, such as the proportion of activities or investment that takes place outside the home country. The striking difference among firms lay in another direction – in the state of mind of the managers. 'The attitudes men hold are clearly more relevant than their passports.'[27]

Three states of mind were identified by Perlmutter: ethnocentric, polycentric and geocentric. They are never seen in pure form; some measure of each is present in all organisations. Their characteristics, as ideal types, are set out in Exhibit 5.5 and explained below.

■ *Ethnocentric or home-country alignment*
  Regarding one's culture as superior to others is an ethnocentric attitude. A manager may assert with conviction, 'Of course I don't think like that!' Simultaneously the firm may order simple components from its overseas subsidiaries, leaving the trickier finishing to be done at home. Explanations are offered in terms of foreign nationals not yet being ready or being unreliable. Generally, business is conducted according to home-country practices, in the home language. 'Outposts' are run by expatriates on temporary postings. Finding it difficult to deal with foreign managers, headquarters ensures that its own are placed in key positions.
    There are many ethnocentric, or *monocultural*, MNEs, perhaps the majority. For instance, the proportion of foreign-born board members of the United States' Top 500 companies in 1991 was 2.1 per cent, the same as ten years earlier. In France, 50 per cent of chief executives of large companies come from six *grandes écoles* and few have international experience.[28] As for companies, McDonald's *knows* the best way to run quick-service restaurants. Therefore it appoints and trains its staff according to standards and rules laid down at headquarters. Training often involves a visit to the McDonald's University. Plants in the United Kingdom owned by Brother, Nissan, Sharp and Toyota typically have Japanese nationals in overall charge and running the production and engineering functions. Accounts and personnel are handled by locals. The advantage of having the same procedures throughout the world should not be underestimated.

| Exhibit 5.5 | Orientation of headquarters to subsidiaries in three types of MNE |

Organisational feature	Ethnocentric	Polycentric	Geocentric
Complexity	High in HQ, which makes main decisions; low in subsidiaries	Varies among subsidiaries	Complex and interdependent
Authority	HQ	Local	Collaborative
Monitoring and control	Home standards applied throughout	Local	Agreed universal standards applied locally
Rewards and incentives	High in HQ; low in subsidiaries	Wide variation	Matched to worldwide and local objectives
Communication	Downwards from HQ	Little	Many paths among subsidiaries
Identification	Home-country	Host country	International and national interests
Continuity	Home-country recruitment for foreign postings	Local people developed for own country management	Best people for key positions throughout the world

■ *Polycentric, or host-country alignment*

Polycentric firms incorporate the notion that host-country cultures are difficult to understand and local people know what is best. Therefore, the branch should be allowed as much local character as possible within the MNE's targets. Rarely are home-country managers placed in top positions in overseas subsidiaries. The polycentric MNE is, therefore, a group of companies that have a high degree of operating autonomy. Such an approach can have its problems if conflict is allowed to develop. When in 1995, the British end of Royal Dutch/Shell, having obtained clearance from the government, began to tow the obsolete Brent Spar rig towards its planned dumping point in the Atlantic Ocean, the strongest public protests arose in Germany. There were attacks on petrol stations and a consumer boycott. The company's German and United Kingdom subsidiaries became involved in a public row.[29]

■ *Geocentric, or world-orientation*

Perlmutter argues that the geocentric attitude is beginning to emerge. Its ultimate goal is a worldwide approach both in headquarters and in the subsidiaries. Collaboration is important, creating worldwide standards for the company products with local variations where agreed. Local managers are expected to manage their operations effectively but always within the total context. Promotion of managers is done on merit, not nationality. ABB is viewed by many observers as a geocentric enterprise, *see* Exhibit 5.6.[30]

Exhibit 5.6 Finding the best people for the geocentric company

Created in a 1988 merger between the Swedish ASEA and Swiss Brown Boveri, ABB Group employs some 215 000 people in 40 countries. In 1997, its sales were thirteenth in the *Financial Times* European 500. Yet the Zurich headquarters employs merely 171 people.

Percy Barnevik, now chairman, succeeded in building the global corporation. To do so, he said, ' ... you need to start early because it takes a long time. ... building a global company is not easy to copy.' His aim as chief executive, building the global structure, was almost complete. He added, 'The main task now is to bring more executives from emerging countries in Eastern Europe and in Asia into the higher levels of the company.' More than 40 per cent of ABB staff are in these countries. Patience is required in developing managers who can think and act globally.

About 500 elite managers, selected according to cultural sensitivity, pass through a series of assignments in different countries. They are charged with binding the organisation together and ensuring that information and expertise pass around the world. Although a few other companies, such as Shell and IBM, have such people, few are available. Barnevik continued, 'Also it's better to grow up with ABB values. It's difficult to digest our culture if you have spent 10 or 20 years in another company.'

Simon argues that the modern MNE no longer produces in one country and trades with another.[31] It has become an integrated system, capable of sourcing products from many sites while passing funds between semi-independent business operations in many countries. For many, the international transactions are less to do with goods and more to do with transfers of advanced technology. It is inevitable that large MNEs will become culturally diversified. The question for the geocentric organisation is not whether loyalty to the business will, or must, overcome ethnicity or nationality. Instead, managers in such MNEs should learn to tolerate diversity and come to terms with conflicting loyalties. These comments echo those of Adler, noted in Chapter 1.

Cultural differences

Having noted Perlmutter's analysis of ways for MNEs to consider differences, we can go on to ask what they are. Cross-cultural research has identified many issues relevant to managers and organisations. A few are noted here.

Attitudes to time

We can look at two aspects, the pace of life and temporal style. We observe that the pace of life seems to vary from nation to nation, many jokes being based on national stereotypes. Vecchio reports results which suggest an objective truth behind these opinions. Exhibit 5.7 gives the rankings of pace observed in six nations.[32]

More significant is Hall's separation of temporal frames into monochronic and polychronic.[33]

Exhibit 5.7	Indications of the pace of life in different countries		
Accuracy of bank clocks	*Walking speed*	*Post Office speed of service*	
Japan	Japan	Japan	High
United States	United Kingdom	United States	
Taiwan	United States	United Kingdom	↑
United Kingdom	Italy	Taiwan	↓
Italy	Taiwan	Indonesia	
Indonesia	Indonesia	Italy	Low

■ *Monochronic, or linear time*

When time is conceived monochronically, it is a measurable, objective standard having equal units. Time passes by the tick of the clock and without reference to events. Activities are arranged linearly. People concentrate on the job, and stress the completion of tasks, schedules and procedures. They are accustomed to short-term relationships. This habit of thought is prevalent among northern Europeans and North Americans, members of large organisations and males.

■ *Polychronic time*

With a polychronic style, people pay attention to several things at once, interspersing activities as and when needed. They are subject to distraction and change of plan and regard time commitments as objectives. The need for promptness depends on the significance of the relationship, each of which is potentially for life. Hall showed that polychronic time frames are to be found in southern European, Amerindian and many Asian cultures, smaller organisations, and among women.

We should remember that these explanations concern ideal-types. Examples of each can be found within any nation, organisation or even individual. As Exhibit 5.8 suggests, the juxtaposition of two incompatible assumptions leads to difficulties! Within the MNE, these difficulties include the problems of trying to get people from different backgrounds to work together on time-constrained projects.

Communication context

In some groups, known as *high-context* cultures, people pay much attention to the context in which communication occurs. Social setting, social status and non-verbal behaviour are recognised and understood as part of the message. Each part of a business transaction is seen as a step in building the relationship. Trust and the harmony of the group are valued. In a *low-context* culture, on the other hand, business correspondence and other messages will focus on the exchange of facts and data. Meaning is derived from words. Clarity and brevity are important for the transaction; relationship building takes place outside the immediate context. During the preparations for the Gulf War, the United States General Schwarzkopf learned to spend many hours in philosophical discussion with members of the Saudi royal family, realising that it was the way the group came to decisions.[34]

Exhibit 5.8 Monochronic meets polychronic time

Scene: Jones' general store in Llanarmon-yn-Lal.

Mrs Jones: Good morning, here again for the weekend? What can I get you?
Mrs Ledger: Good morning. I'll start with two pounds of carrots and four of potatoes.
Mrs Jones: Good morning Mr Roberts, what can I do for you?
Mr Roberts: I'll have two pounds of potatoes with my paper.

Mrs Jones brings enough potatoes for both, weighs them and takes Mr Roberts' money. Begins to weigh carrots …

Mrs Jones: [*In Welsh.*] Hello, Mrs Evans. Nice to see you again. How's your daughter? Just be wanting your paper is it?
Mrs Ledger: I thought you were serving me.
Mrs Jones: I am, dear, I am. [*Puts carrots in bag and takes coins from Mrs Evans.*] Now what else would you like?

Scene: Bank in same village.

Cashier: Who's next?
Mrs Ledger: Will this bill be settled by Tuesday if I give you cash?

Attitudes to rules and legal agreements

Managers of MNEs frequently comment on different attitudes showing themselves in situations such as contract negotiation and enforcement. We can look at two examples:

■ *The buying process*
Managers from Europe and North America are used to the legal notion of *caveat emptor* – let the buyer beware – applied to buying real estate. When considering a business acquisition, they conduct a thorough investigation before completing. The target company is expected to cooperate. In Japan, the onus of diligence is on the seller who must show good faith and satisfy all reasonable expectations that the buyer would have. *Caveat emptor* is not followed in Asia and Latin America so that detailed investigations can be seen as insulting.[35]

■ *Contract enforcement*
Western managers view contracts as the basis of all transactions and seek to formalise those of significant value. Their enforceability through the courts or arbitration provides security. Choi contrasts this with East Asia where the reputation of the individual or the organisation plays a much more important role. 'Losing face' is to be avoided and the sense of personal obligation is strong.[36]

Management policy in different cultures

Many organisations espouse standard policies for issues such as the welfare and safety of staff. Janssens and others compared perceptions of safety at three plants of a United States, MNE.[37] They found that it was perceived differently in Argentina, France and the US. In the last two countries, the individualist culture was reflected in the expectations for managers to take control. They were seen as responsible for finding the balance between production and safety. In the collectivist culture of Argentina, however, blue-collar workers saw production and safety as everyone's responsibility. MNE policies need to recognise local cultural differences.

The above paragraph mentions an important idea in cross-cultural studies – individualism versus collectivism. It is among the dimensions established in one of the most ambitious and famous pieces of research in this field, that carried out by Hofstede.

Hofstede's cultural dimensions

Many studies have been limited in scope because they have compared two or three nations along a predetermined dimension such as attitudes to time, space, rules, control and so on. Differences have been found but, since these were the only ones that were looked for, assessment of whether other factors might be more important is not possible. In contrast, the Dutch scholar Geert Hofstede applied a wide-ranging questionnaire to 116 000 IBM employees in some 70 countries.[38] He then used statistical methods to draw conclusions from the data:

> Factor analysis *looks for patterns of answers that suggest relationships among the questions. Hence if those who answer Question 25 positively tend also to answer Question 37 positively and 51 negatively, and vice versa, we can infer that these three questions refer to aspects of the same underlying factor.*

Such methods led Hofstede to discover four such underlying factors, or *cultural dimensions*. These are summarised in Exhibit 5.9, which also names countries that scored high or low on each scale. Although there is no room here for detailed comparisons, the lists clearly show variable patterns among countries. While some may be similar on one or two dimensions, they turn out to diverge on others. Two points about the country names need to be emphasised. They only appear if IBM had an operation at the time of Hofstede's study and they only relate to IBM employees.

The differences warn us against two traps. First, we must avoid stereotyping statements like, 'People in South-East Asia ...' Second, we should also beware of taking Hofstede's results as describing a fixed state of affairs. This is the 'permanent present' trap exemplified by anthropologists' habits of reporting in the present tense.[39] While we readily recognise cultural changes in our own society, our ignorance often makes us think of other ones as much more stable. Rugman and Hodgetts note, for instance, that Japan had the highest *individualism* score among countries in the Orient (although not so high as in the West) and the trend is probably becoming more pronounced in that country.[40]

In spite of difficulties of time and interpretation, Hofstede's work remains an important milestone. Many researchers have followed the work, sometimes using the same scales to extend investigation of the four cultural dimensions.[41] Hofstede himself has worked on many other studies. Looking more closely at people in East Asia, one project revealed a plausible fifth factor labelled *Confucian dynamism*. This refers to differences between long- and short-term time orientations.[42]

Others have examined the question of how similar countries are to each other. Although it was stated above that countries varied widely, analysis can show that each is more similar to some and more distant from others. Cluster analysis looks

Exhibit 5.9   Hofstede's dimensions of cultural differences

Power distance
How far is unequal distribution of power, and hence distance between people, accepted?

Low power distance –
   Independence is valued
   Managers consult staff
   Organisations have flat pyramids

High power distance –
   Subordinates follow instructions
   Control is close
   Hierarchies have many layers

Austria, Israel, Denmark, New Zealand, Ireland, Norway, Sweden

Malaysia, Panama, Guatemala, Philippines, Venezuela, Mexico, Ecuador, Arab countries, West Africa

Uncertainty avoidance
How much do people feel threatened by ambiguity and seek to minimise or avoid it?

Weak uncertainty avoidance –
   Activities tend to be unstructured
   Managers take risks
   Dissent is acceptable
   Initiative encouraged

Strong uncertainty avoidance –
   Dependence on rules
   Means found to avoid risk
   Decisions based on consensus
   Security is important

Singapore, Jamaica, Denmark, Sweden, Ireland United Kingdom, Malaysia

Greece, Portugal, Guatemala, Uruguay, Belgium, Japan

Individualism
How far do people look after themselves and their immediate family only?

Individualist –
   Stress on self and self-sufficiency
   Focus on initiative and leadership
   Individual security

Collectivist –
   Group affiliation and decision making
   No one wants to be singled out
   Belongingness

Australia, United States, United Kingdom, Netherlands, New Zealand, Canada, Italy

Guatemala, Ecuador, Panama, Venezuela, Colombia, Indonesia, Pakistan

Masculinity
How far do 'masculine' values dominate society?

Masculine –
   Growth seen as important
   Achievement = wealth and recognition
   Challenge important

Feminine –
   People and environment important
   Cooperation is valued
   Quality of life

Japan, Austria, Venezuela, Mexico, Ireland, Jamaica, Germany, United Kingdom

Sweden, Norway, Denmark, Netherlands, Costa Rica, Yugoslavia, Finland, Chile, Portugal for groups who tend to have similar scores on the underlying factors. For instance, drawing on the work of Hofstede and others, Ronen and Shenkar[43] found that countries fell into eight clusters with four misfits. The clusters were labelled: Anglo; Arab; Germanic; Far Eastern; Latin American; Latin European; Near Eastern; and Nordic. The four fitting no group were: Brazil; India; Israel; and Japan.

While cross-cultural research raises as many questions as it answers, it does awaken us to the notion of cultural similarities and differences. Generalisation, as with clustering, is useful as a starting point yet we must be aware of its dangers. For example, Luce reported:

> Viewed from afar south-east Asia strikes many as a relatively homogenous group of countries. Moves to integrate the region through the seven-member Association of South East Asian Nations (Asean) have reinforced the view ... Companies with direct experience in more than one Asian country, however, take a strikingly different view. South-east Asia is in fact probably one of the most diverse regions in the world ...[44]

■ Developing global managers

The growth of MNEs has increased the demand for international managers. Yet many report on the shortage of people with transportable skills and the frequent failures where postings are cut short or the manager performs ineffectively.[45] Adler and Bartholemew explain these problems in terms of the lag between firms' global strategies and the human systems required to carry them out.[46] They argue for improvements both in the skills of individuals and in the management of human resource systems. These statements raise broad questions of management training and development to which we shall return in Chapter 15. We shall focus here on the narrower aspect of preparing managers for international assignments.

Many of the problems associated with taking up international posts apply equally to managers changing jobs within or between organisations inside one country. Black, Mendenhall and Oddou make this point in proposing a comprehensive model that combines the job change and the international difficulties.[47] Figure 5.6 is based on this model. It divides the process of adjustment to the new work situation. Two phases are identified – preparatory and on-location.

Preparatory adjustment

This process begins before even the individual is identified. It seeks, as far as possible, to provide overseas managers who are well adjusted and likely to succeed. Selection is critical. The organisation needs to choose managers as much for their likelihood of coping as their technical competence for the anticipated job. Having been selected, good training will build on prior experience to ensure that the individual has accurate expectations about the job and its environment. It is known that managers with previous overseas experience are more likely to succeed again.

Training is likely to contain a substantial element of cross-cultural work. This is particularly relevant to managers. We noted in Chapter 1 how they spend so much of their time communicating. Fluency is more than linguistic. It involves an acknowledgement of cultural differences and building the ability to send and receive messages in 'other-culture' terms.

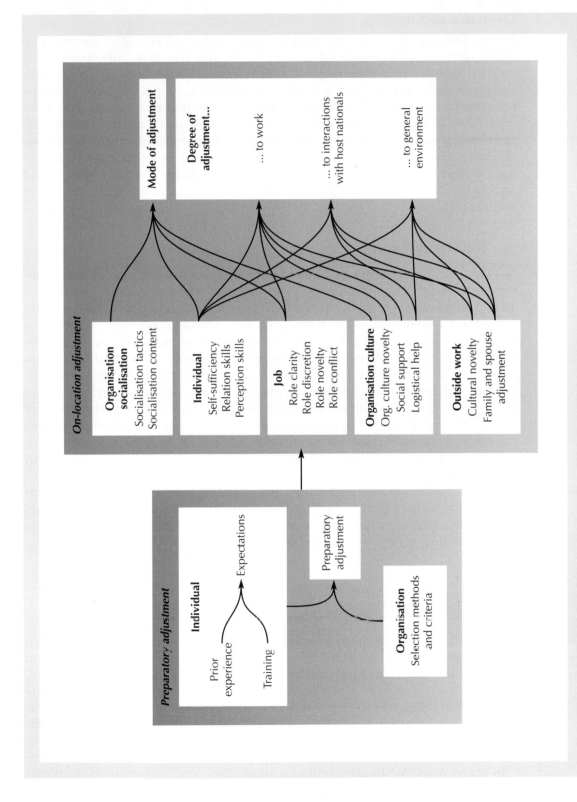

Fig. 5.6 Preparatory and on-location adjustments in international posting

On-location adjustment

Despite preparatory efforts, the manager has to adapt on arrival at the new job. There are five classes of factors that affect fitting-in at this stage. Adjustment itself has two aspects – mode and degree. Mode refers to how the manager copes with the gap between expectations and actual requirements. It can be closed either by behavioural changes on the manager's part or by adaptation of the role to suit the capabilities already possessed. The degree of adjustment is a measure of how far the manager adjusts to three facets: work, relating to host-country people and the general environment. Only if there is reasonable accommodation to all three will the manager be able to succeed. The arrows linking the boxes in the right-hand area of Fig. 5.6 trace Black and others' propositions about how adjustment factors affect success.

■ Differences at work

Nowhere might differences in attitudes to management create more urgent problems than on an aircraft flight deck. Helmreich and colleagues surveyed more than 13 000 pilots employed by 25 airlines in 16 countries.[48] They were interested in values and attitudes related to work, such as teamwork, leadership, response to stress and organisational culture. The results showed commonality in communication, teamwork and attitudes toward stress but strong cross-cultural differences when it came to command interactions, and tolerance for rules, routines and procedures. Exhibit 5.10 lists first the 'universals' – items endorsed by at least 85 per cent of pilots from all airlines in all countries. Then follow items where there were differences among the groups of pilots according to country. The percentages show the range of agreement with each statement.

   The authors concluded that the pilots varied dramatically in their preference for an egalitarian versus a hierarchical command style, and for flexibility and autonomy versus adherence to, and compliance with, rules and set procedures. Their findings supported Hofstede's four dimensions shown in Exhibit 5.9. The study alerts airline managers to doubts over the value of operating procedures and the question of how to best deploy pilots from different nations.

Conclusion: managing the global corporation

For better or worse, the business world is becoming dominated by MNEs. In contrast to earlier times, the MNE gains its strength from bypassing markets and replacing them with internal transactions. This trade is in goods, services and, increasingly, the transfer of technical knowledge to be applied throughout the world. Information technology is very important. Its role in processing and communications has made the MNE ever more efficient. At the same time, it has spawned new worldwide industries to satisfy demands for both hardware and software. Computer systems are powerful homogenising forces.

   In many ways, MNEs are agents for good. They can contribute to economic development of poor regions and the spreading of education, health and so on. At

Exhibit 5.10 Pilots agree on many things but have different attitudes to them.

Attitudes universally endorsed:

■ good communication and crew co-ordination are as important as technical proficiency for flight safety;

■ the captain's responsibilities include co-ordination between cockpit and cabin crews;

■ the pre-flight briefing is important for safety and for effective crew management;

■ the pilot flying the aircraft should verbalise plans and be sure the information is understood and acknowledged;

■ pilots should monitor each other for signs of stress and fatigue.

Attitudes varying by national culture:

■ crew members should not question the decisions or actions of the captain except when they threaten the safety of the flight (15% – 93%);

■ if I perceive a problem with the flight, I will speak up, regardless of who might be affected (36% – 98%);

■ written procedures are required for all in-flight situations (15% – 84%);

■ the organization's rules should not be broken – even when the employee thinks it is in the company's best interests (22% – 76%).

the same time, we have seen how these global corporations possess great economic power. This has come to worry national governments who fear the MNEs' ability to switch technology, to form joint ventures or to close down operations without significant constraint. Liberalisation of trade may continue, or the world may crystallise into blocs, each with its proportion of giant MNEs, protected by barriers against the others.

As it develops, the MNE retains its ethnocentric character or develops along more diverse lines. The true geocentric organisation is rare although some companies are beginning to adopt this perspective. Whatever attitude prevails, the organisation has to face and cope with cultural diversity. The ethnocentric organisation has to make bridges between expatriate managers and local employees; the polycentric business has to link national divisions to headquarters. The world view within the geocentric firm is perhaps the most problematic. Are managers expected to 'forget' their backgrounds and adopt the new company culture? Perhaps this is both meaningless and impossible. Managers of such companies have to find their own ways of coming to terms with bridging the cultures across which they function.

The failure rate of managers posted abroad imposes unnecessary costs on international companies and their staff. Increased cultural sensitivity is needed if managers are to succeed. Cross-cultural research suggests agendas for programmes of training and other activities that can contribute to successful adjustment.

Quick check up *Can you ...*

- Define globalisation;
- Identify five convergent and five divergent forces;
- Recall the industries in which the world's largest corporations operate;
- Explain triad;
- Name six reasons why firms become MNEs;
- List four routes to internationalisation;

- Distinguish LSA from FSA;
- Name Perlmutter's three states of mind;
- Separate monochronic and polychronic time;
- Outline Hofstede's dimensions of cultural difference;
- Name two phases of a manager's international adjustment.

Questions

Chapter review

5.1 Discuss the forces that, it is suggested, are pushing the world apart or pulling it together. Can you add to the list? What is your conclusion about the balance?

5.2 Explain how an MNE responds to a combination of firm-specific and location-specific advantages.

5.3 What are the main types of cultural difference identified in the text? Can you think of other factors or examples that could be valuable?

5.4 Compare Perlmutter's classification of MNEs with Adler's set of managerial attitudes given in Chapter 1.

Application

5.5 Return to Mrs Ledger's experience in Exhibit 5.8. Apply the ideas of time and context to each stage of the transactions to build a cultural interpretation of the events.

5.6 Review Glenmorangie's FDI policies in the light of the ideas in the chapter.

Investigation

5.7 Study an MNE, from Fortune's Top 500 or elsewhere, to assess the extent to which it 'thinks globally and acts locally'. Use a range of sources to examine factors such as integration, location of operations, nationality of senior managers and dealing with customers. Why does it act as it does?

Cultural differences at NDM[49]

Denso is the leading manufacturer of electrical and electronic automotive systems, ranked 260th in the 1996 Fortune 500. Toyota is its largest shareholder and customer, yet the company supplies most assemblers throughout the world. Profits in 1996 were ¥90 billion on sales of ¥1,423 billion. From its headquarters in Aichi prefecture, the heart of the Japanese motor industry, Denso runs a business employing more than 40 000 staff in 11 domestic plants and 42 companies and 9 sales offices in 21 overseas countries.

The company owes its continuing success to applying research and investment to solving customers' problem themes of efficiency, performance and safety. Fixed investment runs at 9 per cent of sales and another 7.3 per cent goes into research and development. Much process development work is done in-house to stimulate innovations not available on the market and to avoid sharing learning with potential competitors. One manufacturing line at Kota is 1170 metres long and has just one direct worker doing a job that would be too expensive to automate. Quality standards are very high with engine control modules failing final tests only once or twice per month.

Established in 1992, NDM Manufacturing at Telford, Shropshire is a joint venture, 75 per cent owned by Denso and 25 per cent by the Magneti Marelli division of FIAT. There are 550 employees making vehicle air-conditioning equipment. Telford was chosen so most suppliers could be within a target two-hour drive.

Kazunobo Ageishi, NDM's managing director, spends four to six hours a day talking to associates (employees). This is more than twice the time he would take in Japan where people would be told what to do and would understand. In Britain, more time is taken for discussing and explaining. The aim is to sustain a no-blame problem-solving culture and to continually improve work practices.

In a study of managers in 10 Japanese-owned companies in the United Kingdom, Alan Jones, general manager at NDM, compared British and Japanese styles of management. Part of the reason for lower satisfaction among United Kingdom managers in Japanese-run firms is that they have difficulty in interpreting the non-verbal expressions of their superiors. This makes them very unsure of their bosses' opinions of them. Furthermore, Japanese managers tend to break down their subordinates' jobs into routine activities that British managers do not find sufficiently demanding.

Having a worthwhile job is more important to British managers than to their Japanese colleagues. The individualism of the former, their need to prove themselves and the perceived link between job demands and promotion are the suggested explanations. Meanwhile, if a Japanese finds the job not wholly satisfying, it will be tolerated as part of a total development programme. Jones concluded that Japanese managers should do more to make staff aware of cultural differences.

Questions

1 Denso's president claims that the firm is a 'truly global corporation'. Do you agree?

2 What are Denso's FSAs and LSAs?

3 Explain Jones' reported cultural differences in terms of the ideas set out in the chapter.

4 Jones' last remark suggests that staff should adapt to working for a Japanese manager. Is this reasonable?

Bibliography   Ohmae, Kenichi (1990) *The Borderless World*, London: Fontana, and *The Evolving Global Economy*, (1995) Boston, Mass.: Harvard Business School Press, capture many questions surrounding MNEs today. For current debates on aspects of international business, try the working papers published from the university web site addresses mentioned in the references. On diversity, a good addition is Trompenaars, Fons (1997) *Riding the Waves of Culture: Understanding diversity in global business*, Second edition, Nicholas Brealy.

References

1. Oram, Roderick (1995) 'UK export-led recovery: Distillers set up their drinks in Asian bars', *Financial Times*, 21 February, 14; Oram, Roderick (1995) 'In search of whisky's lost generation', *Financial Times*, 6 April, 20; Jennings, Patricia (1996) 'Single malt boosts Macallan', *Daily Telegraph*, 2 April; Oram, Roderick (1996) 'Glenmorangie changes the blend', *Financial Times*, 15 May; Wilson, Andrew (1996) 'Exports keep spirits up at Glenmorangie', *The Herald*, 24 May; Laforce, Marguerite (1996) 'Marie Brizard prévoit des bénéfices cette année', *Les Echos*, 3 June; Springett, Pauline (1996) 'Guinness offers a new strategy to spirit world', *Guardian*, 27 Sept, 21.
2. Nakamoto, Michiyo (1996) 'WTO's liquor tax ruling unsteadies Japan', *Financial Times*, 8 October, 7.
3. Rugman, Alan M. and Hodgetts, Richard M. (1995) *International Business: A strategic management approach*, New York: McGraw-Hill, 433.
4. Perlmutter, Howard V. (1995) 'Becoming globally civilised – managing across cultures', *Financial Times*, 1 December, xii.
5. Kobrin, Stephen J. (1995) 'Beyond symmetry: state sovereignty in a networked global economy', *Working Paper*, 95–8, Wharton School: University of Pennsylvania: http://www.gsia.cmu.edu/afs/andrew/gsia/bosch/kobrin/kobrin.html
6. Elliott, Larry (1996) 'Putting trade in its place', *Guardian*, 27 May.
7. UNCTAD (1995) *Trends in Foreign Direct Investment*, Geneva: United Nations Conference on Trade and Development.
8. Levitt, Theodore (1983) 'The globalisation of markets', *Harvard Business Review*, **61** (**3**) May–June, 92–102.
9. Data is drawn from 'Fortune's Global 500: the world's largest corporations', *Fortune*, 4 August 1997, F1–40; http://www.pathfinder.com/fortune/global500/500list.html
10. Based on data given by Rugman and Hodgetts (1985) *op. cit.*, 71.
11. Ohmae, Kenichi (1995) *The Evolving Global Economy*, Boston, Mass.: Harvard Business School Press.
12. Stopford, John M. (1994) 'The impact of the global political economy on corporate strategy', *Working Paper*, 94–7, Wharton School: University of Pennsylvania: http://www.gsia.cmu.edu/afs/andrew/gsia/bosch/stopford/stopford.html
13. For example, Daft, Richard L. (1994) *Management*, Third edition, Fort Worth, Tex.: Dryden Press, 94.
14. Oldfield, Clare (1996) 'The V&A ties up classic deals with licensing', *The Sunday Times*, 12 May.
15. Dempsey, Judy (1996) 'Bertelsmann unit, Mitsui in licensing agreement', *Financial Times*, 11 January.
16. 'Un joint-venture en projet en Chine pour Eridania Beghin-Say', *Les Echos*, 17 June 1996; 'Air Liquide: nouveau joint-venture en Chine', *Les Echos*, 18 June 1996; 'Marcegaglia definisca la joint venture in Cina',.*Il Sole 24 Ore*, 25 June 1996.
17. Whitebloom, Sarah (1996) 'Marks & Spencer's woolly jumpers going to meet their maker', *Guardian*, 18 October, 22.
18. Dunning, J.H. (1979) 'Explaining changing patterns of international production: in defence of the eclectic theory', *Oxford Bulletin of Economics and Statistics*, **41**, 269–96.

19. Burton, John and Buxton, James (1996) 'Scotland wins £1 billion Korean factory', *Financial Times*, 8 October, 9.
20. Vecchio, Robert P. (1995) *Organisational Behaviour*, Third edition, Fort Worth, Tex.: Dryden Press, 625.
21. Denfeld Wood, Jack (1995) 'Culture is not enough', *Financial Times*, 8 December, II.
22. Vecchio (1995) *loc.cit.*
23. Riordan, Christine M. and Vandenberg, Robert J. (1994) 'A central question in cross-cultural research: do employees of different cultures interpret work-related measures in an equivalent manner?', *Journal of Management*, **20** (**3**) Autumn, 643–71.
24. McKenna, Stephen (1995) 'The business impact of management attitudes towards dealing with conflict: a cross-cultural assessment', *Journal of Management Psychology*, **10** (**7**) July, 22–27.
25. Marsh, David (1995) 'Positive effects of a culture clash', *Financial Times*, 15 May, 11.
26. Hofstede, G.(1993) 'Cultural constraints in management theories', *Academy of Management Executive*, **7,** 81–94.
27. Perlmutter, Howard V. (1969) 'The tortuous evolution of the multinational corporation', *Columbia Journal of World Business*, **4**, 9–18.
28. Woolridge, Adrian (1995) 'Survey of multinationals – from multilocal to multicultural – this way for the rainbow corporation', *The Economist*, 24 June, 70.
29. Summers, Diane (1995) 'PR consensus finds Shell at fault. Opting for a U-turn over Brent Spar only made the nightmare worse say the publicity experts', *Financial Times*, 23 June, 11; Southey, Caroline and Corzine, Robert (1995) 'Gummer attacks Brent Spar U-turn: European partners are accused of "caving in"', *Financial Times*, 23 June, 18.
30. 'The ABB of management', *The Economist*, 6 January 1996, 64; Wagstyl, Stefan (1997) 'Own words: Percy Barnevik, ABB and Investor', *Financial Times*, 8 October. There is more on ABB in Chapter 12.
31. Simon, Herbert A. (1994) 'Is international management different from management?', Carnegie Mellon University Working Paper: http://www.gsia.cmu.edu/afs/andrew/gsia/bosch/simon/simon.html
32. Levine, R. and Wolff, E. (1983) 'Social time: the heartbeat of culture', *Psychology Today*, March, 28–35; quoted in Vecchio (1995) *op. cit.* 626.
33. Hall, Edward T. (1969) *The Dance of Life*, New York: Anchor-Doubleday.
34. Dumaine, Brian (1992) 'Management lessons from the general', *Fortune*, 2 November, 104.
35. Chu, Wilson (1996) 'The human side of examining a foreign target', *Mergers and Acquisitions*, **30** (**4**), January–February, 35–9.
36. Choi, Chong Ju (1994) 'Contract enforcement across cultures', *Organisation Studies*, **15(5)**, 673–82.
37. Janssens, Maddy, Brett, Jeanne M. and Smith, Frank J. (1995) 'Confirmatory cross-cultural research: testing the viability of a corporation-wide safety policy', *Academy of Management Journal*, **38 (2)**, April, 364–72.
38. Hofstede, Geert (1980) *Culture's Consequences: International differences in work-related values*, New York: Sage.
39. Carrithers, Michael (1992) *Why Humans Have Cultures*, Oxford: Oxford University Press, 8.
40. Rugman and Hodgetts (1995) *op. cit.*, 135.
41. For instance, Morris, Michael H., Davis, Duane L. and Allen, Jeffrey W. (1994) 'Fostering corporate entrepreneurship: cross-cultural comparisons of individualism versus collectivism', *Journal of International Business Studies*, **25 (1)** Spring, 65–89; Harrison, Graeme L. (1995) 'Satisfaction, tension and interpersonal relations: a cross-cultural comparison of managers in Singapore and Australia', *Journal of Managerial Psychology*, **10 (8)** August, 13–19.

42. Hofstede, Geert and Harris Bond, Michael (1988) 'The Confucius connection: from cultural roots to economic growth', *Organisation Dynamics*, **16** (**4**), 4–21.

43. Ronen, Simcha and Shenkar, Oded (1985) 'Clustering countries on attitudinal dimensions: a review and synthesis', *Academy of Management Journal*, **28**, September, 449.

44. Luce, Edward (1995) 'SE Asia – singularly different', *Financial Times*, 4 December, 12.

45. Houlder, Vanessa (1995) 'Cultural exchanges – roving executives with truly transportable skills are in short supply', *Financial Times*, 5 April, 19; Marquardt, M.J. and Engel, D.W. (1993) 'HRD competences for a shrinking world', *Training and Development*, **47** (**5**), 59–65.

46. Adler, Nancy J. and Bartholemew, Susan (1992) 'Managing globally competent people', *Academy of Management Executive*, **6** (**3**), 52–65.

47. Black, J. Stewart; Mendenhall, Mark and Oddou, Gary (1991) 'Towards a comprehensive model of international adjustment: an integration of multiple theoretical perspectives', *Academy of Management Review*, **16** (**2**), 291–317.

48. Helmreich, R.L.; Merritt, A.C. and Sherman, P.J. (1996) 'Human factors and national culture', *ICAO Journal*, **51** (**8**), 14–16.
http://www.psy.utexas.edu/psy/helmreich/nasaut.htm

49. Naclerio, N. (1995) Report on JTEC site visit to Nippondenso Kota Plant http://www.itri.loyola.edu/EP/nipponde.html, 30 August; Marsh, Peter (1995) 'Managers uneasy over cultural divide', *Financial Times*, 9 October, 6; Rich, Motoko (1995) 'Digging in and flourishing – second round', *Financial Times*, 19 October, viii; Marsh, Peter (1995) 'Insider's view – cultural diversity at a Japanese–Italian joint venture in Shropshire', *Financial Times*, 25 October, 22; Denso company information on http://www.denso.co.jp/index-e.html

Chapter 6

Social responsibility and ethics

Chapter objectives

When you have finished studying this chapter, you should be able to:

- explain why social responsibility has emerged as an important issue for organisations;
- identify stakeholders; compare arguments for and against recognition of their interests;
- describe and illustrate four main social responsibility strategies;
- summarise deontology, utilitarianism and virtue ethics; show how these apply to management decisions;
- resolve ethical dilemmas through the application of these principles;
- outline how organisations should plan their approach to managing social responsibility and ethics programmes;
- assess your own views on social responsibility and ethics.

Being socially responsible and staying in business[1]

Pulp mill waste emissions in Scandinavia have fallen by 90 per cent in ten years, following pressure from environmental groups in market countries, especially Germany. Cuts have been achieved in liquid effluent, including chlorine, and waste gases such as sulphur dioxide. The improvements come from developments in the bleaching process, the use of different chemical agents and better waste management. Threats to the delicate ecosystems of the region's lakes have diminished.

The pulp companies have had to spend many millions on these changes, expenditure that is difficult to justify in a highly competitive, cyclical market. Pulp prices, having fallen to $380 per tonne in 1993, rose to $750 two years later before falling to $550 in 1997. Fortunately, competitors in North America, Brazil and Indonesia are facing the same political forces.

Pressure does not abate. Groups are now targeting the industry's forestry management. Environmentalists argue that insensitive practices threaten biodiversity and endanger many species from birds to lichen and mosses. The companies are responding with more protection, and better staff training to deal with protest. They also emphasise that they are still

catching up after much reckless felling in the nineteenth century and that regeneration rates easily exceed harvesting. To scale down at home and import more wood, say from the states of the eastern Baltic, could make things worse as little is known of how forests are managed in those countries.

National and EU directives setting recycling targets also exert pressure. These usually place the responsibility for recycling on producers. For large exporters from low population countries this poses a particular problem. Mills producing from wood are best sited near to forests, but, if they use waste, closeness to major population centres is an advantage. Finland's Enso-Gutzeit built a newsprint mill in Germany to use waste, a more sensible strategy than transporting the bulk back to its origin. Recycling, by companies such as Raturpapper in Stockholm, is, at 50 per cent, well developed. Yet total paper and board production in Sweden uses only 15 per cent of recycled fibres compared with 50 per cent in Germany and 95 per cent in Hungary. Paper and pulp make up 13 per cent of Norway's total exports. Its largest company, Norske Skog with 15 per cent of European newsprint capacity, sells 70 per cent of its output abroad.

Introduction

Few managers these days fail to acknowledge the wide societal impact of business. Hence few refuse to face questions about how they should influence, control and restrain it. We have seen, since the growth of large corporations at the end of the nineteenth century, gradual shifts away from strong entrepreneurialism and reliance on the unfettered economic market. In most European countries, companies have come to be seen as public property with non-owners having a legitimate interest in influencing the decisions that their managers make. As illustrated by the opening case on Nordic paper companies, governments use their powers to regulate corporate behaviour in many ways and there are numerous groups who press their viewpoints upon organisations.

Organisations are, therefore, engaged in a continual interaction with an environment that is wider than the market. Harvey[2] calls this an 'influence market', populated by all sorts of interest groups, lobbyists, quasi-judicial regulatory bodies, government officials and ministers and other organisations. It is more complex and uncertain than the classical market, varying from firm to firm, time to time, and from country to country. These variations appear clearly in the paper industry; the political framework within which the industry operates is changing rapidly and each firm is affected differently depending on its scale, location, technology and so on.

Recognising at least that governments will take greater measures to control business unless it 'puts its house in order', the question for managers moves on from *whether* they should admit to social responsibility to *how much*. Answers to these questions influence managerial action. At one end of the scale, the statements of free market economists such as Milton Friedman are well known – being socially responsible is to follow a fundamentally flawed doctrine. Firms should do the minimum they are required to do and no more. 'Business is business'.[3] At the opposite end, those favouring greater responsibility, such as Harvey, argue that firms could, and should, do much more. Managers do not, and should not, feel powerless when faced with societal problems over which they have some, even if small, influence.

Social responsibility is grounded more deeply than simply doing good business within the influence market. In their decision making, managers face ethical issues. Frequently these are so implicit that they are not recognised as such but, in choosing one course of action against another, managers are making moral judgements. They are, moreover, displaying leadership which, since managers occupy positions of influence, must bring with it moral responsibility. Therefore, ethical choices are important for individuals and groups within the organisation. The second part of the chapter is devoted to a discussion of ethics in business.

Social responsibility

▎ *Social responsibility is the obligation of managers to choose and act in ways that benefit both the interests of the organisation and those of society as a whole.*

While this definition has the advantage of brevity, a closer look shows that it is not, on its own, a means of answering the question, 'Are we a socially responsible organisation?' We can raise three issues for clarification:

- *Who is included?*

  While there is a growing consensus that all organisations should do their best to avoid detrimental impacts on the natural environment, there is less agreement about whom and what else ought to be included in the 'society as a whole'. Consumer rights have become well established in advanced economies, taken seriously by leading companies and underpinned by legislation. On the other hand, few companies concern themselves with disadvantaged people even though the disadvantage may be an indirect outcome of their own activities. We can give two instances. First, a supermarket may drive local shops out of business. Although many gain from the switch, some customers will find difficulty in reaching the new store. This is not seen as the company's problem. Second, there are congestion costs to which all contribute and for which people are only beginning to feel responsible. Only the private aspects of these costs, that is delays to one's own fleet, are built into company transport policies. The social costs, delays to other people, are left for others to worry about.

■ *Complexity of decisions*

As we shall see in Chapter 11, it is often difficult for managers to select the best course of action for an organisation. Given that assessing the impact of any action upon the wider society is a far more exacting task, what chance do managers have of getting it right? A firm may decide not to close a plant in a region where unemployment is high, deciding that community interests demand that it be given 'a last chance'. Such action may save jobs in the short term but may put other areas of the business at risk. Furthermore, it may reinforce a local habit of reliance on outdated skills and employment patterns. Then, when the plant is eventually closed, the catastrophe is worse.

■ *Winners and losers*

Part of the decision-making problem is the choice of who is to benefit from its outcomes. Social programmes, for instance, do not come free. Who pays for the community involvement of companies such as Grand Metropolitan? This global business allocates £17 million to charity work in the United Kingdom. It is a policy that hardly benefits a customer in Copenhagen or a distributor in Dublin. Although it may seem pointless to spread the benefit thinly amongst all the countries where GrandMet operates, it is a clear example of managers choosing to benefit some groups at the expense of others. Managers argue that the policies add more from improved motivation and image than they cost. Rather than losing, everyone can gain. Lord Sheppard, Chairman of GrandMet, compares his company's charitable gifts with the £900 million spent throughout the world on marketing. Both benefit the company. In addition, Sheppard sees the community involvement of managers as 'a big part of career development ... better than a thousand management courses'.[4]

Companies respond to these questions in different ways. The opening case was set in the context of the protection of our physical environment. The Body Shop,[5] *see* Exhibit 6.1, pursues a social policy extending far beyond ecological issues. It tries to make a real difference to the lives of people it deals with throughout the world. Central to its themes are a belief in trade with developing countries, rather than aid, and a recognition that money is rarely the sole motivator of people. These values have their basis in the outlook of the organisation's founder, an outlook that has developed and changed with her experience of leadership. Successful socially responsible leaders manage to transmit their ideals to others. This binds organisation members into a cohesive, recognisable whole.

Although The Body Shop stands out as an example, in other cases the benefits are not clear cut. Many maintain that business should not encompass social responsibility at all. The debate is nicely balanced with four main arguments on each side.

Exhibit 6.1   The Body Shop: building on ideals

More than 40 countries host the 1200 outlets of The Body Shop. It sells a range of cosmetic products inspired by traditional manufacture using natural ingredients. Formulations are not tested on animals. Packaging is simple and recycled, marketing is low key with very limited advertising.

The company expresses the ideals of its founder Anita Roddick and the many franchise holders and employees who have, since 1976, enjoyed its growth within a culture that has taken more and more interest in the natural environment, sustainable development and the lot of fellow mankind. According to Tom Peters, Roddick stands out as a visionary thinker. She has, 'A set of beliefs that really are the essence of what she's about. ... She really does live that set of beliefs, and it happens to have been tremendously effective commercially in a very, very difficult industry.' In the late 1970s, the industry had come to be seen by some as exploiting women, torturing animals, damaging the environment and self-promoting on the basis of huge exaggerations.

The Body Shop seeks to create bonds with its employees, franchisees and customers through deeper links than the commercial or employment contract. It aims to create a sense of passion about world issues and encourages people to join in action. Staff are assisted to join in community work and have been given paid breaks to work in Romanian orphanages.

Companies that espouse high levels of social responsibility invite criticism from new directions. An example was the August 1994 report by American journalist Jon Entine which criticised The Body Shop's relations with its franchisees and third-world suppliers. Unused to defending itself against such attacks, The Body Shop had some difficulty in refuting the claims that Entine made. Later, it reported that the controversy had had little effect on sales. Slackening of growth around this period was attributed to increased competition in the company's largest division, the United States. Imitators of the successful formula included Body & Bath Works which, taking advantage of low store opening costs, expanded rapidly.

■ Arguments for social responsibility

The arguments in favour of social responsibility stem from the power and importance of organisations in modern society. This means they are repositories of power and skills that can make a difference. The four arguments are presented as though spoken by a proponent:

- *Potential to do good*
  'Modern businesses have high technical, managerial and financial capability. Indeed, many multinational companies have more resources than the governments in whose territories they operate. Therefore, since their actions could have a decisive impact upon social problems we should require them to behave responsibly.'

- *Anticipation of emerging problems*
  'If organisations had displayed greater responsibility in the past in areas such as equal opportunity, safety, quality and financial probity, there would have been

less need for the tight regulation that many governments feel obliged to apply nowadays. It follows that more socially responsible behaviour now, such as in respect of ethical advertising, tax and duty payment and information security may avoid government intervention in these problem areas.'

After allegations of corruption in dealing with the authorities, both Banco Bilbao Vizcaya in Spain and FIAT in Italy formulated specific policies concerning how they are to manage such relationships in the future.[6]

- *Investment should yield benefits for all*
  'Profitability in the long term depends on a favourable social, economic and physical environment. Policies from conservation to training mean that extra spending now can lead to more riches later, including *benefits for the organisation itself*. Good values mean good business.'

- *Unavoidable responsibilities linked with rights*
  'Notwithstanding whether businesses ought to show responsibility, there is no doubt that business is intimately involved in any society. Society grants rights and privileges to organisations, such as legal protection or the freedom to open or close facilities within established constraints. A civilised society requires rights to be exercised responsibly.'

Arguments against social responsibility

Arguments against tend to start from the classical economic model but can also be broadened into expressions of fear about the power of businesses managed by a self-appointed elite. Again, the cases are put as though spoken a proponent:

- *Purpose of business*
  'The purpose of business is to make profit. Markets work because the sum of individual transaction decisions between buyers and sellers is the best way to allocate resources. The needs of groups from local residents to third-world suppliers should only be considered by business managers when such action yields clear improvements in business efficiency and effectiveness. Unless an organisation is established with explicit social goals – for instance an arm of government or a charity – it should not become involved with them.'

- *Capability of managers is limited*
  'Since businesses are economic institutions, they should develop the competence to pursue economic goals. Social goals take them into fields where they have no particular capability. They only sidetrack managerial attention.'

- *Power should be restricted*
  'Business already has too much power. If harnessed for good ends, use of this power can be beneficial. Yet there have been many cases where businesses have manipulated weaker groups and governments. In a democratic society, it is better, in principle, if power is not concentrated in the hands of a few.'

- *Legitimacy is confined to the organisation's legal purposes*
  'Owners and managers are unelected. How can managers be held responsible for the allocation decisions that they make? The market system is the ultimate test of the enterprise's economic performance but, without elections, there is no sanction

on the societal performance. Without a political process, where managers are sub-jected to tests of public opinion, how would conflicts of interest be resolved?'

Stakeholders

For those organisations that accept some degree of social responsibility, there are two central questions: whose interests are to be served and how far should the organisation go in serving them?

If managers are to consider the interests of parties other than those formally owning or placed in charge of an organisation, there must be a mutual recognition that these parties stand for something that is important. This legitimacy, which is the right to a stake in the organisation, comes from a variety of sources. These are: economic necessity; the legal framework in which the organisation operates; and the values espoused by the organisation and its members. Managers can, there-fore, exercise some choice over whom it recognises as a stakeholder, that is, whose interests are to be taken into account. We can summarise these points in the fol-lowing definition:

> *A stakeholder is an individual or group, inside or outside the organisation, who has a meaningful stake in its performance.*

Figure 6.1 represents the important stakeholders of Norske Skog, the leading Norwegian forest products company mentioned in the opening case of this chap-ter. Each has its own interests that differ from, and sometimes conflict with, the interests of other groups. For instance, managers serve the economic interests of

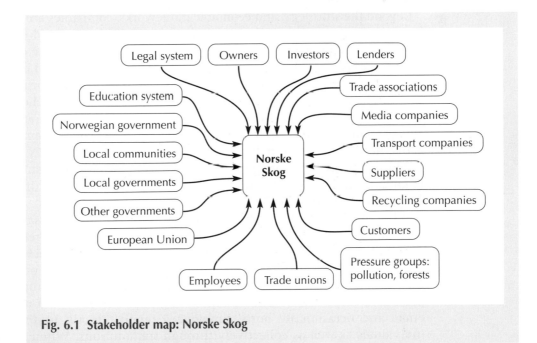

Fig. 6.1 Stakeholder map: Norske Skog

owners and other investors by aiming for a satisfactory return on investment while maintaining the stability of the business for long-term success. Employees expect good pay as well as work satisfaction, job security and good prospects. To some extent, these aspirations conflict with those of the owners and investors.

Other stakeholders join with the company in creating its value chain, which is the system of processes through which products are made, distributed and sold to the customer. With the increasing integration of these chains, *see* Chapter 19, the dependency of each component on the progress of all the others becomes more apparent. They are each stakeholders in the other. Customers are also stakeholders to the extent that they depend on the company products. If, for example, Norske Skog makes a special paper for a customer, then the latter become dependent on the paper company for the supply. The more difficult it is for the customer to switch, the greater the economic dependency.

The legitimacy of local and national government interests in the many countries in which Norske Skog operates has two bases. First, there is the legislation covering areas from fair trade practices to product and process safety. Only foolhardy companies do not take such responsibilities seriously. Second, governments take an interest in the progress of major companies because they are significant components of national economic performance and, through employment, location and purchasing policies, can aid or hinder development in different regions. Here, the relations between the Norwegian government in particular and the company will be close. For example, the company will expect the government to maintain a transport infrastructure appropriate to its needs while the government will expect to be briefed on strategic plans and decisions affecting the nation. We saw in Chapter 5 how MNEs maintain such relations in all countries in which they have a presence. Norske Skog has paper mills in Austria and France and customers in 70 countries.[7]

Beyond the strict legal and economic frameworks, companies are subject to pressures from groups advancing causes ranging from product safety and environmental protection to equal opportunity and fair trade. The case study identifies recent pressure from groups concerned with the interlinked issues of wildlife protection and forest management. The strength of this advocacy is such that some argue that it is as if the trees themselves have become stakeholders.

The last group to consider achieves recognition, not from any claims they advance, but from the discretion of the owners or managers themselves. We saw above how Grand Metropolitan gives to charity. Other examples are: Coca-Cola, supporting many social programmes around its home city of Atlanta, Georgia; and Pilkington, well known for similar activity in St Helens in North-West England. Although some would claim that this is merely 'good business', there is an element of philanthropy in such gifts. The companies do not necessarily see them as investments and do not demand analysis of any direct economic return.

A final point can be made about Fig. 6.1. It is labelled a *stakeholder map* yet is little more than a listing of the groups having an influence on Norske Skog. Clearly some influences are two-way, such as between the company and other parts of its value chain. Additionally, some groups exercise direct or indirect influence, and occasionally both. Employees relate directly to the company as individuals as well as collectively through trade unions. When the reasons for interaction have a legal basis, such as the employment contract, the influence can be exerted through the legal system of the country concerned. Influence maps can be developed to aid a deeper understanding of such linkages. Figure 6.2 suggests how two of the areas could be presented. The left hand half explores the relationships between the company and groups in Norway. The right hand half covers the employee–trade union link and shows how relationships can be usefully labelled.

Social responsibility strategies

Whatever conclusions we could reach on the social responsibility arguments, it is clear that organisations are increasingly committing themselves to act responsibly.[8] We can classify these actions into four types, recognising that they really form a continuum of behaviour from obstructive to proactive, *see* Fig. 6.3. Since the actions are deliberate, they can rightly be called *social responsibility strategies*.

Obstructive

An organisation following an obstructive strategy will tend to deny responsibility for its actions and resist change that it can only see as disadvantageous. The policy is also known as *stonewalling* or a *reactive* policy.

> *In March 1993, Volkswagen recruited from General Motors a team led by José Ignacio Lopez de Arriortua, head of global purchasing. He had gained a high reputation for reducing supply costs. Later, Lopez and others were accused of taking with them GM's secrets. VW spent many months denying the possibility, its chairman saying that the evidence had been planted. Anyhow, the secrets would be of no use to VW! GM brought a civil action for damages in a Detroit court while prosecutors pursued the criminal investigation in Germany. VW argued that the civil case should be heard in Germany. In the end, rather than take its chances in Detroit, VW agreed to a settlement of the civil action.*

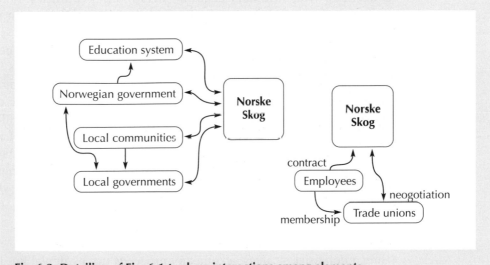

Fig. 6.2 Detailing of Fig. 6.1 to show interactions among elements

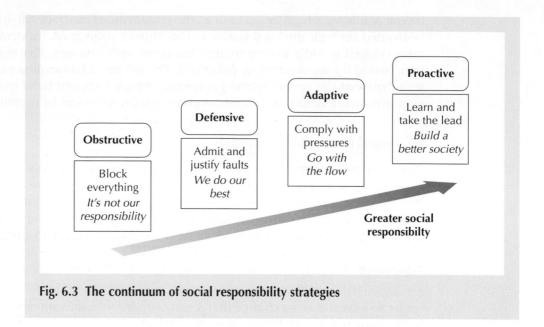

Fig. 6.3 The continuum of social responsibility strategies

> *Announced in early 1997, this meant a payment of more than $100 million and a VW commitment to buy at least $1 billion worth of components from GM. Lopez and three others resigned or were suspended as the criminal investigation proceeded.[9]*

Another back-to-the-wall campaign has been fought by Albright & Wilson, the leading producer of phosphates. These substances are valuable as washing aids, food additives and fertilisers. Their use in washing powder was first banned in the Great Lakes region of the United States and Canada in 1972. This was because they stimulated algae growth that in turn took all the oxygen from the water. In Europe, there are bans or controls in Austria, Germany, Italy, Norway and Switzerland with voluntary codes in several other countries. Phosphate powders are now little used in the EU market, although they still account for 6 per cent of the total phosphate used in the United Kingdom.

Yet the restrictive policy may be mistaken. There are three reasons. First, phosphate-free detergents are not so effective in hard water areas. Users, therefore, pour more bleach, brighteners, dyes and perfumes down the drains, causing other forms of pollution. Second, the detergent replacement, a mixture of an aluminium compound, zeolite, and PCA, a petrochemical, may be more harmful to the natural environment than has been imagined. Third, the removal of phosphate from sewage, much easier than drawing out the zeolite/PCA mixtures, brings with it dangerous heavy metals and can produce reusable pellets. Both Albright & Wilson and Kemira, a Finnish chemical company, commissioned studies that, while not claiming to be conclusive, suggest that moves to further restrict phosphates are misguided.[10]

Defensive

Using a defensive strategy, a company proceeds not by denial but by manoeuvring to justify its position and avoid being saddled with extra responsibility. The stance is to do everything that is legally required and no more. The strategy uses legal actions and public relations campaigns to prove compliance. In 1995, Shell was criticised first for wanting to sink the Brent Spar oil platform in the North Atlantic, then for changing its mind, and finally for its failure to explain the reasons for its actions.[11] Later, Shell found itself defending its operating and investment policies in Nigeria. It announced further investment with the Nigerian National Oil Corporation just as the country was suspended from the Commonwealth for its government's human rights record. The treatment of the people of the Delta Region was a central issue. Shell took full pages in many national dailies to defend its case, see Exhibit 6.2.[12]

Adaptive

Under an adaptive social responsibility strategy, the company accepts that it is accountable for its actions, although this acceptance is often the result of pressure brought by external groups. In the case of the Brent Spar, Shell had carried out detailed studies of the best way of disposing of the equipment and had received a licence from the United Kingdom government to go on with the sinking. It was only after strong pressure from environmental groups, led by Greenpeace, and a customer boycott and political pressure felt most strongly in Germany, that the company abandoned the scheme and had the rig towed to a Norwegian fjord to await a decision on its dismantling. Shell's approach had focused on a technical optimisation of the decision within economic and regulatory constraints. It had failed to consider the emotional and violent response, including fire bombing of filling stations, that occurred once the disposal got under way. In the end, the company decided to have the 14 500 tonne platform cut into pieces to form the foundations for a new quay near Mekjarvik in Norway.[13]

Exhibit 6.2 **Shell: putting the case against charges of irresponsibility**

IF WE'RE INVESTING IN NIGERIA
YOU HAVE THE RIGHT TO KNOW WHY

Shell plans to invest in the Nigerian Liquefied Natural Gas Project. Some say we should pull out. And we understand why. But if we do so now, the project will collapse. Maybe for ever.

So let's be clear about who we'd be hurting. Not the present Nigerian government, if that's the intention. The plant will take four years to build. The revenues won't start flowing until early next century. Of course the government of that time would suffer, but why should anyone want that?

The people of the Niger Delta would certainly suffer – the thousands who will work on the project, and thousands more who will benefit in the local economy.

And the environment would be hurt, because this plant will bring real benefits, with a great reduction in the need for gas flaring by the oil industry.

Whatever you think of the Nigerian situation today, we know you wouldn't want us to hurt the Nigerian people. Or jeopardise their future.

After Brent Spar, Greenpeace apologised for feeding the public false facts. This time, we thought you deserved to hear the truth.

Proactive

The proactive company takes the lead. It looks carefully at the relationships between its activities and the interests of its stakeholders. Then it responds to these interests without pressure being applied. We can again quote examples from Shell, *see* Exhibit 6.3.[14] Clearly, such practices show that a company is behaving responsibly in relation to stakeholders and help to resist accusations of malpractice. The advantage comes not just from good behaviour itself but from being seen by stakeholders in this light. The movement for external verification, for example through the creation of a European Association of Social and Ethical Accounting, is supported by proactive companies.[15] Norske Skog produces socio-economic accounts as part of its annual reporting.

The four responsibility strategies, summarised in Fig. 6.3, represent organisations whose attitude varies from 'the business of business is business'[16] to 'we are responsible for all the consequences of our actions'. As on other questions discussed in this book, organisations do not always make the same response. The examples from Shell illustrate how one firm can react differently to questions of waste disposal, Third World politics, local conservation and employment. Shell may indeed argue, 'We do our best', or, 'We can only go with the flow', or, on occasion, 'We are helping to build a better society', but such reactions are sometimes not enough for the advocates of greater responsibility. For instance, after the news of the Nigerian investment, Anita Roddick announced that Body Shop employees should no longer use Shell products and her company would put pressure on Shell's stakeholders to reform the oil giant.[17]

■ Altruism or enlightened self-interest?

Does social responsibility mean that businesses should be motivated by altruism, the selfless commitment to the benefit of others? Our examples suggest that such cases would be rare. If social responsibility was defined narrowly as corporate altruism, most firms could not claim to be responsible at all. Motives are the keys to under-

Exhibit 6.3 Becoming proactive

Shell's refineries occupy many hectares of ground. Much of it is unused, serving solely to separate points where dangerous substances are processed and stored. For many years, the company has employed conservation officers to advise on the best way to manage this land as, in effect, conservation areas for wildlife. Through such activities, it hoped to demonstrate its good citizenship.

Yet Shell's image has been tarnished. Acknowledging that some of its troubles have been of its own making, Shell has begun moves to become proactive across the broad front of its activities. In 1997, it published revised business principles, including for the first time a statement in support of human rights. It also fears that problems may have arisen from the narrow cultural base of its senior managers; most are British and Dutch men. It plans to increase the number of women in top positions from 4 to 20 per cent in five years. Moreover, since some 80 per cent of employees come from outside The Netherlands and the United Kingdom, Shell knows it must achieve greater diversity.

standing altruism. Yet, since most business leaders use their political skills to present a decision to different stakeholders in different ways, we are left to speculate.

It is more realistic to consider business decisions taken for the benefit of wider stakeholders stemming from *enlightened self-interest.* We have looked at many examples that can be interpreted in this way. Many senior managers admit to the change of emphasis. David Buzzelli, environment director at Dow Chemical, pointed out that no one in the 1970s chemical industry could have built a career on environmental friendliness. Now the company, the world leader in chlorinated compounds, is leading discussions of the role of chemicals in a greener world. Dow produces many compounds with benign, valuable applications but others are: raw materials for napalm, widely used in the Vietnam war; bleaching agents, applied in textiles and paper but producing harmful dioxins; and solvents that are both toxic and not biodegradable. Greenpeace argues that Dow's environmental policies are not proactive but merely methods of marketing, public relations and keeping on the right side of officials.[18]

Enlightened self-interest is much more than using sponsorship to build public images. Green policies yield business opportunities and powerful active companies have begun to persuade governments to pass relevant legislation, which, incidentally, favours their business prospects. The Montreal Protocol is an intergovernmental agreement banning the use of CFC aerosol propellants and refrigerator gases because of their harmful effect on the ozone layer. The policy was backed by the major suppliers Du Pont and ICI, partly because they were already well advanced in the development of substitutes. Since the ban, the number of suppliers of suitable refrigerants in the EU has fallen from more than 20 to 4.

Examples from Germany show that there are many business opportunities. More than 2500 companies gain more than half their income from recycling and green technologies. There is also restriction. From 1991, drinks for the German market had to be supplied in refillable bottles. This helped to protect small local brewers.[19] In 1995, the government announced it was banning imports of textiles containing Azo dyes. These dyes have caused cancer in the workers who use them but there is no evidence of any harm to wearers. They are widely used in India whose large export industry sees Germany as second only to the United States as a customer. Trade-based quotas are being phased out under the rules of the World Trade Organization, but restrictions on safety grounds will remain lawful.[20]

These examples suggest the range and variety of potential benefits for the socially responsible organisation. Here is a brief round up:

- creating markets for environmentally friendly products or process technologies;
- supplying products and programmes for disadvantaged groups;
- influencing governments through direct lobbying or swaying public opinion;
- recruiting, motivating and retaining good employees;
- staff training assignments in community programmes;
- enabling owners and managers to see funds diverted to their favourite organisations;
- providing a favourable image as a defence against possible accusations of malpractice;
- creating or sustaining an impression of having high ethical standards in business dealings;
- attracting ethical investors.

While we can readily observe action, we cannot easily sort out the reasons why organisations choose their policies. If we return to our definition of social responsibility, we can see that, in situations of choice, it identifies *obligation both to the organisation and to society*. The obligation may have become more accepted and the balance between organisation and society may be shifting. Understanding why, however, requires us to get inside the hearts and minds of every manager. This alters the focus from corporate social responsibility to the choices made by individuals.

Ethics

The study of ethics centres on choices facing the individual. Further, to the extent that the individual participates in a group whose members have the same views, we can speak of the ethics of the group. As we shall see in Chapter 17, the relationship between a person and a group is two-way. The person joins with others in forming the group and brings his or her individuality to it. Simultaneously, membership of the group changes the individual, shaping values and therefore stimulating or restraining behaviour. To the extent that there is cohesion among members, we can speak of group values and behaviour. The groups may be very large, such as when we speak of religious ethics as sets of moral principles which guide the lives of millions.

The connection with corporate social responsibility follows. In the first part of the chapter, we saw how responsible behaviour can be seen as a rational reaction to external pressures – the influence market as mentioned in the introduction. But arguments based on adaptation to the business environment can never explain why one firm turns out to differ from another. Why managers, individually or as a group, choose one action or another is answered by examining the ethical principles to which they adhere. Studying ethics in management, therefore, means we must study both the basis of individual choice and how a group or organisation ensures that its standards are followed in decision making.

What is ethics?

Of many possible definitions, we shall use the following:

> *Ethics is concerned with the code of values and principles that enables a person to choose between right and wrong and therefore select among alternative courses of action.*

It follows that an ethical issue is one where there is a choice between alternatives and these alternatives will bring benefit or harm to others. One response to this line is to ask, 'Doesn't this apply to most issues, since real choices mean at the least giving benefit to some as opposed to others'. To answer this point we need to draw a boundary to cut out cases where ethics is not relevant. First, there are personal decisions that have no impact upon other people. Generally, the books I read, the time I waste and the dreams I dream have no effect upon others and are purely independent choices. It is only when they have consequences for other people that these choices become ethical. Second, influences on others must be neither remote nor trivial. It is possible to draw chains of cause and effect from almost any human action to any other in the future. One could argue, for example, that if I buy a new washing machine I may be joining others in representing an increase in demand leading to, say, rising prices and eventual disadvantage for others. On the other hand, if I do not buy the model, someone loses a little income. Clearly, no one is saying that I should follow this reasoning but there are other more significant circumstances that echo this choice. Should people campaign for the retention of the corner shop while shopping at the supermarket? Should I drive into town or take the park-and-ride? Should companies support suppliers through lean times? Should firms buy nationalistically?

The third limitation looks to the law as a codification of the ethics of the society as a whole. The law is part of the framework set up by the state that enables society to function. Furthermore, it underpins the role of government in its many activities carried out for the common good. As Argandoña[21] points out, business and markets would be impossible without the rights and duties given to individuals and agents, the establishment of 'rules of the game', and so on. The law sets out what to do in many circumstances and, in as far as the law is just, it must be obeyed.

There is an argument that following the law is all that one has to do, and no more. Yet this may be inadequate for two reasons. In the first place, there are many areas of life in which the government chooses not to legislate, because of unenforceability, a desire to 'roll back the boundaries of the state' or because change has made previous laws go out of date. Doing only what one is forced to do, which might be called 'yuppie ethics',[22] springing from extreme notions of personal freedom, would lead to a breakdown of many social processes. Something more than law is needed.

The second problem is that legal systems differ in different countries. Argandoña distinguishes between legality and morality:

> If the legislation ... is different but is just, it must be followed because, by so doing, one contributes to the common good. If there is no law, or if it is not in accordance with moral criteria, one must always follow the moral criteria.[23]

For instance German and Portuguese companies operating in both Germany and Portugal follow the relevant national environmental legislation. This is true except when, with greater permissiveness in Portugal, they find in all conscience that they should not observe it. Then they should apply moral criteria.

The difference between law and morality is important. Many human actions are subject to law, and therefore to ethics, since adherence to the law is a moral duty. Others are subject to ethical rules and not to laws as the latter are absent. Additionally, there are those private, free choice, acts that are subject to neither. Figure 6.4 labels the three domains of action, suggesting ill-defined boundaries that tend to change in time.

■ Ethics in management

Ethics is about: norms; values; rights and responsibilities; sharing; fairness; obligation and exchange. It is more than just understanding the rules and how they apply to cases. It includes study of the origins of the rules and how they are developed and elaborated through experience of their application. Therefore,

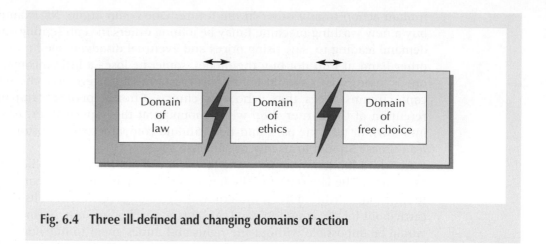

Fig. 6.4   Three ill-defined and changing domains of action

being part of a community that both establishes and maintains a set of moral rules is a matter of concern. An organisation is such a community, one of whose purposes is to establish rules by which its members make decisions. Whether this happens formally, through the setting out of codes of conduct, or informally through the gradual diffusion of the principles of the leaders, depends on the organisation itself. Establishing such controls will be discussed at the end of the chapter. First we must check to see whether and how managerial decisions have ethical implications. We take the line that management ethics is not a separate branch of ethics. Managers face different applications to other people, for example in advertising, recruitment, international trade and industrial safety, but the moral questions they face are fundamentally the same. They have to decide what is right according to a set of principles.

The organisation context is important. As we saw in Chapter 2, one school of thought analyses the organisation as a bureaucracy. This functions most efficiently when carrying out clear rules. Once these have been established at the top, the role of members is to implement them. If the rules are found to mutually conflict, the problem goes up the chain for resolution. From the point of view of ethics, it is as though the law/ethics boundary of Fig. 6.4 has moved towards the right so that the whole domain of action is covered as far as possible by written rules. These enable people in the organisation to avoid ethical dilemmas. A social security office is an example that aims to cover most of its choices by reference to rules. Even here, however, some instances are referred to adjudicators who have to judge whether individuals qualify for this or that benefit.

At the other extreme we can conceive of a very 'loose' organisation, full of entrepreneurial spirit, whose members are encouraged to treat each deal as it comes according to their personal judgement. Of course, the law is not broken but, besides that constraint, the 'law of the jungle' prevails. In Fig. 6.4, this is equivalent to pulling the ethics/free choice boundary to the left to shrink the domain of ethics.

Yet neither of these perspectives is realistic. The ideal bureaucracy is impracticable and the loose organisation, if it is to be an organisation at all, must have some common code governing practice. Anyhow both have implied moral positions – 'Follow the rules' or 'Follow the market'.

Ethical dilemmas

Most managers recognise that they wrestle with ethical dilemmas. Dilemmas arise because the interests of different parties involved in, or affected by, decisions are in conflict. One finds that benefiting one party cannot be achieved without disadvantaging another. At this point the manager has already made the first moral decision, that it is right to include the interests of the selected parties in the decision at all. In the loose organisation discussed above, following the market implies that no one has rights beyond those either implied by market transactions, as buyers and sellers of property, labour and so on, or as contained in the law, for instance, third parties covered by safety legislation. The bureaucratic organisation can go almost to the other extreme, stating that, in the interests of equity, all decisions affect all members and clients. They must be applied to all in the same way.

A further difficulty for managers, as for other people such as doctors and lawyers who take on responsibilities that affect others, is that they are acting as agents for the organisation. They are carrying out organisational rules and decisions that may have personal implications that they have to resolve. The following case illustrates:

> *You are in charge of a section of an office. In your spare time you play in a band, both relaxing and earning good money. Heavier work responsibilities have meant you have had to gradually reduce your band commitments. At the year end, your manager tells you that you are a valued, vital member of the team who performs well above average but there is to be no pay rise because of a government freeze. In recognition of your efforts, however, the manager offers to help you spend more time with the band by 'looking the other way' if you want to leave early on Fridays to travel to out of town bookings.*

At first sight, this situation would pose little difficulty for many people. They may say that leaving early breaks the contract of employment, the manager should not make this offer and, therefore, you should not accept it. Others would appeal to the moral implications of the contract of employment, a fair day's work for a fair day's pay, and suggest that the manager is simply correcting the harm done by not giving a salary increase. Yet others would argue against the unfairness of granting a specific exception for one employee when all should be treated even handedly.

Naturally, further details would be required before we could explore the case further. We can, however, see the general point that there is no single principle that can be applied in this setting. Some appeal to equity, others to strict rule adherence. Generalising, we can suggest that using a single principle is rarely satisfactory. More likely is the sort of questioning, 'If I were to follow this rule, then I might recommend this course of action. On the other hand, if I were to follow ...'. We can picture the process as something like Fig. 6.5. It is the process of fitting principles and lessons from similar cases to the case in question. In developing a view of the case, people start by looking for principles that may have a bearing upon it. They then assess the extent to which the principles match the situation, possibly by referring to cases that are similar – 'Oh it's rather like ...', or, 'They had something like this in XYZ the other day ...'. There is, therefore, a triangular judgement to be made, between the principles, cases that display similarities but are not the same, and the case in question. Having weighed the arguments generated by this process, a person makes a decision and moves to action.[24]

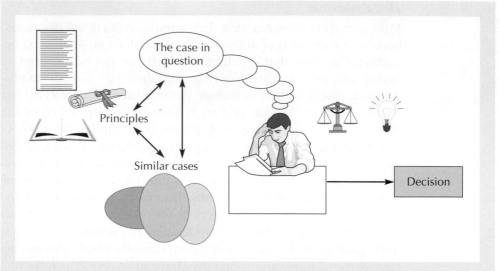

Fig. 6.5 Ethical analysis: fitting principles and similar cases to the problem in hand

In contrast to the goal-orientated decision processes explained in Chapter 11, this appears to be a messy process. Although outlined as a series of steps, there is no suggestion that a person can slavishly follow a formula, as a bureaucrat might, to reach a decision. On the contrary, the result emerges as a process of subtle judgement among the forces unique to the circumstances and may indeed involve several people.

■ Ethical principles

We now reach what most see as the core of ethics, coming to grips with the principles themselves. What is their nature? There are many traditions and classifications of such principles, the two dominant being *deontology* and *utilitarianism*.[25] A third approach, *virtue ethics*, concentrates on the type of person one ought to be rather than on establishing a set of rules. All have applications in management.

Deontology

By its origin, deontology is the science of duty. It now refers to the method of directing our thinking according to basic ideals that are almost universal in character. This caveat of 'almost' is included because, while rules, when set out, are intended to apply always, it may be that exceptions are discovered. For instance, one may willingly support a principle that pharmaceutical companies should not produce drugs that could harm people. Yet there are many products that carry a risk of harmful side effects for some users. In these cases, it is up to the producers to post warnings on packets and advise doctors and pharmacists how to avoid supplying the drugs to those who would be at risk.

One of the greatest philosophers, Immanuel Kant, created much of the foundation of deontology. His *categorical imperative, see* Exhibit 6.4, can be used as a guide

> **Exhibit 6.4** **Immanuel Kant: one of the great contributors to the study of ethics**
>
> Immanuel Kant (1724–1804) is held by many to be the most influential thinker of modern times. A German born in what is now Kaliningrad in Russia, Kant studied and worked at the local university first in classics, then in science and mathematics. He became professor of logic and metaphysics in 1770, continuing to teach until retirement in 1797. The *Critique of Pure Reason* (1781) set out Kant's views on the basis of how humans come to know things. Truths are either *analytic*, based on pure logic, or *synthetic*, based on observation. 'This red cup is a cup' is an example of the former, while 'This cup is red', being an observation, is in the latter category. From these beginnings, Kant created a structure of categories of knowledge.
>
> *Metaphysics of Ethics* (1797) explained Kant's system of ethics, which is again based on reason. Since we are rational, we must do our duty out of respect for the moral law. Kant identified two types of moral law: the hypothetical imperative, which decides the method of reaching a desired outcome; and the categorical imperative, which determines action because it is right and necessary. The latter is the universal basis of morality. It can be summarised as: 'One should never act unless one is willing to have the principle behind the act become a universal law.'
>
> Kant wrote in other fields, notably astronomy, politics and religion. Because of his controversial religious views, the King of Prussia banned him from teaching the last subject for five years from 1792.

for moral choice. We can illustrate its application by looking at bribery. Is it right to pay a bribe to gain a business contract? The purpose of the bribe is to gain preferential treatment, putting others at a disadvantage. If such action is right for one, then it is right for everyone, a conclusion that the person offering the bribe would not support. Justification for offering bribes cannot be universalised. They are, therefore, unethical.[26]

Deontology has appeal in its simplicity and universality. Difficulties arise when people discover exceptions or when a case appears to be subject to conflicting principles. To illustrate the former we may suggest that 'Always tell the truth' is a good rule. Yet there are plenty of circumstances, from contract negotiation to playing poker, where such behaviour is not expected. For the latter, we can contrast 'Follow the just law' with 'Respect life'. Is it justifiable to break the speed limit when taking a sick person to hospital? These examples point to weaknesses in deontology. It does not consider consequences of actions, focusing only on foregoing principles.

Utilitarianism

In contrast, the utilitarian approach does look at consequences. The *moral course is the one that provides the greatest good for the greatest number*. This reasoning has been widely accepted in administration and business. It offers grounds for capitalistic market systems and the existence of business organisations themselves. These, according to economists, combine to provide the greatest good for the greatest number, at least when measured in money terms. In government there has been the development of cost–benefit analysis, first concentrating on money value and then extended to measure social costs and benefits of public projects and investments. All these find their ethical foundation in utilitarianism.

Criticisms of the utilitarian approach are threefold. First, there is the possibility of unfair distribution of the benefits of any action. It could be that minor advantages for many are hidden by major disadvantages for a few, the latter having to 'bear the brunt' of whatever is proposed. In response, the rule could be adapted to prevent anyone being worse off, either by not allowing any action that disadvantages anyone or ensuring that the losers are fully compensated. This is *distributive ethics*, the basis for many management polices, for instance redundancy payment schemes. Yet, as seen in the notorious Ford Pinto case,[27] *see* Exhibit 6.5, a general policy of resolving difficulties by compensation payments is questionable.

The second criticism is that utilitarianism addresses itself to separate acts and does not yield general guidance about what is right and wrong. Times and circumstances change the morality of actions. Further, it may be possible to imagine some wrong actions that, resulting in no apparent losers, must be right. This is the equivalent of the so-called 'victimless crime'. Is it wrong to run unregistered software on my computer when I only do it as a pastime and I wouldn't buy it if I had to? Is it ethically wrong to make false claims in advertising when one can show that nobody suffers? Is it wrong to use inside information to buy or sell a very few shares on the stock exchange? If there are truly no sufferers from each of these acts, the utilitarian is in difficulties. The deontologist, on the other hand, would say, 'You must not use unregistered software unless you were prepared to have a world where registration had no meaning. Then there would be little software supplied!'

Exhibit 6.5   The Ford Pinto: $11 for a product improvement, $200000 for a life

Ford launched the Pinto in 1970 as an urgent response to rising competition from imported small cars. In rear-end crash tests shortly before the launch, engineers found that the petrol tank could fail easily, although its design met the prevailing safety standards. The defect was discovered after assembly line tooling had been made. Senior managers decided to proceed with manufacture even though the company had a patent on a much safer design. Change would have cost millions through retooling and delays.

A new safety standard had been under discussion since 1968. Realising that the Pinto design would not meet this standard, Ford lobbied hard to have its introduction delayed. In this it was successful, 'Standard 301' was adopted in 1977. Another controversial aspect of the case was a cost–benefit study carried out inside the company and presented to the National Highway Traffic Safety Administration. It showed that introducing an $11 dollar improvement to prevent tank rupture was not economical. The total cost of $137 million far outweighed the benefit of fewer deaths and injuries estimated at $49.5 million. In the latter figure were included 180 deaths at $200000.

Critics challenged both the calculation and the principle behind it. They asserted that between 500 and 900 extra people suffered burn deaths in Pinto crashes as a result of avoidable tank failure. Ford settled many cases out of court. The Pinto sold at the rate of 500000 units each year.

The third criticism of utilitarianism is its complexity. While having the great advantage of putting forward a single principle, it suffers from difficulties with 'the greatest good'. How is it to be measured and who is to decide what is good? While the approach seems both democratic and practical in principle, it breaks down when confronted by the extent and depth of real circumstances. Consequently, many managers use judgement, checklists and rules of thumb to simplify issues and therefore cope. How they make choices under these conditions depends on what sort of person they are.

Virtue ethics

Rather than looking at moral principles, virtue ethics asks the question: 'What sort of person ought I to be?' Stretching back to the Greek Aristotle, the virtue tradition has the advantage of seeing morality as a set of attitudes and behaviour established among groups or societies. Further, it underpins and justifies the idea of moral education, which is training people to behave according to a society's views of what is right and wrong. Training in virtue is possible if there are a role model, motivation and the opportunity to perform in practice. This is as important in parenthood. Disciplining children serves many functions from protecting them from danger to guiding their moral development. In organisations, those who see management as a professional practice require all managers to accept common goals and ideals of good behaviour. Codes of practice and other policies, covered later in the chapter, follow from this line.

There are two reasons why a person might behave virtuously. First, there are practical advantages in being seen to be honest, fair, strict, friendly, dependable, upstanding and so on. If nothing else, being known for virtue reduces transaction costs. One can close deals quickly, gain credit and have promises accepted without other parties seeking guarantees or carrying out investigations. Further, one is accepted into a club or community of like-minded people that operates both efficiently and pleasurably. Therefore we note, 'The banker's word is the banker's bond', and the expressions of shock when someone is found to have betrayed trust. Nowhere was this more sharply illustrated than in the series of company failures in Japan at the end of 1997. On 17 November, Hokkaido Takushoku, a big commercial bank, went under with huge debts. Pictures of tearful directors, apologising for their breach of faith with depositors, were broadcast around the world.[28]

The second reason relates to the sort of person one wants to be. Self-perception, say of being a loyal friend, a good parent (or faithful child), a sound team-player, a clear thinker and so on, accounts for much of what people think they are. Self-esteem amounts to regard for a set of virtues.

These examples immediately raise problems with virtue ethics. They point to the relativist nature of good and ill, in the first case allowing it to be determined group by group and in the second putting the burden on the shoulders of the individual. Another difficulty arises when two virtues conflict. I may be part of a society that condemns certain behaviour as wrong, for example making a disturbing noise in the park. Simultaneously I may see myself as a tolerant person. Does my tolerance prevent me from condemning minor noise infractions by others? Such problems abound in business. There are problems in reconciling empowerment and control, personal development and getting the job done. We return to these points in Chapter 12.

Illustration

We can briefly illustrate how ethical thinking brings issues together. The question is the thorny one of whether we should tell the truth, this time in business. Hamilton and Strutton[29] explain that two fundamental problems connected with honesty in business are preventing violations of standards and being uncertain about what the standards are. For instance, firms sign contracts promising to pay invoices within 30 days. Yet they do not settle until later. Since such a breach is common, do the standards apply? If 30 days is 'merely a guide', then no standard is breached.

The guidelines that are offered are that honesty is required either when the other party expects it or when it supports the firm's known reputation for honesty. Details of the possibilities are set out in Fig. 6.6. They are based on a mix of ethical approaches. The deontologist would look for maxims to be generalised. For instance, it would be possible to say, 'In situations where recipients of our information (such as advertising) will depend on the truth of that information, then we must tell the truth'. The utilitarian position is illustrated by a realisation that dishonesty may result in costs, say in litigation and compensation for breach of contract. The virtue view is, 'We must do what we said we would do', or, 'The reputation of the organisation depends on consistently telling the truth'.

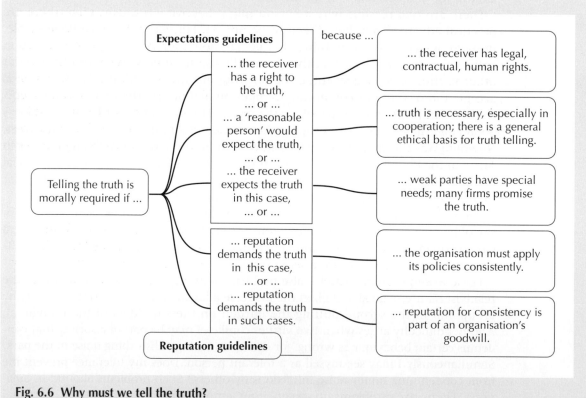

Fig. 6.6 Why must we tell the truth?

Managing social responsibility and ethics

Clearly, exhorting managers to recognise the wider picture or behave virtuously will not do. Behaving consistently in these areas is as important to many organisations as the continuing pursuit of financial targets. Compliance to standards can be achieved through the following methods: training; advocacy; codes of practice; and encouraging whistle blowing.

Training

Training is covered in detail in Chapter 15 so we will merely outline its function here. Two outcomes of training programmes are relevant – the appropriate skills to recognise and analyse problems in the field of responsibility and ethics and the changed attitudes towards these issues. If nothing else, training programmes may sensitise managers to the implications of their decisions and therefore convert them from *amoral* (blind or indifferent) attitudes to moral ones. As with the accomplishment of all such proposals, training programmes need to be related to managerial jobs and be backed up with motivation from senior management.

Advocacy

An advocate in the domains of ethics and social responsibility is a specialist in the study of such problems. This person may be employed as a guide to the resolution of difficult questions or may be expected to challenge current thinking and practice throughout the organisation. Advocates spread ideas about good practice or act as devil's advocates. Furnham[30] supports the notion of expert analysis. He notes that, drawing on the conventions of the medical and human science professions, ethics committees are being established to consider everyday business situations. Yet Furnham criticises these because their main purposes are to diffuse responsibility for awkward decisions and to stave off, avoid or deaden the impact of legal actions. Few have had an impact on the sense of responsibility of individual managers.

Codes of practice

Codes of practice have long been common in professions, being applications of the virtue ethics tradition. Exhibit 6.6 summarises the key points from the code of the Institute of Purchasing and Supply in the United Kingdom. Many companies have similar, or even stronger, rules for their purchasing staff. Breaches attract heavy penalties.

Exhibit 6.6 Code of Practice for purchasing managers: key points of the IPS recommendation

■ *Declaration of interest*
Members should declare any personal interest in any transaction.

■ *Confidentiality and accuracy of information*
Information gained in the course of business should not be used for personal gain; information given should be true and fair.

■ *Competition*
Arrangements with suppliers which prevent the operation of fair competition should be avoided.

■ *Business gifts*
Gifts, other than small tokens such as diaries and calendars, should not be accepted.

■ *Hospitality*
Mutual hospitality is an accepted courtesy yet the member should not be put in a position where the hospitality itself influences a business decision.

■ *Uncertainty*
If there is doubt as to whether a gift should be accepted or not, then it should be refused.

The question of professional (that is, ethical) behaviour is not confined to managers but also to clients, regulators, government officials and so on. A practicable code of conduct refers to all employees and to specific behaviour that should be followed or avoided.

Whistle blowing

What should you do if you see that a colleague or superior is involved in misconduct? The formal position might be that it is your duty to report it. Yet the realities of organisational life mean that, faced with pressures to conform and with the fear of loss of earnings or job, many employees ignore the symptoms of trouble. The enquiry into the 1988 explosion on the Piper Alpha oil platform, when 167 lives were lost, reported that workers feared for their employment if they raised safety issues that might embarrass their superiors. A sales manager with Colonial Mutual Insurance was dismissed after repeated attempts to interest senior managers in his reports of breaches of regulations.[31]

In the end, those who complain may feel forced to reveal unethical behaviour to authorities or other outsiders. Whistle blowing refers to this action.[32] As has been suggested, the cost and risk to the individual make whistle blowing very difficult. Recognising its value in stemming malpractice, however, both governments and enlightened companies have made moves to encourage it. Companies such as Esso and NatWest Bank have set up confidential 'hot lines'. Public Concern at Work is a British charity set up to give advice to those who feel compromised. The leading legislation is in the United States where the False Claims Act and other laws safe-guard whistle blowers' employment rights and provide for compensation and reward. Pressure is growing both among European governments and within the EU for related legislation. A difficulty may arise from the high scale of rewards. A financial officer with Los Angeles-based United Technologies received $22.5 million after exposing fraud in helicopter contract invoicing. Such sums may prompt disaffected managers to make allegations out of frustration or revenge.[33]

Conclusion: social responsibility and ethics

Corporate social responsibility and the ethics of managers meet at several points. The organisation is the means by which stakeholders, both internal and external, achieve their aims. Their influence is reconciled by managers' interpretation of the validity of those aims and the pressures that the stakeholders are able to exert. Clearly, managers' individual ethics play their part in this process.

Another aspect of the interaction is that managers' values both shape, and are shaped by, their organisational experience. Founders and leaders are important. Beyond these, however, there is a complex web of culture, people and events among which the manager learns and develops. This growth can be haphazard or the deliberate diffusion of consistent management practice. Whatever the means, we should not be surprised that the resulting social responsiveness is one aspect of the unique face which an organisation presents to the world.

Why bother? Aside from saintliness, Connock and Johns are among those who stress the practical value. Ethics makes for effective organisations and good management. Acknowledging that there is a measure of self-interest on behalf of managers, they conclude that ethical leadership:

■ is good for business;

■ makes organisation members feel good about what they do;

■ helps senior managers pursue the organisation's interests and shape and guide its destiny;

■ reflects growing societal desires not to harm others and engage with the problems of the disadvantaged;

■ matches emerging societal expectations of how organisations should conduct themselves.[34]

■ Exercise: A manager's ethical dilemma – the mailing list

The information given in Exhibit 6.7 comes from real events.

Exhibit 6.7 **Thomas's doubts**

For many years Thomas has run his own import–export business. He depends on his ability to create and spot opportunities and build trust with both suppliers and customers. One of Thomas's clients told him that he had been approached by an acquaintance recently made redundant as senior sales manager of a main competitor. He offered to sell the firm's mailing list.

Thomas had advised not to buy on the grounds, 'Knowing the way the competitor works, I would be surprised if a comprehensive up-to-date list would be available, even within the company.'

I pressed Thomas, arguing, 'That's an easy way out. You advised rejection for practical reasons.'

Thomas continued, 'Very well, if he is prepared to sell a list so readily, he is not the sort of person I would want to deal with.'

Again, I argued that this was hardly a moral position. Pressed, he would not concede that one should appeal to contractual, legal or moral arguments.

Questions for discussion

1 Summarise the ethical issues in the case of the mailing list.

2 Was I correct in suggesting that Thomas had not taken a moral position?

3 Should the manager's old organisation be informed? Or anyone else?

■ Ethics Test: Marketing

What is your response to the practices outlined on this page? Think about each and note your response.

(a) A supermarket is using a hidden camera to observe shoppers' behaviour. The camera is directed by the observer, working in another part of the building. From time to time the store layout is modified to try to see what factors influence buying decisions.

(b) You have found that your boss is cheating on travel expenses. You suspected this for some time but recently came across a copy of a claim left on the photocopier. You know that some journeys were not made at all and overnight stays did not take place in the hotels stated.

(c) Your agency is placing advertisements that use women dressed in underwear. There are three accounts, for:
  (i) lingerie, placed in a women's magazine;
  (ii) motor cycles; placed in a trade journal;
  (iii) bed linen; placed in daily newspapers.

(d) Your firm sells financial products from life insurance to personal pensions. It generates sales leads by telephoning or stopping people in the street. Staff pretend to be conducting a survey.

Turn to page 264 to see how you compare with other students.

Quick check up *Can you ...*

- Define social responsibility;
- Outline four arguments for social responsibility ...
- .. and four against;
- Define stakeholder;
- Summarise four corporate responsibility policies;

- Define ethics;
- Illustrate deontology, utilitarianism and virtue ethics in management;
- List four means to ensure compliance to ethical standards.

Questions

Chapter review

6.1 Summarise the arguments for and against social responsibility.

6.2 What are the classes of ethical ideas that can be brought to bear on a management dilemma?

6.3 What benefits are available to the socially responsible organisation?

Application

6.4 What connections can you draw between ethics and social responsibility?

6.5 What do you think is the best method of encouraging whistle blowing, if indeed it should be encouraged?

6.6 Return to the opening case to analyse its dilemmas from an ethical position.

Investigation

6.7 Study an organisation to assess the extent to which it displays social responsibility. Why does it do this?

6.8 Use a few interviews to gain insights into how far managers tell the truth at work. Summarise and explain their views of cases when they feel they need not.

Irresponsible advertising from Benetton?[35]

CLOSING CASE

Established in 1965, and run by three brothers and a sister, Benetton is one of the world's most successful clothing companies. It buys more raw wool than anyone, knits, stitches and dyes in highly automated owned and subcontractor factories in Italy and sells through thousands of franchised agents and retailers. Operations in this 'virtual' manufacturing and distribution system are both flexible and tightly controlled as needed in the high volume fashion industry. Benetton has succeeded by separating this internal culture of efficiency and hard work from the external image of an exciting company where things happen.

Luciano Benetton is responsible for advertising. Rather than display typical products or stores, campaigns use issues. 'Every theme we choose has to be recognised all over the world by a single image. There's no point in choosing an image that means something only in Italy and nothing anywhere else. Many of the images come from television. Like television news. In a way, we're like a television news service. By itself the theme of news is not new but what is new is that it's used like this by a company. Organisations think that, on balance, this approach certainly has raised our visibility.'[36]

Benetton spends a modest 4 per cent of turnover on communications. Yet the rows created by the shock tactics of the campaigns add much more. Images have included the death of an AIDS victim, floods in the Developing World, a nun and priest kissing, a dead Bosnian soldier, and another soldier carrying a Kalashnikov and human femur. There were 800 complaints to the UK's Advertising Standards Authority about a poster featuring a baby. The theme is issue-led brand recognition, used less controversially by The Body Shop. Sponsorship supports the approach; the Benetton team has been very successful in Formula One. Luciano argues, 'Not showing the product will become more and more common'.

But what to show instead? Most who wear Benetton are under 25 years old. They like the feeling of disapproval, of authorities making the company take posters down, of media refusing to accept some images. Benetton customers receive high quality products from world-class factories. Yet wearing Benetton is chic rebellion.

Questions

1 Who are Benetton's stakeholders?

2 What arguments can be assembled for and against Benetton's publicity policy? Would different stakeholders take different views?

Bibliography

Comprehensive and accessible discussions of the issues in this chapter are to be found in: Harvey, Brian (ed.) (1994) *Business Ethics: A European approach,* Prentice Hall; and Hoffman, W. Michael and Frederick, Robert E. (1995) *Business Ethics: Readings and cases in corporate morality,* McGraw-Hill.

References

1. Carnegy, Hugh (1995) 'Governments get tough – The use of recycled fibres is set to grow', *Financial Times: Survey of Nordic Pulp and Paper,* 28 June, 4; Fossli, Karen (1995) 'Prices have begun a sharp recovery', *ibid.,* 5; Brown-Humes, Christopher (1995) 'Substantial improvements, at a price – Environmental issues', *ibid.,* 8.
2. Harvey, Brian, (1994) *Business Ethics: A European approach,* Hemel Hempstead: Prentice Hall, 3.
3. Eighteenth-century proverb.
4. 'One-minute briefs: Caring in the community', *Management Today,* March 1995, 16–18.
5. Ward, Stephen (1993) 'You must be green – and squeaky clean', *Independent,* 23 August, 15; Franssen, Margot (1993) 'Beyond profits (The Body Shop Canada's social policy)', *Business Quarterly,* **58** (1), 14–20; Romano, Gerry (1993) 'Crazy times call for crazy organizations: Management analyst Tom Peter's management restructuring scheme', *Association Management,* **45** (11), November 30; Buckley, Neil (1995) 'The Body Shop warning hits shares', *Financial Times,* 3 May, 24.

6. Sasseen, Jane (1993) 'Companies clean up', *International Management*, **48** (**8**) October, 30.

7. 'Norske Skog va investir 2 milliards de francs à Golbey', *Les Echos*, 17 April 1997; http://www.norskeskog.no

8. Pizzolatto, Allayne Barrilleaux and Zeringue, Cecil A. II (1993) 'Facing society's demands for environmental protection: management in practice', *Journal of Business Ethics*, **12** (**6**), June, 441–7.

9. 'Why José's dream-car matters: General Motors and Volkswagen', *The Economist*, **328** (**7821**) 24 July 1993, 65–6; 'Pistols at dawn: General Motors and Volkswagen', *The Economist*, **328** (**7822**) 31 July 1993, 64; Flint, Jerry (1993) 'Der Zuricher', *Forbes* **152** (**5**), 30 August, 80; Tran, Mark (1997) 'Carmakers settle the espionage dispute', *Guardian*, 10 January, 22.

10. Luesby, Jenny (1995) 'Lather over laundry – The case made for reinstating phosphates to detergents', *Financial Times*, 7 June, 13.

11. Summers, Diane (1995) 'PR consensus finds Shell at fault. Opting for a U-turn over Brent Spar only made the nightmare worse say the publicity experts', *Financial Times*, 23 June, 11; Southey, Caroline and Corzine, Robert (1995) 'Gummer attacks Brent Spar U-turn: European partners are accused of "caving in"', *Financial Times*, 23 June, 18.

12. The *Guardian*, 11 and *Financial Times*, 11; both 17 November 1995; Wollacott, Martin (1995) 'A world forced to keep bad company', *Guardian*, 18 November, 27.

13. Corzine, Robert and Dempsey, Judy (1995) 'Shell stunned by Brent Spar anger', *Financial Times*, 17 June, 2; Lascelles, David, Dempsey, Judy and van der Krol, Ronald (1995) 'Brent Spar dents oil giant's pride rather than profit', *Financial Times*, 20 June, 13; Boulton, Leyla (1995) 'Shell seeks temporary berth for Brent Spar in Norway', *Financial Times*, 29 June, 10; Corzine, Robert (1995) 'Shell and that sinking feeling', *Financial Times*, 5 July, 14; Ostrovsky, Arkady and Burt, Tim (1998) 'Brent Spar: Oil rig to be rebuilt as ferry quay', *Financial Times*, 30 January.

14. Harverson, Patrick and Corzine, Robert (1997) 'Case study: Nike and Shell', *Financial Times*, 31 October; Corzine, Robert (1998) 'Shell: More top jobs for women', *Financial Times*, 13 January.

15. Gosling, Paul (1995) 'Setting the standards for fair trading practices', *Independent*, 10 May, 27.

16. Attributed to John Calvin Coolidge, whose United States presidency spanned the boom years 1923–9.

17. Vidal, John (1995) 'How good ethics will pay off in the long run', *Guardian*, 18 November, 27.

18. Boulton, Leyla (1995) 'A delicate balancing act – Dow Chemical benefits from making green issues a business concern', *Financial Times*, 28 June, 18.

19. Editorial (1995) 'How to make lots of money and save the planet too', *The Economist*, **335** (**7917**), 3 June, 75.

20. Murthy, R.C. (1995) 'Germany slams the door', *Financial Times*, Supplement: India 17 November, 9

21. Argandoña, Antonio (1994) 'Business, law and regulation: ethical issues', in Harvey(1994) *op. cit.*, 124.

22. An example of *psychological egoism*, see Hoffman, W. Michael and Frederick, Robert E. (1995) *Business Ethics: Readings and cases in corporate morality*, McGraw-Hill, 17. Broadly, this view focuses on what is, that is people are self-interested, whereas ethics is concerned with what ought to be.

23. Argandoña (1994) *op. cit.*, 129.

24. This discussion is developed from van Luijk, Henk (1994) 'Business ethics: the field and its importance', in Harvey (1994) *op. cit.*, 12–31.

25. For an application in retailing see Uusitalo, Outi and Takal, Tuome (1995) 'Retailers' professional and professio-ethical dilemmas: The case of finnish retailing business', *Journal of Business Ethics*, **14**, 893–907.

26. There are other arguments against bribery. This one is picked out to illustrate the categorical imperative. For a full discussion and criticism, see Hoffmann and Frederick (1995) *op. cit.*, 28–33.

27. Hoffman, W. Michael (1995) 'The Ford Pinto' in Hoffman and Frederick (1995) *op. cit.*, 552–9.

28. 'And then there were 19', *The Economist*, **345** (**8044**), 22 November 1997, 125.

29. Hamilton, J. Brooke III and Strutton, David (1994) 'Two practical guidelines for resolving truth-telling problems', *Journal of Business Ethics*, **13**, 899–912.

30. Furnham, Adrian (1995) 'Of business ethics and litigation', *Financial Times*, 6 February, 12.

31. Norton-Taylor, Richard (1995) 'Corporate whistle blowers set to receive protection they deserve', *Guardian*, 6 December, 20.

32. Leob, Marshall (1995) 'When to rat on the boss: the costs of snitching can be high. Here are some guidelines for when you should – and shouldn't – speak up', *Fortune*, **132 (7)** 2 October, 183; Norton-Taylor, Richard (1995) *op. cit.*

33. Tran, Mark (1995) 'Compensation and cost of mental turmoil', *Guardian*, 6 December, 20.

34. Connock, Stephen and Johns, Ted (1995) *Ethical Leadership*, London: Institute of Personnel and Development, 222–3.

35. Sullivan, Ruth (1995) 'Dropping the shock for the new', *Marketing*, 20 April 12; Wright, Robin (1994) 'Benetton's "shock" tactics only irk the moral minority', *Campaign*, 25 March, 23; Tomkins, Richard (1995) 'Risk and reward (Benetton Sportsystem's controversial advertising campaign)', *Financial Times*, 27 July, 14.

36. Quotations from Rocco, Fiammetta (1995) 'Woolly thinking', *Telegraph Magazine*, 2 December, 24–32.

Chapter 7

Managing for quality

Chapter objectives

When you have finished studying this chapter, you should be able to:

■ define quality, recognise the range of definitions in use and show how meanings differ between buyers and sellers of goods and services;

■ clarify the importance of quality – its impact both upon costs and market advantage;

■ identify the costs of quality; show how an organisation can gain by changing the balance among them;

■ outline the contributions made over the past 50 years by some leading advocates of the quality message;

■ evaluate the role of product and process standards and suggest why the latter have gained ground at the expense of the former;

■ explain Total Quality Management as a mix of philosophy, processes and techniques; outline its limitations;

■ demonstrate the use of charts and other forms of data presentation in the investigation and communication of quality issues;

■ summarise the key features of benchmarking for establishing standards and evaluate the associated benefits and problems;

■ explain Taguchi's work in proposing the ideas of robust quality and dominance.

OPENING CASE

Crockery to bone china: Churchill moves up market[1]

Founded in 1794, Churchill China is a £50 million business based in Stoke-on-Trent, the centre of the United Kingdom ceramics industry. In 1989, the company, with 90 per cent of the inexpensive end of the tableware market, had a reputation for 'cheap and cheerful' designs. These were often sold in boxed sets through general retail and discount stores. It was a position vulnerable to import competition.

Throughout the early 1990s, Churchill aimed to move into the more profitable middle market. For instance, a new *Port of Call* range by fashion designer Jeff Banks was launched in July 1995. Demanding higher quality, the middle market includes contract business known as hotelware which has a high proportion of repeat orders. Churchill made deals with major brewery and catering chains. As large estates of 'wet' pubs convert to food sales, this sector is booming. Operating margins in hotelware are around 18 per cent against 7.5 per cent for tableware.

Growth has included exports, for instance through a seven-year agreement with Allied Buying Corporation, a network of 50 United States hotelware distributors. Stephen Roper, Churchill's chief executive, had considered moving some production to China to take advantage of low production costs. Rising incomes in Japan, Korea and Taiwan are leading people to forsake the rice bowl in favour of tableware in Western style. Yet, with Japanese production costs too high and Chinese quality too low, Roper decided there was plenty of scope for export from Stoke to fill the gap. Consequently, the company has invested in new production processes to improve margins and quality.

The 1994 purchase of Queens took Churchill into the fine bone china sector. Here the policy has been to cut the product range from 3000 to 800 items, relocate production into a new plant at Stoke and replace outdated management systems. In 1995, Queens lost £81 000 on sales of £5.2 million. Yet the process improvements and shifts in the range towards more modern, informal styles were expected to quickly bear fruit.

Introduction

Over the past twenty years or so, the critically significant importance of quality has been recognised as industry after industry has been challenged by innovation and international competition. While manufacturing and service organisations that could not keep up have suffered in the new climate, those that have absorbed the quality message have prospered. Success has bred success as customers respond to rising standards and have their demands satisfied like never before.

We see in Churchill a common strategy followed by companies. Recognising that labour-intensive production of goods for the mass market is threatened by cheaper imports, they have to choose whether to automate to pull down these costs or change their products towards those that require a higher degree of skill and experience to match the rising demand for quality of service. Many companies too small to accomplish the former have sought to augment their quality of design, manufacture and service to stand among the best. Churchill's new customers wanted tougher and reliable tableware. Another industry with many small and medium firms is knitwear. Here, those that thrive apply specialist knowledge in focused markets such as Pringle's expensive cashmere sweaters or Hainsworth's bespoke uniforms.

What does moving up market mean when it comes to quality? Indeed, what does quality mean to the supplier and buyer? We need to start with definitions, showing that quality may not mean the same to both. Then we can look at policy issues and standards. Finally, we shall examine implementation and how quality questions can be analysed.

What is quality?

Let us start by referring back to a story introduced in Chapter 4. This is the one about the company ordering 10 000 items with a specified defect rate of 0.02 per cent. The supplier, keen to match specification supplied two containers. One had 9998 good items and the other the two defects. The story was used to make a point about the development of myth. Yet it also brings out one aspect of quality.

The tale is based on the notion of *conformance to specification*. This is, however, only one interpretation of the idea of quality. For instance, people may say the quality of cheese from the supermarket is inferior to *Carron Lodge*, a Cheshire cheese sold only through specialist shops. The latter regularly wins prizes at county shows. On the other hand, they may find the former cooks perfectly well. This introduces the notion of suitability, or *fitness for purpose*, an alternative idea to conformance. If you want to make a sauce for plaice Florentine, then a mass produced mild Cheddar will do. On the other hand, when served after the dessert, something better, possibly served on one of Churchill's Queens plates, is required. The cheese, in other words, must be fit for the purpose.

Other aspects of quality are included in Exhibit 7.1. All apply equally to the supply of goods and services. This is even true of the last item, quality in service, that at first seems to apply only to the service encounter.[2] Yet, depending on context and culture, service is often central to customers' opinions of the quality of manufactured goods. For instance, Williams showed that Australians and Japanese judge seafood differently. For the latter, business and personal relationships were a significant component of the perceived quality of fish supplied by an Australian exporter.[3]

One feature of the items in Exhibit 7.1 is their apparent incompatibility. For instance, tailoring a product to suit a customer's requirements in terms of special use or aesthetic values runs up against the benefits of uniform standards required by large-scale production and marketing. Quality is defined differently by customers and producers. How are these differences to be reconciled?

Quality defined

To operate as a business, managers need a practicable definition that combines attributes and standards with the purpose to which the product is to be put. As Crosby argues, 'Quality has to be defined as conformance to requirements, not as goodness... The setting of requirements may simply involve only answers to questions. Requirements, like measurements, are communications.'[4]

Exhibit 7.1 Dimensions of quality

Quality in use
Performance – will it do the job?
Safety – with no hazards?

Quality as features or grade
Zanussi FJ1093 Jetsystem RS: Rinse sensor; half-load; child security ...
Ballantine's £250 sweaters from the *finest cashmere wool.*

Quality as reliability
Reliability – risk of failure in use
Serviceability – easy attention
Durability – life before wear-out.

Quality as conformance
Are agreed specifications and imposed standards met?

Quality as aesthetics
The sensory attributes – 'That is a very good design/ piece of music/ book/ ...'

Quality personally defined
Does it match the person's individual requirements?

Quality of service
Reliability – precise and dependable
Responsiveness – prompt attention to individual needs
Service environment – facilities and the appearance of staff
Confidence – manner, knowledge and trustworthiness of staff
Empathy – caring staff, offering personal attention.

In stressing *conformance to requirements*, Crosby is emphasising two features. First, quality is about matching, that is conforming to, some standards. Second, these standards, or requirements, have to be established and communicated in some way from their origin, be it customers or another external source. If we are talking about individual service, it may be possible to adjust operations for each client. On the other hand, mass production and free markets work because standards have been discovered, created or imposed across whole industries.

Quality is, therefore, about setting standards and conforming to them. Successful managers make accurate evaluations of customer expectations and match these with their companies' capabilities. A formal definition, adopted by both the British Standards Institution and the American Society for Quality Control,[5] captures the range of issues.

> *Quality is the totality of features and characteristics of a product or service that bear on its ability to satisfy stated or implied needs.*

Why is quality important?

The story of a supplier sorting defects from good items emphasises how Japanese companies built a reputation for supplying quality goods. The remarkable progress of leading Japanese consumer goods manufacturers is, further, more solid evidence. Quality is a strategic factor that works through virtuous cycles to improve marketing and operations. These are shown in Fig. 7.1. At the left, the *quality improvement programmes* combine product improvement, matching customers' needs more closely, and process improvements, ensuring better conformance. Improved product quality increases demand and enables the firm to charge higher

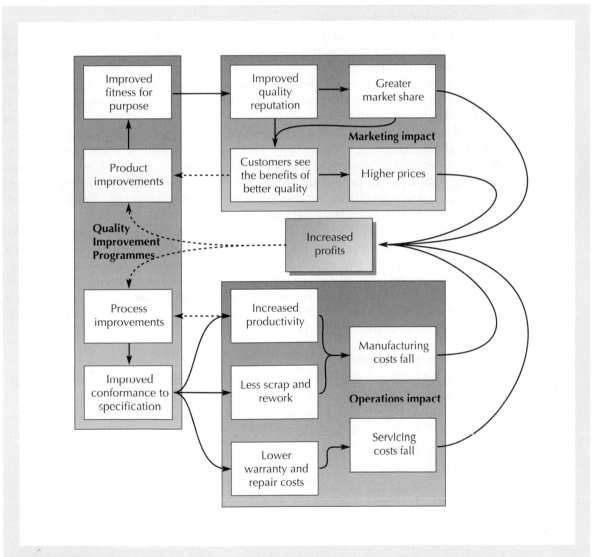

Fig. 7.1 Virtuous loops in quality improvement

prices for the extra value offered. An extra loop represents the way customers learn about quality and the firm's response by feeding back their demands into further product improvements. Achieving customer satisfaction is not, therefore, a one-off process; rising standards create demand for even higher standards in the competitive marketplace. Inside the organisation, process improvements have direct impact on costs. They also show an extra loop as the habit of continual development is self-reinforcing. The main loop of Fig. 7.1, however, leads to increased profits. This provides funds for further quality improvement.

Managers in Japanese firms have recognised these interactions since the 1950s.[6] It may be difficult, initially, to accept that improving quality will lead to improved productivity but the fewer delays, mistakes and rework more than pay for themselves in terms of rises in net output. In an empirical study of 184 New Zealand manufacturers, Maani and others showed that improving quality enhances operational performance and productivity.[7]

Taking a narrow view of simply cutting spoilage, Deming used an example to make the point that quality and productivity are closely linked.[8] He referred to a production line running with 11 per cent defective output, a level that top management was unaware of. The line was well controlled, showing consistent performance over time. The main cause of the defects was that both operators and inspectors did not understand sufficiently the kind of work that was acceptable or unacceptable. To them, 11 per cent was normal. A special study came up with a practical definition of work standards. This was posted for everyone to see. Defects fell to 5 per cent. The corresponding benefits, shown in Table 7.1, were achieved at little cost. Through producing 95 instead of 89 good items from every hundred units, the line's productivity rose by more than 6 per cent. Deming noted, 'Customer happier. Everybody happier'.

As Deming's example shows, defects are not free. Someone is paid to make them, resources are used and opportunities of making sales are lost. There is a danger in overstating this argument. We must not interpret the example as suggesting, in Crosby's words, that *Quality is Free*.[9] The reasoning should be that there are many operational situations where improvement in quality will bring with it reduced operating costs, so much so that there will be net gains to the organisation. This justifies *investment* in quality.

Quality in service operations

Services echo the manufacturing line of Deming's case. Rework when things go wrong adds cost for no one's benefit. In service settings, things are complicated because standards are ill defined and difficult to implement. Yet the satisfied cus-

Table 7.1 Quality up, costs down

	Defects before change: 11%	Defects after change: 5%
Total cost	100	100
Number of good items	89	95
Cost per item	1.12	1.05

tomer will not only do more business in the future but recommend the firm to others. On the other hand, the dissatisfied customer will not only directly reduce profitability but will deter new customers. Besides these interactions with customers, poor service is demoralising for staff as they spend time handling complaints and are demotivated if nothing is done to relieve them. Lister provides data on the consequences of poor service.[10] Depending on the industry:

- For each complaint there may be 26 unresolved problems.
- Of those who do complain, between 50 and 70 per cent will do business again if their complaints are handled effectively.
- Dissatisfied customers will tell between 10 and 20 people whereas satisfied customers tell between 3 and 5.
- Problems with service dominate why customers stop doing business, *see* Fig. 7.2.

The problem is often less a question of motivation but more one of leading the way. Although '… everyone is doing his best', the 'best efforts are not sufficient'.[11] Unless they are pointed towards consistently improving quality, best efforts cause a random walk. This is a journey where the direction of each step is random. As Fig. 7.3 suggests, it is a good way of getting nowhere.

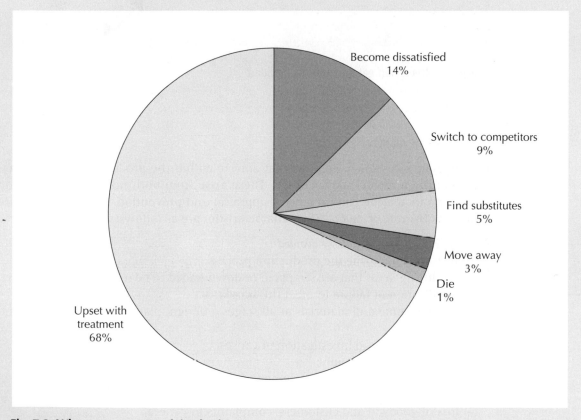

Fig. 7.2 Why customers stop doing business

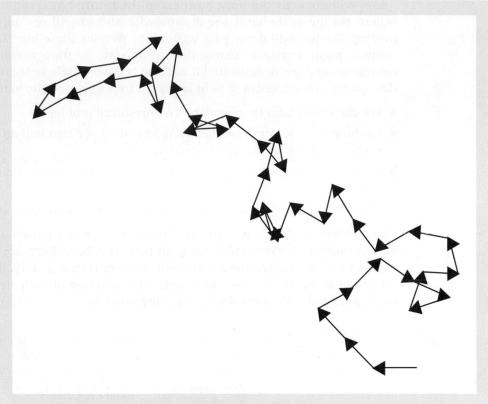

Fig. 7.3 Keen staff get nowhere if unguided

Costs of quality

Rather than focus solely on costs that appear within the production process, analysts identify a much broader range. These arise from both nonconformance and the efforts to achieve conformance – appraisal and prevention. Together these are known as the *costs of quality*. Their characteristics are as follows:

■ *Failure – waste that could be avoided*
  Defects arising during the production process:
  – producing items that are scrapped, or downgraded to be sold as second quality;
  – rectification of failure to meet the standard;
  – waste of time and materials at all stages – design, planning, manufacture and delivery;
  – re-inspection and investigation of causes.
  Defects found after supply:
  – repair, extra servicing, replacement under warranty;
  – handling of returned items;
  – loss of goodwill and customers' complaints in general;
  – consequential losses leading to litigation;

- financial compensation apart from litigation;
- further inspection, investigation and administration.

■ *Appraisal – stopping defects going further*
Checking for defects:
- inspection of materials bought in or produced internally;
- final inspection of products and services;
- quality audits to assess the quality control system;
- vendor rating – quality audit of suppliers' standards and procedures;
- equipment and processes devoted to inspection;
- the costs of quality appraisal, control systems and organisation.

■ *Prevention – eliminating waste*
Reducing or eliminating defects:
- identification of customer quality requirements; producing specifications for components, assemblies and services;
- optimising the balance between prevention, appraisal and failure costs;
- building-in quality to all products. The cost of quality research, good design and prototyping;
- training of staff to appreciate their contribution to quality, especially failure prevention;
- administration of quality programmes.

The total cost of quality is the sum of all the elements identified above. As Rust points out, however, many costs are overlooked because the accounting system is unable to trace them.[12] While some organisations will be satisfied with a concentration on appraisal, recognising that some defects will 'get through', many have found benefits from increased prevention efforts.

> *Tennant is the world's largest manufacturer of floor sweepers and scrubbers.[13] Concerned about quality in an environment of increasing competition, senior managers set out to refocus the business on quality and productivity. An assessment found it was in position A of Fig. 7.4. Failure costs represented half the estimated 17 per cent of revenue that was being spent on quality. Through increasing attention to fault prevention, Tennant improved customer satisfaction. Simultaneously, the change resulted in a halving of quality costs with a shift towards prevention and away from correction.*

In Fig. 7.4, Tennant shifted from A to B and then C. This is an example of a general relationship between the ability to match quality to customers' expectations and the direct quality costs. Where the quality capability is low, as at A, failure costs are high and dominate the total. With improving capability, both failure and appraisal costs can be cut, resulting in better performance overall. Whatever the starting point, advocates of continuous improvement argue that improvements are always possible. The costs of quality should continue to fall as the organisation learns new approaches within an ever more exacting environment. Yet enthusiasm may wane. A cost of quality programme at Xerox achieved excellent savings over seven years; yet by then the big improvements had been achieved and its protagonists had moved on.[14]

In other cases, quality improvements can pay for themselves quickly. Whirlpool found that a sticking bearing in a dryer was accounting for 2.33 per cent of its calls

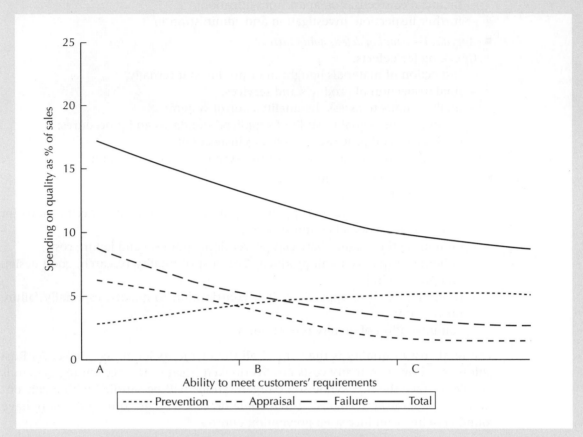

Fig. 7.4 Cutting the total cost of quality by choosing a different balance

for service under warranty. These annual costs were running at $1.3 million. A study found that improving the bearing material cost just half a cent per machine or less than $5000 a year.[15]

Yet quality is not free. An improvement programme requires investment since the spending on prevention will *precede* the benefits from reduced failure and appraisal costs. Figure 7.5 picks up this dynamic link. It outlines typical cash flows during a major change. During the first two years there will be a bulge in spending on prevention, including new systems, designs, equipment and training. After this investment has peaked, all categories begin to fall.

The two main thrusts of a quality plan are, therefore, prevention and appraisal. We have seen that failures are to be avoided. This is the so-called ZD or zero-defects policy. It should be recognised, however, that the *cost of avoiding all failures may be prohibitive* and the technology to do so may not be available. If failures do occur, the organisation must make an effective response, especially if the problem occurs after the product is supplied to the customer.

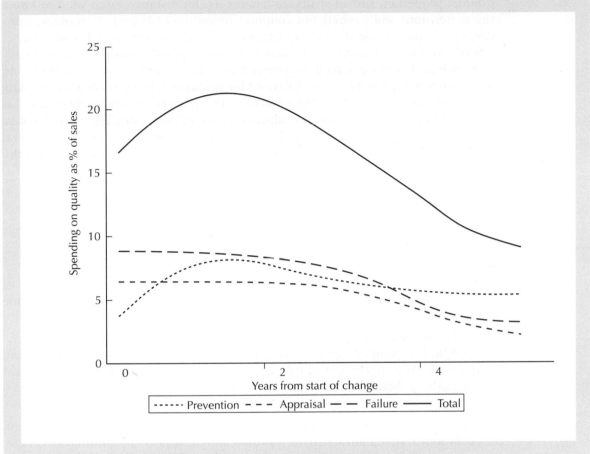

Fig. 7.5 Cash flow during a major quality change programme

Quality standards

Behind the 'stated or implied needs' of our quality definition are standards. How are these discovered and incorporated into trade? It could be that every contract included a detailed specification but for most products in most applications this would severely restrict free trade. Most buyers and sellers are content to use common standards that have grown from local and industrial customs through national agreements to international conventions. The European Union, for example, has made common standards one main plank in its construction of the single market.

Assay offices represent an early attempt by governments to regulate a trade. Then they were established to prevent unscrupulous traders from diluting gold with base metals. Gradually, national organisations emerged, such as the British Standards Institution (BSI), Deutsche Institut für Normung (DIN) and the American National Standards Institute. This made it possible for commonly manufactured goods to be interchanged and for users to know in advance details of product properties. British structural engineers, for instance, used BS 4 to know the dimensions and strengths of common rolled steel I-beams. Nowadays, standards cover products as diverse as film speeds, flame proofing, pencils and paint.

While often formalised in national and international organisations, industry standards and norms emerged by several routes: agreement between suppliers and users, such as the emerging specifications for digital television; success of a leading design or brand, IBM's PC being notable in this respect; or almost by chance, as evidenced by the dimensions of wallpaper, cloth, railway track and vinyl records. Product standards are frequently backed by statute, often at the international level. There are many EU regulations covering product specifications from the strength of vehicle seat belts to the noise emitted by domestic lawn mowers.

Several drawbacks with product standards can be noted:

■ *Limited scope*
Technical constraints and change mean that they relate to only a limited range of products in circulation.

■ *Limited applicability to assemblies*
Standards can apply to some components but not to complete assemblies. It is, for example, hardly of interest to know that the bolts inside a washing machine are made to BS dimensions.

■ *Applied only to some properties of a product*
BS 476, for example, specifies testing methods for fire resistance of building materials. The attachment of this label to a batch of, say, decorative panels will say nothing about their acoustic or other properties.

■ *Complexity*
The historical multiplicity of standards almost denies the point of having them. Although BSI and similar organisations aimed to provide national coverage, many purchasers continued to issue specifications based on their special needs. Government purchasing, especially of military equipment, became subject to rules such as the 05 standards of the Ministry of Defence and NATO's Allied Quality Assurance Publication.

Since many items of military hardware were very complex and had to have quality built into every component, defence procurement authorities required suppliers to have their manufacturing processes open to external audit. Indeed, when small companies manufactured supplies for the MoD, they were allowed to progress from stage to stage only when an external inspector was present. From the frustration, confusion and costs of this system, and the burgeoning number of standards in the civil sector, grew a new approach, concentrating on the processes themselves.

■ Process standards: through BS 5750 to ISO 9000

BS 5750 focuses on processes. Recognising problems with product certification, it is a practical, national standard usable by organisations of all sizes. If quality is built in at every stage, and evidenced by relevant documentation, then the whole system will produce quality output. Compliance with the provisions of the standard leads to inclusion in the *Register of Quality-assessed United Kingdom Companies*.

Unannounced checks are made about four times a year. Exhibit 7.2 outlines the general and specific provisions of the various sections of BS 5750.

Sponsored by the European Union, the ISO 9000 series comprises five sections (9000 to 9004) based largely on BS 5750 which it effectively replaces. Again, it is a process standard, this time developed with the express intention of achieving uniform and fair practice throughout the EU. It has gained acceptance outside the continent, first through foreign companies seeking to do business in the EU and then through their own suppliers and partners. Some 60 countries have recognised it formally but the push behind its acceptance comes from companies for whom it cuts out the confusing and conflicting standards met within international trade. There are more than 30 000 certified organisations.[16]

The question raised by the switch to process standards is whether typical product quality is affected by them.[17] ISO 9000 leaves three problems outstanding:

■ *Universality means average*

Norms achievable across many organisations are already being achieved by excellent ones. For them, the value of ISO 9000 lies solely in providing a further lever to raise the standards of some of their suppliers. Dickson noted, 'The

---

Exhibit 7.2 BS 5750

General provisions

■ Good quality organisation; clear responsibilities.

■ Regular, systematic reviews to identify problems; changes audited to confirm problems resolved.

■ Quality system integrated with other key functions: design, research and development, subcontractor management, manufacturing and supply and installation.

■ Planning of new approaches to testing and assessment.

■ Monitoring all measuring and testing equipment; results recorded.

Specific provisions

■ Design activity, including: development programme; code of practice; studies of new methods; communications and interfaces with other departments; preparation and control of drawings, specifications, procedures and other instructions; incorporation of appropriate statutory provisions; studies of new materials; validation of the reliability of engineering and value studies; design review; incorporation of feedback from previous designs. (If supplying to another's designs, this section is the customer's responsibility.)

■ Managing relations with subcontractors and suppliers; appraisal of capability and performance; agreements on inspection procedures; all arrangements documented.

■ Manufacturing clearly controlled; work instructions and operational procedures.

■ In-process quality appraisal: sampling and acceptance rules; options for failed work.

■ Final test procedures; personnel, conditions and control.

fuss over European-wide certification – notably complaints by small and medium-sized suppliers about the time and money spent on acquiring the quality standard ISO 9000 to appease their demanding customers ...'.[18]

■ *Narrow definition*

By concentrating on supply process consistency, ISO 9000 ignores dimensions of customer satisfaction that many would include in a broader definition of quality. Possibilities are speed of response, customisation and continuous improvement. These extra service elements often dominate customer satisfaction.

■ *Products*

Moving products from the centre of the stage allows for wide coverage for registration and does not restrict innovation. In taking this approach, however, ISO 9000 does not guarantee any particular product. Makers of lead balloons can be certified if they make them consistently according to the specified procedures!

While the last point suggests that absurd positions may arise, it is worth making the point that ISO 9000 is not intended to replace product standards. They remain relevant in many industries. The two aspects are linked, for an organisation seeking product approval is likely to require process registration as a prerequisite of an appraisal.

Some organisations face a further problem associated with the growth of the ISO 9000 scheme. Certification may have an unwelcome side effect in forcing them to adopt a degree of bureaucracy. The need to define and specify processes in formal documents, and then *adhere to these specifications*, may run counter to the prevailing culture. Good management is required to blend discipline with the flexible and creative culture that may be desired.

Total Quality Management

Just as quality has various definitions so does Total Quality Management. In essence, TQM brings together the ideas we have covered so far in this chapter and links them to detailed methods and techniques that follow. In that sense TQM is a philosophy of quality that links policy and operational practice. Identifying the need for quality products in the competitive marketplace is just the first step. More difficult, however, are setting of appropriate goals and the mobilisation of the whole organisation towards achieving them.

Of the three elements of TQM:

■ *Total* suggests full commitment of everyone in the organisation and a coverage of every aspect of all processes.

■ *Quality* means continuously meeting customers' requirements.

■ *Management* implies an active process led from the top.

For our discussion, therefore, we shall use the following definition:

> *Total Quality Management is a process of involving everyone in an organisation in continuously improving all products and processes to achieve, on every occasion, quality that satisfies customers' needs.*

The definition has four key implications that we shall examine further. They are:

■ involving everyone in the company through teamwork, trust and empowerment;

■ continuous improvement;

■ identification of customers and their needs, and then focusing on them;

■ using tools and techniques to jointly resolve quality problems.

Teamwork, trust and empowerment

The holistic approach of TQM distinguishes it from conventional approaches where the responsibility is assigned to a 'quality department'. For some, it even goes beyond the Quality Circle, *see* Exhibit 7.3, which can be seen as management delegating some quality responsibilities while retaining most of the control. The holistic goal is commitment and sharing of the quality issue among all employees so that the contributions of each are both recognised and influential. At Denso, for example, a QC meeting is unlikely to be seen as an interruption to 'real work'. This and other leading Japanese companies, such as Matsushita and Kansai

---

Exhibit 7.3 Quality circles

Quality Circles have made major contributions to the success of Japanese companies. Conventionally, staff are organised into groups of, say, 6 to 12. Training and guidance in the concepts of quality and problem-solving techniques are given by middle managers. At regular meetings a group selects problems to work on and solve. It sets its own targets, not only for quality improvement but also for related issues such as production flow, planned maintenance, working conditions and safety.

Among many variants, QCs may:

■ have people from one or several work groups;

■ have people from one or several levels in the organisation;

■ have a nominated leader or decide to rotate the leadership role;

■ be stimulated by a scheme offering rewards for suggestions.

From the first QC in Japan in 1962, the number has expanded to, perhaps, 100 000 registered with the Union of Japanese Scientists and Engineers. (There are an estimated 1 000 000 further circles not formally recorded.) In the early 1990s, Yamaha had 700 circles, Toyota 6700 and the medium-sized Toppan Printing 150 among a mere 2000 workers. More than 13 million Japanese people participate, always voluntarily and usually outside working time. Each QC generates about 50 suggestions a year. The movement is seen as a driving force behind the continuous improvement of products and processes.

The QC fits well into the Japanese organisational culture with its emphasis on the group, as opposed to the individual, its lifetime loyalty (at least in major firms) and lack of serious demarcation of job roles. Although tried in the West with some success, the different context makes the idea difficult to transfer. Organisations face either the struggle to create favourable conditions or the temptation to remove or dilute some key principles that make QCs work.

Electric, do not see TQM as a separate set of activities different from the running of the business.[19]

Chapter 14 shows how empowerment can only occur when people are well trained, given access to relevant information, know and use the best techniques, are involved in the decisions and receive appropriate rewards. Many quality problems relate to materials, designs, specifications and processes and have little to do with poor employee performance or organisation. Yet these same employees are usually well aware of the shortcomings of the production system and can be valuable in finding solutions.

■ Continuous improvement

Many programmes for change are based on the notion of restructuring the system and moving it from one state to another. As discussed in Chapter 14, large changes are difficult to install and are frequently resisted by those most affected by them. Furthermore, in the uncertainty of complex operating systems, it is not always clear in which direction great steps ought to be made. To cope with these problems, advocates of continuous improvement, or *kaizen*, see striving for quality as an endless journey rather than a trip to a known and fixed destination. Actions involve experimentation, adjustment and minor improvement to every detail. In the *kaizen* philosophy, employees expect small developments and do not see them as challenges to existing working practices and relationships. Continuous questioning of the status quo means that no one stays happy with it for long.

Imai is a leading advocate of *kaizen*. To him, every person's work should comprise two parts – continuation and improvement.[20] The former, which Imai calls maintenance, refers to the current work. People must know what to do and follow the standard. The second part, improvement, means finding a better way of doing the job and raising the standard. It also happens that people find new ways of doing jobs without raising the standard. Imai argues that this behaviour should be seen as deviation rather than improvement because the key factors of quality, cost and delivery have not been affected. For improvement to take place, the standard must be raised. *Kaizen*, then, implies continuous challenges to the standards in every job.

As suggested in Fig. 7.6, most of the work at shop floor level is directed towards continuation. The role of managers is to take on more responsibility for improvement. Imai suggests a set of questions to act as guide when problems occur. Did it happen as a result of:

■ Having no standard?

■ Having an inadequate standard?

■ Not following the standard?

■ Staff not trained to follow the standard?

When problems arise, the manager's job is to find out what has happened, using the above questions. A better standard or method can be worked out. This, in Imai's view, is most important. Standards guide both continuation and improvement. There can be no quality without it. With it, recurrence of problems can be prevented

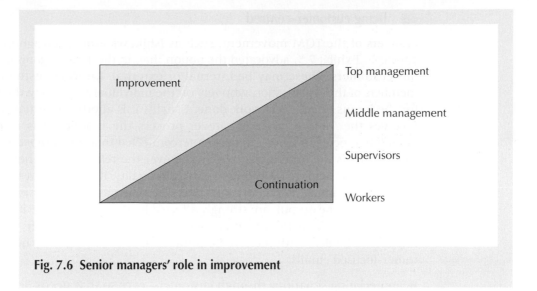

Fig. 7.6 Senior managers' role in improvement

and the variability within all processes can be limited. Quality improvement in Japan can be seen as a story of continual establishment and adaptation of standards.

Closely associated with this commitment to involvement in the detail of standards and their improvement is *gemba*. *Gemba* means the place where the activity takes place. It can refer to: the shop floor; the customer's offices where a salesperson is calling; the customer's site where an installation is being made; the screen or drawing board where an engineer is working out a design; or the hotel reception area, bedroom, restaurant or sauna. Imai sets out the improvement process based on five *Gemba* principles, *see* Exhibit 7.4.[21]

Many solutions can be made in the first two steps. Yet the real solutions are achieved only after the last ones are taken. Otherwise, managers not using the discipline remain fire-fighters. The principles have implications for the roles of senior managers. They should be there to remove restraints on *Gemba*, that is to help people lower down the hierarchy to investigate and solve problems without excessive constraints. Since managers are ultimately responsible for everything that happens in *Gemba*, they need to stay in touch and become involved when problems arise. Hence the opening maxim, 'Go to *Gemba* first and right away!' To Imai, the problem with most managers is that they believe their workplace is their desk.

Exhibit 7.4 **The five principles of *Gemba***

1   When an abnormality occurs, go to Gemba first and right away!
2   Check with *Gembutsu*. *Gembutsu*, in Japanese, means something you can touch, such as machine, material, failures, rejects, unsafe conditions, etc.
3   Take temporary countermeasures on the spot.
4   Find and remove the root cause.
5   Standardise for recurrence prevention.

■ Being customer-centred

Pioneers of the TQM movement, such as Ishikawa and Juran whose biographies appear in Exhibit 7.5, advocated the notion that, in the TQM organisation, everyone has customers. These may be internal or external. Internal customers are other members of the organisation who rely on the individual next along the quality chain for the inputs to get their work done. Usually, it is another internal customer who receives the 'output' from whatever process the individual is responsible for. Sometimes, people's work can be so interconnected that they are *mutually dependent*, that is each is the other's customer. Whatever the relationship, they are all part of quality chains, *see* Fig. 7.7. When it comes to quality, it follows that the internal customer is very much like an external one. The difficulty of the customer's work, and the quality of the output, are strongly affected by the quality of the input.

As for external customers, it is obvious that the TQM company will require *all employees* who deal with them to be committed to satisfying their needs. Being customer-focused entails:

- appreciating situations through customers' eyes so that needs, especially hidden ones, are anticipated;

Exhibit 7.5 Ishikawa and Juran; two quality pioneers

Kaoru Ishikawa

At Tokyo University, Professor Ishikawa advocated quality ideas in the 1930s. He founded the Union of Japanese Scientists and Engineers which became the focus of Japan's quality developments as its economy recovered after the war. He developed the idea of customers being both internal and external to the organisation and popularised the fish bone diagram and other techniques.

Ishikawa saw that Western management practices could not be grafted easily on to Japanese habits. He was a pioneer of Quality Circles, seeing the group as crucial in learning. His first were at Nippon Telegraph and Cable in 1962; the number passed one million by 1978.

Joseph M. Juran

From a background in statistics in the United States, Juran had strong influence on Japanese managers, being linked to Ishikawa's UJSE. Employed in Japan during the reconstruction, he recognised how workers' illiteracy hindered quality improvement. Large businesses had already started 'reading circles' led by supervisors and others with the necessary skills. Juran took advantage of this situation by having his ideas published as cheap learning materials for such groups. The pamphlets were even sold through newspaper kiosks. For the reading circle based on Juran's material, it was a short step to the Quality Circle.

Back in the United States, Juran founded the Juran Institute to spread his ideas about partnerships and teamwork, internal customers and problem solving. For him, quality meant *fitness for purpose,* a broader definition than *conformance to specification,* which he regarded as very limiting. Juran lectured into his nineties.

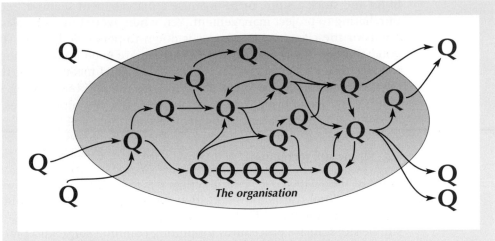

Fig. 7.7 Quality chains link internal and external customers

- listening to customers, especially the detail of what they want;
- understanding possible ways of satisfying customers' wishes;
- providing the appropriate response.

Exhibit 7.6 illustrates how leadership, when customer focus is concerned, can be so negative. The point of the tale is that it represents customer service failure. Any discussion of who is responsible for the problems is put on one side. Further, the manager does not see the impossibility in a mass service organisation for a small elite of managers to deal with customers. The TQM business acknowledges this and, rather than criticise the inadequacy of recruits, develops its people to achieve high standards. This means leadership, training, standards and rewards.

With their attention to detail, leading retailers can teach a great deal about customer orientation for the whole organisation. Writing on excellence, Peters likens retail, in the classroom or the showroom, to a performance art. True, to locate,

---

Exhibit 7.6 **The blaming trap**

A senior railway manager once told me, 'The trouble is that the people in this organisation who deal with the public are the people at the bottom'. We went on to discuss something else. Later, I thought about the implications of the assertion. The critical points of contact between travellers and railway staff are not at ticket sales or general enquiries but when a passenger has a difficulty or complaint. Then, the manager is implying, 'the sort of people we employ' on the shop floor (porters, train crew and so on) are ill-equipped to handle the problems. If only the complaints were immediately handled by intelligent and articulate staff (like the manager himself) passengers would be better satisfied.

In many organisations, the front line people have low status and pay.

build and stock a store, or to organise a management seminar, require skills from purchasing to project management. Yet, when everything is in place, and the shop opens or the class begins, success is down to personal delivery. Just as there are good and bad actors and actresses, so there are good and bad shopkeepers, receptionists, ticket collectors and teachers. Being good means giving the customer the best of what they want every day. 'You are the absolute master, ruler, tsar,' says Peters. 'You alone bring that space, or those five restaurant tables, to life. Ninnies or saints, fearful or fearless, management can't hold you back.'[22]

Tools and techniques

Later in the chapter we shall investigate some important tools for solving quality problems. Imai warns, however, that too much stress can be laid on the need to learn the techniques.[23] He believes that most quality problems can be resolved by simple steps. Imai's procedures for putting common sense into practice are:

- *Go to Gemba*.
  This is the most important rule.

- *Standardisation*.
  Standards are the basis of both continuing activity and improvement. If there are no standards they should be introduced. If the standards are failing, they should be modified.

- *Don't get it, don't make it, don't send it*.
  Based on the premise that quality is everyone's job, one should be determined not to receive rejects, create them or pass them on.

- *Speak with data*.
  Collecting data is the starting point of analysis. People should be prepared to measure before changing anything.

- *Ask why*.
  Problem solving means asking why as often as necessary to find the root cause. Only then can the problems be eradicated.

While some argue that quality cannot be sustained without sophisticated techniques, the focus of the TQM organisation is less on measurement and more on the use of simple approaches to support continuous improvement. Rather than use detailed recording and statistical analysis at the end of the production process, it may be more effective to enable a process worker to take some simple measurements earlier on. Immediate corrective adjustments are possible. Matching the complexity of quality tools with the training and experience of the users is a vital part of involving people at all levels. Tools are clearly a necessary but not sufficient basis for a TQM programme.

Limitations of TQM

At its core, Total Quality Management is a simple idea. The search for competitive advantage through quality is best sustained by applying basic ideas right across the organisation. Yet, in spite of strong arguments for quality programmes, many companies have not carried out change successfully. What are the constraints and problems?

Costs

When we examined the costs of quality and changing the balance among them, we came across the idea that quality programmes would eventually pay for themselves. 'Quality is free' because the total costs of prevention are less than the costs of failure. This begs two questions. First, what happens in the firm once it has cut its costs of failure? Further gains will become more difficult to achieve and may be difficult to justify in financial terms. Second, quality programmes are an investment. Figure 7.5 showed how total quality spending may have to rise before it falls.

These financial arguments account for some constraints on quality developments. Unless substantial benefits can be achieved very quickly, a firm with a shortage of financial resources may prefer to invest in other areas of business development.

Human resources

Dawson sounds several warnings when discussing changes in technical and social processes during the introduction of a TQM programme.[24] He first points out that TQM is not a panacea. Many plants have problems that need to be resolved either as a prerequisite of a quality programme or separately from it. Further points concern social issues:

- There may be problems within the work groups during the transition. To participate in TQM, through Quality Circles for example, is voluntary. Yet to work under the restructured operating system is mandatory. Those employees who, because of pre-existing problems, find it impossible to join in will not support the change. The TQM development may, therefore, make current social tensions worse.

    From the employee's point of view, non-involvement could be quite rational. A factory worker with a dull job may see getting to the end of a shift as the prime aim. Then work can be forgotten until the morrow. Why staff adopt these attitudes, and whether they can be changed, is a subject for Chapter 16.

- Employee involvement may be difficult to mobilise at first and may have to be considered as an eventual objective. Cultural, language and structural constraints create barriers:

    Culture and language

    At one Pirelli plant in Adelaide, Australia, there were language differences among shop floor workers, many of whom were recent immigrants. These hindered the deep levels of communication which cooperation requires, a problem that would not arise in the remarkable homogeneity of Japanese society.

    Structure

    The relevant structures at shop floor level include plant layout and the shift system. Both may hinder participation in TQM, either through physical or temporal separation of individuals and groups. In such circumstances, workers will have grown used to relying on supervisors for co-ordination and they are likely to see TQM in the same light. Night shift workers, often fewer than day staff, often perceive themselves as semi-independent of management and are reluctant to commit themselves to personal involvement.

■ Employee ability may be limited, not only by cultural and language diversity but by general levels of education. Dawson comments that the value of TQM techniques, especially statistics, had been exaggerated. Groups used brainstorming methods at first but relied on one or two members or co-ordinators to produce simple graphical material. A further problem for those left out of the discussions by such barriers was that they were expected to go along with the decisions that were made.

There remains a further question, that of seeing the above points as 'problems' to be solved by omniscient, homogeneous and rational management. Yet TQM, as with other management programmes, is often introduced in an atmosphere of contradiction among managers and uncertain management–shop floor relations. In short, its introduction is a political process.[25]

In a wider context, it may appear that the emphasis on individual and group development, backed up by training, would provide great opportunities for the development of personnel policies and practices generally. Yet personnel functions are not heavily involved. TQM accomplishment is very much an operations activity, often established under a project leader who is a line manager. The stress in many Western companies will be on immediate business results rather than long-term development of employees. A clear exception in the United Kingdom is Rover Group. Heller reports that it is 'plainly reaping the rewards of its long drive'[26] while maintaining high levels of employee satisfaction.

Paradoxically, while several American engineers, scientists and statisticians worked with their local counterparts during the rebuilding of Japan after 1946, their work did not become recognised in their home country until much later. By this time, American and European business had seen Japanese imported products climb from the cheap imitations of 1950 to the outstanding quality of the 1970s and beyond. Belatedly, the teachings of pioneers were recognised and they have moulded the attitudes of a generation first of factory managers and then those engaged in service businesses, government and non-profit organisations. Juran has already been mentioned, but the outstanding contribution came from Deming.

Spreading the word: the work of Deming

Paramount among developers of quality ideas was Deming, *see* Exhibit 7.7.[27] In the 1950s, when scientific management perspectives on control were common in the best companies, ideas of participation were revolutionary. Western industrialists thought that they could not be applied in their concerns. Quality Circles, invented in Japan in the early 1950s, did not reach the United Sates until 1974. Deming's ideas were ignored for so long. Forty years on, many have become incorporated in conventional management training and practice. Nowadays they seem less surprising and, perhaps, rather quaint. In proposing his famous 14 points, *see* Exhibit 7.8, Deming emphasised that they are the permanent obligations of top management, none of which is ever completely fulfilled.[28]

Exhibit 7.7 Edwards Deming: honour in his own land

W. Edwards Deming

From a background in physics and statistics, Deming became responsible in 1939 for mathematics and sampling at the United States Bureau of Census. His methods of statistical control achieved great improvements in the productivity and quality of the 1940 census. This accomplishment led to invitations to train industrial and military personnel and he taught many thousands how to improve quality. His first visit to Japan in 1947 was to prepare a census for the government of occupation. Yet it was in 1950 that he made his mark in Japan with a lecture series on quality control. Eight day-long seminars were attended by eighty per cent of the country's industrial leaders, some 230 people. It was essentially the same course he had delivered to United States personnel during the war.

While Deming based his work on advanced statistical methods, his contribution lay in presenting the ideas in a simple way. He showed the benefits of eliminating waste, doing the job right first time and regarding quality as participative learning rather than merely a system to be installed. Deming advocated the use of statistics to measure process variability, which was the chief culprit of poor quality. He then argued for continual investigation and fine-tuning to incrementally improve the production system. He proposed a framework for this continuous improvement.

The ideas were very influential in Japan, a country locked in poverty making inferior products. The Deming prize, created in 1951, remains the country's leading quality award. Deming became very well known and respected. Yet it was not until 1980 that his work was recognised in his own country. A national television report noted how United States output per capita had steadily fallen to seventh in the world and featured the work of Deming and others in Japanese manufacturing industry. NBC received thousands of requests for recordings and transcripts. So at the age of 80 Deming began consulting with leading United States manufacturers and lecturing to large audiences throughout the country. He died of cancer in 1993.

Deming was eventually listened to because of his experience of Japan and the simple rigour of his problem-solving approach. He pressed for the adoption of informed decision making based on good quality data. He advocated the plan–do–check–act (PDCA) cycle, *see* Fig. 7.8.[29] He called this the *Shewhart cycle* in recognition of the founder of statistical quality control but the Japanese, and others, call it the *Deming cycle*. It is an example of a family of learning cycles of which more detail is given in Chapter 24.

Using the PDCA cycle, managers are encouraged to start with small changes about things that are really important. The approach is set in the tradition of research and trial-and-error experimentation. Actions and reflections are grounded in observed data. The four stages of the continuous PDCA loop are:

■ *Plan*
Base changes on observed data. Decide whether an experiment is needed and how to conduct one.

Exhibit 7.8 Deming's *14 points*

1 *Create constancy of purpose*
Take the long-term view; innovate with materials, methods, services; invest in research, education and equipment of all kinds.

2 *Learn the new philosophy*
Be dissatisfied with current levels of defects, unsuited materials, poor training and management. Learn to be smart.

3 *Ask for evidence of process control along with incoming parts*
Buyers must learn control methods to include them in their orders. Relying on inspection is futile.

4 *Be prepared to reduce the number of suppliers*
Having more than one vendor means extra costs. Buyers should trade off quality and price and not just buy the cheapest.

5 *Use statistical methods to find out, in any trouble spot, what are the sources of trouble*
Judgement always gives the wrong answer when it comes to finding out where a fault lies.

6 *Institute modern aids to training on the job*
Use statistics to discover whether training would be beneficial. A fully trained person can do no better. Unsatisfactory people should be moved.

7 *Improve supervision*
Many supervisors were deplorable. Calling attention to every error is wrong and counterproductive. Supervisors should lead and use statistics to improve the production system.

8 *Drive out fear*
Employees may do jobs the wrong way because they are afraid to ask. Security means an absence of fear. Insecure people will not ask questions, report difficulties or discuss improvements.

9 *Break down barriers between departments*
Barriers hinder achieving the common goal: customer satisfaction.

10 *Eliminate numerical goals, slogans, pictures, posters, urging people to increase productivity, sign their work as an autograph, etc., so often plastered everywhere in the plant*
'ZERO DEFECTS' posters do not lead to people doing better jobs. Numerical targets lead to frustration, merely indicating management's lazy attempts to convert budget promises into shop floor action.

11 *Look carefully at work standards*
Consider whether quotas and numerical targets bring the claimed benefits. They make people forget quality. Deming rejected the practice of Management by Objectives.

12 *Train employees in simple, powerful statistical methods*
Deming's belief in statistics as a medium for investigation and communication made him see that it should be part of everyone's training. Experts should guide the rest.

13 *Vigorously retrain people in new skills*
Match developments in models, processes, materials, machinery, rules and so on.

14 *Top management must push every day on the above thirteen points*
Development is everyone's job. Leaders must take full responsibility for necessary changes.

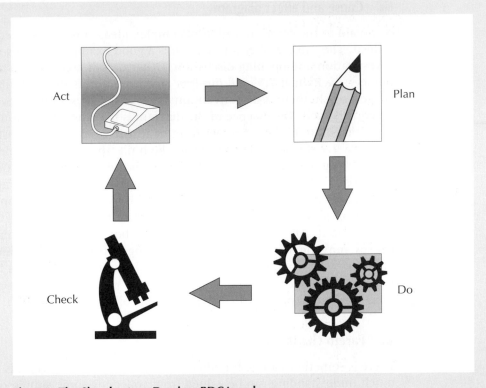

Fig. 7.8 The Shewhart, or Deming, PDCA cycle

- *Do*
  Make the change or do the experiment.
- *Check*
  Observe the effects of the change or experiment.
- *Act*
  Study the outcomes and establish the lessons to be learned. Confirm the change, or otherwise. Interpret the experiment. Start planning again.

The cycle is not original. As with many of his ideas, Deming's contribution was to draw them together and apply them both rigorously and vigorously to the quality question.

Techniques for quality investigation

Deming argued that data is vital to improving quality. Yet the temptation to use advanced statistical techniques must be resisted if participation is to be encouraged. To avoid the trap, several simple tools and charts have been devised to stimulate problem awareness and breakdown, and act as valuable records of group discussion.

Cause and effect diagrams

As an aid to the communication of complex ideas, a well-designed chart is difficult to beat. The cause and effect diagram is a good example. It helps when starting an investigation and opening discussion. Other names are *Ishikawa diagram*, after the pioneer, *see* Exhibit 7.5, and *fish-bone diagram*, after its form. While often drawn to suggest a fish, there is no conventional method of presentation. Stars or sprays will do equally well. The essence of the diagram is to record discussion and ideas. It is a practical aid to thinking and need not be restricted to quality questions.

Figure 7.9 shows how a chart may be built up during a problem identification session. Egg damage in a supermarket is on the agenda for a group. This is noted on a board and ideas, as they emerge, connected to it. The top diagram shows four suggestions for causes. The centre suggests how further ideas can be noted as the discussion proceeds. The bottom diagram records yet more thoughts and tidies the arrangement. An informal convention uses boxes to represent main limbs where causes may lie with the small bones suggesting some detailed sub-reasons. Therefore, the diagram summarises ideas of cause and effect in a hierarchical way. Having established a visual agenda, a team, or Quality Circle, can use the fish-bone diagram to plan further investigation, collect data and so on.

Pareto charts

There is sometimes a role for advanced statistical analysis. Yet it is remarkable how much understanding can be gained from collecting some simple records and summarising them in an uncomplicated way. This is what the Japanese call *speaking with data*.

To illustrate, let us imagine we are concerned about product faults in a plant rolling sheet steel for customers making washing machines and the like. Asking around, we may be told, 'We get many surface markings because …', or, 'It's quite common to find …', or, 'Sometimes it's as though …'. Staff will be aware of some issues but are unlikely to agree on the main causes. For instance, their assessment is likely to be dominated by the problems that have cropped up most recently. Judgement of which faults were most common over, say, a twelve-month period, would be unreliable.

The next step is to collect data. Instead of recycling scrap material without examination, we would assess the imperfections of each piece. (In fact, one would expect this to be normal procedure in a steel rolling mill.) The point of the exercise is to look more closely at the reasons for failure in order to make some sense of them. Juran was one who taught how Pareto charts can be used at this stage. This form of presentation shows the frequency of events in ranked order.

Figure 7.10 gives the results for the mill in two surveys a year apart. We can see that strides were made in the reduction of failures, especially those caused by roll marks in the steel. Yet pock marks in the surface remained the most serious problem, dominating the others in terms of material spoiled. The Pareto presentation helps to focus the problem-solving effort. In the TQM firm, it is normal to record critical parameters, not merely to appraise whether products are acceptable, but also to continually understand and improve the process. Kobe Steel Company

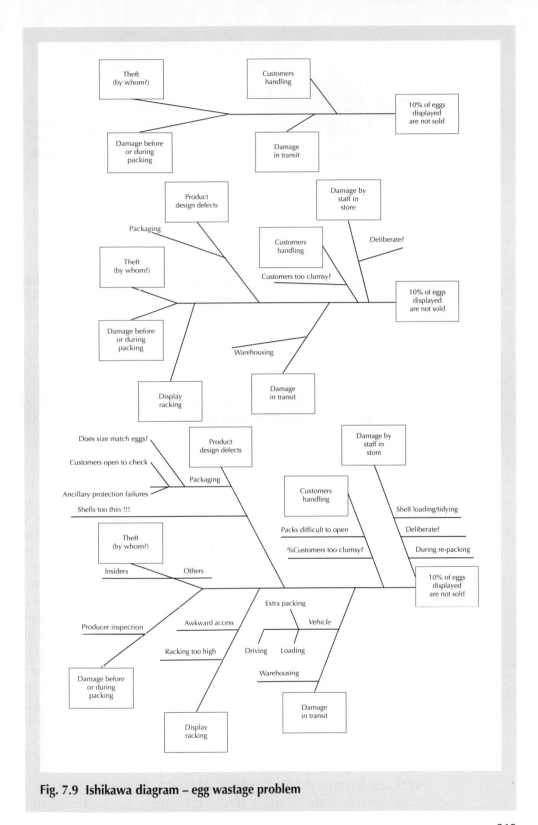

Fig. 7.9 Ishikawa diagram – egg wastage problem

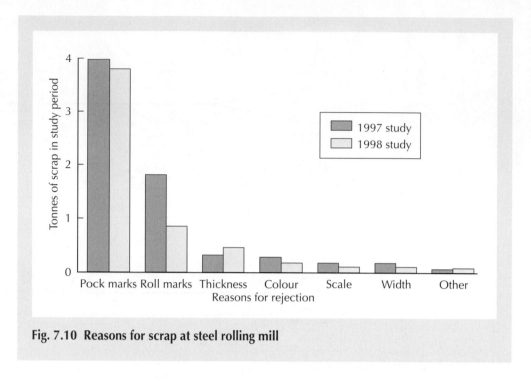

Fig. 7.10 Reasons for scrap at steel rolling mill

combined such internal appraisal with an external comparison with rivals' products to focus its efforts on improvement.[30]

Control charts

In a target-shooting competition, the 'chart' is produced directly by the process. In the first series, two competitors produce the results shown in Fig. 7.11. The left-hand contender, LH, has scored four inners with the rest of the ten shots spread around the next ring. The rival, RH has produced a tight cluster with none in the centre. If hitting the inner is the only way to score, then LH leads 4–0 and is the better quality shot. Yet whom would you back for the next series?

Next time, RH can improve by adjusting aim, either by aiming 'a little to the right and down a bit' or by adjusting the gun sight. On the other hand, LH can do little. It seems the aim is good with some unsteadiness. This competitor suffers from random variations (nerves?) which cannot be overcome by sight adjustment. LH showed maximum performance in the first series.

This example illustrates an approach to process quality control – laying out the results on charts. For a business application, we have a sanding machine that finishes timber furniture components. The critical parameter is thickness. One way of tracking the process is to take samples of five components every 15 minutes. How can we speak with this data?

Before going on to look at general cases, we can study one outcome, shown in Fig. 7.12. The measurements are recorded on a time chart. Note that all the raw data are written down. Summarising with means and measures of dispersion unnecessarily loses richness. In our case, there are echoes of the shooting range

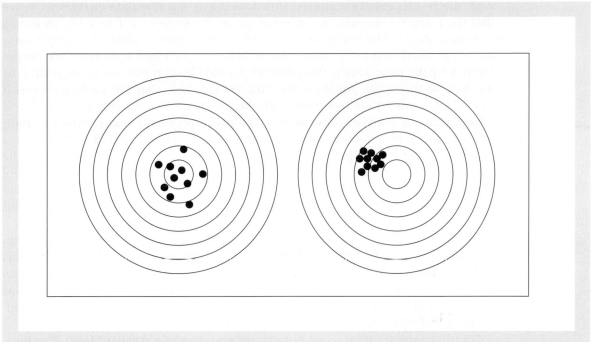

Fig. 7.11 Whose shooting is the best 'quality'?

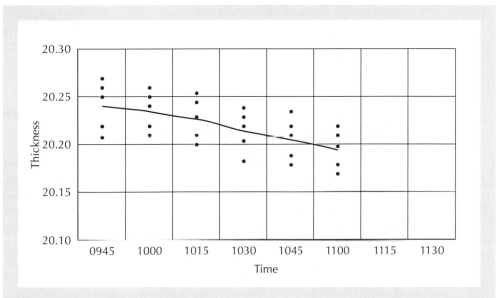

Fig. 7.12 Thickness of sanded timber panels

with the results closely scattered. Just looking at the raw data enables us to see that the machine produces a consistent group of samples each time but its setting is drifting slowly. The impression is confirmed by summary data: the sample average is sketched in and the range varies between 0.05 and 0.06 mm. We do not know why the panels are getting thinner. It could be that someone is adjusting the machine or that a component is wearing. We conclude that the sanding process is capable of consistent quality output but the setting needs investigation.

Note that there are always small variations in processes that cannot be eliminated. Deming reported an example of an employee at the Nashua Corporation, a producer of carbon paper, *see* Exhibit 7.9.[31] It would have been better for the employee to collect and measure samples, take a mean value and, using a control chart, decide whether any adjustment was necessary. If the variations were unacceptably large, the process should have been improved. Taguchi's approach to this issue is discussed below.

We have omitted the question of whether the sanding or spraying machines actually produce quality products. Study of this aspect requires targets and limits to have been set in advance. These boundaries form the framework for *control charts*, proposed first by Shewhart in 1924. Shewhart's statistical approach was aimed at separating common causes from special causes in process variation. Deming acknowledged that this formed the basis of much of his later work.

Control charts are used to set out process variables in a standard form. The horizontal axis shows time and the vertical axis represents a variable. This could be any property such as length, weight, electrical resistance, viscosity and so on. The vertical axis shows the target value and two *control limits*, upper and lower. These are usually set well within the *specification limits* outside which the product would be unacceptable. Typical control chart patterns are shown in Fig. 7.13. As with other charts, visual inspection can reveal a great deal and suggest the actions set out in Table 7.2.

Exhibit 7.9 Adjusting randomness out

The carbon was sprayed onto the paper through an adjustable nozzle. The employee running the process would measure the amount on the paper and, in the light of whether there was too much or too little, would open or close the nozzle. Was there anything wrong with this?

Even with a perfect process, random variations mean that half the product turns out below the mean and half above. And this is true whether or not the mean is fixed on the target value. Taking single sheets and adjusting the spray process in response to them meant that the operator was trying to adjust *randomness* out of the system. In fact it was found that this behaviour merely added variation.

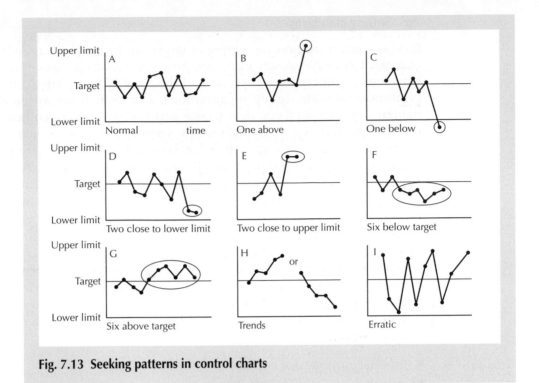

Fig. 7.13 Seeking patterns in control charts

Table 7.2 Responding to different control chart patterns

	Observation	Conclusion
A	Normal	Close to target – no action.
B **C**	One outside control limits	Take further samples to see if result freakish or part of emerging pattern.
D **E**	Two near control limits	Note danger signs. Take further samples before adjustment.
F **G**	Six to one side of target	Well within control limits but process not set properly. Establish why off target before adjustment.
H	Trends	Check cause of drift and repair or adjust. Increase frequency of monitoring to confirm problem cured.
I	Erratic	Process not good enough to operate within chosen limits. (Difficult to pick out trends and act as in B to H.)

Setting standards

Process control requires the setting of targets and control limits. Where do these originate? We have already examined how standards were established to mediate between customers' varied wishes and the need of many companies to achieve economies of scale. Inside organisations, however, there are many activities hidden from the market's view whose performance has a significant impact on overall results. How does an organisation know how well it is doing?

One answer lies in the growth of *benchmarking*. This is not mere imitation. It is about taking the best features from all other organisations and combining them in improved ways. Encompassed in the definition are two modes. The more straightforward one is done within the industry. The organisation monitors rivals' products and processes to enhance its own. Outside the industry, imaginative comparisons can be made between corresponding functions. For instance: ICL has measured its training methods against those of the Royal Mail; a United States regional airline compared its aircraft turnarounds with motor racing pit stops; the government has compared its tax and benefits office practices with the successful telephone-based insurance company Direct Line.[32]

Beyond quality itself, benchmarking can produce ideas across all management practice:

- Internal and external *products*;
- *Operational processes* used in the production and distribution of these products;
- *Infrastructure* including people, capital assets and other resources and how well they are used;
- *Management processes,* especially strategy and the management of change.

A key issue is picking the target or partner for a study. Exhibit 7.10 summarises some selection criteria.[33] The process can run into problems with other companies, particularly fierce rivals. Yet much information is available from three sources: it is published; products can be examined or experienced; and customers are often willing to compare rivals' offerings. Main gives some advice for use when approaching other organisations:[34]

- *Don't go fishing*
  Limit scope to areas that need improvement.

- *Send out the people who face the problems*
  Let people see for themselves. Raising awareness is a step along the path of change.

> Benchmarking is the practice of recognising and examining the best industrial and commercial practices in an industry or in the world and using this knowledge as the basis for improvement in all aspects of the organisation.

Exhibit 7.10	Picking the target	
Target organisations	**Advantages**	**Disadvantages**
Other in-house organisations	Ready access to information	Insufficiently convincing; biased
Domestic and foreign competitors	Much information accessible; very convincing	New information not easy; resistance; concern over leaks
'National class' of excellent organisations	Innovative; cooperation most likely	Different operating environments
'World class' of excellent organisations	Highly informative and innovative	Cultural differences hinder transfer; costly; time consuming

- *Consider exchange*
  The target may be involved in its own benchmarking. Exchange is possible; one should not ask questions that one is not prepared to answer. Commonly, a study is welcomed by the target organisation.

- *Steer away from legal problems*
  Avoid discussing price, market share and new product development with rivals.

- *Keep obtained information secure*
  An organisation that provides information may be alarmed if it is passed on.

Benchmarking can be both an eye-opener and a stimulus to action. When studying engine repair processes, British Airways found that technicians on Japanese Airlines took 40 minutes to turn round a 747 while its own people took 3 hours. The process also has its limits, however. It works well for high performance companies. Yet for moderate performers, the exercise may only generate confusion and low morale. There are plenty of basic actions they can take, from team building to improving links with customers, before they start to worry about becoming world class.

Quality in use

While many designers had an intuitive grasp of including extra strength or capacity in products, Taguchi developed methods of analysing optimising *robust quality*. This refers to *quality in use*, which is the performance of a product when it has been used, misused, overloaded (a little), knocked about in service, not overhauled on schedule, and so on. Customers assess products as much by how they perform outside the specification as how they conform to it in the first place. Naturally, designers attempt to overcome the effects of degradation by building in extra strength at key points. But, as Taguchi and Clausing emphasise,[35] many problems come not from weaknesses in individual items but from the interactions between slight variations in one item with others with which it forms systems.

> *In one case, it was asserted that minor deficiencies in the foundations of a new power station hall allowed the alignment of an electric generator set to move a few thousandths of a millimetre out of true. The vibrations significantly increased the rate of bearing wear and damaged the generator windings.*[36] *Taguchi's argument may have followed the following lines here. The generator building should be built properly. Yet unexpected conditions could allow the foundations to move. Therefore, good design of the electrical equipment should recognise this and be robust, that is operate successfully in spite of slight variations.*

Through the work of Taguchi and others, Japanese engineers became familiar with the design of experiments to test the robustness of their products. In 1989, Genichi Taguchi was awarded MITI's Purple Ribbon from the Emperor of Japan for his contribution to the development of industrial standards. His strength lay in applying statistical methods, not to quality *control*, where they had already found wide application, but to improving products and processes. A family of techniques, called 'Taguchi methods' has grown up. Yet Taguchi did not like the use of the term, especially when applied to standard statistical methods. Others acknowledge his contribution but criticise his use of statistics as inefficient and cumbersome.[37] Taguchi's own contributions focused on:

- making products robust compared with environmental conditions;
- making products insensitive to variations in their own components;
- minimising variation in manufacture.

To illustrate these points we can take an example from home economics, *see* Exhibit 7.11.

▨ Dominance

Juran proposed the idea of dominance. Depending on the process, quality frequently hinges on just one element. Therefore, that part of the process must be

---

Exhibit 7.11 Robust muffins

A food company is creating a new muffin mix. Staff in the laboratory can formulate mixes and test them under ideal conditions. Yet success depends to a great extent on quality in use, that is whether the mix will work well in domestic environments. Here oven temperatures are unreliable and baking time often a guess.

The mix that gives the best muffin under experimental conditions may not be the one that should be sold. Alterations in the formulation may produce a slightly inferior muffin. Yet it may be more robust in that the mix delivers an acceptable output over a wide range of temperatures and times.

A Taguchi experiment would then vary the *design factors* – the amounts of plain flour, baking powder, salt, egg and milk powders and sugar – and assess the sensitivity of the outcome to the *environmental factors* already mentioned. An endless series of trials is possible. Taguchi showed how data from trials could be arranged to discover a robust design efficiently.

the one that is most effectively controlled. Dominance, according to Juran, falls into four classes: set-up, machine, operator and component. For instance, there are some processes such as printing where the quality depends almost wholly on the set-up. In structural welding, on the other hand, operator skill is dominant. Table 7.3 outlines further examples and explanations. Different methods of appraisal relate to different conditions of dominance. Clearly, if more than one factor arises, then more than one type of appraisal is needed. But this would not be a robust process.

Conclusion: quality is (nearly) all

Two things about the so-called 'quality revolution' are surprising. First, it took until well into the 1980s before it was recognised in the West as a critical element in competition. Second, it was then taken up (and often dropped) so quickly. Perhaps many managers' key skills lie in jumping on bandwagons!

Basic lessons have been learnt; it is now accepted that quality is not produced by inspection and that it is not the cure for all ills. Now that such basics are integrated into everyday managerial common sense, some argue that quality is just good management. Yet this is to forget that quality is more than exhortations to see everyone as a customer or make zero defects a way of life. It refers to a set of processes, tools and techniques that can be applied to improving particular parameters of products, those that relate to fit, use, reliability and so on. For leading organisations such as Denso and Matsushita, TQM lies at the heart of their activities, identifiable yet integrated with all others. To succeed, organisations could follow what Binney identified among leading European companies:

Table 7.3 Features of dominance

Dominance	Explanation	Control needed	Examples
Set-up	With stable processes and reliable equipment, set-up is the key task.	Inspect first piece to check setting; inspect last to conform nothing went wrong.	Machining, printing, counting money using good equipment.
Machine	Tools wear, machines warm up, environment changes: all can cause drift.	Continuous control using charts for records.	Spray painting, glass making, weaving, wood machining are sensitive to minor changes.
Operator	Variations in skill and experience show through into output differences.	Comparing performance using charts.	Baking, brush painting, cooking, dress making.
Components	Quality influenced by component variations.	Inspection of inputs; control parameters early in process.	Assembly plants; processes using natural ingredients.

- leaders should be forthright and assertive about quality, yet listen to questions and problems about how it can be improved;

- managers should provoke involvement rather than demand it and impose solutions;

- quality should be integrated into the core of the business – activities from recruitment and training to measurement and evaluation should support it;

- all should learn, experiment, don't blame and learn some more.[38]

There is a drawback to Binney's exhortations. In using words such as *forthright, assertive, provoke* or even *should*, he is not alone in revealing attitudes about the role of leaders in TQM. Should they appear to be so forceful? One could ask, 'What happened to ideas of empowerment and participation?' Chapter 16 investigates styles of leadership to find what approaches may be most appropriate to the introduction of TQM.

Quick check up *Can you ...*

- Define quality;
- Clarify why quality is important;
- Summarise the costs of quality;
- Distinguish product and process standards;
- Give a definition for TQM;
- Describe a Quality Circle;

- Translate *kaizen* and *gemba*;
- Summarise three limitations of TQM;
- Trace the Deming cycle;
- Sketch Ishikawa, Pareto and control charts;
- Outline the benchmarking process;
- Suggest why people may resist the introduction of TQM.

Questions

Chapter review

7.1 Explain why there are so many definitions of quality and how a manager can respond to them.

7.2 What are the costs of quality and how would you explain these to a confectioner?

7.3 Assess the strengths and limitations of TQM.

7.4 Why was the work of Deming and Juran accepted in Japan some 30 years before recognition in the West?

Application

7.5 Why did Churchill (*see* opening case) change its product quality policy? What characteristics of tableware are important to its customers?

7.6 Identify quality dimensions for the products you have on your desk or in your bag or pockets. To which do national or international standards apply?

Investigation

7.7 How can a supplier of domestic gas or electricity use quality to improve its competitive position? Compare rival companies to support your points.

The Madras cheque-clearing system[39]

In the Madras area there are about 800 branches of some 50 banks. Cheque clearing is the responsibility of the National Clearing Cell, a division of the Reserve Bank. Since 1987, the process has been automated around a high-speed reader-sorter system (HSRSS) for cheque data capture, linked to a mainframe computer. Cheques paid in at one bank and drawn on another are processed by the NCC. The system sorts the cheques by bank and branch code and prints reports, including the balances for each bank.

The HSRSS reads data from the magnetic ink character recognition band along the bottom of each cheque. As with United Kingdom cheques (which use optical characters) basic data is pre-printed. This covers serial number, account number, branch code and so on. The payment is encoded by the branch after the customer has presented the cheque. Those that have incorrect codes, or are of poor quality, are rejected by the HSRSS. They are then sorted and their data is entered into the system by hand. Two batches of cheques are returned to each branch. Those accepted by the machine are fully grouped while the other has to be separated by the branch. Therefore, a faulty cheque is sorted twice.

The efficiency of the system depends on the HSRSS acceptance rate. Following complaints from banks about the amount of labour-intensive work they were expected to do, it was found that the cheque reject rate was about 10 per cent. The manual work was leading to high error rates in data processing which in turn created reconciliation problems among the banks. They realised that the shift to computer processing had not resulted in the promised benefits.

In defence, the NCC manager pointed to the peculiarities of cheques presented in Madras and the high proportion that originated elsewhere in India.

After about a year of debate, steps were taken to improve NCC's internal processing. The tuning of the HSRSS equipment was adjusted and the whole operating area was cleaned to remove all traces of dust. This reduced the rejects by 1 per cent. Simultaneously NCC sent new instructions to the banks to improve the data encoding but this had little effect.

The next step was for NCC to inspect all incoming cheques and attempt to repair the bad ones. While this succeeded in cutting another 2 per cent from the reject rate, it was only achieved at high labour expense. The intervention was abandoned.

Finally, the NCC decided to investigate the encoding procedures at the branches. Training of staff was carried out by five NCC staff across a sample of 50 offices. For two months little happened, but, as more branches were trained, the reject rate fell to 4.5 per cent. The training programme was extended, new operators had to be taught and all branches had to designate one person with the responsibility of ensuring that only quality cheques were sent to NCC. People from the branches visited the HSRSS operation to learn of the impact of proper encoding on the whole operation. These steps led to great improvements but rejects refused to come down to the international norm of 3 per cent.

Further studies analysed the errors in more detail. It was realised that the bank branches were answerable for only one of the five information fields encoded on each cheque. The others were the printers' responsibility. Quality was not good enough. At a meeting at NCC, the printers agreed to submit a hundred-cheques for proof checking. Print runs could run into millions. To minimise machine idle time after set-up, the NCC, in its turn, promised to return the test batch, with a report, in half an hour. Some printers agreed, others did not. Later, it was found that those who had cooperated produced rejects at fewer than 1 per cent. Soon, the others fell into line and the total reject rate fell to 2 per cent.

The NCC manager then set about standardising the new procedures. It was found that the standards could be met by different personnel, rotated around jobs, thus proving that the standards were 'people proof'. A regular series of meetings with the banks was started. It shared opinion on operations and discussed suggestions for further improvement.

The project covered the work of thousands of employees. It had the backing of senior management. What had begun as a response to problems of poor service led to a transformation in competence levels and empowerment of employees. There was a significant reduction in costs, although that was not the intention. The labour devoted to sorting was cut, most cheques were sorted automatically and reconciliation errors fell to negligible levels.

Questions

1 Identify examples of the costs of quality in the HSRSS.

2 Use an Ishikawa diagram to express the causal links in NCC's service quality problem.

3 If you were investigating the causes of failure of the system, what sorts of data would you collect and how would you present it?

4 What would have been the relevance of a benchmarking study in this case?

Bibliography Perhaps the most readable works by a leading advocate are Crosby's *Quality without Tears: The art of hassle-free management*, New York: McGraw-Hill, 1995, or *Quality is Free: The art of making quality certain*, New York: New American Library, 1993. Classics are Juran's, *Juran on Planning for Quality*, New York: Free Press, 1988 or Deming's, *Out of the Crisis*, Cambridge: CUP, 1988.

References

1. Midas (1995) 'Far East is potty about our china', *Mail on Sunday*; News Digest (1996) 'Churchill China advances 42%', *Financial Times*, 27 March; 'Churchill China is boosted by popularity of eating out', *Birmingham Post*, 27 March; 'Churchill China – Quality pays off', *Investors Chronicle*, 12 April.
2. Zeithamal, V.A., Parasuraman, A. and Berry, L. (1990) *Delivering Service Quality: Balancing consumer perceptions and expectations*, New York: Free Press, 26.
3. Williams, Steve (1995) 'Cross-cultural contextual differences in perceptions of seafood quality', *Asia Pacific Journal of Quality Management*, **4** (**1**).
4. Crosby, Philip B. (1984) *Quality without Tears*, New York: McGraw-Hill, 60.
5. British Standards Institution (1987) *BS 4778 Part 1* Section 3; Johnson, R. and Winchell, W.O. (1989) *Production and Quality*, Milwaukee, Wis.: American Society for Quality Control, 2.
6. Ho, S. (1993) 'Transplanting Japanese Management Techniques', *Long Range Planning*, **26** (**4**), 81–9.

7. Maani, Kanubiz E., Putterill, Martin S. and Sluti, Donald G. (1995) 'Empirical analysis of quality improvements in manufacturing', *Asia Pacific Journal of Quality Management*, **4** (**1**), http://www.mcb.co.uk/services/articles/documents/apjqm/maani.htm

8. Deming, W. Edwards (1981) 'Improvement of quality and productivity through action by management', *National Productivity Review*, **1** (**1**), reprinted as Reading 7 in Latona, J.C. and Nathan, J.(eds) (1994) *Cases and Readings in Production and Operations Management*, Needham Heights, Mass.: Allyn and Bacon, 223–36.

9. Crosby (1984) *op. cit.*

10. Lister, Richard (1994) 'Beyond TQM …', *Management Services*, May, 8–13.

11. Deming (1981) *op. cit.*, 223.

12. Rust, Kathleen C. (1995) 'Managing the costs of quality', *Management Accounting*, **77** (**2**), August, 33–7.

13. Gador, Brad (1989) 'Quest for quality – Tennant Company, Minneapolis, MN', *Target*, Fall, 27–9.

14. Carr, Lawrence P. (1995) 'How Xerox sustains the cost of quality', *Management Accounting*, **77** (**2**), August, 26–32.

15. Swanson, Edward T. and Jambekar, Anil B. (1995) 'A technology choice for noise reduction: a quality management case study', *International Journal of Quality and Reliability Management*, **12** (**7**), September–October, 44–56.

16. Henkoff, R. (1993) 'The hot new seal of quality', *Fortune*, 28 June, 116–17.

17. Ho (1993) *op. cit.*, 87.

18. Dickson, Tim (1993) 'Management quality street cred – TQM is struggling to make an impact in Europe', *Financial Times*, 20 October, 16.

19. Westbrook, Roy (1995) 'Organising for total quality: case research from Japan', *International Journal of Quality and Reliability Management*, **12** (**4**), April, 8–25.

20. Imai, Masaaki (1992) 'Solving quality problems using common sense', *International Journal of Quality and Reliability Management*, **9** (**5**) 71–5.

21. *Ibid.*, 72–3.

22. Peters, Tom (1994) 'Theatre on the retail stage', *Independent on Sunday: Business*, 6 March, 26.

23. Imai (1992) *op. cit.*, 74.

24. Dawson, Patrick (1994) 'Total Quality Management', in Storey, John (ed.) *New Wave Manufacturing Strategies*, London: Paul Chapman, 103–21.

25. McCabe, Darren (1996) 'The best laid schemes of TQM: strategy, politics and power', *Industrial Relations Journal*, **27** (**1**), March, 28–38.

26. Heller, Robert (1995) 'The heart of the quality matter', *Management Today*, June, 25.

27. Levy, Claudia (1993) 'W. Edwards Deming dies; his lectures on quality control fuelled Japan's rise', Obituary, *The Washington Post*, 21 December; full text on http://deming.eng.clemson.edu/pub/den/files/demob.txt

28. Deming (1986) *op. cit.*, 229–35. Various versions and interpretations of the points can be found. For example: by Deming himself, (1985) 'Transformation of Western style of management', *Interfaces*, **15** (**3**), 6–11, (1986) *Out of the Crisis*, Cambridge, Mass: MIT Press, 23–96 and (1991) 'Philosophy continues to flourish', *APICS – The Performance Advantage*, **1** (**4**); Aguayo, R. (1991) *Dr Deming: The man who taught the Japanese about quality*, London: Mercury, 121–2. Curiously, Aguayo has 16 points in his list of 14!

29. Deming (1986) *op. cit.*, 88.

30. Dale, Barrie and Asher, Mike (1989) 'Total quality control: Lessons European executives can learn from Japanese companies', *European Management Journal*, **7** (**4**), 493–503.

31. Quoted by Schmenner, Roger W. (1993) *Production/ Operations Management*, Fifth edition, New York: Macmillan, 122–3.
32. Trapp, Roger (1994) 'Benchmarking moves on to bench-testing', *Independent on Sunday: Business*, 9 January, 13.
33. Ohinata, Yoshinobu (1994) 'Benchmarking: The Japanese experience', *Long Range Planning*, **27** (**4**), 48–53.
34. Main, Jeremy (1992) 'How to steal the best ideas around', *Fortune*, **126** (**8**), 19 October, 104.
35. Taguchi, Genichi and Clausing, Don (1980) 'Robust quality', *Harvard Business Review*, **68** (**1**), January–February, 49–59.
36. At the time of writing, legal proceedings were expected.
37. Box, G., Bisgaard, S. and Fung, C. (1988) 'An explanation and critique of Taguchi's contributions to quality engineering', *Quality and Reliability Engineering International*, **4** (**2**), 123–31.
38. Binney, G. (1993) *Making Quality Work – Lessons from Europe's leading companies*, London: Economist Intelligence Unit.
39. Sudhakar, Kaza (1994) 'Reject rate reduction at the Reserve Bank of India', in Dean, James W. and Evans, James R. *Total Quality: Management, Organisation and Strategy*, St. Paul, Minn.: West Publishing Co., 167–8.

8

Enterprise

Chapter objectives

When you have finished studying this chapter, you should be able to:

- define entrepreneur and distinguish between enterprise and small business;

- describe the scale and importance of the SME sector in the United Kingdom and outline comparisons with other countries;

- evaluate the extent to which entrepreneurs can be distinguished from the rest of the population and describe the usefulness and limitations of such approaches;

- analyse why and how government policies towards SMEs are shifting from stimulating start-ups to picking winners and encouraging growth among them;

- explain the function of intrapreneurs and how some firms succeed in stimulating their activity;

- identify key management problems constraining the success of owner-managers, suggesting how they can be overcome.

The rise of Intrason[1]

When Patrice Flippe and his wife set out in 1984, with a capital of FF20 000 (£2200), they could not have foreseen that a decade later their enterprise would have created the world's most advanced miniature hearing aid. At 29, Flippe had little business experience. After dropping out of medical studies, he had taken dental technician training more from interest than need. Meanwhile, he supported himself from street selling. After four years at the *Fédération française de l'audition* (Hearing Association), sporting an earring and being unable to stand hierarchies, the aspiring entrepreneur took the plunge and founded Intrason. Producing conventional in-ear devices, the company thrived, reaching sales of FF11 million by 1989.

At the start of the 1990s, Flippe moved into top gear to create a new device. The small business was transformed by bringing in other managers and investors. In came Flippe's brother-in-law, Christian Friconnet, who had experience at Moulinex and Bébé Confort, and a Briton, Desmond Greener, who was an expert in the hearing aid business. Venture capitalist companies took up 49 per cent of the shares and a loan of FF2.2 million came from a government technology fund. In four years, the enterprise invested FF12 million to create the 'Alpha'. During this time, Flippe took out a FF12 million key man insurance policy on the life of the company's technical director, without whom the product could not have been developed.

Ready in 1994, the Alpha was a true high technology device. Its eight parameters were matchable by computer to each patient's hearing. Smallest in its class, it was invisible once placed in the ear. Tiny power consumption gave the battery a twelve-day life.

The future is bright for such products. There are some 40 million aurally impaired people in OECD countries, of whom five million live in France. Yet high prices mean that only 700 000 have prostheses. The deafness market is growing as the population ages and many young people carelessly damage their hearing.

Having a unique product is not enough; distribution is vital. Lacking its own network, Intrason appointed distributors in 1992 in the United States, followed by Belgium, Italy, Germany and Spain. Then came the coup of a five-year agreement in Japan. Turnover in 1995 reached FF33 million, expected to double the following year. Export orders were estimated at FF450 million for the next five years.

Abroad, the Alpha was not sold made up. Intrason supplied kits containing the key technical components. Local agents make the mould to fit the patient's ear. Retail prices were three times the price paid for a kit. To avoid missing this potential profit, Intrason needed to quickly develop its own world network to really push its product in the market against competitors such as Starkey, Siemens and Philips.

FF50 million was needed to fund the network. Flippe thought hard about a stock market flotation, yet the rules on disclosure were unattractive. He preferred to remain the sole boss and was careful to keep to just below the 50-employee threshold at which a works council would be required under French law. Yet he wanted to realise the goodwill value of Intrason, which he estimated at FF60 million. The Flippes dreamt, 'We can begin with a year or two's holiday sailing round the world.' In early 1995, a company specialising in small businesses was instructed to arrange a sale. Before the end of 1996, having tripled their value, the venture capitalists were due to sell their investments.

It was likely that the business would be absorbed by a large group, Japanese or American. The Flippes' continued involvement would depend on negotiations. Bubbling with new ideas, the entrepreneur foresaw a national network in France along the lines of Krys or other chains of opticians. The Alpha was selling at FF2200 francs to French hearing specialists who charged their customers FF7800.

Introduction

In using the terms 'enterprise' and 'entrepreneur' in the story of Intrason, we have met two words that have come to preoccupy many politicians, managers and scholars. For governments throughout the world, a problem has been to kindle the 'enterprise culture' which is seen as both stimulating growth and generating new jobs. Often, the term 'rekindle' may be more relevant because of the common feeling that the spirit of enterprise has been lost. For the manager, enterprise has become associated with innovation and dynamic adaptability. In large organisations, leaders have sought how to reproduce the same lost spirit to revitalise their sagging hierarchies. For scholars, the words pose something of a puzzle. We seek answers to questions from 'Who are entrepreneurs,?' and 'How are they created?', to 'What government policies encourage their activities and nurture their businesses?'.

Popular books on enterprise fall into two categories. The 'How to do it' book focuses on setting up a small business, almost from scratch. Chapters cover initial market surveys, the first visit to the bank, the purchase of the basic equipment and so on. Clearly, many entrepreneurs establish small businesses but then what happens? Some businesses disappear, some remain small, and a very few thrive to become the large corporations of the next generation. The second category is 'How I (or they) did it'. These represent *post hoc* descriptions with some attempts to draw general conclusions when several case histories are brought together. What these sources reveal is that entrepreneurs are involved in businesses of all kinds and sizes, not always small. This illustrates that the terms enterprise and small business, so frequently taken as synonymous, are not interchangeable.

This chapter takes neither the 'how to do it' nor the 'how I did it' approach. We can learn from the experience of practitioners yet, as with so many other aspects of management, this must be enriched with the results of research and reflection. In aiming to blend and enrich these two aspects, the chapter draws on both the experience and the research traditions. It starts by examining the nature of enterprise and small business. Then it looks at their origins and how development can be stimulated through public policy. Finally, there is a review of entrepreneurs as managers facing problems.

What do *enterprise* and *small business* mean?

Reference is often made to the small firm and the enterprise as if they were the same. Indeed, this merging is bound up in the label *Small and Medium Enterprise* used to describe any business whose size is below a defined level. We shall begin our discussion by distinguishing between the two ideas.

Enterprise and entrepreneurs

Enterprise, and associated terms with the same root, are used in many ways. For example, when discussing the notion of 'enterprise culture' from a sociological perspective, Burrows points out the lack of an agreed definition; the idea slips between a movement and a petit bourgeois class label related to self-employment.[2] Others take enterprise to simply mean 'business' and entrepreneurs the people who perform that role. To many, however, entrepreneurs are more special than this. Deakins compares a range of views that are summarised in Exhibit 8.1.[3] While there is a consensus that the entrepreneur is a key element in the economy, divergence between two main lines of thought continues. One concentrates on willingness to accept risks while the other stresses the innovatory function. Putting these together, we can summarise by saying that entrepreneurs:

- Are agents of adjustment. This means that, in being flexible in their choice of business and the way they conduct it, they both lead and satisfy the adjustment needs of the whole economy.

- Apply innovative ideas, changing the way businesses convert inputs into outputs.

- Go beyond replicating the current processes in the market. They find new marketing processes to reach new customers or satisfy existing customers in new ways.

- Take risks.

In each of these aspects, the entrepreneur breaks new ground, usually seeking incremental rather than great change. In this way the person is a calculative risk taker yet not an out-and-out gambler or fool. Yet many entrepreneurs lack formal skills in risk management. Deakins illustrates this in a study of how small firms insure aspects of the business. More than 90 per cent of a sample of 76 took out

---

Exhibit 8.1 What is an entrepreneur? Five perspectives

The intermediary is alert to profitable opportunities for trade. The opportunity arises from information not possessed by others yet which is freely available. The intermediary's advantage is alertness, for otherwise there are no special skills required. (Kirzner)

The originator goes beyond being alert to imagining opportunities. This is a special skill involved in not only finding openings amid uncertainty but in identifying their potential and assembling resources to exploit them. (Shackle)

The innovator relies on aptitude to develop new technology. This gives a temporary advantage over other firms who can eventually respond by extending or replacing the innovation. There is some difference with the intermediary, who may look to exploit the innovations of others, and the originator, whose function may equally lie in marketing as in technology. (Schumpeter)

The risk taker gains profit as the reward for carrying risk. This person assesses the uncertain future and ventures in business according to that judgement. All business faces risk that cannot be covered by insurance. This is the risk of being in business itself. (Knight)

The co-ordinator makes judgements and co-ordinates resources. Central to this view is access to resources without which the entrepreneur could not function. This means capital. As the economy changes, the co-ordinator is first to adapt, matching changing supply and demand. In fact, co-ordinators make the economy work. (Casson) insurance to cover motors, property and public and employer's liability. There are, of course, statutory and contractual requirements in these areas. Fewer than 10 per cent, in contrast, had insurance for health and life, personal accident, travel, key persons, professional indemnity or patents and copyright.[4] This shows that they took risks that they could have insured against. It is, however, unclear whether the firms were unaware of the possibilities or had decided not to insure because the premiums were too high. The data, however, underlines the point that the risk is real. The entrepreneur is investing personal resources, including taking chances on health and personal accidents, for economic gain. As one commented, 'Insurance is all very well, but the real risk is losing everything'.

Summing up, *an entrepreneur is a person who shows willingness and ability to take reasonable risks for gain in business or commerce.* Following on, *enterprise is the behaviour shown by entrepreneurs, which is taking reasonable risks using personal resources.* Note that the definitions say nothing about the size or type of business activity. As we shall see, being an entrepreneur involves using a wide range of management skills in a variety of sizes of business.

Small business

A small business is usually defined by some arbitrary criterion such as sales or number of employees. Unfortunately, such criteria, being established to cover all cases, ignore the firm's perception of size as compared with the norms for its industry. For instance, Hendry and others studied a sample of firms in which the one with most employees (355) saw itself as a small independent bakery, while a visitor bureau (44) and software company (130) each perceived themselves as large for the industries they were in.[5] In competitive terms, some nominally small businesses are large and vice versa.

Relativist definitions of size do not suit governments or other agencies seeking to develop policies favouring small businesses. Even discussing a sector such as that comprising *Small and Medium Enterprises (SMEs)* is inappropriate. There are two reasons. First, with 500 employees having emerged as a widely accepted upper limit of the SME range, some 99 per cent of all firms are included. Second, the character and problems of a firm with several hundred staff will be very different to one with a handful. A more detailed taxonomy is needed. The European Union uses three sub-categories of SMEs, illustrated in Table 8.1. This gives data for the United Kingdom's almost three million businesses.[6] With the proportion of employees in large UK firms having fallen from 43 per cent in 1979, the country has moved close to the average of the EU. The latter's 15.7 million firms are divided into: 14.5 million micro-enterprises; 1 million small firms; 70 000 medium and 12 000 large.[7] Employment is roughly equally split among micro-firms, SMEs and large firms.

Among firms in the micro, small and medium categories, there is a mixture of those owned and managed by the same people and others where ownership and management are separated, as is normal in much larger organisations. Gibb argues that the essence of small business lies in the former, that is firms that are owned and run by the same people. We can expect them to require and develop entrepreneurial attributes. Yet there will be some small businesses whose owners are not entrepreneurial or who take little active part in the business, employing professional managers instead.

Table 8.1 Firm size, numbers and share of employment: UK 1991

Label	Number of staff	% UK firms	% UK employment
Micro	up to 10	92.5	28.2
Small	11–100	6.8	22.2
Medium	101–500	0.6	16.8
Large	over 500	0.1	32.8
		100	100

Entrepreneurs, therefore, tend to be found in the large number of micro and small firms. Exceptions are twofold. Some grow their firms into large ones while others find their way to the top of existing companies. The latter, the so-called *intrapreneurs* who display entrepreneurial attributes within large businesses or institutions, are few.

Distinguishing between those SMEs that are unlikely to change, and those with growth potential has become important to governments. Job creation comes from growing firms. Governments throughout the world have begun to recognise this point, although the problem of identifying potential remains. We can give some examples of policy, although variable definitions mean that numbers are not directly comparable. A study among the 18 countries of the Asia Pacific Economic Cooperation (APEC) group showed the importance of SMEs in member economies, especially in manufacturing. One third of manufacturing establishments, with 50 per cent of that sector's employment, are held by SMEs.[8] Japan's SMEs number 99.1 per cent of the country's 6.5 million businesses, and account for 77 per cent of employment.[9] Some five years after the velvet revolution in Eastern Europe, SMEs accounted for 60 per cent of employment in Poland, 55 per cent in Hungary and 50 per cent in the Czech Republic. The number of SMEs in Bulgaria rose from 23 000 in 1989 to 360 000 by 1994.[10]

What makes an entrepreneur?

Some people are naturally more entrepreneurial than others. Furthermore, they show the tendency more at different times of their lives and in different situations. Explanations vary from those concentrating on personality traits to those that examine the relationships between a person and the social environment. An extension of the latter point is the question of how much entrepreneurship can be learned, and therefore taught. For instance, it can be argued that one function of business training is to give people confidence to take on responsibilities, therefore removing a personal barrier. We shall examine personal, social and situational factors.

■ Personal factors

Researchers have examined personal traits for clues to explain many aspects of human behaviour including leadership, *see* Chapter 16, and entrepreneurship. For the latter, the approach has been summarised by Deakins.[11] He ranks the following traits in order of importance in the make-up of the entrepreneur:

- *Need for achievement*
  Monetary gain is not the sole driving force behind entrepreneurs. They gain satisfaction from solving problems and taking responsibility for their outcomes.

- *Desire to be in control of environment and destiny*
  This is the preference for being one's own boss rather than being employed (and directed) by another.

- *Willingness to take risks*
  The consensus on this point has already been noted.

- *Need to be independent*
  This is the wish of not having to rely on, or be responsible to, others.

- *Unconventional personality*
  This is the feeling of being out of place in a large firm.

- *Capability for innovation*
  Innovation can relate to any aspect of the business.

Some studies have tried to establish whether such traits distinguish entrepreneurs from the rest of the population. Are entrepreneurs really different to others? Clearly some factors are required of all successful managers, especially the important need for achievement and desire to be in control. For not only are managers directly responsible to other officials, and hence occupy dependent roles, but also they are responsible for others, exercise freedom and take risks.

A further question concerns whether entrepreneurs are born or made. If such traits are needed by both managers and entrepreneurs, then entrepreneur development should have much in common with management development. In other words, many aspects of entrepreneurial behaviour can be acquired through learning and experience. People's ability to learn is the key skill separating the successful from the rest.

Answers to these questions could be useful, for example, in predicting whether an individual is likely to succeed. The approach, however, has been criticised by Chell and others.[12] As with other aspects of human activity, it is inappropriate to pick out just one or a few factors when entrepreneurs are clearly characterised by their diversity. In addition, factors in the social and economic environments, which may have a greater effect than personal differences are ignored by this approach.

■ Social factors

Beyond personality, there is evidence that social factors influence the likelihood of a person becoming an owner-manager.[13] Evidence includes:

- peaks in the age profile of the self-employed;
- the best single predictor of self-employment is whether the family has included some form of the same;
- self-employment is more prevalent among married than among single people;
- self-employment follows from social marginalisation and is more common in some ethnic groups.

While such factors may be noted as more typical of entrepreneurs than others, they do not help much with the question of what makes an entrepreneur. For instance, from correlational data, one could argue that marriage encourages self-employment in some way. The danger is the same evidence supports the opposite argument – self-employed people are more likely to get married!

Age profiles

The interaction of personal and social factors is illustrated by data on the age of the self-employed. One study found almost half business starters were aged between 30 and 45.[14] Others identified two peaks in the age profile of self-employed people, namely 35–44 and over 65.[15] A different approach compared the growth rate of small privately owned companies with the age of their directors. The companies, with a minimum turnover of £2 million, were beyond the start-up phase. Figure 8.1 gives a growth index with 100 as the mean value. We can see that companies with younger directors grew more quickly, whether the measure used was profit, turnover or employment. A further explanation of the effect can be sought in the way directors' motivation changes. Hunt's scale compares drive for achievement against the drive for comfort, with zero meaning they are equally important. The tendency for older directors to prefer comfort can be seen in Fig. 8.2.[16]

Although the measures and age groupings in such surveys do not correspond, they all point to changes with age. We can suggest that the peak among the 'thirty-somethings' depends on their having gained sufficient experience to set up in business while retaining the drive for achievement. The second peak among over 65s is explained by their minimal chances of formal employment. Small-scale self-employment supplements pensions.

Family businesses

Self-employment runs in families. This is not only because ownership is inherited but seems to follow from values and skills that parents give to their children. Inheritance may be a mixed blessing. There is evidence to support the adage, 'Rags to rags in three generations'. Abbott and Hay show that the growth rates of family firms tended to slow as second and subsequent generations took over, *see* Fig. 8.3.[17] They conclude that offspring tend to 'harvest' the businesses more than the founders. Costa makes the same observation. Just 8 per cent of family businesses reach the third generation. Decline in family businesses is not inevitable, however. Examples such as the Mogi family, engaged in making soy sauce since 1630, show how careful attention to strategic and succession planning is required.[18]

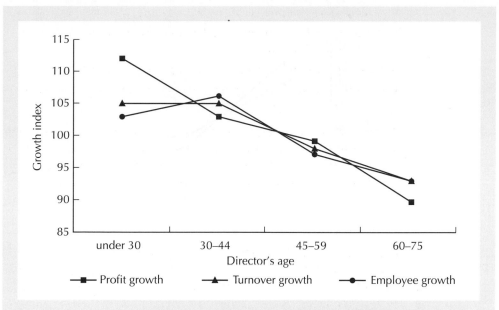

Fig. 8.1 Growth in profit, turnover and employment compared with directors' ages

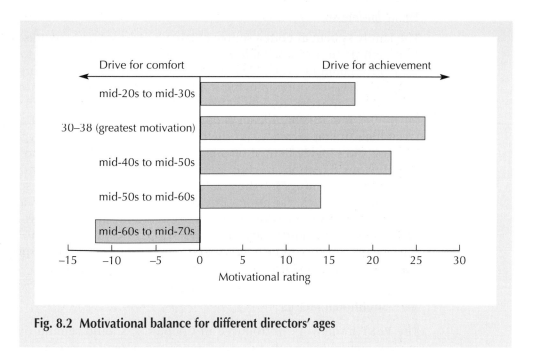

Fig. 8.2 Motivational balance for different directors' ages

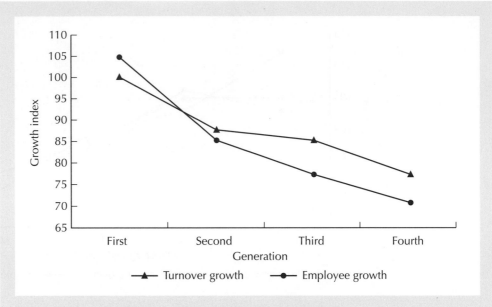

Fig. 8.3 Rate of growth of generations of family businesses

Ethnic businesses

The family system as both a source of labour and contact networks is important for some ethnic minorities. Table 8.2 gives self-employment rates for groups in the United Kingdom in 1986.[19] They can be compared with the majority, Whites, who had relatively low unemployment and self-employment, indicating a preference for, and easier access to, jobs. Afro-Caribbeans experienced high unemployment but found few feasible business opportunities. Pakistanis and Bangladeshis also faced high unemployment. Yet their rate of self-employment suggested that small business did provide limited openings for the large numbers who had lost jobs in the previous recession. In contrast, for Indians, self-employment seemed to provide enough openings for those affected. Ward concluded that social differences accounted for such variations in experience. Asians typically used family and ethnic networks to provide flexible resources and market access, for example in the clothing and knitwear industries supplying international markets. Afro-Caribbeans, on the other hand, relied much more on product specialisation (for instance, record and fashion shops, hot bread) and local markets.

■ Situational factors

The PEST framework, introduced in Chapter 3, should remind us of many other environmental factors that may influence the potential of a business. Drawing on the work of Mason,[20] the most important factors are:

■ an industrial structure that favours small independent units;

■ employees working in problem solving occupations with close contacts with customers;

Table 8.2 Unemployment and self-employment rates for ethnic groups in the United Kingdom

		Business participation rate	
All groups 11%		**High**	**Low**
Unemployment rate	High	Pakistanis/ Bangladeshis 23%	Afro-Caribbeans 5%
	Low	Indians 19%	Whites 11%

Figures indicate percentage of working age population in self-employment in 1986

- clusters of technically advanced small firms;
- high awareness of small business activities;
- banks and financial institutions attuned to the needs of small businesses;
- available help and advice;
- an affluent population providing a market;
- social attitudes favouring individualism.

Based on the list, a variation among regions in the rate of new business formation would be expected. In Great Britain, South-East England shows the greatest increase while North-West and South-West England, Wales and southern Scotland have the lowest.[21] Items in the list can be seen as 'pull factors', which draw the entrepreneur towards the opportunity to set up a new venture, and 'push factors', which propel people away from traditional activity. In South-East England, for instance, the fast growing sectors of finance, property and professional services have acted as pull factors for entrepreneurs. In other areas, situational effects from unemployment to government subsidies have pushed many towards setting up businesses. Cleveland is an area where government policies appeared to succeed.

> *At the end of the 1970s Cleveland began to experience high unemployment following decline of its large-scale manufacturing industries based around chemicals and steel. Lack of appropriate skills, capital and a tradition of small firm ownership kept the area in deep recession. During the 1980s, however, there was a significant rise in the number of new firms, heralding the new enterprise culture. Yet, as Keasey and Watson note, many new businesses offered services, from hairdressing to car repairs, that depended on the local market. This rapid increase in self-employment in marginal occupations came from unemployed workers with no other prospects. While this may have brought tempo-rary relief to them, offering income higher than state benefit but lower than previous levels, it hardly formed a basis for new growth firms of the future.[22]*

The effect of the social and cultural environment is clarified when international comparisons are made. Italy and Spain are noted for industrial districts favouring SME development. For example, the Valencia region has districts specialising in toys, wooden furniture, carpets, marble products, ceramics and so on. On the other hand, many countries, from Japan to Romania, have barriers to the spread of enterprise.

> *Business, and social attitudes in Japan, for instance, resist individualism. Government policies protect growing businesses rather than accept that some will fail. Entry to the stock market is severely restricted. Established institutions, from banks to potential partner companies, prefer not to deal with new ventures. The society as a whole frowns on individualism. School education encourages conformity and university level courses on entrepreneurship are rare.[23] Romania illustrates problems in many countries faced with structural change. The 'mentality' and lack of skills of the people, especially managers of state firms, combines with absence of models of successful entrepreneurship to act as constraints to new business start-ups.[24]*

Operating environment

The list of factors also points to the operating environment as favouring or hindering entrepreneurs. Since they find roles as agents of adjustment, innovators and risk takers, they will be more likely to succeed in situations that require these capabilities. This implies complex and uncertain supply markets, product markets and technologies. Larger, more stable organisations do better in simpler and more certain environments. These points are summarised in Fig. 8.4.[25]

Encouraging the entrepreneur

In many countries since about 1980, there has clearly been an increase in self-employment. For example, SMEs in the United Kingdom increased from 1.8 million to almost 3 million during the 1980s. This measure of the stock of firms hides the important flows in and out of the sector during the period. We can say that births exceeded deaths by some 1.2 million. Because some businesses merge with others, however, not all deaths are failures. Furthermore, a few grow sufficiently to exceed the upper limit of the SME definition.

Typically, government policies have been focused on stimulating formation. Failures, excepting Japan noted above, have been left to the market. Recently, however, governments have recognised that only a few SMEs grow quickly and provide the precious new jobs sought in the economy. We are beginning to see a shift in policy towards helping such firms.

■ Births and deaths

Many firms start small and remain so, struggling to survive on low turnover. Eventually, many cease to function. Although covering only about two-thirds of all firms, Value Added Tax returns are often used as indicators of trends. Figure 8.5, for example, uses VAT data to show how registrations exceeded deregistrations throughout the 1980s.[26] Average growth rate was 3 per cent, made up of 14 per cent births and 11 per cent deaths of firms existing at the beginning of each year. This aggregate data hides variations between sectors. There was a 120 per cent increase (that is, more than doubling) of firms engaged in financial and other services whereas production, construction and transport were close to the average of 22 per cent. Two sectors, agriculture and retail, saw a fall.

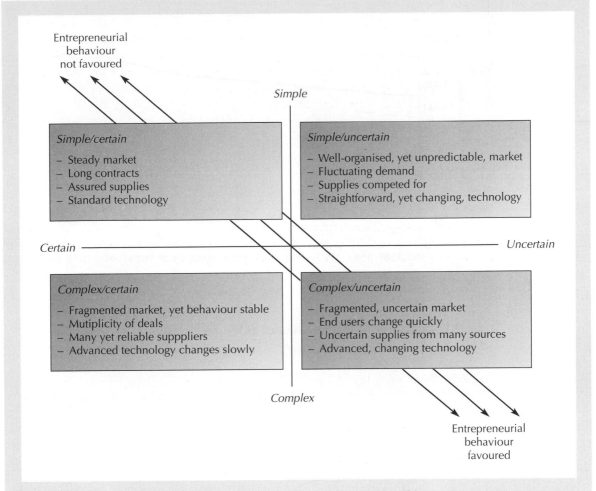

Fig. 8.4 Operating environment characteristics matched to entrepreneurship

Another way to examine the lifespan of companies is to compare the likelihood of death with the firm's age. Figure 8.6 again uses VAT data to make this comparison.[27] It can be seen that young firms have up to 9 per cent chance of deregistering within six months. The figure falls steadily as firms mature. (The data does not consider delays in deregistration so the peak at 12–18 months is likely to be the result of earlier failure.)

Other studies use data on receiverships and insolvencies to assess closure rates. The regular Barclays Bank survey noted the apparent contradiction in 1996 between a fall in receiverships and insolvencies and an increase in closures for other reasons. In a rising economy, the former 'true' failures would be expected to decline. Simultaneously, many other micro-businesses close as people leave self-employment to become paid employees.[28] These flows into and out of the stock of businesses are volatile. A rise in failures may relate less to the current economy and more to a peak in formation three or four years earlier.

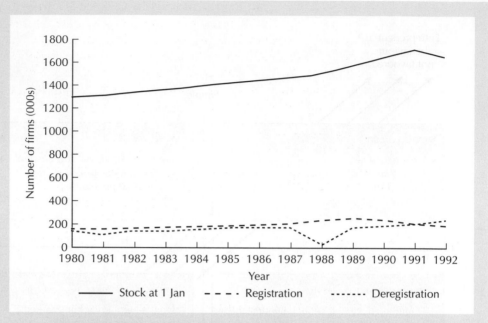

Fig. 8.5 Birth and death of firms indicated by VAT registrations

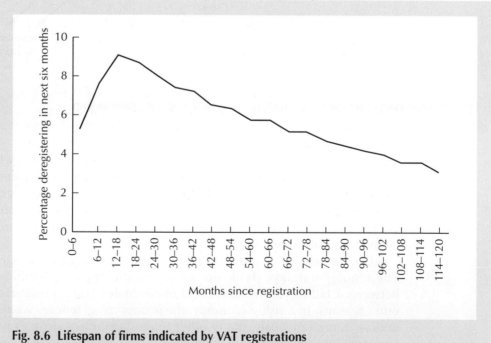

Fig. 8.6 Lifespan of firms indicated by VAT registrations

High rates of new firm formation may look impressive as evidence of an 'enterprise culture'. Yet many do not survive the first year and most fail within three. The preoccupation with start-ups has overlooked the consequent rise in failures with their effects on entrepreneurs, their families and their creditors. There is also the question of how far new, subsidised firms displace other enterprises that may themselves have been established only a few years earlier. Therefore, as important as the number of start-ups is their quality, that is their potential for survival and growth.

■ Growth

Once any starting subsidies have been absorbed, SMEs can face higher costs than their larger rivals. Finance, for example, tends to be more expensive since SMEs have no access to the main equity markets and lenders charge premiums to cover their extra risk. The benefits of limited liability are often illusory as owners are required to cover loans with personal guarantees or secure them against family property. Furthermore, in industries with economies of scale in functions from purchasing and operations to distribution and marketing, the larger firm will again have the advantage. How, then, can the entrepreneur succeed?

Keasey and Watson identify four conditions where the small firm will gain advantage:[29]

- *Industries without economies of scale*
  From domestic repairs to high fashion, many industries lack scale advantages. This may be because of process technology or insufficient market demand. For example, car assembly has scale advantages yet small segments of the market are served by low volume production. Here luxury, nostalgia or high performance niches provide work for Rolls-Royce, Morgan and TVR. Customising, restoring and rebuilding are niches populated by many small firms.

- *Opportunities favour entrepreneurial behaviour*
  As shown in Fig. 8.4, complexity and change in the business environment means that flexibility within the firm will enable it to chase opportunities. Entrepreneurial behaviour is sometimes displayed by large firms with flexible systems and outlooks. Yet size is an obstacle to be overcome. The owner-entrepreneur, on the other hand, has the incentive and speed of decision making that are required. An example is the 'spin-off' contract based on research findings of large companies or other institutions that are unsuited to their own development plans.

- *Acceptance of lower returns*
  With many SMEs not having to provide detailed financial reports, it is not clear how their average financial performance compares with other firms. It is evident, however, that many SMEs, especially the very small ones, survive at the expense of poor working conditions, long hours and moderate pay and pensions. Involvement of family, including children, is frequently seen in shops, restaurants, hotels and small holdings.

- *Regulatory framework*
  The less stringent financial reporting rules, reduced taxes and non-applicability of some employment legislation mean a gentler legal environment for small

businesses. In addition, governments make some attempts to counter the advantages of large companies in business transactions. These range from overseas sales promotions to penalising slow payers.

Given the possibility of exploiting entrepreneurial advantages, it is perhaps surprising that only 3 per cent of new firms show high growth and create many jobs.[30] There seem to be differences between the few firms that grow rapidly and the majority that remain small throughout their lives. Fundamental factors include the entrepreneurs, their motivations, sources of finance and strategies and practices of management. This raises the possibility of picking winners, a policy that would be advantageous to the government and business advisers as well as the managers themselves. Unfortunately, failing firms frequently show the same characteristics as the very successful ones! Picking winners remains about as easy as in steeplechasing. Among the mix of personal and business factors, it is often the unique idea that makes all the difference. In the opening case, we saw that it was only after six years of trading that Patrice Flippe came up with his big idea and persuaded venture capitalists to join in. Without the product, he could not have been a 'winner'.

Growth among medium-sized firms

'Supergrowth' is also rare among medium-sized companies. One survey of 500 independent family-owned companies in the United Kingdom found 70 that had increased sales by 60 per cent over three years.[31] Compared with the group as a whole, the latter had better qualified senior managers, spent more on training and had introduced changes and techniques adopted by larger competitors and customers. These included: more frequent product updates; shortened delivery times; interdisciplinary problem-solving teams; cross-functional product development; value engineering to design out costs; and reverse engineering to study the costs of rivals' products. In short, the rapidly growing medium businesses are better managed than average.

Harrison and Taylor studied some 200 high-growth medium-sized companies in Germany and the United Kingdom for the 15 years up to 1995.[32] Their results emphasise the importance of marketing and continued innovation. Successful medium-sized firms do not take on established rivals directly. Instead, they find market niches that are ready for innovative products and where entry is aided by speed, flexibility and customer service. Additionally, they protect these niches through patents, licences for distribution or long-term contracts with important customers. Following initial success, diversification, *see* Chapter 10, is important to avoid reliance on one product, one customer or one region. Yet this must be controlled so that new products and markets are closely related to present ones. Finally, the entrepreneur must be prepared to pull out. As competitors come in and market growth tails off, it may be best to sell up and look elsewhere for innovatory opportunities.

These studies support the view that medium-sized (in German, *Mittelstand*) businesses are often the engines of growth in the economy. In ten years, the 200 firms studied by Harrison and Taylor created between 50 000 and 100 000 jobs and invested more than £2 billion. Governments would like to encourage even greater success. Yet whether their winning ways can be discovered in advance remains a problem.

■ Government support

We shall not detail government initiatives for stimulating the start-up and growth of SMEs. This is because they are continually changing, their impact is unclear and they vary so much between nations. There are, however, some common themes. The shift of focus from start-ups to continuance has already been noted. Non-sustainability is a problem encountered in many countries. For instance, commenting on the proposed sell-out of Intrason to a foreign rival, Le Parmentier noted, 'It's a story of a France that knows how to create high-tech products but is incapable of transforming such innovations into international winners'.[33] For France read Britain, Denmark, Sweden, the Netherlands and so on.

Encouraging, removing constraints and creating infrastructure

Governments offer support to starting and growing firms according to local perceptions of needs. They do this as part of their role in sustaining economic growth but also for wider social and environmental reasons. For instance, while much of the employment and regeneration focus in the United Kingdom is on areas of urban decline, others argue that the rural economy also needs help for diversification. According to the Country Landowners Association, this should be achieved through three policies: encouraging SME formation and growth by providing advice, opportunities and pump-priming finance; removing constraints including excessive regulation; and developing infrastructure, especially communications and utilities.[34]

The same themes of encouragement, removing constraints and enabling through infrastructure are repeated throughout the nation and the world. Such policies are shown in sharp relief in South Africa where SMEs are a relatively small part of the formal employment picture and are, for the most part, in the hands of white owners. SME development is expected to be an instrument of social change for, as the government acknowledges, ' ... small business support will for a considerable time also have to focus on the particular needs of black enterprises and the ways to overcome the remaining consequences of that legacy [of big business domination and the uneven distribution of wealth].'[35]

The SME scene in many countries is dominated by a collection of projects, schemes, clubs and institutions intended to offer support, advice and connections. Some are government agencies while others are local organisations sponsored by the state. Examples of the former are the United Kingdom Department of Trade and Industry and its equivalents in other nations. The latter are illustrated by the well-established Chambers of Commerce in France, Germany and Japan. It is often reported that one problem for SMEs is the diversity of sources of assistance and the skill required to find a route through the maze.

Despite the plethora of projects, governments usually have little power to directly create and sustain SMEs. Apart from budgetary constraints, they must avoid aiding new businesses at the expense of existing ones. Two recessions, marking the start and end of the 1980s, meant closure for many small businesses. Since entrepreneurs often operate at the margins of the economy, they are particularly sensitive to downturns. Furthermore, since many work through complex networks of contacts, they tend to fall when things go wrong like lines of dominoes. Hence the common plea, 'Government should remember that the best way it can assist small firms is by creating a stable macroeconomic environment'.[36]

Intrapreneurs

Intrapreneur is a term coined to describe employees who display entrepreneurial qualities while preferring to remain within the framework of an established organisation. Unfortunately, there is little consensus on what these qualities are. In using a case approach to compare successful entre- and intrapreneurs, Jennings, Cox and Cooper identify the latter as those who have proved success at manage-

---

Exhibit 8.2   Two successful managers; but are they intrapreneurs?

Michael Guthrie (1941–present)

In the 1960s, Guthrie left catering college and, after a spell in a university catering department, joined Mecca as a trainee manager. He was attracted by the challenge, prospects and the culture of doing things well. Guthrie progressed through assistant and general manager, to director, then divisional managing director and finally chairman. He led Mecca from being a subsidiary of Grand Metropolitan, through a buyout to a full listing on the Stock Exchange in 1985. Its three divisions, entertainment and catering, social clubs and holiday centres, employed more than 7000. Mecca met problems after a rash acquisition and Guthrie was replaced when the firm was taken over by Rank in 1990.

By 1994 he was running the private company, Brightseasons, owners of Pizzaland, Bella Pasta and Pizza Piazza. When this business was to be sold, he planned to leave and start another venture.

Guthrie is known as a very confident person; some see him as arrogant. He reports his success as due to having energy, finding life exciting and enjoying the recognition of others when he did a good job.

Sir Antony Pilkington (1935–present)

Pilkington joined the family firm at 24 after boarding school, a Cambridge history degree and two years as a Coldstream Guards officer. At 32 he became flat glass marketing manager and then progressed rapidly to director level. When 45, he took the chair of the group, Pilkington plc. This is the world's leading glass company.

The family company's success in recent years has been built on innovation, especially through the exploitation of float glass technology. Sir Antony saw chairmanship as requiring him to maintain the family dynasty through operating the business successfully. One of the reasons the family firm has survived since 1826 is the way it manages succession. Family members who come in have to prove themselves before being promoted. Several have been asked to find another job.

ment by rising to the top of major companies. Some, like Michael Guthrie, had risen incrementally through the corporate hierarchy while others, such as Sir Antony Pilkington, had been groomed for leadership of the family firm, *see* Exhibit 8.2. These are highly competent, strongly motivated managers. According to Jennings and others, they show a more cautious approach than entrepreneurs, interested in developing and consolidating their businesses step by step.[37] Yet it is difficult to see intrapreneurial features in Pilkington, who may be the last of the family dynasty and could be said to have failed.[38] Furthermore, Guthrie is a risk-taker, regarded by some as a 'serial entrepreneur' driven by the 'buzz' of conducting deals and a wish to be respected in the city.[39]

For other authors, to see an intrapreneur merely as a successful manager is to miss the point. Intrapreneurs' special qualities are especially needed in larger firms operating in the complex/uncertain environments of Fig. 8.4. Large, established firms do not fit these environments well. They tend to:

- make cumbersome plans;
- possess rigid structures and systems;
- limit personal autonomy and creativity;
- use controls that hinder innovation.

Carrier defines intrapreneurship as *the taking in charge of an innovation by an employee or other individual working under the control of an enterprise*.[40] An innovation is any change leading to an improvement of performance.

Recognising how growth and change tend to stagnate, some companies have launched programmes to promote intrapreneurship. Pinchot defined three possible roles:

- *The inventor* creates the new idea, whether it be for a product, process or other change.
- *The product champion* helps with overcoming resistance to change through becoming committed to the idea and having the position and experience to press ahead with the project.
- *The sponsor* is a senior manager who recognises the value of the idea and uses position and organisational politics to secure resources and give it a chance of survival.[41]

Although presented here as separate, the roles can be combined in one person. The product champion and sponsor, for example, do not have to understand technical details beyond being able to judge whether the idea has a chance of succeeding. These roles are vital, however, as difficulties of pushing ideas through hierarchies without sponsorship cause many inventors to either give up or leave.

Programmes to stimulate intrapreneurship include creating flexible teams and offering appropriate rewards. They have not always been successful. Kodak dropped its attempts after disappointing results.[42] Others, such as Hewlett-Packard and 3M,[43] *see* Exhibit 8.3, have succeeded. Given that their purpose is to overcome formal constraints, it is at first surprising to see that successful intrapreneurship programmes require appropriate planning to sustain them. Yet an intrapreneur programme:

- encourages teamwork;
- concentrates on results;
- rewards innovation and risk taking;
- tolerates mistakes and learns from them;
- maintains flexibility and an orientation towards change.

Exhibit 8.3 Success for 3M's intrapreneurship policy

Post-it Notes started in 1977 after Art Fry took advantage of 3M's policy of allowing scientists to spend up to 15 per cent of their time on self-selected projects. He applied a colleague's rejected discovery, a glue that was impermanent, to a problem that was frustrating him. At church, page markers frequently fell out of his hymnal!

Fry won the backing of 3M's Commercial Office Supply Division and became responsible for taking the idea to market. The product caught on in 3M's own offices but early sales were poor. After all, why should potential buyers pay for such pads when staff can use scraps of paper? The solution was to flood one market, Boise, Idaho, with free samples. Customers were hooked. Demand grew quickly. Now Post-it Notes are worldwide best sellers.

Fry was promoted in 1986 to corporate scientist, the highest technical grade.

Intrapreneurs and SMEs

The question of intrapreneurship arises in growing SMEs as innovators other than the owner-manager begin to emerge. Carrier argues that distinctions between large and small firms are such, however, that the issues must be considered from a different viewpoint in each case. On the face of it, small firms' friendlier and more flexible structures, together with more personalised relationships, should enable better working partnerships to emerge. Yet the compatibility of the intrapreneur with the owner-entrepreneur becomes the key issue. If a trusting relationship can be nurtured, the entrepreneur must maintain a working atmosphere with matching strategies and rewards. The unwillingness of many to have their ideas challenged and to let go of controls can make matters difficult. Yet they need to be aware of the dangers of rejecting, and losing, an intrapreneur. Exhibit 8.4 summarises the different concerns of large firms and SMEs with respect to intrapreneurs.[44]

Managing the SME

Having compared the characteristics of entrepreneurs and intrapreneurs and outlined some government policies directed towards encouraging the success of SMEs, we shall complete the chapter by raising important management questions.

Exhibit 8.4 Contrasts for intrapreneurs in large organisations and SMEs

Large firms	SMEs
Structural context	
Size disadvantage in detecting intrapreneurs and removing barriers; some firms now organise in small units to overcome this problem.	Intrapreneur's ideas must complement owner-manager's. Will co-star be accepted? Working relations can be miserable if trust is lacking.
Relationship context	
Intrapreneurs at odds with line managers; objectives incompatible, politics and status issues tiresome. Anonymity in early development advantageous.	Success depends on entrepreneur's open-mindedness, confidence and willingness to protect the intrapreneur from premature criticism. Anonymity impossible.
Rewards	
Promotion often offered mistakenly; more autonomy and freedom preferred.	Promotion viewed positively; it extends scope, increases autonomy and is a move closer to owner-manager.
Strategic processes	
Formal strategies demonstrating support for intrapreneurship needed.	Strategy and emergence of intrapreneur intertwined. Formalisation to incorporate intrapreneurial activity.
Consequences of dissatisfaction	
Leave; set up in competition; join a competitor; take key staff.	Leave; set up in competition; join a competitor; take key staff. Consequences more serious in smaller firm.

These relate to management and technical expertise; information; international business; finance; and planning

■ Management expertise

It is often argued that the most serious difficulty facing the SME is the shortage of skills. For instance, there is the observation that small firms make less use of information systems, including being unable to obtain and use software to suit their particular needs, and engage less in international business. These activities, it is stated, require management resources beyond those normally available. Compared with its larger rivals, the SME is also hampered by lack of other skills, especially in marketing and cash management. Some, however, are available under government sponsorship.

Entrepreneurs frequently apply expertise and experience gained in previous employment. They often set up in industries or markets in which they had been working. To illustrate some issues in the switch-over, we can look at Jones-Evans' study of technology-based firms. The 'technical entrepreneurs' who run these businesses are important since their SMEs are often identified as having substantial growth potential. Clearly, management requires technological expertise but success depends on how this is combined with business acumen. Jones-Evans identified four types of technical entrepreneur depending on their occupational background:

■ *Research*
  Involved in scientific or technical development in a university or non-profit research centre.

■ *Producer*
  Engaged in product or process development in a commercial environment, probably a large company.

■ *User*
  Peripheral involvement in technological development through roles such as marketing or end-user applications.

■ *Opportunist*
  Experience gained in a non-technical organisation, therefore no technical expertise.[45]

Entrepreneurs were assessed for relevant technical and management expertise. They tended to cluster in the cells shown in Fig. 8.7. Very few fell into the other cells, even the ideal 'high–high' combination shown by the star. The small number of technical entrepreneurs who were stars owned the firms with the greatest potential. Jones-Evans emphasises that the amount of experience is not so important as its relevance to the current or proposed business.

■ Using information systems

Expertise applies not only to setting up the business but in coping with external innovation and change. Nowhere has this been more apparent than in information where some SMEs establish an edge over their rivals. Naylor and Williams investigated the use of information systems (ISs) among 30 SMEs in Merseyside. Seven firms showed that even small firms can use ISs beyond basic transactional applications. Exhibit 8.5 gives two examples that bought computers to carry out routine administration yet found, after installation, unplanned ways of using them. These more successful SMEs used their information systems to change operations and extend their markets. The study concluded that managers' ability to interact with the IS in creative ways was vital; success followed continual innovation to integrate applications into the whole business.[46]

While it is possible for SMEs to win in the IS application race, overall involvement in the sector is low, especially at the small end. In 1996, government data showed that 40 per cent and 6 per cent of medium-sized firms used e-mail and the Internet respectively. Only half these proportions of small firms were users.

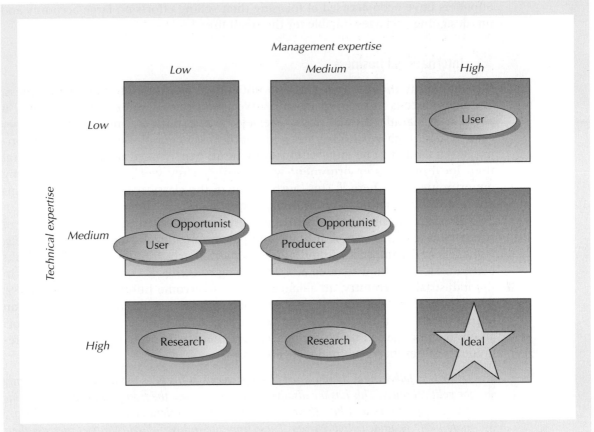

Fig. 8.7 Experience array comparing management and technical expertise of technical entrepreneurs

---

Beyond basic IT applications in SMEs

Firm B, with 20 employees, distributed welding and related engineering equipment. It introduced a basic information system to monitor its operations yet the major gains were unplanned. Using the new spreadsheet facility, the sales manager saw how many customers were buying just one product from the wide range. Taking the twelve largest accounts, he aimed to increase their spending by selling them different lines. A discount scheme was offered. In one year, sales to these customers doubled.

Firm K, with 80 employees, is the leading United Kingdom manufacturer of shower surrounds. In a careful information system plan, it anticipated benefits in administration, sales and short-term forecasting. The greatest gains arose, however, from being able to introduce a five day delivery guarantee throughout much of Europe, while at the same time increasing output and improving the control of stocks and work in progress.

Suppliers have been accused of focusing their selling efforts on large accounts and not designing packages suitable for the small firm.[47]

■ International business

It is commonly thought that SMEs do not engage much in international business. Yet experience is mixed. For instance, Westhead quotes surveys showing only 4 per cent of manufacturing firms in Merseyside as exporters compared with 70 per cent of small high-technology firms in South-East England. He found that exporting SMEs tended to be larger and run by more experienced people who felt that their local business environment was 'hostile'. They were pushed into seeking opportunities elsewhere.[48] This 'push' is one of the classical explanations for firms engaging in international business, *see* Chapter 5.

Apart from exporting, SMEs increasingly use joint ventures as the means of strengthening their position at home and penetrating developing overseas markets. Donckels and Lambrecht found alliances particularly frequent in building links between SMEs in industrialised and developing countries.[49] For the entrepreneur in the industrialised country, an alliance helps to overcome hurdles of market access, limited capital and political risk. The developing country counterpart, usually also an entrepreneur, gains technology, and technical and management skills. The authors go on to argue that, in such relations, entrepreneurs do best to team up with entrepreneurs rather than multinational enterprises.

> *The MNE, following a standardised global strategy, is likely to use local alliances mainly for political safety. This has the disadvantage of restricting the transfer of learning into the developing country and has, therefore, an element of exploitation. Ethical principles are more likely to guide entrepreneurs. Those from the industrialised countries increase their commitment if they find the project to be socially worthwhile. Transfer of learning is part of this commitment. For the developing nation, the growth of the SME sector is vital. Many economies rely too much on a few large corporations with a micro-business sector working in the informal economy. A sizeable population of SMEs would bridge the gap.*

Alliances between partners in nations at different stages of development can work very well. In business among developed countries, on the other hand, SMEs tend to be much more cautious. They prefer well-known partners and avoid cooperative agreements entailing high investments and risk. The latter point arises when partners are seen as potential competitors. Preferred alliances are, for example, with complementary firms that can share distribution channels to mutual advantage.[50]

Alliances and other international business opportunities are constrained by many factors, not the least of which is the difficulty of obtaining and using information. To counter the emerging advantage of MNEs in their control of market and operating information, the 'Group of Seven' (G-7) governments have launched a project to increase the participation of SMEs in global business. Its three strands are:

- a global networked information system covering international activities and experiences;
- systems to improve the efficiency of SMEs in functions such as data interchange, billing and payments;
- trials of international electronic commerce.

■ Managing finance

Most SMEs have difficulties in obtaining and managing finance. Consequently, many are undercapitalised and look to banks to provide a succession of overdraft arrangements. Compared with the average, small firms rely more on short-term loans, trade debtors and trade creditors. Their balance sheets show fewer fixed assets.[51] Almost the first business challenge is to find a way out of the cycle of high interest rates, lower profits and restricted growth. Undercapitalisation means not only exposure to sudden failure but also pressure to make poor decisions such as accepting barely profitable work or missing openings to purchase materials in bulk.

Banks

While banks are the first port of call for funds, it is often reported that entrepreneurs are dissatisfied with their service. Some can bypass restrictive or coercive lending rules by applying to initiatives such as the Loan Guarantee Scheme. These are, however, not available to all types of business and many are asked to provide personal guarantees or the backing of family property.

Chaston shows that differences in the *perceptions* of service quality, *see* Chapter 7, are important sources of dissatisfaction. In determining quality, banks stress accuracy and dependability while the SME would place willingness to help and prompt service at the top of the list. A further problem is the way that United Kingdom banks responded to the 'enterprise culture' by advertising and promoting service standards that were not, in practice, delivered.[52] Problems have abated as banks have improved. For example, they are now more likely to offer more stable 'term loans' instead of the unpredictable overdraft. They require collateral on only one fifth of start-up loans.

Debtors

It is often reported that some large businesses obtain working capital by delaying payment to their smaller suppliers. Depending on the survey, the average United Kingdom payment period is reported between 50 and 77 days. This compares with the 30 days widely accepted as 'terms of trade' and a European Union average of 61 days. Other companies argue that deliberate delay is neither good business nor good ethical practice. Yet only 12 per cent of SMEs say they are paid within the 30-day period.[53]

There is a continual debate on whether there ought to be a statutory duty to pay promptly and a right for creditors to charge interest. The United Kingdom government has avoided following other EU governments, such as Italy and Spain, with legislation. There is a general reluctance to criminalise aspects of contract law and problems with enforcement are foreseen. A small business needs its cash immediately, rather than awaiting a court order after it has folded. Instead, other measures are being promoted by the government and business groups:

■ a new British Standard, BS 7890, to form the basis of legally binding contracts;

■ the Prompt Payment Code of the Confederation of British Industry;

■ pressure by government departments on persistent late payers, including publication of 'black lists';

- reporting on policy and practice in annual reports;
- making access to the Small Claims Courts easier to recover debts.[54]

Beyond these examples of banks and trade debtors, small businesses face many other problems of financial management. There is a lack of interest and awareness of finance among entrepreneurs, who, as we have seen, start out with the intention of exploiting innovations in technology or marketing. Better preparation and training, combined with access to good, low-cost advice, may improve the longevity of many micro- and small businesses.

Planning

The role and value of planning in SMEs, especially for owner-managers, are a problem. On the one hand, it is evident that many small businesses do produce plans. This can be explained by their being needed when seeking funds from banks or venture capitalists or gaining grants from government agencies. Deakins is not alone in seeing the necessity for at least elementary plans as a major advance over less formal discussions with bank managers.[55]

Producing plans because one has to convince a lender, however, is different from being committed to planning. As we will see in Chapter 9, planning is concerned with guiding and integrating the business and monitoring its performance. It is a process that must be both logical and flexible. We can see in Firms B and K of Exhibit 8.5 that they had planned their information systems to serve certain business needs yet could change as they learnt that new possibilities became available.

In spite of the gains in performance available from planning, Richardson argues that many small firms are unable to overcome the following misconceptions and barriers:[56]

Misconceptions

- planning is for large firms with plentiful resources;
- relevant knowledge is to be obtained outside the organisation;
- the process requires special expertise and a structured, formal approach;
- benefits do not arise immediately;
- the output is a set of budgets spanning several years.

Barriers

- unwillingness of owner-managers to delegate and to learn and guide simultaneously;
- the pressure of the here-and-now;
- unavailability of current business information, especially financial. Obtaining regular flows requires a degree of analytical expertise that is often absent.

Progress is achieved by countering the misconceptions and overcoming the barriers, possibly through external training or other interventions. Given the apparent formality and inflexibility of it all, it is not surprising that many entrepreneurs intuitively resist planning, especially if it means making explicit written statements. Yet if the firm is to grow successfully, it must face at some point the need to switch to using a wider group of professional managers. Formalising planning is part of this change.

Conclusion: the intertwining of enterprise and the economy

Starting from an examination of the nature of enterprise, this chapter investigated what it means to become and be an entrepreneur. It showed that, while entrepreneurs were common in small businesses they could also be found in large ones. In the latter case, employers, recognising the need for flexibility in facing their environments, have policies to stimulate entrepreneurial activity.

Entrepreneurs and SMEs are needed by the economy both to make it work and to provide many innovations that will form the businesses and create the employment of the future. The need is reciprocal, because SMEs need, above all, a steadily growing economy to continually generate openings without running into the recessions when marginal businesses suffer more severely. Government policy in stimulating the mystical 'enterprise culture' focused heavily on start-ups at the expense of high failure rates later. Now policy is becoming more discriminatory, seeking to back the few growing firms with high potential. Yet picking these winners is not easy.

Success is clearly linked to the competence of entrepreneurs. The problem for many companies is that they rely too heavily on the expertise of this one person. They score highly on flexibility and commitment yet fail on productivity, investment and continual innovation. SME investment in staff training, for instance, tends to be at a lower rate than in larger companies.[57] From the nation's point of view, it may seem satisfactory to have a flexible business sector that can ebb and flow with the economic tide. Yet their efficiency is also very important. Weak performance of SMEs hinders whole chains when they are heavily involved as subcontractors such as to the final assemblers of domestic appliances or vehicles, which compete globally.

Quick check up *Can you ...*

- Distinguish entrepreneur and intrapreneur;
- State three SME categories used by the EU, giving some data on the sector;
- Name three classes of factors used to explain why people become entrepreneurs;

- Give four conditions when small firms can gain advantages;
- State three important roles for the intrapreneur;
- Summarise Jones-Evans' model of technical entrepreneurship;
- Outline the problem posed by debtors to SMEs.

Questions	*Chapter review*

8.1 What are the similarities and differences between businesses run by entrepreneurs and SMEs in general?

8.2 What are the arguments for and against the statement, 'Entrepreneurs are born and not made'?

8.3 Explain the roles associated with intrapreneurs and suggest why they are so important in overcoming resistance to change.

Application

8.4 Using the information in the opening case, assess how far Flippe fits with the various models and categories of entrepreneur described in the chapter.

Investigation

8.5 Draw on sources such as the 'Enterprise' pages of serious newspapers, to investigate key factors in the business environment that help or hinder SMEs. Explain how far government policies have an effect on these factors.

8.6 Draw up a brief schedule based on the 'What makes an entrepreneur?' section of this chapter. Use it to interview an owner-manager to build a picture of one person's reasons for being in business.

CLOSING CASE

Storwell[58]

For ten years Storwell has specialised in the speedy delivery of high quality, keenly priced storage boxes. These are designed for stocking, filing and archiving of office materials, medical records and X-ray films. Recent additions to the range are bins for disposal of aerosols and broken glass. All products are made in tough corrugated board whose white, outer face carries the Storwell brand name and blank grids for lists of contents.

The business was founded in 1987 by its directors, Allan and Sandra Weddell. Neither had experience of small business nor was entrepreneurship running in their families. Allan had joined Lawton's office supplies company as sales representative in 1972. By 1982 he was divisional sales manager responsible for stationery and storage products. He found the job interesting at first. He cut the number of

lines from 4500 to 300 while increasing the sales of higher margin, branded lines. So, while volume began to fall, profit rose. Yet, by 1986 at the age of 40, Allan was dissatisfied. It was difficult to motivate and keep staff, especially as their numbers were reduced and territories expanded. Tight controls had become irksome. He felt the business should be launching new products but the directors were reluctant to make the needed investments. There was no prospect of further promotion.

In 1986 Allan was invited, through a consultant, to be interviewed for a similar job at a rival company. On the way home he began to reflect on a question he had been asked: 'Why are you working?' At Christmas that year the family, the parents and two children in early secondary school, took stock. Sandra, who had worked in the Inland Revenue office before becoming a full-time mother, was finding it difficult to find good full-time employment. They wondered if they could set out on their own. The children were cautious. One observed how 'business seemed to make people unhappy'. After careful budgeting, however, the family agreed it could get by on half of the current expenditure if it needed to.

Storwell was registered in March. The business needed £30 000 to start, half from personal savings and half from an overdraft secured against shares inherited from Sandra's grandfather. Premises were to be rented at first. Allan resigned in June and started trading in September.

The Weddells' plan was to aim for national sales of a narrow product range. The boxes were stronger and cheaper than those offered by Lawton's, Eastlight and Fellows, makers of Bankers Box. Direct sales cut out the distributors' margin. Sales staff were to visit customers, supported by leaflets and mail shots. Two former Lawton's colleagues were brought in as commission-only sales representatives. Allan knew that the health sector had good potential so, from his prior experience, he wrote personal letters to buyers at each of the country's 380 major hospitals. About half the business now comes from the National Health Service. Schools, in contrast, were disappointing. Their orders were small and repeats slow. Mail shots to other markets used purchased mailing lists but these proved disappointing.

The business was launched at a good time. In spite of the first year sales being half of the budget, Storwell had three good years before the recession. While this slowed things down, a profit has been made every year. The 1990s growth has been steady. The Weddells have recently been able to buy the freehold of a larger warehouse, take foreign holidays and support the children in higher education.

Storwell's operations consist of buying in bulk from board manufacturers, storing and despatch. Each day, Allan makes up the consignments ready for collection by the parcel service. Sandra stays at home, also the office, to take calls and do the administration. Having budgeted for 80 days debtors, she is pleased that the average time for payment is around 45. Working hours for Allan and Sandra are reasonable as there is no business in the evenings or at weekends. During the day, however, someone has to be in the office all the time. Sales are now entirely by mail, telephone or fax.

In conversation, the Weddells claim little knowledge of designing and making corrugated cases. In this industry it is normal for customers to discuss their needs with the board companies, which then produce prototypes. The X-ray and disposal boxes, added to the original range, were developed this way. There are no plans to move into other types of product.

Nowadays the Weddells recognise that their business gives them a satisfactory standard of living. They are beginning to plan retirement. 'Ten years ago we both needed interesting jobs. Now we have them and they provide a comfortable income. Will one or both of the children want to come in? Should we appoint a manager? Should we sell out?'

Questions

1 When asked about risk, Allan replied, 'There was little chance of it failing.' What does this tell you about the Weddells' attitude to risk? From the case and your wider knowledge, how could and can the business fail?

2 Comparing this case with theories in the chapter, how do you account for the Weddells' entrepreneurial behaviour? On what skills has success been built?

Bibliography

Deakins, David (1996) *Entrepreneurship and Small Firms*, Maidenhead: McGraw-Hill, gives a broad review of the issues covered in this chapter. Keasey, Kevin and Watson, Robert (1993) *Small Firm Management*, Oxford: Blackwell, concentrates on the economic and financial aspects from both firm and government perspectives. Both focus on the United Kingdom. The 3M home page is worth a visit. Start at http://www.mmm.com/profile/innov.

References

1. Le Parmentier, Arnaud (1996) 'Intrason, l'histoire d'une PME qui devrait passer sous contrôle étranger', *Le Monde*, 17 January, 14.
2. Burrows, Roger (1991) 'The discourse of the enterprise culture and the restructuring of Britain', in Curran, James A. and Blackburn, Robert A. (eds) *Paths of Enterprise: The future of small business*, London: Routledge, 29.
3. Deakins, David (1996) *Entrepreneurship and Small Firms*, Maidenhead: McGraw-Hill 8–14.
4. Deakins (1996) *op. cit.*, 24–5.
5. Hendry, C., Jones, A., Arthur, M. and Pettigrew, A. (1991) *Human resource development in small to medium sized enterprises*, Research Paper 88, Warwick Business School, University of Warwick, 6.
6. Department of Trade and Industry (1994) *Small Firms in Britain 1994*, London: HMSO.
7. Nelson, Edwin G. and Taylor, John (1995) 'New ventures and entrepreneurship in an Eastern European context: a training and development programme for managers in state-owned firms', *Journal of European Industrial Training*, **19** (**9**), 12–22.
8. Study by Philippines University of Asia and the Pacific reported at APEC conference, 14 March 1996.
9. MITI (1995) *Outline of the small and medium enterprise policies of the Japanese Government*, Small and Medium Enterprise Agency, MITI, October. Size boundaries in Japan are defined according to sector. A small manufacturing firm has up to 20 employees, whereas a small commercial or service firm no more than 5.
10. Desnø, Annick (1996) *SME development: regional factors and the role of foreign direct investment*, CCET Newsletter, Paris: OECD.
11. Deakins (1996) *op. cit.*, 17–18.
12. Chell, E., Haworth, J. and Brearley, S. (1991) *The Entrepreneurial Personality*, London: Routledge.
13. Keasey, Kevin and Watson Robert (1993) *Small Firm Management: Ownership, finance and performance*, Oxford: Blackwell, 10–11.
14. Deakins (1996) *op. cit.*, 52.
15. Keasey and Watson (1993) *op. cit.*, 10.
16. Abbott, Steven and Hay, Michael (1996) *The 1996 Pulse Survey – survival of the fittest*, London: Arthur Andersen/Binder Hamlyn.
17. *Ibid.*, 6.
18. Costa, Shu Shu (1994) '100 years and counting', *Management Review*, **83** (**12**), 32–4.
19. Ward, Robin (1991) 'Economic development and ethnical business', in Curran and Blackburn, *op. cit.*, 59.
20. Mason, C. (1991) 'Spatial variations in enterprise: the geography of new firm formation' in Burrows, R. (ed.) *Deciphering the Enterprise Culture: Entrepreneurship, petty capitalism and the restructuring of Britain*, London: Routledge.
21. Department of Trade and Industry (1994) *op. cit.*, 12.
22. Keasey and Watson (1993) *op. cit.*, 85–8.
23. Terazano, Emiko (1995) 'Daring to go it alone', *Financial Times*, 20 June, 18.

24. Nelson and Taylor (1995) *op. cit.*, 21.
25. Based on Gibb, Allan (1988) 'The enterprise culture: threat or opportunity?' *Management Decision*, **26** (**4**), 5–12.
26. Department of Trade and Industry (1994) *op. cit.*, 55.
27. *Ibid.*, 57.
28. 'Small business becomes tougher', *Financial Times*, 3 September, 1996.
29. Keasey and Watson (1993) *op. cit.*, 97.
30. Storey, D.J. (1994) *Understanding the Small Business Sector*, London: Routledge, 113–15.
31. Coopers and Lybrand (1994) *Made in the UK – Middle Market Survey*.
32. Harrison, John and Taylor, Bernard (1996) *Supergrowth Companies: Entrepreneurs in action*, Oxford: Butterworth–Heinemann.
33. Le Parmentier (1996) *op. cit.*, 14.
34. Country Landowners Association (1996) Policy statement.
35. Government of South Africa (1995) *National Strategy for the Development and Promotion of Small Business in South Africa*, White paper, para 2.3.3.
36. *Guardian* (1996) 'A lifeline for small firms – but they need macro-economic help even more', Leading article, 12 March.
37. Jennings, Reg, Cox, Charles and Cooper, Cary L. (1994): *Business Elites: The psychology of entrepreneurs and intrapreneurs*, London: Routledge; Rankine, Kate (1996) 'On a quest to the new Mecca – Michael Guthrie has known highs and lows in the City', *Daily Telegraph*, 12 October.
38. King, Ian (1996) 'Pilkington glass full up', *Guardian*, 13 July.
39. Northedge, Richard (1996) 'Rise of the serial entrepreneur – Once may not be enough', *Daily Telegraph*, 9 October.
40. Carrier, Camille (1994) 'Intrapreneurship in large firms and SMEs: a comparative study', *International Small Business Journal*, **12** (**4**), April–June, 54–61.
41. Pinchot, Gifford (1985) *Entrepreneuring*, New York: Harper & Row.
42. Hirsch, James S. (1990) 'Kodak effort at "Intrapreneurship" fails', *Wall Street Journal*, 17 August, B1.
43. Mitchell, Russell (1989) 'Masters of innovation: 3M keeps its new products coming', *Business Week*, 10 April, 58–63; More examples and explanations are given by 3M on http://www.mmm.com/profile/innov
44. Carrier (1994) *op. cit.*
45. Jones-Evans, Dylan (1996) 'Experience and entrepreneurship: technology based owner-managers in the UK', *Industrial Relations Journal*, **27** (**1**), 39–54.
46. Naylor J.B. and Williams J. (1994) 'The successful use of IT in SMEs in Merseyside', *European Journal of Information Systems*, **3** (**1**), 48–56.
47. Ryle, Sarah (1997) 'Time we went walkies on the net, Gromit', *Guardian*, 7 January, 18.
48. Westhead, Paul (1996) 'Exporting and non-exporting small firms in Great Britain – a matched pairs comparison', *International Journal of Enterprise Behaviour & Research*, **1**(**2**), 6–36.
49. Donckels, Rik and Lambrecht, Johan (1995) 'Joint ventures: no longer a mysterious word for SMEs from developed and developing countries', *International Small Business Journal*, **13** (**2**), January–March, 11–26.
50. Kaufmann, Friedrich (1995) 'Internationalisation via cooperation – strategies of SME', *International Small Business Journal*, **13** (**2**), January–March, 27–33.
51. Storey (1994) *op. cit.*, 215–16.
52. Chaston, Ian (1994) 'Rebuilding small business confidence by identifying and closing service gaps in the bank/SME relationship', *International Small Business Journal*, **13** (**1**), October–December, 54–62.

53. Rapp, Roger (1996) 'Delays in payment fail to improve', *Independent*, 19 February, 18.
54. Gosling, Paul (1996) 'Minding your own business', *Independent on Sunday*, 27 October.
55. Deakins (1996), *op. cit.*, 222.
56. Richardson, Bill (1995) 'In defence of business planning: why and how it still works for small firms and "corporations of small business units"', *Small Business and Enterprise Development*, **2** (**1**), 41–57.
57. Marsh, Peter (1996) 'The ebb and flow that hampers Midlands: DTI says small companies suffer low productivity, investment and innovation', *Financial Times*, 11 July.
58. Thanks to Allan and Sandra Weddell, Directors of Storwell.

How did you score on the marketing ethics test? (See p. 188)

The questions are based on Lane, J.C. (1995) 'Ethics of business students: some marketing perspectives' *Journal of Business Ethics*, **14**, 571–80. Lane surveyed 412 Australian business students, noting means and significant differences among subgroups.

(a) Customers are unknowing subjects of a research experiment. It should not occur but 73 per cent of the students approved. Marketing students were more likely to approve.

(b) You should blow the whistle. Only 42 per cent of the sample would do this; 25 per cent would not; 2 per cent would resign and the rest were undecided.

(c) Depending on the details, using women models in lingerie adverts is justified but not in the other cases. 96 per cent of students agreed for lingerie; 39 per cent approved for motor bikes (with 52 per cent against and the rest undecided); 68 per cent approved for bed linen (with 21 per cent against and the rest undecided). Males were significantly less critical of the last two cases.

(d) 51 per cent approved of 'sugging' – selling under the guise of market research. It is unethical and against the professional body's code of practice. 31 per cent were against and the rest didn't know. Males aged 22–26 were significantly less critical.

Part 3

PLANNING AND DECISION MAKING

He's a real nowhere man, sitting in his nowhere land, making all his nowhere plans for nobody. *John Lennon and Paul McCartney, British Musicians*

Let him who desires peace prepare for war. *Vegetius, Roman writer*

Whenever you see a successful business, someone once made a courageous decision. *Peter Drucker, Austrian writer*

PART 2	CHAPTER 8	CHAPTER 7	CHAPTER 6	CHAPTER 5
THEMES IN MANAGEMENT	Enterprise	Managing for quality	Social responsibility and ethics	Global business: bridging nations and cultures

PART 3	CHAPTER 9	CHAPTER 10	CHAPTER 11
PLANNING AND DECISION MAKING	Planning: coping in an uncertain environment	Strategic management: looking to the long term	Decision making: choosing from alternatives

PART 4	CHAPTER 15	CHAPTER 14	CHAPTER 13	CHAPTER 12
ORGANISING LARGE GROUPS	Human resource management	Managing organisational change	Organisational design: matching the situation	Organisations: principles, models and outcomes

Planning is the first stage of the cycle of planning, organising, implementing and controlling. This forms the thread that runs through Chapters 9 to 24 of the book. In Part 3, the focus is on planning and decision making. To begin, Chapter 9 relates planning to uncertainty arising in the environment. Managers seek appropriate ways to handle what is essentially unknown. The result of the process is a statement of goals and objectives with the means how they are to be achieved.

Chapter 10 deals with strategic planning and management. This means broad planning and implementation in the long term. The chapter shows how the plans of managers at various levels vary in scope and time horizon and explains how they should be fitted into a whole. It also recognises that plans go awry and managers should prepare for the worst.

Along with many other management tasks, making plans involves choices. Indeed, for many commentators, decision making is the core of management. Chapter 11 presents and compares two models that portray this process. Yet it is more than abstract calculation. The chapter examines the important roles played by individuals and groups and how they can so often go wrong. Finally, problems frequently require creative solutions. Therefore, managers are faced with the question of how to simulate and harness creativity within the decision framework.

9

Planning: coping in an uncertain environment

Chapter objectives

When you have finished studying this chapter, you should be able to:

- define a plan and explain the planning process, showing how it relates to the uncertain environment;
- explain levels of planning in the organisation and the links between them;
- classify the types of uncertainty faced by managers and outline how managers respond through forecasting and contingency and crisis planning;
- clarify the purposes of objectives and constraints, goals and mission statements, suggesting why each is needed;
- describe the main problems with, and barriers to, the use of objectives within organisations;
- set some practical processes, appraisal and operations management techniques, within the planning context;
- outline the scope and function of the Business Plan for SMEs;
- support and illustrate the purpose of contingency and crisis planning when unanticipated changes occur.

Uncertain year for Halewood[1]

Employees at Ford's Halewood plant on Merseyside greeted 1997 with a feeling of uncertainty. In mid-January senior managers proposed to union representatives that, to cut costs, operations should be scaled back from two shifts to one. The company, it was said, sought to remove more than 400 jobs from among the 4500 employed on assembly and 1100 making gearboxes. The move was part of a wider strategy to reduce costs in the company's European operations. These had lost £280 million in the third quarter of 1996.

The current Escort model, built also at Valencia in Spain and Saarlouis in Germany, was in decline. Since quality problems at Halewood meant that its output served only the United Kingdom market, the plant was heavily dependent on the Escort's home sales. At its peak, the car had taken 12 per cent of the United Kingdom market. Yet only 129 000 were sold in 1996, about a 6 per cent share. Halewood's highest output had been 200 000. For almost two years, however, there had been periods of short-time working as demand did not recover. Saarlouis was also in difficulties.

A new Escort model was to be launched in 1998. In the highly competitive middle market, profit margins are always thin. Ford was considering whether to cut the number of assembly sites to two, in which case Halewood would switch to another model or close. Low labour costs in Merseyside were not sufficient to offset Halewood's below average productivity and unfavourable location. It may be that a lower volume model with many variants, such as a people carrier, would better suit a low investment, low labour cost setting. Investing in new equipment for the Escort, and then operating it on one shift, would be wasteful.

The government and local agencies had worked with Ford to persuade suppliers to establish satellite plants close to the Halewood factory were the new Escort to be built there. This would have been a *supplier park* whose just-in-time deliveries would follow the rhythm of Ford's line. Not only was the government concerned with local unemployment but also with the chronic unfavourable balance of trade in the automotive sector. Importing a further 125 000 Escorts would not have been good news.

Two weeks later, Ford announced that the new model was not to be built at Halewood. The number of jobs to go within the coming months was 1500. For the rest, plans had not been completed. Therefore, uncertainty over the Escort had been replaced with uncertainty over keeping any of the plant open. Unions reacted by organising a strike ballot among all 30 000 British workers. This move, according to European division chairman Jac Nasser 'sharpened the mind' of the management. Within a further fortnight, he announced that Halewood had been earmarked for the sole source for a new 'people carrier' after 2000. Short-term redundancies were to be scaled back from 1300 to 980 and made voluntary. Plans, according to Nasser, had not been changed. Significant additional investment in the plant would attract, he hoped, a government grant of around £70 million.

By the end of March 1997, the government announced £15 million of regional selective assistance to safeguard jobs at Halewood. Jobs would be saved if the new vehicle output reached the planned 100 000 to 150 000, in line with current Escort production. Yet even this plan was changed. By January 1998, Nasser announced that Halewood had been chosen as the site for building the new Jaguar X400 saloon from 2001. The plant would become part of Ford's Jaguar subsidiary based at Coventry. The £300 million investment would safeguard the 2900 current assembly jobs, and create more opportunities once production started. While this was good news for employees and the local district, some recognised the high risk involved. With its new models, Jaguar was moving into a very competitive market sector and would depend heavily on export success.

Introduction

The term *uncertainty* used in the title of the opening case is often used to refer to a future whose prospects are gloomy. Here some staff, and possibly all, were expected to lose their jobs. The opposite kind of future, with business booming and staff being taken on, gives employees a sense of certainty. What they mean is that they face their own futures with more optimism; they expect their jobs to continue.

From the managers' point of view, however, prospects of growth or decline each present uncertainty. If they cut production only to see sales pick up, they will incur unnecessary costs. If they maintain current output only to see the finished car park fill with unsold models, they will soak up working capital for no extra revenue. And what should individual departments do? Should personnel stop recruiting, engineering delay new installations, or purchasing scale back its orders? Or should they all strive to squeeze that extra unit of production out of the lines?

While most managers do not want to spend time idly contemplating future possibilities, they do need to decide where they want the organisation to be in the future and how to get it there. At Halewood, output had been scaled down through short-time working. Now the new levels of output were confirmed, the scaling down was to be made more permanent. Managers had to work together to make this happen. Dates and numbers had to be agreed both among the management functions and with the important stakeholders – trades unions and suppliers.

At a higher level, the case gives us hints of senior managers making decisions about production of the new model. With the launch less than two years away, work on this project would already have taken five years. Decisions on where to make the car, requiring among other information estimates of likely sales and costs, were imminent. All these policies are carried out and co-ordinated through plans. We have a sense of different time scales and different levels in the management hierarchy. Yet we must not become too attached to the idea of a planning machine, ticking away and co-ordinating activities as in the ideal bureaucracy. Organisations are seldom fully co-ordinated like this, especially when it comes to long range, or strategic plans that have to cope with great uncertainty. Further, as Mintzberg observed, managers seldom engage in reflective, systematic planning, *see* Chapter 1. They do plan, but tend to do so 'on the fly', fitting it in amongst all their other activities.

What is planning?

We are all planners, more than we might imagine. As individuals, we put together menus, make shopping lists, set out essays and revise for examinations, schedule our holidays and make arrangements for our retirement. When in a group we often discuss where to go and what to do. We hope that at least one person has a sense of direction to steer us, and another person a sense of time if there is a deadline. Often, plans are informal, including many in business. Whether formalised or not they give shape and purpose to our lives and enable us to gather resources and cooperate with others in achievement of ends. In larger organisations, plans are usually formal. A useful definition is:

> *A plan is an explicit statement of intention that identifies both objectives and the actions needed to achieve them.*

Note that the statement has two aspects. First, there are objectives. If these were the only elements of a plan then it would amount to no more than a statement of wishes. The second aspect, the statement of actions, spells out the tasks required, including who is to carry them out, when and so on. Objectives without actions are the province of the weak leader who expresses intention but has not the power to carry it out. Actions without objectives mean that the organisation is moving from day to day like some rudderless ship hoping for favourable seas.

The term *objective* presents some difficulty for the management student because it is frequently used interchangeably with terms such as *goal, aim* and so on. Some authors differentiate between shades of meaning while others, and many managers, are less formal. For the moment, we shall stick to the one term, objective. This is a statement about the future state that the organisation wants to achieve. As we shall see below, good objectives identify both this state and *the time when it is to be reached*. In brief:

> *An objective is a defined, measurable result that can be achieved within a stated time.*

The planning process

Following from the definition of a plan,

> *Planning is the process of setting the objectives of an organisation and the means for their achievement.*

While it is sometimes suggested that planning is the primary management function from which all activities follow, it is not a process independent of other managerial activities. For example, it goes hand in hand with control. The former sets the direction and points the organisation along its route; the latter ensures that the direction is maintained or, if that proves impossible, it warns of the need to choose a new direction. Taken together, planning and control form a cycle with four elements shown in Fig. 9.1. While in practice it represents a continuous loop, we can start to read the diagram in a clockwise direction starting from *Formulate plans*. The planning process involves this stage and initiates the next – *Carry out plans*. Control includes two elements – comparison and correction. Comparison requires observation of the outcomes of the implementation, or carrying-out, stage to discover how closely its results match the plan. The last stage, *Take corrective action,* depends on the mismatches between the plan and its achievement. Changes can be made to the way the plan is being carried out (*Review implementation*). Alternatively, if the gap is such that the plan itself needs review, then it can be adapted (*Review future plans*). This idea of a cycle of planning and control is a widespread, recurring one in management. This chapter and the next explain the planning aspects of the cycle. For the control elements that imply feedback to complete the loop *see* Chapters 23 and 24.

Figure 9.1 also illustrates the hierarchical nature of planning. To carry out plans at one level in the organisation usually means the creation of a series of more detailed planning and control cycles at the next lower level, and so on. The diagram

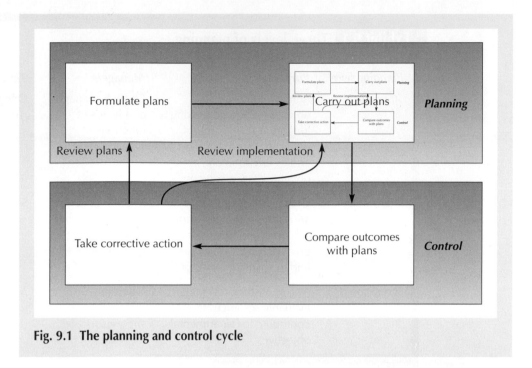

Fig. 9.1 The planning and control cycle

illustrates the links as a set of nested loops. Each *carry out* box contains a complete loop at the next level down. Here the number of loops is limited only by the printer's capability! For instance, when rival mobile telephone companies, Vodaphone and Cellnet, agreed a £42 million joint investment to upgrade communications throughout the Scottish Highlands, they began a series of nested planning and control loops. One team had to plan sites for up to 180 masts, working with local interest groups to minimise impact on the natural environment while maximising effectiveness. Others had to design the network, place construction orders and plan commissioning. Meanwhile, the two companies were developing their own competing marketing and service channels to reach the dispersed population. All this work had to be phased in as the geographical coverage spread.[2]

Levels of planning

For the purposes of our discussion, three planning levels can be identified although in practice there may be more or fewer. Typical terms are *strategic, intermediate* and *operational levels.* They are shown in Exhibit 9.1, which also suggests the managers who are responsible and the time scale covered by each plan. Note that senior managers display a broader scope in their plans, both in terms of areas of the business and time span covered. The latter aspect is important. It is said they have different *planning horizons* (also known as *time horizons*).

▉ *The planning horizon is the time that elapses between making and executing a plan.*

Longer time horizons imply that strategic planners face greater uncertainty than intermediate or tactical planners. Not only are forecasts likely to be less detailed

	Exhibit 9.1	Three levels of planning

Planning level	Purpose	Managers	Time horizon
Strategic	Achieving business objectives through making long-term relationships between the organisation and its environment; obtaining key resources.	General managers and heads of functions.	One year to 10 years or more.
Intermediate	Giving direction to, and allocating resources among, sub-units and functions to give each clear objectives and to ensure co-ordination.	Middle managers working together and also with their departmental teams.	Six months to two years.
Operational	Accomplishing tasks with available resources to contribute to departmental objectives.	Operating unit managers, supervisors and individual staff.	A few hours to one year.

over a longer period but, put more simply, there is more time for unexpected events to occur.

The plans at the three levels have differing purposes. In general, more senior managers are expected to face outwards, that is incorporate the uncertainty of the environment into their planning. In giving directions to lower hierarchical levels, they seek to absorb some of this uncertainty. Intermediate and operational plans can be more specific and concrete because they cover shorter periods and relate to the objectives of the next higher level that should already have been clarified. Agreement over objectives reduces uncertainty for managers. The senior managers help to insulate the operating core of the organisation from environmental uncertainty. At the operations level, some linking, or boundary spanning, roles are assigned to specialist departments. Examples are marketing or purchasing.

Links between levels

Effective planning is based on the co-ordination and linking of plans between levels. There are links that work both upwards and downwards:

■ Downward links occur when managers at each level establish guidelines for their subordinates. As with other plans, these include statements of objectives and resources available for their achievement. Therefore, a *means–ends chain* is established in which each level provides the means to achieve the ends of the next higher one. This is illustrated by the mail-order film processing company of Fig. 9.2. The operations director is responsible for the strategic objective to increase company profits over a period of three years. Figure 9.2 shows how the objectives of two other managers act as means to this end. The manager of the processing plant has, among others, the objective of reducing running costs. Another level below, a supervisor aims to find new ways of scheduling staff to reduce labour costs.

■ Upward links are seen in the way managers apply information on the capacity and capability of their departments in formulating plans. Otherwise, plans would be unrealistic. For instance, the operations director of Fig. 9.2 does not agree to an objective just because its achievement would satisfy the needs of external stakeholders, such as a holding company. It must also imply a recognition that the higher profits can be achieved within the three-year time horizon.

Integration of planning involves both types of link. Senior managers provide leadership, setting out the directions the organisation should follow. This is known as *top-down planning*. At the same time they consult with their teams to find out what is feasible and what ideas the members have for change. This is called *bottom-up*

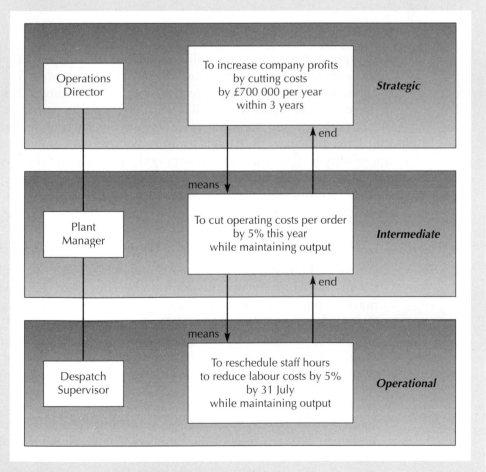

Fig. 9.2 Hierarchy of objectives and constraints

planning. Integration of these styles can be achieved informally although, in large organisations, there may be formal planning cycles and linking methods such as Management by Objectives.

Planning under uncertainty

Lest we overemphasise the notion of planning systems running like clockwork, we should examine the relationship of uncertainty to planning in a little more detail. Organisations are continuously challenged to achieve success in spite of the actions of competitors, governments and other major influences in their environments. They plan partly to face this uncertainty. This is not to try to eliminate it, as in the five-year plans of Soviet economies, but to recognise it and develop appropriate policies. In relatively stable environments, a single, integrated plan may be relevant and achievable. On the other hand, where great uncertainty abounds, the organisation must be prepared to adapt, using contingency plans in the light of emerging difficulties.

■ Types of uncertainty

Regarding the environment, Milliken defined uncertainty as *an individual's perceived inability to predict an organisation's environment accurately*. This arises from two sources. First, the necessary information may be lacking. This would affect all managers in the business in similar ways. Second, the person may not be able to sort out relevant and irrelevant data. This is a reflection of the individual's capability.[3] One difficulty, illustrated by the opening case at Ford, is that the term uncertainty is frequently used to refer both to facts about the environment and to individuals' interpretations.

From her starting definition, Milliken proposed that there are three types of uncertainty.

■ *State uncertainty*

   Difficulties of both data collection and perception cause problems when it comes to knowing about the current environment. This makes prediction doubly difficult. For instance, in our opening case, Ford had good data on market share of the Escort model. This comes from car registrations and is shared throughout the industry. The company knows less about purchasers' attitudes towards its products and how such results suggest future buying decisions. Links are difficult to establish. Although long experience would be a good guide, the company would be uncertain whether the downward sales trend was set to continue.

   Sometimes state uncertainty is concerned with timing. This relates to circumstances typified by, 'We are sure that something is going to happen but we can't say when'. The building of the Channel Tunnel caused this difficulty in many organisations. Construction had started and stopped several times over more than a hundred years. Eventually, as its project progressed, Eurotunnel managers became more and more certain that it would open for business. Delays in the supply of rolling stock, however, meant that the time for running the full service was not known until late. This led to problems for ferry operators and port authorities. They had to plan investments and schedules without knowing when they would have a new competitor.

■ *Effect uncertainty*
The second difficulty for the manager is in trying to assess the impact of future environmental changes on the organisation. For instance, global companies such as Ford have to cope with fluctuating exchange rates and government financial policies as well as the strategies of their competitors. While the company has experience of operating under these conditions, it will always be unsure of the effect of major changes.

■ *Response uncertainty*
Finally, the manager has difficulty in predicting the outcomes of any decision. How will various forces in the environment respond? At Ford, given that the Escort model was to be replaced, the company may reduce prices in an attempt to secure or build market share and ensure that residual stocks are disposed of. Likely customer and competitor responses to such policies are difficult to assess. A further issue was the response of the staff. Managers may have expected some unrest at the plant but could not predict the reaction of workers at other factories. Would sister factories at Bridgend and Dagenham witness strike action or other demonstrations of solidarity if redundancies were announced at Halewood?

In any situation, perceptions of the different types of uncertainty surround the manager's decisions. In the last example, the managers could not predict the trades unions' responses but would have a fair estimate of the loss of output in case of a strike occurring. Rather than wait to see whether a strike might occur, they took the initiative in bringing forward the announcement of future (unchanged) production plans.

▨ Forecasting to counter uncertainty

Faced with uncertainty when planning, managers have two choices. First they can try to reduce it, either by improving the quality of forecasts or, when doubt stems from their own lack of capability, through training in interpretive skills. Second, they try to absorb unexpected changes in the environment through a pattern of contingency plans. We shall study the second later in the chapter but first we shall look at the role of forecasting. Exhibit 9.2 illustrates the need for a long-range forecast.[4]

Forecasts underpin all planning. They may be based on implicit thinking habits or on specially designed models that bring together streams of data into a program or algorithm. Usually the planner has a *time horizon* in mind. This relates to the period between making the plan and its coming into action. A forecast of passenger movements in 2005 differs from the supervisor working out today's route for a delivery van. Although varying in scope, forecasts at each of these levels have much in common. Two broad classes, qualitative and quantitative, together with examples, were discussed in Chapter 3. We shall look here at a practical application.

■ A forecasting example: electricity generation

Electricity is a special kind of product that cannot be stored easily. Production and distribution companies, therefore, place great emphasis on forecasting. They use a mixture of quantitative and qualitative techniques to predict demand with time horizons ranging from a few minutes to many years. Illustrations of how this is achieved, and the uncertainty that managers face, are given in Exhibit 9.3.

Sudden fluctuations can be dramatic. Figure 9.3 shows the time series of demand through the evening of 4 July 1990. The moderate summertime base load of about 26 000 MW has some remarkable peaks. This was the occasion of the World Cup soccer semifinal between England and Germany. The three increasingly unpredictable surges occurred at half-time, full-time and the end of the penalty shoot-out.[5] The largest leap in demand was 2800 MW, equivalent to a modern large power station.

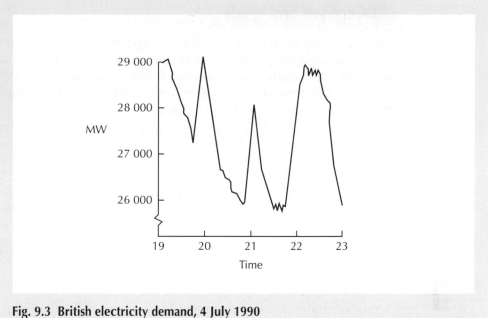

Fig. 9.3 British electricity demand, 4 July 1990

Medium and long-term forecasting are also critically important to the generators and distributors. They want to create budgets as well as take a longer view for the planning of new networks and power stations. The distribution company MANWEB[6] found that during the 20 years to 1990, sales changed as follows: an average annual increase of 1.5 per cent to industrial customers; sales to commercial units increased by 4.1 per cent per annum; domestic consumption remained stable. A time series extrapolation of each sector would be a first stab at future forecasting. However, the company experienced a 15 per cent fall of sales to industrial customers in 1980–1 when there was a significant recession. It also recognises the effect of the weather and the relative prices of other energy sources in those markets where there is competition. The identification of such causal links in its market sectors means that time series forecasting is not good enough. Causal forecasting, using time series extrapolations of underlying variables, to give clearer pictures of the future.

While forecasting techniques have become more sophisticated over the years, especially since the arrival of computer modelling, we should remain cautious about their value. No matter how clever the models, an organisation will never eliminate uncertainty about the future. Unforeseen events are inevitable. Good planners allow for these with contingency plans only to be enacted when needed. We return to these later in the chapter.

Objectives and goals

We have noted the difficulty for the management student in that the term *objective* is often used interchangeably with goal and aim, both in the literature and by managers. One distinction, however, is common and useful. Whereas objectives are specific statements with a time scale, goals refer more generally to desirable ends without measures of value or time.

■ *A goal is a future state that the organisation is trying to achieve.*

Goals are useful when it is meaningful to express the desired state yet impracticable to suggest when it is to be achieved. The goal of Halifax, the converted building society, is to become 'the UK's leading personal financial services company'.[7] Given the uncertain environment, especially in relation to strategies of competitors, it would be rash to include a date in this statement. Usually, goals relate to broader ideas and higher levels of the organisation. They are often summarised in its mission statement.

■ Mission statements

A mission statement is a generalised statement of the organisation's purpose. It can be seen as capturing its *raison d'être*. Johnson and Scholes[8] explain that a useful mission statement may incorporate the following:

■ *Vision*
A view of the desired future of the organisation;

■ *Strategic intent*
The main intentions of the organisation including:
– main activities;
– position sought in each aspect of activity;
– the values that support and constrain the activities.

While some organisations produce detailed mission statements covering the above factors, others prefer brief phrases. Matsushita, whose brands include Panasonic and Technics, does both. It includes: a brief statement of vision – *an electronic enterprise unlike any other in the world* – a summary of strategic intent; an exhortation to all employees to join in; and a slogan to capture the sense of mission.[9] Exhibit 9.4 picks out key details. There is more on mission statements in Chapter 10.

■ What are objectives, goals and mission statements for?

Objectives, goals and a sense of mission bring important benefits within the organisation and send messages to wider audiences. Within the organisation, they provide:

■ *Unity of direction*
Objectives support a sense of direction. They focus members' attention on targets and give an opportunity to co-ordinate effort in achieving them. Without such clarification, each manager may interpret situations differently and find it difficult to act in unison.

Exhibit 9.4 **Matsushita's mission**

Matsushita will be an electronic enterprise unlike any other in the world.
  It will achieve this through:

■ demonstrating the value of the decentralised management system;

■ creating new business and products – adding to key business areas;

■ focusing on software development;

■ innovation in manufacture to achieve harmony with the global environment and to cut lead time throughout the supply chain;

■ promoting global management;

■ pursuing value in sales through increased specialization, higher productivity and accelerated growth.

To achieve progress, the President made the following requests:

■ 'Each employee should become "a driving force for progress" working hard with a strong sense of mission.'

■ 'By setting personal goals and striving to achieve these goals, each employee should work to recognize his highest potential, towards self-actualization.'

The company adopted the 1998 management slogan: 'Take Action for Progress'.

■ *Basis of plans and decisions*
Good objectives help in the production of good plans. They help in choosing priorities, since some objectives will be more urgent or more vital to a company's success than others. Identification of these 'must-do' objectives separates them from others that can be postponed if resources are unavailable.

Objectives offer criteria that can be applied in decision making. Many techniques of operations management, for example, depend for their application on a framework of objectives. Cost is often the overriding criterion. For example, scheduling techniques seek to achieve delivery times at least cost.

■ *Motivation*
The process of objective setting includes encouraging employees to consider, and commit themselves to, the ends of the whole organisation. Beyond building initial commitment, achievable objectives offer the individual a sense of personal achievement. As we shall see in Chapter 16, motivation needs more than a statement of objectives. Yet, without one, motivation would be worthless.

■ *Basis of control*
Through clarifying the performance that is expected, objectives become the basis for control. Used in the bottom right-hand cell of Fig. 9.1, they are the criteria on which comparisons between outcomes and plans are made. Therefore, they determine what is to be measured as well as setting the corresponding performance standards.

Beyond these internal purposes, declarations of objectives and goals are often addressed to wider audiences. When incorporated into mission statements, they signify legitimacy to stakeholders from investors to customers and suppliers. It is intended that these interest groups then regard the organisation in a favourable light and accept its function. The Body Shop is a successful global business that incorporates the values of its founder, Anita Roddick. Strong, clear statements of the company's aims cover not only what business it is in but also how it wishes to carry it out and whom it prefers to recruit as employees or suppliers. Examples of Roddick's own business values, which are incorporated in the goals of The Body Shop, are given in Exhibit 9.5.[10]

Good objectives

From the definition given above, we can see that a good objective should be couched in terms that are quantitative, both in measuring the outcome and the length of time before achievement. Furthermore, since objectives represent formal agreements over means and ends, they should be written. In summary, the tests of a good objective are threefold:

- is the desired result clearly stated?
- is it possible to measure whether the result has been achieved?
- is the time scale made clear?

The examples given in Fig. 9.2 all satisfy these tests. For instance, the plant manager is committed to reduce the ratio of operating costs to orders by 5 per cent. We can infer that the ratio has been established by control systems that collect costs and count orders. The time scale for the change is also set down.

Figure 9.2 brings out a further aspect related to objectives, namely *constraints*. From the example of the despatch supervisor, we see that the objective is 'To reschedule staff hours ... *while maintaining output*'. It would be easy for a line manager to cut staff hours if output was also permitted to fall. The italicised part of the statement, however, mentions a constraint on the cost cutting. Activity must remain at its previous level. Constraints such as this set the limits within which the objective must be achieved.

Constraints can be stated or implied. Explicit references are made to remove doubt in key areas; implied constraints arise from the shared understandings among managers, that is the culture and conventions of the organisation.

Exhibit 9.5 Body *and* Soul: public assertions legitimate The Body Shop's goals and methods

'... as far as I am concerned the business has existed for one reason only – to allow us to use our success to act as a force for social change, to continue the education and consciousness-raising of our staff, to assist development in the Third World and, above all, to help protect the environment.'

'We want to spark conversations with our customers, not browbeat them to buy.'

'One of our main responsibilities is to allow our employees to grow, to give themselves a chance of fulfilling themselves and enhancing the world around them.'

'I have never been able to separate The Body Shop from my own personal values.'

■ Problems with objectives

Conflict

In contrast to the examples of single objectives used so far, managers are usually faced with multiple objectives that may be in conflict. This is the managerial equivalent of jugglers 'keeping all plates in the air'. Most can juggle with one, focusing attention and energy upon its movement. The task becomes more challenging with more plates, yet less attention can be given to each. Then keeping one going is often at the expense of another's fall.

Conflict may be direct. For example, when choosing outputs managers have to balance efficiency and effectiveness, or work speed and quality, or profit margin and sales volume. On the other hand, conflict may be indirect as when activities compete for a constraint. Examples are: two contracts requiring the same item of plant; several customers asking for delivery simultaneously; or too many deadlines for the manager to meet.

Measurability

The achievement of some managerial tasks is difficult to measure. Many managers have to combine such tasks as ensuring that short-term schedules are achieved with other aspects such as developing staff and work teams, improving quality and work processes, and so on. Having a mix of measurable and unmeasurable objectives creates the temptation of concentrating on the former in order to look good. There is the related problem of *measurementship*, where employees deliberately set out to agree low objectives so they can appear good at the period end review.

Means–ends confusion

Difficulties arise when the objective becomes an end in itself and its contribution to the wider effort is forgotten. This is especially true if achievement is the basis of rewards to an individual, department or organisation. There have been many cases of stakeholders or leaders demanding improvements in particular aspects of performance and forgetting that these may be achieved at the expense of equally vital objectives or constraints. In extreme cases, much human ingenuity is devoted to reporting success and hiding failure. For example, in the public sector, policy accomplishment is often through special programmes or 'drives' that fail to incorporate a 'bottom-up' engagement of staff. Who, then, is to blame the junior officers in cases such as Bumblebee in Exhibit 9.6? Commenting on this example, Duckworth said, 'So what's the problem with targets? Nothing in principle. They are a well-tried means of creating organisational focus, mobilising people and providing a concrete measure of success. The problem arises when instead of the target being simply a way of calibrating the delivery of substance, meeting the target itself becomes the goal.'[11]

Change

According to the formal description set out here, each objective, however minor, contributes to the general master plan of the organisation. This immediately raises the question of what happens when circumstances change. In stable environ-

Exhibit 9.6 Bumblebee: fact or fantasy?

Operation Bumblebee was an anti-burglar initiative of the Metropolitan Police. Independent research commissioned by the Home Office found, however, that while there were fewer burglaries, the number of crimes of 'criminal damage' had shot through the roof. Enthusiastic officers seemed to reclassify burglaries into another category in order to meet Bumblebee's targets.

ments, planning can be done with confidence but, if they are unstable, no sooner is the plan created than it is out of date. Therefore, the idea of a master plan for an organisation is a shaky one. Furthermore, at the individual level, detailed objectives lose their value if subject to change outside the manager's control. Pursuing an objective may become irrelevant. Such situations need continual review and a more flexible approach to setting objectives and plans.

Problems with planning

Extending these points on problems with objectives, we can note common practices that hinder successful planning. These are:

- *Inappropriate use of planning specialists*
  Given the complexity that planning can often involve, there is a temptation to delegate much of the activity to specialists. Only they, it is thought, can assemble and handle the range and quantity of data that is needed. This may be satisfactory as long as the specialists' role is to support the line managers responsible for putting the plans into practice. Often, however, a planning department becomes large, self-interested and distant from the line managers. Planning becomes an end in itself with a stress on technical expertise and use of techniques for their own sake. The plans, once delivered to the line managers, are immediately filed in their bottom drawers.

- *Lukewarm top management commitment*
  Senior managers must not only provide the direction for the business, they must also encourage and become involved in the process. It should be something that all managers do. Reasons for lack of involvement could be low morale, conflict among directors, a too powerful strategic planning group or the dominance of one charismatic leader.

- *Lack of planning expertise*
  Many managers have limited experience of collecting and interpreting data related to plans. To them, planning techniques may appear intimidating, or they may be content with simple recipes that give less than the best results. Line managers must, however, both cooperate with and lead planning specialists, ensuring that reality is brought to what would otherwise be abstract modelling of the company's future.

Planning in practice

Given the need to establish levels of planning, an organisation needs to consider how the planning process is to both function within units and pull them together. We can review some approaches, starting with various means of formally integrating plans throughout the organisation. Management by Objectives was developed to enable all staff to define and integrate their objectives and plans and subsequently control their performance. At a more technical, operational level, flow charts, Gantt charts and PERT illustrate how operational plans are formulated and implemented. *Strategic planning,* which in many ways is the origin of all other plans, is dealt with in the next chapter. To round off the review of practice, we shall look at the nature and purpose of the business plan in small and medium-size enterprises.

■ Management by Objectives

Management by Objectives is one of a family of processes that attempt to integrate individual with departmental and organisational objectives. Its aim is to motivate staff through participation in the steps of goal setting, decision making and, to close the cycle, feedback. At the heart of the system is the negotiation of a 'performance contract' which has the following elements:[12]

- *Participation in the setting of objectives.* This, the most difficult step, is intended to strengthen motivation through mutual agreement. Where work teams are involved, all members are invited to join in the process. Not only does it build commitment from staff but part of the contract is that the manager will supply the necessary resources. Hence there is commitment from all sides.

- *Action plans.* Plans set out the courses of action needed to reach the agreed objectives. As each manager and subordinate or group sets out action plans, they are integrated into broader plans at higher levels through a process of adjustment, often helped by an adviser from outside the department. The plans may span periods of six months or a year, depending on the interval between reviews, and include milestones. These are review points marked out along the way.

- *Progress reviews.* Reviews can occur frequently and informally during the planning period, especially at milestones, and formally towards the end. Rather than reinforce commitment to action plans that may be overtaken by events, the reviews are also opportunities to adjust objectives so that they remain relevant and achievable.

- *Appraisal.* Overall performance is appraised annually both for individuals and work teams. Out of the evaluation of success and failure come opportunities to identify ways of improving and needs for personal development. Meanwhile, the evaluation forms a platform for the next round of objectives. One controversial question is whether this stage should be linked to the system of salary review and promotion.

These stages are illustrated in Fig. 9.4, which is based on the example used for Fig. 9.2. Potential benefits of MbO (confusingly, the initials MBO are now used for Management Buy-Out) come from the attention it gives to plans and participation at all levels and their integration. Therefore we can see that it fits in with a particular, participative leadership style to be discussed in Chapter 16.

The formality of MbO is inappropriate in situations of continual change, when management performance is poor or organisational culture resists participation. Furthermore, the accent on formal goals means that appraisal can focus too much on assessing success and failure rather than more modern ideas of continuous team building as a key to high motivation. These pros and cons are summarised in Exhibit 9.7. They can be illustrated by reference to the use of MbO in government administration, where the apparent stability of many departments suggests that a formal, participatory planning system could be valuable. Yet its effectiveness is restricted by the short tenure of leaders, complex and overlapping goals of many public programmes, and constraints of employment contracts. With the drive to 'privatise' both the activities and cultures of public administration, MbO is perceived as out of step with contemporary thought.[13]

After its inception in the 1950s and an enthusiastic commitment by many organisations, the formal use of MbO has declined in recent years. Many remain

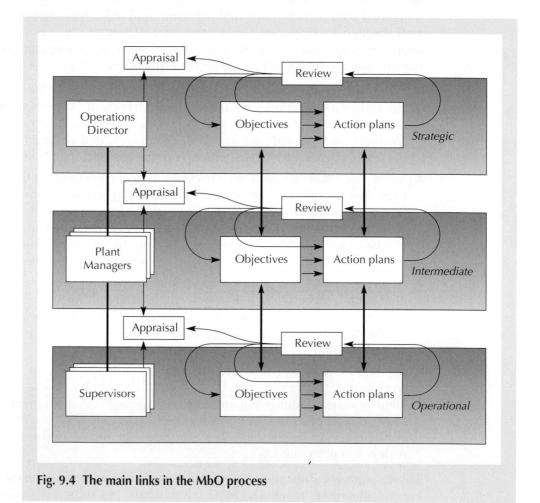

Fig. 9.4 The main links in the MbO process

Exhibit 9.7 Advantages and disadvantages of Management by Objectives	
Advantages of MbO	*Disadvantages of MbO*
Alignment of goals at all levels and across functions.	Not suited to constantly changing conditions.
All participants agree the activities needed to attain shared goals.	Cannot overcome an organisational culture of low participation.
Increased motivation from participation, consensus and perceptions of fairness.	Poor relationships between staff and managers may be worsened.
Improved performance.	Means–ends confusion leads to too much paperwork and little action.

committed to its good aspects. These are the focus on results and the regular appraisal of staff at all levels. The difference between current appraisal methods and MbO is that they now avoid rigid commitment to detailed objectives and action plans. Moreover, organisations themselves have become less rigid with fewer layers. Managers and staff tend to be better qualified and are often better trained. These trends mean that the paperwork of grand systems is replaced by more informal processes.[14] Affected by overtones of bureaucratic rigidity, even the name of MbO had been changed to titles such as 'Staff appraisal' or 'Goal acceptance programme'.[15] There is more on teams and motivation in Chapters 16 and 17.

■ Operational planning

Operational plans are usually short term and, because they involve the commitment of resources, they require a degree of precision not required at the strategic or intermediate levels. For example, weekly production and delivery schedules have to be drawn up, orders have to be placed on suppliers, staffing requirements have to be compared with whom is available, and so on. Specialists in management science have improved the standard of these planning tasks through techniques devised to suit the problems that regularly arise. An early example of planning the flows of coal from pit to power station was illustrated in Exhibit 2.9.

As with plans at other levels, operational plans can be divided into *standing* and *single-use* plans. Standing plans are sets of rules and procedures designed to be used several times, for instance in routine service or manufacture. Their purpose is to regularly achieve targets of efficiency, quality, service and so on. Single-use plans, on the other hand, are set out to achieve a one-off goal, such as the construction of a new plant or the reorganisation of a business. Since the activity is unique to the organisation, it involves more uncertainty. It is common to employ outsiders to advise on or manage these changes. Examples are management consultants specialising in, say, mergers, or civil engineering contractors for whom scheduling of construction projects is routine.

Graphical tools have been widely used to work out and illustrate such planning, although more complex cases are usually handled by computer programs. We can illustrate three here – flow charts, Gantt charts and PERT.

Flow charts

Flow charts are widely used in production and operations planning to sequence tasks and decisions. By breaking complete processes into stages corresponding, say, to departmental or individual responsibilities, they are used to instruct staff on how to proceed. Furthermore, they contribute to process simplification when each stage can be examined to see if it is necessary to the whole procedure. A sample of instructions is shown in Fig. 9.5.[16] It is taken from a car repair manual that uses flow charts and other diagrams instead of the more common verbal approach. This chart uses diamonds to represent binary (yes–no) decisions with good (OK) or no-good (NG) outcomes. Tasks are shown in boxes, each of which is cross-referenced to other sequences in the manual. Its advantage is in simplifying complex process and, in this case, helping users with limited reading skills.

While flow charts are good for setting out sequences and links, especially when decision points are involved, they do not incorporate the time dimension. Hence it is impossible to tell whether two tasks can be carried out simultaneously or estimate the time needed for the whole process.

Gantt charts

Gantt was a pioneer who worked with Frederick Taylor at the Midvale steel works, *see* Chapter 2. In response to problems of scheduling, he developed the now widely used bar chart that carries his name. Examples are seen on the walls of production and despatch units where orders are allocated to machines or vehicles on an hourly or daily basis. Holiday planning charts are also found in many offices. Gantt charts can represent either standing or single-use plans.

The Gantt chart has a row for each order, item of equipment, room, person or whatever is being scheduled. Columns represent time divided into appropriate units. In the example shown in Fig. 9.6, a series of orders, labelled 101 to 105, have to pass through two processes A and B. The time that each needs for each process is known but the manager has to decide the sequence in which they will be carried out. In the upper part of the diagram, the orders are scheduled in according to their numbers. In the lower half, the planner applies a rule of thumb, based on doing the shortest tasks first or last, to enable the total time for all the orders to be reduced.[17] The example shows how testing of alternatives can be carried out in advance and the optimum found. Real-life cases are more complex than the one illustrated here. Schedulers have to combine many items of plant and varying levels of staff to process what may to the outsider seem an infinite variety of orders. Frequently, computer programs will search for best plans, either through trial and error or through the application of well-known decision rules. Alternatively, managers seek to reduce complexity before attempting to schedule tasks.

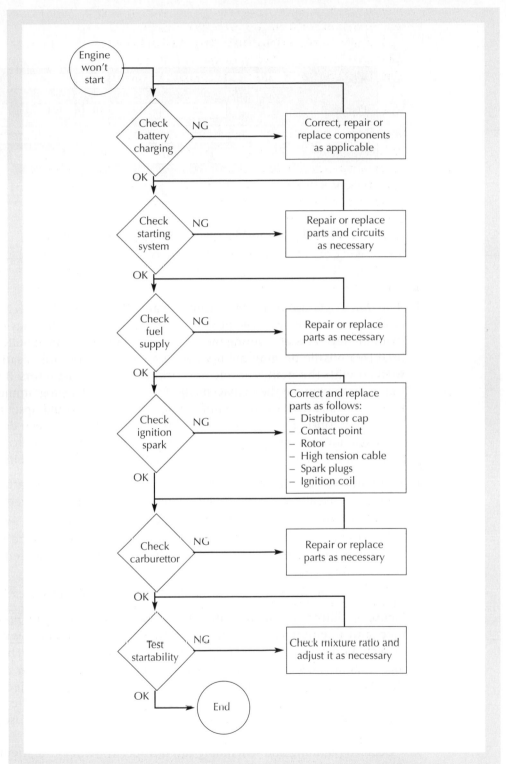

Fig. 9.5 Flow diagram of sequence used to correct engine starting problem

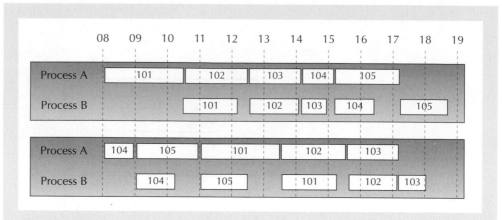

Fig. 9.6 Gantt chart illustrating application in process scheduling

PERT

Suited to single-use plans, Programme Evaluation and Review Technique grew out of the need to manage huge projects made up of many thousands of activities and spanning several years. During the 1950s and 1960s, the United States Navy's Polaris undersea missile programme involved more than 3000 organisations. The Navy worked with the main contractor, Lockheed, and consultants Booz, Allen and Hamilton to improve the management of this and similar programmes. They sought to schedule all activities and identify those whose delay would upset the whole plan. In addition, since many of the component activities had not been done before, they wanted to incorporate the effects of uncertainty in the planned outcomes.

The first output of a PERT exercise is a network. This is created in stages:

1 Divide into elements or work packages. Each represents a bundle of work which is usually the responsibility of one manager or subcontractor.

2 Identify the sequential links among the work packages. For example, 'Before pouring the concrete for the new bridge, shuttering must be fixed, reinforcing mesh must be ready for fitting, the access road reinforced and the crane positioned.'

3 Produce a network which represents the choices made in stages 1 and 2.

Figure 9.7 illustrates an application in the construction of some prototype electro-mechanical equipment.[18] Fifteen work packages, labelled with names and expected durations, have been set out in a network diagram. Three milestones, one each at the start and finish, and one at a half way review point, complete the layout. Inspection shows that the total time for the project is decided by the sequence ABDEHIJKLMPQR (the blue rectangles). This is the so-called *critical path*. It is critical because a delay in any of its elements will cause a delay to the whole project.

Detailed planning and scheduling can now occur, with extra attention being paid to the critical activities. When the project goes ahead, progress can be compared with the plan and adjustment made continually. The approach also allows man-

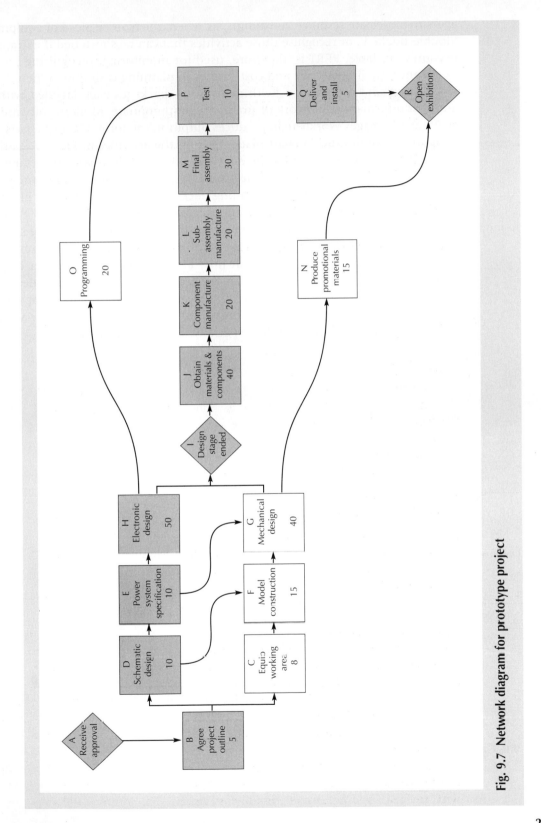

Fig. 9.7 Network diagram for prototype project

agers to anticipate resource constraints, as when a person or piece of equipment is 'double-booked', or recognise those activities that can be shortened if extra money becomes available. PERT is, therefore, used for monitoring, recognising problems in advance, trading off time and cost, and even planning cash flow. When the project is large and complicated, with many work packages each labelled with time and cost information, network diagrams are inappropriate. Modern software, such as Project Manager Workbench, produces output in the form of Gantt charts.

Figure 9.8 shows such a chart made up from the activities in Fig. 9.7. Dark blue bars represent the times when the activities on the critical path must take place. The pale blue activities, on the other hand, have *slack* or *float* represented by the white spaces. Output from the planning package will produce charts like this as well as tables showing resource allocations, cost budgets and so on.

PERT and related techniques have become powerful tools for making single-use plans. In spite of these decision aids, however, finding the optimum balance among objectives of cost, time, cash flow and risk remains a matter of judgement.[19] We should also remember that the technique, like all others, depends on its underlying assumptions and the quality of data used. Estimates of times for work elements that are new to the organisation are subject to greater variation. These should be watched carefully, especially if on the critical path.

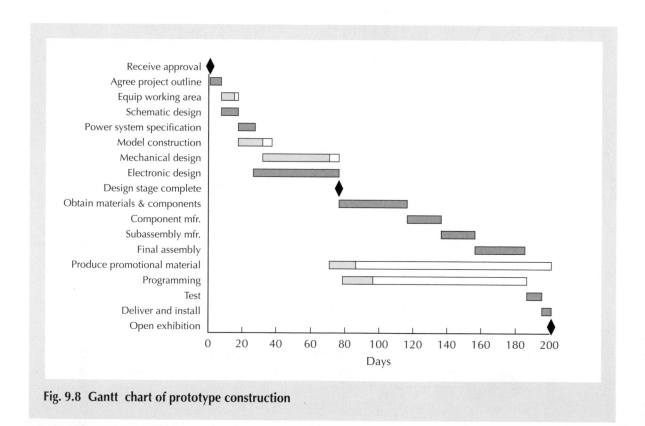

Fig. 9.8 Gantt chart of prototype construction

■ The Business Plan

The Business Plan is a term now frequently used to refer to the document produced at the start-up, or in the early days, of a small enterprise. Its special nature relates to the purposes for which it is produced:

- raising loans from banks or share capital from investors;
- obtaining grants from suitable agencies;
- guidance and control within the business.

The last point is common to all business, so the particular design of the business plan tends to focus on fund raising. Most agencies and banks now require one, at least in outline, before investments are considered. Deakins welcomes this change from the normal practice of the 1970s when 'back of an envelope' sketches of ideas were all that were required by sympathetic bank managers.[20] Yet this observation also suggests that, without pressure from the providers of funds, business plans would not be produced. This is in spite of exhortations to the entrepreneur to produce the plan for the business and not for the outside party.

The sense of instrumental, or tactical, behaviour by the entrepreneur is reinforced by the prescriptive nature of the requirements of some agencies. One problem is that among banks and bank managers the specifications can vary. Further, while the banks do request guarantees in case of doubt, other investors, such as venture capitalists, do not do so. Instead, they ask for even more information!

An outline of the elements needed in a business plan, with a sequence in which they can be put together, is shown in the PERT diagram of Fig. 9.9.[21] The diagram suggests that key elements are:

- self appraisal – the entrepreneur's skills, knowledge and resources;
- product idea – the nature of the new offer to the marketplace;
- market evaluation;
- production plan;
- plans for corresponding functional areas where necessary;
- financial plan including spreadsheets giving expected cash flows and end of period accounts;
- a sensitivity test of the key factors on which the business hinges – what is the down side?
- addressing the plan to the relevant audience.

There are many guides, for example, from the main clearing banks, that give details of each of these stages and other suggestions for inclusion.[22] At this stage we have presented the business plan as summarising a series of practical steps that the entrepreneur may already have decided upon before formalising them in this way. Formal or not, decisions on questions from product choice to production methods, or from pricing to personnel, require a good deal of strategic thinking. They will be raised again in the next chapter.

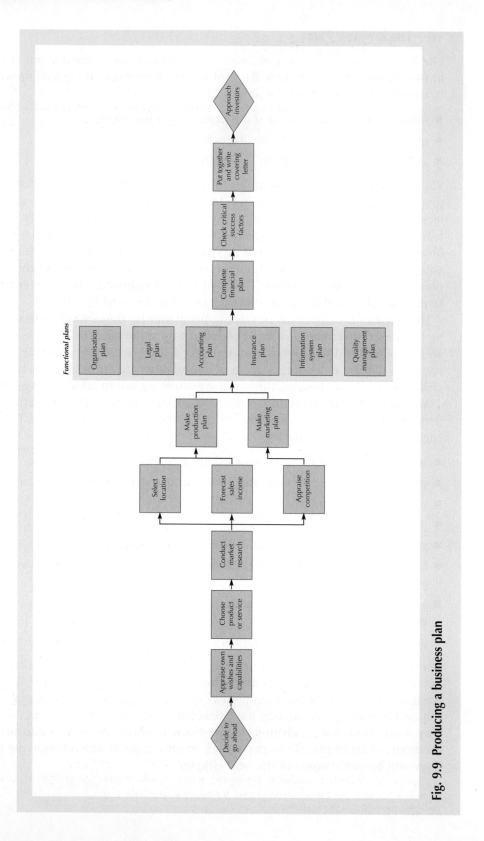

Fig. 9.9 Producing a business plan

Contingencies and crises

Robert Burns wrote, 'The best laid schemes o' mice an' men gang aft a-gley'.[23] This is just as true today. Even the best managed companies find that things go wrong because their environments change in unexpected ways, they do not achieve their targets or they simply make mistakes. The so-called 'Murphy's laws' capture the problem succinctly:

- anything that can go wrong will go wrong;
- some things that cannot go wrong will go wrong;
- when things go wrong, they will do so at the worst possible times.

Good planners prepare as far as possible for these cases. For example, if sales of a product were to fall 25 per cent below expectations, they may have prepared *contingency plans*. These are plans that are to be used only if circumstances warrant them. For instance, more effort could be put into sales, production capacity could be switched to other lines or some parts of the plant could be closed. Clearly, cost and time prevent a plan being made for every eventuality so they are only created for significant cases. IBM's problems at the Atlanta Olympic Games seemed to stem from hurried preparation and inadequate contingency plans, *see* Exhibit 9.8.[24] Such

---

Exhibit 9.8   **IBM's plans *gang a-gley***

Info '96 was the system provided by IBM for the Atlanta Olympic Games. It was a high risk project: if it went well, few would notice; if badly, negative publicity would result.

In the first week of the games, the age of a 21-year-old athlete was given as 97, a French fencer was said to have run faster than Michael Johnson, one boxer seemed to be 60 cm tall while another topped 7 metres! Yet these 'glitches' were minor compared with what happened behind the scenes. Twelve international news agencies, who had each paid $10 000 for the results service, were fed inaccurate and late data. Deadlines were missed; newspapers came out with incomplete results. Some athletes relied on the service to tell them starting times only to miss their events and be disqualified.

The IBM Operations Center was a 1000 square metre windowless hall in a location kept secret for fear of terrorist attack. There was no shortage of hardware including four mainframe systems, 80 mini computers and 7000 lap-tops. Many of the last were manned by volunteers whom IBM blamed for the initial errors. After these mistakes, the company flew in expert reinforcements with the effect of making the pressure cooker atmosphere worse. With no spare hotel rooms, the new staff had to put up on bunk beds in the Center.

In addition to its operations, IBM had paid $40 million to be an official Olympic sponsor. It had invited senior managers from client companies to the Games and had planned a tie-in media campaign. The advertising was dropped.

IBM saw that it had failed to run enough simulated tests on its ambitious exercise in integrated communications. Eventually things improved and there was barely a problem during the last week of the event. Other problems at the Games, from the terrorist bomb to Atlanta's chaotic transport system, overtook the negative publicity. Subsequently, IBM won the contract for Sydney in 2000.

---

lack of preparation seems all too common, either for failures in single projects such as Info '96 or when there are threats to normal operations. The enquiry into the disastrous fire at King's Cross underground station found that London Underground had virtually no formal procedures to deal with such occurrences.

Contingency plans can involve minor changes, such as devoting extra resources to activities that fall behind a project plan or altering schedules when a customer changes an order call-off. At the operational level, such adjustments are commonplace, planners continually updating instructions as new information comes in. Other events can be more threatening to the organisation's survival and, while an organisation cannot prepare in detail for every eventuality, they rehearse *crisis management* procedures. Fire drills and bomb alerts are well-known examples. British Airways has contingency plans for more than a hundred forms of crisis; Procter & Gamble has manuals on every desk in the marketing and communications departments and employs *agents provocateurs* to test its defences.[25] When centralising its computer control at a new site in 1996, the financial institution, Société Générale, studied the risks of threatening actions, such as a break-in, in order both to minimise them *and* to plan backup systems and procedures.

Crisis plans may be well rehearsed for anticipated threatening situations. In general, however, good management involves centralising all control on a well-trained team. Their task is to obtain as much information as possible, act as the only spokespersons for the organisation and act quickly and decisively to bring the crisis under control. Many learnt from Johnson and Johnson's Tylenol experience. Some bottles of this leading North American equivalent of the pain killer Anadin were found to have been deliberately contaminated with cyanide. The company immediately withdrew every bottle from the market, changed the packs to make them tamper proof and launched a media campaign to explain what had happened. Sales soared and market research saw a gain in brand loyalty. In 1985, Perrier, having found traces of benzene in its bottled water, followed the same policy. Sales very quickly returned to normal. The BSE crises of 1995 posed serious problems for many companies in the United Kingdom beef market. McDonald's smarter response enhanced its customer support, *see* Exhibit 9.9.[26]

Compared with the normal loyalty of customers who are satisfied with products and service, if something goes badly wrong and the company handles it

---

Exhibit 9.9 **Customers beef about beef**

In 1995, as the debate over 'mad cow' disease grew in intensity, McDonald's tried for 3 months to persuade its customers that its beef was safe. Along with its main rivals, it did not use offal or meat mechanically stripped from carcases. Then, in March 1996, when the government belatedly admitted that there could be a link between BSE and Creutzfeldt-Jakob disease (CJD) in humans, the company stopped its Big Macs. This response was not to 'scientific evidence' but to consumer emotion. It took five days to arrange for alternative supplies to be brought in from the continent. Rivals Burger King, on the other hand, decided to wait until it had alternative provisions ready before switching. The outcome was a reported increase in McDonald's 70 per cent market share.

courteously and effectively, loyalty can rise substantially.[27] On the other hand, companies with a reputation for covering up face an uphill task when crises arise. The vain attempts of Yorkshire water to explain away its difficulties are summarised in Exhibit 9.10.[28]

Responding, therefore, to the lessons of Murphy's laws, companies should, through planning:

- minimise the possibilities of things going wrong;
- minimise the impact if things go wrong;
- have alternatives available if things go wrong;
- have well-trained teams available if crises arise.

Conclusion: statements of ends and means

We began the chapter by showing that planning is an everyday activity in which we are all engaged. We do this mostly intuitively although, for more important and complex tasks, we may work more formally. Contingency plans are included by habit, as carrying an umbrella or the cash for a taxi. Crises are coped with by extra effort or calling for help.

Things get more complicated in organisations because they require many people to pull in the same direction while remaining ready to change direction. For many organisations, formal, carefully worked out, plans are necessary. Yet they will not suit others, especially the entrepreneurial firm whose advantage lies in its flexibility. The art of planning is to achieve a balance.

Three layers of planning were identified in the chapter. The operating level needs objectives and plans to focus its stream of decisions on ordering, scheduling, task allocation and so on. These are framed in the context of higher level plans that provide the operating level with enough stability to proceed. Strategic planning, the subject of the next chapter, bridges the gap between the need for a manageable operations system and an environment that changes uncertainly.

Exhibit 9.10 Less water, more profit

Faced with a 'once in a hundred year drought', water rationing was introduced throughout Yorkshire in 1995. There were fears for health as towns and cities such as Halifax and Bradford began to run dry and stand pipes were set up. In August, Yorkshire Water dismissed the notion of using road tankers as impossible. Yet, within a month, 700 vehicles a day were carrying supplies from the North. The company chairman claimed to be not taking baths yet a newspaper reported that he regularly visited relatives in another region just for that purpose. It turned out that shortages had been forecast some twenty years earlier and little had been done. Yorkshire Water had applied for drought orders in 5 of the previous 8 years. When profits rose by 48 per cent in 1995, many felt that the company was taking too much advantage of its monopoly position.

At the heart of plans are objectives and goals. Making them explicit, in statements from departmental plans to organisational mission statements, offers important benefits. They provide unity of purpose, motivation and form the basis of control. Furthermore, in linking levels in means–ends chains, they offer the opportunity to co-ordinate the work of the whole. Clearly, there are problems with objective setting and planning. For the former, we noted conflict, confusion between means and ends, and change. The latter is hindered by having too many specialists sometimes lacking expertise, and absence of senior management commitment. Yet many prefer to sort out these difficulties at the planning stage rather than wait until things go wrong later.

Although some approaches, such as Management by Objectives and its successors, seek to link all functions and layers of the organisation, there are other methods that focus on particular aspects of planning. At the operations level, for example, techniques such as flow and Gantt charts and PERT have found widespread application. For the new or small enterprise, the business plan is often drawn up at the behest of investors and other outside stakeholders. Finally, given that even the best laid plans go wrong, many organisations protect themselves against the consequences of failure. Contingency and crisis plans are prepared and tested by wise managers.

Quick check up *Can you ...*

- Define the terms plan and planning;
- Distinguish between an objective and a goal;
- Sketch the planning and control cycle, showing links between levels;
- Define uncertainty, listing three types;
- Suggest four internal benefits of objectives;
- Summarise the threefold test of a good objective;

- State what may be addressed in a mission statement;
- Name three problems with each of objectives and planning;
- Summarise the MbO process;
- Outline three operational planning techniques;
- Distinguish between contingency and crisis planning.

Questions   *Chapter review*

9.1 Define planning and explain the main components of the planning process.

9.2 With what aspects of uncertainty do managers have difficulties with and how do they respond?

9.3 What goes wrong with objectives and planning and how might these difficulties be overcome?

Application

9.4 Suggest goals and objectives for an emergency service such as fire or ambulance.

9.5 Explain how Gantt charts or PERT could be used in planning an important social event such as a wedding or an institution's centenary celebrations.

Investigation

9.6 Examine the mission statements provided by several organisations in the private and public sectors. Many are available with annual reports. Identify and comment on the stakeholders to whom the statements appear to be addressed.

9.7 Study an organisational crisis that has been reported in the newspaper recently. Assess how well the crisis was managed and how far contingency planning could be used to improve the response to future crises.

Planning a season at Jaeger[29]

The Jaeger division is one of the strongest in the Coats Viyella group, Britain's largest clothing manufacturer. This success is built on Jaeger's strong brand recognition, modern design, high quality and commitment to customer service.

Operations at Jaeger are vertically integrated in that it both manufactures and retails its goods. Knitwear is highly automated which means that labour cost differentials have not caused production to be moved to developing countries. More than 90 per cent of goods are made in the UK. The home market has some 230 outlets and exports reach 45 countries. Shops are directly owned sites, department store concessions and franchises. They are reached by direct supplies or through wholesalers.

In common with other leading companies in fashion retailing, Jaeger has moved away from having simply two annual sales seasons, spring and autumn, towards a more continuous replenishment of stores with new designs. In effect, this means five seasons, there being two, early and late, in the spring.

Eleven months is the time taken from conception of a range to the supply of the first batch to the shops. This is found to be the minimum time for everything to be done. Starting the process as late as possible is in the company's interests because it will be more confident of fashion trends.

Design starts with colour. For a spring range, colours are chosen in December and January and discussed with fabric suppliers. Mid-February is the time for the merchandising manager to decide upon the direction of the range. February to May sees cloth selection and ordering of sample lengths. From 1 April to the middle of June, Jaeger goes through fabric modelling and sampling. Designing and modelling of garments occupies May and most of June, while fabric is being obtained for pattern cards and swatches. By 1 June, the merchandise director and product managers review the design work. This leaves one month for pilot and sample orders to be placed and filled. Meanwhile, the company buys cloth. Fabric has a long lead time so 70 per cent of purchase orders are placed by 10 May with the balance by 10 September. Suppliers find the last date quite late.

For the new range, Jaeger's factories make production plans based on sales estimates by 20 July, agreeing delivery dates by the end of that month. This means that the sales department can begin to accept firm orders during August. Before any are received, however, Jaeger has itself to place firm garment requisitions on its own factories. It does this by 1 August, ordering one quarter of estimated sales on the first of each month until November.

The 1 August is also the decision date for information about the range, including prices. Samples, ordered in June, arrive at the warehouses on 10 August and selling starts in earnest ten days later.

Managers right to the top receive weekly reports of progress to remind everyone of the decisions that are due and who has to make them.

Questions

1 What kinds of uncertainty are faced by Jaeger and how does the business respond to them?

2 Select from the case study examples of the levels and kinds of planning used at the company. How are they linked into a whole?

3 Show how a Gantt chart can be used to express the information given about this and other seasons. (Note: You may have to add your estimates to the data to complete your chart.)

Bibliography

A useful study of planning in many types of organisation is Richardson, Bill and Richardson, Roy (1992) *Business Planning: An approach to strategic management*, Second edition, London: Financial Times Pitman Publishing. Numerous titles offering guides for small business include: Salter, Brian (1997) *The Essential Guide to Business Planning and Raising Finance*, Thorogood, and Record, Matthew (1997) *Preparing a Business Plan*, Second edition, How to Books.

References

1. Barrie, Chris (1997) 'Ford wields Halewood axe', *Guardian*, 13 January, 17; Milne, Seamus (1997) 'Ford lifts Halewood threat', *Guardian*, 8 February, 22; Halsall, Martyn (1997) 'Two key car plants rescued', *Guardian*, 28 March, 22; Wolffe, Richard and Simonian, Haig (1998) 'Ford: Jaguar's new baby brings joy to Halewood', *Financial Times*, 7 January.

2. Editorial (1996) 'Mobile phone firms plans masts in Highlands', *The Herald*, 11 November.

3. Milliken, Frances J. (1987) 'Three types of perceived uncertainty about the environment: state, effect and response uncertainty', *Academy of Management Review*, **12**, January, 133–43.

4. Manchester Airport plc (1993) *Runway 2: Planning Application Supporting Statement*, July, mimeo.; Cobham Resource Consultants and Consultants in Environmental Sciences Ltd (1993) *Runway 2: Environmental Statement – Non-technical Summary* Manchester, Manchester Airport plc, July, mimeo; Naylor, John (1996) *Operations Management*, London: Financial Times Pitman Publishing, 288, 304–5.

5. National Grid Company plc (1994) *Highways of Power*.

6. Kleinwort Benson Limited (1990) *Mini Prospectus*: *The Regional Electricity Companies Share Offers*, 21 November, 23–4.

7. Halifax Building Society (1997) *Transfer Document*, Halifax, January, 19.

8. Johnson, Gerry and Scholes, Kevan (1997) *Exploring Corporate Strategy*, London: Prentice Hall, 223–7.

9. Morishita, Yoichi, President of Matsushita (1998) *Summary of Management Policy for 1998*, 9 January: http://www.panasonic.co.jp/corp/message/policy98-e.html.

10. Roddick, Anita (1991) *Body and Soul*, London: Ebury Press, 24–5, 123 and 251.

11. Duckworth, Gary (1994) 'Meeting targets could knock you right off course', *Marketing*, 13 January, 6.

12. Swiss, James E. (1991) *Public Management Systems: Monitoring and Managing Government Performance*, Englewood Cliffs, NJ: Prentice Hall.

13. Poister, Theodore H. and Streib, Gregory (1995) 'MBO in municipal government: variations on a traditional management tool', *Public Administration Review*, **55** (**1**) January–February, 48–56.

14. Fletcher, C. (1993) 'Appraisal: an idea whose time has gone?', *Personnel Management*, September, 34–7.

15. Vecchio, Robert P. (1995) *Organizational Behaviour*, Third edition, Fort Worth, Tex.: The Dryden Press, 222–5.

16. Nissan Motor Co. (1982) *Nissan Prairie Model M10 Series Service Manual*, Tokyo: Nissan Motor Co.

17. Naylor (1996) *op. cit.*, 312–4.

18. Naylor, *ibid.*, 353–64.

19. Icmeli, O., Evenguc, S.S. and Zappe, C.J. (1993) 'Project scheduling problems: a survey', *International Journal of Production and Operations Management*, **13** (**11**), 80–91.

20. Deakins, David (1996) *Entrepreneurship and Small Firms*, London: McGraw-Hill, 222.

21. Based on an idea in Sinopolis, Nicholas C. (1994) *Small Business Management*, Fifth edition, Boston, Mass.: Houghton Mifflin.

22. For example, Barrow, C. (1989) *The Small Business Guide*, London: BBC.

23. *... often go wrong*; Burns, Robert (1759–1796) *To a mouse*.

24. Garrett, Alexander (1995) 'No medals for Atlanta's corporate sponsors', *Observer*, 4 August; Carlin, John (1996) 'And you thought Britain had a bad Games', *Independent*, 5 August.

25. Cannon, Tom (1997) 'From the top', *Guardian: Jobs and Money*, January 25, 29.

26. Editorial (1996) 'Big Mac and little ministers', *Daily Mail*, 25 March; Oram, Patrick (1996) 'Consumers put the bite on burgers', *Financial Times*, 26 March.

27. Armstrong, Stephen (1996) 'So much at steak', *Guardian: Media*, 25 March.

28. 'We're sorry but there's still no water', Editorial, *The Northern Echo*, 11 April, 1996.

29. Young, G. (1985) Untitled seminar paper in McAlhone, B. (ed.) *Directors on Design*, London: The Design Council; Buckley, Christine (1996) 'Coats Viyella to shed jobs', *The Times*, 15 March; also see Coats Viyella's Jaeger page at
http://www.coats-viyella.co.uk/jaeger.htm

10

Strategic management: looking to the long term

Chapter objectives

When you have finished studying this chapter, you should be able to:

- define strategy and identify the key features of strategic thinking;

- outline how attention to strategy has developed over the past 50 years;

- describe and illustrate the main stages of the strategic management process for a strategic business unit;

- give details of the requirements of strategic analysis, selection and implementation;

- evaluate a mission statement;

- explain how SBUs fit into corporate level strategy using the notion of portfolio management;

- summarise important limitations of the formal strategic management approach and their implications.

Nokia connects[1]

From its 1865 origins in forestry, still Finland's largest industry, Nokia grew and spread until, by the early 1990s it had become a sprawling, loss making, conglomerate company. Paper products had grown downstream from the forestry; in the 1960s Nokia had entered rubber and cables; the 1980s saw electronics. There were costly moves into consumer electronics and computers most of which were quickly disposed of.

Then, led by a young team headed by 41-year-old Jorma Ollila, there came a dramatic transformation. The loss making businesses were sold and the businesses refocused on telecommunications. By 1995, 90 per cent of revenues came from this industry; Nokia's mobile equipment, with a 20 per cent share, was second in the world to Motorola. The company's share price had risen twenty fold and it accounted for some 40 per cent of the capitalisation of the Helsinki stock market. Ollila and his team became important symbols of international success in an economy struggling to recover from recession. Unemployment in Finland was 17 per cent.

Commentators attributed success to the skill and vigour of the leadership, whose average age was 42. Ollila knew the business, having been promoted from the telecommunications division. The 1992 reorganisation into three divisions – telecommunications infrastructure, mobile telephones and electronics and cables – had concentrated the business on growing markets. Nokia was able to seize the opportunity of expansion in the infant industry because, along with rivals Motorola and Ericsson, it had manufacturing capacity coupled with global distribution channels. These leaders had more than 70 per cent of the 1995 mobile telephone market. There were some 60 million subscribers, expected to grow to 350 million by 2000. Ownership in Norway and Sweden was 25 per cent of the population.

Apart from the purchase of the United Kingdom company Technophone in 1992, most of Nokia's growth had been created internally.

While its spending on research and development was low (7 per cent of sales, against 20 per cent at Ericsson) it achieved a high return on this investment. Two thirds of products were less than three years old. Nokia's early commitment to the GSM technical standard paid off when it was adopted throughout Europe. Ollila preferred a focused R&D programme maximising returns if the outcomes are successful. Both Nokia and Ericsson grew their businesses from a base in Nordic countries where common technical standards were adopted early. There were setbacks for both in 1995 when a new distribution of United States network licences went mainly to companies favouring the CDMA operating system that was incompatible with GSM. The United States was using almost entirely analogue systems and a rapid change to the superior digital was expected.

Internally, Nokia was having to cope with rapid growth. Employment in the mobile phones division had trebled in three years to 9000. Telecommunications was looking to add 5000 to the 6000 it had in 1994. The divisions were trying to keep their structures as flat as possible, maintaining rapid decision making and enthusing new staff with the open culture. 'The Nokia Way' had core values of high customer satisfaction, respect for the individual, achievement and continuous learning. This meant much training, especially for foreigners who are not used to the informal style of management prevalent in this company.

Indications of future struggles for Nokia came in 1996 when sales and profits fell. The share price tumbled from FM 340 to 190. Product prices fell in maturing markets. The company's warehouses in the United States were overstocked yet in other markets it could not keep up with demand. Looking ahead, there were fears that global companies such as Alcatel (France), NEC (Japan), Northern Telecom (Canada), Philips (The Netherlands) and Siemens (Germany) would use even lower prices to try to push up their small market shares. Nokia's response was to cut costs even further to maintain production volumes and to streamline its range of 40 products while continuing to add high value new ones. Anticipating convergence of technologies within five years, it was relying on the growth of data transmission, launching the 9000 Communicator. This combined telephone, personal organiser, notepad, fax, e-mail and Internet access in a case little bigger than most mobile phones.

One cloud threatens the whole industry – health. Few electrical devices are held as close to the brain for any length of time as the transmitter in a mobile telephone. Studies among Norwegians and Swedes, as well as among groups where usage has been high for some time, have proved inconclusive. Scientists agree that research has fallen behind the rapid growth in use and doubts do exist. Nokia and other companies claim that there is no danger from the tiny one watt transmitters. Digital phones use less power and emit higher frequency, less penetrative signals. Worried users can buy separate earpieces and microphones.

Introduction

The opening case offers some explanations of how a loss-making firm making products from tyres to toilet paper could rise to join the leaders of one of the world's emerging industries. In some ways it should never have happened. Nokia should have been beaten to the tape by firms already established in consumer electronics or telecommunications. Where were the giants of the triad countries? Alongside the Swedish company Ericsson, Nokia had not had, until recently, a base inside one of the great trading blocs. The rest had failed to, or decided not to, compete effectively in the growing marketplace.

The strategy followed by Nokia ensured that it was able to take advantage. The case brings forward important elements of strategic management – choosing the right direction and ensuring that the organisation follows it. Ollila and his team had chosen a focus for the business and sold those activities that did not relate to it. They took a long-term view by investing in both R&D and marketing, applying experience gained in the advanced Nordic market. They built on strengths in distribution and used manufacturing capacity to produce a stream of new products. Having an appropriately decentralised structure with a culture that supported service, flexibility and decision making meant that growth could be accommodated without the organisation becoming weighed down with administration.

Yet the position of Nokia could also be seen as fragile. It had not won the strategic race once and for all. This is rerun every year under new rules. New competitors come in, new technologies emerge. Growing prizes mean that stronger rivals enter; the European GSM gave advantages whereas the developing CDMA system in North America put Nokia temporarily out of the race. Diversified global rivals may be able to withstand the pressure of a health scare in mobile phones. Nokia, so deeply involved in this industry, would be more vulnerable. It is no surprise that rumours, strongly denied, of a merger between Ericsson and Nokia began to circulate at the end of 1996.[2]

■ Strategic thinking

Here we have a picture of strategy in the making. There are three themes that can be picked out:

- *The long term*

  Thinking strategically means raising one's eyes from day-to-day problems to consider how the relationship between the organisation and its environment is shaping up for the long term. Chapter 3 showed how the environment changes in many directions. The strategist looks for patterns, which often at first comprise weak signals or 'straws in the wind'. Having formed a judgement on trends, the search begins for how the organisation should act for the best. In large organisations, internal change can be slow and costly so being able to think as far ahead as possible is valuable.

  We cannot define *long term* precisely. It depends on the speed of change. 'A week is a long time in politics.'[3] The mobile telephone industry was very young and the rate of innovation of new products and services was high. Rivals were poised to enter. It would become a different industry in three years time so that is long term. In contrast, for development managers in the pharmaceuticals industry, where product ideas take at least five years to come to market, three years is just like tomorrow.

- *Big issues*

  Filtering issues of importance from the mass of detailed data is a skill possessed by good strategists. While good management often stems from a willingness to be involved in detail, strategic thinking means converting a deep awareness of trends into an overall picture of the world and how the organisation should relate to it. When, in 1992, Ollila and his team looked at Nokia, they saw there was no way that the business could succeed in all the sectors it was involved in. Furthermore, the wide spread of interests was preventing them from being successful in any of them. They quickly selected an industry where the pattern of emerging events seemed to favour the company provided it concentrated its resources to take advantage.

- *Interdependency*

  The strategist is able to place the big issues on a mental map. Understanding the way that each links to the others enables the manager to see the map as it changes. A price war in a small market may not last long and, not being a *big issue*, would not qualify as strategic. Yet it may be a warning of the unfolding pattern of rivals' behaviour. Action to resist further inroads, for example, when Nokia invested in more cost and price reductions, could cause a competitor to think twice before attacking another, more significant market.

  Interdependency also shows through when it is realised that different companies pursue different strategies. If they are well managed they will each have studied the business environment and come to different conclusions about the best way to proceed. This stems from three factors: different perceptions of uncertainty; unique capabilities; and organisation cultures that support or resist relevant changes.

Strategic management

Strategic management is the systematic application of strategic thinking to the development of the organisation. It is important because it looks to the basic issues that influence long-term success. In this chapter we shall see how organisations create and use strategic plans. These processes and their usefulness are, however, controversial. Therefore, before we look at them in detail, it is worth examining the origins of this recent and changing practice.

■ The emergence of strategic management

The emergence of the explicit application of strategic thinking in organisations occurred in the second half of the twentieth century. While the ideas can be traced from the great leaders of early history to the first half of the century, their growth and deliberate application in business emerged from the war experience of many who later became leaders, *see* Exhibit 10.1. At the same time, there was a flurry of books and papers on the subject.

Greeted with a wave of enthusiasm for planning, especially at the headquarters of large multi-product businesses, the spread of strategic thinking has been neither uniform nor free of controversy. Several schools of thought have emerged, each with its own foundations and arguments about what organisations should do for the best. Losing the sharp focus on overall planning of the 1950s, strategic management has become an *eclectic* field. This means it borrows as much from economics and finance as it does from politics and behavioural science. This change has arisen from disillusionment with general prescriptions and the failure of complex planning when circumstances change so rapidly.

Koch traces six phases that describe the trends in strategic management.[4] Shown on a time-line in Fig. 10.1, they are as follows:

1 *Corporate planning*

   Large companies with many products were the first to become involved. Drucker's *Concepts of the Corporation* and *The Practice of Management*[5] were both influenced by the experience of General Motors, Sears Roebuck, Ford, IBM and other American giants. Alfred Sloan had applied strategic ideas to reorganising General Motors in 1921. He created a structure with central planning and decentralised operations that was widely emulated. Sloan waited until 1963 before publishing his *My Years with General Motors*.[6] Chandler's *Strategy and*

Exhibit 10.1 **Business borrows terms from the armed forces**

Military strategy is the planning of war. Generals regard strategy proper as broad planning for a campaign, that is at army group level or higher. When several allies and services are involved, thus requiring both political and military direction, the process is called *grand strategy*. Below army level, *operational strategy* covers divisions and brigades. The direction of small units is *tactics*.

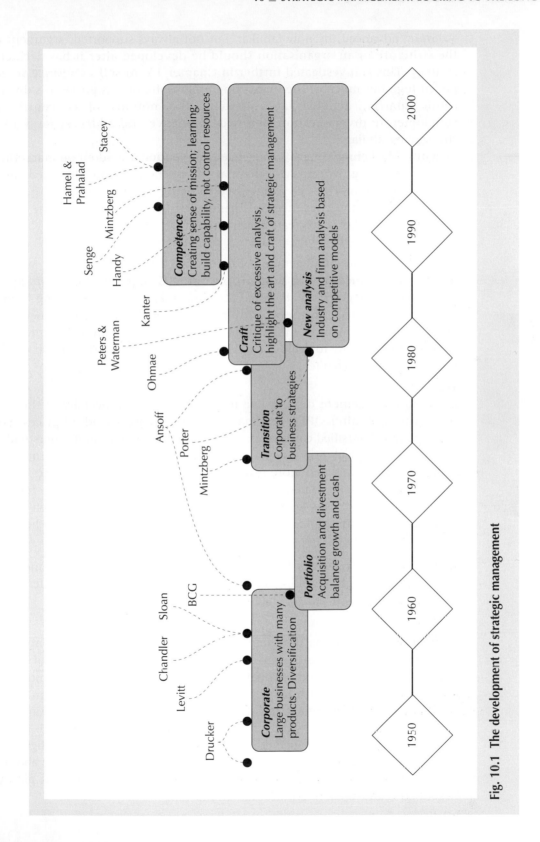

Fig. 10.1 The development of strategic management

Structure[7] advanced the now familiar, but not always supported, argument that the structure of an organisation should be developed after it has decided its strategy. This is investigated further in Chapter 13. Ansoff's *Corporate Strategy*[8] pulled together much of the underlying philosophy of this phase. His diversification matrix, detailed later, brought the notions of concentric and conglomerate diversification to a wide audience and added synergy to the strategic vocabulary.

Levitt's 'Marketing Myopia'[9] challenged conventional wisdom on marketing as selling that had grown up with the mass production system. He urged companies to become market-led as opposed to being dominated by the perceived needs of production efficiency. This parallelled Drucker's case that the primary purpose of business is 'to create a customer'.[10]

2 *Portfolio planning*

Taking further the management of diversified firms, Henderson,[11] with colleagues who joined him at Boston Consulting Group, developed and applied ideas such as the *experience curve* and the *growth-share* matrix. Differing from the earlier broad strategy, the new consultants advocated a detailed microeconomic analysis of each business unit within its sector. The method then prescribed what should be done to achieve a balanced portfolio. There is more on the BCG model later in the chapter.

3 *Transition*

Portfolio management did not live up to its promise, especially in the 1970s recession years after OPEC had managed to increase world oil prices. Some large, widely diversified companies were badly hit. Siemens and others had created large central planning departments that did not produce the anticipated benefits. Planners turned more towards business level analysis. Critics, such as Mintzberg,[12] showed that successful senior managers were less the reflective strategists and more people of intuitive action. They depended as much on 'soft' information and anecdotes as on hard data and financial analysis. They spent much of their time talking and listening and wrote and read little.

After this opening trajectory from the corporate to the business and individual leader level, strategic thinking has fragmented into several complementary schools, running in parallel. We shall give the remaining three here:

4 *Craft*

Mintzberg, by observing how senior managers spent their time, changed the direction for many strategists. Ohmae, writing about leaders of Honda, Matsushita, Toyota and other Japanese companies, showed how intuition, creativity and obsession with being the best were more significant than skills at data analysis.[13] Later, Ohmae has stressed the demands that globalisation places on strategists and how they must combine cross-cultural thinking with financial modelling. Kanter[14] developed the notion of empowerment and highlighted the need to be able to overcome resistance to change. Handy[15] also wrote about the links between policy, accomplishment and structure, stressing that planning should be as much based on intuition as analysis.

Mintzberg has continued his series of critical works stressing the failure of 'big planning'. In *The Rise and Fall of Strategic Planning*,[16] however, he does not condemn planners as having no useful purpose but places them in supporting roles.

5 *New analysis*

Porter's influential *Competitive Strategy* gave a new vigour to the application of the economic theory of the firm. Presenting a model of competition in which firms within industries vie for advantage while at the same time keeping out new entrants, Porter provided both simple explanations of why some firms are successful and some valuable analytical tools. He brought into strategy the terms *generic strategy* and *competitive advantage* that he used for the title of his more rigorous sequel.[17] Competitive strategy provoked a healthy debate over whether the search for a rigid single strategy in an attractive industry was the best policy. There is more on Porter's work later in the chapter.

Peters and Waterman also attempted rigorous analysis in writing *In Search of Excellence* which first appeared in 1982.[18] A comparison of leading companies looked for the management ingredients that distinguished them from the rest. Almost as it was published, however, critics pointed out that the chosen excellent companies were beginning to disappoint. There is more on this work in Chapter 2.

6 *Competence*

Our last phase is the growth of interest in the embedded skills of the organisation. The role of the centre in this setting is as *parent* of the subsidiaries, that is coach and leader, creating growth and ambition and skills that can be applied whatever industry or market the organisation is facing. Senge's *The Fifth Discipline*[19] advocates the *learning organisation*, although the achievement of this plausible idea has been disappointing. Details on learning are given in Chapter 24. Hamel and Prahalad wrote the influential *Competing for the Future*[20] to argue that it is not the current mix of products and markets that gives a firm a secure future. Instead, it possesses *core competences* that it can enhance and apply to an unending stream of future activities. Here are three examples: Nike's core competence is not offering high quality shoes but design and marketing; Sony's lies in miniaturisation; and, at its core, McDonald's offers convenience. Effective management of competences, which means being able to nurture them and transfer them from one area of activity to another, forms the foundation for future success. In other words, core competences create *sustainable competitive advantage*.

Stacey is among those who question the assumptions on which the formal planning process has been constructed.[21] He draws on chaos theory to advocate management processes that learn and interact and are able to adapt to the real nature of the environment – instability. Chapter 24 has more about the application of chaos theory.

■ What is strategic management?

While the above authorities each have different emphases, they share a common theme. Strategic management is a process that guides the long-term development of the organisation. We shall picture the process as having four core activities: analysis, selection, implementation and control. The stages can be summarised as:

- Strategic analysis is the stage of data collection and interpretation. The manager assesses how well the organisation is doing within its changing environment. Questions are asked about the value that the organisation offers to all its stakeholders. There is an appraisal of the resources available and how well they are arranged to provide this value.

- Strategy selection involves the generation of possible choices for the future. Then, the chosen strategy will build on the capabilities or strengths of the organisation compared with the environment. It will look to develop and exploit relative advantages and sustain them over time.

- Strategy implementation means taking the chosen pattern and ensuring that it is carried out through the organisation. In large businesses this may mean a hierarchy of strategies – corporate, business and functional – that fit together rather like the plans of Chapter 9.

- Strategic control is required just as control is needed in any management process. Since every aspect of strategy is in a state of flux, managers need to continually monitor the outcomes of their choices to adapt the policies or the way they are carried out.

A thumbnail sketch of the process is shown in Fig. 10.2. This has much in common with the planning and control model given in Fig. 9.1 but is set out this way to enable us to develop details of strategic management. Before looking at the details, however, we need to set the process in the context of the whole organisation.

Corporate, business and functional strategies

Just as planning has interlinked levels, *see* Chapter 9, so does strategic management. Strategists think in terms of three levels, corporate, business and functional.

Corporate strategy is concerned with the question: What businesses should we be in?

It looks at the business as a whole and considers the combination of businesses, seen in terms of products, markets, nations, technologies and so on that best suits the long-term aims of the stakeholders. We noted that strategic thinking was for-

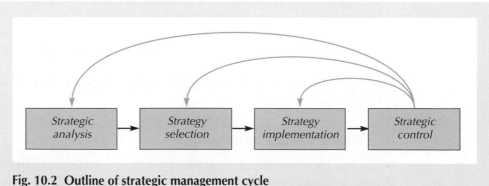

Fig. 10.2 Outline of strategic management cycle

mally applied first to the large, multidivisional corporations that somehow needed overall direction. Their divisions, frequently large firms in their own right, were spread across industries and nations. Each faced different challenges and each was presented with different opportunities. Planners had to decide where to invest funds for the best return, where to build or acquire new businesses, and where to pull out if prospects were poor. They were managing a *portfolio* of businesses. An example of corporate strategy, summarised in Exhibit 10.2, is the acquisition of the United States makers of Dr Pepper and 7-Up soft drinks by Cadbury-Schweppes.[22]

While corporate strategy remains vital, the results of overemphasis on this aspect were the cause of dissatisfaction. In their planning, managers had forgotten the need to plan each unit within the portfolio. This is rather like the general running a campaign as though it were a war game. Counters representing armies or divisions are pushed around on a large-scale map. Meanwhile, if the officer corps is inexperienced, the services not well integrated, and the troops lack proper equipment, what happens on the ground bears little resemblance to the grand strategies of headquarters.

Nowadays, strategists think of the corporate whole as made up of *strategic business units*. SBUs can be considered as businesses in their own right, responsible for a limited product range supplied to a defined market. While one of the functions of headquarters is to integrate relevant activities of its SBUs, each is semi-independent for the purposes of *business-level strategic management*.

> Business strategy is concerned with the question: How do we succeed in this particular business?

This question is asked of every SBU. For example, among other activities, AB Volvo has SBUs in car assembly (Volvo Car Corporation), lorry building and construction equipment manufacture. As VCC's contribution to the corporate strategy of AB Volvo, it is required to plan a new range of cars, including specialist 'niche' models. At the same time it is to reduce the risk involved in development and the drain on corporate cashflow by working through partnerships. Therefore, it has an agreement with Mitsubishi to build a saloon in the Netherlands and another with TVR for an innovative convertible and coupé.[23]

Strategists often go down one more level, thinking in terms of functions. As with the means–ends chain of planning in general, *functional strategies* are the means by which business strategies are carried out.

Exhibit 10.2 **Softly, softly: Cadbury-Schweppes enters the American market**

Cadbury-Schweppes' purchase of the Dr Pepper and 7-Up brands confirmed the company's desire to grow in the attractive soft drinks industry. Its route avoided head on competition with the leading colas, Coca-Cola and Pepsi-Cola. The deal tripled the company's share of the American market to 16 per cent and took it to 9 per cent globally. Dr Pepper, one of the fastest growing soft drinks, would be promoted abroad where consumers are seeking a greater variety of flavours.

> *Functional strategy is concerned with the question: How does this function contribute to the business strategy?*

BMW has managed to capture the niche for cars for up-and-coming managers and professionals. Its products have the aura of being desirable yet not unattainable. To achieve the transformation from a 1960s company making Italian bubble cars under licence, BMW has pursued consistent and steady product development, manufacturing and marketing strategies. It first pitched for the executive market below Mercedes with 2-litre saloons; the 7-series followed and took on its rival directly; then came the 3-series of smaller cars. Manufacturing has consistently focused on quality, at the expense of higher costs. Marketing has created an air of exclusiveness and desirability even though annual output has reached about 600 000 units.[24]

Figure 10.3 summarises the three levels, using BMW as an example. Depending on the level in the organisation, the focus of strategy ranges from achieving an overall balance in the business to optimising the contribution of each section. To examine the strategy management process in more detail it is best to start at the business level. This is long-term management of the strategic business unit. In large businesses, this will take place in the framework of corporate strategy while in smaller ones there will only be one SBU. In this case, corporate and business strategy will be the same.

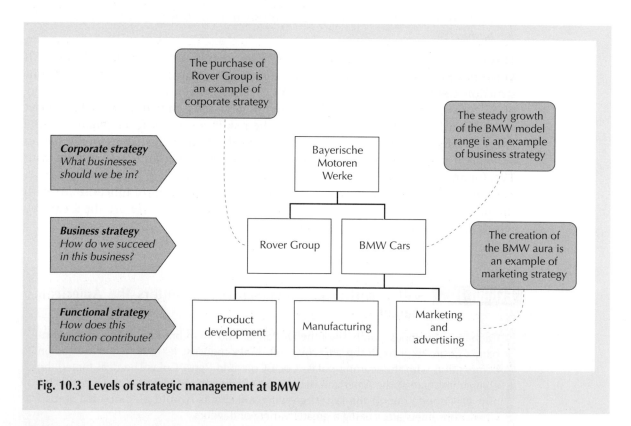

Fig. 10.3 Levels of strategic management at BMW

Business strategy

Figure 10.4 is an expansion of the sketch shown in Fig. 10.2. It shows the elements of each stage of the strategic management process, how they link to form a chain, and how strategic control enables, through feedback of information about outcomes, the elements to be reviewed and changed. We shall consider each in turn.

■ Strategic analysis

This stage, sometimes called *situational analysis*, can be seen as a strategic check up. Managers take a good look at their mission, the environment in which they operate and their organisation itself. Here we shall start with mission, but the analysis should be seen as a continual, integrated process and each element cannot be checked without awareness of the others. In other words, strategic direction, environment and the organisation form a tightly interrelated system.

Mission and goals

Chapter 9 showed how the direction of an organisation is expressed in terms of mission, goals and objectives. The mission is an expression of what it is for, why it exists and what role it seeks in the world. Many organisations have produced *mission statements*. There is often the question, however, of whether these are propaganda or a true expression of the 'sense of mission' which lies at the core of success. This sense covers all aspects from the path sought by the organisation overall to the way that individual members are expected to behave. Koch estimates that half of Japanese firms have this sense yet only 10 per cent of those in the United Kingdom.[25]

To check on a mission it is useful to test its internal consistency and the extent to which it is accepted by all. The Ashridge Mission Model is a valuable tool. A strong sense of mission 'exists when the four elements of mission link tightly together, resonating and reinforcing each other.'[26] Applied to the furniture retailer IKEA[27] in Figure 10.5, the model uses four parameters: purpose, values, strategy and standards of behaviour. The founder of IKEA, Ingvar Kamprad, had a strong belief in the way any business should be conducted and this he incorporated in his 'testament' which guides the business today.

We can use the mission model to carry out two aspects of the check up. First, are the elements of the model consistent? We see clues at IKEA, for example in the way low cost is not just delivered at factory and store level but designs are made for use throughout the world. There is little attempt at local variation. Even directors travel economy. Another example is the way the Swedish identity is maintained. Informal working relationships, typical of Sweden, are reinforced by the leadership style of managers, dress codes and office layouts. Almost the entire design team is Swedish.

The second test looks at whether the goals are consistent with the two other elements in the appraisal stage – resources and environment. This is the mission–environment–resources test to which we return below.

311

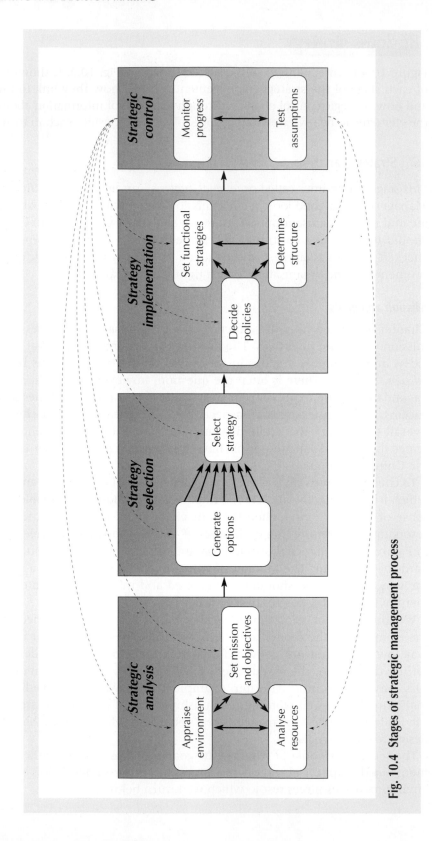

Fig. 10.4 Stages of strategic management process

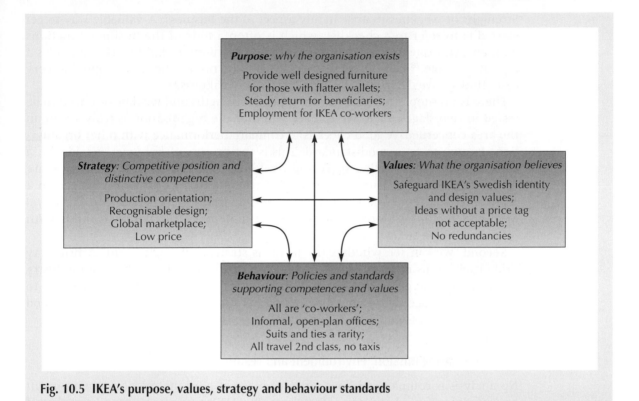

Fig. 10.5 IKEA's purpose, values, strategy and behaviour standards

Assessing the environment

In Chapter 3 we learned how the environment could be investigated and interpreted. From the strategic perspective, it can be categorised into opportunities and threats. These mean just what they say:

> **Opportunities** *are features of the environment that favour the organisation provided it is able to take advantage of them.*

> **Threats** *are features of the environment that will cause the organisation not to achieve its goals if it cannot resist or avoid them.*

The operating environment presents the most obvious opportunities and threats, say from the actions of a competitor or change at an important customer. Yet managers must also investigate the wider environment if they are to succeed in the long term, which is the purpose of strategic management.

Appraising the organisation

A practical and detailed check up of the internal workings of the business is based on looking at its strengths and weaknesses. As with opportunities and threats, these mean just what they say:

> **Strengths** *are favourable internal characteristics that the organisation can apply to achieve its strategic goals.*

> **Weaknesses** *are internal characteristics that hinder or limit goal achievement.*

Strengths or weaknesses arise in any aspect of the business. A valuable way to get started is to refer to a checklist, which is often a tour of the business functions with an extra category for management and organisation. Exhibit 10.3 provides a typical example.[28] Although the checklist is long, not all the items apply in every case. How do we decide what is a strength or a weakness?

There is no simple rule that can be applied. Strengths and weaknesses need to be tested in two stages. First, we can see whether the organisation is truly strong in the area concerned. A good check is to compare performance with other organisations known to set a good standard. This is the process of *benchmarking*. Ideally, a comparison is made with a successful rival but, since they do not willingly share information, the measure can be against the standard of a firm engaged in a related activity. For instance, ICL compared its training methods with the Royal Mail and a United States regional airline matched aircraft turnarounds with motor-racing pit stops.[29]

Second, we can see whether the factor is strategically significant. A firm may pride itself on its excellent stock control. Unfortunately, it may be in an industry where rivals are 'good enough' and, in any case, stock control is not relevant to gaining advantage over them. Taking two extreme examples, it is crucial in food retailing but of less importance in banking or broadcasting.

Comparing mission, environment and resources

No analysis is complete without an assessment of how the mission, environment and organisation's resources interrelate. The MER test can be readily applied if strengths, weaknesses, opportunities and threats are set out in a single table, the well-known SWOT analysis. SWOT should be put to work. Many managers (and students) are satisfied if they can produce long lists in each category but this is to forget the advice given above. Three or four key factors in each enable a meaning-

Exhibit 10.3 Checklist of strenghths and weaknesses

Management and organisation	Finance	Marketing	Operations	Human resources	Research and development
Management quality; Staff quality; Experience; Structure; Planning, information and control systems	Profit margin; Capital ratios; Stock ratios; Credit management; Return on capital; Risk; Costs	Market share; Advertising effectiveness; Channels of distribution; Customer satisfaction; Service reputation; Sales force turnover	Location; Capacity; Age of facilities; Purchasing; Quality management; Efficiency	Skills and qualifications; Union relations; Turnover; Absenteeism; Job satisfaction; Grievances	Basic research; Development capabilities; Research programmes; New product introductions; Process innovations

ful investigation of their interdependence. Figure 10.6 shows a SWOT layout for the furniture SBU of IKEA.[30]

Having set out the SWOT elements, comparison is made among them to answer questions such as: Does the company have the resources and willingness to take advantages of opportunities? Do threats pose risks against which the business is unguarded? Lines, as shown in Fig. 10.6, can be drawn among elements of the SWOT as ideas about relationships grow. We shall pick out one set (show as heavy lines) from the many that can be found. One of IKEA's strengths is its low operating costs based on selling large volumes from a standard product range. Pushing costs down further enables further penetration of current markets and makes entry to

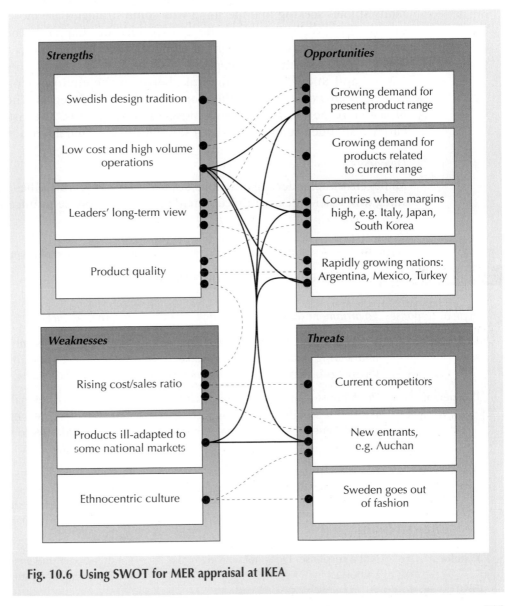

Fig. 10.6 Using SWOT for MER appraisal at IKEA

new ones attractive. Possibilities are nations where current distribution is inefficient or where economic growth is rapid. Unfortunately, standardisation means poor adaptation to the needs of some markets. IKEA would sell more in Germany and the United States if its beds and seats were bigger, Austrians prefer corner settees in their arrangements. Local companies may exploit this weakness, matching IKEA's methods while offering more 'local' ranges. In spite of the threats, however, we can conclude that the expansion strategy implied in the company's mission is built on a realistic match between resources and environment.

Other tests of environment–organisation fit

Apart from this approach to fit based on the SWOT analysis, there have been many studies seeking to understand why some strategies are more successful than others. The 'excellence' approach was explained in Chapter 2. The notion of suitable *generic strategies* was brought in earlier in this chapter and is considered later. We shall give one further example.

Miles and Snow[31] studied the links between the environment, organisations' value systems and the way they formulated their strategies. They named three proactive responses as *defenders, prospectors* and *analysers*. The last group, *reactors*, barely responded at all. Exhibit 10.4 sets out the key characteristics of the types.

Defenders

Managers of defender organisations display their conservative beliefs through pursuing low-risk strategies in secure markets. Their response to uncertainty is to shy

---

Exhibit 10.4 Responses to environmental uncertainty

Type of response	Environment sought	Internal features
Defender	Good at producing limited product range and serving a narrowly defined market. Openings beyond current market not sought.	Internal processes and structure change little. Concern over current efficiency and quality.
Prospector	Produces stream of new products and constantly searches for new market opportunities. Challenges competitors.	Accepts fall of internal efficiency caused by persistent change of products and entry to new markets. Research orientation.
Analyser	Operates in stable and changing product/market sectors. Stays close to customers.	In stable sectors, aims for efficient processes and fixed structures. In changing sectors, studies competitors and imitates their best designs.
Reactor	Not a response. Does not actively make a choice.	Changes only under strong environmental pressure.

away from it, concentrating on serving their narrowly defined markets most efficiently. Strategy focuses on maintaining this effort. Investment in risky new technology, unless it can be applied to the improvement of existing processes, is avoided. This approach is likely to be successful while the chosen technology and the identified markets remain relevant.

Chapter 8 suggests why many SMEs are likely to be defenders. In the closing case, Storwell relies on a clearly defined home market that it satisfies better than its rivals. Yet the business would suffer if 'paperless' archives were realised. Some large organisations are defenders, too. In the restructuring of financial services organisations, for example, some United Kingdom building societies have eschewed the opportunity to become public companies. Examples include Nationwide, which would feature in the Top 100 public companies if it converted. It relies on the traditional personal savings and loans market. Here, high efficiency enables the society to compete successfully with banks.

Prospectors

Prospectors' strategies include searching for new opportunities and taking higher than average risks to achieve them. They are influenced by entrepreneurs, either founders or current leaders, and intrapreneurs. They are more commonly found in emerging industries. When an established industry is attacked by new technologies, the new firms will be prospectors and the existing firms will be defenders. Direct Line showed the characteristics of a prospector when it expanded in the car insurance market, *see* Exhibit 10.5.[32]

Prospectors are not rash. In a study of biotechnology firms in Britain and Germany, Weisenfeld-Schenk showed that prospectors are no more inclined to take on higher risks than the rest.[33] Instead, they *perceive* risks as less high and, given that, approach them in a similar way.

Analysers

Analysers are characterised by 'following the leader', whether a defender or prospector. They either let the prospectors take the risk of developing new

---

Exhibit 10.5 **Direct Line: a prospector enters**

Direct Line, established in 1985, changed the way the British public buys insurance. Founder Peter Woods quickly developed his idea of telephone sales of car insurance into one of the country's most successful firms. Through aiming his business at low risk customers, Woods cut prices. He became one of the nation's highest salaried people. By the early 1990s, Direct Line, with 40 per cent of the market and low costs, seemed unchallengeable. Success continued after takeover by the Royal Bank of Scotland. Profits reached £112 million in 1994–5. By this time, however, competitors with broader market bases had entered. Eagle Star and Norwich Union set up similar operations, eliminating the broker's commission. AA Insurance, which is a broker, cut its own costs and prices. By 1996 there were some 58 companies offering direct insurance. As profits began to fall rapidly, Direct Line turned from prospector to defender, seeking ways of further reducing costs and improving customer retention.

products and opening new markets or evaluate the conservative strategies of defenders. Either way they seek to imitate the best features without infringing intellectual rights such as patents. These organisations do not seek the reputation of leading innovators. Yet they do bring benefits to consumers in terms of providing stiff competition. The reaction of Direct Line's rivals shows their nature as analysers, *see* Exhibit 10.6.[34]

Reactors

Reactors respond little to environmental pressures. They may not have the habits of studying the environment thoroughly, or making sense of it. Alternatively, they may have internal problems and strong resistance to change at all levels. Many argue this is what happens when excessive government protection allows business to atrophy.

Defenders, analysers and prospectors can all be successful provided their strategies fit with their environments. Reactors are outperformed except in industries subject to close regulation.

Strategy selection

Strategic analysis gives a picture of the capabilities of the SBU and the state of its environment. This forms a platform from which the process of strategy selection can begin. A classical decision model, which is covered further in Chapter 11, would present that as a choice from among alternatives. Therefore, before the choice is made, a number of alternatives have to be considered. As Chapter 11 goes on to explain, creating choices and choosing from among them are likely to be intertwined. For clarity, however, we shall look at them as though they were sequential.

There have been many cases of businesses transforming themselves over several years. In the automobile industry, for example, BMW transformed itself from an assembler of bubble cars, Toyota had, in the 1960s, a reputation for turning out 'rust buckets' and Honda did not make cars at all. Yet such transformations are rarely possible unless the company picks the right strategy. Choices can be expressed in terms of *grand strategy*, *directions* and *means*.

Grand strategy alternatives

The grand strategy represents the overall direction the business is going to follow. Three alternatives are presented in Exhibit 10.7. Many businesses, especially small ones, follow a *stability* strategy. This means that the business will go along more or less

---

Exhibit 10.6 Rivals study Direct Line's progress

During the first ten years of Direct Line's life, many rivals acted as analysers, waiting to see if its success would be sustained. Hastings Direct was set up in 1996 by Chiyoda Fire and Marine, one of Japan's Top Ten insurers, 38 per cent owned by Toyota. It intended not only to attack the United Kingdom market but to analyse how to sell cover directly in its soon to be liberalised home market. Japanese companies feared foreign competitors with new methods.

in the current pattern. If markets expand, so will the business, but it will not seek to expand faster than that. A stability strategy will pay off in stable conditions where the business can devote its efforts to improving its efficiency while not being threatened with external change. Finally, there are many organisations constrained by regulations or the expectations of key stakeholders. This is especially true of the public sector and many non-profit organisations. Schools, for example, usually serve their local community; charities are frequently set up to perform defined charitable purposes.

Growth strategies are followed by businesses that see themselves as strong and doing well. Their managers may prefer higher risks and be motivated to expand, for many equate business size with success. Furthermore, in a volatile environment, growth may provide a cushion against a downturn in fortunes or a barrier against the development of a rival.

Retrenchment means drawing back. Falling demand in main markets, pressure on costs through having a poor location, or the loss of key personnel may make it desirable for a business to scale back. Retrenchment may be the only means for the organisation to make the internal improvements necessary to face an increasingly competitive environment. In this light, it is often seen as a temporary expedient before the business adopts a growth or stability strategy starting at the new, lower level. In the ultimate, however, retrenchment could lead to closure.

The use of retrenchment as an interim strategy suggests a further point about the three grand strategies: they can be used in combination. They can be sequenced, for instance growth followed by stability, or pursued simultaneously in different parts of the SBU. For example, stability in the current product line may be looked for while the company prepares to launch a replacement. The case of Ford's new Escort model at the beginning of Chapter 9 is an example.

Exhibit 10.7 **Selection of grand strategies**

Grand strategy	What?	Why?
Stability, or consolidation	Continues with same products, markets, processes. Focus on steady all-round improvement.	Seen to be doing well. Prefers low risk and little change. Stable environment. Stakeholders may impose limits.
Growth, or building	Seeks to add new products, markets and processes, or Looks for major increases in current activity.	Wants to do much better. Prefers higher risk and change. Managers motivated to expand. Volatile environment. Stakeholders have high expectations.
Retrenchment, or withdrawal	Recognises need to cut back on range of products or markets. Seeks to improve current processes through cutting back.	Recognises things are going badly. Threatening environment. Managers opt for survival policy. Stakeholders dissatisfied with current activities.

Directions: internal or external; product or market

The second basic question in considering alternatives is whether the change is to be internal or external. The internal direction means the firm does things itself. It implies change in the volume of output of current products or the introduction of new ones that it has brought forward. Gaining new markets is achieved by direct entry. The external direction, on the other hand, means joining with other organisations to achieve the strategy. Examples include merger, divestment and joint ventures.

These strategies can be presented on the product-market matrix that Ansoff introduced in 1965.[35] In the basic model, Fig. 10.7, two growth directions from a stability strategy are shown – product development and market development. Compared with stability, product development means increasing the product range while continuing to serve current customers. Examples are BMW or Honda adding cars to motorcycles, the Midland bank offering new types of insurance to account holders or any supermarket introducing newspapers, clothing or a pharmacy. Under market development, on the other hand, the organisation sticks to its product range, but offers it to new customers. Examples include new territories, such as exporting, or new segments such as the promotion of malt whisky to younger consumers. In each of these development strategies the business builds from a base that it knows to be strong; it knows its customers or knows its products. They are sometimes referred to as *concentric diversification* since, although there is an element of moving away from the stable state, there remains a strong link to it.

Concentric development seeks to take advantage of *synergy*, the idea that the whole can be greater than the sum of the parts. It is sometimes referred to as the '2+2 = 5 effect' although we should recognise the possibility of synergy being negative. Joining individuals or work groups together does not always result in

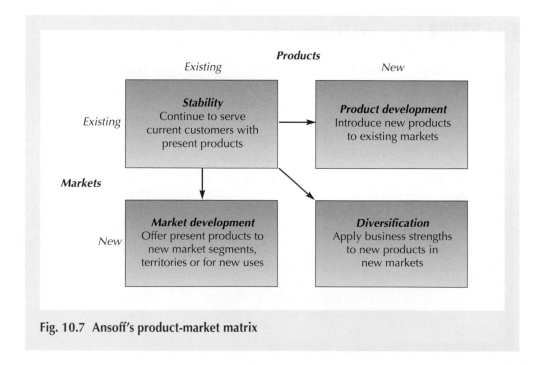

Fig. 10.7 Ansoff's product-market matrix

harmony! Concentrically diversified companies seek synergistic relationships among units as follows:

- *Market synergy* – sales of one product reinforcing sales of another; sharing distribution channels; applying brand names across many products and so on.
- *Operating synergy* – filling out product ranges to occupy spare capacity; sharing infrequently used resources; recycling.
- *Technological synergy* – sharing product or process technology among divisions; exploiting patents throughout world markets.
- *Financial synergy* – allocating funds among units to gain the best return; using financial strength to raise new capital at low cost.
- *Management synergy* – applying core competences learnt in one sector to another; transferring managers with special skills to areas where they are most needed.

In contrast, diversification (sometimes known as *conglomerate diversification*) means abandoning the current product-market base altogether. The business may find little opportunity in concentric moves and seeks completely new lines to which to transfer its competences. This is a risky strategy because the number of unknowns is higher and there is an element of 'burning the boats'. Since the effect of such diversification is to set up a new SBU, this strategy really involves the corporate level. Perhaps the best known conglomerate business in the United Kingdom in recent years has been Hanson Trust. The founders, who became Lords Hanson and White, saw their talent as acquiring and improving companies that had somehow lost their competitiveness. Links among SBUs were less important than turning each unit around. In the early 1980s, acquisition opportunities were cheap. By the 1990s, however, conglomerates were paying such high prices that gaining a return was no longer possible. 1995–6 saw Hanson *demerge*, that is sell most of its international, chemical, insurance, energy, retailing and tobacco interests to focus on building materials and equipment. By a circuitous route, it had become a concentrically diversified company.[36]

Ansoff presented his model at a time when the accent was on expansion and diversification was in vogue. More recently it has been recognised that the strategic management of other changes is equally important. Figure 10.8 shows how the expansion view of Fig. 10.7 can be reflected to show a retrenchment view also. Here, the product-market directions suggest two directions for cutting back – reducing the product range or the customer base. There is also the possibility of cutting both simultaneously when a business has poor prospects and makes a general retreat down to a level at which it can survive and rebuild.

Each directional cell of Fig. 10.8 suggests the internal and external dimensions. The internal examples involve changes of pace of current operations. Alterations can be: the volume and range of products from existing facilities; the capacity of these facilities; developing or withdrawing from markets and so on. Using the external direction, the business deals with other organisations, buying or selling operations or establishing or leaving joint ventures and other agreements.

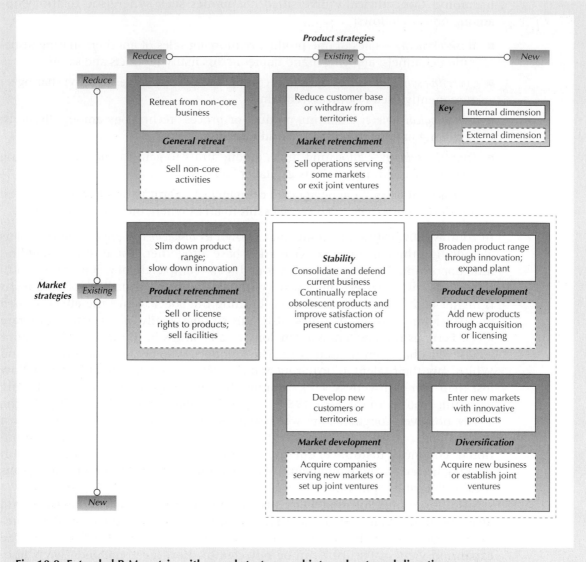

Fig. 10.8 Extended P-M matrix with grand strategy and internal-external directions

Means: how does the business compete?

In competitive environments a company must make basic decisions about how it is to do battle with its rivals. We can examine Porter's work here. Taking a perspective originating in economic analysis, he proposed that it should adopt one of three strategies: differentiation, cost leadership and focus.[37] Their characteristics are set out in Exhibit 10.8.

Differentiation

Following this strategy, the SBU offers added value for factors that it expects its customers to appreciate. Examples are Savile Row suits, Rolls-Royce cars,

Exhibit 10.8 Porter's competitive strategies

Strategy	Features	Resources and skills
Differentiation	Distinguish products from rivals through superior quality, service, speed or response time, or strong brand image. Customers must value benefits more than the extra they have to pay.	Marketing stresses features as value; Effective operations; Design; Research and development; Reputation for providing superior standards.
Cost leadership	Attracts customers by operating more efficiently than rivals and hence charging low prices. Customers must be sensitive to price but standards must be acceptable.	Marketing stresses price as value; Tight cost control; Efficient process development; Product design focused on low costs.
Focus	Differentiation or cost leadership strategies aimed at limited target segment, usually a 'niche' market.	Marketing concentrates on chosen niche; Differentiation or cost leadership in operations as appropriate.

Glenmorangie malt and Hilton hotels. All these are distinctive products that charge a higher price than cheap suits, cars, spirits or lodgings. Note that to be successful with the strategy, the extra value offered must be valued by the customer more than the extra cost it takes to provide it.

Cost leadership

Cost leaders strive to offer lower priced products than their rivals while keeping other aspects of value up to a sufficient standard. Some roadside restaurants, such as Little Chef, attract the traveller through offering attractive meals at low prices. Here the menu and service design, building construction and layout, and tight control systems concentrate on providing meals of acceptable standard at low prices. Budget motel chains such as Travellers' Lodge or Campanile keep costs down with small rooms and a reception area that doubles as a breakfast counter.

Focus

Using a focus strategy, a business concentrates on a subgroup of the market such as a district or buyer group. It tailors its offering to this group using either differentiation or cost leadership. SMEs often thrive by offering speedy service to particular buyers, *see* Storwell in Chapter 8, or they may, through avoiding the expensive overheads of large firms, undercut their prices.

Porter argued that businesses ought to follow one of what he called these *generic strategies*. Failure to do so results in being 'stuck in the middle', having no advantage, and eventual failure. Others have shown, however, that firms can combine cost leadership and differentiation and be successful.[38] Examples are McDonald's and Direct Line. We saw above how the latter sold car insurance by a new speedy and convenient method that, through focus on the low-risk market segment, turned out to be much cheaper than its rivals. Porter's arguments are not now taken as inflexible rules, but notions such as differentiation have entered the language of strategy and form useful aids to debate.

Strategy implementation and control

As Fig. 10.4 shows, putting strategy into practice involves a mixture of: confirming or adapting the organisation structure; making detailed policies including those for each function; and ensuring there is a control system that allocates resources, motivates staff and provides timely information on deviations from planned progress. Putting strategy into action, however, will not happen of its own accord. Senior managers need to display effective leadership, bring together the above elements, persuade others of the benefits to be gained from change and ensure that all share the mission the organisation has set for the future. We saw how Jorma Ollila at Nokia was able to gather and lead a strong team who in turn led the rest of the organisation through its transformation. Topics such as leadership, structure and information systems are covered in later chapters. The last stage of the management process, strategic control, is discussed in Chapters 23 and 24.

Corporate strategy

At the corporate strategy level, organisations consider the mix of SBUs that they have under their control. The need to maintain a balance among these elements is a requirement of large multi-business companies and also organisations such as universities. The latter seek a portfolio of activities that will accommodate a full range of students. Yet universities have difficulty with the competing demands of departments for resources. It is the same for business. Until the former sold Rover Group to BMW, British Aerospace and Saab both manufactured cars and aircraft. How could they decide what to invest in each? The BCG matrix is the best known of a family of models which help in answering such questions.

The Boston Consulting Group matrix, shown in Fig. 10.9, presents the SBUs on a two-dimensional array with scales representing industry growth rate and market share. Comparing SBUs that are in high or low growth industries, and possess high or low market share, creates four categories to make up the corporate portfolio.

We can first refer to the upper grid of Fig. 10.9. *Stars* have high market share in high growth industries. They are important because not only are they doing well but they have potential for further expansion. Since this will need investment in, say, larger capacity plant or distribution channels, the star requires cash to be put in. As its industry becomes more mature and growth slows, less investment will be required and the star will transform itself into a *cash cow*.

Cash cows are strong businesses in slowly growing industries. Low investment means not only that these SBUs should be profitable but also that they should generate surplus cash as they age. From the corporate point of view, cash cows can be 'milked' to provide funds for investment in stars and newer, riskier businesses known as *question marks*.

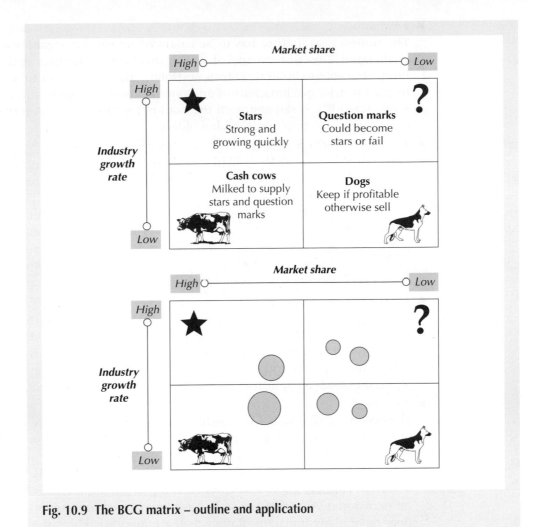

Fig. 10.9 The BCG matrix – outline and application

These businesses, with small shares of rapidly growing sectors, are risky. Question marks can go either way. Investment can develop them into stars or they may make the wrong choices and fail. The business should not, however, shy away from having some question marks in its portfolio, for in them shine the glimmerings of future stars.

Finally, the *dog* is a weak business, having a small share of a slowly growing market. The BCG protagonists argued that, unless a quick recovery could be achieved, a retrenchment policy should be followed.

The lower grid shows how a business with six SBUs could be presented. Each circle represents one unit with diameter corresponding to size. The lone star would be expected to become even brighter as it grows in future years. There is a healthy cash cow producing surplus cash for the star and question marks. Two dogs might be disposed of.

This plausible and beguiling model, with others in similar vein, has received much criticism over the years since its introduction. Key points can be summarised as follows:

■ *Finance*

The notion that finance has to be balanced *within* the organisation has been challenged. Investors, many of whom are huge groupings such as pension funds, are able to build their own portfolios. They prefer not to leave decisions to the internal machinations of any one business. If a company is, in effect, a single star SBU, it can approach the market for investment. Alternatively, cash cows can return surpluses to shareholders.

■ *Measurement of high and low*

Defining and measuring growth and market share are difficult enough. Then come further problems of assessing whether either is high or low. BCG suggested originally that a high growth be more than 10 per cent per annum and a high market share meant that the SBU was at least 50 per cent larger than any of its rivals.[39] This meant that only market leaders (and comfortable ones at that) could appear in the left-hand cells and, since 10 per cent is uncommon, only a few of those would be stars. Most discussion of the approach ignores this point and treats the scales as judgements.

■ *Prescription*

Many, including some of the original advocates, have treated the model as prescriptive. That is they look to it for a view as to what should be done: 'Cash cows should be milked, dogs should be liquidated'. It is clearly inadvisable to base strategy on the rough calculation of two dimensions. The assumption that all businesses in all industries should receive the same treatment is groundless.

■ *Imagery*

Popularity of the model was enhanced by its simple, folksy imagery. Cows effortlessly produce milk while dogs are rather sad and useless creatures. Note that these are American dogs; the term in the New World has overtones of 'cur' that are not recognised among European dog lovers. Yet this imagery can be reversed. Farmers know that cows do not produce milk endlessly. They require an occasional visit from the bull. Cash cows need investment, too. Similarly, dogs have many functions. Rather than a mangy weakling, the dog in Fig. 10.9 is a guard, preventing prospectors from trespassing on a weak segment as a prelude to a full-scale attack.

In spite of such weaknesses, the portfolio concept lives on. Yet now it serves to help debate rather than prescribe what should be done. This trend is not unusual. Many models familiar to strategists have been promoted as the 'one best way' to approach their task. After disillusion has set in, however, they may leave a ghost in the form of a useful idea or a piece of jargon. In any case, weak models do not invalidate the process itself. Strategic management has its stout defenders who, for instance, argue that it is better than 'no planning'.[40] Yet, to close the chapter, we must look at some other criticisms that point to the limits of its benefits.

Limits to strategic management

Criticisms of strategic management have ranged across both its practice and principles. For the former, for instance, follow-up studies based on models in use have shown that they have led to poor decisions. Weaknesses in portfolio models are but one example. The principles of strategic management have also been probed by those who found, for example, that many firms succeed without formal plans. We shall outline two of the main limits here.

Forecasting

Chapter 9 showed that, faced with uncertainty, managers have two choices. First, they can try to reduce it, by improving forecasting and interpretive skills. Strategic forecasting looks towards long-time horizons, often obscured in a haze of incomplete information. Despite this difficulty, there is pressure to come up with firm statements about the future. It is no surprise that these tend to be cautious. Economic forecasts are a good example. Kay noted that they have a tendency to cluster around a safe guess. For instance, in predicting inflation, analysts usually pick a figure between the current rate and the long-term average. Furthermore, they persistently revise their forecasts. Kay reported that the International Monetary Fund, not for the first time, changed its forecasts for average growth in 1996 *three times during the previous year*. Economists could do better if they were invited to state the ranges within which they expected the outcome to fall. But clients and the media continually look for single 'headline' figures.[41] With analysts dithering so much in the short term, what hope for strategic forecasters?

The second approach is to generate a range of contingency plans. This means that if the first choice plan is thwarted for some reason, a second, 'Plan B', is available, and so on. Even here, however, there is a problem. How can the organisation be sure it has an alternative to suit any eventuality? Logically, not knowing the future means it cannot. But many organisations find that testing plans against a range of possible futures helps to ensure they are robust. This is the purpose of creating scenarios.

Scenarios

The approach extends an understanding of relationships to create a sense of what might happen. Following pioneering work by Shell,[42] many companies have come to use *scenario planning* to bridge the gap between the unknowable and the possible. A scenario is a *description of a possible future environment*. It is more than a haphazard collection of trends but a coherent, rich story of a future world. Studies of the past will point to interrelationships that are required in order to make the description internally consistent. The scenario is not a forecast; it is a way of perceiving the future and then exploring its implications. Orwell's *Nineteen Eighty-Four*, written in 1948, was not a forecast. Its success arose partly from its scenario, the believable description of a world that might come to pass.

Companies invite teams of managers to build two or three scenarios as narratives of how events might unfold. Through comparing these possibilities with their analysis of their current business, participants are shaken out of their day-to-day environment and frequently come up with new strategic thinking. They can then assess whether they are likely to cope with the changes that would be required. British Airways reported success with mixed teams of managers, who built scenarios after interviewing others about past changes and future expectations. The company sees scenarios, two of which are sketched in Exhibit 10.9, as analogous to pilots' flight simulators, preparing managers for many eventualities.[43]

Emergent strategy

Mainstream management thinking remains committed to a structured and analytical approach to problems. Its advantages in fields from operations management to credit control are evident. Large businesses could not operate without the efficient procedures that management scientists and others have created. In strategic management, however, many now recognise that analysis has been overemphasised and, as in scenario planning, flexibility, insight and innovation are at least as important.

Do senior managers produce single strategic plans? It seems not. In large businesses faced with rapidly changing environments, there is no place where all strategic decisions are collected. Barwise explains, 'In a fast-changing environment, successful strategies tend to emerge from a series of decisions, often initiated by mid-level managers close to markets and technologies. There may well be no detailed written strategy at all'.[44] According to Mintzberg and other writers who have studied what they actually do, chief executives are not systematic planners. They use information from many sources, often through *ad hoc*, oral interactions. They do not sharply separate planning, implementation and control as stages suggested in models such as Fig. 10.3. This does not mean that Fig. 10.3 is wrong, rather that it is not a full description of what happens.

When there is uncertainty, some of the *intended strategy* is not put into effect. Events that were unexpected need new decisions and these contribute to *emergent strategy*. The middle managers come up with ideas that are generated by their learning about markets and technologies. The two streams of decisions come together to form what actually takes place, the *realised strategy*. Figure 10.10 summarises the relationships.

Exhibit 10.9 Wild Gardens and New Structures: two scenarios for the airline business

Wild Gardens

Market forces unleashed. Asia grows quickly. US in long recession. UK government divided over Europe. EU grows eastward but without single currency. Brussels replaces national governments in airline negotiations. Open skies over Atlantic routes and free access to some domestic airports.

New Structures

Governments have more control. Asia grows slowly. European integration and single currency. Integrated air traffic control and high speed railways. More commitment to the environment. US taxes increased, defence spending cut. Security crisis in Asia, unrest in China. Investment in Asia reduced.

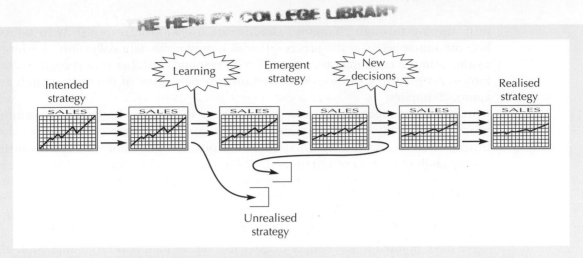

Fig. 10.10 **Intended, deliberate and realised strategies**

Strategy emerges, therefore in a sequence of steps like a waltz on a crowded floor. There is an intention, to proceed counter clockwise according to a set of rules. But as opportunities for movement open and close, the partners have to change. The emergent path traced by their feet depends on this changing environment interpreted through their own creativity. In strategic thinking, such proceeding by steps is known as *logical incrementalism*, a term coined by Quinn.[45]

The implication of this idea of emergence is that strategy is not the process of long-term management of an organisation. Instead it represents the outcome of often complex social, technical and political decision making. It is simply another aspect of management. Does this mean that all the talk of vision, SWOT and directions is misplaced? Mintzberg argues not, for organisations pursue,

> ... *umbrella strategies: the broad outlines are deliberate while the details are allowed to emerge within them. Thus emergent strategies are not bad and deliberate ones good; effective strategies mix these characteristics in ways that reflect the conditions at hand, notably the ability to predict as well as the need to react to unexpected events.*[46]

Mintzberg goes on to argue that planners should be less concerned with perfecting plans in every detail and more involved with coaching managers in strategic thinking and to find originality where it has been hidden. The craft aspects of helping strategy to emerge need to be emphasised.

Conclusion: order or chaos

The last points pull our chapter together. We set out to explore the process of strategic management as a search for fit between the organisation and its environment. If only this could be achieved, it seemed, then the orderly, productive relationship would benefit all the stakeholders of the organisation. Yet strategic management is uncertain and dynamic. It is concerned with keeping the organisation moving through changing, chaotic situations. One response is to try to become much better at the process, that is improve the data collection, the forecasting and the organisation's own ability to respond. Another is to recognise that long-term planning cannot be carried out in the degree of detail that such an approach implies.

Strategic management is also about being in charge. In formal planning processes not only is there the impression that managers are preparing for the future, there is also the legitimation of the position of senior managers whose responsibility for it is not questioned. These factors make espousal of the formal process so attractive. Strategic management is somehow superior management. Yet, while the senior managers may talk strategy, they make a stream of decisions based on a mix of technical rationality and intuition. These form the emergent strategy, how the organisation actually behaves in the long term.

We have pointed to the danger of golden rules, of panaceas to be applied in all cases. For instance, one doesn't simply milk cash cows and dispose of dogs. These days, rules have become more circumspect. We are a long way from, 'Diversify or die!' To put strategy briefly, however, the following rules from Doyle are handy:

1 Strategy must fit the environment;

2 Successful strategies erode; what fits the environment one day may not do so the next;

3 Effectiveness is more important than efficiency: doing the right thing is crucial;

4 Speed is important; doing the right thing must happen early;

5 Organisation and culture are more important than strategy.[47]

Quick check up — *Can you ...*

- Define strategic management and outline its cycle;

- Name three features of strategic thinking;

- Summarise six phases in the emergence of strategic management;

- Identify three levels of strategy;

- State what SWOT stands for;

- Explain the MER test;

- Identify the four strategies from the Miles and Snow study;

- Name the steps of strategy selection;

- Draw Ansoff's product-market matrix;

- Distinguish Porter's generic strategies;

- Explain the BCG matrix and suggest four limitations;

- Suggest two limits to strategic management.

| Questions | *Chapter review* |

10.1 Define strategy and summarise the main components of the strategic management process.

10.2 Outline the main trends in the development of strategic thinking.

10.3 Explain, using your own examples, what Porter meant by generic strategy.

10.4 What are the main strategic directions available to an SBU?

10.5 Use your own illustrations to explain Ansoff's growth matrix and how it can be extended to cope with retrenchment.

Application

10.6 Use a MER analysis to assess the position of an organisation with which you are connected. Does it suggest any problems?

Investigation

10.7 Using an industry report, which may be available in your library, compare the generic strategies of several companies in the same industry. Assess how far they compete directly or avoid it through differentiation.

10.8 Create two scenarios around the idea of being a university student fifteen years from now. What lines of thinking might the scenarios suggest to the strategist?

Dorling Kindersley's strategic vision[48]

CLOSING CASE

Dorling Kindersley publishes educational and reference manuals for adults and children. Its distinctive style, using clever graphics and photography, has been a key to success. Co-founders Peter Kindersley and Christopher Dorling started out to produce highly illustrated reference books for the market that was more visual than most publishers appreciated. The partners launched three titles for Christmas 1974. Two broke even with around 50 000 sales, and one, Hedgecoe's *The Book of Photography*, sold a million. Initially Dorling Kindersley sold by licensing titles to other publishers. This was how they entered the important United States market and, in translation, other important countries.

In 1982, DK began its own imprint. An early success was *The First Aid Manual* that has reached five million sales and is still selling strongly. This was soon topped by the best seller *Family Medical Guide*, now reaching six million copies in 15 languages. In 1987 children's books saw the *Windows on the World* series. Dorling retired in 1987, selling his half share to Reader's Digest. This relationship was not fruitful and soon Kindersley was looking for another publisher to take a stake. In 1991 Microsoft bought a 26 per cent stake, offering a promising link into electronic publishing. Yet that did not work out and, at the 1992 flotation, Microsoft's share was diluted to 18 per cent. It sold out at a handsome profit in 1995.

Meanwhile DK had to learn for itself how to produce CD-Roms. The first list came out in 1994 with all titles developed in-house. Only 12 titles each year were planned. Recognised as high quality by fellow professionals, the CD-Roms met problems in the market, especially from price competition in the United States. DK is less dependent on that one market than its US rivals and uses the struggling retailers less. It has healthy sales through DK Family Library and bundling with sales of PC equipment.

A global philosophy has fuelled expansion. With the high graphical content, publishing in several languages is practicable. The early 1990s also saw DK Inc. set up to publish directly in the United States. Its growth has been rapid. DK Inc. created a large cartography team to work on atlases and travel guides. DK Family Library is a direct channel using agents selling to friends through party plans and so on. There are now some 8500 agents in the United States and 7500 in the United Kingdom. Home demonstrations of CD-Roms quickly hook parents. The new customers do not visit bookshops and therefore the market is widened. Growth in other countries is mainly by co-publishing but more titles do not seem to create much growth. German publishers are very conservative and French ones idiosyncratic. DK is considering whether to use formal joint ventures or go it alone. Some other expansion has been by small acquisitions to gain needed expertise. In 1995, DK bought Henderson, publisher of children's pocket money books and, in 1996, Hugo Language Books for £1.2 million.

Quality and innovation have always been at the core of the business. New technology was pioneered and DK went into CD-Roms early. Kindersley shows no reverence for the book as such, pointing out the benefits of a database over a 20-volume encyclopaedia. Furthermore, DK has never seen itself as a service to authors. It is a book creation and sales business. Publishing decisions are led by the market. The company neither publishes on editor's hunches nor does it bring out a long list in the hope that some will do well while

the rest are remaindered. DK's titles follow extensive market testing both with booksellers and overseas co-publishers. This approach means that the company's list, with some 90 adult books and twice that number for children, is very short in comparison with other publishers. On the other hand, 90 per cent of all titles are still in print. Each is treated as a best seller and none is left to fend for itself. Average sales reach 250 000 for the adult range and 150 000 for the children's.

The recession of the 1990s left many publishers struggling but DK expanded steadily. Turnover rose from £42 million in 1991 to £174 million five years later, 5 per cent per annum ahead of the strategic plan. In spite of a corresponding rise in employee numbers to 1600 in 1996, DK retains the buzz of the small entrepreneurial firm. Groups of four or five work on a book, including editor and designer. There may be 20 on a multimedia project. Each person's participation is recognised and is named in the list of credits. Staff in the book division average 31 years old and multimedia 27. Commitment to quality is unstinting. Projects cost between £250 000 and £1 million, or an average of £1200 per page. The best authors are drawn in; leading institutions, such as the Royal Horticultural Society, the British Medical Association or their overseas equivalents, are invited to endorse the work. In spite of a stock market valuation in the hundreds of millions, the company does not spend lavishly on its senior staff. Directors fly economy and Kindersley himself often cycles to work.

Following positive reports by analysts in the previous autumn, 1997 opened with less rosy prospects. Sterling had appreciated 9 per cent against the United States dollar during the previous year. Dollar sales, already under competitive pressure, were worth less. DK's costs, on the other hand, rose, mainly in pounds. Shares, having risen from 165 in 1992 to a high of 645, fell to 430.

Questions

1 Go through the case and underline each strategic issue mentioned. Assemble these issues into a SWOT framework, checking that they are relevant.

2 What does the case state or imply about the company's mission? Outline what its mission statement might look like.

3 Assess how well DK satisfies the MER test. Can you foresee any difficulties?

4 DK's generic strategy is differentiated and focused. How vulnerable is this strategy to competition?

Bibliography

For further, if often advanced, reading on any of the schools of strategy you may use the references given throughout the chapter. Leading texts on strategy include Johnson, Gerry and Scholes, Kevan (1997) *Exploring Corporate Strategy*, London: Prentice Hall and Lynch, Richard (1977) *Corporate Strategy*, London: Financial Times Pitman Publishing. Crainer, Stuart (1995) *Key Management Ideas* and Koch, Richard (1995) *The Financial Times Guide to Strategy* (both London: Financial Times Pitman Publishing) give valuable overviews. Journals, including *Management Today*, *Long Range Planning* and *Management Decision*, cover many aspects of strategic thinking.

References

1. Carnegy, Hugh (1995) 'Scared of growing fat and lazy', 10 July; Carnegy, Hugh (1996). 'North star seeks another way to shine', 17 June; Carnegy, Hugh (1996) 'Technology: Mobile phones brain teaser', 16 July; Cane, Alan (1995) 'Little room at the top in the mobile market', 14 July; Brown-Hulmes, Christopher (1996) 'Nokia says goodbye to the golden days', 1 March; all *Financial Times*.
2. 'Rumeurs de fusion entre Nokia et Ericsson', *Les Echos*, 19 December, 1996.
3. Attributed to Harold Wilson, United Kingdom Prime Minister, *Oxford Dictionary of Quotations*, 1965–6, 574 (18).
4. Koch, Richard (1995) *Financial Times Guide to Strategy*, London: Financial Times Pitman Publishing, 6–9.
5. Drucker, Peter F. (1972, originally 1946) *Concepts of the Corporation*, New York: Times-Mirror; (1955) *The Practice of Management*, London: Pan.
6. Sloan, Alfred P. (1986) *My Years with General Motors*, Harmondsworth: Penguin.
7. Chandler, Alfred (1962) *Strategy and Structure: Chapters in the history of American industrial enterprise*, Cambridge, Mass.: MIT Press.
8. Ansoff, H. Igor (1965) *Corporate Strategy*, New York: McGraw-Hill.
9. Levitt, Theodore (1960) 'Marketing myopia', *Harvard Business Review*, July–August.
10. Drucker (1955) *op. cit.*, 52.
11. Henderson, Bruce (1984) *The Logic of Business Strategy*, Cambridge, Mass.: Ballinger.
12. Mintzberg, Henry (1973) *The Nature of Managerial Work*, New York: Harper & Row.
13. Ohmae, Kenichi (1982) *The Mind of the Strategist*, Harmondsworth: Penguin.
14. Kanter, Rosabeth Moss (1989) *When Giants Learn to Dance: Mastering the art of strategy, management and careers in the 1990s*, London: Unwin.
15. Handy, Charles (1989) *The Age of Unreason*, London: Arrow.
16. Mintzberg, Henry (1994) *The Rise and Fall of Strategic Planning*, London: Prentice Hall.
17. Porter, Michael E. (1980) *Competitive Strategy*, New York: Free Press; *idem* (1985) *Competitive Advantage*, New York: Free Press.

18. Peters, Thomas J. and Waterman, Robert H. (1989) *In Search of Excellence: Lessons from America's best-run companies*, London: Harper & Row.

19. Senge, Peter M. (1990) *The Fifth Discipline: The art and practice of the learning organisation*, New York: Doubleday.

20. Hamel, Gary and Prahalad, C.K. (1994) *Competing for the Future*, Boston, Mass.: Harvard Business School Press; *see also* the useful web site of Hamel's company, Strategos: http://www.Strategosnet.com

21. Stacey, Ralph D. (1993) *Strategic Management and Organisational Dynamics*, London: Financial Times Pitman Publishing.

22. Oram, Roderick (1995) 'Cadbury makes $2.5 billion offer for Dr Pepper: Gamble for soft drinks market share poses stiffest challenge yet for UK group', *Financial Times*, 27 January, 19.

23. Simonian, Haig (1995) 'Volvo takes a gamble with untried partner', *Financial Times*, 26 September, 24.

24. Simonian, Haig (1995) 'Survey of Europe's most respected companies (11). A desirable icon of the age – Profile, BMW', *Financial Times*, 19 September, IV.

25. Koch (1995) *op. cit.*, 236.

26. Campbell, Andrew and Young, Sally (1991) 'Creating a sense of mission', *Long Range Planning*, 24 (4)10–20.

27. Carnegy, Hugh (1995) 'Struggle to save the soul of IKEA', *Financial Times*, 27 March, 12; Richards, Hale (1996) 'IKEA founder still part of the furniture – Ingvar Kamprad has built a dynasty that will survive his departure – when he decides it's time', *The European*, 22 February.

28. Based on Daft, Richard L. (1993) *Management*, Third edition, Orlando, Fla.: The Dryden Press, 224.

29. Trapp, Roger (1994) 'Benchmarking moves on to bench testing', *Independent on Sunday*, 9 January, 13.

30. Villarno, Lalo Agustina y Pilar (1996) 'La distribucion tiembla ante el avance de los "category killers"', *Actualidad Economica*, 5 February; News item (1996) 'Un chiffre d'affaires en croissance de 8% dans le monde', *Les Echos*, 27 September; Paine, Ines Garcia (1996) 'IKEA enciende la luz de alarma en las empresas del mueble', *Actualidad Economica*, 11 November.

31. Shortell, Stephen M. and Zajac, Edward J. (1990) 'Perceptual and archival measures of Miles and Snow's strategic types: a comprehensive assessment of reliability and validity', *Academy of Management Journal*, **33**, December, 817–32.

32. Brierly, Sean (1996) 'Red phone in dire need of a new line', *Marketing Week*, 28 June; Mortished, Carl (1996) 'Tempus; Insurance – Direct Line', *Daily Telegraph*, 30 November.

33. Weisenfeld-Schenk, Ursula (1994) 'Technology strategies and the Miles & Snow typology: a study of the biotechnology industries', *R&D Management*, **24** (**1**), January, 57–8.

34. Sunderland, Ruth (1996) 'Japan blow to Direct Line', *Mail on Sunday: Financial Mail*, 24 November.

35. Ansoff, H. Igor (1965) *Corporate Strategy*, New York: McGraw-Hill.

36. Jackson, Tony (1996) 'Big can still be beautiful: Although the Hanson era is at an end, a new breed of conglomerates has prospered by adding value', *Financial Times*, 1 October; Bennett, Neil (1996) 'New Hanson will build on strengths', *Sunday Telegraph*, 29 December.

37. Porter (1980) *op. cit.*

38. Miller, D. and Friesen, P.H. (1986) 'Generic strategies and performance: an empirical examination with American data. Part 1: Testing Porter', *Organisation Studies*, **7** (**1**) 37–55; *idem* (1986) 'Porter's (1980) generic strategies and performance: an empirical

investigation with American data. Part 2: Performance implications', *Organisation Studies*, **7** (**3**) 255–62.

39. Henderson (1984) *op. cit.*, 56–61.

40. Richardson, Bill (1995) 'In defence of business planning: Why and how it still works for small firms and corporations of small business units', *Small Business and Enterprise Development*, **2**, 41–57.

41. Kay, John quoted in Leading Article (1995) 'Economics as futurology', *Financial Times*, 5 October, 23.

42. Schwartz, Peter (1996) *The Art of the Long View: Planning for the future in an uncertain world*, New York: Doubleday; for discussion of Shell's own scenarios, start at http://www.shell.com/b/b2_03.html

43. Skapinker, Michael (1995) 'Plane talking – BA is using scenario planning to prepare executives for the unexpected', *Financial Times*, 24 February, 16.

44. Barwise, Patrick (1996) 'Mastering Management 15(2): Strategic investment decisions and emergent strategy', *Financial Times*, 16 February.

45. Quinn, J.B. (1980) 'Managing strategic change', *Sloan Management Review*, **21** (**4**), 3–20.

46. Mintzberg (1994) *op. cit.*, 25.

47. Doyle, Peter (1996) 'From the top', *Guardian: Management section*, 16 November, 23.

48. van de Vliet, Anita (1996) 'Dorling Kindersley's limitless vision', *Management Today*, December, 50–4; Freeborn, Tim (1996) 'A multimedia massacre', *Daily Mail*, 18 December; Cowe, Roger (1996) 'Textbook business turns knowledge into profits', *Guardian*, 17 September; Rodgers, Paul (1996) 'My first million', *Independent on Sunday*, 7 April; www.dk.com

11

Decision making: choosing from alternatives

Chapter objectives

When you have finished studying this chapter, you should be able to:

■ explain the causes of increasing complexity facing modern decision makers;

■ compare risk, uncertainty and ambiguity in problem settings;

■ describe the different types of decision made in organisations and match different styles to them;

■ set out and explain the steps of the rational and administrative decision models, comparing the applicability of each;

■ describe the main decision traps facing individuals – heuristics, framing, escalation of commitment and overconfidence; show how these may be avoided;

■ assess the value of having groups involved in decision making;

■ identify the symptoms of groupthink and polarisation and how a manager may prevent them;

■ recognise creativity and show how it can be cultivated in the organisational context;

■ construct mind maps and decision trees as aids to decision making.

Air traffic control: streams of complex, risky decisions[1]

At the London Air Traffic Control Centre (LATCC) at West Drayton, there are two control rooms. One deals with all movements into Gatwick, Heathrow and Stansted airports. Of these, Heathrow is the busiest with 1300 daily incoming flights peaking at more than 80 per hour. The other room oversees all commercial flights over England and Wales.

Air traffic controllers (ATCs) follow movements on large radar screens. Each aircraft is shown by a dot to which is attached its call sign and destination. ATCs cope with routine instructions and emergencies. The latter range from priority landings for planes with sick passengers to coping with dangerous incidents. With the 1.6 million commercial flights in British air space growing at about 5 per cent annually, air safety is the most important task for the nation's 1800 controllers. An important feature is maintaining separation distances. International agreement sets vertical intervals, or flight levels, in increments of 1000 feet, and lateral distances within a level at 5 miles. Close to airports, these gaps may be reduced. As aircraft prepare for landing, they are given permission by the ATCs to descend from level to level as they approach. If traffic is heavy, the aircraft are directed towards a 'hold' or 'stack' where they circle, one at each level, until a landing slot becomes available.

Where aircraft come together, as in holds, there is an increasing risk of collision, especially through human error. Heathrow normally has two holding areas, Biggin Hill and Ockham. On 22 November 1996, a controller cleared a Boeing 757, circling at Biggin Hill, to descend from 11 000 to 9000 ft. having overlooked the presence of another that had been at 10 000 ft for 10 minutes. This may have been due to both planes being of the same type and airline. Fortunately, the crew of the descending aircraft saw the second below and were able to level at 10 400 ft before climbing back to 11 000 ft. Some 40 per cent of

mistakes by controllers allow aircraft to get too close. Among pilots, non-compliance with ATC instructions and deviations from set levels each account for 30 per cent of errors.

Improving the efficiency of flow is vital. In Europe, airport congestion is the greatest single threat to continued expansion in the region. Of Europe's 29 major airports, 25 will have a serious runway capacity shortage by 2005. In 1995, 19 per cent of flights were delayed by lack of slot capacity, costing £2 billion. Yet safety must remain paramount. Automation is being introduced but experts believe that future ATCs will still make the major decisions on speed, direction, height and separation. The controller must be kept 'in the loop' rather than pushed to one side as tasks are taken over by machine.

Controllers learn to make decisions based on a mental picture of a dynamic situation, presented visually and by voice. Although paperless systems are being tested in Finland and Sweden, most centres still keep written records. The familiarity of handwritten 'flight progress strips' reinforces the controllers' visualisations. Maintaining the skills is vital. Three times in the past 15 years power failure has hit LATCC. Controllers, having a mental picture of the traffic, stopped take-offs and entries from overseas and gradually emptied the skies until remaining flights could be routed without radar.

The following events show how vital human decision makers are in non-routine situations, in spite of their weaknesses. At 0720 on 10 June 1990, a scheduled flight, BA5390 with 81 passengers and 6 crew, left Birmingham for Malaga. At 0733, it was climbing through 17 300 ft when there was a bang as a windscreen panel blew out. The commander would have been sucked out had not a steward grabbed his legs and, aided by colleagues, held on to them until after landing. Having regained control, the co-pilot descended quickly to 11 000 ft before making a distress call.

Unfortunately, the noise on the flight deck meant that he was unable to hear the acknowledgement of the signal during the descent and there was some delay in establishing two-way communications. Several other pilots intervened, offering to relay the weak radio signals. Six minutes elapsed before the contact was clearly established. Then came this exchange:

LATCC: Speedbird 5390. London Control 132.8. I hear you strength five, sir. Go ahead now.

BA5390:   Roger, sir, we have had an emergency depressurisation and er requesting radar assistance please for nearest airfield.

LATCC: Er Speedbird 5390. Roger. Can you accept landing at Southampton?

BA5390:   Speedbird er 5390 I am familiar with Gatwick – would appreciate Gatwick.

LATCC: Er Speedbird 5390. Roger. If you make a left turn now, sir, direct to Mayfield.

BA5390:   5390. If you can direct me into Southampton. Affirmative.

LATCC: OK, Sir. Would you prefer Southampton or Gat- er Gatwick? ... Er Speedbird 5390. Confirm you wish to route to Southampton.

Untrained in, and unaccustomed to, emergencies because of their rarity, the ATC on duty mistakenly presented the beleaguered co-pilot in his chaotic, noisy cockpit, with choices of what to do. Yet the co-pilot needed firm directions to the nearest safe landing. These were given once the request came through. Several minutes were lost at a time when seconds were important.

Approaching Southampton, control was passed to the airport tower. It was only then that the co-pilot was able to report the extent of the accident:

TOWER: 5390. We've been advised it's a pressurisation failure. Is that the only problem?

BA5390:   Er negative, sir. The er commander is half sucked out of the aeroplane. I understand ... I believe he is dead.

Lack of preparedness may also have led to another problem, insufficient runway length. At 0746 this was the exchange:

BA5390:   ... Could you please confirm the er length of your runway at Southampton is acceptable for a One-Eleven?

TOWER: Yes, it is acceptable for a One-Eleven and I'll give you the figures very shortly.

BA5390:   Er as long as we have er at least two and a half thousand metres I am happy.

TOWER: Er I'm afraid we don't have two and a half thousand metres. Neither do Bournemouth. We have a maximum eighteen hundred metres.

BA5390:   5390 that is acceptable.

With the co-pilot unfamiliar with Southampton, the tower controller 'talked him down' until the runway was in sight. Landing occurred at 0753. The fire service pulled the commander back into the aircraft and took him to hospital. He had been on the aircraft roof for 20 minutes. Happily, despite wrist and arm fractures, frostbite and shock, he survived.

Introduction

Air traffic controllers make decisions that have an impact on the safety of travellers every minute of their working day. Cooperating with pilots in practised routines, they are used to the smooth flow of traffic through their air space. They cope with complexity through learning and rehearsal. It is when difficulties arise, however, that they are expected to show their mettle. Faced with extraordinary situations, the accuracy and timeliness of their decisions take on greater importance. Although acting in emergencies can itself be rehearsed, their very unfamiliarity presents unusual challenges. Human judgement and discretion take over from formal routines. It is not surprising that some people cope better than others.

Simultaneously, other managers are making decisions about the future of the whole ATC system. Whether the focus is current economic performance or increased capacity or safety, planners have to study deeply how and why controllers choose from among alternative courses of action. This can then trigger the search for improvement.

This case study points us to some key issues confronting managers making decisions. They include complexity, risk and the fact that choices are often shared by several people who bring different skills, information and perspectives. Decisions, moreover, do not stand alone. Each forms part of a flow; it is affected by those that have already been made, and influences and constrains those that are to follow. The next section considers these issues from the manager's point of view. Then the chapter looks at decisions themselves, introducing two models that describe the process and the roles of individuals and groups within it. Finally, since it is often valuable to come up with original solutions to problems, the function of creativity is examined.

Managers making decisions

The word decision has appeared often during the preceding chapters. Sometimes it can be presented as a simple yes or no choice such as is presented in an algorithm. Another decision maker may have little information, and even less time, yet may be pressed into choosing from several courses which have not been tried before. Sometimes the consequences of error are small, at other times they are catastrophic. Another possibility is that the full effects are never established. From an entrepreneur spending a few hundred on advertising to the people of Sweden narrowly voting, in May 1994, to join the European Union, the direct consequences of many decisions cannot be ascertained.

What do all these acts share? To answer is to define decision making:

■ *Decision making is the act of choosing from among alternatives.*

If it were that simple, there would be little more to be said. Yet, as we have already seen in respect of planning and strategy, the act of choosing takes place in the context of a process. We must recognise that a decision must be made and define it within its context. We must set up alternatives to pick from, for a poor decision is often the result of being presented with just one proposal. 'Take it or leave it' are the sole options. A later section covers this *decision-making process* in more detail. We shall start, however, with its context to see the challenges presented to modern managers when faced with the responsibility for making decisions. The context includes complexity, risk, decision traps, and managers' problem-solving styles. These issues are shown 'surrounding' the manager in the *mind map* of Fig. 11.1. This is a tidied version of the one used to plan the chapter, *see* Exhibit 11.1.[2]

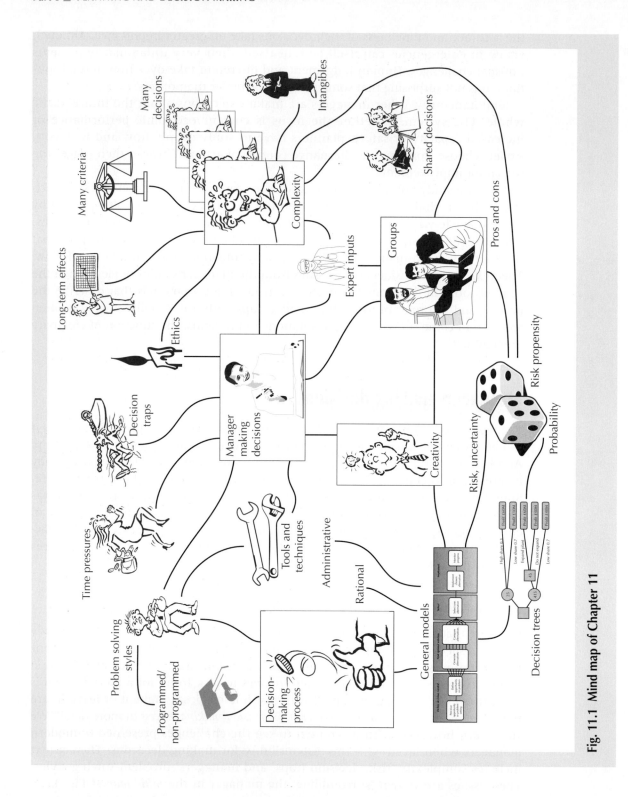

Fig. 11.1 Mind map of Chapter 11

Exhibit 11.1 **Mind maps**

Sketching ideas and links in a mind map is a valuable habit for any student or manager. There are few rules. Words or pictures represent ideas. Lines, possibly weighted, show connections among the ideas. Some areas can be emphasised by outlining; in Fig. 11.1 boxes pick out the main themes of the chapter.

Nothing is shown in detail. The aim is to start with a haphazard sketch and refine it to show the shape and relative importance of information and ideas. Since mind maps are more compressed than normal notes, the one-sheet picture helps us to pick out links and form new ideas.

Mind maps can be used for taking and consolidating notes from many sources. They work at an early stage before ideas have been sorted.

Stuck for somewhere to start? Put down a few ideas; link them; add a few more; leave it for an hour; think of some more links; make some tea; start again ... Try it!

Complexity

Decisions are rarely tidy. Frequently, as with the BA5390, they have to be made under just about the worst circumstances where complexity threatens to overwhelm the manager. The reasons for complexity are as follows:

■ *Many decisions*

Single decisions do not usually make systems work. They contribute to a flow, just like streams. Some follow others in regular order; others form parallel currents, backwaters and little eddies. Air traffic control functions because of teams of operators exchanging information with pilots and other control centres, making decisions, and issuing instructions based on them. The stream of ATC decisions relates both to each aircraft's movement and the interrelated movements of other flights. Normally it runs smoothly but sudden changes create eddies when instructions have to be changed.

■ *Long-term effects*

It is not only the decisions that flow. Often a routine decision can create ripples that spread through an organisation and have a long-lasting effect. For instance, in a board mill, one supervisor came across two workers fighting in the cloakroom. Following agreed procedures, the supervisor immediately suspended the men and had them escorted from the premises. Subsequent investigation found that one had been bullying and the other had decided to 'sort him out' Colleagues protested against the second's dismissal. The dispute rumbled on for months with output of a profitable line curtailed.

■ *Many criteria*

It is normal for decision makers to face multiple criteria, often imposed by different groups of stakeholders. Chapter 6, for example, pointed to the multiple influences over choices such as whether to expend more effort on recycling of materials or worn out plant. The manager's problem is that, in the end, a choice may well please some and annoy others.

■ *Shared decisions*

Yet another people problem arises from the sharing of many decisions. It is uncommon for one manager to act independently. Good leaders often share decision making to bring people along. Yet groups sometimes behave in unexpected ways when making decisions and usually slow the process down.

Slowness is seen acutely in international agencies. Jean-Jacques Dordain, head of strategy and international policy at the European Space Agency (ESA), warned, 'The United States makes a new satellite in 18 months. We are not even able to decide on a project in 18 months'. Waiting for government decisions was a serious problem as they depended on many different countries.[3]

■ *Expert advice*

The complexity faced by managers is increased when they have to take advice from specialists. Not only can this be time-consuming but the manager also has to deal with contradictory advice. Referring to external guidance, a former finance director of ICI reported, 'When the peak of an economic boom or recovery is approached, the merry-go-round of advice rotates faster and faster, with more and more advisers climbing on board to tell companies what to do'.[4] Profits, dividends, target rates of return are either too high or too low depending on who is arguing.

■ *Intangibles*

Later in the chapter, we shall see how a rational decision-making process relies on stating both objectives and outcomes in consistent, measurable terms. Yet many decisions involve subtle judgements and have effects on intangible factors such as staff morale, company image or customer satisfaction.

■ *Ethics and values*

Chapters 5 and 6 illustrated many aspects of international business where conflict between personal and organisational values poses ethical dilemmas for the manager. Family, group and national loyalties may cut across the formal mission of the multinational business, especially if it is an ethnocentric one. The rationalisation of the European car industry is bedevilled by national attitudes. When Renault, still 45 per cent owned by the French government, announced that it was to close its only plant in Belgium, the company was accused of deliberately selecting a foreign operation to axe. After a visit from the Belgian king, Albert II, the president of the European Commission added his voice to others, led by the country's prime minister, in the protest.[5] In such circumstances, how should the local managers at the Vilvoorde plant have behaved? As loyal employees of Renault, should they have given the trades unions information to help them with their cause?

■ *Risk propensity*

Risk propensity is the willingness of a decision maker to gamble when facing a decision. Some managers treat every decision cautiously. Their fear of making mistakes means that they will exaggerate the chances of failure and understate the chances and benefits of success. They avoid the big mistakes. Other managers are willing to take risks, often choosing courses of action intuitively and quickly. Entrepreneurs and intrapreneurs do achieve great successes from this approach but are also more likely to incur losses and ruin.

The culture and rules of an organisation influence risk propensity. This effect can be seen in City financial trading, illustrated in Exhibit 11.2.[6] The idea, and its companions uncertainty and ambiguity, are so important that it is worth looking at them in more detail.

■ Risk, uncertainty and ambiguity

Ideally, managers would have all necessary information to hand before making a decision. Yet, as always, the world is less than ideal. Figure 4.1 showed for example, that both change and complexity in the business environment combine to increase uncertainty in managers' perceptions of it. Since many aspects are unknowable, the manager has to accept that a decision may not resolve a chosen problem and future events may follow unexpected tracks. Four conditions, shown in Fig. 11.2, can be identified. These depend on the sort of information available and whether the decision is guided by clear objectives.

- *Certainty*

  A condition of certainty exists when *a manager has all the information needed to make a decision*. A distribution manager, for example, should know the number of vehicles, the location of warehouses and customers, running costs per kilometre and so on. From this data, and knowing that the objective is to minimise total cost for a given level of customer service, the manager has techniques to schedule the vehicles. Many operations research techniques depend on this level of certainty. Yet few decisions approach this ideal and most of these are confined to the operating level of the organisation. It is a mistake to treat decisions as though they were based on certainty whereas in reality they are not.

- *Risk*

  A condition of risk exists when *a manager has clear objectives and information yet knows that outcomes are subject to chance*. When the European Space Agency's Ariane V rocket, with a valuable commercial payload, exploded in June 1996, some may have argued that the mission should never have been attempted. Yet

Exhibit 11.2 Incentives encourage risk taking

Following the loss by NatWest Bank of £50 million through alleged unauthorised trading, an article by an economist at the Bank of England received wide attention. It suggested that bonuses paid to traders in the risky derivatives and futures financial markets might increase the business risk. A bonus system designed to motivate a risk averse trader to take more risks may simultaneously encourage one who is risk tolerant to go too far. In some cases, lump sum bonuses tied to profit targets would push staff into taking chances to reach the target knowing that, if things went wrong, they stood to lose little personally.

In its supervisory role, the Bank of England has to ensure that banks can always cover their risks. It was considering whether to include details of bonus schemes in its future assessments of banks' policies.

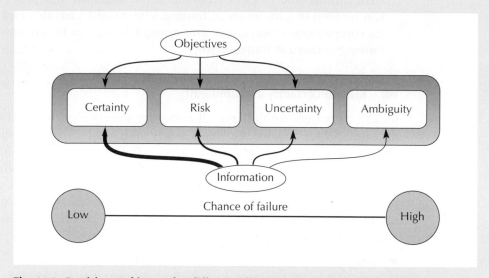

Fig. 11.2 Decision making under different objectives and information conditions

experience gives ESA managers and their customers a good idea of the risks of failure. They can, therefore, cover themselves on the insurance market, which also has access to the same risk information.

Risks are stated in terms of probabilities, of which there are two types. *Objective probabilities* are odds that are worked out from reliable historical data or experiments. (Note that the term *objective* is used here as an adjective to mean detached or unprejudiced.) Before launching a new chocolate bar, for example, a manufacturer may use data from earlier products or test marketing in a limited area to provide relevant information. *Subjective probabilities* are estimates based on experience and judgement. Returning to the ESA example, records may show that 1 in 20 launches goes awry. If there were no changes in rocket design and launch procedures, this data, 5 per cent, would represent the objective probability of failure next time. On the other hand, scientists change designs to increase rocket power and reliability. The effects of these changes cannot be measured exactly. Therefore, a 3 per cent failure risk might be a reasonable subjective probability estimate.

■ *Uncertainty*

A condition of uncertainty arises when *a manager has limited reliable information about choices and future outcomes*. For instance, Chapter 5 showed that, in international business, uncertainty arises at all levels from the interactions among people of different cultures to the political level of changes in national governments. Under such circumstances, managers strive to reduce uncertainty through plans and countermeasures. Yet it cannot be eliminated. Managers often have to accept that decisions are needed under less than ideal conditions. Good judgement enables them to be successful with questions such as, 'Although it is impossible to assess the outcomes exactly, shall we go ahead anyhow?'

■ *Ambiguity*

A condition of ambiguity exists when *a manager faces an ill-defined problem, has unclear objectives and lacks information about choices and future outcomes*. This echoes uncertainty with added difficulties. In the normal run of events such conditions do not present themselves (or managers choose to ignore them). If things are not going so well, however, managers may recognise they are facing a *mess,*[7] *see* Exhibit 11.3.

Unclear and conflicting objectives, poor information, fuzzy problem boundaries and sudden change are characteristics of messes. Resolution often requires more than calculating optimum results but fundamental organisational change. We return to this in Chapter 14.

Decision traps

Ambiguity often arises when problems and objectives are unclear, suggesting great complexity and change in the situation. Yet personal traits can also affect clarity and hence lower the quality of decision making. Among the most common of these decision traps are heuristics, framing errors, escalation of commitment and overconfidence.

■ *Heuristics*

Many people follow rules of thumb, or heuristics, when they make decisions. This is a realistic approach for, faced with a vast number and variety of decisions we invent rules to simplify them. I mow the lawn every week, buy my shoes at Clark's, book flights through Airline Network, search the web with Alta Vista and never bid *no trumps* with a singleton. The notion of heuristics also includes learning. The rules are revised in the light of experience. Therefore, I mow the lawn more frequently in the spring and less in a dry summer.

Vecchio identifies two judgemental heuristics, or strategies, that people frequently rely upon.[8] Unfortunately, they often mislead people into making the wrong choices because the intuitive rules take them beyond the information they have been given. First, the *availability heuristic* reflects how accessible relevant informa-

---

Exhibit 11.3 **Ackoff warns that problems depend on perception**

'Problems have traditionally been assumed to be *given* or *presented* to an actor much as they are to students at the end of chapters in text books. Where they come from and why they are worth solving is implicitly assumed to be irrelevant to consideration of how they should be solved or what their solutions are. Books dealing with the methodology of research and problem solving seldom give more than a polite nod to problem generation, identification and formulation. They move impatiently to problem solving'.

'...problems are *taken up by*, and not *given to*, decision makers. ...'

'What decision makers deal with, I maintain, are messes, not problems. ... A mess is a system of external conditions that produces dissatisfaction.'

tion is to a person. For instance, asked to estimate the proportions of adult Americans and Germans who have passports, people in Stratford-upon-Avon will guess the former to be much higher. They generalise from unreliable perceptions of the numbers coming to their neighbourhood. In fact, about 10 per cent of United States citizens and about 90 per cent of Germans have passports. Similarly if asked to guess the proportion of British passport holders (50 per cent), answers will be biased by whether respondents have one themselves.

The second bias comes from the *representativeness heuristic*. This is based on one's sense of resemblance between events or objects. Ask a child to sort a tray of Lego and you will be surprised by the categories chosen. Would you use shape, thickness, colour, size, taste, number of studs, newness or who gave it as a present? In applying this rule of thumb, a person judges how well an object or event fits into a category and then makes decisions according to the category. This can be a basis of prejudice, as Exhibit 11.4 shows.

■ *Framing errors*

Framing errors arise from the influence on interpretation, and hence decisions, of the way information is presented. Shortly after Graham Swift won the 1997 Booker Prize for his novel *Last Orders*, a row erupted over the failure of the author to acknowledge similarity with William Faulkner's *As I Lay Dying*. None of the judges had read the earlier work so, as one critic put it, they had either undervalued *Last Orders* by 'failing to appreciate the true resonances' or overvalued it by 'missing the comparison'. Appreciation of its value depended on whether the work was perceived as an 'original reworking of a classic text' or plagiarism.[9]

In business, advertisers frame product claims carefully to influence consumers' choices. One disinfectant kills 99 per cent of all known household germs and the 'One 2 One digital mobile phone service covers 80 per cent of Great Britain's population, from the South Coast right up to Scotland'.[10] Reframed statements would say: 'Domestos fails to eliminate 1 per cent of bugs and may miss any not normally found in the house or that we don't know about'; and 'One 2 One cannot reach 20 per cent of the British population from the South Coast to Scotland'. Naturally, neither is used.

Exhibit 11.4 A test of representative heuristics

I have a friend who teaches in a university. He is small in build, rather shy and publishes poetry occasionally. Which is your best guess of his field of expertise – Chinese studies or psychology?

If your answer was Chinese studies you have fallen into the trap of representative heuristics. You saw the personal profile as fitting more closely the stereotype sinologist than psychologist. Yet you ignored two critical items of statistical information. First, there are many more psychologists than sinologists. Second, someone who teaches in a Business School is more likely to come across the former. On either criterion, psychology is the superior answer. Put them together and the case is overwhelming.

On the other hand, if you saw the personal profile as fitting psychology ...

■ *Escalation of commitment*

Known colloquially as 'tossing good money after bad', escalation of commitment refers to people's unwillingness to change a course of action in spite of evidence that their decision has been incorrect. An organisation can become stuck with spending more resources hoping to achieve an outcome that is becoming less likely. The original DOS operating system for personal computers was jointly developed by IBM and Microsoft. Recognising that Microsoft was developing Windows to replace the outdated DOS, IBM rushed to develop its own substitute, OS/2. Windows took more than three quarters of the market while OS/2 had a small share. Later, as Microsoft was introducing Windows 95, IBM announced a new version of its own product. Many foresaw that it also would be a failure.[11]

Many individuals find that giving up is personally and socially difficult. Adding to these factors are those originating within the organisation. Summarised in Fig. 11.3, they combine to provoke escalation. Yet continuation is sometimes almost unavoidable. Drummond and Hodgson[12] point out that, while persistence often results from emotional factors and fear of failure, it is not always irrational. They caution against expecting too much. Citing a case of a local government department, moreover, politics may mean that reversing a decision is worse than carrying on.

■ *Overconfidence*

Overconfidence exposes people to unnecessary risks. We see this frequently in sport where some players develop reputations for taking more risks than others.

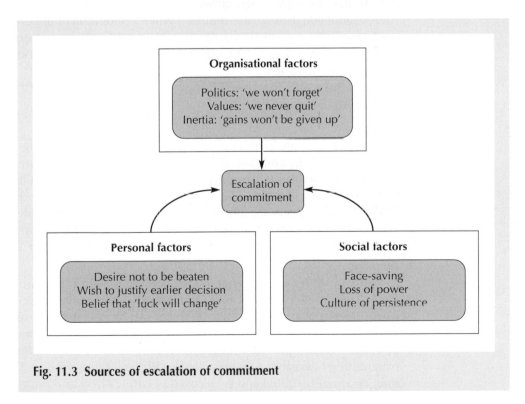

Fig. 11.3 Sources of escalation of commitment

Should the golfer drive over the hotel on the seventeenth hole at St Andrews or the poker player raise holding three knaves? When these 'long shots' pay off, legends are made; when they fail, they are soon forgotten.

Regular and familiar tasks encourage confidence, but not overconfidence, as each person develops a sound assessment of what is needed. Oddly, it is when tasks are less familiar and more difficult that overconfidence becomes a problem. Inexperienced managers need to guard against the reassurance given to them by their qualifications when they move into unfamiliar territory. They should critically examine every element of their decision, from initial information through to implementation, to see whether they have overestimated their own capabilities.

Managing risk and overconfidence are also problems when decisions are made by groups. We shall, therefore, return to these later in the chapter.

■ Problem solving styles

The different degrees of risk, uncertainty and ambiguity associated with decisions can be summarised by dividing them into two classes first proposed by Simon.[13] *Programmed decisions* occur in situations that have occurred often enough to enable managers to create decision rules to cover them. Many operating systems, from stock control to order processing, work almost entirely through decision rules. The operator's skill is to process routine material as quickly as possible while being on the lookout for anything unusual. As indicated in the opening case, air traffic control achieves high standards of efficiency and safety because almost all decisions are programmed.

Non-programmed decisions are required when conditions of uncertainty and ambiguity prevail. These decisions tend to be unrehearsed, infrequent and have important consequences for the organisation. They are typical of strategic management and crisis management.

Corresponding to the two types of decision, we can identify two problem-solving styles:

■ *Thinking*
  Some managers prefer to approach problems using a thinking style. They look for precision, logic and objectivity. Clearly, these people will prefer routine tasks in which the ability to carefully assemble and weigh reliable information is an asset. Numeracy and the ability to break a problem down into elements are key skills. Such managers are most comfortable with programmed decisions although they could also work on non-programmed ones if they were not too ambiguous. The thinking style is that of the *technocrat*, explained in Chapter 1.

■ *Intuition*
  In contrast, other managers approach problems with a predominantly intuitive style. They prefer complex and changing situations that offer opportunities to use judgement and follow 'gut feelings' about the way things will turn out. Rather than break problems down into workable elements, these people look at patterns to seek opportunities for intervention. They are comfortable with non-programmed decisions whereas, faced with colleagues who prefer to think, they may become frustrated and be accused of carelessness and imprecision.

As with many management ideas, these styles represent extremes of a continuum. This means that many managers use mixed styles which they can adapt from time to time according to circumstances.

Decision making

Two models of decision making are frequently referred to by authorities – the classical and the administrative models. While they have superficial similarities, we must recognise that they originate from different traditions and were created for different reasons. We shall look at each in turn.

Classical model

The conventional approach to describing decision making, often called *classical decision theory*, makes certain fundamental assumptions that, as we shall see, have their limitations. These assumptions are:

- objectives are clear and agreed;
- problems are clearly defined;
- the manager seeks full information on all possible alternatives before making any choice;
- criteria for evaluation can be unambiguously drawn from the objectives and problem definition;
- decision makers will make logical decisions to satisfy objectives as well as possible.

Figure 11.4 shows the steps set out according to classical decision theory. The approach in the model is to represent decision making as an optimising choice from an exhaustive list of alternatives. Implementation and monitoring follow as with all well-founded management processes. Here we see four stages in total, although the number can be varied according to the way they are broken down.

1 *Define decision need*

How does a manager know when to make a decision? Following the quotation from Ackoff in Exhibit 11.3, needs are rarely presented 'on a plate'. The early writer Barnard, *see* Chapter 2, pointed out that there were three sources – instructions from superiors, reference by subordinates or the initiative of the manager.[14] All these result from someone 'taking up' the issue. Whatever the source, decision needs are defined according to the perception of those involved. If the paint is flaking off the door, that is only a problem to those who prefer doors to be nicely painted.

A further point concerns the basis of the decision need. It can lie in an *opportunity* when someone recognises that something positive could be achieved. Alternatively, it can come from a *problem*, that is someone is dissatisfied and wants something fixed. Therefore, a passing painter sees the door as an opportunity for employment, while the householder worries about a further drain on the budget. However it is defined, bringing out the decision need triggers the rest of the process.

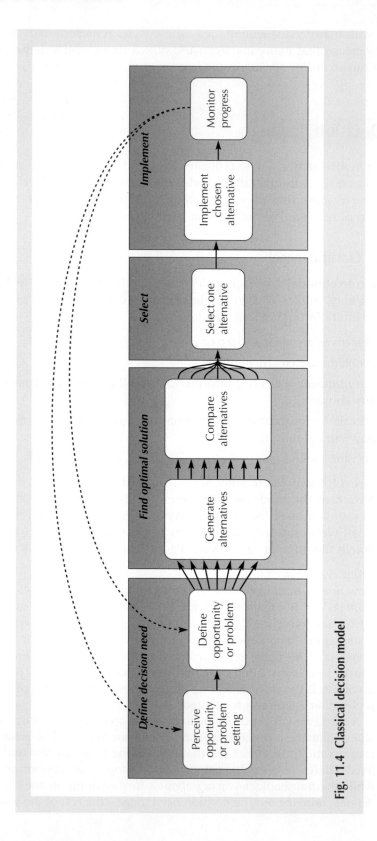

Fig. 11.4 Classical decision model

2 *Find optimal solution*

The classical approach to finding an optimal solution relies heavily on the assumptions listed above. Rationally, one must explore all possible alternatives before coming to a conclusion about which is the best. Hence we can conceive of two stages, generation and comparison. They do not imply an infinity of choices for the constraints that surround the problem definition will usually mean that the number of possibilities is limited. Yet a good example of rising numbers is the *travelling representative problem*.

The travelling representative problem can be stated succinctly. Given that a 'rep' has to visit several places during a tour, what is the shortest (or quickest) route? (*see* Fig.11.5). With 3 places there are just 6 routes, with 10 there are 3 628 800 and with 100 places the number soars to 10^{156}! Search methods proposing near optimal solutions have been put forward but there is yet no known method of homing in on the optimum other than using computer power to try all combinations.[15] Apparently unreal with large numbers, this problem comes up often in business. A despatcher may plan a lorry tour with 30 or 40 drops. Related problems come up in information network designs where hundreds of connections may have to be made.

3 *Select*

The selection stage is straightforward in the classical model. With clear objectives and full information about the problem, the choice of the best is automatic. Selection can be seen simply as an adjunct of the previous stage.

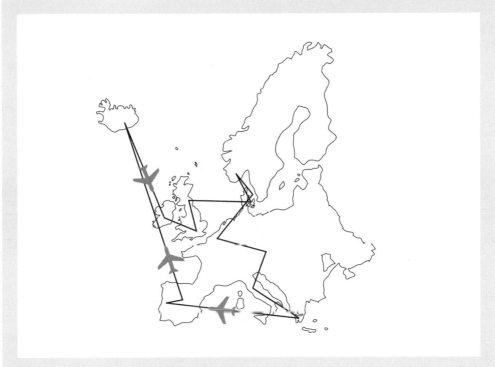

Fig. 11.5 The rep's tour. Yet is it optimal?

4 *Implement*

The chosen course of action is the one that will be put into effect. Note also that there must be subsequent evaluation to test its success in taking the opportunity or solving the problem. This may cause changes to the process, especially in the way the decision need is identified.

Decision trees

To illustrate, a well-known method showing how the process follows on from a selected opportunity or problem is the decision tree. This is an aid in situations where a series of choices may be foreseen. A manager may make a decision, some events follow, another decision is required, some more events follow, and so on. The tree allows the manager to explore the consequences of the first choice through these subsequent events. Further, it is possible to build in allowances for chance, that is the risk that events may turn out in different ways.

Figure 11.6 shows a partly constructed decision tree. Our manager, looking for the best profit, has to choose between several strategies, A to Z. Some of these may have several variants, for example Z has sub-strategy 2. Starting from the left of the diagram, we sequence them as shown. Squares represent the decision points and lines the outcomes. Then we include the risks. For choice Z2, for example, the manager cannot tell what the outcome is to be but perceives three possibilities. A circle represents the uncertain event and the idea is to draw a line from the circle

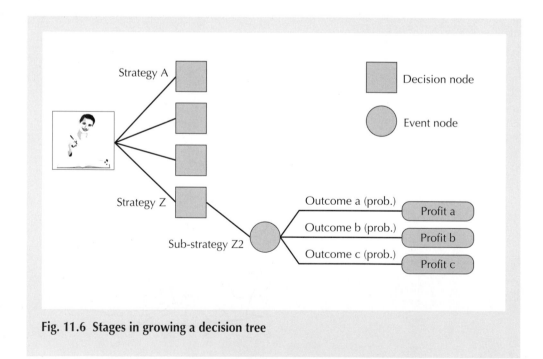

Fig. 11.6 Stages in growing a decision tree

representing each possibility. The profits listed at the right correspond to each of them. The diagram is extended until all branches have been explored.

The next stage is to evaluate the tree to find the series of decisions that are worth the most. This is done by working *from right to left*. That means stating a cash value to each final result. At each circle, assign a probability to each chance at that point. These can be objective probabilities if based on tests or historic trends, or subjective if they come from judgement. The expected value at each circle can then be found by combining the estimated values and their probabilities:

■ *Expected value = Probability$_a$ × Value$_a$ + Probability$_b$ × Value$_b$ +......*

Branches also emerge from squares. Since these depict decisions, the highest valued offshoot is chosen.

A worked example is shown in Fig. 11.7.[16] The mind map at the left of the diagram sketches the starting point. The company is deciding what size to build a new plant. After construction, marketing effort will be increased but it is not clear what its impact will be. For simplicity, we shall say there is a 0.3 (30 per cent) chance of high revenue and 0.7 of little change, a low revenue. A small plant would satisfy the low market estimate but if sales did take off, a further problem would present itself: should the company expand the small plant? Building small and expanding later is more expensive than building large straight away.

The decision tree represents the choice and event nodes. At the right-hand side, the outcomes show the income for every possible combination of decisions and events. These are entered as shown. Then, working from right to left, the 'expected value' of each node can be calculated. Thus, for the large plant:

■ *Expected value$_{LP}$ = 0.3 × 60 + 0.7 × 10 = 25 million*

At the decision node concerning whether to expand the small plant in the light of rising sales, clearly the choice would be made to go ahead. The value of this node is £45 million. This gives us the value of the small plant:

■ *Expected value$_{SP}$ = 0.3 × 45 + 0.7 × 40 = 41.5 million*

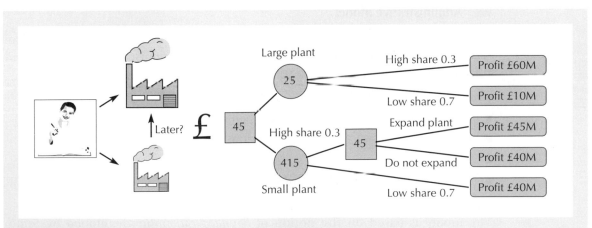

Fig. 11.7 Worked example – mind map to decision tree

Values at each node can be entered as shown. Modelling this mind map into the form of a decision tree has enabled us to calculate the values of each option presented to the manager *in the light of subsequent decisions and risky outcomes*. Not only did the model aid in structuring the problem but it also provided a set of rules for finding the optimum systematically. These two features are to be found in many useful aids to decision making.

Problems with the classical model

The classical model has been popular with scholars and teachers partly because it is normative. This means it sets out how a decision should be made and does not necessarily conform to how managers actually make decisions in practice. The response of some scholars could be, 'What they should do is what matters. If only they followed the rigour of the model, their decisions would be improved!'

It is an uphill struggle. Improved modelling techniques, supported by powerful computers, have given a push towards reason and away from intuition. Yet examination of the assumptions underpinning the model shows its limited application. First, as Ackoff argued, there are many messes with ill-defined problems and unclear objectives. Second, it is almost impossible to consider all alternatives. Finding, and then evaluating, them would require too much effort. Information is not free so, in the end, the manager has to rely on limited and imperfect knowledge. Third, many cases go beyond the complexity that operations research techniques can cope with. Fourth, managers have neither the skills, nor the inclination, to perform heavy calculations. Fifth, social, cultural and political settings may restrict a manager's choice. They may, therefore, not be prepared to make the 'logical' decisions that the classical model demands.

We can conclude that managers are often unable to make rational decisions even were they inclined to do so. It is not surprising, therefore, that alternative models of the process have emerged. The behavioural theory of decision making contrasts with the normative classical approach in that it sets out to describe managerial behaviour. The *administrative model* is the product of this theory.

■ Administrative model

The administrative model describes how managers make decisions in the difficult settings we have discussed earlier in the chapter. It recognises the difficulties identified in the preceding section. In summary, these are:

- objectives are unclear and have not been agreed;
- problems have not been clearly discerned;
- managers' search for information on alternatives is limited;
- decision criteria have not been established in advance;
- the vagueness of criteria and information mean that managers are not committed to optimising decisions.

The model is based on the notion of *bounded rationality* developed by Simon and others in the 1950s and now an accepted part of decision theory.[17] Bounded rationality means that people set limits on how rational they can be. The boundary may arise from a stream of previous decisions. For instance, Simon pointed out that a doctor with seven years training and ten years practice does not ordinarily spend time thinking whether he or she should be a physician or not.[18] Values pose another constraint. At The Body Shop, for instance, there is a policy of no redundancy while others argue that ethics should be brought closer to the core of all decision processes. Exhibit 11.5 summarises one approach.[19]

Because of the problems processing vast amounts of information, namely attention, memory, comprehension and communication, managers will also *satisfice*. To satisfice is to *choose the first alternative that meets minimum decision criteria in spite of the possibility of there being others that are better*. For instance, a manager is looking for a convenient place to stay overnight in Brussels. A telephone call to the centrally located Ibis hotel establishes that there is a room and its price is within the company's budget. The manager makes the reservation. The decision is good enough.

Figure 11.8 lays out the stages of the decision process in the satisficing, bounded rationality mode. Having defined the decision need as before, the manager faces making a choice on incomplete information and with barely developed criteria. Therefore, looking for alternatives runs parallel with developing these criteria. The manager, so to speak, learns his or her way into the task. Uncovering alternatives suggests criteria and vice versa. Selection is also incorporated, for as soon as a satisficing alternative appears, it is chosen. If none emerges then the search is extended.

An example of the way decision criteria are allowed to emerge as the process evolves comes from investment decision making. For appraising new capital outlays, several procedures are well known. Generations of business students have been taught IRR (internal rate of return), NPV (net present value), payback period and ARR (accounting rate of return). They know that no technique is superior to the others in combining ease of understanding and use with validity in modelling the essence of complex problems. Wilkes and others[20] show how firms, especially larger ones, use several methods. Sometimes several were used on the same assessment, in other cases different approaches were used for different projects.

Exhibit 11.5 Building ethics into the formal process

Working to build a practical ethics programme into the daily work of a large organisation, Navram Associates found that the model they had constructed with senior managers was beyond the reading level of about a quarter of all staff. They designed an alternative that could be used by all. At any step in a decision process, ideas can be run through PLUS filters to check their ethical standards. PLUS is a mnemonic for:

■ Policies – is the idea consistent with policies, procedures and guidelines?

■ Legal – is it acceptable under relevant legislation?

■ Universal – does the idea match the organisation's universal principles?

■ Self – does it fit my own definition of honest, right and fair?

Nearly every decision has an ethical component. PLUS helps bring them to light.

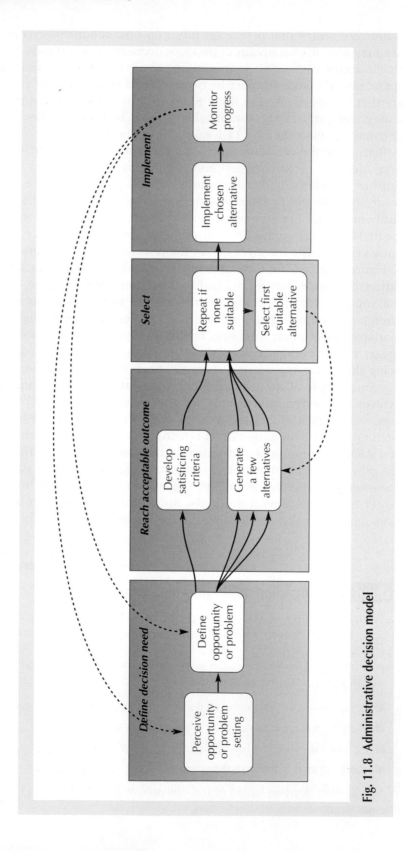

Fig. 11.8 Administrative decision model

Using several methods at once is a cautious way of avoiding major pitfalls. On the other hand, some techniques may be more suited to some types of problem, for example large or small, property or other assets. Furthermore, managers may choose methods that favour their own proposals. It appears that investment decisions are based on rational techniques. Yet, to the extent that the choice is a matter of judgement among the conflicting outcomes of these techniques we see judgement and intuition come into play.

Groups in decision making

Chapters 16 and 17 look closely at the behaviour of groups and the role of the manager as leader. Clearly, this is a critical role since the manager can influence how much a group participates in the decision process. We can, however, look at groups from another angle. The question is more general: to what extent do groups help or hinder when it comes to making decisions? There is hardly an issue here for, like other aspects of management, decision making is an organised, social activity. The question is less whether groups should be involved, but how and for what sorts of decision are they best suited. It is important, then, to understand the issues raised below so that a manager uses the group appropriately. Having compared their advantages and disadvantages, we shall comment briefly on how groups can be managed to best effect.

▨ Advantages of groups

Exhibit 11.6 sets out the benefits and drawbacks of group decision making, matching the points roughly to the general pattern of the decision model. Some could appear in more than one category, however. It can be seen that the group can gain at almost every stage although pitfalls, too, must be avoided.

When facing decisions, groups have advantages over individuals because they can bring wider perspectives to both the problem and the value framework that is to be applied to the selection of a solution. Drawing these together at an early stage forestalls later difficulties that could arise were the interests of certain stakeholders ignored, or important information forgotten. The sharing of ideas should also enrich the tasks of generating alternatives and modelling, evaluating and choosing among them. At the point of selection, it may be advantageous to share responsibility, especially if large sums or great risks are involved. Finally, the group's processes can increase the satisfaction of participants and help to build commitment to putting the result into effect.

▨ Disadvantages of groups

Whereas a group with appropriate membership and organisation *may* bring with it great advantages, managers need to be wary of the corresponding drawbacks. Perhaps the most obvious is cost. Bringing people together for a couple of hours to make a decision may cost hundreds of pounds, far greater than the cost of one

Exhibit 11.6 Pros and cons of group decision making

Advantages of groups	Disadvantages of groups
Building a system of shared values: Pooling perspectives and values as part of cultural change	Differences may be exaggerated; Status differences may limit sharing
Defining decision need: Pooling adds to information base	Confusing interpretations; overload
Generating and evaluating alternatives: Specialisation; sharing skills in interpreting, modelling techniques, etc.	Higher cost if process inefficient or time wasted on routine tasks
Choosing solution: Clarifying ambiguities reduces uncertainty; Sharing decision-making responsibility	Groupthink; Polarisation; Diffusion of responsibility
Implementing solution: Participation creates commitment to the outcome; Motivation through the social process	Escalation of commitment; Poor processes can be demotivating

manager's time. The extra cost needs to be recouped through a better quality decision and a smoother implementation as those who have to put it into effect have already taken part in the process.

In complex, non-programmed decisions, the group processes may appear to slow the rate of progress. This may arise if stages such as establishing criteria or even selecting the problem result in serious disagreement. Later, attempts to incorporate the knowledge and perspectives of a wide range of stakeholders may result in a serious information overload for participants. Frustration felt by members in such circumstances can be so demotivating that they allow unsatisfactory compromises and do not develop the necessary commitment to the outcomes. Paradoxically, it is in the most complex and uncertain cases that groups are most necessary and have the greatest potential. The difficult issues need to be sorted out.

Beyond these general points about disadvantages, there are particular difficulties that must be confronted, namely groupthink and polarisation.

Groupthink

Intrigued by the notorious venture of the Bay of Pigs, *see* Exhibit 11.7, Janis began to ask how a group of senior military personnel and civilian administrators could make such a rash decision. Although selected for qualities of intelligence, motivation and abilities at decision making, it seemed that when people worked in a group, they abandoned their skills. This was groupthink.

Exhibit 11.7 The Bay of Pigs

On 17 April 1961, a force of 1500 exiles attempted a covert invasion of Cuba at the Bay of Pigs. In spite of air and naval support from United States forces, it was a failure. The hoped-for popular uprising within the country did not materialise. 1173 were taken prisoner. The following year, President Kennedy agreed to ransom most of them for $53 million in food and medicine. The incident strengthened the ties between Cuba and the Soviet Union and harmed relationships between the United States and friendly Latin American and European nations.

The disaster occurred in spite of hundreds of hours of planning by a presidential special advisory committee and training of the forces by the CIA. Kennedy and his advisers had approved a plan based on wishful thinking. Expecting a quick overthrow of President Castro, they played down the risks and failed to consider the consequences of failure.

Janis defined it as, 'a mode of thinking that people engage in when they are deeply involved in a cohesive in-group, when the members' striving for unanimity overrides their motivation to realistically appraise alternative courses of action.'[21] He suggested it was a kind of disease that infected otherwise healthy groups. Members' desire to maintain consensus overrides the need to seriously explore alternatives. Why?

The eight main symptoms of groupthink, according to Janis, are:

- *An illusion of invulnerability* gives members a sense of power, reassures them about danger signals and encourages them to take excessive risks.

- *Rationalisation* enables the group to dismiss evidence that contradicts its emerging consensus.

- With an *illusion of superior morality*, the group does not question its own motives yet outsiders are considered evil, to be treated with suspicion.

- *Negative stereotypes* of leaders and powers outside the group mean that negotiating with them is regarded as futile. Since their opposition is expected, they are easier to cast aside in the decision making. Kennedy's group believed that Castro's air force was so weak that a few obsolete American bombers could easily eliminate it.

- *Pressure to conform* results in those who express momentary doubts being immediately brought into line or ostracised.

- Using *self-censorship*, victims of groupthink remain silent about any misgivings and convince themselves of the insignificance of their worries. Several of Kennedy's advisers later wrote of their regrets at not having objected more strongly.

- *An illusion of unanimity* follows from the previous symptom. The group assumes that silence means that members are willing to go along with the prevailing view.

- *Mindguards* sometimes take it upon themselves to interpret the leader's thoughts to the rest of the group and control the flow of information. Several members, including the President's brother, attorney-general Robert Kennedy, took it upon themselves to restrict the flow of critical information into the Bay of Pigs group.

Behind the symptoms, researchers have identified four basic causes of groupthink. First, there is the existence of what may otherwise be considered a valuable trait, *group cohesion*. Strongly bonded groups can be either positive, if working well, or negative, if the symptoms begin to appear. Second, there is the danger of *group isolation*. Many of them work in secret. Unfortunately, this works both ways. Limiting the outward flow of information means that potential advisers and critics do not know enough to be able to offer sound advice. Third, a leader may unwittingly bias the course of events: expressions of authority will increase pressures to conform; procedures of meetings, such as agenda setting and style of discussion can be manipulated; an early expression of preferences may dampen debate; and pleas for consensus building will restrict critical discussion. Fourth, all members are likely to feel the stress of an important decision. It is natural to look for ways such as underlining the positive and rationalisation of action to alleviate it. These causes are manifest as the groupthink symptoms.

Like any infection, remedies for groupthink are best directed at removing the cause, although dampening down the symptoms may also bring benefits. Since a working group would not wish to reduce its cohesion, efforts should be made to reduce isolation, for example by bringing in outsiders at every opportunity and allowing members to debate issues with trusted subordinates. Furthermore, leaders should learn to be impartial, let it be known that criticism and argument are expected, state their preferences only after they have participated in debates and give ample time to reflect on the final decision. For important decisions, it is worth having a final meeting at which everyone is invited to express residual doubts before the conclusive choice is made.

Polarisation

Most of us assume that work groups exert pressure to draw radical members towards more cautious views. In other circumstances, they persuade the excessively cautious to be more ambitious. In either case we believe that groups have a moderating influence. Through a series of experiments in the 1960s, however, Stoner showed that this assumption was unsound.[22] *Risky shift* is the phenomenon in which groups subscribe to riskier positions compared with their individual members. Other experiments and observations confirmed Stoner's discovery and sought to explain it. They also found that some groups moved towards a more cautious position than the members would take on average if acting alone. This leaning was labelled the *cautious shift*. What was happening?

There are several social and psychological explanations that we do not have the space to detail. Summarising, it is clear that many attitudes, beliefs, values, judgements and perceptions are intensified in group discussions. Groups, therefore, tend to move to extremes depending on the initial inclination of the members. Let us say that a group of managers is meeting to discuss whether to attack a rival's market. A predisposition to caution will lead to a very tentative policy, perhaps a request for further market research. On the other hand, a group that starts by thinking the proposal to be 'quite a good idea' may end up betting half the company's resources on its success.

Discussion, therefore, does not lead to moderation but to *polarisation*. Evidence suggests that, when individuals discuss ideas, they shift towards what they think matches the values of the group. Perceiving a culture of risk taking, cautious people will begin to advocate taking more chances. This shift will, in turn, encourage those who were originally risk-takers to become more so, and so on. Discussions become biased, information is perceived selectively and rationales for one position or the other are reinforced.

The context of the decision is important. Vecchio points out that, in business and career planning the dominant culture favours risk taking, almost seeing it as a prerequisite for success. Consequently, risky shift is a common occurrence. In the area of social and personal life, however, groups of families and friends will urge caution on individuals who face important decisions. Examples include weighing medical risks, which are approached more cautiously by a group than by individuals,[23] and risk avoidance in arranged marriages.

Avoiding pitfalls

For a manager responsible for effective decision making by a group, a basic skill is to use awareness of the pros and cons to good effect. It is good practice, for example, to restrict cost by setting limits on meeting schedules. Having agreed membership and agendas, avoiding groupthink and polarisation is important. Again, recognising and responding to their symptoms is a mark of good group leadership. Changing the pattern of group meetings, for example by breaking into small groups, enables more reticent members to make contributions and restricts the effect of dominance caused by higher rankings in the organisation. We shall return to this question in Chapters 16 and 17.

Creativity

Many opportunities or problems, especially those messy ones requiring non-programmed decisions, offer opportunities for creative solutions. Clearly, creativity is relevant to the generation of alternatives, for the more and better the potential choices the better will be the outcome. Yet it is also relevant to other stages, for instance in the many ways to unravel the mess into problem definitions and working out detailed routes to implement solutions. Its importance to organisations cannot be overstated because, in the end, competitive edge arises from doing things better than one's rivals and that often means thinking of these things first. Creativity is, therefore, important in product and process innovation, which are covered in Chapter 21. Here we shall look at its general relevance to decision making both by individuals and in group settings. 'Whatever creativity is, it is part of the solution to a problem.'[24]

What is creativity?

It is very difficult to demonstrate creativity, for, as de Bono says, 'Any valuable creative idea is always logical in hindsight'.[25] When the Venetian traveller Marco Polo visited China in the 13th century, he was surprised to find that the Chinese had used single-gate *flash locks* on the 1600 kilometre Grand Canal for about a thousand years. These meant that every rise could only be small. Huge efforts were required to pull boats against the stream and much water was wasted. The two-gate *pound lock* system was introduced in China about that time and, according to later travellers, was quickly perfected.[26] The idea reached The Netherlands in the 14th century. With hindsight, we recognise the pound lock as logical, just as the wheel before it and most other developments later. The danger is then to argue that, since the lock is so logical, not discovering it represents a failure of logic and has little to do with creativity!

Of course this is a false argument, for de Bono goes on to show that hindsight colours our perception. Things that are obvious in hindsight are not necessarily so *in foresight*. Creativity is to do with seeing things ahead and not reasoning about them afterwards. Since post-event explanations will always suffer from this difficulty it is best to recognise it as it happens. Whenever you might say to someone, 'That's a good idea!' you will have recognised creativity but you can't quite say what it is. 'True creativity often starts where language ends.'[27]

■ Creative individuals

Many people believe themselves to be uncreative and tend to point to famous artists, designers and so on as examples of highly creative individuals. Whether anyone lacks creative ideas is controversial for some argue that it is our habit not to recognise or apply the ideas that make the difference. Chopra argues that around 95 per cent of our 60 000 thoughts per day are the same as yesterday's: the challenge is to break out of automatic response mode and take up some of that 5 per cent.[28]

Vecchio summarises many research studies of personal differences.[29] United States research found that beyond 10 years old, females are more creative than males. This is the reverse of the case in India, underlining how culture plays its part in defining appropriate behaviour. Peak ages are the 30s, with scientists in the 30–34 range and artists 35–39. Afterwards, creativity does not vanish but output declines.

Looking at personal characteristics, studies bring out independence, breadth of interests and the search for fulfilment. Having studied creative managers, Raudsepp concluded that, compared with others, they:

■ looked to the long term rather than immediate gain;

■ had a great deal of energy;

■ found the status quo irritating;

■ persevered;

■ followed hobbies and special interests;

■ held that day dreaming was not a waste of time.[30]

These points raise questions for organisations that see the creativity of their employees as a critical resource. Recruiters need to understand how to assess individual creativity. One method is to observe responses to problem-solving tasks. Another is to create or apply standard tests. Recruitment is covered in Chapter 15.

■ Cultivating creativity

Extending the notion that creativity is dampened by habits and cultural constraints, methods for enhancing it stem from the idea of temporarily releasing individuals and groups from them. Perhaps the best known technique is brainstorming. In a group session, members are asked to concentrate on a problem and come up with as many unusual solutions as they can, pushing these ideas as far as possible. To make the meeting work, certain 'rules' have become accepted, *see* Exhibit 11.8.

The most important rule in Exhibit 11.8 is the enjoinder not to evaluate ideas as they emerge (or half emerge). It is common to hear creative suggestions put down with a 'That's no good because ...' response before they have had time to grow.

Brainstorming has many variants. Seeds, such as randomly selected words, can be thrown into the meeting as starting points. In other cases the group may work on a list of *forced comparisons*, say between the question and a randomly selected problem or situation. These are helpful in individual brainstorming which, unexpectedly, is often reported as more productive than when done in a group.

A good personal skill is to 'listen for' ideas that might appear during times of relaxation and jot them in a special notebook at the first opportunity. The thoughts can then be sorted and grown using tools such as the mind map, Fig. 11.1, or de Bono's *PMI*.[31] *Plus*, *Minus*, *Interesting* is a method of recording perceptions, assigning weights to different possibilities and, for some, an aid to decision making.

Whether for individuals or groups, fostering creative thinking in organisations requires that attention be given to:

- tolerance of risk taking and failure;
- tolerance of a range of personalities;
- autonomy;
- open communication;
- appropriate measures of output and related personal rewards.

At the organisational level, many firms have become concerned at the way cultures sustain conformity and complacency. Dress codes often symbolise such attitudes. In an attempt to break them down, some American companies

---

Exhibit 11.8 **Good brainstorming practice**

- A leader should set up the meeting, announce its fixed length, encourage participation by all and suggest new beginnings if one train of thought has been followed for too long.
- Group members should be drawn from a range of disciplines and experience.
- The atmosphere should be informal and participants should be encouraged to joke about crazy proposals.
- There should be no evaluation of ideas during the session.
- A large board is helpful. In any case, a record of ideas, either tape or notes, should be studied afterwards for good ideas.

Exhibit 11.9 Formal Fridaywear

Through branches of United States companies, the casual wear day has spread to Japan. There some companies now prefer creative and individualistic traits, rather than the traditional life-long loyalty, and are seeking ways to stimulate them. While many have resisted, others have taken dressing down to excess, causing some employers to ban golf clothes and jeans. Inevitably, a new fashion, *Fridaywear*, has appeared on both sides of the Pacific. Previously, Japanese managers wore only suits or golf outfits. Now stores are offering head-to-toe co-ordinated collections for those without the confidence to do their own matching.

---

introduced casual days when staff were invited to wear informal clothes. Yet this policy has had unexpected side-effects, *see* Exhibit 11.9.[32]

Conclusion: the right alternatives and choices

Central to the managerial process, decisions range from the programmed routine to sorting out the non-programmed mess. Messes have uncertain boundaries, incomplete information and no consensus over objectives. Yet decisions about messes tend to be more significant in the long term and a good manager can display value through taking effective action in such circumstances. Uncertainty and ambiguity are compounded by risk. Different managers have varying propensities to take risks and will tend to evaluate situations in optimistic or pessimistic ways accordingly. It is up to organisations to ensure consistency in the management of risk.

Decision making involves making the right choices from among appropriate alternatives. Many authorities advocate the use of a formal decision process in which aims, alternatives and choices are developed rationally. The prescriptive classical, or rational, method represents something of an ideal but it is weak in that it does not account either for the cost of obtaining the vast amount of information or for the time required to agree aims in advance. In contrast, the administrative model comes closer to the way managers behave in practice. They recognise the impossibility of knowing all alternatives and of reaching the advanced consensus over problem definition and objectives and, instead, satisfice. With information becoming cheaper, we may see a shift towards incorporating more of it in decisions but there will always be a tension between the contrasting models.

Decision traps lurk, whether for the individual or the group. Training can help managers avoid the personal traps such as heuristics, framing, escalation of commitment or overconfidence. These can also affect groups, although they also have difficulties of groupthink and polarisation.

Valuable at all stages is creative skill. Studies show that creativity varies among cultures and according to a person's age, gender and other personal traits. On the other hand, a good manager should see that all staff are creative to some extent. The challenge is to release inventiveness from time to time. Organisations, in the end, depend on inventing the new at least as much as doing the old well.

Questions *Chapter review*

11.1 List the causes of increasing complexity for decision makers, giving an example for the owner of an SME and the local manager of an ethnocentric MNE.

11.2 What are the conditions needed before an operations research model can be used in the rational decision process?

11.3 When would you expect individual decision making to be superior to group decision making and when inferior?

Application

11.4 Would the air traffic controller in the BA5390 crisis have used elements of either decision model given in the chapter? Explain.

11.5 What do you think are the arguments for and against the introduction of casual clothes days? What conclusion do you draw from these?

Investigation

11.6 If you can attend a formal meeting, make notes on how decisions are reached, comparing them with views expressed at the outset of the discussion. What was the influence of the leader in the meeting? Relate your notes to the discussion of groups in the chapter.

11.7 Construct a mind map of a case study you have worked on previously, such as Nokia or Dorling Kindersley in Chapter 10. Explain whether the process caused you to notice any new angles or avenues for further investigation.

■ Overconfidence test

We noted that overconfidence exposes people to unnecessary risk. So recognising it in yourself is important. How can you tell? You can look at your past behaviour but people tend to remember successes and forget mistakes. Asking friends may be a guide, but they will be biased too. Try this quiz instead.

Rules

The idea here is not to get 'spot on' but to give a fairly good answer. The questions are tough and you're not an expert but you probably can guess. Each of the ten questions asks you for three numbers. In the first column put your best guess, which is the answer you would give if you were in a conventional quiz. In the other two columns write your confidence range that you are very sure – 90 per cent sure – includes the correct answer. For the bottom of the range, you are quite sure that the correct answer is higher; for the top, you are quite sure it is lower. Remember you're trying to be about 90 per cent sure so don't give silly limits either way. Then the test would have no point.

There is one example, guessing the FTSE to be at 3900 and the range 3500 to 4250.

	Best guess	Min	Max
What was the London FTSE-100 index on 12 March 1997?	3900	3500	4250
In what year did Lewis Carroll write *Alice in Wonderland?*			
For how many years is a French senator elected?			
How many bedrooms has the London Hilton hotel?			
What was the 1994 turnover of the South Korean company Samsung?			
How long is the Panama Canal?			
When was the *Superbowl* inaugurated in American football?			
What is the height of *Mont Blanc*, the tallest mountain in the Alps?			
How many United States presidents preceded F.D. Roosevelt?			
What was the French franc/sterling tourist rate on 10 March 1997?			
When was Ludwig van Beethoven born?			

Scoring

Check the answers on Page 369. To score, ignore your best guesses. Gain one point if the correct answer falls within your range, otherwise zero.

Comparison

Since the standard was for 90 per cent sure, you should reach 9 points. Scoring 8 or less means you are overconfident.

Lots of misses? You're in good company. Russo and Schoemaker,[33] who devised this form of quiz, tested more than 1000 managers from around the world. Fewer than 0.5 per cent scored one miss or none. Most had 6 or more!

You felt stymied by lack of expertise? On their special subjects, experts were found to do slightly better; they missed 5 on average. Naturally, their answers tended to be closer but they narrowed their confidence ranges too.

Personal message?

Think twice, be less sure and get some more information before making decisions.

Risky decisions at Merck[34]

The leading pharmaceutical business, Merck and Co. Inc., invests annually about $2 billion in R&D and capital projects. Most of it goes into long-term high risk projects for which conventional cash flow analyses are unsuitable. The breadth of uncertainty is so great that single estimates of, say, sales, exchange rates, market launch dates and so on would be worthless.

Merck has developed its own risk analysis models based on Monte Carlo simulation. The model takes probability estimates of input variables and produces a corresponding probability profile of the outputs. Two applications are in research planning and exchange rate hedging.

Research planning

Only 1 in 10 000 candidate chemicals makes it through to becoming a prescription drug. Investment costs are huge so the company is interested in income over the whole period of about 20 years while the formulation is protected by patents. Risks include failure to pass safety trials of all kinds, difficulties in manufacture, the chance that a rival may reach the market first or enter later with a more effective formulation, market resistance and the appearance of side effects after introduction. Some of these risks can be assessed from experience (objective probability) while others are little more than informed guesses (subjective proba-

bilities). The research planning model combines these with macroeconomic assumptions to provide probability profiles of cash flow and return on investment.

Revenue hedging

As a global business, Merck trades in many currencies. Hedging involves trading in actual currency or options to buy or sell in order to reduce the impact of unfavourable shifts in rates. The hedging model uses a 5-year planning horizon taking into account expenditure and revenue in local currencies and projections of exchange rates. Again, all the data are expressed in terms of probability distributions. The model enables rapid comparisons of different hedging strategies and informs managers of the currency risks to which the company is exposed.

What do managers do with the models? Merck's chief financial officer, Judy Lewent, explains that the models do not make decisions. Instead, they give managers an assessment of risk and return that is drawn from their own judgements of the future environment. 'The models are not some black box that completely ignores the great wisdom of management and tries to mechanise the decision making of the business. They understand both the potential and their limitations.'

Questions

1 Using the categories described in the chapter, compare the decisions faced by the LATCC air traffic controllers and the managers at Merck.

2 In spite of Lewent's denial, there are dangers in increased reliance on complex models. Relate the case study to the stages of the decision-making process to work out what these might be.

3 One problem with environment models is that managers can assume that rivals use them too. How can they incorporate this knowledge and what extra problems may arise?

4 What impact might modelling have on group decision making?

Bibliography

Jennings, David and Wattam, Stuart (1994) *Decision Making: An integrated approach,* London: Financial Times Pitman Publishing gives a broad introduction to the subject at different managerial levels and from many points of view. For work on the intriguing idea of lateral thinking, try any of the 45 books by Edward de Bono.

References

1. Noxon, Julian (1996) 'Delays loom for advanced European ATC systems. (air-traffic-control)', *Flight International*, 4537, 21 August, 11; 'AEA slams European ATC performance', *Flight International*, 4526 ,5 June, 8; Learmount, David (1995) 'The future's controller: air traffic control in the foreseeable future will continue to depend heavily upon direct human input', *Flight International*, 4493, 11 October, 39–43; Harper, Keith (1997) 'The peril in Britain's skies', *Guardian*, 3 October, 17; Department of Transport (1992) Report on the accident to BAC One-Eleven, G-BJRT over Didcot, Oxfordshire on 10 June, 1990 – Air Accident Report 1/92 London: HMSO.
2. Buzan, Tony (1995) *Use Your Head*, Revised edition, London: BBC Books; Mind Tools Ltd (1996) *Improved note taking with mind maps*: http://www.mindtools.com/mind-tools.html
3. Willan, Philip (1996) 'Network Europe: Europe stuck on launch pad', *The European*, 21 November.
4. Clements, Alan (1995) 'Put in a spin by financial advice – amid a welter of conflicting opinions, the corporate point of view can be lost', *Financial Times*, 24 July, 8.
5. 'Europe's great car war', *The Economist*, 8–14 March, 1997, 91.
6. Buckingham, Lisa (1997) 'City told to curb bonuses', *Guardian*, 6 March, 17; Davies, Daniel (1997) 'Remuneration and risk', *Financial Stability Review,* quoted in 'A bit rich', *The Economist*, 8–14 March, 1997, 103.
7. Ackoff, R.L. (1974) 'The systems revolution', *Long Range Planning*, **7** (**6**), December, 2–5.
8. Vecchio, Robert (1995) *Organizational Behaviour,* Third edition, Fort Worth, Tex.: The Dryden Press, 403–5.
9. Millar, Stuart (1997) 'Literati back borrower Swift', *Guardian*, 10 March, 3.
10. Advertisement, *Guardian*, 10 March, 1997.
11. Sherman, Stratford (1994) 'Is he too cautious to save IBM?', *Fortune*, 3 October, 78–88.
12. Drummond, Helga and Kingstone Hodgson, Julia A. (1996) 'Between a rock and a hard place: a case study in escalation', *Management Decision*, **34** (**3**), 29–34.
13. Simon, Herbert A. (1977) *The New Science of Managerial Decision Making*, Englewood Cliffs, NJ: Prentice Hall.

14. Barnard, Chester I. (1938) *The Functions of the Executive*, Cambridge, Mass.: Harvard University Press, 190.

15. Amin, S.; Fernandez-Villacanas, J. L. and Cochrane, P. (1994) 'A natural solution to the travelling salesman problem', *British Telecommunications Engineering*, **13** (**2**), 117–22.

16. Adapted from Coles, Susan and Rowley, Jennifer (1995) 'Revisiting decision trees', *Management Decision*, **33** (**8**), 46–50; *see also* Mind Tools at http://www.mind tools.comdectree.html

17. March, James (1994) *A Primer on Decision Making*, New York: Free Press, 8.

18. Simon, H.A. (1976) *Administrative Behaviour*, Third edition, New York: Free Press, 68.

19. Navram Associates (1994) *The Big PLUS in Ethical Decision Making*: http://www.navram. com/Newsletter/94-04/04-94a.html

20. Wilkes, F.M., Samuels, J.M. and Greenfield, S.M. (1996) 'Investment decision making in UK manufacturing industry', *Management Decision*, **34** (**4**), 62–71.

21. Janis, Irving L. (1982) *Groupthink*, Second edition, Boston, Mass.: Houghton Mifflin, 9.

22. Stoner, J.A.F. (1961) *A comparison of individual and group decisions involving risk*, Master's thesis, MIT Sloan School of Management, quoted in Vecchio, Robert (1995) *op. cit.*, 410.

23. Vecchio (1995) *op. cit.*, 412.

24. Aldiss, Brian W.(1990) *Bury My Heart at W. H. Smith's: A writing life*, London: Hodder & Stoughton.

25. de Bono, Edward (1988) *Letters to Thinkers: Further thoughts on lateral thinking*, Harmondsworth: Penguin, 188.

26. United East India Company (1655) *Beschrijving van't Gesandschap der Nederlandsche Oost-Indische Compagnie aan Den Grooten Tartarischen Cham, nu Keyzer van China*, Amsterdam.

27. Koestler, Arthur (1989) *The Act of Creation*, Harmondsworth: Penguin.

28. Success consultant Deepak Chopra quoted in Landale, Anthony (1997) 'Into the new year and daring to be different', *Guardian*, 4 January, 11.

29. Vecchio (1995) *op. cit.*, 418.

30. Raudsepp, E. (1978) 'Are you a creative manager?', *Management Review*, **58**, 15–16.

31. de Bono (1988) *op. cit.*, 79; *see also* http://www.mindtools.com/pmi.html

32. Terazono, Emiko (1995) 'Japan tries on Fridaywear', *Financial Times*, 26 May, 12.

33. Russo, J. Edward and Schoemaker, Paul J.H. (1990) 'The overconfidence quiz', *Harvard Business Review*, **68** (**5**) September–October, 236.

34. 'Mastering Management 5.6: Risk analysis at Merck', *Financial Times*, 24 November, 1995.

Overconfidence test answers (questions on p.366)

The FTSE was 4444.3 and the other answers are:
1865; 9; 600; £36 billion; 80 km (50 m); 1966; 4807 metres (15 772 feet); 31; 8.90; 1770.

Part 4

ORGANISING LARGE GROUPS

This island is almost made of coal and surrounded by fish. Only an organising genius could produce a shortage of coal and fish in Great Britain at the same time. *Aneurin Bevan, British politician*

Like fingerprints, all marriages are different. *George Bernard Shaw, Irish writer*

One must never lose time in vainly regretting the past nor in complaining about the changes which cause us discomfort, for change is the very essence of life. *Anatole France, French writer*

It might be said that it is the ideal of the employer to have production without employees and the ideal of the employees is to have income without work. *Fritz Schumacher, German economist*

PART 3			
PLANNING AND DECISION MAKING	**CHAPTER 9** Planning: coping in an uncertain environment	**CHAPTER 10** Strategic management: looking to the long term	**CHAPTER 11** Decision making: choosing from alternatives

PART 4				
ORGANISING LARGE GROUPS	**CHAPTER 15** Human resource management	**CHAPTER 14** Managing organisational change	**CHAPTER 13** Organisational design: matching the situation	**CHAPTER 12** Organisations: principles, models and outcomes

PART 5			
ORGANISING SMALL GROUPS	**CHAPTER 16** Leadership and motivation	**CHAPTER 17** Groups and teams	**CHAPTER 18** Communication in management

Since management is concerned with 'getting things done through people', working with groups and individuals is a dominant feature of the role. Therefore, covering this large field, Parts 4 and 5 are devoted to the social aspects of management. Part 4 is concerned with establishing and changing organisations. The study begins in Chapter 12, which contains definitions and states the fundamental tensions between the need to differentiate and integrate functions. Charts are introduced and these are used to compare different organisational forms.

Chapter 13 draws on the open systems perspective to investigate how formal structures relate to situational factors such as uncertainty, globalisation and technology. The limitations of this contingency approach are also drawn out. Although every situation is unique, this should not mean that similarities are ignored.

Chapter 14 addresses the question of change. Within every organistion, there are forces promoting and resisting adaptation to evolving circumstances. While change is necessary if the organisation–environment fit is to be maintained, a continual flux may be as harmful as not changing at all. Consequently , the evolution of structures can be seen as alternating periods of stability and upheaval. The chapter investigates how managers can stimulate adaption when it is needed.

The discipline of Human Resource Management links issues for the whole organisation to considering individuals and small groups. For the former, the chapter covers human resource planning and policies for appraisal, welfare, pay and industrial relations. The latter perspective arises when their impact upon individuals begins to be understood. Individuals and small groups are the theme for Part 5.

12

Organising: principles, models and outcomes

Chapter objectives

When you have finished studying this chapter, you should be able to:

- clarify what is meant by organising and outline how differentiation and integration have to be reconciled;

- describe four key issues that need to be considered in organising, namely: hierarchy, specialisation, centralisation and co-ordination;

- explain the existence of line and staff organisations;

- evaluate the use of organisation charts, process models and rich pictures in representing organisations;

- illustrate and compare functional, divisional, matrix and network forms;

- show how multinational enterprises face particular problems of organisation.

Siemens AG: integrating a worldwide portfolio of businesses[1]

Ranked twenty-fifth in the world, Siemens is a decentralised global business with more than 45 per cent of its 379 000 staff employed outside Germany. In spite of stagnation in the domestic market, 1996 saw worldwide orders reach DM 100 billion for the first time. Siemens sees itself as committed to 250 business fields within the electronic and electrical industries. It has sustained its growth with product innovation, process development and customer service.

At the start of 1997, the company had its own organisations in 189 of the world's 193 countries. These ranged from small agency offices to giant manufacturing plants spread throughout the most important economies. In the United States there were 400 offices, 80 plants and 40 research and development units. How does the company organise its effort to innovate and focus operations while, simultaneously, presenting a local 'Siemens' face to each customer?

At the highest level, reporting to the managing board, responsibility for the worldwide business lies with 16 groups. As Fig. 12.1 shows, 14 of these are part of the Siemens company and two, Nixdorf and Osram, are legally separate businesses owned by Siemens. At headquarters there are corporate departments. Spread throughout the world, regional

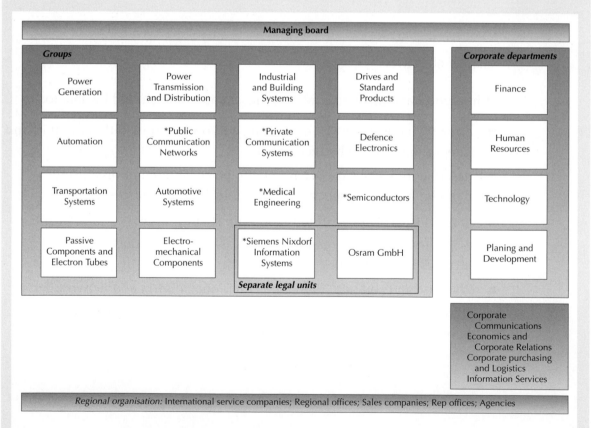

Fig. 12.1 Seimens AG – board and business groups

units are responsible for local sales and service on behalf of the whole organisation.

Some business groups, regional businesses and headquarters units are themselves huge organisations. For example, Siemens Nixdorf, formed by merger in 1990, has sales of DM 13.6 billion in 58 countries. Some 34 per cent of the 34 100 employees work outside Germany. Siemens Nixdorf serves its customers through 10 business units, as shown in Fig. 12.2. Each has a presence in the triad regions – Europe, America and Asia–Pacific. They are supported by headquarters units responsible for finance, employees, corporate strategy and system strategy.

Siemens' main board is responsible for co-ordinating all the activities. For example, it has to decide where to focus research and development activity to provide the innovations on which future business will be based. Almost 8 per cent of sales is spent on R&D, supporting 44 500 staff throughout the world. Of this sum, 70 per cent is spent in the five operating units shown with an asterisk in Fig. 12.1. This emphasis is based on the recognition that microelectronics is the key to competitive advantage. The years 1993–6 saw Siemens, already a leader in Germany, double its rate of registration of inventions.

Some critics argue that the business has become too difficult to manage and should be separated into high-technology and low-technology companies. Yet the board sees this as an artificial split, stressing the value of integration in global markets. Beyond internal development and innovation, however, it continues to reshape the business through acquisitions, disposals and joint ventures. To illustrate, among many changes in 1996–7 were joining with the Thai company CP to build a new chip plant in China, selling the high-performance printing operation, and setting up a separate company for the technical lighting business. This last change was to ease the establishment of further joint ventures.

Beyond changing the portfolio, the board is improving all activities. In 1993, it started the TOP (Time Optimised Processes) movement to push for improved customer satisfaction, productivity, innovation, new market openings, and a corporate-wide culture change. TOP targets are to increase productivity by 30 per cent and halve the length of innovation and purchasing cycles.

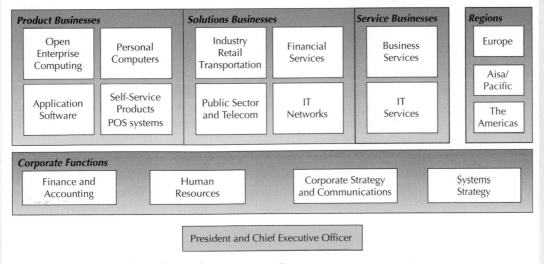

Fig. 12.2 Siemens Nixdorf Informations systeme AG: corporate management

Introduction

Commensurate with its global reach, Siemens faces the problem of structural design on a grand scale. Some stakeholders, worried about the gap between their company and the best performers in the sector, notably ABB and General Electric, press for reorganisation. Challenged on the idea of a split into separate electronic and electrical divisions, chairman Heinrich von Pierer replied, 'I ask myself why nobody puts that question to my friend Jack Welch (chairman of General Electric). The reason is he achieves excellent earnings. This must be the only reason, because it is much easier to question the presence of synergies at GE than at Siemens'.[2] For von Pierer, synergy means that many business units benefit from links and would be worse off outside the group. Infrastructure projects in Asia, for instance, entail bulk orders covering a wide range of electrical and electronic products and services.

Siemens' strategy is to satisfy the needs of its customers by producing packaged solutions. For a new power station in a developing country, for example, there will be work for many groups shown in Fig. 12.1. The company wants to present a single face to the customer yet divide its manufacturing and service operations into efficient, focused units each of which achieves the highest standards of quality and productivity. Bridging strategy and operations is the problem of organising. We can define this as follows:

> *Organising is the arrangement of all elements of an organisation to achieve its strategic objectives.*

We can see that the definition implies choice. Clearly, there are many possible configurations of Siemens' business units spread across 250 sectors and 189 countries. Like most organisations, there is a tension between the need to deploy resources into identifiable departments, the notion of *differentiation*, and the requirement to link them in patterns that match customers' needs, the idea of *integration*. The structure is important here. Close linkages allow the business to take advantage of economies of scale yet they can, in practice, be very difficult to manage. For instance, many organisations gain through having a headquarters unit responsible for purchasing. Yet, unless this activity is confined to the largest buying contracts, the benefits of drawing it together can be lost in extra administration and slower service. Centralisation, therefore, is another question to be resolved by senior managers.

Organising is never a once and for all task. Just as we picture strategic management as a flow of decisions producing an emergent strategy, organisation structures emerge as adaptation to change. This means that their form can, at least in part, be explained by their history. While most groups at Siemens are wholly integrated into the single business, SNI and Osram are legally separate yet wholly owned companies. This arrangement follows from the way SNI was formed by merger and Osram was a major acquisition. Through acquisition and disposal, the form of the business is continually being reshaped.

The points made here are among the fundamental ideas that apply to all organisations, whether businesses, government agencies or in the voluntary sector. The rest of the chapter details these principles and shows how they work out in practice. In the following two chapters, organisational structures are related to wider questions such as environment and change. We shall also point to some deeper challenges to their existence in their modern, hierarchical form.

Principles

In this section, we shall examine four key issues in organising, namely hierarchy, specialisation, centralisation and co-ordination. None of these is new. As shown in Chapter 2, Fayol was concerned with much the same questions. To illustrate the general nature of the issues, we shall compare Siemens with a voluntary organisation. Measured by turnover or employment, The Network,[3] described in Exhibit 12.1, was only a few millionths of the size of the German MNE. Yet the same sorts of questions arise in the small and large organisations.

Exhibit 12.1 **The Network: the satisfaction of sharing**

The Network was a skills exchange established in the premises of Merseyside Council for Voluntary Service (MCVS), a charitable trust in the centre of Liverpool. Facilities included a small office with a telephone, a workshop and lounge. Any person, employed or unemployed, could become a member by signifying some 'offer' of skill or time and some 'want' to be satisfied. There was no payment in money, exchanges did not necessarily take place reciprocally and the basis of all transactions was reasonable give and take. The group who established The Network expressed its aims in terms of a need to find practical solutions to the problems of rewarding work. They felt that a resource exchange could offer the member many non-economic functions of employment – time structuring, sharing and widening experience, a sense of usefulness, personal status and enforcing activity. Further, a successful operation would lead to changed attitudes in the wider society, towards work, the unemployed and welfare benefits. The 12 founder members originally hoped for a large-scale operation in an area where the number of registered unemployed was around 100 000. They saw the key operational problems mainly in terms of coping with a large membership. Instead of this extensive impact, however, a smaller organisation with average membership of 130 emerged. The jobs done for others ranged from typing to transport and dog handling to dressmaking. Besides exchanges, members were involved in group projects, workshops and social events.

The weekly members' meeting, with rotating chairman and minutes secretary, was the decision-making body. Day-to-day running of the organisation began with a members' rota. After a year of operation, however, this arrangement was supplemented by members becoming, for one month at a time, a full-time, paid co-ordinator. Financial support came from various foundations via MCVS as guarantor. Concerned by his fiduciary duty to ensure that the funds were spent wisely, the MCVS secretary exercised considerable influence over the way The Network was run, insisting on detailed financial records. Given that this person's signature was required on all drawings from the bank, the members felt obliged to comply.

■ Hierarchy

In Chapter 2 we noted Weber's studies of bureaucracy. He saw it emerging from the change from traditional authority to the rational and legal system of organisation and control. In Weber's view, bureaucracy established a relation between people at the top, such as company directors or elected politicians, and their subordinate officials. The legitimacy of the top people arises from an external source, such as ownership, appointment or election, while the rights and duties of others in the organisation come from delegation. Weber would have had these rights prescribed in written rules. Many organisations, however, do not stick to this strict approach. While the rules are embodied in people's job descriptions, the pace of change is such that written documents cannot keep up. Members are expected to continually rethink and renegotiate their tasks. Nevertheless, the ideas of authority, its delegation, and corresponding responsibilities are important ones.

> *Authority is the formal right of a manager to act as a manager, that is to plan, decide, give instructions, allocate resources, and control, to achieve the aims of the organisation.*

Barnard was one of the first to point out three features of authority:[4]

■ In a formal organisation, authority resides in the *position* and not the person. As chief executives of Siemens and General Electric, both von Pierer and Welch are expected to exercise authority related to their roles. While they have wide discretion, their decisions are constrained by the policies of their company boards and the legal frameworks within which they operate. Similarly, The Network chairman should exercise that role according to the rules of the group guided by knowledge of good practice in the conduct of meetings.

■ Authority must be accepted by subordinates. The idea that authority originates outside and can be imposed upon those within rarely works for long. In its discussion of leadership and power, Chapter 16 shows that acceptance is important. The manager's authority vanishes if the subordinates refuse to follow. Nowhere is this difficulty seen more acutely than in politics. Here, power, either positional or personal, can quickly evaporate, as illustrated by Exhibit 12.2.

■ Authority can be delegated. *Delegation is the transfer of authority* from one level to another. Delegation to the lowest feasible level is supported in many organisations for it provides maximum flexibility, responsiveness to customers and can improve

---

Exhibit 12.2 Vanishing power

In a struggle after the death of Mao Zedong in 1976, the Gang of Four ousted the moderates led by vice-premier Deng Xiaoping, who went into hiding. Hua Guofeng was installed as party chairman and head of government yet soon he had the Gang arrested on treason charges. During Hua's stopgap administration, Deng recovered his former influence and progressively challenged Hua. Deng's protégés were gradually installed in key politburo positions to the extent that, in 1982, Hua and senior colleagues were removed. They had lost the support of the party and the people. Although not officially holding the highest offices, and gradually retiring from those that he did fill, Deng remained highly influential until his death in 1997.

the motivation of all involved. There are, however, some limits on what can be delegated. In many countries, certain decisions are restricted to officials such as company directors and their equivalent. Only a company board can approve accounts and directors are responsible for safety practices. The Network struggled with this tension. On the one hand, members wanted wide discretion to spend the grants allotted to the group yet, on the other, MCVS had given undertakings to ensure that spending was according to its charitable aims and every penny could be accounted for.

Closely tied to authority is the notion of responsibility. It mirrors authority in that *responsibility is the duty to act according to the authority that has been delegated*. If the above criteria mean that managers have legitimate authority to act, then that is what they must do. Normally, managers are given responsibility that matches their authority. If responsibility is excessive, the manager's job becomes very difficult, relying on persuasion rather than giving firm orders. Then, if things go wrong, there is the possibility of scapegoating, that is blaming unfairly. As Fig. 12.3 suggests, if the balance swings the other way, there is the possibility of a manager using power for personal, wasteful or, ultimately, tyrannical ends.

Line and staff

While it may seem that it is unsound to appoint managers without formal authority, such practice is common. With managers having to deal with an increasing range of specialisms, from engineering to employment law and systems to personnel development, more of these tasks are taken over by separate individuals and departments. They are 'off-line', so to speak. The *line managers* concentrate on tasks that are directly related to the main activities of the organisation. In a manu-

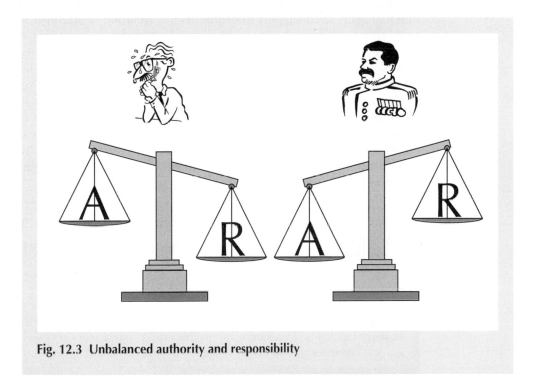

Fig. 12.3 Unbalanced authority and responsibility

facturing company, these could be obtaining materials, production, selling and distribution. In a hospital, line activities are the medical and nursing units. *Staff departments* cover all those functions that support the line managers in their tasks. Note that the term 'staff' has a special meaning in this context, somewhat different to its more common usage.

We should beware of relying on this apparently clear-cut distinction for there is much scope for interpretation. The link between the line and staff managers can range from superior–subordinate in the same department to an advisory link between colleagues in different departments or even from an outside consultant. Why establish such a complex arrangement?

The origins of so-called *line and staff* organisations are in military practice. A fighting unit would frequently have staff officers attached to provide specialist knowledge and skills. One function would be to gather and interpret intelligence using skills in examining aerial photographs or using foreign languages. The advantage is that scarce specialists can be deployed where needed without having to clog the traditional command structure.

The practice was taken up in the civilian sphere. Often, staff departments operate at all levels in the hierarchy, providing vertical channels of communication for specialist, technical information. The corporate functions at Siemens Nixdorf serve as staff advisers to the CEO, the senior line manager. In practice they do not have to consult with the chief on every detail. Usually they will exchange information and instructions directly with their counterparts in the business units. The systems strategy function at headquarters may issue instructions to corresponding functions within the businesses on matters related to the acquisition and development of company-wide software. Exhibit 12.3 gives a further example of the line–staff distinction, this time from the pharmaceutical industry. Here the technical complexity of manufacture means that line managers need support from staff teams. Rotation of scientists between line and staff functions helps to build experience and teamwork.[5]

There are dangers with the growth of staff roles. Godfrey and others[6] warn against line managers delegating responsibility for a key activity to staff managers, whose role should be limited to advising on, and handling, its technical aspects. Their example, given in Exhibit 12.4, is taken from health care management yet could just as well apply anywhere. There are many instances of quality improvement programmes failing because they have been seen by senior line managers as essentially *technical* solutions to problems and therefore the province of specialists. Note how the director of quality management is made accountable for the programme yet has not the authority to carry it through.

Exhibit 12.3 **Line and staff roles in pharmaceutical manufacturing**

The manufacturing scientist can rotate from staff process positions into technical manufacturing areas that provide participation in line management. These supervisory positions give the scientist a thorough understanding of process safety, quality, productivity, and employee issues that affect the daily production operation. The varied experiences that scientists bring to this role are invaluable for effective interaction with support departments that assist in meeting market demands.

> **Exhibit 12.4** **Responsibility without authority**
>
> 'In health care, executives initially intent on quality management as a strategy easily become distracted by new threats from purchasers, crises in physician relationships, restructuring, mergers, capital needs, and a thousand other short-term demands. Try as they might to hold fast to the agenda of improvement, [senior managers] can easily yield to the temptation of delegating the quality management initiative to others.
>
> 'Over-delegation can occur in disguise. No executive who has read the quality literature ever says to the staff quality director, "I am expecting you to handle this change, so that I can attend to other matters." Instead, the language is of "full support," "generous budgets," and "regular reviews." But, by other salient tests, the work of leadership may not have changed at all. Has the Chief Executive's daily calendar really changed so as to make quality the strategy of the organization? Have behaviours among senior managers evolved so as to teach, support, and sustain the breaking down of barriers, the customer focus, the "process-mindedness," and the new use of statistical thinking without which quality management is only rhetoric? Do organization-wide quality strategies exist? Are they managed? Are they, in fact, the top priority, or not?
>
> 'Many executives who have over-delegated the change process do not appear to realize it. No wonder; no one tells them. It would be a rare, courageous, and perhaps short-lived "Director of Quality Management" who would make an appointment with the CEO to say, "I have been thinking, boss. The job you gave me, and are expecting me to carry out, I now realize, is, in fact, your job. You are holding me accountable for changes in culture, behaviour, strategic priority, and organizational methods that only you ... can really deliver. In the end, you may think that I let you down; but it's the other way around."'

The director was left without support. In another organisation, the staff department could win too much support and begin to act in an arrogant way, overestimating its own importance. Self-serving attitudes may grow as the staff managers forget that their primary task is to support the line.

▨ Specialisation

It has been widely accepted that work can be carried out more efficiently when employees specialise. In this way they can focus their attention on a limited number of activities and hone their skills accordingly. Organisations are developed around this principle, although how it is applied in each case depends on the choice of senior managers. The Network displayed the beginnings of specialisation in an emerging organisation. Evidently not all members could take the chair, keep the minutes or conduct administrative tasks. These tasks were shared among those who were willing and able to take on the burden. Siemens has problems of specialisation on a much larger scale. The company chose to build its business units around technological groupings with, for example, all computing or all power generation being put together. Yet there could be a case for specialisation by region or by type of customer. How MNEs resolve the tension among these approaches is brought up later in the chapter.

Within business groupings, each level is split into further specialities until, at the operating level, there are departments for supply, operations, sales and distribution and so on. The benefits of efficiency seem to be available right down to the single task. Yet, as explained in Chapter 16, there are limits to these gains. In the ultimate, specialisation leads to low motivation as workers would be expected to carry out merely one repetitive and boring job. Scientific management can be taken too far. Therefore, many companies are replanning their organisation to develop teams throughout the structure. As with many aspects of organisational design, the problem concerns not whether specialisation is good or bad but finding its right pattern and degree.

■ Centralisation (and decentralisation)

Related to the questions of authority, responsibility and specialisation is the one concerning centralisation. This pertains to the level in the hierarchy at which decisions are made. In a centralised organisation, they tend to be made by those near the top, whereas decentralisation means that authority is passed to lower levels. In the latter, there is less monitoring of employee decision making and performance.

To assess the degree of centralisation of an organisation is especially difficult. This is partly because, since decentralisation has acquired a positive image in both managers' and commentators' minds, many claim its existence while actual behaviour shows otherwise. Furthermore, the possibilities for decentralisation vary from firm to firm and from time to time. Crisis, for example, leads to centralisation. This is because crisis management procedures, *see* Chapter 9, often require that all aspects of the emergency are handled through a single 'command and control' office.

Trends are also difficult to perceive. In recent years, many authorities have espoused policies of decentralisation to match developments such as flatter organisation structures and the recruitment of more capable employees. Reality is, as usual, more complex than such simple models, for opposite trends coexist within the same organisation. For example Siemens, in common with many global companies, has progressively developed policies for centralised purchasing. This takes advantage of improved prices and better control of quality through consolidated, long-term commitments. Meanwhile, increasing the geographic spread to almost 200 countries requires Siemens' service organisations to move more closely to customers than ever before. Such an organisation cannot be controlled in detail from one office in Germany, however large and efficient it may be.

Figure 12.4 summarises the advantages and disadvantages of centralisation. The benefits lie in gains in economic performance through administrative cost savings, taking advantages of scale and avoiding wasteful conflict and competition among units. Decentralisation, on the other hand, offers the following: decisions closer to the point where they are needed; more flexibility; and benefits to employees such as higher motivation and chances to broaden experience. A wise organisation will consider these issues in relation to each aspect of its policies. For example, strong arguments can be advanced for centralising the following activities:

- allocation of capital investment and R&D expenditure;
- managing international cash flows;

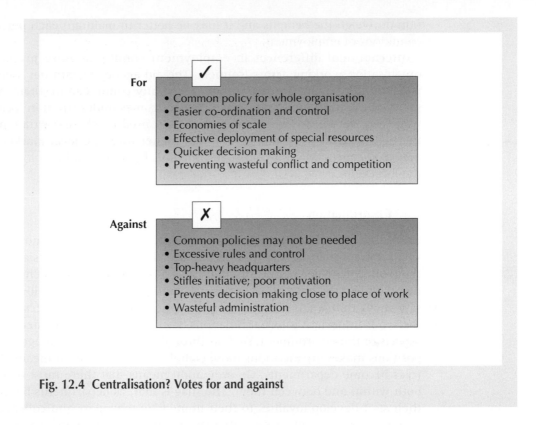

Fig. 12.4 Centralisation? Votes for and against

■ design of information systems;

■ purchasing of major items;

■ development of senior managers;

■ setting conditions of employment.

Meanwhile, here are some tasks that may be better decentralised:

■ management of day to day operations;

■ links to national and regional industry organisations;

■ small-scale purchasing;

■ sales;

■ recruitment;

■ training of locally recruited staff.

Since Siemens' expenditure on fixed investments and R&D both run at more than 8 per cent of company turnover, allocating the spending among business units must be a decision for the main board and its advisers. Yet it would expect the management of approved projects to be carried out by teams within the businesses. In human resource management, companies may gain through setting standard conditions of employment. This aids harmony among staff and simplifies transfer of middle and senior managers among units. Yet such a policy begins to break down when the group merges with new businesses. The costs of harmonisation outweigh the benefits and it may be better to maintain each person's original conditions of employment.

International differences in employment conditions raise problems for any organisation working across frontiers. The aid agency Oxfam has a commendable policy of not paying the senior manager in any country more than five times the salary of the most junior employee. Yet this comes under strain in locations where wages are very low. The international scales used for the expatriate manager sets the nightwatch's wage at a level much higher than the local market would suggest. Polycentric MNEs avoid such problems by leaving all employment issues to the local unit.

■ Co-ordination

Co-ordination refers to the *need for staff to act in unison*. This is not difficult in the small entrepreneurial set-up. Here, all but the most trivial decisions are made by the owner-manager who continually adapts the business to its changing environment. Unless the entrepreneur behaves haphazardly, co-ordination is implicit. We saw above that when organisations grow they tend to spawn specialist roles. These carry out important internal functions, such as accounting, or deal with different aspects of the environment, such as through regional sales managers. Adding such positions makes organisations more complex. Further growth means that specialist roles become departments. Co-ordination means that there must be collaboration both within and between them. The snag is that, as departments become stronger, their staff develop loyalties to their immediate managers and colleagues. Barriers between departments are created so that the management of work flow across them becomes more difficult. Witness how professionals, such as teachers, doctors or engineers, often speak of their units or departments as though they were in competition with others with whom they are supposed to co-operate.

What means are available to achieve co-ordination? Figure 12.5 illustrates four basic methods: line management, liaison staff, information systems and cross-functional teams.

Line management

Line managers, working within an appropriate hierarchical structure, are fundamental in achieving order. We shall see later in this chapter how the structure can take several forms. These, in turn, can be related to the circumstances in which each is likely to be more successful. Fundamentally, an approach that relies on structure sees co-ordination as a critical responsibility of managers at each level.

Liaison staff

Co-ordination difficulties for line managers arise from the complexity and number of tasks that have to be linked. One solution is the appointment of liaison, or linking, staff whose function is to connect the work of several individuals or departments. A common sight in factories dedicated to batch production is the *progress chaser* who, clipboard in hand, follows orders from process to process ironing out snags in the flow. Managed from a central production control unit, these

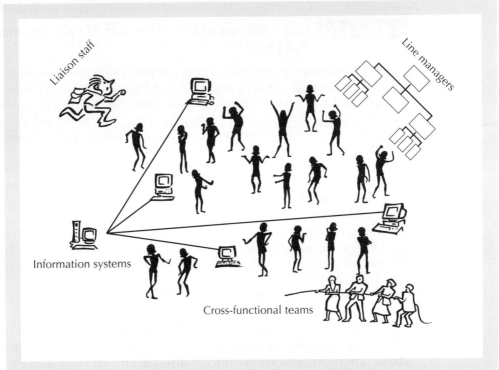

Fig. 12.5 Ways of getting people to co-ordinate their work

staff are attached to none of the manufacturing sections. They rely on personal drive, persuasive powers and detailed knowledge for their authority.

At The Network, it was at first hoped that co-ordination would be achieved by volunteers each taking on the task for a week at a time. This led to neither continuity nor consistency. Consequently, members took on the role for longer periods and were paid small salaries in return for agreed weekly hours.

At a broader level, leading companies making ranges of consumer goods rely on product, or brand, managers to co-ordinate each line. Exhibit 12.5 illustrates the tasks that can be involved. Note how links are made both with other managers in the organisation and with outside agencies.[7]

Information systems

Information systems offer the capability of transmitting huge quantities of information through and between organisations irrespective of hierarchical and departmental divisions and geographical separation. Such arrangements are being introduced by both large corporations and SMEs. Daryl Industries is the UK's leading producer of shower and bath screens, employing some 90 staff on three sites in Merseyside. In 1996 it began to develop open systems to integrate tasks, such as product modifications and final assembly schedules, which are difficult to control. The computer network would make this information available to up to 30 staff concurrently.

> ### Exhibit 12.5 One company's view of the role of category manager: link person
>
> This is a challenging mixture of both category and brand management, offering the autonomy to play a leading role in the development and growth of our quality portfolio. You'll also have the chance to mastermind the launch and commercialisation of both existing and new brands on the back of our phenomenal success. Your impact on the business will be immediate, encompassing a whole range of strategic initiatives in line with present and future customer-orientated objectives.
>
> Working within a multi-functional team, you'll define and evolve detailed category development programmes, carefully positioning and monitoring brands so that each is poised to make maximum impact in terms of distribution, market share, volume and profitability.
>
> Integrating your skills with customer managers, marketing/commercial management and external agencies, you'll oversee the development of marketing communications material and other below-the-line activities to fully support your planning and launch of new products.

Information networks also allow staff dispersed throughout many layers and sites of a large organisation to share data, possibly by access to a common data base. They can also communicate directly and cheaply using modern software such as Lotus Notes. The effect of the freer flow of information means that managers' role as information carriers is curtailed. There is more on this aspect of information systems in Chapter 22.

Cross-functional teams

A cross-functional team, known sometimes as a *task force* or *working party*, is set up to solve a problem involving several departments. The members bring the perspective and expertise of their own functions to bear on the shared problem. For instance, at Rover's Swindon plant, production managers were concerned about the best specification of glove to be worn by staff when handling panels jammed in machines after a line failure. There were risks of cuts and abrasions from sharp corners. Each production manager is personally responsible for safety and is expected to resolve questions such as this. Several of them decided to get together to work with invited advisers and potential suppliers. The goal was a solution common to all sections. It would simplify supplies. Incidentally, even this outcome was a stop-gap since the best way to approach such risky tasks is to avoid the need for them. As they said at Rover, 'We should design them out'.

Task forces and working parties are often temporary. More permanent arrangements include standing committees that meet regularly to co-ordinate activities. Daryl, for example, has a team of managers meeting occasionally to review the performance of its information system and explore ways to improve it. As we shall see later, teams can become so important and numerous in some organisations that they are represented in their permanent structures – the so-called matrix organisations.

Co-ordination in voluntary organisations is vital as the involvement of members is an important part of retaining their commitment. Typical of small voluntary groups, The Network used its weekly meetings to make all-important decisions from spending several thousands on a new project to choosing which colour to paint the snack bar ceiling. This would be regarded as excessive co-ordination in all but the smallest organisations.

Representing organisations

When asked to describe their organisations, many managers will immediately reach for the well-known organisation chart, such as in Fig. 12.1 and 12.2. This picture tells us something about the organisation, including our respondent's status within it! Organisation charts are representations, or *models*, of organisation structures. They show the set of relatively permanent links among officials. The models work if the links are what we are interested in. Like all good descriptive models, they tell us what we want to know and leave out other details. Yet there are also many things that they do not tell us. We learn little of what happens, of how the system behaves. For instance, important features not shown include: relationships that cut across the normal hierarchy; power distances between levels; information flows; committees and other group activities; and details of each manager's responsibilities.

Let us illustrate this difficulty by looking again at The Network. A useful skill when examining an organisation for the first time is to sketch something related to the mind-map of Fig. 11.1. In this context, such sketches are known as *rich pictures*. Figure 12.6 is a representation of The Network in this form. On a single sheet, it tries to capture the main elements of the organisation and the processes that are undertaken within it. This example was used after our initial study both to record our first impressions and, in a tidier and enlarged layout, for communicating to the group, 'This is the way we see you'. The unconventional form of the rich picture, however, means that it cannot communicate much without verbal support. The notes in Exhibit 12.6 summarise the introductory points of a presentation made to a meeting of members and sponsors.

■ Representing structure and process

In trying to capture multiple aspects of what happened at The Network, Fig. 12.6 sacrifices detail of any one issue. Like other models, it is a simplification, here designed to support and record an initial understanding. It leads to further questions, both about relationships and how things work. To proceed, we tend to use two further models, often designed to represent structure and process.

■ *Structure* refers to those features of the organisation that are fixed. Besides the hierarchy, these include features, such as plant and buildings, systems from information technology through to working rules, and the basic culture shared by members. Being unchanging, they share the property that they can be depicted with static models such as charts, sketches and manuals.

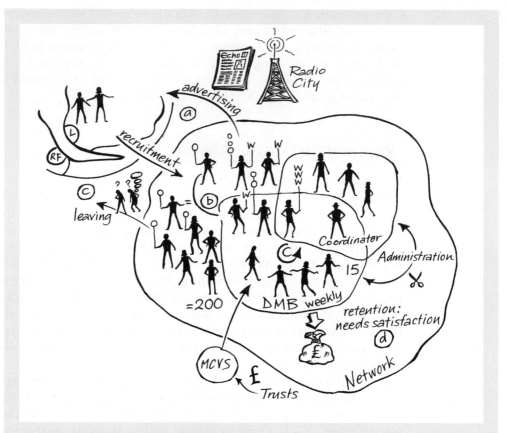

Fig. 12.6 The Network skills exchange

Exhibit 12.6 Notes to support the rich picture of Fig. 12.6

The Network sought to recruit new members through free advertising and promotion spots in local media (a). When prospective members arrived they were invited to declare 'offers and wants' (O and W) which were compared in a matching system (b). Decisions were taken at the weekly decision-making body (DMB) which included a rotating chairman, the co-ordinator, the MCVS secretary and up to 12 volunteers. Volunteers, not always the same ones, covered administration with the co-ordinator. There was evidence of conflict between the two groups. The DMB dispensed funds and MCVS guarded them. The Network knew little about members who left or those who visited and did not join (c). They assumed people stayed on because their needs were being satisfied (d).

■ *Process* refers to those features of the organisation that are continually changing. They include flows of goods, cash and information.

We should note that these categories are not clear cut. Nothing in organisational life stays the same for ever. We can, therefore, talk about structural change and the processes used to achieve it. Deciding what is fixed and what changes is not a new problem. The Greek, Heraclitus (546–483 BC) saw the cosmos as in a constant state of flux. Hence to pin down what it actually is presents a great difficulty. To him is attributed the statement, 'You cannot step in the same river twice'.

Ideas about structure and process go hand-in-hand in describing systems. A structural statement about the Rhine could be, 'The river is the longest in Europe, rising in Lake Constance and reaching the North Sea south of Rotterdam.' A process statement is, 'In 1986, a factory fire caused 30 tonnes of pesticide to leak into the river, rendering lifeless more than 100 km.' Countering Heraclitus, the structural statement does describe the same river over a long period. On the other hand, the process statement follows the Greek thinker: as each moment passes the river changes irreversibly.

Structural models of organisation have already been introduced and are used extensively in the rest of this chapter. To illustrate a process model, we can draw on one routine noted in Fig. 12.6, recruitment. The process is represented by a flow through several stages. In Fig. 12.7 we see the process as practised by the group in its early days. Anxious to build up membership and launch its system of exchanges, The Network would press potential recruits for information about themselves and the extent they could participate in the core process. This was daunting to many who had dropped in out of curiosity. It risked reinforcing feelings of isolation and inadequacy. Furthermore, The Network did not arrange for

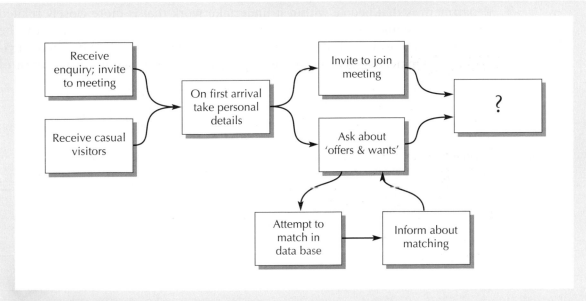

Fig. 12.7 Recruitment process at The Network

any particular follow-up if immediate matching could not be offered. Our advice was to take things more slowly, recognising that voluntary organisations build up their membership as much through social bonding as an appeal to practical advantages. Figure 12.8 illustrates the alternative process for a first contact. There would be no urging to join or participate in the exchange system; the main aim would be to ensure that the person would come to the next meeting. By not forcing the pace, recruitment would be more successful.

Process models are common in all fields of management from strategy to operations. They are used to describe and analyse planning, processing and controlling sequences and appear throughout this book. The approach is fundamental to the practice of Business Process Reengineering, which is explained in Chapter 14.

Forms of organisation

Organisation charts are descriptions of structure. They are useful in studying formal relationships and staff deployment between departments. They use the two dimensions of the chart to depict:

■ Hierarchy – the number of levels and the chain of command;

■ Specialisation – the division of tasks between managers and deciding who is responsible for linking their work at each level.

These dimensions can be used to depict various organisational forms. Whichever is chosen by an organisation, it is an attempt to resolve the balance between the need to specialise while simultaneously achieving co-ordination. The organisational design both *differentiates* and *integrates*. In principle, many choices are available. Staff of the large organisation are split into departments. The idea of a department is that people within it undertake work that is more closely related than with members of other departments. The snag is that these links can be drawn in many ways and can change as new situations arise. The functional, divisional and matrix structures are approaches that have adapted the notion of

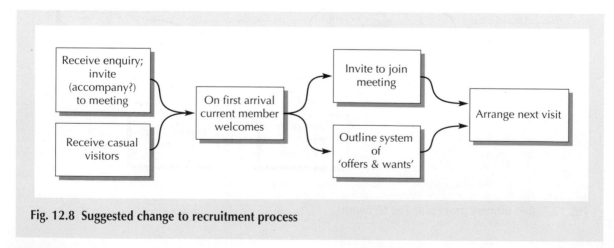

Fig. 12.8 Suggested change to recruitment process

hierarchy and formal reporting to different circumstances. We shall examine these below, together with newer, network forms that have emerged from the need for flexible organisations in the environment of global competition.

Functional form

Organisations planned along functional lines place together people who are applying related technical skills to similar tasks. They are based on disciplines such as production, marketing, finance or personnel. Figure 12.9 is an example of a company creating functional departments at three levels. First, the whole business is split into production, personnel and so on. At the next level, the production department is separated into sub-departments according to the disciplines indicated. At the third level, further functional separation occurs. Structures within departments other than production would also be shown in a full chart, but there is no space to show their subsections here.

The advantage of functional departments is the enhanced co-ordination from the affinity that staff with similar skills feel with one another. Such departments develop in growing SMEs as each manager takes on assistants to cope with the increasing workload. Disadvantages, on the other hand, come from the narrow outlook which may develop among departmental members whose concern with the specialism may outweigh broader considerations of the success of the company as a whole. It is also difficult to measure the department's performance because it

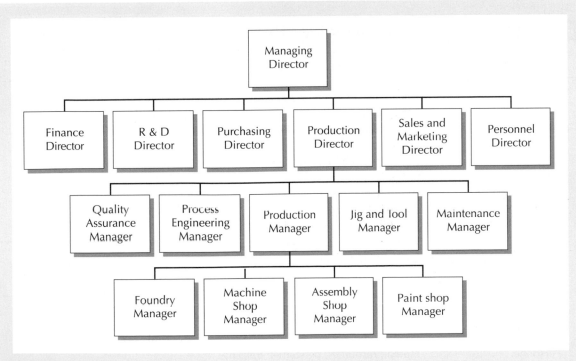

Fig. 12.9 An organisation divided according to function at three levels

will not be responsible for the delivery of identifiable products. Especially in the case of large functional departments, the structure emphasises differentiation at the expense of integration.

Hospitals often have functional departments, based around medical and paramedical specialities. This arrangement rightly encourages the professional development of staff within each discipline and the need for departmental heads to have specialised knowledge. On the other hand, hospitals have a history of interdepartmental rivalry with professional interests being advanced at the expense of the system as a whole. Exhibit 12.7 lists the functional departments, known as directorates, within Huddersfield NHS Trust. The horizontal line is placed in the list to separate the medical and paramedical directorates from the business functions. The former can be said to be primary activities, delivering services directly to clients, while the latter are the support activities. The switch to increased operational control of medical functions by general managers has created much tension in the health service.

▉ Divisional form

The invention of the divisional, often called the *multi-divisional*, form is attributed to Sloan who reorganised General Motors this way, *see* Exhibit 12.8.[8] The unifying theme of the division is its output. Each division operates as if it is almost an autonomous business within the whole organisation. This type of organisation is valuable when:

Exhibit 12.7 **Directorates of Huddersfield NHS Trust**

Directorate	*Responsibility*
Surgery	All surgical activity; accident and emergency; audiology; orthoptics.
Medicine	Medical, including elderly in Royal Infirmary; general out-patients.
Mental health	Mental illness; learning difficulties; clinical psychology; child and adolescent psychiatry; community psychiatric nurses.
Children's and women's services	Paediatrics; child health; obstetrics; gynaecology; family planning.
Clinical support	Anaesthetics; radiology; pathology; pharmacy; intensive care unit; theatres; therapy.
Elderly	Geriatric medicine; geriatric units.
Community	Community nursing clinics; community dental services; health centres; family planning services.
Finance	All financial functions.
Business development	Planning and development; information; contracting.
Operations management	Estates; site management; support services; medical photography.
Personnel	Human resources; personnel; training.
Nursing and training	Professional nursing guidance; nursing training; quality leadership.

> **Exhibit 12.8** **Alfred P. Sloan at General Motors – pioneer of the divisional form**
>
> Alfred P. Sloan (1875–1966) became president of General Motors in 1923 and chairman in 1946. He was made honorary chairman on his retirement in 1956. He is remembered for the influential *My Years with General Motors* (1963).
>
> When Sloan took over, General Motors was struggling in the face of competition from Ford's Model T. Sloan replaced GM's bureaucratic, centralised organisation with one based on product divisions, quite the opposite of the way Ford was organised. Thus, the world saw Chevrolet competing with Cadillac. Internally Sloan maintained a delicate balance between centralisation and decentralisation.
>
> The divisional structure was an outstanding success. GM's United States market share, 12 per cent in 1923, exceeded 45 per cent by 1980. The federal structure meant that executives could avoid the detail and focus on divisional performance targets and overall direction. General Motors became a model of management for the large corporation. Today, more than 85 per cent are estimated to be structured this way.
>
> The delicate balance began to be lost in the 1960s, however. A web of committees and groups emerged and there were continual power struggles. The finance function became so powerful that tight targets and narrow measures of performance stifled innovation. GM began to be paralysed by what had made it strong.

- the size of each division is sufficient for it to be able to provide its own specialisms, such as accounting and personnel; and

- the work of each division is relatively independent so that their operations do not have to be closely co-ordinated.

There are three themes found in the setting up of divisions – products, geography and customers. We can exemplify each in turn.

Product-based divisions

Many large organisations are organised on this basis. Its advantage lies in the unification of effort towards the supply of a particular bundle of goods and services. Figure 12.10 shows the organisation structure created at the Vítkovice Works in Ostrava, Czech Republic shortly after the revolution of 1989.[9] The reorganisation was to prepare for privatisation of this large steel company. Employing more than 20 000 people in total, the seven product divisions can be seen within the two main sections of the business, namely basic iron and steel making and heavy engineering. They became self-contained factories on the shared site, each serving different types of customer. There was, however, an exception to the focus on products. While the responsibility for operations within each division should in principle be autonomous, the sales and marketing remained in a central unit. With so much output being exported, the company was unwilling to duplicate international sales functions. This continued the tradition from before the revolution when foreign sales of all Czech companies had been handled through a single government agency. The division 'Vítkovice Plant' was also a remnant of the previous

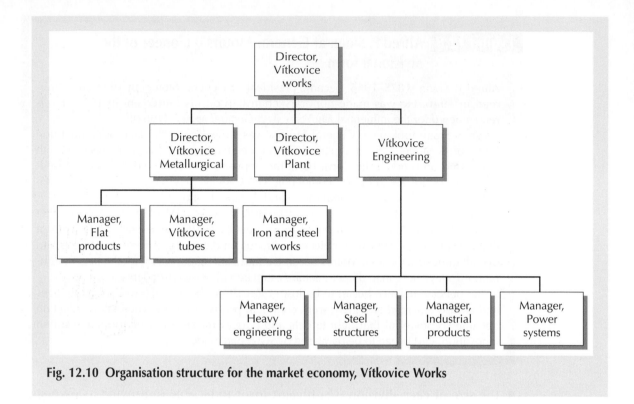

Fig. 12.10 Organisation structure for the market economy, Vítkovice Works

regime. Its responsibilities were the retraining of redundant staff and programmes to clean up environmental pollution.

Geographically-based divisions

Geography is a common basis for structural design, especially in large companies whose operations are widely dispersed. Service companies, from transport to retailing, can offer the same group of products to customers in many locations. They may then be best organised by region. British Airways has geographic divisions, such as BA Manchester; the separate divisions of large bus operators such as Badgerline run services in different towns, often keeping the names of previous companies; the electricity company MANWEB organises its maintenance operations by district.

Differences between regions push managers towards organising geographically so that the business can respond more effectively to local conditions. We saw in Chapter 5 how international organisations face variations in cultural settings and economic conditions which can have strong influences on every aspect of marketing, employment, finance and so on. Oxfam's charitable work in central African countries, for example, has to take into account famine and the displacement of peoples from one country to another. In Brazil, on the other hand, work is among disadvantaged groups within a country whose economy is among the world's top ten.

Customer-facing divisions

Our last variant of the divisional form is one where the organisation tries to match customer differences in its structure. This approach is useful when customer groups demand dissimilar products or require them to be supplied in distinct ways. The business can then compete more effectively against a rival that targets principally one of its customer groups. BT switched from a geographical to a customer-oriented organisation when it was privatised in 1991. Exhibit 12.9 describes the main departments that were set up then. Business Communications and Special Business were the areas where competition was becoming more intense.[10] Within five years BT had formed alliances with many overseas partners. This meant further developments in organisational design that nonetheless confirmed the principle of organising the business into worldwide customer facing units rather than according to region. Among several new divisions formed were Global Systems Integration, International Operations and Global Alliances and Joint Ventures.[11] At the time of the proposed merger with MCI, a United States telecommunications business, it was planned to manage the United Kingdom core business as a wholly owned subsidiary company. BT saw these changes as the most effective way of serving important global customers, especially MNEs, while continuing to develop its work in its most important national market.

■ Hybrid forms

We have presented each basis of departmentalisation in its ideal form. In practice, however, organisations stray from the ideals, adapt them according to circumstances. This point is shown in the example of the Hospital Trust structure of Exhibit 12.7. It can be seen as a mixture of customer-facing and functional designs

---

Exhibit 12.9 **BT's organisation in the early 1990s**

'As part of a major reshaping of the Group, a new organisation structure was introduced on 1 April, 1991 aimed at serving customers in BT's chosen markets more effectively.

'BT is now organised into three customer-facing operating divisions: Business Communications, Personal Communications and Special Businesses, and a number of support units ...

'Business Communications and Personal Communications provide the primary interface between BT and its customers, whether business or residential, for the provision of United Kingdom and international calls, exchange lines and equipment supply, while the Special Businesses division is responsible for providing customers with [private circuits, managed networks and mobile communications].'

The support services are:

Worldwide Networks, for the UK and international trunk networks;

Products and Services Management;

Development and Procurement;

Finance, Personnel and other services.

at the same horizontal level. Organisations, moreover, may use different criteria at each level in the hierarchy. Figure 12.11 illustrates a supermarket firm. It has a functional structure at board level, then two levels divided geographically and mainly product departments within the store.

Organisation design is often a compromise. Whichever principle is used to unite staff in teams, this will be at the expense of other linkages that may have been created under another principle. For example, BT moved in 1991 from a regional to a customer-facing structure. In urban areas where all types of customer appear in abundance, it will be relatively easy to maintain service levels to both. In remote rural areas, on the other hand, a district may have a few domestic subscribers and even fewer businesses. Here it would be foolish to have separate installation teams for the two types. BT's customer-facing divisions would best cope with the intense competition found in an urban area; meanwhile, some sort of sharing may be needed in rural situations.

The multidivisional form, Sloan's legacy, is the commonest structure seen in today's large organisations. Yet, in our comments on General Motors in Exhibit 12.8, we began to see its weaknesses when it gets bogged down in complex webs of rivalry and control. GM's sluggish response to the rise of the compact car in the United States is but one symptom. More competitive and dynamic times may require more entrepreneurial, flexible forms.

■ Matrix form

The problem of seeking to integrate organisations in several ways simultaneously has led some companies, especially large ones, to consider having dual lines of authority. For instance, firms engaged in large project work in civil engineering or aerospace found that it was difficult to achieve the kind of team integration required for these projects while operating with a traditional departmental structure. The solution involved staff reporting to both their permanent functional manager and, for the duration, to the manager of the project team.

Figure 12.12 shows how Vítkovice set up major change projects that cut across the newly formed product divisions whose normal operations run on uninterrupted by the projects. These included introduction of new products and processes, new arrangements for transport, reorganisation of plant heating systems and so on. Each change was led by a Project Manager supported by teams drawn from appropriate divisions. We see in our simplified diagram that Projects A and B cut across three divisions while C involved all four. For the purposes of the project work, which would take up an agreed proportion of each team member's time, responsibility would be to the Project Manager. Otherwise, it was to the normal departmental manager.

The criss-crossing lines of authority and responsibility are a feature of the *matrix organisation*. Our example is of a temporary matrix as horizontal connections are formed and broken as each project is started and wound up. In some MNEs, on the other hand, matrix structures are made permanent. They face the dilemma of co-ordinating the work of managers in different countries along both product and geographic dimensions. The company wants to integrate the supply and demand for each product line on a world scale while, at the same time, it wishes to co-ordinate different activities in each country from the point of view of finance and

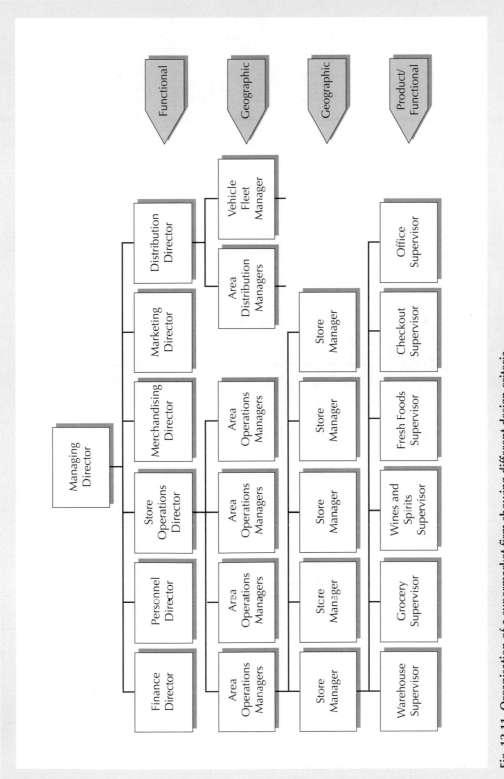

Fig. 12.11 Organisation of a supermarket firm showing different design criteria

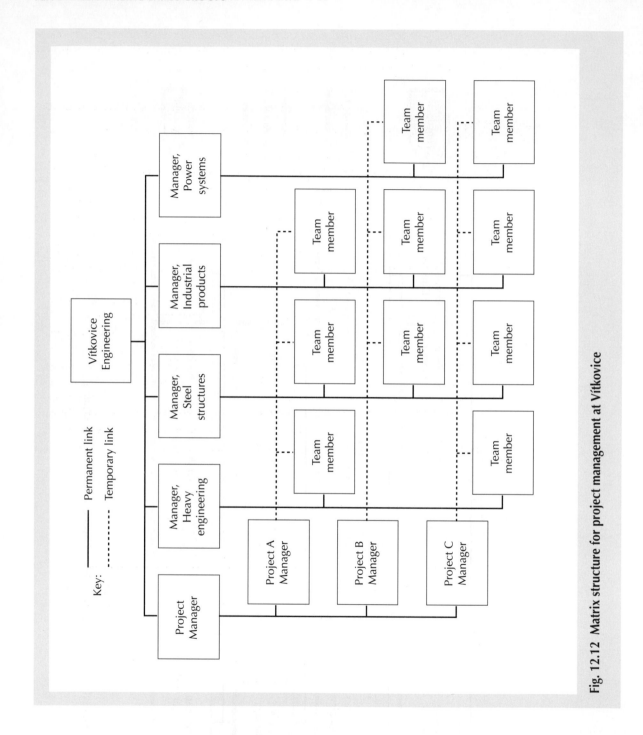

Fig. 12.12 Matrix structure for project management at Vítkovice

taxation, employment, training and so on. In some cases, the company needs more than two dimensions to resolve the complexity. The case of Electrolux is shown in Fig. 12.13, supported by Exhibit 12.10.[12]

Exhibit 12.10 **Co-ordinating across three dimensions at Electrolux**

The 'major appliances' (or 'white goods') product division of Electrolux is widely dispersed into about 500 business units. Each is a nationally based company with its own balance sheet and profit and loss account. The white goods division has some 43 factories in 15 countries grouped in three 'product areas', namely cold, hot and wet. Within the product areas, the national 'product divisions' have at most two factories each. Generally, the factories do not duplicate production so each is responsible for the supply of its lines for all markets where the item is sold. There are 135 marketing and sales companies in 40 countries, their work co-ordinated by one of two international marketing co-ordinators.

Electrolux operates in a polycentric way. It sees the country managers as having an important role in co-ordinating territory activities and ensuring that the company is seen as a 'good citizen'. They deal with national issues such as relations with large retail customers and trades unions and overseeing national salary structures. Figure 12.13 gives a simple example of the structural relationships referred to here. Country X, assumed to be in Europe, has production facilities for hot (cooking) and cold (refrigeration) appliances. Since goods are supplied to both the home market and overseas, the sales and marketing activity in country X reports to both international marketing managers. All activities within country X are co-ordinated by its country manager..

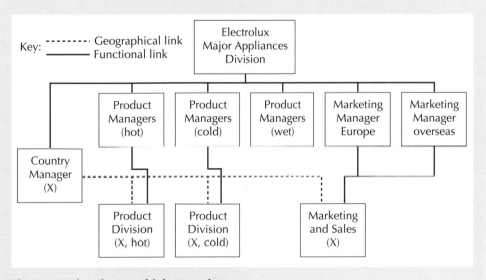

Fig. 12.13 Eletrolux's multiple reporting

The arrangement at Electrolux is, therefore, designed to integrate both operations and strategy making activity along three dimensions:

■ Country managers monitor performance of production and sales companies in their territories.

■ Product area managers are responsible for product design and development, deciding where each is to be made and planning output flows in liaison with the marketing groups.

■ Marketing managers control sales and marketing including the co-ordinating of brands (such as Electrolux and Zanussi) and promotion across frontiers using satellite television and other cross-border media.

The claimed advantages of the arrangement lie in good co-ordination and allocation of responsibility. These, however, are at the expense of internal tensions between the various managers and co-ordinators. Many questions and problems do not fall readily into the remit of one or the other type of manager. At Electrolux, managers are expected to resolve these problems quickly by direct contact.

This example of a fully fledged, permanent matrix design emphasises both the advantages and disadvantages of such structures. These are summarised in Exhibit 12.11. Problems arise because the basic axiom of each person in the organisation having a single supervisor is breached. This was one of Fayol's principles explained in Chapter 2. The change can lead at least to stressful ambiguity and, at worst, to destructive power struggles among managers. We should not forget, however, that such difficulties also frequently arise in the simpler departmental structures we discussed earlier. Structures do not of themselves create well-managed organisations, but well chosen ones can create favourable conditions. More than anything, success depends on the skills and willingness of the managers to interact within them in a positive way.

Exhibit 12.11 Advantages and disadvantages of a matrix organisation structure

Advantages	Disadvantages
Integration of important functions such as sales and marketing, production and project management	Conflict between managers over range of responsibility
Improved information flow	Some doubt about whether more information is at the expense of its quality
Flexibility in response to changing market and competitive environments	Possible loss of efficiency through extra managerial overhead
Coordination at appropriate levels in the organisation	Conflict that has to be referred to higher levels for resolution
Managers report directly to those who are responsible	Stress caused by having several bosses with potentially conflicting interests

For some organisations, such as Electrolux, the matrix organisation is seen as the only way to co-ordinate large groups effectively. Others have found that the excessive complexity leads to such loss of efficiency that detailed co-ordinating of operations by central managers is dispensed with. Texas Instruments, for example, gave up its matrix structure in the early 1980s in favour of a simpler structure to loosely co-ordinate more independent business units. These units are expected to decide what co-ordination is necessary and make the relevant arrangements themselves. In 1995, Royal Dutch Shell gave up the multidimensional matrix structure it had used for 35 years. The complexity of defining operating companies by geography, sector and line of business led to creeping bureaucracy with excessive efforts in co-ordination and many powerful regional 'fiefdoms'.[13] In contrast, Ford introduced a matrix structure in 1993–4 to support its new integrated global business strategy.[14]

While these last examples of matrix structures are all MNEs, we should not ignore the possibility of much smaller organisations adopting this form. Although sometimes not labelled a matrix, the general notion of a grid of lines of authority can be found in private and public sector organisations seeking to integrate along more than one dimension. School teachers, for instance, are usually organised into departments according to discipline – maths, humanities, sport etc. Yet teamwork by level – lower school, upper school or, in a larger unit, year groups – is also required. Then there are pastoral care teams, and so on. Describing the arrangement as a matrix organisation may over-complicate the emerging patterns. In university business schools, however, managers see the co-ordination of subjects, courses and levels as problematic and often express the organisation as a matrix structure.

As we have seen, not all MNEs use a matrix. One way out of the problems of the excessive centralisation of the pyramid is the development of network structures.

Network structures for MNEs

We have so far presented the MNE as having a strong head office co-ordinating any number of subsidiary companies around the world. Siemens is in 250 fields and 189 countries. Co-ordination needs to be according to commonalities in product, raw material, technology, region and so on. Divisional or matrix structures help to resolve the problem but, as the examples show, bring others in their wake. Ghauri suggests that the focus on a single 'centre' may be part of the problem. He notes examples of the growth of several centres within the same firm. MNEs with head offices in small countries, such as Sweden, are moving in this direction. Small home markets mean that subsidiary companies can have higher turnover than the parents that spawned them.[15]

Figure 12.14 compares the conventional model with the emerging network firm. In the firm on the left, the organisation is based on the idea that subsidiary units are directly linked to, and controlled by, head office. This is the form created by Sloan at General Motors and copied often since. In the network structure on the right, several subsidiaries, A, B and C, act as centres for others. The latter group may or may not have direct contact with headquarters.

Interdependence within a country or region depends on local conditions. In the traditional model, local links are weak. There may be some trading among sub-

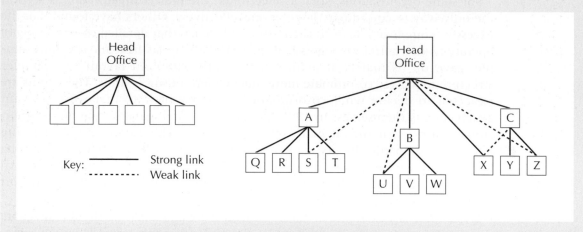

Fig. 12.14 Emergence of regional centres in a multinational enterprise

sidiaries but the structure is essentially designed to serve the needs of the centre. As it develops, the subsidiary may find that the balance of pressures from head office, other regional subsidiaries and local government changes. For instance, it may find advantages in directly trading among regional companies. Otherwise, fitting in with local rules and regulations may become paramount.

These new network structures are not means for headquarters to delegate functions to regional centres. They emerge through development and adaptation to local conditions. Subsidiaries of Swedish firms in South-East Asia, having turnover many times higher than their parents, become more powerful than head office. They frequently have their own R&D and product development programmes. Two examples from Ghauri of subsidiaries in the Philippines are shown in Exhibit 12.12.

We may ask why headquarters would allow subsidiaries to gain semi-independent status. The answer lies in their success. For instance, Electrolux in the Philippines is one of the most successful units in the whole group. From its excellent manufacturing facilities, it exports to other subsidiaries in the region. The products are more suited to local conditions than European designs. Given this success, headquarters has decided not to intervene in dealings among regional companies.

While Ghauri paints a picture of Swedish MNEs discovering a new form, we should take his observations cautiously. Others have argued that executives in MNEs find the structure of Swedish corporations ambiguous. Interpretations vary from a preference for matrix structures to being chaotic.[16] Yet, as more MNEs find their home bases less important, the development of federated structures may strengthen.

Network, virtual and spherical organisations

Since the 1980s, a new form of organisation has begun to achieve success. This is founded on the idea of disaggregation – separating major functions into separate companies linked by a small core organisation. Rather than having design, manufacturing, distribution, sales and marketing and customer service under one roof,

> ### Exhibit 12.12 Leaving home: Sandvik and Electrolux in East Asia
>
> Sandvik's subsidiary purchases its materials through Singapore. Supplies from Sweden are channelled through Singapore. The regional office also decides whether to buy from other firms rather than through head office. Although counter to official policy, Singapore has emerged as a regional centre. It receives and consolidates financial reports from eight countries. Head office looks at the performance of the regional office rather than the national operations.
>
> In 1980, the Electrolux local subsidiary imported components from the parent or affiliated companies around the world. Gaining experience, it not only began to buy locally but worked on developing suppliers' competence so they could make more items to Electrolux's specification. After seven years, 85 per cent of components were bought locally and the Philippines vacuum cleaner was quite different to the one made in Europe.

some of these functions are supplied by separate organisations. Support functions, from engineering maintenance to information systems, are also included in this trend towards slimmer, more flexible structures.

Organisations have always subcontracted specialist functions, from advertising to auditing and recruitment to removals. The network firm subcontracts as much as possible, keeping to itself the core competence that gives the whole network its strength. Benetton (*see* Chapter 6) designs, makes and sells its clothes through a global network of contracted manufacturers, distributors and franchised retailers. Its core is design and marketing. Benetton built its business by seeking partners and joining with them. Other networks are formed by breaking up rigid structures and opening them to competition. Privatisation of services in United Kingdom local governments means that contractors now clean the streets, manage the theatres, tend the parks and process the information.

Network organisations have advantages in:

■ sharing resources and risk;

■ matching complementary core competencies;

■ increasing actual or perceived size;

■ reaching new markets.[17]

Setting up and running a network firm demands new skills among managers. For example, Miles and Snow saw the job of manager increasingly taking on that of broker. They identified three new roles for the manager as broker: architect to design the network, both structure and processes; cooperator to seek out and initiate links; and developer to extend the arrangements into new fields.[18]

Others are less enthusiastic. Although they recognise the possibility of new organisational forms, they argue that they will not develop unless the related problems of leadership are recognised and overcome.[19]

Virtual organisations

Overlapping the notion of networked organisation is the virtual organisation. Made possible by the emergence of high quality communication systems, virtual organisations allow teams to be formed and tasks to be done anywhere.[20] Groups can be spread over a wide area. It becomes more difficult to answer the question, 'Where is this company?' A key motivation in Western countries is to cut costs. For example, engineering design carried out in the Philippines costs less than half the rate in the EU. A report on engineering design for companies in Scotland's Highlands and Islands[21] shows how a local virtual organisation, with design teams working flexibly from home, can match subcontracting overseas in terms of cost and cycle time. Advantages and disadvantages of virtual organisations are summarised in Exhibit 12.13.

A virtual organisation can be set up and operated by one firm. Alternatively it can be shared by a network of contractors and joint venturers. Unfortunately, the terms network and virtual tend to be used interchangeably.

Spherical organisations

Building on their earlier work, Miles and Snow[22] argue that effective brokerage skills are not enough for success among tomorrow's network firms. They point to the difficulties of matching internal resources to the rapidly changing demands of the network. More flexibility is needed. The metaphor of the pyramid must be replaced by that of the sphere. The former is the epitome of stability, authority and a firm face to the environment. The sphere is different. When presented with an opportunity it can quickly rotate, offering to the initiator all the company's resources. Whoever receives the original request becomes responsible for processing it and seeing it through to completion. Figure 12.15 illustrates the contrast between these metaphors.

Miles and Snow extend the image of a rotatable organisation into a network. Technical and Computer Graphics is a cluster of 24 small companies whose 200 staff earn a total revenue of £30 million. It is known as a significant innovator in electronic equipment. New product ideas are handled by a process of 'triangulation' as shown in Fig. 12.16. This means setting up a partnership between a TCG

Exhibit 12.13 **Virtual organisations: advantages and disadvantages**

Gains from ...	Yet problems with ...
productivity;	relying on existing expertise;
lower direct costs and overheads;	training very difficult;
speed and responsiveness;	building and retaining knowledge;
higher levels of expertise;	costs rather than results orientation;
overcoming time-zone constraints;	not a preferred lifestyle for some staff.
organisational flexibility to match customer needs;	
preferred lifestyle for some staff.	

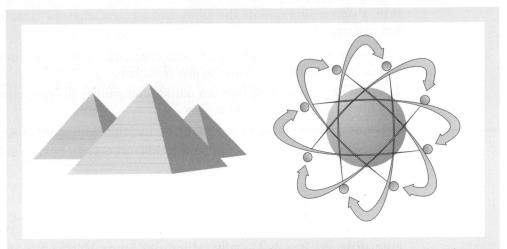

Fig. 12.15 The image of the rock steady pyramids contrasts with the ever moving sphere

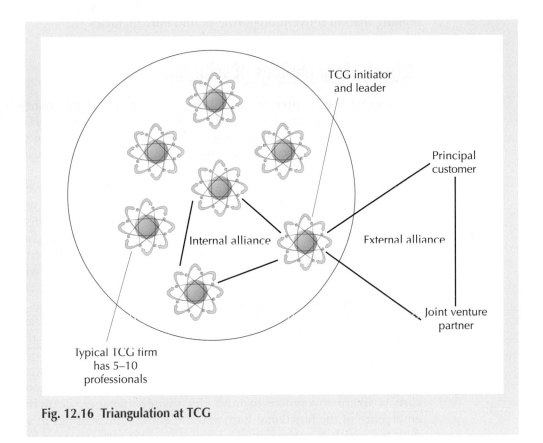

Fig. 12.16 Triangulation at TCG

firm, a similar firm outside the group and a potential major customer. The process has five stages:

1 Identify the market niche. Each firm constantly searches for new opportunities and rotates itself in response to any that arise.

2 Find a development partner. An outside company with complementary resources is invited to share costs and profits.

3 Locate a major customer to join the partnership with an advance order.

4 Draw in other TCG firms into internal alliances, again by triangulation.

5 Develop the triangles in new directions.

For those of us who are used to thinking in more conventional terms, metaphors like the spherical organisation and triangulation are difficult to cope with. Yet many companies are gaining from offering network flexibility. TCG is a medium enterprise yet it sells globally. Miles and Snow believe the metaphor can be extended to other, larger organisations. They refer to Nike, Motorola and ABB as pioneers in the process of managing links among flexible supply and distribution networks. Always, however, they point out that management is much more challenging than in conventional, rule-bound bureaucracies.

Conclusion: choices of structure

We opened the chapter by saying that Siemens faced an organisational design problem corresponding to its global scale. In finding its (temporary) solution, the company recognises practical problems of the cost of changing what exists. The structure of each company is like this – a blend of the mess of history and notions of the ideal.

What are these notions? In this chapter we have identified the existence of hierarchy in which authority and responsibility are combined. Line and staff roles are means of overcoming some weaknesses of a single pyramid structure. They allow the introduction of specialists without overloading the line. Another important choice is the relative weight of centralisation and decentralisation of decisions. Having divided the whole into appropriate units, the firm must work out how it is to co-ordinate all activities.

When explaining the way a group is organised, it is common for managers to reach for an organisation chart. While acknowledging their value in briefly summarising the way different roles are linked, we also recognise the limitations of these models, yielding only a partial picture of 'what is going on'. Nevertheless, the chart is an ideal way of expressing and comparing different structural forms.

Organisational structure can be related to maturity. In the smallest SME, the structure is likely to revolve around the owner-manager. Growth then sees the emergence of the functional form and the entrepreneur brings in specialists to help with tasks such as engineering or accounting. This may serve the business well for a long time but such structures begin to creak when the firm finds it is engaged in supplying different products to different markets. Co-ordination around the product rather than the management discipline becomes more important. The divisional structure with each unit, in effect, a miniature business, comes into its own.

Growth, change and globalisation have challenged the pre-eminence of the divisional form. The matrix is an extension, trying to reconcile the pulls of several dimensions by having several hierarchies on a two- or three-dimensional grid. At this size and complexity, however, it seems that all organisations run the risk of becoming bogged down in problems of co-ordination and conflict. For some, introducing the matrix may be a refreshing way of supporting new initiatives. On the other hand, those who have had a matrix for too long find that it can spawn too many committees and too much politics.

Perhaps the time has come to dismantle these elaborate structures. Studies of network, virtual and spherical organisations suggest that more flexibility can result from their small scale and the function of managers as brokers instead of leaders or administrators.

We must close on a note of warning. Discussion of organisations can, as in this chapter, begin and end with comparison of different hierarchical forms. We have not raised questions of the legitimacy of hierarchy itself. Critics include Handy, who takes a moral stance. 'Managers,' he argues, 'have been brought up on a diet of power, divide and rule. They have been preoccupied with authority rather than making things happen. ... Though the world is a good one for professional executives, they are a minority of the human race.'[23] The hierarchy, therefore, brings most benefit to those who are in it. The next chapter looks a little more at questions such as this.

Quick check up — *Can you ...*

- Name four key issues in organising;
- Define:
  - authority,
  - responsibility,
  - delegation,
  - differentiation, and
  - integration;
- Distinguish between line and staff roles;
- List four main means of co-ordinating organisational work;
- Give examples of structure and process;
- Sketch functional, divisional and matrix structures;
- Summarise the features of a virtual organisation;
- Name the three brokering roles of Miles and Snow.

Questions

Chapter review

12.1 Use your own examples to illustrate the four key issues in organising.

12.2 Explain with examples the three main bases for organisational divisions.

12.3 Why are some MNEs changing to the matrix structure while others are shying away from it?

Application

12.4 Use the information on Siemens and SNI in the opening case to explain what sort of organisation these are and suggest why.

12.5 Sketch a rich picture of the information in the Siemens case. In relation to organisation design, what issues does it suggest?

Investigation

12.6 Study an organisation that has recently announced a reorganisation. Comment on the reasons given for the change and the benefits you might expect to see.

Ethics test: 'It's not your department'

Ben, a young graduate, had been recently appointed manager of a department producing ceiling panels and door linings for the building industry. The raw material was 2.4×1.2 metre boards of asbestos cement. Now no longer in use, asbestos fibres were mixed in the cement to give strength and fire resistance. Dry fibres are dangerous when breathed in large quantities over a long period. They cause asbestosis, a disease leading to a lung cancer, mesothelioma. Stringent safety precautions apply in all such plant. Air quality has to be regularly checked for the incidence of the fine fibres.

The company's engineers prided themselves on the dust extraction equipment surrounding the saws and panel finishing equipment. It usually cost more than the basic machinery. Although managers felt the Asbestos Regulations were too strict, company policy was to keep the air cleaner than the lowest limit. Men could, therefore, work without having to wear masks. Yet the engineering department was also responsible for the air quality monitoring.

Ben observed them on their visits every second day. They spent about fifteen minutes each time, making counts at regular spots. Ben would talk to them about how the test equipment worked and how results were recorded. Yet he was puzzled that the readings were put down in a notebook and later transcribed to the official forms. One day, a pallet of scrap material slipped from a fork lift truck at the time the air tests were being taken. The engineer commented that this would put the result over the limit.

Ben stood in for his boss at a management meeting the following week. As usual, the test records were among the agenda papers. He noticed that those for the day of the pallet incident were inside the safe limit, as were all readings throughout the site. Having expressed his concerns to his boss the next day, he was told, 'Don't worry about it. It's not your department'.

Ben was unsure of what to do. He had suspicions, no evidence and a boss who didn't seem concerned. Is safety not his department? What would you have advised?

Super Bakery – an organisation in the big league[24]

Founded in Pittsburgh in 1983 by former Steelers' running back Franco Harris, Super Bakery has achieved a national presence in its chosen market. Operating as a virtual corporation, it focuses on the doughnut segment of the school lunch menu using four strategies. First, reversing the trend to cancel unhealthy doughnuts from school menus, it offers a new product, the Super Donut, which is low in calories and vitamin enriched. Second, refrigeration permits national distribution. Third, Super Bakery outsources selling, manufacturing and distribution to independent contractors. It retains a master baker to work on product improvement, regional sales managers to support the independent sales agents and a small office to process orders and payments. Fourth, the company offers advice to customers, who are distributors and school authorities, on improving standards and lowering costs.

Super Bakery's turnover, expected to reach $10 million in 1995, means that it is large compared with outside bakeries but small when gauged against trucking companies. Not surprisingly, it found it could exert control over doughnut production scheduling and quality. Less easy, however, was negotiating improvements in shipping performance. Its attempts to negotiate service guarantees, including penalties for failure to comply, have not been successful, although they do aid in clarifying expectations.

Super Bakery worked with 12 trucking companies in four years before reducing the number it used to three. These were the ones most willing to work on improved service through, for example, redesigning packaging to maximise loads and minimise damage. Information on orders is relayed to the truckers earlier so they can plan their routes. Compared with sales, freight costs have fallen from 10 to 6 per cent in five years.

In spite of having so much work carried out by other companies, Super Bakery retains control. This is vital as deliveries must be neither early nor late. Most school authorities do not have refrigerated warehouses. Allocation of orders to production plants and trucking companies is done by Super Bakery. All customer contact is through its office. Systems of monitoring and control of flow and costs have been introduced. There are regular surveys of customer satisfaction. Problems are initially taken as difficulties to be shared. Super Bakery seeks trusting relationships with contractors so that they can jointly work on overcoming them. Results for 1994 were impressive: 93 per cent of orders complete and undamaged (target 95); 94.6 per cent on-time delivery (target 95).

Questions

1 Express the information in the case as a rich picture. (Remember, this is an informal sketch, on one sheet, in which you try to express your interpretation of the case.)

2 Why is Super Bakery so successful?

3 Although Super Bakery is nominally an organisation, should it be seen as one?

Bibliography

Besides *The Empty Raincoat*, Charles Handy has written many titles on organisations, including *Gods of Management* (1979), London: Pan and *Beyond Certainty* (1995), London: Century. A detailed review of structures is to be found in Child, John (1988) *Organisations: A guide to problems and practice*, London: Paul Chapman or Mintzberg, Henry (1979) *The Structuring of Organisations*, Englewood Cliffs, NJ: Prentice Hall.

References

1. Teresko, John (1996) 'Rethinking the basis of technology', *Industry Week*, **245** (**13**), 1 July, 42; 'Siemens va restructurer sa branche techniques d'éclairage', *Les Echos*, 27 November, 1996; Bardacke, Ted (1996) 'Siemens and CP in chip plant deal', *Financial Times*, 13 December; Siemens home page: www.siemens.de; Siemens Nixdorf home page: www.sni.de

2. Minchau, Wolfgang (1996) 'Siemens: A troubled conglomerate driving up productivity', *Financial Times*, 7 November.

3. Senior, Barbara and Naylor, John (1984) 'A skills exchange for unemployed people', in Koopman-Iwema, A.M. and Roe, R.A. (eds) *Work and Organisational Psychology*, Lisse, Swets and Zeitlinger, 98–116.

4. Barnard, Chester I. (1938) *The Functions of the Executive*, Cambridge, Mass.: Harvard University Press.

5. Merck & Co., Inc. (1997) Information for job applicants.

6. Taken from Godfrey, Blan; Berwick, Don and Roessner, Jane (1997) *How Quality Management Really Works in Health Care*, The Juran Institute, http://208.17.213.71/juran/articles/article001.html

7. United Distillers (1997) Job advertisement, www.united.distillers.co.uk/udp2.htm, 24 February

8. Crainer, Stuart (1994) 'Management pioneers and prophets – Alfred P. Sloan', *Financial Times*, 14 November, 10.

9. Macák, František (1991) 'Re-structuralization and privatization of the Vítkovice Works of Ostrava', *Vítkovice 91*, 4, December.

10. S.G. Warburg and Co. Ltd (1991) *British Telecommunications public limited company, Offer for sale*, London, 21 November, 9.

11. BT (1997) *BT and MCI in Concert – Circular to BT Shareholders*, London, British Telecommunications plc, 7 March, 8.

12. Lorenz, Christopher (1994) 'Management: How to bridge functional gaps', *Financial Times*, 25 November, 14.

13. Corzine, Robert (1995) 'Shell to shed 1200 jobs in shake-up: Anglo-Dutch group plans radical restructuring', *Financial Times*, 30 March, 1; Lascelles, David (1995) 'Barons swept out of fiefdoms; Shell's far-reaching shake-up is dramatic but necessary', *ibid.*, 19; Lex (1995) 'Reshaping Shell', *ibid.*, 20.

14. Lynch, Richard (1997) *Corporate Strategy*, London: Financial Times Pitman Publishing 725–6.

15. Ghauri, Pervez (1992) 'New structures in MNCs based in small countries: a network approach', *European Management Journal*, **10** (**3**) 357–364.

16. Czarniawska-Joerges, Barbara (1993) 'Swedish management: modern project, post-modern implementation' *International Studies of Management and Organization*, **23** (**1**), Spring, 13–27.

17. Morgan, Stephen J. (1995) 'Virtual corporations offer real advantages', *Executive Issue*s, **6** (**3**), Summer, Aresty Institute, Wharton School, University of Pennsylvania.

18. Miles, Raymond E. and Snow, Charles (1992) 'Managing 21st century network organisations', *Organisational Dynamics*, Winter.

19. Willis, Gordon (1994) 'Networking and its leadership processes', *Leadership and Organization Development Journal*, **15** (**7**), 19–27.
20. Davidow, W. and Malone, M. (1993) *The Virtual Corporation*, New York, Harper Business.
21. Ki-Net Ltd (1995) 'New organisational structures for engineering design', *Report to the Highlands and Islands Enterprise Board*, Nairn, Michael Wolff Associates, http://www.ki-net.co.uk/ki-net/index.html
22. Miles, Raymond E. and Snow, Charles (1995) 'The new network firm: A spherical structure built on a human investment philosophy', *Organisational Dynamics*, Spring, 5–18.
23. Handy, Charles (1994) *The Empty Raincoat: Making sense of the future*, London: Hutchinson.
24. Davis, Tim R.V. and Darling, Bruce L. (1995) 'How virtual corporations manage the performance of competitors: the Super Bakery case', *Organisational Dynamics*, Summer, 70–5.

Organisational design: matching the situation

Chapter objectives

When you have finished studying this chapter, you should be able to:

- justify contingency theory and relate it to universalist and particularist perspectives;

- demonstrate and criticise how structure and performance have been matched to situational factors;

- explain and illustrate three situational factors in the environment, namely uncertainty, globalisation and technology;

- untangle the ties between strategy, interdependence and culture, and organisational design;

- show why organisations must differentiate their structures and the means by which they can order interdependent functions;

- set out the limitations of the contingency approach to organising;

- apply these ideas to explain the structural forms discussed in the previous chapter.

Abbott's structural dilemma[1]

Ranked 129th on Fortune's 1996 list of United States companies, Illinois-based Abbott Laboratories has been in health care for more than a century. Some 40 per cent of 1996 sales of $11 billion were generated outside the United States. Abbott's strategy is to grow while maintaining its reputation for consistent financial performance. Chairman Duane Burnham points to four elements of this strategy – internal R&D, market expansion, external collaboration and acquisition. Commitment to the first two is shown by the spending of $1.2 billion on R&D, the primary driver of growth, and the addition of 600 people to the international sales force. Collaboration and acquisition cover the full range of market research, licensing, manufacturing and entry to new business areas. TAP Holdings, for example, is a joint venture formed in 1977 with Japan's Takeda Chemical Industries. Sales in 1996 exceeded £1 billion and it is one of the fastest growing pharmaceutical companies in the world.

In the mid-1990s, senior managers were wrestling with the problem of how to reconcile two alternative organisational models that had grown up. It was in the late 1960s that Abbott first split itself into three product-based divisions – pharmaceuticals, hospital products and nutritional preparations. Each operated as a self-contained business including R&D, manufacturing and marketing. A fourth division, Abbott International, handled all operations outside the United States. It was organised on geographic, as opposed to product, lines.

Parallel to the four divisions, however, a new business emerged. Formed in 1973 by bringing together several disparate activities, the diagnostics division has become a world leader with sales of $2.4 billion. Contrary to the other businesses, it is managed globally, using its own personnel and not working through Abbott International. Therefore, two approaches to running international business appear within the same company.

Abbott could live with this difference for another 25 years were it not for changes in the environment. These have stimulated an internal debate on the best way forward. The first change has been towards global product development in the healthcare industry. Intent on cutting launch costs and speeding the rate of market entry, companies look to co-ordinate trials of new drug formulations in all major markets. The same is true of hospital products for which launching in the United States and subsequent trials abroad mean delays and expensive modifications. This trend, then, pushes companies towards having global product divisions.

The second change pulls companies in the opposite direction. Healthcare purchasers in the United States are consolidating their activities, either because of merger or through buying groups. Co-ordination is occurring across product ranges. This means that suppliers such as Abbott look towards building company-based relationships rather than focusing on selling each line independently. Abbott has to find a way of linking its divisions' marketing in its home market. One benefit is the possibility of synergy among products of different divisions. For instance, Abbott has an HIV diagnostic test, a nutritional product for AIDS sufferers and a drug, Norvir, which shows promise in reducing HIV to undetectable levels. To achieve such linkages, Abbott has created a separate marketing unit to build closer ties with key customers.

Should the home business become more like the international? Or should the international mirror the home on a global scale? These questions are difficult for a successful company. Some senior managers point to the costs of change to achieve marginal benefits. Others point to the dangers of meddling with a flourishing arrangement that everyone understands. Abbott has some 60 per cent of the sales of rivals Johnson & Johnson yet realises 75 per cent of its profit. Post-tax return on sales, at 16.6 per cent, is 4 per cent ahead of its rival and it manages to spend 10.9 per cent on R&D, against 8.2 per cent.

By 1997, Abbott had globalised development of drugs and diagnostic systems. Every step from clinical testing to government approval and marketing was managed on an international basis. It saw its broad diversity as a strength, giving opportunities to achieve synergies between businesses. The company brings together professionals from different units and disciplines to share ideas and experiences as a base for further technological advances, integrated product families and joint marketing programmes.

Introduction

In Chapter 12 we examined the basic principles that may influence the choice of organisation structure. We also set out the most common of these, illustrating how one or the other is used by different firms. From this starting point, there is a temptation to look for commonality and then search for prescription. This leads to the notion of optimisation. Choosing a structure might become a question of understanding key factors, comparing with successful firms that possess these factors and copying these rivals' structures. We may be tempted to say, 'SMEs should be organised along the lines of ...' or, 'International banks need global treasury operations because ...'

Practice suggests this approach may be wrong. While some may detect a drift towards, say, decentralisation or creation of matrix structures, others point to as much movement on the opposite tack. Chapter 12 showed how some MNEs are establishing matrix structures while others are abandoning them. In addition Abbott Laboratories is not the only company incorporating two different structures for related global businesses.

We can illustrate by picking up the biological analogy. Naturalist David Attenborough points to the changing emphasis in *ethology*, the study of animal behaviour, from the species to the individual.[2] Such work is typified by zoologists Christophe and Hedwige Boesch, who spent ten years getting to know each of a group of sixty chimpanzees in an Ivory Coast forest. Each has much in common with its neighbours, yet it is individuality that is crucial in explaining behaviour and, say, reproductive success. In a similar way, Abbott Laboratories faces a choice among the limited number of alternatives available to the species 'global pharmaceutical company'. These have been tried and used or discarded by others. Abbott can learn from its own and their experiences. Yet it faces its choice in its own way and it will come up with a unique arrangement in response to the demands of its situation.

This is the *contingency approach* to organisation design. It recognises that the organisation is a complex, open system that exists in a complex and changing environment. There is no optimal design. Instead, the choice made by managers will be the one that is preferred. It depends on unique perceptions and interpretations of the situation and the constraints of what has gone before. The mix of hierarchy, flexibility, centralisation, working teams and so on will be unique and every principle may appear somewhere in the structure. In short, the contingency approach recognises common elements and themes but stresses the differences that make every situation unique.

Can the outsider say anything constructive? We can if we study these contingencies. We are looking to say something along the lines of, 'If the company finds itself in these circumstances, then it would be better if the organisation structure had the following features'. An example might be, 'If a global, multi-product electrical and electronics company, such as Siemens, tried to operate with a single, functional hierarchy, it would not be successful'. While we could claim this example to be true, it is only a beginning. To do better we must review studies that have examined the relationships between many situational variables, organisational form and success. This chapter, therefore, examines some leading examples. We shall look at how structure can be related to features of the environment: uncertainty, globalisation and technology. Then we shall consider internal issues such as strategy, departmental interdependence and culture. Finally, we shall study some important criticisms of the approach.

Environmental impact on organisational design

The role of theory

Researchers, seeking generalised relationships between environment and organisation design, face a daunting task, *see* Fig. 13.1. Not only must investigators decide which aspects of environment and organisation they are comparing but they have to establish yardsticks for measurement. Furthermore they have to work out measures of success. Then, having made the appropriate comparison between environment, organisational design and firm performance, they may find difficulty in establishing that it was the design decision that caused the performance outcome. Assuming this causal link can be established, researchers may call a halt. They may be satisfied with saying, 'Over the past ... years, it appears that those organisations that faced the following features in their environment would have been more successful if they adopted the following structures'. The risks of converting their results into a predictive theory, one that makes statements about the future, are high. The fate of the inductivist turkey of Chapter 1, or Peters' and Waterman's 'Excellence' theory in Chapter 2, show the danger.

Managers are in a different position. As hinted in Fig. 13.1, they are concerned with the future effect of their decisions. Therefore, they seek an element of prediction, 'If we organise ourselves along these lines, the following will occur ...'. To make the inductive leap from the past to the future involves experience and judgement as well as a sound understanding of what the studies were about.

Environmental uncertainty and organisation

Two important studies that compared the effects on the organisation of uncertainty and change were those conducted by: Burns and Stalker, into diverse bases of internal structure; and Lawrence and Lorsch, who applied the more specific ideas of differentiation and integration.

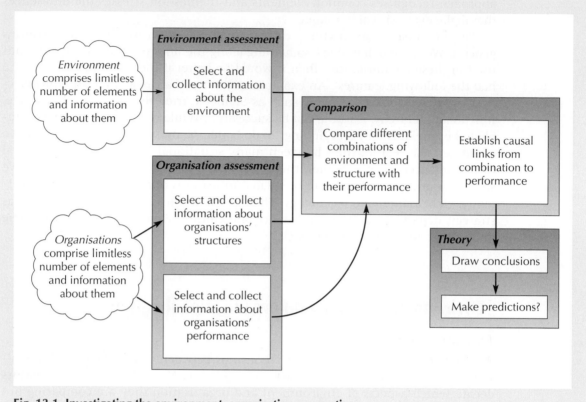

Fig. 13.1 Investigating the environment–organisation connection

Burns and Stalker

British behavioural scientists Burns and Stalker[3] examined how well firms adjusted to changing environmental conditions. From the late 1950s, they looked in detail at electronics manufacturing companies in Scotland, comparing them with other firms in Britain. While this now seems a small-scale study conducted long ago, its importance lies in its pioneering nature and the way the ideas it brought out have permeated management thinking.

The key contribution of Burns and Stalker's work lies in their typology for characterising organisations. *Mechanistic organisations* tend to have rigid structures in contrast to *organic organisations* that are flexible in structure and adaptive to change. It is important to note that these are ideal types. Real organisations will be somewhere between the extremes and we should place them according to how strongly they match the relevant characteristics. Exhibit 13.1[4] lists the clues we would use to pick out mechanistic or organic organisations.

From the lists in Exhibit 13.1, it can be seen that mechanistic organisations have:

■ clearly defined, specialised tasks to be carried out by defined methods;

■ a specific hierarchical structure in which knowledge is assumed to be centred at the top; vertical communication stresses instructions and control;

| Exhibit 13.1 | Features of mechanistic and organic organisations |

Characteristic	Mechanistic	Organic
Employees' task definitions	Precise, narrow	Imprecise, broad
Link from personal contribution to organisation's purpose	Obscure	Clear
Task flexibility	Limited	High
Rights and obligations	Explicitly set out	Vague
Locus of control	Hierarchical	Self-control
Channels of communications	Vertical	Lateral, as needed
Nature of vertical communications	Orders, instructions	Advice, information
Expected loyalty	To organisation	To project and work group
Knowledge required of employee	Narrow, related to specified job	Broad, professional
Personal prestige	Related to position in hierarchy	Built on personal contribution

- emphasis on loyalty to the organisation and obedience to superiors.

In contrast, the organic organisation has:

- open definitions of roles with continual adjustment of the contribution of each person;
- recognition that expertise is widely distributed and not related to hierarchical position;
- communication of information and advice flowing in whatever direction is necessary;
- commitment to the shared purpose of the organisation and prestige drawn from individual contribution.

Burns and Stalker also studied the environments that their businesses were operating in and assessed how successful they were. They found that:

- in stable environments, mechanistic organisations tended to be more successful;
- in unstable and uncertain environments, organic organisations did better.

The implications of the matching are important. We should not react to the descriptions of mechanistic and organic by saying that the first is bad and the second is good. In today's changing business environment, we should expect many successful organisations to be organised along organic lines. Yet, at the same time, there are many whose environments change little from year to year. Taking on the characteristics of Weber's bureaucracy, they strive for efficiency as opposed to flexibility and, in so doing, relate to their environments most successfully. From McDonald's restaurants to branches of the Inland Revenue, these organisations serve customers with unchanging needs and do so mechanistically.

As has been suggested, organisations will not match closely either ideal type. Further, they may be mixed, for example, running operations in a mechanistic style and R&D organically. Finally, they may change from one to the other as they relate to different aspects of the environment. BT, for example, experiences different uncertainty in its business and domestic markets and would require customer service organisations to match.

Lawrence and Lorsch

First published in the United States in 1967, the work of Lawrence and Lorsch[5] is better known than that of Burns and Stalker. It drew on the latter and to a lesser extent on the work of Woodward (*see* below under technology) to pose the following questions:

1 *How are the environmental demands facing various organisations different, and how do [they] relate to the internal functioning of effective organisations?*

2 *Is it true that organisations in certain or stable environments make more exclusive use of the formal hierarchy to achieve integration, and, if so, why? ...*

3 *Is the same degree of differentiation in orientation and departmental structure found in organisations in different industrial environments?*

4 *... Does this influence the problems of integrating the organisations' parts? Does it influence the organisational means of achieving integration?*[6]

The study began with six organisations in the plastics industry. All were divisions of major chemical companies and faced similar, dynamic environments. Lawrence and Lorsch looked at their internal structures in terms of their degrees of differentiation and integration. They studied how four basic departments – production, sales, applied research (often called development) and fundamental research were fitted together.

Differentiation was defined as *'the difference in cognitive and emotional orientation among managers in different functional departments'*. This means that dissimilar work required people with unlike backgrounds, levels of education, frames of reference and so on. The researchers saw that managers varied according to: attachment to goals (tightly focused or broad); time orientation (for example, longest for fundamental research, shortest for sales); interpersonal relations (people-oriented in sales, task-oriented in production); and formality of structure (high in production and sales, low in research).

Integration was defined as *'the quality of the state of collaboration that exists among departments that are required to achieve unity of effort by the demands of the environment'*. Integration does not mean that departments come together by erasing differences, that is, it is not a process of reducing differentiation. Instead, integration must match the degree of differentiation. When making decisions, firms need to have appropriate means to resolve conflict and achieve co-ordination.

The plastics industry at the time found itself in a rapidly changing environment. Progress in scientific knowledge was accelerating; product and process innovation was brisk; the market structure was changing and demand was growing quickly. Successful firms had to cope with a variety of changes yet cope with them in a coherent way. Lawrence and Lorsch found that:

■ The divisions that did best were those whose internal structures permitted high differentiation while simultaneously promoting matching integration.

This point was reinforced when the researchers added four further firms to their study. Two in the food industry faced an environment that had medium levels of uncertainty; two in the container industry enjoyed the most stable environment of all. Again, the authors looked to see which of the firms were more successful and concluded that:

■ Organisations needed to match their internal differentiation to the complexity of their environment – more complexity meant higher differentiation; and

■ More differentiation meant that they must pay more attention to integration.

How was integration achieved? Table 13.1 summarises the integrative devices found in three more successful firms. It lists, in order of importance, the mechanisms used in each firm. The plastics company had a special department among whose primary roles was integration of the basic functions. Additionally, it had many integrating teams drawn from across departments. Direct contact was also encouraged and seen as important. Therefore, the most differentiated business also had the most elaborate set of formal integrating methods. The food company had a less complex approach. Here, managers were given integrating responsibilities and temporary teams were established when problems demanded them. Finally, the

Table 13.1 Differentiation and integrative devices in three high-performing organisations

	Plastics	Food	Container
Degree of differentiation	High	Medium	Low
Main integrative devices	Integrative department	Individual integrators	Direct managerial contact
	Permanent cross-functional teams at three levels of management	Temporary cross-functional teams Direct managerial contact	Managerial hierarchy Paper system
	Direct managerial contact	Managerial hierarchy	
	Managerial hierarchy	Paper system	
	Paper system		

container business relied mainly on its hierarchy, supported by some instances of direct contact and a paper system to resolve routine questions such as scheduling. Since it required little differentiation, the formal hierarchy of command was found adequate for most purposes. In Burns and Stalker's words, its mechanistic organisation matched its stable environment.

Lawrence and Lorsch concluded by drawing general lessons for organisational design. We can pick out two here. Figure 13.2 summarises what the notion of differentiation means. Faced with variety in the environment (two aspects are represented by the blue circles) it is most effective if the organisation responds with a structure that allows separate departments to deal with each environment. The first differentiation error occurs when it tries to handle too much variety with one department while the second occurs if it creates two departments when only one is needed. Possible examples from the history of Abbott Laboratories are added for illustration.

Figure 13.3 then summarises integration. The examples at the top and bottom of the list show effective cases. If differentiation is small, the normal hierarchy can be a satisfactory integrator; if large, a special unit may be needed. Failures occur if either the hierarchical or special unit approach is used inappropriately.

More on organisation and environment

There have been many other studies of the links between organisation and environment, underscoring the view that a unique blend of factors exists in every situation. Widely known are the investigations of Kanter into the ability of United States businesses to innovate. In *The Change Masters*[7] she compares sets of firms that are more or less receptive to change. Her *segmental* and *integrative* management policies are not unlike mechanistic and organic. In the segmental corporation, there was a sense of control of internal boundaries. Pressure from

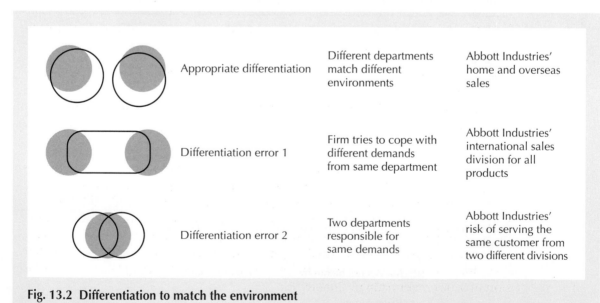

	Appropriate differentiation	Different departments match different environments	Abbott Industries' home and overseas sales
	Differentiation error 1	Firm tries to cope with different demands from same department	Abbott Industries' international sales division for all products
	Differentiation error 2	Two departments responsible for same demands	Abbott Industries' risk of serving the same customer from two different divisions

Fig. 13.2 Differentiation to match the environment

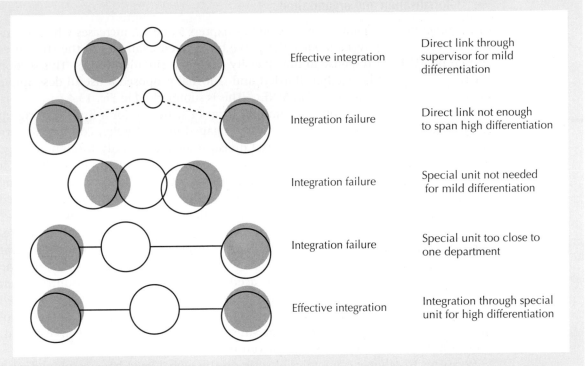

	Effective integration	Direct link through supervisor for mild differentiation
	Integration failure	Direct link not enough to span high differentiation
	Integration failure	Special unit not needed for mild differentiation
	Integration failure	Special unit too close to one department
	Effective integration	Integration through special unit for high differentiation

Fig. 13.3 Integration: effective and ineffective

other departments, and the external environment, was perceived as a threat. In integrative organisations, on the other hand, success came from flexibility. They had more 'surface' open to the environment, rather like Miles and Snow's spherical structure of the last chapter. This meant that more people, with greater skills, interacted with the environment. Managers of these innovative organisations required three key skills:

- political – persuading colleagues to provide resources and information and offer support;
- team leading – establishing and encouraging participation in flexible teams;
- coping – that is not being afraid of change and being able to take advantage of change opportunities.

When Giants Learn to Dance[8] explores the internal workings of large corporations trying to understand how innovation is nurtured. Echoing Lawrence and Lorsch, Kanter found that success came from differentiating those areas devoted to innovation from the mainstream of the business. Given the dominance of the latter, innovatory people and teams would not last long without such insulation. Again, the art is to allow the differentiation yet set up effective means of integrating new ideas into the mainstream. We can see similar ideas, with examples, in our discussion of intrapreneurship in Chapter 8.

Globalisation and organisation

Environmental uncertainty, as explained in Chapters 5 and 12, increases when organisations engage in international activity. We have given examples of the structures chosen by MNEs in response to the diversity that their situation brings. This section gathers these strands together. Bartlett and Ghoshal proposed a useful descriptive model for structural types found in MNEs.[9] This is summarised in Fig. 13.4.

The international division is a common form of structure for a firm opening up its international business. It enables those engaged in the foreign country activity to group their effort. The international division, being the only foreign activity, needs no global co-ordination. Also, since its activity is essentially home-based, it does not seek to be responsive to local conditions with special products or selling processes. Abbott Laboratories' organisation of the 1960s had three home-based product divisions with international sales being handled by a separate unit.

International subsidiaries frequently evolve from the international structure. Direct foreign investment may be the trigger, especially in those countries that demand local participation. Anyhow, firms cannot go on supplying staff from the home base, a constraint that is quickly faced by firms based in small countries such as in Scandinavia. The parent company retains control through having appointed the senior manager in the unit and using a formal set of planning and control processes. Abbott has many overseas subsidiaries formed by direct investment, acquisition of local companies or joint ventures.

Pressures to achieve economies of scale on the global level have combined with the effect of globalisation in consumer industries to make many MNEs change to global product structures. The company plays down local differences, recognising that differences in national cultures count for little compared with the advantages of integration. We have noted BT's shift to global product groups and Abbott's desire to develop pharmaceutical solutions on a global scale. Some companies,

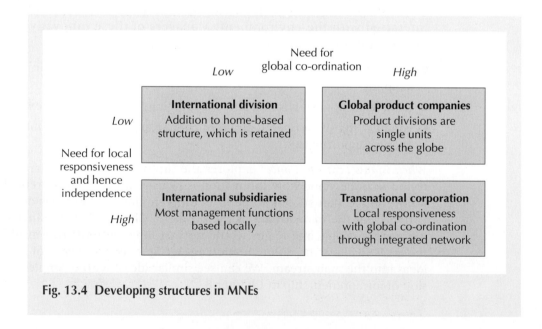

Fig. 13.4 Developing structures in MNEs

such as retailers Benetton, The Body Shop and IKEA, choose to ignore those local differences that are important to industry rivals. For these companies, however, policies of global integration on functional lines are based on a recognition that there is a large enough homogenous market to enable them to thrive.

Finally, we have the structure that combines local responsiveness with global co-ordination. Bartlett and Ghoshal call this the *transnational corporation*. Matrix structures are embodiments of this combination. Two-dimensional matrices may result from blending the local orientation with worldwide ordering along product, market or other functional lines. More than two-dimensions are apparent when more than one function is included in the linking. Electrolux is a well-known example of this approach. In the 1990s, Abbott Laboratories was toying with co-ordination along both product and customer dimensions and giving up the dated split between the home market and overseas.

■ Technology and organisation

Woodward was another researcher who sought to develop a contingency model of organisation. Instead of a general model of environmental uncertainty, she studied the links between process technology, organisation structure and firm success. Her classic study of 92 manufacturing firms in south Essex during the 1950s[10] led towards a new thinking about production organisation. *See* Exhibit 13.2. for a brief biography.[11]

Woodward collected data on many aspects of operations, management and measures of success. Data included, for example, the percentage of total costs allocated to payment of employees, the number of levels in the hierarchy and the *span of control* of supervisors and senior managers.

> *The span of control is the number of subordinates who are directly responsible to a manager or supervisor, that is who occupy the next lower level in the hierarchy. Firms often try to even out responsibilities among staff at a particular level by taking span of control into account. Other factors, such as spatial dispersion or technical content also come into play. Woodward's comparisons used averages for each firm.*

Exhibit 13.2 | Joan Woodward – practical academic

Joan Woodward (1916–71) gained practical experience as operations and planning manager in a wartime munitions factory. In September 1953, a small Human Relations Research Unit was established at South East Essex College of Technology. Using both its own and United States aid funds, the British Government was anxious to accelerate the growth of social science applied to commerce and industry. Technical colleges, being close to local industry, were seen as ideal bases for some of this work. Woodward led the team during the 5 years' fieldwork and then moved to the Department of Mechanical Engineering at Imperial College, London. Here she conducted detailed follow up studies of control. She was appointed Professor of Industrial Sociology in 1969.

Woodward concluded that, according to similarities among key organisational variables, the different systems of production fell into three clusters whose characteristics were broadly similar. These she called *unit and small batch, large batch and mass*, and *process* systems. Eighty firms occupied these categories while the remainder combined two of them. The categories are summarised in Table 13.2. Examples are given of the sort of firm to be found in each case.

Table 13.3 summarises some of the many observations made. The differences between the systems are striking. For example, first-line supervisors in large batch and mass companies could look after many more staff than their counterparts in the other systems. This can be explained, however, by the different nature of supervision. The routine jobs of this type of factory would almost run themselves, once the supervisor and engineers had made relevant plans. Tasks in the jobbing shop, on the other hand, involved more variety and uncertainty. Work to be done and the way it was to be carried out would, largely, be planned as it went on. There was more worker–supervisor interaction. At the other end of the scale, the few subordinates of process plant supervisors are accounted for by their having largely been replaced by machines.

If results such as these were the only output of the work, then it may not have been regarded as particularly significant. So far, we can see that Woodward

Table 13.2 Emerging groupings of Woodward's 92 firms

	Unit and small batch production (jobbing)	Large batch and mass production (line)	Process production
Outputs	Single items or small batches to customers' orders; prototypes; large items built in stages.	Large batches, possibly on assembly lines; mass production	Batches of chemicals in flexible plant; continuous flow of chemicals in dedicated plant
Critical function	Product development	Production	Marketing
Examples	Making cranes; small print jobs	Automobile parts; printing magazines	Paint making; oil refining

Table 13.3 Selected data on firms with different production systems

	Jobbing	Line	Process
Mean number of levels in hierarchy	3	4	6
Percentage of costs allocated to wages and salaries	40	35	15
Mean span of control of first-line supervisors	22	49	13
Mean ratio of managers and supervisors to all staff	35	17	7

described the firms in one area of the country and fitted them into clusters according to similarities among their production systems. She went further than this, however. In collecting data about the *success* of firms in the sample, Woodward investigated what features distinguished the better performing firms from the worse. In doing so, she was seeking whether it was possible to make statements about the ways firms *ought* to be organised, that is to develop a *normative theory* of the organisation of production.

The way Woodward presented the data is illustrated in Table 13.4. The first line shows the span of control observed in the 25 continuous process firms. These had already been divided into those that were more successful, average and less successful so the other lines show the more and less successful groups. We can see that more successful process firms had spans of control that were close to each other and to the median of the group as a whole. The less successful firms tended to be scattered. Woodward's observations of other organisational factors showed similar patterns, with the more successful firms being more similar to each other and closer to the mean values. This pointed the way to the normative theory.

> *The figures relating to the span of control of the chief executive, the number of levels in the line of command, labour costs, and the various labour ratios showed a similar trend. The fact that organizational characteristics, technology, and success were linked together in this way suggested that not only was the system of production an important variable in the determination of organization structure, but also that one particular form of organization was most appropriate to each system of production. In unit [jobbing] production, for example, not only did short and broadly based pyramids predominate, but they also appeared to ensure success. Process production, on the other hand, would seem to require the taller and more narrowly based pyramid.*[12]

Such conclusions leave us a long way from a general theory of organisation. Woodward, to achieve rigour in her research, was taking a narrow perspective. She took the production systems in each company as given and did not investigate, for example, whether each was appropriate to its market situation. Furthermore, there was no allowance made for the historical development of each company – structures often exist because they have always been that way. Despite these comments, however, the study did enlighten the debate about the implications of different types of process technology. Not only did it develop a way of identifying different technical characteristics but it added to the argument that there is no one best way to organise.

Table 13.4 Spans of control of first-line supervisors in continuous process firms

	Number of people controlled					Firms
	<10	11–20	21–30	31–40	Median	
All firms	6	12	5	2	13	25
More successful	1	5	–	–	–	6
Less successful	1	–	1	2	–	4

We have presented process technology as an 'environmental influence' upon organisation design. This is reasonable only if we regard the technology as 'given', beyond the immediate control of management and determined by outside factors. Clearly, however, managers make choices about both organisation and technology. They are integrated. We shall see in Chapter 17 the significance of this *socio-technical systems* view on job design. At the moment, we can see that technology lies somewhere between the external factors of Burns and Stalker and Lawrence and Lorsch, and the internal factors we shall now examine.

Internal factors in organisational design

An important debate of the last quarter of the twentieth century has concerned the relationship between strategy and organisation design. We shall open this section with this debate and then move on to two other important issues, interdependence and culture.

▄ Strategy and organisation

A naive view of the relationship between strategy and organisational design is that the former should precede the latter in a logical way. This view sees design as part of the means through which strategic choices are carried out. It is well summed up by Lynch:

> *From a* prescriptive *strategy perspective, the purpose of an organisation structure is to allocate the work and administrative mechanisms that are necessary to control and integrate the strategies of an organisation. Thus work is allocated to functions, such as finance and marketing, and recombined in divisions or departments, with power being distributed accordingly. ... Importantly, in this definition the strategy is developed first and only then is the organisational structure defined. For the prescriptive strategist, organisational structure is a matter of how the strategy is* implemented: *it does not influence the strategy itself.*[13]

In this view, the stage 'Determine structure' is some way from the start of the process we first met in Fig. 10.4. It is part of the means of rationally implementing the chosen strategy. Yet a second look at Fig. 10.4 may make us consider that the structure is also part of the earlier analysis stage. Asking how resources are organised, and how well the organisation fits in with current strategy and environment, come early in the formal strategy process. Furthermore, Fig. 10.10 points to the *emergent* nature of strategy. In spite of the best laid plans, strategy is adapted and honed according to events, people and other resources. Lynch summarises the contrast:

> *From an* emergent *strategy perspective, ... the relationship between strategy and structure is more complex. The organisation itself may restrict or enhance the strategies that are proposed. The existing organisational structure may even make certain strategies highly unlikely. For example, an informal, free-flowing structure might be better able to generate new strategic initiatives than a bureaucratic structure.*[14]

Beyond merely seeing structure within resource analysis, this emphasises the strategy process itself. Since strategy is the result of management decisions, the way managers are organised, linked with the perceived role of strategic management within the organisation, has an important impact on the way it emerges.

Figure 13.5 develops Fig. 10.10 to summarise the two explanations. The upper diagram presents the rational, prescriptive case: there is a causal link *from* strategy *to* structure. In the lower picture, on the other hand, as the intended strategy becomes the realised strategy, so the present structure is adapted. Changes to strategy and structure interact, each partially causing the other. These are the basic positions: what about the evidence?

Strategy precedes structure

The most influential advocate of the prescriptive explanation is Chandler. He studied growth and change in United States businesses between 1850 and 1920.[15] He found that, as companies grew, they created a general office, to plan and co-ordinate activities, supported by various specialised departments. The general office, taking the long-term view, established the company strategy that was then carried out through, among other things, designing a suitable structure. Chandler always distinguished between strategy formulation and its accomplishment. He defined structure as: 'The design of an organisation through which the enterprise is administered'. Chandler was impressed by Sloan's work at General Motors and advocated the decentralised, divisional structure for the large, multi-product businesses that were emerging during his era.

As time passed, multidivisional corporations became more diversified and decentralised. In these businesses, linkages between divisions became difficult, if

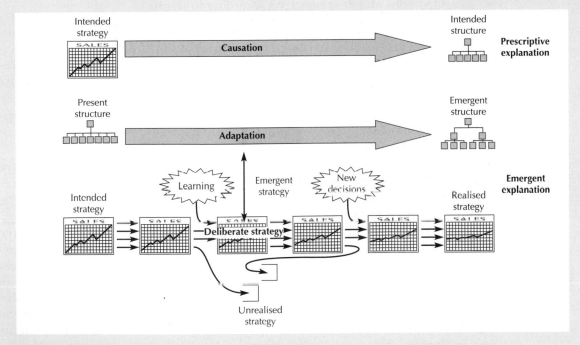

Fig. 13.5 Two explanations of the strategy–structure link

not impossible, to achieve. These are the modern conglomerate companies. Chandler did not investigate the implications of such wide diversity. Others, however, have asked whether putting such contrasting activities into the same group adds any value. The cost of the company headquarters may outweigh other gains.

Williamson's theoretical work in economics concluded that *well-managed* diversified companies could work better than if each division was independent.[16] He advanced two reasons based on the difficulties of capital markets such as the stock exchange. First, since they scan many opportunities, outside investors do not gather much information about any one company. They are, therefore, unable to consider any strategy in depth. Second, information revealed to investors inevitably reaches competitors. This means that companies tend to announce as little as possible, making the private investor's task harder. To emphasise this problem, subsidiaries of large corporations do not have to reveal any information at all.

Having justified the existence of what he called *holding*, or *H-form*, companies, Williamson went on to consider their structures. The optimal structure:

- was based on free standing units, separated from others in the business. These are the strategic business units (SBUs) explained in Chapter 10;
- allowed each to be as autonomous as possible. Normally this means each being a profit centre;
- permitted efficient monitoring of each division's performance;
- enabled allocation of cash flows to the best opportunities. This is the heart of the 'portfolio' approach to corporate planning;
- supported strategic planning led by the central unit;
- rewarded units and their managers according to results.

Clearly, Williamson saw structure as the means to carry out the strategy of conglomerate diversification. In these he joined Chandler in the structure-follows-strategy argument. Williamson's work on comparing firms with related diversification (M-form) with H-form companies became well known and helped those seeking to justify conglomerate growth. Later researchers have argued that too much attention is paid to structure. In concluding a study of medium and large United Kingdom firms, Weir is 'sceptical of the importance of internal structure in explaining firm performance. The adoption of the M-form structure does not ... ensure superior profitability ...'.[17] Interestingly, many diversified companies have recently been perceived as failing. Slogans such as 'Demerger to release shareholder value' or 'Refocus management on core business' have replaced the 'Diversify or die' message.

In contrast to the broad view of a multidivisional corporation, others have examined structures to implement business strategies within functional departments. Research and development is one taxing area. Explanations of differences in performance between firms are sought, to some extent, in variations in the way the function is organised. Bailetti and Callahan argue, 'To support a successful business strategy, the acquisition and development of technical and non-technical skills must be driven by the congruent assembly of organisational components rather then by the internal characteristics of individual components within the firm'.[18] They are saying two things relevant to our discussion. First, the way people are organised is at least as important as the skills of the people themselves. Second, the arrangement of people in the organisation comes after the business strategy has been chosen.

Interlinking strategy and structure

Contradicting these arguments, Mintzberg is a leading advocate of the knitting of strategy and structure. To show the way elements of an organisation fit together, he conceived of six basic components. Different patterns of these parts correspond to organisational types met in practice.[19] Set out in Fig. 13.6, they are:

- *Operating core* producing the goods or services;
- *Middle line* managers connecting the operating core with the apex;
- *Strategic apex* running the whole organisation;
- *Technostructure* designing and controlling the processes, (e.g. engineers, accountants, information specialists);
- *Support staff* providing direct services to the operating core, (e.g. office, transport, canteen, cleaning);
- *Ideology* binding the whole together.

According to Mintzberg, six fundamental organisational configurations are to be found. Each is dominated by one component part. For instance, the entrepreneurial organisation is dominated by the strategic apex, the owner-manager. Furthermore, the primary means of co-ordinating work within the organisations differ. The entrepreneur, for example, co-ordinates through direct supervision.

Table 13.5 brings these points together. We shall elaborate just two of the examples. The machine organisation is one where the basic work is routine, usually

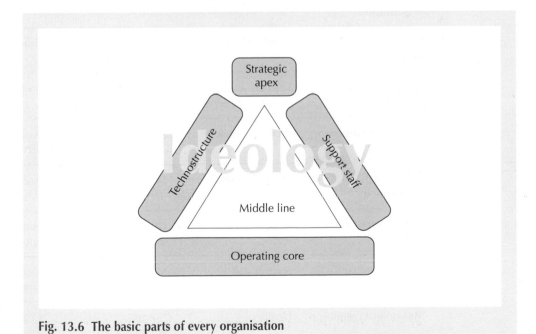

Fig. 13.6 The basic parts of every organisation

dominated by a production line. The technostructure is the element that assures success in such situations. In contrast, in the professional organisation, the highly skilled staff of doctors, lawyers and so on work directly on its output. The organisation is only as good as its professionals so the operating core is critical. Since the key staff are expected to work without supervision, co-ordination among them is achieved by having common qualifications. Practice and the values supporting practice are aligned.

As with other organisational models, we should stress Mintzberg's intention that these are ideal-types. Real organisations lie somewhere between the definitions and may display different patterns in different functions.

The configuration model is useful in studying organisational change. Whether the change is planned as part of strategy or occurs during mutual adaptation, it will be needed whenever a mismatch between the configuration and the situation appears. One example is a firm of consulting structural engineers and surveyors. It was a well-developed professional bureaucracy in which each of the nineteen partners 'looked after' a set of clients and led small teams of well-qualified staff. While each had high respect for the others' professional competence, status among partners was based on seniority and prestige of the client sets. During a period of industry upheaval, when demand for traditional work was falling and competitors were reorganising, this firm had great difficulty in changing itself. Partners were unused to processes of mutual adjustment that are needed in innovative organisations. Tasks such as winning new clients, rather than waiting for references from other agencies, and forming joint ventures, which had become fashionable in the industry, threatened the traditional 'pecking order' and led to loss of trust.

Table 13.5 Dominant elements and main means of co-ordination in Mintzberg's six types of organisation

Mintzberg's configuration	Dominant element	Main means of co-ordination	Examples
Entrepreneurial organisation	Strategic apex: the owner-entrepreneur	Direct supervision	SME
Machine organisation	Technostructure	Work standardisation	Assembly line; fast service restaurant
Professional organisation	Operating core	Skills standardisation	Auditing practice; school
Divisionalised structure	Middle line	Output standardisation	Hotel and catering group
Innovative organisation	Support staff	Mutual adjustment	Biotechnology company
Missionary organisation	Ideology	Norms standardisation	Charity; political party; pressure group

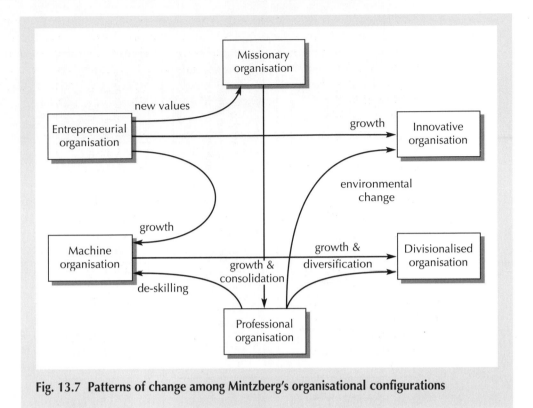

Fig. 13.7 Patterns of change among Mintzberg's organisational configurations

This change, from professional to innovative organisation, is but one shift that might be needed if the fit between structure and strategy is lost. Several others are sketched in Fig. 13.7.

■ Interdependence and organisation

The second internal contingency influencing structure is interdependence – the extent to which departments depend on each other to carry out their functions. This question was implied in the previous discussion of M-form and H-form divisionalised structures. The M-form has divisions that have something in common and could benefit from sharing resources, processes, information and so on. Achieving the links, however, is not so easy, forcing many firms to go to great lengths to ensure that they happen. This takes us back to the complex matrix structures set up by the giant MNEs.

Here we shall take the question of interdependence down the scale to examine how it relates to the basic functional structure. In setting up departments, the functional structure cuts across work flow. The extent to which this happens is a measure of departmental interdependency. It has three forms – pooled, sequential and reciprocal-shown in Fig. 13.8. These forms correspond to three technologies first proposed by Thompson. More general than those proposed by Woodward, the categories apply both to manufacturing and service activities.[20] They are:

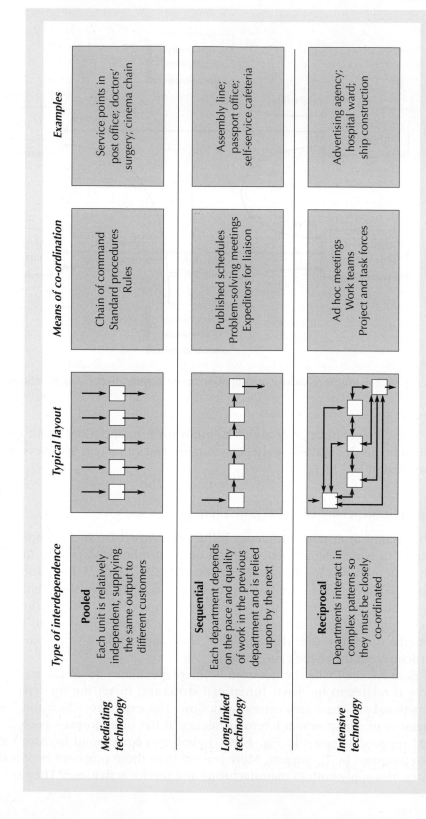

Type of interdependence	Typical layout	Means of co-ordination	Examples
Mediating technology — **Pooled** Each unit is relatively independent, supplying the same output to different customers		Chain of command Standard procedures Rules	Service points in post office; doctors' surgery; cinema chain
Long-linked technology — **Sequential** Each department depends on the pace and quality of work in the previous department and is relied upon by the next		Published schedules Problem-solving meetings Expeditors for liaison	Assembly line; passport office; self-service cafeteria
Intensive technology — **Reciprocal** Departments interact in complex patterns so they must be closely co-ordinated		Ad hoc meetings Work teams Project and task forces	Advertising agency; hospital ward; ship construction

Fig. 13.8 Pooled, sequential and reciprocal technologies

432

- *Mediating technology.* The common processes are used by otherwise independent units to serve either customers in different places or different categories of customer. Standardisation is the key co-ordinating mechanism. Designing each process or piece of equipment once, and then using the same throughout a large organisation, permits economies of scale to be achieved. For instance a bank maintains security and efficiency through common operating procedures and equipment. Yet this may not satisfy the needs of every customer and the rigidity of the system may make it difficult to adapt.

- *Long-linked or sequential technology.* Assembly lines are the clearest examples of this type. Each stage is dependent for its work on the stage that precedes it so planning is critical. Apart from the line, there are many other examples of manufacture or service that use sequential processing. These systems have traditionally been unresponsive to change although modern methods of scheduling and applications of information systems have made them more flexible.

- *Intensive technology.* Here skills and experience are continuously applied at each stage to achieve mutual adjustment. Rather than the work being predetermined, what is done depends on the outcomes of the previous stage. Examples are hospitals where decisions about a course of treatment are constantly revised in the light of the patient's response. A high degree of interpersonal co-ordination is required to maintain this level of adaptability.

Different parts of the business may need to be co-ordinated in different ways, depending on their technology type. For example, Hennes and Mauritz is a successful chain of clothing retailers based in Stockholm. It is expanding into other European countries where it faces stiff competition in its chosen 'fashion at value for money' niche.[21] In common with rivals such as Marks & Spencer and C&A, functions such as design, buying and marketing are highly centralised. We can use such a company to illustrate Thompson's typology.

Figure 13.9 shows how different patterns of co-ordination are required for different activities 'flowing across' the organisation. For example, we can distinguish between the serial interdependence of operations and the reciprocal interdependence required in planning new fashion ranges or store openings. Scheduling and expediting within a conventional hierarchy are appropriate for the former. The latter, on the other hand, needs project managers supported by task forces, possibly in a matrix structure.

Including suppliers in the diagram raises a further point. Leading retailers are increasingly involved in forging close links with their suppliers, either for quick call-offs of goods or for closer involvement in product innovation. Co-ordination, therefore, extends beyond the formal organisation boundary. Thompson's work suggests that the method of co-ordination is again contingent on interdependency. Current supplies activities are sequentially interdependent. Therefore, they are managed by contracted schedules, rules for calling-off and staff whose task it is to iron out problems. On the other hand, involving suppliers in designing new ranges means, minimally, a deeper level of reciprocal interdependence. It may go as far as including outside members on development teams. In these ways, the supply chain is managed as a whole.

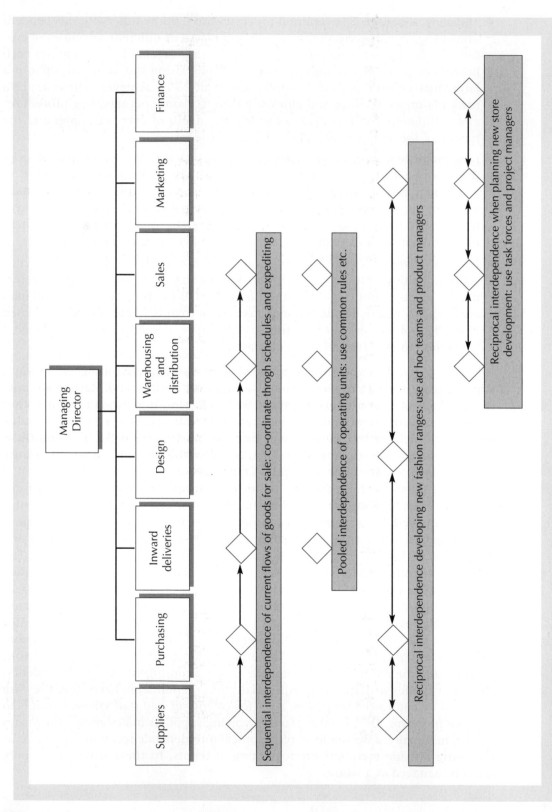

Fig. 13.9 Functional co-ordination in centralised retailing company

Culture and organisation

To start a discussion of the relationship between culture and organisation we can reach for Hofstede's work, introduced in Chapter 5. In particular, Exhibit 5.9 shows that, in some cultures, such as Malaysia, Venezuela and West Africa, there is high power distance. This means that hierarchies have many layers, subordinates heed instructions and there is close control. Low power distance cultures, on the other hand, value independence among staff. Firms in Denmark, Ireland and Sweden have flatter hierarchies with much consultation between levels.

A cultural perspective is also a way of comparing different organisations and even functions within them. This corresponds to the cognitive and emotional orientations used by Lawrence and Lorsch. In short, we would expect organisation structures to be contingent upon culture. What effect does this have in practice? Two examples, from Sweden and Germany, appear in Exhibits 13.3 and 13.4.

In Exhibit 13.3, Czarniawska-Joerges is pointing out that other aspects of management, apart from structural preferences, differentiate Sweden from elsewhere.[22] Yet, lest one gets stuck in the trap of imagining the nation as fixed in a particular democratic model since the 1930s, she stresses that management orientation is changing. Shifts in emphasis from production to marketing have been accompanied by contradictions. Preference for flexible service has continued while it seems that social relationships are becoming more formal. Salespeople are reverting to addressing customers with the more polite form (the second person plural) and it is no longer shameful to use titles such as Professor before one's name.

More rapid change was forced on many organisations after the collapse of East European regimes around 1990. Following research in Germany after reunification, Sweeney and Hardaker point out that two levels of culture need to be examined: national and organisational.[23] Differences in the former justified cross-cultural training to dampen down anxiety and frustration for new managers. Yet they argue that the main dissimilarities experienced were organisation-specific. Managers from the West were posted to new jobs in the eastern Länder and locals experienced huge changes. Exhibit 13.4 summarises what happened.

Exhibit 13.3 Sweden's modern organisations

'As perceived by executives in multinational companies, the structure of Swedish corporations is ambiguous. This is sometimes interpreted as a preference for matrix structures, and it is sometimes simply perceived as being chaotic. Decision-making processes are slow. This, again, is interpreted by some authors as the result of a striving for technical perfection and by others as a routine aimed in effect at preventing action. Control processes are experienced, paradoxically enough, as informal but tight. Also, although the importance of consensus is obvious, this is variously interpreted as a cultural trait, or as a conscious choice of democratic procedures ...

'"No bureaucracy at all," sighs an Italian who has just made an important deal in a telephone conversation. "Why don't these people say what they mean?" wonders, in turn, an American who participated in a typical consensus-reaching meeting where everyone was speaking around the matter and the meeting ended at apparently the same point where it began.'

Apart from showing how persons can be left out in times of great upheaval, Sweeney and Hardaker remind us how important it is to consider individual behaviour within the structural framework. A structure in one context may work very well not because it is somehow perfect for the job but because the members have found ways of making it work. Transplanted into another cultural setting, a generation of managers with different experiences may not be able to 'fix it'. We will return to this point when discussing the informal organisation below.

Another way of examining whether culture is a contingent factor is to compare matched organisations in different countries. Results are mixed. Mullins[24] summarises three studies; one compared Canada, the United Kingdom and the United States and two looked at Germany and the United Kingdom. The first found no effect. Yet the two Germany–UK inquiries suggested otherwise. In the first, British companies seemed to spawn more specialist functions than their German counterparts. This possibly related to differences in specialisation within the education systems and the strong influence of professions in the UK. The second did not discover specialisation as an issue but explained variations through managers seeing their roles and authority in contrasting ways.

Criticisms

In common with other theories about management and organisations, contingency theory has had several criticisms: on practical grounds, it may not be all that useful; the studies on which it is based are few; its selection of factors can play down the impact of human behaviour; and it does not address the question of management legitimacy within a unitary model. Each is covered in the following discussion.

■ Limits of the contingency approach

The contingency approach relates situational factors and organisational design to performance. In this chapter we have followed studies that have seen organisational design as an important intermediary feature, as shown in Fig. 13.10. The management idea could be, 'Pick the right structure and we can cope with the situation'. Warnings, shown as 'Stop' symbols in Fig. 13.10, should, however, be put up around this argument. They are listed below. Letters refer to items in the diagram:

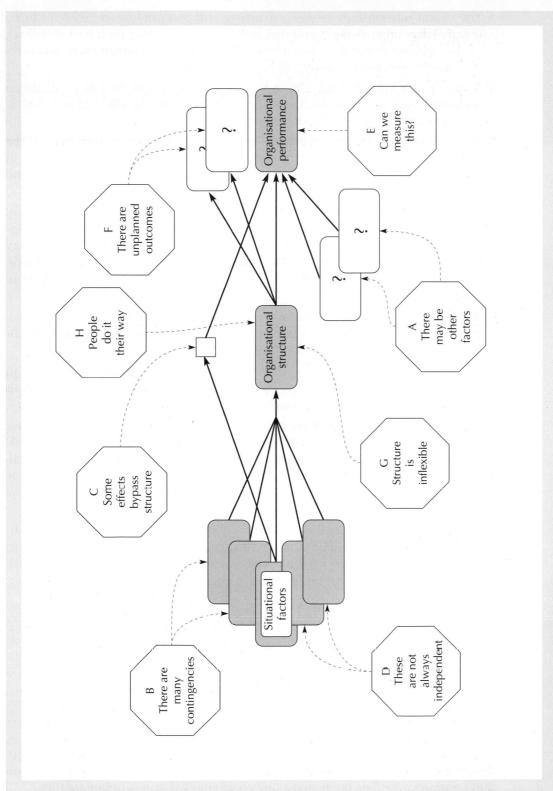

Fig. 13.10 Warning signs for the contingency approach

A The causal relationships between structure and performance are difficult to tie down. Many other changes, internal and external, also play their part. Feedback in the opposite direction is also a possibility. Firms may change their structures in response to outcomes instead of as a cause of them.

B Many factors influence whether a structure is successful. Just as predicting a patient's response to a cocktail of drugs is problematic, the effect of any combination of factors will be difficult to establish.

C Some situational factors have direct impact on performance and 'bypass' the structural effect. For example, the choice of process technology will need to match the needs of the market in terms of product variety and quantity. Beyond influencing structure, it will directly affect results.

D The situational factors are assumed to be outside the control of the organisation. Yet, when an organisation is large enough, it will exercise considerable influence over its environment. Forcing the environment to adapt to its needs may be a superior policy to changing the structure. A notable example is the behaviour of a firm having a monopoly. Customers will fit in with the system, and not the other way round.

E All the studies reported here have used performance as the dependent variable. For comparison, they have assumed that the same results, for example profit or growth, apply to all organisations. This is unlikely.

F Structural changes will have consequences other than the measures mentioned in paragraph E. Unanticipated effects include changes in attitudes among individuals and work groups. In turn, they may make a chosen structure succeed or fail.

G The costs of reorganisation are such that changes occur infrequently. As we shall see in the next chapter, change is more likely at times of crisis when serious mismatches become clear. Otherwise, structural change may be gradual, taking place when opportunities arise. Examples could be the retirement of one or more key managers or the opening of a new department. In either case, the structural form is likely to lag behind the ideal.

H Structure and performance will not wholly depend on the contingency conditions expressed in such impersonal terms. People interpret the rules implied in any organisational design in many ways. Each case is unlike any other. We shall develop this point in the next section.

If the contingency approach has succeeded, it has shown managers that there is no one best way of designing an organisation's structure. To overreact, that is to stress the unique nature of each case, is to ignore similarities. We should remember that the empirical work identifies both sides, the differences and the similarities. Therefore, by understanding the contingencies that are likely to be important, a manager can learn from the past and incorporate experience into structural design.

The informal organisation

One difficulty with organisation charts is the way they can shift from attempts to describe what exists to attempts to prescribe what ought to be. The assumption that some organisations interacted along chart lines led others to imitate them. 'All messages must be sent through the proper channels!' Yet one continual outcome of the research effort over 50 years has been the recognition that the formal structure represents wishful thinking. Real managers learn how to make almost any structure work by building up informal networks and cutting corners when it is advantageous to do so.

This is the informal organisation. Personal links between machinist and manager, chauffeur and chairman, or secretary and superintendent are built as alliances to share information, exchange favours and get the work done. In times of little change, the informal network delivered and the basic hierarchical form remained unchallenged. Later, as the pace picked up and organisations became larger and more diverse, the strains began to show and the informal organisation was no longer able to compensate. Barsoux' interpretation of what happened next is shown in Exhibit 13.5.[25]

Organisation structures are only a means to an end. They are enabling mechanisms, allowing the energy and initiative of people to be channelled in cooperation. If an organisation is badly designed, it will hinder success. If, as one would hope, it is designed to suit the situational factors, it will enable success. But enabling is different from guaranteeing. This comes from the energies and direction of the people themselves. A problem with the argument of Barsoux is that matching informal networks will not build a successful organisation. Not only would this merely replicate the needs of the past but making a map of informal arrangements does not make them work.

One study of MNEs showed what happens when decentralisation with fewer hierarchical layers is introduced.[26] Such businesses come to rely on personal networks for informal horizontal communication. Further structural changes can interrupt these flows, which can then work against the formal system. Managers at the centre have to balance their wish to control against the benefits of creating a working environment where personal links flourish.

This leads us to another difficulty with Barsoux' view of the informal organisation. He assumes it to be benign. It counters weaknesses in the formal structure as well-motivated managers get on with things through personal networks. Why

Exhibit 13.5 Making it work – informally

'It then dawned on managers and management thinkers that the informal organisation was quite good at capturing and channelling corporate energy. These looser configurations clearly made things happen, switched people on and sustained corporate competitiveness.

'If the informal organisation was where the company's real energy lay, why not redesign the formal organisation to look more like it? This realisation led to a host of new organisational forms ... Fluidity was the underlying theme. These organisations were characterised by the fact that they were adaptive, team-based, project-driven, with semi-permeable boundaries. ...

'We must beware of assuming that structure has a logic of its own, independent of the people who make up the organisation.'

should we assume this? The network could equally be malignant, slowly etching away the carefully built structure. Symptoms could be: resistance to change; nagging inter-departmental rivalry; permanent jockeying for position; unwillingness to carry out tasks that do not make a manager look good; lack of co-ordination in crisis situations; and lack of control. These are features of an organisation that is falling apart.

Responses to these fears should avoid attempts to stamp out either politics or informal networks. After all, both are facts of organisational life. We should see that the formal structure does matter and there is no substitute for making it better.

Unitary and pluralist views

Many sociologists have recognised two contrasting ways of perceiving an organisation – unitary and pluralist.

■ The *unitary* perspective sees the organisation as an assembly of people acting as a team with a common sense of purpose, willingness to share work and co-ordinate effort under an agreed leader. Accepting this point of view, managers place great emphasis on communication, creating a team spirit, selecting staff who fit in, and matching rewards to appropriate effort. In particular, senior managers see it as their function to create an organisation that will enable everyone to pull together.

■ The *pluralist* perspective sees an organisation made up of competing individuals and subgroups. Each has its own sense of purpose, direction of effort and leader. Under the pluralist assumption, managers tolerate the existence of differences, of rivalrous groups, of distorted communications and of people limiting their commitment to the job. The organisation has to acknowledge these differences and support a system of bargaining. People are unwilling to work but will consent to do so provided the deal is right.

Elements of both perspectives appear in real organisations. No one believes that a large corporation can work on unitary principles alone, although the language used by leaders often suggests that they can! Similarly, a business run on pluralist lines without any appeal to a shared purpose would hardly be a business. Recognising the limits of the unitary model has implications for organisational design. There is no one best way. Yet the contingency view still suggests that managers have to find the structure appropriate to the situation. It is unitarist. Notions such as hierarchy, the 'manager's right to manage' and the legitimacy of serving the common goal are not challenged.

Critical perspective

Critical theory takes a more radical and humanistic stance than shown in the above debate. It criticises management theory for emphasising instrumental rationality. This means that ends (such as business success) are unquestioned and means (such as creating a structure) are legitimated by the ends. While there is nothing inherently wrong with this approach, concentrating on the means leads to acceptance of power, position and status. These in turn yield high incomes for those fortunate enough to do well out of the 'system'.

Alvesson and Willmott[27] urge a more critical and reflective perspective. They point to one effect of hierarchies. Managers expend much effort in constructing favourable images of themselves and what they do. One use of management 'language' is to *mystify the hierarchy* to make it seem that its negative effects are not present and all members benefit from its existence. The talk is of 'flattening', 'empowerment' and 'flexible work teams' whereas things continue much as before. The authors quote the case of a Swedish computer company, *see* Exhibit 13.6.[28]

The contrast between the 'official' line of flatness and the admission of Sten's role suggests that this employee had not fully reflected on what was happening. The talk was a subterfuge to ensure compliance. Nor is this an isolated instance. Sometimes the claims are less subtle. From 1990, the National & Provincial Building Society underwent a 'transformation into a process-driven organization'. In a report on the change process,[29] two of the consultants involved confidently noted that, by 1993, 'The hierarchical organisation had ceased to exist'. At the time, the N&P employed some 4500 people! It became part of the Abbey National bank in 1996.

Conclusion: common themes or differences?

We noted in Chapter 2 how the universalists, epitomised by Fayol, sought management ideas and skills applicable across all sorts of organisation. The first impact of what we can now call contingency studies was to challenge this approach. Organisations seemed to succeed in spite of being very different. Researchers went further than this, however. They pursued links between fundamental factors and optimal ways of organising. If these factors are present then it is most appropriate to organise in a stated way.

Among the most significant situational factors picked out in the environment are uncertainty, globalisation and technology. Inside, they are strategy, size, interdepen-

---

Exhibit 13.6 **Believing in a flat hierarchy**

'Employees were repeatedly told that the hierarchy was extremely flat, with only two grades – subsidiary managers and consultants – and no intermediate grades. ... Social relations within the firm were represented as non-hierarchical, close, friendly and family-like.

'One consultant ... was asked to compare it with his former workplace. [He acknowledged that] at his present workplace there was a flat structure. "My only boss is Alf (Subsidiary Manager)," he said. Later in the interview, he was asked about possibilities for exerting some influence in the allocation of assignments. It turned out that his last assignment had been given to him by Sten, without his being asked whether he was particularly interested in it. The researcher then asked if Sten, a consultant, had managerial responsibilities and received the answer, "Yes, he works directly under Alf." In practice, then, it seemed that Sten functioned as a middle manager with semi-formal status as second-in-command.'

dence and culture. Studies have identified possible 'If ... then ...' links. The snag is that these are very difficult to model in practice and the cocktail of factors makes each situation unique. This takes us to the opposite of the universalist view – the particularist. Stated bluntly, each case is unique and cannot be compared with others.

The contingency approach tries to balance the two views. It recognises the special features of every situation while also searching for commonality. In doing so, it provides understanding and gives clues on how to proceed in practice. For instance, it does alert managers to the factors that are likely to be important and enables them to see why and how organisations must differ. Structures may be modified for different parts of the same business and they almost certainly must change with time.

Broader criticisms introduced in the chapter relate to the risk of ignoring what might be called 'real behaviour'. The informal organisation may support the formal structure acting as the grease preventing the joints from seizing. Yet for grease read acid, eating away the structure; the informal organisation can also prevent things from working. Perhaps more fundamental is the recognition that organisations do not merely support the interests of one group. The pluralist perspective encourages us to think of them as riddled with rivalry. Yet this work rarely challenges the legitimacy of the hierarchy itself and the roles of managers within it. Critical theory seeks to expose managers' espousal of flattened hierarchies and flexible work teams as just empty talk. Such notions are weapons in managers' battle to maintain the status quo.

Quick check up *Can you ...*

- Summarise the types of organisation identified by ...
  - Burns and Stalker;
  - Lawrence and Lorsch;
  - Woodward;
- Sketch the six components of Mintzberg's organisational model;

- Name Thompson's three categories of interdependency;
- List eight warning signs for the contingency approach;
- Define informal organisation;
- Distinguish between unitary and pluralist views of organisations.

Questions | *Chapter review*

13.1 What are the main features of the contingency approach to organisation?

13.2 Compare the work of Burns and Stalker, Lawrence and Lorsch, and Woodward to bring out the similarities and differences between their results.

13.3 How can the main structural forms described in Chapter 12 be justified by reference to situational factors?

Application

13.4 What are the situational factors most relevant to the Abbott Laboratories case? How will changes in these continue to influence the company's development?

13.5 The closing cases for Chapters 12 and 13 feature structures extending beyond conventional boundaries. What implication does contingency theory have for these initiatives?

Investigation

13.6 Explain and illustrate Thompson's ideas on interdependence in an organisation with which you are familiar. From this answer suggest what improvements might be made.

Building quality links with suppliers[30]

In the automobile industry, relationships between assemblers and their suppliers have been changing from adversarial to cooperative. A short-term orientation concentrating on cost is being replaced by long-term partnerships based on a Japanese model. These emphasise: cost reduction through working with fewer suppliers; quality improvement through sharing responsibility; productivity improvement through fewer faults and joint improvement programmes.

Ford has been involved in the partnership idea for more than a decade. The link with Chemfil exemplifies the new form of close relationship. Under the 'Total Fluid Management' (TFM) agreement, Chemfil manages fluids at the Taurus/Sable assembly plant in Chicago and eight others in the region. Chemfil is a Tier I supplier: either it supplies and manages all the fluids or, if it does not make some of them, it contracts Tier II companies to fill the gap. Items include phosphate sprays to wash car bodies before painting and solutions for spray booth cleaning. Timothy Gillies, the Chemfil representative, is responsible for more than fluid supplies and stocks. He is accountable for the quality of the output from the processes. This means he must control the mixtures and equipment settings. Waste products must be disposed of to standards set by Ford and regulatory authorities. Odours must be acceptable to Ford's personnel.

How is the relationship managed? We can look at goals, both organisational and individual, the role of information, and changing organisational boundaries.

Organisational goals, outlining each partner's commitment, are set out in a TFM handbook. Written in a tone that underpins cooperation, it lists the main goals as quality, productivity and cost reduction. The first is most important. To cater for developments, the handbook explains how changes to specifications will be managed. Financial benefits from continuous improvement will be shared equally. Interaction and trust are thus sustained.

Individual goals put into effect the partnership goals. Ford empowers its workforce and the Chemfil representative to contribute to operations management and improvement. The handbook requires Gillies to teach Ford people about the chemicals and train them in their use. In return, Ford staff, including shop-floor workers, train Gillies in the statistical process control (SPC) techniques that are used. Such close links are very unusual.

Sharing knowledge is seen as most important. All understand the significance of quality in maintaining position in the market. Continuous improvement is rewarded. Ford has an annual profit sharing scheme and savings from suggestions are shared with individuals who put forward ideas.

Information to support co-ordination and control is freely shared. Under SPC, relevant charts and sampling techniques have been jointly worked out. They are used both by Gillies and the Ford employees. SPC enables Gillies to compare fluid consumption with cleaning results. Abnormalities signal failure and there is an agreed 'reaction plan' to recover quality. Beyond immediate response, Gillies can change the process to improve quality or cut costs. Changing mixture strength, or redirecting the way it is applied, lie within his remit. SPC shows the results. Improvements, if sustained, can be jointly implemented. The continuous improvement activity goes ahead without red tape.

Instead of charging the price of its supplies, Chemfil is paid per car. This has advantages for Ford in making costs predictable and focusing management's attention on quality. Gillies tracks chemical costs with simple spreadsheets. If changes, internally or externally, mean that Chemfil starts to earn too little or too much profit, there are agreed mechanisms for negotiating change.

Having a representative permanently on site is not new. But the Ford–Chemfil link signals an important change in traditional company boundaries. Gillies has access to much more information about Ford than hitherto. He investigates processes leading up to the cleaning stage and learns about product performance in the marketplace. Ford also relies more on Chemfil than previously. It uses Gillies' spreadsheets when negotiating contract renewal and expects Chemfil to handle all business with Tier II contractors.

Immediate benefits to both parties are clear. Ford gains quality at lower cost; Chemfil wins more business with more gain possible through improved control of Tier II supplies. Yet negative consequences are possible. Ford gradually cedes operating knowledge of a critical process; Chemfil has to bear more management costs to administer its own supplies and those of other contractors. Furthermore, Chemfil may face increased product liability risk. What is its obligation in a law suit over product recall or environmental damage? Such costs are difficult to account for and may not be covered by the price-per-car arrangements.

Successful partnerships overcome these problems. The Taurus won several quality awards and became the best selling vehicle in its class. Ford and Chemfil are satisfied with progress.

Questions

1 What situational factors pushed Ford and Chemfil into setting up their new partnership?

2 Are supplier partnerships flexible responses to dynamic environments or bids to dampen down change?

3 Relate the way the link operates to the ideas on configuration and interdependence put forward in the chapter.

4 Considering the way informal organisations grow, what are the risks of the official goals of the link being undermined at the operations level?

Bibliography

Any of the studies described in the text provide insights into the work of contingency theorists and the difficulties that have to be surmounted. Referenced in the text, these include Burns and Stalker (1961), Chandler (1962), Kanter (1983), Lawrence and Lorsch (1986), Mintzberg (1979), Thompson (1967) and Woodward (1971). An authority on organisational design and contingency theory is Child, J. (1988) *Organisation: A Guide to Problems and Practice,* Second edition, London: Paul Chapman.

References

1. Waters, Richard (1995) 'Two's company – Abbott Laboratories, debating the best way to run an international business', *Financial Times*, 7 July, 17; Burnham, Duane L. and Hodgson, Thomas R. (1997) *1996 Annual Report to Shareholders*, Abbott Park, Illinois: Abbott Laboratories Inc.
2. Attenborough, David (1990) *The Trials of Life*, London: Collins/BBC, 8.
3. Burns, Tom and Stalker, G.M. (1961) *The Management of Innovation*, London: Tavistock.
4. Based on Burns and Stalker (1961) *op. cit.*, 5–6.
5. Lawrence, Paul R. and Lorsch, Jay W. (1986) *Organisation and Environment: Managing differentiation and integration*, Boston, Mass.: Harvard Business School Press.
6. Lawrence and Lorsch (1986) *op. cit.*, 16.
7. Kanter, Rosabeth Moss (1983) *The Change Masters*, New York: Simon & Schuster.
8. Kanter, Rosabeth Moss. (1989) *When Giants Learn to Dance*, New York: Simon & Schuster.
9. Bartlett, C. and Ghoshal, S. (1989) *Managing across Borders: The transnational solution*, Boston, Mass.: Harvard Business School Press.
10. Woodward, Joan (1971) *Industrial Organisation: Theory and practice*, London, Oxford University Press.
11. Dickson, Tim (1994) 'Management: pioneers and prophets – Joan Woodward', *Financial Times*, 8.
12. Woodward (1971) *op. cit.*, 69–71.
13. Lynch, Richard (1997) *Corporate Strategy*, London: Financial Times Pitman Publishing, 624.
14. Lynch (1997) *loc.cit.*
15. Chandler, Alfred D.(1962) *Strategy and Structure*, Cambridge, Mass.: MIT Press.
16. Williamson, O. E. (1975) *Markets and Hierarchies: Analysis and Antitrust Implications: A study in the economics of internal organization*, New York: Free Press.
17. Weir, Charles (1995) 'Organisational structure and corporate performance: an analysis of medium and large UK firms', *Management Decision*, **33** (**1**), 24–32.
18. Bailetti, Antonio J. and Callahan, John R. (1995) 'Specifying the structure which integrates a firm's skills with market needs', *R&D Management*, **25** (**2**), April, 227–40.
19. Mintzberg, Henry (1979) *The Structure of Organisations*, Englewood Cliffs, NJ: Prentice Hall.
20. Thompson, J.D. (1967) *Organisations in Action: Social science bases of administrative theory*, New York: McGraw Hill.
21. Carnegy, Hugh (1995) 'Swedish fashion retailer proves model performer', *Financial Times*, 23 February, 36.
22. Czarniawska-Joerges, Barbara (1993) 'Swedish management: modern project, post-modern implementation', *International Studies of Management and Organisation*, **23** (**1**) Spring, 13–27.
23. Sweeney, Eamonn P. and Hardaker, Glenn (1994) 'The importance of organizational and national culture', *European Business Review*, **94** (**5**), 3–14.
24. Mullins, Laurie J. (1996) *Management and Organisational Behaviour*, Fourth edition, London: Financial Times Pitman Publishing, 386.

25. Barsoux, Jean-Louis (1995) 'Management: The importance of the creative spirit – The organisational structure is only a means to an end', *Financial Times*, 26 April, 19.

26. Marschan, R, Welch, D. and Welch L. (1996) 'Control in less-hierarchical multinationals: the role of personal networks and informal communication', *International Business Review*, **5** (**2**) April, 137–44.

27. Alvesson, Mats and Willmott, Hugh (1996) *Making Sense of Management: A critical introduction*, London: Sage.

28. *Ibid.*, 101–2.

29. Hurcomb, John and Chapman, Paul (1997) 'Organizational learning at National & Provincial Building Society', *Knowledge and Process Management*, **4** (**1**) March, 34–48.

30. Zeller, Thomas, L. and Gillis, Darin M. (1995) 'Achieving market excellence through quality: the case of Ford Motor Company', *Business Horizons*, **38** (**3**) May–June, 23–31.

14

Managing organisational change

Chapter objectives

When you have finished studying this chapter, you should be able to:

- define organisational change, demonstrating the origins of change drivers;
- show how organisations grow through periods of stability and change;
- relate the types and nature of change in organisations, separating planned and reactive modes;
- demonstrate the origins of attitudes towards change and their symptoms;
- show how force field analysis can be used to assess the balance between change and resistance, suggesting why managers do not change when they should;
- assess the various tactics to overcome resistance;
- explain why changes effect the whole organisation yet show how difficult holistic change can be in practice;
- outline the assumptions and techniques, and evaluate the effectiveness, of organisational development;
- describe the key features of reengineering and comment on its application.

Opening case: people chemistry in R&D[1]

Following acceptance of Glaxo's £9 billion bid in 1995, Glaxo Wellcome became the world's largest drugs company. Critical to the success of the project was the integration of the constituent companies' R&D functions. The plan was to put together the best of the prior development portfolios in a new structure different to those of Glaxo or Wellcome. Dr James Niedel, Director of R&D, said, 'We saw the integration as an opportunity to change fundamentally the R&D organisation and process. This is a science-driven company; if we are successful in R&D, the company will be successful'. The target is to treble productivity and bring three new medicines to market each year from 2000. Industry standards now rank one or two as impressive. Glaxo and Wellcome had been achieving little more than one between them.

Previous giant mergers in the pharmaceutical industry – SmithKline Beecham, Bristol-Myers Squibb and Rhône-Poulenc Rorer – had not treated their research departments in the same way as other functions. General advice is to act quickly to take advantage of disruption, expectations of change, and hopes and fears of individuals. Fearing the impact of low morale, the big players had treated research staff with kid gloves, introducing change more gradually.

Glaxo Wellcome acted immediately. An integration team drawn from both companies reviewed all 160 development projects and related jobs in six months. Of these, 90 had been in Wellcome although that business had been only half the size of Glaxo. This mirrors the latter's more focused and decisive style of managing R&D: either cut a project or fund it fully. Strict criteria were applied across the board: unmet medical need; scientific rationale; commercial potential; strategic fit; and development feasibility. There were 93 survivors grouped into seven main areas: respiratory; central nervous system; gastro-intestinal and metabolic; antiviral; cancer; cardiovascular; and immunology. The scrapped projects did not mean withdrawal

from any key area targeted by the company. The risk is high. Of 100 compounds entering development, only 10 achieve registrations and, of these, only three recover their costs.

All admit that staff morale was very low during the summer of 1995. Yet it improved once everyone knew whether they would be staying or leaving. Dr Niedel commented, 'I think people see that we did this with honesty and integrity. The ones who remain say, "This was a rotten time and we wish we hadn't gone through it, but a stronger company has emerged."'

Wellcome projects did well in the review. This underscores opinion that Glaxo made its bid partly because it was concerned with gaps in its own innovation stream. It had relied on the wonder drug Zantac for too long. In the end, the combined R&D staff was cut from 11 500 to 9700. Spending, however, was to be held constant as the company had decided to invest heavily in automation and engage in more joint ventures. An example of robotics investment was a biological screening system handling 50 000 samples a week being replaced by one capable of 50 000 per day. On collaboration, chairman and chief executive Sir Richard Sykes acknowledged, 'We cannot hope to do all the R&D on our own'.

The new global R&D organisation replaced the regional structures in both companies. European and North American activities had been run separately with insufficient co-ordination. The six to eight layers typical of the old style were cut to four with many middle managers being made redundant. For the first time, commercial managers were to be members of R&D decision-making bodies.

By May 1997, the company announced that it was on line to launch three new drugs a year from 2000. The annual report reveals the critical nature of the innovation 'pipeline'. Sales in 1996 rose 6 per cent to £8.3 billion. Respiratory medicines, at £1.8 billion, had overtaken gastro-intestinal. The latter category was dominated by Zantac, which fell for the second year running. The basic United States patent on this highly successful product was to expire in 1997. Having represented 43 per cent of Glaxo's sales in 1994, and 23 per cent of Glaxo Wellcome in 1996, competition from generic copies was expected to push sales below 10 per cent of the total. No other major patents were due to expire until after 2000.

Introduction

Although product development needs many years, time was not on the side of the managers of the R&D function at Glaxo Wellcome. The merger had raised expectations among many stakeholders. All knew that Zantac, so long Glaxo's cash cow, could not be milked for ever. The new business had to combine the work of many thousands of scientists to beat the innovation performance achieved by the separate businesses. Meanwhile, costs were escalating, competitors were combining and purchasers increasingly resisting new, expensive drugs unless they showed significant advantages.

Change is often resisted. Frequently, R&D is treated differently in reorganisations for fear of scientists' ultimate sanction. They can simply stop thinking. A company merger is the easy step. Carrying out the consequential changes is always tougher. Some leaders shy away altogether, leaving different divisions to carry on as before. Glaxo Wellcome decided it must act decisively and quickly.

A vital part of management is carrying out change. This means answering the following: why the changes are needed and resisted, what changes are needed; and how the changes are to be put into effect. These three questions form the broad structure of this chapter. Before examining the why question, however, we need a definition.

In Chapter 4 we introduced Rhenman's distinction between reversible and irreversible environmental changes. Essentially, the former represented cyclical or random variations while the latter meant permanent changes. In response, the organisation handles the reversible kind through operational methods such as spare capacity, stocks and queues. Just like the tide, these problems rise and fall. Irreversible changes are different. They represent a new situation. As they build up, the organisation must make some permanent adaptation if it is to continue to match the environment. Hence we may see changes from minor product modifications to major acquisitions or sell-offs. Comprehensive or piecemeal, these are what we mean by organisational changes.

> *Organisational change is an irreversible adaptation of any feature of its structure, personnel, products or processes.*

The R&D function at Glaxo Wellcome introduced changes in abundance: it brought in a new structure; it promoted some staff and let others go; it discarded some programmes while pushing on with others more promising; and it changed the way projects were evaluated and managed. Within each of these changes, there would be dozens of others requiring more detailed attention. In the end, someone would have to produce a new telephone book, alter the cost codes, reorganise the warehouse or refurbish offices and laboratories.

Change management requires the full range of managerial planning and control skills. Yet a report by the consulting arm of KPMG Canada showed that organisations generally do not have a systematic, integrated approach to change. In a survey of Canada's top companies, 53 per cent of respondents reported moderate to low success rates. Lack of fusion was the failing. All the pieces must be fitted together for the whole to work well. Important tasks are communication, resource allocation, encouraging involvement, overcoming resistance, monitoring and reinforcement. Their balance depends on circumstances. 'Just like the Rubik's cube, you cannot win until all the squares are in place, but the combination of the squares varies.'[2]

Growth and change

Clearly organisations change as they grow. In a well-known model of growth, Greiner proposed that each follow a typical path. At each stage of the process, there is an ideal structure. For example, large companies generally need more formal arrangements than do SMEs. As each stage ends, a crisis or period of transition occurs before the next stage is begun. We can imagine a series of spurts separated by periods of relative calm.

Greiner's model is usually shown on a two-dimensional chart as shown in Fig. 14.1.[3] Since, however, the two axes, size and age, are correlated in Greiner's view, the second dimension adds little and the growth path appears as a straight line. The stages of growth and crisis are as follows:

■ *Growth through creativity*
At birth, issues of structure are rarely raised. The direct involvement of the founder-entrepreneur provides the creative drive to carry the organisation forward. As the workload increases, however, the leader, or leaders, find it difficult to consider every problem in detail. Hence they reach the well-known *crisis of leadership*.

■ *Growth through direction*
The leadership question is resolved by the appointment of professional managers. They introduce formal procedures, departments appear and specialisation grows. Having capable specialists creates its own problems, however. Their desire for greater self-direction may be resisted by the same managers who introduced the functional specialisms in the first place. This tension leads to the *crisis of autonomy*.

■ *Growth through delegation*
Delegating more responsibility to capable staff surmounts the autonomy problem. More delegation implies looser control, however, and managers find different divisions and functions pulling in contrary directions. The organisation meets a *crisis of control*.

■ *Growth through co-ordination*
Control problems are attacked through putting more effort into co-ordination, or integration in Lawrence and Lorsch's terms. Methods include all of those discussed in the previous chapter. One consequence, which we saw in the example of Shell and several other MNEs, is the proliferation of management channels,

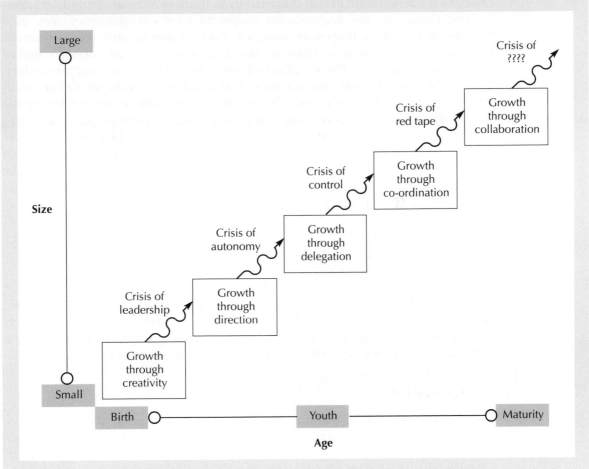

Fig. 14.1 Greiner's description of organisational growth and change

---

Red tape

Throughout the United Kingdom and the Empire, it was traditional for administrators to tie bundles of documents with red tape. Hence this derogatory name for excessively bureaucratic methods.

---

groups and committees. Complexity replaces control as the key problem. The organisation may be strangled as it faces a *crisis of red tape*.

■ *Growth through collaboration*
Greiner proposes that the crisis of red tape be resolved by simplification of procedures and reliance on the initiative and self-control of well-trained managers. In such a mature organisation, structures are seen as less important. The model is completed by speculation about the next crisis to face the typical organisation.

Greiner's model is useful in that it invited us to think of alternate periods of stability and change as the organisation adapts to new circumstances. Yet, as a description of events, it appears outdated. Greiner was writing well before the emergence of the virtual organisation; information systems had not been applied to horizontal control; and *downsizing* had not entered the managerial vocabulary. In the light of the previous chapter, we should also beware of the level of generalisation incorporated in the model. Clearly many organisations do not follow the path shown. Most never grow from SMEs. Others that do grow follow other paths, face different crises and finish with sections at different stages of development. We should take from the model, however, the sense of intermittent change. At each stage in its life, a successful organisation creates structures and processes to make it successful. Their very success makes them resist change, thus delaying and amplifying the subsequent crisis.

Forces and resistance

We can explore the nature of change through thinking about forces pressing upon the organisation, its divisions, subdivisions and individuals, and resistance generated by these same groups and people. As we shall see, the balance between the forces and resistance settles whether and how much change occurs.

Forces for change

The forces for change arise both in the environment and inside the organisation. Chapters 3 and 4 showed how irreversible environmental changes cause problems. For the most part these cannot be resisted. The exception occurs when the business has sufficient power to manage the environment to its own advantage. Examples include monopoly suppliers or government protection from competition. Others know that they must continuously adapt or disappear.

Within the organisation, change stems from internal processes and decisions. Managers may change the company or departmental goals, innovation may establish new directions, employees and their trades unions may make new demands on the way to share the benefits of their efforts.

Performance gap

As suggested in our earlier chapters, perception is important in understanding the ways managers might respond to these trends. The need for change can come from identifying a *performance gap*. This is a mismatch between what is wanted and current or forecast outcomes. It can arise either from shifts in what managers consider desirable, that is a raising of ambition, or from failure or decline in current business. If the gap is recognised, managers will seek action to close it. Glaxo Wellcome knew that the end was in sight for its wonder drug. Zantac had earned this name both for its effectiveness as a treatment and for its contributions to company profits. Yet the company needed to do more than repair the Zantac gap. Rising stakeholder expectations demanded more. The two elements of the performance gap are shown in Fig. 14.2.[4] The lower part shows how, without new for-mulations, sales of existing products would stabilise and begin to decline, gradually taking performance below the recent 4 per cent growth trend. The upper part shows the effect of rising stakeholders' expectations after the merger. The total gap, amounting to one third of sales in 2002, led the R&D managers to set such an ambitious pace of innovation.

Complacency

There is a danger in thinking that the need for change is obvious. We would expect managers to show alacrity in closing the performance gap. Yet many do not. Kotter puts this down to weaknesses in leadership. Changes fail because staff do not share a sense of urgency. He notes that some boardroom debates resemble those of an academic common room. Ideas are discussed for their own sake with no intention of action. Kotter's six typical examples of complacency appear in Exhibit 14.1.[5]

Parkinson put it another way. In his ironic essays, he exposed the shortcomings of organisations through suggesting that they worked hard at failure. In Exhibit 14.2, he describes the symptoms of a disease he called 'Injelititis'.[6]

■ Types of organisational change

Nadler and Tushman[7] have provided a useful typology that we can use to further explore types of change and responses to them. In the 2 × 2 array, shown in Fig. 14.3, the vertical axis divides the origins of change into those that are planned in response to anticipated forces and those that the organisation is obliged to make

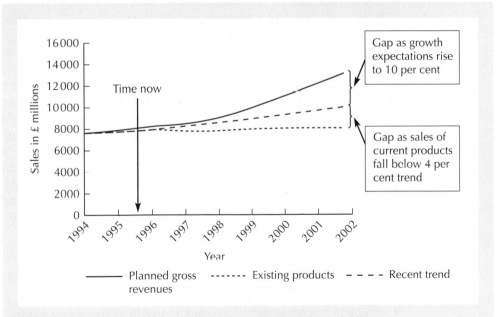

Fig. 14.2 Prospects for Glaxo Wellcome as current products decline

---

Exhibit 14.1 Recognising complacency

- There was no highly visible crisis: money was not being lost, employees were working full shifts. Yet the business was in slow decline.

- Meeting room screamed, 'Success!' Soft carpets and a ten-metre antique table passed on the subliminal message, 'We're winners! When is lunch?'

- Standards were low; managers said profits were up by 10 per cent that year. They ignored the 30 per cent fall over 5 years and recent 20 per cent rises among rivals.

- Managers focused on functional goals; marketing had indices, production had schedules. Only the chief executive was responsible for overall performance. No one else felt responsible.

- Rigged control systems made it simple to attain functional goals. Typical for marketing was the easy, 'Launch a new advertising campaign by 15 June.' Market share was not a target.

- The only feedback was internal. Most employees never dealt with dissatisfied customers, angry investors or frustrated suppliers.

Exhibit 14.2 Successful failure, according to Parkinson

'Little is being attempted. Nothing is being achieved. And in contemplation of this sorry picture, we conclude that those in control have done their best, struggled against adversity, and have finally admitted defeat. It now appears from the results of recent investigation, that no such failure need be assumed. In a high percentage of the moribund institutions so far examined, the final state of coma is something gained of set purpose and after prolonged effort.'

---

after the event. Labelled *proactive* and *reactive* these separate those organisations for which deliberate planning is the way forward from those that prefer, or are compelled, to survive through flexibility. Neither is superior. We should remember that planning suits the larger organisations in relatively certain environments. Reaction is the habit of the entrepreneur.

The horizontal axis refers to the scope of change from small, incremental steps to major strategic changes. Again, neither approach is superior. Occasionally a series of minor adjustments may be appropriate. This is logical incrementalism. In others, small steps may not be enough and major moves are required.

The cells of the model pick out four types of change:

- *Tuning* – incremental change made in anticipation of future events – exemplified by programmes such as *kaizen*, that is continuous operational improvement, or training programmes to keep staff up to date.

- *Adaptation* – incremental change made in response to events – illustrated by entrepreneurial responses to competitors' irreversible actions such as entering or leaving the market.

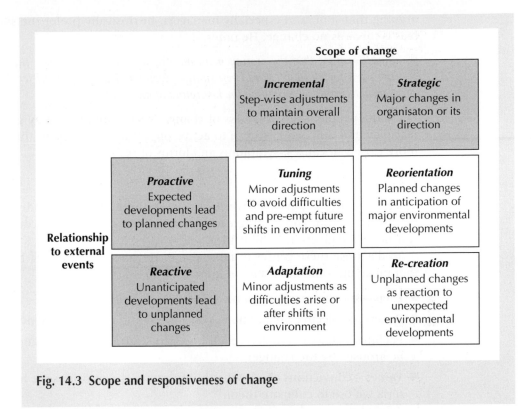

Fig. 14.3 Scope and responsiveness of change

- *Reorientation* – change made having anticipated environmental events – embodied in Glaxo Wellcome's reorganisation of its R&D effort to bridge the expected performance gap. This is strategic management.

- *Re-creation* – unplanned change demanded by unexpected events. Often involving a severe crisis, this cell is represented by Shell's struggle to come to terms with rising pressure from environmentalists, *see* Chapter 6.

The four types are ranked in order of rising complexity, potential impact, and risk. It will not be surprising, therefore, that they will be met with increasing degrees of resistance.

■ Resistance

Effective management of change requires understanding the resistance that frequently meets it. Fundamentally, resistance is a personal matter although it can be expressed by groups, organisations or whole societies. Each scientist at Glaxo Wellcome would have mixed hopes and worries in many ways. For one, the expectation of joining a new work team may have been refreshing. For another, adjusting to a new boss may have meant uncertainty and awkwardness. As Nicholson and West put it, 'Uncertainty and danger constitute the darker opposite side to challenge and opportunity'.[8] This sounds neatly symmetrical, suggesting that for every opponent there is a matching proponent. Yet Furnham denies this, arguing that staff, and especially managers, intrinsically prefer the status quo. The bias is towards no change. He notes:

> *Small wonder that the management mantra for the 1990s is that 'the only constant is the need for change'. And even smaller wonder that staff at all levels appeal for 'a period of stability' following the last round of manoeuvres.*[9]

For some people, their wariness of change is so strong that they go beyond complacency and dull acquiescence to active opposition. To explain this we must look more closely at causes, symptoms and forms of resistance.

Causes

Since resistance is personal, we seek understanding from the individual's point of view, that is from considering each person's state of mind. Six common causes of resistance are given in Exhibit 14.3.

To diagnose these causes in more detail, Hultman suggests the following factors that make up someone's state of mind:

- Facts – statements that can be checked using evidence;
- Beliefs – subjective assumptions, conclusions and predictions about the situation;
- Feelings – senses of anger, relief, hope, frustration and other emotions that may be aroused by the change;
- Values – convictions about what is important, the priorities we have and the criteria we use to compare them.[10]

Exhibit 14.3 Causes of resistance to change

Cause of resistance	Beliefs, feelings and values behind them
My needs are already being met.	Without *feelings* of motivation, change is responded to negatively.
It will now be harder for me to meet my own (unstated) needs.	Facts may be less important than *values* (assumptions, conclusions, predictions) that follow from them.
The risks outweigh the potential gains.	*Beliefs* about the risk will be subjective and may be wrong.
I think there is no justification for the change.	Leaders may use outside threats to disturb complacency but they may not be *believed*, *values* will be challenged and *feelings* of discontent may be aroused.
I don't like the way they propose to do it.	People may not so much resist the change itself as the means by which it is introduced. 'No consultation!' is an oft-heard cry when *feelings* are hurt.
I don't believe it will be carried through.	*Disbelieving* outcomes or the commitment of others to make the change will generate negative *feelings*.

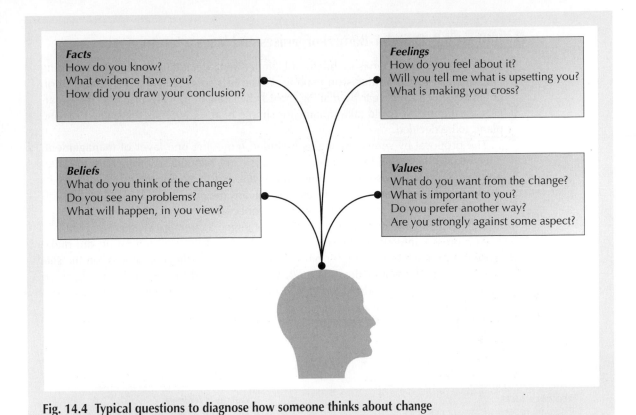

Fig. 14.4 Typical questions to diagnose how someone thinks about change

The comments in Exhibit 14.3 show how looking into the state of mind enables resistance to be better understood. Figure 14.4 shows typical questions that can be used to probe a person's grasp of Hultman's four factors – facts, beliefs, values and feelings. This simple picture provides a handy framework for investigation. It is a good idea to use the model as a template to set out responses to the questions. Snapshots of each individual can then be compared. A brief example of events at Daimler-Benz will illustrate the point. *See* Exhibit 14.4 for the background and Fig. 14.5 for a diagnosis of Dr Werner's resistance to change.[11]

Since we might expect senior managers to share the same facts in this situation, we look for suggestions of divergence on interpretation of these facts. Further, Werner did not hold the same beliefs about the Mercedes-Benz company as did his colleagues. His values in relation to business and his own role impeded agreement. For instance, in one letter to the board he stressed how the company's image had already suffered noticeable damage. Finally, we should not be surprised by managers' emotional involvement. Although we do not have the inside story, reference to a power struggle gives us a hint of acrimonious debates, subtle manoeuvres and aroused indignation.

Symptoms

How can we spot resistance? It takes many forms, both active and passive. Exhibit 14.5 suggests some examples of symptoms in each category. Recognising the ways in

Exhibit 14.4 Daimler-Benz reorganises and loses a top manager

In early 1997, the supervisory board of Daimler-Benz decided to introduce sweeping changes to streamline decision making. Observers suggested that DM400 million could be saved each year by making the 23 divisions more responsive to their markets. At the time it could take months for simple matters, such as the budget for one plant, to be decided.

The proposal by senior managers included removing one layer of management. This meant eliminating the two boards of subsidiary Mercedes-Benz. The semi-independence of Mercedes-Benz, lasting nine years, had been strongly defended by its chairman, Helmut Werner. He wished to safeguard the position of Europe's most profitable car maker, seeing the change as risky, unnecessary and unlikely to succeed. Yet, having lost the power struggle with group chief Jurgen Schrempp, Werner resigned.

At a press conference, Werner acknowledged that the reorganisation did make sense but he saw no role in it for himself. An amicable settlement, at least on the surface, was vital for both sides. Aged 60, Werner planned to refocus his energies on leading the Hanover World's Fair 2000. Continuing support of Daimler-Benz as sponsor and exhibitor was assured.

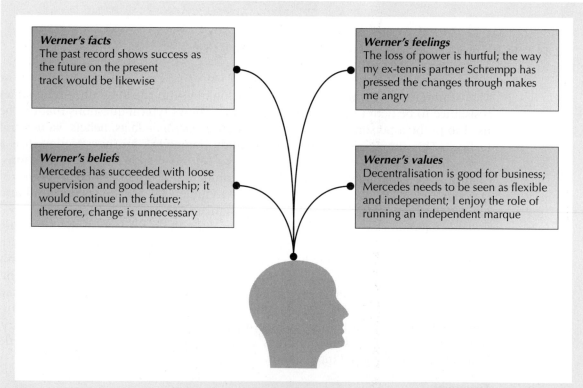

Werner's facts
The past record shows success as the future on the present track would be likewise

Werner's feelings
The loss of power is hurtful; the way my ex-tennis partner Schrempp has pressed the changes through makes me angry

Werner's beliefs
Mercedes has succeeded with loose supervision and good leadership; it would continue in the future; therefore, change is unnecessary

Werner's values
Decentralisation is good for business; Mercedes needs to be seen as flexible and independent; I enjoy the role of running an independent marque

Fig. 14.5 Fighting a battle against change

which people oppose change and how these relate to their state of mind offers clues on how to overcome it. For example, managers often diagnose lack of support for change in terms of staff not having the facts. So they stress communication, seeing it as a means of reaching a common perspective. The resistance may, however, be more deep seated. If differences in values are the cause, then no amount of fact sharing will overcome them. Managers would be wrong in seeking a unitarist solution while they should be responding to the pluralist nature of the circumstances. A unitary perspective encourages managers to seek alignment among all concerned. Resistance is perceived as deviance from norms to be cured by information and persuasion. The pluralist approach, on the other hand, accepts that differences are normal and makes progress through negotiation. Change is caused by bargaining. This was shown in the Daimler-Benz case. Clearly the parties could not reach a working accommodation and the story ended with a negotiated settlement.

■ Force Field Analysis

Force Field Analysis had its origin in the work of the pioneering behavioural scientist Kurt Lewin.[12] He put forward the idea that change occurs when *change drivers* collectively overcome *restraining forces*. The analysis can be used as part of the planning process or later, as part of the means of putting the plan into effect. Often presented in a diagram, *see* Fig. 14.6, the analysis is simply a summary of forces. It can be useful to assign a score to each force (1 = weak, 5 = strong) and scale the arrows to enhance the impact of the presentation.

Although the scores should only be taken as a rough guide, the 10–12 against should warn the manager of the perils of trying to push on with the scheme. Clearly it would have been better to anticipate some difficulties at the planning stage yet, with the go-ahead having been given, what actions are suggested by the force field to fine tune its accomplishment?

We can mention two approaches for the plan outlined in Fig. 14.6. First, introduce the change in stages, possibly with a pilot system run for one type of

---

Exhibit 14.5 **Active and passive resistance related to different states of mind**

	Active resistance	Passive resistance
Facts	Distort or use facts selectively; produce more complex interpretations; bring in experts	Withhold or delay information
Beliefs	Argue; challenge interpretation	Appear to agree but do nothing
Feelings	Ridicule proponents; spread fear	Withhold support; cold-shoulder
Values	Advocate alternative values; start rumours	Feign lack of interest

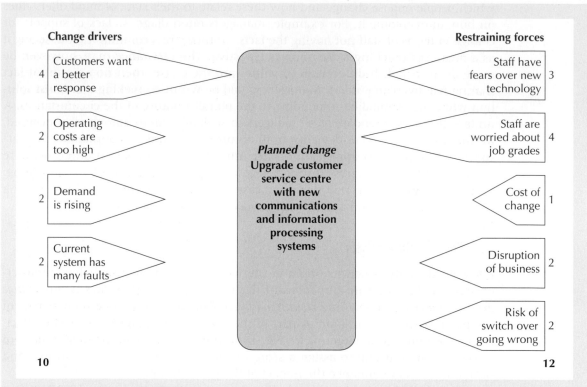

Change drivers

4 | Customers want a better response

2 | Operating costs are too high

2 | Demand is rising

2 | Current system has many faults

Planned change
Upgrade customer service centre with new communications and information processing systems

Restraining forces

Staff have fears over new technology | 3

Staff are worried about job grades | 4

Cost of change | 1

Disruption of business | 2

Risk of switch over going wrong | 2

10

12

Fig. 14.6 Using Force Field Analysis when introducing a new service system

customer. Although this would slow the process and increase its cost, it may have favourable impact on other forces. Better and more interesting work offered with the new system may induce a demand from other sections that they should join in. This is a new change driver. The demonstration could also reduce staff worries about the new technology and would surely cut the risk of failure. Training can overcome the fear of new technology. Restraining forces would, therefore, be weakened. The second approach changes the balance by bargaining. For example, the staff worries over job grades could be countered by offering guarantees. A promise of higher pay for those who take on the new work may increase the demand for training and ease system introduction. Therefore, by changing the number and weighting of the forces on each side, the manager can alter their balance in favour of the project.

▩ Overcoming resistance

Commonly cited as the weakest link in the change process is communication. The KPMG survey showed that, while 72 per cent of respondents had a communications policy in place they were not satisfied with its consequences. Barely half (54 per cent) felt that managers kept employees well informed. Further, only 37 per cent felt that people had a clear, realistic understanding of how they, and their jobs, would be affected by the change.[13] In the light of such experience, it is not surprising that managers see the need to increase the number of team meetings, briefings, newsletters and so on.

Yet this is only part of the story. Kotter and Schlesinger showed that communication is one of six options used, possibly in combination, to overcome resistance.[14] Exhibit 14.6 lists them and notes the circumstances when they are best applied. In drawing up the list, Kotter and Schlesinger make an important point about communication. While it is always necessary, relying on it as the sole tactic will only work where the resistance to change arises mainly from lack of information. As we saw above, dispute over facts is but one cause of obstinacy.

Facilitation and support are valuable when resistance arises from feelings of fear or anxiety. Staff may be concerned about having to do tasks in different ways or occupying new roles. The stress that can arise in such circumstances should not be underestimated. For example, changes to work practices among train crews meant that many guards took on customer service functions for the first time. These included selling (as opposed to checking) tickets and making announcements. Several had great difficulties in adjusting. Special training and counselling may help. Managers should also ensure that alternative roles are available for those who cannot make the switch.

Both *participation* and *negotiation* seek to overcome resistance through including in the decision-making process those who are affected by the change. Rather than focusing on facts, these processes try to overcome negative feelings and beliefs and

Exhibit 14.6 Tactics for overcoming resistance to change

Tactic	*Circumstances*
Communication	■ There is a strong technical element.
	■ Staff need detailed information to appreciate the need for change.
Facilitation and support	■ Resistance arises from problems with adjustment.
Participation	■ Staff need to develop a sense of ownership and belonging.
	■ Contributions and suggestions are sought from a wide circle.
	■ Staff may be able to organise active or passive resistance.
Negotiation	■ A group knows it has power to hinder the change.
	■ The group thinks it will lose as a result of the change.
Manipulation and co-optation	■ Other tactics have been unsuccessful.
	■ Opportunities present themselves for token representation.
Coercion	■ A crisis means action is urgent.
	■ Other tactics have been unsuccessful.
	■ Leaders of change have the power to push it through.

respond to value differences. Participation involves drawing members into discussions about change, soliciting their suggestions and delegating decision making to individuals and work groups. Drawing on the unitary perspective, it seeks solutions that represent a gain for all parties. Yet the scope for influence is usually controlled by management who retain the right to make the final decisions. Negotiation, on the other hand, means more formal bargaining between two parties. Each recognises that the other has power to influence events. A pluralist perspective applies. Often, a gain for one side represents a loss for another. Therefore, for the process to work, both must be prepared to make concessions. A common example is the bargaining between managers and unions over changes in job structures because of new technology. Negotiation is not confined to industrial relations, however. In reorganising functions or divisions, top management may be drawn into negotiation with the losers. This is how the board-level dispute at Daimler-Benz was brought to a close.

Differences between participation and negotiation can be blurred in practice. Some large organisations have formal procedures for both. Health and Safety Committees, established by statute in the United Kingdom, are often presented as examples of participation. The notion is that managers and staff get together to jointly study issues and come up with mutually beneficial improvements. Yet the same people, managers and workers' representatives, may also meet in negotiations over pay and working conditions. Unions are tempted to use the safety rules as a bargaining counter. On a power station construction site, for example, unions threatened to withdraw safety representatives. This meant that work could not continue lawfully. The unions used power in one arena to extract concessions in another.

Manipulation is a common practice among managers anxious to get their way. It means controlling the flow of information and other resources to increase the chances of success. *Co-optation* is also manipulative. Significant opponents can be drawn in to the change process through token appointments to steering committees and similar panels. In absorbing them in this way, their opposition may be dampened and they cannot later claim they were not consulted.

Coercion refers to managers using their power to force staff to change. Those who resist are told to accept or face sanctions. These can be loss of prospects, transfer to the organisation's 'salt mines', or dismissal. Coercion is seen as a last resort although its use in a time of crisis may be accepted. Frustrated at lack of adaptation to changing circumstances, some companies appoint senior managers with reputations as 'hatchet wielders'. An illustration is shown in Exhibit 14.7.[15]

Exhibit 14.7   A new force at Air France

In 1997, Air France faced a brief strike by the main union among its 2800 pilots, the Syndicat National des Pilotes de Ligne, SNPL. Its commercial impact was limited by the non-participation of smaller unions and some SNPL members. Even so, the company lost passengers, revenue and reputation. Christian Blanc, the president of Air France, looked to long-term gains however. It was the third time he had refused to yield under a strike. Its collapse placed him in a more powerful position to press on with changes to the battered, loss-making business. One commentator remarked, 'It is a method that has its risks but it has until now allowed him to overcome many obstacles'.

Hsieh and Bear point to the sense of crisis and fluidity during the first hundred days of office of a new chief executive.[16] Connections snap, information channels dry up and power bases collapse. In short, uncertainty prevails. The new chief is placed in a very powerful position and can act decisively. Care is required, however. It took a hundred days for Napoleon to progress from exile in Elba to the Battle of Waterloo.

Top management

The support of senior management is vital in overcoming resistance to change. Not only will it symbolise its importance to the whole organisation but it will have practical value when resources are being reallocated among departments. The changes at Glaxo Wellcome are an example of a major change that could not have been put through without commitment from senior managers. Those whose pet projects were being closed needed to see that the decision was legitimate and supported from the top.

Naturally, one may ask, 'Don't the top people always back change?' Table 14.1 suggests that this is normal, at least according to senior managers![17] Yet we can note the number of cases where full backing was not given. One reason is that top people can lose interest and delegate change projects, sometimes to the wrong departments. McCabe reports a case where the introduction of Total Quality Management failed.[18] The managing director had launched the project with a great fanfare. News about participation and negotiation were announced in a special 'Bulletin'. Other problems then made him hand leadership to the engineering director, whose style did not favour discussion and involvement. Planning committees subsequently excluded the unions. Suggestions from the shop floor were rejected or ignored. Staff sensed that the directors did not have a clear and unified approach towards TQM. Ignorant of the proposed changes and lacking trust in management's intentions, they felt justified in opposing the development.

Table 14.1 Managers' priorities in change projects

	Yes	No	Unsure
Success was seen as a priority throughout the organisation	84%	7%	9%
Managers focused on a few key issues at one time	75%	13%	12%
Managers changed their priorities to stress the change process	73%	11%	16%
Managers worked with staff to align personal priorities and job activities	77%	8%	15%
Top management gave sufficient time to ensuring success	88%	3%	9%

What needs changing?

Change can arise or be introduced in any part of the organisation. It can also affect any part of it. Recognising this stems from an appreciation of the systems perspective introduced in Chapter 2. Figure 2.2 showed the business functions linked with elements of the environment to form a transformation system. A more general systems model was developed by Kast and Rosenzweig.[19] Adapted in Fig. 14.7, the model presents the system with five subsystems: goals and values; structural;

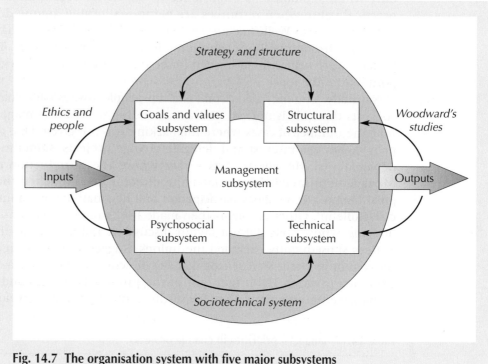

Fig. 14.7 The organisation system with five major subsystems

psychosocial (or people); technical; and management. Such is the close interaction among these systems that we should not expect changes in one to be possible without adjustments elsewhere. Let us remind ourselves of some connections:

■ Chapter 2 introduced the work of Trist and Bamforth at the Tavistock Institute. When introducing mechanised coal-getting equipment in the 1940s, managers of the National Coal Board underestimated the intimate relationship between the people and technology down the pit. The Tavistock group found the connections so strong that it was better to consider them as an integrated *sociotechnical* system.

■ The work of Woodward, explained in Chapter 13, illustrates the links between the technical and structural subsystems. Different process technologies were found to be best managed with different structures. Nowadays, with the rising interest in managing flows along whole supply chains, team-based structures, supported by information systems, have been found to work well.

■ Chapter 13 also discussed the links between strategy, within the goals and values subsystem, and structure. The latter is both a means of implementing the strategy and a cause or constraint on the way it is developed.

■ The values of the organisation, expressed as a system of ethics, interact with the people subsystem. Ethical standards guide staff and, simultaneously, are generated and adapted by them, *see* Chapter 6.

Many changes cut right across all subsystems. To its advocates, TQM should have wide effects. McCabe's study of Total Quality Management failure, discussed above, showed that it is not a neutral, technical procedure. Power, politics, structure and attitudes are critical issues in its introduction. Dawson's investigation inside a Pirelli plant in Australia highlighted both people and structural issues in its introduction.[20] Language difficulties among shop floor workers, many of whom were recent immigrants, hindered the deep levels of communication that cooperation requires. Structural factors, from workplace layout to the shift arrangements, also hindered the growth of teams. Night workers in particular had grown used to relying on supervisors to co-ordinate work and were unwilling to engage in group meetings. Given the depth and complexity of changes that are implied by the introduction of TQM programmes, it is not surprising that many disappointments occur. Respondents to the KPMG survey reported that, of seven major change initiatives, TQM was most frequently unsuccessful.[21]

Figure 14.7 presents the organisation as an *open system*. This means that it is continually exchanging resources, outputs, information and influences with its environment. Other forms of the open system model have varying numbers and arrangements of subsystems but the message is essentially the same: all components are interdependent. This implies that changes introduced in one part of an organisation will have impacts elsewhere which make the result differ from the intended one.

Burnes summarises some weaknesses with open systems.[22] While it is a major contribution to understanding change it is also very abstract. There is no practical guide to sorting out the complex network of causes and effects. To be useful to managers, there must be some more concrete guidance that can be put into effect. Faced with this complexity, Burnes focuses on the psychosocial subsystem, arguing that the core of change lies with individuals and groups. To change anything requires their action, cooperation and consent. It is only through an organisation's members that the goals, structure, technology and management are converted from abstract notions into concrete action. This argument means that changing people lies at the heart of organisational change.

For others, adapting subsystems will always be sub-optimal. Extending the tradition of systems and management science, they argue that the skills and tools are now available to cope with the complexity. It must be possible to make comprehensive changes. These counter-philosophies are exemplified by Organisation Development and Reengineering.

Organisation development

Noting the special importance of individuals and groups in any change, we shall now examine a range of interventions in the social processes of organisations. Organisation development (OD) is not a technique but rather a family of approaches that are concerned with improvement through people. There are many possible definitions corresponding to views of the range of topics to be included. Vecchio argues that, while any facet of an organisation is a legitimate target of OD, the focus is on people rather than structure or technology.[23] Some authors stress the cultural aspect. French and Bell emphasise the culture of work teams.[24] Burke contrasts the deeper cultural changes envisaged under OD with other quick fixes that have but limited effect.[25] We shall define OD as:

> *a planned, organisation-wide programme*
>
> *managed from the top*
>
> *to increase organisation effectiveness and future capability*
>
> *through specific interventions in the practices of the organisation*
>
> *which apply knowledge and techniques from behavioural science.*

Note the key features of the definition, one on each line. The programme is planned and applied across the whole organisation; it is run and supported by senior management; its purpose is effectiveness and capability in the long term; it identifies and uses specific interventions; these interventions are based on knowledge from the fields of psychology, sociology and management. In short, it is an informed approach to improving organisations through changing people.

Phases of the OD process

Since OD focuses on the people element of organisations, specialists appreciate that success is difficult. The measured, three-phase approach put forward by Lewin gives a framework for understanding the change process and putting it into effect. The steps, illustrated in Fig. 14.8, are as follows:

■ *Unfreezing*

Unfreezing, or breaking the mould, means creating the conditions under which change is possible. First, there must be diagnosis of the need for change. We have already raised this question in this and previous chapters. Identifying a performance gap, exemplified by the Glaxo Wellcome case, is one approach. The need may also be discovered through deeper diagnosis of the organisation's culture, discovering values and behaviour that, while not having an immediate impact on financial results, suggest long-run difficulties. The second aspect, overcoming resistance to change, comes early on Lewin's agenda. Diagnosing the sources and strength of resistance enables responses to be incorporated early into any change plan.

Organisations have to tolerate some level of dissatisfaction. This echoes the earlier discussion of Greiner's model which showed that they alternate between periods of relative stability and sudden change brought on by a crisis. They

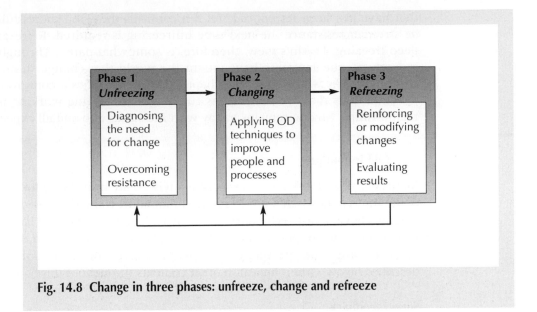

Fig. 14.8 Change in three phases: unfreeze, change and refreeze

cannot change continually for the advantage of little adaptations will be outweighed by the costs incurred. Beer proposed a means for deciding whether a change is desirable.[26] He argued that the need is a function of: dissatisfaction with the present (D); a recognisable end-state (S); and a plan (P) for achieving that end-state. The shift should only be introduced when the gains are great enough, that is:

■ *Value of change* [= f (D, S, P)] > *Cost of change*

These issues must be addressed before the go-ahead is given.

■ *Changing*
The change, according to OD practice, is a systematic attempt to correct deficiencies uncovered during the diagnosis phase. The plan may call for action in specific areas such as training, recruitment or communications. Otherwise, it may have effects across the whole organisation, as with a major restructuring. Examples of what practitioners, echoing medical practice, call *interventions* appear in the next section.

■ *Refreezing*
The newly created structures, processes or techniques become the norm during the refreezing phase. Unless steps are taken to reinforce change, and make minor adaptations in the light of experience, people and groups have the habit of returning to old practices and arrangements. It is normal for OD specialists to monitor the effectiveness of their interventions so that, as with any properly managed activity, feedback can be used to adapt and learn.

The imagery of Lewin's framework encourages us to think of change as shifting from one stable state to another. Such thinking may cause further problems, however. The benefit of the refreezing phase seems to lie in confirming the changes that have just been introduced. Yet if it confirms these too successfully, there will be stronger resistance the next time unfreezing is required. Refreezing becomes deep freezing. Lewin's view, therefore, is somewhat dated. Through the quality movement, the Japanese have taught the world that change should be seen as continuous. As we discussed in Chapter 7, *kaizen* implies a continuous stream of developments that are not seen as challenges to existing working practices and relationships. No one remains happy with the status quo and all expect change.

■ OD techniques

Managers, often working with specialist advisers, are responsible for selecting appropriate interventions, that are techniques that address the diagnosed deficiencies. As we saw above, many techniques can be assembled under the OD banner. Table 14.2 shows the range of possibilities linked to subsystem and level in the organisation. Since we are concentrating on the people aspects of change, six examples are described below. Others appear in other contexts throughout this book.

Survey feedback

A widely used method for the whole organisation is to administer questionnaires or carry out interviews with employees. The topics relate to the problems diagnosed earlier in the process. The approach differs from conventional surveys of staff opinion in two important aspects:

Table 14.2 Examples of OD interventions related to subsystems and levels (Individual, Group and Organisation)

Subsystem	Intervention	Level	Chapter
Goals and values	Setting goals	I,O	9
	Planning	G,O	9
	Introducing strategic change	O	10
Structural	Designing new structures	O	13
	Analysing roles	I,G,O	Below
	Creating flexible organisations	O	13
Sociotechnical	Designing jobs	I,G	17
People	Arranging survey feedback	O	Below
	Team building	G	Below
	Life and career planning	I	Below
	Improving quality of work life	I,G,O	Below
	Counselling	I	Below
Management	Improving interdepartmental relations	O	12
	Designing reward systems	I,G,O	17
	Decision making	I,G,O	11

- As far as possible, everyone in the organisation is surveyed. This helps to develop a sense of sharing of results and their interpretation.

- Instead of the outcomes being seen only by senior managers, everyone in the organisation is provided with responses. This means they can be used freely in discussions, in educational programmes and to support decisions.

Surveys can be confined to the diagnostic phase but implementing them in this way can also be seen as the first step in change. By letting all staff know how they stand in relation to each other, other planned interventions, such as those mentioned below, can be more effectively targeted.

Team building

The most commonly used method at the level of groups, team building is designed to increase the effectiveness and satisfaction of people who work in them. Project teams set up within matrix organisations are examples where such exercises may be valuable. One approach is for an OD specialist to meet each member to investigate how they feel about the group. Then a meeting is arranged, probably away from the workplace, in which discussions and exercises focus on ironing out problems and improving relationships. Exhibit 14.8 shows the value of team building when a change marks a radical departure from previous practices.[27]

Role analysis

The Eisenach case shows how other techniques combine with team building to add to the success of a group. One is role analysis, which is the systematic clarification of roles and allocation of them among group members. The interdependence among tasks in, say, a car assembly area means that conflict about who is responsible for

---

Exhibit 14.8 **Team building at the heart of rebuilding a business**

Until the fall of the Berlin wall in 1989, there had been little change in 20 years at the East German Automobilwerke Eisenach (AWE) plant. In spite of AWE devoting some ten thousand workers to producing 100 000 Wartburg cars annually, the waiting list had risen to 17 years! After unification Opel (General Motors) became the new owners. The plant was quickly converted to Vectra assembly. Full production of Astra and Corsa models followed. Opel moved away from traditional mass production techniques, placing people at the core of the new production system. With about 200 teams of between 6 and 8 staff, Eisenach has become one of the most productive plants in Europe. One fifth of the previous personnel produce almost twice the output.

Change was eased by local people's disappointment with their recent past. They were willing to accept anything new. Yet work teams do not build themselves. Opel management had to coach, advise and assist in times of difficulty. They could build on the comradeship of AWE's 'work brigades' of the old system. These had been used to tackle problems *after* they arose. Yet training in group problem analysis and decision making are crucial if problems with lean production and quality are to be prevented at the front line. Efforts are made to foster group cohesion outside work. The company provides funds to support activities such as family days, hiking and children's parties.

what will immediately cause difficulties. Role analysis does not mean that they have to be fixed. The group, however, has to recognise what is required and develop means by which the tasks are allocated and rotated. At Eisenach, all team members are trained to carry out all jobs within the work station. Beyond that, however, they are encouraged to spend time in other units, thus increasing experience and flexibility.

Life and career planning

Training is often provided for individuals after a narrow analysis of their immediate job needs. When seen in the broader OD context, however, specification of training needs might be one outcome of life and career planning. In this process, people are encouraged to develop and express personal goals with strategies for integrating these goals with those of the organisation. There is, however, a view that such training is expensive and wasteful. People who gain better qualifications are poached by rivals. Yet Dearden and others suggest that this is a myth.[28] They report that, on average, employers who provide training, including qualification training not directly related to the current job, are slightly less likely to lose the staff than employers who do not. Companies known for commitment to long-term staff development, such as the retailer John Lewis Partnership, train the people they want to keep. They believe they stay because of it. Dearden's group conclude that it is the fear of poaching, rather than the fact of it, that restricts investment in non-specific training.

Quality of work life

There are links between quality of work life and career planning. Not a specific technique, it is a philosophy of improving the climate in which work occurs. It may identify the need for less conflict and greater job satisfaction through participation.

Counselling

The second of the techniques that concentrate mainly on the individual, counselling offers non-evaluative feedback. Its aim is to help individuals better understand what it is like to work with them and, through this, assist them to attain their goals. As with other methods in the OD framework, the purpose is to improve future performance.

■ Achieving success

What makes OD interventions successful? According to one survey of 245 consultants, the risk of failure is high, with 47 per cent of projects unsuccessful.[29] Exhibit 14.9 draws upon recommendations from this study and work by French and Bell.[30] It summarises the conditions that are needed for any OD intervention and how the appointment of a suitable change agent, or consultant, can contribute to success.

Exhibit 14.9 Successful OD adoption and the role of an effective change agent

Conditions for success ...	... include the appointment of an outsider who ...
Support from top management and opinion leaders.	... reports to a senior person and is fully supported.
It is accepted that the system needs change.	... is chosen on the basis of relevant skills.
Early successes in the OD programme demonstrate that it is working.	... uses multiple interventions, probably in sequence.
No criticism of those who are expected to undergo 'improvement'.	... is discreet.
Proper co-ordination of the OD programme.	... has a high degree of access to people and resources.
Careful measurement of outcomes.	... shares results; admits and overcomes difficulties.

■ **Evaluation**

While it is easy to argue that, along with all significant management activities, the effects of OD interventions should be evaluated, it is in practice very difficult to achieve reliable measurements. Vecchio points out three sources of difficulty – experimental design, time span and measurement scales.[31] Since these are problems common to many aspects of management, it is worth looking at them in some more detail.

Experimental design

The nub of this problem is that there is only one organisation and only one set of interventions. The OD programme is, in effect, a single case study. At the simplest level of evaluation, a review comes after the OD programme, collecting views of participants on whether things have improved. Strictly, it will not be possible to say whether and how far the OD programme accounted for the observations reported. People may, for example, have simply become more optimistic.

Slightly superior is a design that makes observations both before and after the OD period. This provides a base line against which the post-event results can be compared. Yet difficulties remain: it is still not certain whether the OD caused the changes; the pre-tests may have changed the participants' sensitivity to surveys, OD and other changes; in the post-event follow-up, respondents may feel they have to report improvements.

In such circumstances, scientists will propose experimental designs that include the random assignment of people to groups. They are given various combinations of pre-test and OD programme, or neither, so that the biases mentioned above can be controlled. We must recognise, however, that such group designs are expensive and, anyhow, usually impossible when we are considering programmes spanning whole organisations.

Time-span

Referring back to our definition, the aim of OD is to improve the long-term performance of organisations. Therefore, it seems sensible to monitor outcomes over a lengthy period, first to show whether they occur at all and second to check that things do not slip back to where they were before. Apart from obvious difficulties related to experimental design, the lapse of time between intervention and survey raises two further problems. First, it will become progressively more difficult to link any change with the OD itself. Second, if one intention of monitoring is to adjust the programme in the light of problems, the information may arrive too late for anything to be done. As we see in Chapter 23, feedback with a long delay can be quite useless.

Measurement scales

Although it might not reveal the causes, using the same attitude scale at different stages before and after an intervention change would appear to give reliable indicators of that change. For instance, someone may be asked, 'Do colleagues in the finance department keep you well informed on budget matters?' A reply of 'Agree' at one stage and 'Strongly agree' later shows that an improvement has been made. Or does it? The snag is that the tape measure is both elastic and flexible. There are three possibilities:[32]

■ *Alpha change* indicates that the scale remained stable and there was a favourable change in the attitude towards the finance department.

■ *Beta change* means that the respondent changed the length of the scale, that is the tape stretched or shrank. This could arise if, during the OD intervention, the person learned much more about the finance department, possibly recognising that it could do little more with its current resources. The previous 'Agree' may mean the same as the post-event 'Strongly agree (all things considered)'.

■ *Gamma change* refers to shifts in the meaning of the scale itself. Again, this may be caused by the OD, for example it may have included a programme of training in finance. Hence, the first response may have been based on the quantity, frequency or timeliness of financial information, while the second may refer to whether particular items are included and presented in useful ways. Since the attitude scale now measures a different construct, the results are no longer comparable. It is as though one is trying to tell how much a child has grown by measuring the waist one time and the arm length the next.

Given all these difficulties, it is not surprising that evaluation of OD is an approximate exercise. Yet such an approach corresponds to one of its tenets: its mission is to help people to achieve personal fulfilment through their work. Therefore, it is sensible to rely on personal assessments of whether progress is being made. Managers, however, usually want more than this. They are investing in personal, group and organisation development and want to know what sort of return they are getting. Porras and Berg summarised 35 published studies, a so-called *meta-analysis*.[33] Researchers had used both outcome measures, such as productivity, absenteeism, profit and so on, and process measures, such as perceptions of trust, leadership, motivation and decision making. Their key results were:

- Whatever measures were used, OD provided improvements. Using output measures, these were stronger at the group level, followed by organisation and individual levels. The process measures suggested that individuals gain most often.
- The most successful techniques were the team building and survey feedback. These are widely used. More successful than any individual technique, however, were interventions that used four or more in combination. Being prepared to use an *eclectic* approach is a key to success.

Commenting on the meta-analysis, Vecchio notes that practitioners will tend to report results in the most favourable light, avoiding publicising failure.[34] Yet there is general support for the idea that OD works. A remaining question is whether it works in all organisations. OD practitioners bring with them values favouring trust, openness and sharing. In many organisations, already receptive to these notions, OD based changes will be welcomed. The snag is that in cases of a high level of distrust and conflict, the OD will be rejected. Thus we meet another management curiosity: in settings where OD would bring the greatest benefit, it is least likely to work.

Reengineering

For many organisations pressed with the need for major, comprehensive change, there is not the time for long-range programmes of OD to take effect. Moreover, the changes they need are more radical than improvements to current practices could yield. They need what Nadler and Tushman called *re-creation*. The current term for fundamental change to all systems within the organisation is *reengineeering*, or, since the focus is on process improvements to better serve customers, *business process reengineering* (BPR). As with OD, there is incomplete consensus of what BPR is, but the following features are commonly advanced:

- practitioners take a process view;
- in principle, they redesign the business starting with a 'clean sheet' and creating the ideal;
- the whole system discards old habits and adopts new methods;
- BPR sees stability as abnormal, continually seeking improvements;
- 'stretch' targets are set, looking for major breakthroughs in factors such as performance, profit, quality and costs;
- leaders seek ways of decentralising decision making and control;
- team work among multi-skilled members is favoured.

The stress on process flow, which usually runs across conventional hierarchies, is central to the BPR ideal. Leading proponents Champy and Hammer[35] argue that the link between products and success needs to be turned round. Good products do not lead to success, they argue, but successful businesses deliver good products. Therefore, managers must get *processes* right.

Information technology has been an important influence. Inspired by ideas drawn from systems engineering, and supported by advances in information systems capacity, reengineering has often concentrated on the 'hard' aspects of management. These are questions such as product and process design, work flow layout and control, supported by work team organisation. 'Softer' aspects, such as attitudes, values and culture, are played down. These are expected to adjust to the new realities of whatever processes are devised.

■ Does reengineering work?

One problem with understanding reengineering is the language used by its supporters. Words and phrases such as fundamental, relentless, radical restructuring, dramatic improvements and discontinuous change abound. Hammer's often-quoted saying, 'Don't automate, obliterate',[36] epitomises the view that it is better to do without operations than to make them more efficient. Yet he has also stressed the sense of urgency and use of power with phrases such as 'root out resistance', combatting those who do resist with the 'back of the hand' and 'shooting the dissenters'. This imagery suggests that BPR is best driven by aggressive managers riding roughshod over human sensitivities. Yet, in spite of this, the language of revolution is tempered by the espoused need to involve all in the change. Hammer and Stanton admit that ignoring people's concerns is a common way to fail.[37]

So what is the reality? Revolution or hyperbole? Crainer quotes several examples where figures are impressive. In one case, an insurance company cut costs by 40 per cent, reduced staff turnover by 58 per cent and shortened claims handling time from 28 to 4 days. In another, IBM saved £1.8 million.[38] Yet such selective cases can be misleading. The insurance company must have been very bad to start with; IBM's gain was mainly through automation, which could have happened without attaching the BPR label. Willcocks is more circumspect. Using Hammer and Champy's three measures of 'significant breakthrough' – 20 per cent gains in both profitability and revenue and 10 per cent cut in cost – he found only 18 per cent of a sample of 168 United Kingdom companies had succeeded in their interventions.[39] Yet almost half had reported success in their own terms, suggesting they were setting considerably lower targets. The approach in practice was much more pragmatic than that put forward by its champions.

Mumford and Hendricks, in what they call 'the story of the rise and fall of business process reengineering' recount 'a tale of fashion and fads, of unfulfilled promises and financial catastrophes'.[40] Under pressure to cut costs to meet competition from offshore manufacturers, struggling United States companies gladly grasped BPR. Even those doing well jumped on the 'downsizing' band wagon. The authors chart a wave of uncritical enthusiasm followed by backlash and disillusionment. They find the roots of failure in three areas:

- *The tendency to copy.* Security for embattled managers is found in following others. This is disastrous when faults with the leader are yet to appear and if the following firm does not need the same therapy.

- *The absence of a theory.* Pioneers have since admitted that rhetoric replaced theory. Yet, without the latter, there is little chance of giving guidance on management or evaluating experience. It is sometimes said that engineering works because it works. That is the only test. Engineers reply, however, that good theory makes engineering so much better.

Exhibit 14.10 BPR: factors in success and failure

Success factors	Reasons for failure
Management	
Human issues stressed;	Little interest in human issues;
Training supports changes;	Poor training;
Clear goals;	Powerful opposing interests;
Continuous, incremental change;	Looking for too much too soon;
Rapid project completion shows progress;	Not building on successful changes;
Communication with all stakeholders;	Stakeholders not informed;
Top management commitment.	Insufficient commitment from leaders.
Process change	
Best people for change teams;	Best people not used;
Train teams;	Poor methods and approaches;
Teams given enough time;	Lack of time for project work;
Invest in IT support;	Weak information systems;
Stakeholder participation;	Stakeholders not involved;
Customer needs at centre;	Customer needs out of focus;
Concentrate on key processes;	Choosing easy or minor processes;
Incorporate learning at each step;	Little learning;
Bring in experienced advisers.	Inexperience in analysing processes.
Staff	
Empowerment and autonomy;	Unwillingness to accept autonomy;
Communicate gains to all;	Poor communication during change;
Develop team work;	Inadequate team skills;
Avoid complexity;	Proposals too complex;
Guarantee future where possible.	Resistance because reengineering seen as means of cutting staff.

- *The use of consultants.* Without detailed methodology, consultants were left to invent their own, often old techniques recycled to suit the new fad.

The main thrust of Mumford and Hendricks is that people had been forgotten. This was in stark contrast to their explicit incorporation in the sociotechnical systems tradition. Proponents, however, argue that the critics arbitrarily select bad cases. When BPR is done well, and people are included, results are impressive. 'It is not something that happens to people – it is what they do.'[41] 'Reengineering is not dead. It just needs more professional engineers.'[42]

Many with experience share the pragmatic view. They regret that the language of revolution has 'oversold' the idea of holistic change, which is change directed at the whole system. It may have attracted too many managers and organisations who yearn for a return to the worst excesses of Taylorism and look for a means to justify coercive action. The counter-argument is that moderation and balance will win in the end. This is shown in Exhibit 14.10, which is based on the views of a forum drawn from this 'moderate' school.[43] On reflection BPR may be seen as less than revolutionary and more a timely reminder, stimulated by advances in information technology, of the need for a holistic approach to change.

Conclusion: change

We began by defining change as any irreversible alteration to any part of the organisation. Its origins may be internal, arising from an emerging performance gap or alterations in the perceptions of stakeholders. Alternatively, it may be external, resulting from the dynamism of the environment. Following Nadler and Tushman, small planned changes are the easiest to handle with large unplanned ones being the most difficult.

The change process is not continuous. Greiner suggested that organisations alternate between periods of calm and crisis, with each crisis presaging change to another form. This is supported by Lewin's model, which gives us a generalised process of putting change into effect. Unfreezing makes change possible and, at the end, refreezing confirms the new pattern.

Lewin also gave us the field theory of change. It will occur when the change drivers are more powerful than the restraining forces. At either the planning or implementation stages, managers can usefully use Lewin's model to assess possibilities and work out ways of combatting resistance. There are many causes and symptoms of resistance. Fundamental are people's uncertainty, perceptions, emotions and values. Sensitive understanding and handling of these issues are skills in the management of change.

Many managers rely on communication and blame its failure when resistance does not subside. Yet Kotter and Schlesinger show that other tactics can be appropriate, depending on circumstances. Questions of what to change, by how much and in what time span are important here.

The chapter was completed with two examples of change approaches that have received much attention. Neither OD nor BPR is a technique. Both are umbrellas for a range of interventions to be used singly or in combination. They enable us to contrast the soft and hard approaches to change management, for their philosophical bases differ. OD is an extension of the human relations school. Supporters place people at the heart of organisations and argue that long-term development of the people subsystem will build the most effective whole. Foci are attitudes, perception, expectations and behaviour. The humanistic feel of OD can be seen in the way practitioners and researchers are often content to evaluate interventions from the perspective of the participants themselves. BPR, on the other hand, is at the other end of the spectrum, at least according to its more exuberant advocates. We have shown, however, that in practice it marks less of a revolution and more another advance in the struggle to take a holistic approach. The fusion of sociotechnical systems thinking and information systems capability accounts for whatever permanent gains are going to be made from its introduction.

Whether we like it or not, change occurs and we must adapt to survive. As Nicholson put it,

> The riskiest thing of all is the no-change option. If you change, you may get it right, you may not get it right. If you don't change, that is bound to be wrong. A simple rule of thumb is that if it was working for you five years ago, whatever it is, assume that it can't be today, and certainly won't be tomorrow.[44]

> **Quick check up** *Can you ...*
>
> - Name the five steps of Greiner's growth model;
> - Define performance gap;
> - Sketch the change typology of Nadler and Tushman;
> - List Hultman's four factors that sum up someone's state of mind faced with change;
> - Summarise force field analysis;
> - Give six tactics for overcoming resistance;
> - Specify the five subsystems of Kast and Rosenzweig's general systems model;
> - Define OD;
> - Identify the steps of Lewin's change framework;
> - Name five OD techniques for the 'people' subsystem;
> - State three roots of BPR failure, according to Mumford and Hendricks.

Questions

Chapter review

14.1 What events stimulate organisational change? Classify these under the categories provided by Nadler and Tushman.

14.2 Summarise, using a *rich picture* or otherwise, the ways in which managers can understand the forces restraining change in an organisation.

14.3 What tactics are available to a manager contemplating changing some aspect of the organisation? Give examples of the circumstances when each may be most appropriate.

14.4 Compare OD and BPR as means of carrying out change. Identify the strengths and weaknesses of each and relate them to situations in which they might be used.

Application

14.5 Carry out a force-field analysis of the Glaxo Wellcome case. Do you agree with the assertion that, when it comes to change, R&D is likely to be a special case?

Investigation

14.6 Koch wrote a guide for new bosses to cover their first 100 days.[45] Based on the material in this chapter, what guidance could you offer to a new leader you can identify? You might choose anyone from production manager to parish priest or Prime Minister to Pope.

14.7 Do you think it is right for employees to resist change? Examine this question by a practical investigation, either based on reports of a dispute or by interviews.

Reengineering the Royal[46]

The Leicester Royal Infirmary is one of the United Kingdom's largest teaching hospitals. In 1995 its 4200 staff served 360 000 outpatients, 57 000 in-patients and 115 000 in accident and emergency. Under the semi-independent status of a health trust, the hospital wants to become the nation's best. Radical change is difficult because: patients present a huge variety of demands; process responses to demands are fragmented; centres of power in hospitals are not well represented within formal structures; autonomy to make changes is limited by the government; and career structures are controlled by national conventions and agreements.

In spite of the constraints, managers decided to embark on a radical rethink. Conversion to Trust status was a stimulus and the hospital was selected as a pilot site for the national 'whole hospital reengineering' programme. This looked to redesign for bringing about huge improvements in care, teaching and research. BPR champion Michael Hammer acted as unpaid adviser.

The programme started in September 1992 with five projects in outpatients' services. Of these, three looked for improvements without fundamental change to system design. Yet the cumbersome bureaucratic processes were what needed attention and the projects were unsuccessful. Dramatic gains, however, came from the two investigations that redesigned processes from scratch. Managers learned that only fundamental redesign of services across the hospital would cause significant improvements.

Since the initial studies, some 50 staff, drawn from the 'best and brightest' have been seconded to BPR teams. The normal period lies between six and nine months while their former work is covered by other departments. The chief executive devotes 40 per cent of his time to BPR. Patients are involved, both in helping to redesign processes and, through a Patients' Council, assessing the quality of the changes from a patient's point of view. New

processes are, therefore, rigorously evaluated before implementation.

Within two years all the main healthcare processes were redesigned. Themes selected included: 'entry', 'visit' and 'stay' of patients; clinical support functions such as 'medication' and 'diagnostic testing'; and operations management functions such as 'distribution' and 'stock management'. The results show great improvements in performance.

In an early study of the neurology department, the aim was to achieve 'one-stop visits' which would carry out all tests and provide results without the patient having to return. The changes enabled procedures to be completed in five hours, as opposed to eight weeks, and cut administrative costs by 40 per cent. Supply time for hearing aids, from first notification of hearing loss to final fitting was cut from a year to four weeks. Routine outpatient tests produce results in 40 minutes instead of 79 hours. Admission times for emergency patients were reduced by 70 per cent. Some groups of in-patients now spend half the previous time in hospital. Annual savings in waiting times for in-patients amount to 300 years.

Hospital managers have always faced the problem of resolving, with professional bodies, who carries responsibility for standards and conduct. Reengineering challenged the relative certainty of traditional hierarchies with their accepted methods of control. It emphasised new roles in team work. The first trial was set in the musculo-skeletal process. Teams are drawn from disciplines such as the operating theatre, occupational therapy, physiotherapy and rehabilitation. Seven staff and four managers each spent three and a half hours working with a facilitator. The idea was to classify work into seven categories, as in Exhibit 14.11. The method used colours, the *Workset palette*, to identify the types of work each person thought they should be doing and emphasise differences between managers' and job-holders' perceptions. The colours provided a vivid metaphor for

Exhibit 14.11 Workset palette used to clarify roles

Label	Type of work	Example
Blue	Must be done by the person in a prescribed way to a clear standard.	Calibration of diagnostic equipment.
Yellow	Outcomes are personal duty; detailed means undefined.	Ensure that patients are informed of process.
Green	Adaptable according to the reactions and needs of others.	Helping team members when they are busy.
Orange	Shared responsibility for results.	Co-ordinating outpatient schedules.
Grey	Incidental to the job.	Filling in for another department.
White	Making improvements beyond the current formal duties.	Monitoring performance to suggest changes.
Purple	Job holder's presence required but leads to nothing useful.	Going to large meetings.

discussion. For instance: it was found that different team leaders discharged their jobs in different ways; the group could check that all blue work was allocated to someone, leaving nothing to chance; and members with affinity for some types of work could be steered towards it, thus increasing job satisfaction.

Patient groups and professional bodies have been very supportive of the changes and the hospital won the HP Golden Helix Award for the best healthcare initiative in Europe. Managers have learnt that excellence without basic redesign of operational processes is not possible and commitment from senior staff is vital. Change is difficult in an organisation that runs continuously. The question of managing today while inventing tomorrow needs to be covered.

Questions

1 Explain the reasons for the claim made in the case that radical change is especially difficult in a National Health Service hospital.

2 Carry out a stakeholder analysis of the Leicester Royal Infirmary, bearing in mind that it is a teaching hospital. What impact might stakeholders have on changes to patient care processes such as those described here?

3 If you were advising the chief executive of The Leicester Royal Infirmary on a force-field analysis, what issues would you raise?

4 The programme used both BPR and OD techniques. As the case is described, would you agree that the programme was successful in sociotechnical systems terms?

Bibliography Specialist books on managing change include Burnes, Bernard (1996) *Managing Change,* Second edition, London: Financial Times Pitman Publishing, which contains alternative approaches, such as action learning, and case studies of Nissan, Rover, Vickers and Volvo. For book length treatments of specific approaches, try: Cummings, Thomas G. and Huse, Edgar F. (1989) *Organization Development and Change,* St Paul, Minn.: West Publishing Company; and Hammer and Champy or Davenport, T. H. (1993) *Process Innovation: Reengineering work through information technology,* Boston, Mass.: Harvard Business School Press.

References

1. Cookson, Clive (1995) 'New formula for the chemistry set: The most important element in the Glaxo Wellcome merger has fallen into place with a new structure for R&D', *Financial Times,* 9 November, 25; Green, Daniel (1997) '"On track" to growth objectives', *Financial Times,* 3 May; Glaxo Wellcome *Annual Report 1996*; see also www.glaxowellcome.co.uk
2. KPMG (1996) *Managing Change Survey,* KPMG, Canada; also at ftp.kpmg.ca/ pub/hr/surveys/change.pdf
3. Greiner, Larry E. (1972) 'Evolution and revolution as organisations grow', *Harvard Business Review,* **50** (**4**), 37–46.
4. Based on data from: Barclays de Zoete Wedd (1997) *Glaxo Wellcome – High growth/low growth – which is right?* London: BZW, 2 April.
5. Kotter, John P. (1996) 'Kill complacency ... (excerpt from "Leading Change")', *Fortune,* **134** (**3**), 5 August, 168–70.
6. Parkinson, C. Northcote (1957) *Parkinson's Law or the Pursuit of Progress,* London: John Murray, 95.
7. Nadler, David A. and Tushman, Michael L. (1990) 'Beyond the charismatic leader: Leadership and organisational change', *California Management Review,* **32** (**2**); *idem* authors (1989) 'Organizational frame bending: Principles for managing reorientation', *Academy of Management Executive,* **3** (**3**), August, 194–204.
8. Nicholson, Nigel and West Michael (1988) *Managerial Job Change,* Cambridge: Cambridge University Press, 5.
9. Furnham, Adrian (1995) 'Innovate and be damned', *Financial Times,* 7 September, 11.
10. Hultman, Kenneth E. (1995) 'Scaling the wall of resistance', *Training & Development,* **49** (**10**), October, 15–18.
11. Gray, Jeremy (1997) 'Daimler-Benz to profit by change', *The European,* 23 January, 15; see also www.daimler-benz.com/index_e.htm
12. Lewin, Kurt (1951) *Field Theory in Social Science: Selected theoretical papers,* New York: Harper.
13. KPMG (1996) *op. cit.,* 6.
14. Kotter, John P. and Schlesinger, Leonard A. (1979) 'Choosing strategies for change', *Harvard Business Review,* **57**, March–April, 106–14.
15. 'P.K.' (1997) 'Air France: division syndicale' *Le Figaro: économie,* 25 May, 1.
16. Hsieh, Tsun-Yan and Bear, Stephen (1996) 'The first 100 days', *Management Decision,* **34** (**5**), September, 30–1.
17. KPMG (1996) *op. cit.,* 5.
18. McCabe, Darren (1996) 'The best laid schemes o' TQM strategy, politics and power', *Industrial Relations Journal,* **27** (**1**), March, 28–38.
19. Kast, F.E. and Rosenzweig, J.E.(1974) *Organisation and Management,* Second edition, Tokyo: McGraw-Hill Kogakusha, 112.

20. Dawson, Patrick (1994) 'Total Quality Management' in Storey, John (ed.) *New Wave Manufacturing Strategies*, London: Paul Chapman, 103–21.

21. KPMG (1996) *op. cit.*, 3.

22. Burnes, Bernard (1996) *Managing Change: A strategic approach to Organisational Dynamics*, Second edition, London: Financial Times Pitman Publishing, 178–9.

23. Vecchio, Robert (1995) *Organizational Behaviour*, Third edition, Fort Worth, Tex.: The Dryden Press, 659.

24. French, W.I. and Bell, C.H. (1995) *Organization Development: Behavioural science interventions for organization improvement*, Fifth edition, Englewood Cliffs, NJ: Prentice Hall, 28.

25. Burke, W. Warner (1987) *Organization Development: A normative view*, Reading, Mass.: Addison-Wesley, 9.

26. Beer, Michael (1980) *Organization Change and Development: A systems view*, Glenview, Ill: Scott Foresman.

27. Haasen, Adolf (1996) 'Opel Eisenach GMBH – Creating a high-productivity workplace', *Organisation Dynamics*, Spring, 80–5.

28. Dearden, Lorraine, Machin, Stephen, Reed, Howard and Wilkinson, David (1997) *Labour Turnover and Work-Related Training*, London: Institute of Fiscal Studies; see also www1.ifs.org.uk

29. Burke, W. Warner, Clark, Lawrence P. and Koopman, Cheryl (1984) 'Improve your OD project's chances of success', *Training and Development Journal*, **38**, September, 62–8.

30. French and Bell (1995) *op. cit.*

31. Vecchio (1995) *op. cit.*, 664–8.

32. Golembiewski, R.T., Billingsley, K. and Yeager, S. (1976) 'Measuring change and persistence in human affairs: Types of change generated by OD designs', *Journal of Applied Behavioural Science*, **12**, 133–57; Thompson, Richard C. and Hunt, James G. (1996) 'Inside the black box of Alpha, Beta and Gamma change: using a cognitive-processing model to assess attitude structure', *Academy of Management Review*, **21** (**3**), July, 655–90.

33. Porras, J.I. and Berg, P.O. (1978) 'The impact of organisational development', *Academy of Management Review*, **3**, 248–66.

34. Vecchio (1995) *op. cit.*, 670.

35. Hammer, Michael and Champy, James (1993) *Reengineering the Corporation: A manifesto for business revolution*, London: Nicholas Brearley.

36. Hammer, Michael (1990) 'Reengineering work: Don't automate, obliterate', *Harvard Business Review*, **68**, 104–12.

37. Hammer, M. and Stanton, S. (1994) 'No need for excuses', *Financial Times*, 5 October, 20.

38. Crainer, Stuart (1996) *Key Management Ideas*, London: Financial Times Pitman Publishing, 155.

39. Willcocks, L. (1995) 'Does IT-enabled Business Process Reengineering pay off? Recent findings', Working Paper RDP95/4, Templeton College, Oxford: Oxford Institute of Management.

40. Mumford, Enid and Hendricks, Rick (1996) 'Business process reengineering RIP', *People Management*, 2 May, 22–9.

41. Lumb, Richard (1996) 'Case for the defence: 1 – Not a fad, not a failure', *People Management*, 2 May, 26.

42. Oram, Mike (1996) 'Case for the defence: 2 – Five stars guide the way forward', *People Management*, 2 May, 29.

43. Peltu, Malcolm; Clegg, Chris and Sell, Reg (1996) 'Business Process Re-engineering: The human issues', Proceeding of Forum at ESRC Business Processes Resource Centre, University of Warwick, 30 April; *see* bprc.warwick.ac.uk/forum4.html

44. Nicholson, John (1996) 'Thriving on change', *Making Sense of Management*, Programme 5, BBC1 Television, 3 November.
45. Koch, Richard (1994) *The Successful Boss's First 100 Days*, London: Financial Times Pitman Publishing.
46. Bevan, H. (1996) 'Managing today while creating tomorrow: The paradox of a reengineering journey', Working Paper HWP 9630, Henley Management Group; Belbin, Meredith; Watson, Barrie and West, Cindy (1997) 'True colours', *People Management*, 6 March, 36–41.

15

Human resource management

Chapter objectives

When you have finished studying this chapter, you should be able to:

- define, and describe the role of, human resource management and explain how it fits into the whole organisation;
- distinguish between hard and soft approaches to HRM, outlining the ideologies on which they are based;
- outline the nature and purpose of human resource planning, showing how it links with recruitment and selection to satisfy the organisation's staff needs;
- explain the purpose of performance appraisal and how it leads on to training and development;
- compare the training and development approaches to the extension of people's talents;
- summarise the design and purpose of different pay schemes, suggesting circumstances where they may be applied;
- demonstrate changing attitudes towards involvement in employee welfare;
- review how employee relations policy has changed in recent years;
- clarify four critical questions facing managers with HR responsibilities: cultural differences; ethics of HRM practice; special issues within small and medium enterprises and equal opportunities.

Scheme for skills at the Skipton[1]

Founded in 1854, the Skipton Building Society was, by 1996, the fourteenth largest in the United Kingdom. From the head office in the small country town from which it takes its name, the Society faced increased market competition and more stringent control by national bodies set up to oversee financial institutions. To prosper while maintaining continuity, the society decided upon several concentric growth strategies, illustrated by the following examples from 1996. To broaden its customer base, the Skipton bought Britannic Assurance's mortgage portfolio and made a deal to sell mortgages through the 800 estate agents' offices owned by Winterthur Life. A controlling stake in southern estate agency Connells further extended geographic cover. Taking a majority stake in the Dealwise share-dealing service signalled entry into stockbroking. An agreement with GA Life, the life insurance company, enabled the society to combine a savings account with a portfolio bond.

Such growth meant that all staff needed greater knowledge of financial products combined with enhanced selling and administrative skills. Growth exacerbated both the problems of skill shortage in the Skipton area and succession difficulties in some key managerial roles.

To support change, the Skipton decided in 1993 to augment its investment in the development of its people. Aided by consultants, the society selected the key management characteristics critical to achieving business goals. These were placed in three categories: interpersonal skills; thinking skills; and energies, including adaptability and personal effectiveness. Focusing at first on 40 head office managers, the human resources team, again advised by consultants, devised a development centre programme to measure managers' skills. Tests and exercises included: occupational personality questionnaires, to assess each individual's self-perception; group discussions; presentations; in-tray studies; ability tests; and structured interviews. The process was so thorough that only six managers could work through the development centre at once. Since four were run each year, the number of managers was constrained.

At the outset, it was made clear that attendance was voluntary without hidden agendas. Although some successful managers did not take part, many found the process helpful in enhancing performance and increasing the chance of promotion. A member of the human resources team gave full feedback to each participant. Then, in cooperation with the line manager, a personal development plan was agreed. The plan was a range of activities addressing the areas selected for development. Examples have included: formal courses; one week job-swaps; longer secondments to other parts of the organisation; and project work. Group workshops enabled participants to share experiences, build relationships and motivate those falling behind. A resource centre holds management development material. Formal courses featured in many plans. Beyond the immediate management group, many staff studied for professional qualifications.

A danger in small, stable organisations is limited opportunity. Advancement is only to fill 'dead men's shoes'. In spite of its moderate size, the Society encourages career mobility by advertising all vacancies internally. Sickness and maternity leave offer opportunities for secondments, letting staff take on senior roles outside their normal discipline. In this way, the flatter organisation structure has offered enhanced career mobility, in contrast to the experience of many organisations. Job grading structures have been simplified to four broad bands. This again aids switching among roles.

Practical ways to improve the business have been sought through the 'Eureka' suggestions scheme, which offers rewards for good ideas. Business process reengineering has been used to reexamine many traditional tasks and managers are expected to contribute to teams working on such projects.

Senior management commitment has been essential to the development programme. They look to sustain commitment and opportunity through a policy of internal appointments. This will reinforce the friendly and informal culture that prevails. Of the 50 headquarters managers passing through the development centre, only one has resigned. Individuals recognise the advantages of a personal development plan. Liz Stephens had been working on hers for two years before being promoted to manager level. She cited the extra confidence and recognition gained in the process as contributors to her advancement. In a survey, 84 per cent of staff agreed that the Skipton Building Society cared about their development.

Introduction

The Skipton Building Society believes that its prospects depend mostly on its people. Following the philosophy of organisation development explained in Chapter 14, the society sees the best way to change is to encourage staff to develop themselves in preparation for the needs of the changing world of financial institutions. No longer able to offer people 'jobs for life', it recognises that preparing them for the future is critical in terms of recruitment and retention of the best. Meanwhile, it will provide a pool of talent and experience from which the next generation of senior managers can be drawn.

Managing the development of people, commonly known as *human resource management*, involves many practices mentioned in the case study. We have planning, recruitment, appraisal, pay assessment and training and development. These core activities of most HRM functions will be described in the first part of this chapter. As a context for HRM practice, however, there are problems and issues about which there are questions and doubts. Four of these take up the major themes of this book: ethics, quality, international contexts and the practice within SMEs. Human resource managers are also taxed by questions of equal opportunities and we shall illustrate these by looking at the role and rights of women in employment and management. First, however, we shall consider what HRM is.

What is human resource management?

At a deeper level than issues of practice in HRM lies the question of what it is. As we shall see later in the chapter, there are considerable variations in the way the function in seen in different parts of the world. Even within nations, however, opinions vary. Truss and colleagues[2] note two distinct descriptions of HRM, soft and hard. The difference arises from whether the emphasis in the HRM label is placed on the *human* or the *resource*. Broadly, the former, soft HRM, is related to the human relations movement, the growth of individual talent and McGregor's Theory Y (*see* Chapter 2). Hard HRM, on the other hand, is based on planning the resource in the same way as any other, fitting with the needs of the environment incorporated in the business plan, and McGregor's Theory X. A mind-map of these points and their consequences appears in Fig. 15.1.

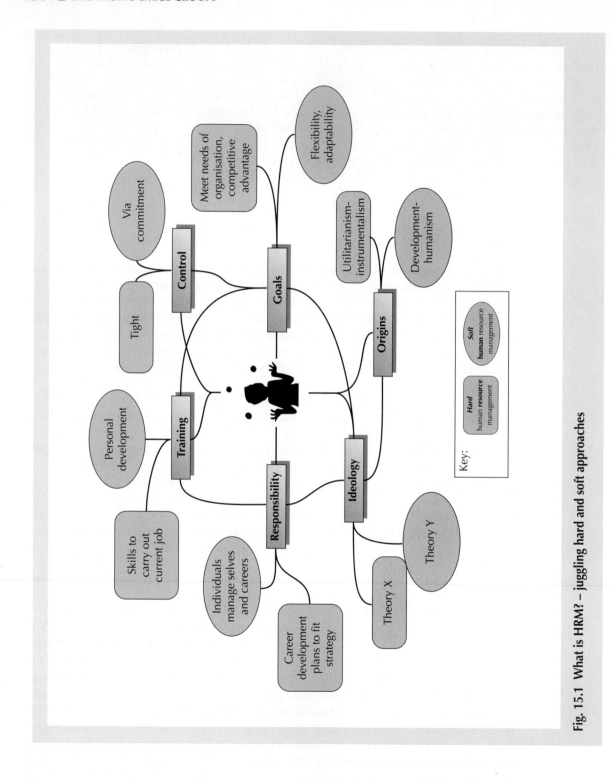

Fig. 15.1 What is HRM? – juggling hard and soft approaches

As with many management models, the hard and soft approaches can be seen as the opposite ends of a scale. Many organisations display facets of both. In an in-depth study of eight leading British companies, Truss and colleagues looked to see the extent to which one or other approach predominated. They found that many managers embraced the dual aims of the soft model, which are business development combined with personal growth. Yet this was mostly management rhetoric. Training is a good example. '[It] was taking place in the organizations, [yet] the *aim* of much of this training was not the development of the individual as an end in itself, but ensuring that individuals had the skills necessary to carry out their jobs in such a way as to improve organizational performance. One side-effect of this training could be individual development, but it was not an explicit aim.'[3] Other managers seem to reject the soft model altogether. Siebert and colleagues refer to, 'toadyish professionals ... too ready to make a distinction between developing individuals and conducting business'.[4]

The soft approach is exemplified by the so-called Harvard framework[5] in which the outcomes of HRM are:

■ *In the short term* – commitment, competence, congruence and cost-effectiveness.

■ *In the long term* – individual well-being, organisational effectiveness and societal well-being.

Note how the Harvard model envisages a positive-sum game. All interested parties, people, organisations and society can win if they take part. The hard approach sees HRM as a set of processes that link business strategy to human behaviour at work.[6] The aim is to carry out business policies in an optimal way from the organisation's point of view. It means managing:

■ personnel flows – that is recruitment, development and leaving;

■ work systems – job design as part of total process design;

■ reward systems – incorporating notions of fairness and motivation;

■ employee relations – links between the organisation and groups of staff.

The Skipton Building Society case illustrates these points. There is clearly a wish to see career development as something guided by the individuals themselves. Ideally, senior managers create opportunities both for development and for a choice of promotions. Staff choose the direction and extent of their participation. Meanwhile, the society is having to press on with strategic change. It is looking to its HRM strategy to deliver a stream of managers who can operate in the new, competitive market environment. Practice includes both self-control and harder aspects such as team bonuses matched to sales targets and performance appraisal by managers and peers. The tension is clear.

It is not easy to translate 'motherhood' statements such as, 'We totally depend on our people', into processes that can be carried out by staff in the personnel department. HR managers have to convert such aims and constraints, some of which are externally imposed, into practice. In doing so, they move from the rhetoric of the soft model to the practices presented more clearly in the hard version. In so doing, HRM moves more closely to personnel management, a term that has gone out of fashion. While HRM incorporates notions of both strategy and practice, personnel has connotations of putting business policies into effect. Although personnel is nominally out of fashion, studies show that most organisations eschew a strategic approach, concentrating more on conventional personnel practice.[7] One recent shift has been to bring responsibility away from the personnel specialist. Nowadays, many organisations have returned to the idea of line management accountability. The HRM function is there to provide specialist advice and support.

Activities of the HRM function

Taking the hard, practice-oriented view of HRM, we can use the following definition:

> *Human resource management is the creation, development and maintenance of an effective workforce, matching the requirements of the organisation and responding to the environment.*

The definition, seeing the people subsystem in the context of the whole organisation and external influences, covers the processes laid out in Fig. 15.2. The diagram expresses the three broad activities of HRM occurring in a continuous

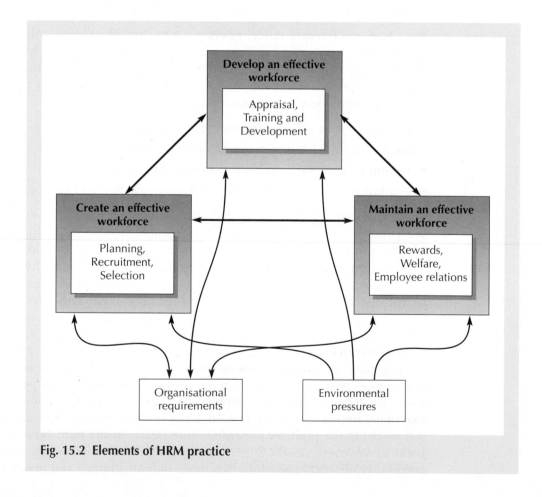

Fig. 15.2 Elements of HRM practice

cycle. Within each of the creation, development and maintenance categories there are process elements as shown. We shall begin with creating the workforce and its first element, planning.

Human resource planning

Planning focuses on the complete approach to satisfying needs for human resources. Processes such as recruitment and promotion are expensive investments, often difficult to reverse if errors are made. Hiring staff on an *ad hoc* basis puts at risk continuity and development of the whole team. A planning approach tries to counter these difficulties both through analysing current needs and anticipating future changes. Environmental or business developments can quickly lead to a mismatch between ideal and actual staffing levels. Exhibit 15.1 shows how environmental change, here in the political policy arena, can create new issues for the human resource manager.

In another example we can note how the strategy of creating external alliances demands new staff expertise. Collaborative supply relations are affecting many more firms in a wide range of industries. While there is no one way to form and maintain these alliances, clearly they involve closer and deeper relations between partners. Typically, a major purchaser, such as an automobile or consumer goods manufacturer, will reduce the number of suppliers and then engage in more detailed links with the remainder. These include vendor rating schemes, cooperation among technical staff, and more frequent auditing of processes, quality and costs. Further developments take companies into joint design and problem-solving, exchanges of staff at all levels, integration of control systems, and so on. A

Exhibit 15.1 Nuclear Electric: manpower planning under uncertain political conditions

Nuclear Electric is responsible for the construction and operation of nuclear power stations in the United Kingdom. Although it awards contracts for construction to civil engineering companies, it requires, during construction, a mix of design, supervisory and commissioning engineers of its own. When the station is complete, its needs change to operating engineers who have different skills again.

To maintain continuity of employment among engineers of various disciplines, the company used to rely on a steady construction programme. Indeed, a programme constraint was the supply of staff to put it into effect. In the late 1980s, however, it became clear that the government might not place any new orders, a policy confirmed during the following decade. Nuclear Electric had to work out how to complete its current construction programme and decide what to do with its staff once it was complete. In its analysis, the company examined the skills, age and other details of all its engineering staff. It offered severance terms to those it could no longer employ and retraining opportunities to others who could eventually become operating engineers. Since Nuclear Electric was the main employer of such experts in the country, it was not feasible to recruit new people directly through the labour market.

consultants' survey stressed, 'Working with suppliers is becoming more important ... supply of materials, products, and expertise ... represents a relatively greater proportion of the cost and lead time which are key elements in competitiveness'.[8] Yet management performance is often poor.

Collaborative relations have implications for HRM. Not only do the skills of current 'boundary spanning' staff, such as the purchasing department, have to be enhanced, but many more staff become involved in dealing with people 'outside'. We introduced the idea of new 'brokerage' roles in Chapter 12. For some, this will be the first time in their careers that they have engaged in such activity. Clearly, there are implications for training and development in the need to build a high level of trust between the parties. Moreover, there are cases where the HRM policies themselves begin to be transferred from one company to another. Marks & Spencer, for instance, has a strong HR culture and has for many years been prepared to advise its suppliers on HR practice. This goes beyond trying to ensure that suppliers conform to the same ethical standards; the more powerful and knowledgeable partner can share its expertise on the best forms of training, quality programmes or the impact of relevant new legislation. In so doing it can help each supplier to deliver what it wants, that is a reliable flow of products of the highest quality. From the supplier's point of view, however, pressure to introduce new HR policies may clash with the traditions and practices of the company and could act as a constraint on the development of the alliance.[9]

Whatever its context, the outcome of the human resource planning process is a detailed analysis of the staffing requirements for the organisation. Included in the plan will be a statement of how the gaps are to be filled. As shown by the scheme drawn up by the Skipton Building Society, the gaps may be filled by a mixture of recruitment and development of suitable personnel. Recruitment may be internal or external and will, anyhow, be followed by an appropriate amount of training.

Recruitment

The second element of creating a workforce, recruitment, means finding staff whose attributes match available jobs. Figure 15.3 sketches a simplified flow model of the recruitment and selection procedure. The first steps are to decide whether a new person is required. This means defining the requirements of the job and clarifying that it cannot be done by current employees, or removed altogether. Following this, efforts are made to ensure that sufficient candidates of appropriate calibre come forward for selection. Meanwhile, the firm must consider how the choice is to be made. For all but temporary or casual appointments, there is usually a series of filters to remove less suitable prospects until a short list is presented for the final choice. Filters may include checks on qualifications, skills and experience, physical and psychological tests and so on.

The aim of recruitment is to encourage suitable applicants to apply. Therefore, it should not look to maximise their number. Steps should be taken to filter out unsuitable people even at the initial stage of advertising. Gone are the days when 'Boy wanted. Apply within' would be regarded as adequate. Not only is there no information as to the nature of the job but the notice is clearly unfair. Recruitment, therefore, needs to be realistic and fair.

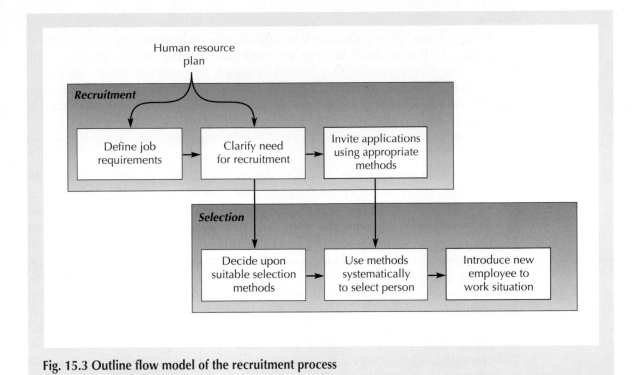

Fig. 15.3 Outline flow model of the recruitment process

Project Officer

£17055–£18180 (3 Year Contract)

The Council's Regeneration Plan provides a framework for addressing the economic and community needs of the Borough. An officer is required to help develop and implement a range of regeneration projects, working with community organisations, agencies and funding partners. You will have particular responsibility for projects in and around Okehampton and you will be responsible for the Council's efforts to promote the development and use of public transport.

You will have four years relevant experience, a good understanding of rural development issues and a proven ability to work independently in conjunction with local communities.

For an application form and job description, please contact ...

Realism

For the first point, an organisation can help itself by publishing exact information about the job. For instance, if there are attributes or qualifications that are definitely required of applicants, they should be stated. The example shown on p. 491 illustrates good practice.[10] Within a small 6 × 10 cm space, the council outlines the post and specifies both the attributes it is seeking and key terms of the contract. It is normal to expand on these in the mailing prepared for enquirers.

Fairness

Recruiting procedures must be fair. Not only are there legal requirements in many countries but many managers and organisations recognise ethical considerations too. There is not the space to explore the range of issues such as positive discrimination (or affirmative action) and how they appear in different nations. We shall confine ourselves to two common pitfalls in the United Kingdom setting. First, *direct discrimination* occurs when an organisation unlawfully interferes with the rights of a person because of race, colour, sex or religion. Apart from two exceptions, personnel practice must not use these criteria. The exceptions are: *authenticity*, for example, in acting or clothes modelling, where gender can be specified, or religious education; and *personal service*, such as childcare or home nursing. Note that, in the United Kingdom, age can be specified in recruitment. The second pitfall is more subtle. *Indirect discrimination* occurs when an organisation's behaviour has unintended consequences that restrict the rights of groups of people. In recruitment, bias can be introduced innocently, for example, through choice of language or media for advertising. At the board mill in Queensferry in the 1980s it was normal to 'ask around the shop floor' when recruiting for unskilled vacancies. This had the advantage of producing applicants for interviews who were known to current staff. They would, therefore, be appraised of what the work was like. Managers' lives were made easier by this informal process; there was little paperwork and expense, and jobs could be filled within days. The problem was that the method was indirectly discriminatory. The net was being trawled across the people whom current workers already knew. Therefore, the racial mix (or lack of it) within the plant tended to reproduce itself, although it no longer matched that of the town.

■ Selection

Selection completes the stage of creation of the workforce. It involves choosing new employees from among the pool recruited. Since the validity of selection methods is, at best, moderate, good practice means a combination is used to improve the chances of success. A well-designed application form presents candidate information in a way that allows unsuitable ones to be eliminated. For

---

Validity refers to how closely the results of a selection test match a person's later job performance.

instance, people can be rejected because they are unqualified, cannot start immediately or simply do not complete the form. A clear form also helps where
applicants have to be ranked. In times of high unemployment, it is common to
hear from many people who satisfy the basic criteria. Ranking should be done
with care to avoid indirect discrimination. If, for example, closeness to the place of
work is used, racial bias may be introduced.

Interview

The interview is the most widely used technique and sometimes the only one. It is
important to avoid the defects of the *unstructured* interview. Here, there is neither a
prepared schedule nor systematic scoring. Its flexibility can be an advantage but also
a major weakness. The snag is that many managers believe they are good interviewers and, lacking systematic responses to results, rely heavily on the process itself.
The validity of unstructured interviews is low. They can stray into discussion of irrelevant or personal issues that, meeting the prejudices of the interviewer, lead to poor
decisions. In challenges to selection bias that have been brought under equal opportunities legislation, it has been difficult to defend the practice.

To use the interview as effectively as possible, a plan should be made ahead of
time. In the *structured* interview, a series of job-related questions is asked of all
candidates. Exhibit 15.2 shows four categories of information with examples from
a supervisory job. Some of this data could be elicited before the interview but it
may be useful to check or ask for clarification. The four categories of Exhibit 15.2
should not be regarded as definitive. In the selection of apprentices or young graduates, an organisation may be as concerned with potential as with current abilities.
In such cases, qualifications and references will be important and the interviewer
may probe attitudes to learning.

Although the structured interview may seem to have advantages, its rigidity
restricts contact among participants. As Chapter 18 shows, conversation involves
parties in two-way flows, alternately speaking and listening as the interaction
unfolds. This is effective use of the face-to-face channel. A good interviewer,
therefore, uses some structure, but must allow flexibility for fruitful communication.

Having a panel of interviewers, although expensive, helps in removing personal
bias. In any case the structured interview provides a formal basis for recording
results that can be referred to if the outcomes are challenged later.

Selection tests

While structuring improves the interview validity, they remain far from perfect.
This has stimulated the search for other forms of selection. Tests include written
assignments and simulation exercises. The former can be used to assess intelligence, aptitude, attitudes and personality. Cooper, Baker and Maddocks note
marked increase in the use of occupational tests in the United Kingdom.[11] This has
arisen from their apparent reliability and ease of use. Yet there are dangers of
abuse of these psychometric measurement techniques. Questions have been raised

---

Exhibit 15.2 Structured interview schedule

Question category	Information sought	Example from machine shop supervisor
Situational	The applicant's ability to handle the range of challenges met on the job.	What would you do if you saw an employee wrongly removing a machine guard?
Job knowledge	The applicant's knowledge of practical, technical, legal, etc. aspects of the job.	Can you explain to me the various grades of tungsten carbide?
Job simulation	The applicant's ability to carry out critical aspects of the job.	What instructions would you give if you were asked to arrange for … to be done?
Personal requirements	The applicant's ability to fit the job needs such as hours, travel, location and so on.	Are you willing to work nights if asked to do so?

---

concerning the obligation of testers to the test takers. Many of the latter have been reported as unhappy with the experience. In the United States, legal challenges have been brought over the intrusiveness and relevance of some tests. Ethical standards should ensure: that candidates are treated fairly and with dignity; that staff are competent to apply the tests and give feedback on results; and that the tests are valid for selection.

McHenry takes up the last point.[12] Noting the rise in use over 20 years from 10 to 75 per cent of companies in the United Kingdom, he fears that many tests in use are ineffective and biased on gender and cultural grounds. Many have been imported from the United States and calibrated using norms established there many years ago. For instance, one test has the statement, 'I very much like hunting'. This is answered true by 70 per cent of American men but only 10 per cent of British. There are marked differences among other nations. Gender biases are shown by statements such as, 'I think I would make a good leader of people'. Does the fact that men say 'Yes' twice as often as women mean that they are twice as likely to be good leaders? Or are women more modest about their abilities? Anyhow, should men and women be compared against the same or different norms? These questions cannot be answered here but we can conclude that tests need to be used with great care by professionally competent people.

Furnham notes widespread scepticism among managers. The supply of consultants, and rising demand among HR professionals anxious to look clever, have stimulated the growth of psychometric testing. Many studies have examined the validity of links between results and job performance. This is especially difficult in long-term predictions as when a firm is recruiting people for managerial careers. What is the best predictor of potential? Furnham quotes one study that examined middle-aged, middle ranking managers:

> *The list of factors thought to be relevant was long: which school they went to; position in the family; age of first mortgage; sport preferences, etc. In fact, this study found that for those middle-aged Britons the best predictor of managerial success was at what age they first travelled abroad: the younger the better.*[13]

The explanation for this odd result lies in suggesting that, in the days when travel was more expensive and difficult, it was the adventurous and curious parents who took their children overseas. Possibly, these parental characteristics lead to children's success later in life. The story, however, illustrates the difficulty of validation. The link only emerged in retrospect and could hardly have been predicted. Moreover, it is a statement about the past; easier travel and less xenophobia surely make the result inapplicable to the future.

Notwithstanding the difficulties, the hope of finding a few carefully researched questions that will predict good job performance is not as far fetched as it may sound. Telephone interviewing is usual in the catering and leisure industries where large numbers of seasonal workers have to be recruited quickly. Exhibit 15.3 explains how Lego was helped by Gallup to staff its new theme park.[14]

Exhibit 15.3 Picking perfect people

Before opening its theme park at Windsor in early 1996, Lego had to choose 600 seasonal staff from 5000 applications. It is common in such circumstances to invite candidates to open days which include short interviews in groups of three or so. This is both expensive and ineffective. Advised by the Gallup Organisation, 12 of Lego's staff were trained to conduct telephone interviews to screen the applicants. Gallup has worked for 30 years on relating interviewee's responses to the qualities judged to make a difference to customers. According to Vernon Pryce, managing consultant for Gallup, people feel they can bluff through many questions. Asked about working with children, they will reply that, of course, they are happy. Yet Gallup asks a very specific question. 'People who have a real yearning to work with children, successfully, responsibly, on a sustained basis over ten hours will answer that question very very differently from someone who does not have that affinity,' explained Pryce. Lego was satisfied that its more rigorous screening produced a workforce that was well matched to the work and showed lower labour turnover than expected.

Assessment centres

Assessment centres are commonly used for selecting managers and higher grade technical personnel. The curious name refers to the place where candidates are assembled, sometimes for several days. They are tested and engage in social exchanges with potential colleagues and superiors. The tests involve a series of managerial simulations, such as in-basket exercises, role plays and group tasks, as well as psychometric tests and interviews. A panel of trained assessors observes how each candidate makes decisions as well as their interpersonal and communication skills. Beyond selection, variants on assessment centres can be used for appraisal and promotion. In the opening case, The Skipton Building Society used a centre to discover its managers' development needs.

Clearly, as with all HRM practices, recruitment and selection must be done with care. Not only is there a question of cost of failure in the light of a bad decision but the process builds an implicit contract between organisation and candidate. People agree to go through selection procedures and, in return, expect them to be valid and fair. It is good practice to explain the procedure to candidates before it starts.

Nowhere are the costs of recruitment and selection highlighted more clearly than among military pilots. It is impossible to know before training whether a person will succeed. The problem for the Royal Air Force is to minimise wastage while maintaining an adequate supply of pilots of the right standard. Since training involves considerable personal investment, the RAF ensures that those who do not make the grade are directed to other valuable roles. Exhibit 15.4 traces the process.[15]

Performance appraisal

We now move on to consider staff development. As shown in Fig. 15.2, this has two elements, appraisal and training and development. Performance appraisal means evaluating people in their jobs to make reasoned personnel decisions. These cover pay, promotion, training and development, counselling and human resource planning. Although formal systems are being extended to cover more managers and supervisors, they are little used for junior staff from clerical to shop floor workers. In these cases, assessment tends to be based on direct measures such as output and quality, often backed up by a bonus scheme.

Appraisal interviews form the cornerstone of many formal systems. These raise many of the questions of fairness and consistency explained above. Interviews need, therefore, to be set in a framework of planning, training and control. Planning an effective and equitable system means answering the following questions:

■ *What is the purpose of the appraisal scheme?*
  Appraisal is usually seen as much more than a manager's assessment of a person's progress. In encouraging an exchange, there are opportunities to improve relationships, share problems and therefore enhance the performance of the team. Sometimes, appraisal results are used for assessing pay increases although such practice cuts across the ideal of frank discussion.

Exhibit 15.4 Integrated selection and training in the RAF

The Royal Air Force needs to maintain a planned ratio of pilots to aircraft. Pilots both fly and act as officers; they must have appropriate skills and be leaders of others. Initial selection for this demanding role is based on tests and interviews. All who pass move on to courses of initial officer training and basic flying. Then there are three streams: Fast Jet; Multi-Engine; or Helicopter. The Fast Jet role is the most demanding. These trainees move on to Advanced Training and then Operations Conversion. Each stage builds up the accumulated investment in the pilot, who can fail at any point. The cost of training one fast jet pilot is estimated at £1.5 million.

■ *Who should be appraised?*
While extending appraisal to all staff helps to break down barriers, it is often seen as impractical to cover more than managers and supervisors.

■ *Who should appraise?*
Immediate managers are usually involved although the inclusion of more senior people could improve communications and spread a sense of fairness. Also advocated is all-round appraisal, known as '360 degree feedback', under which responses are gathered from those who depend on a person's performance. These include colleagues at the same level, subordinates and even suppliers and customers. One sample showed the use of 360 degree appraisal in fewer than half of large United Kingdom companies, although the number was growing.[16] Advocates point to, for instance, differences between perceptions of others and how we perceive ourselves. Men tend to overrate themselves in self-appraisal whereas women tend to the opposite. Since the most successful people have a self-image close to how they are seen by others, closing the gap should be good development. Critics, however, point to the expense of the method and the stress caused in a few companies when it is linked to pay.

■ *What training and preparation do appraisers need?*
Training and plans are required to ensure consistency among all appraisers. For example, three general orientations towards assessment have been identified. These are based on traits, outcomes and behaviour. Although widely used, trait-orientated appraisal is the weakest and most susceptible to prejudice. Concentrating on personality traits, such as charm, stated ambition or initiative, is hardly connected with job outcomes. Outcome-orientated appraisal examines how objectives were set and achieved. While having the appearance of rationality, this approach has the disadvantage of referring to individual goals thus making comparison among staff difficult. Using this approach for pay review is especially problematic. Behaviour-orientated appraisal concentrates on behaviour relevant to the job. Its use is, in principle, the most effective. Yet the establishment of reliable dimensions is time consuming and is only likely to be worthwhile in large organisations with many similar jobs.[17]

■ *When should appraisals be conducted?*
Although, as we note in Chapter 16, speedy feedback is an important element of motivation, annual appraisals are the most common. This frequency enables and encourages managers to conduct the process thoroughly. Intervals should, however, match the nature of the organisation, the scheme and the people involved. There may be more than one session per year in dynamic situations or for staff who are inexperienced, have been recently appointed, or have shown inadequate performance.

■ *Who sees the results?*
Open reporting, that is sharing results openly, may inhibit frank discussion between boss and subordinate. On the other hand, too closed a system may reduce confidence of participants in its fairness. It is normal, therefore, to share reports among appraisee, appraiser, appraiser's manager and an independent monitor whose role is to assess how the scheme is working. Appraisees are often given the opportunity to read the report before completion and add comments before signing.

■ *What about monitoring?*

Monitoring occurs at both the detailed and broad levels. Agreements for change made between boss and subordinate are recorded and followed up in 'action plans' before the next round. Examples include training opportunities or changes to the way work is carried out. More broadly, the independent monitor has to check that practice is consistent, fair and lawful.

Training and development

Identification of training and development needs is one outcome of appraisal. Indeed, for the 'soft' HRM organisations committed to organisation development, it will be seen as the most important. Training is *the provision of guided experience to change employee behaviour, attitudes or opinions.* According to Mullins, its benefits are as follows:

■ greater confidence, commitment and motivation of staff;

■ recognition and greater responsibility parallelled by improvements in pay;

■ feelings of personal satisfaction and achievement with enhanced career prospects; and

■ improved availability and quality of staff.[18]

To this list we can add, from the trainee's point of view, enhanced job mobility.

Implied within the definition of training is the notion that change is to be related to the job. Planning a training programme, therefore, starts with a comparison between the attributes needed to do the job effectively and those already possessed by the employee. This *training needs analysis* identifies specific gaps. In turn, the training plan is designed to fill them.

In principle, therefore, each trainee is different. Each needs an individualised plan. Managers then face the problem of supplying a bespoke service to each person within budget constraints. In practice, a compromise is reached in which employees are given standardised training packages in spite of their not needing every element of them. While wasting some resources this may be the most efficient method of supply. Worse occurs when training is given to staff as a sort of reward in spite of their not needing it at all. Lloyds Bank wasted 40 per cent of its effort largely because individuals received it when it was thought to be 'their turn'.[19] Experienced trainers find that up to 10 per cent of clients on external courses register at the first session but attend few of the following activities. They see the events as informal holidays in a comfortable location.

Training takes place either at the workplace, *on-the-job training,* or away from it, *off-the-job training.* The advantages and disadvantages are summarised in Exhibit 15.5. Off-the-job methods are often criticised because of the difficulty of bringing back learning directly into the workplace. Unless the training is planned in parallel to other changes, there is a risk of immediately unlearning the ideas and skills that have been given. A combination of on- and off-the-job modes should ensure retention and optimise the application of new skills. For this to happen, the training should:

■ occur in settings similar to the job;

■ enlarge the trainee's experience;

Exhibit 15.5 Comparison between on-the-job and off-the-job training

	Advantages	*Disadvantages*
On-the-job training	Learning directly applicable. May not need specialised trainers. Trainee contributes to output. Cheap.	May offer only narrow experience. Bad habits passed to the trainee. Trainee may inhibit productivity.
Off-the-job training	Suitable for tasks not currently practised. Vital when trainees' errors may risk disaster or be expensive. Offers wider experience and practice in unusual situations. Training experience may be more readily planned and directed.	Difficult to match to individual's needs in the job setting. May need expensive development and testing if to be effective. Expensive to operate. Attendance at special training. centres used to reward performance, not to meet need.

- offer challenges not normally encountered by the trainee;
- enable learning of underlying concepts rather than 'recipe following';
- be offered when the employee can best appreciate and use the programme's benefits;
- use a tempo suited to the employee's rate of learning and capacity for reflection.

For example, in training a clerk in the use of new software, off-the-job training may be advisable so it can be delivered by experts without interruption. A set of modules can teach procedures, explain the reasons for them and allow the participant to practise. As the programme advances it may switch to the work situation, giving the trainee access to the software for live use. Other instances of off-the-job training are simulators for airline pilots. Compare these with on-the-job practice for car drivers. In the former, much has to be done before pilots can take over a real aircraft. In the latter, most people come to the driving school knowing well the context of the task. The learner has to rehearse a set of skills that have to be combined and made intuitive before being able to pass the test.

Cultural differences in training

Designing training programmes from job-based analysis can lead to narrow prescriptions if the short-term behavioural approach is overemphasised. For example, bank trainees are taught all the processes that working in a branch entails. Yet the service function must go further than simply counting cash or checking customers' accounts. Service in banking involves relating to customers at the personal level. Generally, Western employers try to achieve this through influencing employees' *attitudes*. For example, they stress that 'the customer is always right' and being pleasant is always the best way. Training programmes may include how to handle awkward situations. Within this general framework, however, staff are encouraged to express their own personality in the way they give service. In common with other leading retail organisations, banks rely on effective selection and guided development to produce staff with appropriate interpersonal skills.[20]

Contrast this with the way service training is traditionally given in Japan. Figure 15.4 is based on one of many sketches in the training manual of the Hiroshima Sogo Bank.[21] The book features dozens of instructions on how to behave in service settings. Greetings, addressing clients, colleagues and superiors, and many other aspects of social behaviour are set out in detail. Formal social processes are, of course, much more important in Japan than in most Western countries. Therefore, employers stress *behaviour* in their training.

Limitations of training needs analysis – the development perspective

The above remarks mention that training based simply on needs analysis sets arbitrary limits on the scope and time scale of expected benefits. The wider perspective, usually called development, sees the need to enhance competences beyond those presented by the immediate job. Bergenhenegouwen and colleagues identify four levels of competence that are relevant to how people carry out their work:[22]

- *First level*
  Knowledge and skills that enable the occupation, job or task to be done properly.

- *Second level*
  Intermediate skills applicable in a wide range of job situations. These include things like social and communicative skills, general technical and vocational insights, organisational qualities and basic approaches to work situations.

- *Third level*
  Values, standards, ethics and morals of the person, the organisation and any professional group to which he or she belongs. These are learnt by the person through insights, experiences and education. They are expressed through things like a special mentality, a specific view of the world, and distinctive opinions about culture, worth and traditions. This is one's own personal and professional frame of reference.

Fig. 15.4 To pour tea, half fill each cup. Then top up in reverse order

■ *Fourth level*

Deeper-lying personal characteristics, such as groundedness, image of self, motives and the source of the enthusiasm and effort that goes into work. Hardly visible to others, these factors nevertheless strongly influence how a person acts in work situations.

The first level corresponds to the behavioural training mentioned in the Hiroshima Sogo bank example. The second is closer to the development of attitudes favoured in Western banks. The third is exemplified by professional development programmes that are less directly related to the immediate task. Much of the Skipton Building Society programme is concerned with developing managers who have a 'personal and professional service' frame of reference. The fourth, deepest level can only incidentally be affected by training programmes so that Bergenhenegouwen and colleagues recommend that such traits be looked for at the selection stage. The authors go on to question how a competence orientated development programme may be steered. In response they refer to the notion of organisational core competences and suggest that the challenge for HRM professionals is to link these to individual development.

Motorola requires all employees to complete at least 40 hours' training each year. For managers, the emphasis is on doing international business. Motorola recognises that competitive advantage, even for a high-technology firm, will flow from being able to deal in different cultures. Sales in India are expected to overtake those in the United States by 2005. It has developed new learning programmes such as an MBA spread between five business schools. Since the future is for products and markets, the key is to develop managers who can cope with whatever the future brings. Flexibility is more important than developing skills related to a defined job.[23]

Rewards

The third block of Fig. 15.2 covers the means of maintaining an effective workforce. The first of these we shall examine is the reward system. HRM staff are involved in setting up a system of payment and other benefits which combine general design principles and relate to factors within and without the organisation. Lockyer suggests the factors summarised in the systems map of Fig. 15.5.[24] Note how this is based on Fig. 14.7. Relevant issues within the organisation arise in all subsystems – goals, structure, technology and people. The diagram also identifies four key environments that the system of rewards must take into account. These are both the business and labour markets, the legal framework and influence groups such as trades unions. Finally, a pay and benefits system should be designed so that it works well. It should be efficient and internally consistent so it does not generate disputes and problems. Moreover, it should contribute to the achievement of business objectives.

Limited space means that, in the rest of this section, we shall focus on payment systems. This is not to say that other benefits are unimportant to the employee. In certain countries they are clearly more important than the term 'fringe' benefits would suggest. Costing up to 30 per cent of total labour costs, they may include payments for medical insurance and pensions and help with housing, schooling, childcare, further education and transport.

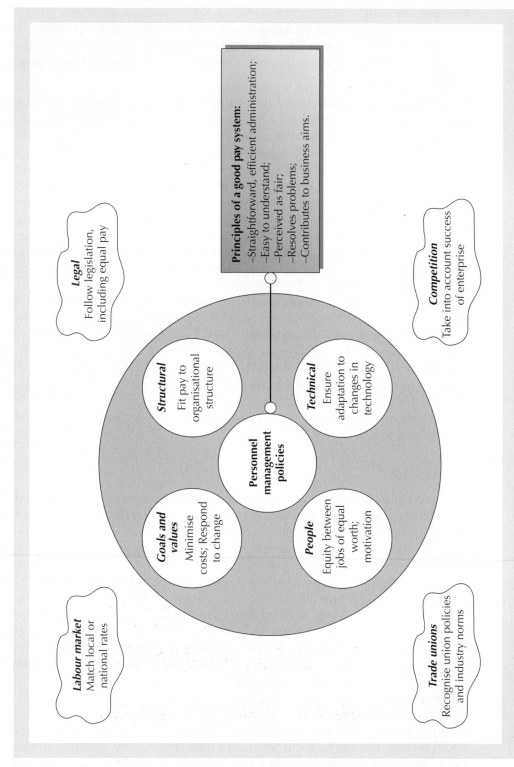

Principles of a good pay system:
–Straightforward, efficient administration;
–Easy to understand;
–Perceived as fair;
–Resolves problems;
–Contributes to business aims.

Legal
Follow legislation, including equal pay

Competition
Take into account success of enterprise

Structural
Fit pay to organisational structure

Technical
Ensure adaptation to changes in technology

Personnel management policies

Goals and values
Minimise costs; Respond to change

People
Equity between jobs of equal worth; motivation

Labour market
Match local or national rates

Trade unions
Recognise union policies and industry norms

Fig. 15.5 A good pay system fits the organisation and its environment

Lockyer also notes a shift in emphasis away from rewarding employees according to negotiated collective agreements. New pressures have arisen from the integration of HRM into business strategy, including:

- *the reduction of labour costs through more-efficient and flexible patterns of work organisation and division;*
- *the introduction of more-flexible and efficient technologies;*
- *increased control over the employee, to reduce the gap between potential and actual performance, to generate employee commitment rather than compliance;*
- *a move towards the individualisation of employment relations.*[25]

While these items can all be found in Fig. 15.5, the key point is the way the emphasis is changing. An inconsistent pattern of flexibility, individuality and expectations of commitment, combined with teamwork, cultural change and close control, has come to replace the traditional collective agreements of the past. Pay schemes are increasingly seen as a tool of management rather than a bargain between management and employees.

Fixed and variable payment schemes

The demands placed on a payment system, including efficiency, fairness, motivation, flexibility and so on, make it hardly surprising that every organisation comes up with its own formula. Conventionally, schemes have been compared according to whether pay is fixed or variable. Fixed pay schemes are the dominant form: about three quarters of United Kingdom employees are paid this way. Most of these are based on time. In other words, payment is by the hour, week or month and does not vary according to effort. In quota-based schemes, sometimes called in factories *measured day-work*, staff are paid a fixed rate when they have achieved an agreed work quota irrespective of the time taken. They operate as if they were subcontractors.

Variable pay has two broad types according to whether alterations relate to characteristics of the person, or to his or her effort. In the former, which we can call input schemes, additional rewards can be matched to length of service, skills or other behavioural factors that the company regards as important. Performance output schemes match pay to achievement of work goals. The oldest and simplest of these is piecework under which employees are paid for each item produced, the rate traditionally being set by negotiation with the supervisor or, more recently, by work-study. Piecework survives among outworkers, who again act as if they were subcontractors, and among many sales staff. In each case, success can be directly related to the person's efforts. It is unsuited to work paced by machines, such as production lines, or where there is a high degree of interdependence among members of a team.

Levels of aggregation

Another consideration in scheme design is whether each person should be treated separately or rewards should be shared among teams or, possibly, the whole organisation. This problem arises from one of the tensions mentioned above: the desire to stimulate personal effort and commitment compared with group cooperation or loyalty to the whole business. We often find a bit of both. Sometimes, weekly or monthly individual incentives are combined with annual bonuses shared by all. The annual bonus is sometimes the only incentive. Boot's the Chemist, for example, declared that it would share £34 million from its 1996 profits among more than 50,000 staff. This amounted to an extra 4.6 weeks' pay.[26] One snag is the impossibility of relating personal commitment to collective outcomes.

Exhibit 15.6	Pay schemes for individuals, work groups and the whole organisation

	Individual	*Work group*	*Whole organisation*
Fixed rate by time or for a work quota	Hourly rate; measured day work; job rate; annualised hours; annual salary.	Quota-based payments to work teams.	Standard rates across the whole organisation.
Input-based variable	Seniority or merit pay; skill-based pay; qualification-based pay; suggestions and other reward schemes.	Skill, contribution to the group; peer assessment based	Discretionary profit-sharing and share bonuses to individuals based on competence, potential contribution or scarcity.
Performance-based variable	Piece work; payment by results; performance-based pay.	Team bonuses.	Share options, joint ownership and profit-related pay available to all.

Combining fixed and variable pay with three levels of hierarchy produces a typology of pay schemes illustrated in Exhibit 15.6.[27] Many variations and hybrid schemes mean that the table is just an outline of what is found in practice. The complexity of many arrangements, some of which have grown up over decades, is illustrated by the pay of train drivers, *see* Exhibit 15.7.[28]

Pay structure

Whatever the practical details of the whole pay scheme, the question of deciding how much to pay each person remains. This means finding a balance among the HRM objectives discussed above. Negotiation, either with each employee or through trades unions, is one approach. Yet it creates a continual sense of crisis and change and sets rates according to bargaining power as opposed to shared understandings of job factors. The result is an *ad hoc* series of agreements with many inconsistencies. The next section deals with a formal approach that is widely accepted as fair.

> **Exhibit 15.7 Driving a bargain**
>
> Until the privatisation of British Rail, drivers were paid according to nationally agreed scales. A basic, pensionable salary of about £12 000 per year could be topped up by six or more allowances to £15 000. A further £6000 to £7000 overtime pay meant that the average package came to a little over £21 000. The extras included merit pay, flexibility allowances, mileage bonuses, bonuses for 'knowing the road' (that is learning more routes), driving fast trains, walking time and so on.
>
> After passenger services became the responsibility of 25 franchised train operating companies, personnel managers looked to new pay schemes with the following aims: simplification of job grades and pay components; versatility through flexible hours and benefits; incentives to take on more training, development and education; and participation in business success. For example, Midland Main Line agreed to cut the average working week and pay a basic £20 850. In return, drivers gave up most enhancements and agreed to work more flexibly.

Job evaluation

Job evaluation is a process of comparing all the jobs in the organisation both with each other and with benchmarks outside. It can be used to set both fixed and variable rates. The starting point is often a collective agreement on the nature of the process and how it will be carried out. Investigations are conducted either by small panels drawn from among managers and staff representatives or by outside consultants. Panels arbitrate in reviews. Sainsbury used them as part of a change project to develop a more consultative management style.[29]

The most straightforward method of evaluation is *job ranking*. Using the general criterion of benefit to the organisation, the panel lists all jobs in rank order. Then, key jobs spread throughout the list are chosen for rating. Pay rates are decided either by negotiation or surveying the labour market. This task is not for the evaluation committee which has to be seen as remaining neutral. Using the benchmark rates, however, the rest of the jobs are filled in by extrapolation.

In large, dispersed organisations, the committee would not be familiar with all jobs. Here, *job classification* improves upon ranking by setting out a list of bands or classes into which all jobs have to be fitted. Each band is given a description with examples. The pay review sets the rate for each band with the possibility of variations for merit or long service. Job classification is common in government and large commercial organisations. One snag is that fitting the bands involves comparing dissimilar jobs and leads to many appeals for regrading.

Answering some of these difficulties, a *point plan* assigns points to predetermined attributes, for example, skill requirement, responsibility, effort and working conditions. These may be subdivided. Scoring takes place on agreed scales and the totals become the points values to be used in ranking.

Job evaluation gains by bringing methods of pay determination out into the open. Some managers may rue the loss of flexibility offered by more *ad hoc* arrangements. For instance, lack of flexibility may make it difficult to keep a valued employee who receives a better offer from elsewhere.

Welfare

The second element of maintaining an efficient workforce is welfare. Practices in this area have often grown out of the philanthropic or human relations approaches to HRM. In a mid-twentieth century factory, for example, the staff welfare unit would: supply work clothes at low prices; offer loans to families in difficulties; provide counselling and health advice; act *in loco parentis* for apprentices; and maintain links with sick or retired staff. Nowadays, especially in smaller or less traditional organisations, many of these functions are left to others. Line managers, colleagues and friends may or may not find the time.

The question for the HR manager, working to support the business strategy within a tight budget, is how far should an employer be responsible for the welfare of employees and their families. Let us take the example of stress. Many applaud the introduction of high performance manufacturing systems based on the ideas of lean production, teamwork and quality circles. Cappelli and Rogovsky show how these changes demand better decisions, a higher pace of working and more commitment from employees.[30] In short, there is more stress. Should the employer be concerned with avoiding excess stress or mitigating its effects?

Among organisations learning how to help their staff cope with stress are the non-government organisations (NGOs) engaged in overseas aid. It was estimated that some 200 NGOs were involved in relief during the 1994 Rwandan civil war. Some of these were small and ineffective. They sent inexperienced workers out to central Africa for two or three weeks at a time. Yet many agencies throughout the world had problems in finding staff who could go at short notice and speak French. Stress can hardly be avoided. One study showed, unsurprisingly, that witnessing suffering is the major cause. Yet other factors, such as poor communications and rivalry with expatriate colleagues, also play their part. Moreover, staff complain about bad field management, poor selection practices, lack of career development, poor appraisal and inadequate training. Clearly, these can be influenced by the employer, who should also provide debriefing and counselling for workers on their return.[31]

Employee relations

It is easy to imagine that relations with employees as a whole have declined in the face of the individualisation of HRM practices. The term *Industrial Relations* refers to patterns of bargaining and consultation between collectives – employers, or groups of employers, on the one hand and trades unions on the other. Ideological reservations among the latter meant that their initial response to the 'new' HRM was confusion and resistance. More recently, the change has been accepted in spite of reservations. Maintaining their role of defending members' interests, unions in many countries have adjusted their stance towards the new styles of management. Unions have recognised that strategies for improving quality and encouraging innovation do bring long-term benefits to members. They increasingly advocate action to improve training and career opportunities. Thus, the United Kingdom's Amalgamated Engineering and Electrical Union supports its members in new style plants such as at Toyota, Nissan and Sony. In Germany, the large union IG Metall has taken a lead in responding to the development of team-work and other new practices.[32]

Perhaps the most notable feature of unions in Western countries over recent decades has been, with one or two exceptions, the decline in membership. This has been greatest in countries where adversarial national collective bargaining had been their main function. Table 15.1 compares union membership for some OECD countries.[33] It suggests that the roles of unions in these countries used to differ and are moving in many directions. As a theme not shown in the figures, however, we can say that cooperation and engagement have replaced conflict. To what extent this represents a change of philosophy or a tactical retreat in the light of declining membership remains to be seen. In some sectors of some economies, unions remain strong and militant. In France, for example, the low density in the whole workforce disguises the strength in nationalised industries and government service.

How does this look to the HR manager? Traditionally, industrial relations has fallen into two parallel functions – negotiation and consultation. Negotiation, or collective bargaining, covered wages and conditions and was depicted as a zero-sum game where the issue was how to 'share the cake'. Joint consultation, on the other hand, was based on a unitary model where both sides worked together to

Table 15.1 Union membership as percentage of workforce

	1980	1994
Australia	48	38
Canada	36	36
Finland	70	72
France	18	10
Germany	36	33
Italy	50	40
Japan	31	24
Netherlands	35	23
Norway	56	58
Portugal	61	30
Spain	25	10
United Kingdom	50	36
United States	22	17

discover ways to 'bake a bigger cake'. Structures for both could run from the department up to national level, since disputes could be referred upwards in the hope that they might be resolved. The sluggishness of these systems, however, coupled with the rise of plant-level bargaining, meant a decline in use.

Ramsay notes that, nowadays, consultation commonly coexists with bargaining at plant level. It often spawns special committees focusing on specific remits. The HR manager may, therefore, be part of health and safety committees, productivity and quality groups and so on. In most European countries, works councils are established either by statute or, in Sweden, by national agreements. The Social Chapter may eventually spread the practice through the whole European Union. Objectives for joint consultation, as seen by management, may include one or more of the following:

- strengthening of communication channels;
- cooperation in facing competitive or other environmental threats;
- restricting the scope of union activities to the point of exclusion;
- enlisting the cooperation of local union officials against the national union's wishes;
- offering (token) participation in decision making.[34]

In some of these aims there lie the seeds of failure. Ramsay notes three that are commonly found:

- the committee deals only with trivial issues – tea, towels and toilets;
- a powerless committee attracts little interest;
- the process breaks down because problems are too severe or the parties' expectations differ too much.

The problem of marginality is seen by some authors as widespread among works councils throughout Europe. Others find that beneficial outcomes are possible provided the approach is genuine and not simply a gesture. Ramsay's summary of good consultation appears in Exhibit 15.8.

Exhibit 15.8 Features of good consultation practice

- Consultation occurs before change – otherwise it becomes manipulation;
- Committee momentum requires an ambitious agenda;
- All members require research and secretarial support;
- Representatives should report back fully to avoid isolation of the process;
- Training of managers and staff is necessary;
- Management members must be sufficiently senior to demonstrate serious commitment;
- Agreed actions should be swiftly put into effect; reasons for rejection should be given clearly and promptly;
- Unions should be kept informed even if they are not directly involved; trying to bypass them is risky.

Questions for the human resources manager

We shall now turn to a brief review of some critical questions facing HR managers, linking them to the themes of this book. They relate to national differences, ethics, SMEs and equal opportunities.

■ Are national differences important?

Clark and Mallory are among many who show that HRM varies between nations.[35] Although a common term may be used to describe the management of the employment relationship, there are many differences in meaning. The growth of HRM from personnel management appeared in the United States of the 1980s as that country sought to overcome perceived failures in its industries. The nature of HRM reflected managers' attempts to recapture the American Dream and its operations fitted the culture of the nation. The 'new HRM' is American.

Hofstede's work, *see* Chapter 5, invites us to see countries in cultural clusters. On this basis, we would expect the American model to transfer most readily to other countries in the Anglo cluster, notably the United Kingdom. Models of HRM processes and practice do not fit so well in mainland Europe. Each nation 'understands' HRM in different ways. For example, in France the state still plays a major role in shaping the framework. This is both through the legal context and the state's involvement in many large organisations where unions are also very influential. Liberalisation is led from the centre. Outside big business, however, HRM as a movement seems to have had little impact.[36]

In contrast to this 'stumbling' model of development, frequently influenced by the experiences of foreign firms, HRM is a home-grown product in Germany. It comes from a long tradition of practical application, research and teaching. HRM stresses the value of human resources in gaining competitive advantage and integrates HR and corporate strategies so they reinforce each other. Ideas of partnership and strong representation by employees at all levels remain central to the way things work.[37] In Sweden, the strongly collective tradition counters moves to individualisation found in other countries, especially the Anglo group. Expressed through the strength of trades unions, this feeling is even stronger in Denmark which, like Finland, is a country where union membership has not been declining.[38] These examples suggest that, while there are pressures towards convergence of policy and practice in HRM, important differences between nations and cultures will remain. Beyond the European shores, we expect the gaps to be greater.

■ Is HRM ethical?

Obviously, the answer to this question is yes – HRM is here to help people. Or is it? One problem with the question is the lack of agreement over what HRM is. We have just looked at international differences and there is the contrast between soft (human) and hard (resource) approaches explained earlier in the chapter. To make progress, Legge suggests we evaluate HRM according to how it approaches three features: flexibility; team building, empowerment and involvement; and cultural management.[39]

Under each feature we can spot winners and losers. Flexible working may suit very well the people close to the core of an organisation but at the expense of those at the fringe, on casual contracts. Empowerment has worked well in many firms but in others it merely increases stress and blame if things go awry. Changing cultures may be done with the best intentions. Yet, with high unemployment, we must ask whether culture change programmes secure real commitment or mere compliance. Is soft HRM real? Furthermore, is it really about developing people as people?

What do ethical ideas have to contribute to this debate? In Chapter 6 we looked at the Kantian, Utilitarian and Aristotelian schools.

- Kant's categorical imperative requires any principle to be capable of generalisation. Further, actions must respect the dignity of individuals and be acceptable to them. Self-interest is immoral. To Kant, hard HRM, however well intentioned, would be immoral. It uses people for an end, such as the success of the organisation. Soft HRM, based on mutuality and the development of all employees as an end in itself, passes the test. But this would be true only if all employees were treated alike. Core and periphery models of employment are ruled out. Culture change programmes that involve the manipulation of one group by another are also off limits.

  One difficulty for Kant's laws is the potential clash between two rules. What about 'I must look after the interests of owners' against 'I must look after the interests of employees'? It is difficult to construct a more general rule to choose between the two so we may fall back on looking at consequences. This means the utilitarian approach.

- Utilitarians judge the morality of actions according to their outcomes. Choice must be based on the greatest good for the greatest number. To this aim, some *distributive* ethicists would add that nobody must be worse off.

  This gives hard HRM some hope. In spite of the stress and loss that HRM policies bring to individuals, managers have the duty to follow paths that provide the greatest good for the majority. Competitive advantage ensures business survival, stimulates innovation and doubles the average standard of living every 10, 20 or 30 years depending on which country you live in. Further, questions of distributive ethics can be handled if steps are taken to correct the disadvantages for the losers through counselling, retraining, switching jobs or redundancy payments.

- An Aristotelian stresses goodness or virtue. This means offering everyone the possibility of realising their moral, social and mental potential within the broader community. Clearly, employment cannot do this on its own but it must follow practices that help growth on its way.

  Genuine soft HRM, full of ideas about learning and development may qualify. But what of staff employed in unskilled jobs with little training? How much more is there for them than the trade of labour for payment? Even for professionals there are great difficulties for this virtue ethics. Systems of reward encourage interpersonal competition. Promotion is at someone else's expense.

Moreover, stimulating commitment from ambitious people leads to workaholic behaviour, burnout and negative consequences for employees' development in their family and community roles. Many modern HRM practices, therefore, would not figure well on the Aristotelian scoreboard.

We can see that genuine soft HRM may be seen as ethical from several points of view. On the other hand, it is difficult to justify hard HRM unless you are an out-and-out utilitarian. Yet maybe that is the way the world is going.

■ Are SMEs a special case?

Hendry and colleagues show that SMEs face problems due to their small size or narrow focus in terms of processes, products or markets.[40] Many well-run SMEs follow up-to-date HRM practice with mixtures of soft and hard approaches. One critical problem they face is excessive reliance on key personnel, whose skills may be in very short supply. Fear of losing them is real. Of these, reliance on the leader is usually the most serious. The entrepreneur has to consider succession, which is how the business is to remain viable after he or she withdraws.

There are several problems for entrepreneurs who might consider HR policies in relation to succession. The first lies in understanding what management development means. Since, for the most part, they have had to learn by doing, they tend to assume that others learn the same way. This is, however, rarely feasible. People who follow cannot have the same experience as the enterprise's founder, so preparing people to take over must involve another sort of training and experience. The second problem is the very close personal identification between the entrepreneur and the enterprise. Therefore, devolving key tasks such as marketing or technology is very difficult. In consequence, Hendry and colleagues found little evidence of succession planning among SMEs. Unfortunately, if consideration of this question is blocked, managers find it difficult to create any coherent HR policies for the wider group of managers and other employees.

■ How does HRM respond to equal opportunities issues?

Most Western countries have legislation ensuring equal employment rights for all citizens. We cannot consider all aspects of its impact as the number of variations is endless. Depending on the state, it may be unlawful to discriminate on grounds of gender, race, religion, nationality or age. To illustrate ethical and practical problems for HRM, we shall focus on gender. Two decades ago, there were few women in influential positions in government, business or most other areas of organisational life. In the 1990s things seemed to change. The United Kingdom Labour government, elected in 1997, had 18 women ministers. These days, many large

> The *glass ceiling* is the invisible barrier that prevents women from rising to the top of organisations. The term is also used to cover minority groups.

corporations, university departments, charities, newspapers and SMEs are run by women. While there are still fewer than there ought to be, many commentators feel that at last the glass ceiling has been smashed. It is possible to point to enough women in senior positions to use as role models. Equality of the sexes is only a matter of time. Now that women are accepted, it is as though the system is waiting for the flow of graduates from business and professional education to move into the ranks. A third of all managers and administrators and 40 per cent of professionals are female; women figure heavily in business start-ups not only in Britain but in China, Germany, Singapore and the United States. Nearly all Japanese currency traders are women. Worrying, though, is the proportion of company directors which, in the United Kingdom, has crept up to just 3.3 per cent. From this last figure, others argue that the glass ceiling has not so much been smashed as raised.

There is a difference between female managers and feminine management. The few exceptional figures of the 1970s and 1980s, for instance Prime Minister Margaret Thatcher and a scattering of senior judges, were said to behave as 'men in disguise'. That is they practised 'masculine' management. Nowadays, successful women still show many attributes of successful men: good with people; taking well-judged risks; self-reliance; energy; and the need to prove oneself. Differences are subtle: women are better time-managers, better able to accomplish several tasks at once and are more flexible. They are often less interested in the trappings of power such as size of office, chauffeur-driven car or class of air travel. Other concerns often attributed to women, such as openness, integrity, equal rights and representation are really feminine traits that are often also displayed by men.[41]

What does this mean for HRM? Monitoring the representation of women in management positions would identify defects in recruitment and development procedures. Provided equal opportunity is sincerely offered, achieving equality among the management cadre is only a matter of time. Unfortunately, such a rosy picture cannot be painted lower in the hierarchies of many industries. Glass ceilings combine with glass walls, which are barriers between professions and even roles in the same organisation. Some 80 per cent of hairdressers, cleaners, caterers and clerical workers are women compared with 0.8 per cent of surgeons. The reality is frequently at odds with the claims of equal opportunities employers. Biswas and Cassell investigated the state of HRM in a hotel in northern England, *see* Exhibit 15.9.[42]

From the business point of view, there is considerable pressure to follow the status quo. The good hotel wins through reproducing a sense of homeliness. This is partly conveyed by modelling the traditional domestic division of labour, placing women in caring roles with men to do the heavy jobs. At the same time, a hotel needs to sell its services to, predominantly, business*men*. Receptionists and sales staff succeed through fulfilling glamour roles. Hence the culture of the industry includes having women matching both caring and selling stereotypes.

The dilemma for HRM is clear. Fitting HR with corporate strategy means fitting the expectations of the market. This means both men and women occupying gendered roles to meet customers' expectations. This is incompatible with any equal opportunities policy. The notion of recruiting the right person for the job is undermined if the 'rightness' is seen mainly in terms of a person's sex. In defence, the

> ### Exhibit 15.9 Sex stereotypes in an English hotel
>
> With 100 beds, the city centre hotel was part of an international chain. In spite of its size it did not have a formal equal opportunities policy, either explicit or implied in the HRM policy. Typical of the industry, employment practice meant having a core of 50 full-time staff supported by part-timers and casual workers.
>
> At the hotel there was evidence of sexual discrimination: women, usually older, were preferred for breakfast service to promote the image of comfort and homeliness; at reception, the stress was on appearance; and all but one porter was male, the token woman finding it difficult to be taken seriously and often being given the light jobs. Perhaps more problematic was the way in which women cooperated in reinforcing sex stereotypes. Chambermaids, for instance, believed that housekeeping was a female reserve, and all accepted that the night receptionist should be male. Both women and men seemed content with the gendered notions surrounding their roles. Exceptions had to develop their own survival strategies. Women in the 'macho' environment of the kitchen or men in the domestic department adopted behaviours more commonly found in the opposite sex.

business may say that it is merely responding to the social environment and to behave otherwise would be futile. Yet, in law, a defence based on such role definitions would fail.

Conclusion: the paradox of HRM

At one level, HRM can be perceived as a set of techniques for creating, developing and maintaining an effective workforce. It can be seen to have grown out of conventional personnel management functions that were responsible for recruitment and selection, training, setting up reward systems, industrial relations and staff welfare. The accent changed with the move towards planning and the integration of these tasks into the organisation's strategy. Then, HRM changed its stance from caring and development to optimising and integrating human resources. This position is stressed in the so-called *hard* HRM where the accent is on the *R*. Planned reduction in staff and how it can be achieved, a topic for which we have had no space, is clearly related to the way HR and business plans are tied together.

In this chapter we have mainly used an Anglo-American perspective although enough has been said to show that HRM is strongly influenced by national systems and socio-cultural environments. Variations between nations mean that there is no universal understanding and MNEs need to tailor their policies to meet local needs. Coping with differences also raises ethical questions such as how far one should go along with local conventions in such areas as employment. Looking more broadly, far from appearing to be free of ethical difficulty, HRM is full of questions. Beyond national contrasts, we have referred to the contrast between hard and soft approaches to show how the former hardly stands up to ethical questioning. In detail, too, there are questions of selection testing and policies towards equal opportunities. The role of HR managers in promoting equal opportunities is, perhaps, obvious. Yet, as the paradoxical strategy at the hotel in Exhibit 15.9 showed, policy is never so clear cut. Strategic goals, which either have been or ought to have been clarified, do not bridge the chasm between attitudes of staff and customers and legislation. In this and other difficult areas, managers often prefer to leave matters in an ambiguous, messy state. HR managers are no longer able to provide straightforward support to managers on staff questions such as recruitment and welfare. In becoming an instrument of business policy, HRM now shares the complex, incoherent questions faced by the rest of the management team.

Quick check up   *Can you ...*

- Define HRM;
- Name the three elements of HRM practice;
- List four features of the hard and soft approaches;
- Sketch a model of the recruitment process;
- Outline the issue of validity in selection;
- Give examples of indirect discrimination;
- Identify the four elements of a structured interview schedule;

- Summarise the activities in an assessment centre;
- Define training;
- List four benefits of training;
- Tabulate the benefits of on-the-job and off-the-job training;
- State what is meant by levels of aggregation in pay schemes;
- Name two methods of job evaluation;
- Explain the term *glass ceiling*.

Questions   *Chapter review*

15.1 Draw and annotate a diagram showing the main HRM processes of an organisation within the business environment.

15.2 Relate training and development as approaches to the growth of people's capabilities.

15.3 Compare on- and off-the-job training, using your own examples to illustrate circumstances where each may best be used.

Application

15.4 Analyse in ethical terms the position of managers at the hotel of Exhibit 15.9. Whose interests should HRM serve?

15.5 To what extent do you think soft or hard HRM was practised at the Skipton Building Society? What effects do you think increasing competition may have on this position?

Investigation

15.6 Find out how a small business recruits new staff. By interviewing a person in charge, establish why they use the chosen method. Comment on its efficiency and whether it risks contravening equal opportunities legislation.

15.7 Through interviewing a sample of employed people, discover the principles upon which their pay and other benefits are worked out. Compare the design of the schemes to assess how far they are likely to be effective.

Do we expect too much of aid workers?[43]

Nurse Ann Smith was in charge of a Red Cross feeding centre in Huambo, Angola, when, with 53 other aid workers, she was robbed and taken captive by rebel forces. Released after several days, she was sent by lorry and cargo aircraft to Luanda. There, the Red Cross ensured that the staff, 30 of whom were its employees, stayed in the same hotel and had plenty of time to discuss events before being flown to Europe. For Ann Smith, 'This was terribly important. The only people I have spoken to properly about this are those who were out there with me'. Like many in her position, she finds it difficult to tell others who 'can't possibly understand'.

Formal debriefing took place at Red Cross headquarters in Geneva before Smith's return to the United Kingdom. She was offered counselling and had a few weeks' leave before undergoing a physical and psychological check-up.

Experiences such as these are becoming more commonplace. Personnel managers meeting workers returning from Somalia found themselves listening to responses they felt inadequate to handle. As the list of disasters, and the number of agencies, has lengthened, so has the number of problems grown.

While the Red Cross has sent people to stressful and dangerous areas for many years, only recently has it started to consider systems for care and support. Influential have been the growing body of research into stress

management and the ways the armed forces and emergency services help their people cope with trauma.

To ensure that field workers are better prepared for their assignments, the British Red Cross has strengthened its personnel practices. One-hour selection interviews have been replaced by one-day assessment centres. The aim is to find better communicators and team-workers. Pre-departure briefing has been extended to seven days and includes stress management and cross-cultural training. A specialist agency, InterHealth, has been brought in to provide medical checks and counselling both before and after assignments.

Paul Eames, overseas personnel manager for the British Red Cross, has more plans. He wants to see a career structure and job security replacing the short-term contract system. This has grown in response to uncertain funding but makes it difficult to build up experienced teams. Eames also wants to improve management training and clarify the roles of field managers.

Field managers' first responsibility is to look after staff health and security. Otherwise, their work would be useless. Yet one remarked, 'It is quite common to work all hours God gives in reaction to the crisis, and because you are going into areas where the infrastructure has collapsed, there are few distractions'. It is not surprising that many return drained. Expatriates come home yet often feel guilty about the local people they must leave behind. One Oxfam manager explained, 'When we pulled out of Kigali, all we could do was share the office money among the Rwandan staff and say we hoped to employ them again some day'.

Questions

1 What factors in the environment contribute to the personnel practices that have developed among NGOs working in overseas aid?

2 Suggest a design for a one-day assessment centre for a charity recruiting staff for central Asian emergency relief.

3 The effects of trauma have been vividly illustrated by cases in recent years. To what extent should organisations be responsible for its effects on employees?

Bibliography

For a comprehensive review of HRM, Towers' *The Handbook of Human Resource Management* discusses its contexts and practices and provides seven lengthy case studies. Clark's *European Human Resource Management* compares philosophy and practice in seven EU countries. Details of both are in the references. With more information on HRM processes is Tyson, S. (1995) *Human Resource Strategy*, London: Financial Times Pitman Publishing. A full coverage of the critical debate appears in Storey, John (1995) *Human Resource Management: A critical text*, London: Routledge.

References

1. Worts, Chris (1996) 'Building a society with special skills', *People Management*, **2** (**2**), 25 January, 36–8; 'Skipton teams up with GA Life to launch instant-access portfolio', *Money Marketing*, 31 October 1996; 'Skipton buys mortgages', *The Northern Echo*, 3 October 1996; 'Skipton steps into world of share dealing', *Yorkshire Post*, 10 September, 1996.

2. Truss, Catherine, Gratton, Lynda; Hope-Hailey, Veronica; McGovern; Patrick and Stiles, Philip (1997) 'Soft and hard models of human resource management: A reappraisal', *Journal of Management Studies*, **34** (**1**), January, 54–73.

3. *Ibid.*, 69.

4. Siebert, Kent W., Hall, Douglas T. and. Kram, Kathy E. (1995) 'Strengthening the weak link in strategic executive development: Integrating individual development and global business strategy', *Human Resource Management*, 1995, **34** (**4**), 549–67; summarised in (1996) 'A centre-stage role for executive development', *Management Decision*, **34** (**5**), September, 51–2.

5. Beer, M., Spector, B., Lawrence, P., Mills, D. and Walton, R. (1985) *Human Resource Management: A general manager's perspective*, New York: Free Press.

6. Hendry, C. and Pettigrew, A. (1990) 'Human Resource Management: an agenda for the 1990s', *International Journal of Human Resource Management*, **1** (**1**), 17–44.

7. Kane, Bob and Palmer, Ian (1995) 'Strategic HRM or managing the employment relationship?', *International Journal of Manpower*,**15** (**5**), May, 6–21.

8. Marsh, Peter (1996) 'Companies fall down on "people issues"', *Financial Times*, 18 November, 11.

9. Hunter, Laurie, Beaumont, Phil and Sinclair, Diane (1996) ' A "partnership" route to Human Resource Management', *Journal of Management Studies*, **33** (**2**), March, 235–57.

10. West Devon Borough Council (1997) Advertisement, *Guardian*, G2, 21 May, 29.

11. Cooper, John N., Baker, Barry R. and Maddocks, Jolyon S. (1996) 'Occupational testing practice: sustaining testing processes through CPD: a case study', *Journal of European Industrial Training*, **20** (**7**), July, 3–9.

12. McHenry, Robert (1997) 'Tried and tested', *People Management*, 23 January, 35–7.

13. Furnham, Adrian (1995) 'A performance that can tip the balance', *Financial Times*, 18 December, 10.

14. 'Picking the right people', *20 Steps to Better Management*, Programme 12, BBC1 Television, 12 January 1997.

15. Moffat, J. (1992) 'Three case studies of operational research for the Royal Air Force', *Journal of the Operational Research Society*, **43** (**10**), 955–60.

16. Donkin, Richard (1996) 'Jury out on all-round appraisal', *Financial Times*, 9 October.

17. Mullins, Laurie J. (1996) *Management and Organisational Behaviour*, Fourth edition, London: Financial Times Pitman Publishing, 644.

18. *Ibid.*, 635.

19. Tragg, Roger (1995) 'New culture, new ideas: Consultants apply commercial thinking to the public sector' , *Independent on Sunday*, 24 September.

20. Saigol, Lina (1997) 'On with the counter revolution', *Guardian: Jobs and Money*, 15 March, 2–3.

21. Hiroshima Sogo Bank (1994) *Watashitati no tekisuto [Our textbook]*, Thirty-second edition, Hiroshima Sogo Bank, Personnel Training Section, 114.

22. Bergenhenegouwen, G.J., ten Horn, H.F.K. and Mooijman, E.A.M. (1996) 'Competence development – a challenge for HRM professionals: core competences of organizations as guidelines for the development of employees', *Journal of European Industrial Training*, **20** (**9**), 29–35.

23. Bradshaw, Della (1995) 'Chips off the old block', *Financial Times*, 13 November, 15.

24. Lockyer, Keith (1996) 'Human resource management and flexibility in pay: new solutions to old problems?', in Towers, Brian (editor) *The Handbook of Human Resource Management*, Second edition, Oxford: Blackwell, 298.

25. *Ibid.*, 299.

26. 'Boots pay bonus', *Guardian*, 16 June 1997, 16.

27. Lockyer, (1996) *op. cit.*, 286.

28. Greenhill, Richard (1997) 'All change', *People Management*, 1 May, 22–5; Brown, Barry (1997) 'Getting there', *People Management*, 1 May, 25–6.

29. Williams, Alan and Dobson, Paul (1996) 'Culture change through training: the case of Sainsbury', in Towers, *op. cit.* 416–31.

30. Cappelli, Peter and Rogovsky, Nikolai (1995) 'What do new systems demand of employees?, *Financial Times: Mastering Management*, 24 November, II.

31. Pickard, Jane (1996) 'Stopping disaster from ruining lives', *People Management*, 25 July, 32–4.

32. Based on Beaumont, P.B. (1996) 'Trade unions and human resource management', in Towers, *op. cit.* 115–30.

33. OECD (1997) *Employment Outlook*, Paris: OECD; *The Economist* (1997) 'Beer, sandwiches and statistics', 12 July, 90.

34. Ramsay, Harvie (1996) 'Involvement, empowerment and commitment', in Towers, *op. cit.*, 223–58.

35. Clark, Timothy and Mallory, Geoff (1996) 'The cultural relativity of human resource management: Is there a universal model?' in Clark, (ed.) *European Human Resource Management*, Oxford: Blackwell, 28.

36. Jenkins, Alan and van Wijk, Gilles (1996) 'Hesitant innovation: the recent evolution of human resources management in France', in Clark, *op. cit.*, 65–92.

37. Scholz, Christian (1996) 'Human resource management in Germany', in Clark, *op. cit.*, 118–51.

38. Schuer, Steen (1996) 'Denmark: Human resource management under collective bargaining: The sociological perspective', in Clark, *op. cit.*, 185–214.

39. Legge, Karen (1996) 'Morality bound', *People Management*, 19 December, 34–6.

40. Hendry, C., Jones, A., Arthur, M. and Pettigrew, A. (1991) *Human Resource Development in Small to Medium Sized Enterprises*, Research Paper No. 88, University of Warwick Business School.

41. Porter, Henry (1997) 'Smashing the glass ceiling', *Guardian*, G2, 26 May, 2–4; Wilkinson, Helen (1996) 'Cracks in the glass ceiling – a new generation of women believe they will win equality in the boardroom, not the common room', *Observer*, 2 June.

42. Biswas, Rashmi and Cassell Catherine (1996) 'Strategic HRM and the gendered division of labour in the hotel industry: a case study', *Personnel Review*, **25** (**2**), February, 19–34.

43. Pickard (1996) *op. cit.*

Part 5

ORGANISING SMALL GROUPS

I believe in benevolent dictatorship provided I am the dictator. *Richard Branson, British entrepreneur*

Insanity in individuals is something rare – but in groups, parties, nations, and epochs it is the rule. *Friedrich Nietzsche, German philosopher*

'Whom are you?' said he, for he had been to night school. *George Ade, American writer*

PART 4	CHAPTER 15	CHAPTER 14	CHAPTER 13	CHAPTER 12
ORGANISING LARGE GROUPS	Human resource management	Managing organisational change	Organisational design: matching the situation	Organisations: principles, models and outcomes

PART 5		CHAPTER 16	CHAPTER 17	CHAPTER 18	
ORGANISING SMALL GROUPS		Leadership and motivation	Groups and teams	Communication in management	

PART 6	CHAPTER 22	CHAPTER 21	CHAPTER 20	CHAPTER 19
IMPLEMENTING POLICIES AND PLANS	Managers and information	Innovation: from ideas to customer benefits	Marketing: managing relations with customers	Operations management

P art 5 is concerned with the role of the manager in leading and guiding individuals and small groups. Leadership is an important capability, although what it is, where it comes from, and how it is put into effect are controversial. Chapter 16 compares ideas on leadership before going on to examine its mirror, motivation. Again, this area is controversial, having generated many theories concerning the nature of work rewards and their link to performance.

Management is a social activity, often conducted in work groups and teams. In Chapter 17, these terms are defined and compared to provide an understanding of their origins and how they function. Effective teams depend on how they are constituted and the processes they use to reach decisions and overcome conflict. In the global context, cultural diversity makes the operation of teams more complex.

Communication is often seen as the glue binding working relationships. Chapter 18 presents the process model of communication and applies it to questions of enhancing skills, especially in listening and writing. In the organisational context, there are many means of making improvements, although these are hindered by problems of jargon and, especially, over-load. Improved organisational communications may be the answer but the chapter sounds a note of caution. It may be that those in power do not wish to share accurate information. Instead, the intention of many messages may be to keep people in the dark.

Chapter 16

Leadership and motivation

Chapter objectives

When you have finished studying this chapter, you should be able to:

- define leadership and explain how it differs from management;

- outline five sources of power for leaders and managers; explain how it can be delegated through empowerment;

- compare four types of leadership theory – trait, behavioural, contingency and transformational – giving examples of each;

- demonstrate the importance of motivation in the generation of work performance;

- explain how rewards for effort may be intrinsic or extrinsic;

- compare three main classes of motivation theory, showing how they can be summarised in the Porter–Lawler model;

- apply and illustrate theories in the context of job design and performance-related pay.

Opening case: peace, joy and results for Juve[1]

Fans have no doubt that Marcello Lippi made a difference. Appointed manager of a football club frustrated by lack of success, he led Juventus to win the Italian league and cup in his first season, become European champions in his second and, in his third, reach a second European final and regain the Italian league title.

After the European success, Lippi broke with conventional wisdom and radically rebuilt his squad. His hand was forced by changes in the transfer market after the Bosman case and the huge fees offered by English clubs for Vialli and, especially, Ravanelli. Other members left too. How was the reshuffle accomplished so successfully? 'One of the characteristics of this squad is that no one feels unimportant. ... five or six players, because of their charisma, their personality, their class and experience will always play if fit. ... When a player signs for Juventus, he doesn't ask "But I will always play, won't I?"'

Lippi's approach to training shows in the way the team plays possession soccer at high speed. Coaching focuses on ball work, passing and moving quickly off the ball. While believing his methods to be superior, Lippi is very tactful about other teams. Typically, he will admit that losers were 'a little unlucky'. This manner comes easily to the 49-year-old whose good looks resemble Paul Newman's.

Tactics are important but Lippi's strongest asset is his astute treatment of players. Lippi is very aware of players' human qualities. Of Frenchmen Zidane and Deschamps, he says, 'They are very different types of player, but as people they are as similar as two drops of water, possessing a rare intelligence and a rare humility, a willingness to put themselves at the disposal of others.' On taking charge, he announced he wanted to make his team *Baggioindipendente*. This was interpreted by some as a snub for the star Roberto Baggio who had had a brilliant 1994 World Cup but was feeling the pressure of expectations. Yet the comment revealed Lippi's sensitive reading of the signals. He was going to create a team which shared responsibility. In another instance, this time from the heat of a match, Ravanelli was seen to gesture angrily towards the manager. After the game, Lippi commented that the remorseful striker must have been pointing at someone in the crowd behind the dugout.

When appointed, the club's president Umberto Agnelli, had asked Lippi to do nothing more than restore a sense of peace and joy and the results would follow.

Introduction

What makes some athletes into good leaders? Some stars on the field fail in management while others who never win a medal become excellent, successful coaches. Those who succeed do so in many different ways, depending on their character, the organisation and the circumstances in which they find themselves. Compare Marcello Lippi, holding billions of lire to spend in the transfer market, with the efforts of Jack Charlton. One of the stars of England's 1966 World Cup success, his managerial career could only be described as moderate until he took over the Irish national side. Then he managed to mould a set of average players into a very successful team. The interaction between the leader and the rest of the group created something greater than their individual records would have suggested.

Bob Geldof, too, is a remarkable Irishman. Responding to the famine in Ethiopia, he drew together many disparate groups to create huge music events, Band Aid and Live Aid. Known for blunt speech, he told Britain's prime minister, 'I don't think that the possible death of 120 million people is a matter of charity. It is a matter of moral imperative'. Through his persuasion, producing, conning and cajoling, some of the world's largest and most delicate egos assembled on the same stage and in the same studio. The 1984 record, *Do they know it's Christmas?* sold seven million copies. Its revenues, with those from the simultaneous 1985 Live Aid concerts in London and Philadelphia which were broadcast throughout the world, reached £60 million.[2]

In their own ways, Lippi, Charlton and Geldof displayed leadership to make groups of people reach beyond their individual capacities. This is one of the most talked-about topics in management. In this chapter we will examine the nature of leaders and how they work with and motivate others.

Motivation is to an extent the mirror of leadership. Leaders motivate followers; followers are motivated by leaders. Yet people are also motivated by other factors that arise within themselves or their environment. A star footballer plays for the manager, the team, the fans, the sport and himself. The second part of the chapter explores explanations of what stirs people to effort.

Leadership and management

Leadership is the process of influencing people towards achievement of organisational goals. This short definition contains three key features about which authors agree – goals, people and influence. It demonstrates that leadership is a social process in that it involves interaction with others to achieve ends. Furthermore, the process can be an exchange, for, within a group, the role of leader can switch from person to person as circumstances develop.

Surely, we might respond, this is the same as management? In reply, we can say that, while both include doing things through other people, they are different. Management, for example, is concerned with questions of choosing goals, solving problems, interpreting control signals and spotting developments in the environment. Leadership provides inspiration, risk-taking, creativity and change. The power available to managers arises from their position as managers while, for leaders, it arises from within themselves. Sir David Barnes is chief executive of the United Kingdom pharmaceutical company Zeneca. He leaves to others the 'hands-on' management of this world leader in agricultural biotechnology and generic research. His role is 'providing the leadership, ensuring appropriate allocation of resources, giving a sense of direction and values; making the company live'. He is also very concerned about business ethics and takes a lead in maintaining the highest standards.[3]

Senge pities senior executives who have little to do. They neither make nor sell things so they are left with putting through yet another reorganisation. Yet they should lead he argues, 'Leadership is a phenomenon, not a position. It's absolutely nothing to do with hierarchy. Leaders are people who move ahead and who have some influence over others. They are not necessarily in any position of authority'.[4] In Senge's ideal *learning organisation*,[5] leaders emerge from among empowered teams of middle managers. Exercised from the top only, leadership can be fatal. Drawing such ideas together, Capowski suggests that management and leadership differ in that one comes from the head and the other from the heart.[6] Figure 16.1 sets out the qualities of the two phenomena. We should remember, however, that a mix will be found in any individual.

Both management and leadership involve power. Power is usually defined as *the potential to influence the behaviour of others*. Note the word potential. This suggests a set of resources that a leader can deploy when exercising influence over others. Power is resource; leadership is a process that involves exercising power. Power can be built and expanded until the leader chooses to exercise it.

Apart from the definition used above, it is worth noting two other usages of the word power. First, it often carries connotations of independence. The sentence, 'You are not my boss and therefore you cannot tell me what to do', is an assertion of this feeling. Second, power is so closely related to control that the two words are used interchangeably. In this book, however, control is used in a more limited way, as detailed in Chapters 23 and 24.

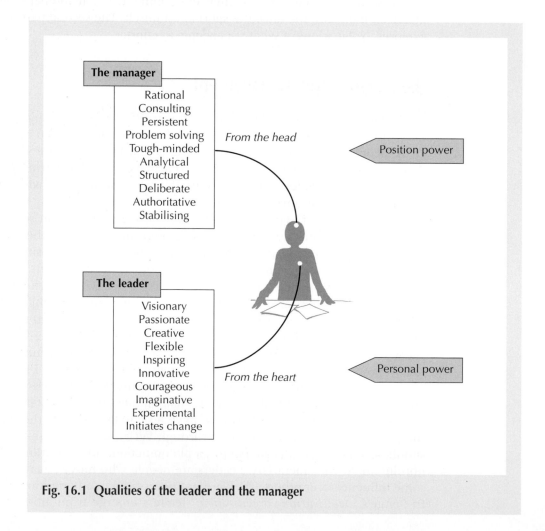

Fig. 16.1 Qualities of the leader and the manager

To analyse power in the organisational context, French and Raven[7] proposed five categories. For our discussion, we shall group them in two sets. These depend on the origins of power – formal position or personal characteristics.

■ Power from formal position

Here, the source of the manager's power is the organisation. Three forms – legitimate, reward and coercive – are used to influence others' behaviour in the direction of goals.

Legitimate power

Legitimate power arises from a person's role or position in the organisation. Also known as *position power,* it is based on formal authority, linked to the position. Since the hierarchy itself can be shown to have been legitimately constituted with rules governing the exercise of authority, the occupants of each position have the right to exercise corresponding power. Although it is natural to look upwards in the hierarchy for those who wield it, power can arise anywhere. For instance, the parking attendant or gate keeper are authorised to give instructions to anyone within their areas of responsibility. In railways, the rules place the signaller in charge of the line and the guard in command of the train. Not even a director of an operating company can overrule their legitimate decisions.

Reward power

Reward power is based on the perception of a subordinate that the leader can reward those who comply with instructions. These can be monetary benefits ranging from immediate payments to bonuses and promotion in the future, to privileges, praise, and factors such as allocation of more interesting and responsible work. The opportunity for managers to offer such incentives underpins practices related to work motivation that are discussed later in the chapter. Clearly, for managers who cannot offer rewards, or for subordinates who are not interested in the ones that can be offered, reward power does not exist.

Coercive power

Mirroring reward power, coercive power is based on the perception of a subordinate that the leader can punish those who do not comply with instructions. Punishments may be financial, such as fines or restricting pay increases, allocation of unpopular tasks or work rotas, removal of support, reprimands or even dismissal. Fear of coercion may be as strong a driving force as the coercion itself. Whatever its type, the strength of coercive power depends on the willingness of managers to apply it and staff to accept its use. If used arbitrarily and excessively, the effect is to create an alienated and resentful workforce. Therefore, enlightened management will exercise sanctions only when it feels its hand is forced by indiscipline.

■ Power from personal characteristics

In contrast to power drawn from external sources, personal power arises from the characteristics of the individual, especially knowledge and personal traits. Since we are now considering power that belongs to a person, rather than to an organisational position, we can see that personal power is the resource of the leader. The two types, expert and referent power, complete the five-fold list of French and Raven.

Expert power

Expert power arises from others' perceptions of a person's special knowledge or expertise. For it to be a real source of power, evidence of its existence must be accepted by others and it must be relevant to the circumstances. For instance, when seeking a lead on a question of employment law, a senior manager may turn to the human resource specialist. On the other hand, one would not rely on a chartered accountant to repair a puncture! Usually, expertise is confined to a narrow function or specialism and may be confirmed by qualifications.

Referent power

Personality characteristics, which engage in others a sense of identification, respect or admiration, are the source of referent power. Even to strangers, referent power can be based on reputation. This power is clearly seen in charismatic leaders who encourage emulation of their behaviour.

Whatever the type of power, and in many cases managers and leaders are able to exercise a combination, we have stressed that it depends on the *perceptions* of others. Therefore a person may be able to bluff by creating the impression of power although it does not exist. Yet a different person may not be able to convince others that it is real. Then attempts to influence them will fail.

Abuse of power

A balance needs to be struck between the exercise of power by the manager and leader and the followers' acceptance of it. Power can be abused when the leader exercises it at the expense of others. For example, large pay rises given to senior managers, at the same time as shop floor wages are frozen, show the leader not taking responsibility to provide adequately for all. A departmental manager can look good by over-delegating, that is by overloading staff with work. The manager is rewarded by climbing the hierarchy while the rest suffer from burn out.

Sankowsky shows how abuse is a particular danger with charismatic leaders.[8] Followers reinforce the leader's position through seeing the leader as being one or more of the following:

■ omnipotent – nurturing and guiding;

■ mystic – knowing the way and the answers;

■ heroic – moving mountains for the good of all; and

■ pure in spirit – driven by ethical values.

When such leaders, often with grandiose visions, are 'found out' not only may the business have failed but followers suffer distress ranging from anger and anxiety to cynicism and self-blame.

■ Empowerment

Since the 1980s, the term 'empowerment' has entered the managerial vocabulary. It usually means that staff can act according to their own choice within a context of general direction. According to Waterman, 'People know what the boundaries are; they know where they should act on their own and where not. The boss knows that his or her job is to establish those boundaries, then truly get out of the way'.[9] Sir Ernest Harrison spent 30 years at the top of Racal making it into a leading supplier of defence products and, on the way, multiplying its value 411 times. He believes in leadership and empowerment. 'I love people who have intensity,' he says, 'who anticipate trouble and take action.' A former subordinate commented, 'Harrison is an excellent boss. He gave me my head in virtually everything. If he trusts you, he trusts you'.[10]

Carefully managed, empowerment can yield benefits at all levels of the organisation. We should note, however, that empowerment depends on the people's perceptions of how much power they and others have. Therefore, a group of workers will not feel empowered unless they see their manager as both having control and being supportive. Perceiving an influential manager means that resources and influence are available and the group will be taking responsibility for meaningful decisions.[11]

The idea of a 'chain of empowerment' looks straightforward and is backed by a democratic ideology. It is, however, fraught with problems. Instead of the traditional methods of controlling organisations through rules, the idea suggests a constantly adapting framework in which power is taken up by staff according to their ability, perceptions and the needs of the situation. We saw an example of the last point in the previous chapter. Soft human resource management encourages staff to create their own development plans. In other words, they are empowered to manage their own training which the employer pays for. Yet, when there is pressure on cash and strategy demands a change of direction, *hard* HRM comes in to impose a succession plan and specify needed competences.

Extra difficulties arise in public service organisations where there are many powerful stakeholders and the government fears failure. Kay distinguishes between constructive and destructive accountability. He favours the former, which gives people freedom to make decisions but holds them fully responsible for their consequences. The latter, in contrast, is a process of supervision that undermines the responsibility of operational managers for their actions without attaching it clearly to someone else. In 1995, after escapes from Parkhurst high-security prison and other failures, Michael Howard, the Home Secretary in the United Kingdom government, dismissed the head of the Prison Service, Derek Lewis. As the subsequent enquiry showed, Lewis' freedom to make operational decisions had been curtailed by excessive supervision and control. He refused to resign, not accepting responsibility for events at Parkhurst because so many of his proposals had been overruled.[12]

Theories of leadership

Alongside the study of management, leadership has been the subject of investigation almost from the time one person exercised influence over another. Using models, from Caesar to Castro and Mao Zedong to Mandela, one school of thought looks to innate abilities possessed by those who stand out from others. We shall start with this *trait* theory, now regarded as too simplistic, and compare it with others that have been developed in the past half century. Figure 16.2 sets them out on a rough time line.

▨ Trait theory

While it has been accepted that leadership traits are both inherited and can be acquired through training and experience, there is little consensus on what these traits might be. Studies have covered physical attributes, social background, intelligence, personality, motivation, focus on tasks and social participation. In a typical study, Dulewicz and Herbert[13] tracked a sample of 72 managers from a 1988 general management course held at Henley Management College. At that time, participants were split, according to their rate of advancement, into 'high flyers' and 'low-flyers'. Almost all the high flyers became directors of their organisations. They were distinguished by exceptional scores on eight characteristics: risk-taking; assertiveness and decisiveness; achievement motivation and competitiveness; together with the conventional managerial skills of: planning and organising; controlling; managing staff and motivating others. These traits are a combination of personal attributes and management skills.

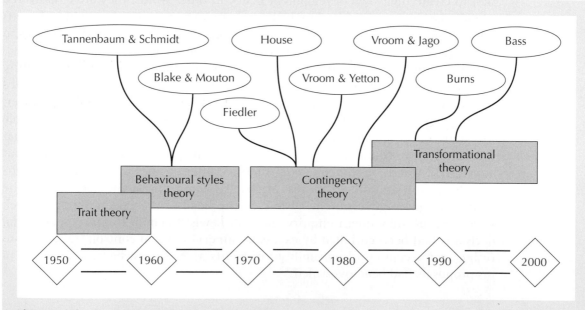

Fig. 16.2 The development of leadership theories

National differences

The trait theory begins to break down in cross-national studies, suggesting that context is also important. Bertin-Mourot and Mauer looked at the career paths of the chief executives of 200 large companies in three European countries.[14] Some results appear in Exhibit 16.1. They show several similarities such as: the bosses averaged 57 years; they had been appointed around the age of 50; they were all male; and they were almost always from the home nation. Differences among the three countries showed in the leaders' backgrounds, with an especially sharp distinction between the French and the others. French leaders started their business careers later than their German or British counterparts but spent less time getting to the top. More were appointed directly from outside (*parachutés*) than from within. As we saw in Chapter 1, academic management education dominates in France. After school, four out of ten had been to the elite establishments, *la Polytechnique* (l'X) or *l'École Nationale d'Administration* (l'ENA). Such paths imply that the heads of large French enterprises are, compared to the two other nations, those who know their businesses the least. Such differences led the researchers to conclude that a European model of ideal leadership traits is a long way off.

Gender

Another question often raised is whether men and women possess different leadership traits. In a study of educational administrators in the United States, Moss and Jensrud found that females were judged by subordinates to be slightly more effective leaders than males. The researchers offered two possible explanations. First, women in the West tend to develop those values and skills that support an empowering, facilitating leadership style. This style is preferred by both men and women,

Exhibit 16.1 Career paths of business leaders in three European countries

	France	Germany	United Kingdom
Career: start age	31	26	22
time to the top	16	23	29
>20 years	17%	37%	36%
<5 years	50%	36%	36%
Promoted from within	33%	76%	82%
Background: from owning family	$\frac{1}{3}$	$\frac{1}{4}$	$\frac{1}{4}$
Experience		$\frac{2}{3}$	$\frac{1}{2}$
Higher education	40% from l'X and l'ENA		
Foreign nationals	2.5%	2.8%	1.3%

although, as we shall see below, it is not always the most effective. The second possibility arises from the difficulty that women still face in achieving promotion. Those who overcome barriers may be more competent than average male colleagues.[15]

In many ways leaders are successful because they are different. For instance, comparing the backgrounds of soccer managers Charlton and Lippi may reveal little to someone wanting to choose another person to fill a vacancy. This suggests that we should concentrate less on innate or learned traits and more on what people do, their behaviour.

■ Behavioural theory

Interest in the behaviour of leaders was stimulated by the systematic comparison of autocratic and democratic types by Lewin and colleagues from the 1930s.[16] They found that groups performed differently:

■ Autocratically led groups worked well so long as the leader was present. Members, however, were unhappy with the leader's style and tended to express hostility.

■ Democratically led groups did nearly as well. Members had positive feelings with no hostility. Efforts continued even when the leader was absent.

The directive–participative continuum

This either/or dichotomy proved too inadequate in describing real managers. The work was refined by Tannenbaum and Schmidt, who produced their well-known continuum reflecting different degrees of subordinate participation.[17] This model, shown in Fig. 16.3, shows different mixes of boss and employee participation. In suggesting that leaders may adjust their styles according to the character of subordinates and the demands of the situation, Tannenbaum and Schmidt clearly saw leadership as something that could be learned from experience.

Thinking that either directive (autocratic) or participative (democratic) leadership is superior should be avoided. For example, if time is short or conditions are difficult, as in a crisis, the directive leader will do better. On the other hand, if subordinates are trained in decision-making skills and are willing to take responsibility, a participative style will be suitable. Information may also present a difficulty. If the manager has the relevant information, the time taken to brief the subordinates may exceed the advantages in morale and motivation to be gained from participation.

The Leadership Grid

Various studies confirmed the above dimensions and suggested others. Best known is the work of Blake and Mouton.[18] In 1961, they published a two-dimensional grid using axes for *concern with people* and *concern for production*. Later, they added another axis, motivation. In the original grid, they identified five leadership styles. Since the two axes were labelled with scales from 1 to 9, these styles came to be known as 1,1; 1,9 and so on. They are shown on the first layer of Fig. 16.4.

The purpose of Blake and Mouton was to encourage people who are not steeped in psychological theory to recognise their own styles. This would be a

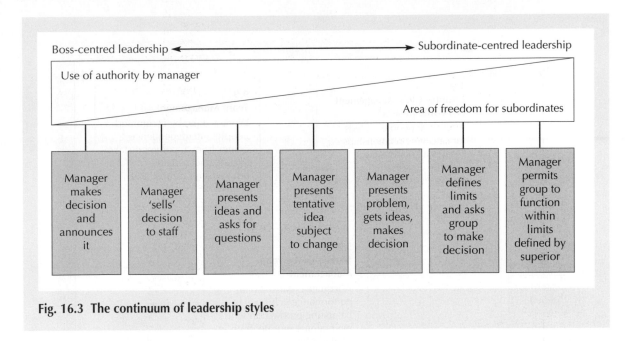

Boss-centred leadership ←——————————————→ Subordinate-centred leadership

Use of authority by manager

Area of freedom for subordinates

| Manager makes decision and announces it | Manager 'sells' decision to staff | Manager presents ideas and asks for questions | Manager presents tentative idea subject to change | Manager presents problem, gets ideas, makes decision | Manager defines limits and asks group to make decision | Manager permits group to function within limits defined by superior |

Fig. 16.3 The continuum of leadership styles

springboard to developing more effective ones. In their later work, the motivational dimension, suggested by the second layer in Fig. 16.4, separated leaders according to whether they were driven by fear of failure (–) or a desire to succeed (+). Through this they identified other common types, especially people who moved between two or more styles. The *paternalist* oscillates between the whip-cracking 9,1– and the people pleasing 1,9+. This person really wants to be liked by people yet needs to be highly coercive when faced with the possibility of failure. In another example, the *opportunist* changes like a chameleon, operating according to the needs of the moment and rarely revealing his or her true colours.

In the last paragraph, we pick up a thread first drawn in the discussion of traits. There is more to leadership style than the character of the person. The needs of the situation, the influence of culture, and the expectations of subordinates all seem to play a part. This takes us towards the notion of contingency.

▨ Contingency theory

In developing a contingency model, the normal method is to compare leadership effectiveness across a wide range of work situations. We shall illustrate the approach by referring to the work of Fiedler, Vroom and Yetton, and House and Dessler.

> A *contingency factor* is any condition in any relevant environment to be considered when designing an organisation or one of its elements.

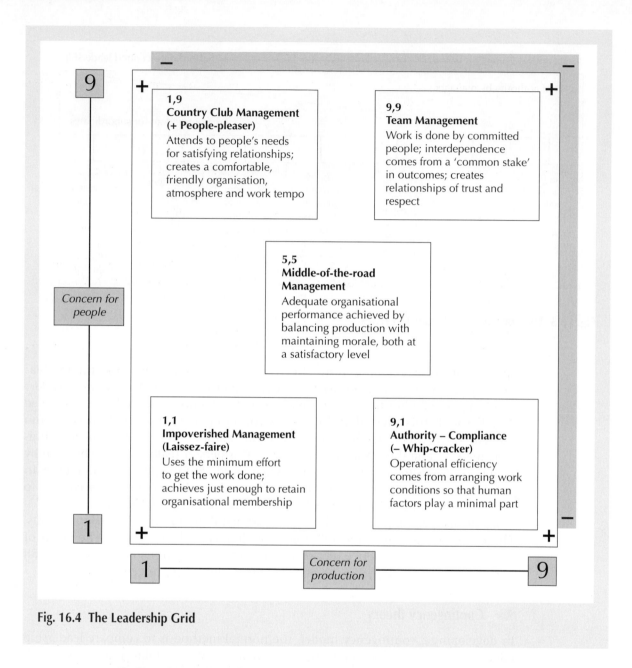

Fig. 16.4 The Leadership Grid

Fiedler's contingency theory

Having observed the different styles used by leaders, Fiedler and his colleagues sought to match them with favourable situations.[19] If the characteristics of the latter could be observed, then the ideal leader could be chosen. They looked at the effect of relations with subordinates, clarity of task structure and the amount of formal position power given to the leader's role. Through putting these possibilities together in different ways, they reached the following conclusions:

- *When the situation is either*
  very favourable (good interpersonal relations, clear task structure and strong position power), or
  very unfavourable (poor interpersonal relations, unclear tasks and weak position power), then ...
  a task-orientated leader will be more effective. This means applying clear direction and control.

- *When the situation is*
  intermediate (moderately favourable with mixed characteristics), then ...
  a people-orientated leader with a participative approach will be more successful.

Although this result may be puzzling at first, it can be explained as follows. In clear water, all that is needed is for someone to take the helm to provide direction. After that everyone knows what to do and is willing to do it. When there are many difficulties, the leader is required to provide clarity and establish control. The poor interpersonal relations will not matter to the task-orientated person. Finally, the intermediate position will benefit from human relations intervention. With appropriate skills, the leader can help the group resolve difficulties, clarify tasks and build commitment. The theory helps us understand why the hard taskmaster sent in to turn round a failing situation can be less valuable once things begin to improve.

Vroom and Yetton contingency theory

Vroom and Yetton[20] focused their model on a narrow question of leadership – which style to adopt in decision making. They proposed that the decision and its setting are characterised by three aspects:

- decision quality refers to its impact on performance;
- decision acceptance, refers to the willingness of the group to put it into effect; and
- the time needed for the decision to be made.

The authors proposed five main decision styles for the leader, set out in Table 16.1.

Having established the types of decision, Vroom and Yetton proposed a series of seven questions to help decide which type of decision style is best. These are set out as a rather complicated algorithm, shown in Fig. 16.5. Answering each question in turn takes the manager to the most appropriate style. Figure 16.5 shows the full algorithm for completeness. Most readers will not need to investigate it in any detail. Instead, they can grasp the general idea of relating styles to contingent factors.

Let us say that the manager of a telephone order office is concerned that one of the clerks handles fewer orders than the rest. After observation, the manager is confident that the clerk lacks product knowledge and is unfamiliar with every aspect of the computer stock control system. Clearly the answer to question 1 is yes and the manager feels there is enough information to work out a remedy – further training. Questions concerning subordinate acceptance would then be

Table 16.1 The five decision-making styles of Vroom and Yetton

		Process	Decision
Autocratic	A1	L uses available information	L makes decision
	A2	L seeks information from subordinates	L makes decision
Consultative	C1	L shares problem with subordinates individually	L makes decision which may or may not reflect subordinates' views
	C2	L shares problem with subordinates as a group	L makes decision which may or may not reflect subordinates' views
Group	G	L shares problem with subordinates as a group	L focuses discussion but does not impose will

faced. For training to work, the clerk must accept the decision, yet the manager is certain that it would be accepted if offered. Therefore the manager can adopt any of the non-participative styles A or C, depending on whether consultation over the details is needed.

The model is valuable for diagnosing a decision situation. In this way it is more practical than others put forward in this section. It is further supported by other studies and by its application in the design of management training programmes.[21] The model has been modified by Vroom and Jago. By the addition of further choice questions answered on five-point scales, scores indicate the appropriate style.[22]

It is also important to note that Vroom and colleagues refer to alternative styles that might be chosen by one manager according to circumstances. This contrasts with the work of, say, Tannenbaum and Schmidt, who saw styles differing between managers, each of whom should follow one consistently.

Path-goal theory

The path-goal theory, developed by House and others,[23] applies the expectancy theory of motivation which we meet later in the chapter. In essence, the approach reaches directly towards the motivation of individuals. It sees they are motivated by two beliefs: more effort will lead to improved performance; and such performance will generate positive rewards and avoid negative outcomes. Leaders can influence subordinates by recognising and satisfying their expectations. In particular, they should make it clear that:

■ subordinates' needs will be satisfied if they perform effectively; and

■ leaders can provide support in terms of direction, guidance, training and other assistance that might be lacking.

The job of the leader, therefore, is to tailor the payoff available for each person to his or her expectations and to make it easier for each to achieve the work objectives. While Fiedler argued that different leaders are needed in different

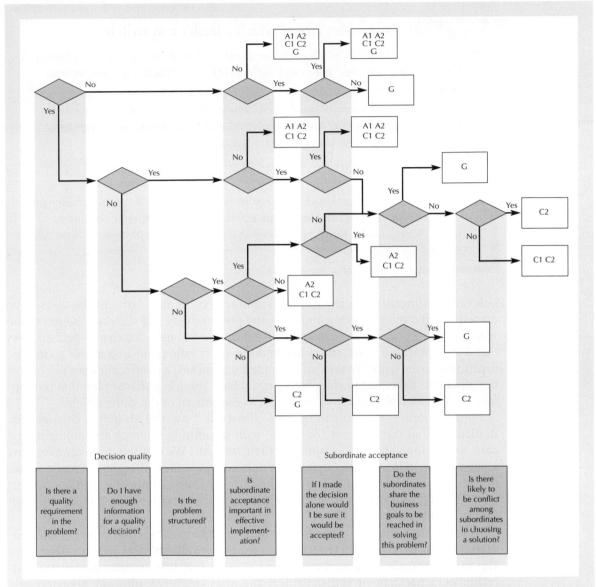

Fig.16.5 Leader's decision-making style: seven questions

circumstances, House's model sets out different leadership styles that match situational factors. Listed in Exhibit 16.2, they can be learnt by the same person.

The two main situational factors included in the path-goal theory are the characteristics of the personnel and the work environment that they share. Personal characteristics include factors such as ability, skills, needs and motivation. For instance, one person may derive great satisfaction from teamwork on projects. In response, the leader may select and organise work to offer that satisfaction. Another, in contrast, may be self-centred and prefer to work alone. Again, corresponding rewards, from payment to work itself, could be arranged.

| Exhibit 16.2 | Four styles among which a leader can switch |

- Supportive leadership implies an approachable, friendly manner and displaying concern for employees' needs and welfare. The leader creates a team, treating others as equals.

- Directive leadership describes the boss telling subordinates exactly what they have to do. The leader plans, sets goals and standards of behaviour and stresses the importance of following rules and regulations.

- Participative leadership means consulting with subordinates and taking their views into account before making a decision.

- Achievement-orientated leadership is seen when the leader sets clear, challenging goals, stresses high quality performance and seeks improvement over current levels. Such a leader shows confidence in staff and works with them to learn how to meet the targets.

Relevant contingencies in the work environment cover the clarity of the tasks to be carried out, the rules covering authority and responsibility and the organisation of the work group. The leader must adapt accordingly. For instance, for clearly defined tasks that a well-practised work group has to do, there is little point in a leader giving the instructions over again. To take an example from cricket, a good team does not expect the captain to direct each fielder before every ball. There is a shared plan that the captain, in discussion with the bowler, adjusts as the pattern of the game unfolds.

Four examples, shown in Fig. 16.6, illustrate how the elements fit together. Remember that the leader is concerned with smoothing the *path* and adjusting the *goals* so that individuals may optimise their rewards. We can see, for example, how a good leader differentiates between a subordinate's lack of technical knowledge, in the first example, and lack of confidence, in the second. The leader's actions mean clarifying the path or building the person's confidence to follow the path that is already clear.

Applying the path-goal and other contingency approaches seems practical and sensible. Yet, lest we accept these recipes too readily, we should note possible objections. The various theories, and we have looked at just a few, lead towards perceiving leadership as a package of skills. Critical theorists, for examples *see* Alvesson and Willmott[24], show how management theory often deals with the problem of legitimacy by trying to hide it in metaphors. Leadership, in the end, is still about getting people to do things that they may otherwise prefer not to do. The contingency approach, in particular, is less about finding out what leaders are like and more concerned with getting those in charge to select appropriate behaviours. The brand labels, such as *supportive*, *participative* and *achievement*, offered by this supermarket of manipulative styles hide their true function. This is to apply technique to dehumanise human relations.

■ Transformational leadership

As an antidote to the calculative and tactical approach embodied in what he termed *transactional leadership*, Burns put forward the notion of *transformational leadership*.[25]

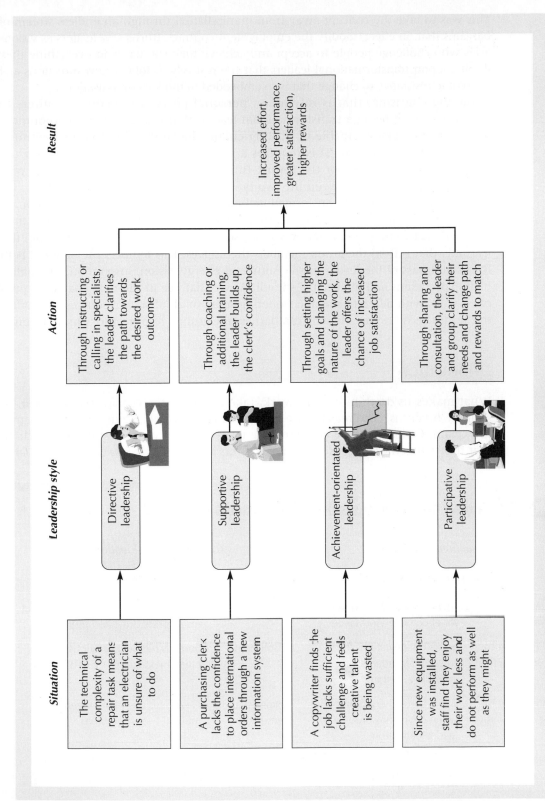

Fig. 16.6 How an effective leader changes behaviour to suit contingencies

This was to take the concept away from manipulation through an endless stream of bargains that, in effect, modify the employment contract. Burns saw leaders as visionaries who challenge people to accept and achieve high standards in everything they do. It is upon transformational leaders that the rest rely to follow new directions and overcome resistance to change that is so embedded in modern organisations.

Having charisma, that is relying on personal power to encourage others to follow, is part of being a transformational leader. Within the modern corporation, however, the person capable of making change has to be able to do so within a functioning organisation. This requires a subtle combination of concern for the present as well as vision for the future. Burns' work was developed by Bass, who set out the differences between the two types of leader as in Exhibit 16.3.[26]

Others link the idea of transformational change with the learning organisation, as explained in Chapter 24.[27] Action learning involves the explicit questioning of their own actions by group members. Advocates see transformation as emerging from this learning, that is from the group members themselves. This tempers the views of both Burns and Bass of the leader as sole source of energy, vision, inspiration, rationality, high expectations and intellectual stimuli. As we shall see in the next chapter, groups often work with different members offering some or all of such resources. The effective leader becomes the one who can harness the group's resources to achieve change.

Motivation

What makes us do things: go to work, take a higher degree, practise snooker, or support Juventus? The reasons are many and complicated. Sometimes we attempt to explain. Other times we act with little thought of why. Motivation is a catch-all that draws together all these reasons. It refers to *internal processes and external forces*

Exhibit 16.3 Transactional and transformational leaders compared

Transactional leader		*Transformational leader*	
'Do what is required'		'Go the extra mile'	
Contingent rewards	Manages exchange of rewards for effective performance	Charisma	Offers vision and sense of mission; instils pride, trust and respect
Management by exception (active)	Seeks out deviations from rules and standards; takes corrective action	Inspiration	Spreads high expectations using clear messages to focus attention
Management by exception (passive)	Takes corrective action only when deviations brought to leader's attention	Intellectual stimulation	Advocates use of intelligence, rationality and problem solving skills
Laissez-faire	Avoids responsibility and dodges making decisions	Individual consideration	Acts as coach and advisor; treats each person as an individual

that direct behaviour. Studying motivation is important to managers. They know that staff work well if they are well motivated, although, as Mullins stresses, they must also recognise the need for competence![28] The link is shown by:

■ *Performance = f (Competence, motivation)*

Frustration

In the work context, as in the rest of life, needs and expectations are often unfulfilled. When people come up against barriers, a good leader helps them overcome them. Either they strive harder to resolve the problem or select alternative goals or tasks. These are constructive responses to barriers. Too often, however, feelings of frustration get out of hand and people respond aggressively, regressively, with fixation or by withdrawal, *see* Fig. 16.7. The manager as leader must learn to recognise and redirect such destructive behaviour. Often described as symptoms of low morale, they are not to be ignored but taken seriously.

Motivational theories

Figure 16.8 provides an outline model of motivation. People have basic needs or expectations which, if they are not satisfied, stimulate behaviour directed towards their satisfaction. Reward, that is satisfaction of the needs or expectations, follows successful behaviour. The model also allows for feedback, that is the person learns about success and can follow the behaviour again. The model helps us tease out three groups of theories about motivation. First, there are those that focus on underlying human needs. These *content theories* encourage managers to think about how far they can satisfy people's innate needs through employment. Second, *process theories* relate more to employees as conscious individuals gauging how to maximise benefits through their jobs. This is the rational world of *Homo economicus* – economic man. Third, we have *reinforcement theories* that link desired behaviour to rewards and hence encourage employees to continue acting to the benefit of the organisation. Figure 16.8 shows how each of these fits with a particular stage of the motivation model.

Authorities distinguish between two types of reward:

■ *Intrinsic rewards* derive from the process of performing a particular function. Accomplishing a complex task, overcoming a serious problem or resolving a difficulty bring feelings of satisfaction. They arise from pleasing oneself.

■ *Extrinsic rewards* are provided by someone else. They include increases in pay and responsibility. They stem, therefore, from pleasing someone else. Although frequently provided by a manager, colleagues can also offer extrinsic rewards through their appreciation.

As with other theories of management, we can find the roots of motivational theory a century ago in the development of scientific management. Recall from Chapter 2 that Taylorism worked on the 'competence + motivation' formula given above. Competence was achieved through specific training. As for motivation,

> Frustration refers to negative feelings that result from unfulfilled needs or expectations, or failure to achieve a goal.

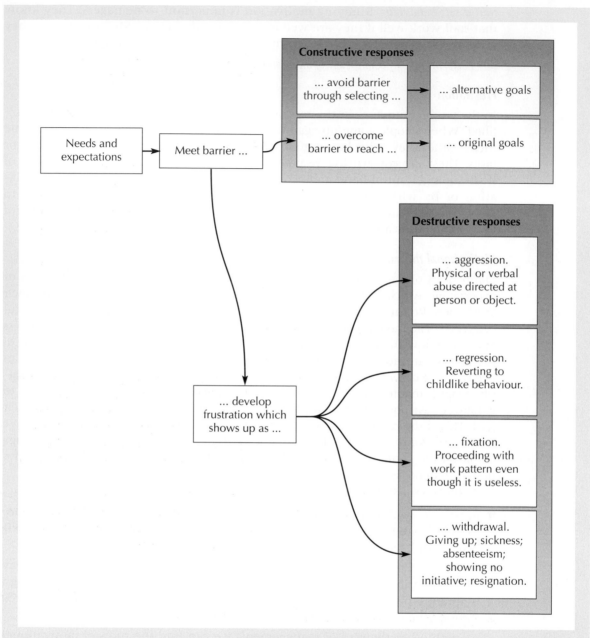

Fig. 16.7 Constructive and destructive responses if needs are unsatisfied

Taylor assumed that man was driven by economic needs. Payment per tonne drove the men to higher productivity. Hawthorne challenged that basic assumption, starting the search for more subtle factors that motivated work behaviour. The debate was influenced by developments in psychology. Members of the behavioural school held that all human activity could be traced to conditioned reflexes and habits based upon them. Although the movement started in the United States, perhaps the best-known behaviourist was Pavlov, *see* Exhibit 16.4.

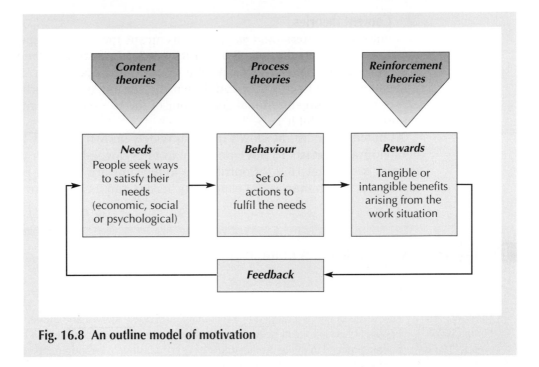

Fig. 16.8 An outline model of motivation

An implication in the behaviourists' work is that how to gain rewards is learnt from experience. The picture is further complicated, however, by work implying that motivation can be inherited. One study compared 34 pairs of identical twins who had been raised separately and had reached their forties.[29] The results showed a strong genetic component to intrinsic motivation. If true, they imply that the managerial task of influencing motivation is more difficult than previously thought.

Given the many strands in the development of studies of motivation, it is not surprising that multiple theories abound. None gives a full explanation so the manager does best by understanding the nature of each and judging its applicability accordingly. It is to these theories that we shall now turn.

Exhibit 16.4   Pavlov – best known for his dogs

Ivan Petrovich Pavlov (1849–1936) became professor at the Imperial Medical Academy in St Petersburg in 1889. He is remembered for his studies of conditioned reflexes in animals, especially dogs. He studied the effect of repeatedly ringing a bell when food was given. Eventually, the bell triggered salivation even though the food was not present. For his work in many branches of psychology and physiology, Pavlov received the Nobel Prize in 1904.

His *classical conditioning* contrasts with *operant conditioning* identified by Thorndike and Skinner. In the latter, the likelihood of a voluntary response can be increased if it is followed by a reward.

Content theories

Content theories stress *what motivates*. This means they look for specific things that motivate. Central to the search are inner needs, their strength and the way these are expressed in the goals that people follow. The hope is that, if managers can understand these needs, they can design the reward system both to satisfy them and to meet the organisational goals. Four of the best-known content theories are summarised in Exhibit 16.5.[30]

As noted in the list, Maslow's theory is widely known. Maslow is one of the few behavioural theorists to have an entry in encyclopaedias such as Britannica or Encarta, *see* Exhibit 16.6.[31] Contributing to his fame are the ease of explanation of his theory, its common-sense plausibility, its age and its American origins. The last

Exhibit 16.5	Content theories of motivation	
Theory	*Summary*	*Comment*
Maslow's Hierarchy of Needs (1943)	Five levels of needs arranged in a hierarchy. People not conscious of needs but normal people proceed to make predictable climb from bottom to top: physiological ⇨ safety ⇨ affection ⇨ esteem ⇨ self-actualisation.	Widely known and influential because simple and plausible. But note that Maslow made original proposal after studying mentally ill patients. There is little supporting evidence from studies of people at work.
Alderfer's Modified Hierarchy of Needs (1972)	Condensed Maslow's list into three levels – existence, relatedness and growth. Suggested a continuous rather than a strict step-by-step progress. Frustration at one level may lead to regression to the next one down.	An attempt to overcome some of the weaknesses of Maslow. Experiments showed that existence needs were more important if they were less fulfilled but did not support the notion of a rising hierarchy.
Herzberg's Two Factor Theory (1950)	Two different factors affect motivation at work. *Hygiene* factors prevent dissatisfaction but do not promote more satisfaction even if provided in abundance. *Motivators*, or growth factors, push the individual to greater performance.	The contribution of Herzberg was to recognise that the opposite of *dissatisfaction* is not satisfaction but *no dissatisfaction*. Both hygiene factors and motivators are important but in different ways. His theory is based on field studies and has direct implications for job design.
McClelland's Acquired Needs Theory (1985)	McClelland proposed that some important needs are not inherited but are learnt. Most frequently studied are the needs for achievement, affiliation and power. People with strong needs in these categories are often found in the roles of entrepreneur, team co-ordinators and top managers of large hierarchies.	Compared with other content theories, McClelland's work looks more towards senior managers' development. Rather than focus on management skill, he argues that attention should be given to developing the drive for achievement.

points mean that it has been included in training courses and business school curricula for several generations! The pyramid of Fig. 16.9 shows the way the theory is usually presented. Having satisfied their workers' basic physiological, safety and belongingness needs through work arrangements which offer satisfactory wages, job security and cooperative work groups, managers are attracted by the idea that motivation comes from responsibility, autonomy and the esteem of others. Not only might these stages be true, but it matches what many want to believe. 'I am motivated by interesting and stimulating work', a manager might say, 'therefore it is good that others are influenced likewise'.

Whether drawing upon Maslow or Alderfer, or common sense, many companies believe that work performance can be improved by appeals to employees' higher order needs in spite of the tasks being inherently dull and repetitive. Fun is advocated at Ben and Jerry's Ice Cream whose 1996 annual report took the form of a colouring book complete with pack of crayons. The company encourages staff to form 'joy gangs' to work out ways to bring more joy to the workplace and develop a sense of belonging.[32] The Body Shop appeals to the needs for social interaction and self-esteem by assisting staff to join charity projects in their local communities.

Although many continue to find the hierarchical models attractive, they have been largely superseded.[33] Herzberg's original work was based on interviews with 203 accountants and engineers. Its outcome, dividing factors into two classes, was an important step. Managers learn to distinguish hygiene factors from motivators, *see* Fig. 16.10. The hygiene factors must be up to expected levels: the pay should be adequate; the office comfortable; or the working conditions reasonably clean and quiet. There is no point in paying excessively, having luxurious offices or overinvesting in clean and quiet workshops. According to Herzberg, what really draws staff along is the chance to achieve the motivators: achievement; advancement; responsibility; recognition; and work itself.

Exhibit 16.6 Abraham Maslow: provided a language to describe motivation at work

Abraham Harold Maslow (1908–70) studied psychology at the Universities of Wisconsin and New York before starting his teaching career at Brooklyn College in 1937. In 1951, he became head of the psychology department at Brandeis University, where he stayed until retiring in 1969. Finding current psychology to be too theoretical and concerned with illness, he developed his step-by-step theory in which, as each level is achieved, the motivation to reach the next is activated. Maslow sought to describe the progress of a healthy person. This idea of incremental personal growth forms the basis of humanistic psychotherapy, often manifested as group therapy. This supports individuals in their development from stage to stage.

Maslow believed that all can have 'peak experiences' that induce very positive and powerful feelings and may strongly influence future behaviour. Yet he believed there to be few self-actualised people, who have them more often than the rest. Using a set of 14 characteristics to distinguish them, he cited presidents Lincoln and Jefferson as examples.

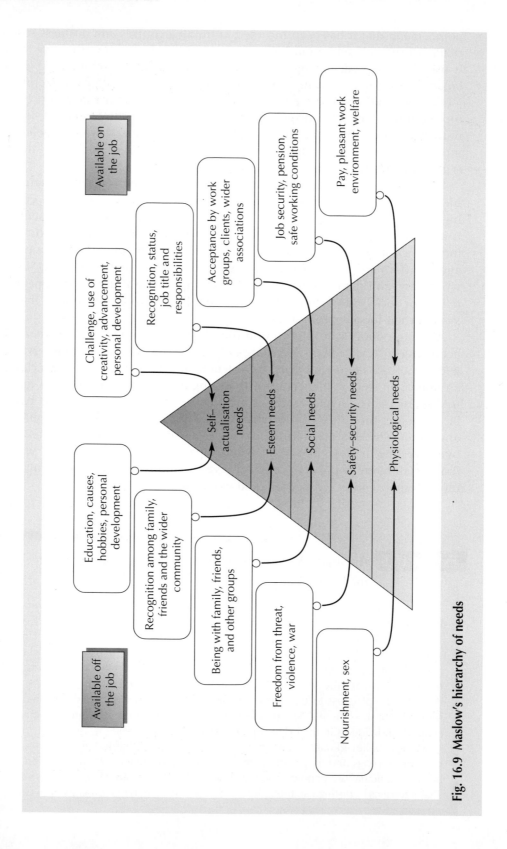

Fig. 16.9 Maslow's hierarchy of needs

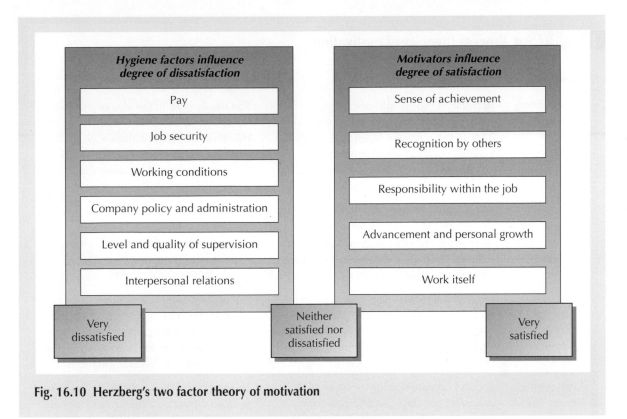

Hygiene factors influence degree of dissatisfaction	Motivators influence degree of satisfaction
Pay	Sense of achievement
Job security	Recognition by others
Working conditions	Responsibility within the job
Company policy and administration	Advancement and personal growth
Level and quality of supervision	
Interpersonal relations	Work itself
Very dissatisfied	Neither satisfied nor dissatisfied	Very satisfied

Fig. 16.10 Herzberg's two factor theory of motivation

Process theories

Rather than examine innate traits, process theories aim to link several variables that make up motivation. They tend to be more complex than content theories because of the multiple perspectives used. Each school of thought is diffuse and is not identified with single authors in the same way as content theories. We shall, however, look at some important examples, mentioning leading authorities where appropriate. Four main approaches are based on the notions of equity, expectancy, job characteristics and goal setting, *see* Exhibit 16.7.

Equity Theory

Equity Theory matches the notions of 'a fair day's work for a fair day's pay'. It really focuses on perceptions of inequity in the output/input ratio whose effect may be similar to the hygiene factors of Herzberg. Inequity leads to tensions and motivations to restore the balance. There are several possible responses for the person affected by feelings of inequity:

■ *Change outcomes*: ask for more pay, different working conditions, or formal recognition with office, job title and responsibilities to match.

■ *Change inputs*: reduce (or increase) effort, attendance, commitment, training and so on.

Exhibit 16.7	Process theories of motivation

Theory	Summary	Comment
Equity Theory (Adams 1960)	Recognises individuals' perceptions of how they are treated compared with others. They assess a ratio of inputs (e.g. education, experience, effort and competence) to outcomes (e.g. pay, prospects, benefits, recognition). People try to reduce inequity.	The theory links to the idea of group norms, found to be very important in the Hawthorne Studies. It also shows that motivational forces are contingent on the local situation. Apart from this, it gives little practical guidance.
Expectancy Theory (Vroom 1964, Lawler 1973)	Motivational strength depends on expectations of work outcomes and associated rewards. It increases if both increase. Incorporates different people's assessments of tasks and rewards and how they may change over time.	Focuses on the individual's perceptions of the situation. Explains changing motivation in the light of circumstances. The theory is supported by common sense and empirical results.
Job characteristics (Hackman and Oldham, 1980)	Job characteristics – skill variety, task identity, task significance, autonomy and feedback – are most important. They contribute to critical psychological states that in turn lead to outcomes.	Places job design at the centre. The interpretation of job characteristics is 'mediated' by each person, but Hackman and Oldham were looking for key factors independent of individual variations.
Goal-Setting Theory (Locke 1984)	Focuses on participation as the route to achieving personal ownership of goals. Motivation follows from: *pointing* towards a target; *encouraging* effort in moving towards it; *promoting tenacity* in the effort in spite of problems; and *permitting the creation of strategies and plans*.	This is a broad theory that clearly applies to those motivated by goals (and perhaps not to others). Studies emphasise the importance of feedback of information on progress. Underpins formal systems such as Management by Objectives and employee participation generally.

- *Distort perceptions*: distort the perceived difficulty or importance of jobs, or the rewards that flow from them.
- *Quit*: find a new job with closer balance.

Shrewd leaders consider both the group norms of equity and individual deviations from them. As illustrated by the bank wiring room in the Hawthorne Studies, group norms can be difficult to change. Leaders often try, however. They may use role models such as the famous Stakhanov. When problems arise among work group members, the leader has to work to reduce their scale or impact. Schemes

Aleksei Stakhanov (1906–77) was a Soviet miner whose output continually overshot the norms. In the 1930s, Stakhanovites searched for means to simplify and improve work processes and were rewarded accordingly. Hero of the Soviet Union, many pictures and statues of Stakhanov appeared during the Stalin years.

such as job evaluation enable organisations both to maintain a balance and demonstrate that they are intent on doing so. Yet organisations often have difficulties, especially if they operate in the global labour market. In considering whether to sign Paul Ince from Milan's Internazionale, Liverpool Football Club had to consider the effects of his pay demands, reputed to be £40 000 per week at Inter, on the club's carefully structured wages policy.[34]

Expectancy Theory

Expectancy Theory follows from the view that people are influenced by the expected outcomes of their behaviour. One way of thinking of this is shown in the analysis of decision trees in Chapter 11. Here, the manager calculates the results of each possible action and selects the most favourable. In contrast to such formal models, individual choices based on expected outcomes will be intuitive, continuously adjusted, frequently based on false assumptions and often difficult for an outsider to understand.

Vroom was the first to develop an expectancy model explicitly related to motivation in employment.[35] In it, he applied the key ingredients of expectancy (the link between personal effort and outcomes) and valence (the anticipated satisfaction from outcomes). The model was later modified by Lawler, who divided expectancy into two stages, E-P and P-O as shown in Fig. 16.11.[36]

From the manager's point of view, it is worth noting the link between this theory and the path-goal model of leadership set out earlier in the chapter. To sustain motivation, the manager's tasks are three-fold. First, match the subordinate's competence to the demands of the job so that the E-P expectation is high. Second, design incentive schemes that link work performance to rewards. Third, ensure that the available rewards are those that employees want. As suggested in Figure 16.11, it may be possible to offer a range of rewards, for example some short term and some long term, to respond to different staff or the changing needs of each

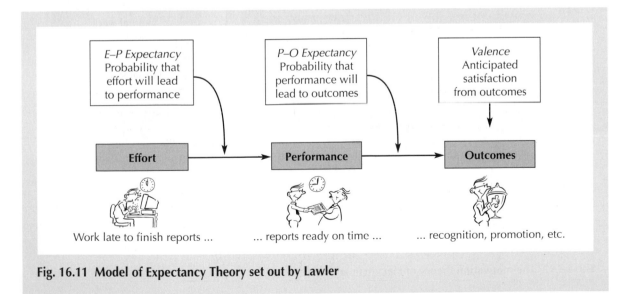

Fig. 16.11 Model of Expectancy Theory set out by Lawler

person. A fixed menu becomes boring. A successful colleague remarked, 'Being named Salesperson of the Year loses its gloss after the third time'.

Job characteristics

Hackman and Oldham searched for general factors within job tasks that would lead to high motivation.[37] Their model links core job characteristics through critical psychological states to results, as shown in Fig. 16.12. Note that the main focus is on features outside the individual. Furthermore, the model does not suggest that work satisfaction leads directly to high output. Instead, both are the result of favourable psychological states as shown. Differences among individuals are recognised in the 'mediating factors' that influence the links but are not central to the approach. The theory aims to offer practical guidance for managing all staff in one occupation, for example, assembly workers, supervisors, police and so on. For instance, the policy of *job enrichment*, dealt with later in the chapter, is underscored by its approach.

Goal-setting Theory

Goal theory starts from the premise that goals play a large part in determining behaviour. Some studies suggest that people who work to agreed output or time standards perform better than those who are exhorted with statements such as, 'Do your best'. However, Yearta, Maitlis and Briner report that most research on goal setting concerns just one aspect. This is the link between goal difficulty and

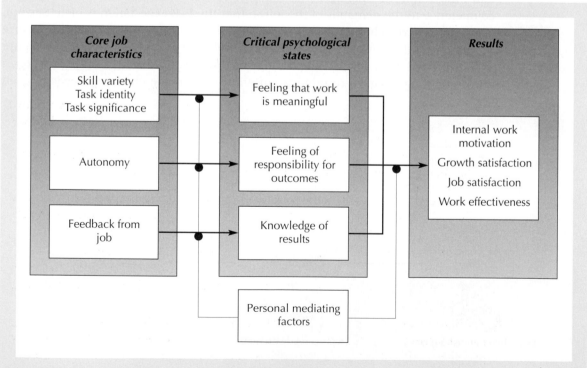

Fig. 16.12 The motivation theory of Hackman and Oldham

performance.[38] It is found that, given adequate levels of ability and commitment, difficult goals will produce better performance than easy goals. Yet, whether linking performance with goals or with participation, almost all research has taken place in laboratory conditions and has examined single-goal settings, something rarely met in practice. A further problem with the results is that experiments include clear measures of performance which often do not apply. Yearta and colleagues, in contrast, examined a real organisation, interviewing some 170 scientists and supervisors in a research centre. They found that performance declined when a goal became more difficult. It seemed that people simply switched to goals where they could make more progress and hence experience positive satisfaction. Further, in this complex setting, any link between participation and increased performance was weak.

The opening case of Chapter 1 includes a comment frequently made by school inspectors. Children's motivation falls when their learning goals are set too low. Clearly, in this case and in others, it is important to select goals that are attainable but not too easy.

Therefore, plausible though it may be, the manager should apply the goal-setting model with caution. Tough goals may not stretch employees. This weakness may explain the frequent disappointment with the effects of bonuses and other performance-related pay schemes. This is not to say that participation in goal setting is a bad thing. There are other reasons why managers and staff should get together to resolve plans, if only to avoid unrealistic expectations. These are covered in the discussion of Management by Objectives in Chapter 9.

■ Reinforcement Theory

Reinforcement Theory relates to the idea of *operant conditioning* mentioned in Exhibit 16.4. Putting on one side content or process explanations of motivation, it concentrates attention on the link between behaviour and consequences. Reinforcement is defined as *any effect that causes behaviour to be repeated or inhibited*. This can be positive or negative. The taste of champagne makes me want to sip some more; eating raw capsicums gives me stomach ache and makes me avoid them.

In practice we can identify four types of reinforcement that depend on the mix of desired and undesired employee behaviour and consequences:

■ *Positive reinforcement* describes a satisfying consequence from following a desired behaviour. Ranging from a simple 'Well done' to changes in pay and prospects, such actions increase the chance of similar behaviour being repeated.

■ *Avoidance learning* refers to the removal of unpleasant consequences as a result of desired behaviour. If, after some problems, an employee improves the standard of work, the supervisor may stop criticising or watching very closely. This is sometimes called *negative reinforcement*.

■ *Punishment* means negative consequences for undesired behaviour. It may range from criticism over poor quality work to formal sanctions for indiscipline. One problem is that it can be given without guidance as to how to achieve acceptable standards. Managers should try to make punishment constructive.

■ *Extinction* involves the withdrawal of rewards in the light of undesired behaviour. Responses such as ostracism by colleagues, or withdrawal of praise or pay increases by managers, may result in the undesired behaviour fading away.

Many argue that the most important lesson from Skinner's work is the manager's role in positive reinforcement. It not only shapes behaviour but teaches norms and enhances the receiver's self-esteem. Managers should recognise that the way it is given is as important as the fact. Reinforcement should:

■ contain as much information as feasible;

■ happen as soon as possible;

■ recognise achievability, responding to small gains as well as large;

■ stem from the top;

■ be unpredictable and irregular, maintaining the element of surprise.[39]

The last point shows up in Exhibit 16.8, relating alternative payment schemes to ideas of positive reinforcement. Daft notes that variable ratio and interval schedules can be the most effective because of infrequent reviews and the persistence of employee behaviour between them.[40]

■ A comprehensive model

Starting from the simple model of Fig. 16.8, we have studied a number of perspectives on motivation in employment. Clearly, each takes a different approach depending on

Exhibit 16.8	Positive reinforcement through payment schemes		
Reinforcement schedule	**Effect on behaviour when used**	**Effect on behaviour when withdrawn**	**Example**
Continuous: reward after each occurrence	Rapid learning of desired outcomes	Rapid decline	Sales commission
Fixed-interval: reward according to passage of time	Average results with irregularities	Rapid decline	Typical clerical worker: monthly payments
Fixed ratio: reward at given increments of output	High and stable performance	Rapid decline	Fruit picking (payment by weight); piece work
Variable interval: rewards based on assessments at unpredictable intervals	Moderately high and stable performance	Slow decline	Awards based on random inspections of employees' work
Variable ratio: rewards based on random work samples	Very high performance	Slow decline	Random checks on sales calls leading to sales bonuses

its origin and which aspect of motivation is being investigated. The various theories, however, can be woven into a broad model, suggested by Porter and Lawler.[41] This combines aspects of content, process and reinforcement. Figure 16.13 shows the model with annotations giving links to some theories we have discussed in the chapter. Note how the model starts with process ideas of equity and expectancy. It links these to satisfaction through content ideas such as the nature of rewards. Two important feedback loops identified by Porter and Lawler are shown. First, there is the employee's assessment of the valence of rewards. This brings in Reinforcement Theory. If learning shows that satisfaction obtained is not high enough, subsequent effort will be diminished. Second, there is learning about how clearly the desired outcomes follow from performance. This is a combination of the E-P and P-O relationships of Lawler's model given in Fig. 16.11. Other loops could be added.

We should not make too much of Porter–Lawler as a comprehensive model. Its core remains a process view that cuts across at least some of the other perspectives. For instance, Porter and Lawler adhere to the idea that satisfaction is a result of the chain leading from effort through performance to reward. Clearly, this conflicts with the views of Herzberg for whom job satisfaction is a motivator. The model, however, is valuable in summarising the various strands of theory. It shows that each theory differs not through contradiction but because they examine different parts of the jigsaw. Each cell of the model suggests a constructive point for the manager, as shown in Exhibit 16.9.

Motivation in practice

There are numerous possibilities for practical examples. We shall, therefore, concentrate on two aspects of the lessons summarised in Exhibit 16.9. First, job design considers the relationship of individuals to their work. Clearly drawing on the

---

Exhibit 16.9 **Nine lessons on motivation for the manager**

1 Ensure that rewards are valued by staff.

2 Find ways to encourage staff to perceive the links from effort to rewards.

3 Through job design, make it possible for high effort to lead to high performance.

4 Select and train people with appropriate competence.

5 Coach staff to understand what is expected of them in their roles.

6 Agree measures to assess performance.

7 Maintain reward systems that match the desired performance.

8 Ensure that rewards are seen as equitable.

9 Continuously study and monitor staff satisfaction.

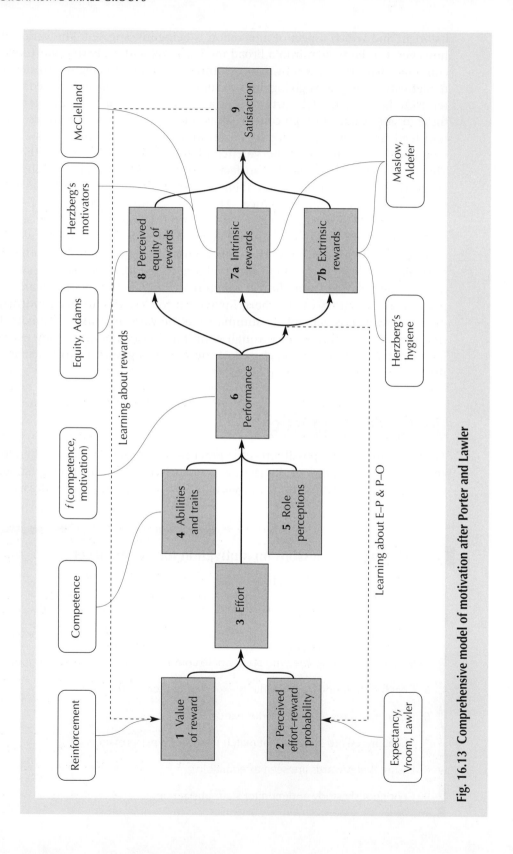

Fig. 16.13 Comprehensive model of motivation after Porter and Lawler

human relations tradition, advocates of motivation through job design argue that performance and satisfaction are both available from good applications. Second, we shall consider the value of variable pay as a motivator. This represents a return to notions of economic man.

■ Job design

Job design is *the identification and arrangement of tasks which together form a job*. It is clear that boring jobs carried out under harsh conditions are demotivating. At the other extreme, jobs that have too much variety, uncertainty and challenge can also demotivate if they make inequitable demands on the people who are expected to do them. Good job design seeks the happy medium. It searches for a balance between job demands and the capacity of staff to satisfy them. There are two basic approaches to achieving a balance – matching people to jobs and matching jobs to people.

Matching people to jobs

One of the effects of industrialisation was that the design of many jobs became dominated by technology. Assembly line jobs arose because many manufacturers felt obliged to seek lower costs in the light of intense competition. Although the growth of robotics meant that some of the most repetitive jobs were mechanised, many humans continue to work as automatons. Apart from assembly, other fields have related difficulties. Surveillance tasks are very dull yet require constant vigilance. These functions arise through necessity and remain because means of automation have yet to be devised. People are expected to fit in.

Given that such unsatisfactory jobs exist, what can managers do to relieve some of their negative consequences? There are three possibilities:

■ *Establish clear expectations.* During recruitment, the nature of the job should be made clear to candidates. It is better to announce 'the most tedious job in the world' than to pretend that it is full of enticing possibilities. Personnel managers in car assembly plants find that many new recruits leave within a few months. Those who stay beyond this period, however, remain for many years. They are comfortable with a simple, predictable job. Unfortunately, knowing in advance whether someone will make the adjustment seems impossible.

■ *Job rotation.* Moving people among tasks at intervals may prevent mental stagnation. It may also bring physical relief if each involves different muscles or posture. Clearly, a balance is needed between the advantages of rotation and its costs. Change has to be organised, training provided and disturbance taken into account. Moreover, the benefits of job rotation are, as shown in the story, very limited.

■ *Earning relief.* Some employers have experienced success through offering *contingent time off (CTO)*. In an eight-hour day one group was producing 160 units

Staff at the Museum of Anatolian Cultures in Ankara change their position at every break. One said, 'I'd rather stay in one place. In that way I would have one boring job instead of four.'

with a 10 per cent reject rate. Managers and staff agreed to a new daily target of 200 plus 3 for every rejected unit. Within a week, output exceeded 200 and defects fell to 1.5 per cent. Staff were free to leave after the daily quota. The average work time became $6\frac{1}{2}$ hours.[42] Although this example says much about the poor state of affairs that must have existed before the change, it is clear that the workers were enticed by the possibility of earning time off. In their circumstances, this must have been an important motivator. In spite of such reports, however, CTO agreements are unusual.

Matching jobs to people

The limited possibilities of adapting people to jobs have led many organisations to the reverse view. Jobs must be adapted to match people's capabilities. Drawing on ideas of socio-technical systems, the nature and boundaries of the job are considered along with the needs of the people. Productivity and needs satisfaction are dual aims of the two main thrusts – enlargement and enrichment.

Job enlargement creates involvement and variety if several tasks that had been divided are combined into a single job. In a simple case, the work of four clerical staff, each handling a separate stage of order processing, may be reorganised so that each does all steps on one quarter of the orders. In other cases, the process design may need to be altered or extra equipment obtained. For instance, to replace an electrical equipment assembly line, each worker would have to be given a complete set of tools and assembly jigs. As with job rotation, critics point out that combining a few boring jobs does not of itself make a job interesting. Yet, if the cycle time is increased substantially by combining a dozen or more tasks, feelings of boredom and frustration may recede as a sense of achievement is reintroduced.

Job enrichment means redesigning the job with the express intention of increasing its motivational content. Hackman and Oldham placed job design at the core of motivation. As we saw in Fig. 16.12, core job characteristics were key ingredients of critical psychological states that in turn influenced performance and satisfaction. All of the job characteristics can be changed through job design:

- *Skill variety*: the range of skills in use can be increased. For example, planning, leading, communicating, recording and monitoring can be developed within the context of manual jobs.

- *Task identity*: enabling a person to complete a whole task with a meaningful outcome. This could range from a complete assembly to looking after all the requirements of a customer instead of referring queries to specialists.

- *Task significance*: designing the job so that its outputs are important to the work of others. Encouraging staff to see colleagues as customers is an important message in quality management.

- *Autonomy*: allowing discretion over job pace, sequence, checking and so on. This is related to the notion of empowerment. There are operational limits to the possibilities for individual discretion. Many modern employers, however, have developed the idea of group autonomy where a few people share control over the work. This is covered in the next chapter.

- *Feedback from job*: providing information on how well a person is doing.

■ Performance-related pay

Matching pay to performance has a long tradition, especially among workers whose output can be fairly well related to their own efforts. Under systems such as piecework or commission rates employees from carpenters to carpet sellers earn bonuses directly related to measured units. There are many schemes. For instance, the percentage of variable earnings can range from 100 for an outworker to between 10 and 20 for an employee in a typical factory setting. In many instances, however, the idea of an employee being personally responsible for output has declined. Work is increasingly carried out by machines, or at least paced by their rhythm. Moreover, work for many is a collective activity and the group is the unit that determines output.[43] For example, someone engaged in selling consumer goods may work hard to achieve personal targets while ignoring the rest of the selling team. Concentrating on sales may be at the expense of not building long-term relationships, picking up bad debts or pressing operations to make too many special deliveries. To counter this, Allied Carpets relates sales bonuses not only to carpets sold but to customer satisfaction ratings.

As with all motivation, the essence here is three-fold. First, rewards should be related to factors under a person's control. Second, they should be related to the authority delegated to the job. Third, relevant performance elements should serve as the basis of rewards. Therefore, if a salesperson has the authority to negotiate discounts, bonuses should conform not to sales volume but to gross profit achieved.

Incentive pay schemes are more than motivators. They double as communicators, suggesting to employees what things senior managers think are really important in the organisation. More important than any mission statement, telling staff that bonuses relate to turnover, profit margin or quality is a strong message. Oliver underscores this view when she points out that typical bonuses in the middle ranks of major organisations amount to between 1 and 4 per cent of salary.[44] Clearly, the bonus symbolises objectives rather than directly stimulating extra striving for a couple of per cent more salary.

Although many organisations have introduced *performance-related pay* (PRP) schemes, results are mixed.[45] Oliver reports that managers do not place it high on their own lists of motivators. It trails in ninth place behind challenge and interest (1), authority and freedom to get on with the job (2), high basic salary (3) and other rewards such as formal recognition, job security and the opportunity to learn. Notable, however, were the responses of the same managers about their employers' views. They felt that employers placed PRP as second, behind challenging and interesting work.

This represents a serious mismatch between employer and employee perceptions. From this and similar studies, many conclude that a link between incentive pay schemes and corporate performance is tenuous.[46] Apart from sales commission, for which there is a long tradition, extrinsic motivators such as pay have a short-term effect and schemes degenerate within a few years.

The evidence is controversial. There is little to support PRP's alleged benefits. Yet there is little to deny them too. Clearly, some companies believe in the advantages and, if they are yet to materialise, continually refocus their schemes. Oliver notes that rewarding teamwork is an emerging trend. In 1990, BP Exploration, with 2500 staff on and around the North Sea fields, had introduced an annual bonus based on the results of the whole company. Recognising its feeble link with motivation, a new team-based plan was brought in from 1993. Bonuses, averaging 9 per cent with a maximum of 15, are paid to teams whose performance exceeds predefined standards. These are set higher than normal budget levels to encourage 'stretch'.

For others, the risk of demotivation from badly designed or implemented schemes looms large. Some plans have demotivated 10 people for each one they have motivated. Some individuals object more directly. The Chief Constable of Hampshire, John Hoddinott, for instance, declined a government appointment because of its PRP element. He explained, 'The notion that I will work harder or more effectively because of PRP is absurd and objectionable, if not insulting.'[47]

Conclusion: follow the leader ... partly

This chapter discussed the interlinked ideas of leadership and motivation. They are connected because part of the leader's intention is to motivate others while followers are partly motivated by the actions of the leader. The one reflects, but is not the reverse of, the other.

We studied how leading and managing differ. It is worth drawing the distinction even though both can be practised by the same person. A valuable perspective is to compare the use of power by leaders and managers. Both use it, although the leader can draw on more power sources, especially those not provided by formal position in a hierarchy. Empowerment is the process of delegating power to subordinate individuals or groups, but only some types of power can be passed down in this way.

Early research on leadership concentrated on personal traits such as competence, appearance and drive. Later studies moved away from this 'Born not made' question to define leadership as behaviour. There are several behavioural models exploring different aspects but none conclusively. As with other aspects of management studies, the difficulty of capturing many variables in a single theory of leadership meant the emergence of contingency theory. This recognises that leadership styles could be tailored to match circumstances. By implication, managers can be given skills to recognise the needs of a situation and trained to adopt the relevant style. More recently, interest has swung away from the building of some skills in all managers to understanding the exceptional leader. This is the person who possesses them strongly. Increasing uncertainty and competition mean that there has never been greater demand for the person who makes all the difference – the transformational leader.

In the employment context, motivation combines with competence to deliver work performance. Many believe that people devote effort for a combination of intrinsic and extrinsic rewards and satisfactions. Yet the links are complex with many theories explaining the patterns. Content theories look to the satisfaction of needs as the starting point. People work better if the work is satisfying. Other theories see satisfaction as an outcome of work. Behavioural theories suggest that people are driven to achieve meaningful goals, seek equity or maximise their expected returns. In all of these, the person's perception is central. How they give meaning to the results of their work is the key to explaining their motivation.

Reinforcement Theory takes this a little further, adding in the notion of learning. People's perceptions, both of rewards and of expectations of their being gained, are influenced by their experience of what happened last time round.

Ideas of leadership and motivation have many applications. The chapter closed with two examples: job design and performance-related pay. Both have shown mixed results. Job enrichment, for example, offers opportunities to many at the expense of unwelcome stress for the few. PRP works for a few but seems to have failed in many instances. Frustratingly for managers, the theories we have covered do not come down on one side or the other. Yet they provide the tools which can be used to analyse practical proposals and understand their likely consequences.

Quick check up   *Can you ...*

- Define leadership;
- Identify the five kinds of power proposed by French and Raven;
- Name four broad classes of leadership theory;
- Lay out the continuum of Tannenbaum and Schmidt;
- Sketch the leadership grid;
- Summarise three contingency theories of leadership;
- Relate the essence of transformational leadership;

- Define motivation;
- Give three classes of motivation theory;
- Name four content theories;
- Name four process theories;
- Explain operant conditioning;
- Define job design, giving five examples of matching people and jobs.

Questions

Chapter review

16.1 Make lists of the main themes of each theory of leadership covered in the chapter. Use these to draw up a table showing the main similarities and differences among them.

16.2 Explain the types and sources of power available to the manager and leader.

16.3 Is it better for a leader to adopt a fixed or flexible style?

16.4 To what extent do you support the argument that motivation is a mirror of leadership?

Application

16.5 Assess the arguments for and against performance-related pay in the light of various theories of motivation.

Investigation

16.6 Compare the portrait of Marcello Lippi, given in the opening case, with other successful sports coaches you know about. What gives them their legendary leadership status?

16.7 Select a service industry for the study of job design. Assess the extent to which job rotation, enlargement or enrichment are, or could be, used to encourage motivation of employees.

Messing about in lifeboats[48]

The Royal National Lifeboat Institution dates from 1854 when the National Institution for the Preservation of Life from Shipwreck changed its name and began to receive a subsidy from the Board of Trade. The subsidy brought with it government involvement in management. By 1869, however, voluntary funds had improved to such an extent that it was agreed that the government would withdraw both subsidy and representation from the Committee of Management. Since that time, the RNLI has been supported entirely by voluntary contributions. It spends £60 million annually on its fleet of 427 lifeboats stationed around the shores of the United Kingdom and Eire. It responds to 7000 calls for distress, saving more than 1600 lives. Demand has grown at more than 5 per cent each year since 1980. By 2000 it plans to be able to reach any point 50 miles offshore in $2\frac{1}{2}$ hours.

About 83 per cent of revenue goes into operations, the rest into income generation and administration. Major costs are salaries for the 750 full-time staff and investment in new boats. The organisation, however, is heavily dependent on its volunteers. There are roughly 4000 lifeboat crew. These are men and women who are prepared to leave home or work the moment their alarm sounds to spend an indefinite time on a rough sea. Furthermore, they give much of their free time to training. Payments are limited to expenses and lost earnings while they are in action.

The RNLI is a charity. Tens of thousands of people are involved in revenue raising through 1800 financial branches throughout the two countries of the British Isles. They do it because they deeply admire the crews' work, enjoy fund raising and believe that their efforts make the difference when it comes to saving lives. Some branches are small, for instance the one in Chester has just ten permanent members.

Flag days and similar events gather money and keep the charity's name in the public eye. This is important since about 60 per cent of the RNLI money comes from legacies. In the United Kingdom, this income stream has declined each year by up to 5 per cent. The cost of sheltered accommodation for the ageing population means that, while the number of legacies has remained steady, the size of each gift has dwindled. Among United Kingdom charities, the RNLI's income ranks sixteenth.

The permanent staff have a crucial role in motivating crews, shore helpers and fund raisers. They offer a 24-hour back-up service to every station and meet other groups at times to suit them. They learn to treat volunteers as much as customers as a workforce. Yet they must be firm in ensuring that procedures are followed, standards are maintained and the stations operate efficiently and effectively.

Training is a core activity for crews. Men and women volunteers will only form a high-performing team if they have the confidence and skill to handle a high-specification boat. With fewer people from these islands going to sea for a living, the RNLI has to build its own expertise rather than drawing it from elsewhere. Training at the station during an inspector's visit used to be enough; now members volunteer to take time out for week-long courses. They must learn and practise navigation and boat handling, including capsizing, night rescue, helicopter winching and emergency beaching.

Achievement is recognised. Sometimes a crew member receives an award for bravery while all volunteers can receive official recognition for distinguished service. More important, though, is the spreading of news of collective achievement either of a lifeboat station or a fund raising group.

The RNLI prides itself on high standards in every aspect of its activities. The lifeboats are built to stringent specifications and are fitted with the best equipment. It argues that a state-run rescue service would have few volunteers and, therefore, much higher costs. Members set great store by the voluntary spirit of the whole institution and resist any change. The RNLI is giving its nations very good value for money.

Questions

1 From what you know of fund raising, discuss the extent to which the motives of RNLI volunteers differ from those who support other charities.

2 Using what you have learned about motivation, show how would you persuade someone to join a volunteer lifeboat crew.

3 Is voluntary work the same as employment, except for the pay?

4 What key lessons would you recommend to business people as a result of studying the RNLI's motivational methods?

Bibliography

A wider treatment of theories of leadership and motivation, including several not covered in this chapter, can be found in Mullins' *Management and Organisational Behaviour*, details in the references, or Vecchio, Robert P. (1995) *Organizational Behaviour*, Third edition, Fort Worth, Tex., The Dryden Press.

References

1. Aspden, Peter (1997) 'Peace, joy and Marcello Lippi', *Financial Times Weekend Section*, 24/25 May, XI.
2. Limerick, David C. (1990) 'Managers of meaning: From Bob Geldof's Band Aid to Australian CEOs', *Organizational Dynamics*, Spring, 22–3.
3. Brierley, David (1996) 'Business portrait of Sir David Barnes: Keeping Zeneca on the side of the gods', *The European*, 12 December.
4. Quoted in 'The poor suffering busters at the top', *Business Age*, 1 May, 1996.
5. Kofman, Fred and Senge, Peter M.(1993) 'Communities of commitment: The heart of learning organizations', *Organizational Dynamics*, Autumn, 4–23; Senge, Peter M. (1990) *The Fifth Discipline: The art and practice of the learning organization*, New York: Doubleday.
6. Capowski, Genevieve (1994) 'Anatomy of the leader: Where are the leaders of tomorrow?', *Management Review*, March, 12.
7. French, J.R.P. and Raven, B. (1968) 'The bases of social power' in Cartwright, D. and Zanier, A.F. (eds) *Group Dynamics Research and Theory*, Third edition, London: Harper & Row.
8. Sankowsky, Daniel (1995) 'The charismatic leader as narcissist: Understanding the abuse of power', *Organizational Dynamics*, Spring, 57–71.
9. Waterman, R.H. (1988) *The Renewal Factor*, New York: Bantam Books, 75.
10. Bevan, Judi (1996) 'Hard work, hard play Harrison', *Sunday Telegraph*, 8 December.
11. Parker, Louise E. and Price, Richard H. (1994) 'Empowered managers and empowered workers: the effects of managerial support and managerial perceived control on workers' sense of control over decision making', *Human Relations*, **47**(**8**), August, 91–108.
12. Kay, John (1995) 'Sharing responsibility is to pass the buck', *Financial Times*, 17 November, 13.
13. Dulewicz, Victor and Herbert, Peter (1997) 'How to spot high-flyers: What makes a successful general manager?', Henley Management College.
14. Cohen, Emmanuelle (1996) 'Comment devient-on dirigeant', *Le Figaro économique*, 9 April, 21.

15. Moss, J. Jr. and Jensrud, Q. (1995) 'Gender, leadership, and vocational education', *Journal of Industrial Teacher Education,* **33** (**1**), 6–23.
16. White, R.K. and Lewin, R. (1960) *Autocracy and Democracy: An experimental inquiry,* New York: Harper.
17. Tannenbaum, Robert and Schmidt, Warren H.(1958) 'How to choose a leadership pattern', *Harvard Business Review,* **36**, May–June, 95–101.
18. Blake, Robert R. and Mouton, Jane S. (1985) *The Managerial Grid,* Third edition, Houston, Tex.: Gulf; Flower, Joe (1992) 'Human change by design: Interview with Robert Blake', *Healthcare Forum Journal,* **35** (**4**).
19. Fiedler, Fred E. (1958) *Leader Attitudes and Group Effectiveness,* Urbana, Ill.: University of Illinois Press; Fiedler, Frederick E. and Chalmers, M.M. (1974) *Leadership and Effective Management,* Glenview, Ill.: Scott, Foresman & Co; Fiedler, Fred E. (1984) *Improving Leadership Effectiveness: The leader match concept,* New York: Wiley.
20. Vroom, Victor H. and Yetton, Philip W. (1973) *Leadership and Decision Making,* Pittsburgh, Penn.: University of Pittsburgh Press.
21. Field, R.H. and House, R.J. (1990) 'A test of the Vroom–Yetton model using manager and subordinate reports', *Journal of Applied Psychology,* **75**, 362–70.
22. Vroom, Victor H. and Jago, Arthur G. (1988) *The New Leadership: Managing participation in organisations,* Englewood Cliffs, NJ: Prentice Hall.
23. House, Robert J. (1971) 'A path-goal theory of leadership effectiveness', *Administrative Science Quarterly,* **16**, September, 321–38; House, Robert J. and Dressler, G. (1974) 'The path-goal theory of leadership' in Hunt, J.G. and Larsen, L.L. (eds) (1974) *Contingency Approaches to Leadership,* Urbana, IU.: University of Southern Illinois Press.
24. Alvesson, Mats and Willmott, Hugh (1996) *Making Sense of Management,* London: Sage 91–109.
25. Burns, James M.(1978) *Leadership,* New York: Harper & Row.
26. Bass, Bernard M. (1990) 'From transactional to transformational leadership: Learning to share the vision', *Organisational Dynamics,* **18**(3), 19–31; Bass, Bernard M. (1985) *Leadership and Performance beyond Expectation,* New York: Free Press.
27. Limerick, David, Passfield, Ron and Cunnington, Bert (1995) 'Transformational change: Towards an action learning organization', *The Learning Organisation,* **1** (**2**).
28. Mullins, Laurie J. (1996) *Management and Organisational Behaviour,* Fourth edition, London: Financial Times Pitman Publishing, 480.
29. Furnham, Adrian (1995) 'Management: Shave off the beard and don a toupée', *Financial Times,* 20 February, 11.
30. For more details *see* Mullins (1996) *op. cit.,* 489–99.
31. 'Maslow, Abraham Harold', *Encarta* (1993) Microsoft; *Encyclopaedia Britannica* (1996).
32. Coles, Joanna (1996) 'Tubs who is cream of the crop', *Guardian,* 28 December, 3.
33. Houlder, Vanessa (1995) 'Managers: Pioneers and prophets – Abraham Maslow', *Financial Times,* 9 January.
34. Ross, Ian (1997) 'Ince leaves Italy for Liverpool', *Guardian,* 3 July, 31.
35. Vroom, Victor H. (1964) *Work and Motivation,* New York: Wiley.
36. Lawler, E.E. (1973) *Motivation in Work Organizations,* Brooks Cole.
37. Hackman, J.R. and Oldham, G.R. (1980) *Work Redesign,* New York: Addison-Wesley.
38. Yearta, Shawn K., Maitlis, Sally and Briner, Rob B. (1995) 'An exploratory study of goal setting in theory and practice: a motivational technique that works?', *Journal of Occupational and Organizational Psychology,* **68** (**3**), September, 237–52.
39. Creech, Regina (1995) 'Employee motivation', *Management Quarterly,* **36** (**2**), Summer, 33–9.
40. Daft, Richard L. (1997) *Management,* Fourth edition, Fort Worth Tex.: The Dryden Press, 541–2.

41. Porter, L.W. and Lawler E. E. (1968) *Managerial Atributes and Performance*, Homeward, Ill.: Irwin.

42. Kreitner, Robert (1992) *Management*, Fifth edition, Boston, Mass.: Houghton-Mifflin, 324–5.

43. 'Mastering management: Why piece work went out of fashion', *Financial Times*, 19 July, 1996.

44. Oliver, Judith (1996) 'Cash on delivery', *Management Today*, August, 52–5.

45. Carnell, Bob (1995) 'Panacea? Not even a placebo: performance related pay', *Management Accounting*, **73** (**1**), January, 32–3; 'Management: Is performance-related pay worth it?', *Financial Times*, 22 July, 1996.

46. Rines, Simon (1996) 'Trigger happy: The vast majority of employees feel insecure in their jobs and cite employer complacency as a real problem', *Marketing Week*, 5 July; Nelson, Bob (1996) 'Dump the cash, load on the praise', *Personnel Journal*, **75** (**7**), July, 65–8.

47. Oliver (1996) *op. cit.*

48. Miles, Brian (1997) 'Where pay has no part to play ...', *Management Today*, January, 5; Armstrong, Neil (1996) 'Legacy funding – Finding the will to stop the decline and fall', *Precision Marketing*, 16 December; RNLI home page www.indigo.ie/rnli

17

Groups and teams

Chapter objectives

When you have finished studying this chapter, you should be able to:

■ define the terms group and team and use examples to illustrate the types found in organisations;

■ account for why people join groups, demonstrating the effect of motivation and notions of distance and social exchange;

■ defend managers' reasons for setting up work groups and cross-functional teams;

■ outline some theories related to group formation, development and the roles people occupy within them; point out the limitations of these theories;

■ explain important factors affecting group performance – composition and cohesiveness – and show how they can resist undermining and handle conflict;

■ illustrate models and theories by reference to problems of cross-national teams and group rewards.

Work teams at Volvo[1]

Some European firms have consistently striven to create semi-autonomous work groups. They have been influenced by people-centred production traditions, markedly in Sweden and The Netherlands. Learning from the unrest of the 1960s and 1970s, Volvo has been among the leaders. Although its pioneering car assembly plants at Kalmar and Uddevala have closed, the use of teams remains widespread, notably in the subsidiary company, Volvo Truck Corporation. VTC is a multinational enterprise manufacturing vehicles from 7.5 to 42 tonnes. The truck market has witnessed pressures to reduce costs parallelled by increasing demands for customised products. The response of VTC has been to remove hierarchical layers and cut the proportion of indirect staff while making production more flexible. Central to the policy are efforts to develop a different type of worker and work system. Unions are supportive. One official stated, 'You cannot work with a traditional work organisation on our line. You must have another type of person, another type of skilled worker than in traditional single machine systems. We cannot do exact work instructions for our type of machines, so you must work in another way, you must trust people, you must educate people, you must give them more responsibility to see over the whole system.'

In most of the Skovde plant, traditional output-based incentive schemes have been replaced by rewards based on competence ladders, such as in Table 17.1. This outlines how staff can progress from level to level as they learn more responsible roles. Within the plant, however, different sections have had to develop their own approaches. The foundry, for example, has a capital-intensive single flow process. Functions such as melting, core making and heat treatment have up to 50 men. Within subgroups, they practise some limited job rotation but the scope for job enrichment is constrained by the technology.

Table 17.1 Competence ladder at VTC Skovde

Level	Status	Approximate time to reach
A/B	Induction, trainee	3 weeks
C	1 job	2–6 months
D	3–4 jobs	1 year
E	6–8 jobs and team leader	2 years
F	Inspector	3 years
G	Relief operator	3–5 years
H	Instructor	> 5 years

After casting, items such as engine blocks and crankshafts pass to the machine shops. Here, the highly automated equipment needs to be kept running at optimal level. Teams of staff at different steps on the competence ladder work flexibly to achieve this aim. When things are running smoothly, they also carry out indirect tasks such as material supply, examining quality problems, housekeeping and work allocation.

In another plant at Koping, team working was brought in when new machines were installed. Teams of six have no formal leaders. Their responsibilities include controlling absenteeism, planning, material control and handling, overtime and task allocation. A production manager commented, 'Team working was not necessary before when there was one person to one machine. When you are working in a larger environment with several machines you have to work in a group and you need social skills.' Managers report that productivity has risen, with 40 to 90 per cent gains in machine efficiency. They admit that the new system places greater demands on staff and there is more stress. Yet absenteeism, traditionally a stress indicator, declined from 15 to 12 per cent in the two years after the change.

The assembly plant at Tuve has two production areas. High volume vehicles are put together on standard assembly lines. Customised vehicles are assembled in one of six dock areas where work cycles last some four hours. In theory, dock team members can rotate their jobs every cycle, depending on their position on the competence ladder. Production leaders and some specialist roles, however, do not rotate. These leaders usually select operatives for their teams. Requirements are health, loyalty, 'a desire to be a good employee' and, above all, the ability to work with others. In turn, managers have selected the team leaders with the assistance of psychological profiling.

Shop floor attitudes at VTC have changed. A Skovde plant manager commented, 'Today, we have a very interested and a very skilled workforce in all systems ... we do not need tough guys here any more, it is OK to have a brain.' Change has parallelled a rise in the number of women blue-collar workers. Staff agreed that behaviour had improved. One manager saw the justice in not discriminating against half the population, adding, '... it gives you another climate. Suddenly the guys shave in the morning, they have taken down the pin up pictures. Suddenly it is more friendly, it gives you another atmosphere.'

Notwithstanding their success in some sections of VTC, work teams have not spread through the whole production system. Barriers to change include: the conservative attitudes of some managers; the demands of technical efficiency, especially for high volume standard products; and the cultural environments of each plant. Lacking the history of collaborative relations found in Sweden, foreign VTC plants, such as in Belgium and Scotland, do not have mechanisms to support the introduction of team working.

Introduction

News about the introduction or failure of work teams in manufacturing plants creates mixed reactions. Some see a heroic failure in the closure of Volvo's pioneering car plants at Kalmar and Uddevala.[2] Worker autonomy along Volvo lines is seen by Womack and others[3] as utopian and a nostalgic expression of craftsmanship values. They point to Toyota and other Japanese firms to demonstrate how teams should be used as part of the lean production system, not as alternatives to it. In the Japanese approach, teams are tightly restricted in a setting dominated by management, an arrangement that is not possible in many other countries. Others see team working as part of the search for balance. If they do not squeeze out the last drop of efficiency that is because the firm has found the middle ground between that objective and improvements in labour turnover, absenteeism and quality. As the case of VTC shows, there is no panacea. Each plant or section must find its own solution related to the technology, the people and their traditions.

Beyond setting up and working with groups, managers spend much of their time working in them. Groups are important features of every organisation. How well they work has a substantial effect on the total performance. As well as means of getting things done, groups can offer social satisfaction to members. Due to this dual function, it is essential for managers to understand how groups emerge, are sustained and succeed or fail. In this chapter, we examine how and why groups form, the processes through which they might develop, the main influences on their performance and typical issues to be found in modern organisations.

What are groups and teams?

Clearly, people are social animals. They have a long history of association to achieve their ends, whether it is to gain great things through pooling resources or simply the satisfaction of the need for social contact. We shall detail the reasons in a moment but first let us have definitions:

> *A group comprises at least two people, who continually interact with each other, have something in common and recognise that they are members of the group.*

Although cast broadly, this definition rules out many possibilities. The key ideas are interaction, sharing and perception of the group's existence and membership. Not included, therefore, are examples such as: people travelling on a bus (something in common but no interaction); a customer and shop assistant (interaction but no continuing commitment); or an unsuccessful party (people with little in common).

The term *team* presents more of a problem. As implied in the opening case, it is widely used to refer to a work group although with special overtones which suggest coherence, harmony, practice and training. Mullins states that a successful group needs a spirit of unity and cooperation, continuing rather curiously, 'Members of a group must work well together as a team.'[4] In the context of shop-floor work, Osborne and colleagues defined the *self-directed work team* as a highly trained group jointly responsible for one stage of the production process.[5] At other levels, managers find themselves parties to cross-functional teams designed to resolve intergroup difficulties. These ideas make us see that a team is a special kind of group:

> *A team is a group chosen from members with complementary capabilities so that together they can achieve a planned purpose.*

Note the ideas of choosing, complementary capabilities and goal-seeking. A successful student quiz team does not contain the four most brainy members of the faculty. It needs a balance between those who can quote Shakespeare and those who can name the drummer in an obscure band. In business, Kodak is one company that uses cross-functional teams to work on problems that get stuck in the conventional organisational structure, *see* Exhibit 17.1.

Teamwork makes all the difference in many sports. Here, ideas of coaching, communication and personal strengths such as vision and self-belief have long been recognised. Such ideas are now being drawn into management as the autocrat gradually makes way for the team leader. Will Carling, who captained the English rugby union team, set up Insights, a motivational consultancy.[6] Then came rugby's turn to learn from business, described in Exhibit 17.2.[7]

Exhibit 17.1 Kodak's commitment to teamwork

A film product development team included not only Kodak's research and manufacturing engineers, and marketing specialists, it invited in customers such as top cinematographers and film-makers. The resulting EXR colour film won an Academy Award and gained the lion's share of its market.

To streamline its annual report, the company built a team from three of the units involved in its production as well as printers, graphic designers and postal staff. More than $100 000 was saved in the exercise.

Beyond such task-orientated cross-functional teams for problem solving or one-off projects, Kodak is also looking to teams as the unit for organisational learning. This needs training, sharing of goals and a change of attitudes towards improvement. Kodak's black and white film manufacturing unit was transformed by these methods. From a number of rivalrous groups blaming each other for misfortune, it has returned to profit.

George Fisher, chief executive officer, has led the change with a more participative management style. Information on progress is shared widely.

Exhibit 17.2 Pride of Lions

The British Lions team, made up of players from the United Kingdom and Ireland, normally assembles every four years. Its 1997 tour was the first visit to South Africa since the end of apartheid. Management had just one week to prepare the squad before it left. Tactical discussions were interspersed with leadership and team development training normally taught to executives. One reason was the risk of unfavourable comments about off-the-field behaviour, similar to those made about touring soccer and cricket teams. Players who were not chosen for the star games had to hide any dissatisfaction from the press and behave themselves.

The last meeting of the course was the most significant. Here, all players, managers and assistants formed small groups to work out a code of conduct and means of sustaining spirit over two months. All undertook to share rooms with others they had never met before or knew little. Players who were not selected for any game agreed to join the pre-match alcohol ban. A disciplinary procedure was established. All 21 points of the code were given to the 47 squad members when they left London. Unexpectedly, the Lions won the international matches 2–1.

Formal and informal groups

Groups and teams are common in organisations. People are often assigned to them. They are set up to achieve certain ends which provide the common theme that members will share. Examples are maintenance units, customer service teams, research groups or aircraft crews. As we noted in the discussion of groups and teams, an effective work group will build shared values and ways of working so that both the organisation's ends and members' needs are satisfied. The negative side is that they may not. A work group that does not function well can be agony for its members and useless for the organisation.

Since organisational work involves cooperative effort, all members are part of at least one formal group. In a model that has been widely quoted, Likert proposed that, rather than see the hierarchy in terms of links among individuals, it could be perceived as a set of groups.[8] Managers act as link pins to bind them together, *see* Fig. 17.1. Its simplistic nature, however, means the model has not been further developed. Although valuable in reminding us that managers are members of at least two groups, it fails to capture the complexity of the groups that they can join. Departmental subgroups, cross-functional teams, working parties and project groups are but some of the arrangements met in practice. Likert would be hard pressed to represent these.

Formal groupings are but part of the story. Informal ones arise from the social intercourse natural in all organisations. Informal groups are all those that are not deliberately set up to further the organisation's aims. Membership, therefore, is voluntary and likely to be based on people finding something in common. Some groups can focus on specific tasks or activities, such as an office hiking club, while others consist of looser clusters of people who like to meet occasionally to share grumbles or rumours over a drink. There is no reason to assume that informal groups work for or against the interests of the organisation. In many cases their function is beneficial, such as creating better working relations or allowing the release of tension. On the other hand, they can be centres of resistance to change. The output restriction among some work groups in the Hawthorne Studies is a famous example of an all too common experience.

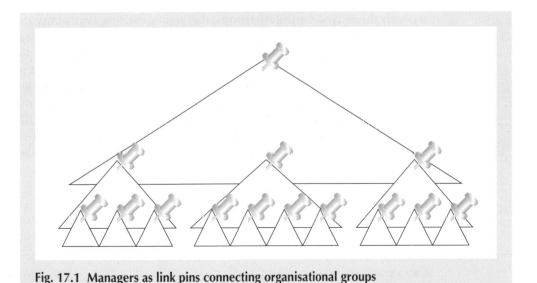

Fig. 17.1 Managers as link pins connecting organisational groups

Open and closed groups

We can also distinguish between open and closed groups. The former will frequently change their membership as people move in and out. Their internal structures are also likely to fluctuate as members take up various roles including that of leader. Closed groups, on the other hand, have a defined membership and often have a well-established internal structure. We may expect many formal groups in the organisation to be closed.

The work teams at Volvo Truck Corporation are good examples. In most cases they had defined membership and some fixed structure, although efforts were made to rotate some roles to give flexibility and maintain motivation. Being closed risks stagnation. Manz and Neck coined the word *teamthink* to refer to this effect: it means the occurrence of groupthink within self-managed teams.[9] Conformity replaces effectiveness.

> *Groupthink:* caused by members of a cohesive in-group placing unanimity above realistic appraisal of proposals. *See* Chapter 11.

Among professional and technical staff, closed groups are best for tasks such as long-term planning. Once the group is some way into the project, it is difficult to bring in newcomers. Again, many groups benefit from the infusion of new ideas brought by a new entrant. An open arrangement for creative groups may, therefore, be advantageous.

Group formation

Given the varied nature of groups, it is not surprising that many different explanations have been proposed for why people join them. Voluntarily joining an informal group, for example, will be a different process to being placed in a formal team by a manager. Many groups develop spontaneously when patterns of work bring people into frequent contact. From the manager's point of view, these can have advantages in helping to smooth the work flow or disadvantages in resisting change. Rather than leave matters to chance, a sensible manager may allocate staff. In so doing, it would be wise to place people in those teams that they would have joined voluntarily. To do so, an understanding of group formation is essential.

People joining groups

For a clue about why people join groups, we can refer to the ideas of motivation explained in Chapter 16. Among the many theories on this point, that of Alderfer offers a helpful start. He proposed a list of motivators with three items:

■ *Existence* – people join employing organisations to gain income to cover their basic needs. When at work, they form support groups or join trade unions to defend their employment rights.

- *Relatedness* – needs for affiliation and emotional support are, for many, satisfied through mutual exchange within a group. These benefits are sometimes only noticed when they are removed. One unemployed person remarked, 'When I was at work, I hated the sniping, nagging and gossip that went on. Yet when I lost my job I found I missed it terribly.'[10]
- *Growth* – groups help in the realisation of difficult tasks. Therefore, they offer enhanced feelings of accomplishment. For new people at work, acceptance in a group brings opportunities to learn from others and builds self-esteem.

Beyond the idea of joining groups in general, however, is the question of why people join particular groups. In other words, why are certain clusters of people drawn together? Two important aspects are distance and similarity.

Distance

It is clear that the formation of groups is influenced by opportunities to interact. People who live close at hand, travel together, or work in the same unit, have plenty of chances to develop closer ties than those who do not come into contact. Proximity can be represented by physical distance, as in groups of workers in a section, or psychological distance. The latter can be pictured as a mental map of the organisation, sketched in Fig. 17.2. The map represents: links among colleagues; distances among them; and all kinds of barriers. An example of a link is found among staff who regularly contact others across the world. They report feelings of closeness although they never meet. Barriers can separate staff on the same site or even in the same room. Differences in status, backed up by formal status symbols, are often important here.

Fig. 17.2 Mental map of physical and psychological links and barriers

Although distance is often the result of chance events, it is clear that managers can make interpersonal links one factor in layout design. Consider a short line, say 25 metres long, attended by seven staff each engaged in one step of a process. It could be kitchen equipment assembly or kit toy packing. Such lines are usually set out in straight lines, as in A of Fig. 17.3. This is ideal if the line is balanced, that is all workers require exactly the same time to do each cycle. Unfortunately, in the more common case of an imbalance, the arrangement makes work sharing difficult through hindering communication. Hence a coherent work group may not coalesce. U-form layouts, as shown, may improve matters. Although people are no nearer, arrangement B may be an improvement as they can see each other easily. C, on the other hand, places the workers closer and avoids the barrier of the machinery. However, they now face away from colleagues.

Similarity

The sayings 'opposites attract' and 'birds of a feather flock together' seem to contradict. Yet, as Vecchio shows, these may be describing different aspects of group formation. It is widely accepted that people will be drawn together if they:

- share similar *attitudes*;
- have different *needs* that complement each other, and
- possess matched *abilities*.[11]

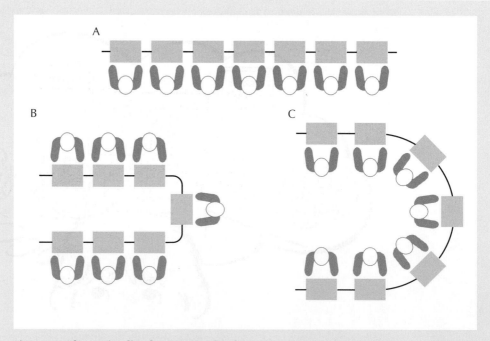

Fig. 17.3 Alternative line layouts to stimulate group formation

> Jack Sprat could eat no fat.
> His wife could eat no lean.
> And so between the two of them,
> They licked the platter clean.

Mr and Mrs Sprat illustrate complementary needs with a shared attitude of parsimony. In many successful partnerships, we find people who share the same goals and values. Yet one, say, is an expert at administration, while the other excels at innovation and marketing.

An alternative to the theory of attraction views the individual's attachment to a group rather than to another person. In *social exchange theory*, Thibaut and Kelley argued that people assess the rewards and costs resulting from being the member of any group.[12] They compare the outcomes (reward minus cost) both with their expectations and with what they think is available elsewhere. If the answers to both questions are unsatisfactory, they quit. Other combinations of answers indicate continuing membership yet at varying levels of commitment. Figure 17.4 expresses three further states as outcomes of an informal algorithm. Opposite the quitter, the *full member* is wholly satisfied and committed to continuing member-

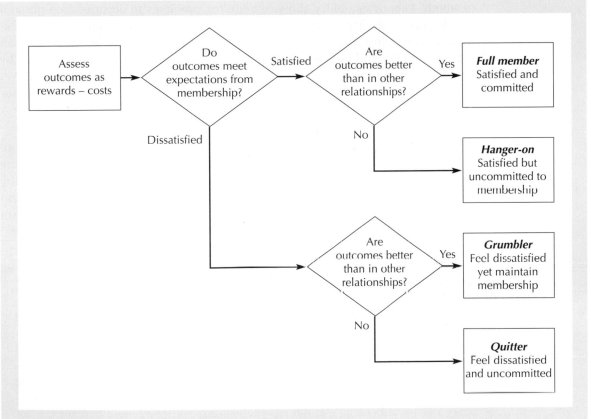

Fig. 17.4 Group membership as optimising social exchanges

ship. The *hanger-on* is only waiting for a chance or excuse to move on. The *grumbler* remains, dissatisfied with the group but knowing there is nothing better.

In many voluntary organisations, people join for practical reasons. They need help or an outlet for their energies. Yet their involvement may outlast their reasons for joining. Exhibit 17.3 gives an example of the Stroke Association.[13]

Managers setting up groups

In spite of expressed concerns for the humanisation of work, the accent in group formation from the management point of view is instrumental. In other words, work groups are set up as a means of achieving optimal output levels, not as an end in themselves. We should expect considerable variation in their design, depending on what is to be achieved. The opening case showed how, even within one plant of VTC, teams of manual workers were established differently in response to various technologies. Other contingencies range from national culture to the impact of individual personalities. Thompson and Wallace distinguished three dimensions – technical, governance and normative – that help to explain why managers establish work groups on the shop floor.[14]

■ *Technical*
  Team working is often introduced as a means of changing the Taylorist division of labour. Labour flexibility allows scheduling problems to be smoothed out and enables responsibility for process control, stocks and housekeeping to be delegated to the group. Teamwork also incorporates a capacity for learning that can improve quality and productivity together. Its introduction may be facilitated by new technology, as in the VTC Koping machine shop of the opening case. Yet the Skovde foundry showed the limits of this approach when applied to automated production lines.

■ *Governance*
  In current management rhetoric, team working represents a shift away from hierarchy towards empowerment of employees. In most cases, however, the degree of control ceded is small. The functions that are delegated arise from the technical requirements of new processes rather than the goal of participation itself. Three issues arise: how much power is delegated; the process of team leader selection; and how the team fits into the wider management of the plant.

Exhibit 17.3 The multiple functions of patient support groups

The Stroke Association is a charity that both offers support for patients and carers and sponsors research into the disease. Most members of the local branch join for instrumental reasons. Often referred to the group by doctors, they look for help when a family member becomes a victim. Yet many stay on well after the patient has recovered or died. In finding themselves able to understand, they reap the rewards of being able to share their experiences with new members and give assistance. The group also offers a sense of belonging at a time of loneliness. For some, these benefits are not available elsewhere.

Although Volvo is regarded as a pioneer, studies suggest that its work teams have little impact beyond their immediate surroundings. We might call them demi-semi-autonomous.

■ *Normative*
Groups have often been seen as means of deepening employees' identification with the goals of the enterprise. Rather than let informal groups resist change, goes the argument, it is better to establish and train formal ones. Team working is a modern expression of such a policy. Through careful selection of teams and their leaders, management hope to dampen some of the difficulties of motivation, conflict and diversity present in any workplace. Developing team players is a central theme of much management development. In its various centres, VTC saw the development of work groups, and related initiatives such as new pay structures, as means of building employees' support for quality and productivity enhancement.

Although the above examples relate to the shop floor, groups are to be found at all levels. Studies have covered all layers from board meetings and consultative councils downwards. With continuing pressure to make organisations work as well as possible, it is important for managers to understand group processes as a prerequisite to improving them.

Group processes

Groups are dynamic. Not only can we think of the group as a whole changing, but also we can examine how individuals perform different functions at different times. Sometimes they lead, on other occasions they follow the rest, and so on. We shall start by describing two well-known perspectives on group development and roles. Then we shall comment on their limitations and look at a more recent alternative view.

Group development

Of many studies of stages that groups pass through as they develop, Tuckman's list is the best known.[15] Choosing rhyming labels for the four stages of development doubtless helped to popularise the model:

■ *Forming*
A new group of people comes together. Caution is the watchword. People behave according to their anticipation of acceptable behaviour and attempt to focus on the task. For a formal group, this may be given by management; for an informal group the task may be 'protest' or 'have a party'.

■ *Storming*
Members come out of their shells enough to express and appreciate their conflicts and the difficulties of their task. Hostility and confusion frequently appear.

■ *Norming*
The group works out how to come together as an effective unit. Members begin to match their capabilities with aspects of the task in hand.

■ *Performing*
Group roles are defined and shared. The group begins to work cooperatively on its task using the above definitions. This is when the group becomes a team.

The time taken for the stages could vary from a few hours to many weeks. We should also note that groups need not always follow the sequence strictly. A formal management group, with people who have worked together previously, may start at the norming stage and only revert to forming and storming if new members come in or a new leader emerges.

Tuckman's model can be illustrated by a party. With few people knowing each other, the first hour could be spent forming. Unsure of themselves and their surroundings, guests stand around nervously, discussing 'the weather'. Later, as things warm up, some begin to talk more animatedly, joking with some and arguing with others. Groups form and, as they norm, they begin to perform. They relax, dance, joke, and discuss politics. The host's role is critical, both in the design of the party and managing the process. Is there music? Are there separate rooms for dancers and non-dancers? Are there to be charades and, if so, must one take part? Are there icebreakers to shorten the forming and dampen the storming? If such points are unclear, and the storming becomes uncomfortable, some may leave early.

Group roles

Within work groups, members play roles whose nature depends on their positions within the group and the wider organisation from which they are drawn. Personal factors also come into play. Therefore, a person who has the longest experience among those assigned to a cross-disciplinary problem-solving team may be given the role of leader. Another person, anxious to get on with the job, may begin by trying to set an agenda and find out facts about the problem.

> A role is behaviour in a social context.

Well known among classifications of group roles is the work of Belbin.[16] He observed how group members in simulations made different contributions according to their personalities and abilities. The team's success depends on how they fit together. The range of roles is shown in Table 17.2. According to Belbin, the list gives us insight into the sort of people who are needed if a team is to be successful. Those who cannot fill one or other of the team roles, as opposed to offering personal qualities such as expertise or humour, will not aid the team building.

Belbin weakens his argument by admitting that not all roles are needed in all groups. Furthermore, some people can offer more than one, For example a combined monitor-evaluator and completer-finisher, *see* Table 17.2, could be a sober, hard-headed person who is also capable of tying up loose ends.

Limitations

The work of Tuckman, Belbin and others has been criticised by Herriot and Pemberton.[17] They argue that our understanding of teams is hindered by the persistence of two myths:

Table 17.2 Valuable team members

Role	Features	Positive qualities	Negative qualities
Implementor	Conservative, dutiful, methodical	Organising, common sense, hard work, self-discipline	Inflexible, deaf to untested ideas
Co-ordinator	Calm, self-confident, controlled	Treating all contributions fairly; sense of objectives	No more than average intellect or creativity
Shaper	Excitable, outgoing, dynamic	Drive; opposes inertia, complacency, self-deception	Provocative, impatient
Plant	Individualistic, serious, unorthodox	Genius, imagination, intellect, knowledge	Impractical, dreamy, ignores protocols
Resource investigator	Extroverted, enthusiastic, curious, communicative	Makes contacts, checks out new ideas, responds to challenges	Loses interest after initial obsession
Monitor-evaluator	Sober, unemotional, prudent	Judgement, discretion, hard-headedness	Lacks inspiration, cannot motivate
Team worker	Social, mild, sensitive	Responsive to people and settings; promotes team spirit	Indecisive in crisis
Completer-finisher	Painstaking, orderly, conscientious, anxious	Follows-through; perfectionist	Worries about small matters; reluctant to let go

■ The *All Friends Together* myth, derived from the human relations tradition, proposes that people work better once they know and accept each other well. This implies that once the team processes have been sorted out, effective performance on the task will follow.

■ The *Stages of Team Development* myth implies that teams must pass through various initiation steps before work can start.

Evidence supports neither. In organisations, teams rarely spend time on process before plunging into the task. Then they alternate between making progress and considering better ways of going about it. There is no fixed pattern since tasks vary so much in familiarity, complexity, time pressure and information requirements. Herriot and Pemberton also emphasise the drawbacks in Belbin's work we mentioned above. In particular, the categories were developed not in work but from observing managers involved in business simulation exercises at a training centre. Their alternative model, shown in Fig. 17.5, offers a more comprehensive summary of the relationships among context, process, tasks, roles and outcomes.

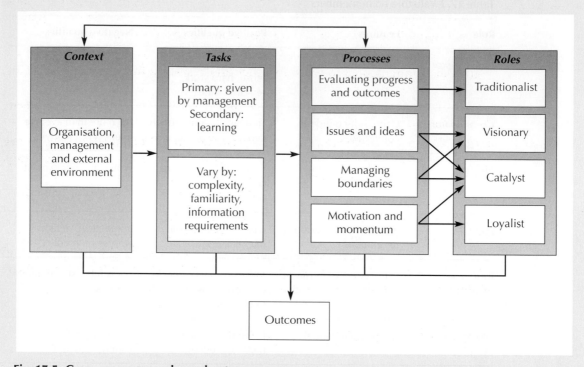

Fig. 17.5 Group processes, roles and outcomes

The broad outline of the model shows that tasks are determined by the context in which the group works. In order to fulfil the tasks, the group must engage in certain processes and these processes determine the roles that are needed. Furthermore, the processes interact with the context in a dynamic way. Examples include the resources and support provided by the rest of the organisation, the time pressure, and the degree of autonomy permitted. In return, the team will attempt to influence the context, buffer itself against fluctuations in policy and resources, promote its cause and make alliances with other groups.

Among team processes, Herriot and Pemberton identify four that are needed for achieving the task and enabling the team to learn. Shown within the main boxes of Fig. 17.5, they are always needed but in different proportions according to the nature of the task. To accomplish these processes, there are four roles, but more broadly defined than by Belbin:

■ *Traditionalists* work dispassionately on facts, making logical decisions. Situations requiring subjective judgements and involving personal factors are avoided. They are good at running existing systems while being weak at responding to change.

　– Traditionalists are important when it comes to *evaluating progress and outcomes*.

■ *Visionaries* like to be analytical but prefer settings with less information. They see the big picture, devising new systems and projects. Detail does not interest them and they avoid personal feelings and emotions.

- Visionaries are needed to spot *issues* in the broad picture and generate *ideas* for *managing boundaries*. This means fitting in with the whole organisation, scanning the environment, drawing in extra resources and so on.

■ *Catalysts* prefer to develop their own and others' skills and talents. They are good at getting people to work together and resolving interpersonal problems. They dislike routine and conflict.
- Catalysts are good at making *ideas* come to fruition and are vital in *managing boundaries*.

■ *Loyalists* act pragmatically to help colleagues and clients. They look to the common good, seeking ways to make things work efficiently and harmoniously. They may not notice change and avoid conflict.
- Loyalists keep up *motivation and momentum* to ensure the task is completed.

The final part of the model relates to outcomes. The primary function of the group is to accomplish its task. An important secondary outcome is learning. All elements of the model contribute to the group's outcomes. The authors argue that context is the strongest factor in success with the group's capability at managing its boundary the most underrated.

Factors influencing performance

In the previous section, we began to discuss the composition and cohesiveness of groups. The work of Tuckman described, in general terms, how a group might develop. Belbin examined roles that members might occupy. The weakness of both of these stances is that they do not explicitly concern themselves with the question of performance. Herriot and Pemberton responded by showing a path from context to roles through task and process. We shall now look in more detail at performance. Issues are: the influence of group composition and cohesiveness; how they face up to efforts to undermine them; how they handle conflict; and how to assure success.

The composition of the group

Size

What is the optimal size of a group? In his whimsical essay on the life cycle of councils and committees, Parkinson noted that they have a tendency to grow, and as they grow they divide into subgroups where the real decision making power lies. What is now known as The Cabinet, the central organ of government in the United Kingdom, has moved through this cycle five times in history, *see* Exhibit 17.4.[18]

Although written with tongue in cheek, Parkinson's tale brings out two points. First, as groups grow, problems arise. They are more difficult to handle, require more supervision and meetings will suffer from lower attendance and lack of attention. It is often observed that they break up into sub-meetings at each end of the table. Rivalry among factions becomes more noticeable. The group closest to the centre assumes more power. The second point is that there is no optimal size.

Exhibit 17.4 A 'history' of The Cabinet

At its incarnation in Mediaeval England, the Council of the Crown had five members but its hereditary membership soon reached a level of between 30 and 50. By the mid-17th century it had grown to 140. Then, in century steps, it grew to 220 and 400. By 1950, when granting hereditary peerages had almost ceased, the House of Lords numbered 850.

By 1300, an inner group had formed. The Lords of the King's Council were fewer than ten and remained so until Tudor times. In 1504, there were 41, rising to 172 by the last meeting.

The Privy Council developed from the King's Council. Starting with nine members, it reached 20 in 1540 and 44 by 1558. 1723 saw 67 members and the 20th century saw its numbers grow from 200 to 300.

By 1615, the Cabinet Council had taken over the reins. Starting with eight members, it reached 12 by 1700 and 20 a quarter of a century later.

In 1740 another inner group emerged. The Cabinet began with five members. The nineteenth century saw its numbers steadily rise from 12 to 20. After that, membership has been held in the range 18 to 23. Naturally, throughout this period many have complained of Prime Ministers running an Inner Cabinet of trusty confidants ...

The number of people required depends, as we saw above, on the processes that are needed and these in turn depend on the group's task. Parkinson, however, concluded that the optimal size of a national cabinet should be eight. This was the only number between 6 and 22 that had *not* been chosen by any nation!

Vecchio notes the following serious points about group size:[19]

■ Organisations settle on between five and seven as an ideal number for full participation by each member. For simple, formal tasks, larger numbers can be chosen. (Another study put the average in North America at 10.[20])

■ As groups grow, members become more tolerant of authoritarian and directive leadership. Participation is inhibited.

■ Larger groups need formal rules and procedures if they are to be effective. In spite of these rules, they take longer to reach decisions than small groups.

■ Job satisfaction declines with group size.

■ Productivity declines with group size. Increased co-ordination difficulties and falling member involvement mean that work groups of twelve typically produce less than two groups of six.

■ Social loafing, or free-riding, becomes a problem with larger groups. Recognising the inefficiency of the group and the infeasibility of sanctions, some individuals feel that their slack can easily be taken up by others.

Composition

For the group to function effectively, its members must have sufficient resources that are relevant to the task. Discussing Cabinets, Parkinson argued for members with resources of specialised knowledge. 'Four may well be versed, respectively, in finance, foreign policy, defence and the law. The fifth, who has failed to master any of these subjects, usually becomes the chairman or prime minister.'[21]

As we saw in our discussion of decision making in Chapter 11, diversity of membership is important in ensuring creativity in group problem solving and avoiding groupthink. Yet when the group need to focus on a clearly defined task, similarity of outlook may be better. That is why self-managed work teams are often permitted to select newcomers when replacements are needed.

Diversity, therefore, must be treated cautiously. The mix of group members must relate to the task in hand. Variety is not of itself advantageous if the extra dimensions brought by additional members are irrelevant. Moreover, leadership roles must be held by those who are the most competent.

Cohesiveness

We can define cohesiveness as a measure of how much members are attracted to, and wish to remain with, a group. Here we can add to our previous discussion of why people join and remain. Six means of sustaining cohesiveness are given in Exhibit 17.5.

Strong work groups have drawbacks. In general, more cohesive groups perform better and provide more satisfaction to their members. Yet, their perceptions of the benefits of group membership may make them more resistant to change.

Preventing undermining

All work groups, intentionally or accidentally, are susceptible to being undermined. Depending so strongly on building up an atmosphere of trust among people from disparate backgrounds, they risk being hit by negative behaviour

---

Exhibit 17.5 Sustaining group cohesiveness

- *Social attraction* – people take pleasure in each other's company or are attracted to the values and goals of the others in the group.

- *External threats* – sharing a mutual enemy or competitor can be an important source of cohesion. Members realise that sticking together is the best way to succeed.

- *Isolation* – being cut off from others enhances the sense of interdependence in facing external forces.

- *Size* – as discussed above, small groups tend to be more cohesive. Yet they may not be large enough to encompass all shades of opinion or areas of expertise.

- *Complementary skills* – groups comprising members with a range of skills will succeed, provided that the balance of skills is relevant.

- *Rewards* – as we noted in the last chapter, reward systems may not only directly motivate but convey information on the sort of behaviour management wishes to see. Incentive schemes based on group results, rather than individual performance, will be important.

patterns and attitudes. Slobodnik and Slobodnik identified eight of these 'team killers' that can erode the work of a group.[22] These are shown in Table 17.3 alongside a list of potential remedies.

Many symptoms from the team killer list were evident in a case reported by Chaudron, summarised in Exhibit 17.6.[23] This article is unusual in that it gives details of a failure. The company name is almost the only element not revealed. The problem-solving team had been set up without clear guidance or enough power to carry out its brief. As circumstances unfolded, it would have been better to have these points clarified. Yet we should recognise the difficulty for five middle managers to agree to do this once things have begun to go wrong.

Table 17.3 Team killers and associated remedies

Team killer	Remedy
False consensus: mistaking silence or vague assent for consensus	Encourage challenge to ensure that all can accept the outcome
Unresolved overt conflict: when a few members regularly have rowdy arguments, others may make allowances just to avoid the war	Encouraging recognition of the problem; agreement on procedures for discussion to which all must subscribe
Underground conflict: conflicts played out through covert action can seriously damage group health; they create a climate of distrust	Making disagreements overt; appointing a neutral arbitrator
Not reaching closure: getting stuck in long discussions without results gives a team a bad reputation	Prior agreements on how decisions are to be made; breaking into subgroups to make progress
Calcification: the pattern is fixed in stone, each member playing the same role in every meeting	Deliberately rotating roles such as leader, recorder and so on; forming different subgroups
Uneven participation: dominance by a few and passivity by the rest means that the team's resources are not well used	Devising means of 'gatekeeping' to give everyone a say; ensuring that everyone is invited to add input
Unaccountable to others: empowerment of a group can give rise to feelings of being answerable to no one	A group should not be set up unless its line of accountability is clear
Customer forgotten: satisfying the wishes of group members may mean that unrepresented external or internal customers are forgotten	If there is a danger, appoint a customer representative; alternatively assign the customer perspective to at least one member

Exhibit 17.6 How not to set up an effective quality team

The company of 150 staff made a clear profit supplying items to customers such as Motorola and Texas Instruments. These and other customers had conducted favourable audits. One quality team was set up to improve the manufacture of one line of equipment. Production problems were compounded by customers complaining over delays.

The team had five middle managers from manufacturing, engineering, sales, service and accounting. Meetings, averaging three hours per week for a year, were well attended. They occurred during the lengthy, 60–80 hour weeks of these busy managers. After the period, their seniors realised the team had failed to reach its target and called in consultants for advice.

The consultants observed the team at work and interviewed members separately. They also applied a standard survey of team effectiveness. They found the team to be frustrated, angry and tired out. They had been interested in the quality problem but were now 'stuck in the mud'. Senior managers had attended meetings but had been rebuffed.

What had gone wrong?
The consultants identified the following external causes:

- no quality measurement therefore only anecdotal evidence of the problem;
- no direction on purpose;
- little senior management involvement from the beginning;
- lack of management support;
- organisation structure working against the team;
- poor production scheduling;
- no improvement incentives.

There were also internal group problems:

- no measurement of progress;
- no early team building;
- poor interpersonal relations with frequent rows;
- wrong team membership – too many engineers and an inexperienced accountant;
- haphazard training – some attended seminars, others did not;
- mismatch between heavy responsibility and little authority.

The consultants put forward three choices: disband the team on the grounds that the members had no energy to restart; cut the project's scope and team membership; or reorganise the company around its three product lines. The last would make a cross-functional team unnecessary. None was chosen. Chaudron reported, 'Alas, this company suffered from a common malady called consultant d'jour.' A new expert was brought in. A new scheduling system was installed and the quality team disbanded without any thanks for its efforts.

■ Conflict

We can see in Table 17.3 that two of the team killers are conflict, covert and overt. Not only does this directly hinder progress but it increases anxiety for members and dilutes their commitment. Yet conflict is not something to be avoided. Clearly, some interpersonal conflict is always present and, through the definitions of their roles, some members will find themselves opposed to others. They may represent, for example, different projects among which the group has to decide.

So, two types of conflict, based on personal factors and stakeholder interests, are to be expected. The third type concerns the structure and processes of the group itself. Especially in a group whose members are just finding their feet, disagreement over the way things should be done can have damaging effects. Such a group may be unable to make progress to resolve or accommodate the normal personal and stakeholder differences.

Inter-group conflict

Conflict also appears among groups. Generally, managers prefer this not to happen. They want groups to cooperate in achieving the goals of the organisation. This is especially true if the work of the groups is interdependent; the output of one is received by the second as a 'customer'. Yet conflict among groups arises for as many reasons as conflict among individuals. This gives us a warning about all groups, whether they are boards of senior managers or self-managed work teams. They can avoid or absorb interpersonal conflict yet at the expense of introducing something more severe.

Inter-group conflict results from practical and perceptual difficulties as follows:

■ *Scarce resources.* When several groups compete for the same inputs, for instance people's time, equipment, investment funds or space, fighting can become fierce. In the cramped office complex, two project teams both spotted an unused room as an ideal base to store and use their documents and other materials while their work lasted. Senior managers were faced with favouring one or the other. This choice would signal which they thought was more important.

■ *Lack of clarity.* Unclear working assumptions in an atmosphere of poor communication create problems for any group. Its needs for internal effectiveness may cause it to determine its own terms of reference, including responsibilities that other groups also claim.

■ *Perceptions and attitudes.* A problem-solving group may perceive that its work is more important than any other. In consequence, it expects senior managers to pay great attention to its recommendations. Furthermore, it may claim first call on the time of any of its members. From different viewpoints, other groups may adopt the same attitudes. If managers intervene to clarify these differences, they may make them worse.

■ *Goals.* If the goals of group members differ from others in the organisation, conflict results. For instance, when asked to report on security arrangements in a rambling office building, a staff group focused its attention on the concerns of employees, especially when working late. They sought to prevent access by intruders and provide safe exits to the car park. Management, on the other hand, had perceived theft of office equipment as the more serious problem.

Successful groups

As we have seen, group work of various kinds has been around for a long time. What is new is the rising interest in group work at the operating level. Pressures to reduce costs and increase flexibility have combined with a humanistic zeal to improve job satisfaction. Self-managed work teams are the result. But how can success be assured?

High-performance work teams

Although we have studied some general models of group formation and development, they give little guide in particular circumstances. The opening case study showed how each situation is unique. One approach is to gather clues from the differences in performance of teams in the same organisation. This can be as great as 100 per cent.[24] Is it possible to learn from the so-called *high-performance work teams*? Clearly, some organisations believe so and try to spread the learning across their organisations. Rover Group, in its drive to improve quality throughout its manufacturing system, used the learning from successful pioneer groups to develop the quality teams that followed.

Avoiding pitfalls

Another approach is to avoid pitfalls. Bergmann and de Meuse suggest that many plants may not be ready for teamwork. Unless all staff are able to adapt to a new relationship, the venture is doomed.[25] Tudor and others, estimating a 50 per cent failure rate, propose basic means of securing cooperation. Unless they take place, the change will meet resistance and probable failure. Preparation should be along the following lines:

■ good initial presentation by committed senior managers;

■ consultation with unions or other representatives;

■ gradual team building with new rules, communication channels and other procedures;

■ attention to employee motivation;

■ guarantees over job security;

■ training.[26]

Horses for courses

One problem with all types of teams is that they have become fashionable. The temptation is to establish them when they are not needed. On the shop floor, for example, the team may be little more than a unit of job rotation, as in the foundry at VTC Skovde. There is a danger of pseudo-empowerment, where the job enrichment on offer is confined to deciding upon who does which boring task. It is difficult to argue that this is better than allocation by a supervisor.

Among professional and technical staff, cross-functional teams have recently gained prominence. Offering open communication and autonomy, they contribute to higher creativity, better decisions and job satisfaction. Using the example of product development however, Andrews argues that these teams are not suited to all decision situations. Although ideal for 'blue sky' thinking about completely new products, developments of current ranges may best be handled through traditional structures.[27]

Groups in practice

The point that groups pervade organisations has been made several times in this chapter. While there is much in common among them, the differences are also significant. A permanent self-directed work team on the shop floor will differ from a temporary project team and the senior management board. The organisational and national settings add further variation. To demonstrate issues concerning groups in practice, therefore, we will focus on two examples. These are how groups can be set up within multinational companies and the link between reward systems and team performance.

■ Culture and teamwork

Myers and colleagues have studied the impact of different management styles on the effectiveness of cross-national teams.[28] Building on the work of pioneers such as Hofstede, they chose to focus on European countries. First, they showed that thinking of a homogeneous European style was unrealistic. Using questionnaire data from 2500 respondents, four contrasting styles were identified:

- *Consensus*
  Found mainly in Finland and Sweden, this style stresses team spirit, effective communication and attention to detailed organisation. Consensus, generated at open meetings, leads to job satisfaction.

- *Common goal*
  Typified by managers in Austria and Germany, these people favour technical expertise applied in harmony to achieve a clear goal. It is acceptable to have an authoritative leader to achieve this. Controls are advantageous.

- *Managing from a distance*
  Confined to French participants in the survey, these managers like to be left alone to do their work as they see fit. Consensus is seen as unimportant. There is little attention to consistency of action with middle managers experiencing high levels of uncertainty. Resentment builds up among subordinates.

- *Leading from the front*
  Common among managers from Ireland, Spain and the United Kingdom, leadership is seen as an individual performance. Both Latin and Anglo-Saxon cultures adhered to the belief that charisma and skills of individuals make a great deal of difference to corporate success. Explanations, however, differ. Spanish top managers may resent any restriction on their status, while the British and Irish are pragmatic and results orientated.

Myers and colleagues give several situations where the different styles will lead to problems in cross-national teams. To illustrate, we shall focus on one – the need to promote discipline at meetings. In a meeting run under the *consensus* style, it will be important for all to show that they are moving in the same direction. To this end, there will be detailed discussion of the agenda points and deviation into wider issues will not be tolerated. If operating under *working towards a common goal*, the agenda will have been set with the sole intention of reaching decisions. Again, deviations are unlikely to be condoned. If *managing from a distance*, there is likely to be much debate across many issues. Each person will be pursuing a personal agenda. Even if decisions are made, implementation is unlikely unless further contact occurs after the meeting. Finally, a *leading from the front* meeting will also have much discussion on issues beyond the agenda, particularly if led by a Spaniard. The British and Irish would tolerate this provided there is a prospect of a conclusion.

One could argue that the ethnocentric multinational has merely to spread its own style irrespective of where it is operating. Were it to do so, the problem would be moved, not solved. The company still has to engage with suppliers, agencies, trades unions and so on. Each of these will expect interaction along national lines. A German expects a two-hour meeting to cover up to three important agenda items. A group from southern Italy would take all day. These and other problems of different expectations are illustrated in the example of Exhibit 17.7.

Myers and colleagues recommend a return to basics, arguing for the establishment of ground rules to achieve commonality while allowing for national variations. The experience of Intel also supports ground rules. A study of its successful international teams stressed the importance of setting clear expectations and defining clear goals, roles and responsibilities. A strong corporate culture provides a point of reference to bind the team together. Among members, positive attitudes, common goals and good communication skills were significant.[29] In addition, to these characteristics, Odenwald points to the extra dimensions of leadership. The leader must: tolerate ambiguity; be flexible, persuasive and patient; build consensus; coach; and expect change.[30] All advocate specific training for leaders and members of international teams.

Exhibit 17.7 Difficulties of cross-national cross-functional teams

A French multinational organisation sought to implement its mission of customer care and service quality through a matrix structure. Its effectiveness depended heavily on the links between the line of business managers and the country managers.

Conflict became the norm. A typical case was the running argument between business managers who wanted standard pricing throughout Europe and country managers who preferred a differential policy, depending on local conditions. Everyone saw the issues and the strength of the arguments. The problem was the way such debates were conducted.

Meetings were a problem. French senior managers would invite the regional and business managers to address particular problems. Germans expected to reach a decision. The French saw meetings as talking shops, appearing to reach agreements but sometimes announcing a different line later. The British, often in frustration, would concentrate only on their responsibilities, following courses of action which suited them. These opposed, at times, directions from above. The Scandinavians expressed disquiet. They felt that, without meaningful discussion, real commitment to resolving the team issue could not emerge.

■ Rewarding team performance

We briefly noted the emergence of team performance rewards near the end of Chapter 16. Individual performance-related pay has failed to provide hoped-for results in many cases, so attention has turned to pay and other rewards for the whole team. Armstrong notes how innovative United Kingdom companies are increasingly adopting the idea.[31] Yet results seem mixed. In a survey conducted by the Institute of Personnel Development, over half of those respondents that had adopted team pay were confident that performance had improved as a result. Unfortunately, only 22 per cent could quantify the gain.

Shop floor group incentive schemes follow a general pattern. Bonuses are linked to output or time saved on team tasks. In contrast, for managerial, technical and office staff, there was little in common save some means of distributing sums among members. Sometimes there are fixed criteria. For instance, Pearl Assurance relates bonuses to speed, accuracy, and customer service and satisfaction. The last criterion is commonly used in financial service firms. Other organisations use more open criteria. The Benefits Agency has its local managers assess teams' contribution to overall performance. It is normal to pay bonuses as a percentage of basic salary.

Armstrong notes that team-based pay works best if teams:

- work to their own targets;
- have a high degree of autonomy;
- comprise staff whose work is interdependent (otherwise the team would have no point);
- have stable membership so that each knows what to expect from the rest;
- are well established, used to working flexibly to meet targets;
- are made up of multi-skilled team players.

There is anecdotal evidence of employee preference for team reward schemes, especially where they have replaced discredited individual performance-related pay. Like so many innovations, they should not be introduced in isolation. Pearl Assurance combined its scheme with empowerment, upward appraisal of managers, regular feedback and non-financial rewards.

Clearly, team rewards are given to all members according to an agreed formula. Indeed, we should add the criteria and methods of measurement to Armstrong's list. Yet the group formula may not match any individual's needs. Matching is one of the points made in the previous chapter. Subsuming of the individual's interests into those of the group is a disadvantage of the reward system and raises further questions on what some would see as a rush to set up work teams everywhere.

Disadvantages

The complex relationship between people and their work groups is disturbed by moves towards shared rewards. From the individual's point of view there may be several drawbacks:

- Teams can enter a downward spiral. Falling expectations mean the best staff will not join.

- More effective employees migrate towards the strongest teams, especially if they can choose. (*See* the assembly plant at VTC Tuve in the opening case.) Reassigning work among teams, or even breaking them up, will be resisted.

- Team pay, according to the above list, works best in mature teams. Yet can it be assumed that staff in such teams will be motivated in this way?

- Some staff find team pay illogical and damaging to self worth.

- There will be pressure to conform and accept the speed of the slowest. People will not be able to gain more than what is acceptable to the average.

- Since individual performance is no longer measured, those who are willing to extend themselves in return for recognition may be demotivated.

Finally, we should note that schemes have been brought in to reinforce commitment to group working. On the shop floor, to establish costs and output is usually straightforward. Among professional staff, however, how are the gains from 'greater cooperation' to be quantified? If the bonuses do make such a difference, one could ask why were staff not cooperating previously?

Conclusion: getting the most out of an old idea

Semi-autonomous, self-directed, high performance, cross-functional and cross-national work teams are notions that have entered the managerial language in recent years. All have the potential both to contribute to the organisation's goals and to enhance the individual's working life through learning and enhanced satisfaction. We should be cautious, however, about seeing groups and teams as entirely new. What is new is the increased interest in getting the most out of them.

It is useful to differentiate between group and team. The former refers to any collection of people with something in common. The latter, by analogy with sport, implies selection, matched capabilities, cohesiveness, practice, coaching and leadership. Moreover, a team is goal-seeking. In the new shop floor operating systems, self-managed work teams are introduced for their potential gains in output, productivity and quality.

Mankind's social nature means that groups form, as it were, on their own. They can be seen to satisfy motivational needs and are more likely to emerge among people who come into close contact. In employment, therefore, there will be many criss-crossing informal groups. Although they do not necessarily work against the organisation's interests, managers often seek to strengthen formal structures to counter or limit their influence. If managers set up the teams, they feel they can affect their norms in relation to output, quality, ethical standards and so on.

When it comes to group processes, applicable theory is weak. Not only is it undeveloped but the complexities of any work situation are huge. Although there are several models of the stages of group formation and others of the roles that members take up, none can be used to describe or prescribe what a group should do. Managers should be aware that context, task, team processes and roles all have their impact on outcomes.

Groups and teams have limitations. Set up for inappropriate purposes, they can waste resources. They can also present difficulties in becoming powerful resistors of change. Furthermore, some individuals may become demotivated. As they see it, discussion may waste time and the group norms may be set too low. For them, coping with the conflict within and between groups may not be worth while.

Quick check up *Can you ...*

- Tell apart groups and teams;
- Explain two further dimensions used to broadly classify groups;
- Apply Alderfer's list to suggest why people join;
- Give two reasons why particular clusters form;
- Outline Thompson and Wallace's three reasons for setting up shop-floor work groups;
- Name Tuckman's labels for group development;

- Summarise Belbin's model of group roles;
- Sketch the group process model of Herriot and Pemberton;
- List six ways of sustaining group cohesiveness;
- Explain what is a 'team killer';
- Suggest four reasons for inter-group conflict;
- Outline reasons for and against work group performance-related pay.

Questions

Chapter review

17.1 Using your own examples, distinguish between: group and team; open and closed; formal and informal.

17.2 Why do managers set up temporary or permanent cross-functional teams? Relate your ideas to the matrix organisation.

17.3 What is a high-performance work team? How might managers use such teams to improve the whole organisation? What difficulties might arise?

17.4 From the management point of view, is it better to encourage strongly cohesive working groups?

Application

17.5 Critically assess the value of performance-related pay in group situations.

17.6 The chapter draws on Alderfer's theory from Chapter 16 to explain an individual's motivation for joining a group. Examine a range of other theories from that chapter to see whether they offer alternative explanations.

Investigation

17.7 Through interviewing people on their membership of voluntary or informal groups, illustrate the notions of distance and social exchange. Establish how and why they joined and why they maintain their attachment.

Tax office teams[32]

In 1992, the Board of the Inland Revenue began a change programme to cut costs, improve compliance and provide better customer service. Customers were defined as taxpayers, other government agencies and agents such as accountants and solicitors. Two basic functions, tax assessment and collection, were brought together into newly arranged offices. Each major town now has a single point of contact. Staff numbers have fallen by about 20 per cent to 55 000 and offices are down from 768 to 542. These figures are planned to fall further as procedures are simplified. Reductions have been mainly natural or voluntary. Staff costs amount to 1.5 per cent of tax collected.

Following the merger of six units, Portsmouth now has one of the largest revenue offices in the United Kingdom. An early move by manager Chris Chant was to set up a task group to consider whether and where team working was appropriate and how it should be approached. Mistakes in other public sector organisations, such as the Post Office, had soured industrial relations. More than 94 per cent of staff are members of the PTC – the Public Services, Tax, and Commerce Union.

The group proposed that, with managers and staff having little experience of the issues, teamwork should be piloted in a few areas using volunteers. Gradualism means that, 18 months after the merger, about 75 of the 600 employees were working in self-managed work teams.

With the number of management layers between chairman and staff now reduced to four, decentralisation is the order of the day. The five managers who report to Chant work as a self-managed team, referring much less frequently to head office than in the traditional Revenue style. They make decisions on re-organisation within agreed guidelines such as, 'Staff must be involved'. There are other task groups looking at problems of merging the six former offices. One group has examined how to convince taxpayers that the Revenue does not see everyone as a potential scoundrel. Another is looking at the processes for dealing with the self-assessment of individuals. Throughout 1997, all offices faced uncertainty over the public response to the new system.

These groups are made up of staff from all grades. Chant wants to offer people the chance to work to their full potential. In such a big office, there will be people who could do more senior jobs than his own. He adds, 'Giving them these chances ... is about using their potential for the benefit of the business – and also giving them the opportunity to enjoy what they are doing.'

In spite of the optimism over change reported from Portsmouth, others suggest that morale in the Inland Revenue is low. The London School of Economics investigated the performance-related pay scheme and found that two thirds of staff were less willing to cooperate with colleagues than before.[33] Perhaps this explains the slow progress at Portsmouth?

Questions

1 Compare Chant's method of introducing self-managed work teams with the guidelines and experiences discussed in the chapter.

2 Given that most Inland Revenue offices carry out the same functions in different areas, what are the limitations on the effectiveness of local task groups and how might these be overcome?

3 Having agreed with the PTC branch that team working should be 'purely voluntary', how could Chant and the other managers step up its rate of introduction?

4 What lessons could the Portsmouth team learn from developments such as VTC or Pearl Assurance?

Bibliography

Beyond the sources listed in the references, with Mullins especially thorough, the following may be available in the library: Wickens, Peter (1987) *The Road to Nissan: Flexibility, quality, teamwork*, London: Macmillan; Adair, John (1986) *Effective Teambuilding*, London: Gower; Belbin, R.M. (1993) *Team Roles at Work*, Oxford: Butterworth-Heinemann; and West, Michael A. (1994) *Effective Teamwork*, London: British Psychological Society.

References

1. Thompson, Paul and Wallace, Terry (1996) 'Redesigning production through team working: case studies from the Volvo Truck Corporation' *International Journal of Operations and Production Management*, **16** (**2**) February, 103–20.
2. Sandberg, A. (1995) 'The Uddevala experience in perspective' in Sandberg, A. (ed.) *Enriching Production*, Aldershot: Avebury.
3. Womack, J.P., Roos, D. and Jones, D.T. (1990) *The Machine that Changed the World*, New York: Rawson Associates.
4. Mullins, Laurie J. (1996) *Management and Organisational Behaviour,* Fourth edition, London: Financial Times Pitman Publishing, 216.
5. Osborne, J.D., Moran, I., Musslewhite, E., Zegger, J.H. and Perrin, C. (1990) *Self-directed Work Teams*, Homewood, Ill: Irwin.
6. Houlder, Vanessa (1995) 'Kicking for team goals', *Financial Times*, 14 June, 19.
7. Merrick, Neil (1997) 'The Lions share', *People Management*, 12 June, 34–7.
8. Likert, Rensis (1961) *New Patterns of Management*, New York: McGraw-Hill.
9. Manz, Charles C. and Neck, Christopher P. (1995) 'Teamthink: beyond the group-think syndrome in self-managed teams', *Journal of Managerial Psychology*, **10** (**1**), January, 7–15.
10. Naylor, John and Senior, Barbara (1988) *Incompressible Unemployment*, Aldershot: Avebury, 26.
11. Vecchio, Robert P. (1995) *Organization Behaviour,* Third edition, Fort Worth, Tex.: The Dryden Press, 443.
12. Thibaut, J.W. and Kelley, H.H. (1959) *The Social Psychology of Groups*, New York: Wiley.
13. Further information on this charity is on http://glaxocentre.merseyside.org/stroke.html
14. Thompson and Wallace (1996) *op. cit.*
15. Tuckman, R.W. (1965) 'Developmental sequence in small groups', *Psychological Bulletin*, **58** (**6**), 384–99.
16. Belbin, R.M. (1981) *Management Teams: Why they succeed or fail*, Oxford: Butterworth-Heinemann, 76.
17. Herriot, Peter and Pemberton, Carole (1995) *Competitive Advantage through Diversity*, London: Sage.
18. Parkinson, C. Northcote (1957) *Parkinson's Law or The Pursuit of Progress*, London: John Murray, 31–43.
19. Vecchio (1995) *op. cit.*, 446–7.
20. 'Noted' *Industry Week*, **244** (**12**), 19 June 1995, 11.
21. Parkinson (1957) *op. cit.*, 32.
22. Slobodnik, Deborah and Slobodnik, Alan (1996) 'The "team killers": behaviours, attitudes and patterns of interaction that undermine effectiveness of work teams,' *HR Focus*, **73** (**6**) June, 22–3.
23. Chaudron, David (1995) 'An effective quality team. Not!', *HR Focus*, **72** (**8**), August, 6–7.
24. Scott, K.D. and Townsend, A. (1994) 'Teams: why some succeed and others fail', *HR Magazine*, **39** (**8**), August, 62–7.

25. Bergmann, Thomas J. and de Meuse, Kenneth P. (1996) 'Diagnosing whether an organization is ready to empower work teams: a case study', *Human Resource Planning*, **19** (**1**), March, 38–47.
26. Tudor, Thomas R., Trumble, Robert R. and Diaz, Joanna J. (1996) 'Work teams – why do they often fail?', *SAM Advanced Management Journal*, **61** (**4**), Autumn, 31–9.
27. Andrews, Katherine Zoe (1995) 'Cross-functional teams: are they always the right answer?', *Harvard Business Review*, **73** (**6**), November–December, 12–13.
28. Myers, Andrew, Kakabadse, Andrew, McMahon, Tim and Spony, Gilles (1995) 'Top management styles in Europe: implications for business and cross-national teams', *European Business Journal*, **7** (**1**), Winter, 17–27.
29. Solomon, Charlene Marmer (1995) 'Global teams: the ultimate collaboration', *Personnel Journal*, **74** (**9**), September, 49–53.
30. Odenwald, Sylvia (1996) 'Global work teams', *Training and Development*, **50** (**2**), February, 54–7.
31. Armstrong, Michael (1996) 'How group efforts can pay dividends', *People Management*, 25 January, 22–7.
32. Arkin, Anat (1997) 'Tax incentives', *People Management*, 20 February, 36–8.
33. Kellaway Lucy (1997) 'Why bad management is all in the genes', *Financial Times*, 16 June.

18

Communication in management

Chapter objectives

When you have finished studying this chapter, you should be able to:

- define communication and show its importance in every manager's job;

- explain three perspectives – psychological, social constructionist and pragmatic – used in understanding communication processes;

- set out the process model of communication, showing the effect of noise and the purpose of feedback;

- demonstrate ways of becoming a better communicator, especially in listening and writing;

- clarify the purpose of communication in organisations, highlighting practical ways of improvement;

- show how communication can be hindered by jargon, sexist language and overload; outline how a manager can respond;

- comment critically on the notion that organisational communication is about sharing accurate information.

Fossilised communications[1]

The 756 staff of the Natural History Museum are organised into 10 departments. These are five sciences – palaeontology, mineralogy, botany, entomology and zoology – and five business functions – library and information services, development and marketing, exhibitions and education, corporate services and visitor services. The museum's roots lie in Sir Hans Sloane's 1753 bequest to the British Museum, from which it became independent in 1963. Now it occupies some 60 000 square metres of splendid but sprawling buildings in central London. Most of the £46 million revenue, which includes £28 million from the government, is spent on staff costs and building maintenance.

The size and scope of the museum are impressive. Exhibitions range from cases of bones to interactive displays of earthquakes, robotic dinosaurs and the ascent of humankind. Staff range from internationally renowned scientists to those catering for the annual 1.8 million visitors. The museum stands with Alton Towers, the Tower of London and Legoland among the nation's Top Ten paid-for attractions. With growing numbers and rising reputation, prospects are good.

Yet, in 1990, the picture was less rosy. Money was tight. Admission charges, introduced in 1987, brought fears of a declining spiral of rising costs and falling revenues. Appointed director two years previously, Neil Chalmers began a major restructuring programme. This was intended to modernise, improve and refocus on core themes of the museum's work. Job cuts, although achieved voluntarily, had a massive emotional effect. Many employees felt betrayed and insecure.

To develop external publicity, Jane Bevan was brought in to the new post of public relations manager. She soon found that much work was needed on internal communications. The embedded tradition of semi-autonomous, hierarchical departments discouraged communications between, and even within, groups of staff. Isolation spread cynicism and distrust, especially during a time of change. Snobbery based on grade or intellectual arrogance was common. Junior staff often felt cut off.

Bevan started with an employee attitude survey, having agreed the principle with both Chalmers and the staff unions. To underline the openness of the process, results were supplied to all staff. Concerns were divided into those related to particular departments and those covering the organisation as a whole. Since work on the latter category would have greater impact and be less personal, it was given priority.

By 1995, a steering group had been set up to oversee change. Membership cut across departments. Included were junior managers in key business areas, union representatives, health and safety officials and administrators. The group chose to work on four areas, as follows.

Newsletter

The survey showed a strong demand for an internal newsletter that was not being filled by the current *Museum News*. This was a weekly summary of important information gathered and circulated by the personnel department. It was not an effective means of two-way communication. Change was not easy. Managers were afraid of a more popular version becoming scurrilous; staff distrusted management propaganda. The outcome was a new bimonthly 12-page magazine with news, features and information. It worked. Readers pressed to increase its frequency and change to full colour.

Team-briefing

Team briefings had been introduced in 1990. Designed to cascade management information throughout departments, they were not working well. While the survey revealed that 30 per cent found the system very useful, 14 per cent had had no briefings at all. The original training had not been followed up and many who had been on the course had since left or lost interest. Bevan's response was to run new workshops for 95 managers to share good practice. Since most staff had the use of a computer, it was also planned to support briefings with e-mail.

Staff suggestions

The survey showed that, while the suggestions scheme had been running for many years, staff remained unsure about its procedures. Suspecting this was mainly a publicity problem, Bevan explained the scheme in the new magazine. Her view was confirmed when the article triggered as many suggestions as in the previous year. The magazine publicised successful proposals.

Information 'hot spots'

Although departments had noticeboards, Bevan wanted several sites where broad information would be available. At these points, staff could pick up the newsletter and see advertisements for new ventures such as staff forums.

Beyond the work of the steering group, there have been other innovations. The staff forum is a bimonthly event designed to encourage two-way communications. For instance, Chalmers had an open question time addressing employees' concerns. These hour-long meetings attracted audiences of 75 to 120. In another development, the museum's intranet began to be used to share information widely. In its first few months of operation, an internal news system was tried and all employees given immediate access to the minutes of union–management meetings. An improved internal directory of staff responsibility and expertise was created.

Introduction

So there it is. You've had your 'sneak preview' of Fig. 18.1 even before it's come up in the text. So you know it captures the essence of the problems in the case study. It shows the fossilised old hierarchy, the snobbery of the seniors, the juniors cut off and the spiralling finances. Or perhaps you'd decided not to read the case yet? No matter, it's only a little story of how an organisation can ossify. And how new energy can rejuvenate it. A newsletter (initially opposed), team briefings, suggestions scheme and hot spot information points were none of them new. What was new was the commitment by a team to show they could work.

Don't worry if you started in the middle. You are probably among friends. Newspaper designers have known for years that people don't start at page 1 line 1. You know your paper. You flip to the sport, the lottery numbers, the television listings, the flats to rent, the stock market details or even the crossword. Entry points are elements that get you into the paper and then to read the rest. Editors need you to turn over every page so they can tell the advertisers (half or more of the revenue) that they have *readers*. That's why even the free sheets that jam your door when you have been on holiday carry news material. Funny how we look at the local snooker results or read how it rained in Alice Springs. When it comes to a book like this, we know you're unlikely to read it end to end. So the chapter names, pictures, headlines and index offer you entry points and help to steer a route once you are in.

The story of the Natural History Museum case flows roughly from top to bottom

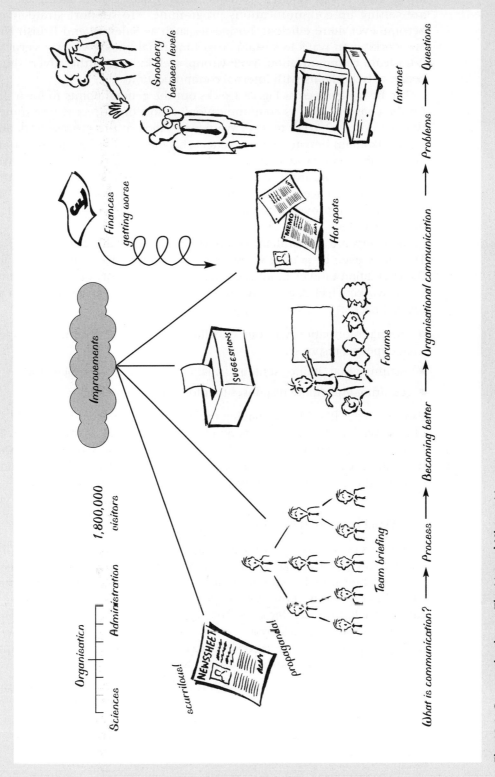

Fig. 18.1 Communication at The Natural History Museum

in Fig. 18.1. It is by no means unique. Many organisations, facing similar problems, are setting up communications programmes. To support strategic change and become ever more efficient, businesses such as Safeway and British Nuclear Fuels are working on ways to sustain cross-functional links, two-way vertical flows and intra-team communication. WPP Group, well known in the advertising world, has begun to help clients with internal communications.[2]

The heavy line across Fig.18.1 picks out the general points to form the headlines for the chapter. What is communication? A sort of process where some people tell things to others? Well, maybe. We need to look at the process in depth. Then we can think about how to become better. This means both becoming better personally and learning how to spot and fix problems in the organisation. Lastly, we must look again at what communication is. What is this about integrating communications strategy? Do managers really want to share, or are improved methods of communication really improved methods of conning people? Well, the Jurassic jury is still out on that one.

Managers are not brilliant communicators. After all, most of them are human. They may even be getting worse. Stimulated by easy e-mail, 'vanity publishing' is the circulation of ever more documents in the interests of 'open' communications. Office workers feel stressed. A survey by consultants Synopsis showed some growing bad habits:

■ issuing information without signalling purpose, significance, intended audience or expected response;

■ assuming that, if once sent, information is read and absorbed; and

■ requiring immediate responses to information requests.[3]

Exaggeration? Possibly. Yet having the most messages wins you a gold star in some offices. We'll come back to this flood towards the end of the chapter. This story is here to catch your attention and to suggest to you how much of a problem communication can be. Now let us quit this style, with its one word sentences. Let us consider the issues more soberly.

■ What is communication?

Definitions of communication can be broad – capturing a wide range of behaviours – or narrow – concentrating on a specific process. For some, it includes any understanding transmitted from one to another. For others, only intended meanings are treated as communication. We also have the question of roles. For some, communication is what the sender does; for others, the dialogue between originator and audience has to be considered.

Trenholm suggests we consider three *perspectives* on what communication is.[4] These can be summarised as follows:

■ The *psychological perspective* depicts communication as a process in which two or

> A *perspective* is a coherent picture drawn from a single point of view.

more people exchange information through the transmission of messages as coded stimuli. In this picture, good communication is about accuracy. Analysis would test how far the ideas produced in the receiver's mind match those intended by the sender. While this seems sensible, it has the disadvantage of overstressing accuracy at the expense of creativity or fun. It does not allow for the socio-cultural environment.

■ In the *social constructionist perspective*, communication is fundamental to a group's process of making sense of the world. Elements of culture, including symbols, habits, traditions and rules, form a constructed reality. This does not mean we live in a world of arbitrary make-believe. Nevertheless, people see it through 'personal lenses' that present them with images to be interpreted. Communication, therefore, is about sharing these interpretations. If you have difficulty with this, you will not be alone. For if everything becomes relative to a person's interpretation, what is left of 'reality'? On the other hand, organisations are socio-cultural constructs and we ought to acknowledge how reaching a consensus of what an organisation is will be an advantage.

■ The *pragmatic perspective* presents communication as a pattern of interdependent behaviour. Interaction is the key notion. It is as if we cannot understand what is going on in *Macbeth* Act III Scene 2 unless we have both followed the earlier part of the play and know something of Scots history. In organisations, we cannot make sense of communication patterns unless we have at least a summary of 'where everyone is coming from'. Among difficulties with this perspective lies its boundlessness. Stories never start. *Macbeth* really requires us not to know Scots history but the Tudor view of Scots history. And that means understanding Tudor history, and so on.

Switching among these perspectives gives us insight into communication in organisations. The next section on process, however, is based mainly on the psychological model. We consider the question of how we transmit our ideas to others and, in return, find out about theirs.

The communication process

From the psychological perspective, communication is the *exchange of information through swapping coded messages*. Contained in the definition are the ideas of: exchange, that is a two-way process; swapping, suggesting both parties have active roles; and coded messages, implying conversion from one code to another and transmission through media.

The process can be modelled using the stages set out in Fig. 18.2. Here we see a telephone interaction between two people, the sender and receiver. The sender has an idea and intends to transmit it to the receiver. To do this, the sender translates the idea into a form that is both meaningful and can be transmitted as a message along a channel. The receiver then interprets the message into a meaningful form. The active receiver may acknowledge the message, for example through an 'Aha', to confirm receipt and suggest common understanding. This is feedback.

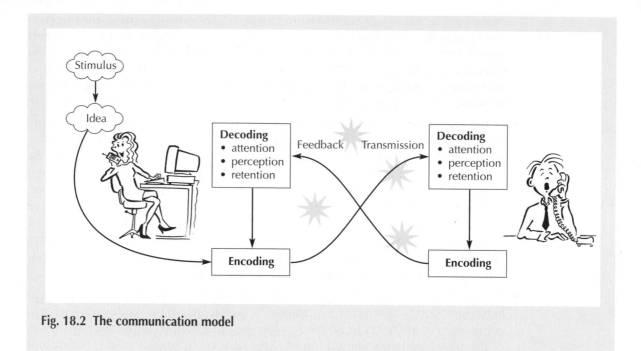

Fig. 18.2 The communication model

Unfortunately, possibilities of distortion appear at all stages. Translation and interpretation, normally called *coding* and *decoding*, are points where things go wrong. Furthermore, as the star bursts show, interference from *noise* may disrupt the message at any point. Let us look at these steps in more detail.

Encoding

Let us say that the sender, Angela, has an idea that she wants Bertie to know about. This idea might arise in Angela's mind or result from an external stimulus. In either case, Angela begins with the process of encoding. This means translating the idea into a set of symbols that can be transmitted. The set is usually a natural language common to Angela and Bertie. It has specific symbols learned by Angela, Bertie and others in their group. The size of this group can range from a few persons to billions. A recent study showed there to be some 10 000 languages in the world. Exhibit 18.1 outlines some key findings.[5]

Language is a powerful communication tool. What makes it work are rules, summarised in Exhibit 18.2, that enable the user to pass on routine information or say things never said before. It is very flexible. Yet a good communicator is aware of the rules, applying them intuitively. Without becoming an expert in the detail, we should recognise not only that communication is based on shared knowledge of these rules. It is also set in the pragmatic context of the relationship between sender and receiver. In the encoding process, the sender makes assumptions about the receiver's capacity and willingness to receive the message. For instance, although both parties have the same language, such as English, the parties will probably converse in a special subset

Exhibit 18.1 The world's biggest and smallest languages

Many languages have no written form and have few speakers. Bikya, from Cameroon, is spoken by one person; in a nearby village, Bishuo is spoken by a father and son. The chart shows the numbers who speak the Top Ten as first or second languages. Counting countries whose official language is English, it leaps to first place with 1730 million.

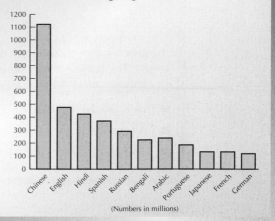

(Numbers in millions)

using dialect, jargon, family words and so on. Easily noticed in speech, such variations convey with the message notions of social status and group membership, friendship or formality, sincerity or cynicism and so on. 'Shet thi 'ed, an' mind thi own business, else I'll fetch the gaffer to thee! Pull up ther', an' le's 'ev un out on't. We be all Wind agyen! Everybody else ull a done afore we begins! Hang on to that chayn, Fodgy! Now, then! ALL together! Ugh!' In this way, a century ago, the drop stampers at Swindon Railway Works drew a white-hot ingot from the furnace.[6]

Although offering great potential to the good communicator, the flexibility of natural languages also creates problems. This is especially true for those, like the March Hare, who say, 'Then you should say what you mean'.[7] There is rarely a one-to-one link between a word or phrase and a meaning. In fact, for many words, the opposite is true. *Like*, for example, can take up eight parts of speech from noun and verb to preposition and interjection. It is included in the famous sentence, 'Time flies like an arrow', illustrated in Exhibit 18.3. The comment of Groucho Marx sums up the difficulty: 'Time flies like an arrow. Fruit flies like a banana'.

Encoding has to take into account the risks of misunderstanding from ambiguities like the ones illustrated here. In informal conversations, there are ample opportunities to check and repeat messages. In formal reports, on the other hand, greater care is needed in their preparation. A reader will not tolerate badly constructed, repetitive material.

Exhibit 18.2 Lanuguage's rules

■ *Phonological* – rules concerning sounds and their combinations;

■ *Semantic* – rules over links between sounds and meanings;

■ *Syntactic* – rules for the construction of phrases and sentences;

■ *Pragmatic* – rules relating words, phrases and sentences to context, for example culture, behaviour, history and relationships.

Exhibit 18.3   Same words, many meanings

Time flies like an arrow

The intended sense compares time passing quickly (flight is a metaphor) with the speed of an arrow (a simile). Confusion begins when we realise that arrows fly towards targets. The statement now suggests time to be a count down to our destiny.

Other meanings that may follow grammatical rules, but be nonsense in practice, are:

■ Measure the speed of flying insects as you would that of an archer's missile;

■ A certain species of flying insect prefers a well-known brand of chewing gum;

■ An American news journal moves through the air in a straight line.

■ Media

Media, or channels, carry the message. The term *media* is often used to refer to the mass media designed to carry messages from the few to the many. Yet media include all methods from face-to-face meetings to letters and memoranda and from newsletters to electronic bulletin boards. We saw how staff at the Natural History Museum learned to use media to convey messages in different ways to different sets of receivers. Simple messages, such as notices of meetings, could be posted on the hot spot bulletin boards. More difficult and subtle questions had to be mulled over in team briefings or debated at the management forum.

These ideas have been formalised by Lengel and Daft. They found that, like a pipeline, media channels differ in their capacity to convey information. They can be classified according to the richness of the information they can cope with. *Channel richness* is the measure of information that can be transmitted during a communication event. Figure 18.3 shows the hierarchy of channel richness.[8]

The richness measure is not a technical figure to be measured in bytes per second. It is a combination of three important characteristics:

■ the number of cues handled simultaneously;

■ the availability of rapid, two-way feedback; and

■ the possibility of creating a personal focus for the communication.

As Fig. 18.3 shows, the richest channel involves physical presence. This is because: many cues, from voice to body expressions, can be handled simultaneously; two-way feedback is spontaneous; and the focus is personal. Therefore, it is best used for sharing deep understanding of problems and situations. At the other end of the scale, impersonal static channels offer few cues, slow feedback and no personal relationship. Printed media work best if confined to straightforward messages that can be assimilated quickly.

The model of Lengel and Daft also brings out two causes of communications failure. These result from using unmatched channels for messages. A *data glut* arises from a deluge of cues whereas a *data deficit* comes from a dearth of them. Looking back at the communication methods introduced at the Natural History Museum enables us to gauge their effectiveness in these terms.

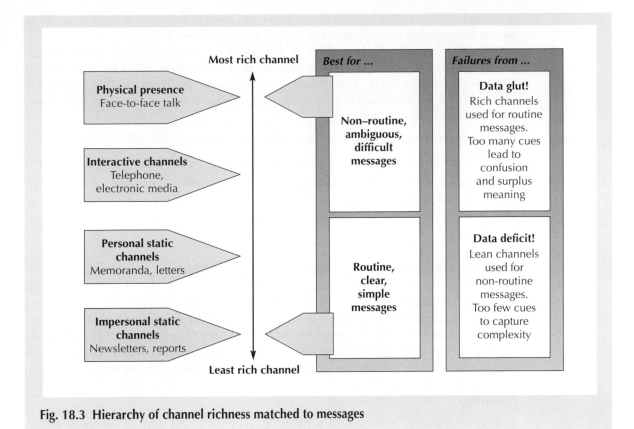

Fig. 18.3 Hierarchy of channel richness matched to messages

Data deficit

The original newsletter had been seen as an impersonal, one-way channel to distribute approved information around the staff. Although restricted to employees, the breadth of the audience meant that the content was limited to clear and simple messages. At its relaunch, the complexity of some messages was increased. Having more pages allowed for sectional interests to be covered and more detail included. Further, soliciting responses was an attempt to allow two-way communication, resisted by some managers who feared the introduction of scurrilous reporting.

Suggestions schemes also suffer from data deficit. They run in many organisations, frequently being revitalised as interest wanes. Yet, given the complexity of problems on the shop floor, it is possible that the best suggestions for improvement are untapped. Staff are unable to condense their ideas into simple messages ready to be placed in the box. This is the problem of data shortage. Compare the suggestions box with a quality circle. In the latter a group of staff spend many hours working on alternatives to current practices.

Data glut

Regular team briefings are face-to-face sessions with groups arranged as in Likert's link-pin hierarchy, *see* Chapter 17. At the museum, they followed a wish to keep all staff informed of changes. Use for downward communication only may be a waste of a rich channel. Other organisations, however, have promoted briefings as valuable means of gathering the responses of staff to management's policies.

Data glut is common in meetings. For example, managers are prone to use group sessions to make routine announcements. These should be transmitted along less rich channels. The museum's management forums would succeed if they allowed debate; they would fail if managers were to cover little more than the content of the newsletter.

Decoding

Decoding refers to *the process of giving meaning to the received message*. It is an active process set in the context of the link between sender and receiver. We can look at decoding in three steps – giving attention, perception and retention.

Attention

Attention is important because, without it, no communication can occur. Several tactics can be used to enhance it. The receiver will attend if the message is important. Therefore, relating it to personal goals or needs is advantageous. For instance: receivers will focus on those parts of a report that affect them; or we concentrate on the weather forecast for our area. Another approach is for the sender to engage the receiver spontaneously. This is done by including novel, vivid or surprising stimuli. Examples range from public speakers' changes in tone of voice to sensational headlines in the tabloids.

Perception

Perception is at the heart of giving meaning. Like the other steps in communication this is a learned process. The way we perceive data is given to us by our culture. It is also an active process in which we impose meaning on the signals we pick up. Through selection among the data and relating them to each other, we construct an internal representation of the world.

Creating shared perceptions is, according to the social constructionist perspective, a key function of communication. Otherwise, difficulties arise when people perceive things in different ways. Optical illusions illustrate the point. Figure 18.4 is based on a set of illusions by Botwinick, published a century ago. Here you may see a young or old man. (The former's chin is the latter's nose.) Illusions are not always intended to confuse. Artists have long used 'tricks' such as perspective and colour to overcome the two-dimensional limitations of their media. As Fig.18.5 shows, the *trompe-l'oeil* lines on web pages bring this application right up to date.

Managers should recognise that perceptual differences are natural. People will interpret message stimuli in their own ways. Expecting and looking for these differences, especially how they vary among individuals, groups, organisations and cultures, helps to make a good communicator. Good practice includes:

■ adapting the message and channel to the receiver's needs and capacity;

■ organising the message well;

■ relating new information to old. There can be references to earlier parts of the message or to knowledge already possessed by the receiver.

Fig. 18.4 Son or husband?

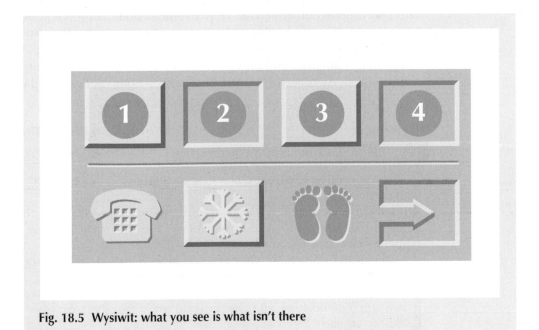

Fig. 18.5 Wysiwit: what you see is what isn't there

Retention

In time, sometimes only a few seconds, the receiver may forget the content of the message. The sender can help in this by encouraging retention. Methods include pointing out the need for retention, summarising, repetition of key message points and suggesting means that the receiver might use. Good teachers use these strategies. Students may be familiar with mnemonics such as 'Never eat Shredded Wheat', for the points of the compass, or 'Little boys better call no one foul names' for the elements from Lithium to Neon.

■ Feedback

One-way channels have a serious disadvantage. The sender does not receive any indication of the receiver's response to the process. Two-way channels allow for *feedback*, giving the sender at least some knowledge of how effective the communication has been. As we saw in the Lengel–Daft model, richer channels offer plenty of feedback cues while the less rich ones do not.

We could think of the conversation in Fig. 18.2 as having been initiated by Angela to send Bertie a message. Yet the roles of sender and receiver very quickly reverse. Unsure of a point, Bertie formulates a question. In asking it, he becomes the sender and Angela the receiver. We can thus think of a good conversation as a dance, *see* Exhibit 18.4.[9] Angela and Bertie must work together to make a good conversation. And, again like dancing, they can learn through practice.

■ Noise

Noise is any interruption of the normal flow of understanding between the parties. This broad definition covers more than sound noise. In a telephone conversation, for example, we may readily point to faults in the equipment: crossed lines, interference and poor sound quality are sometimes the cause for complaint. Distractions in the offices at either end also add data for one party to filter out. There is, moreover, noise in each person's head. This ranges from sudden recall of the work one

---

Exhibit 18.4 **Conversation as dancing**

'To understand how to make a conversation a genuine two-way experience, think of it as dancing.

'When you dance ... you work as a partnership, responding to each other's movements and trying not to tread on each other's toes too much. The idea is to cooperate rather then compete so you feel satisfied by the experience.

'It's about each person having the opportunity to express their point of view, explain their needs, and make their thoughts and feeling clear.

'An unsatisfactory conversation feels more like a game of table tennis, where the aim is to score points and for one person to win at the other's expenses. Conversations like this are about competing rather than cooperating.

'An open conversation is ... a duet rather than two solos.'

has to do later to physical barriers caused by overload or tiredness. In all, noise can interfere with any part of the cycle.

How can noise be overcome? Experts often think of the quality of a transmission in terms of the signal to noise ratio. The higher this ratio, the easier it is for the receiver to pick out the message data from the background. Clearly, the ratio is improved by increasing the signal or cutting the noise.

Increasing the signal

Computers and fax machines are often programmed to transmit messages twice. Only if the two correspond is the message confirmed. This is an example of *redundancy*, where messages deliberately contain more information than is needed in case *glitches* add or remove a few bytes. Natural languages display redundancy in large measure. The surplus sounds, characters, words and phrases have the advantage of overcoming transmission errors. For instance, if there was no redundancy, we could never tell if a word was mispelt (misspelt).

Sometimes redundancy in messages is deliberately increased. Experiences of noise interference in early wireless telegraph systems led to the introduction of codes to spell out key information such as aircraft call signs. 'Charlie Foxtrot Victor' is an example. Other codes cut redundancy to use limited channel capacity fully. Hand signals grew up where the normal aural medium was overwhelmed by noise. In the 1880s, the American Stock Exchange operated as an informal outdoor market in the centre of Manhattan. Brokers congregated on the street while their clerks, with telephones, sat above on window sills. Although the market moved indoors in 1921, the hand signals persisted until a wireless computer network was introduced in 1996.[10]

Figure 18.6 demonstrates the effect of character redundancy. You can't be sure about the symbol at the top of the picture until you realise it is repeated in the message below. This illustration shows the human capacity to reconstruct messages if much of the signal is missing.

Unfortunately, we sometimes make the wrong reconstruction, Figure 18.7 shows two faces. (Sorry! It's a vase.) This well-known example has been used in many experiments. For instance, picking out faces or vase is influenced by the colour of the two areas. Yet we cannot say for sure until a little more data is added.

Clearly, the redundancy in a two-way informal conversation is higher than that accepted in a formal report. This again illustrates the need for careful preparation before communication occurs.

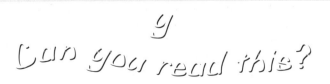

Fig. 18.6 Seeing shadows

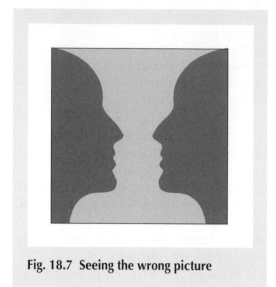

Fig. 18.7 Seeing the wrong picture

Reducing the noise

As a first step, one can consider cutting distracting external noise. For sound, sources are obvious and can be worked on. Visual noise includes all sorts of external distractions plus stimuli related to the medium. In the printed form, we often see inappropriate use of symbols, fonts, colours and so on. These need to match the message. As suggested above, noise can arise within messages. Rich channels carrying many parallel messages can be confusing if these are contradictory. Posture and face may not match the content of the message. It is as though the vicar smiles through the funeral.

■ Non-verbal communication

Contradiction between intended and unintended messages is a problem of non-verbal communication. This refers to the exchange of messages through actions and behaviour rather than through words. Although most attention is focused on formal, verbal interaction, non-verbal communication is an important part of messages in rich media.

Non-verbal communication differs from verbal in several important ways. First, it may be unintentional, such as 'preening' when males meet attractive females. In humans this is often seen as straightening the tie or cuffs, touching the hair or even retying shoelaces! Second, the 'languages' of non-verbal communication do not correspond to verbal languages. The sign in Fig. 18.8 means 'OK' in the United States and 'Excellent, really excellent' in The Netherlands. In France, it means something worse than 'You are worthless' while it would puzzle many Britons. Third, non-verbal communication is especially powerful for conveying some emotions such as grief The eyes are strong indicators of emotion. Fourth, non-verbal communication contains several dimensions that may, or may not, work in harmony. These are:

Fig. 18.8 Hand signals have different languages

■ *Body language*
Consisting of facial expression, gestures and posture, body language conveys messages from sender to receiver often without either thinking about them. For example, the receiver's attentiveness is confirmed by gaze, upright posture and hand signals. These are examples of *kinesics*, often minor movements that many people think of when referring to body language. Four other sub-categories have been added:

Proximics – the ownership and occupation of interpersonal space;
Chronemics – the time that lapses between verbal exchanges;
Oculesics – eye contact; and
Haptics – body contact.

To illustrate some cultural differences in these forms of communication, Exhibit 18.5 looks at the proximic and haptic behaviour around the 'space bubble'.[11]

■ *Paralanguage*
Paralanguage is the way we speak, as opposed to the words we use when doing so. Variations include: changes in the speed, tone and other voice qualities; special sounds from groans to rapid catching of breath; and hesitations or silences to gather thoughts or impose dramatic effect.

■ *Physical appearances*
Appearances, both personal and of one's surroundings, convey messages. A manager can use the office arrangements to convey signals ranging from power to informality. Do you sit face-to-face, separated by a desk? Or are you invited to share a corner with easy chairs? To many, the first suggests that the manager is conscious of position and intends to discuss a serious matter. The latter, in contrast, implies an intention to 'have a chat'.

> ### Exhibit 18.5 | Space invaders
>
> Spaniards like back slapping, Argentinians grip your arm and Americans delight in bone-crushing hand shakes. People from many Asian and northern cultures find such effusive gestures uncomfortable.
>
> The 'space-bubble' of Oriental, Nordic, Anglo-Saxon and Germanic people extends to about a metre. This zone is barred to strangers, although half the radius applies to close friends and relatives.
>
> Mexicans happily come within half a metre of strangers during meetings. When at this distance, they are ready to discuss business. Faced by such a space invader, however, British managers tend to back off beyond the metre line. Finding themselves back in the 'public zone', the Mexicans think the British don't like them or don't want to do business. They find discussing confidential matters over a gap greater than a metre to be like talking through megaphones.
>
> The Japanese are particularly sensitive about personal space. Anglo-Saxons, Nordics and Germans tolerate closeness uneasily. In East Asia, apart from Indonesia, distance is a sign of respect. Latins, Arabs and Americans interpret closeness as evidence of confidence while distance infers loss of approval.

Suspicions

Some people are suspicious and critical of making non-verbal communication the subject of analysis and managerial training. Learning to interpret unintended messages will only increase the dominance of some artful people over those who are not in the know. Yet sales training includes interpreting gestures. If a customer leans forward on the edge of the chair, interest has been aroused. Sitting back suggests boredom. An open posture shows willingness to talk while crossed arms or legs reveal defensiveness. In the last case, experienced sales people would not try to close a sale.

Another criticism is that sending out false cues to support untrue messages increases the possibility for manipulation. Political leaders are trained in techniques to improve their apparent sincerity. The exceptional Margaret Thatcher was, among other things, coached to lower her tone of voice as she grew from the shrill education secretary of the 1970s to the Prime Minister of the 1980s. Otherwise, politicians are usually such bad performers. Comparing the skill of actors with the clumsiness of ministers on the stump or at the dispatch box, Ratcliffe differentiates between gesture and body language. Gesture is deliberate. Body language is the involuntary give away.[12] Hence our leaders stress points with rehearsed table thumping gestures. The Soviet leader Khrushchev famously used his shoe to do this at the United Nations. Other politicians try to make points with their arms folded. This defensive, self-defeating male kinesic gives away the emptiness of their case.

One counter to suspicions of error, power and manipulation is that we send and receive non-verbal signals anyway. Studies suggest that people respond to body language 55 per cent of the time and to tone of voice 38 per cent. The actual words are worth a mere 7 per cent.[13] Should not the argument be to rely more on body language? This seems too extreme. Perhaps a good approach would be to reinforce what we do intuitively. Look for consistency between verbal and non-verbal communication. If the latter suggests that something is amiss, probe a little further. Being attentive in this way is a skill we should know. Trenholm recommends that we should:

- pay attention to non-verbal cues;
- decode non-verbal messages cautiously;
- review our own non-verbal messages to see where they are inappropriate;
- remember the invasive and threatening potential of non-verbal messages.

Becoming a better communicator

Communication skills are important for any manager today. Many studies show that managers spend up to 80 per cent of their working days in this activity. Although the accent in the psychological model is on the efficiency of transfer of information *from* the sender *to* the receiver, we could look at it the other way round. How successful is the receiver at gathering information from the sender? As with the illustration of a conversation as a dance, both roles are vital. This section, therefore, starts with listening before looking at an aspect of sending so far glossed over – writing.

Listening

Clearly, averaged across all oral communication settings, there are more listeners than senders. That means we spend more of our time listening than speaking. Yet most formal training is given for the latter activity. Three reasons suggest themselves. First, communication is thought of as presentation. This is a one-way process, as in public speaking. Second, audiences think it easy to make an immediate evaluation of the speaker while the reverse is rarely possible. Lastly, we assign responsibility for the effectiveness of the transaction to the presenter. Failure is the speaker's fault.

There are many business situations where good listening skills make all the difference. Diplomacy is said to be about achieving one's aims while letting the other party do all the talking. From encouraging staff to overcome a personal setback, to selling the latest design of widget to a busy customer, diplomatic listening pays dividends.

Take the listening test in Exhibit 18.6. (This is designed as a quick diagnosis so don't worry if you find some questions ambiguous. The aim is to gather a general impression.)

If you gave positive answers to half or more of the list, you are normal. That means, like the rest of us, you have some poor listening habits. It used to be said of people, 'A great talker, they could sell anyone anything'. The modern sales person, however, uses less 'gift of the gab' and spends less time trying to build a personal relationship with the client through irrelevant chat. Buyers are more cautious, better informed and more closely controlled than ever before. The seller must now learn the buyer's needs quickly and this can hardly be done while talking. Listening habits that improve selling, *see* Exhibit 18.7, apply equally well to other business or social conversations.[14]

Exhibit 18.6 Listening test: tick each box that applies to you

When engaged in a serious conversation with a colleague, customer or friend, do you ever:

☐ Glance at the time while the other is speaking?

☐ Complete the other person's sentences?

☐ Think, 'I want to say something but I'll wait until it's my turn'?

☐ Find eye contact difficult?

☐ Interrupt when the other is struggling to make a point?

☐ Think, 'I've heard this all before'?

☐ Anticipate what the other is about to say?

☐ Find your thoughts frequently distracted?

☐ Wonder what the other has just said?

☐ Work out your response while the other is talking?

☐ Feel you know the issue before the conversation has started?

☐ Find it difficult to get the other to speak?

Writing

Generations of employers and managers have complained about the poor writing skills possessed by young people. One American survey found that 41 per cent of printed business communications were poorly written.[15] This is variously blamed on the death of compulsory Latin or the dominance of television. Computers offer the chance to improve some aspects of writing. Not only do they make it easier to rewrite poor work at little cost but they offer support through spelling, grammar and style checkers.

Written media lack channel richness on the Lengel–Daft scale. The capacity of the channel is low and there is no chance for feedback. Encoding, therefore, concentrates on incorporating far less redundancy in the message compared with oral media. Furthermore, the encoding anticipates the reader's decoding skills. In the publishing world, many issue style guides. These are not concerned with the rules of syntax but set out general policy and clarify details where alternatives are possible. For example, Exhibit 18.8 is taken from the guide issued by the publishers of this book.[16] At journals such as *The Economist*, they help contributors and editors achieve a consistent approach to the magazine's well-educated, international readers. The outcome is known to be clear, varied and to the point. It both commands attention and suggests authority.

Many companies, concerned about the quality of written communication, run courses and give guidance. The following suggestions, frequently offered, would

Exhibit 18.7 Listening skills

1 *Block out distractions*. Arrange meetings when and where interruptions are least likely. Surroundings familiar to you may distract a relative stranger. Do you really need that James Dean poster or Venus Flytrap?

2 *Tune in*. Clear your own mind of distractions. (If something else is on your mind, delaying the event may be better.) Face the other person square on if possible. Show that you are interested in the subject. Show you are interested in the person.

3 *Encourage the other to talk*. One way is to say, 'Go on', 'Tell me more,' or even 'And?'. Another is to summarise something the other has just said. 'So it wasn't a problem with the paint ...'.

4 *Pick out the highlights as you go along*. In some settings jotting a note may be best, especially if details such as numbers are involved.

5 *Learn to use open-ended questions*. Open-ended questions elicit other than one-word responses. Compare the closed, 'Did you finish the job?' with 'How do you feel now that your first project is over?'.

6 *Try to reach feelings and facts*. Discussing responses to the facts gives us an idea of why the speaker thinks these facts important. Compare the following responses to, 'I could really do with a day off.' Either the generous, 'Yes, go on, I'll cover for you tomorrow', or the probing, 'You could do with a day off ...'. (Note that 'Why' would be intrusive.)

7 *Watch the body language*. Observe the other's body language to check whether they feel comfortable with the conversation and its setting. Check your own, too, but don't try to manipulate.

8 *Give feedback*. Feedback, focusing on the highlights, can be given to help the conversation along. The other's confidence is raised if you show you have understood. Showing attentiveness confirms that you find the subject matter important. Summarise what has happened, not what you anticipate.

9 *Ask for feedback*. Summarise what you are taking away from the conversation, asking for clarification of key points or things you might have misunderstood.

Exhibit 18.8 Financial Times Management preferences

■ -ise not -ize spellings;

■ dates in the form 15 November 1993;

■ spell out numbers under 10;

■ single quotes (double within single);

■ use 1 not (i) for numbered lists;

■ use (a) or a, not a) or A for lettered lists, etc.

also prove valuable to any student. Unfortunately, they are difficult to act upon:

- *Use simple language.* Long words in complex phrases and sentences put readers off.

- *Start with the most important information.* Readers expect summaries at the start of reports; they want to know a letter's content from the first paragraph.

- *Don't sacrifice communication to rules of composition.* Conformance to rigid rules defeats communication. This does not mean that 'anything goes'. People will object if you can't spell *business*. Furthermore, the style habits of the organisation should be followed but not slavishly.

- *Write concisely.* Brevity consistent with clarity and completeness is the target.

- *Be specific.* Vagueness undermines any impression of accuracy and clarity you are trying to create.

- *Check the document carefully.* Proofreading is a difficult task but one should at least avoid the major errors. Note that computers do not detect them all. Having another person do the checks is a good idea, *see* Exhibit 18.9.

Exhibit 18.9 **McDisaster averted**

A colleague asked me to look over the printer's proofs of his book chapter. At this late stage, only the smallest corrections were possible. The work assessed 'MacDonald's' policies in relation to the natural environment. Although the company's name occurred almost a hundred times, editors and typesetters had not noticed the error. I had to point out that the product is really the Big Mc.

Communication and organisation

Communication and organisation are closely connected. In Chapters 12 and 13 we saw how one principle of organisational design was to place closer together those staff whose work interlocked. This was to reduce the length of the communication chain. Design will, however, only resolve communication issues to a limited extent. Whatever the structure, the organisation has to ensure that information can flow in all directions, vertical and horizontal. Here, we shall consider the first of these, in both downward and upward directions. Horizontal links are examined in Chapter 22. Then we look at another type of flow, which travels along any path – the grapevine. Lastly, we shall look at the role of meetings in organisations.

Downward communication

Managers often feel aggrieved when they hear reports such as, 'No one ever tells you anything', or, 'I don't know what is going on'. Although some may mean, 'I never listen to anything', or, 'I don't agree with what is going on', managers will often respond with a review of the communication system. In larger firms, the desire to exercise more control over the way downward communication works leads to the establishment of centralised communication functions. Often these are adjuncts of the public relations or personnel sections. At the Natural History Museum, inadequate downward flows were overcome by improvements to moribund existing systems, such as the newsletter, notice boards and team briefings. A new centralised function, staffed with new people, can revitalise structures that have fallen into disrepair.

Another approach is to add a channel. Although the United Kingdom opted out of the European Union's Social Chapter, many firms decided to adopt its principles in all countries. Unilever was criticised by some shareholders for being too eager to comply. Defending the action, chairman Niall Fitzgerald argued that acceptance meant two minor policy changes. First, 'Works councils provide helpful additional channels of communication with employees'. (The second policy covered uniform parental leave[17]). Other examples are electronic media. Yet we have already commented that these might add noise and redundancy instead of offering a new, rich channel.

■ Upward communication

Successful organisations need good upward and downward communication. This is difficult to achieve especially in large firms. Yet it is vital if only because sound decisions often depend on gathering sound information from grass-roots level. There are several methods of stimulating upward communication: intelligence gathering units; attitude surveys; suggestion schemes; and informal meetings.

Intelligence gathering

Structures of the armed services, designed to pass instructions downwards, are poor at collecting and interpreting information picked up by the troops. Debriefing prisoners, for example, can often yield valuable information provided it is pieced with other snippets. Recognising this problem, armies have long-established intelligence branches where special skills in languages, technology and analysis are applied to data. One of the best-known British intelligence officers was T.E. Lawrence (1888–1935). His leadership ability, linguistic skills and knowledge of the region helped him, in 1916, to unite the Arabs against the Ottoman Turks. He led the Arab army into Damascus two years later. Today, other branches of military intelligence, such as MI5 and MI6, gather and interpret data from all around the world.

Attitude surveys

Companies often replicate the military experience. For instance, personnel specialists will interview leavers to assess their attitudes. From these *exit interviews*, they assess factors from pay and conditions to attitudes within particular work groups. The same department is often responsible for broad attitude surveys. Conducted at regular intervals, these are means for senior managers to gauge how shop-floor attitudes are changing. The directness of the survey eliminates distortion by the middle ranks.

Suggestion schemes

Suggestion schemes are means for managers to gather ideas. Some yield large flows from which occasional inspirations yields valuable benefits. The scheme at

| Exhibit 18.10 | Overwhelmed by suggestions |

The new scheme switched its attention to problems of integrations and means of winning new business. At the launch, promises were made to recognise each suggestion and give feedback within 8 weeks. The scheme has the full backing of the chief executive Mike Blackburn. Although the flow rose to 34 000, swamping the office set up to administer it, Blackburn stays involved. Two thirds of proposals are duplicates and attract a small token prize. Blackburn or another director signs responses to the rest. Original but impractical ideas are acknowledged with a £5 voucher. Suggestions with more merit generate higher prizes and entry in a quarterly awards assessment. This event, again led by Blackburn, receives publicity throughout the business. One cashier proposed a change in credit scoring that should lead to £10 million more annual business, while another saved £200 000 on telephone enquiries. Without the scheme, such suggestions may have been permanently stuck in the hierarchy.

the Halifax bank was reviewed after the 1995 merger with The Leeds. Its focus on cost-cutting had possibly restricted responses to around 3500 each year from 26 000 original staff. Administration was clumsy and slow with some responses taking more than 18 months. Exhibit 18.10 describes the change.

Informal meetings

Many advocate that there is no better means for gathering information than by looking around. *Management by Wandering Around* (MBWA) was made famous by the founders of Hewlett Packard. It has had many imitators. The forums at the Natural History Museum are another form of meeting, although the numbers attending probably restrict the chances of debate. The difficulty with such methods is that they do not guarantee to reveal important information. In addition, they tend to sideline middle managers who may not feel part of the process.

The grapevine

The *grapevine* is the informal information channel that is found in all organisations. It often bypasses formal systems compared with which it is faster and sometimes more accurate. After all, if it did not satisfy some needs it would not exist! Because so many of its messages are transferred face-to-face, it is a rich medium with strong influence on participants. Therefore, especially when seen from the social constructionist or pragmatic perspective, the grapevine is very important.

Its richness and immediacy are reasons that might tempt managers to use the grapevine, or at least try to manage it. They can, for instance, cultivate 'listening posts' for themselves. Alternatively, they may spread rumour or news to achieve their own ends. These approaches suffer if the grapevine is unreliable. Although a typical three quarters of information may be true, the problem is to know which. To limit such undesirable effects, managers should improve other forms of communication. When key decisions are made, for example, they should be shared, using formal channels, without delay.

Running meetings

Running a meeting is an important skill. Although they have a variety of purposes, meetings often form a vital link between staff and the organisation. This is especially true for those who work off site, such as sales and services crews, outreach workers, home workers and managers of store chains. Yet, in spite of their frequency, many do not seem to work. Common complaints are that meetings are boring, are a waste of time, lack direction, never achieve anything, go over old issues, are incoherent, do not focus on my problems, or offer an opportunity for the boss to give a lecture.

In Chapter 17 we studied how, as meetings grew beyond 10 or more, there was increasing tolerance of directive leadership and a need for formal rules. The communications aspects of a meeting should, therefore, support this approach. Valuable elements are as follows:

- *Have a real meeting.* Ensure that the same results, such as giving instructions, could not be achieved elsewhere.

- *Issue an agenda in advance.* Beyond giving information on time and place, the agenda allows people to prepare themselves.

- *Invite only those who are needed.* Others become frustrated and may be disruptive.

- *Give undivided attention.* Prevent interruptions and distractions.

- *Prepare.* Ensure that information is available. Have an idea of what you want to achieve. Brief key colleagues in advance.

- *Encourage contributions from all delegates.* Use questioning skills to develop participation.

- *Keep to the agenda.* Especially important when people from different cultures attend, keeping to the agenda is a way of maintaining momentum.

- *Conclude and summarise.*

Overcoming problems

Our review of communication and organisation outlined the links between these two elements. Although easing the flow of communication seems to help to make organisations work better, many are increasingly worried about the rapidly increasing volume. As with new six-lane motorways, the traffic soon grows to fill the space. Besides this management issue, other problems arise in developing personal communication skills. We shall start with two of these, jargon and gender.

Jargon

Semantics, the study of the meaning of words, throws up many stories of the causes and consequences of misunderstanding. Difficulties are to be expected in international business but jargon is perhaps a more subtle problem. This language of a class, profession, sect or organisation has a social construction function. It provides opportunities for ready communication among members of the group, thus reinforcing the notion of group membership. In academic disciplines, foreign

---

Exhibit 18.11 **International exchange**

Professor of Sociology from Aachen:

'It is strange that English-speaking academics, when referring to the concept of 'world view', use the German word *weltanschauung*. You know the term we have started to use in Germany for this concept? *World view*!'

---

words such as *gestalt* or *anomie* become popular when one's own language will not quite do. They reinforce the sense of the in-group, *see* Exhibit 18.11.

Jargon is everywhere. Information specialists, in their *virtual reality, surf web pages* using *hyperlinks*; they know their wares – *soft, hard, course, people, free, share, pay* and *net*; and, for them, *PostScript* is a page design language. In business, instead of making a plan, some *dimension a management initiative. Political correctness* in education requires *disadvantaged learners* not to fail. Instead, they *achieve a deficit.* Having *gained insufficient credits*, they may still receive an award provided they *achieve the necessary exit velocity.* Some such words and phrases spread and enrich general usage. Others wither. In business communications avoiding jargon is impossible. The skill is to tailor its use to the awareness of the audience.

Gender

There are differences between sex and gender. The former is a biological definition based on physical attributes. Gender, on the other hand, is not strictly biological. Socialisation usually encourages people to learn the values and behaviour of the gender role corresponding to their sex. The problem for critics is that, in Western society at least, sharp dichotomies have grown up in both sex and gender definitions. Men should occupy male gender roles and display masculinity; women should occupy female gender roles and display femininity.[18]

Sexist communication has been criticised for contributing to the glass ceilings and walls in organisations. Among occupations, *chairman, statesman, businessman* and *foreman* have implied various degrees of power, while *cameraman, airman, fireman, middleman* and even *highwayman* have suggested some reserved occupations. While many say that such words are understood to refer to both genders, critics argue that they have a subtle effect on role images. Women are not seen to be chairmen, statesmen or highwaymen. The problem spreads beyond individual words into the imagery and metaphor used throughout the organisation. Alvesson and Willmott argue that the language used in jokes or for discourses about corporate strategy contains 'strong elements of masculinity that act to strengthen male identities and thereby reproduce asymmetrical gender relations in organisational life'.[19]

The authors are careful to point out, however, that, since both men and women vary so much, both sexes experience advantages and disadvantages from the present situation. In the main, however, women come off worse. Sexist vocabulary often overlaps with speech habits that reinforce notions of (male) power, *see* Exhibit 18.12.[20]

Exhibit 18.12 You may call me 'Sir'

The modes of address that differentiate managers from workers were the subject of a survey by the Manufacturing, Science and Finance Union. Responses were received from 557 workplaces that together employ more than a quarter of a million people.

On average, 33 per cent of managers expect to be addressed as 'Sir' or by their title. Regional differences were marked. In the North and in Wales the proportion was 45 per cent, falling to 15 per cent in the South West.

Many found managers' interpersonal skills inadequate. Sixteen per cent had been shouted at in public and 23 per cent openly criticised. Moreover, 39 per cent had never been thanked by the senior people in their organisation.

Eradicating sexist language from vocabulary will have two benefits for the ethical manager. Not only will possible bias be removed from communications but the manager may be forced to challenge *his* personal stereotypes.

Overload

In the introduction, we briefly noted a survey by Synopsis showing some bad communication habits of managers. Another survey, among 1000 large international companies, was conducted by Gallup. The results, shown in Exhibit 18.13, measured the daily deluge of messages.[21] Meredith Fischer, vice-president of communications at Pitney Bowes, said, 'It is as if the communication demands are driving the work and the conduct of business, and not the other way round'. He suggested that 'traffic police' might be used to sort and filter information for colleagues and guide them through the jams.

Computer Associates, one of the world's largest software companies, acted to stop employees constantly checking their e-mail. Logging on was restricted to three times each day. Other approaches include limiting all messages to one screen or imposing a notional charge on departments to cover the computing costs.

The rapid growth of electronic mail is expected to swamp all other media within a few years. Companies must clearly develop policies to manage. Not only must these stem the flood but they must also cover three further issues:

■ Privacy – Are employers at liberty to read employees' e-mail?

■ Legal liability – It is known that people are less cautious and diplomatic in e-mail than in paper letters or memoranda. Storing such messages may lead to legal problems.

■ Security – Sharing information means more leakage of confidential data.[22]

Exhibit 18.13   Communication: more is not better

A typical middle manager sends or receives 178 messages or documents each day. Almost three quarters of all staff say they feel overwhelmed by the number of messages they have to handle; 84 per cent are distracted three or more times per hour. Secretaries face more than 190 letters, e-mail, faxes, telephone calls, voice messages, sticky notes, pager messages, courier deliveries and internal mail.

Many employees have more than 100 e-mail messages awaiting them in the morning. Gaining a recipient's attention becomes ever more difficult. Messages are sent several times, thus increasing traffic. First, there is e-mail, then a fax of a print-out, followed by a copy in the post. Finally, the sender rings to check receipt.

Teamwork is another reason for increased information loads. Sixty per cent of office workers were on a team, with 51 per cent on more than one. An assistant is often assigned to keep all members up to date; this means many messages, often in different formats.

Rather than replace existing tools, new communications technologies are added on. Yet the preferred method of external communication remains the telephone, at 79 per cent. For internal communication, however, e-mail, at 66 per cent, has come to dominate.

The lack of attention to this depressing picture was confirmed in the study. Sixty-nine per cent of large companies were reported as having no communications policy. Moreover, only 14 per cent of employees stated they would 'almost always' ask a recipient how they would like to be sent the information.

The limits to truth

Much discussion of communication in organisations treats information unquestioningly. We can recall that the psychological perspective considers the challenge of transferring understanding from one person to another *with the minimum of distortion*. Consequently we look to match messages and media with training in sending and receiving for those involved. But what if the messengers were setting out to avoid the truth or, at least, paint a one-sided picture?

When discussing upward communication, managers reveal fears that they may not be told all they should. *Forbes* magazine interviewed eight senior executives in the United States to find out how they coped with the problem. Exhibit 18.14 notes some of their comments.[23] The responses show the managers to be aware of the problem. Yet they feel that the extra provision they make more than counters it. According to Larson and King, however, much of this is unrealistic. Many managers advocate open communication while rewarding kneebending and punishing dissent. Studies show how individuals are motivated to create favourable impressions; therefore they hide weaknesses and emphasise strengths. Recipients have a natural tendency to accept information that supports their beliefs and reject that which is negative or critical. So good news travels quickly while bad news is distorted or blocked.[24]

Exhibit 18.14 Eight managers' routes to the truth

- ■ 'The women are the catalysts for telling the truth round here. Men are brought up to be discreet. Otherwise, they get into fights.' (Female chief executive.)

- ■ 'Alarm bells ring when someone says it's so complicated I can't explain it to you. I just don't believe them.'

- ■ 'I have a phone that is not screened by anyone.'

- ■ 'People tend to tell you the good news and not speak honestly about problems. I don't let them off the hook. I've got to make it wrong not to talk about problems.'

- ■ 'A staff complaint that I parked my car in a disabled spot reassured me that people who work for me aren't afraid of me.'

- ■ 'Suggestion boxes all over our offices do bring about a level of truth.'

- ■ 'Don't rely on intuition. There's nothing like the facts.'

- ■ 'To get to the truth, go to its source.'

Beyond personal reasons for misinformation, Alvesson and Willmott argue it arises from the nature of organisations themselves. From their bleak perspective that organisations can be seen as sites of psychological imprisonment, they question whether structures of communication reinforce oppression.[25] In other words, does communication serve to present power difference, such as capitalism, hierarchy and management itself, as natural and beneficial rather than arbitrary and harmful?

Drawing on the work of Forester, two dimensions are identified. First, there is the question of whether distortion is inevitable or unnecessary. Second, there is its origin. Does it stem from the choices of individuals or is it embedded in the social order of the organisation? Combining these dimensions gives us the 2 × 2 matrix of Fig. 18.9. The matrix brings out four sources of communication distortion:

- ■ Cell 1 refers to the communication model set out earlier in the chapter. The distortion arises inevitably as individuals and channels reach the limits of their processing capacities. This is noise.

- ■ Cell 2 refers to distortion arising from specialisation. We have shown how managers work hard, at least officially, to overcome this problem through trying to improve the upward, downward (and sideward) flows. These efforts can be seen to be futile, however. The problem arises not from poor connections but from the nature of the organisation itself

- ■ Cell 3 shows distortion as an action chosen deliberately by the individual. Here the limits to 'open' communication are tested when a manager justifies deception or half truth because they will achieve the required ends. Depending on the direction down or up, the subordinate is persuaded or the wrath of the boss avoided. In societal terms, this is propaganda.

- ■ Cell 4 covers cases where information is distorted for reasons justified by the social order, which is the hierarchy. 'We cannot reveal costs because we need to

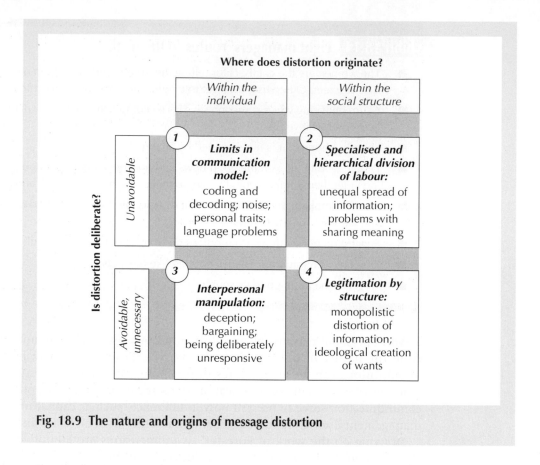

Fig. 18.9 The nature and origins of message distortion

bargain', or, 'The basis of overhead allocation is confidential' are typical statements of the genre.

From their critical theory standpoint, Alvesson and Willmott argue that Cell 1, the domain of the psychological perspective, is the least interesting. To understand the function of communication means taking a broader, pragmatic approach. This means looking critically at why communication takes place and expecting that there will be a degree of distortion in many of its practices. Cell 4 ought to be the place where work starts,

Conclusion: responsible communication

We began the chapter with a common enough illustration. A survey of opinion shows that employees complain of being poorly informed. This triggers a review in which channels are revitalised, replaced or reinforced. Meanwhile key agents, especially line managers, are trained to be better communicators. They learn about verbal and non-verbal communication, selection of media whose richness matches the message and how to tailor their presentation to suit the needs of the audience, avoiding jargon and sexist language. Above all, they are trained to listen. As a result, more information flows more smoothly between people and through the organisation.

There are dangers at every turn. The fearsome one is overload. Channels do not replicate, they add. Traffic becomes heavier with each technical innovation. Communication resigns as servant to reign as master. Resisting the flood is difficult. Imposing limits seems fraught with danger. If an efficiency doctor prescribes 'e-mail access three times a day after meals' the purpose of the service is lost. Rather than waste time on screen, staff will return to the telephone or fax for urgent business. Other problems cover staff suspicions over detailed supervision of correspondence and the possibilities of legal action based on evidence from careless e-chat.

A deeper question concerns what communication is. Is the ideal to be seen as sharing of understanding among all parties? Critics say this is both impossible and undesirable. It ignores both human nature and the oppressive reality of organisations. Both provide ready reasons for distortion in communication. Only if people can fully trust each other can they afford to tell all. Since they do not, we find that good news flows faster than bad and subordinates plot to keep the boss out of the know. Furthermore, the interests of the organisation are served by maintaining an information differential between those in power and those who have to be persuaded to operate lower down. Those at the top do not want to reveal all and those at the bottom are conditioned not to expect it. Open communication has its limits.

Given these suspicions, why not call a halt, asserting that becoming a better communicator is wasted effort? The reason for pressing on is that organisations do not have to fail their employees. Ethical managers, believing in a responsible, participative style, will want to be good communicators. Leading, directing, coaching and controlling all require the capacity to present ideas clearly. They also require the corresponding skill of listening. Trust can be built. Staff will tell the boss more if bad news is received as openly as good. According to IBM folklore, after losing $10 million in a risky venture, a young manager was summoned to the office of founder Thomas Watson. Despondently, he said, 'I guess you want my resignation.' Watson replied, 'You can't be serious. We just spent $10 million educating you.'[26]

Quick check up   *Can you ...*

- Name three perspectives on what communication is;
- Define communication from one of these perspectives;
- Sketch the communication model;
- Define channel richness;
- State the steps of decoding;
- Distinguish body language from paralanguage;
- Suggest ways of handling non-verbal communication;

- Give five of the nine listening skills;
- State four means of encouraging upward communication;
- Explain the term grapevine;
- Outline the problems of jargon and gender in language;
- Suggest two approaches to coping with noise;
- Summarise the criticism by Alvesson and Willmott of the communication model.

Questions	**Chapter review**

14.1 Explain and illustrate the three perspectives on communication suggested by Trenholm.

14.2 Describe the communication model for interpersonal communication, explaining how it can be used for diagnosing problems.

14.3 List the difficulties with upward communication in organisations. How effective do you think the solutions proposed in the chapter are likely to be?

14.4 What are the implications of improved communication systems in organisations?

Application

14.5 Review the attempts to improve links at the Natural History Museum in the light of the process perspective of communication. What extra light do the other perspectives throw on the picture?

14.6 We have seen some firms establish controls over communication channels because of message overload. Examine the ethical issues arising from such action.

Investigation

14.7 Examine any publication designed for people within an organisation, professional group or common interest group. Identify any jargon. What are the advantages and disadvantages of using language in this way?

CLOSING CASE

Selling products or solutions[27]

Act 1: Selling a product

Representative: That's a fancy looking cup. What's it for?

Customer: Thank you. Our team won the quiz league this season.

Representative: Ah. Well, you'll know the 5 premier and football league clubs with an X in their name?

Customer: No. I'm in for history, geography and that sort of thing.

Representative: Well ask the lads on your staff if they know. ... But I see You're busy so we mustn't waste your time ....

Customer: (*You* are doing so very effectively)

Representative: ... so I will come to the point. As you know. we have a proud tradition stretching back to before yours and my time of offering top rate service to our clients. I am sure you'd be interested in our latest all-in-one shampoo. It's just designed for cleaning businesses like your own. You have to do lots of square footage in a very short time. The shampoo is more concentrated than all the others so it dries more quickly and the customer can use the room pretty well straight away. We've even designed a special adaptor that will suit most cleaners so I'm sure it will suit yours . ... Trials in Spain show that the time spent scrubbing can easily be cut by 10 per cent. ... The packaging is particularly secure and attractive. ... The bottle can be recycled ... (ten minutes in all).

Customer: Well it's delightful to hear everyone's improving. I would like to read about the details. Would you leave the literature with the receptionist on your way out? I'll phone you when I've had a chance to think about it.

Representative: You'll be better if you call by next Friday. That's the last day of the introductory offer I was talking about. (And it's the last day for working out this month's bonus.)

Customer: OK I'll let you know.

Act 2: Selling a solution

Representative: What would it mean if you had a shampoo you could use almost up to the minute that customers wanted their offices?

Customer: We could get more done in the early mornings. (The staff could each do an extra half-hour. Part-timers could do with the extra money.)

Representative: And what about a shampoo that's so effective you can cut the scrubbing time by nearly 10 per cent?

Customer: Well, we'd have to see. It might help a little. Ten per cent isn't much. (But possibly a great deal in those large government offices. I could afford to pay a little bonus.)

Representative: Do your machines leave the occasional damp patches on the floor for an hour or so? Would you like to avoid that?

Customer: Yes. We must always strive to look professional. (Customers complain about this.)

Representative: And you are now committed to environmental purchasing? (I checked on the way in.)

Customer: We prefer all our materials to pass the standard and packaging to recycle.

Representative: We don't launch a product unless it can pass. Tell me, do you use the Emca ZA machine? (I checked that on the way in too.)

Customer: Yes. Why?

Representative: Well, we've designed a small adaptor to measure the shampoo more carefully. It will regulate the flow and avoid those damp patches. They're easy to fit. But if you would like to place a trial order, I'll call next week and fix up half a dozen machines free of charge.

Customer: What's the price of the shampoo?

Questions

1 What sales tactics are the salespeople using in Acts 1 and 2? Which seller is likely to be successful?

2 Compare the two conversations in terms of Trenholm's three perspectives.

3 How do the conversations compare with any recent experiences you have had as a customer?

Bibliography Among the books you find under 'communications' in the library, many are devoted to the sender's skills of clear writing, speaking, presenting and so on. Setting communication in context, however, are: Dimbleby, Richard (1992) *More than Words*, London: Routledge; and Stanton, Nicky (1996) *Mastering Communication* Basingstoke: Macmillan.

References

1. Prickett, Ruth (1997) 'Alive and kicking', *People Management*, 15 May, 28-31.
2. Killgren, Lucy (1997) 'Internal affairs', *Marketing Week*, 3 April.
3. *Financial Times*, 10 July, 1997.
4. Trenholm, Sarah (1995) *Thinking through Communication: An introduction to the study of human communication*, Allyn and Bacon; *see also* http://maine.maine.edu/~zubrick/trenl.html
5. Carvel, John (1997) 'Global study finds the world speaking in 10 000 tongues', *Guardian*, 22 July, 5.
6. Williams, Alfred (1969) *Life in a Railway Factory*, Reprint of 1915 edn, Newton Abbott: David & Charles, 213.
7. Carroll, Lewis (1865) *Alice's Adventures in Wonderland*, Chapter 7, A Mad Tea-party.
8. Daft, Richard L. (1997) *Management*, Fourth edition, Fort Worth, Tex.: The Dryden Press, 563–4.
9. BT (1997) *Let's Dance: How to get more out of life through better conversations*, London: British Telecommunications, 7–8.
10. Davies, Erin (1996) 'The Amex's old hand signals give way to computers', *Fortune*, **134** (**8**) 28 October, 52.
11. Lewis, Richard D. (1996) 'Space at a premium', *Management Today*, September, 105–6.
12. Ratcliffe, Michael (1996) 'Gesture, posture and pose: everybody's acting nowadays', *New Statesman*, **126**, (**4322**), February, 41.
13. Arthur, Diane (1995) 'The importance of body language', *HR Focus*, **72** (**6**), June, 22–3.
14. Based on: British Telecommunications (1997) *op. cit.*; Phillips, Rick (1996) 'Listening your way to more sales', *Sales Doctors Magazine*, 15 July; http://www.salesdoctors.com
15. 'Writing the bottom line', *Personnel*, August 1990, 4–5.
16. Financial Times Management (1998) *Preparing Your Manuscript: Guidelines for authors*, 2.
17. August, Oliver and Bassett, Philip (1997) 'Unilever defends its social chapter stance', *The Times*, 7 May.
18. Giesen, Erika (1996) 'Communication and gender lessons', http://cyberschool.4j.lane.edu/People/Faculty/Duke/CoMMG/lessons/Lessons.htm
19. Alvesson, Mats and Willmott, Hugh (1996) *Making Sense of Management: A critical introduction*, London: Sage, 113.
20. Smith, David and Higgins, Sarah (1997) 'Call me "Sir", demand British bosses', *The Sunday Times: Section 3 Business*, 13 July, 1

21. Uhlig, Roger (1997) 'Office workers sinking under tide of technology', *Daily Telegraph*, 24 June; *Electronic Telegraph*: http://www.telegraph.co.uk; McGookin, Stephen (1997) 'Better communication: managing information flow', *Financial Times*, 7 July; http://www.ft.com

22. Houlder, Vanessa (1997) 'Failing to get the message. E-mail's advantages could be lost by staff misusing it', *Financial Times*, 17 March.

23. Conlin, Michelle (1997) ' The truth', *Forbes*, **159** (**3**), 10 February, 20–1.

24. Larson, Erik W. and King, Jonathan B. (1996) 'The systematic distortion of information: an ongoing challenge to management', *Organisational Dynamics*, **24** (**3**) Winter, 49–61.

25. Alvesson and Wilmott (1996) *op. cit.*, 116–17.

26. Larson and King (1996) *op. cit.*

27. In this fictitious case you will probably recognise real behaviour. It was suggested by Phillips, Rick (1996) 'All I want is an unfair advantage', *Sales Doctors Magazine*, 25 November; http://www.salesdoctors.com

Part 6

IMPLEMENTING POLICIES AND PLANS

Saying is one thing, and doing another. *Proverb*

Aesop was writing for the tortoise market. Hares have no time to read. *Anita Brookner, British novelist*

It is all about technique. The great mistake of this century is to put inspiration and creativity first. *Vivienne Westwood, British fashion designer*

I am the very model of a modern Major-General,
I've information vegetable, animal and mineral,
I know the kings of England, and quote the fights historical,
From Marathon to Waterloo, in order categorical. *W.S. Gilbert, British librettist*

Part 6 is about doing. Converting words into action is the job of the functional manager, be it in operations, marketing or design and development. Chapter 19 explains the importance of managing operations in any organisation. Often known as the 'technical core', operations usually accounts for most of its employment and cost. The chapter picks out common themes, such as the effect of volume on processes. It sets these ideas in the context of manufacturing and service provision, pointing to similarities and differences.

Many believe that business begins and ends with marketing. Chapter 20 explains the way it is developing to build closer relationships with customers. This growing closeness, combined with the alleged power of brands and advertising, makes marketing the most visible and criticised of functions. The chapter closes with an evaluation from the perspective of ethics and social responsibility.

Chapter 21 continues the theme of action by studying how organisations can convert their wish to innovate into a flow of new products and processes to keep ahead of competitors. As Westwood suggests, the process of converting ideas into marketable products is as much about management skill as about the original inspirations.

None of the elements could work without information. Chapter 22 explores the impact of the information age on managers, demonstrating how it offers the potential for improved performance. It also brings with it hazards, such as the information overload and mindless accumulation of data experienced by Gilbert's 'modern Major-General'.

Chapter | 19

Operations management

Chapter objectives

When you have finished studying this chapter, you should be able to:

■ define operations management and explain its scope;

■ distinguish between manufacture and isolated service and other types of service;

■ explain how volume is the key influence on process design and layout decisions;

■ show how scale and customer involvement relate to service process design;

■ identify the factors to be considered in location selection and show how these influence different types of enterprise;

■ explain the way capacity planning establishes a framework within which scheduling decisions are made and outline three approaches to production scheduling;

■ give reasons for the existence of inventories and queues and show how good operations management can turn them to advantage.

Cost versus speed at Courtaulds Textiles[1]

Courtaulds Textiles, whose 1996 turnover was £1000 million, is the second largest clothing and fabrics producer in the United Kingdom, and the leader in lingerie and underwear. Its brands include Gossard, Y-fronts and Lyle & Scott. The company is organised into four product divisions: Lace & Stretch Fabrics; Lingerie & Hosiery; Casualwear & Underwear; and Furnishings. It has plant in 16 countries, although two thirds of the worldwide staff of 20 000 are employed in the United Kingdom. Facing the competitive pressure of imports from low-cost countries, especially the Far East, the company has been reducing its home production of standard spun and woven products. Of 31 mills engaged in these activities in 1990, only four remained by 1995. At the same time, the remaining United Kingdom production has been shifted towards more complex items such as stretch fabrics and lace where consistent quality requires good technology and experienced staff.

About one third of sales go to Marks & Spencer, whose international expansion places increasing demands on maintaining good supplies. Such private label customers, which also include Laura Ashley, place a premium on speed, flexibility of service and rapid introduction of new designs. They no longer look for seasonal ranges in the leading stores; they want to see lines that are changed continually. If a garment sells well, more stock is required almost instantly. This policy demands a service lead time of two or three days, impossible to meet from far off countries whence sea transport takes more than a month.

Courtaulds Textiles' North American division of Dawson's International followed a different policy to Courtaulds. It had invested to compete head-on with imports of low priced garments such as sweatshirts and T-shirts. Courtaulds has struggled but gained. Dawson's has been unprofitable throughout the 1990s. Both the GATT and the North American Free Trade Agreement mean that its prospects are poor. The Uruguay round of the GATT will give further advantages to Third World textile production as quota restrictions are gradually dismantled.

Introduction

The choices facing manufacturers, such as Courtaulds Textiles, and their customers are common. The basis of competition has shifted from minimum price based on large manufacturing volumes to a mix of all the six PQRRSS factors introduced in Chapter 3. These are: price, quality, reliability, responsiveness, service and speed. In addition, globalisation means that the number of potential suppliers in many industries has greatly increased. Such issues are the concern of operations managers who, through both their strategic and day-to-day decisions, have to offer an optimal blend of goods and service to their customers. Doing operations well is a key part of maintaining competitiveness.

We saw in Fig. 2.2 how the core of an organisation can be seen as a chain made up of a series of primary activities. Together they form a transformation process that takes a range of inputs and converts them into outputs made available to the customer. In creating specialised functions, firms generally separate the operations activities from sales and marketing. This mirrors a break between those activities lying wholly inside the system boundary and the sales and marketing tasks whose purpose is boundary spanning. Naturally, managers must pay attention to the integration of all these primary tasks. In this chapter, we focus on the operations core, referring to links with other value chain elements at appropriate points.

Key issues in operations management

Operations is essentially a transformation process. Its role can be defined as:

> *to plan, organise, operate and control a transformation system that takes inputs from a variety of sources and produces outputs of goods and services at times and places defined by internal or external customers.*

What are the issues faced by operations managers when considering the transformation processes? Concerns extend to both the strategic and operating levels. At the former, managers consider product design, facility location and process design. Then, within this strategic framework, the manager is faced with questions ranging from medium and short-term capacity management and scheduling to the control of inventories and queues. Figure 19.1 shows how the operating system converts resources into products by using capacity and resources that it has set up. The three areas of concern are linked, so that each has to be changed in the light of feedback information on output performance.

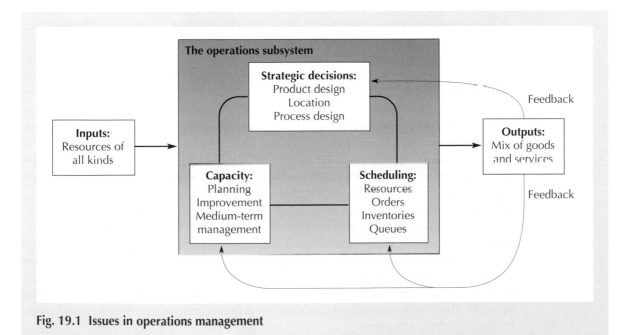

Fig. 19.1 Issues in operations management

■ Manufacture and service distinctions

Figure 19.1 also shows that the output of the operations function is a mix of goods and services. There is a long tradition of distinguishing between the two types of products, distinguishing the physical from the ephemeral and denigrating the inferiority of the latter.[2] Others have given attention to processes rather than products. Peters, for example, says, 'Would you believe that 96 per cent of us ply service trades? ... 79 per cent of us work in the service sector ... and of the 19 per cent still employed in so-called manufacturing, 90 per cent do service work (design, engineering, finance, marketing, distribution and so on).'[3] From the process point of view, organisational life is dominated by service.

There is such an overlap between manufacturing and service business that to classify operations into these categories is not particularly fruitful. Most so-called manufacturers include customer service functions, for example, despatch, promotion and after-sales service. Furthermore, many service functions are organised along similar lines to manufacture. Examples range from pension management to equipment repairs. Aircraft engine maintenance illustrates:

> *Aircraft maintenance is carried out by specialists. Not only is it important for the airline to have a short down time for maintenance but a predictable time is also needed. Major components such as engines are not, therefore, maintained* in situ *but are exchanged for replacements that have already been serviced. The engines can then be taken apart and rebuilt under factory conditions after the aircraft has resumed flying.*

Despite these overlaps, there is a useful distinction that we can use in our discussion of operations management. This is based on whether the customer is present. If not, operations take place under what we could broadly call 'factory conditions' where manufacture and service show much in common. We can call this *manufacture and isolated service*. When the customer is present, we have *personal service*. The service aspects of these operations are often called 'back office' and 'front office' respectively.

Figure 19.2 compares the flows of resources through the two operational arrangements. In both, the operational process is separated from the effect of environmental uncertainty by buffers designed to absorb fluctuations in demand. In manufacture and isolated service, stocks (also called inventories) may be used to separate the core process from the supply and customer environments. Typically, stock is present both before and after the process, but this can be a sub-optimal view. Planning methods, such as OPT and JIT discussed later in the chapter, look to smooth processes and reduce inventory. Personal service is different. Stocks are not possible so the buffers are surplus capacity or queues. Extra resources like these are known as slack.

Both manufacture and service organisations are strongly influenced by scale. Large scale enables producers to use facilities that have been especially designed for their function and tuned to achieve optimal efficiency. Economies of scale are evident in manufacturing and isolated service operations such as paper making, chemical plant, sewing machine assembly and film processing. Among personal services, the effect is seen in telephone banking, supermarket retailing and some forms of higher education.

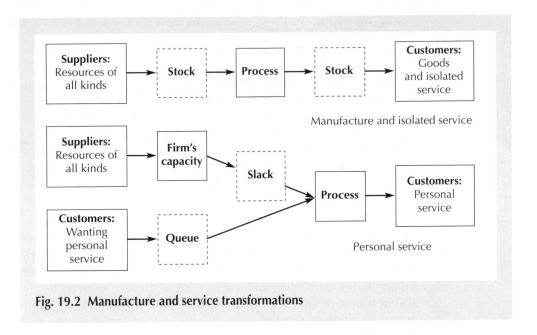

Fig. 19.2 Manufacture and service transformations

Small-scale operations, often called *jobbing shops*, gain their advantage from offering variety and flexibility. In manufacturing and isolated service, such firms are in printing of invitations, dressmaking, binding of theses and building specialised vehicles. Jobbing personal service businesses offer medical care, exclusive dining or hair cutting.

Exhibit 19.1 classifies operations according to both the degree of customer involvement and scale. Key operational tasks differ. Personal service requires that attention be paid both to interpersonal skills, that is an understanding of the needs of the customer in relation to the way the service is provided, and to some technical skills. Manufacturing and isolated service, in contrast, are not so concerned with personal interaction and depend more heavily on technical skill in managing the production system.

Exhibit 19.1	**Service and manufacturing operations affected by scale**	
	Services supplied in the customer's presence stressing interpersonal skills	*Manufacturing or isolated service stressing technical skills*
Small scale	Personal service: medical advice, manicure, child minding	Jobbing: building, *haute couture*, computer repairs
Large scale	Mass service: banking, trains, supermarkets	Mass production: vehicle assembly, newspapers, pension management

In spite of the contrasts, operations systems have many issues in common. As illustrated in Fig. 19.1, they are broadly concerned with:

- At the strategic level:
    Product and process design; facility location;
- At the intermediate level:
    Capacity planning;
- At the day-to-day level:
    Scheduling orders and resources; inventories or queues.

Planning the operations process

Whether it is a newspaper shop or a brewery, operations will take place within a planned facility. The starting point could be seen as product design, for unless a product decision has been made, there can be no progress on establishing how to supply it. Yet the link should not be seen as merely sequential as *process capability* is an important design constraint. Product decisions, arising from interactions of the design function with marketing and production, are covered in Chapter 21. Here we shall concentrate on layout issues alone.

■ Process layout

In the design of facility layouts, many factors have to be considered. These include the range and scale of the operations and the way they are to link with complementary processes within the value chain. The prime difference is between:

- *manufacture and isolated service*, where the concern is with the way goods flow through the production process; and
- *personal service* in which the customer enters the facility area and attention switches to questions such as queues, convenience, comfort and the way the work environment contributes to sales.

We shall start with manufacturing and isolated service, where there are five basic processes: fixed position or project; jobbing; batch; line and continuous processes. Figure 19.3 shows their main features. Many firms combine one or more of these into so-called *hybrid* production systems.

Fixed-position, or project layout

The fixed-position layout is required when the item being made, or serviced, remains stationary. The staff, materials, and other resources are brought to the work area when they are needed. Industries from civil and marine engineering to film making and research centres use such layouts. This is because of the uniqueness, complexity or sheer weight and volume of the items they produce. For instance, civil engineering contractors are engaged in the supply both of unique products, such as roads and bridges, and of those that they produce in batches, such as houses.

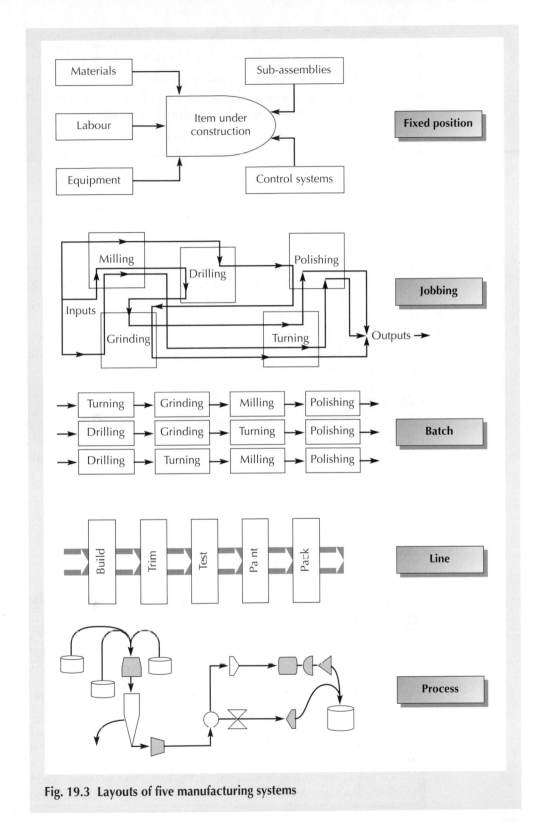

Fig. 19.3 Layouts of five manufacturing systems

Difficulties that arise in fixed-position layouts include:

- limitations of space for safe working and material storage;
- the flow of materials to their installed position is difficult to plan and implement;
- the number of staff required and the rate of use of materials varies, so services from accommodation to transport are difficult to plan;
- hazardous processes are troublesome to isolate;
- many projects involve working out of doors or at remote sites, thus imposing extra costs and risks of delay;
- supervision and inspection are difficult.

These problems can be alleviated by carrying out as much work as possible away from the assembly position or site. In heavy engineering such as the manufacture of oil rigs, the policy is to make subassemblies indoors and bring them to the site only when needed. This approach is limited only by constraints in the transport system. When United Kingdom public sector house building moved to large-scale, off-site assembly, however, many of the above difficulties emerged, as shown in Exhibit 19.2.

Techniques for scheduling and control of projects differ from those discussed later in this chapter because they apply to single items, rather than flows of output. They are discussed in Chapter 11.

Jobbing shop layout

In the jobbing factory, work is carried out on many single items or small batches, each of which is under a different contract. In principle, the type and sequence of tasks are unlimited but the sensible jobbing company will specialise in some way. It will either restrict the acceptance of orders or put out work it cannot handle to subcontractors. Specialisation may be:

- By facilities. The jobber may have facilities such as printing machinery, lathes or saws which means that certain classes of work can be taken on. Competitive advantage flows from expertise.

Exhibit 19.2 The rush to rehouse

The system building movement of the 1960s illustrates the difficulties of a rapid switch to off-site assembly without proper control of manufacture and supervision of installation. Tower blocks were built in many towns and cities. The low cost and rapid construction were attractive to local authorities pressed by housing shortages and budget constraints. Room-sized concrete panels, reinforced and insulated during factory manufacture, were put together on site. Built-in rubber seals were intended to make them watertight. But problems of dimensional accuracy and careless assembly meant that the seals let in the rain. This led to dampness in the flats, the growth of black mould and rusting of steel reinforcing bars. After ten years, investigations began to show that many structures were seriously defective. Most have been demolished.

■ By knowledge of customers or markets. The jobber seeks work connected with a particular product area or customer. Advantage is built around this customer focus.

> *Motor car repairs display each type of specialisation. Tyres are changed at depots that stock a range of sizes and have invested in efficient changing and balancing equipment. Many repair shops, on the other hand, offer comprehensive service focused on a named range of models. There are specialists for Rolls-Royce, VW, old MGs and so on.*

For layout decisions, jobbing shops have little obvious work sequence. Since orders are unpredictable and the corresponding sequence of operations equally so, there is no linkage of machinery into a production line. We would find a range of general purpose equipment surrounded by space for storage of partly finished work. The example in Fig. 19.3 shows the flow routes of three different contracts passing through up to five machining departments.

This grouping of related machines and tasks into departments is called a *process-based* or *functional* layout. Flexibility is achieved at the cost of close control of flow by supervisors or production controllers. They arrange for orders to pass among the groups, or departments, as required. Because of uncertain loads in any department, jobbing shops tend to fill with part-finished orders. The large stocks of work-in-progress make them seem cluttered.

Batch production

Batch processing is a step up from jobbing in terms of scale. Compared with jobbers, batch firms concentrate on larger quantities of a narrower product range. The process-based layout is still common. With increasing scale, however, it becomes economical to dedicate a family of machines and a team of specialists to each product or product range. As shown in Fig. 19.3, the product-based layout represents the beginnings of the dedicated production line. Batch firms are often torn between the flexibility offered by the process-based system and the efficiency that comes from specialised lines. The balance between the two can shift as changes occur in the business environment. IBM found this to its cost, *see* Exhibit 19.3.[4] Group technology, a hybrid system discussed later, addresses this problem by finding a new balance between flexibility and efficiency.

Exhibit 19.3 **Removal of robots at IBM, Greenock**

In 1986, IBM at Greenock spent £6 million to set up a robotic assembly line for PC monitors. Yet, by 1993, the company had decided to dispense with the robots and increase the line manning. Before 1993, some 25 assembly staff, with their robots, produced 550 monitors per shift. Afterwards, 50 assembly workers made 700. IBM gives the reasons for the change as the rapid pace of technological development and the different safety standards that had been imposed in different countries. Both factors caused the product variety to increase and the line was not flexible enough to cope. To alter the product on the line, it had to be shut down and all the tools and holding mechanisms had to be changed. Now, the only remaining robots pack the finished items into cartons for shipment.

Line production

Mass production owes its efficiency to a combination of mechanisation and specialisation. The assembly line is both the symbol and the outstanding achievement of industrial engineering. Its purpose is to produce standard designs in large volumes. These are sufficiently high and stable to justify the huge equipment investment. The ultimate line produces just one item. In practice, however, many are designed to cope with a limited range of related products. Lines, created around conveyors, use purpose-built equipment and specialised staff. Each stage in the system operates at the same rate so that buffer stocks are not required between stages. Line speeds can be changed according to market demands. When this happens, the challenge for operations managers is to ensure that the equipment capacity is satisfactory and personnel are assigned to tasks in the most efficient way. This is *line balancing*.

Ford's first moving assembly lines, for the Model T, had work carried out while the product was fixed to the line and moving with it, *see* Exhibit 19.4.[5] Compared with previous methods, it was successful for the following reasons:

■ The skill required was reduced. Jobs were divided into elements each requiring a small cycle time, sometimes as low as 30 seconds. This reduced the training time for workers.

■ It stimulated careful attention to the optimisation of work methods that became integrated with the line design and the associated equipment specifications. Work stations could be designed to be highly efficient. For example the four or five nuts on a car wheel could be tightened to the correct torque simultaneously using an electric or pneumatic spanner.

■ It reduced the stock of work in progress. Feeder lines, acting as tributaries to the main line, could be balanced to deliver at the rate required and therefore avoid excessive stocks.

Exhibit 19.4 **Henry Ford (1863–1947): the inventor of the line**

Henry Ford (1863–1947) is usually acknowledged as having been the first to introduce the modern line. He did not, however, invent it. For example, Ford knew of its use at Chicago abattoirs and the Whitney factory where ideas of standardisation and volume production were applied to the production of muskets. Ford's contribution was to recognise the opportunity presented by the line to create a mass market in affordable cars.

In 1896, Ford was in business with an old friend, Frederick Strauss. They produced petrol engines but, at the same time, Ford secretly built his first car. He began his own company in 1903 and launched into the process of building a standardised product. Between 1908 and 1927, 15 million Model Ts rolled off the lines. At the peak, in 1920, the rate was one a minute. Efficiency through specialisation was everything. For instance, in 1913, Ford's magneto assembly line reduced the labour content per item from 20 minutes to 5. By 1914 a vehicle line had reduced assembly time from 12.5 to 1.5 man-hours.

Ford lost his touch in the 1920s. As other makers, such as General Motors, began to compete through refinement, model variations, service and credit, Ford strove more intensely than ever to reduce costs through specialisation and standardisation. To him is attributed the statement, 'They can have any colour they like as long as it's black'. This was the fastest drying colour.

Process production

Process, or continuous process, manufacturing is carried out for products such as chemicals, oils, polymers, paper, glass, beer, cement and some foods. These differ from line products in that they are measured by *dimensions,* such as mass or volume, rather than by counting units. Plant is characterised by large scale and high capital costs. Changes to capacity are often only available in large increments so that close attention needs to be paid to market demands before investments are made. For instance, in brewing for the mass market, increments of about 90 million litres per year are required if the plant is to maintain economies of scale.

Plant layout is determined by the nature of the product. Special machines have balanced capacity to allow the product to flow through the plant without delay. Such would be the case in an oil refinery where there is little room to store intermediate products. Balance enables operations managers to achieve optimal efficiency and match customer demands. Attention must also be paid to reliability and safety.

The transmission networks of utility companies, such as gas, water, electricity and telephone, can be thought of as very large, and widely distributed, process plants. Their purpose is to maintain interconnection, either from sources to consumers or, in telephones, between any pair of users. High reliability and safety are achieved both by component design and by *redundancy*. This means there are many duplicated routes and items of equipment. The isolated service operations of banks are another example requiring high reliability and security in data transmission, as illustrated by Exhibit 19.5.

Hybrid production systems

Many companies make products for which none of the above ideal-types of production system quite fits. They may either have different approaches at different stages of manufacture or be working at the borderline between two systems. Biscuit making is an example of joining two processes: ingredients are mixed in batches while the biscuits themselves are moulded, baked, coated and packed on dedicated production lines.

Exhibit 19.5 Redundancy in Kredietbank's information network

In the early 1990s, Kredietbank, the second largest bank in Belgium and a leader in European Currency Unit clearing, was concerned with the risk of service interruption. International banking operations, which include risk management, foreign exchange and money market transactions, funds and credit transfers, as well as ECU clearing, require continuous processing. In Kredietbank's case, the centres were Brussels, London, New York and Hong Kong.

There was no main computer in Hong Kong, its work required permanent connection to Brussels. Kredietbank used redundancy to lower the risk of interruption. It used both a private line and the InfoLAN commercial network, with quick automatic switching between, to maintain service integrity.

Exhibit 19.6 Group technology: keeping it in the family

CIP makes bronze water nozzles and similar machined components. To increase throughput while maintaining flexibility, it decided to change to group technology. Machines had been arranged in a process layout with products passing from department to department. The left hand half of Fig. 19.4 outlines the arrangement, the thickness of the lines connecting the machines indicating the heavy flows of items over long distances. The right hand half shows how the machines were rearranged to cater for three 'product families', although constraints meant that two machines, 180 and 303, had to be shared. Material flows were cut and the new arrangement enabled teams to work more closely together to resolve problems. This means that CIP changed both elements of its socio-technical system.

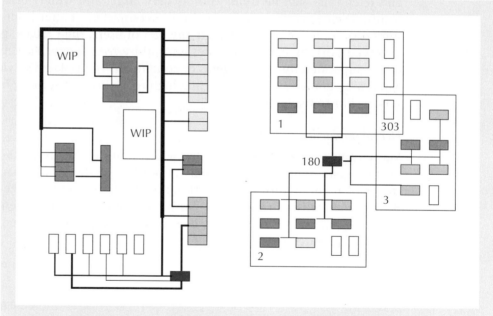

Fig. 19.4 CIP – layout before and after change

Group technology or *cellular manufacturing* stands at the borderline between batch and line production. A batch producer can gain some advantages of the line through clustering products into families. Exhibit 19.6 shows the change at Champion Irrigation Products.[6]

Service process design

Not only are service operations influenced by scale, they are also strongly affected by the degree of involvement of the customer. Compared with conventional personal service, we have already noted that one possibility is to carry out much of the task away from the customer in 'factory' environments. Another direction is to curtail the amount of service provided personally. This is the move to self-service. These changes, *isolation* and *detachment,* are shown in Fig. 19.5.[7] Also shown are the effects of volume, leading to *standardisation* or *customisation* depending on whether the service is growing or shrinking. Scale and customer involvement suggest, therefore, six types of service provision:

- *Service Shop*
  Each customer's needs are treated individually but the service takes place without the customer being present. This enables the back room to be organised as a jobbing shop.

- *Service Factory*
  This is the service shop operating at large scale. The range of services available is standardised and they are offered through *gatekeepers*. These are staff whose role is to bridge the gap between the customer and the 'back room'. The service factory may be organised as a batch production plant.

- *Professional Service*
  Service is supplied in the presence of individual customers by professionally trained personnel. Examples include doctors, counsellors, beauticians and music teachers.

- *Mass Service*
  Mass service operations replicate the supply of professional services on a large scale. They are carried out in the presence of groups, or even crowds, of customers. Examples include some higher education, large-scale retailing, television and concerts.

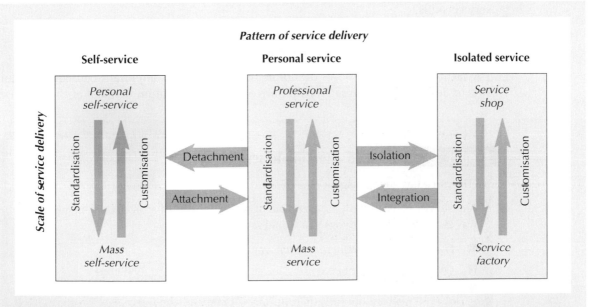

Fig. 19.5 Six service patterns

■ *Personal Self-Service*

These systems are developing from the desire to combine the needs for personal service with the cost and availability advantages of self-service. The sector is not well developed and awaits growth in the application of expert systems and person-computer communications technologies. 'Intelligent' ticket machines are an example of the trend.

■ *Mass Self-Service*

Detachment has been achieved through the removal of human servers and the lowering of physical, psychological and technical barriers between customers and the service. Examples range from retail stores to dispensing machines. These all work well if they are easy to use and present sufficient information.

The two dimensions of scale and customer involvement have strong influence on service system design. The labour intensity of small-scale operations means that managers are continually concerned with overcoming the effects of labour cost increases while maintaining quality. Because of the unpredictable nature of the tasks to be carried out, staff must be flexible and offer a variety of service on request. Large-scale operations, on the other hand, seek efficiency through reducing the reliance on labour. The challenge is to establish and maintain the feeling of good quality service under such conditions. Physical surroundings are important and there must be sufficient staff to offer personal contact when needed. Where personal contact does occur, training and motivation aim at high quality, repetitive delivery. Successful large-scale organisations, such as the major retailers, pay great attention to the detailed steps of customer transactions and train their staff accordingly. Exhibit 19.7 is taken from the staff training manual of Superdrug, the major retailer of household and personal care products.[8]

The focus on the customer must be maintained at the contact point of the isolated service operation. Effective and efficient gatekeeping requires personal service skills.

Layout of personal and self-service systems

The fact that personal services cannot be held in stock has important consequences for system design. The organisation can only cope with maximum demand at the expense

---

Exhibit 19.7 **Detailed attention to service**

'The price has gone up again'

A customer walks up to you, complaining that the price of a product is higher than it was last week. List the things you would say and do.

■ *Listen to the complaint in a polite way.*

■ *Offer to check the price.*

■ *Explain the increase and suggest a cheaper alternative, if possible.*

■ *Report to management if the customer has found an item cheaper elsewhere.*

of spare capacity at other times. Examples are the rush-hour train or the crush at the theatre bar. Queues are not wholly outside the control of the organisation. Having understood the ways in which queues form and are sustained, the manager should try to limit their extension beyond acceptable lengths and influence the perceptions of those who are in the line. The way in which a service provider manages queues offers it an opportunity to display to customers positive aspects of its attitudes towards them. A clear, active and fair approach to queue management is a key element of good service.

The involvement of the customer in service has other implications for layout design. Especially in self-service, a layout must be attractive and convenient for customers. Good layout is an important element of sales promotion.

We shall examine the issues of queues and service layout in the next sections.

Balancing demand and capacity

The personal service system rarely achieves equilibrium between demand and capacity. Before examining queues we can consider what scope there is for balancing demand or capacity. Demand can be influenced by restricting access at peak times to customers who have reserved, paid a premium or fall into a special category. Capacity changes come from:

■ flexibility: employ multi-skilled staff with extras at peak periods;

■ adapting the service, switching from *customised* to *standardised* service;

■ switching to self-service from personal service, the processes of *attachment* and *detachment* of Fig. 19.5;

■ sharing capacity with other organisations;

■ automation of some operations to reduce service times.

Many service organisations follow one or more of the above policies. For instance, restaurants use differential pricing between lunch and evening and weekday and weekend; promotional offers may run from Mondays to Thursdays; they may offer a fixed-price quick service lunch menu and a fuller one at dinner; reservations may be advised on weekend evenings; some events may be 'privileged diners only'; staff are employed according to anticipated demand.

In carrying out the balancing policies, managers must recognise constraints that exist both in the market and in their operating system. These include:

■ negative responses to complex pricing structures;

■ the danger of cheapening the service in the eyes of full-price customers;

■ perceptions of unfairness by some customers;

■ quality;

■ limits to flexibility in service design.

The extent to which the balancing policies work is influenced by the traditions of each industry. Many customers expect restaurants to vary their policy at different times, although perhaps not at The Ritz. The convention of higher fares on commuter trains is well established. Yet higher prices for some long-distance train tickets on 'Fridays, certain Saturdays in July and August, and 23 December' are not well understood and cause frustration for some travellers. Complex charging structures for telephone calls and electricity are also not easy to grasp.

■ The queuing problem

While some smoothing of demand and capacity can occur, imbalances are common in personal and self-service systems. Unless capacity is very high, variability results in queues. Given this difficulty, the basic challenge is to reconcile:

■ a service capacity that keeps waiting lines down to a tolerable length while not inducing excessive costs, and

■ the risk of creating dissatisfaction among customers, or even a loss of their business if excessive service times lead to their 'voting with their feet'.

Performance against these objectives can be assessed as follows. First, operations managers accept that there needs to be some spare capacity at the service points. In other words, the ratio:

$$Service\ capacity\ utilisation = \frac{Service\ time\ demanded}{Service\ time\ made\ available}$$

is less than 100 per cent. Second, the effectiveness of managing queues can be judged from their average length, measured either by number or waiting time. This is a less than perfect means of assessing customer responses because, as we shall see, different individuals experience queuing in different ways.

Figure 19.6 sketches a typical relationship between waiting time and capacity utilisation. An attempt to increase service capacity utilisation, for instance by reducing the number of service points in use, inevitably leads to longer queues. This effect becomes more acute as utilisation approaches 100 per cent. One approach for providers is to aim not to exceed a service threshold, as shown in Fig. 19.6, and adjust the service capacity accordingly.

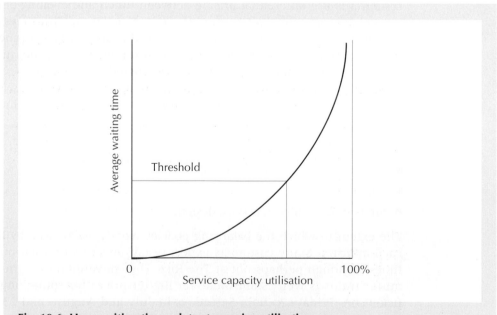

Fig. 19.6 How waiting time relates to service utilisation

■ Managing queues

Queues occur in many service situations. Beyond standing in a line, they include waiting:

- for service to arrive: in a restaurant, after a breakdown or in a sick bed;
- for an item to be mended;
- in an electronic queue: terminals or telephones;
- over a long period: to enter a hospital, join a golf club or obtain a visa.

In industries where queues are commonplace, the successful organisation will be one that shows its customers that it is aware of, and responding to, the situation in a positive way. Four questions can be noted: the acceptable length; avoidance; differentiation; and changing the waiting experience.

Acceptable queue lengths

Factors affecting acceptability vary from individual to individual and from case to case:

- *The significance of the wait.* Some people have more time than others; they are prepared to wait for some services more than for others, possibly because these services are more important or there are few alternatives. For instance, it is accepted that there is to be some waiting time for a free hospital bed in non-urgent cases, although there is little consensus over how long this interval ought to be!

- *Perception of queue length.* Customers perceive the length of a line in different ways. For instance there is the difficulty of comparing a short but slow-moving line with a longer one that is moving more quickly. Queue structures can, therefore, have an impact on customer response. Another issue is the sense of urgency felt by the customer. Lining up for a railway ticket well ahead of departure will be a more comfortable experience than when the train is about to leave.

- *Information.* Besides the time lost in the line, another customer anxiety is uncertainty. Some organisations relieve this problem by informing customers of the likely period of the wait. For this policy to be successful, customers need to be confident that the estimates of delays are accurate and that there is a commitment by the organisation to keep to them. Theme parks such as Disneyland incorporate signs in the queuing areas with such information.

- *Competition.* Standards may be set by competitive forces in industries where service quality can be defined as including the time spent waiting. As part of their strategies to gain in the important business market, many airlines are offering fast or automated check-ins to premium-price passengers. In supermarkets, delays at the crowded checkouts were one reason behind Tesco's advertising campaign of late 1994, an example of which appears in Exhibit 19.8.[9]

Exhibit 19.8 Competing over waiting lines

If there's ever more than one other customer in front of you at the checkout we'll aim to open another until all our tills are open.

TESCO *Every little helps*

■ *Priorities.* Competition may encourage organisations to discriminate among customers and replace the common first-come-first-served rule. Alternative priority criteria include:

- urgency, for some medical cases while others wait;
- consequences, fire and other emergency services answer any call but, in case of overload, they are allocated according to the potential consequences of the crisis – for instance to large public buildings;
- special customers, for instance those who place large orders or buy premium services, such as first class tickets.

Queue avoidance

A sensible alternative to the pressure and problems resulting from queuing is to avoid them through some form of regulation system. This will aim to limit demand for service, either to cut it altogether or to shift it to more favourable times. One policy is to use price premiums at peak times but, as we have noted this is a relatively blunt weapon. Reservations have been adopted in various industries; in some they are commonplace while in others they are not expected. Declining demand for cinema seats in the United Kingdom meant that few customers thought of booking. The recovery of the 1990s, however, meant that reservation systems were reintroduced. Chains such as UCI showed how to gain advantage from offering a good service, *see* Exhibit 19.9.[10]

A further difficulty for some customers is that a reservation system may increase the delay in receiving service. A person with an urgent need may prefer to queue straight away rather than make a later appointment.

Exhibit 19.9 UCI's growing reservation system

United Cinemas International operates 28 cinemas throughout the United Kingdom. It has installed, in Manchester, a computer-answering system that is designed to answer 95 per cent of calls in less than 20 seconds. Customers make up to 23 000 calls per day using a range of Freephone numbers, each of which enables the computer to recognise from which cinema catchment area the call originates. The system replaces cinema offices with up to four operators which at busy times lost many enquiries through engaged tones or long waits. More than 60 per cent of sales at some cinemas were by telephone.

When answering, the operator's screen shows the programme of the caller's local UCI with prices and availability. After booking, all details are transmitted to the customer's cinema where tickets and receipts are prepared for collection. The facility is staffed for almost 100 hours per week. At other times, a touch-tone telephone can be used to make reservations.

Sales rose about 6 per cent in the year after the system was installed. Since the cinemas were connected to the network in stages, it was possible to separate the effects of the better service from the impact of the films being shown.

The policies for queue avoidance laid out in this section imply the need to keep demand below capacity. While many businesses view excess capacity as wasteful, others will compete through promising that it will always be available. McDonald's and other quick-service restaurants, for instance, have high capacity, simple technology and flexible staffing that enable them to offer fast service effectively under a wide range of demand conditions.

Queue differentiation

The most common form of queue operates on a first-come-first-served basis. This system is generally operated and accepted where there is only one service point, such as small shops, banks and so on. When there are several servers, complications arise, particularly where the layout and atmosphere of the serving area conflict with the need for orderly lines to form. Competition at a crowded bar is an extreme example. Several arrangements are possible for more than one channel:

■ *Multiple lines to full-range servers*
This is the typical standard supermarket checkout or the arrangement found in many banks. All servers offer the full service and customers join any queue. Where the variability of service time among customers is high, customer frustration can become acute as queues move at different speeds. The problem is exacerbated for those with few purchases. Customers may switch lines.

■ *Multiple lines to specialised servers*
One common way of separating lines is to have some servers dedicated to particular transactions such as selling stamps in the post office or quick checkouts for those with few purchases, or paying cash, in the supermarket. Gains come from efficiency associated with specialisation and reduction in customer anxiety caused by multiple queues with widely varying service times. A disadvantage is that some customers may see other lines empty while they are still waiting. Furthermore, excessive specialisation of the servers means that some customers have to wait in more than one queue to have their needs attended to. This is the experience of outpatients in some hospitals who may have to move from queue to queue for several tests. Some hospitals, in introducing 'patient-centred care', bring services to the patient as required.

■ *Single line to multiple servers*
Perceived by many to be the fairest method, customers are served in order of joining. This arrangement has been introduced into many offices and banks and applies in telephone systems. When demand is high, the queue can seem long, although it can move quickly. The arrangement requires a waiting area set out to maintain the queue organisation and that the servers are all able to provide the full service.

There are several hybrid arrangements. For instance, banks combine single lines to multiple servers for most business, with specialist counters for some transactions.

Changing the experience of queuing

As with all service business, excellence will only be achieved if the perspective of the customer is fully considered in planning the queuing process. This clearly includes the customers' perceptions of having to wait.

Exhibit 19.10 Factors that make waiting seem longer

Queuing seems longer if it:

- occurs before the process rather than during it   ↑↑↑↑↑
- has an uncertain duration   Under
- is unexplained   firm's
- seems unfair   control
- feels uncomfortable
- involves idleness   Shared
- concerns anxious people
- is for a service of low value   Under
- is done alone   customers'
- comprises people whose current attitudes are unfavourable control
- incorporates customers who always perceive waiting negatively ↓↓↓↓↓

Both Maister[11] and Davies and Heineke[12] propose sets of hypotheses concerning personal queuing which draw together the above discussion, *see* Exhibit 19.10. Note that some aspects are more under the operations manager's control than others. For instance, customers' attitudes and value systems cannot easily be changed by the firm. It will succeed by learning as much as it can about them before tailoring its service to suit. Using these ideas as a basis, managers should consider the following actions:

- Reducing the anxiety that comes from uncertainty. Informing customers of the likely length of the wait both enables them to plan what to do meanwhile and gives the impression that the managers care about their circumstances.
- Influence the perception of queuing time by distracting customers. Distractions include drinks in a restaurant, Mickey at Disneyland, videos in the post office, coffee at the garage and ensuring that complementary parts of the service are not too fast, *see* Exhibit 19.11.[13]

    There is also the well-known story of the up-market New York hotel where customers complained of having to wait for the lifts. Grumbles became fewer when full-length mirrors were installed on each landing.

Exhibit 19.11 Walking as a distraction

The baggage reclaim hall at Dallas – Fort Worth airport is close to the gate area. Passengers have a short walk to collect their luggage but usually arrive first. At Los Angeles they have to walk much further and arrive after the luggage. Dallas passengers grumble more about luggage delays.

- Identify stressful elements of the environment and take steps to relieve these. Problems include room temperature and noise. The latter may, of course, be caused by the queue itself!

- Make the queuing time part of the service by taking orders, handing out registration forms or briefing customers about what to expect.

- Use numbered tickets to maintain the principle of first-come-first-served while allowing people to leave the queue. For instance, this is done at the delicatessen counter within supermarkets.

Whatever the queue structure and management policies chosen by an enterprise, it is essential to show to clients that the operation is *under control*. There is nothing more disheartening for the anxious customer than to feel that events are following their own course.

Service facility layouts

In discussing layouts, we have concentrated our attention on the waiting line. While this is a critical issue in the design of service layouts, we must not forget that the customer is present in other aspects of the service operation. Retail stores and shopping centres use design to create environments that are both efficient and stimulate demand through their presentation.

Store and shopping centre layout

Retail managers have, through years of experience, developed many tricks of the trade to promote sales. For example, it is expected that goods presented at eye-level are more likely to sell, as are goods displayed towards the ends of rows of shelves. These rules of thumb are reinforced by research studies using direct observation of customer behaviour and analysis of sales. Leading supermarket chains now plan their layouts centrally. They allocate some 50 per cent of shelf space to own-label goods, perhaps 40 per cent to the leading proprietary brands and 10 per cent to other brands that may well have some local following.

Store design is a critical component of company image and influences shoppers' perceptions of value. Compare the small cramped aisles of the discounter with the spacious layouts of the leading, quality-orientated superstores. Each attracts customers through messages concerning its price–quality image. Dividing a large store into sections, each with its own ambience created by scale, colours and smell, is an extension of the design philosophy. For instance, Safeway creates in-store bakery departments with an identity that supports the company's image of high quality goods at reasonable prices.[14]

Designers of shopping centres have not only to consider safe and comfortable conditions but also seek to persuade leading companies to take space within the development. Indeed, developments are often not started until such agreements are in place. Another aim is to achieve a mix of stores so that customers can be confident of having their needs satisfied 'under one roof'. This may appear to limit competition among the outlets but most are subject to indirect competition from other retailers as each pursues some diversification of its range. For the smaller operator, the negative effects of competition can be outweighed by the benefits from the 'pull' of the so-called anchor stores, the branches of major chains.[15]

Facility location: push and pull

The location decision involves an assessment of cost and service factors. Many optimisation models, *see* Chapter 11, have been proposed as decision aids but we shall just outline the main questions to be considered. It is useful to distinguish between *push* and *pull* factors in the decision.

Push factors, arising from dissatisfaction with a current location, trigger the organisation to consider alternatives. They include:

■ poor service from current site;

■ labour problems;

■ competitors with better locations;

■ site costs such as rents and property taxes;

■ shortage, or surplus, of space;

■ regulatory actions related to safety, effluent, noise or planning issues;

■ a wish to release capital;

■ unusual events or risks such as flood and fire.

Many moves are over short distances, allowing for continuity of employment and access to current markets. Compared with the average moving rate for manufacturers of 3 per cent each year, larger plant moves less frequently. Those with more than 100 people move at the rate of 1 per cent, which corresponds to once every 100 years![16]

The push factors stimulate the decision process, then the pull factors come into play. They represent a set of forces that draw the organisation to one place or another. The choice may involve several stages that, in practice, are intertwined. At a very broad level, an international business looks for a trading bloc, nation or region in which to create a new facility. Then, within the region, it will pass on to detailed issues of site selection. In practice, these steps are run together because the number of sites that are available is small.

Pull factors include:

■ economic policies of governments and blocs such as the European Union;

■ different risks associated with one country as opposed to another;

■ raw materials and energy sources;

■ location of markets;

■ transport links and communications infrastructure;

■ climate and quality of life;

■ labour costs, supply and training opportunities;

■ competitors and allies;

■ availability of sites, including local subsidies and inducements.

The relative significance of the above factors may alter with time. Consider, for example, the changing perspectives of Volkswagen over a period of 60 years outlined in Exhibit 19.12 and the map of Fig. 19.7.

Exhibit 19.12   Volkswagen's location decisions

One of the earliest large-scale car assembly plants to be planned in a wholly new location was that of Volkswagen at Wolfsburg where construction began in 1938. The site was by the Mittelland canal, close to *autobahnen* and railways. Wolfsburg was, however, deliberately chosen to avoid disturbing existing industrial complexes and busy traffic flows. Workers were to be housed in a new town of about 100 000 people for which room had to be allowed. As it happened, the new town was not built immediately. After production restarted and expanded after the war there was considerable commuting. For instance, in 1953, 3000 employees (14 per cent) were travelling daily the 80 km from Hannover. Further expansion plans could not be accommodated at Wolfsburg so, from the mid-1950s the company expanded elsewhere, first at Hanover and then in other places in North-West Germany.

Gradually, the motor industry has become globalized. For the producer, it is no longer a question of where in a country a plant should be located but where in each trading bloc. Volkswagen now has a complex network of links among its worldwide production facilities. Figure 19.7 shows the flows among its major sites outside Europe.

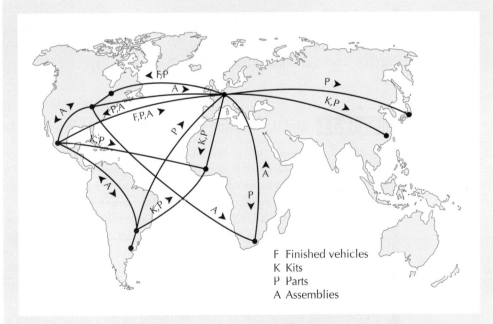

F Finished vehicles
K Kits
P Parts
A Assemblies

Fig. 19.7 Links in Volkswagen's global manufacturing system

There is no location factor that dominates every case. When examining particular industries, however, different ones come to the fore. For example, there has been concern among car assemblers, component suppliers and electronics companies over trading bloc import tariffs and quotas. This has led to many deciding to establish manufacturing facilities in the European Union and the North American Free Trade Area.

Global corporations have great freedom in deciding where to locate. Access to resources or markets is very important, *see* the case of Kodak[17] in Exhibit 19.13. Studies of medium firms more closely tied to regional or national sources of supply or markets show that government tax reductions and other inducements tend to have only marginal effects.[18] The availability of suitable labour is frequently quoted by all types of firm.

■ Retail location

Since retailers require visits from customers, the weighting of considerations changes. More emphasis is placed on many *micro* issues in site selection that are not of interest to the factory or warehouse operator. The sales performance of sites even a few metres apart can differ substantially.

Bowlby and others[19] suggest that, for the retailer, the ideal decision sequence gradually narrows the search from area to identified premises:

- *Geographical area*
  Related to area demand or part of achieving full national coverage

- *Site identification*
  Often among a few that are available

- *Micro issues*
  Detailed examination to cover issues that influence performance. Important factors are: catchment area population; competition; access, especially for passing trade; costs; and planning controls.[20]

Exhibit 19.13 **Kodak: locating within the EU and close to markets**

In the 1960s, Kodak built a new plant for the supply of film materials at Chalon-sur Saône in central France. It is now the largest employer in the region, with some 2600 permanent and 300 temporary staff. The key factor in the original decision was the financial assistance offered by the French government in promoting its regional policy. Further, labour was available and there was a plentiful supply of water. Today, Chalon and Harrow, near London, are the company's principal plants in Europe.

Expansion at Chalon since the 1960s has been encouraged by several strategic factors. The autoroute system connects the area with major markets from Spain to Germany. Communications have become more important as firms seek to get closer to markets.

Continuing support comes from the region's policy of stimulating growth in imaging, visual and photographic industries. For instance, there are links with Dijon University on both training and research projects.

Capacity management

Capacity management relates to matching the size of a facility with demand. This is a two-way process in which both the scale of the facility and the size of demand should be managed or, at least, influenced. The issues can be examined from short-, medium- and long-term points of view. In the short term, balancing is tactical. Routine adjustments are made to sway individual orders and adjust output within the framework of a given facility and other resource commitments. In the medium term, the firm plans to cope with the bulk of orders it expects to receive without analysing any one. It looks for means of adjusting resources such as personnel and subcontract activity, again within the fixed facilities. In the long term, all aspects are variable. The scale of the facility can be altered and the organisation needs to make choices with respect to market and product policy. We shall look at these aspects of capacity decisions, starting with the long term.

Capacity in the long term

Choosing long-term capacity is one of the riskiest decisions an organisation has to face. Not only is the business relying on its ability to modify itself over several years but it is making the decision without knowing what its competitors are likely to be doing over the same period. It could be that all make the same decisions during a boom period and end up facing overcapacity in their dedicated process plants during decline. This happened in the European chlorine business, *see* Exhibit 19.14.

Figure 19.8 summarises the role of the capacity planning decision. Within the framework of the organisation's strategic plan, capacity requirements are influenced by three choices. The marketing policy identifies the expected sales volume and whether it is smooth or seasonal. Furthermore, it is concerned with how and where the customers are to be supplied. The operations strategy is linked to marketing and concerns range, batch sizes, speed of response and so on. The make or buy decision addresses the question of having at least some capacity provided by subcontractors or associates.

Exhibit 19.14 **Decline in chlorine demand in Europe**

The five years up to 1993 saw a 15 per cent decline in European demand for chlorine. This resulted from the elimination of its application in paper bleaching and the steady reduction in the use of chlorofluorocarbons and chlorinated solvents. PVC takes 39 per cent of the European chlorine output but this product has, in turn, become an issue with environmental groups. PVC usage in packaging will suffer as governments introduce recycling targets.

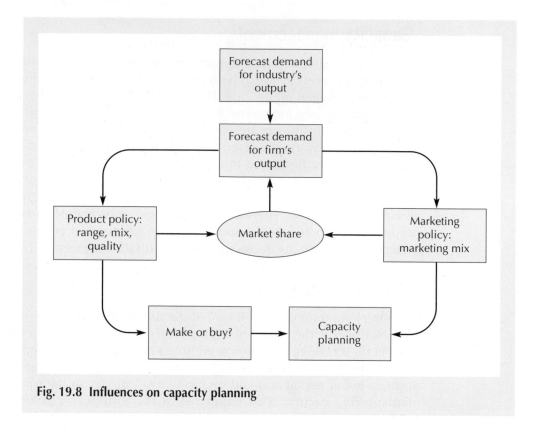

Fig. 19.8 Influences on capacity planning

Forecasting demand over a long period is subject to the sources of uncertainty identified in Chapter 9. In the case of air travel, for example, planners have identified an underlying annual growth of between 7 and 8 per cent. Manchester Airport[21] took this approach in justifying its proposed second runway, *see* Exhibit 19.15.

Learning

Forecasts of trends in capacity also apply to the supply side of the balance. While some facilities have a capacity that, without major change, is fixed, others are susceptible to steady improvement. This is usually called *learning* as managers and employees gradually discover how to make their facility work effectively. Improvements of between 15 per cent and 30 per cent have been reported for each doubling of cumulative output, at least in the short term. This means that the hundredth item only requires between 70 and 85 per cent of the time taken for the fiftieth. The two hundredth item is reduced by the same ratio again.[22]

The existence of the same effect in the long term is controversial. Render and Heizer[23] quote the example of the Model T Ford. Costs seem to have fallen by 14 per cent for each cumulative volume doubling. But the data observed is the showroom price. Ford may have reduced his prices because of cheaper raw materials, larger scale of production and, probably more important, the emerging competition from General Motors. Depending on the industry, many process innovations

> ### Exhibit 19.15 Forecasting demand for runway capacity at Manchester Airport
>
> Manchester Airport is the third busiest in the United Kingdom after Heathrow and Gatwick. In 1992 it handled 11.7 million passengers (mppa). There are some 100 airlines offering 170 charter and scheduled services. The airport has a single 3048 metre runway served by three terminals, two passenger and one freight.
>
> Demand is forecast to rise to 22 mppa by 2000 and 30 mppa by 2005. These figures imply compound growth rates of 8 per cent until 2000 and 7 per cent thereafter. Based on an average of 100 passengers per air transport movement (ATM), corresponding ATMs are forecast to be 220 000 in 2000 and 300 000 in 2005. The runway achieves a 'best in class' performance of 42 ATMs per hour. This output is not achieved at all times of the day nor all year. Peak daily demand occurs from 0700 to 1000 and 1600 to 1930. Summer demand, especially for charter movements, is higher than in the winter. Furthermore, the runway is closed from time to time. Planned closure is for maintenance, usually at night, while unplanned closure can happen any time. This causes a complete shut down of the airport.
>
> Management estimates, however, that the 300 000 ATMs in 2005 will require a capacity of at least 60 per hour. If this were the case, the annual capacity utilisation would be 57 per cent.

originate not within firms but in research institutes or equipment suppliers. In other cases, they are easily copied. Therefore, process innovations may be available to all producers, large and small. Learning is enhanced if firms work on increasing their rate by training and disseminating innovation. There is more on innovation in Chapter 21.

Where it does occur, learning has implications for capacity planning. It may:

- result in better use of capacity;
- enable lower cost budgets;
- change schedules as some tasks are speeded up;
- yield demand increases and further market opportunities.

Capacity in the medium term

In the medium term we are looking to make some changes to flexible parameters within the built plant capacity over periods of weeks or months. In a factory, it may mean the recruitment of a second shift; a retailer may extend the hours of opening or increase the number of tills to augment throughput. As shown in Fig. 19.9, this process is *aggregate planning*. It forms a bridge between the long-term capacity plan and detailed schedules. It combines medium-term sales forecasts, which can be established with more confidence than the long-term ones with knowledge of current capacity. Arrangements can then be made for the processing of anticipated orders.

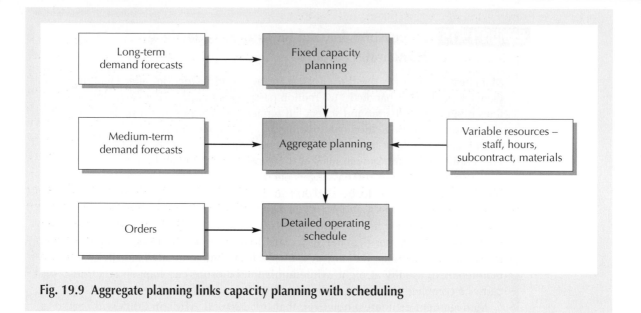

Fig. 19.9 Aggregate planning links capacity planning with scheduling

Scheduling: short-term operations management

The scheduling task takes place in the context of the aggregate plan and is designed to ensure that customers' orders are delivered according to promises. In our review we shall compare the apparent chaos of the jobbing shop with modern approaches to scheduling batch and line production. In two of these, OPT and JIT, efforts are made to cut inventory levels to save costs and space, and shorten the system response time. Inventory is the bugbear of many manufacturing systems and we will conclude our discussion with its purposes and disadvantages.

Scheduling the job shop

In jobbing shops, with their ad hoc layout designed to be as flexible as possible, the scheduling task is most difficult. In practice, they get the work done using a mixture of: rough planning based on priority rules such as 'first-come-first-served' or 'longest processing time first'; having surplus capacity; expecting individual employees to use their initiative to progress orders; and the employment of progress chasers. The last, as their name suggests, intervene to keep things moving. While many jobbing shops seem chaotic as a result, we should remember that they win their business through offering flexibility. They can change both their rate and type of output, often at short notice.

Scheduling batch production

Batch production units could work in similar ways. Indeed, as many have grown from jobbing shops, they have a history of doing so! Yet the increase in order size and the emerging focus on a more limited product range make the development of formal scheduling systems worth while. Among the best known are Manufacturing Requirements Planning and Optimised Production Technology.

Manufacturing Resources Planning

MRPII is not one method, rather a family of approaches based on the same general principles. Its name originates in the earlier MRP, Materials Requirements Planning. MRPII is a means of planning all manufacturing resources, cascading down from the aggregate plans to giving detailed instructions to every function involved in the supply of customer orders. The instructions include raw materials supply, staff allocation and machine scheduling. Extensions allowing for tool preparation, maintenance planning and financial analysis are possible. Work of this complexity lends itself to information system applications and many software specialists have produced MRPII programs.

Figure 19.10 is a flow chart that traces the stages of the MRPII process. The core of the system is the Master Production Schedule. Continually updated, it links the aggregate plans and customer orders to plans for materials and shop-floor capacity. This enables the purchasing function to obtain general stocks or items matched to each order, depending on the buying policy. At the same time, capacity requirements planning makes detailed plans for known orders and somewhat more flexible plans for those that are anticipated a little later.

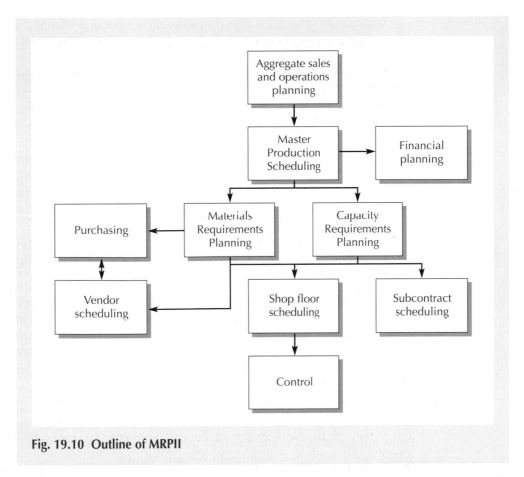

Fig. 19.10 Outline of MRPII

While recognising that MRPII systems operate with sophisticated information technology, we should note that MRPII is not automatic. The software contains algorithms to resolve local sequencing problems and will warn managers of, say, overloads at key points. Yet the basic decisions have to be made by managers. A scheduling office will be manned by a few experienced staff who know the production process well and have diplomatic skills needed to cope with friction when plans are changed. Considerable benefits from the introduction of MRPII have been reported, although only the minority of projects are wholly successful. In these cases, Spreadbury[24] notes how manufacturing efficiency and on-time delivery can rise to above an excellent 95 per cent.

Problems with MRPII

In contrast to Spreadbury's optimism, several surveys[25] point to failure. It is not clear whether these amount to reductions in performance of the whole production system or a lack of achievement of high expectations which have been set out at the start of MRPII projects. Failures lie in both the technology of the operating systems and the way they are managed. The technical power and complexity of MRPII are potential sources of weakness. Introducing such systems requires major changes in behaviour throughout the operations functions.[26] Luscombe shows how staff used to traditional planning systems tend to undermine MRPII when problems arise.[27] The sales department backs a rush order from a valued customer although the system declares that it cannot be supplied. Then senior managers do not have the commitment to stand up to the resulting complaint.

Other failures may be technical or lie at the interface between system design and users. One study of a Liverpool manufacturing plant investigated a system that had been built up in an ad hoc way over a period of 17 years. There were clear technical difficulties in the planning and control modules that enabled the managers to blame 'the system' for any difficulties. The company manufactured three product lines in the same plant, yet the markets for each were very different. Further, it had not given sufficient status or support to the scheduling office. The person responsible for the MPS had the same rank as a first-line supervisor.[28] Examples such as this show that introduction of new ways of working risk failure if complementary changes to jobs and structures are not made.

Does the apparent need to push sales 'to fit in with' schedules represent a return to a production orientation for the business? Luscombe answers in this way:

> To give all customers the best possible service all the time, much better planning and control is required than has previously been possible. There was never any difficulty in rushing one urgent job through production to satisfy a particularly demanding customer. The price was in the poor delivery performance, inability to forecast despatch dates, high production inventory costs, and long lead times that were accepted as the norm for the bulk of customer orders.[29]

The key to successful implementation lies in recognising that an approach such as MRPII is not a technical 'fix'. If treated in this way it becomes a rigid, bureaucratic extra burden which managers find they have to override to regain the flexibility which successful batch production systems require.

Optimised production technology

Another criticism of MRPII schemes has been directed at their attempt to manage the whole production system in detail. The more complex the system, the more difficult this task becomes. Is there no other way to cut lead times and inventories and therefore improve performance? According to Goldratt and Cox, several basic ideas of the way plants are planned and organised are wrong. They challenge three key assumptions:

- capacity to be balanced with demand, followed by attempts to maximise the use of the capacity;
- incentives to be based on the utilisation of workers in the tasks they have been set;
- activation and utilisation of resources amount to the same thing.

These assumptions mean that the drive at the shop-floor level is to keep as much as possible running for as much as possible of the time. Yet much of this effort does not lead to progress. Why? The answer is that in practical manufacturing there are a few *bottlenecks* that limit the throughput of products. Otherwise, there is a great deal of slack. Hence there are only a few key points on which managers should concentrate. Maximising the use of all resources, including paying incentive bonuses to workers who are not working at bottlenecks, is no good. All that happens is a build up of partly finished items waiting for their turn at the bottlenecks.

It was around this realisation that Goldratt created the *Theory of Constraints* and developed the software system known as *Optimised Production Technology*.[30] Depending on the business, different constraints dominate, as shown in Exhibit 19.16. In identifying and concentrating on these features, Goldratt shows how to simplify the scheduling of complex systems.

Inventory reduction is an important benefit. It comes first from recognising bottlenecks and second from batch size reduction, as shown in Exhibit 19.17.

Exhibit 19.16 Bottlenecks and constraints

Operation	Constraint (in environment)	Bottleneck (in operations system)
Brass ware manufacturer	Supply of castings from foundry	Any process, e.g. turning, milling, plating
Retail shop	Access; parking; deliveries	Number of checkouts
Open-air pop festival	Roads near site	Food and water supplies; toilets; number of sets
Chocolate factory	Raw materials supplies	Any processing plant; distribution system
Hospital specialising in transplants	Donors	Operating theatres and equipment; recovery beds; trained teams

---

Exhibit 19.17 **Improving the bottleneck means improving the whole system**

Work upstream of a bottleneck, if done too early, does not contribute to delivery on time. Whereas an hour lost at the bottleneck is an hour lost from the whole system, an hour saved at a non-bottleneck saves no time. Mounting stocks of partly finished goods are the only outcome.

Batch size reduction can reduce inventories and improve deliveries. Imagine 1000 items passing through two bottlenecks A and B. If A takes 4 hours then it seems that B can start 4 hours after A. But what if the batch size is reduced to 250? B can start one hour after A starts provided that four smaller deliveries are made from A to B. Depending on distance, this simple change may involve some higher costs. Yet it will take 3 hours out of the time to supply the order. Furthermore, it will reduce stocks as the product goes through more quickly.

Gardiner *et al.*[31] summarise the impact of OPT:

- complexities better understood;
- fewer resources scheduled;
- early warnings of problems given;
- lead time reduced;
- areas for improvement identified;
- advances over other systems are gained;
- measures of performance aligned.

OPT does not eliminate scheduling; it focuses it. Companies have used OPT with modified MRPII so that only bottlenecks are scheduled in detail.[32]

Just-in-Time

Originating in the renowned Toyota Company, *see* Exhibit 19.18, just-in-time systems are widely used in line manufacture and assembly systems. They are seen as ideal for high volume repetitive operations although they have been adapted for batch and even jobbing shops.[33] The purpose of JIT is to minimise stocks of work in progress and to keep all materials in motion through the production system. Therefore, besides cutting the cost of stockholding, competitive advantage is sought through work simplification and the reduction of throughput times. JIT depends on the ability of firms to:

- create subassemblies just as they are needed in the final assembly shop;
- make components just in time for fitting to subassemblies;
- receive bought in items at the time they are needed.

JIT is different to conventional production planning with its philosophy of using a planned schedule to *push* materials through the process. It *pulls* work through the system. The rules prevent any stage from working before its output is needed. Having deliveries at least once a day implies small batches and little stock.

Exhibit 19.18 The origins of *kanban*

JIT grew in Japan by linking many series of small factories each with hundreds, rather than thousands, of employees. Each plant made daily deliveries to its successor, the quantity being the exact amounts required for the following day's production. For this to be stable and efficient, all the suppliers knew the monthly production schedule set by the final assembler. This last company became the 'drummer' setting the rhythm for the flow of supplies through the system.

Kanban is a term used for the way the information is recorded and process rates regulated. The name refers to the card attached to each component bin in the original system. Development of the kanban system was helped by the proximity of the factories. For example, until Toyota began to develop overseas plants in the 1980s, all its plants were located in the Aichi prefecture, a district close to Tokyo.

Toyota, led by Taiichi Ohno as Manufacturing Director, was a pioneer of kanban. Its performance after the sudden oil price rises of 1973–4 stimulated the interest of rivals both in Japan and elsewhere. Another company, Toyo-Kogyo, whose brand is Mazda, was almost bankrupted by the same oil shock. Its recovery had much to do with its introduction of the Toyota production system that was already regarded as good practice throughout the country. Ford's close connection with Toyo-Kogyo began when it bought a 25 per cent stake in 1976. Then followed an intensive programme of training of Ford managers in Japanese techniques.

The approach goes beyond stock minimisation, however, to continuous improvement and incorporation into other business functions. To operate flow systems with little stock implies a family of techniques and methods that must be brought together. Among these is Total Quality Management, *see* Chapter 7. The disruption to the flow arising from poor quality work is felt more acutely if there is little spare stock. Therefore, quality standards at all stages must be raised.

As has been suggested, JIT works both within and between manufacturing organisations. For example, large car assemblers such as Peugeot Talbot have integrated their suppliers into partnership sourcing agreements that include arrangements for JIT supplies. Hills Precision Components is situated close to Peugeot's Coventry plant. Orders for fascia assemblies are transmitted by electronic data interchange twelve times daily. Each specifies models, colours, left- or right-hand drive and so on. The fascias are assembled from a range of standard components and delivered within two hours.[34] Suppliers are building factories near the assemblers to minimise delays. Concern with local road links is evidenced by the objections raised by Nissan Motor Co. to the proposal by Sunderland Football Club to build its new stadium near to its plant. The company feared that match day congestion would upset the tight schedules of JIT deliveries from seven local manufacturers. The new ground was built elsewhere.[35]

Inventory management

Inventories, or stocks, are the goods that the organisation transforms in the production process. Usually there are three types:

■ *Raw materials*: these are the physical resources that are to form the products after processing. Examples include the metal, timber, stone and paint of the construction firm or the meat, bread and drink of the bistro.

■ *Work-in-progress*: this is the collection of items moving through the production process, being sometimes worked upon but commonly idle, waiting for the next stage. Partly constructed buildings and half-cooked meals are the WIP of the civil engineer and the restaurant.

■ *Finished goods*: these are products whose manufacture is complete but have yet to be sold. For instance, builders hate to have a stock of unsold houses and, for the bistro *patron*, the display of quick snacks becomes a headache if it remains unsold.

Inventory management is a tricky task. On the one hand we must recognise that inventories are important to the functioning of many organisations. Shops must have stock to sell. Manufacturers need supplies to satisfy that rush order. Inventory is conventionally seen as contributing to the assets of a firm – the more stock, the greater the firm's worth. On the other hand, progressive firms increasingly see stock as dead weight. It ties up capital that could be more usefully put to work elsewhere. The art is to carry enough stock to meet manufacturing and customer service targets, such as 99 per cent service levels, but to carry no more.

High inventory levels hide many problems in scheduling. The Japanese *kaizen*, continuous improvement, is applicable here. The approach is to make small reductions in stock levels and solve the problems that emerge. These could range from poor forecasting to poor quality and maintenance at a bottleneck stage. This incremental approach must take place within an inventory management strategy that sets out the way levels are to be maintained and regulated. We have already looked at three of these that come under the general category of *dependent inventory control*. MRPII, JIT and OPT systems include dependent control because they are driven by known customer orders. In principle, there is no stock that is not needed for orders. Excess above the minimum only arises from defects in the scheduling or manufacturing processes.

Many businesses operate stocks under greater uncertainty. These range from the retailer to the jobbing manufacturer. They each seek to respond to customer demands within a shorter time than it takes to obtain raw materials. Since demand is random, these firms carry stocks unrelated to orders. Hence the control is known as *independent inventory control*. We can imagine an inventory holding system, such as a warehouse or the shelves in the book shop, together with a control system. The latter monitors inputs and outputs, as shown in Fig. 19.11, and uses decision rules to obtain more supplies when needed. There are many such rules, depending on circumstances. One, the fixed quantity procedure, is illustrated in Fig. 19.12. The graph is a time plot of the holding of one item. Fixed quantities of replenishments are used when it is economic to order in standard batches. These may be cartons, containers, or train loads. The procedure works as follows:

■ the inventory is replenished from time-to-time with the *fixed order quantity*;

■ replenishment occurs at irregular intervals. The falling lines in Fig. 19.12 suggest demand to be irregular;

■ new orders are placed when inventory falls to the *reorder level*;

■ delivery of the orders follows a delay called the *delivery lead time*.

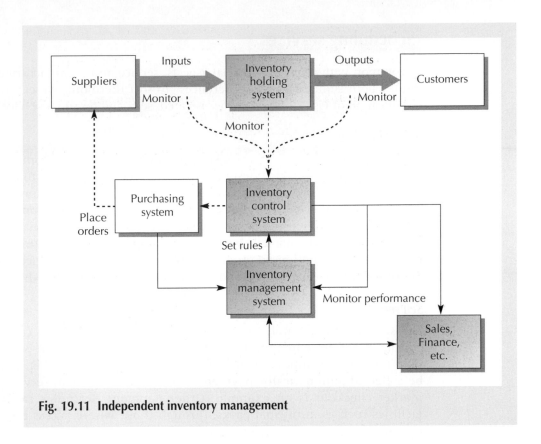

Fig. 19.11 Independent inventory management

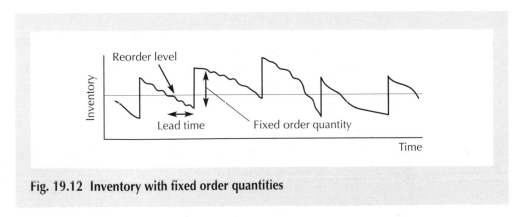

Fig. 19.12 Inventory with fixed order quantities

The reorder level is high enough to limit the risk of there being a stock-out before delivery but not so high as to make stock levels excessive. Several formulae are available to calculate order quantities and reorder points within the different control procedures. These are based on cost data whose accuracy is difficult to justify and should only be used as starting points. Improvements are made in the light of experience under the *kaizen* philosophy.

Scheduling services

In common with other operational aspects, service and manufacturing scheduling display both similarities and differences. To sort these out, we can return to the classification of Fig. 19.5 to consider isolated, self- and personal service.

Isolated service

Isolated, or back office, service takes place away from the customer. Therefore, a critical part of the service design is the interface with the customer. This is, in effect, either personal or self-service so the isolated service function is always combined with another pattern that acts as the front office. Questions of scheduling these aspects are discussed below. Behind the front office service, many mass service operators have adopted the practices of repetitive manufacture, adapting the principles of, say, optimised production technology, into the service arena. Federal Express, a world leader in parcel delivery, is a case in point, *see* Exhibit 19.19.

Self service

Self-service outputs rarely need scheduling. The provider offers capacity that the customer will use when required. In the ideal case, there is no personal interaction, the user consumes any amount of the facility any time. Yet, unless fees can be collected automatically, payment systems need personal service. The supermarket checkout is an example. Other payment examples range from free facilities such as municipal parks, through those where access requires a fixed payment, such as cable television or toll bridges, to cases such as telephones where billing is automatic.

Exhibit 19.19 **Federal Express as a distributed service factory**

The hub and spoke system of Federal Express carries half the overnight packages in the United States. It is an example of the way transport can be thought of in flow-process terms. It is, in effect, a distributed service factory with personal or self-service links with the customer.

Each evening, freight aircraft fly parcels along inward spokes to FedEx's sorting hub at Memphis, Tennessee. Here they are sorted and loaded for the outward trip to arrive by early morning. A late afternoon consignment from the main European capitals has a guaranteed delivery by 10.30 am anywhere in North America. The system works by having clear fixed flight and sorting schedules supported by parcel tracking software. Plane loads out of Memphis are thus defined well before the parcels arrive for sorting.

Computer developments mean that more than 25 000 United States businesses have direct access to the information system to track their own parcels and time consignments accurately. For example, Laura Ashley clothes shops are restocked within two days, thus cutting out the risk and expense of local warehousing. Federal Express has more than 460 aircraft and delivers over two million packages a day. Excess demand is coped with by delaying consignments on lower grade services.

Personal service

Personal or *direct* service, poses special problems for the operations manager. Why is this?

- Demand for direct service is variable and cannot be levelled as with a master production schedule. Queues will form unless the operator has high, or rapidly adjustable, service capacity.

- Customisation is normal in many service activities. This means that job variety is high.

- The presence of the customer impedes adherence to any schedule that may have been planned. For example, the customer may ask for, or need, a change of service half way through.

Having laid out the facilities and designed the service process, the service manager can attempt to influence demand or fine tune capacity and service levels. Reservation or appointment systems work in some circumstances. Otherwise, where demand is variable and unregulated, how can a business adjust to maintain a high standard of customer service? It uses a combination of anticipation and changes in staff and service levels.

Telephone home shopping is an example of mass personal service. In such bureaux, the capacity is established to cope with anticipated demand but local, short-term adjustments are always necessary. Figure 19.13 shows the pattern of

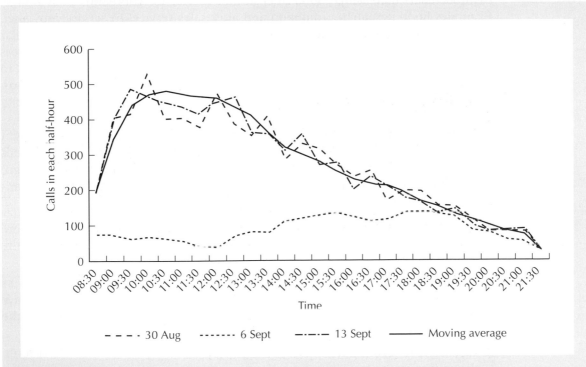

Fig. 19.13 Calls received at credit referencing and query office

calls received at a large credit referencing and query office. Calls received during each half hour interval are shown for three consecutive Saturdays in 1997. Two Saturdays, 30 August and 13 September, are typical of a consistent pattern, closely matching the quarterly moving average. Whatever the day of the week, the staff on duty are planned to cover the average call rate plus up to 10 per cent. Adjustments to the normal cover are made for known contingencies such as public holidays. On each day, random peaks are coped with by delaying breaks and adjusting the times spent with each customer. There is more information on the control of bureau capacity in the opening case of Chapter 23.

Schedules matching recent patterns are thrown into disarray when events with unpredictable consequences occur. Demand on 6 September was typical for many service operations that Saturday. This was the day of the funeral of Diana, Princess of Wales. So many people participated at the event, or watched television, that business was quiet. Retail sales for the month fell by about 1 per cent as a result of the 'Diana effect'.[36]

Conclusion: managing primary functions

Operations management is concerned with the primary functions of the organisation, which are the transformation of inputs into products. While there are notable differences between goods and services, in their supply we find many features in common. Tough competition in the supply of goods means that manufacturers increasingly look to customer service for competitive advantage. Examples lie in despatch, promotion and after-sales service. In service provision, many organisations find benefits in arranging back office operations along similar lines to manufacture. We saw, therefore, that rather than use the goods–services distinction, it is more useful to distinguish between operations according to whether the customer is present. Back office services have much in common with manufacturing while front office services have special problems of capacity and queues.

In the competitive environment, organisations gain through offering the right mix of price, quality, reliability, responsiveness, service and speed. To achieve this aim, tasks specific to the operations function are: product and process design; selecting locations; capacity management; and activity scheduling, including managing inventories and queues:

- The strongest influence on process design is volume. The larger this is, the more likely will the organisation be able to dedicate special purpose facilities to the operation.
- Facility location depends on how closely the organisation needs to stand to its market. Both push and pull factors influence location decisions, the former stemming from dissatisfaction with existing sites, the latter accounting for the new locality.
- Capacity planning is carried out in stages from the long term to the short term, depending on the factors that can be adjusted.

■ Scheduling involves short-term capacity management. Inventories and queues uncouple the technical core of the operations system from the changing environment. They enable the core to limit the cost of flexibility but imply that both elements, inventories and queues, must be well managed in the successful enterprise.

Quick check up   *Can you ...*

- Define operations management;
- Explain the difference between front and back office;
- List five manufacturing systems layouts;
- Identify six patterns of service provision;
- Give three arrangements of queues with more than one service channel;
- Suggest five ways to change the experience of queuing;

- Provide four examples of each of push and pull location factors;
- Outline MRPII and JIT;
- Name the assumptions challenged by OPT; give four examples of constraints;
- Summarise why inventory management is required;
- Suggest three reasons why it is difficult to schedule personal service.

Questions

Chapter review

19.1 What are the main types of production plant layout and how do they relate to the goods that are made?

19.2 Explain the impact of scale on manufacturing and service process layouts.

19.3 Draw up a table summarising the key features of MRP, OPT and JIT systems.

19.4 What are the main elements of an operations system and how do they interact?

Application

19.5 Consider how the PQRRSS factors apply in the case of Courtaulds Textiles. What are their implications for textile production in countries with high labour costs?

19.6 Using the material in Exhibit 19.12, investigate the considerations for vehicle plant location in the 1930s and now. Why has anything changed?

Investigation

19.7 Observe and compare the formation and management of queues at service facilities known to you. How could the facilities be improved?

19.8 Report on the reasons for the siting of any one manufacturing or service facility in your area.

Ethics Test: Location

Should a plant, such as the MHO refinery, be forced to move if it cannot cut emissions to near to zero? If so, where should it go?

Metallurgie Hoboken-Overpelt[37]

MHO is known throughout the world for refining metals from gold to lead. Its plant at Hoboken, Belgium employs 2500 staff to process 125000 tonnes of lead each year. In 1973, ten cows and horses died of lead poisoning after grazing near the plant. Chemical analyses of the soil found lead concentrations of 800 to 9000 parts per million (ppm), while dust on the factory roof measured 72500. Accepted safe levels are 40 ppm. Forty years of production, with each year blowing around 30 tonnes up the chimney, had resulted in dangerous accumulations of toxic metals.

A government commission found that people living near the plant had high concentrations of lead in their blood. Children are particularly sensitive. Some had more than three times the recommended safe maximum. Workers' health data was not revealed by a reluctant MHO management. By 1978, protesters were active and the scale of the problem was well known.

The government considered moving all the population at a cost of 2.5 billion francs. Moving the plant would cost four times as much. A compromise was reached, a green belt established and all the contaminated soil had to be removed. Furthermore, emission and cleanliness standards were tightened. Little changed. Restrictions were stiffened yet, in 1991, lead and cadmium emissions exceeded World Health Organization standards. Fear for the loss of 2500 jobs weighed more heavily than risk to health.

CLOSING CASE

Engineering and manufacturing, Oiso[38]

E&M-Oiso is a manufacturing plant of the NCR Corporation located some 65 km from Tokyo. It has 550 employees developing and assembling cash registers, point of sale terminals and financial terminals. The first two product groups are sold throughout the world.

In principle, the plant works by building to order. There is an aggregate production plan drawn up as 'a hedged version of marketing's sales forecast'. It considers factors such as capacity and lead times for subassemblies and suppliers' availability and delivery times. Risk is involved and has to be managed since sales never turn out to match the forecast. The monthly plan is based on firm orders. Variability in the flow of orders has to be matched with flexibility. Kanban systems are used to regulate the assembly of products to customers' orders. Certain processes, however, have long lead times that would not allow quick enough supplies.

Such lead times exist in the printed circuit board manufacture where the capacity of the surface mount technology is limited. The solution is to build controlled lots of basic boards for stock. When firm orders set the kanban system in motion, these boards can be withdrawn for further components to be built on. Therefore, there is a mixture of 'push' and 'pull' production scheduling. This achieves delivery requirements without the need to add SMT capacity.

E&M-Oiso uses Computer Integrated Manufacturing to manage the JIT programme. Its aim is to minimise lead times. Having set schedules that aim to have components arriving at assembly just when they are needed, the CIM system captures data on the status of all orders to ensure that they are progressing satisfactorily. All items carry bar codes.

The company works closely with its 192 suppliers to gain and share benefits from the JIT system. It sees relationships with these companies as sharing responsibilities for minimising the cost of ownership of bought-in components. Suppliers are involved in the process of design for manufacture.

Daily delivery is not required in the JIT system. Attention centres on those items that make up most of the value. Parts have been split into four categories from A-prime to C. The A-prime items are just 3.4 per cent of the number but represent some 70 per cent of the value. They are all in the JIT programme which is to be extended to the whole A category. JIT will then cover 85 per cent of parts by value.

Of the 192 suppliers, only three are offshore. The company wants to increase this number. The tight schedules make such sourcing difficult. Not only are shipping times longer but risk is higher. Offshore supplies will have to be based more on the aggregate forecast than on actual orders and this will create inflexibility.

Visualisation is seen as important in the presentation of performance results. Data on weekly results, such as delivery performance, are prominently displayed in consistent graphical formats throughout the plant. Even the untrained eye can recognise the degree of goal attainment. While details are given of who is responsible for each element of the output, the intention is not to allocate blame but to contribute to team building and continual improvement. The company believes that cooperative performance depends on common knowledge.

Questions

1 Based on the discussion in Chapter 19, what do you think are the key factors in location decisions for this company?

2 Identify the type of production systems likely to be found at E&M-Oiso. Suggest applications of MRPII, OPT and JIT ideas in this situation.

3 What are the production and supply risks involved with offshore sourcing into Japan?

Bibliography Many points covered in this chapter are covered in more detail in Naylor, John (1996) *Operations Management*, London: Financial Times Pitman Publishing. Recommended for further reading are: Slack, Nigel *et al.* (1998) *Operations Management*, Second edition, London: Financial Times Pitman Publishing; and Goldratt, E.M. and Cox, J. (1989) *The Goal*, London: Gower. The latter has stimulated much original thought in the operations area.

References 1. Cole, Robert (1994) 'Textile survivors pick up the thread: UK firms setting up abroad and cutting lead times to survive', *Independent*, 11 January, 27; Stevenson, Tom (1995) 'Shrinkage at Courtaulds Textiles', *Independent*, 3 August; Questor (1995) 'Courtaulds feeling stretched', *Daily Telegraph*, 3 August; Courtaulds Textiles (1997)

Annual Report and Accounts http://www.corpreports.co.uk/sectors/textiles/cour-taulds/courtaulds.htm

2. In *The Wealth of Nations* (Methuen edn., 1981) Adam Smith classed the work of servants as 'barren and unproductive'.
3. Peters, Tom (1984) 'Hit and run strategy for hypercompetition', *Independent on Sunday, Business News*, 9 October, 22.
4. Hallahan, S. (1994) 'All hands to the production lines', *The Times*, 29 July, 15.
5. Crainer, Stuart (1994) 'Management: pioneers and prophets – Henry Ford', *Financial Times*, 7 November, 12.
6. Kumar, K.R. and Hadjinicola, G.C. (1993) 'Cellular manufacturing at Champion Irrigation Products', *International Journal of Operations and Production Management*, **13** (**8**) 53–61.
7. Developed from a four-element model given by Schmenner, R.W. (1993) *Production/Operations Management*, Basingstoke: Macmillan, 18–22.
8. Superdrug (1993) *Success: Customer Care and Service Skills Programme*, Unpublished company materials.
9. Tesco plc (1994) Media and handbill campaign, November.
10. Morton, Nuala (1994) 'Cinemas dial box-office hit', *Independent on Sunday, Business News*, 17 July, 8.
11. Maister, D.H. (1985) 'The psychology of waiting lines', in Czeipel, J.H.; Solomon, M.R. and Surprenant, C.F. (eds) *The Service Encounter*, Lexington, Mass.: Lexington Books Heath D.C.
12. Davies, Mark M. and Heineke, J. (1994) 'Understanding the roles of the customer and the operation for better queue management', *International Journal of Operations and Production Management*, **14** (**5**) 24–31.
13. Render, Barry and Heizer, Jay (1994) *Principles of Operations Management*, Boston, Mass.: Allyn and Bacon, 356.
14. Jenkins, Ray (1993) 'The evolution process of the in-store bakery', *Paper No.379, Proceedings of British Society of Baking*, 76th Conference, October.
15. Anderson, P.M.(1985) 'Association of shopping centre anchors with performance of a non-anchor speciality chain's stores', *Journal of Retailing*, **61** (**2**) 61–74.
16. Data for the United States from Schmenner (1993), *op. cit.*, 440.
17. Ridding, John (1995) 'Survey of Burgundy: Incentives brought Kodak to Chalon – Why the US photographic giant set up in the home of 19th century film pioneers', *Financial Times*, 10 April, 29.
18. For example, *see* Artikis, G.P. (1992) 'Financial factors in plant location decisions', *International Journal of Operations and Production Management*, **13** (**8**), 58–71.
19. Bowlby, S., Breheny, M. and Foot, D. (1984) 'Store location: problems and methods', *Retail and Distribution Management*, **12** (**5**), 31–3.
20. Governments throughout Europe are restricting the growth of out-of-town shopping. *See* Lawson, David (1995) 'Resistance grows in Europe', *Financial Times*, 29 September, 15.
21. Manchester Airport plc (1993) *Runway 2: Planning Application Supporting Statement*, July, mimeo.; Cobham Resource Consultants and Consultants in Environmental Sciences Ltd (1993) *Runway 2: Environmental Statement – Non-technical Summary*, Manchester: Manchester Airport plc, July, mimeo.
22. Henderson, B. (1984) *The Logic of Business Strategy*, Cambridge, Mass.: Ballinger, 49–50.
23. Render and Heizer (1994) *op. cit.*, 306.
24. Spreadbury, A. (1994) 'Manufacturing resources planning', in Storey, J. (ed.) *New Wave Manufacturing Strategies*, London: Paul Chapman Publishing, 154.

25. For example: Waterlow, G. and Monniot, J. (1986) *A Study of the State of the Art in CAPM in UK Industry*, London: SERC/ACME, 1986; Whiteside, D. and Ambrose, J. (1984) 'Unsnarling industrial production: Why top management is starting to care', *Industrial Management*, March, 20–6.

26. Sillince, J.A.A. and Sykes, G.M.H. (1993) 'Integrating MRPII and JIT: A management rather than a technical challenge', *International Journal of Production and Operations Management*, **13** (**4**), 18–31.

27. Luscombe, M. (1994) 'Of course I'm committed to MRPII but...', *Management Services* March, 12–13.

28. The study was conducted in 1994 by a colleague at Liverpool John Moores University. Turnover of this branch plant of a large combine was some £50 million. *See* Naylor, John (1996) *Operations Management*, London: Financial Times Pitman Publishing, 319–20.

29. Luscombe (1994), *op. cit.*

30. Goldratt, E.M. and Cox, J. (1989) *The Goal*, London: Gower.

31. Gardiner, Stanley, C., Blackstone, John, H. and Gardiner, Lorraine, R. (1993) 'Drum-Buffer-Rope and buffer management: impact on production management study and practices', *International Journal of Operations and Production Management* **13** (**6**), 68–78.

32. Spencer, M.S. (1991) 'Using *The Goal* in an MRP system', *Production and Inventory Management Journal*, **32** (**4**), 22–8.

33. Harrison, A. (1994) 'Just-in-time Manufacturing', in Storey, J., *op. cit.*, 181.

34. Gooding, C. (1993) 'Technology: On the road to a slicker operation', *Financial Times* 22 July, 16

35. 'Company News', *Financial Times*, 23 January, 1993, 4; Tighe, C. (1993) 'Nissan and Sunderland FC cry foul in a local derby', *ibid.*, 15 October, 1; 'Sunderland gives stadium approval', *ibid.*, 11 March, 1994, 7.

36. Segall, Anne (1997) 'Spending recovers as Diana effect wears off', *Electronic Telegraph*, **901**, 11 November; ... 'High street sales hit by mourning for Diana', *Electronic Telegraph*, **873**, 14 October: http://www.telegraph.co.uk:80/et.

37. Schokkaert, Erik and Eyckmans, Johan (1994) 'Environment', in Harvey, Brian (ed.) *Business Ethics*, London: Prentice Hall, 195–7.

38. Based on: Tanabe, Masaru (1992) 'Making JIT work at NCR Japan', *Long Range Planning*, **25** (**5**), 37–42.

20

Marketing: managing relations with customers

Chapter objectives

When you have finished studying this chapter, you should be able to:

- outline the functions of marketing in the organisation;
- evaluate the product life cycle as a model of market behaviour;
- explain five different ways businesses approach markets;
- define marketing research; describe the key activities of understanding customers and segmenting markets;
- show how businesses build relationships with customers;
- define the term *brand*; show where brands have become a battlefield and decide who gains or loses from them; assess the advantages of brand development;
- evaluate marketing from the point of view of ethics and social responsibility.

Focus on cameras[1]

Facing a 30 million unit world market that has been, at best, static, leading camera makers have followed two strategies. First, they cooperated in the 1995 launch of the Advanced Photographic System which uses film in self-loading cassettes. These are smaller than conventional 35 mm packs, thus allowing further miniaturisation of the camera. APS film never leaves the cassette; each shot is addressed so that it can be found for reprints without being marred by dust or sticky fingers. The system also promises varied picture formats and quicker processing. Second, the manufacturers cut dependency on camera sales by diversifying into printers, photocopiers and related optical equipment. Canon, Minolta and others now rely on cameras for less than a quarter of turnover.

Many see the market for the camera-film system as dying, in spite of APS. As in other fields, the future is digital. Fuji and Kodak, who make both components of the current system, stand to lose more by a switch. While they are locked in a row over Kodak's access to the Japanese film market, both are developing mass-market digital cameras. So far, three factors have constrained the switch. The first is resolution. Casio's QV10, launched in 1995, offered 350 000 pixels for each shot, compared with the equivalent 20 million for 35 mm film. While most PC screens cannot beat Casio's standard, the difference shows up in printing. The second constraint is the need for a computer to view the results. This requires users to master software such as MGI's PhotoSuite. The third problem is price. In 1997 kits started at £300. Even the £2000 Fuji DS-300 could manage just 1.25 million pixels.

Worldwide sales of digital cameras in 1996 were 1.3 million. Casio, traditionally not a camera maker, timed its launch just as the Japanese demand for personal computers and use of the Internet took off. It gained 47 per cent of its home market followed by Fuji on 12 per cent. According to Mr Kobayashi, owner of Japan's leading consumer electronics stores, buyers sought to make more use of their PCs or become involved in desk top publishing. The 'I want' customers, buying for fun, began to attach pictures to e-mail, or make greetings cards. The 'I need' customers made images for their small businesses to be used in products or advertising on the Internet. Neither group represents the consumer market.

The mass market will not be attracted if the system is too complex or expensive. Most people do not want to send pictures over the Web. Benefits such as instant results seem attractive, but these are available from £20 Polaroid cameras. Yet, as with other goods that incorporate electronic data capture and storage, performance is increasing and prices are falling. Few 1997 cameras beat 1 million pixels. A much higher resolution system for less than £150 could be available in three years. Were high street processors to invest in equipment to allow users to select, edit and print pictures without waiting for hours for results, more consumers would be drawn in. With such developments, demand for digital cameras could exceed six million by the year 2000.

Introduction

Of all the business functions, marketing is the one that most clearly connects the organisation with the outside world. True, other functions also perform such boundary spanning. For example, finance manages relations with banks and money markets, purchasing links with suppliers, and HRM both engages in industrial relations and maintains contacts with the labour market. Above all, however, the primary role of marketing is boundary spanning. It is concerned with maintaining relations with customers.

Our opening case study, summarised in the rich picture of Fig. 20.1, illustrates the scope of the issues in which marketers become involved. The conventional camera makers knew that sales were sluggish. Some had been applying their established *brand images* to new product ranges such as photocopiers and medical equipment. Meanwhile, within the camera market, they needed something to stimulate sales. Each company had spent years of development on increasing the flexibility and convenience of cameras while reducing their size and weight. This had become a battleground in the competitive war in which they were engaged. Yet the results were not all advantageous. As sales slowly recovered from the 26 million trough in the mid-90s, many consumers were buying the cheap, throwaway models that meant less profit for those whose brands carried reputations of automation and precision.

In the drive to add more convenience, the 35 mm format had itself become the constraint. The APS, requiring wide agreement among the rivalrous camera and film makers if it were to be accepted by a cautious public, offered further enhancement in reliability and convenience. Yet critics saw the changes as offering little more than an extension of the *product life cycle, see* Exhibit 20.1.[2] APS sales were expected to replace 35 mm within the overall ceiling of 30 million or so.

> A *brand image* represents the set of beliefs that people hold about a brand.

Possibly distracted by their commitment to APS, leaders were surprised by the speed of the take off of digital photography. Casio was the first to take advantage. There seemed to be a new market, for temporary imaging, that the industry was not aware of. Photography had long since seen itself as producing a permanent record of authentic or artistic images. Yet, as Fig. 20.2[3] suggests, challenging the permanent assumption opens new possibilities. Business people were the first to reach for digital. Entrepreneurs from web site creators to estate agents have found uses for the new technology. Early sales were not at the expense of film cameras. The potential was uncertain but some, including Fuji, thought it to be huge. As people learned to play with light and shade, focus and framing, the new technology could reawaken an interest in photography generally. Furthermore, the opportunities for add-on products seemed unlimited. The scope and scale of the new opportunity presented new uncertainties for marketing managers. Who would buy? What did they want? Where would they buy? How much were they prepared to pay? Such are typical questions for all products. Yet, in cameras, few had any idea of the answers.

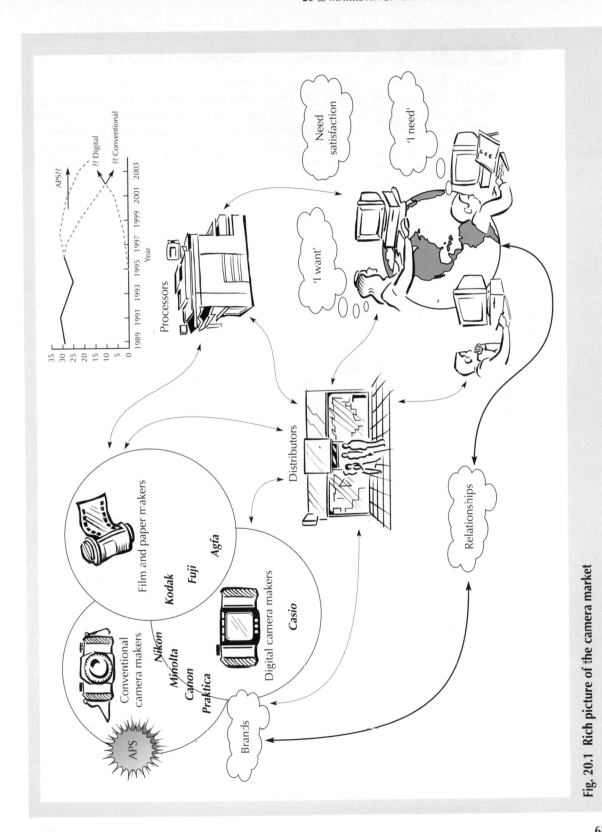

Fig. 20.1 **Rich picture of the camera market**

Exhibit 20.1   Strengths and limitations of the product life cycle

The product life cycle is a time series model describing changes in sales. Used in the right way, the PLC gives valuable insight into how markets develop. The model is usually presented in four phases – introduction, growth, maturity and decline. There are corresponding marketing tactics. Advertising is needed during introduction and early growth to gain acceptance and maximum market share. As sales mature, there is increasing competition and the emphasis changes to pricing policy. Finally, as sales tail off promotion through special offers and discounts takes over. One means to extend the PLC, shown by the dashed curve to the right, is by relaunching the product with new features.

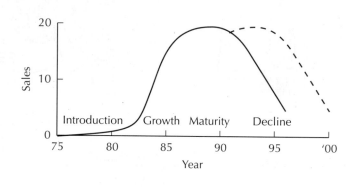

As with many simple models, the PLC has its weaknesses. First, it does not apply in all cases. The demand for some products hardly changes at all. Others, such as Beecham's Powders, have been around for so long that it would be a rash person who forecast when decline is to set in. Second, the patterns of the past may not give a guide to the future. The car industry was used to the PLC of models that needed replacing every few years. As development costs rose, the time between model changes was increased. Recently, however, intensive competition and new design approaches have tended to cut the cycle time again. This leads on to the third difficulty, unpredictability. The PLC suggests how sales of a new product may behave, yet it is useless if we are looking for forecasts for any time in the future. The graph to the left shows the fraction of American firms' equipment investment spent on IT. Who can guess the future shape of this curve?

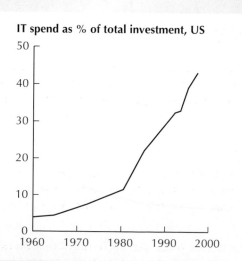

IT spend as % of total investment, US

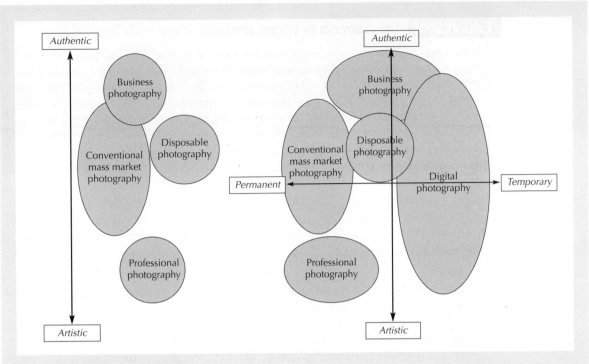

Fig. 20.2 Digital adds a new dimension

After outlining and defining marketing, this chapter examines the key issues brought out by the case study. These are knowing the market environment, building relationships with customers and creating brands. Finally, since marketing is the most visible of functions, it attracts the most questioning and disapproval. We must discuss, therefore, whether ethical marketing is both possible and desirable.

What is marketing?

Many think of marketing as a clever form of selling. The marketing approach in business involves a commitment to satisfying the needs of customers. It incorporates both a set of values, concerning market orientation, about the way business should be conducted and a set of processes that put them into practice.

Market orientation

Several authors investigate the orientation shown by marketing managers as they consider stakeholder interests, especially those of customers, the organisation and society. Kotler and colleagues identify five alternative approaches.[4]

■ *Production*
  Stressing production arises from the view that customers prefer products that are both widely available and affordable. Management's focus is on efficiency. *See* the example in Exhibit 20.2.[5]

Exhibit 20.2 **The dilemma of excess demand**

When asked about the competition between rail and road transport in his country, the General Manager of Pakistan National Railways replied, 'The question is not whether the roads are a problem for Pakistan railways. I am unable to cope with the load which is laid upon me. In the passenger sector I am responsible for fifty per cent of the traffic yet the demand is twenty per cent more than that. In the freight sector, the figures are similar. I do not have the equipment to carry the demand. Road transport, therefore, is not a problem for me.'

Note how the manager uses the first person to present himself as the embodiment of the railway company. He reveals his production orientation both by denying the significance of competition and in the choice of words he uses to describe his problems.

■ *Product*

The product orientation concentrates on supplying products that offer the best quality, performance and innovative features. Captured in the quotation attributed to Emerson, this mode of thinking continues to dominate some industries, none more so than pharmaceutical manufacture, where most believe that science counts. *The Economist* asserted, 'Breakthroughs in the laboratory capture headlines, but drugs companies that devote the best of their grey cells to the search for the next blockbuster are in danger of neglecting the business basics.'[6] Even some of the largest companies could greatly improve their marketing and distribution management. Why has this apparently obvious point been neglected? *The Economist* cites companies with cultures founded and dominated by scientists working within a market with little price competition.

'If a man write a better book, preach a better sermon, or make a better mousetrap than his neighbour, though he build his house in the woods, the world will make a beaten path to his door.'

Source: Ralph Walde Emerson

■ *Selling*

Here the assumption is that customers will not buy on a large enough scale unless the organisation devotes substantial effort to selling and promotion. Perceiving the limitations of using inefficient distributors to sell goods in growing markets, some manufacturers were attracted by vertical integration into retailing. One example is Bata, described in Exhibit 20.3.[7]

The selling approach is also used with *unsought items*. These are items that the customer does not think of buying but becomes interested in once the benefits have been pointed out. A classic example is the *Workmate,* whose development and selling are described in Chapter 21.

Exhibit 20.3 Bata's empire under threat

Traditionally, the key to success in the shoe business had been a highly efficient manufacturing system coupled to an extensive distribution network. Tomáš Baťa (1876–1932) was a self-made man who built his shoe business to become one of Czechoslovakia's largest enterprises. He pioneered the application of modem work methods and the provision of decent working and living conditions for employees. The tradition was continued by his son, Tom, after the family, fearing Nazi occupation, moved the business to Canada in the 1930s. By 1997, the company employed 57 000 staff in 65 factories and 4500 shops. The latter were supplemented by over 100 000 independent retailers and franchisees. The family had recovered some operations in the Czech Republic, including the flagship store in the centre of Prague.

During the 1980s, however, there had been rapid change. The key factor in the industry was no longer selling from a low-cost manufacturing base. Marketing came to the fore. Strong, distinctive and innovative brands, such as Nike and Reebok, were sold through large retailers in shopping centres or on the edge of town. Tom Baťa admitted, 'Whereas at one time our retail operation was primarily a means of distributing the products of our manufacturers, in these more sophisticated types of outlets, no manufacturer could possibly produce the variety of products which the consumer would like.' In spite of opposition from strong-willed family members, trustees and managers, the company was being forced to respond to the new situation.

■ *Marketing*

Nike and Reebok, mentioned in Exhibit 20.3, made the breakthrough in marketing. This means that they found out the needs and wants of target customers and satisfied them better than competitors. In contrast to selling, which starts with the product and the system to supply it, marketing begins with understanding the customer. Meehan and Barwise define market orientation as 'an externally focused, organisation-wide value system that puts customer needs and preferences at the centre of all decision making'. They show that companies with such a value system do better than average, in whatever market or technology they are engaged.[8]

■ *Socially responsible marketing*

Growing out of the marketing concept, socially responsible marketing responds to the ethical issues raised by marketing practice. These range from the way information about customers is collected and used to the need to be truthful in the way products are promoted. We shall return to these questions later in the chapter.

Drawing these points together, we can define marketing as follows:

> *Marketing is the process that identifies and anticipates customer requirements and satisfies them responsibly, in the face of competitive pressure, to meet organisational objectives.*

This definition means that the marketing manager focuses on exchange with that important element of the environment – customers. There are wider considerations, too. Fig. 20.3, which is developed from Fig. 3.3, shows the interaction with customers along with these, other features. The organisation supplies its products to customers, either directly or through distributors. Mirroring the sales and supply chain is the process of *market research*. This gathers information on relevant aspects of the environment, from the needs of customers to the behaviour of distributors, competitors and other actors and stakeholders. Other items shown in the diagram are the way the organisation promotes its sales, for example through advertising and other means, while competitors do likewise. Many markets are influenced by regulators. Instances range from price or profit controls by government agencies to voluntary codes of conduct in advertising. Beyond formal regulation, other stakeholders, such as consumer groups and those concerned with care of the natural environment, exercise pressure in the marketplace.

Marketing research

The first part of the marketing definition refers to identifying and anticipating customer requirements within an environment that usually contains competitors. This is the province of marketing research. We can define it as *the collection and analysis of data about any problem in the field of marketing.* There are four aspects to the function:

■ to identify opportunities and problems in the marketplace;

■ to help in planning marketing activities;

■ to monitor marketing performance; and

■ to learn, that is to improve understanding of the marketing process.[9]

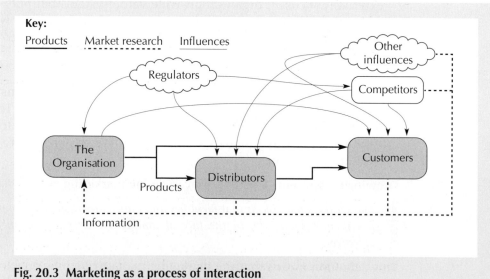

Fig. 20.3 Marketing as a process of interaction

The scope of marketing research can be wide. Some groups or agencies specialise in one aspect, such as measuring advertising effectiveness or retail spending, while others cover most aspects of the discipline. The scope of such studies can be summarised as follows:

- *Market research*: demand for new and current products; local and international markets. (Note that *market* research refers to finding out about markets. The more general term, *marketing* research, is concerned with the marketing process.)
- *Product research*: comparison among rivals; testing demand; analysing problems; packaging.
- *Promotion research*: effectiveness of selling methods; motivation; sales force management.
- *Distribution channel research*: selecting channels; locating distribution centres, dealers and agents.
- *Pricing research*: elasticities; attitudes; forecasting.

Data

Central to any study is the collection of data. Researchers commonly distinguish between two types, according to the sources from which it is drawn:

- *Primary data* comes from direct contact with customers, buyers, users or other actors within the marketing system.
- *Secondary data* is not drawn directly by its user, nor is it specific to the user. It may have been collected for reasons and by means that the user would not have chosen.

Secondary data, although easy and cheap to obtain, has limited value, *see* Exhibit 20.4.[10] Marketing studies often start with a review of secondary data that can form a context for the design and carrying out of the more difficult and expensive primary data collection.

The collection of primary data starts not with a scan of what might be available but from asking what managers want to know. All aspects of the marketing system can be the targets of studies, for example distributors, advertisers and especially customers. We can use the last to illustrate some problems of primary data collection.

Understanding customers

Like opening a Russian doll, understanding of customer behaviour is many-layered. We shall refer to three here. First, many organisations routinely collect data on whom customers are, what they buy and when they buy. While detailed analysis was once only possible when there were few customers, information systems now allow studies to be carried out when there are many more. Leading retailers have, through loyalty schemes, built up huge data bases that record the spending patterns of their customers. Even small and medium enterprises have found that sales analysis gives them a better appreciation of which customers are important to them, *see* Exhibit 20.5.[11]

Exhibit 20.4   Secondary data on security systems

One advantage of secondary data is its abundance. Any information from any source – within the firm, official agencies, commercial providers or casual origin – can be fruitful. It is often cheap and can be obtained quickly. Notwithstanding these advantages, secondary sources are often poor substitutes for direct involvement with the customer.

The table compares the rate of car theft in European countries and the United States. A car is broken into every 20 seconds in Britain. Insurers pay out some £500 million each year to settle theft claims. There is no convincing explanation of why this crime is so much higher in Britain than elsewhere.

This and more detailed data is readily available to makers of cars, car radios, alarm and tracker systems, immobilisers and so on. But what does it tell them about the market for new security devices? Unfortunately, on its own, it says very little.

	Cars (millions)	Thefts per 1000 cars
UK – England and Wales	22.4	22.7
UK – Scotland	1.9	15.5
UK – Northern Ireland	0.5	14.6
United States	133.9	11.5
France	25.1	11.4
Italy	30.0	10.2
Norway	1.7	10.0
Belgium	4.2	9.0
Spain	16.2	7.0
Netherlands	5.6	6.1
Portugal	2.6	3.2
Germany	40.5	3.2
Switzerland	3.2	2.9
Austria	3.6	1.4
Total	291.4	128.7

Exhibit 20.5 Using an information system to know about customers

Mersey Equipment distributes equipment for welding and related trades. It has 16 staff. When it bought a small computer system, the firm expected benefits from faster invoicing and cash flow. Yet it was the spreadsheet facility that brought pay-offs. Using it for sales analysis, the managers could look at trends for each product line and individual customer, leading them to change their stock range and pricing structure.

The second layer of understanding starts to unravel *why* customers make purchases. Exhibit 3.4 gave an instance of sales of the disinfectant Dettol.[12] Through estimating price and advertising elasticities, marketing managers showed that increasing both prices and promotional expenditure would raise profits. With such detail, a marketing manager can be more confident about planning. Yet the data gives no more than behavioural observations, suggesting what responses are expected from price and advertising stimuli. It does not, so to speak, get under the skin of the customer to find out why these responses occur.

> *Elasticity* is an economist's measure of the sensitivity of a product's sales to changes in a feature such as price, performance, quality, advertising and so on.

The third layer, therefore, is concerned with customers' attitudes. The conventional view in marketing is that changes in attitudes lead to changes in purchasing behaviour. To see the implications of this, we can again refer to Dettol.

> *The researchers wanted to know* why *sales increased from higher advertising expenditure. Remember that the product is used both for cleaning surfaces and sanitary ware and for personal hygiene. In a survey of customer attitudes, the marketing team found that more people were seeing Dettol as a strong, trustworthy and reliable disinfectant than before the advertising campaign. On the other hand, the already favourable image as an antiseptic had hardly changed. This shift in the brand image could be related back to the emphasis in the advertisements themselves.*

Difficulties with attitudes

Examining changes in attitudes is more difficult than observing changes in behaviour. Sales data gives a simple measure of the latter. Yet if focusing on attitudes, the marketing researcher has to study shifts in both attitudes and behaviour to understand the connections. The plausibility of the link from attitudes to behaviour hides a serious flaw, however. Favourable attitudes towards products may not affect buying behaviour. You may be impressed by the humour of Guinness commercials, the green credentials of Body Shop, the strength of the Volvo's safety cage or the service standards of Cathay Pacific. Indeed, you may concede that these companies provide good value *for those who deal with them*. Yet you may never buy their products yourself. Excellent promotion may make you intend to buy but this is but one factor affecting the actual purchase decision. In the end, you may do something else with your money.

A further difficulty arises from looking for the source of attitudes. We can assert that attitudes are the result of beliefs. In turn, beliefs are affected by experiences ranging from advertising to previous encounters with the brand or product. For instance, you may acknowledge that Guinness is a good product cleverly advertised. Yet you may not like the taste. While marketers may be tempted, therefore, to investigate beliefs and how they are formed, they then face even greater difficulties in linking them through to sales and profits.

Many companies, especially innovative ones, have given up theorising about behaviour and the application of broad survey techniques to uncover its causes. Instead they are taking a more holistic perspective, emphasising qualitative research. *Focus groups* bring together invited consumers to discuss all aspects of marketing. *Storytelling, see* Exhibit 20.6, is a relatively new approach to probing behaviour and discovering feelings.[13] In each case, broad surveys give way to in-depth studies of a few customers. The purpose is to gain flashes of insight rather than measure marginal shifts in response levels.

Exhibit 20.6 Following customers home

Known for the *Quicken* range, software company Intuit built its business through offering easy-to-run finance packages for individuals or small businesses. Customers are less interested in technology than making their lives more convenient. Intuit tests new products on small groups of people, four-fifths of whom do not use its products. Employees often visit people's homes to find out how people organise their finances when left to themselves. *Follow Me Home* is a research method where company staff watch over customers' shoulders as they try to install and use Intuit software. They leave behind cassette machines for users to record comments or complaints.

Market segmentation

A key use of customer data is in matching customers to products. For instance, in many cities restaurants are offering American, Chinese, Greek, Indian, Italian, Mexican and Turkish cuisine. Each specialises in one or two lines, and thereby appeals to that market segment interested in its style. In other industries, firms offer a product range, each part of which aims at a different customer group. News International segments its newspaper market by country and readers' needs. The *Sun* and *The Times* are just two of many titles it produces throughout the world.

Segmentation has three elements:

- define and understand the market in terms of realistic segments to which products can be offered;
- through product differentiation, create a range of offerings to suit the segments;
- promote the products using appropriate selling methods.

The ultimate of this process is *customisation*, which is offering a unique product to each customer. As we saw in Chapter 19, many businesses, from architects to fashion houses, already achieve this. Most customers, however, cannot afford such luxuries. To supply them, the key is to find ways of creating differentiation while maintaining low supply costs. The product range is limited not only by the production system but by the extra cost of making choice available to consumers. Exhibit 20.7 gives an example of how differentiation may be getting out of hand.[14]

Exhibit 20.7 Product clutter

Boot's stocks 75 kinds of toothbrush, not counting colour variations, and 240 kinds of shampoo. John Lewis carries 12 kinds of kitchen scissors. Philips produces 13 kettles and 24 irons. Nike offers 347 separate varieties of training shoe. There are least 110 different types of personal stereo on sale in the United Kingdom.

Segmentation in practice

Segmentation has become standard practice for companies that market to large numbers. There were two conventional ways of doing this:

- Location segmentation is important when consumption patterns are determined by where customers live, work or otherwise spend their time. On a local scale, the position of some shops will influence their success, if they depend on passing trade. Tobacconists, sandwich shops and newsagents are examples. On a broader scale, customers for utilities have traditionally been segmented geographically. Technological and regulatory changes, however, have recently broken down such barriers. Digital technology erodes the monopoly of regional broadcasters. Separating product and transmission charges enables gas consumers to buy from anyone.

- Socio-economic segmentation is based on the notion that consumption patterns can be related to differences in basic personal variables such as age, gender and income. Government income statistics are published using groupings such as A, B, C_1, C_2, D and E. Given the wealth of data on the distribution of such groups throughout nations, it is not surprising that marketers build their own analysis around the same classifications. Demand for some products can be broadly related to such categories. Yet others display a poor match. It remains meaningful to talk of, say, an 'ABC$_1$ newspaper', but the categories have little to say about the consumption of roller skates or rock music. This emphasises the difficulty of using secondary data in marketing research.

Segmentation by lifestyle

Rather than start from classes based on secondary data, research and media agencies now choose clusters according to observed consumption patterns. For instance, young people living in cheap rented accommodation around universities have more in common with each other than do their parents. Although they may be children of professional or manual workers and come from the town or the countryside, their spending habits will be similar. They are likely to drink much wine yet buy little life insurance.

Identifying sets by behaviour is known as segmentation by *lifestyle*. Groups are discovered from marketing research data using statistical measures of similarity. Details of the technique, cluster analysis, are beyond our scope save to say it is based on associating individuals according to their patterns of questionnaire answers or actual consumption. Different agencies come up with their own patterns to which they often attach labels evoking the essence of each cluster. For instance, some of one media agency's groups appear in Exhibit 20.8.[15] Note that only extracts from longer descriptions are shown. The agency knows about much more than cola, crisps and credit cards!

Armed with lifestyle data, the marketing manager can focus on potential customers better than ever before. The Littlewoods Organisation both uses and sells marketing information built up from its long involvement with the consumer market through mail order and football pools. Its *Super Profiles* market targeting system began with the 1981 census and is constantly revised. The 23 million United Kingdom households divide into ten lifestyles. Each has up to six 'target markets' making a total of 36. Clusters are the smallest building blocks of this system. 150 of them represent collections of between 0.55 and 1.5 per cent of households.

Figure 20.4 sets out part of this hierarchy. The 'metro singles' lifestyle refers to affluent single people living mainly in the South of England. They live in high-quality rented accommodation close to 'where the action is'. Within this lifestyle, three identifiable target markets account for 80 per cent. One of these, 'young professionals living in bedsitters', makes up 2.09 per cent of all households and is split into eight clusters. Cluster number 095, for instance, comprises some 56 000 young professional workers living in either Greater London or cities in the North West. They rent flats privately and have very low car ownership.

Exhibit 20.8 Some lifestyles from Carat, a media agency

Broadsheet browsers

These medium to heavy readers of quality newspapers watch commercial television for less than two hours a day. Compared with average adults, they are twice as likely to have taken a United States holiday but consume less cola and crisps. Twenty-eight per cent use credit cards more than six times each month.

Media hermits

Watch little commercial television but are infrequent newspaper readers. It is hard for advertisers to reach them.

Media junkies

These people are keen on independent television, read lots of newspapers and consume more cola and crisps than average. Infrequent pub goers, almost 40 per cent are worried about their weight. Some 5 per cent use credit cards more than six times per month.

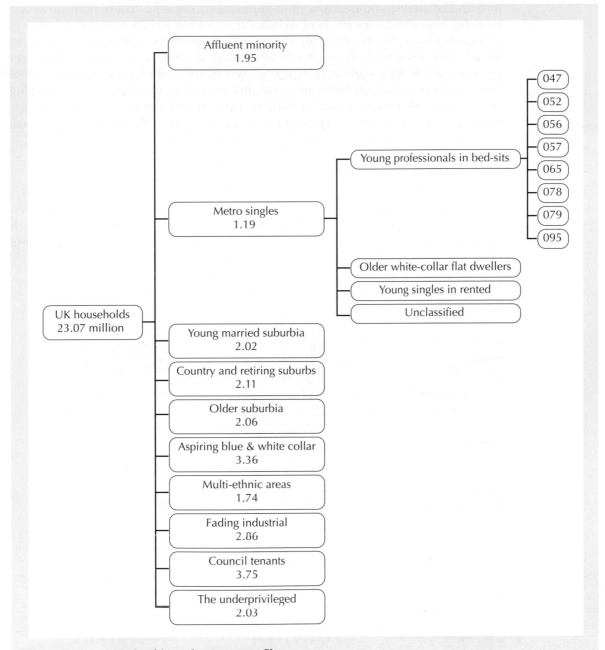

Fig. 20.4 Segmentation hierarchy: Super Profiles

Limitations of lifestyle

Rather like improving the sharpness of photograph prints, analysts attempt to identify clusters with ever finer resolution. Yet their groupings remain aggregates of people whose habits seem broadly similar. Clearly, the selection of the groups depends on the criteria being used to separate them and these in turn are related to both the quality and quantity of the original survey data. There may, however, be differences among members of a cluster that are not picked up yet are critical to a potential user. Cluster 095, for example, has members who may, on average, drink more wine and eat out more often than the population as a whole. Yet among them will be asthma sufferers, guitarists, football players, primary school teachers, vegans, foreign nationals, philosophers and so on. Users of the profiling system will only benefit if their particular requirements can be linked to the clustering criteria. Therefore, a vegetarian products company will not gain if questions about meat eating are never asked.

Freakish patterns

As clusters are refined, an increased risk of freakish patterns emerges. A team from the University of Manchester Institute of Science and Technology compared answers from 30 000 respondents to the British General Household Survey with their birth dates. Some results are shown in Fig. 20.5.[16] Two explanations for these outcomes are possible:

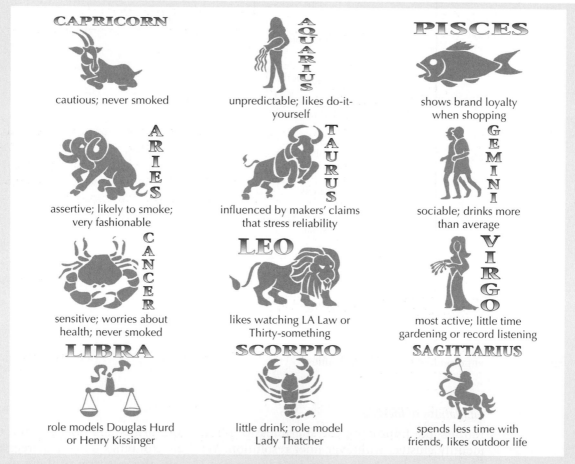

CAPRICORN
cautious; never smoked

AQUARIUS
unpredictable; likes do-it-yourself

PISCES
shows brand loyalty when shopping

ARIES
assertive; likely to smoke; very fashionable

TAURUS
influenced by makers' claims that stress reliability

GEMINI
sociable; drinks more than average

CANCER
sensitive; worries about health; never smoked

LEO
likes watching LA Law or Thirty-something

VIRGO
most active; little time gardening or record listening

LIBRA
role models Douglas Hurd or Henry Kissinger

SCORPIO
little drink; role model Lady Thatcher

SAGITTARIUS
spends less time with friends, likes outdoor life

Fig. 20.5 Star signs and lifestyles

- consumption habits are influenced astrologically; or
- the correlations arose by chance.

Before rejecting the astrological link, we should recognise that half United Kingdom adults consult their horoscopes at least once a week. It is possible, therefore, that people are influenced through learning about the way people with their signs are supposed to behave. In other words, they are affected not by the stars but by astrologers. An illustration might be, 'Scorpios are loyal and deep yet vindictive, ruthless and jealous'. Astrology could be the subtlest form of marketing!

Segment size one

The variation of questions that could be asked of marketing databases is endless. Also, the databases are gathering and storing more data. Cluster sizes are becoming smaller so that the firm looking, say, for 'childless people who like to holiday abroad and list walking and theatre among their leisure interests' can be offered a short, yet high-quality mailing fist. Eventually, the cluster size comes down to one. With powerful information systems, it becomes unnecessary to aggregate data at all. In principle, each research question can be answered by scanning personal profiles according to relevant criteria. Marketers seek to cater for the needs of each individual by gathering data on, and responding to, their unique preferences.[17] This takes us on to the notion of relationship marketing.

Building relationships with customers

Partly from having only a vague understanding of who customers were, much effort in mass marketing has been focused on winning customers with less attention being paid to keeping them. Competitiveness was based on getting the market to respond to clever manipulation of the 4Ps. These are the four competitive strategies conventionally seen as available to the marketing manager, *see* Exhibit 20.9.

Exhibit 20.9 The 4Ps of marketing

- *Product*
  Design of new products, extending the life of current ones; brands, packaging and associated services.
- *Price*
  Pricing policies and their links to costs and competition.
- *Promotion*
  Communication – advertising sales promotion, public relations; personal selling.
- *Place*
  Distribution channels; logistics, including stockholding. location of outlets

Despite careful segmentation, these strategies are crude instruments: products only approximate to customer needs; pricing effects are difficult to track; much promotional effort is wasted; and stocks and outlets do not satisfy everyone. They are increasingly seen as outdated. Emphasis has shifted to *adding value through the quality of the relationship between firm and customer*. Loyal customers come back many times and, when they do, they spend more. Aijo summarises the trends that have forced this change on companies.

> *Increase in affluence, buyer's market, trade and investment liberalization, globalization, technological innovations, computer and telecommunications developments (information revolution), etc. have combined to create a state of unlimited customer choice, a higher level of competition (sometimes called hypercompetition) and an ever-increasing pace of change. Companies find themselves having simultaneously to lower their costs, improve efficiency, raise the level of quality and service, as well as speed up innovations and the innovation cycle.*[18]

> A *paradigm* is the framework we use to view, understand, and explain the world.

For marketers, the paradigm shift incorporates a new emphasis on service as a competitive weapon. They have learnt from experience both in conventional service industries and in industrial marketing. In the latter, where there are relatively few buyers and sellers for many products, understanding and solving a customer's problems has long been a key marketing strategy. Now, all businesses are recognising they must get closer to their customers. At the heart of the paradigm is the notion of partnership with customers, and rapid response. Can this be achieved in the consumer market? Certainly, advances in information systems make such a goal look attainable. As Crainer points out, 'When it comes to creating loyal customers, the database is king.'[19]

■ Relationships and episodes

Relationship, or 'one-to-one', marketing is based on treating each customer as an individual. Products are matched to his or her needs, thereby building a permanent relationship. Ravald and Gronroos distinguish between a relationship and the episodes from which it is built. 'An episode can be defined as an event or interaction that has a clear starting point and an ending point and represents a complete exchange. In an episode there can exist several interactions, such as check-in, room and breakfast during a stay at a hotel, where the stay represents the actual episode'.[20] Then, like a soap opera, the relationship between the customer and the hotel develops from the series of episodes.

To understand what happens when an interaction occurs, therefore, we must look into both the episode itself and the way it develops the relationship. The total value of the episode to the customer is determined by the benefits compared with the costs of gaining them. This can be represented, roughly, by the equation:

Total episode value = (Episode and Relationship benefits) − (Episode and Relationship costs)

Two important implications can be drawn from the equation. First, managers should work to increase the benefits of episodes and the relationship while reducing the costs that the customer has to face. The latter fall into three categories:

■ direct costs are money payments to maintain the relationship, including subscription fees, insurance premiums and bank account charges;

■ indirect costs are incurred by the customer because of failure. These include costs of a breakdown, delays in delivery or correcting errors in accounts;

■ psychological costs are mental burdens on the customer such as uncertainty over the supplier's performance, the need to solve problems in the relationship, or worry over whether the relationship is the best one.

The second implication comes from the interaction between episode costs and relationship costs. Sometimes a poor episode can be balanced by a positive perception of the relationship. For instance, poor service on one occasion may be tolerated if a complaint is well handled and the overall relationship is satisfactory. Customers with positive views of a supplier will be tolerant of occasional lapses. On the other hand, a positive relationship can only be built from a series of positive episodes. Therefore, the two elements of the model interact closely.

The emergence of relationship marketing, RM, has highlighted the cost side of the value equation. Perceived value, from the customer's point of view, can be increased if the costs are reduced. To achieve this, the supplier must understand each customer's needs in detail. Clearly, efforts on the direct costs, to lower the price and increase purchase convenience, are but the first step. Improvements can also be made to the indirect and psychological costs. For instance, when a steel stockholder cannot supply a requested material or a just-in-time supplier anticipates a delay, the customer experiences indirect and psychological costs that could be avoided.

Building relationships

The idea of episodes building into a relationship is a useful one if we are to understand RM. It implies that the parties are involved over a period. Time is only one element, however. Kotler and colleagues see RM as 'creating, maintaining and enhancing *strong* relationships with customers.[21] Maintenance and enhancement are achieved through multiple episodes, but what does it mean to develop strong relationships? Three approaches are proposed:

■ Offering financial benefits – such as vouchers or discounts for regular purchasers. Examples of frequent flier and reward programmes are given below.

■ Adding social benefits – increasing social bonds through learning about customers and their needs. The idea is to think of customers as *clients*, treating them less as ciphers and more as individuals. For example, instead of a customer having to deal with many departments, high street banks now assign one person to look after all aspects of their accounts. Staff introduce themselves as 'personal banking advisers'.

■ Creating structural ties – furnishing customers with special equipment or technical support to ease regular use of the supplier's products. Many warranty or after sales arrangements include these features as do contracts with Internet service providers.

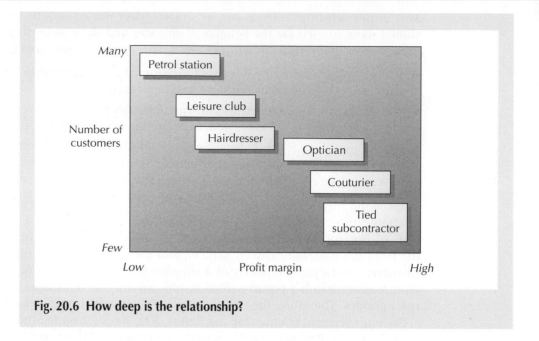

Fig. 20.6 How deep is the relationship?

In practice, what organisations are able to do, and what customers are willing to accept, depend on the business environment. As mentioned above, close relationships are common in many industries. Kotler and colleagues show how profit margins and number of customers influence the depth of relationships that can be achieved. Figure 20.6 sets out some examples using these two scales. The greatest depth of involvement is shown by the darkest shading. It is illustrated by a specialised supplier, such as an engineering consultancy, that has few customers and seeks a high profit margin. To maintain its position, the subcontractor works closely with the customer to find ways of delivering better value. In contrast, the shallowest interaction is represented by the petrol station. Selling takes place through self-service (even payment may be automatic) and there is no after-sales follow-up. In between these extremes we see other examples. One point to note is that not all companies follow the same strategy. Several are seen among opticians, for example. Those with high price and service develop traditional relationships with regular customers, while others seek to operate more like supermarkets.

In a study of consumer relationships, Pressey and Matthews identified four factors that influence their depth.

■ *Contact*
Personal contact in transactions facilitates RM. This suggests that the approach will work best where contact is frequent and the customer continues to require the service.

■ *Power*
Links with balanced power support RM. The experience of industrial marketing shows that the most stable relationships occur when the parties share power as opposed to one coercing the other. Power is equal when each party selects the other and is able to choose an alternative.

■ *Professionalism*

Encounters requiring or involving professional behaviour assist RM. A seller shows professionalism in offering expert advice and engendering trust. Furthermore, where transactions involve sharing a high degree of technical information, a common outlook will be valuable.

■ *Involvement*

When the customer is personally involved, RM is supported. A high level of involvement by both parties leads to high commitment, sharing of information and a continuing link.[22]

Comparing these factors across four retail service sectors, namely hairdresser/barber, optician, recreation centre and supermarket, the authors found that conditions favouring RM existed in the first three but not in the fourth. Yet, as we shall see below, supermarkets seem determined to build marketing strategies using RM principles.

Customer loyalty programmes

We can see the emergence of the RM paradigm in customer loyalty programmes. Schemes offering discounts and vouchers for repeat purchases have been around for a long time. Their application has, however, been stimulated by the availability of information systems. Frequent flier programmes are presented as offering rewards to regular customers. Yet, as Exhibit 20.10 explains, airlines gain as much from information as from increased turnover.

We can see how well planned programmes meet Kotler's criteria for successful RM. They offer: financial benefits through prizes or vouchers; social benefits if the airline routinely responds to passengers' special needs, such as for meals or seating position; and structural links through simplified booking procedures and priority

Exhibit 20.10 **The loyal air force**

Frequent flier programmes, such as Virgin's *Freeway* or Sabena's *Qualiflier* have become important factors in building customer loyalty. They have spread rapidly from their 1980s origins in the United States. Members earn points or *air-miles* which can be exchanged for flight tickets or other incentives. Virgin offers flying lessons, trips in balloons or stays at health clubs. Sabena also offers points with purchases of duty-free goods and if customers book in at partner hotels.

One reason for success is that there is little price competition on tickets. About a quarter of European business travellers decide on their carrier because of loyalty points. American Airlines boasts 16 million members for its Advantage plan.

Although schemes may cancel each other out in their immediate impact, the real benefit to airlines lies in the information they deliver. Since more than 85 per cent of travellers book through agents, companies have known little about their customers, not even their addresses. Now, airlines gather details on the travel patterns of those who use them often. The firm that can make the best use of this data stands to gain.

access to busy flights. Clearly, the *depth* of the relationship will depend on how episodes develop. At a basic level, more episodes yield more rewards. Trust will be enhanced, however, if it is clear to the customer that shared information is handled professionally and the travel service is correspondingly enhanced.

Relationship marketing in retailing

Supermarkets are among many retail chains to develop loyalty cards as a competitive weapon.[23] In return for about 1 per cent discount on purchases, shoppers reveal details of their shopping habits and, by implication, aspects of their lives. This information forms a platform for further relationship building:

- The accent is on *customer share* and not on market share. If a firm satisfies all the needs of 10 per cent of the population, it will do better than satisfying 10 per cent of the needs of the whole population. It will be more efficient and resistant to competition. Through studying the buying patterns of its most important customers, the retailer seeks to ensure that it always has their goods in stock.

- Promotional effort can be concentrated on those most likely to respond. A mail shot announcing a new flavour of *Whiskas* can be targeted on those with cats at home.

- The database supports diversification. Recognising customers' frustration with the location and opening hours of banks, Tesco used its *Clubcard* to found a new money service. This is but one of many possibilities opened by access to detailed customer data.

The pattern has been repeated, with variations, throughout the world. Firms have begun to cooperate in schemes, as with the 'co-branded' Visa cards. In The Netherlands, a traditional fear of credit means that people tend not to hold cards. However, if a group of retailers offer affinity cards providing both loyalty privileges and credit, the package is more acceptable. In Portugal, Continente, a hypermarket, joined with 150 firms to offer a Visa card with a low annual fee. Participants gain 1 per cent on groceries and between 2 and 25 per cent in other participating stores. Some 100 000 users were signed up in the first year, 1995. For a country where only 8 per cent of adults used a card, this was impressive. Trading laws restrict the use of discount points in Germany making an emphasis on non-financial privileges even more important. In Japan, where space is in such short supply, loyalty cards mean free parking.[24]

Do loyalty cards work?

Will the adoption of RM principles lead to long-term success? In spite of their apparent advantages, the benefits to supermarkets may be illusory. At the practical level, many analysts are gloomy over the medium-term prospects in the low-margin supermarket industry. Tesco, which was first in the United Kingdom market, may have covered its start-up costs with increased sales. Rivals Sainsbury, having initially described Tesco's scheme as an electronic version of trading stamps, lost 15 months. On the day Sainsbury finally launched its Reward card,

Tesco was able to announce an upgrade to include a current bank account.[25] Sainsbury's marketing director claimed that Reward would raise sales by 3 per cent, although Matthews pointed out that few commentators believed this figure.[26] The plan was for four-fifths of the weekly nine million customers to use a Reward card. This compared with 8.5 million already using Tesco's.

Loyalty programmes yield temporary advantages to innovators who reach the market first. Later, as others copy, the gains may be cancelled. In the supermarket industry, the ties that can be created remain weak. Low margins mean the financial benefits of membership are small. Social and structural ties are, at best, peripheral. A study by Nielsen, a market research company, showed that more than a third of United Kingdom householders shopped at several stores to obtain the best prices with a fifth identifying special offers as important. Other factors affecting choice were location and ease of parking. Therefore, the marginal benefit of loyalty cards was unlikely to tie down the so-called 'promiscuous shopper'. [27]

The growth of loyalty programmes adds fuel to criticisms of marketing. These include sustaining high prices, adding to the costs of promotion and distribution, acting deceptively and disadvantaging some customers to benefit others. As we shall see, these points are not always supported by evidence. Yet they do concern those firms who seek to act responsibly. So why are cards so important to those issuing them? The answer lies in the value of the information on customers and consequently helping to build the retailers' brands.

Building brands

A brand is an ownership mark. In the marketplace the term is used to describe the names or symbols that identify and differentiate some products from others. Labels from Beecham's to BP and Saab to Sony conjure up powerful brand images in consumers' minds. Their importance comes from the fact that many people prefer packets carrying the labels Cadbury's or Carlsberg instead of Charlie's Chocolates or Bertie's Beer. The value of brand names often represents a significant proportion of the assets of a business. One consultancy estimated the name Marlboro to be worth more than £27 billion.[28] What price Guinness, Grant's or Glenfiddich? The value of names is partly the result of the cumulative investment made in them. Manufacturers constantly nurture, control and defend their meaning. In many countries they are recognised as intellectual property to be protected both by the common law and rules on trade marks and copyright. An entrepreneur can neither make Levi's jeans nor use a name, font or logo close to those used by Levi Strauss Co. This does not normally prevent a Mr Levi from making photocopiers as long as he does not engage in *passing off*, that is pretending they are associated with the famous brand.

> *Brand image* refers to the set of beliefs that people hold about a brand.

To avoid problems of imitation and to prevent the slide of a word into common use, brand owners continually support their names with advertising, promotion and packaging, and an occasional legal action. While still registered as trade marks, Biro, Fibreglass, Hoover, JCB, Jeep and Thermos have lost some of their worth through fame and common use. In 1996, Kellogg spent £188 million in Europe to defend and differentiate its products from the two main threats of own-label and Cereal Partners, the joint venture of Nestlé and General Mills. Breakfast cereal consumption is rising in most EU countries, led by the United Kingdom. Here the average person ate 250 bowls in 1997, more than three times the rate in Germany, and some 12 per cent more than in 1993. In the UK, Kellogg spent £75 million, including £11.7 million on Corn Flakes, the nation's leading brand. Part of the endeavour was to protect and enhance the meanings of names such as Frosties, Rice Crispies and Special K. In spite of these efforts, its United Kingdom market share fell from 50 to 45 per cent in three years.[29]

■ Manufacturers versus retailers

Kellogg's decline has been matched by the rise of own-label breakfast cereal sales, especially in the United Kingdom. While we often think of brands as manufactured goods, we must remember that service providers have long recognised the potential of names and trade marks. Banks from Rothschild's to HSBC, holiday firms from Thomas Cook to Centerparcs or media businesses from Bertelsmann to the BBC all have names with sterling reputations. None more than the great retailers since Bloomingdale, Boot, Fortnum and Mason, Gucci, Macey, Marks & Spencer were nothing if not great developers of brands. Another great name was F.W. Woolworth, *see* Exhibit 20.11.

In the consumer market, many predict the death of manufacturers' brands in favour of the retailers'. Some companies, listed in Exhibit 20.12, already sell most or much of their packaged goods in this form.[30] Two points are notable in the list – the predominance of United Kingdom firms and the few who have reached 50 per cent Among the leaders, Marks & Spencer is known for its high quality and pricing while Aldi and Tip are discount arms of larger groups. Interpreting such data is crucial to manufacturers and retailers alike. For the former, there is the choice between refusing to supply for retailers' private labels or looking to such business for a steady flow of large orders. For the latter, decline in manufacturers' brands could leave them isolated. Yet will they decline and, if so, how far?

Exhibit 20.11 Woolworth's life cycle

Frank Winfield Woolworth (1852–1919) opened his first 'five and ten cent' shop in Pennsylvania in 1879. With his brother, he built a chain of hundreds of similar stores in North America and Europe. After 1950, rising prices, changing habits, loss of focus and competition from specialists put the trading formula out of date. Overseas chains were sold and the last United States store closed in 1997.

Exhibit 20.12	Percentage sales of own-label packaged goods – Europe's Top Ten	
Marks & Spencer	UK	98%
Aldi	Germany	83%
Tip	Germany	75%
Sainsbury	UK	67%
Waitrose	UK	65%
Tesco	UK	56%
Morrison's	UK	50%
Safeway	UK	46%
Asda	UK	43%
Casino	France	37%

In the United Kingdom, the private label market is 27 per cent, followed by Switzerland (23 per cent), Germany (15 per cent), France (13 per cent) and Turkey (10 per cent). Euromonitor, a market research firm, has identified several that contribute to the United Kingdom market's switch to own-label. The interaction among them is shown in Fig. 20.7. This is a *causal model* whose arrows show the interactive links in a dynamic situation. Here, the links are all positive. They show how changes in each factor positively influence others, leading to an overall growth in private label sales.

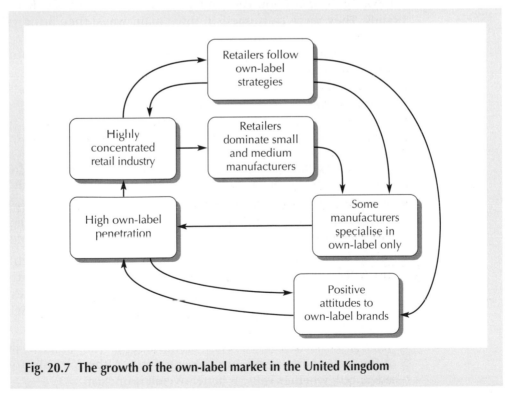

Fig. 20.7 The growth of the own-label market in the United Kingdom

With one store per 1400 people, the United Kingdom has a highly concentrated industry with dominant chains. For instance, the four leading supermarkets take more than half the grocery turnover. Promotion strategies over many years, led by Marks & Spencer, have created positive consumer attitudes to retailers' brands. This contrasts with their traditional cheap image in much of Europe and North America. Meanwhile, the leaders have come to dominate small and medium manufacturers, many of whom have chosen to specialise in private label production. The gradual phasing out of second-tier brands means that shelves often carry just one manufacturer's brand – Cadbury, Heinz, Kellogg, Nestlé and so on – alongside the retailer's own. Whether the model of Fig. 20.7 can be applied to the whole EU depends on its completeness. For instance, compared with the whole market, retail concentration in Europe is low. Leading manufacturers, however, have built pan-European operations. Furthermore, if retailers were to become more powerful, the Commission may investigate anti-competitive behaviour. This means a negative loop would be introduced to the diagram.

■ Who benefits from brands?

Is the struggle between manufacturers and retailers a war with the consumer caught in the crossfire? Put more broadly, are brands generally in the public interest? Whom do brands benefit? Evidently, they benefit their owners. Otherwise, they would not exist. Furthermore, the owners claim that they only exist to satisfy consumers. Or is it that marketers use brands to exploit consumers and manipulate markets to their own advantage?

Drawing on many sources, Ambler concludes that the evidence is in favour of brands. They serve consumers in three main ways: they bring value for money; they are the means through which quality is improved; and they offer psychological satisfaction.[31] Since these arguments tell us much about the nature of marketing, we shall look at their details.

Economic benefits

The economic benefits of brands arise from their importance in the sales transaction. In particular, brands:

- *Support competition*. Imagining a market without brands is difficult. How would one choose between goods if they had the same descriptions and packaging?

- *Provide choice*. Consumer surveys show that variety is rated highly by shoppers. The increase in the size of grocery stores is partly to give greater choice. New products, and therefore greater choice, usually come from the leading brand manufacturers.

- *Reduce risk in the transaction*. Names provide assurance to regular customers. If the price is higher than the cheapest goods, it may be worth paying for the greater confidence. When assessing quality, the consumer relies on the methods and cues listed in Exhibit 20.13. The reputation of brands will become more important the more the buyer has to rely on credence.

- *Improve consumer value*. Overall, brands offer a wide range of prices that satisfy different buyers' needs in different ways. Although this argument is often advanced, whether value is better overall is unclear.

Exhibit 20.13 **How consumers appraise quality**

- Search – ascertained by inspection, e.g. fruit, cloth, timber.
- Low experience – quickly discovered from limited use, e.g. beer.
- High experience – only established after prolonged use, e.g. domestic appliance.
- Credence – not apparent in use but depends on belief, e.g. pain killers, engine oil.

Functional benefits

Functional benefits describe innovation and improvements in quality that may be stimulated by brands. In this respect, brands offer:

- *Different value to different customers.* Rising incomes have led customers to search for products that closely fit their particular needs. This in turn has stimulated new product development. This accounts for the trend to customisation in many markets from cars to personal computers, or kitchens to holidays.

- *Differences in quality.* Quality differences arise both through continual improvement of existing product ranges and new product innovation. Brands must improve to match consumers' rising expectations. Innovation is a means for manufacturers to defend their brands against own-label.

- *Reliability.* We noted how branding is part of relationship marketing. It is in the supplier's interests to ensure the customer is satisfied with every transaction. Reliability factors range from safety in use to full measures in packaged goods.

- *Subsidise arts and sports and the media.* Advertisers pay at least half the cost of newspapers and magazines and for all of the 'free' media such as commercial-television. Through these, or more directly, brands support the arts, civic programmes and sport. To the extent that consumers enjoy these activities the subsidy benefits them.

- *Ensure fitness for use.* A key idea in marketing is that customers buy to satisfy a need. Successful brands survive because they can provide satisfaction in the long term.

- *Are widely available.* Availability is crucial if demand is to be created and met. Strong brands are the most widely distributed. For instance, being 'within an arm's reach of everyone' makes Coca-Cola the world's most valuable brand.

Psychological benefits

Psychological benefits arise in the mind of the consumer rather than in the product itself. Marketers are sometimes accused of creating brand images to represent 'quasi-persons' and so provide a false satisfaction from their use. Yet many consumers clearly care less about function than they do about style. Some (rational?) consumers buy every available product report before making a choice. Others do not. Whether this is natural behaviour, or weakness in the face of the barrage of advertising, is an issue we shall deal with later. Psychological satisfaction from purchases is, clearly, important. Brands contribute because they:

- *Simplify consumer choices.* Although proliferation of brands may seem to add confusion, a recognised brand simplifies the choice for a regular user. This is especially true for complex products, such as cameras or computers, where the name replaces the need for extensive product knowledge. Part of the process is providing the customer with a new vocabulary to use when thinking about brands. For example, Kodak coined 'clicknology' and Audi used 'vorsprung durch technik' in markets where German was not used.

- *Bring social benefits.* Many brands help to satisfy needs for social approval, personal expression or self-esteem. This is especially true for so-called 'badge' products that signal rank, self-image and social attachment. Lacoste golf wear establishes membership of an identifiable group; Benetton another.

- *Help consumers feel good.* In the end, customer satisfaction depends on how they feel about their purchases. A 'brand personality' helps a consumer to realise a sense of self An example is Land Rover whose brand image has been developed to appeal to consumer values as shown in Exhibit 20.14.[32] The emotional support offered by friendly brands, such as the Mr Muscle and Mr Sheen cleaning products, is important. It often lies at the heart of building loyalty through trust.

Exhibit 20.14 Land Rover's appeal to self-concept

Brand image	Consumers look for a vehicle that ...
Individualism	... is individual and distinctive
Authenticity	... is a genuine 4 × 4 vehicle
Freedom	... allows you more freedom
Adventure	... gives you a sense of adventure
Guts	... is well-built and robust
Supremacy	... has the best off-road performance

How broad can a brand be?

Compared with retailers, positive attitudes towards manufacturers' brands are often based on perceptions of expertise. After all, how can a retailer know about goods ranging from textiles to tomatoes? The answer of the leading retailers is that they do have the expertise, although it is hidden from the customer. Marks & Spencer, Aldi and Tip recognise buying skills as a key to competitive advantage. Yet the broad question remains: how far can a brand be 'stretched' across a range of products?

Brand extension, the process of launching new products using the reputation of existing ones, is widely practised. Although about 3000 new products are launched in the United Kingdom grocery market each year, only seven of the leading 100 brands were less than 10 years old. They are listed in Exhibit 20.15. This data supports the common observation that most new products appear under existing

Exhibit 20.15	Flourishing new brands

Always
Clover
Dolmio H
Heinz Weight Watchers
Müller
Pringles
Radion

names. With rapid innovation rates in some product lines, the brand establishes continuity through changes. We can envisage the brand linking life cycles into a chain of continuing sales, *see* Fig. 20.8. Some 65 per cent of detergent products available in 1996 had been launched within the previous five years. Thus the 'Superwash' brand would be replaced by New Superwash, and then by New Improved Superwash before returning to Original Superwash. Meanwhile, variants may include Low Temperature, Automatic, Coloured, Sensitive Skin, Bio, Travel or Liquid.

Although an attractive strategy in many cases, brand extension has drawbacks:

■ Some names are both brands and product descriptions. If they are closely associated with the latter, the range of brand extension is limited. This is a reason that Coca-Cola only refers to a narrow range of flavoured drinks.

■ Brand extensions may be restricted. With clothing and boots, managers of Marlboro and Camel have stretched their brand images away from the declining, in the West at least, cigarette market. An anticipated European Union directive will ban this form of indirect advertising.[33]

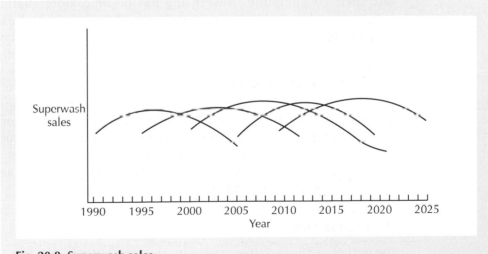

Fig. 20.8 Superwash sales

■ The risk of a favourable image being tarnished increases if it is applied to many disparate products. Among brands that have recently emerged on the global stage, contrast the narrow focus of Benetton and IKEA with the breadth of Virgin, *see* Exhibit 20.16.[34] The international recognition achieved by the Virgin brand is remarkable. Apart from the airline, however, the rest of the business is tiny by world standards. It runs two risks. The first is becoming involved in a business that fails to embody Virgin's values of quality and friendly service. The second is the over-dependence on the entrepreneurial leadership of Richard Branson.[35]

Marketing, ethics and social responsibility

Marketing is often the most visible and controversial among the functions of management. Critics point to cases of partly true advertising being used to promote unwanted or unnecessary goods. For the defence, however, these problems are presented as the excesses of the few. Most marketers, it is argued, act in the public interest. After all, one cannot charge bankers with antisocial behaviour simply because of a few loan sharks.

Part of the problem lies in different perceptions of what marketing is for. If we rely on the definition of Kotler and colleagues, which asserts that marketing is simply the science of transactions, then a utilitarian approach will suggest that marketing is ethical. That is, if we accept the benefits of capitalism and markets, then any approach to improving the performance of markets will be in the interests of all. Therefore, probing and interpreting customers' motives so as to satisfy their needs is a legitimate activity. The difficulty arises from the application of this principle. Interpretation of what is responsible behaviour in applying it have gradually been extended. For example, marketing research has justified deeper prying into peoples' lives, and especially the underlying thoughts and feelings that motivate their consumption. Advertising has become more subtle, invasive and, sometimes, subliminal. It has created demand for products in the interests of satisfying needs. Yet without advertising, these needs might never have existed. Such actions, it is asserted, are all in the interests of improving marketing.

Therefore, while the marketing manager may seek to behave ethically within the business definition of what the marketing function is for, it is left to others to ask the uneasy questions of its legitimacy. Exclusive reliance on the principle of consumer satisfaction creates problems both for consumers and for the rest of society. Selling tobacco satisfies a need. Yet this is obtained at the expense of smokers' future health and the pockets of those who have to treat their illnesses. Countering the approach based on utility, Nantel and Weeks are among those who call for the use of deontology, that is starting with principles.[36]

Fair exchange

The notion of fair exchange underpins the ethics of transactions. There has been a gradual change in societal attitudes from *caveat emptor* (let the buyer beware)

Exhibit 20.16   Virgin's elastic brand

Businesses using the Virgin brand range from airlines and railways through financial services and cola to cinemas and music. Some are wholly owned subsidiaries in a complex structure; others work under joint ventures or management agreements. The breadth of this range counters much marketing wisdom which argues that finding a common image suited to all these operations is difficult. Yet Richard Branson, known for innovation, risk taking and publicity stunts, sees friendly customer service as the core skill for the future. He seeks to expand in those sectors where customers show some dissatisfaction and Virgin can make a difference. Branson embodies his products – clear, no frills, trustworthy – in the eyes of youth and young adults. These are groups he understands.

Virgin Atlantic, founded in 1984, found a niche in the tough long-haul business. When the no-frills Virgin Express, a separate company from Virgin Atlantic, took over Euro Belgian's flights from its Brussels hub, there were many complaints. Yet these came from European business travellers unaccustomed to the cheap-and-cheerful service; there were plenty of other passengers attracted by fares up to 50 per cent lower than state-owned rivals.

The music business, however, shows up one hazard of elastic branding. Since its sale to Thorn EMI in 1992, Branson cannot use the Virgin name on recordings. On return to this industry, he had to use the V2 label instead. Virgin Radio, another successful venture, was sold to Capitol in 1997.

Commentators have rated several new ventures as risky:

- Virgin Cola, launched amid flamboyant publicity in 1994, took 3.1 per cent of the United Kingdom take-home market in 1997. This compares with 50 and 20 per cent for Coca-Cola and Pepsi respectively.

- Virgin Cinema, 45 per cent owned by the group, operates a mix of cinemas. It is gradually restyling and branding the older operations inherited from MGM. Some say the switch was made too soon.

- Following the 1991 privatisation, Virgin took on two rail operating franchises. Whether it could make a difference to the services depended on being able to change culture and technology. Most of the staff transferred from British Rail and new rolling stock was only on the drawing board. The transition period was a problem with many speed limits and Railtrack rebuilding the network. Punctuality and reliability were deteriorating.

- Virgin Direct, started in 1995, is a 50–50 joint venture with AMP, a financial services firm. It offers pension and savings plans.

- In 1997, the group was planning a joint venture, Vie, with up to 100 chain stores selling cosmetics. Jeans were to follow in 1998.

The Virgin brand is very well known and is well regarded overall. A Mintel survey ranked the group's trustworthiness high, beaten only by British Airways, Co-operative Bank, Abbey National and Marks & Spencer. Yet one survey showed Virgin was among the least trusted financial services providers in the country, while Marks & Spencer was the most trusted. Other studies, however, place it among the most successful.

towards *caveat venditor* (let the seller beware). In other words, there has been a shift in favour of consumers' interests over the suppliers'. Consumer sovereignty is the basis of the modem capitalist system. Through exercising informed choice, the consumer both expresses the principle and makes markets work.

Some firms have responded to consumerism and its consequences by perceiving markets as battlegrounds. They will behave to the minimum standards required by law and try to maximise their power over the buyer. Yet, following Kant's universal principle, we can see that marketers should exercise more responsibility than this. Since sellers in one context are buyers in another, Kant would point out that sellers must not treat customers in ways in which they would not wish to be treated themselves. A firm should not despatch poor quality or unsafe goods to a Third World market if it would be disappointed if a supplier did the same to it.

In this view, ethics obliges vendors to make transactions as fair as possible. But how to put this notion into practice? Smith proposes a three-part consumer sovereignty test:[37]

- *Consumer capability*

  To what extent is the consumer vulnerable and how does this affect decision making? It is accepted, for example, that children are more so than adults and many countries restrict marketing activities focused upon them. Parents are too familiar with 'pester power', where children harass them into buying branded football boots or merchandise from the latest Disney. The difficulties surrounding this question were highlighted by the judge of the long-running 'McLibel' action mentioned in the closing case of this chapter. In his summing up, Mr Justice Bell accused McDonald's of exploiting children through its advertising. Yet where do parents' and advertisers' responsibilities meet? A famous line from British advertising – 'Don't forget the Fruit Gums, mum' – would not be allowed under current anti-pestering rules. In Sweden, the government barred television advertising to the under-twelves, although the European court prevented it from blocking satellite commercials.[38]

  The vulnerability of adults is more controversial. The United States has rules to protect the recently bereaved from predatory funeral directors while trade associations in other countries have codes of practice of varying effectiveness. In the United Kingdom, giving misleading advice on transfers from company-based to personal pensions has led to fines for some large companies. Even mutual life insurers, companies owned by their policy holders, joined in the practice. Friends Provident, a large mutual, was fined £450 000 by the Personal Investment Authority for 'extremely poor progress' in sorting out its 6428 cases of mis-selling.[39]

- *Information*

  The fairness of transactions is underpinned by both parties having adequate information for their decisions. This does not mean that both should have the *same* information. That would imply the seller revealing secrets about, say, costs that would yield advantages to competitors. Such facts are relevant to the seller's willingness to sell but not normally to the buyer's willingness to buy. The seller's duty, therefore, is not to offer misleading information and, further, to reveal information that could influence the purchaser's decision. The sweeping changes to United Kingdom rules governing the sale of investment products were brought about because many in the industry were not conforming to this standard. Although acting as 'financial advisers' many brokers or agents were selling savings and insurance contracts according to the commission they could obtain. It was a rare agent who advised a client either to refrain from buying or to invest in products such as National Savings, where no commission is payable.[40]

- *Choice*

  It may seem odd that market leaders should not reap the rewards of their efforts from rising market share. Yet dominance and monopoly have been shown to have economic disadvantages that can be underlined from the ethical point of view. Fairness requires that both parties enter the transaction willingly. This condition is less likely to hold under monopoly conditions. A customer should be able to switch to another supplier if others are more reliable, fair or honest. Therefore, in spite of the pressure to push up sales, marketers should not seek to monopolise markets; nor should they unreasonably force up switching costs for customers who need repeat purchases; nor ought they restrict channels of distribution in order to maintain high prices.

  Perfume houses had for many years defended their practice of refusing to supply unauthorised 'grey' distributors on the grounds that their products needed to be displayed and sold by experts. In fact they were exploiting strong brand loyalty among the heaviest users, middle-aged women, and the system held prices high. Now new brands, aimed at younger women and men, have shaken up these cosy relationships. Examples include Tommy Hilfiger, Ralph Lauren and, above all, Calvin Klein. In the United Kingdom, wider distribution and discounting meant that sales value in real terms fell by 4 per cent in the five years to 1997. The rate of fall was expected to double in the next quinquennium. Figure 20.9 shows the leaders in each category. Some, such as CKone, are bought by both sexes.[41]

Although tests like this could cover all transactions, its focus is on consumer relationships where there is likely to be a power imbalance between buyer and seller. In this field, the consumer sovereignty test can be used to evaluate marketing practices.

Fundamentally flawed?

Some are less optimistic. Reviewing both the general impact and specific practices of marketing, Alvesson and Willmot[42] take a much more critical stand than those who look to codes of ethics to improve matters. To them, marketing is fundamentally flawed. A negative consequence of viewing relationships as transactions is to depersonalise them. The effect is to convert the seller into an instrument of distribution and the buyer into an instrument of consumption. A danger emerges of portraying all social interactions as 'marketised' transactions. One outcome is that the valuing of people is substituted by the valuing of objects; people's identities become increasingly linked to their status as consumers.

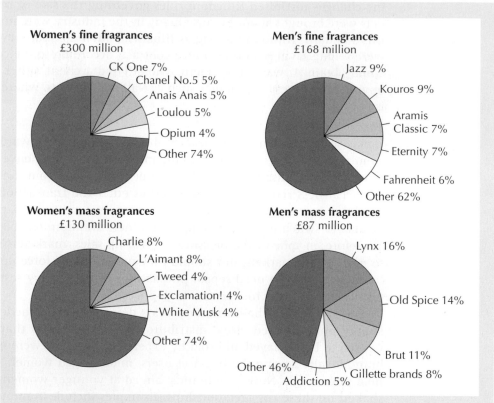

Fig. 20.9 Leading perfume brands in the United Kingdom, 1996

The notion of *lifestyle*, supported by the development of relationship marketing described above, implies self-expression and self-conscious individuality. People are encouraged to dress, speak, eat, drink and otherwise behave according to models implanted, and not 'discovered', by marketers. We can use the example of bars. On the one hand, an Irish pub in Italy is a bit of fun. On the other, Italian people, particularly younger ones, are encouraged to participate in a 'reality' of whose existence there is no guarantee. Meanwhile, they reject equally valuable norms and habits. Just as the smartest places to be seen in London are espresso houses, the place to be in Rome is *Paddy's Bar*.

Advertising and consumption

Alvesson and Willmott are further concerned about the support given by marketing to mass consumption. The outpouring of advertising reinforces the impression of consumption as an end in itself. While one can support the function of advertising in encouraging a person to select one product as opposed to another, a side effect is to legitimate consumption as a whole. The authors, rather, place this as the most important effect. Advertising makes consumption itself normal and desirable. It becomes the *raison d'être*.

Through mass media, and more recently through closely targeted mail shots, advertising serves to institutionalise envy and build anxieties. A simple example from relationship marketing will suffice. To gain discounts on most frequently dialled telephone calls, customers (who used to be called subscribers) are invited to join BT's *Friends and Family* scheme. The intention behind lowering prices for frequent users may be admirable. Yet the company has taken to mailing scheme members with analyses of how much they saved and *how much they would have saved if they had acted differently*.[43] Details of numbers are included. In another promotion, BT offers further discounts for scheme calls made *over and above* the average bill for the previous four quarters. This form of anxiety-based persuasion is all too common in direct mailing.

Deception

Deception is a common accusation levelled at marketers. Indeed, many methods are taught and used which are aimed at undermining consumers' will by inducing them to act habitually (brand loyalty), impulsively ('Go on, spoil yourself') or distractedly (through piped music or confusing messages). Kotler and colleagues classify deception into three categories, pricing, promotion and packaging:[44]

- Deceptive pricing includes the widespread practice of advertising 'factory' or 'wholesale' prices or discounting from a notional 'recommended retail' or list price. Discounts may be offered subject to unstated conditions. The true cost of loans, or the start-up costs of savings schemes, may be disguised amid a mass of small print and 'technobabble'.

- Deceptive promotion covers: overstating of a product's features, performance or benefits; luring a customer to a shop or sale by advertising bargains that are out of stock; or running rigged competitions. In selling insurance, many representatives have been accused of overestimating the risk and exploiting unstated fears. Advertisers have long seen themselves as having a limited licence to exaggerate. This so-called 'puffery' is seen in the not so subtle Heineken's 'refreshing the parts other beers can't reach' or the more explicit 'Guinness gives you power' used in anglophone Africa.

- Deceptive packaging includes exaggerating the contents through package design or misleading labelling and size information. Reducing the coating thickness or size of a chocolate wafer is a common response to increased manufacturing costs.

Sensible marketers avoid deception since it destroys relationships in the long term. Furthermore, they recognise that most customers treat product claims sceptically, even when they are true. Levitt makes the case for a little deception, for 'without distortion, embellishment and elaboration, life would be drab, dull, anguished and at its existential worst ...'[45] The snag is when does distortion become dishonesty, or embellishment and elaboration turn into eluding and evasion?

Conclusion: responsible marketing

Our opening case outlined typical features of marketing in the global consumer environment. To succeed, companies must learn about the markets they both operate in and seek to enter. At the same time, they must track the behaviour and innovation of possible rivals to ensure they do not lose out to developments. The marketing perspective is that an organisation best fits its environment if it continues to satisfy its customers' needs on a long-term basis. Marketing is about maintaining links between inward looking business functions and the outside world.

This idea, at least in its formal expression, has been current for barely half a century. Levitt's notion of marketing myopia was published in 1960. It presaged a surge of interest in markets and customers, aided by the growth of information systems and driven by the desire to be 'customer-led'. Manufacturers were the first to build global brands, using them alongside technological prowess to expand. Globalisation of service companies followed. In each case, winners combine technology, brand management and organisation skills.

Marketing research illustrates the development of customer orientation. Notions of market segments were crude, often accepting government classification of populations according to the income of the head of the household. Now that computers can support huge database analysis programs, the possibilities offered to researchers appear endless. Indeed, the possibility of handling detailed information in so many ways challenges the value of segmentation itself. The trend is to treat each customer individually, even in the mass market. In spite of all the numbers, however, the question of why customers behave in the ways they do remains unanswered. Observing behaviour is easy; understanding motivation is not.

The growth of marketing offers the organisation great power in its relations with consumers. Notions of using relationship marketing and brands to hold on to customers' loyalty sound innocent enough. From the marketing perspective, we have seen how brands bring general benefit. Yet the possibilities of manipulation and exploitation are ever present. Even common practices such as test marketing, where a sample of consumers is offered new products to see whether they will take to them, can be criticised on the grounds that they are unknowing participants in an experiment. The marketer must make sure that transactions are fair.

The visibility of marketing has placed it among the most criticised of business functions. At one level, we saw how brands, in principle, work in the common interest. Probing further, however, we uncover many ethical questions. Optimists suggest that codes of ethics can support responsible marketing. Pessimists, on the other hand, see our current conceptions of consumers and consumption as flawed. Since its effect is to encourage excess, a fundamental rethink of the role of marketing is needed.

Quick check up   *Can you ...*

- Sketch the product life cycle and assess its usefulness;
- Set out five alternative market orientations;
- Define marketing;
- Define and list four aspects of marketing research;
- Distinguish between primary and secondary data;
- Connect segmentation with relationship marketing;

- Name the four Ps of marketing and outline why they are being superseded;
- Link relationships with episodes;
- Define brand and name eight benefits of brands;
- Give examples of brand extension;
- Summarise Smith's consumer sovereignty test.

Questions

Chapter review

20.1 Outline the main purposes of marketing research, illustrating your answer with a flow diagram.

20.2 What are the arguments in favour of brands? Illustrate with your own examples.

20.3 Discuss the advantages and disadvantages of applying the same brand to a range of products.

20.4 Prepare and illustrate arguments against the consumer sovereignty test for responsible marketing practice.

Application

20.5 Direct marketing, by post, telephone and electronic mail, is becoming more common as organisations recognise its potential. What issues should be included in a code of ethics drawn up to guide such activity?

20.6 Use recent publications to assess the current state of the manufacturers versus retailers brand battle.

Investigation

20.7 Identify five organisations that, in your view, match the orientations described early in the chapter. Suggest why each takes its particular stance.

20.8 Investigate how firms in a consumer market not discussed in the chapter are developing the notions of relationship marketing. Examine why they are doing this and comment on whether they are likely to succeed.

Joburgers[46]

With 20 000 outlets around the world, are there too many McDonald's? Apparently not. Although franchisees worry about rivals in their vicinity, putting more stores into a market increases market share, sometimes spectacularly. Peoria, Illinois, has a population of 113 000. In 1981, McDonald's, with 10 stores, had 40 per cent of the market, double that generated by the five stores of its nearest rival, Hardees. By 1991, however, Hardees had grown to 40 per cent from 18 outlets, while McDonald's, with 11, fell to 28 per cent. Big Mac then decided to fight back. By 1995 it had boosted its store count to 29 while Hardees cut to 17. Market share topped 50 per cent while sales volume, cash flow and profit per restaurant also grew. Having learnt the lesson of market penetration, as opposed to optimising the position of each store separately, McDonald's is buying and refurbishing the properties of weak competitors.

The United States has 25 burger bars and 11 pizza parlours per 100 000 people. In second place, with five and two respectively, comes Japan, with the United Kingdom a close third. Rising competition in its home market, where it has a 45 per cent share and 7 per cent of the population visits every day, has forced McDonald's to push more into overseas markets. Two-thirds of openings are outside America. Foreign operating profits overtook domestic ones in 1995 to take 54 per cent of $2.6 billion. Average takings per overseas restaurant rose 7 per cent to $2.42 million, while at home they were down slightly at $1.54 million.

In 1996, a specialist consultancy, Interbrand, rated leaders according to market share, global spread, customer loyalty and how far their brands could stretch. McDonald's narrowly beat Coca-Cola to first place. It is one of the few truly global brands. Its reputation makes it possible to achieve the reach it manages at home. Some 5 per cent of Australians are daily customers.

The company's ethnocentric culture and management practices support brand attributes recognised in most places where the company operates. Through common standards and values, with some flexibility to adapt to local partners and customer tastes, McDonald's maximises its strength and minimises its costs. In achieving a global presence, it has consistently and deliberately pursued its ground rules. These cover protection of the brand image, site development, customer satisfaction, franchise management and adherence to the McDonald's business philosophy.

The formula works. And when the legendary reputation for food quality, quick service, clean surroundings and family values with care of children does not win people over, the company is prepared to use its muscle. When local communities complain over too many take-aways, McDonald's promises to generate up to a hundred jobs with training for school leavers and special attention to the needs of disadvantaged groups. When two unemployed environmental activists distributed leaflets complaining about its farming, packaging and employment practices, McDonald's got bogged down in the longest libel action in British legal history. After 313 days in court, it was awarded £60 000 damages. In South Africa, where it had allowed its trade mark registration to expire, a local trader applied to use the name. Other traders were already using 'MacDonalds'. It lost in the Supreme Court in 1995 but won an appeal a year later.

The South African market, however, was not proving easy to crack. Though McDonald's won its legal case on the grounds it was a well-known name, this fame proved to be only among the minority white population. Furthermore, during the apartheid years, strong local brands and two other foreign brands, KFC and Wimpy, had developed. While quick service and attention to the needs of children were appreciated, McDonald's standard menu was not. It had judged the market to be not different enough to need offerings such as India's Maharaja Mac, made with mutton. The South African market splits on racial lines. Most blacks favour chicken, which accounts for two-thirds of fast food; McDonald's chicken burgers are too pricey and plain. Whites like beef, but lots of it; McDonald's quarterpounder (120 grams) is puny beside Steer's 200 gram 'Big Steer'.

Questions

1 How, in marketing terms, does McDonald's differ from most other 'hamburger joints'?

2 Why is the company reluctant to vary its menu for local markets?

3 Several attempts to extend the McDonald's brand have failed. Is the company stuck with its formula?

4 Where should McDonald's stand on the continuum of social responsibility?

Bibliography

For a thorough coverage of marketing, Kotler, Phillip; Armstrong, Gary; Saunders, John and Wong, Veronica (1996) *Principles of Marketing: The European edition*, London: Prentice Hall, is recommended. Further discussion of issues raised in this chapter appear in the journals, for instance: *International Journal of Retail and Distribution Management, European Journal of Marketing* and *Marketing Week*.

References

1. Milner, Mark (1997) 'Focusing on the wrong picture', *Guardian*, 22 February; Lang, Amanda (1997) 'MGI software set to snap up digital photo market', *Financial Post*, 25 February; Annells, Jonathan and Waters, Richard (1997) 'Snapshot of a new technology', *Financial Times*, 1 March.
2. Data from 'Assembling the new economy', *The Economist*, 13 September, 1997, 105–11.
3. 'Digital snap', *The Economist*, 30 August 1997, 63–4.
4. Kotler, Philip, Armstrong, Gary, Saunders, John and Wong, Veronica (1996) *Principles of Marketing: The European Edition*, London: Prentice Hall, 14.
5. Tulley, Mark (1994) 'Great Railway Journeys of the World', *BBC2 television*, 17 February.
6. 'Too clever by half', *The Economist*, 20 September 1997, 99.
7. Simon, Bernard (1995) 'Quiet revolution at Bata Shoe – The paternalistic mould is being broken', *Financial Times*, 28 March; *idem*, 'Bata in transition: The group is still strong but recent upheavals may be only a start', *Financial Times*, 6 June; *idem*, 'Bata executives quit in strategy row: Triple resignation blamed on disagreements with Czech-born figurehead over retail side', *Financial Times*, 9 October; Lednicky, Václav and Matusikovà, Lucja (1996) 'A contribution for the Batal's management system recognition', *Selected Research Papers*, Faculty of Economics, Technical University of Ostrava, 89–92; *see also* http://www.bata.com.

8. Meehan, Sean and Barwise, Patrick (1996) *Do market-oriented businesses perform better?*, Working Paper 96–103, Centre for Marketing, London Business School.

9. Kotler *et al.* (1996) *op. cit.*, 214.

10. 'World champion', *The Economist*, 13 September 1997, 36.

11. Naylor, J.B. and Williams, J. (1994) 'The successful use of IT in SMEs on Merseyside', *European Journal of Information Systems*. **3** (**1**), 48–56.

12. Cannon, Tom (1992) *Basic Marketing*, Third edition, London: Cassell, 156–71.

13. Lieber, Ronald B. (1997) 'Storytelling: a new way to get close to your customer', *Fortune*, 3 February, 102–6.

14. Fielding, Helen (1994) 'Spoilt for choice in all the clutter', *Independent on Sunday*, 6 March, 23.

15. Thapar, Neil (1994) 'Advertisers usher in classless society', *Independent on Sunday Business News*, 6 March, 1.

16. Chaudhary, Vivek (1997) 'Market researchers look to stars', *Guardian*, 16 September, 8.

17. 'Relationship marketing: reaping the benefits of IT', *International Journal of Retail and Distribution Management*, **23** (**11**), Winter 1995, xii–xiii.

18. Aijo, Toio S. (1996) 'The theoretical and philosophical underpinnings of relationship marketing: Environmental factors behind the changing marketing paradigm', *European Journal of Marketing*, **30** (**2**), February, 8–18.

19. Crainer, Stuart (1996) *Key Management Ideas*, London: Financial Times Pitman Publishing, 167–8.

20. Ravald, Annika and Gronroos, Christian (1996) 'The value concept and relationship marketing', *European Journal of Marketing*, **30** (**2**), February, 19–30.

21. Kotler *et al.*, (1996) *op. cit.*, 450.

22. Pressey, Andrew D. and Mathews, Brian P. (1997) 'Facilitators to relationship marketing in the retail context'. *Marketing without borders: Proceedings of the Academy of Marketing Conference*, Manchester, 8–10 July, 757–68.

23. Miles, Richard (1997) 'Boots takes the loyalty pledge', *Guardian*, 7 August, 18.

24. Bird, Julie (1997) 'Customer loyalty – How to keep them faithful the world over', *Precision Marketing*, 26 May.

25. Cowe, Roger (1996) 'Supermarket plays trump card', *Guardian*, 18 June, 18.

26. Matthews, Virginia (1996) 'Loyal to what end?', *Marketing*, 29 August, 34–6.

27. Nielsen, A. C. (1996) 'Customer loyalty – The issue for the 90s', *The Researcher*, A. C. Nielsen.

28. Fletcher, Winston (1997) 'Ad lib: Words designed to bring added value', *Financial Times*, 11 August.

29. Stuart, Liz (1997) 'Troubled Kellogg pressurises JWT', *Marketing Week*, 3 April; Willman, John (1998) 'Fast food spreads amid changing lifestyles', *Financial Times*, 27 March.

30. 'Continued success assured in Europe', *The Grocer*, 26 April, 1997.

31. Ambler, Tim (1997) 'Do brands benefit consumers?', *Pan'Agra Working Paper*, 97–901, London Business School.

32. Bull, Nick and Oxley, Martin (1996) 'The search for focus: Brand values across Europe', ESOMAR Seminar, Berlin, **203**, 9–11 October, 189–207; quoted in Ambler (1997) *op. cit.*, 47.

33. Griffiths, John, Harverson, Patrick and Timmins, Nicholas (1997) 'The government's "twin track" strategy of pursuing a ban on tobacco', *Financial Times*, 11 June.

34. Ramesh, Randeep (1997) 'Can Virgin put the West Coast back on track?', *Independent on Sunday*, 16 February; 'NatWest and Virgin suffer from lack of public trust', *Marketing Week*, 3 April 1997; Farrelly, Paul (1997) 'Virgin to launch cosmetics chain', *Observer*, 11 May; Robison, Peter (1997) 'Cheap 'n' cheerful takes off', *Independent on*

Sunday,11 May; Cheary, Natalie (1997) 'Virgin Cola faces Iceland setback', *Marketing Week*, 22 May; Smith, Alison (1997) 'Richard Branson: A genius for publicity', *Financial Times*, 4 August.

35. 'What's in a name?' *The Economist*, 11 January, 1997.

36. Nantel, Jacques and Weeks, William A. (1996) 'Marketing ethics: is there more to it than the utilitarian approach?' *European Journal of Marketing*, **30** (**5**), May, 9–19.

37. Smith, N. Craig (1995) 'Marketing strategies for the ethics era', *Sloan Management Review*, **36** (**4**), Summer, 85–97.

38. Tylee, John (1997) 'Should advertisers take "pester power" seriously?', *Campaign*, 18 July, 11.

39. Brown-Humes, Christopher (1997) 'Friends Provident: record £450 000 fine over pensions mis-selling', *Financial Times*, 1 October.

40. Diacon, Stephen R. and Ennew, Christine T. (1996) 'Ethical issues in insurance marketing in the UK', *European Journal of Marketing*, **30** (**5**), May, 67–80.

41. Melkie, James (1997) Price-cutters cast cloud over perfume houses', *Guardian*, 27 September, 9.

42. Alvesson, Mats and Willmott, Hugh (1996) *Making Sense of Management*, London: Sage, 119–28.

43. BT (1997) *Your personalised BT savings review.*

44. Kotler *et al.* (1996) *op. cit.*, 38.

45. Levitt, Theodore (1970) 'The morality (?) of advertising', *Harvard Business Review*, **48** (**3**), July–August, 84–92.

46. Pike, Matthew, Sheath, Ray and Carey, Jim (1995) 'Burger bulldozer', *New Statesman and Society*, 24 March, 28; (1995) 'Big Mac's folly', *The Economist*, 1 July, 59; (1996) 'Macworld', *The Economist*, 29 June, 61–2; (1996) 'Developing a truly international brand and company', *International Journal of Physical Distribution and Logistics*, **26**(**7**), July, 19–21; Samuels, Gary (1996) 'Golden arches galore', *Forbes*, **158** (**11**), November, 46–48; Branch, Shelley (1996) 'McDonald's strikes out with grownups', *Fortune*, **134** (**9**), 11 November, 157–60; (1996) 'Broad, deep, long and heavy: assessing brands', *The Economist*, 16 November, 72–3; (1997) 'Johannesburgers and fries', *The Economist*, 27 September, 107–8; Willman, John (1998) 'Fast food spreads amid changing lifestyles', *Financial Times*, 27 March, 7; *see also* http://www.mcdonalds.com

21

Innovation: from ideas to customer benefits

Chapter objectives

When you have finished studying this chapter, you should be able to:

- explain and illustrate the differences between invention and innovation;

- recognise the risks involved in innovation and discuss how they can be coped with;

- show where the benefits of innovation arise and how they increase a firm's value;

- demonstrate how innovation applies to all aspects of a product;

- outline the innovation process; summarise the difficulties in managing it in the organisational context and suggest how they can be overcome;

- compare arguments for the source of innovation, whether it rests in the individual, the organisation or the environment.

Clockwork radio[1]

Trevor Baylis had had a career ranging from a film stunt man and circus escapologist to installer of swimming pools. The idea for a clockwork radio came to him in 1991 while watching a programme on the spread of AIDS in Africa. The cost of batteries in many cases meant that radio could not be used for community health education. After three months of spare time in his workshop, Baylis, coupling a hand drill to a motor, had made a dynamo power a small radio. Having shown that the idea would work, he set about building a prototype. Primary energy was stored in a steel spring, just like wind up toys. The spring drove, via a gearbox, a generator whose voltage was controlled by a diode.

Baylis was surprised that the system had not been invented before. Realising it might be used for all sorts of electrical devices, he applied for a patent, not for the clockwork radio, but for 'electrical generators'. With his idea protected, Baylis began to look for commercial partners. Rejection followed rejection. One suggested that a 75 kilogram mechanism would be needed to give four minutes running time! His break came after the idea was featured on the BBC television programme *Tomorrow's World*. One viewer catching the tail end of the Friday broadcast was Christopher Staines, an accountant with experience in acquisitions and mergers. He spent the night working out a business plan, faxing it to Baylis the following day. By Monday he had obtained the worldwide rights for development.

Baylis, an inventor and not a businessman, realised he had taken his idea as far as he could. Staines, with his business acumen and connections in South Africa, brought in Rory Steer who was to play a key role in commercialisation. Another interview, this time on a Johannesburg radio station, was heard by Hylton Appelbaum, of Liberty Life Group. This fund invests in worthy projects, especially if they involve disadvantaged groups. After several meetings among Appelbaum, Baylis, Staines and William Rowland, the president of Disabled People of South Africa, Liberty agreed to put up £750 000 for development. The United Kingdom Overseas Development Administration also provided £143 000 support. DPSA became a partner in the embryonic company.

Developing the prototype into a production model was not easy. It looked as if the components could not be made small enough. Then market research revealed that the radio must be big, heavy and loud! This realisation enabled the spring to be enlarged, the gearbox simplified and a reasonable playing time achieved.

Highlights of Baylis's first visit to South Africa were an emotional welcome at the new Baygen plant and a meeting with President Mandela. While he had invented several other devices for disabled people, this was Baylis's first commercial success. The achievement was enriched by the employment of both able and disabled people in manufacture.

The sales launch was in November 1995. Of robust construction, the Baygen Freeplay radio receives clearly on AM, FM and SW. Twenty seconds of winding offers 40 minutes of listening. It has won design awards and has been endorsed by more than 20 humanitarian aid organisations. Several of these buy it at the wholesale price of £19. The factory produces some 20 000 radios each month, insufficient to meet demand. Ironically, the widespread publicity made the radio very popular in the developed world. Not only does it have practical benefits for campers or yachting folk, but it has become an object of desire. It went on sale at Harrod's in London. A clockwork torch is also on the market. Talks have been held with toy manufacturers, such as the American Battelle, and Sony and Samsung, with their expertise in miniaturisation. A small radio was launched in 1998.

Introduction

Trevor Baylis's story relates experiences undergone by many inventors. He had an appealing idea that, as he admits, may have been had by many people before him. In his case, however, he had the determination and skill to make a prototype that worked. Then came the difficulty – commercialisation. Sceptical engineers and companies turned him down and it was only through perseverance and good fortune that the clockwork radio came to market. Although immediately successful, we cannot yet judge the long-term future for the Freeplay. Baygen has been unable to lower production cost to the levels he had hoped. This means that sales to collectors in the first world, where the radios retail at £80, are subsidising distribution to the original intended market. So far so good.

For another invention that also carries the 'Why didn't I think of that?' association and has clearly been a commercial success, we can go back to the 1960s and the development of the *Workmate*.

Ron Hickman was another inventor working independently of any manufacturing company. The *Workmate Mark I*, of 1968, was the culmination of years of spare-time effort. Like Baylis, Hickman approached manufacturers. His targets included Black & Decker, Burgess, Polycell, Record and Stanley. In spite of presentations at senior management level, the idea was rejected, usually because it had no potential. Having failed to license his invention, Hickman decided to produce the bench himself. With component manufacture subcontracted, a small team was recruited for assembly and despatch. By 1972, annual sales had reached 14 000, mainly through mail order. Meanwhile the inventor was developing the *Mark II*, a version with more features including variable heights and swivelling clamping pins. By this time, however, Black & Decker was interested. Hickman decided to license his patents and trade mark to the American company in return for a royalty of 3 per cent of sales revenue. The *Workmate's* product and brand have become well known in many parts of the world.[2]

While both examples describe the lone inventor seeing something that others could not, these stories illustrate many issues surrounding innovation in all organisations, whether small or large. Someone comes across an idea that may yield commercial (and social) benefits. That is often 'the easy bit'. From then on, gaining acceptance while working out ways of converting prototypes into production versions can be a battle. Some companies do this much better than most. Others barely try, preferring to buy inventions either from people such as Ron Hickman or by acquisition of innovative companies. We shall be assessing different approaches to the management of innovation throughout this chapter.

Our examples also give us clues about the sources of new ideas. Those for both the Freeplay and Workmate came from unexpected quarters. Neither Baylis nor Hickman had experience of manufacture or marketing of their inventions. They simply sensed that what they created would sell. It was a producer orientation. Companies that invest heavily in innovation do not work this way. They start with the market. Their approach is to spot opportunities and direct their efforts towards exploiting them continuously. This is where we will launch our investigation.

Innovation in context

We have argued that, because of rapid changes in the environments of most organisations they must change to survive. This includes changing the products that they offer to customers and the processes by which they supply them. For most, standing still is not viable. They must innovate, that is bring new offerings to the market. Innovation is not the same as invention, which refers to the creation of an original idea.

■ Inventions are ideas that may or may not develop into new products or processes that best satisfy the needs of customers. They are the fruit of creativity, which was discussed in Chapter 11.

■ Innovations are ideas that are developed into new products or processes. They result in changes that customers recognise as new.

The relationship between the two is shown in Fig. 21.1. Inventions frequently trigger the innovation process although not necessarily. Innovation activity may originate in other ways. For example, managers could spot a market opportunity that they do not have the capacity to fulfil. This begins a focused search for new products or processes. Alternatively, managers might identify a problem requiring

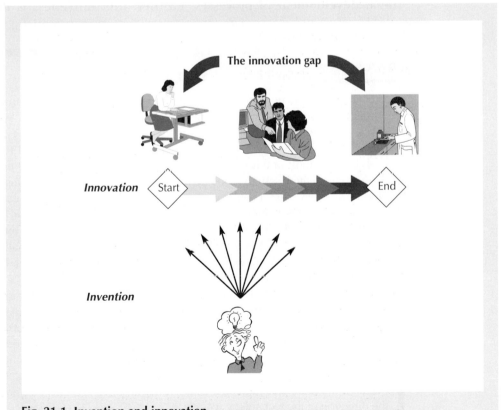

Fig. 21.1 Invention and innovation

a product redesign or process enhancement. Clearly, fresh ideas are needed not only at the start but at all phases of innovation. Therefore, we can see creative thinking, or inventiveness, as illuminating the whole cycle.

The transformation of ideas into new products is uncertain. Two problems arise for the manager, risk and lag. The risk involved in backing an invention arises from failure along the way. While estimates vary, perhaps only one in five product ideas becomes technically viable. Of these, fewer than one in 20 become market successes. Hence the odds against winning are worse than 100:1! The second problem is the lag between invention and innovation. This is known as the *innovation gap*. The television, zip fastener and heart pacemaker all took more than 20 years from invention to commercial exploitation. On the other hand, the ball point pen and videocassette recorder came out in a sprightly six years.[3] Clearly, a better understanding of the innovation process will assist management to both shorten the innovation gap and reduce the risks of failed investments. Hasselblad might have avoided an expensive failure through a more cautious appreciation of these questions, as explained in Exhibit 21.1.[4]

Products and processes

It is worth noting that the above definitions refer both to products and processes. Although the test of innovativeness must ultimately lie in the number and value of new products brought to market, organisations must back them up with a continual development of processes. Further, innovativeness is not confined to

---

Exhibit 21.1 | **Hasselblad: tiny snapper in the digital pond**

Hasselblad is a name respected by both photography professionals and astronauts for its medium-format, 6 × 6 cm, cameras. With sales of 1700 million Swedish crowns (£130 million), it has about a fifth of the world market of 65 000 units. The company spends 10 per cent of turnover on research and development. In the 1990s, Hasselblad was devoting most of this effort to digital technology. Early work was encouraging. An image management system found application in transmitting and storing images for the world's press. In 1993, company president Stefan Junel decided to create a digital version of its famous camera. Yet, by 1996, the company had given up. The image management system was sold. Technologist Junel was replaced by marketing expert Goran Bernhoff brought in from OKB, a Swedish glass company. Finally, Hasselblad's owners, part of the Wallenberg family empire, sold the business to a buyout consortium of banks and company managers.

Why the withdrawal? The new owners wanted more profit at lower risk. They were looking towards a flotation on the Stockholm stock exchange. Advisers Andersen Consulting warned that good, cheap, digital photography was further away than Hasselblad had imagined. Major players, such as Kodak, were spending heavily on research. Anyway, Kodak used Hasselblad bodies as platforms for their technology. Hasselblad's own £5 million budget was miniscule in comparison. The company's declared intention was to keep a close watch on developments and only return when the direction of the technology was clear.

operations management. It can be applied throughout all aspects of the value chain. For instance, many product ideas fail because it proves impossible to supply them with consistent quality. It was only when the Baygen team realised that the market preferred big radios that it abandoned the frustrating search for ways of making an efficient miniature clockwork generator.

Inventors and innovators

The examples of Baylis and Hickman also illustrate that the roles of inventor and innovator are different. They require different skills. For an inventor, the key aptitude is creativity. This means recognising and applying some of the 5000 original thoughts each of us has every day. The innovator possesses a wider range of entrepreneurial and managerial skills. These include planning, persuading investors and others, leading a team and pressing on in spite of opposition.

Within organisations, this is the intrapreneur described in Chapter 8. As we saw, Trevor Baylis lacked some important skills needed to bring his radio to market. These were provided by Staines and others. Ron Hickman, on the other hand, found he had to undertake the whole innovation process before a major company would believe in his invention.

Innovative cultures

The risks intrinsic to innovations mean that successful firms engage in a variety of them. Not only do these affect diverse products and processes but they each involve a different degree of change. On the one hand, continuous improvement implies a series of incremental steps while, on the other, radical change is exemplified by the adoption of new product or process technologies. Although we might imagine that organisations choose between one and the other, studies have found that firms undertake both or neither. Kanter showed how the capacity to innovate is related to organisational culture.[5] Further, change-orientated firms tend to have more programmes, from training and team working to quality circles and brainstorming, designed to encourage and back their staff in innovation. Therefore, innovation is not a process undertaken intermittently or in one or two areas of the organisation. If the culture is supportive, it is likely to be widespread.

■ Societal benefits

Innovation in products and the processes that supply them is a large element of our rising standard of living. It may seem odd, but official indicators do not show this. The modern television, with its digital sound, teletext and remote control, is barely comparable with one of a generation ago. Clothes are more resistant to losing their colour and need less ironing. Telephones are clearer, faster and carry more services. All these, and many more, make us better off. Yet by how much? To calculate this effect, Hausman proposed the idea of a 'virtual price'. This is what the customer would have been prepared to pay had the innovation occurred at some time earlier. Take mobile telephones, for example. Since they are very different from conventional telephones, comparing their prices with those of their predecessors gives a false picture of changes over, say, 20 years. And since their use is widespread, the effect is significant. To estimate it, one should compare cellular telephone prices with the virtual price that people would have paid had they been available 20 years ago. Hausman estimated that, in 1996, the mobile telephone alone had improved Americans' welfare by an unmeasured 0.3 to 0.6 per cent.[6]

Although broad estimates, the figures support what we already know. If our incomes were to stabilise so that we could only buy the same quantity of goods each year, we would steadily become better off. This is because products are more reliable, are of better quality and include features that previous products did not. This change is a representation of the real value of innovation and is one indication of why people will pay more for it. It can even happen to a traditional product such as corned beef, *see* Exhibit 21.2.[7]

What is a product?

New varieties of corned beef will bring extra profits only if they are accepted in the marketplace. This should make us question what Princes Foods is selling and how the new flavours and packs improve the offer to customers. What is innovation in marketing terms? To answer this question, we must look more closely at the nature of a product. Kotler and colleagues explain that designers and planners think of products on three levels, shown in Fig. 21.2:[8]

■ The *core product* is what the customer is really buying. It describes the fundamental benefits expected by the customer. Note that benefits are what counts. A person buys cleaner clothes, labour saving and convenience, not a washing machine.

■ The *actual product* is the set of features that, in rival products, are combined to provide the core benefit in different ways. Possibilities include quality, features, styling, packaging and branding, although their importance will differ according to the application. A washing machine may feature programme flexibility, drum capacity, easy loading, and energy saving; its styling may suggest convenience,

---

Exhibit 21.2 **Innovation for a corny product**

Corned beef accounts for about a third of canned meat sold in the United Kingdom. Sales, worth about £80 million, had been declining for many years. It was seen by producers and distributors as a traditional product. Consumers were dominated by sandwich eaters, mostly men between 40 and 65.

Market leader Princes Foods, a subsidiary of Mitsubishi, planned to arrest the fall, whose annual rate had reached 6 per cent. In its first market research for years, the company found enthusiasm for new flavours. In 1997, to appeal to the sandwich group, it launched 200g cans with onion, mustard and sweet pickle. Other line extensions were 'finest corned beef' and a low-fat, low-salt version. Finally, a larger 340g spicy variety was for hot dishes. The increased range was expected to correct the 'underfacing' (lack of allocated shelf length in self-service stores) compared with other canned meats. With premium prices backed by an advertising campaign, the innovation was expected to increase sales by at least 25 per cent within two years.

safety and reliability while fitting into the modern kitchen; and different brands have varying quality reputations. Apart from ensuring security of delivery, packaging may have little significance.

■ The *augmented product* comprises the set of extra benefits and services that give a product an edge in the marketplace. These may include delivery, installation and set-up, warranties and after-sales support. Sales of leading washing machines are supported by national networks for maintenance and repair.

A product, therefore, is more than the set of features described in its physical form, or, for a service, an outline of the process. From a free installation kit and box of *Superwash* to a friendly follow-up call from the distributor, the augmentation can be as important as the basic good or service. In marketing terms, innovation can refer to the improvement or complete redesign of any aspect of the whole product. Examples in the augmented product zone range from extended warranties to a free maintenance visit after 12 months.

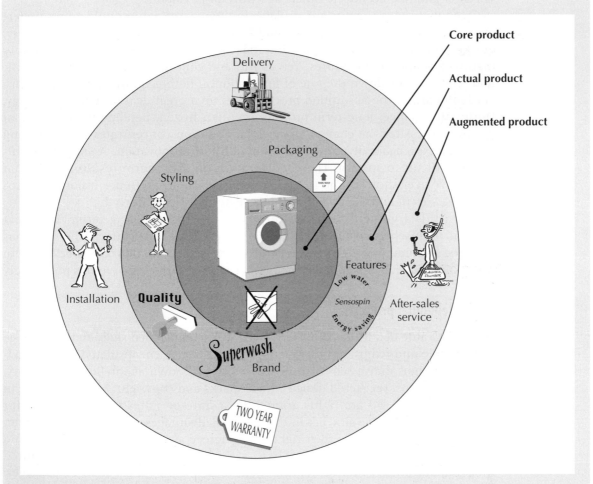

Fig. 21.2 Elements of the core, actual and augmented product

▬ The market for invention and innovation

We have seen how innovation benefits society in general and customers in particular. Through the latter, who are prepared to pay more for new and improved products, innovative firms can become more profitable. Here we should note that all firms innovate to some extent, for if they do not change at all they are doomed. Those we call innovative, however, change more than most and change in the right direction. If innovation does create real value for society, customers and firms, we would expect this benefit to be evaluated in some way. There are two approaches, to value the firm and to value the innovations themselves. First, when businesses are bought and sold on the market, those with a good innovation record command higher prices. These represent how much the knowledge embedded in the business is worth. Being able to innovate is a competence that some firms are known for. Second, included in the worth of the business are its assets of intellectual property. These assets are created through the registration of inventions, designs and names. Firms are granted exclusive rights to use or dispose of the assets, including the possibility of granting licences to others in return for payment.

Given that rights to ideas are available in the market, why should a firm undertake research and development itself? Frequently, acquisition may be cheaper, quicker and more profitable than internal innovation. There is greater certainty than with brand new ventures. Yet, as Hitt and colleagues[9] have shown, acquisition tends to slow down the rate of innovation in both acquiring and target firms. For both parties, the absorption process takes up a great deal of time and energy. During the change, long-term projects are often frozen, pending the outcome of negotiations. After the change, managerial attention concentrates on integrating the businesses, again diverting their attention from innovation. A supportive culture is difficult to sustain. The concentration on short-term results means that firms have ever shorter time to achieve adequate returns. Hence innovation programmes are cut and the policy to acquire externally is reinforced.

Given this argument, it is not surprising that, in the long term, firms that commit themselves to internal innovation do better. An alternative that has emerged in some industries in recent decades is to form alliances specifically to share knowledge. Innovation becomes external. We shall return to this point later.

▬ Intellectual property

While the value of a firm is often enhanced by the embedded skills and knowledge of its people and teams, cumulative innovation is also encapsulated in the products and designs that it sells or uses. These assets, known as intellectual property, comprise patents, registered designs, trade marks and copyright. While differing in their application, all are rights granted by a state or states to exploit ideas for defined periods. Their value lies in the business advantages which flow from them. Prudent owners announce their rights using agreed symbols, such as ®, ©, ™ and ℠, and corresponding notices. These are not strictly needed in the United Kingdom but other countries require them to be placed on products or packages. Breaches of protection are civil wrongs for which the owner must seek remedy.

Leading companies defend their rights vigorously, *see* Exhibit 21.3.[10] Smaller companies, facing risky and expensive court proceedings, are often advised to grant licences in exchange for royalties. Some details of the types of protection are given in Exhibit 21.4, while Exhibit 21.5 shows some examples.[11] International treaties mean that United Kingdom practice broadly matches most other countries.

Exhibit 21.3 Intel inside

Intel, the microchip maker, has spent over $100 million suing any company threatening its intellectual property rights. These underpin Intel's dominant position, from which it receives more than 20 per cent of the price of every personal computer.

Exhibit 21.4 Ways to protect intellectual property: United Kingdom

Patents

A successful patent application must satisfy three conditions: it must be new, that is its details must not have appeared in public anywhere in the world; it must not be obvious in the light of previous inventions; and it must have a practical application. If approved, the state grants the right to prevent anyone copying for up to 20 years. In return, the Patent Office publishes details, usually 18 months after the application. Application costs about £225; the subsidy that keeps this figure low is recovered by annual renewal fees.

One difficulty for an applicant is to know if the invention is really new. The Patent Office runs a search service to check this. It estimates that £22.5 billion is wasted annually by duplicate research in Europe alone. Eighty per cent of the world's technical information is to be found in patents.

Designs

Any product with an original shape or configuration gets the automatic protection of design right. The right lasts for 10 years from the date the product first goes on sale, or 15 years from the date of creation, whichever ends the sooner. Design rights come into existence at the moment of creation and are useful in that they do not have to be registered. Better protection is afforded by formal registration through the Patent Office. In registered designs, surface patterns and decoration can be included, besides shape and configuration. To qualify, the design must be new and have significant eye appeal.

Copyright

Copyright applies to materials such as books, plays, music, dance, works of art, photographs, diagrams and computer programs. The right extends to 70 years after the author's death. An agreement between the Society of Authors and the Publishers Association allows for short extracts to be quoted, with acknowledgement, from books or articles under the principle of 'fair dealing'. Music, songs and pictures are not covered by this dispensation.

►

Exhibit 21.4 *(continued)*

Trade marks

A trade mark is any sign that can identify the products of one business from those of another. The 1994 Trade Mark Act extended the scope of a mark from words and devices to three-dimensional shapes, sounds and smells. Advertising jingles and theme tunes could be covered, for example. The world's oldest trade mark, number 1, has been held by Bass the brewers since 1876.

International protection

Globalisation of trade increases the importance of protecting intellectual property in many countries. Treaties and other agreements help with this process. For instance, a United Kingdom patent only applies within the UK. The European Patent Convention covers all EU countries and several others. The Community Trade Mark, CTM, was started in 1996 to cover the whole European Union with one registration. More widely, the Patent Cooperation Treaty has more than 100 signatories. Using these international systems, although expensive, is cheaper than making separate applications in each country.

Exhibit 21.5 **Protective action at the United Kingdom Patent Office**

In 1996, the leading companies to be granted UK patents were Ford (105), Mercedes (100), Daimler-Benz (95) and Honda (91). Telecommunications was the busiest sector with 8 per cent of the 11 000 applications.

Design registrations in the vehicle sector, at 346, are low. Manufacturers can register the shape of a whole vehicle but not individual parts. This rule allows others to manufacture spare parts provided they are not protected by other rights such as patents or trade marks.

Unilever, with 231, was the company registering most trade marks. Since early 1996, the Patent Office has permitted individuals to register their own names as trade marks, provided they are distinctive enough. Alan Shearer, the international footballer, registered his name in the category of clothing, including boots, shoes and slippers. Anyone seeking to use it must negotiate a licence.

Registration of trade marks in insurance and financial services more than doubled in the years 1994–6. First, there was a speedy growth of telephone services such as Direct Line and First Direct, each of which sought a distinctive brand name. Second, the entry of retailers such as Marks & Spencer, Tesco and Virgin pushed the established companies to re-examine their brands. Too many had relied on a narrow thesaurus of words such as mutual, permanent, provident, life and Scottish.

The innovation process

To examine the innovation process we shall take a narrower definition than one that covers all changes that might improve customer satisfaction. After all, process improvements in some elements of the value chain, while bringing benefits to the firm, will have only an indirect effect on customer satisfaction. Examples are reducing costs of computing through better maintenance practices or finding new suppliers for general materials. Here, however, we shall concentrate on one aspect, namely product development.

In service industries, product and process are often indistinguishable. In many cases of personal service, the product is the process. What is often not appreciated is the closeness of the two in manufacturing. Not so long ago, it was typical for product designers to work out their ideas and then pass the results 'over the wall' to the process engineers in the factory. The latter would have to work out ways to make the designs. Modern ideas of parallel engineering and manufacturability recognised the waste that this behaviour causes. With rising concern for the environment, the question of disassembly and recycling has also emerged as an issue.

The product development process for a manufactured item is outlined in Fig. 21.3. We can see that this is closely related to the rational decision-making process of Fig. 11.4. There are three main connections. First, the developers need an aim. This is expressed in an agreed brief. When the development or design is being carried out by a contractor, such as an architect or design consultant, the brief forms the contract between the parties. Second, the innovation proceeds by a mixture of creating alternative ideas and comparing them with the brief. In the end, several 'good ideas' are taken forward for selection and testing. Third, selection is made from several alternatives. This is where differences compared with the decision process arise. Selection and testing face more uncertainty in development. Sometimes selection from a short list may be carried out by the client. For example, an architect would present several alternatives, each of which satisfies the original brief, and ask the client to make a judgement. On the other hand, for goods to be manufactured in large volumes over a long period, a series of prototypes will be made. They will be used to assess manufacturability and may help with test marketing.

With consumer goods, test marketing usually requires full-scale operations in a controlled market for several months, if not years. Although expensive, test marketing yields benefits if mistakes are avoided. Yet there are two further drawbacks other than cost. The first is that they do not show up well in hindsight. If the product is eventually successful, the time devoted to the test represents loss of revenues that could have been earned with an earlier full-scale launch. On the other hand, if the test points to failure, the development money appears to have been wasted. Worst of all are erroneous test results. Positive test results may not be borne out by eventual performance. Then marketing managers will be looking for new jobs. False negative results, on the other hand, would mean cancellation of what would have been a viable product. Then, no one will know

The second drawback is the way tests reveal information to rivals. Kotler and colleagues note the case of Carnation *Coffee-Mate*, which was test marketed over a period of six years prior to its United Kingdom launch. This gave ample time to

> Manufacturability refers to a design's ability to consistently and profitably meet specifications. These include performance, reliability, availability and quality.

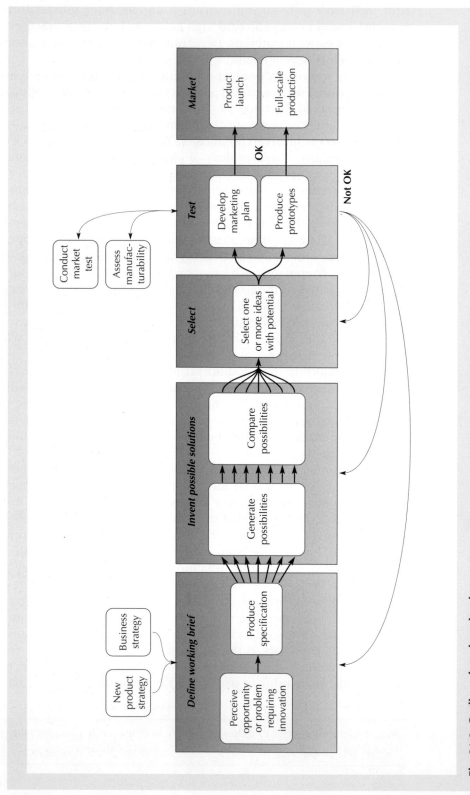

Fig. 21.3 Outline of product development process

Cadbury to develop and launch its own product, *Marvel*.[12] To counter such difficulties, firms may test products in remote markets, or only try out some aspects of them such as tastes or other ingredients. They try to disguise their intentions.

Alongside many other examples, manufacturability is a problem in confectionary. Many chocolate bars can be made in the laboratory but producing and distributing them to consistent quality is more difficult. The test market, therefore, confirms that industrial-scale production is possible. Cadbury's *Astros* were launched in Europe in 1997 to compete with *Smarties* (Nestlé) and *M&Ms* (Mars). The product was to be for 'mindless munching' among the teenage market. Under the name *Asteroids*, the product was already sold in South Africa. *Astros* followed closely on the heels of *Fuse*, *see* Exhibit 21.6.[13]

■ Is inventiveness necessary?

History has seen the remarkable contributions, not only of those we have featured here but of many other inventors. It may, therefore, seem odd to ask whether inventiveness is needed to kick start the innovation process. Some assert that it is not. Creative solutions can be found systematically rather than waiting around for flashes of inspiration. Going further, they would argue that inventiveness is constrained by our paradigms acting as psychological barriers to seeing the new.

A remarkable contribution came from the USSR. From 1946, Genrich Altshuller worked in the patent department of the Soviet navy. Although he had been

---

Exhibit 21.6 **Chocolate makers' pro*fuse*ness**

After its launch in September 1996, Cadbury's *Fuse* went to the top of the charts for non-moulded chocolate bars. In a few weeks, it settled into joint second place alongside *Mars* and behind *Kit-Kat.* Chocolate consumption in the United Kingdom, at 8 kg per head, is second only to Switzerland. Many teenagers eat three to four bars daily. The market is large yet crowded, ever changing and gradually stagnating. The big three, Cadbury, Nestlé and Mars, have 75 per cent of sales by value.

Like its rivals, Cadbury is always looking for new brands. Only 1 in 100 formulations reaches the market. The brief for *Fuse* targeted the 16–34 age group. It specified a product that sounded healthy and substantial, was snappy rather than soft and cloying, and could be eaten as a snack in the car without provoking a dry cleaning bill. Development took five years during which 250 ingredients were tried. Flavours from cherry and almonds to coconut and pineapple were rejected because they provoke strong love or hate responses. For the mass market, testing showed the most popular ingredients to be chocolate, caramel, raisins and peanuts with a wafer biscuit. Caramel was too sticky so fudge was selected. The other items, used sparingly, hint at wholesomeness without interfering with the dominant chocolate flavour.

Development and launch cost £11 million, half of which was spent on a new production plant. The product was so successful that this investment was recouped in three months. This is the quickest return since *Wispa* in the early 1980s. Meanwhile, Mars, whose bar was launched in 1932, began a £9 million advertising campaign to fight back.

exposed to methods, such as brainstorming, intended to overcome psychological barriers, he considered that these did not contribute to understanding the innovation process. While little was known about the process, he realised that its *results* could readily be observed in the files of the patent office. Therefore, they must be susceptible to analysis from a technological point of view. Through classifying solutions according to how far they departed from current ways of doing things, Altshuller discovered that 90 per cent of patents were for solutions within current paradigms. Put another way, more than 90 per cent of problems faced by engineers had already been encountered and solved in analogous form. For instance, the problems of cleaning filters, stripping sunflower seed shells and splitting diamonds along minute cracks are related and can be approached using similar methods.

Altshuller and colleagues examined 1.2 million patents of which 40 000 were studied in detail. This work led to the method of Inventive Problem Solving, known by its Russian acronym, TRIZ. It has been applied to problems as varied as product development, service provision and manufacturing. For most unresolved questions in such areas, a solution is already available. TRIZ provides a systematic way of finding it. For instance, one branch shows how to cope with contradictions, the problem of making one aspect of a product or process better at the expense of another. Exhibit 21.7 gives an example of a razor. TRIZ generalises from this to show how conflicting functions in many areas can be separated spatially or sequentially.[14]

Developed under the Soviet system, procedures such as TRIZ do not stand out as exemplars to be followed. Yet their failure may be blamed more on inappropriate and inconsistent objectives than on basic technical principles. Similar activities are to be found in many companies, which scour patent applications for evidence of rivals' intentions. This is why some avoid early publication unless they fear that a competitor is close to the same invention. As mentioned in the closing case, Hitachi follows this line.

Managing innovation

We must be careful not to interpret Fig. 21.3 as a regular set of steps from an initial idea to a saleable product. In practice, innovation proceeds neither in a straight line nor so smoothly. Stages run into each other and there are many opportunities for iteration and feedback as choices are seen to founder when tested against the criteria of market acceptance or manufacturability. A further problem appears when we recognise that the development work usually involves teams composed of specialists drawn from different departments. We covered the ways in which teams can be

Exhibit 21.7 Cutting the compromise

To be as effective as possible at cutting hair, a razor needs to be as sharp as possible. The more finely honed it is, however, the greater the risk of cutting skin. In the days of unguarded 'cut-throat' razors, this problem was resolved by compromise, making the blade reasonably sharp but not excessively so. The modern method is to spatially separate the two functions – cutting and guarding so that each can be done as well as possible.

organised in Chapters 12 and 13. Some form of matrix structure is common in project-orientated organisations. Not only must teams be formed in this way, their composition varies as the process moves through its various phases. The interaction between the innovation process and the organisation structure is, therefore, dynamic. Figure 21.4 shows what might happen to one project as it is developed from its starting point to the product launch. Here, the organisation has followed common practice in separating the functions of Basic Research from Development. The project flows between departments, often with two or three working on it simultaneously. It is to be expected, therefore, that the innovation needs to be integrated. The person responsible is often called a product or project manager.

In spite of the apparent gains to be had from closer integration, especially of development with both marketing and production, many organisations face problems with achieving it. Aaby and Discenza point to two fundamental reasons behind this:[15]

■ Many managers have little understanding of technology (often the development and production functions). This means they do not know how to fit it into the organisation, how technologies fit together and, therefore, how they relate to marketing.

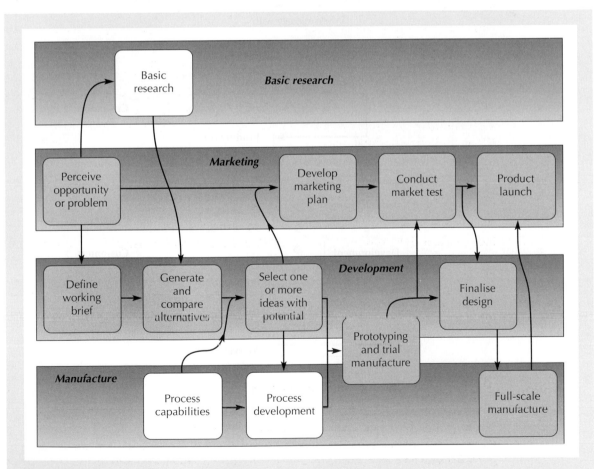

Fig. 21.4 Product development involving several organisational functions

■ Many barriers stand between marketing and technology management. For example, managers will have different educational backgrounds and the functions will be organised in different and exclusive ways.

Therefore, finding organisations where the production and development functions are close is common, as in chart 1 of Fig. 21.5. Separated by an organisational barrier, the marketing department makes limited contributions. It supplies market research data on customer wants and informs on the results of any test marketing. Shifting design and development closer to marketing, *see* chart 2, runs the risk of

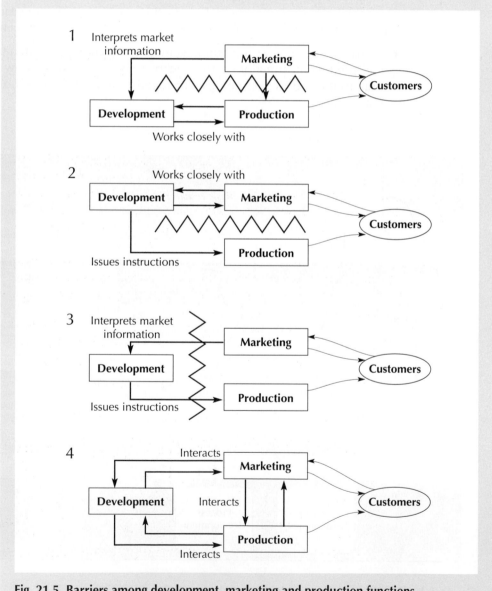

Fig. 21.5 Barriers among development, marketing and production functions

them creating designs without full consideration of manufacturability. Matters can be worse. In chart 3, fears of premature leakage of development plans to rivals mean that development work is carried on in secrecy. Chart 4 suggests a balance. This underlines the need for integrated work teams.

This example of the marketing–production–development triangle is but one of many instances of blockages to innovation in organisations. How is it that some firms are more successful than others? Many studies have looked for factors to explain this question. Drawing on the work of Slappendel,[16] we can classify these into three levels:

- The *individualist* perspective sees people as the main source of change in organisations.

- The *organisational* perspective assumes that innovation is largely determined by the characteristics of the organisation itself. Explanations cover the influences of structure and rules to the shared values and attitudes of members.

- The *environmental* perspective suggests that innovation arises in, or is stimulated by, the environment.

Individuals as sources of change

Work on the individualist perspective was exemplified by the 'What makes an entrepreneur?' question of Chapter 8. This approach looks for traits, which are personal qualities that result in someone being predisposed to certain behaviour. Here it is innovation. Slappendel points out, however, that while looking for traits has some validity when trying to understand the behaviour of a person acting independently, weaknesses show up when individuals within organisations are considered. Success comes from both inventors and those who can push change through and round the barriers that all organisations seem to build. Chapter 8 noted Pinchot's study showing that developments follow from having innovators, product champions and sponsors.

Instead of the hierarchical approach of Pinchot, Chaharbaghi and Newman[17] present three roles needed at different phases of the innovation process. They match the phases of Lewin's change model. They are shown in Fig. 21.6, which has been adapted from Fig. 14.8.

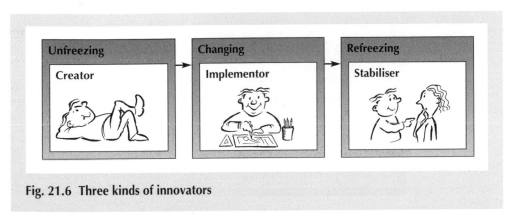

Fig. 21.6 Three kinds of innovators

■ *Innovating creators* are involved in invention. They envisage what could be; they make new connections and see new patterns; they test and develop the new logic of what they invent. While creators are important, only a few are present in most organisations.

■ *Innovating implementors* manage the change. They apply creativity to making the invention work in the organisational context. There are usually more implementors than creators but they are still in the minority.

■ *Innovating stabilisers* refreeze the organisation into a stable system after the change has been brought in. These are the people who produce the new product, start the new personnel policy or consolidate the presence in a new market. Stabilisers account for most of the people in the organisation.

As usual with models, Chaharbaghi and Newman point out that the three roles are stereotypes and people can display mixed characteristics. Their advantage is that they enable organisations to recognise the balance needed to bring about innovation. Lacking an appropriate blend, innovations may never be sparked, be snuffed out, or simply fade away. We should note also that innovation involves every person in the organisation.

Selecting individuals

With organisations giving priority to innovation, they must consider how they can achieve a balance among the three roles identified above. They might look to selection. Fletcher evaluates how the methods normally used in personnel selection may be applied to the search for innovating creators.[18] These are shown in Exhibit 21.8.

All methods have weaknesses. Using biographical data, whether collected in advance or elicited at an interview, assumes that the past is a guide to the future. Yet whether people have shown innovative capability will not solely depend on their personal traits. In prior roles, they may have lacked either opportunity or motivation. The third approach, presenting candidates with unusual situations, has come into vogue in recent years. Yet it may be as much a test of lucidity or leadership as inventiveness. 'Not building Lego towers again!' some candidates may groan. The fourth method, psychometric testing, is attractive in principle. Yet, to be effective, tests must be extensively tested to check whether their predictions

Exhibit 21.8 **Searching for innovating creators**

■ Study biographical data, from application forms and references.

■ Ask interviewees to describe whether and how they have changed things, or produced new ideas, in the past.

■ Present candidates with unusual situations and ask them to respond rapidly.

■ Apply psychometric tests, such as *KAI*. This one separates adaptors, who work within a current paradigm, from innovators, who try to break out of it.

are accurate. Since innovativeness is such a difficult characteristic to observe and measure, it is doubtful whether such calibration is possible. Fletcher concludes that selecting for innovation is very difficult. In any case, selection is merely one step in development. Innovativeness must be nurtured and encouraged and the organisation must take risks for it to flourish.

■ Organisations as the incubators of change

The organisational perspective looks to characteristics such as size, strategy, structure, systems and technology as determinants of innovation. Slappendel reminds us of the dangers of taking such an approach too far. We must not fall into the trap of treating the organisation as if it had a reality independent of the people within it. This makes it unwise to argue that such-and-such a characteristic is the cause of low or high innovation. On the other hand, some studies have found links. We shall pick out two examples, size and complexity.

Size

It is often assumed that large organisations find it difficult to sustain innovation. This is not always the case as some have recently become large because of their innovative success. These will, therefore, still carry the memory of how to innovate and retain managers who are prepared to take risks. Microsoft and other large information companies are good examples. Dougherty and Hardy, however, argue that it is the large, mature organisations that have difficulty.[19] Their explanation is as follows.

While resources in these organisations undoubtedly exist, they tend to be spread in a piecemeal fashion. They depend on implementors to take ideas and show how they can work. Those who achieve this, predominantly operational and middle level managers, do so through their personal networks and experience. Within large organisations, these powers are relatively ineffective and are easily thwarted by changes in senior management personnel and policy. Dougherty and Hardy, therefore, point to the conservative power structures of large organisations to explain why they can be so sluggish.

Complexity

Although complexity can be defined in many ways, we shall use the term to refer to the degree of structural differentiation that arises from the number and variety of tasks to be carried out. This is in line with the approach of Lawrence and Lorsch discussed in Chapter 13.[20] An organisation facing such complexity will need a range of specialists devoted to the various tasks. Through external contacts, these people are likely to bring in new ideas. Beyond this, the variety of experience and attitudes will itself foster the take-up of innovation. According to this argument, more complexity stimulates more innovation.

A counter-argument arises from the way complexity can lead to conflict. While many new ideas are introduced, an atmosphere of conflict will make adoption of change unlikely. In addition, the organisation may not have learnt from the second part of the Lawrence and Lorsch study: organisations that are more differentiated must ensure matching integration. As we saw earlier in the chapter, the number of functions involved in the introduction of new products and processes places a premium on effective co-ordination.

Fiol argues that contradiction can be a mixed blessing.[21] She suggests that effective management of innovation requires contradictions to be kept in balance and interlocked during the change process. Simply stimulating conflictive interactions, however, will not lead to collective creativity. Without balance, one of two simple yet unsatisfactory outcomes may occur. There is either a complete breakdown in communications or one party achieves dominance over the rest.

Best practice

Differences among firms in the same industry suggest that organisational factors play a strong part in effective innovation. Krause and Liu conducted a detailed benchmarking study among 15 large international companies in the chemical, pharmaceutical and telecommunications industries. They pinpointed 13 best practices which are summarised in Exhibit 21.9.[22]

Exhibit 21.9 **Best practices in R&D innovation**

■ Strategy formulation and communication
  - Clear strategies well communicated to R&D organisation
  - Formal techniques used to identify core technologies

■ Funding and investments
  - R&D investments made from multinational perspective
  - Basic research funded from corporate level; development funded by business units

■ Organisational and cultural issues
  - Basic research at small number of centralised, specialised facilities; development activity decentralised, close to business units
  - Cross-functional teams for both basic and applied research projects
  - Formal mechanisms for interaction both among R&D staff and between them and others

■ Performance evaluation
  - Analytical tools used for project selection and monitoring
  - Most important measure is the rate of transfer of technology from R&D to business units

■ Personnel development
  - All levels in the R&D organisation have effective career development
  - Graduate recruits come from diverse universities and from other companies when needed

■ Cooperative links
  - Some basic research is carried out internally but there are many outside links
  - External links are formally monitored.

It is worth expanding on some details of this study, not just for what they show about innovation, but also because they confirm important points about the selection and management of all work teams. Teamwork styles differentiated the most successful companies from the rest. They recognised the need for business unit participation in development. Whereas basic research teams had technical leaders, development teams were jointly managed by technical and business leaders. Teams were selected formally to achieve a balance of members' technical and group skills. This contrasts with the less successful companies. Here, although there was much collaboration, it was informal. Scientists tended to do most research alone, supported by technicians. People from marketing or manufacturing were only involved late in the process.

Personnel policies varied. Best practice paid attention to career development and recruitment from a variety of sources. Relying on recruitment from a few favoured university departments, a habit among several less effective companies, led to several difficulties. Opportunities to interview exceptional candidates from elsewhere were not taken. Furthermore, using a few sources limited the diversity of candidates and restricted the vital global perspective.

The way funding is managed gives important signals to staff about the way they should act. The fourth point shows that long-term R&D is best funded from the centre while resources for development come from business units. The highly performing companies recognise the tensions between risky, long-term investments in basic science and short-term returns from development. The burden of the former, seeking to develop core technologies, should not fall on individual divisions. Development, on the other hand, needs to be tied in closely to the programme of the division that benefits from it. Resolution of this tension is also seen in the fifth point, where the physical location of the research facility matches its basic or applied purpose.

The environment as the source of change

The third of our perspectives examines the extent to which innovation arises in the environment. The origins of this point of view lie in ideas either that some nations or cultures are more creative than others or other environmental factors are at work. Let us look at some examples.

East versus West

It is often argued that competition in the future will be based on the ability to create and use knowledge. As we shall see in Chapter 22, the growth of 'knowledge management' experts shows a recognition of its economic value. Yet knowledge in the conventional sense of assembling large quantities of data, the style of Western business, may not be what is required. Intuitive, or tacit, knowledge, nurtured in Japanese companies, may be more important. Tacit knowledge refers to the learning that is embedded in teams. These are the collective rules-of-thumb, hunches and skills passed on from trainer to apprentice, team leader to new starter, or middle manager to graduate trainee. Japanese firms, with national traditions of life-long employment, respect for seniority and collective ideals, may be much better at creating, sharing and maintaining such knowledge than Western organisations.

Does reliance on tacit knowledge make organisations more creative? Nonaka and Takeuchi argue that this is the case and propose that all firms can learn from the Japanese experience. Yet relying less on explicit data may not serve Japanese firms well, especially as they move outside their national base where tacit knowledge is more relevant. The Honda *City*, a car regarded as a major innovation for the 1980s and 1990s, incorporated much intuition but not enough market research. Global sales averaged 40 000 and the model was withdrawn in 1994 after they had fallen to just 3800.[23]

Variations among nations

Arguing that competitive advantage ultimately depends on innovation, Porter identified four factors that appeared to account for different rates in different countries.[24] As shown in Fig. 3.5, these are:

■ *Factor availability*
Beyond the widely recognised needs for raw materials, workers and infrastructure, Porter notes the importance of scarce, specialised resources. Successful firms and nations will devise means of responding to these shortages. For instance, the United States has long been committed to automation to overcome the effects of high labour costs. The same is seen in Japan where there is also a habit of space saving. It is no surprise that the company with the highest reputation for miniaturisation of consumer electronics is Japanese, namely Sony.

■ *Home market*
Porter argues that the scale of the home market is less important than the sophistication of customers. Pressure for improvement from knowledgeable customers is an important force for innovation. This creates a virtuous circle. Restaurants in Belgium and France, for example, are good because their customers know what a good restaurant is. And, as the standard rises, so does the expectation.

■ *Support industries*
Clusters of support industries stimulate innovation because of the flows of information and people among the firms. Best known in modern times is Silicon Valley where many famous innovating companies stand within walking distance of each other. Globalisation, however, means that clusters need not be as physically close as the leather industry in Italy or ceramics in The Potteries of England. An example of a global industrial network, biotechnology, is given in Fig. 21.7 and discussed below.

■ *Rivalry*
Porter stresses the advantage of competition in stimulating investment, cost reduction and all-round improvement. This is partly because weak firms fail but mainly because none has protection against strong local competition. This acts as a permanent stimulus to innovate.

When experienced in combination, these features make for a very competitive environment. The advantage to the firms involved is that their management skills are sharpened. In the global business environment, they achieve an advantageous position over rivals operating in less stimulating circumstances. It is worth comparing this framework with Porter's earlier work on competitive advantage which suggested firms were better off isolating themselves from the full rigours of competition. Building barriers to industry entry or retreating into niches were favoured recommendations. The later argument represents a switch from products and locations to knowledge and innovation as key factors.

A good illustration of the stimulating effect of competition was provided by Bertschek.[25] She examined the effects of imports and incoming foreign direct investment (FDI) on the innovation of firms in Germany in the mid-1980s. With falling trade barriers, most industrial sectors were facing greater competition from imports and FDI. Consequently, domestic firms had to become more efficient, using innovation as an important route. Bertschek showed that both product and process innovation were related to the rising competition.

Global networks

Studying clusters or networks of firms on a national basis may be shortsighted. This is especially true of industries where knowledge is a critical resource and the major firms operate on a global scale with few economic barriers. Powell and colleagues argue that the biotechnology industry is like this. It has a global, expanding and complex knowledge base. Risk is high and many firms spend more than 25 per cent of sales revenue on research. In this field, 'the locus of innovation is found within the networks of interorganisational relationships that sustain a fluid and evolving community.' Firms collaborate in all sorts of ways, from R&D to marketing, but the former is fundamental. Figure 21.7 shows the rapid growth in collaborative research projects. There are more than 1200 small biotechnology firms in the United States alone.[26]

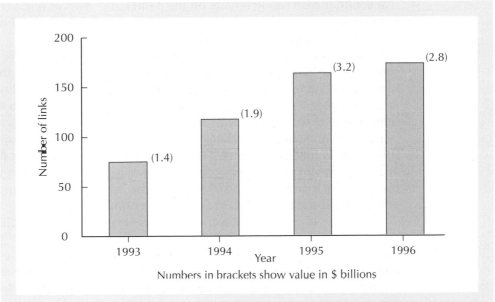

Fig. 21.7 New R&D projects between small biotechnology and large drugs companies

---

Exhibit 21.10   **Swimming against the tide of biotechnology**

Merck, with its reputation for in-house innovation, eschews cooperation. It spends 5 per cent of its R&D budget outside its own laboratories, compared with 20 per cent or more among its major rivals. Merck's scientists believe others do it because they are not clever enough to come up with ideas of their own. It is a strategy, however, increasingly criticised by analysts:

■ the chances of commanding even a small area of biotechnology are slender;
■ it is possible to buy small firms, with their ideas, at bargain prices;
■ subcontracting research makes costs transparent and imposes internal discipline.

It is normal for firms in this industry to have multiple partnerships. To achieve and sustain them, two learning processes occur simultaneously. 'First, firms are increasingly using ties to enhance the inflow of specific information, resources and products. Second, firms are becoming much more adept at and reputed for the general practice of collaboration with diverse partners.'[27]

One of the few companies not to have plunged heavily into collaboration is Merck. It fears that the excellence of its own research work can only be diluted by collaboration, *see* Exhibit 21.10.

Conclusion: the vital process of innovation

Throughout this chapter we have demonstrated the importance of innovation. It has been presented as a complex and subtle process requiring the contribution of teams rather than solely relying on the pioneering spirit of one person. The inventor may kick the process into life but it requires other skills to carry it forward, especially in large organisations.

Clearly, sound investment in innovation brings its rewards. We have seen how society as a whole is usually better off when products and associated processes are improved or new technologies are brought into play. Benefits flow to individuals and firms from the way they increase intellectual capital, protected by patents and other forms of registration.

Difficult questions for managers are whether innovation can be delivered to order and, in any case, where it originates. The TRIZ process was backed for many years by a Soviet government concerned that its economic system was not keeping up with developments in the West. None the less, systematic learning from others offers ways for organisations to avoid reinventing the wheel.

As for the sources of innovation, studies seem to point in different directions. For some, freeing the individual spirit is an important element. This stems from concerns to increase the rate of invention. Methods to stimulate ideas were discussed in Chapter 11. Yet here we have shown that these will not succeed within an organisation whose structure and culture are unfavourable. Finally, firms must not underestimate the environment both as the cause of healthy competitive pressure and as offering possibilities for interorganisational collaboration.

Quick check up *can you ...*

- Give examples of invention and innovation;
- Define innovation gap;
- Name the three product levels identified by Kotler;
- List four types of intellectual property;
- State the three conditions for a successful patent application;
- Summarise the rules of copyright;

- Define manufacturability;
- Give the five main stages of the product development process;
- List the three roles, according to Chaharbaghi and Newman, needed at stages of the innovation process;
- State the four factors that Porter uses to account for variations in innovation among nations.

Questions

Chapter review

14.1 What approaches are used to explain why some firms are more innovative than others?

14.2 Explain why and how the market values intellectual property such as patents and trade marks.

14.3 Is the innovation process a means of overcoming the lack of inventiveness in an organisation?

Application

14.4 Using a consumer magazine such as *Which?* or *What Camera?* investigate the relevance of the product definition of Fig. 21.2.

Investigation

14.5 Compare the experiences of Trevor Baylis and Ron Hickman with another modern inventor, such as James Dyson,[28] or one from history, such as James Watt.

'Look at Hitachi and see the future'[29]

The company motto, given in the headline, symbolises Hitachi's commitment to long-term development. Number one electronics and electrical group in Japan and thirteenth in the *Fortune 500*, it is truly a global company. In the tough market conditions of 1997, revenues were ¥8523 billion, yielding tiny net profits of ¥88 billion. There were some 330 000 employees in a network of more than 70 companies. Figure 21.8 gives other selected data.

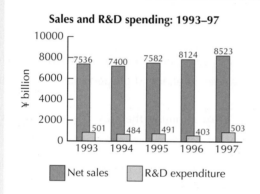

Sales and R&D spending: 1993–97

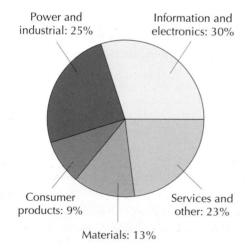

Sales by divisions: 1997

Power and industrial: 25%
Information and electronics: 30%
Consumer products: 9%
Services and other: 23%
Materials: 13%

Fig. 21.8 Some financial data from Hitachi

Underpinning its corporate strategy, Hitachi's research goal is to meet corporate policy and societal needs through development of original science and significant patents. Table 21.1 lists some research programmes with the time scales within which they are expected to deliver results. The company has built its bank of intellectual property in high technology areas. Since 1963, for example, it ranks fourth after IBM, General Electric and AT&T in the number of registered United States patents. From 1985, Hitachi's earnings from licences have exceeded the fees it has paid to others.

The business employs 20 patent lawyers, kept busy by the 15 000 applications made annually. This represents a fall of 30 per cent from the 1980s. Patenting policy has changed to focus on fewer registrations, concentrating on ideas with potential for cross-licensing deals. These are areas where Hitachi may be pushed out by competitors' registrations. If it perceives no external threat, however, the company avoids the disclosure required when filing applications and prefers to keep its technology secret for as long as possible.

In 1997, Hitachi employed almost 17 000 staff in 35 research facilities. About one in twelve of these had doctorates. There were nine corporate research laboratories, listed in Table 21.2. These accounted for 24 per cent of R&D expenditure as shown in Fig. 21.9. Funds come in three categories: corporate headquarters pays for studies that are more than five years from the market; business divisions commission research with a horizon of three to five years; and work that is expected to be marketed within two years is conducted in the divisions' product development facilities.

Of the laboratories listed in Table 21.2, Central Research and Advanced Research have the largest proportions of their funds provided centrally. The £23 million budget of the latter comes entirely from corporate headquarters. The aim is to generate fundamental break-

Table 21.1 R&D programmes, with time horizons

3 to 5 years	5 to 10 years	10 to 20 years	Over 20 years
Neural networks on microchips to mimic learning	Computers, linked by radio, obeying voice instructions	High capacity, high speed, superconducting chips Neural computers learn and reason Single atom switches	Biocomputers that can repair themselves
Multimedia offices	Virtual reality communication across networks	Widespread language interpreting software Flat high definition television screens	Intelligent cities wired with fibre optics
Very high speed magnetic levitation trains		Underground magnetic levitation goods conveyors Energy from nuclear fusion	

Table 21.2 Hitachi's corporate research laboratories

Laboratory	Fields	Staff
Central Research, Tokyo	Fundamentals of IT and microelectronics	1300
Hitachi Research, Hitachi	Macro-systems; media; materials	1300
Mechanical Engineering, Tsuchinza	Mechatronics; energy systems	700
Energy, Hitachi	Nuclear power; computational science	350
Production Engineering, Yokohama	Automation; mass production for electronics	600
Systems Development, Kawasaki	Artificial intelligence technology and software	700
Image & Media, Yokohama	Audio-visual and multimedia systems	380
Design Centre, Tokyo	Design for lifestyle and visual identity	180
Advanced Research, Hatoyama	Basic physics, biotechnology, software and materials	170

throughs as important as the transistor. Staff are encouraged to present papers at symposia and mix with the world's leading scientists.

R&D spending of all kinds is seen as essential to the company's future. Throughout the 1990s, efforts have been made to focus spending more closely on market-driven projects. *Tokken*, or special research, teams have been managed for 30 years to work on urgent or important projects. The approach has been bottom-up with proposals of junior scientists vetted by higher levels. Teams have created supercomputers, semiconductors, disks, displays, power plants and intelligent robots. They support Hitachi's reputation for technological excellence. Yet this has resulted in an egalitarian and indi-

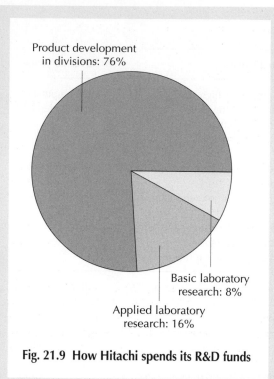

Product development
in divisions: 76%

Basic laboratory
research: 8%

Applied laboratory
research: 16%

Fig. 21.9 How Hitachi spends its R&D funds

vidualistic style. Concerns have been expressed over researchers' links to market development. Rivals such as Matsushita, Sharp and Sony have done better at commercialisation.

In a switch of emphasis, selecting corporate projects has been made the responsibility of the business planning division and not the laboratories. The Strategic Business Projects (SPROT) system brings together staff from accounting and finance, sales and marketing, and R&D to make overall choices. The tokken philosophy continues for projects with time horizons beyond five years, while *tokkai*, or special development, projects expect commercialisation within three years or so.

Hitachi views the world as a single market, selecting optimal locations for facilities, including R&D. It believes its strength can only be sustained by investing in high growth regions and forming alliances with first-rate partners. For instance, in the semiconductor sector, 1997 saw agreements with Acer, Microsoft, Mitsubishi and Texas Instruments.

Questions

1 How does the structure of Hitachi's R&D effort compare with the ideas explained in the chapter?

2 Why not patent basic research?

3 What are the advantages and disadvantages of the policy change to SPROT?

Bibliography Readily accessible reports on innovation in many countries are available from the World Technology Evaluation Centre at Loyola College, http://itri.loyola.edu/ep. The United Kingdom Patent Office is an excellent source of information on intellectual property rights. Companies with interesting sites including innovation are 3M, http://www.mmm.com, and Siemens, http://www.siemens.de.

References 1. Gourlay, Richard (1995) 'Working like clockwork', *Financial Times*, 8 August, 13; Arthur, Charles (1995) 'Wind-up radio is a hit', *Independent on Sunday*, 13 August; 'It may be a wind up but it's no joke!', *Inventors' World*, Winter, 1995 http://www.wdi.co.uk/invworld/wint95/home.html

2. Roos, M.J. (1984) 'Workmate', in Lowe, Julian and Crawford, Nick (eds) *Innovation and Technology Transfer for the Growing Firm*, Oxford: Pergamon, 48–55.

3. Lowe and Crawford (1984) *op. cit.*, 37.

4. 'New technology is no snap', *The Economist*, 11 October, 1997, 125: www.hassel blad.com

5. Kanter, Rosabeth Moss (1983) *The Change Masters,* New York: Touchstone.

6. Hausman, Jerry (1997) 'Cellular telephones: new products and the CPI', NBER Working Paper 5982, March, quoted in 'And now prices can be virtual too', *The Economist,* 14 June, 1997, 122.

7. Cawley, Richard (1997) 'Princes brings fresh interest to corned beef', *The Grocer,* 19 July.

8. Kotler, Philip, Armstrong, Gary, Saunders, John and Wong, Veronica (1996) *Principles of Marketing: The European edition,* London: Prentice Hall, 546.

9. Hitt, Michael A., Hoskisson, Robert E., Johnson, Richard A. and Moesel, Douglas D. (1996) 'The market for corporate control and firm innovation', *Academy of Management Journal,* **39(5)**, October, 1084–119.

10. Jackson, Tim (1997) *Inside Intel: How Andy Grove built the world's most successful chip company,* London: HarperCollins, quoted in Jackson, Tim (1997)'Paranoia pays off', *Guardian: Online,* 30 October, 1: http://www.inside-intel.com/

11. Trapp, Roger (1994) 'Trademarks shape up: protection for a product's form, sound or smell opens new areas of dispute', *Financial Times,* 2 November, 35; *see also* the Patent Office's site on http://www.patent.gov.uk

12. Kotler *et al.* (1996) *op cit.,* 525.

13. Stuart, Liz (1997) 'New Cadbury brand to challenge Smarties', *Marketing Week,* 26 June; Arnot, Chris (1997) 'Dazed and fused', *Guardian: Weekend,* 10 May, 51; Hall, Amanda (1996) 'Chocs away at Cadbury', *Sunday Telegraph: City News,* 8 September.

14. Domb, Ellen, King, Bob and Tate, Karen (1995) 'Systemic innovation: inventing on purpose instead of waiting for the lightening to strike', *Journal of Innovative Management,* Winter, 65–70.

15. Aaby, Nils-Erik and Discenza, Richard (1995) 'Strategic marketing and new product development: an integrated approach', *Marketing Intelligence and Planning,* **13 (9)**, September, 30–5.

16. Slappendel, Carol (1996) 'Perspectives on innovation in organisations', *Organization Studies,* **17 (1)**, Winter, 107–29.

17. Chaharbaghi, Kazem and Newman, Victor (1996) 'Innovating: towards an integrated learning model', *Management Decision,* **34 (4)**, July, 5–13.

18. Fletcher, Clive (1997) 'Keep an open mind on selecting for innovation', *People Management,* **3 (5)**, 6 March, 55.

19. Dougherty, Deborah and Hardy, Cynthia (1996) 'Sustained product innovation in large, mature organizations: overcoming innovation to organization problems', *Academy of Management Journal,* **39 (5)**, October, 1120–53.

20. Lawrence, Paul R. and Lorsch, Jay W. (1986) *Organisation and Environment: Managing differentiation and integration,* Boston, Mass. Harvard Business School Press.

21. Fiol, C. Marlene (1995) 'Thought worlds colliding: the role of contradiction in corporate innovation processes', *Entrepreneurship. Theory and Practice,* **19 (3)** Spring, 71–90.

22. Krause, Irv and Liu, John (1993) 'Benchmarking R&D productivity', *Planning Review,* **21 (1)**, January–February, 16–23.

23. 'Now you know', *The Economist,* 27 May, 1995, 58.

24. Porter, Michael E. (1990) *The Competitive Advantage of Nations,* New York: The Free Press.

25. Bertschek, Irene (1995) 'Product and process innovation as a response to increasing imports and foreign direct investment', *Journal of Industrial Economics,* **43 (4)**, December, 341–57.

26. 'Mercky waters', *The Economist,* 24 May, 1997, 93–5.

27. Powell, Walter W., Koput, Kenneth W. and Smith-Doerr, Laurel (1996) 'Interorganisational collaboration and the locus of innovation: networks of learning in biotechnology', *Administrative Science Quarterly,* **41 (1)**, March, 116–45.

28. Dyson invented and commercialised the *Ball Barrow* (1975), the plastic garden roller (1977) and the bagless vacuum cleaner (1993); Ahmed, Kamel (1997) 'Inventor scores a first as Britain cleans up in Europe', *Guardian*, 1 February, 21.

29. Boulton, William R., Meieran, Eugene S. and Tummala, Rao R. (1995) 'Hitachi's R&D structure', Chapter 3 in Boulton, William R. (ed.) *Japanese Technology Evaluation Centre Report on Electronic Manufacture and Packaging in Japan*, JTEC, Loyola College, *see* http://itri.loyola.edu/ep/c3s6.htm; Hitachi (1997) *Financial Report and Message from the Chairman and the President;* data on Hitachi and its research laboratories is available on http:///www.hitachi.co.jp

Chapter 22

Managers and information

Chapter objectives

When you have finished studying this chapter, you should be able to:

- show how the information age presents new challenges to managers in their roles as information workers;

- distinguish between data and information, explaining how the latter is used;

- specify the factors that make information useful to managers;

- classify the types of information system that have grown up, discerning MIS and DSS;

- relate systems strategy and planning to organisational strategy, noting why so many investments seem to fail;

- explain the interaction between information systems and management – especially their relationships with centralisation, co-ordination, new structures, managing knowledge and the changing roles of many organisational members;

- outline associated ethical issues, including those raised by artificial intelligence and the misuse of data by employees.

Channel One[1]

Formed by merger in 1997, Förenings-Sparbanken is one of the largest full service banks in the Nordic region. It has 1300 branches in Sweden and interests in other countries. Before the merger, Sparbanken had begun to move towards paperless banking with the launch of its intranet. This system, named Channel One, was intended for all 9000 employees to share information. Previously, staff had used a collection of more than twenty loose leaf binders to answer queries on procedures such as processing loans or reporting theft. Now, the query system allows keyword searches of data with a delay time of less than two seconds.

Another use for Channel One is to send news and instructions to identified groups such as branch managers or lending clerks. There is also a news group for staff to raise and discuss problems of bank procedure. The questions, with replies, are available for all to see. The 'Forum' news group is the most popular application.

Preparations for the merger meant that installation of the intranet has not reached all 11 000 work stations. Yet its impact has been significant. The responsibility for reading information has been passed to the receiver who can no longer pretend that it did not arrive.

Swedish customers are used to seeing technological applications in banking. Salary payments are mostly made direct to banks through a wide range of transfer systems. FöreningsSparbanken offers an Internet site enabling funds transfer, bill payments and share transactions. Director of Infrastructure, Goran Lustig, foresaw a time when Channel One would hatch an 'Extranet' permitting customer access to complex product information. He saw IKEA as an analogy. Some of the bank's five million customers would assemble products to suit themselves.

Handling less paper and being able to solve difficult procedural problems more quickly will save staff time. The aim is for them to spend more time building customer relationships.

Intranet: a computer network with access limited to a defined group, usually the staff of one organisation.

Introduction

Throughout Europe, the positive response to corporate intranets contrasts with the scepticism with which many view the public Internet. The latter's information is mostly in English whereas companies can choose the language of their private systems. Furthermore, the Internet suffers from the afternoon slowdown when American users have woken up. Many European companies, therefore, foresee their browsers pointing at private databases and drawing on powerful applications software. Basic intranets can be set up simply and quickly for publishing and document management. Channel One took a four-person team about six months to develop. The risk of failure is limited by the well-tried nature of the technology.

Exhibit 22.1 Linking through information systems

At Cap Gemini, Europe's largest computer services company, some 17 000 staff can simultaneously reach 40 servers to find case studies, design documents and reports, even if they are away from their place of work. Olivetti uses an intranet to link its research laboratories in Italy and abroad.

Companies formed through merger use the systems to help with integration. Norwegian conglomerate Kvaerner is installing servers in Houston, Singapore and Sydney to link its 40 000 employees in 400 offices. These extend the link set up between Oslo and London after the acquisition of United Kingdom company Trafalgar House.

The examples in Exhibit 22.1 show us a fundamental use of information systems (ISs).[2] They enable organisations to operate better, that is to improve the ways current products are supplied to their customers. As we note later, these are *transaction processing systems*. Beyond this, information innovations have created many extensions to Ansoff's product-market matrix. This model was explained in Chapter 10. Figure 22.1, developed from Fig. 10.7, shows how Dorling Kindersley has expanded its business using information technology. Some 8500 distributors

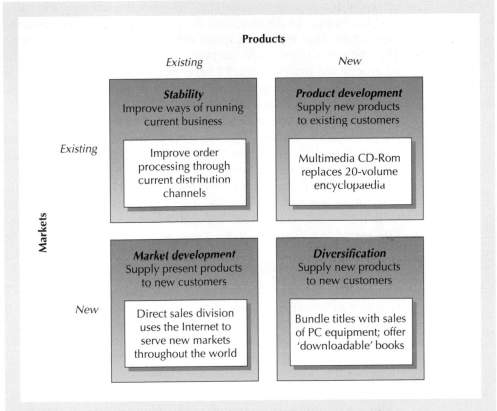

Fig. 22.1 How DK uses information to develop its products and markets

throughout the world could not be reached through an intranet. Therefore, DK uses the Internet to allow direct ordering and settlement of accounts. At the same time, the business has embraced developments in multimedia applications to create new products that match its 'learning' brand image.[3]

Beyond innovations such as DK's, information technology has spawned new industries. Not only is there the business of making, supporting and maintaining computers and their operating systems, but many entrepreneurs have found ways of handling information in new ways. These enable customers to apply, manipulate or be entertained by it. In short, information technology has transformed some industries and organisations in the past 30 years and will continue to do so. To unravel these changes, this chapter examines them from a management perspective. We shall look into how managers use information and develop systems to support these uses. Then we shall consider how organisations have changed in response to the possibilities opened. Finally, lest we fall into the trap of seeing information technology as value free, we will examine some ethical questions surrounding its use in organisations.

The information challenge

The applications mentioned in the previous section concern improved processes, products or reaching new markets. Yet what impact have ISs had on the manager's job? In Chapter 18 we identified the pivotal role of communicating. Some authorities suggest that managers spend about 80 per cent of their time in this activity. Mintzberg has often made the point, '... the job of managing is fundamentally one of processing information.'[4] Therefore, the arrival of systems that support this activity looks an attractive proposition. Yet for many, the achievement has brought limited benefits and huge problems.

Managers are continually supplied with information and use it for all sorts of purposes. However, they find the amount they receive to be uncontrolled and the way it is used is often less than ideal. To illustrate, studies commissioned by Reuters, the supplier of news and on-line information, are summarised in Boxes 22.2 to 22.4.[5] Three surveys were conducted between 1994 and 1996. In each case, there were more than 500 interviews with senior and middle managers in United Kingdom companies. The last round was expanded to cover a further 800 managers from Australia, Hong Kong, Singapore and the United States.

Informal sources and misuse

The results in Exhibit 22.2 make gloomy reading for those who see the information age as bringing in new openness in flows of information in organisations. Moreover, managers reported using informal and private sources rather than rely on formal systems. It is noticeable how little they relied on information professionals to supply them with their needs.

Ignorance of value

Exhibit 22.3 underscores the often observed casualness that firms exhibit in relation to their information assets. Managers are often unwilling to evaluate either

Exhibit 22.2 Use and abuse

Sources of information
Newspapers, journals and word of mouth were most important and most heavily used. Most sources are informal rather than formal systems such as libraries.

Information and job performance
Almost all agreed that free flow is vital to business success.

Information as a political weapon
Two-thirds believe information does not flow freely for political reasons. This is most common in the highly competitive sales and marketing departments and women report it more often than do men.

Sharing or withholding
Managers believe some directors and senior managers hoard information. A third have had needed information withheld from them. One in twenty reported cases where someone more junior had not passed information on to them. Most found they wasted much time seeking information; this was the most common result of someone withholding it.

Corporate policies
Most employers had no formal information policy. There was little evidence that information resources were managed effectively.

the cost of collecting information or its value to them in the way it might underpin performance. The studies also noted how many thought, erroneously, that losses would be covered by insurance.

Exhibit 22.3 An undervalued asset

Information as an asset
Three-quarters rated information as the most important or a very important intangible asset.

Valuing information
A quarter of companies did not track the cost of collecting or maintaining the asset. They either had not considered it, or expected the outcomes to be insignificant or impossible to measure. Firms in the finance sector were best at this. Few foresaw the possibility of making information an entry in the company accounts alongside other goodwill items, including intellectual property such as patents and brand names.

Dependence
Many said loss of key information would be devastating. None insured information specifically, as opposed to information technology, although many managers thought that it would be covered under general insurance.

Overload

The results shown in Exhibit 22.4 confirmed the existence of *Information Fatigue Syndrome* (IFS). This underscores the examples of excessive communication among all staff which were set out in Chapter 18. For managers, having too much information added to the difficulties of an already stressful job. In the survey, this problem was more serious in the Anglo-Saxon countries as opposed to Hong Kong and Singapore. Some looked forward to using more electronic sources in the future. In contrast, one in five managers deliberately collected the minimum, relying on intuition to decide.

It should be noted that overload is not a new phenomenon. In a study 'of Swedish managers in the 1940s, Carlson found that they complained about how the number and size of reports grew. Reading them all was impossible.[6]

Such studies challenge those seeking to improve ISs in organisations. In particular they must recognise that entry to the information age has been a mixed blessing to many managers. While, in principle, data is more plentiful and more readily available, in practice managers perceive overloads for themselves and misuse of it among others. We could suggest that such problems are likely to be more common among middle and senior managers whose roles are more uncertain and 'political'. Yet issues of mismatch and inappropriateness of formal systems persist throughout. For engineers engaged in product development, the information age has brought with it many possibilities such as Computer Aided Design (CAD) technology. Yet Court and others[7] report the following:

■ information inefficiencies cause considerable added costs;

■ engineering design depends heavily on informal communication;

■ engineers rely on suppliers for an increasing proportion of information;

■ personal knowledge and experience are very important.

Exhibit 22.4 **The emergence of IFS, a new health syndrome**

Information overload

One-third received what they feel to be enormous amounts of unsolicited information. Two-thirds stated they need lots of information to be effective.

Almost half believed they were unable to handle the quantity of information they receive. Information overload was blamed by: 42 per cent for causing ill health; 50 per cent for having to take work home; and 61 per cent for sometimes having to cancel social activities. Personal relationships were also placed under strain. Women reported these difficulties more than men.

Finding information

40 per cent wasted time locating information; this distracted them from the main purpose of their jobs.

84 per cent felt forced to collect information.

43 per cent reported that having too much information delayed or halted decisions.

44 per cent thought that collecting information cost their businesses more than it was worth.

Members of design teams, therefore, prefer manual and verbal communication methods and informal storage. Computer-based communication links have hardly made a difference. To search for answers to these difficulties, we must look more closely at the nature of information and how a manager might use it.

Managers and information

A key point is the difference between information and data. Data consists of raw facts, numbers, pictures and so on, that refer to, or measure, some object, process or event. In other words it is a representation of some entity. Information, on the other hand, has meaning. This is given to it by the person who studies the data, interpreting it according to attitudes, values or beliefs that he or she brings. Quiz questions typically test data recall. This is the ability to supply facts such as the names of the largest lake in Hungary or Donald Duck's nephews. In contrast, we can suggest that examination questions ask for information. Figure 22.2 shows how the same image can be data to one person, who has no idea of its context, and information to another. The latter, being familiar with the rules of poker, knows that, whatever card is dealt, this is a good hand.

> Information = Data + Meaning

A manager is presented with a stream of data and information. Clearly, data is available from all sorts of observations, messages and so on. Additionally, as we saw when discussing the two-way communication model in Chapter 18, the manager also picks up information directly from others. Contained in messages are

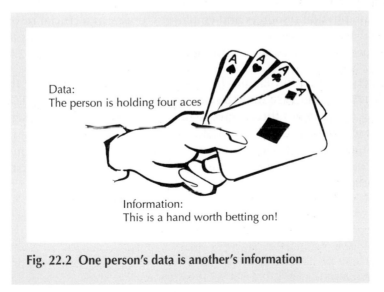

Data:
The person is holding four aces

Information:
This is a hand worth betting on!

Fig. 22.2 One person's data is another's information

both data and the meanings that these others have attached to them. Finally, as the manager makes sense of the world from a personal perspective, the meaning further enriches the incoming flow.

■ Using information

How do managers in organisations use data and information? Through complex, and often invisible and informal processes of sharing, they hope to make themselves, and their organisations, decisive, perceptive and wise. Choo expands these fundamental elements:[8]

- *Decision making*
  The rational decision model of Chapter 11 assumes that sufficient information is available on objectives, alternatives, and the outcomes of these alternatives. In practice, this is rarely possible. While the administrative model recognises that decisions are based on incomplete information, Choo points out that the organisation seeks to maintain at least the semblance of rationality. In any case, the administrative model still requires a supply of some information. Full or partial, the organisation depends heavily on it.

- *Making sense of changes*
  In the dynamic world, organisations have continuously to learn about and interpret change, especially in their environments. To maintain links with customers, suppliers and other stakeholders, managers must be alert for signs of something new. Indeed, we have argued that those who perceive changes earlier and more clearly will gain advantage. The signals are, unfortunately ambiguous and contradictory. A critical task, therefore, is to pick out the most significant features and to share understanding of what they mean.

- *Organisational learning*
  For many authorities, the process of creating, organising and processing information to generate new understanding is the most important aspect. Over a quarter of a century ago, Drucker placed knowledge alongside other critical elements – capital, physical resources and employees' time – as a crucial resource to be managed.[9] He has since revised his view to underline knowledge as *the key resource*, a perspective also associated with the work of Senge, *see* Exhibit 22.5.[10]

Managers have responsibilities beyond building and maintaining their own expertise. They must ensure that the organisation, as a whole, learns. Organisational learning (OL) implies three steps, to draw from Lewin's work described in Chapter 14. These are: unlearning the past; changing; and remembering the new knowledge for application to new products and processes. OL goes beyond the individual coping personally to devising means of sharing common understandings, that is actively sponsoring a learning culture.

Exhibit 22.5 Senge's five disciplines for building the learning organisation

Learning companies will be successful because they can learn and absorb new ideas and practices at all levels. They overcome what Senge calls 'learning disabilities'. To do so, there are five learning disciplines arranged in levels. First, *Personal Mastery* refers to individual motivation to learn. The next three levels, *Mental Models, Shared Vision* and *Team Learning,* show how learning is spread through teams and hence through the organisation. Finally, the fifth level, *System Archetypes,* requires recognition, and hence avoidance, of common blockages that hinder decision making and prevent virtuous growth.

Operating information

Within organisations we can find further uses for information. Examples include assembling it into meaningful financial reports, requesting or settling payments, preparing promotional material such as advertising, or using it for process control. It is in such areas where the greatest advances have been made with computer-based systems. As we noted above, applying computer systems to support managers in their work presents the greatest challenge.

■ Useful information

To support work at all levels, from strategic to operational, information must be useful. How can we assess this usefulness? Robson explains that the usefulness, or value, of information is impossible to measure exactly.[11] Broadly, however, we can say the following:

$$\begin{array}{c} \text{Expected value of any} \\ \text{element of information} \end{array} = \begin{array}{c} \text{Business gain possible} \\ \textit{with the information} \end{array} - \begin{array}{c} \text{Business gain possible} \\ \textit{without the information} \end{array}$$

In other words, information is assessed according to how much advantage it yields. This can be, for example, through reductions in various costs and risks, or additions to current revenues or long-term competitive strength. In retailing, EPOS (electronic point-of-sale systems) offer both aspects. They can cut many operating costs and, through improved sales data, help to sustain strategies such as relationship marketing.

Beyond the cost equation, Robson summarises other ways information can yield benefits. Table 22.1 shows how these relate to its content, timeliness and means of presentation. The importance of these factors varies according to the type of work undertaken by the information user. As the table shows, an operations manager relies on flows whose content is accurate, complete and carries detail corresponding to the complexity of the processes being managed. Strategists, on the other hand, have to cope with incomplete information that is less precise and aggregated into broad summaries of the issues they are considering. Aggregation can mean assembly of data either over a period, so that behavioural patterns can be discerned, or across a range of activities to allow comparisons to be made.

Table 22.1 Information attributes and managers' needs

	Feature	Managing operations	Strategic management
Content	Accuracy	Must be precise	Need not be so precise
	Detail	Detail to match processes	Aggregated
	Completeness	Must be complete	As complete as feasible
	Relevance	To match the needs of the manager	
Timeliness	Currency	As up-to-date as possible	Some delay acceptable
	Response time	Short	Long
	Perspective	Present and immediate past	Future orientated
	Frequency	Regular	As requested
Presentation	Medium	On-line preferred	Mixed media
	Format	Fixed	Flexible
	Conciseness	Concise yet sufficient	

Timeliness is the second factor. Operations managers, whose tasks mainly relate to the short term, require a regular supply of information related to recent or current events. Strategists can accept some lag, although even this should not be excessive. Their perspective requires information pointing to the future. The last category is presentation. Modern ISs are adapted to providing results in different formats; the immediacy of the screen suggests that operations data can be presented in this way. The range, irregularity and uncertainty of strategic intelligence, however, propose a variety of media.

Mangaliso studied how middle managers perceived the usefulness of information for making strategic decisions.[12] Some 90 were responsible for subunits and functions of operating companies within a large multinational enterprise. The main result was that managers see information as useful if it is presented in reasonably aggregated form, is timely and has a scope matched to future time horizons. These three factors should be matched to uncertainty in the environment. For example, instead of waiting for full information, managers in rapidly changing situations preferred it to be supplied quickly, although it was incomplete. Aggregation and timeliness helped these managers to see 'the big picture' and supported their use of intuition and judgement. Mangaliso also notes that many middle managers are dissatisfied with the information routinely supplied to them. They are required to process it like cogs in a machine rather than use it to decide. This difficulty represents the complex effects of ISs on how much decentralisation is needed in the organisation. Although sharing knowledge supports decentralisation in principle, it also offers opportunities to senior managers to keep tighter reins on decision making.

■ Control information

In the next two chapters, we look closely at the nature of control. Clearly, information plays a vital role in all control systems. At first, we may see control as requiring information to be available as soon as possible after the relevant processes have been carried out. This implies, for the operations manager, up-to-date and regular presentation. Strategists can accept some delay as relevant data takes longer to collect and assemble. Possibilities in control, however, go further than this idea of feedback. As we shall see, control can be anticipatory (known as feedforward) or concurrent. In the former case, there is a reliance on forecasts while, for the latter, immediacy of data flow is imperative. The switch from looking backwards to looking forwards represents a key development in ISs for managers.

Types of information system

In Table 22.2 we made a rough distinction between the needs of the operations and strategic manager. This is useful because they are supported by different types of IS. The former typically needs systems to support current operations and associated decisions. The latter, in contrast, are concerned with the strategic decisions of middle and senior managers.

■ Information systems for operations

The early growth of computer-based ISs arose in the replacement of manual processes. Payroll, invoicing and accounting records were common applications, followed by word processing and related office activities. These remain the development routes for most SMEs as they introduce computers.[13] Across all organisations, operations systems can now be placed in three categories:

- *Transaction processing systems*
  These systems record, process and store data associated with all sorts of business transaction. We have met several examples throughout the book. Invoices, despatch notes, purchasing orders, stock lists, bonus payments and many other pieces of data can be produced and recorded in many ways. Information, meaningful to different groups from customers and suppliers to delivery drivers and managers, can be provided. These systems are the basic building blocks of most reports that pass around the organisation.

- *Process control systems*
  As mentioned in the previous section, control of all processes is a vital function for information. Process control systems are increasingly automated to provide reliable monitoring and continuous adjustment. Whether it is sensitive equipment monitoring mixture temperatures in a brewery, or sensors measuring the thickness of chocolate in a biscuit factory, process controllers carry out continuous adjustments to thousands of processes in many plants.

- *Office information systems.*
  These systems were introduced to improve the speed and quality of office work. Word processing and data storage are two common applications. They have

moved on from this basic level to allow on-line transaction processing. In so doing, new ways of doing business have been created. Direct customer service in banking and insurance are leading examples.

Information systems for managers

Information systems for managers are designed to support their work through providing relevant information when they need it. Often promoted by equipment and software suppliers and consultants, they take many forms and offer a range of benefits. Therefore, a problem for both managers and students is making sense of the number of labels given to the different designs and purposes. *See* Fig. 22.3.

Unfortunately, the number of labels increases by the year. Sometimes, new ones describe innovative approaches although often they represent attempts to establish brand identity in the battle among the many software suppliers. The following types of system are in common use:

■ *Management information system*
This term is the one whose definition varies the most. Used broadly, it is seen as the system satisfying all the information needs of management. Others, however, give it more limited scope. Developed from the large data stores in transaction processing systems, a MIS collects and analyses data and produces reports. Its purpose is to help managers solve structured problems.

Decisions based on MISs depend on the application of formal rules in routine situations. MISs improve organisational efficiency by reducing costs and improving processing speed. Their weaknesses lie in their historical orientation and their inability to cope with change. The standardised nature of the reports limited the range of possibilities. Overcoming this by adding more data merely

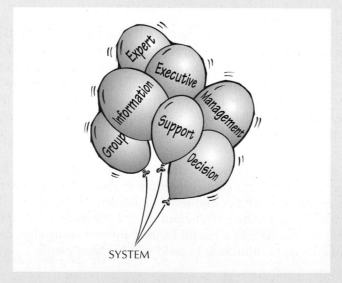

Fig. 22.3 Pick any combination for your information system

makes any item more difficult to find. In response to this growth of the size and scope of reports, Ackoff coined the term *Management Misinformation System*.[14]

■ *Executive information system*

An EIS provides appropriate analyses for senior managers. While including all the features of an MIS, this type of system is designed to produce analyses suited to the needs of those at the top. Their design depends on understanding what is important to this group. The range of internal and external information can be vast. Therefore, the system should provide summaries on request and offer the manager the chance to 'drill down' to extract more detail if required. It is often claimed that EISs can act 'intelligently', such as selecting data that is appropriate to each manager's needs. Yet, as we see in Exhibit 22.6, this promise is difficult to attain and there have been many disappointments.[15]

Exhibit 22.6 **The stumbling EIS**

The promise of the EIS remains unfulfilled. Its intention was to provide corporate managers, at the press of a button, with business intelligence so they could make the best possible decisions. The result of failure is that many continue with paper reports or, if they use computers, summaries prepared by others and sent by e-mail. Jack Welch, chairman of General Electric, is typical of many. He receives most information as faxed reports or simply from listening to people.

Why the disappointment? Reasons include:

■ Inflexibility of software. Users could not change things to suit their needs.

■ Lack of dependability and consistency in basic databases. Many companies, especially if formed by merger, use a range of different information systems. Putting disparate data together is a problem.

■ Slow response times. Databases had not been designed to support EIS queries.

■ Difficulty in learning and use. This is a widespread problem in business applications.

Many managers use desk top personal computers. A Coopers and Lybrand study found more than two-thirds of chief executives of smaller, growing companies used PCs to monitor results such as sales, cash flow and debtors, often daily. Yet they did not rely on their machines to provide trend analysis. In another survey, Allison found almost one half of managers using systems to monitor progress, one third for reporting and communication yet only one in ten engaged in business or trend analysis or manipulating background information.

Others are more optimistic. New generations of software focus on a few functions presented in a user friendly way. Wise Foods, a $300 million United States snack food company, has developed a fast database to support its sales EIS. Weekly analysis is available on-line with a two-day delay compared with previous paper records distributed several weeks after each month end.

Another approach is to establish a 'data warehouse' that can be used by managers connected by an intranet. While the searching work is carried out by a browser similar to those used on the Internet, the intelligence is provided by the user. Such methods have been introduced at Savacentre, the do-it-yourself subsidiary of Sainsbury.

■ *Decision support system*

The DSS is designed to help managerial decision making at all levels through offering a flexible menu of models and decision aids alongside relevant data. Since the decision aids are offered as a menu, their use does not have to be specified in advance. Therefore, DSSs are suited to unstructured problems. A spreadsheet can be used in this way. At its simple level, it can merely present rows and columns of data, say of monthly expenditure against budget. Means and variances are readily summarised.

Going further, however, most spreadsheets, such as Excel, Lotus and Quattro Pro, have built-in models that allow the user to make forecasts using simple extrapolation rules. The user is, therefore, assisted in choosing between several spending policies. However, if a DSS is to be a significant part of a firm's IS provision, it needs to go beyond the standard spreadsheet to add further modelling capability suited to its industry. The complexity and uncertainty of managers' decisions make the design of DSS difficult. Yet some organisations, such as London Underground, have made progress, *see* Exhibit 22.7.[16]

■ *Expert systems*

These systems collect and analyse data on some aspects of decision making and, in the light of the outcomes, offer expert advice. It is in this 'expertise' that they differ from other systems. They look to apply ideas of artificial intelligence in attempts to replicate the thinking processes that skilled workers, professionals and managers use when deciding. The notion is to apply the decision rules that, for example, a doctor uses when making a diagnosis. They can be more reliable than doctors, especially in noticing conditions of which the doctor has had little experience. For instance, many general practitioners in Europe have not seen cases of diphtheria (which has been eradicated) or malaria (which is exotic). Some success has been achieved in areas dominated by technical expertise, such as medicine, geology or mathematics. Progress in areas where interpersonal relations are important has been limited.

■ *Electronic meeting systems*

An EMS helps group work and communication. It will include: parallel communication links joining all members; shared software; and some decision support tools. Further, it may include proprietary software that stimulates brainstorming, records issue analysis and permits voting, as in a Delphi survey.

Exhibit 22.7 Data on the tube

London Underground has created a database holding returns from ticket machines and station gates. Users of the system include train schedulers, station managers, market researchers and so on. Clearly, the varying decisions faced by these managers mean they must aggregate ticket information in different ways. For instance, train schedulers look at route loadings while station managers are concerned with balancing their staffing levels with demands for ticket sales, escalators and entry and exit gates. Planners found, however, that 80 per cent of users' decisions could be supported with standard browsing. The rest required specific solutions designed after bringing users and IT staff together.

- *Group decision support systems*
  Such systems are extensions of DSSs and EMSs, including features of each. Therefore, they extend the information management and aids to decision making of the DSS with facilities for negotiation and communication.

Mentzas is among those to propose taxonomies, which are means of classification of computer-based systems. He uses three dimensions to distinguish among systems according to their uses.[17] They are:

- *Information processing support*
  On-line support for collecting, processing and tracking data that is vital to the organisation.

- *Decision support*
  Support for decisions concerning unstructured problems whose information requirements cannot be specified in advance.

- *Communication support*
  Underpinning the flows of information among several users.

Figure 22.4 presents the three dimensions as a simplified cube. We can read the figure starting from the lower left cell. As computer information systems go, the

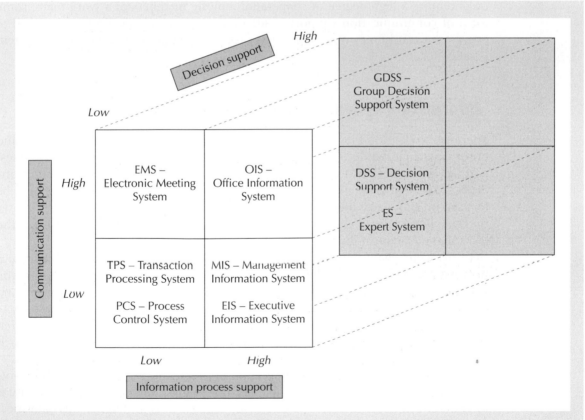

Fig. 22.4 Classifying computer-based information systems

routine TPS and PCS offer moderate information, communication and decision support. Their performance is, of course, superior to the manual or semi-integrated systems they replace. Similarly, the EMS can be seen as a replacement of previous patterns such as personal contact or telephone conferencing. On the Lengel–Daft scale introduced in Chapter 18, we mean that EMS offer greater *channel richness* than e-mail or the telephone while not matching face-to-face contact.

The other types of IS described above can be understood according to their relationships to the TPS/PCS cell. For instance the MIS and EIS enhance information support through aggregation and fitting reports to managers' needs. Further, the OIS is an enhancement of both EMS and MIS as suggested in its description above.

The greatest challenge for designers of ISs for managers arises in the decision support area. We can perceive the DSS and ES as extensions of transaction processing and control. Yet they are not sophisticated enough to provide high information support to unstructured management decisions. The GDSS is presently a DSS supported by various types of group communication software.

The layout in Fig. 22.4 helps us distinguish among the types of IS available and the purposes to which they can be put. While decision support presents the most complex design problems, the diagram does not suggest that any system is superior to the others. Like many aspects of sound organisational planning, each should be used in the circumstances for which it is best suited. For instance, if tasks require a high degree of cooperation among members of a work team, some form of communication support is advantageous. If the system is to be used to ensure the consistency of a production process, then an automatic control system is called for.

Information systems strategy

The push to develop EISs and DSSs comes from the desire to support strategic and other unstructured decision making. Through being able to improve processes, and link them better to other parts of the organisation and environment, managers are both able to add value and reduce costs. Investment, however, should be focused on those activities where the greatest gains are to be made. Chu proposes that managers should concentrate on *critical value activities*, CVAs.[18] These are the tasks that a firm must do well to succeed.

In his value chain model, *see* Fig. 22.5, Porter set out the value activities that a firm uses to do business.[19] Divided into nine primary and support elements, the value chain represents the fundamental processes of the organisation. Depending on the industry, different activities are more important. Not only must these CVAs be done well individually, but, in many cases, competitive advantage is gained through linkages. They are the connections among the cells designed so that each supports the others.

Retailing enjoys a widespread application of ISs. With EPOS (electronic point-of-sale) equipment available to all companies, one might imagine they could all use it to good effect. Yet this is not so. The firms that harness and apply the data most effectively will do best. It will inform all aspects of strategic decision making with rich and up-to-date information. Figure 22.6 shows the value chain links for a

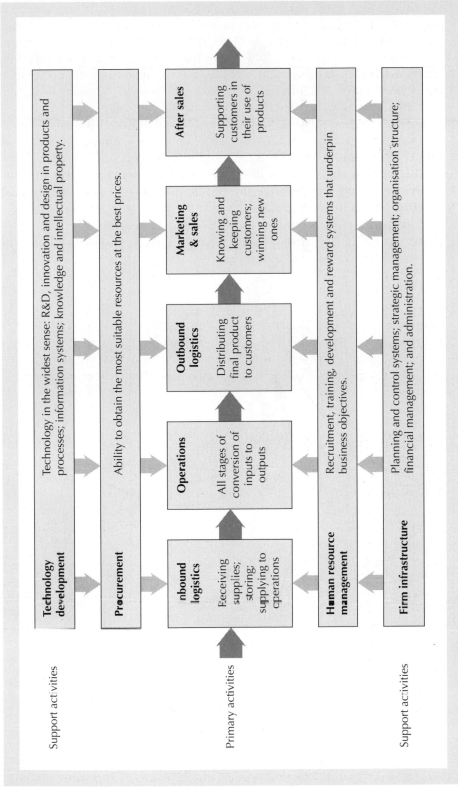

Fig. 22.5 The value chain

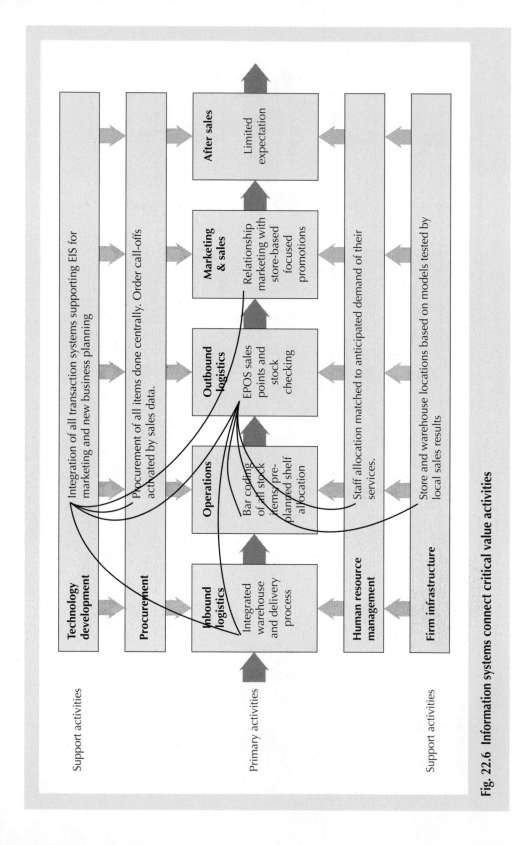

Fig. 22.6 Information systems connect critical value activities

---

Exhibit 22.8 Geographical Information Systems and the gut feeling

Geographical Information Systems provide data to users in the form of maps. Building from applications in town planning, environmental studies and crop management, they now have many commercial uses.

From 1980, Tesco led the United Kingdom retail sector when it set up its Site Research Unit. Employing forecasters, statisticians and other specialists, it combined formal data with 'gut feeling' to find the best store locations. Home-grown computer applications have now been combined with GISs. Staff generate information from both geographic and non-geographic sources, such as EPOS returns. Work now extends beyond location search to support database marketing, plan distribution routes, match promotions to demography, and assess store performance. Mapping and visualisation are important advantages of the GIS software.

---

leading supermarket chain. Sales data is used to: integrate supply and store operations using sales data; create a platform for relationship marketing; manage each store's staff allocations; build models of store profitability related to geographical information; and develop new businesses, such as personal banking. Going further, Exhibit 22.8 shows how Tesco, a market leader, has integrated its own developments with a further type of system, the GIS.

Implementation

Accomplishing IS strategies to sustain such strategic thinking is difficult. Earl identified three hurdles: business strategies are often an inadequate foundation for building; methods are too complicated or time-consuming; and the resulting strategies are not put into effect. In response to these difficulties, many starting points and routes to the goal of integration have been proposed. Earl identified five common modes of IS planning in United Kingdom companies. These are summarised in Table 22.2.[20]

In a survey, managers rated the organisational approach most highly among the five modes. Better results were attained with fewer problems. As with other aspects of strategy making, this result shows the limitations of analytical methods. Pragmatic, learning-by-doing processes often produces better results. Exhibit 22.9 summarises why this is so. It shows that, while planning methods are used, success arises from using teamwork and learning processes coupled to capability for achievement. The step-by-step approach to change worked well provided the organisation was not in such a poor state that it needed a radical overhaul. This argument corresponds to Quinn's *logical incrementalism* perspective on strategic management that we met in Chapter 10.[21]

Failures

Despite studies such as that of Earl, there is little understanding of how to avoid failures in information projects. Hulme notes how many large government projects run into serious trouble. They arrive late, do not work as planned and cost many millions more than expected. Although governments often undertake the largest

Table 22.2 Approaches to IS planning with their pitfalls

	Approach	Advantages	Disadvantages
Business led	IS strategy follows current business strategy	Seems to follow common sense	Business strategy sometimes unclear; IS cannot take advantage of unforeseen opportunities
Method driven	Uses the best available planning method; often through consultants with proprietary procedure	Stresses weaknesses in strategic thinking	Opposition from those who do not want to see current strategy challenged; therefore implementation difficult
Archi-tectural	Specialists use analytical approach to design plans for each aspect of IS	Non-involvement of users except as 'customers'	Detailed designs difficult for managers to understand; therefore unlikely to be accepted
Admini-strative	Follows normal resource allocation procedure – each unit makes annual bid for IS resources	Method familiar and visible; this makes implementation likely	Not strategic; supports 'business as usual'; resources allocation not optimised across the whole business
Organis-ational	IS professionals and users work in partnership using cross-functional teams	Two-way link to business strategy; focus means implementation likely	Managers face uncertain outcomes; projects may not survive change of managers

---

Exhibit 22.9 **The 'organisational approach' to information systems strategy**

- ■ *Themes*
  Work concentrates on a few themes rather than large portfolio of applications.

- ■ *Evolution*
  Change takes place in incremental steps. This reduces risk and allows learning to take place.

- ■ *Teamwork*
  Teams integrate IS thinking with business thinking; forms range from temporary task forces to permanent improvement groups similar to quality circles.

- ■ *Education*
  Teamwork learning is enhanced with training and outside demonstrations.

- ■ *Devolution*
  Specialist information function is devolved to business unit level.

- ■ *Methods*
  Many methods are used as appropriate, including techniques to plan IS, stimulate creativity and analyse systems.

projects, the failure problem is not confined to that sector. United States data shows that fewer than nine per cent of projects in large companies are produced on time, within budget and with all the specified features. Nearly one third are cancelled.[22] In the United Kingdom, NatWest Bank spent £200 million on a branch computer network whose installation took several years longer than expected. An extensive system for EuropCar, the car rental company, failed on its first day.[23]

Projects are entered into with optimism that overestimates benefits while underestimating both risk and time for completion. Beyond these factors, Hulme explains the contribution of procurement methods, pointing to the practice of competitive tendering. This method grew up to ensure honest competition when organisations were buying commodities or relatively simple goods. High technology purchases, in contrast, are complex and uncertain. Both benefits and costs throughout a product's life cannot be established accurately. Potential suppliers provide estimates on which purchasers place a varying degree of reliance. Establishing which bidder offers the best value for money is difficult.

Estimating the cost-benefit of buying new systems from outside has two further difficulties. First, the service does not exist. Unlike a good, which can be examined either in model form or through inspecting a similar one already produced, the service is not available ahead of the selection. Second, its value depends on the quality of the client–provider relationship. Writing a specification for such a dynamic experience is infeasible. Pringle supports these points in listing the most common causes of difficulty with IT services, *see* Exhibit 22.10.[24]

Therefore, unlike traditional purchasing, which chooses on the lowest price to meet a specification, Hulme recommends supplier partnering. Here choice is based on defining the business problem and choosing suppliers whose skills relate to that problem. While procurement is only one aspect of the failure problem, experience in Canadian government purchasing suggests that it is one area where changes will yield benefits.

Information and management

Clearly, ISs are important components of many modern organisations. Apart from small enterprises, many set up an information technology function to manage the hardware and provide expertise to make systems work. Yet these departments run the risk of being too remote from users. With the switch towards distributed net-

Exhibit 22.10 Main cause of dissatisfaction with outsourced IT services

- Too dependent on, or tied into, one supplier.
- Little influence on supplier's service levels.
- Time taken to get service right.
- Management time spent on supplier issues.
- Loss of IT skills; difficult to re-establish in-house function.
- Supplier does not understand business.

works, companies have tried decentralisation to re-establish user control. Haapaniemi reports that two-thirds of the spending now occurs outside the IS department. Unfortunately, this allows a state of anarchy to emerge. Departments buy hardware without an overall plan. Furthermore, it frequently will not work with other departmental systems. Even experts from the IT function are unable to help. The task of maintenance and user support falls to enthusiastic local managers who spend much of their time fixing and adjusting their systems instead of concentrating on their main jobs. With the average company expected, by 2000, to be spending nine per cent of its revenue on IT, mostly in decentralised fashion, a great deal of money can be wasted.

Changing the balance between centralisation and decentralisation is not the only effect of IT within organisations. For example, some have grasped the attractions of improved communications to enhance co-ordination among staff. This can be through breaking down barriers to information flow or through specific programmes such as knowledge management. On the other hand, some see an opportunity to delayer, that is cut the number of levels in the hierarchy. In the environment, not only can ISs gather more information more efficiently, but there are possibilities of augmenting cooperative alliances through systems integration. We shall look at these managerial questions in more detail.

▄ Does IT lead to centralisation?

It used to be accepted that the growth of ISs, based as they were on mainframe hardware, would lead to greater centralisation of organisations. In many functions, such as purchasing for a geographically dispersed operation such as a retail chain or multi-site manufacturer, the IS offered the possibility of full centralisation for the first time. Not only was control from the centre possible but also the available benefits made it desirable.

Today's globally decentralised companies, however, eschew the notion of central command. Many prefer decentralised IS management. Deere, the United States farm equipment maker, abandoned central control of IT in 1995. As a result, it found divisional managers to be more satisfied with IT, meeting project time and cost targets better. Yet this improvement was at a price. Heads of the decentralised units found themselves spending between a quarter and half their time on IT matters. This contrasts with less than a quarter reported by chiefs of centralised businesses.

Given the possibilities of waste in a fully decentralised approach, should an enlightened management search for a balance between the two extremes? Remarkably, taking the centre ground, although common, seems to yield least satisfaction. In one survey rating the IS groups in their companies, 53 per cent of managers in decentralised settings gave a rating of 'very good' or 'good'. This compared with 46 per cent for centralised organisations. Where the policy sought a balance, the score was worst, achieving just 36 per cent.[25]

Managers are responsible for finding the right point on the scale. The trade off in respect of IS management should not be made independently of the business strategy. For instance, one retailer offering instant credit as part of its competitive approach needed to decide customers' risk profiles at the centre. An information system project, attempting to support local decision making, was abandoned because it threatened to become too complex and difficult to use. Instead, investment was directed towards consolidating links between each store and headquarters.

Gurbaxani and Whang pick out different uses of ISs to explain why they can have mixed effects on centralisation.[26] When the *costs of making decisions* are reduced, taking on more of them is possible for any manager. This is centralisation. On the other hand, where the *costs of performance monitoring* are cut, the centre can permit a greater degree of autonomy because it knows better 'what is going on'.

A more sanguine view considers change as a response to the latest disappointment. One IBM manager quoted survey results indicating problems with client/server installations of the early 1990s. In response, IS managers were beginning to re-establish control of critical systems. The trend was being encouraged by new communications and data storage technology and concerns over information security.[27]

Co-ordination

Broadening this debate, Malone and Crowston consider the relationship between IS development and co-ordination, that is the way people work together.[28] To appreciate the argument, we can use road traffic as an analogy for information flow, *see* Exhibit 22.11. What has happened because of the falling cost, to the user, of private road transport? We can sum the effects up in three phases:

- First, some types of travel, such as walking, cycling or travel by bus or train, are replaced by driving. The *modal split* shifts towards private motor transport.
- Second, reduced personal costs mean that people travel further and more often. They visit friends more frequently or simply 'go out for a spin'.
- Third, spatial layout changes as more roads are built and the locations of different activities are set out in zones such as retail, business and leisure parks. Access to these depends for most on being able to use a car. Towns take on new forms.

Clearly, new information systems reduce the cost of co-ordination. As with roads, we can perceive three effects:

- The immediate outcome is the replacement of some human co-ordination activity with IT. Banks, for instance, have replaced many clerks by transaction processing systems. At a higher level, the long-predicted end of middle management may at last be happening as their communication tasks are taken over by computers.

Exhibit 22.11 **Analogy's limits**

An analogy is a loose sort of model. Its purpose is to yield insights into the subject we are investigating. No attempt is made to match the model closely enough to enable, say, predictions to be made. Hence thinking about road traffic helps us to picture some aspects of information flow but we must not take the comparison too far.

A common analogy seen in books is the matching of an organisation to an organism. Brain, sensors and control mechanisms can be perceived. Yet the differences are so great that little of value can be drawn.

■ Later, a second-order effect of cost reduction may be to increase the quantity used. Sometimes this increase may overtake the original saving. Malone and Crowston describe a case where an electronic meeting system helped in the removal of a management layer.[29] After some years, almost the same number of posts had been created in a staff group. The organisation now had the resources to undertake complex analytical tasks that previously it had been unable to do.

■ A third effect may be a shift towards structures that require more co-ordination to make them work. An example is Mintzberg's *adhocracy*.[30] This is a very flexible organisation with many, changing project teams. Communication takes place through decentralised, autonomous networks rather than through hierarchical structures. Examples are the virtual and spherical organisations described in Chapter 12. Technical and Computer Graphics (TCG) and Super Bakery, two companies presented in the chapter, are good examples.

Both TCG and Super Bakery gain their competitive strength from being at the hub of information networks. Having cut transaction costs, ISs allow market relationships to replace internal decision making. Another example lies in computer airline reservations systems. After these were introduced in the United States, reservations through travel agents doubled to 70 per cent. Agents, working through the market, were more efficient than direct booking procedures.

If co-ordination becomes very simple, rapid assembly of task forces to work on any activity for a short time may be possible. Such a virtual organisation could simultaneously satisfy needs for both economies of scale and personal autonomy. Malone and Crowston speculate on whether the trend has any limit. Although there are few examples to test this possibility, many established companies are finding that alliances with others are aided by advances in ISs.

Some twenty years on from the vertical disintegration of airline bookings mentioned above, the Internet threatens the travel agents' advantage by making self-service possible. Meanwhile, travel and hospitality companies are forming horizontal alliances to fill out their services. Brown and Pattinson[31] describe how Radisson Hotels Australia (RHA), a virtual corporation comprising a network of independent operations, extends the Sabre and Galileo flight booking systems to integrate the sales of travel, hotel rooms, car and coach hire and entertainment. The frequent flier programme of Qantas, the Australian airline, allows air miles to be earned by RHA guests. Many forms of data sharing and computer-based communication underpin such links.

Changing patterns of employment

Every human resource management activity relies on, and produces, information. It is central to the way HRM contributes towards organisational integration, building staff commitment, extending and maintaining workforce flexibility and improving quality. Many see that progress towards these aims can be helped through *teleworking*. Working from home is not a new idea. In fact it can be seen as a resurrection of an old one. Employment for most people was dispersed among small units and homes until the industrial revolution brought advantages to scale and concentration. Now governments are promoting a new dispersion to ease traffic jams. Congestion is a serious problem in cities, especially Madrid and Rome where office staff cling to the notion of commuting four times a day, including the long lunch break. Griffiths quotes a study that suggests that information systems will cut United Kingdom lorry and commuting journeys by a fifth in ten years.[32] Government policy is to foster this change, for instance through the European Telework Development Initiative.[33]

ISs allow geographical distribution of work without removing possibilities of easy communication and economies of scale. Teleworking is an umbrella term covering a range of possibilities:[34]

■ *Home working*
In this, the most commonly held view of teleworking, people assume that home working implies the home becoming the sole place of employment. Yet it is more common to find staff working partly at home and partly at other premises, such as the office or at a client's site. Seeing it as operating solely from home, many have pointed to the negative effects. These include loss of employment rights, fewer development opportunities, cuts in income and the absence of the psychological benefits of human contact.

■ *New process designs*
Many customer service processes have been redesigned to bring all relevant information to one desk. Someone calling a home shopping bureau, for instance, speaks to a clerk whose screen presents customer and product details. The task is to receive the requirements and check them against stocks, credit status and so on. Given that the telephone service is spatially decoupled from the rest of the business, it is but a small step to place it in a low cost area. Many of British Airways' customer services are provided from India.

■ *Shared office facilities*
Sometimes known as 'telecottages', small businesses can share offices providing administrative support. On a larger scale, they can act as call centres. A growing network of taxi firms uses a single national telephone number. The equipment, however, recognises the origin of a call and diverts it to the local service office.

■ *Peripatetic employees*
Portable information technologies permit more employees to carry out their work at any location and only occasionally travel to the office. Exhibit 22.12 gives an example of supporting staff who spend most of their time with customers.[35]

Providing the base for an occasional visit is helped by the introduction of 'hot-desking'. One study found that sales and field engineering staff used their office space only 40 per cent of the time. Savings were made using special planning software. It allowed all to have a desk when they needed one but did not allocate them to individuals.

■ *Distributed teams*
Communication systems, such as EMS and GDSS, help the extension of team working among people at different sites. These have become important to support globally dispersed research and development efforts. Examples in this and the previous chapter show companies investing in conferencing and messaging facilities. They save time and travel costs and improve team performance.

Exhibit 22.12 Supporting service

Brian Lerigo is a service engineer for Yorkshire Water. At 7.30 am each day, he uses his notebook computer and modem to pick up his jobs and messages from the company's database. The system uses Lotus Notes. Route planning is helped by a detailed local map on CD-Rom. During the day, Lerigo updates his notes when he passes a local depot. He files a report as the shift ends.

Half of Yorkshire Water's 3000 employees do not work in offices. More than 200 have been equipped with mobile computers linked by modem to the operations centre in Bradford. Training 'practical staff' to compute represented the biggest challenge.

Although worried about the complexities of computing, Lerigo soon became a fan of the new arrangements. Complaints used to take weeks to deal with. For each, he had to go to the depot and write to three departments. Now, a one hour response is typical. As for fears of working without support, being on-line keeps him in touch with colleagues.

Knowledge management

As explained in Chapter 21, the strengths of many organisations are based on their knowledge. Yet many recognise that they do not know what they know. Information with commercial value is dispersed in computer databases, drawers of filing cabinets and even in employees' heads. Work is repeated, and mistakes replicated, because of the difficulties of using knowledge kept elsewhere. Now leading firms are creating a senior post, the knowledge manager. Business schools are creating chairs.[36] Exhibit 22.13 gives some company examples.[37]

There are drawbacks. Computer-based knowledge management systems are limited by the complex nature of the knowledge itself. Explicit knowledge comes

Exhibit 22.13 Nurturing, sharing and valuing knowledge

Dow Chemical has a director responsible for global intellectual assets. Through improved management of its 29 000 patents, it found savings of some £25 million and made plans to increase its licensing income substantially. The starting point was to create a database from patent records, describing each according to 100 possible points. The work was extended through trademarks and copyrights to cover all of Dow's intellectual assets.

Other businesses go beyond formal know-how. Arthur Andersen, the leading accounting and consulting firm, edits and diffuses information about good practice, business contacts and case histories across its computer network. Supplementing this 'official' system, an electronic bulletin board enables staff to post anything they think colleagues will find useful.

Some companies use knowledge management to help in assessing their true worth instead of relying on intuition. Celemi, a Swedish consulting firm, has developed software to assist this. It values its own knowledge assets at £5.2 million, more than twice the figure shown on the conventional balance sheet as words and numbers and can be readily stored and transmitted. The so called 'tacit' knowledge, on the other hand, relates to anything from the subtle aspects of running a tricky process to a deep understanding of cultural values. Nonaka argues that it has little to do with data processing.[38] Stored in the minds of middle managers, it has great strategic value. Yet this is precisely the group that reengineering has sought to replace with computers. Faced with this threat, many managers and specialists seek to use their expert power to maintain their status and employability. Why should they share their knowledge with others?

Organisations, roles and people

As noted above, many organisations create a separate unit to handle the IS speciality. This becomes responsible for maintaining and upgrading hardware, establishing new applications, training its own and users' staff, and many other related activities. Since the range of work covered is so great and changes so quickly, work becomes duplicated and many staff face a range of tasks that colleagues in other departments would not attempt. In 1994, Johnson & Johnson, the leading United States producer of health care products, found that internal clients were dissatisfied with IT services. At the time, Rich Wasilius, the director responsible, was merging four IT departments that had grown up over the years. He found overlapping roles and stretched staff. Many were responsible both for finding opportunities for implanting strategic technology and maintaining current information operations. Among other aspects, the new structure focused on overcoming these problems.[39]

System developments have begun to have marked effects on other organisational roles. Bowles and Blyth note how so much more market information has been generated by transaction processing systems in retailing. The focus of market research had changed. The question, 'How do we find out about ...' has been replaced by, 'How do we put these databases together to make sense of them?'[40] Accountants are not immune. Hilton argues their traditional skills have been eroded by information applications. They had been good at historical reporting. Soon, senior managers and investors will know where a business is without their intervention. Accountants, including those in professional practice, seek a new role. The fear and stress created by pressure and change is not confined to users. Exhibit 22.14 shows how it applies to the specialists themselves.[41]

Managing information ethically

The information age has arrived with most believing in its generally benign effect. For instance, Stonier wrote, '... just as the industrial economy eliminated slavery, famine and pestilence, so will the post-industrial economy eliminate authoritarianism, war and strife. For the first time in history, the rate at which we solve problems will exceed the rate at which they appear.'[42] True, some databases have been misused. Some systems have been invaded by amateur hackers or professional criminals. Others worry about openings for closer surveillance and control. For the most part, however, such activities are perceived as design weaknesses

---

Exhibit 22.14 IT: a safe occupation?

A survey carried out in the United Kingdom by Guardian Financial Services ranked IT staff fourth in a list of those reporting that their jobs were highly stressful. Stress is reflected in a high incidence of sickness, absenteeism and even suicide. Why IT? Managers report that this is an area above others where employers demand more for less. The last decades have been marked by increasing hours of work and pressure to improve productivity. Constant reorganisation and short-term contracts also generate anxiety. Further, the customer–client relationship between users and the IT department makes the latter a ready scapegoat when things go wrong.

More than half of IT professionals are aged between 20 and 35 with the majority being male. In society as a whole, men in this age group are five times more likely to commit suicide than people in any other. Stress measurements need to be seen against this background. Nevertheless, they are high. The Samaritans, a national charity offering emotional support in times of crisis, has set up a web site to serve this high-risk group.

---

presenting challenges to imaginative technologists or questions for an enlightened management to resolve. Nevertheless, are information systems good for us? And can we trust those who manage them?

The big picture

Remenyi and Williams offer a review of broad ethical questions concerning IS development.[43] As mentioned above, the prevailing view is that information systems are beneficial. Yet, in science, there are several examples in modern times of researchers, along with others, regretting the knowledge they have created. Atomic physics was so promising as an energy source yet so misused in weapons. Even when tamed, its detritus leaves problems for future generations. Genetic engineering, carefully controlled in the right hands, promises huge benefits. In offering the potential to clone people, however, it may be horribly misused.

Could the 'information genie' be let out of the bottle? Risks exist in the development of more powerful processors and communications technologies. Opportunities to misuse knowledge, forever present, will grow. We must assume that information will become available to criminals and other adversaries. It is worth reflecting that, before 1939, the Dutch government innocently collected statistics on its citizens' religious adherence. During the occupation, these records helped the Nazis find Jewish people.

The direction of artificial intelligence is also obscure. It is not clear whether research will create a benevolent or malevolent HAL.[44] While seeing how a silicon brain could become a monster is difficult, what is our response to such a machine having independent thought? Remenyi and Williams raise questions such as

---

HAL is the flawed computer that battles with Jupiter-bound astronauts in *2001: A Space Odyssey*. Its name came from the alphabetic characters preceding IBM.

responsibility. In applying intelligence, for example through an advanced form of expert system, a machine would be expected to make errors, just like a human. Who, then, is responsible? Do we accuse the programmer, user or even the machine itself? Although the prospect is some way off, voices are now calling for a debate on these questions. The unfettered rush for commercial advantage may have to be restrained.

Systems size and security

Nowadays, hacking is endemic. The United States Federal Bureau of Investigation estimates that one computer is broken into every 20 seconds via the Internet. The Pentagon's own systems were attacked about 250 000 times in 1996 with about two-thirds managing some penetration. Many hackers do it not for material gain but to beat a challenge. Yet others elicit information for profit. A special investigation by one United Kingdom health authority found 30 attempts every week to access personal files without permission. This scales up to more than 250 000 each year in the National Health Service. Ross Anderson, adviser to the British Medial Association on security warned, ' ...public health information is being sucked towards the centre. The effect is ... aggregation of sensitive data to which ever more staff have access.'[45] With data so valuable in the wrong hands, the temptations placed before staff are very great.

These examples show how readily information can be obtained. Computer security consulting has become big business. Yet we might ask why it is necessary. Should large databases with sensitive commercial, administrative and personal information be created at all? The advantages of aggregation, so apparent to a bureaucrat, should be measured against the risks borne by each 'data subject'.

Use and misuse of data

We discussed, in Chapter 21, some tensions faced by marketing managers when handling information. Reed explains how, conventionally, product managers have relied on market research to reveal trends. Customer databases, the province of retailers, have answered more limited questions such as which people are likely to buy which products. With databases having expanded and deepened, many manufacturers would like to use them to supplement their studies of market share and usage. But that would mean obtaining customers' personal details.

Should the particulars be passed on? The United Kingdom Market Research Society defends the idea that survey data remains anonymous. Yet those involved in direct marketing advocate the notion of 'fair obtaining'. This means that if a person is told why the data is being collected, and is given a chance to withdraw, then trade in the data is permissible. Paying customers for the data through loyalty card discounts seems to support the case. Clearly, however, customers are not told in detail how the data is used.[46]

Personnel

Instead of looking at weaknesses of system design and management, authors such as Banerjee, Jones and Cronan examine the losses caused by unethical behaviour among individuals.[47] Again, they argue that the beneficial effects of proper use are marred by these losses. They harm both organisations and society. Explanations of why people are ethical or unethical, such as proposed by Bommer and colleagues,[48] start from the following factors:

- personal attributes: morals, personal goals, motivation, position and status, life experience, personality and demography;

- personal environment: peer group and family;

- professional environment: codes of conduct, practice licences, professional associations;

- work environment: corporate goals, policy and culture;

- government and legal environment: legislation, government agencies, judicial system;

- social environment: religious, humanistic, cultural and societal values.

In Bommer's model, these factors are related to the decision process, including data gathering and interpretation and assessment of rewards and losses. Banerjee and colleagues criticise the model. It consists of a list of possibilities with no attempt to validate any link. Instead, they focus on the relationship between demographic variables and ethical intention. IS personnel from six organisations were, with senior management's permission, given a questionnaire. Demographics included gender, age, position and length of service. Intentions were measured by the answers of the 139 respondents to scenarios representing issues such as access, accuracy, privacy and property. Examples are given in the ethics test of Exhibit 22.15.

The results of the survey suggest that being male and having longer service are associated with unethical behaviour. Therefore, managers may need to concentrate ethics training on such staff. On the other hand, there were differences among the patterns of response to the seven scenarios. This suggests that ethical attitudes are relative to situations. For instance, in the second case in Exhibit 22.15, employees of a bank may all take a firmer line on Frank's case than an average information person.

Surveillance

Direct monitoring of each employee's work performance is often a by-product of IS development. Taylor and McIntosh take a pessimistic view of this trend.[49] The worker on the supermarket checkout may be unaware, or have forgotten, that the machine provides work rate data to supervisors. After all, the EPOS equipment seems to be there for handling the flow of goods as smoothly as possible. Yet, through comparison of speeds with store averages and other norms, managers can see whether any individual is working at the desired rate. This is the first layer of control. Additionally, the equipment provides information on the proportion of items cancelled by the operator. Through colluding with friends, some employees use this method to steal. Therefore, if an employee is cancelling more entries than average, managers will scrutinise the transactions. They may supplement their investigation with another form of information technology, the in-store camera, to monitor the employee's behaviour. Without denying their duty to reduce the incidence of inefficiency and crime, Taylor and McIntosh conclude by asking whether

---

Exhibit 22.15 **Ethics test: how do you measure up**

As a personal computer user you have bought and used several commercial packages protected by typical licence agreements. You have enhanced your system by writing your own routines that, from time to time, call up the commercial packages. This is legitimate.

Your friends, intrigued by how easy your machine is to operate, asked for copies of your work. These you readily gave but, accidentally, you also copied the commercial programs to the disks. Your friends use your routines and, unknown to you, the packages.

You have acted unethically.

I strongly disagree | 1 | 2 | 3 | 4 | 5 | 6 | 7 | I strongly agree

Frank, a programmer, was in serious financial difficulty. He kept news of this from his employer, a bank. Then came a significant personal tragedy that made him need some extra cash for a short time. Frank decided that to violate his trust at the bank would cause the least harm to the fewest people. Therefore, he changed a reporting program to hide his own account number from daily overdraft reports. Between monthly summaries, this report was relied on to stop further cheque cashing.

Frank's action did not change current balances or controls and his action would have been revealed at the month end. Yet he repaid the overdraft by this time and corrected the change in the program. His statement included a penalty payment for the overdraft. Frank told himself that he had done no one harm. He had run up a small unauthorised loan for which he had paid a high interest rate. It would only have been wrong if he had been unable to repay the sum in time.

Frank's behaviour fell well below acceptable ethical standards.

I strongly disagree | 1 | 2 | 3 | 4 | 5 | 6 | 7 | I strongly agree

---

such practices reinforce the dominant position of managers and gender divisions of labour. In the supermarket, do they sustain the 'well-preserved patriarchy in which (largely) male managers dominate the work of (mainly) women employees'?[50]

Conclusion: wizard or monster?

Seeing managers as information workers offers a sharp perspective on their roles in organisations of the information age. Not only does the new technology offer better ways of doing often tedious work but it presents opportunities to entrepreneurs and others willing to become involved in the creations of new businesses and industries. Meanwhile, the ever growing flood of data threatens to overwhelm staff. Because creating large volumes of it is so easy, its really useful elements are dispersed and unvalued.

In their work, people use information for many purposes. It is useful if it makes a difference to performance, either in transaction processing, decision making, control or in enabling managers to understand more clearly their environment. If relevant, timely and well-presented information is available at reasonable cost, then it passes the value-added test.

We have studied some of the many types of information system, noting in particular the differences between those developed for operations and for strategic management. Taxonomies, such as that proposed by Mentzas, are helpful in distinguishing other purposes. These may be communication, decision and information support. The decision support system may seem ideal to many managers but hopes for high-quality, user-friendly applications have hardly been realised. Many information systems have failed, either from the moment of commissioning or later as their failure to match promises results in their being discarded. Integrating the IS with general strategy is important. So are policies such as logically incremental development and the method of choosing suppliers.

Information systems interact with the practice of management along many dimensions. Among the most significant issues are: the management of knowledge assets; consequences for structure of both the organisation and its allies; and the effect on the roles of many members.

The rapid rise of the information business has brought with it a list of ethical questions. At a societal level, we must consider the dangers inherent in the growth of huge databases. In the right hands they offer great gains. Yet their susceptibility to intrusions cannot be eradicated. At the firm level, how shall managers be guided about what they should and should not do? Marketing is evidently a field where such questions arise but we could equally well have investigated functions such as personnel management including recruitment. Finally, while artificial intelligence seems as remote as ever (although computers approach the brain's performance in some aspects such as speed) development continues with hardly a second thought. Will information systems prove to be monsters?

Quick check up   *can you ...*

- Give a formula that relates data to information;
- State Choo's three main uses of information by managers;
- List four ways information can be useful, according to Robson;
- Name three common information systems for operations;
- Identify the uses of the characters D, E, I, M, S etc. in system labels;

- Give the three dimensions used by Mentzas to classify information systems;
- Identify the forces linking ISs and centralisation;
- Suggest five ways in which ISs change patterns of work;
- Define explicit and tacit knowledge.

Questions

Chapter review

22.1 Define information and explain the features that make it useful.

22.2 Explain and illustrate the differences between MIS, DSS and EIS.

22.3 Summarise the lessons that can be learned for avoiding failure in IS development.

22.4 What ethical issues, for the manager and for society at large, are brought out by the spread of information systems?

Application

22.5 Identify the types of information system in use at FöreningsSparbanken. How do they help to sustain competitive advantage?

Investigation

22.6 Identify some information businesses that have emerged in the past quarter of a century. Investigate how far they have replaced previous technologies or represent parts of totally new industries.

22.7 Interview an experienced manager to find out how he or she thinks information technology has changed the management role. Produce a report relating your observations to ideas given in the chapter.

Improving a telephone service[51]

CLOSING CASE

The IB Group is a Netherlands government organisation. It handles the following: grants and loans for 650 000 current students; repayments by 400 000 graduates; school fees from the parents of 400 000 pupils 16 and 17 years old; the allocation of higher education places; teachers' unemployment benefit; and the organisation of public examinations. The main task is the first – grants and loans.

IB employs some 1500 people: 1300 in the Groningen central office and 200 in 16 satellite offices throughout the country. These out-stations spend 90 per cent of their time on giving information to enquirers about the various finance systems. In 1995, they handled 12 000 incoming calls every day. Enquiries about other services, around 5000, are routed to four call centres. Finally, there are about 3000 calls in and out, typical of an organisation of this size.

During the period 1988 to 1992, staffing at the remote offices had grown three-fold to 150, yet call waiting times and response rates remained unsatisfactory. Daily demand had risen to 7500, with only about 50 per cent answered. Customers called their local office which answered each in turn. At one, a queue might form while others were unoccupied. Unfortunately, incoming traffic could not be diverted. In mid-1992, IB introduced a single 800 number. Calls on this line were passed to a single queue from which they were distributed to the first available clerk in any office. Having calls diverted to a named office was possible and the system was backed up with voice-response for routine information.

Provision of the network, including 150 voice-response lines and automatic call diversion (ACD) equipment, was contracted out. IB's own staff provided the management information system. This is fed data every 10 seconds by the ACD so that current status can be monitored. Additionally, average performance analyses are made available. Results in 1993 showed an immediate improvement in service levels. With no other change, the number of calls handled could be increased by 20 per cent. There was some further expansion of staff so that the daily average of calls handled reached 10 000 in 1993 and 12 000 a year later.

Following the change to the satellite offices, IB brought in corresponding innovations at headquarters. Rather than have staff waste time dialling unanswered numbers, the collections unit began predictive dialling by computer. The line would be switched to a clerk only if someone answered. Keeping in touch in this way cut the work involved in debt chasing, cutting the number of debtors referred to solicitors by 20 per cent.

The changes have benefited IB Group and its customers in the following ways: improved efficiency with savings of about five million guilders each year; improved service quality with faster answering, service integration and out of hours routine voice responses; accurate monitoring of business performance enabling optimal operational scheduling and identification of areas for future improvement. Further plans include the expansion of voice-response services and the facility to display a student's form at any office.

Questions

1 Why did IB seek to improve its operations?

2 What data would you collect to assess the performance of the telephone service?

3 What effects might the information system changes have on the IB organisation?

4 Are any future difficulties possible from the improved performance?

Bibliography   Of the many books on IT, Currie, Wendy (1995) *Management Strategy for IT* considers IS development within the wider business environment. She devotes several chapters to exploring cross-cultural differences. Robson, Wendy (1996) *Strategic Management and Information System*s spends much time on business strategy itself. It is, however, a useful source for material on IS security, legal issues and some ethical questions not covered here. Both books are published by Financial Times Management.

References   1. Kenneally, Christopher (1997) 'Swedes banking on intranet: Sparbanken's Channel One to paperless transactions', *PC Week*. **14 (23)**, 9 June, 39–40; http://www.aragon.se/eq/sparbq1.htm; http://www.sparbanken.se/english/main.html

2. Nairn, Geoffrey (1996) 'IT: Competitive benefits', *The Financial Times Survey of Information Technology*, 6 November, 2.

3. 'Home comforts: Dorling Kindersley sells books via the Internet', *Computer Weekly*, 10 July, 1997, xii–xiii.

4. Mintzberg, Henry (1994) 'Rounding out the manager's job', *Sloan Management Review*, **36 (1)**, Fall, 11–26.

5. Oppenheim, C. (1997) 'Managers' use and handling of information', *International Journal of Information Management*, **17 (4)**, 239–48.

6. Carlson, Sune (1951) *Executive Behaviour – A study of the work load and the working methods of managing directors*, Stockholm: Strömbergs, quoted in Mårtensson, Pär (1996) 'Developing executives' information', Chapter 6 in Lundeberg, Mats and Sundgren, Bo (eds) *Advancing your business: people and information systems in concert*, EFL, Stockholm School of Economics, V1:2.

7. Court, A.W., Culley, S.J. and McMahon, C.A. (1997) 'The influence on information technology in new product development: observations of an empirical study of the access of engineering design information', *International Journal of Information Management*, **17** (**5**), 359–75.

8. Choo, C.W. (1996) 'The knowing organization: how organisations use information to construct meaning, create knowledge and make decisions', *International Journal of Information Management*, **16** (**5**), 329–40.

9. Drucker, Peter (1980) *Managing in Turbulent Times*, London: Pan, 31.

10. Senge, Peter M. (1993) *The Fifth Discipline: The art and practice of the learning organisation*, London: Century.

11. Robson, Wendy (1996) *Strategic Management and Information Systems*, London: Financial Times Pitman Publishing, 368.

12. Mangaliso, Mzamo P. (1995) 'The strategic usefulness of management information as perceived by middle managers', *Journal of Management Studies*, **21** (**2**), Summer, 231–50.

13. Naylor, John and Williams, Jenny (1994) 'The successful use of IT in SMEs in Merseyside', *European Journal of Information Systems*, **3** (**1**), 48–56.

14. Ackoff, Russell (1967) 'Management Misinformation Systems', *Management Science*, **14** (**4**), 147–56.

15. Allison, Ian K. (1996) 'Executive Information Systems: an evaluation of current United Kingdom practice', *International Journal of Information Management*, **16** (**1**), 27–38; Bartholomew, Doug (1997) 'When will EIS deliver? Executive information systems promised to revolutionise the way top management works, but the promise remains unfulfilled', *Industry Week*, **246** (**5**), 3 March, 37–9; Warren, Liz (1996) 'A panoramic view', *Computer Weekly*, 12 December, 46–7.

16. Warren (1996) *op. cit.*

17. Mentzas, Gregory. (1994) 'A functional taxonomy of computer-based information systems', *International Journal of Information Management*, **14**, 397–410.

18. Chu, P.C. (1995) 'Conceiving strategic systems', *Journal of Systems Management*, **46** (**4**), 36–41.

19. Porter, Michael E. (1985) *Competitive Advantage: Creating and sustaining superior performance*, New York: Free Press; Lynch, Richard (1997) *Corporate Strategy*, London: Financial Times Pitman Publishing, 246–51, shows how the concept can be extended to cover the *value system*, a cluster of interrelated organisations.

20. Earl, Michael J. (1996) 'Information systems strategy ... why planning techniques are not the answer', *Business Strategy Review*, **7** (**1**), Spring, 54–8.

21. Quinn, J.B. (1980) 'Managing strategic change', *Sloan Management Review*, **21** (**4**), 3–20.

22. Hulme, Martyn R. (1997) 'Procurement reform and MIS project success', *International Journal of Purchasing and Materials Management*, **33** (**1**), Winter, 2–7.

23. Haapaniemi, Peter (1996) 'Cyber-strategy', *Journal of Business Strategy*, **17** (**1**), January–February, 22–6.

24. Pringle, Davis (1997) 'Outsourcery', *Information Strategy*, **2** (**9**), November, 18–9.

25. 'CEO and CFO satisfaction with IS', *Computerworld*, 12 June, 1995, 12–15.

26. Gurbaxani, V. and Whang, S. (1991) 'The impact of information systems on organisations and markets', *Communications of the ACM*, **34** (**1**), 59–73.

27. Kavanagh, John (1998) 'Centralisation: Moving back to the future', *Financial Times*, 14 March.
28. Malone, Thomas W. and Crowston, Kevin (1994) 'The interdisciplinary study of coordination', *ACM Computing Surveys*, **26** (**1**), March, 87–119.
29. *Ibid*.
30. Mintzberg, Henry, Quinn, James Brian and Ghoshal, Sumantra (1998) *The Strategy Process: Revised European edition*, Hemel Hempstead: Prentice Hall, 708–14.
31. Brown, Linden and Pattinson, Hugh (1995) 'Information technology and telecommunications: impacts in strategic alliance formation and management', *Management Decision*, **33** (**4**), July, 41–51.
32. Griffiths, John (1997) 'IT: More will ease road jams', *Financial Times*, 14 November.
33. European Telework Online, http://www.eto.org.uk/etd/index.htm
34. Taylor, John A. and McIntosh, Helen D. (1996) 'Managing human resources in the information age', in Towers, Brian (ed.) *The Handbook of Human Resource Management*, Second edition, Oxford: Blackwell, 373–93.
35. Phillips, Tom (1997) 'Hard drive, soft water', *Guardian: Online*, 21 May.
36. 'Mr Knowledge', *The Economist*, 31 May, 1997, 84.
37. Mullin, Rick (1996) 'Knowledge management: a cultural evolution', *Journal of Business Strategy*, **17** (**5**), September–October, 56–9; Houlder, Vanessa (1997) 'Knowledge management: the high price of know-how', *Financial Times*, 14 July.
38. *The Economist* (1997) *loc. cit.*
39. Paul, Lauren Gibbons (1997) 'Building a new organisational chart', *PC Week*, **14** (**33**), 4 August, 85.
40. Bowles, Tim and Blyth, Bill (1997) 'How do you like your data: raw, *al dente* or stewed?', *Journal of the Market Research Society*, **39** (**1**), January, 163–4.
41. Lambeth, Jonathan (1996) 'At breaking point', *Computer Weekly*, 10 October, 44.
42. Stonier, T. (1983) *The Wealth of Information: a profile of the post-industrial economy*, London: Methuen.
43. Remenyi, D. and Williams, B. (1996) 'Some aspects of ethics and research into the silicon brain', *International Journal of Information Management*, **16** (**6**), 401–11.
44. Clarke, Arthur C. (1951) *The Sentinel*; Kubrick, Stanley (1968) *2001: A Space Odyssey*.
45. Campbell, Duncan (1997) 'Hypocritic oaths: medical records have lost their way', *Guardian: Online*, 6 November, 7.
46. Reed, David (1996) 'Profiling and market research. To be anonymous, or to be passed on ... that is the ethical question', *Precision Marketing*, 25 November.
47. Banerjee, Debasish; Jones Thomas W., and Cronan, Timothy Paul (1996) 'The association of demographic variables and ethical behaviour of information systems personnel', *Industrial Management and Data Systems*, **96** (**3**), March, 3–10.
48. Bommer, M.; Gratto, C.; Gravander, J. and Tuttle, M. (1987) 'A behavioural model of ethical and unethical decision making', *Journal of Business Ethics*, **6**, 265–80.
49. Taylor and McIntosh (1996) *op. cit.*, 380–1.
50. *Ibid.*, 381.
51. Klok, J., Pauli, E., Roode, R., Saat, P., Stijger, K., Thiadens, T. and Schut, K. (1995) 'Handling a 20 000 calls-a-day telephone environment: the case of a service organisation', *International Journal of Information Management*, **15** (**5**), 389–400.

Part 7

CONTROLLING

Who controls the past controls the future. Who controls the present controls the past. *George Orwell, British writer*

What we have to learn to do, we learn by doing. *Aristotle, Greek philosopher*

PART 6	CHAPTER 22	CHAPTER 21	CHAPTER 20	CHAPTER 19
IMPLEMENTING POLICIES AND PLANS	Managers and information	Innovation: from ideas to customer benefits	Marketing: managing relations with customers	Operations management

PART 7		CHAPTER 23	CHAPTER 24	
CONTROLLING		Control systems	Control and change	

Part 7 completes the cycle of planning, organising, implementing and controlling. As Chapter 23 shows, however, control is more varied than simply making corrections after deviations from plans have become apparent. Better understanding of processes, supplemented by timely control data, enables managers to anticipate difficulties and take action to prevent them. The chapter also points out that control activity is effected through people. Without their cooperation, the cybernetic model of automatic control is worthless.

Another effect of the extension of information systems is the ready access to more data. Although this might support the technocratic approach to management, excessive attention to numbers, especially accounting data, may lead to unbalanced development.

Chapter 24 discusses further problems of control, relating it to power and the behaviour of people and groups. The control dilemma concerns the balance between failure and the need to empower employees to make changes they think are necessary. Tightening of controls only makes things worse. The emerging theory of chaos, suggesting that the future is unknowable, challenges the single-loop model. This means that organisations must learn and the way to do so is, to follow Aristotle, through doing.

23

Control systems

Chapter objectives

When you have finished studying this chapter, you should be able to:

- explain the nature of control in organisations;
- match contrasting views of control with the various schools of management thought;
- set out the purposes of control within the organisational context;
- identify three basic types of control system, explaining the steps that each involves; identify their differences and give examples of suitable applications;
- apply these models to illustrate circumstances when control systems can fail;
- show how control systems can be linked to cover a whole organisation, suggesting some weaknesses with this approach;
- describe and illustrate reasons for effective control;
- compare conventional performance measures with new ideas concerning balance;
- outline the limitations of the cybernetic approach in the human context.

Home shopping services

Home shopping grew out of mail order. In the United Kingdom, a few companies dominate business. In 1995, Key Note estimated that the five leaders accounted for 97.4 per cent sales.[1] The remaining thousand or so sold specialist or premium products to niche markets. The catalogue division of Great Universal Stores, number four in the world, generated revenue greater than £1.2 billion. It had about 45 per cent of the market, followed by Littlewoods with half that amount. Such leading companies take more than three quarters of all their orders by telephone. Connections are free or at local rates. For customers, telephone ordering is easier, delivery is faster, and, when stock-outs occur, alternatives are offered. Compared with the mail, service quality is improved. Operators check customers' credit records on-line so that satisfactory orders are immediately placed in the despatch schedule and picking instructions sent to automated warehouses.

Better service raises expectations. Mail order customers used to be unaware of how quickly their orders were handled. Telephone users, however, want instant attention. They find waiting frustrating. Consequently, telephone bureaux set themselves response targets, or have them set for them. For example, under the regulator's rules, the privatised British Gas is expected to answer care line calls in 30 seconds; the privatised rail companies' national inquiry service must answer 90 per cent of the weekly 900 000 calls before the caller gives up. In home shopping, GUS, Littlewoods and the others need telephone bureaux whose capacity balances their response targets against the cost of having staff idle for much of the time. At peak times, Littlewoods has more than 100 operators at work.

Callers join a single queue and are answered in sequence. The equipment connects them to desks in rotation. The call queue length is displayed prominently in the operating room to warn of excess demand.

Demand varies hourly and daily. Experience enables a forecast to be made for each half-hour interval. Companies recruit and train enough staff to cover the forecast pattern. Yet, as shown in Fig. 19.13, changes occur by the minute. To cope with these short-term surges, the supervisors can:

■ Reduce the time spent with each caller. When time permits, staff remind customers of special offers and pass on other information about the company. When they are busy, they cut this activity.

■ Ask staff to delay their breaks.

■ Call to the manager to divert staff from other activities, although this usually takes several minutes to arrange.

Performance is reviewed at three levels. First, each week, the supervisors receive information on operators' performance levels including the times that each individual takes to handle calls. They are expected to check on operators whose performance appears to be out of line. The accent is on coaching. Discussion usually resolves difficulties. Not overemphasising speed at the expense of quality is important. For the customer, each service episode is significant. The art, at peak times, is to give good quality while maintaining an efficient tempo.

At the second level, the departmental manager is responsible for achieving service standards within cost constraints. Enough staff must be allocated to the operation to enable more than 99 per cent of calls to be answered within 30 seconds. The average wait should be much lower – about three seconds. Such performance has to be achieved within operating cost budgets.

The manager plans the allocation of staff according to latest demand forecasts. Hourly, daily and seasonal fluctuations are estimated from patterns identified in the management information system. The trend is also worked out from this data, modified by the effect of, say, advertising campaigns. Forecasts are updated weekly. In addition, the management information system makes available the following summaries: costs; staff performance compared with standards; average times to answer calls; average length of call; and the number of enquirers who hung up before their calls were answered. Using this information, the manager discusses and adjusts the coming weekly programme with the supervisors.

The third level of control is with the divisional manager who receives summarised performance information each week on all departments including both telephone and mail order. Problems and possible changes are discussed with the departmental managers. Additionally, the divisional manager works with other departments to improve the ordering activity in the longer term. These include: changes to the information system; new order processing methods; improved query handling; clarifying instructions and information given to customers; and the timing of special offers and other promotions.

The divisional manager must consider the increasing use of the telephone, include the use of automated call handling (ACH), and the switch to newer technologies. ACH poses a dilemma. It promises consistent call duration, greater line capacity and 24-hour availability. It also promises to relieve problems for employees handling routine calls under close supervision. Answering more than a hundred calls each day is tedious and stressful work, sometimes leading to 'modern' illnesses such as repetitive strain injury, RSI.[2] On the other hand, customers often rely on the knowledge and helpfulness of human contact. Staff can also deal with unexpected queries. Furthermore, broadening the product range to include new items, such as insurance and other financial services, requires specialist advice at the point of contact.

Automation is also an advantage of the Internet. It beats ACH in several ways, mainly because it is a richer channel. Users can send more information in both directions. Growth has yet to be seen, however, among the groups to whom GUS and Littlewoods appeal in their catalogues.

Introduction

The case study illustrates many aspects of control in organisations. We see that managers at several levels monitor the performance of each bureau and, if it deviates from its targets, they act to bring it back into line. This process of correction of errors, or *variances*, forms the basis of this chapter. Beyond the simple loop of monitoring, comparison with target and corrective action, we can see a hierarchy of control. Each layer monitors the performance of the next. As we look further up the hierarchy, monitoring information is more aggregated and provided less frequently. In the same way, corrective action, which can be immediate at lower levels, is delayed at higher ones. This arrangement is typical of formal control systems.

Within the case we also find suggestions of problems. Although the leading companies try to avoid the stress and demotivation caused by routine answering of calls, there are widespread reports of poor practices. In the United Kingdom, call

> To accountants, the term *variance* refers to the difference between budgeted and actual spending or receipts.

centres have been among the fastest growing employment sectors. With more than 250 000 people already at work, especially in cities in the North where costs are low, many centres echo the 'dark satanic mills'[3] of mass production. Closely supervised staff sit in lines or booths. Like the checkout operator of Chapter 22, the performance of each is monitored remotely. Not only do supervisors watch call handling rates, they eavesdrop on conversations, and they expect staff to ask permission before leaving their desks. On such modern treadmills, control generates a climate of fear.

In this chapter and the next we examine both these aspects of control. On the one hand, as we have argued at various points in the book, it is a poor manager who fails to monitor the outcomes of plans and instructions. Yet control must be exercised humanely and constructively if it is not to be seen as coercive. We shall start by studying control as an application of a rational model, closing the chapter by outlining some difficulties from the behavioural perspective. Chapter 24 explores the limits of the rational model, both in terms of its search for stability and in its playing down of human factors.

What is control?

There are many uses of the term control. From a narrow point of view, we have control meaning coercion or close direction. It is a feature of both 'hard' human resource management, *see* Chapter 15, and the autocratic or directive style of leadership discussed in Chapter 16. Through dominance and close supervision, organisations are 'under control' when they operate as extensions of managers' decision processes. They expect them to respond like the scalpels of *telesurgery*. This is the information age method of doing medical operations. A team of highly skilled surgeons works on a patient at a theatre, possibly on the other side of the world. Their tools include joysticks, robots' arms, cameras and a high bandwidth information link.[4]

Contrasting this close-up, Anthony sees the world through a wide angle lens. He sees planning and control as inseparable aspects of the same activity. In his view, splitting planning from control is too artificial in the organisational context. 'Management control is the process by which managers influence other members of the organisation to implement the organisation's strategies.'[5] In other words, the steps set out in Fig. 9.1 are combined into the one process. This is justified because, 'Although planning and control are definable abstractions and are easily understood as calling for different types of mental activity, they do not relate to major categories of activities actually carried on in an organisation, either at different times or by different people, or for different situations.'[6]

Instead, Anthony identifies three layers of control, each of which contains the loop of Fig. 9.1. Shown in Fig. 23.1, they are: *strategic planning, management control,* and *task control*. The layers correspond to the strategic, intermediate and operational ones of Fig. 9.4. The first, strategic planning, has been covered in Chapter 10. Below in the hierarchy come management control and task control. The former covers interpretation of strategy into action while the latter concentrates on transactions. 'Task control is the process of assuring that specific tasks are carried out effectively and efficiently.'[7] Unfortunately, although this is a useful distinction, it suffers from the very difficulties it was meant to overcome. While searching for a holistic view of control, the three-tier approach runs the risk of losing it. Berry and colleagues point out, '... interlinkages between levels, which are interdependent, are not shown, also the environment in which the organisation exists is omitted from consideration.'[8] In other words, as the knives of Fig. 23.1 show, whichever way we slice the whole, we sever important links.

What does this mean in practice? How should we look at control? We could rely on the process model alone. Yet the home shopping case that opened this chapter tells us about how control is exercised at three managerial levels and about how these levels are linked. Both angles tell us something about control in this organisation. But neither tells us everything. Neither is complete. We must switch between the two, and add in broader views such as the organisation–environment relationships drawn from Chapter 3.

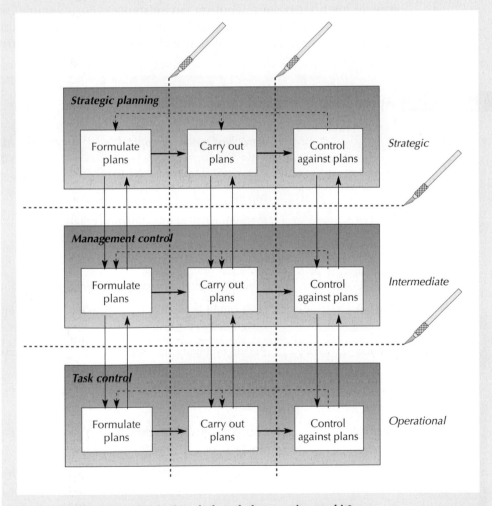

Fig. 23.1 How do we divide the whole to help us understand it?

There is a further problem with merging planning and control into a single idea. What about leading, communicating and other managerial roles and functions identified by authors from Fayol to Mintzberg? An objection to using any of these categories, demanding that management be viewed only as a whole, would make discussion and research impossible. Categories are useful for making sense of the world. Therefore, we shall distinguish control from planning although the same person is often responsible for both. Management is multifaceted. Stacey points out, 'Management is about more than making a decision and taking action – it is also about evaluating the outcome of the decision and its consequent action. In other words, it is also about control and about learning from the consequences of behaviour.'[9.]

Origins of control ideas

Mullins shows how the emerging schools of management thought held different views of the nature of control.[10] Summarised in Exhibit 23.1, we can link these views back to Chapter 2. It is worth noting the modern view, that the choice of control methods is contingent on circumstances. For example, we would expect there to be much coercion, that is external control, in corrective institutions. Exhibit 23.2 describes one of many checks on prisoners returning from work

Exhibit 23.1 Approaches to organisational control

School	Perceived nature of control	Main source of control
Scientific management – Taylor	Stress on detailed control of every aspect of a job	External
Bureaucracy – Weber	Predominance of rules and procedures	External
Administrative principles – Fayol	Management includes control as generic process	External
Human relations – Follett, Mayo	Control should not mean close direction	Internal
Theory Y – McGregor	Self-control is possible if a person is committed to the task	Internal
Management science – Urwick	Accent on inputs and outputs – control stresses linkages	Process
Socio-technical systems – Tavistock	Role of technology in the control of work	Process
Systems and cybernetics – Weiner	Learning from engineering control systems	Process
Systems and chaos – Gleick, Stacey	Limits of formal control – instability	Mixed – limited
Contingency	No single best way to control	As required

assignments outside a camp in Stalin's Russia.[11] The 'zeks' were afraid to do anything that might displease the arbitrary wishes of the guards.

Sources of control

Commenting on the variety of control observed in organisations, Mullins adds, 'It may even be that control systems provide a better means of predicting certain facets of organisational behaviour than the classification of technology.'[12] The schools in Exhibit 23.1 illustrate three assumptions about where control should originate. Classical theorists had no doubt; control is exercised by management and is largely external. Those in the human relations movement saw the opposite. They discovered that, in spite of managers' motivational efforts, from incentives to coercion, individuals and groups exercised great power in setting their own work targets. In this perspective, therefore, control is largely internal. Finally, the systems-cybernetics school saw control as essentially a process problem. Decision making, supported by a flow of relevant information makes a complex process work. Literature on quality management, for instance, pays the greatest attention to this aspect. Oakland defines control as, '... the process by which information or feedback is provided so as to keep all functions on track.'[13]

All three views of control are useful to understanding of the issues. This chapter concentrates on the process view, giving a close-up of the stages of information processing, decision making and action needed to keep processes on track. Questions of internal and external control, and their relationship to organisation and motivation, covered in Chapters 15 and 16, are brought together in Chapter 24.

■ The purpose of control

Having effective control systems offers advantages to the organisation. As Figure 23.2 illustrates, these fall into four categories that we shall now examine.

■ *Achieving objectives*
   Taken overall, control helps the organisation achieve its objectives. As we shall see, formal control systems require managers to state their objectives clearly and consistently. The case of home shopping showed how managers at different levels worked to customer service targets measured for call duration, waiting times and dropouts, and costs.
   We should also remember the uncertainty surrounding all plans. As Burns wrote, 'The best laid schemes o' mice and men gang aft a-gley'.[14] Deviations from

---

Exhibit 23.2 Taking risks for something to trade

'Meanwhile Shukhov had removed both mittens, the empty one and the one with the hacksaw, and held them in one hand (the empty one in front) together with the untied rope-belt. He fully unbuttoned his jacket, lifted high the edges of his coat and jacket ... and at the word of command stepped forward.

The guard slapped Shukhov's sides and back, and the outside of his knee-pocket. Nothing there. He kneaded the edges of coat and jacket. Nothing there either. He was about to pass him through when, for safety's sake, he crushed the mitten that Shukhov held out to him – the empty one.'

expectations may arise from unexpected variations in inputs, hidden process deficiencies, changes in the environment or imperfections in the plan itself. We should not set plans in motion and expect desired results to emerge on their own.

■ *Limiting drift*

While acting upon every minor deviation from a plan is foolish for managers, there is a risk of small errors slowly accumulating eventually to create serious problems. For instance, cuts in service quality flowing from the desire to reduce costs may have little apparent effect in the short term. Yet their long-term effect may be disastrous. This is one reason the rail regulator in the United Kingdom pressed the train operators to improve the quality of their enquiry service. He argued that an effective service was a prerequisite of encouraging more travellers. The declared standard was 90 per cent of calls to be answered. Yet, in April 1997, only 51 per cent had a reply. After three months, and under threat of a fine, performance rose to 82 per cent.

■ *Managing complexity*

While all organisations need control, in the simple ones it can be basic and informal. When large, however, there will be complex structures, often with project teams or matrices imposed on divisions. At this stage, careful attention to control is important if the whole is not to get out of hand. Great Universal Stores has interests in shops, property and so on besides its home shopping businesses. Each will need control appropriate to its setting while linked so that the whole business is manageable.

■ *Environmental response*

We argued in Chapter 3 that irreversible environmental changes pose problems for the organisation. In the time between goal-setting and achievement, turbulent environments can cause disruption making assumptions inappropriate. While the home shopping bureau was practised at coping with random and seasonal fluctuations in demand, managers also knew they had to adapt to trends. Their control system, gathering information about environmental changes as well as cumulative data on customer demand, warned them of areas where they needed new responses.

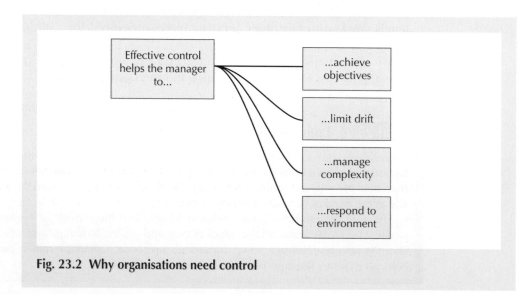

Fig. 23.2 Why organisations need control

Types of control system

Whatever the practical nature of control, or its position in the hierarchy, an organisation needs a process that will ensure that objectives are met, drift avoided, complexity coped with and environmental uncertainty responded to. Taking the open-systems view of an organisation and its processes, we think of a process system (or set of systems) with inputs and outputs. Since the system does not automatically respond to change, it requires continual monitoring and adjustment to keep it on course. This is the function of control. Drawing on the above discussion, we can define it as follows:

> *The function of control is to ensure*
> *that the plan is achieved*
> *in spite of obstacles, variations and uncertainties*
> *in both the organisation and its environment.*

This means that a control system must know the plans, be able to assess performance compared with the plans, and act to correct differences between the two. This control loop is seen in many systems whose survival depends on finding stability. For instance, living systems have many mechanisms conserving the delicate balance needed for life. Of the thousands in the human body, one keeps the brain temperature to within 0.1°C for healthy functioning.

Many natural systems rely on control action following change. They rely on responding to their current state as opposed to anticipating a future one. If our body temperature rises, we pump blood to the skin surface to increase the rate of cooling. We 'glow' *after* exercise. On the other hand, intelligent animal behaviour involves built-in forecasting. To catch prey, the predator moves towards where it thinks the moving target will be. It uses speed and direction information to forecast its position. The relationship between correction and anticipation distinguishes three types of control system: feedback, concurrent and feedforward.

■ Feedback control

Feedback control uses information about past behaviour to correct performance. Cybernetics experts refer to the control activity as based on *negative feedback*. The elements of such control are shown in Fig. 23.3. The process being controlled converts inputs into outputs. It could be any separate process, for example a paint line converts unpainted into painted products. On the other hand, it could be a whole business, converting inputs of economic resources into products and, it is hoped, profits. There are four key features of the model:

■ *Goals*

A precondition of any control is setting out standards. As we shall see, these are made known to the controller as the basis of decisions. For instance, the home shopping bureau had to answer 99 per cent of calls within 30 seconds. Yet this

---

Negative feedback is not an unfavourable response. It means that the control unit responds to errors so as to reverse them.

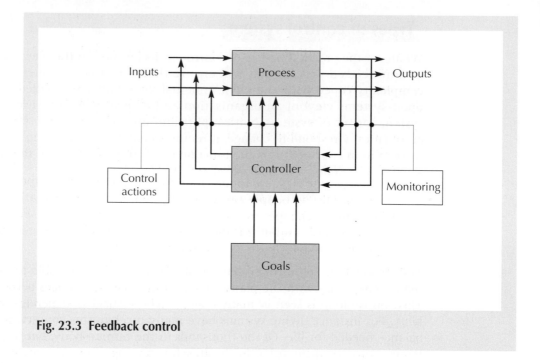

Fig. 23.3 Feedback control

performance was not to be achieved at any cost. The managers had to plan staff deployment to achieve the standard within budget.

■ *Monitor performance*
The second feature of feedback control is measuring process outputs. For many activities, monitoring operates routinely. The queue indicator in the home shopping bureau was an important indicator of current performance.

The case studies of Chapters 9 and 10 provide examples of performance monitoring at the strategic level. For example, Jaeger, *see* Chapter 9, plans its fashion ranges more than a year before it puts them on sale. At intervals throughout this period, managers and staff get together to report on progress.

■ *Comparison*
The third feature of our model brings in the controller. This compares the monitoring results with the goals. If the results are favourable, or close enough to target, then the controller takes no action. Otherwise, the controller acts to counter deficits in the system outputs.

The comparison stage underlines the need for a plan. Tracking progress in the Jaeger design cycle would be of little use if staff were unaware of a plan. The idea is to have sufficient garments in the shops for the launch of each fashion season. Since there are five every year, managers are familiar with the timing of each step in the build up. Having a reliable plan means that things will go well if they stick to it. On the other hand, if work is delayed, they know they must strive to catch up before it is too late.

Intelligent controllers know when deviations in the planned output are significant. In quality control, for instance, small variations in product properties are inevitable. As explained in Chapter 7, these are allowed for by *process toler-*

ances which set upper and lower limits for most parameters. It is worth heeding Deming's story of the printer at Nashua Corporation, *see* Exhibit 7.9. Instead of ignoring minor, random variations, he was fruitlessly trying to adjust them out.

■ *Control action*

The corrective action to be taken depends on the details of the control system. With an automatic controller, the predetermined response is incorporated into the design of the device. A well-known example is a thermostat turning on a heater when the temperature falls.

Note how Fig. 23.3 shows control actions directed at either the process inputs or the system itself. With many machines, such as the heater, the controller is designed only to regulate inputs, here to switch the energy supply. In contrast, a process involving people can be controlled either by regulating inputs or by making minor changes to the way the process itself works. We could see both types at the call centre. In response to rising demand, supervisors would ask for more inputs, that is more staff resources. Alternatively, they would adapt the process by asking operators to spend less time with each client.

Figure 23.3 shows the process with several inputs, outputs, goals and control actions. Although adding extra lines appears at first to complicate the diagram, remember that this typifies most processes. Unlike the simple thermostat, the process controller often has to achieve several goals simultaneously. An added difficulty arises from the inability to observe or measure one or more crucial outputs.

Concurrent control

Often known as real-time or self-control, concurrent control works as closely as possible to the process. Reflecting Anthony's view of the inseparability of process elements, monitoring and adjusting are seen as part of the whole. For instance, if you are sanding a door, you can monitor and adjust your effort without interrupting the rubbing. The call centre operator acts in a similar way. The selling and order taking processes are continually adapted to the client's wishes.

The purist may want to separate the functions of processing and controlling implied in the above examples. Looked at so closely, the process resembles feedback control. At one moment the worker is processing, the next moment monitoring, and so on. Yet from the perspective of the manager, the impression is different. The manager sets the goals and expects the employee to act without further intervention. In contrast to feedback and feedforward control, whose loops run outside the system, the concurrent arrangement has internal monitoring and action. The loops are all within a 'black box', as shown in Fig. 23.4.

> *Black box* refers to a system whose relationship between inputs and outputs is known, although we are not interested in the details of how it works.

Feedforward control

A criticism of feedback control is that it is like closing the stable door after the horse has bolted. Another critic would liken it to driving a car where the wind-

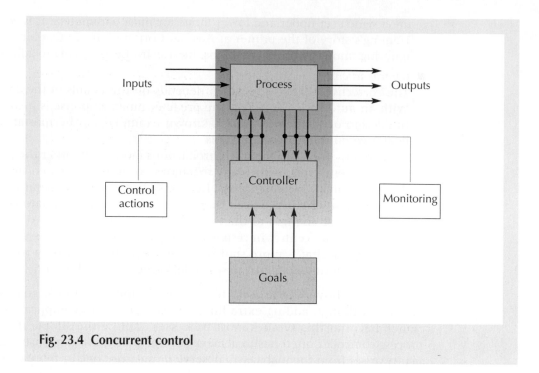

Fig. 23.4 Concurrent control

screen is replaced by a monitor showing the state of the road as it was three seconds previously. To counter such charges, many control systems incorporate an element of feedforward to anticipate problems *before* they arise.

One way to picture feedforward, or *anticipatory*, control is shown in Fig. 23.5. It differs from feedback in one critical aspect. Not only does the controller receive monitoring data on process outputs but these are converted into forecasts of the future outputs if the process continues as it is. A good illustration is the practice of preventive maintenance. In many process plants, it is common to monitor the state of all critical machines including bearings, valves, motors and so on. These tests reveal whether items are beginning to fail. Managers can then arrange to change or repair components before a breakdown occurs. In a more approximate way, car servicing calls for oil changes every 10 000 km or so. To change oil well before its life has expired is cheaper and more efficient than to wait for an expensive bearing failure.

In the telephone bureau, it would be a poor supervisor who waited for process performance to be adversely affected before responding to increased queue length. Continuous monitoring of demand and operator performance enables preventive action to be taken in advance. In air transport, an aircraft leaving Madrid is allocated a landing time at its destination airport in northern Europe and is given a flight plan of its route and height. The crew, taking into account forecast wind speeds for the level at which it is to fly, calculates the correct air speed to ensure it arrives neither ahead of, nor behind, schedule. They compare performance with the plan and make speed adjustments during the flight.

Although feedforward control takes place ahead of changes being required, it is different from planning. The latter considers the question: 'Which direction should

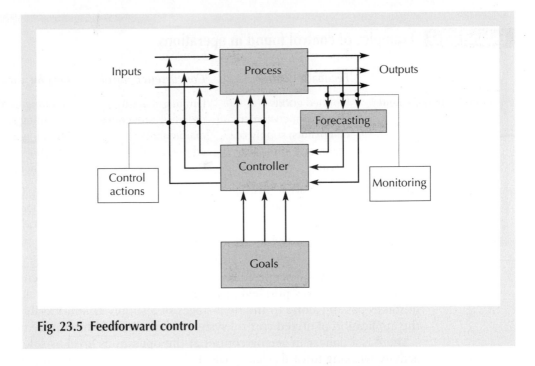

Fig. 23.5 Feedforward control

we be taking and how can we ensure that we take it?' Compare this with feedforward control: 'What early warnings do current outputs give us of future process performance? What should we do now to improve that performance?' Lest the examples given here suggest that the forecasting part of the model works only on output data, we should also recognise that anticipation will also take into account information from other sources. For instance, at the telephone bureau, the management information system combines process data with extrapolations of demand from previous weeks and seasons. This is modified by trend lines based on the effects of advertising by both the company and its rivals. In addition, awareness of exceptional environmental changes is important. Raising tax or interest rates may serve to dampen demand.

While, therefore, three types of control mode are shown here, we should recognise the possibility of variations. Within the general principles of feedback, concurrent and feedforward, differences of detail include: monitoring the inputs and the process as well as the outputs; forecasting all these elements; controlling either inputs or the system, but not both; and being controlled by other systems. Although adding complexity to the discussion risks losing the point, we must consider in a later section how these control systems link into chains and hierarchies. Meanwhile, we shall illustrate the general principles by referring to operations control.

▨ Control of operations

None of the control processes explained and illustrated above is superior to another. We find each used widely in organisations, often in combination. Feedforward control helps to avoid hazards and errors; concurrent control enables

Exhibit 23.3   Examples of control found in operations

	Feedback control	Concurrent control	Feedforward control
Quality management	Finished goods inspection; customer complaints; supply of spares and after-sales service	Limiting work-in-progress; preventive maintenance; empowerment	Assuring quality of incoming supplies; obtaining new equipment; design for manufacturability
Inventory management	Regular stock checks; audits of records	Continuous monitoring	Using sales forecasts to influence purchase and production plans

staff to be given the scope to overcome difficulties as they occur; and feedback control both stresses post-event adjustment and provides a backstop to prevent mistakes passing along to the next stages of a supply chain. Exhibit 23.3 illustrates the application of mixed control systems in quality and inventory management.

There is a danger in seeing control at the operations level as solely a mechanistic activity working towards clear goals. Exhibit 23.3 uses two examples where routine data collection followed by process adjustment is a viable approach. Here, information systems that monitor quality or stocks can warn managers when things are going wrong. Yet these processes depend on being clear about what the goals are and what is to be measured. Problems arise when these are not available. For example, Roper and colleagues found that, among small firms, there were difficulties in deciding what quality standards were appropriate.[15] Exhibit 23.4 gives an outline of the study.

What can go wrong?

When studying processes in practice, the control models give us a set of paradigms against which we can assess the situation. They enable us to pick out faults, for example by checking to see whether all the elements are in place or if they are linked appropriately. Figure 23.6 presents some common examples. Although they relate to the feedforward model, the other models can be also investigated in a similar way.

The faults illustrated arise in four areas: monitoring, goals, control action and forecasting.

- *Myopic monitoring*

  A common fault arises from being unable or unwilling to measure all the process outputs. In the heyday of scientific management, for example, Taylor and colleagues tended to assess output from the number of railway trucks unloaded or weight of pig iron shifted. Yet, as the Hawthorne Sudies discovered, job satisfaction was also an output of employment processes. It was important because of its long-term effect on productivity. Nowadays, following the influence of the socio-technical systems school, managers pay more attention to this factor in job design. Yet measuring it remains difficult.

Exhibit 23.4 SMEs and customers: not seeing the same quality attributes

SMEs may have gained some advantages from registering their procedures under assurance schemes such as ISO 9000. Yet, for the most part, sales are influenced by the way customers perceive their product quality compared with alternatives. Evaluation may include awareness of registration but will also depend on many other factors. There is 'a major disparity between the relative quality perceptions of ... suppliers and their customers.' Roper found that the SMEs gave themselves a higher rating because:

■ they did not identify their true competitors;

■ suppliers and customers stressed different product attributes in their assessments;

■ suppliers made higher estimates of relative quality even on agreed attributes.

Avoiding the expensive outlay, SMEs often lack market research data. This gap allows the first two disparities to arise, accounting for about half of the observed differences. Consequently, many firms strive towards the wrong quality goals and, in so doing, measure output parameters unimportant to their customers.

This is just one example of the 'soft' outputs of many organisational processes. They can relate to the employee or the customer. For the latter, it is easy to count sales but not so easy to assess satisfaction. Some firms monitor the proportion of repeat business, when control is almost too late, while others try to measure it directly using customer surveys. Leading hotel chains, such as Marriott Corporation, follow the good practice of encouraging guests to complete questionnaires when they leave. An extract is shown in Exhibit 23.5.

■ *Garbled goals*
An arbitrary and conflicting set of goals make it impossible for the control system to work effectively. Clearly, to the controller, the goals serve as a yardstick with which performance is to be compared. They should, therefore, be unambiguous and consistent. Multiple goals are a weakness of the application of control models to organisations. We saw in Chapters 6 and 9 that this is typical of situations with many stakeholders. Without refinement, the goals will be unsuited as key elements in the control model.

■ *Curbed controls*
Failure of control systems can also be attributed to the 'action' side of the model. Inability to make the necessary changes results from two sources. First, the controller may have insufficient understanding of how the system works. This may, of course, arise from incompetence or inexperience. Yet complex systems tax even the most experienced controller, especially when unusual circumstances arise. Exhibit 23.6 gives two contrasting examples where competent controllers either failed or succeeded.[16]

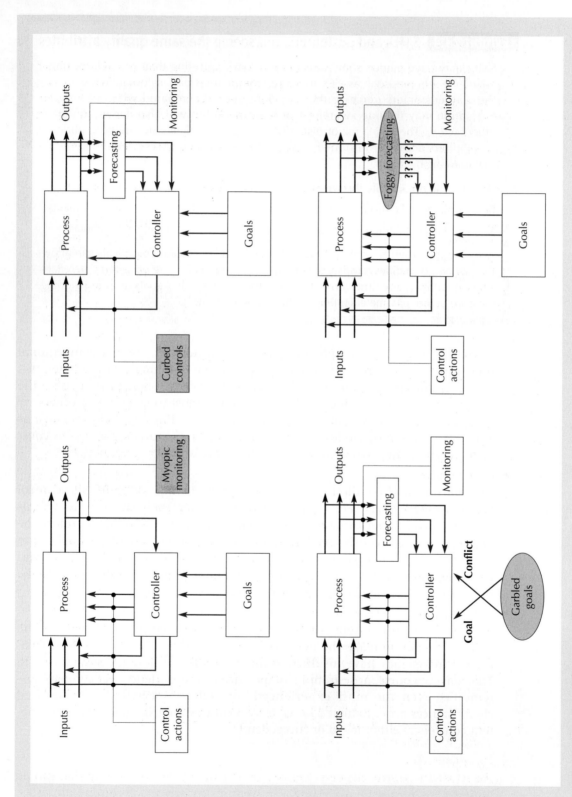

Fig. 23.6 Failures in feedforward control

Exhibit 23.5   Marriott's customer survey

The Marriott Corporation is one of the world's leading hotel chains. It stresses service quality as a basic tenet of its strategy. Whether they have stayed overnight or attended a conference, every guest is invited to complete a questionnaire to evaluate the hospitality. In an accompanying letter, the chairman, Bill Marriott, promises to share the comments with the hotel manager and follow up all comments and recommendations.

The four-page computer-marked form has 36 questions and a space for open-ended comments. The following questions are typical:

12 Please think about the bathroom and bedroom areas of your hotel room and rate the following items:

Overall cleanliness of bathroom	10 9 8 7 6 5 4 3 2 1
Cleanliness of tub and tile	10 9 8 7 6 5 4 3 2 1
Cleanliness of vanity area	10 9 8 7 6 5 4 3 2 1
Supply of bath towels and wash cloths	10 9 8 7 6 5 4 3 2 1
Overall cleanliness of bathroom	10 9 8 7 6 5 4 3 2 1
Condition of carpet in bedroom	10 9 8 7 6 5 4 3 2 1
Condition of bedspread	10 9 8 7 6 5 4 3 2 1
Condition of furniture in bedroom	10 9 8 7 6 5 4 3 2 1

14E Please rate the following items if you ordered from the breakfast menu:

Server's knowledge of menu	10 9 8 7 6 5 4 3 2 1
Server's familiarity with items on menu	10 9 8 7 6 5 4 3 2 1
Friendliness of server	10 9 8 7 6 5 4 3 2 1
Timeliness with which you received your beverages	10 9 8 7 6 5 4 3 2 1
Food prepared the way you wanted it	10 9 8 7 6 5 4 3 2 1
Timeliness of beverage refills during meal	10 9 8 7 6 5 4 3 2 1
Timeliness with which you received check	10 9 8 7 6 5 4 3 2 1
Value for price paid	10 9 8 7 6 5 4 3 2 1

The second reason for not taking action is powerlessness. Little or large, control action means change and, as we saw in Chapter 14, change means resistance. Although the control model suggests an active controller making process adjustment in the light of every variance from planned outputs, the reality of organisations is very different. Perhaps the effort required to overcome resistance is not justified by the expected improvements. On the other hand, there may have been too many changes already. One of the 'secrets' of the Toyota production system is its commitment to stability. The whole supply chain, including many subcontractors, or 'partners', works to the same pace. Kanbans link stages with just-in-time deliveries. Toyota, the final assembler, sees itself as both the 'drummer' beating out the rhythm, and the 'buffer' between the production system and the market. Seeking to optimise efficiency through the chain, it is very reluctant to change the beat.

■ *Foggy forecasting*
Anticipatory control depends heavily on the quality of forecasting that can be built in. In operations, well-known procedures control many routine processes.

Exhibit 23.6 Out of and in control

28 March 1979: Three Mile Island, Harrisburg, Pennsylvania

Following a misunderstanding over whether a valve was open or shut, the nuclear reactor ran out of control for several hours. Fearing radioactive emissions, the authorities evacuated thousands from the locality. Although by all accounts competent, the plant operators were unable to cope with the sequence of events. The control systems continued to function yet presented the staff with too much information too quickly. The design of gauges and dials did not help easy assimilation. No sooner had the crew appreciated one alarm than another went off. At one point more than fifty were sounding.

5 November 1997: Heathrow Airport, London

There were no serious injuries among 114 passengers and crew of a Virgin Atlantic A340-300 Airbus forced to crash land. Approaching Heathrow, the crew was warned that the left-hand undercarriage had failed. Captain Barnby, the pilot, following standard procedure, rolled the aircraft from side to side to try to dislodge it. Then he flew low over the control tower for a visual check that the wheels were stuck. Finally, with ground services prepared to douse the airliner in foam, the pilot managed to land and keep the aircraft upright almost until it had stopped. The passengers escaped within one minute.

Although he had won aerobatic championships, Captain Barnby had not crash landed before. His ability to manage the emergency arose from many hours of practice in flight simulators. To him, 'It was all in a day's work.'

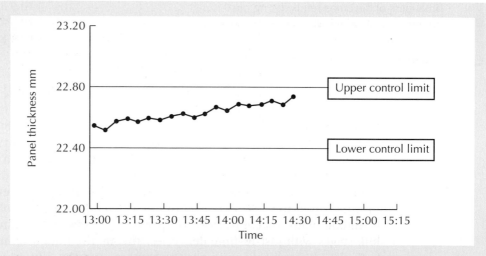

Fig. 23.7 Thickness measurements

For instance, samples taken from the output of a wood sanding machine may show thickness measurements shown in Fig. 23.7. It is easy to see that the dimension will soon exceed the upper control limit and the machine needs adjustment.

Unfortunately, forecasting is rarely so easy, especially when it comes to strategy. Organisations often put much effort into carrying out their strategic plans but are blind to checking whether the premises on which the plans were based remain valid. Picken and Dess build on Mintzberg's arguments that strategies need to change frequently. 'An inflexible commitment to predetermined goals and strategy can prevent the very adaptability that is often the essence of a good strategy. Because goals and objectives are considered fixed and inflexible until the next planning cycle, the organisation typically does not alter either its strategies or its objectives to deal with the realities of a changed environment.'[17] Evidently, a control system must allow for changes in goals, as we shall see in the next section.

Building the control system

Just as there are many configurations of the basic control loop, there are many ways of fitting them together to build the total system. General models of organisations based on layers of nested loops have been put forward. Starting from an analogy with human brain and nervous system, Beer proposed five levels of control, each connected to the ones above, below and alongside. Before looking at this work, we shall briefly consider vertical and horizontal connections.

Levels of control

Levels of control mirror levels of planning in the organisation. Illustrated in Exhibit 9.1 and Fig. 9.2, the planning approach shows how managers at each level establish guidelines for their subordinates. In terms of the control model, the controller is given goals by some 'higher' authority. Yet what if the goals turn out to be unachievable? Then, the possibility of changing them must be considered. Figure 23.8 shows how feedback from the control function can be incorporated into the goal-setting process. Fixed goals are best when the process and its environment are stable. If this is not so, there is more likelihood that the goals should be changed. It is as though we have a thermostat with the intelligence to decide what the temperature should be.

Being able to influence goals, known as *second order control*, is common in successful organisations. They learn through practice, adjusting goals and control systems to become more efficient. We return to learning in Chapter 24. Meanwhile we should note that feedback to higher level goals reinforces the means–end chain explained in Chapter 9.

Links along the value chain

Processes in an organisation have little worth unless they are joined in a chain. We expect, therefore, to see connections among control systems at the same level.

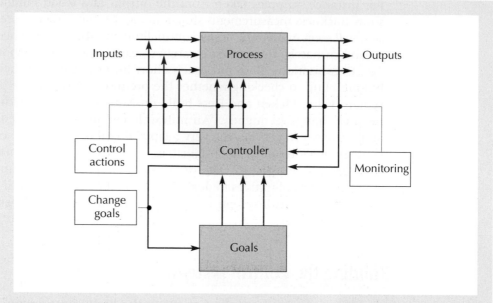

Fig. 23.8 Second order control: the controller influences its own objectives

Figure 23.9 shows three operational processes each complete with its loop. If no attention were paid to co-ordination, as if the three were independent organisations, they would be in danger of instability as small disturbances pass along the chain. The role of the overall controller, therefore, is to stabilise the chain.

■ An integrated whole

Drawing on years of research and practice, Beer proposed a model of the cybernetic organisation.[18] Eschewing organisation charts, he argued the importance of following the dynamics of instructions, decisions, monitoring and information flows. He divided the whole organisation into five subsystems as follows:

1 *System 1* is the basic unit of control.
2 The function of *System 2* is to connect the operational level to a stabilising centre.
3 This centre is *System 3*. Together, these three subsystems, under the control of System 3, seek an internal balance enabling them to operate at maximum efficiency.
4 *System 4* connects the internal activities to the top of the organisation, passing down instructions and channelling feedback. Additionally, it interacts with the environment to collect information used for decision making.
5 Top management, the ultimate thinking and directing centre of the organisation, is represented as *System 5*.

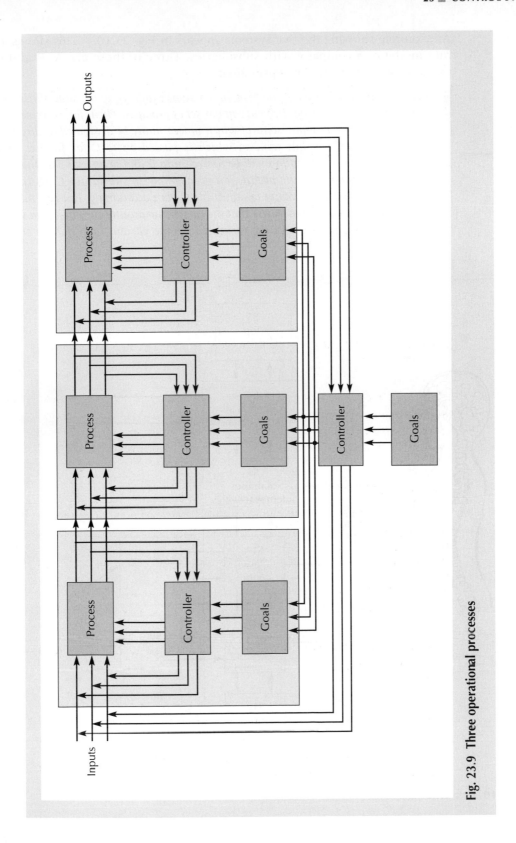

Fig. 23.9 Three operational processes

An example showing the five systems appears in Fig. 23.10.[19] This shows a corporate model of a company with subsidiaries. Three of these are A, B and C. Beer explains how interaction is represented:

> *Consider first production in the firm, and assume that each of the subsidiaries has a role to play in manufacturing the firm's major set of products. Then, for example, subsidiary B manufactures an output, some of which indeed many be dissipated as directed sales to the outside world ... but some of which is passed on to C for further processing. Thereafter, some of this output will be passed on to D and so on. Suppose that something goes badly wrong with the production programme in subsidiary C. Its controller 1C within [System] 2 will attempt to adjust the C plan accordingly. But this may very well be locally impossible, in the sense that the contract to acquire supplies from subsidiary B may have to be varied, and the contract to make various deliveries to subsidiary D*

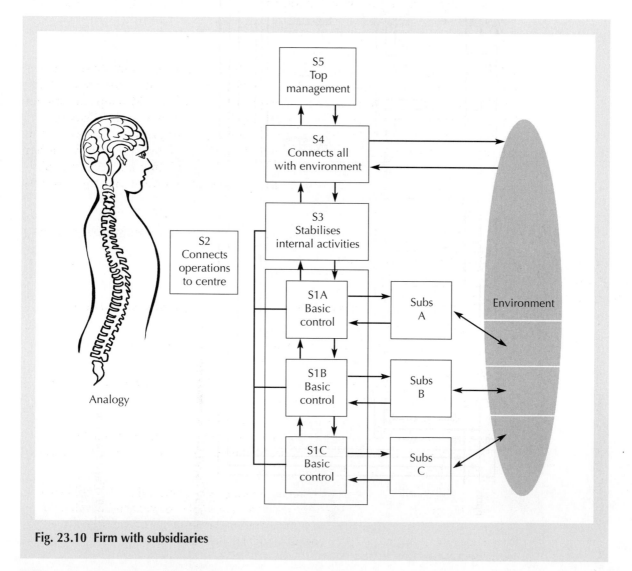

Fig. 23.10 Firm with subsidiaries

> *cannot be met. Controller 1C within 2 must inform controllers 1B and 1D, and all three of them will try and change their plans to suit each other. Needless to say, the trouble may reverberate from B to A, from D to E, and so on.*[20]

In similar vein, Beer continues to describe how Systems 2, 3 and even 4 and 5 become involved in resolving this difficulty. System 3 tries to dampen down the disturbance. Yet, if that proves impossible, it can refer to higher levels to seek a change in policy.

To illuminate the description of hierarchies of control, some of which are automatic, Beer frequently refers to the neurophysiological control of the human body. In Chapter 4, we looked at criticism of the use of weak analogies between organisms and organisations. Through seeing some aspects in common, there is a risk in assuming that all aspects are very similar. Beer, however, defends the use of models for the insight they provide. Since control theory looks for commonality across a range of systems, why cannot one be a model of another? The argument is summarised in Exhibit 23.7.[21]

Limitations

While many applaud Beer's application of cybernetics to organisational management, they remain unsure of its usefulness in practice. Control theory has been successfully applied at the operational level of the hierarchy. Moving it to higher levels, however, has yielded few fruitful applications. Berry and colleagues are doubtful whether Beer's modelling follows the rigour implied by the notions in Exhibit 23.7. They comment, 'The presentation of Beer's work is intuitive rather than carefully argued, but, while it contains much stimulating material, it is difficult to assess how much derives from the models propounded and therefore its validity is not demonstrable.'[22]

Exhibit 23.7 **Models that work**

Four key notions of models:

- *Scaling down* in size and complexity. For instance, Legoland at Billund incorporates a model of a 'typical' English town.

- *Transfer across* – real parts of real things are represented as parts of the model in the appropriate positions.

- *Depiction* – the model behaves in some way like the thing it represents. This may be a model railway set or a flight simulator.

- *Appropriateness* – the model is good if it represents in a relevant way. A model train is made so well that it can represent a real one in a film. Yet, it only represents it in scale appearance. Real trains neither run on 12 volts nor pick up current solely through opposite wheels.

We use models to learn something about the thing we are modelling, but not everything. Cybernetics compares complex systems and looks for general laws that can apply to all. From this point of view, the many similarities between the organism and the organisation justify using the one as a model of the other.

Effective control

So far we have examined the nature of control, various system designs and the problems that can arise. Another point of view is to consider effective control. Effectiveness depends both on features of the system itself and its fit with organisational structure and processes. Figure 23.11 shows these two domains. To the left we have the factors that all useful control systems should have. These are clarity, timeliness, flexibility and accuracy. To the right we see three factors that cover the fit, namely underpinning of decisions, focus on plans and actions and matching the structure. The points in the diagram can be expanded as follows:

Good design of all control systems

■ A *comprehensible* control system produces data that is meaningful to those who manage it. From the simple knobs and scales on a domestic cooker to the many gauges and dials on the bridge of a modern super tanker, the control system must match the processes and the capabilities of people involved. The examples of a nuclear power station and airliner given in Exhibit 23.6 were of control systems of such complexity that their operators required many hours of training. Even with such practice, staff at Three Mile Island had difficulties in understanding signals that were out of the ordinary.

■ *Timeliness* does not necessarily mean speed. A healthy control system produces information as often as needed. A good example can be found in quality con-

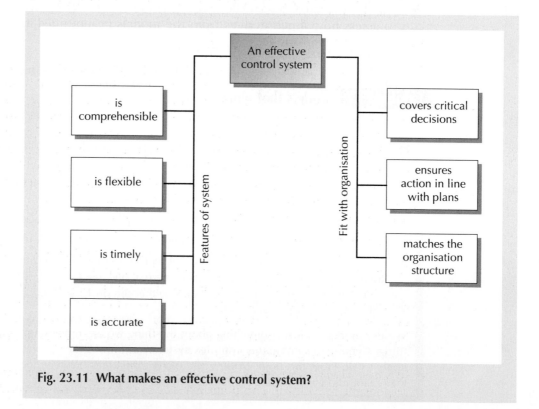

Fig. 23.11 What makes an effective control system?

trol. In the example shown in Fig. 7.13, experience of a manufacturing process suggests that it is sensible to measure relevant parameters every (say) ten minutes. If staff gather unusual results, as in cases B, C, D or E, they can reduce the interval between inspections. This continues until they decide to make adjustments or the process returns to normal.

■ As the above example shows, the control system must be *flexible*. Here, the rule covering inspection intervals is changed in light of experience. Flexibility, moreover, has another aspect. Changes in the organisation's policies or environment must be accommodated. For instance, a state corporation could have a control system designed to track expenditure under yearly spending budgets. This might not be appropriate if the organisation is transferred to the private sector and changes to a different cost management system.

■ To say that a control system must work with *accurate* information sounds like a statement of the obvious. Frequently, however, cases arise where there are incentives to produce inaccurate control information. In a railway repair shop at Derby, job tickets were returned to the office when tasks were complete. These served both to monitor output and enable bonus calculations. However, a prudent charge hand (team leader is a more modern title) might delay sending in some Friday tickets if his group had had a good week. This served two purposes: the spare tickets provided a buffer against a low output during the following week; and levelling bonus claims cut the risk of management investigation. A series of good weeks led to the accumulation of tickets 'in the back of the book'. The practice destroyed the value of tickets for job control so supervisors had to create their own systems of monitoring.

Fitting the control system to the organisation

■ The control system should relate to the *critical decisions* faced by each manager. This statement is also one principle underlying the design of information systems, especially those for decision support. A common statement concerning control is, 'If no one measures it, no one manages it'. Turning this round, we can suggest that managers will pay attention to any variable that they measure. Providing managers, especially senior ones, with unnecessary control information is not only uneconomic but it tempts them to become involved in matters they should have delegated. In a divisionalised company, for example, there is little point if headquarters, having agreed strategies and annual budgets, become involved in day-to-day operations of each unit.

■ The purpose of any control system is to *ensure that action is in line with plans*. A basic monitoring activity will warn the controller of things going wrong. It can be improved, however, if it also suggests ways to improve performance. Careful structuring of information is one way to achieve this end. For example, an executive information system may warn of deviations from budget. It could also offer the manager the chance to gather clues on what to do through interrogating the database for more detail. Sometimes known as 'drilling down', this enables the manager to separate causes more finely.

■ In *matching the organisational structure*, the system provides information to those responsible for control. This point extends the previous one concerning budgets.

If a transport company finds its fuel costs are rising, drilling down into the records may reveal causes, some favourable and some the opposite. Propitious reasons include gaining more business through carrying heavier loads over longer distances. On the other hand, unfavourable ones arise from higher fuel prices, poor vehicle maintenance and unsound driving practices. Drilling down into more detailed records will identify the cause. Details should be reported to the relevant manager.

What to measure: broadening criteria

Many managers think of controls as built around the organisation's accounting system. True, the management of costs, cash and margins are essential in many cases, especially businesses devoted to profit. Yet, as we shall see, the pursuit of such ends to the exclusion of others leads to problems.

Mullins summarises the reasons why finance and accounting systems dominate:[23]

- Stewardship of financial resources is vital. Managers are under pressure to show that their departments or units provide value for money. This is as true in the public sector as in the private. For instance, many local authority departments have to bid every five years for their own work under the procedures known as Compulsory Competitive Tendering. If they fail, competitors may be asked to take over.
- Aims, objectives and targets are frequently expressed in financial terms. Consequently, outcomes are measured and expressed in the same way.
- Money is readily measured and accounts can be very precise. Statements of budgets and performance are easily understood. This commonality allows comparison among many units of a diversified organisation.
- Financial limits and controls are easy to identify with and readily accepted. Rules of authority can be specified without difficulty. For example, a manager may be allowed to spend £10 000 on equipment without reference to seniors.

Clearly, accounting systems appear to satisfy the criteria for effective control set out in Fig. 23.11. They satisfy the general criteria of comprehension, timeliness, flexibility and accuracy. Further, they can be designed to support each manager's critical decisions, providing them with sufficient information, and allowing for further investigation to establish causes and solutions. Yet the style of accounting in most organisations is narrowly focused. Driven by the need to maintain professional standards and pass formal audits, there can be too much accuracy at the expense of usefulness.

All statements in accounts are both backward and inward looking. Management control should be broader than this. Therefore, it should be concerned with wider aims, especially strategic ones. Examples include: enhancing product and process knowledge; broadening the customer base; developing quality; encouraging enterprise; and operating with social responsibility. To cope with such questions, two related approaches have been proposed – the Performance Pyramid and the Balanced Scorecard.

The Performance Pyramid

Proposed by McNair, Lynch and Cross,[24] the Performance Pyramid uses nine dimensions to measure performance. Setting them out in a pyramid, shown in Fig. 23.12, brings out both the vertical and horizontal divisions in the hierarchy. The vertical split divides measures of effectiveness and efficiency. The horizontal bands correspond to levels. At the apex, there is the corporate vision or mission. At the strategic level, the vision is translated into external, market satisfaction measures and internal financial ones. Moving to the next level, the measures are expressed in terms of customer satisfaction (external), productivity (internal) and flexibility (both). Finally, when we look at departments and work stations we see performance measured against quality standards, delivery targets, planned cycle times and the proportion of wastage.

While the pyramid has been drawn up for a typical firm supplying goods, we should note that its details are not meant to be prescriptive. The number of levels and cells can be readily adapted to suit any other form of organisation. A service provider, for instance, would use different productivity measures. Additionally, public service organisations usually include equity among their overall aims. Therefore, they may add this to effectiveness and efficiency when categorising their standards. For instance, since 1994, local authorities in the United Kingdom have been required to publish performance indicators covering many of their services. Exhibit 23.8 shows how equity (fairness of treatment) is included with other factors in the report of one council.[25]

The Balanced Scorecard

The Balanced Scorecard presents a more even view than provided by conventional accounts. The idea is to provide a quick yet comprehensive assessment of a wide range of activities. Kaplan and Norton explain that it 'includes the use of financial measures that tell the results of actions already taken. And it complements financial measures with operational measures on customer satisfaction, internal processes, and the organisation's innovation and improvement activities. These are the drivers

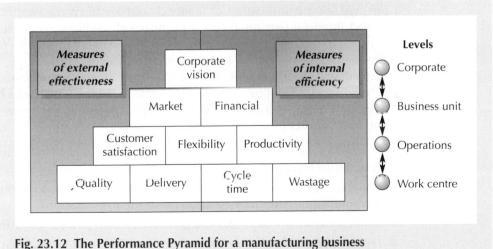

Fig. 23.12 The Performance Pyramid for a manufacturing business

---

Exhibit 23.8 **How did we look after our houses?**

Chester City Council manages some 7500 council homes. Here are some performance indicators concerned with letting and maintenance of this stock.

	1994–5	1995–6
Percentage of homes ...		
... adapted for elderly or disabled people	24.9	23.9
... let to homeless people and families	15.0	21.3
... empty, waiting for new tenants or minor repairs	1.0	0.9
... empty for other reasons	0.5	0.8
Repairs: percentage finished within category target times of ...		
... 24 hours	90	72
... 3 working days	62	64
... 8 working days	76	84
... 60 calendar days	82	57

---

of future financial performance.'[26] Current results are no more important than building the business for the future. Figure 23.13 suggests a typical presentation. The four cards shown correspond to four perspectives:

- *Customers* – how well do we serve them?

- *Internal business* – what are we good at and how good are we?

- *Innovation and learning* – how are we improving to create better value?

- *Financial* – how well are we satisfying those who put up the money?

Many variants of the basic idea of scorecards have been proposed. The essence is practical application in each firm. 'The objectives and the measures of the Score Card are derived from an organisation's vision and strategy.'[27] For instance, a service business may use six cards to evaluate: competitive performance; financial performance; service quality; flexibility; use of resources; and innovation.[28] In all cases, we see a combination of feedback and feedforward control. Here competitive and financial performance are instances of feedback. The last four factors, on the other hand, cover 'inputs' that make the difference for the future. Thus, we best see them as examples of feedforward control.

Kaplan and Norton extended their scorecard idea to propose an enhanced strategic management system.[29] Again, the central theme is to avoid over-reliance on traditional financial controls. Using a range of perspectives helps managers overcome four hurdles of strategy:

- *Translating the vision* – enables broad, appealing mission statements to be converted into objectives with practical meaning at all levels;

- *Communicating and linking* – helps managers develop a shared view through communicating the strategy throughout the organisation;

- *Business planning* – facilitates integration of financial and operating plans;

- *Feedback and learning* – ensures that feedback is used to enhance the strategy process for the future.

Financial perspective		Customer perspective	
Goals	*Measures*	*Goals*	*Measures*
Survive	Cash flow	New products	% of sales from new products
Succeed	Sales and income growth	Responsiveness	% of orders supplied on time
Develop	Growth in market share and ROI	Partnership	Number of partners

Internal perspective		Innovation and learning perspective	
Goals	*Measures*	*Goals*	*Measures*
Technology	Quality compared with rivals	Technology	Development time Success rate
Manufacturing	Speed, cost and waste in process	Process learning	Time to learn new processes
Design	Output efficiency Measures of manufacturability	Product focus	% of products as market leaders
Innovation	Meeting innovation targets	Time to reach market	Compare with benchmarks

Fig. 23.13 The Balanced Scorecard

The ideas of the Performance Pyramid and Balanced Scorecard result from the work of practical people less concerned with creating a general model of control and more with correcting imbalances as they confront them. We can contrast them with the cybernetic approach to control discussed earlier in the chapter. While Beer also grounded his work in practical experience, he was concerned with establishing a comprehensive framework to be used for modelling control processes. The performance measurement approaches, on the other hand, try to steer managers away from modelling and narrow short-term computation. Linked to corporate strategy, they apply both internal and external criteria and combine the short term with the long. Compared with cybernetics, a significant difference is the appraisal of innovation and learning. The ability of control systems to change themselves and their contexts in the light of experience is crucial to long-term success. We shall return to this second-order change in the next chapter.

Behavioural issues in control

Control is bound up with questions of monitoring, motivation, power, leadership and change. We saw in Chapters 14, 16 and 17 how complex these questions are. Although this chapter began by presenting control as a rational activity built on cybernetic principles, it should be clear that the presence of people within such processes means that emotion, perception, attitudes and other factors will have strong influences on their effectiveness. The manner with which control is carried out will be at least as important as the detailed design of monitoring and feedback loops. To close this chapter, therefore, we shall briefly note some behavioural issues. They are selected because we have not detailed them earlier in the book.

Limits to control

Whether organisations aim for centralised or decentralised arrangements, managers will clearly exercise some degree of control. If carefully developed with people's needs in mind, control systems can be regarded as constructive and, therefore, welcomed by members of staff. On the other hand, when they see control as coercive, employees will quickly see how it runs counter to their own needs for fulfilment. Although our rational approach suggests that the effects of negative reactions might be overcome with even more careful monitoring, there are limits to what can be supervised. Further, there is no limit to employees' ingenuity in bypassing the best laid plans if they want to.

Close supervision echoes the patriarchal attitudes of many followers of Taylor. It both results from, and reinforces, a lack of trust between managers and workers. Beynon quotes a senior shop steward at Ford's Halewood plant shortly after production had started in the 1960s. Referring to supervisors who had been transferred from the main plant at Dagenham in Essex, the steward said, 'They thought they could treat us like dirt, them. We were just dirty scousers [natives of Liverpool] who'd crawled in off the docks out of the cold. We'd never even seen a car plant before and these sods had been inside one since they were knee high.'[30] Yet, in Beynon's view, the workers could always get their revenge. Exhibit 23.9

Exhibit 23.9 The wet deck at Halewood, Merseyside in 1970

'In the Paint Shop the car, after an early coat of paint, passes through the Wet Deck where a team of men armed with electric sanders – "whirlies" – sand the body while it is being heavily sprayed with water. ...

'If there was a problem on the Wet Deck, a manning problem, speed-up, if the foreman had stepped out of line, they always had a comeback. They could sand the paint off the style lines – the fine edges of the body that gave it its distinctive shape. And nobody could know. The water streaming down, the whirlies flailing about, the lads on either side of the car, some of them moving off to change their soaking clothes. The foreman could stand over them and he couldn't spot it happening. Three hours later, the body shell would emerge with bare metal along the style lines. They *knew* it was happening.'

quotes one of the many acts of sabotage he reported.[31] In more extreme circumstances, Solzhenitsyn shows how prisoners spent so much effort trying to outwit the efforts of camp guards to apply arbitrary rules, *see* Exhibit 23.2.

Resistance to control

The extent of resistance depends on the balance among the control system design, the people and the circumstances. Mullins, drawing on the work of Lawler, proposes that resistance will be greatest when the control system:

- measures performance in a new area;
- replaces a system that people have an interest in retaining;
- uses standards set without participation;
- does not feed back results to those whose performance is measured;
- does feed back results to higher levels in the organisation;
- provides results to be used by the reward system;
- affects people who are satisfied with the way things are and regard themselves as committed to the organisation's aims;
- affects people who are low in self-esteem.[32]

Control, therefore, is not a dry, technical process that occupies the time of 'bean counters' from quality inspectors to cost accountants. It is controversial. The benefits of control systems are not always self-evident to workers. If, for example, staff are paid bonuses according to output, the inspector at the end of the line becomes the enemy. Each time this person rejects an item, everyone's pay is cut. Again, staff may greet programmes such as empowerment or shifts to 'self-control' with mixed feelings. This is especially true if schemes are backed up with job titles and related status symbols for those 'in control'. They may, as Alvesson and Willmott argue, ' ... simultaneously and inadvertently draw attention to the arbitrary and political nature of corporate arrangements, thus nurturing scepticism rather than tighter discipline'.[33]

Conclusion: control has its limits

The word control is used to describe a function ranging from close supervision to a broad activity encompassing planning, monitoring and adjusting performance. Different interpretations of sources of control further complicate matters. For classical theorists, control is something done by managers. Human relations proponents, on the other hand, argue that it originates within each person over whom supervisors have limited influence. Lastly, systems-cyberneticists consider control as a process.

In this chapter, we have concentrated on the process view. Control is the management of activities to achieve a plan in spite of unforeseen changes arising either inside or outside the organisation. Clearly, this process is needed if objectives are to be achieved and drift avoided. Many managerial settings are so complex and variable that, without it, little of value will be done.

The control process has four steps: setting standards; monitoring performance; comparing performance with standards; and taking action if any difference demands it. Within this general summary, three variants exist – feedback, concurrent and feedforward control. Each has appropriate applications and finding all at work in controlling processes within organisations is normal.

Corresponding to the steps of the control process are reasons for failure. We labelled these as myopic monitoring, garbled goals, curbed controls and foggy forecasting. At one level, it may be argued that these problems should be countered by trying harder. That is, there should be more effort in monitoring, goals should be clearer, and so on. Yet, in these difficulties, we can begin to see the limits of the approach. For instance, resources limit monitoring, goals can rarely be unambiguous and managers have neither the time nor the power to change continuously every aspect of the systems for which they are responsible.

Another limitation arises when we examine proposals for integrated control systems. Linking a hierarchy both horizontally and vertically, as exemplified by the work of Beer, has great appeal to the cyberneticist but has not been introduced widely. On the other hand, horizontal linkages along chains of operating units have been successful. Just-in-time production, often involving links between several companies, has been aided by computer-based communication and control systems.

While we need to recognise the limitations of the control model, this chapter has shown that its use is widespread. We commonly see it in operating units. Here control tasks from quality to inventory or costs to waste are subjected to the monitoring–comparison–action cycle. In other activities, especially higher levels such as strategic management, the rigid approach breaks down. The search for unambiguous performance measures led to an over-reliance on short-term financial controls. These suffer from the problem: 'If no one measures it no one manages it'. Through deliberately taking a broader perspective, approaches such as the Performance Pyramid and the Balanced Scorecard counter this difficulty. In so doing they move away from the mechanistic application of the control loop. The principle of monitoring and comparison remains, but within a context of balancing often contradictory measures. We return to these issues in the next chapter.

Quick check up   *can you ...*

- Define control;
- List four purposes of control;
- Draw models of feedback, concurrent and feedforward;
- Show on your models what can go awry;

- Give seven fundamentals for effective control;
- Outline the Performance Pyramid;
- Describe the Balanced Scorecard;
- List eight reasons why people resist control.

Questions   *Chapter review*

23.1 Explain the purpose of control in organisations, showing why it is important.

23.2 Compare the three basic forms of control system. Illustrate their application using your own examples.

23.3 What is meant by effective control? Clarify the conditions when this is likely to occur.

23.4 Why do people resist the introduction or change of control systems?

Application

23.5 Produce an annotated diagram showing the control systems in the home shopping bureau. Identify areas where you think difficulties may arise and suggest ways of overcoming them.

23.6 Compare the control processes described in the case studies *Engineering and Manufacturing, Oiso* (Chapter 19) and *The Madras cheque-clearing system* (Chapter 7).

Investigation

23.7 Interview a few managers to identify examples of feedback, concurrent and feedforward control. For each example, ask about difficulties in control. Account for any differences you find.

Skandia's scorecard[34]

CLOSING CASE

Skandia, the insurance group, is among several Swedish companies developing and publishing non-financial performance assessments. The movement to value intellectual capital seeks to explain why firms on the Stockholm exchange, in common with many others around the world, are valued at three to eight times their book values. Skandia recognises the importance of intellectual capital, seen as the difference between the financial measure of book value and the company's real market value. Figure 23.14, drawn from the 1996 report,[35] shows the company's perspective. Value enhancement is through the combination of customer, human and organisational capital.

'Skandia's goal is to be the leading and most profitable insurance company in the Nordic countries, and to pursue profitable growth in the global savings market.'[36] To achieve this, it seeks to strengthen its position in Scandinavia, improve productivity, and enhance its products to meet customers' needs. Growth markets are seen in Germany, Japan, the United Kingdom and the United States. Underpinning the insurance activity, the group has reduced its risk,

especially in two activities. These are exposure to catastrophes and to 'long tailed' liabilities that are difficult to assess. For the former, buildings insurance in San Francisco or other earthquake areas are examples. Covering pharmaceuticals instances the latter, where patients may develop adverse symptoms after a long time of use.

Exhibit 23.10, based on the 1996 annual report, gives some data on goal fulfilment. Yet the company takes appraisal further. In his introduction to the report, Lars-Eric Petersson, president and chief executive, argues that making a fair assessment of Skandia's development 'requires a broader description of our business than what can be read in our financial accounting'. Each year, the company supplements its statement to shareholders with an assessment of one aspect of its intellectual capital. 'We have long maintained that our truly sustainable earnings are derived from the interaction between our intellectual capital and financial capital.' For example, through investing in relationships with its eight million customers, Skandia creates mutually beneficial growth in value.

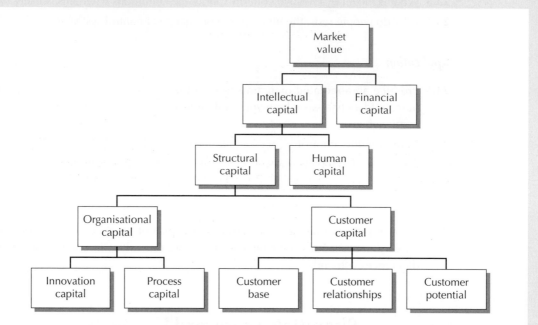

Fig. 23.14 Skandia's value scheme showing the customer and organisation branches

Exhibit 23.10 Skandia Group strategic development from 1992 to 1996

Sums in millions of SKr

	From	To	Annual change %
Life and unit assurance			
Operating profit	204	1522	+65
Premiums written	7205	36424	+50
Assets managed	22671	147175	+60
Market share, United Kingdom, %	3.2	8.5	
Market share, United States, %	1.0	3.8	
Nordic integration			
Market share, %	12	14	
Expense ratio	29	22	
Risk exposure			
Premiums, new non-life business	7904	1398	−35
Technical provisions, non-life	14157	4239	−26
Group finance			
Borrowing	12894	5745	−18

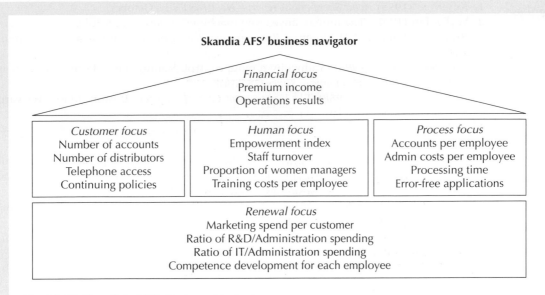

Skandia AFS' business navigator

Financial focus
Premium income
Operations results

Customer focus
Number of accounts
Number of distributors
Telephone access
Continuing policies

Human focus
Empowerment index
Staff turnover
Proportion of women managers
Training costs per employee

Process focus
Accounts per employee
Admin costs per employee
Processing time
Error-free applications

Renewal focus
Marketing spend per customer
Ratio of R&D/Administration spending
Ratio of IT/Administration spending
Competence development for each employee

Fig. 23.15 Skandia's AFS's Business Navigator

For the renewal of human capital, one important task for group management is to seek out the next generation of leaders. There are some 9000 employees with roughly half working in Sweden. In the Nordic countries, of 300 young staff evaluated for leadership potential, a third were added to a list of possible future leaders. In another initiative, an attitude survey makes annual measurements of indices for leadership, human capital and empowerment.

The company sponsors several research projects to extend and consolidate the measures. One subsidiary, Skandia AFS, uses a Business Navigator with some 30 key indicators.[37] This is outlined in Fig. 23.15. The five foci chosen – financial, customer, process, human and renewal – show the influence of the ideas of Kaplan and Norton.

Questions

Although the information in the case study is, as always, incomplete, you should be able to outline answers to the following questions:

1 How well are the measures used by Skandia Group related to its stated strategy? Are there any gaps?

2 Draw a diagram to set out the group's strategy as a Balanced Scorecard or Business Navigator.

3 Do you foresee any difficulties with Skandia's approach to planning, controlling and reporting?

Bibliography Anthony's contributions to management control are worth reading. A good source is Anthony, Robert R. (1988) *The Management Control Function*, Boston, Mass. Harvard Business School Press. Critical discussions of theories and issues, with descriptions of applications in many types of organisation, are to be found in Berry, Anthony J., Broadbent, Jane and Otley, David (1995) *Management Control: Theories, issues and practices*, Basingstoke: Macmillan.

References

1. Key Note (1995) *Home Shopping: A report – No. 016833*, 16 October.
2. Wylie, Ian (1997) 'The human answering machines', *Guardian*, 26 July.
3. Blake, William (1804) *Milton: a Poem in Two Books*, better known as the anthem *Jerusalem*.
4. Houlder, Vanessa (1996) 'Scalpel by remote control: Routine long-distance surgery is increasingly possible', *Financial Times*, 28 April.
5. Anthony, Robert N. (1988) *The Management Control Function*, Boston, Mass.: Harvard Business School Press, 10.
6. *Ibid.*, 27.
7. *Ibid.*, 37.
8. Berry, Anthony J., Broadbent, Jane and Otley, David (1995) 'Approaches to control in the organisational literature', Chapter 2 in same authors (ed.) *Management Control: Theories, issues and practices*, Basingstoke: Macmillan, 19.
9. Stacey, Ralph D. (1996) *Strategic Management and Organisational Dynamics*, Second edition, London: Financial Times Pitman Publishing, 43.
10. Mullins, Laurie J. (1996) *Management and Organisational Behaviour*, Fourth edition, London: Financial Times Pitman Publishing, 594.
11. Solzhenitsyn, Alexander (1963) *One Day in the Life of Ivan Denisovich*, Harmondsworth: Penguin, 107.
12. Mullins (1996) *op. cit.*, 595.
13. Oakland, J.S. (1993) *Total Quality Management*, Second edition, Oxford: Butterworth-Heinemann, 29.
14. Burns, Robert (1785) *To a mouse*; '... often go wrong'.
15. Roper, Stephen; Hewitt-Douglas, Nola and McFerran, Brendan (1997) 'Disparities in quality perceptions between small firms and their customers', *International Small Business Journal*, **15** (**4**), July–September, 64–79.
16. Bignell, Victor and Fortune, Joyce (1984) *Understanding Systems Failures*, Manchester: Manchester University Press, 9–39; Butcher, Tim (1997) 'Pilot averts disaster as Airbus crash-lands', *Daily Telegraph*, 6 November, 1.
17. Picken, Joseph C. and Dess, Gregory G. (1997) 'Out of (strategic) control', *Organizational Dynamics*, **25** (**1**), Summer, 35–48.
18. Beer, Stafford (1994) *Brain of the Firm*, Chichester: John Wiley.
19. *Ibid.*, 130.
20. *Ibid.*, 129.
21. *Ibid.*, 83–4.
22. Berry *et al.* (1995) *op. cit.* 12.
23. Mullins (1996) *op. cit.*, 613.
24. McNair, C.J., Lynch, Richard L. and Cross, Kelvin F. (1990) 'Do financial and non-financial performance measures have to agree?', *Management Accounting*, **72** (**5**), November, 28–36.
25. Chester City Council (1996) *Annual Report and Performance Indicators*, Town Hall, Chester.
26. Kaplan, Robert S. and Norton, David P. (1992) 'The balanced scorecard – measures that drive performance', *Harvard Business Review*, **70** (**1**), January–February, 71–9.
27. Kaplan, Robert S. and Norton, David P. (1996) *The Balanced Scorecard: Translating strategy into action*, Boston, Mass.: Harvard Business School Press, 8.
28. Fitzgerald, Liz (1996) 'Integrated approaches to performance', *Financial Times: Mastering Management*, 12 April, 2.
29. Kaplan, Robert S. and Norton, David P. (1996) 'Using the balanced scorecard as a strategic management system', *Harvard Business Review*, **72** (**1**), January–February, 75–85.
30. Beynon, H. (1973) *Working for Ford*, Harmondsworth: Penguin, 77.
31. *Ibid.*, 140–1.

32. Mullins (1996) *op. cit.*, 609.
33. Alvesson, Mats and Willmott, Hugh (1996) *Making Sense of Management*, London: Sage, 172.
34. Skandia Insurance Company (1995) *1994 Annual Report*; (1997) 'Customer Relationships and growth in value', *Intellectual Capital: Supplement to 1996 Annual Report*, Stockholm: Skandia Insurance; http://www.skandia.se/
35. Skandia Group (1997) *1996 Annual Report, loc.cit.*
36. Skandia Group (1997) 'Organization and strategy', *1996 Annual Report, loc.cit.*
37. Skandia Group (1995) *op. cit.*

24

Control and change

Chapter objectives

When you have finished studying this chapter, you should be able to:

- explain and illustrate the control dilemma;
- identify four control levers, showing the purpose of each;
- apply Etzioni's ideas about power and involvement to control;
- distinguish among bureaucratic, market and clan control, relating these categories to information needs and availability;
- differentiate single- and double-loop learning for individuals and organisations;
- outline how and why people resist learning and suggest how they may overcome this;
- summarise the characteristics of learning organisations, pointing out the difficulties encountered in putting them into practice;
- outline chaos and complexity theory as applied to organisations, drawing out its implications for control.

All eyes on Bausch & Lomb[1]

German immigrants John Jacob Bausch, owner of a tiny optical goods shop in Rochester, New York, and Henry Lomb formed a partnership in the late 1850s. Soon, Bausch discovered by chance that vulcanite, a hard rubber material, was suitable for spectacle frames. Cheap and durable, vulcanite met immediate success. Blockades during the Civil War of 1861–5 restricted imports of traditional materials, gold and horn. Vulcanite was so successful that, in the 1860s, Bausch & Lomb Incorporated sold its retail operations to concentrate on manufacturing. The new factory began with eyeglasses and developed into other precision equipment such as microscopes (1876), photographic lenses (1873) and searchlight mirrors (1890). By 1889, the company had sufficient manufacturing capacity to stop importing spectacle lenses and, in 1915, opened an optical glass plant, to eliminate its dependence on European raw materials.

Optical equipment has many military applications. Sales of items such as binoculars, periscopes and gun sights grew rapidly during the First World War. By 1918, they exceeded $14 million. The 1920s saw a contract from the Army Air Corps to develop a glass to reduce the glare encountered by pilots. Bausch & Lomb responded with its first *Ray-Ban* sunglasses. Introduced to the public in 1937, the original style, known as the Aviator, remains one of the company's leading lines.

Innovation and expansion continued after the Second World War. 1965 saw sales reach $100 million. The first approved soft contact lenses appeared in 1971. Business was going well. Through a process of acquisition and divestment, Bausch & Lomb expanded abroad to the extent that overseas revenues made up half the total. By 1989, sales had risen to $1000 million. Diversification into hearing and pharmaceuticals aided growth in sales, although some of this expansion did not yield the hoped for extra profits. Cutbacks followed as the company refocused its strategy. It developed new markets through many partnerships, for instance the 1992 agreement to develop an optical range to be sold under the Levi's brand. In the same year, Bausch & Lomb was a leading sponsor of the Olympic Games.

In 1996, however, Bausch & Lomb's annual report admitted, 'Our 1996 financial results were as disappointing to us as, we're sure, they were for you.' Static net sales and declining margins suggested a company in difficulties. The stock price had fallen from a 1994 peak of $53 to $32. The company cited 'continuing challenges in our US sunglass business' where the largest distributor had had problems. Traditional lines had declined while sales of new ones had been so successful that they could not be produced fast enough. Bausch & Lomb admitted distribution difficulties: '... as retail inventories of traditional lines come into balance, we are working to ensure that the face of Ray-Ban sunglasses is right ... we want customers to find the right mix of new and traditional styles available in the stores ... .' Managers recognised the need to make '... significant improvements in our internal product supply processes and in our relationships with key vendors so that we can keep up with consumer demand for new styles.' Not only would electronic information from the largest outlets help to match inventory and needs but it would also keep the firm, 'attuned to the consumer trends in the marketplace.'

What had gone wrong with the business whose stated mission is to be 'Number One in the Eyes of the World'? Under the leadership of chief executive, Dan Gill, Bausch & Lomb enjoyed great success between 1981 and 1991. Rapid growth in high margin products led to a five-times increase in the share price. Gill was committed to annual growth exceeding 10 per cent. The company's culture became very demanding and focused on numbers. Shortfalls were received with little tolerance. Goals had to be achieved at all costs. By 1991, however, market growth had slowed and competition was increasing. Gill's strategy of diversification beyond the optical arena through key acquisitions was not paying off. Yet the rigid targets remained. How did managers respond? Picken and Dess give three examples:

■ At the Ray-Ban division, business units frantically launched promotion after promotion to shift stock before quarterly results were reported. In a typical 1993 deal, one Chilean distributor was persuaded to receive six months' stock. Another was carrying nine months' inventory.

■ In 1993, the head of the contact lens division instructed 30 main United States distributors to take up to two years' worth of the older Optima lenses. Otherwise, they would face having their agreements cancelled. They were assured, verbally, that payment would not be required until they sold the lenses. Two refused and lost the business. Shipments to the rest meant that $23 million of sales were booked in the last days of the financial year. During 1994, however, the contact lenses not having been sold, most were returned. Bausch & Lomb received no revenue.

■ International operations faced few constraints. Sales through Hong Kong had been achieving annual growth of 25 per cent. Yet many were never despatched to Asian distributors. Instead, goods were moved to another warehouse whence many found their way into the grey market. This allowed dealers in other regions, such as Europe and the Middle East, to profit from the lower Asian wholesale process.

Unbalanced controls and arbitrary goals

Picken and Dess sum up the failure at Bausch & Lomb: 'There's nothing wrong with stretch targets, management incentives, or an aggressive culture, but organisations must also maintain standards of ethical behaviour and a sense of "fair play".' Managers adversely affected by the grey market would be acutely aware of this. Culture, rewards and boundaries of responsibility were ill defined and lacked alignment. Goals and objectives were cast in stone. They could not adapt to change.

Only after the United States Government's Security and Exchange Commission began an investigation into the contact lens debacle did Gill change tack. He instructed managers to follow more conservative practices, eliminate wheeling and dealing at each quarter-end, cut incentives to distributors and change bonus rules to focus on longer term goals. Gill was forced to resign in December 1995.

Introduction

The downfall of Gill illustrates a problem facing all managers in the modern age. How can they maintain sufficient control in organisations that demand flexibility and creativity if they are to succeed in the dynamic environment? At Bausch & Lomb, Gill used the control system to press for ever increasing performance. Yet the measures used were unnecessarily strict and narrow.

In other celebrated cases, controls have been too slack. For instance, the actions of poorly supervised currency traders have threatened several financial institutions. Exhibit 24.1 reminds us of the actions of Nick Leeson whose deals led to the fall of Baring Brothers, the oldest merchant bank in the United Kingdom.[2]

Exhibit 24.1 Weak safeguards topple Barings

The immediate cause of Baring Brothers' failure in February 1995 was the discovery of unexpected losses. Leeson was involved in huge futures contracts staking some £17 billion of clients' money. He was betting that the Japanese stock market would rise. Although it was Leeson who was convicted of fraud, the case also brought to light weak control both within Baring Brothers and in the external supervisory system.

Leeson was general manager and head trader of Baring's Singapore office from the end of 1992 until the collapse. His authorised dealing was reported as profitable although some critics wondered how such 'risk-free' business could create such margins. In fact, secret account 88888 was used to 'park' trading losses, for example about £23 million for 1993. In that year, the bank reported profits of some £100 million after allowing another £100 million for staff bonuses. Similar profits were announced for 1994 but, by this time, the losses hidden in 88888 had reached £208 million. January 1995 saw the Kobe earthquake further upsetting the Japanese markets. Losses soared to £337 million.

There were failures in financial and management controls at all levels. Here are some examples:

■ Leeson traded both on the bank's behalf and for clients. Yet reporting lines for these two activities had never been clarified. Ron Baker, head of equity business, assumed that he was responsible for the former and Mike Killian, head of global futures and options, covered the latter. But Killian thought that Leeson did not report to him.

■ Auditors had expressed concerns over the front (trading) and back (accounting) offices at Singapore being run by one person, the general manager. Their recommendations were not put into effect. Leeson's wife worked in the back office. Here all trades should have been reconciled and reports sent to London. An audit in 1994 did not find the secret account but initially recommended more regular, weekly, reconciliation. This was later deleted from the auditors' report under pressure from Leeson. He complained about the extra work it would cause.

■ Baring Brothers did not report the extent of its exposure in Japan and Singapore to the Bank of England. Yet the latter should have responded to other warnings. It knew of: the high funding supporting Far East operations; the high profits generated in Singapore; and large risks on the Singapore and Osaka futures exchanges.

In March 1995, after Baring Brothers was acquired by the Dutch bank, Internationale Nederlanden Groep NV, it was able to resume trading.

Simons addresses the dilemma: 'How do senior managers protect their companies from control failures when empowered employees are encouraged to redefine how they go about doing their jobs?'[3] He dismisses a solution based on the machine bureaucracy. Certainly, when standardisation is important, such as in large-scale administration or on the mass production line, rigid controls and close surveillance are feasible. Yet, many managers work in changing, competitive markets where they cannot spend all their time ensuring that others are doing as they tell them. On the other hand, it is unrealistic merely to hire well-qualified staff, design an incentive programme and expect them to produce results. This is especially true if staff face coercive, unrealistic or continually raised targets that threaten their incomes or positions if they fail. Managers at Bausch & Lomb or Baring Brothers, or the workers at Halewood mentioned in Chapter 23, showed how such schemes can be undermined.

The snag for many managers, according to Simons, is that they define control too narrowly. Reliance on the cybernetic model to achieve stated goals is both too restricting and incomplete. Consideration of beliefs, boundaries and interactive controls should supplement it. Summarised in Exhibit 24.2, each of the four 'control levers' has a marked function:

- *Cybernetic systems*
  As explained in Chapter 23, these control systems work on correcting deviations from planned behaviour to keep the organisation on track. Bausch & Lomb, however, illustrates what can go wrong if employees are made accountable for rigid performance goals and are allowed to decide how to achieve them.

- *Beliefs systems*
  Incorporated into declarations such as mission statements, belief systems govern ethical behaviour and good management practice. For example, they encourage notions such as 'placing the customer first', 'pursuit of excellence through innovation' or 'respect for the less fortunate in society'. Such aims may not appear within the narrow goals of a feedback system, yet they can inspire employees to seek new ways of achieving them. As people have been better educated, they have higher expectations from both the organisations they work for and their own careers. They want to increase their contributions but the policies of senior management must enable this.

Exhibit 24.2 Each control lever has a purpose

Control lever	Purpose	Responds to ...	Stimulates ...
Cybernetic systems	To identify and underpin clearly stated targets.	Lack of clarity or shortage of resources.	Achievement
Beliefs systems	To share the organisation's core values and mission.	Uncertainty about overall purpose.	Contribution
Boundary systems	To establish and sustain rules of managerial behaviour.	Lack of clarity; unforeseen temptations or pressures.	Doing things right
Interactive systems	To stimulate dialogue, learning and change.	Absence of opportunities and unwillingness to take risks.	Innovation and change

■ *Boundary systems*

According to Simons, boundary systems are based on the sometimes valuable power of negative thinking. This means that making it clear what *not* to do is sometimes better than telling employees what to do. Operating procedures and rule books ensure that they carry out routine tasks yet restrict creativity. In contrast, boundary systems set minimum standards and identify those activities that are not permitted. They can be expressed in codes of conduct or standards of ethical behaviour. At Bausch & Lomb the grey market should have been prevented. In normal circumstances, managers in the Far East would not have undermined the efforts of colleagues in other regions. Yet the pressures to 'make the numbers' were so strong that unspoken codes broke down. The advantage of codes of conduct is the boundaries are drawn. This is especially important in businesses where reputation takes years to build and can be destroyed by a recalcitrant employee. Major consulting firms, for example, have a rule preventing members from revealing any information about clients, even their names, to anyone.

We can view the interaction between belief and boundary systems as a healthy tension. Together, the inspiration of the belief system, surrounded by the constraints of the boundary system, draw from the limitless range of opportunity a focused picture of the real possibilities that an organisation is prepared to exploit. In the decision-making process, they help to define both alternatives and constraints.

We should not regard the boundary system as solely related to ethics. It may, for example, express the strategic directions that the organisation is unwilling to explore, or the type of employer it wishes to be seen to be. Of the many examples throughout the book, we can mention two here. First, as we saw in Exhibit 21.1, Hasselblad stopped research into digital technology until richer rivals had laid out the ground. Second, in the opening case of Chapter 15, the Skipton's personnel policies avoided any suggestion of 'hard' HRM.

■ *Interactive systems*

Because of the uncertainty surrounding many situations, managers need to be involved with their staff. Through this they can keep the focus on key issues and ensure that organisational learning takes place. Simons identifies four characteristics that set interactive control systems apart from the cybernetic ones:

- constantly changing information;
- information of sufficient potential to demand regular attention from managers at all levels;
- advantages of interpreting complex data in face to face discussions among many staff;
- stimulation of debate about the nature of the data, its assumptions and the actions that result from it.

In short, interactive control systems do not concern themselves solely with correcting deviations from a chosen plan. They are more engaged with asking whether the correct course of action has been chosen. A further question is whether circumstances have changed sufficiently to put prior choices out of date.

There is, therefore, more to control than spreading the plan–act–monitor cycle throughout every organisation. Although suited to routine tasks in a stable bureaucracy, the cycle breaks down in a changing environment. In this chapter we shall be considering these issues, notably responses to control, learning and change.

People and control

The dilemma of increasingly empowered employees in the flexible organisation is summed up by Leifer and Mills. They argue, 'Reliance on traditional, objective controls reduces the flexibility and adaptability necessary to cope with uncertain and equivocal information'. Yet, they point out, coping with this uncertainty through flexibility and discretion increases the probability of control being lost. To overcome this negative consequence, 'it is in the organisation's best interest to develop mechanisms for enhancing commitment, trust and bonding'. To examine this issue in more detail, we shall refer to the work of Etzioni and Ouchi.

■ Power and involvement

In Chapter 16 we noted three types of power arising from a manager's position within the organisation – coercive, reward and legitimate. Etzioni used a similar classification when he studied the use of power for ensuring compliance and therefore control. His typology, which relates power to corresponding involvement of participants, is summarised in Fig. 24.1.[4] First, in coercive organisations, members are unwilling to follow the instructions of those at the top and can only be persuaded to do so by threats of punishment. A prison is an example of this category. Inmates display *alienative* involvement. Second, an organisation founded on utilitarian lines uses economic power to induce participants to act instrumentally. Despite an individual's personal objectives, which it deems to be irrelevant, it achieves compliance through a series of contracts or bargains. The link between employee and organisation is that of 'a day's work for a day's pay'. Typified by the principles of scientific management, the link is known as *calculative* involvement. The third dimension of power is normative. Here most members share the same goals. Having overall goals is valuable if they are seen as a summary or aggregation of those held by participants. Compliance is voluntary as people show a *moral* commitment. Membership of voluntary organisations and movements, including joining religious orders, typifies such behaviour.

There are two further points to be made about Etzioni's views on power and control. First, the three categories are ideal-types. Some suggest that coercive control is typical of prisons, normative control of monasteries and reward control of wage labour in business organisations. It is likely, however, that most real settings will display a mixture of the types. Therefore, we should think of any organisation as exercising power over its members using a mixture of approaches. Figure 24.2 sets out some possibilities. Three organisations approaching the ideal-types are shown close to the points of the triangle. Others illustrate the mixed approach. For instance, in many labour markets the employment contract is not an agreement between equals. Managers can use both reward power (bonuses for achieving

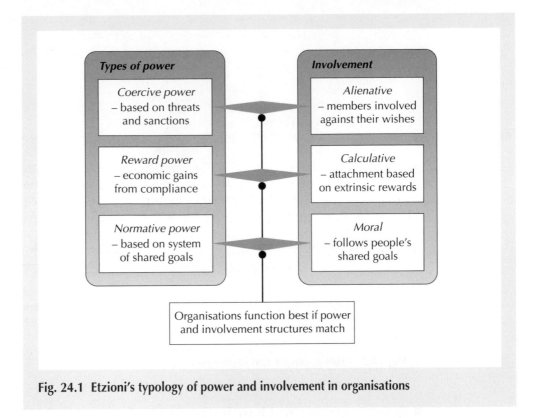

Fig. 24.1 Etzioni's typology of power and involvement in organisations

work standards) and coercive power (through threats of suspension or dismissal for unsatisfactory performance). Other mixtures shown are: a coercive sect, retaining members through a mixture of promises and sanctions; and caring professionals such as nurses, who may forgo some financial reward in exchange for being able to do a satisfying job.

Our second point is that appropriate methods of control depend on circumstances. Involvement and control methods must match. For example, expecting voluntary commitment to management norms from an alienated inmate in a prison would be fruitless. In contrast, coercive control of volunteer charity collectors would not work. Finding the best approach is far from easy. Therefore, in choosing a balance for the organisation represented by the question mark in Fig. 24.2, management must recognise that control is pluralistic. Different people will respond differently according to time, place and other factors.

▨ Bureaucracies, markets and clans

Although Etzioni's work draws attention to the behavioural issues of control, its practical implications are unclear. This is especially true when discussing large organisations. Control problems range from affecting the performance of any individual to achieving targets for entire divisions. Ouchi, for instance, proposed three broad means of controlling the relationships among individuals and groups in all organisations – bureaucracy, markets and clan.[5]

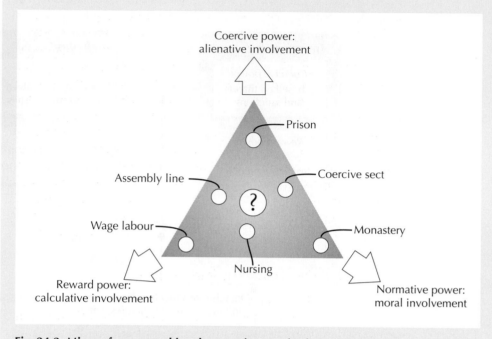

Fig. 24.2 Mixes of power and involvement in organisations

- In the *bureaucracy*, which we investigated in Chapters 2 and 12, control is exercised by specifying the tasks to be carried out by each member. Monitoring systems are predetermined. This is the setting for the formal control model explained in the previous chapter.

- The rediscovery of *markets* is a response to the way large organisations have reached the limits of bureaucratic control. Under the weight of rules, they display *diseconomies of scale*. This means that the difficulties of co-ordination exceed the benefits gained from putting units together. We saw in Chapter 12, how network, virtual and spherical organisations respond to this problem. They are families of small units linked by market, or contractual, relationships. At a small scale, we had examples of Technical and Computer Graphics and Super Bakery. Among global organisations, such as ABB, agreed strategic plans form a network of financial and psychological contracts between divisional managers and headquarters.

- Ouchi recognises the limitations of control through bureaucratic rules or contracts. Many managers occupy roles that entail high discretion. In carrying out their complex and uncertain tasks, trustworthiness will be as important as skill at making 'rational' decisions. Ouchi referred to such sets of relations as *clans*. They rely on shared language, symbols, myths and stories to develop shared values. In other words, a common culture emerges. It both is the outcome of, and influences, the stream of actions taken by organisation members.

Jones and Dugdale draw these points together as illustrated in Fig. 24.3.[6] Each approach has a corresponding control mechanism that focuses on a different aspect of the work: hierarchical control is concerned with tasks and processes;

market control concentrates on resources and outcomes with price being the key factor; and trust (or clan) control fastens onto people's underlying attitudes. There are echoes of Etzioni here, as suggested in Fig. 24.3, although the model is intended to cover a wider range of sizes and forms of organisation.

As with our previous discussion, the three categories are ideal-types. Jones and Dugdale stress that 'enterprises are characterised by various forms of hierarchical, market or trust relationships which coexist'.[7] Here are three examples of this coexistence. First, as Weber showed, bureaucratic organisations rest on the legitimacy of frameworks of rules and power. They are, therefore, underpinned by a set of shared values. Second, market relationships rely on hierarchies of position that empower managers, for example, to conclude agreements. Third, trust cannot be relied upon as the sole approach since the process of forming a common culture is incomplete. Clearly, various levels, groups and people within the organisation have diverging interests. Some elements of hierarchy or markets are always required. We should remember that even the monastery needs hierarchy and rules.

■ Control when knowledge is incomplete

Ouchi argues that, when easily measured outputs emerge from well-understood processes, hierarchies or markets are equally valuable control mechanisms.[8] Then he examines what happens when either or both conditions do not apply:

■ *When outputs are easily measured but processes are not well understood*, using market relationships is better. For instance, many managers employ subcontractors to carry out specialised functions. These range from recruitment services to vehicle maintenance. Since the organisation is inexpert in these fields, yet their results can be readily assessed under straightforward contracts, it pays to use the market mechanism.

■ *When processes are well understood but outputs are not easily measured*, relying on hierarchical control is better. This follows from the importance of employee behaviour in these circumstances. The focus is on *how* they carry out tasks. Although challenged by advocates of privatisation, many argue that the core functions in health and social services should not be left to the market. Cases are so complex and uncertain that co-ordination and control are best carried out through hierarchies rather than markets. In spite of failings in these structures, well-practised staff learn to make them work. Replacing them with markets merely increases the costs of control.

■ *When the process is poorly understood and outputs not easily measured*, neither markets nor hierarchies has much to offer. Here, Ouchi argues for the importance of self-control implicit in the common culture of the clan. The norms and values of the group play leading roles in monitoring performance.

The failures in large-scale information system projects, described in Chapter 22, illustrate the weaknesses of using either markets or hierarchies when knowledge is lacking. Government departments recognised that they had neither the knowledge nor capacity to do the work themselves. Unwilling to rely on hierarchy, they turned to the market for project management. Yet they used conventional competitive tendering, where price was the final determinant, to

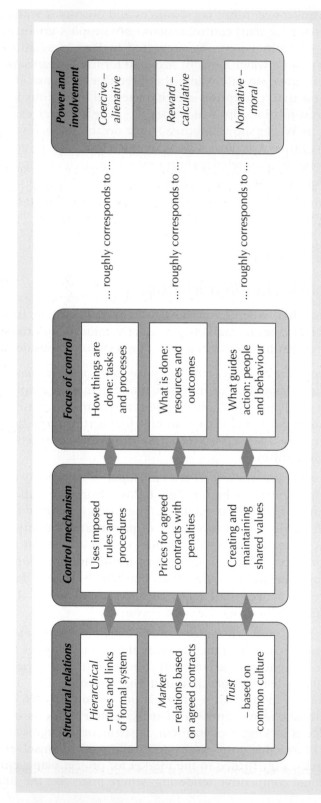

Fig. 24.3 Structural relations and controls

award contracts for very complex tasks. Recently, there has been a search for new ways to manage these contracts. Supplier partnering, already well-established in manufacturing industries, replaces detailed specification with a statement of the business problem. Suppliers are chosen according to how well their skills and experience relate to this problem.

The two dimensions of process knowledge and assessment of outputs suggest a grid as shown in Fig. 24.4. It shows the settings matching Ouchi's three control mechanisms. Additionally, the shading in the diagram links the control mechanisms to information processing requirements. Where these requirements are low, that is tasks are well known and outputs measurements straightforward, information needs are low. Formal control processes are in order and managers and employees use little discretion. Under greater uncertainty, self-management, supported by more information, will be increasingly important.

■ The control dilemma

Control and flexibility present fundamental difficulties for all organisations. Some form of structure is needed to unify disparate elements. Managers have also to exercise some degree of coercion. The cooperative activity required in even the minimal organisation is, therefore, achieved under conflict-laden circumstances. Those responsible for the organisation, who are owners in the case of private enterprise, can never fully count on those to whom they entrust their resources. Stricter control, for example through the introduction of more rules or the replacement of informal agreements by tightly drawn contracts, may cause increased resistance among staff. Even more stringent control is then required.

On the other hand, many organisations have realised the advantage of flexibility and adaptability, although it leads to some loss of formal control. To overcome this

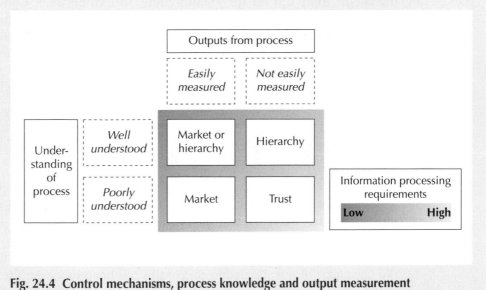

Fig. 24.4 Control mechanisms, process knowledge and output measurement

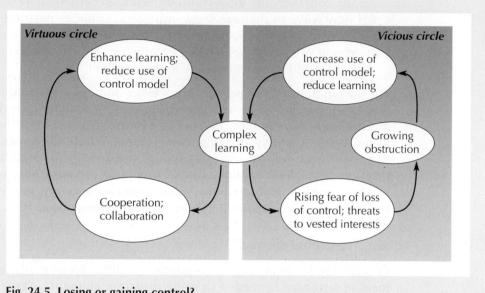

Fig. 24.5 Losing or gaining control?

loss, organisations work to increase commitment and bonding. We have seen throughout the book many examples of policies, from recruitment and training to participation, intended to build loyalties and underpin a common way of doing things.

Managers face a choice between the vicious circle of fear and tightening controls and the virtuous one of trust breeding trust, *see* Figure 24.5.[9] We shall look at the virtuous circle in more detail below. For the moment, let us examine the former. Sometimes, senior managers feel that the choice is not theirs. Faced by the pressures from owners and the increasingly detailed contract specifications demanded by clients, they opt for the vicious circle. In Exhibit 24.3, Cohen describes her experiences when asked to produce a procedures manual.[10] In the short run, such action seems to yield benefits. Yet these are at the expense of flexibility and change. Cohen concludes that manuals 'send out a powerful message of compliance to employees; they are neither expected, nor invited, to offer new or individual ways of doing things'. They cut across schemes for releasing creativity and making flexible responses to changing circumstances.

Control, learning and change

There has to be a better way. How can the virtuous circle be entered and its effect sustained? Many organisations are taking up the idea of *learning*, which is applicable to both the individual and the organisation.

Individual learning

So far, much of our discussion on control has been based on the notion of *simple learning*. The search is for ways to achieve a match between intention and out-

Exhibit 24.3 Closer control of contract cleaning

A well-established contract cleaning company, with branches in most large United Kingdom towns, employed several thousand part-time staff. Each unit reported directly to head office in the South of England. Following a change in 1992, new senior managers were appointed. They were struck by their distance from the operations level. Not only were the branches dispersed but the new team had no experience of cleaning, although members were well versed in contracted services.

Because of this sense of isolation, coupled with pressure from the parent company to raise profits quickly, the managers commissioned a procedures manual. This, they hoped, would provide knowledge of operations and administration practices at branch level. Beyond letting employees know precisely what was expected of them, the manual would support managers' decisions on where to rationalise.

In industries such as cleaning services, contracts are becoming more detailed. They require contractors to specify the tasks to be undertaken for the client. This in turn presses the suppliers to impose on their own staff procedures that are correspondingly precise and detailed. With this statement of 'the one best way', we see a return to scientific management.

To the new managers, this goal was both desirable and achievable. In fact they saw great merit in the procedures manual as a new and refreshing idea. To them, the procedures followed by the organisation were unclear. Inefficiency and corruption were likely. Flexibility had to be replaced by standardisation. The manual was not to be a description of how activities were carried out. It was to form a set of instructions stating the way they must be carried out. The managers justified this because they had set out the best procedures in the manual. This gave them an additional moral imperative, beyond recognising the needs of the market, for coercive control.

come. Kim expands the basic definition of individual learning – the acquisition of knowledge or skill – to show that it conveys two meanings:[11]

- The *acquisition of know-how* which is the ability to produce some action;
- The *acquisition of know-why* which is the ability to conceptualise and generalise from experience.

Many authors have offered models of learning as a set of cycles. For instance, Stacey sets out the two loops as in Fig. 24.6.[12] To the left, his acting–discovering–choosing loop corresponds to the steps of our feedback control models set out in Chapter 23. People learn from observing how their actions, combined with factors outside their control, influenced outcomes. This is simple, or single-loop, learning:

> *Single-loop learning means learning from the results of previous actions to amend the next. The feedback process from action through consequence to subsequent action is done without questioning the underpinning mental model.*

On its own, single-loop learning would keep an individual working effectively so long as the plans remained appropriate. Learning does take place, yet consists of finding better ways of achieving the present goal. Complex, or double-loop, learning involves further questioning, that is extending the *know-why:*

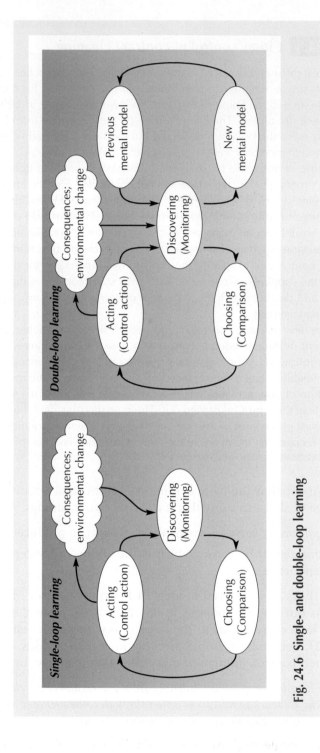

Fig. 24.6 Single- and double-loop learning

> *Double-loop learning occurs when the consequences of actions lead to the mental model behind them being challenged. The results of this may be shifts in the mental model or redefinition of the problem. In so doing, people destroy the old ways of doing things and create new ones.*

Complex learning combines the goal-seeking of the left-hand cycle and the goal-challenging of the right. As Argyris and Schon explain, 'Single-loop learning is concerned primarily with effectiveness, this is with how best to achieve existing goals ... In some cases, however, error correction requires a learning cycle in which organisation norms themselves are modified ... [There is] a double feedback loop which connects the detection of error not only to strategies and assumptions for effective performance but to the very norms which define effective performance'.[13]

Double-loop learning means both using and breaking the mould, and then creating a new one. It appears destabilising and revolutionary yet is necessary for innovation and change. This is a development of the ideas introduced in Chapter 14.

Organisational learning

Argyris and Schon distinguish between individuals undergoing these processes and organisational learning.[14] Employees may follow the rules and routines that have been laid down, whether formally or informally. In so doing they will act as automatons. They may go further than this, however. Using their intelligence, they may look for better ways of doing one or other part of the job. This is individual learning which, in this case, helps the organisation. Yet we know that people will also look for ways to benefit themselves that have either neutral or negative effects for the organisation. The Hawthorne Studies, *see* Chapter 2, are among many that have revealed this sort of behaviour.

So what is organisational learning? At some stage we can imagine the employee sharing the change with other members of the work group or even, if there is a climate of trust, with supervisors. If the proposals are agreed and incorporated into normal practice then we can say organisational learning has taken place. Therefore, besides the problem of discovering new ways of seeing and doing things, organisational learning faces the problem of overcoming resistance. The procedures manual of the cleaning company was seen in a positive light by the new managers yet, once issued by them, would form a significant barrier to further journeys round the learning loop.

Resistance

Stacey explains what happens when most managers engage in budgetary control.[15] Performance variances from budgets are investigated and corrective action chosen. This, along with uncontrollable external changes, influences outcomes in the next accounting period. The process enables managers both to control and to *learn*. They are discovering the consequences of their actions and changing their behaviour as a result. Yet they may not fundamentally question what they do. They see the budget as fixed. In Rhenman's example of two Swedish textile companies, given in Exhibit 24.4, we can compare one that tried harder and failed with another that tried *differently* and succeeded.[16]

Exhibit 24.4   Work harder or smarter?

Faced with pressure from competitors in low-cost countries, Company A automated and rationalised much of its operations. In 10 years, it raised its productivity three-fold. Yet this was barely enough to counteract the unfavourable trend in prices and wages.

Starting from a similar base, Company B faced the threats differently. It changed direction by focusing on a specialised niche at the periphery of the traditional textile industry. Productivity increased only slightly, for the company had to reorganise its production frequently. Yet the enhanced prices commanded by its products more than compensated for increased costs.

The more that managers share values, and hence share a mental model of the world, the more likely they will resist change. Reasons for poor profit performance will be found within the shared view. This may blame external forces. One hears statements from, 'The government should do something about the strength of the currency', to, 'People are simply not buying enough'. Complex learning, on the other hand, involves challenging the mental model, as the managers of Company B did. It managed to 'break out' of its traditional ways. Two loops are working simultaneously in complex learning. The second, more difficult loop, means challenging the way things are, questioning paradigms and searching for solutions that are other than the obvious.

Why do people resist learning? Argyris argued that the answer lies in our fear of breaking the mould. Part of this comes from difficulties with espoused models and models in use:

- *Espoused models* are the mental models we say we use. For instance, managers espouse rational decision making, open consultation, free access to information and the need to plan on the basis of serious research. These models are usually easy to ascertain. They are found simply by asking the people concerned.

- *Models in use* are the models we actually use. So while managers may espouse the above behaviour, they decide off the cuff, limit consultation for fear of 'leaks', and are often in so much hurry that they have little time to think. Clarifying these models is rarely easy. Since they often form them unconsciously, managers will find it difficult to express them.

(Note that instead of models, we sometimes refer to the above concepts as *espoused theories* and *theories in use*.)

The gap between the two models means that we often state one thing and do another. For example, a manager may espouse commitment to equal opportunities yet may judge people according to the crudest stereotypes. Double-loop learning implies a challenge to the model in use. Yet how can one challenge a view, such as a stereotype, that a person is hardly conscious of? It is no wonder that people avoid confronting this issue and, instead, retreat into what Argyris calls defensive routines. One of his studies was of a management consultancy firm, *see* Exhibit 24.5.[17]

Exhibit 24.5 Physician, heal thyself!

Seven partners had broken away from a large firm, hoping to avoid the wrangling and political games they had met in larger organisations. Yet they were disappointed. Faced with threatening problems, they avoided challenging their theories in use. At partners' meetings there always seemed to be one person unwilling to discuss an important issue. Outside the meetings, in the corridors and private offices, these questions were hotly debated.

This process built and reinforced divisions among the founders. The conflict habit soon spread to the rest of the firm.

Fig. 24.7 The mixed message mitigates malaise

Organisations are full of defensive routines through which managers avoid challenges to their theories in use. Figure 24.7 is based on Argyris's explanation of how a manager turns down a subordinate's suggestion or overrules a decision. Espousing democratic ideals and the need to bring out the best in each individual, the boss seeks to save the disappointed employee's face. Yet to tell someone directly that you are doing this is to defeat its purpose. 'What you tell Fred is a fiction about the success of his own decision making and lie about your reasons for rescinding it. What's more, if Fred correctly senses the mixed message, he will almost certainly say nothing. The logic here, as in all organisational defensive routines, is unmistakable: send a mixed message.'[18] In this illustration, we also see a conflict between open communication as an espoused theory and holding back, or deviousness, as a theory in use. To understand further why people behave like this, refer back to the critique of the communication model towards the end of Chapter 18.

How individuals learn

Ideas from core competence to knowledge management suggest a consensus that a key success factor for future organisations will be the ability to learn. Meanwhile, managers experience frustration at the complexity of the process and the resistance to the changes it inevitably brings. Schein, in his studies of culture, leadership and learning, shows how deeper understanding of how individuals learn, combined with studying how they might learn together, can underpin plans for sustaining learning.[19]

Two learning anxieties

Change through learning involves two kinds of anxiety. The first is the fear of the new. Most of us prefer stability and are only prepared for change when we feel most of our situation is stable. Commonly heard are statements such as: I will only take on the MBA when ... my job prospects are clearer/ I no longer work shifts/ the children have started school/ I've restored the house/ I've given up football. Fear of the new also refers to the process itself. From the instructor observing naive keyboard errors to trepidation before the examination, these are threats we can do without.

The second anxiety refers to being left out. In a changing world, we may be worried that the competences we possess will become out of date. Worse than this, we may realise that our skills are already inadequate, possibly because our education is unfinished. To practise law or accountancy, for instance, a graduate must pass the professional examinations. Increasingly, such qualifications are merely the beginning. Double-loop learning, learning how to maintain professional competence through careers, is coming more to the fore.

Given these anxieties, when does learning occur? Schein's proposition yields insight. Using an idea akin to Lewin's force field, he argues simply that the pressure to change must exceed the pressure resisting it. In other words, $Anxiety_2 > Anxiety_1$. How does the instructor, teacher, coach or manager ensure that this occurs? Two approaches are suggested:

■ *Increase Anxiety$_2$*

Here, the manager or teacher increases the fear of not learning so that it overcomes the fear of learning. A common tactic is to threaten the learner. At school an outdated teacher's cliché is, 'If you don't learn this you won't get a job.' Again, a manager, or student, may recognise that lack of information system skills prevents leadership or participation in developments. Reason dictates that the person puts some time into bridging the gap.

Schein warns that we are not always so logical. High $Anxiety_1$ makes us defensive, misunderstand or deny reality, procrastinate and, in the end, fail. Then we blame others. No matter how much threatening or cajoling occurs, how much effort is put into creating a sense of looming incompetence, the individual will resist. Is this the time to give up on the potential learner? Another way beckons.

■ *Reduce Anxiety$_1$*

Here, we focus on making the learner feel easier about the uncertainty associated with learning by providing an appropriate environment. The elements of fear abatement are set out in Exhibit 24.6.

Exhibit 24.6 ■ Reducing the learner's fear of change

- *Psychological safety* – learning will take place with supportive encouragement;

- *A vision of a better future* – leaders and learners can cooperate in creating a positive view of individuals, groups and the organisation;

- *A practice ground* – time away from the job to make mistakes and learn from them;

- *Direction* – naive learners often do not know what is possible for them. Setting out a map is helpful;

- *Opportunities for sharing* – learning in peer groups can reduce the sense of incompetence and offer support in keeping going;

- *Good coaching* – providing learning skills and feedback on progress;

- *Rewards* – rewards for progress are more effective than punishments for failure;

- *A supportive climate* – learners' mistakes should be seen as enhancing their progress and not things to be hidden.

Developing the learning organisation

Having applied the idea of anxiety to understand how an individual approaches learning, Schein proceeds to investigate organisations. The pressure seems to be for them to learn new initiatives, ranging from TQM to OD, or reengineering to empowerment, with increasing speed. $Anxiety_2$ is, therefore, growing so managers need to work on $Anxiety_1$. In other words, how can they lead their organisations to reduce barriers and accept continuous learning? For Schein the answer lies in the *learning culture* whose features are set out in Exhibit 24.7. Others suggest varying numbers of steps and elements, but there is agreement that they centre on participation, free flows of information, culture and self-development.[20]

Listing the features of a learning culture is an easy step. To put them into practice is far more difficult. Schein sees removing barriers as imperative. Only when we can see ourselves and our behaviour as inhibitors of progress can such progress really begin. We can mention three cultural issues: hierarchy, individualism and delusion. First, the traditional hierarchical model, which for many managers is the only one they have, blocks change. By implication it requires managers to create self images of omniscience, omnipotence, decisiveness and certainty. Clearly, many know of their weaknesses. Yet the dominant culture prevents them from admitting it. These feelings resist learning. For if organisation learning is to occur it must start with managers admitting that they do not know everything.

The second inhibitor is individualism. The individual who rises to the top against the odds is often presented as a hero. In contrast, the contented and dependable team player, while often loved and trusted, is neither so admired nor so rewarded. This means that teamwork, so often advocated for improving performance, is regarded as a tedious necessity. Unless its benefits are demonstrable, it is not to be used. The effect of this bias is that competitiveness is regarded as the more natural behaviour. Few see teamwork as the 'normal' way of operating.

Exhibit 24.7 Seven elements of Schein's learning culture

- Shared concern for all stakeholders – staff, customers, suppliers, owners, community.

- Shared belief that all people can and will learn. This is in line with McGregor's Theory Y explained in Chapter 2.

- Shared belief that the environment can be understood and changed. The fate of the organisation is in the hands of its members and therefore learning is worth while.

- Diversity and slack – diversity among people, groups and sub-cultures offers creative tensions and alternatives. Slack allows people to have time to learn away from the total preoccupation with the here-and-now.

- Open communication. While it should be the norm, not every issue, especially personal ones, should be known to all. Communication should support tasks. Practices such as withholding information, or using it in power games, make it impossible to learn.

- Learning to include the ability to think *systemically*. This means recognising the organisation as an open system, as in Chapter 2, with its implications of interconnectedness and complexity.

- Learning to support teamwork. There must be a shared belief that cooperation will be needed and that it will work.

The third barrier comes from the differences between espoused theories and theories in use. Most managers espouse the idea that the long-term development of people is important. Yet many see the real task of managers is understanding the world, and acting in it, through models, numbers, accounts and money. Such theory in use is also seen in business schools. Courses with high 'quantitative' content are regarded as superior, at least by those who take them. They look down on other students, who choose human relations supported by just enough 'quantitative methods' to achieve the approval of university authorities. Job advertisements frequently mention the ability to 'apply analytical skills', 'take personal responsibility' and 'work independently under pressure'. These are the values of the technocrat mentioned in Chapter 1. Being able to handle the short-term reporting and control systems is more impressive than paying attention to morale or employee development. The latter are only turned to when budgetary issues have been settled. And they never are.

Successful learners

In spite of such pessimistic views of why organisations do not change, others point to those that do. Gephart and colleagues give several examples of variations in learning style and identify leadership as a critical feature. Leaders support learning through: acting as role models; providing facilitating systems; encouraging people to offer new ideas; ensuring the spread of new knowledge; providing resources; and sharing leadership.[21]

De Geus, whose career at Shell included work on learning organisations, investigated the characteristics of organisations that have survived for much longer than average.[22] Current data suggests that a typical multinational exists for about 40 years. Yet the Swedish paper and pulp group, Stora, was founded in the thirteenth century. Sumitomo is 400 years old. More junior are the United States' du Pont and the United Kingdom's Pilkington, in their 190s and 170s respectively. These life spans suggest that the firms have demonstrated more than once the capacity to change without tearing themselves apart. Why have they lasted so long?

De Geus distinguishes two types of company, the *economic* and the *living*. The economic company keeps its investment in people as small as required to maintain current returns to owners. Its sole aim is to create wealth for, usually, a small group of owners and managers. In contrast, living companies display four properties: financial conservatism; sensitivity and adaptation to the environment; cohesion within a strong corporate culture; and tolerance of eccentricity within boundaries. 3M exemplifies the last point. It allocates 15 per cent of personal slack time to each of its researchers.[23]

Snags with such studies arise from their *post hoc* nature. We can make three general points. First, they are looking at firms that have succeeded. There is no comparison made with those that have failed and disappeared. Second, they assume that anything that may have caused their success was deliberate and can work again. Third, it could all be down to chance. Summarising another way, if you start with a thousand firms in 1800, and the probability of survival for 200 years is 0.3 per cent, then three firms will still be around in 2000. With hindsight we can search for reasons why the survivors came through. But could we have picked the winners at the outset? Would we be confident that Bausch & Lomb would have survived even the American Civil War? Picking an outsider in the Grand National is a better bet.

A critic in the *Economist* points to several particular limitations of de Geus's study.[24] A central issue is its selectivity. What of those long-surviving firms whose organisations demonstrate inflexible cultures and rigid hierarchies with centralised management? Some prosperous companies from Exxon to Suzuki have this sort of reputation. Rather than focus on learning, Chandler's 1990 study of 200 large firms in several countries linked success with two early investments.[25] Winners were quick to build networks for marketing and distribution and to develop effective management. Products are not necessarily the key; nor is the ability to adapt. In their different eras, both the century-old Standard Oil (now Exxon) and Microsoft have led the way in building organisations to take advantage of economies of scale. Neither is famed for its adaptability, *see* Exhibit 24.8

Studies such as these provide insights into why change is needed and how it can be achieved. Yet the selective case approach, when developed into generalisation, has weaknesses similar to the excellence school explained in Chapter 2. Among other hazards, subsequent failure of a star company places any 'theory' in disarray. For instance, de Geus might have chosen Barings Bank!

Exhibit 24.8 Can't change the organisation? Change the environment!

Q. How many senior managers of Microsoft are needed to change a light bulb?
A. None. They just redefine 'dark' as standard.

The logic of looking backwards to find clues about the learning organisation is also questionable. If organisational environments have really changed so much as to require new structures and practices, then the experiences of firms over the past two centuries cannot shed anything but the dimmest light. To develop a theory for organisations of the future, one needs to go more deeply into their changing nature. Developments in systems science have stimulated ideas about learning. For example, Senge and Fulmer show how investigating and modelling system dynamics extends managers' understanding and their capacity to learn for the future.[26] Others see developments in systems theory, in particular theories of chaos and complexity, as offering a richer harvest. Freedman, for instance, observes, '... the learning organisation has characteristics remarkably similar to the complex adaptive systems that scientists are discovering in nature ...'.[27]

Chaos and change

It had become conventional, in studying the dynamics of systems, to see them as dominated either by negative or positive feedback loops. The former means that the system would dampen disturbances and tend towards stable equilibrium. We are used to the idea of stability seeking, whether it be in our body's maintenance of blood temperature or a finance minister's struggles to keep inflation within targets. The second kind of feedback is positive; it builds on itself to generate explosive growth or rapid collapse. Human population or nuclear plant meltdowns are examples. In these cases the concept of a stable state does not apply.

Bounded instability

Work on the theory of chaos has discovered a third possibility. As a complex negative feedback system is adapted so that it becomes subject to some positive feedback, it passes through an intermediate region in which the forces of stability and instability work together. Sometimes they balance; sometimes one gains the upper hand. This leads to very complex behaviour in which new patterns emerge from very minor disturbances. The region is referred to the *area of bounded instability*. The system is, mostly, still under the control of negative feedback loops. Yet its behaviour patterns are so complex and sensitive that predicting any part of them is almost impossible.

Deterministic

A further point about the behaviour of these systems in the intermediate zone is that they are still deterministic. They are the opposite of random and probabilistic. Deterministic systems are subject to laws of cause and effect. Its predecessors cause each event in a predictable way. Because, however, overall behaviour emerges in so complex a manner, the individual links from cause to effect are lost.

Stacey summarises the consequences of these two statements, '... deterministic, non-linear feedback systems generate completely unpredictable behaviour ... in the long term'.[28] This means that the remote future of any such system is not merely difficult to predict, *it is unknowable*. Behaviour is sensitive to changes too small to be measured accurately. These work through to become large changes later.

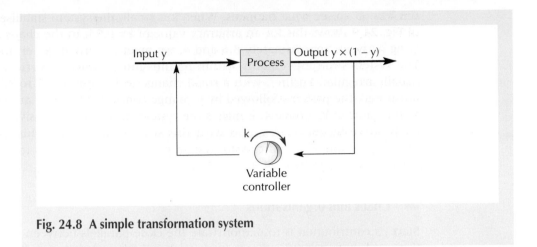

Fig. 24.8 A simple transformation system

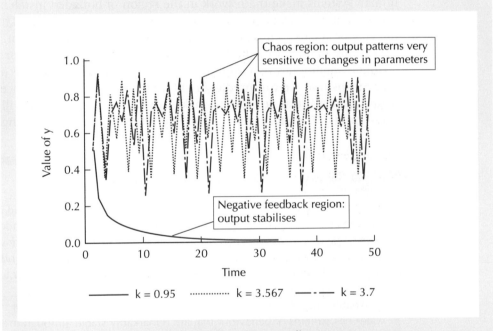

Fig. 24.9 Simulation of system in stable and intermediate zones

Figures 24.8 and 24.9 offer an insight into the way our thinking must change. It shows a simulation of chaotic behaviour. Let us imagine a system that transforms its input in one time period, y_t, into an output in the next given by the formula $y_t \times (1 - y_t)$. The 'controller' of the system feeds back the value of this output to form the input for the next period. On the way, it multiplies y by k. The result is what is known as the *logistic difference equation*, $y_{t+1} = k \times y_t \times (1 - y_t)$.

The remarkable feature of this system is that it can be stable, unstable or chaotic depending on the value of the constant k. We can imagine the controller 'turning the *k* knob' to see what happens. When k is small, the system stabilises. The graph of Fig. 24.9 shows this for an arbitrary value of k= 0.95. In the chaos zone, with k lying between approximately 3.6 and 4, we meet patterned yet erratic behaviour. The system's output remains within bounds but produces a variety of patterns, usually irregular. Further, with a small change in k, from 3.567 to 3.7 in the case illustrated, the patterns followed by y change considerably. They are very sensitive to the value of k. Above 4, k makes the system move into explosive growth based on positive feedback. A graph with this scale cannot show this. A frequently quoted example of a real chaotic system governed by countless feedback loops is the weather, *see* Exhibit 24.9.

■ Chaos and organisations

Stacey's contribution is to demonstrate the close parallels between many organisations and those natural systems, such as the weather, that show chaotic behaviour. This is more than a weak analogy. He shows how the structure and processes of human systems make them work in the region of bounded instability. An organisation is a complex adaptive system. It evolves so that at least part of it operates within the chaotic region. Therefore, the theory of complexity is relevant. Having demonstrated this point, Stacey shows how it has profound significance for managers.

Unknowability has two implications. First, the bounded nature of system behaviour means that we can predict broad limits with some confidence. Second, chaos means that it is not possible to make any prediction of what will happen within these limits. Therefore, leadership should not be about plotting and steering a

---

Exhibit 24.9 **Wise about the weather**

If you were asked to forecast the weather in your district one year ahead, you may reply, 'I haven't the foggiest idea!' On reflection, however, you may be persuaded to try harder. Depending on the season, you may estimate the noon-time temperature with a range (to be safe) of ±20 degrees. You may also observe, 'If it were sunny the previous day, the chances are that it will be fine.' This is because you know the weather follows patterns. In the United Kingdom at least, we tend to have wet and dry spells.

Weather is not random, although it appears to be. The system of moving air and water has patterns of behaviour that are remarkably stable although irregular in detail. The above statements recognised this. They appreciate the patterns and the seasons and that parameters are bounded. The 'rules' prevent snow in the Sahara or years of drought in Iceland. Given these limits, however, weather is unknowable.

Some have presented chaos theory in terms of the question, 'Can a butterfly taking off in a European garden cause a typhoon in Japan?' The theory of complex deterministic systems means that the answer is a qualified 'Yes'. The insect does not cause the typhoon on its own but may influence one in detail. The draught from its wings may be amplified through millions of loops, to which have been added all sorts of other behaviour, leading to the typhoon. We can never know. But we can say that trapping all butterflies will not prevent typhoons. They occur in any case as part of the general climate pattern.

detailed course. It is more like keeping afloat on a heavy sea. Being in control in the traditional sense means having the power to impose the targets and rules and to act on the basis of monitored performance. Instability is different. As Stacey says:

> It is possible, with much effort, for someone, or some small group of powerful people, to predict the outcomes of group, organisational and societal systems and, therefore, to remain 'in control' of them. But this is possible only if such systems are held well within the stable zone of operation, far away from the edge of chaos. The result will be stability, perhaps for a long time, but it will be the death of creativity and innovation and hence, ultimately, the death of the system. If it is to survive, every human system must return to the edge of chaos, where outcomes are unknowable and no one can be 'in control'. So, the system cannot move according to some blueprint, but it will produce emergent new outcomes, and it will be controlled through the process of spontaneous self-organisation itself, unless we, in our desperate attempts to stay 'in control', cause it to tip over into the unstable zone. For managers it is a message about having the courage to let go and let it happen, while vigilantly seeking to avoid tipping an organisation into the unstable zone ... The key seems to lie, not in preparing blueprints, but in trying to understand how to contain the anxiety of operating at the edge of chaos. The true role of the leader of a creative system is, not to foresee its future and take control of its journey, but to contain the anxiety of its members as they operate at the edge of chaos, where they are creating and discovering a new future that none could possibly foresee.[29]

By now we can make a connection with organisational learning. In the chaotic world, successful organisations face circumstances they cannot know in advance. Since the message for members is, 'Do not fool yourself into thinking the future is wholly knowable', they cannot be said to be 'in control' of it.[30] Nor can they subject it to any form of rational analysis or decision making. Therefore, continuing success depends on learning. This is, in Stacey's terms, 'a spontaneously self-organising process from which new strategic directions may emerge'.[31] For him, while the formal, espoused organisation may be some form of bureaucracy, working at the edge of stability means that new forms will emerge to stand alongside or 'shadow' the formal system. He sees such developments as constructive, enabling the whole system to overcome the weaknesses of its formal arrangements. This means more than nourishing the grapevines of informal communications discussed in Chapter 18. Self-organising networks can act, and they can do so without formal authority from the centre.

In the emergence of today's *self-organising organisations*, we may be catching a glimpse of future forms. To describe them, Hock coined the title *chaord*, referring to order out of chaos. They are decentralised, non-hierarchical, evolving, and self-regulating. He says, 'In chaordic systems, order emerges. Life is recognisable pattern within infinite diversity'.[32] A notable example is the one he founded – Visa International, *see* Exhibit 24.10.[33]

> ### Exhibit 24.10 Visa – a global chaord
>
> Dee Hock is credited with inventing Visa International as a *chaord*, a chaotically organised complex system. Visa is not merely a cooperative, jointly owned by its 21 000 member banks. The governing body shapes the shared mission and common standards for operations, information systems and advertising. But it does not control members' businesses. Outside shared commitment to Visa, they compete as they have always done. Visa is a federation with each region and board having substantial authority. Within global standards for the brand, regions vary slogans, advertising and so on. This reflects cultural differences. In mainland Europe, customers use Visa almost solely as a debit card; those in the United States, in contrast, use cards to borrow. With customers unwilling to use cards for debits, the US region sees cheques and cash as its main competitors and promotes its services accordingly.
>
> Members are united by wanting to keep their grip on money transactions in the face of threats of 'disintermediation' from telecommunications providers and software houses. As well as joining Yahoo! on the Internet (another chaordic system), Visa sees 'Smart' cards as its answer to the threat led by Microsoft. In developing nations, for example, poor networks make both magnetic stripe card technology and the Internet unusable. Smart technology allows merchants to authorise sales from the information carried on the chip.
>
> Visa has been successful. It handles more than $1000 billion annually, some 57 per cent of all multipurpose card transactions. Europe accounts for a third of the turnover. There are some 100 million Visa cards in Europe, growing by 14 per cent each year. The largest cluster, numbering about 40 million, is in the United Kingdom; 44 per cent of this nation's households use Visa as the main card compared with 21 per cent using MasterCard. Market share is 80 per cent in the United States.

Conclusion: the limits of control

Although it has applications at the operational level, and offers important insights at all levels, the definition of control as a cybernetic process is too narrow. Building a structure from tight plan–act–monitor cycles can only work in unchanging circumstances. Managers' thinking needs also to embrace ideas of controlling beliefs, boundaries and interactive systems.

A central paradox to be coped with is how to cope with change while not losing control. Reliance on conventional, objective controls risks losing necessary flexibility. Empowering staff to make flexible responses to new situations risks control loss. This is where control needs to be viewed more broadly. The work of Etzioni and Ouchi suggests that a blend among hierarchical, market and trust (or clan) relations is needed. Whichever mix is chosen depends on circumstances, for instance when knowledge is incomplete. Here, the required controls differ from those where the normal assumption of full information applies.

Managers often feel that the choice is not theirs. Circumstances dictate that they tighten up to please owners or their superiors. Hence they enter the vicious circle of increasing fear and ever more stringent controls. It is no wonder that few organisations manage to break this mould for long.

Scholars have advocated the learning organisation as offering hope for change. In exercising the loop pattern, an individual gathers not only know-how but know-why. Argyris, Schon and others have made a bridge to organisational learning, suggesting how such double-loop learning can be disseminated. Such authors generalise their experiences to suggest conditions that either encourage or restrain the growth of the learning organisation. Argyris, in particular, shows how managers call on defensive routines to stave off challenges to the status quo. Yet few studies suggest answers to the question, 'How can we change ourselves into a learning organisation?'

Surprisingly, complexity theory offers a way to bridge the gap. Asserting that organisations are, after all, natural systems, authors argue that many parts of them should and do work in an intermediate zone between order and chaos. Stacey embraces this perspective, not to seek how to return to stability, but to recognise the value of working far from equilibrium. Here, seeing the leader as the person 'in control' is false. Instead, leadership is not about omniscience and omnipotence. It is concerned with assuring and coaching members as they work at the edge of chaos. Together they create and discover the unforeseeable future.

Quick check up *Can you ...*

- State the control dilemma;
- Name Simons' control levers;
- Summarise Etzioni's power–involvement theory;
- Draw diagrams to represent simple and complex learning;

- Separate theory in use from espoused theory;
- List the key features of a learning organisation;
- State the implications of chaos theory for control.

Questions

Chapter review

24.1 Explain Etzioni's power–involvement theory, illustrating its elements by reference to Bausch & Lomb.

24.2 Explain where and why bureaucratic and market control are best used and why they fail.

24.3 Compare single- and double-loop learning, giving examples from your own experience.

24.4 What is meant by a bounded yet unknowable future?

Application

24.5 Illustrate Simons' control levers by applying them to the Baring Brothers' case.

Investigation

24.6 Investigate the function of procedures manuals and similar standing orders in an organisation to which you have access.

24.7 Using a spreadsheet with columns for t, y_t and y_{t+1}, explore what happens to the logistic function when k moves in the chaos zone. What does this suggest to you about organisations?

The transformation of IBM[34]

IBM made its name when mainframe computers carried out processing of payroll, accounts, stock control and invoicing. It became the leader in most sections of the world market. The mid-1980s, however, brought the first recession and from 1991–3, the company lost 117 000 jobs and $16 billion. Investment needs grew while turnover fell. Worse, the many internal rules and procedures, with a management focus on operating costs, seemed to bar the company from ever recovering.

The new head of IBM Corporation, Louis Gerstner, saw the problem not as technological but as one of management. The choice lay between a break up into a collection of autonomous businesses or keep it together and find ways of using the breadth of products and services as the key competitive advantage. Rejecting the former, he set up 13 linked divisions and allowed greater freedom to commercial units. He created a single worldwide sales and service organisation. More than 100 advertising campaigns were consolidated into a single voice with one global agency. Manufacturing and other operational departments became profit centres. Gerstner's aim was to make the horizontal system work through recreating the whole corporation as a network of resources.

IBM-France was a microcosm of the global changes:

■ The business was split into autonomous units matched to product groups. Planning, budgets, performance measurement and so on were then tied to product lines and not according to office or site as before. Where a location, such as a large plant, contained several divisions, the control systems were split.

■ Sales and marketing departments were given great decision-making powers. This change was supported by a *Transaction Management System*. This enabled them to simulate the effects on supply divisions of commercial choices. Control, previously built around rules and procedures, switched to results.

■ Sales staff became specialists according to market and technology.

This suggests that the new control system was built to serve the new strategy and structure. Did it work out this way? Could an organisation employing tens of thousands be changed by decree? Experience promised the worst. Some initiatives had been ignored. For instance, declaring 1987 to be 'The year of the user' had had little effect; exhortations to listen more intently to customers had been in vain. By 1993, IBM was falling apart.

Yet, as new systems are introduced, they are adapted by the stream of events and decisions encountered by managers as they carried out their functions. Managers saw that approaching the new situation using the logic of the old was inadequate. Factory managers replaced their preoccupations with technology to become more involved in financial decisions. Instead of rival departments, all the managers in the factory shared the same objectives. The control system promoted cooperation. Parallel changes at other levels promoted mutual adjustment among factories.

Such changes, however, had second order effects. After setting up the profit centres, objectives and measures of performance by product line were agreed. These revealed the excessive costs of duplication. In the old system, managers' security fears led to most production occurring at more than one site. Once these costs came into the open, managers decided to concentrate production. Put another way, the structure of production was changed. In turn, this nullified one of the new control system's advantages – inter-site comparisons. We see how the control system did not just serve to implement the new strategy. Through revealing results in a new way, it caused the managers to revise it.

A third effect of the move to decentralisation took longer to emerge. After abandoning the system of rules, the autonomy of units has grown. Headquarters has delegated responsibility and removed intermediate layers of management. The aim is to allow unit heads to act as entrepreneurs, responding quickly to change. Control has not been abandoned. In contrast to the 'old IBM' where conformity to budget was paramount, it is now entirely focused on results – indicators of costs, profits

and quality. Beyond changes in the way results are monitored, however, Gerstner has changed IBM's culture. His cultural revolution means that when managers meet a problem, they should not reach for their procedures manuals. They should know in their hearts and minds what to do. Eight principles and a code of ethics have replaced detailed rules.

The 'new IBM' is moving further from hierarchy towards a network of self-organised units. In this complex setting, a control system has more functions than simply correcting variances from budgets. It must support self-organisation in circumstances that are varied, changing and unpredictable.

Trends in the industry have helped IBM's return to health, favouring its products and services. As Gerstner commented, 'We got lucky. It's not often that a company gets a second shot at leadership. But that's all it is, a shot, an opportunity. We still have to compete. We still have to execute our strategy.'[35]

Questions

1 Explain the changes at IBM in terms of Simons' control levers.

2 What insights into the changes does the work of Ouchi provide?

3 Return to the 'structure following strategy' argument of Chapter 13. Which case is supported by the experiences of IBM?

4 Suggest some examples, from the industries in which IBM is engaged, to illustrate the notion that the future is bounded but unknowable.

Bibliography   The works of Argyris, Schon and Stacey, given in the reference list, offer scope for further study. All are difficult. Stacey has taken on the task of interpreting a new science. Argyris has a reputation for 'academic' thoroughness rather than populist exposition. The Society for Organisational Learning has a good web site at: http://www.sol-ne.org/res/wp/index.html.

References   1. Bausch & Lomb Inc., (1997) *1996 Annual Report*, Rochester, NY, http://www.bausch.com/CorporateInfo; Picken, Joseph C. and Dess, Gregory G. (1997) 'Out of (strategic) control', *Organizational Dynamics*, **25** (**1**), Summer, 35–48.

2. Dunne, Helen and Pretzlik, Charles (1995) 'Wife of Barings "rogue trader" held key post', *Daily Telegraph*, 1 March; Jones, George and Gribben, Roland (1995) 'Shock

over bank man's £17 bn bet', *Daily Telegraph*, 2 March; Dunne, Helen (1995) 'The pleasant profits that broke Britain's blue-blooded bank', *Daily Telegraph*, 19 July, 1; Leeson, Nick (1996) *Rogue Trader*, Boston, Mass.: Little, Brown & Company.

3. Simons, Robert (1995) 'Control in the age of empowerment', *Harvard Business Review*, **73** (**2**), March–April, 80–8.

4. Etzioni, A. (1975) *A Comparative Analysis of Complex Organisations: On power, involvement and their correlates*, New York: Free Press.

5. Ouchi, William G. (1980) 'Markets, bureaucracies and clans', *Administrative Science Quarterly*, **25** (**1**), 129–41.

6. Jones, T. Colwyn and Dugdale, David (1995) 'Manufacturing accountability', Chapter 19 in Berry, Anthony J.; Broadbent, Jane and Otley, David (eds) *Management Control: Theories, issues and practices*, Basingstoke: Macmillan, 299–323.

7. *Ibid.*, 305.

8. Ouchi, William G. (1979) 'A conceptual framework for the design of organisational control mechanisms', *Management Science*, **25** (**9**), 833–49.

9. Stacey, Ralph D. (1996) *Strategic Management and Organisational Dynamics*, Second edition, London: Financial Times Pitman Publishing, 398.

10. Cohen, Claire (1995) 'Striving for seamlessness: Procedures manuals as a tool for organisational control', *Personnel Review*, **24** (**4**), 50–7.

11. Kim, Daniel H. (1993) 'The link between individual and organisational learning', *Sloan Management Review*, Fall, 37–50.

12. Stacey (1996) *op. cit.*, 64.

13. Argyris, Chris and Schon, Donald A. (1978) *Organisational Learning: A theory of action perspective*, Reading, Mass.: Addison-Wesley, 20.

14. Argyris, Chris and Schon, Donald A. (1996) *Organisational Learning II*, Reading, Mass.: Addison-Wesley.

15. Stacey (1996) *op. cit.*, 62.

16. Rhenman, Eric (1973) *Organisation Theory for Long Range Planning*, London: John Wiley & Sons, 24.

17. Argyris, Chris (1993) *Knowledge for Action*, San Francisco, Cal.: Jossey-Bass; (1995) 'Action science and organisational learning', *Journal of Managerial Psychology*, **10** (**6**), 20–6.

18. Pickard, Jane (1997) 'A yearning for learning', *People Management*, 6 March, 34–5.

19. Schein, Edgar H. (1992) *Organisational Culture and Leadership:* Second edition, San Francisco, Cal.: Jossey-Bass; (1993) 'How can organisations learn faster', *Sloan Management Review*, **34**, 85–92.

20. Burgoyne, John (1995) 'Feeding minds to grow the business', *People Management*, **1** (**19**), 22–5; Leith, Clare; Harrison, Richard; Burgoyne, John and Blantern, Chris (1996) 'Learning organisations: the measurement of company performance', *Journal of European Industrial Training*, **20** (**1**), 31–44.

21. Gephart, Martha A., Marsick, Victoria J., van Buren, Mark E., Spiro, Michelle S. and Senge, Peter (1996) 'Learning organisations come alive', *Training and Development*, **50** (**12**), 34–43.

22. De Geus, Arie (1997) 'The living company', *Harvard Business Review*, **75** (**2**), March–April, 51–9; ...(1988) 'Planning as learning', **66** (**2**), March–April, 70–4.

23. http://www.mmm.com

24. 'How to live and prosper', *The Economist*, 10 May, 1997, 89.

25. Chandler, Alfred Dupont (1990) *Scale and Scope: The dynamics of industrial capitalism*, Boston, Mass.: Harvard Business School Press.

26. Senge, Peter M. and Fulmer, Robert M. (1993) 'Simulations, systems thinking and anticipatory learning', *Journal of Management Development*, **12** (**6**), 21–33.

27. Freedman, David H. (1992) 'Is management still a science?', *Harvard Business Review*, **70** (**6**), November–December, 26–38.
28. Stacey (1996) *op. cit.*, 313.
29. *Ibid.*, 346.
30. Ballman, Paul C. (1969) 'Managing effectively in chaos', *Human Resource Planning*, **19** (**3**), 11–14.
31. Stacey (1996) *op. cit.*, 349.
32. Durrance, Bonnie (1997) 'The evolutionary vision of Dee Hock: from chaos to chaords', *Training and Development*, **51** (**4**), 24–31.
33. Authers, John (1997) 'Visa card extends lead over rivals in the US', *Financial Times*, 3 January; *idem,* 'Visa acts to attract more US debit card customers', *Financial Times*, 14 August; *idem,* 'Smart with the cards', *Financial Times*, 15 September; Authers, John and Kehoe, Louise (1997) 'Visa links with Yahoo! on web directory', *Financial Times*, 30 July.
34. Moriceau, Jean-Luc (1994) 'La transformation à IBM-France: Rôle et contre-Rôle du contrôle', *Actes du XV^{éme} Congrés de l'Association Français de Comptabilité*, Université de Paris – Dauphine, 771–83; Gerstner, Lou V. (1994, 95, 96) 'Chairman's letter', *IBM Annual Report* http://www.ibm.com
35. Gerstner, Lou V. (1997) 'Address to stockholders', *IBM Annual General Meeting*, Dallas, Texas, 29 April.

Index